COMPl

THE CAMBRIDGE HISTORY OF INDIA

IN SIX VOLUMES

VOLUME III

Turks and Afghans

THE CAMBRIDGE HISTORY OF INDIA

SIX VOLUMES

Vol. I	ANCIENT INDIA ...	Rs. 35·00
Vol. II		*In Preparation.*
Vol. IV	THE MUGHAL PERIOD	Rs. 35·00
Vol. V	THE BRITISH INDIA 1497—1858 ...	Rs. 30·00
Vol. VI	THE INDIAN EMPIRE 1858—1947 ...	Rs. 30·00

(Brought up-to-date by Dr. R.R. Sethi)

THE CAMBRIDGE SHORTER HISTORY OF INDIA

EDITED BY DODWELL

Part I	ANCIENT INDIA	Rs. 4·50
Part II	MUSLIM INDIA	Rs. 6·00
Part III	BRITISH INDIA	Rs. 8·00

(Brought up-to-date by Dr. R. R. Sethi)

...ETE   Rs. 16·00

THE
CAMBRIDGE
HISTORY OF INDIA

VOLUME III

Turks and Afghans

EDITED BY

LT.-COLONEL SIR WOLSELEY HAIG
K.C.I.E., C.S.I., C.M.G., C.B.E., M.A.
LECTURER IN PERSIAN
IN THE SCHOOL OF ORIENTAL STUDIES
UNIVERSITY OF LONDON

1965

S. CHAND & CO.
DELHI—NEW DELHI—JULLUNDUR
LUCKNOW—BOMBAY

PUBLISHED IN INDIA BY S. CHAND & CO., DELHI
BY ARRANGEMENT WITH THE CAMBRIDGE UNIVERSITY PRESS, LONDON.

2nd Indian Reprint
January 1965

*The Syndics of the University Press are
deeply indebted to Sir Dorabji Tata
for his generous contribution towards the
cost of the illustrations in this volume*

S.   CHAND   &   CO.

Ram Nagar	—	NEW DELHI
Fountain	—	DELHI
Mai Hiran Gate	—	JULLUNDUR
Hazratganj	—	LUCKNOW
Lamington Road	—	BOMBAY

PRICE : Rs. 35·00

*Published by S. Chand & Co., Ram Nagar, New Delhi-1
and Offset by Eurasia Offset Printers, New Delhi-1.*

PREFACE

This volume deals generally with the history of India under Muhammadan rule from the time of the earliest invasions of the Muslims to the overthrow of the Lodī dynasty on the field of Pānīpat and the establishment of Bābur the Tīmūrid on the throne of Delhi, and covers the period unfortunately described by that usually careful scholar, the late Mr. Edward Thomas, as that of the "Pathan Kings" of Delhi. Of the five dynasties which occupied the throne of Delhi during this period, from about 1200 to 1526, three were Turkish, or of Turkish descent; one claimed to be of Arab blood, and one was Afghān, but probably not Pathān.

Mr. Thomas's misnomer, after clinging obstinately, for many years, to this period of Indian history, has been generally discarded, and the period is now known as that of the Sultanate, or Kingdom, of Delhi, as distinguished from the Empire of the Tīmūrids founded by Bābur. This distinction is not entirely accurate, or satisfactory, for it suggests that the earlier Muslim rulers were content with a comparatively small kingdom in the neighbourhood of their capital whereas for nearly half a century they ruled virtually the whole sub-continent of India, two at least of them being emperors of India in a truer sense than any of the first four Tīmūrids, and the ruin of their empire covered the greater part of India with a number of independent Muslim states. Nevertheless the term will serve, for imperial rule was not characteristic of the sovereigns of Delhi during the thirteenth, fourteenth, and fifteenth centuries. During the first century of their rule they were consolidating and extending their authority ; then followed half a century of empire, and then the disintegration of that empire.

It is only in respect of Delhi, the historic capital of Muslim rule in India, that it has been found possible to adhere to the year 1526 as the termination of an epoch of that rule. In the case of other states, both Muslim and Hindu, it has been found necessary to carry the local history on, either to the termination of the state's independence or to a period at which it may conveniently be relinquished. The history of the Hindu Kingdom of Vijayanagar, for instance, is continued to 1565, the date of its overthrow by the confederate Muslim Kingdoms of the Deccan ; that of the Muslim Kingdoms of Mālwa, Gujarāt, Bengal, and Kashmīr to the dates of their annexation by Akbar, and that of the independent Kingdoms of the Deccan to 1600, the date of the capture of Ahmadnagar by Akbar's third son, Sultān Dāniyāl.

Chapter I of this volume is introductory, and treats of the conquest of Sind by the Arabs in the eighth century. The Arabs never extended their authority or their influence beyond Sind and Multān, and their rule in those countries was a mere episode in the history of India. Chapter II treats of the Yamīnī or Ghaznavid Cynasty. Mahmūd was a raider rather than a conqueror, but he and his successors were Indian rulers by virtue of their annexation and occupation of the Punjāb, the last of their great possessions which remained to them. Chapter III treats of the first actual Muslim conquerors of Northern India, Mu'ziz-ud-dīn Mùhammad b. Sām of Ghūr, his lieutenants, and his successors, the earlier Slave Kings of Delhi ; and Chapter IV of the rule of Ghiyās-ud-dīn Balban and his worthless son. Chapter V treats of the Khaljī dynasty and the first Muslim conquest of the Deccan ; Chapter VI of the first two Sultāns of the Tughluq dynasty, and the second conquest and revolt of the Deccan ; Chapter VII of the later Sultāns of the Tughluq dynasty and invasion of India by Tīmūr ; Chapter VIII of the Sayyids ; and Chapter IX of the Lodī dynasty. Then follows a series of chapters dealing with independent Muslim Kingdoms, all of which, with the exception of Kashmīr and Khāndesh, rose on the ruins of the great empire of Muhammad b. Tughluq ; Chapter X with Jaunpur ; Chapter XI with Bengal ; Chapter XII with Kashmīr ; Chapter XIII, which has been written by Professor Sir E. Denison Ross, with Gujarāt and Khāndesh ; Chapter XIV with Mālwa ; Chapters XV and XVI with the Bahmanī Kingdom of the Deccan ; and Chapter XVII with the five independent Muslim Kingdoms of the Deccan. Chapter XVIII treats of Hindu states in Southern India, and Chapter XX with those in Northern India ; and Chapter XIX treats of the states of Sind and Multān during their independent existence. Chapter XXI, which has been written by Mr G E Harvey of the Indian Civil Service, deals with the history of Burma between the years 1287 and 1531 ; and Chapter XXII, by Don Martino de Zilva Wickremasinghe, with the history of Ceylon from 1215 to 1527. Chapter XXIII, written by Sir John Marshall, C.I.E., Director General of Archaeology in India, who has also supplied the illustrations to this volume, deals with the monuments of Muhammadan rule in India between the years 1200 and 1526.

A few explanations remain to be offered. The system of transliteration adopted is that used by the Governmnt of India in their

official publications. Except in the chapter on Ceylon diacritical
marks, with the necessary exception of the macron, have been
avoided. The *hamza* is represented, when necessary, by', the letter
ع by,' and the letter ق by *q*. It has not been considered necessary
to distinguish between the letters خ and ﻕ and غ and ﻕ by under-
lining the combinations *kh* and *gh*, and, in order to preserve the
correct pronunciation of names and titles in which the Arabic
article occurs, such forms as 'Alā-ud-dīn and Badī'-uz-Zamān have
been preferred, partly for typographical and partly for other reasons,
to the more scholarly and correct 'Alā-a*l*-dīn and Badī-a*l*-zamān,
or 'Alā'u'-d-dīn and Babī'u-'z-zamān.

In place-names the spelling cf the *Imperial Gazetteer of India*
has, with few exceptions, been followed, but the adoption of *q* as
the equivalent of ق necessitates the substitution of Qandahār for
the better-known Kandahār, and *e*, representing no Arabic or
Persian letter, has been omitted from such names as Fathābād
and Fathpur, the Gazetteer spelling of which serves only to stereo-
type a vulgar and corrupt pronunciation. The name of the great
river of Southern India is spelt *Krishna*, as there appears to be no
justification for the Gazetteer spelling *Kistna*; Ausa has been
substituted for *Owsa* as the name of a town in the Deccan hardly
well enough known to entitle it to the honour of a conventionalized
spelling; and the name of the founder of the Lodī dynasty is spelt
Buhlūl, as there appears to be no reason to preserve the mis-
pronunciation enshrined in the more familiar Bahlol.

In order to avoid, as far as possible, the use of foreign words
the plural of the words *amīr* and *malik* has usually been translated
by 'nobles,' which will not mislead the reader if it be remembered
that there has never been a recognized hereditary aristocracy in
Muslim Kingdoms. The 'nobles' were military officers, or officers
of state with military rank, whose titles, though occasionally revived
in favour of a deserving son, did not become hereditary until the
crown became so weak that a son was able to assume his father's
office and title. In the chapters on the history of the Deccan the
word 'Foreigners,' when spelt with a capital letter, denotes members
of the Foreign party.

A few words, such as *Islam*, *Sultan*, and *Raja* have been treated
as naturalized English words, and written without the macron, except when they form parts of names or titles.

My best thanks are due to Sir John Marshall and Sir E. Denison
Ross for having kindly undertaken arduous work in connection
with this volume in spite of heavy official duties. I must also

PREFACE

acknowledge the assistance of Mr. G.E. Harvey, Mr. S. Krishnaswami Ayyangar, Don Martino de Zilva Wickremasinghe, and Mr W. E. C. Browne, who has prepared the index. In conclusion, I desire to express my gratitude for the advice and assistance which I have at all times received from Professor E. J. Rapson, the editor of Volumes I and II of this history.

W.H.

THE ATHENAEUM
26 March 1928

TABLE OF CONTENTS

CHAPTER I
THE ARAB CONQUEST OF SIND
By Lt.-Colonel Sir WOLSELEY HAIG, K.C.I.E., C.S.I., C.M.G.,
C.B.E., M.A., Lecturer in Persian in the School of Oriental
Studies, University of London

CHAPTER II
THE YAMĪNĪ DYNASTY OF GHAZNĪ AND LAHORE, COMMONLY KNOWN AS THE GHAZNAVIDS
By Lt.-Colonel Sir WOLSELEY HAIG

CHAPTER III
MU'IZZ-UD-DĪN MUHAMMAD *BIN* SĀM OF GHŪR AND THE EARLIER SLAVE KINGS OF DELHI
By Lt.-Colonel Sir WOLSELEY HAIG

CHAPTER IV

GHIYĀS-UD-DĪN BALBAN, MU'IZZ-UD-DĪN KAIQUBĀD, AND SHAMS-UD-DĪN KAYŪMARS
By Lt.-Colonel Sir WOLSELEY HAIG

CHAPTER V

THE KHALJĪ DYNASTY AND THE FIRST CONQUEST
OF THE DECCAN
By Lt.-Colonel Sir WOLSELEY HÁIG

CHAPTER VI
THE REIGNS OF GHIYĀS-UD-DĪN TUGHLUQ AND MUHAMMAD TUGHLUQ, AND THE SECOND CONQUEST AND REVOLT OF THE DECCAN
By Lt.-Colonel Sir WOLSELEY HAIG

CHAPTER VII

THE REIGN OF FĪRŪZ TUGHLUQ, THE DECLINE AND EXTINCTION OF THE DYNASTY, AND THE INVASION OF INDIA BY TĪMŪR

By Lt.-Colonel Sir WOLSELEY HAIG

CHAPTER VIII

THE SAYYID DYNASTY

By Lt.-Colonel Sir WOLSELEY HAIG

CHAPTER IX

THE LODĪ DYNASTY

By Lt.-Colonel Sir WOLSELEY HAIG

CHAPTER X

THE KINGDOM OF JAUNPUR

By Lt.-Colonel Sir WOLSELEY HAIG

CHAPTER XI

THE KINGDOM OF BENGAL

By Lt.-Colonel Sir WOLSELEY HAIG

CHAPTER XII
THE KINGDOM OF KASHMÍR
By Lt.-Colonel Sir WOLSELEY HAIG

CHAPTER XIII
GUJARĀT AND KHĀNDESH
By Professor Sir E. DENISON ROSS, C.I.E., Ph.D., Director of the School of Oriental Studies, University of London, and Professor of Persian

b

CHAPTER XIV
THE KINGDOM OF MĀLWA
By Lt.-Colonel Sir WOLSELEY HAIG

CHAPTER XV
THE KINGDOM OF THE DECCAN, A.D. 1347-1436
By Lt.-Colonel Sir WOLSELEY HAIG

CHAPTER XVI

THE DECLINE AND FALL OF THE KINGDOM OF THE DECCAN, A.D. 1436—1490

By Lt.-Colonel Sir WOLSELEY HAIG

CHAPTER XVII

THE FIVE KINGDOMS OF THE DECCAN, A.D. 1527-1599

By Lt.-Colonel Sir WOLSELEY HAIG

CHAPTER XVIII

HINDU STATES IN SOUTHERN INDIA, A.D. 1000-1565

By S. Krishnaswami Ayyangar, M.A., Professor of Indian
History and Archaeology, and Fellow of the University of
Madras

CHAPTER XIX

SIND AND MULTĀN

By Lt.-Colonel Sir WOLSELEY HAIG

CHAPTER XX

THE NATIVE STATES OF NORTHERN INDIA FROM
A.D. 1000 TO 1526

By Lt.-Colonel Sir WOLSELEY HAIG

CHAPTER XXI

BURMA, 1287–1531. THE PERIOD OF SHĀN IMMIGRATION

By G.E. HARVEY, Indian Civil Service

CHAPTER XXII

CEYLON, A.D. 1215-1527

By Don Martino de Zilva Wickremasinghe, Professor
of Tamil in the School of Oriental Studies, University of
London

CHAPTER XXIII

THE MONUMENTS OF MUSLIM INDIA

By Sir John Marshall, C.I.E., M.A., Litt. D., Ph.D., Director
General of the Archaeological Survey of India

LIST OF MAPS

LIST OF MAPS

LIST OF PLATES

LIST OF BIBLIOGRAPHIES

CORRIGENDA

p. 21, ll. 9, 11, 28, 33, 36, 40, *For* Nanda *read* Ganda.

p. 22, ll. 23, 30, 37, 41. *For* Nanda *read* Ganda.

p. 127, l. 17. *Delete* pure. *Delete* note[1], *and substitute the following* :

[1] Tughluq was the personal name of Ghiyās-ud-dīn, but has been applied, both by Eastern and Western historians, to the dynasty founded by him, as though it were a patronymic. It is usually transliterated Tughlaq, but I follow Ibn Batūtah, who is explicit on the point, and who, though not always a safe guide in the matter of proper names, must have known how the name was pronounced at Delhi in his time.

p. 238, l. 12. *After* provisions *insert* to pursue his advantage.

p. 244, l. 5. *For* in *read* to.

p. 316, l. 35. *For* 1510 *read* 1511.

p. 441, ll. 10, 18. *For* Sadāshivarāya *read* Rāma Rāya.

p. 442, ll. 7, 24. *For* Sadāshivarāya *read* Rāma Rāya.

p. 443, l. 2. *For* Sadāshivarāya *read* Rāma Rāya.

p. 444, ll. 2; 26, 29. *For* Sadāshivarāya *read* Rāma Rāya.

p. 445, ll. 11, 27. *For* Sadāshivarāya *read* Rāma Rāya.

p. 448, ll. 10, 24, 30, 36. *For* Sadāshivarāya *read* Rāma Rāya.

p. 449, ll. 4, 15, 24. *For* Sadāshivarāya *read* Rāma Rāya.

CHAPTER I

THE ARAB CONQUEST OF SIND

THE rise of Islam is one of the marvels of history. In the summer of A.D. 622 a prophet, without honour in his own country, fled from his native city to seek an asylum in the town of Yathrib, since known as *Madīnat-un-Nabī* 'the Prophet's City,' rather more than two hundred miles north of Mecca, the town which had cast him out. Little more than a century later the successors and followers of the fugitive were ruling an empire which extended from the Atlantic to the Indus and from the Caspian to the cataracts of the Nile, and included Spain and Portugal, some of the most fertile regions of southern France, the whole of the northern coast of Africa, Upper and Lower Egypt, their own native Arabia, Syria, Mesopotamia, Armenia Persia, Afghanistan, Baluchistan and Transoxiana. They threatened Christendom almost simultaneously from the east and the west, besieging Constantinople three times and advancing into the heart of France, and but for the decisive victory of Theodosius III before the imperial city in 716 and the curshing defeat inflicted on them near Tours in 732 by Charles the Hammer, the whole of Europe would have passed under their sway. The battle of Poitiers decided whether the Christians' bell or the muezzin's cry should sound over Rome, Paris and London, whether the subtleties of the schoolmen and later, the philosophy of Greece, or the theology and jurisprudence of the Koran and the Traditions should be studied at Bologna, Paris, Oxford and Cambridge.

By the beginning of the eighth century of the Christian era the Arabs had carried their arms as far as the western confines of India and bore sway in Mekrān, the ancient Gedrosia, that torrid region extending inland from the northern shore of the Sea of 'Omān. Immediately to the east of this province lay the kingdom of Sind, ruled by Dāhir, son of the usurping Brāhman Chāch.

An act of piracy or brigandage, the circumstances of which are variously related, brought Dāhir into conflict with his formidable neighbours. The King of Ceylon was sending to Hajjāj, viceroy of the eastern provinces of the caliphate, the orphan daughters of Muslim merchants who had died in his dominions, and his vessels were attacked and plundered by pirates off the coast of Sind.

According to a less probable account, the King of Ceylon had himself accepted Islam, and was sending tribute to the Commander of the Faithful. Another author writes that 'Abdul Malik, the fifth Umayyad, and father of Walīd, the reigning Caliph, had sent agents to India to purchase female slaves and other commodities, and that these agents, on reaching Debul, Dāhir's principal seaport, had been attacked and plundered by brigands.

It is the results rather than the details of the outrage that are important. Hajjāj sent a letter through Muhammad b. Hārūn, governor of Mekrān, demanding reparation, but Dāhir replied that the aggressors were beyond his control, and that he was powerless to punish them. Hajjāj then obtained from Walīd permission to send an expedition into Sind and dispatched 'Ubaidullāh against Debul, but he was defeated and slain and Budail, who followed him, shared his fate. Hajjāj, deeply affected by these two failures, fitted out a third expedition, at the head of which he placed his cousin and son-in-law, 'Imād-ud-Dīn Muhammad, son of Qāsim[1], a youth of seventeen years of age.

Muhammad, with 6000 Syrian horse, the flower of the armies of the Caliphs, a camel corps of equal strength, and a baggage train of 3000 camels, marched by way of Shīrāz and through Mekrān towards Sind, crossing the frontier at Armāīl, probably not far from the modern Darbejī. On his way through Mekrān he had been joined by more troops and the Arabs appeared before Debul, then a seaport situated about twenty-four miles to the south-west of the modern town of Tatta, in the autumn of 711. His artillery, which included a great *balista* known as 'the Bride,' worked by five hundred men, had been sent by sea to meet him. The town was protected by strong stone fortifications and contained a great idol temple, from which it took its name. The siege had continued for some time when a Brāhman deserted from the temple and informed Muhammad that the garrison consisted of 4000 Rajputs and that 3000 shaven Brāhmans served the temple. It was impossible, he said, to take the place by storm, for the Brāhmans had prepared a talisman and placed it at the base of the staff of the great red flag which flew from the steeple of the temple. Muhammad ordered Ja'wiyyah, his chief artillerist, to shorten the foot of 'the Bride,' thus lowering her trajectory, and to make the flagstaff his mark. The third stone struck it, shattered its base, and broke the

---

[1] Not Qāsim or Muhammad Qāsim, as he is sometimes called by European historians. This vulgar error, arising from a Persian idiom in which the word 'son' is understood but not expressed, should be avoided.

talisman. The garrison, though much disheartened by the destruction of their palladium, made a *sortie*, but were repulsed, and the Arabs, planting their ladders, swarmed over the walls. The Brāhmans and other inhabitants were invited to accept Islām, and on their refusing their wives and children were enslaved and all males of the age of seventeen and upwards were put to the sword. The carnage lasted for three days and Muhammad laid out a Muslim quarter, built a mosque, and placed a garrison of 4000 in the town. The legal fifth of the spoil and seventy-five damsels were sent to Hajjāj, and the rest of the plunder was divided among the army.

Dāhir attempted to make light of the fall of Debul, saying that it was a place inhabited by mean people and traders, and as Muhammad advanced towards Nīrūn, about seventy-five miles to the north-east and near the modern Haidarābād (Hydrābād), ordered his son Jai Singh to leave that fort, placing a priest in charge of it, and to join him in the strong fortress of Bahmanābād. The Arabs, after seven days' march, arrived before Nīrūn early in 712, and the priest left in charge of the place surrendered it to Muhammad, who, placing a Muslim governor there marched to Sehwān, about eighty miles to the north-west.

This town, populated chiefly by priests and traders, who were anxious to submit at once to the invaders, was held by Bajhrā, son of Chandra and cousin of Dāhir, who upbraided the inhabitants for their pusillanimity and prepared, with the troops at his disposal, to defend the place, but after a week's siege lost heart, fled by the north gate of the city, crossed the Kumbh, which then flowed more than ten miles to the east of Sehwān, and took refuge with the Jāts of Būdhiya, whose raja was Kāka, son of Kotal, and whose capital was at Sīsam, on the bank of the Kumbh. The inhabitants of Sehwān then surrendered the town to Muhammad, who granted them their lives on condition of their remaining loyal and paying the poll-tax leviable from non-Muslims.

Sir William Muir has observed that the conquest of Sind marks a new stage in Muhammadan policy. The Islamic law divides misbelievers into two classes, 'the People of the Book,' that is Christians and Jews, as the possessors of inspired Scriptures, and idolators. The first, when conquered, are granted, by the authority of the Koran, their lives, and may not lawfully be molested in any way, even in the practice of the rites of their creeds, so long as they loyally accept the rule of their conquerors and pay the *jizya* or poll-tax, but a rigid interpretation of the Koran, subsequently modified by commentators and legislators, allows to idolators only the choice between Islām and death. By a legal fiction which placed the scriptures of Zoroaster on a level with the Old and New Testaments as a divine revelation the Magians of Persia had often obtained the amnesty which was strictly the peculiar privilege of Christians and Jews, but Hajjāj, a bitter persecutor, knew nothing of the lax interpretation which tolerated idolatry on payment of tribute, and in Central Asia idolators, were rooted out. In India Muhammad granted the amnesty to idolators, and in many cases left their temples standing and permitted their worship. At Debul he had behaved as an orthodox Muslim, but his subsequent policy was toleration except when he met with obstinate resistance or his troops suffered serious losses. Thus we find the zealous Hajjāj remonstrating with the young soldier for doing the Lord's work negligently and Muhammad consulting his couisn on the degree of toleration permissible. His campaign in Sind was not a holy war, waged for the propagation of the faith, but a mere war of conquest, and it was undoubtedly politic in the leader of a few thousand Arabs to refrain from a course which might have roused swarms of idolators against him.

The endeavour to follow in detail the movements of Muhammad after the fall of Sehwān bristles with difficulties. The unsatisfactory attempts of historians to reproduce in a script utterly unsuited to the purpose the place names of India, the corruption of their versions of those names by copyists who had never heard and could not read them, and above all the constant changes in the face of the country due to the repeated shifting of the courses of the great rivers which traverse it, combine to confound the student. The general course followed by him may, however, be traced.

From Sehwān he marched to Sīsam on the Kumbh, defeated the Jāts, who attacked his camp by night, and captured their stronghold in two days. Bajhrā, Dāhir's cousin, and his principal followers were slain, but Kāka submitted, and afterwards joined the Muslims.

In accordance with orders received from Hajjāj, Muhammad returned towards Nirūn, there to make preparations for the passage of the Mihrān, the main stream of the Indus, which then flowed some distance to the east of Nirūn and between it and his objective, the strong fortress of Bahmanābād, where Dāhir was prepared to oppose his further advance into the country. He halted on the western bank of the river, opposite to a fortress called Baghrūr by the Arab chroniclers, but was delayed there for some months by scurvy, which broke out among his troops, by a malady which carried off a large number of his horses, and by the impossibility of obtaining boats. Hajjāj sent him sage advice as to the best means of effecting the passage of the river and, what was more to the purpose, two thousand horses and a supply of vinegar for his suffering troops. This last was transported in a concentrated form. Cotton was saturated in it and dried and the operation was repeated until the cotton would hold no more ; the essence could then be extracted by the simple process of soaking the cotton in water. In June, 712, Muhammad crossed the river with his troops without serious opposition from the Hindus.

Dāhir had meanwhile assembled an army of 50,000 horse, and marched from Bahmanābād to Rāwar to meet the invader. The armies lay opposite to one another for several days, during which some skirmishing took place, and on June 20 Dāhir mounted his elephant and advanced to the attack. The battle was sustained with great valour on both sides, but an Arab succeeded in planting an arrow, to which burning cotton was attached, in Dāhir's elephant, and the terrified beast turned and fled towards the river, pursued by the Arabs. The driver arrested his flight in midstream and induced him once more to face the enemy, and the battle was renewed on the river bank. Dāhir charged the Arabs, and did great execution among them until he was struck by an arrow and fell from his elephant. He contrived to mount a horse but an Arab cut him down, and the Hindus fled from the field, some towards Aror, the capital, and others, with Jai Singh, to Bahmanābād, while Dāhir's wife, Rānī Bai, and her handmaids immolated themselves at Rāwar, to avoid falling into the hands of the strangers.

The remnant of the Hindu army rallied at Bahmanābād and offered such a determined resistance that 8000 or, according to another account, 26,000 of them were slain. Jai Singh, loth to sustain a siege in Bahmanābād, retired to Chitrūr and Muhammad captured Bahmanābād, and with it Rānī Lādī, another wife of Dāhir, whom he afterwards married, and Suryadevī and Parmaldevī, Dāhir's two maiden daughters, who were sent through Hajjāj to the Caliph.

After the capture of Bahmanābād he organised the administration of Lower Sind, placing governors in Rāwar, Sehwān, Nīrun, Dhāliya, and other places, and on October 9th set out for Aror, receiving on his way the submission of the people of Muthalo and Bharūr, and of the Sammas, Lohānas, and Sihtas.

Aror was held by a son of Dāhir, called, by Muslim chroniclers Fūfī, whose conviction that his father was yet alive and had but retired into Hindūstān to collect an army encouraged him to offer a determined resistance. Muhammad attempted to destroy his illusion, which was shared by the people of Aror, by sending his wife Lādī to assure them that her former husband had indeed been slain and that his head had been sent to the Caliph's viceroy, but they repudiated her with abuse as one who had joined herself to the unclean strangers. Fūfī was, however, at length convinced of his father's death, and fled from Aror by night. Muhammad, on learning of his flight, attacked the town, and the citizens, deserted by their leader, readily submitted to him.

He appointed a governor and a judge to Aror and marched towards Multān. On his way thither he first reached a fortress to which Kaksa, a cousin of Dāhir, had fled from Aror. Kaksa submitted to him, was taken into his confidence and became one of his most trusted counsellors. Continuing his march north-eastwards he came to a fortress of which the name has been so corrupted that it cannot be identified, but it lay on the northern bank of the Beas, as it then flowed. It was bravely defended for seven days, but was then deserted by its governor, a nephew of the ruler of Multān, who took refuge in Sika, a fortress on the southern bank of the Rāvī. The people, left to themselves, surrendered the fortress and were spared, but the garrison, to the number of four thousand, was put to the sword, and their wives and children were enslaved. After appointing an Arab governor Muhammad crossed the rivers and attacked Sika, the siege of which occupied him for seventeen days and cost him the lives of twenty-five of his best officers and 215 men. When the commander of the fortress fled to Multān and the place fell, he avenged the death of his warriors by sacking it and passed on to Multān. The Hindus were defeated in the field and driven within the walls but held out until a deserter pointed out to Muhammad the stream or canal which supplied the city with water, and this was destroyed or diverted, so that the garrison was obliged to surrender. In the great temple were discovered a golden idol and such quantities of gold that the Arabs named the city 'The House of Gold'. The fighting men were put to the sword and their wives and children, together with the attendants of the temple, numbering six thousand souls in all, were enslaved, but the citizens were spared. Amīr Dāūd Nasr was appointed to the government of the city and another Arab to that of the province, and Arabs were placed in charge of the principal forts.

There is a conflict of authority regarding Muhammad's movements after the capture of Multān in 713, which laid at his feet upper Sind and the lower Punjāb. According to one account he became involved in hostilities with Har Chandra, son of Jhital, raja of Qinnauj, not to be confounded with the great city of Kanauj in Hindūstān, and marched to meet him at Odipur, fourteen miles southward of Alwāna, on the Ghaggar, and according to another he returned to Aror, but his career of conquest was drawing to a close, his sun was setting while it was yet day.

The romantic story of his death, related by some chroniclers, has usually been repeated by European historians, but is devoid of foundation. It is said that when the Caliph Walīd sent for Suryadevī and Parmaldevī, the daughters of Dāhir, he first selected the elder for the honour of sharing his bed, but the damsel protested that she was unworthy, for Muhammad had dishonoured both her and her sister before sending them to his master. Walīd, transported with rage, wrote with his own hand an order directing that the offender, wherever he might be when the message reached him, should suffer himself to be sewn up in a raw hide ahd thus dispatched to the capital. When the order reached the young hero it was at once obeyed. He caused himself to be sewn up in the hide, the contraction of which as it dried would crush him to death, enclosed in a box and sent to Damascus. The box was opened in the presence of the Caliph and Suryadevī, and Walīd pointed proudly to the corpse as evidence of the obedience which he was able to exact from his servants. Suryadevī, having read him a homily on the duty of investigating all complaints made to him before issuing orders on them, confessed that her accusation was false, that Muhammad had scrupulously respected her honour and that of her sister, but that she had had no other means of avenging her father's death. Walīd condemned both sisters to a horrible death. We need not stop to inquire whether they were immured alive, or whether they were dragged through the streets of Damascus by horses until they expired. Both accounts are extant, but the end of the young conqueror, though tragic enough, was not due to an act of romantic and quixotic obedience to a distant and ungrateful master.

Walīd died in 715 and was succeeded by his brother Sulaimān; to whom Hajjāj had given great offence by encouraging Walīd in the design of making his son rather than his brother his heir. Hajjāj was beyond the reach of mortal vengeance, for he had died before Walīd, but the new Caliph's hand fell heavily on his family and adherents. Yazīd, son of Abu Kabshah, was appointed governor of Sind and Muhammad was sent a prisoner to Mesopotamia, where he was imprisoned at Wāsit by Sālih. He could not have fallen into worse hands, for Ādam, Sālih's brother, had been one of the numerous Khārijī heretics put to death by the bigoted and brutal Hajjāj. His murder was now expiated by the gallant young conqueror of Sind and his relations, who were tortured to death by Sālih's orders.

Yazīd died eighteen days after his arrival in Sind, and Sulaimān appointed Habīb, son of Muhallab, to succeed him. Habīb adopted a conciliatory policy, and allowed the princes expelled by Muhammad to return to their states, so that Jai Singh, son of Dāhir, established himself at Bahmanābād, Aror being retained as the capital of the viceroy, whose only warlike operation appears to have been the reduction of a refractory tribe to obedience.

Sulaimān died, after a reign of no more than two years, in 717, and was succeeded by his cousin, the pious and zealous 'Umar II, to whom the toleration of idolatry, even on the fringe of his empire, was painful. He wrote to the princes of Sind, urging them to embrace Islam and earn the temporal as well as the eternal blessings which would follow their acceptance of the true faith. Many, among them Jai Singh, responded.

Junaid, governor of Sind under the Caliph Hishām (724-743), was active and energetic, but unscrupulous. He prepared to invade the territory of Jai Singh, now a Muslim and a feudatory of the Caliph, but when Jai Singh protested against the aggression reassured him. Jai Singh responded by sending to him assurances of his loyalty to the Caliph and the tribute due from his state. Hostilities nevertheless broke out, and Jai Singh was defeated and slain. Each has been accused of perfidy, but Junaid is convicted by his subsequent conduct. When Chach, Jai Singh's brother, fled to Mesopotamia to complain against him 'he did not cease to conciliate him until they had shaken hands, and then he slew him.'

Junaid afterwards carried the Muslim arms further into India; but the places which he captured or menaced cannot now be satisfactorily identified. He was afterwards promoted to the viceroyalty of the eastern provinces of the Caliphate, and was succeeded in Sind by Tammīm, son of Zaid-ul-'Utbā, a feeble ruler distinguished chiefly by his lavish generosity, whose successor, Hakam, found Islam languishing and the people, for the most part, relapsed into idolatory, and was obliged to build for the Muslims two strongholds to serve as cities of refuge, al Mahfūzah, 'the guarded,' and Mansūrah, long the capital of the Muhammadan provinces of Sind, lying a few miles to the north-east of Bahmanābād. He and his lieutenant

'Amru, son of the unfortunate Muhammad, laboured to recall the people to the faith of Islam and to restore the military reputation of the Muslims, and their successors 'continued to kill the enemy, taking whatever they could acquire and subduing the people who rebelled.'

In 750 the 'Abbasids overthrew the Umayyads and sent officers to expel those who had held offices under them in the provinces. Mansūr, who now held Sind, resisted with some success the adherents of the new line of Caliphs, but was at length defeated and driven into the desert, where he perished miserably of thirst. Mūsā, who expelled him, repaired the city of Mansūrah and enlarged the mosque there.

Al-Mansūr (754-775), the second 'Abbasid Caliph, sent to Sind Hishām, who reduced Multān, still in arms against the new dynasty, and captured Qandāīl, which may be identified with Zihrī in Balūchistan, about fifty-seven miles south-west of Gandāva ; and Kandhāro, on the south-western border of the present Bahāwalpur State.

Governor was regularly appointed to succeed governor until Bashar, son of Dāūd, rebelled against the Caliph al-Ma'mūn, who reigned from 813 to 833, and Ghassān, who was sent to suppress his rebellion, carried him to Baghdād, and left as his own deputy in Sind, Mūsā, son of Yahyā, son of Khālid, son of Barmak. Mūsā the Barmecide, an active and energetic ruler, died in 836, but before his death ventured on a step which clearly indicated that the hold of the Caliphs on Sind was relaxing. He nominated his son 'Amrān as his successor, and the significance of the measure was hardly diminished by the formality of obtaining al-Mu'tasim's recognition of the appointment. When provincial governments in the east begin to become hereditary they are in a fair way to becoming kingdoms.

'Amrān made war upon the jāts, whom he defeated and subjugated. He also defeated and slew a fellow Muslim, Muhammad, son of Khalīl, who reigned at Qandāīl, and attacked the Meds of the sea coast of Cutch. Of them he slew three thousand and advanced as far as Adhoī, in eastern Cutch.

The later history of Islam in Sind is obscure, but the religion flourished, and retained its dominion over idolatry. The authority of the Caliphs in the province was virtually extinguished in 871, when two Arab chiefs established independent principalities at Multān and Mansūrah. The former comprised the upper valley of the united Indus as far as Aror ; the latter extended from that town to the sea, and nearly coincided with the modern province of

Sind. Little is known of the details of the history of these dynasties, but they seem to have left the administration of the country largely in the hands of natives and to have tolerated freely the Hindu religion. Their power was maintained by an Arab soldiery supported by grants of land, and though they were in fact independent they retained the fiction of subordination to the Caliphate, for as late as the beginning of the eleventh century, when Mahmūd of Ghaznī was wasting northern India with fire and sword, the Muslim governor of Sind professed to be the Caliph's representative.

Of the Arab conquest of Sind there is nothing more to be said. It was a mere episode in the history of India and affected only a small portion of the fringe of that vast country. It introduced into one frontier tract the religion which was destined to dominate the greater part of India for nearly five centuries, but it had none of the far-reaching effects attributed to it by Tod in the *Annals of Rājasthān*. Muhammad b. Qāsim never penetrated to Chitor in the heart of Rajputāna ; the Caliph Walīd I did not 'render tributary all that part of India on this side the Ganges'; the invader was never 'on the eve of carrying the war against Raja Harchund of Kanouj' much less did he actually prosecute it ; if Hārūn-ur-Rashid gave to his second son, al-Ma'mūn, 'Khorassan, Zabulisthan, Cabulisthan, Sind and Hindusthan', he bestowed on him at least one country which was not his to give ; nor was the whole of northern India, as Tod maintains, convulsed by the invasion of the Arabs. One of these, as we have seen, advanced to Adhoī in Cutch, but no settlement was made, and the expedition was a mere raid ; and though the first news of the irruption may have suggested warlike preparations to the princes of Rājasthān their uneasiness cannot have endured. The tide of Islam, having overflowed Sind and the lower Punjab, ebbed, leaving some jetsam on the strand. The rulers of states beyond the desert had no cause for alarm. That was to come later, and the enemy was to be, not the Arab, but the Turk, who was to present the faith of the Arabian prophet in a more terrible guise than it had worn when presented by native Arabians.

CHAPTER II

THE YAMĪNĪ DYNASTY OF GHAZNĪ AND LAHORE, COMMONLY KNOWN AS THE GHAZNAVIDS

THE Arabs never carried the standards of Islam far beyond the Indus, and though the doctrines of the new faith were accepted by many and familiar to all of the inhabitants of Sind, and Muhammadan dynasties were ruling at Mansūra until A.D. 976 and at Multān until a later date, India in general remained untouched by Islam until the beginning of the eleventh century, by which time the faith had lost its political unity and the control of its destinies had passed from the hands of the Arabian successors of Muhammad into those of independent dynasties acknowledging the Caliph at Baghdād merely as a spiritual head.

In the early part of the tenth century the descendants of Sāmān, a Persian chieftain of Balkh who had accepted Islam, extended their dominion over Transoxiana, Persia, and the greater part of the present kingdom of Afghānistān, but their great empire wanted almost as rapidly as it had waxed and their power gradually passed into the hands of the Turkish slaves to whom they had been wont to entrust the principal offices in their court and kingdom. One of these, Alptigīn, rebelled and established himself at Ghaznī, where he reigned as an independent sovereign, though his successors found it convenient, when they were in difficulties, to acknowledge the Sāmānids, who now held their court at Bukhārā, and to court their favour. Alptigīn was succeeded in 963 by his own son Is·hāq, on whose death in 966 Mansūr I of Bukhārā acknowledged Balkātigīn, a former slave of Alptigīn. Pīrāi succeeded in 972, whose reign of five years is remarkable for the first conflict in this region between Hindus and Muslims, the former being the aggressors. The raja of the Punjab, whose dominions extended to the Hindu Kush and included Kābul, was alarmed by the establishment of a Muslim kingdom to the south of the great mountain barrier and invaded the dominion of Ghaznī, but was defeated.

Pīrāi's rule became unpopular and he was expelled, and on April 9, 977, Sabuktigīn, a slave upon whom Alptigīn had bestowed his daughter's hand, ascended the throne at Ghaznī. He found it expedient to seek, and readily obtained, confirmation of his title from Nūh II of Bukhārā, but thenceforward made small pretence of subservience to a moribund dynasty.

Later Muhammadan historians are prone to represent Sabuktigīn, who never crossed the Indus and led only two expeditions against the Hindus, as a champion of the faith whose chief occupation was the propagation of Islam with fire and sword among the idolators of India. In fact he was fully employed in extending the area of his small state, which at first comprised little beyond the immediate neighbourhood of Ghaznī. In the first twelve years of his reign he extended his frontiers to the Oxus on the north and approximately to the present boundary between Afghānistān and Persia on the west. Two years after his accession Jaipāl, raja of the Punjab, again invaded the kingdom of Ghazni from the east, but terms of peace were arranged, and in 986 Sabuktigīn, whose power had been rapidly growing, invaded his enemy's territory and carried off many captives and much booty. Two years later he againg attacked Jaipāl and compelled him to cede Kābul and much other territory, but these expeditions were undertaken rather as measures of reprisal and for the purpose of securing his dominions than with any intention of propagating the faith.

In October 994 Sabuktigīn, by aiding Nūh II of Bukhārā to expel Abu 'Alī Sūnjūr, a rebel and a leader of the Ismā'īlian heretics, from Khurāsān, obtained the government of that province, to which he appointed as his deputy, his eldest son, the famous Mahmūd. Sabuktigīn died, in August 997, near Balkh, having firmly laid the foundations of the great empire which was to be extended and consolidated by his more famous son.

The nobles of Balkh, in obedience to Sabuktigīn's will, acknowledged as their sovereign his younger son Ismā'īl, but a party favoured the claims of the more able and energetic Mahmūd. Mahmūd wrote to his brother demanding the cession of Ghaznī and promising to retain him as governor of Balkh, but his demand was rejected, and the two brothers, one from Nīshāpūr and the other from Balkh, marched on Ghaznī. In a battle fought near the city Ismā'īl was defeated and compelled to take refuge in the fortress, but his nobles surrendered him to his brother, who imprison ed him for the rest of his life.

Mahmūd was born on November 1, 971, and was therefore twenty-seven years of age when he deposed his brother and ascended the throne in 998. His kingdom at the time of his accession comprised the country now known as Afghānistān, and Khurāsān, or eastern Persia. In the following year he added to it the province of Sīstān. After this success he sought formal recognition of his sovereignty from the Caliph, al-Qādir Billāh, who sent him a robe

of investment and a patent conferring on him the titles Yamīn-ud-
Daulah and Amīn-ul Millah, from the former of which his successors
are known to eastern historians as the Yamīnī dynasty. It was on
this occasion that he is said to have vowed to undertake every year
an expedition against the idolators of India, but intestine troubles
claimed his immediate attention. 'Abd-ul-Malik II, the last Sāmānid
ruler of Bukhārā, was driven from his kingdom in 999 by Abu'l-
Husain Nasr I, Ïlak Khān, Kāshghar, and his brother, Abu Ibrāhīm
al-Mustansir, who had found an asylum in Gurgān, thrice attempted
to establish himself in Khurāsān, where his forefathers had held sway.
Twice he drove Nasr, Mahmūd's brother, from Nīshāpūr, only to be
expelled when Nasr returned with reinforcements, and on the third
occasion he was defeated and fled to the Ghuzz Turkmans, with whom
he took refuge.

It is difficult to follow the long series of expeditions led by
Mahmūd into India in pursuance of his vow, to reconcile the
accounts of historians who contradict not only one another but themselves, and to identify places disguised under a script ambiguous in itself and mutilated by generations of ignorant scribes. The number of
these expeditions is almost invariably given as twelve, but there are
few historians who do not give accounts, more or less detailed, of
more than twelve. The first is said to have been undertaken in 999 or
1000, when Mahmūd, after annexing Sīstān, crossed the Indian
frontier and plundered or annexed some towns, but the authority for
this expedition is slight, Mahmūd had at this time little leisure
for foreign aggression, and the campaign may be regarded either as
apocryphal or as a foray undertaken by some of his officers.

In September, 1001, Mahmūd left Ghaznī with 15,000 horse and
advanced to Peshāwar, where Jaipāl I of the Punjab was prepared to
meet him with 12,000 horse, 30,000 foot and 300 elephants. The raja
was expecting reinforcements and was in no haste to engage before
their arrival, but Mahmūd's impetuosity left him no choice, and on
November 27th the two armies advanced to the attack, discharging
clouds of arrows. Those of the Hindus did great execution, but
the Muslims had the better mark, and their arrows, as well as the
swords of their horsemen, rendered many of Jaipāl's elephants unma-
nageable or useless. The Hindus could not withstand the impetuosity
of the Muslim horse and by noon were in full flight, leaving 15,000
dead on the field or slain in the pursuit. Jaipāl and fifteen of his
relations were captured, and their jewels, including a necklace of
enormous value worn by the raja, formed part of Mahmūd's plunder-

After the battle Mahmūd attacked and plundered Ūnd[1], then an important city, and Jaipāl was permitted to ransom himself for a large sum of money and a hundred and fifty elephants, but as the ransom was not at once forthcoming was obliged to leave hostages for its payment. His son, Anandpāl, made good the deficiency and the hostages were released before Mahmūd returned to Ghaznī, his soldiers speeding them on their way with a contemptuous buffet on their hinder parts.

After Mahmūd's departure Jaipāl, overwhelmed with shame and mortification, bowed to the decision of his subjects, who refused to acknowledge a king who had been a captive in the hands of the Muslims, and, after designating Anandpāl as his successor, mounted a funeral pyre and perished in the flames.

In 1002 Mahmūd was occupied in crushing a rebellion in Sīstān. The leader of the rebels escaped death by means of a ready tongue and when brought before his conqueror addressed him by the then unfamiliar title of Sultān[2]. He was pardoned and rewarded with the government of another district, Sīstān being included in the provincial government of Khurāsān.

In his campaign against Jaipāl Mahmūd had expected aid from Bajra, the ruler of Bhātiya, the modern Uch, who had been on friendly terms with Sabuktigīn, but he had been disappointed and in 1004 he marched from Ghaznī to punish Bajra for his failure to support him. He was stoutly opposed but defeated Bajra before Uch and compelled him to flee for refuge to the jungles on the banks of the Indus, where, to escape capture by the Muslims, he stabbed himself. His head was carried to Mahmūd and a general massacre of his disorganised troops followed. Mahmūd, after plundering Uch, remained there for some time, engaged in making arrangements for the permanent annexation of the state and the conversion of its inhabitants, and it was not until the rivers were in flood in 1005 that he set out on his return journey. In crossing them he lost his plunder and much of his baggage, and was attacked during his retreat by Abu-'l-Fath Dāūd, the ruler of Multān, and suffered considerable loss.

Dāūd was the grandson of Shaikh Hamīd Lodī, who had established himself in Multān and had always cultivated friendly rela-

---

[1] This is the town variously called Hind, Ohind, and Waihind. It is situated in 34° 2′ N. and 72° 27′ E. fifteen miles above Attock, on the west bank of the Indus.

[2] According to another account the Caliph bestowed this title on Mahmūd, who is said to have been the first prince so honoured, but this is improbable, for Mahmūd never used it on his coins but was always content with the designation of Amīr, which seems to have been that by which the Caliph distinguished him.

tions with Sabuktigīn, but his grandson had embraced the doctrines of the Ismā'īlī sect, and was therefore as abominable in Mahmūd's eyes as any idolator in India. In the autumn of 1005 Mahmūd had marched against him, and in order to avoid the passage of the rivers in their lower waters marched by way of Ūnd, in the dominions of Anandpāl, of whose subservience he was assured. Anandpāl, however, opposed his advance, but was defeated and fled into Kashmīr, and Mahmūd pursued his way through the Punjab, plundering the country as he advanced.

The defeat of Anandpāl and Mahmūd's triumphal and devastating progress overcame the resolution of Dāūd, who shut himself up in Multān, and when Mahmūd prepared to form the siege of the city offered as the price of peace a yearly tribute of 20,000 golden *dirhams* and abjuration of his heretical doctrines. The invasion of his northern province by the Turks of Transoxiana under Abu'l-Husain Nasr I of Bukhārā obliged Mahmūd to accept these terms, and he returned with all speed towards the Oxus, appointing as governor of Ūnd, by which place he marched, Sukhpāl, a grandson of Jaipāl, who, having been taken prisoner with his grandfather, had accepted Islam, and was now known as Nawāsa Shāh. We are not concerned with the details of Mahmūd's campaign against the Īlak Khān, who was defeated and driven across the Oxus, but it is an interesting fact that a corps of Indians formed part of the victorious army.

On his return towards Ghaznī in 1007 Mahmūd learnt that Nawāsa Shāh had apostatised, was expelling the subordinate Muslim officers from the district committed to his charge, and purposed to rule it either as an independent sovereign or as the vassal of his uncle, Anandpāl. He marched at once towards Ūnd and ordered those of his officers whose fiefs lay near that district to attack the renegade. They captured Nawāsa Shāh and the treasure which he had amassed and carried him before Mahmūd, who confiscated his wealth and imprisoned him in a fortress for the remainder of his life.

In the following year Mahmūd resolved further to chastise Anandpāl for his opposition to the passage of the Muslim army through his dominions on its way to Multān, and in the autumn of 1008 marched to Peshāwar. Anandpāl, who had been aware of his intention, had appealed for aid to other Hindu rajas, and one historian mentions the rajas of Ujjaīn, Gwalior, Kālinjar, Kanauj, Delhi, and Ajmer as having either marched in person or sent troops to his assistance. The number and consequence of his allies are perhaps exaggerated, but it is evident from Mahmūd's excessive caution that Anandpāl had received a considerable accession of strength and that the army which he led into the field was a very different force from that which Mahmūd had so easily brushed aside on his way to Multān. Among the most valuable of Anandpāl's auxiliaries were the wild and warlike Khokars from the lower hills of Kashmīr.

The Hindu army was encamped between Und and Peshāwar, and Mahmūd lay in camp before it for forty days without venturing to attack it, although each day's delay brought it fresh reinforcements and the only inconvenience which it suffered arose from the difficulty of provisioning so great a force. This was alleviated by the devotion of the men's wives, who sold their jewels to enable their husbands to keep the field.

Mahmūd protected his flanks with entrenchments and instead of following his usual impetuous tactics strove to entice the enemy to attack him in his own strong position. In this he succeeded and the Hindus attacked on December 31. A force of 30,000 Khokars, bareheaded and barefooted and armed with strange weapons, charged both his flanks simultaneously, passed over his trenches, and did such execution among his troops that he was meditating a retreat when a fortunate accident decided the day in his favour. Anandpāl's elephant took fright and bore his rider from the field and the Hindus, believing their leader's flight to be intentional, broke and fled. The battle was now at an end and the pursuit began. The Muslims pursued their enemy for a great distance, slaying 8000 and taking thirty elephants and much other plunder.

The dispersal of this great army opened the way for a raid into India and Mahmūd marched towards the fortress of Nagarkot, or Kāngra, famous for its wealth. So little had his victory and subsequent advance been expected that the fortress had been left without a garrison, and was occupied only by the Brāhmans and servants of the temple, who appeared on the walls and offered to surrender. After some parleying the gates were opened to Mahmūd on the third day after his arrival, and the booty which fell into his hands is said to have amounted to 700,000 golden *dīnārs*, besides large quantities of vessels of gold and silver and of unworked gold and silver, and jewels. With this plunder he returned to Ghaznī and exhibited it, piled on carpets in the courtyard of his palace, to the wondering eyes of his subjects.

A year later he marched to Ghūr[1], a small district in the hills between Ghaznī and Herāt, which had hitherto remained inde-

---

[1] Usually written *Ghor* but Ghūr is correct.

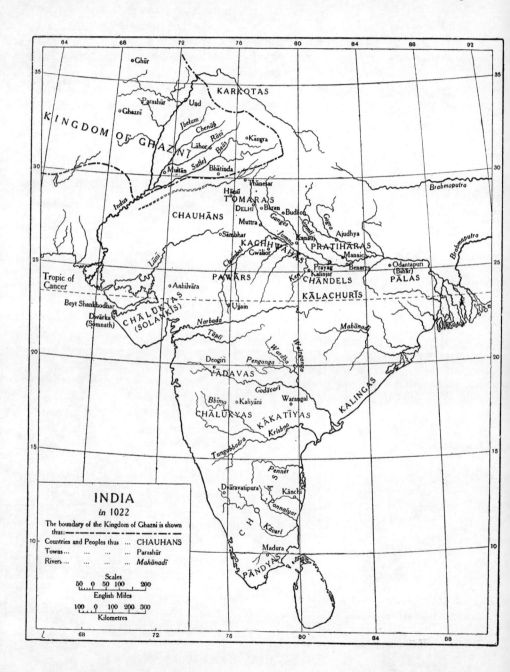

INDIA

in 1022

The boundary of the Kingdom of Ghazni is shown
thus:— ▬ ▪ ▬ ▪ ▬

Countries and Peoples thus ... CHAUHANS

Towns... ... ... Parashūr

Rivers ... ... *Mahānadī*

Scales

50 0 50 100   200

English Miles

100 0 100 200 300

Kilometres

pendent under its Tājik or Persian rulers, defeated its prince, Muhammad *bin* Sūrī, and reduced him to the position of a vassal. This expedition, though not directly connected with the history of India is interesting in view of the subsequent relations between the princes of Ghūr and those of Ghaznī. The former exterminated the latter and achieved what they had never even attempted—the permanent subjugation of northern India.

Later in 1010 Mahmūd again invaded India. There are some discrepancies regarding his objective, which the later historians, who confound this expedition with that of 1014, describe as Thānesar. He probably intended to reach Delhi but he was met at Taräorī, about seven miles north of Karnāl, by a large Hindu army, which he defeated and from which he took much plunder, with which he returned to Ghaznī.

In 1011 he visited Multān, where his authority was not yet firmly established, brought the province under more efficient control, and extinguished the still glowing embers of heresy.

Meanwhile Anandpāl had died and had been succeeded by his son, Jaipāl II, who made the fortress of Nandana[1] his chief stronghold, and in 1013 Mahmūd invaded India to attack him. On hearing of Mahmūd's advance he retired into the mountains, leaving his son Nidar Bhīmpāl, or Bhīmpāl the Fearless, to defend his kingdom. The accounts of the campaign are strangely at variance with one another. According to one Bhīmpāl was besieged in Nandana and forced to surrender while according to another he ventured to meet Mahmūd in the open field, and was with difficulty defeated. Defeated, however, he was, and Mahmūd turned into the hills in the hope of capturing him, but captured only his baggage. Large numbers of the natives of the country, guilty of no crime but that of following the religion of their fathers, were carried off to Ghaznī as slaves, and the remarks of one historian probably reflect contemporary Muslim opinion on this practice : 'Slaves were so plentiful that they became very cheap and men of respectability in their native land were degraded to the position of slaves of common shopkeepers. But this is the goodness of God, who bestows honour on His own religion and degrades infidelity.' An officer named Sārugh was appointed governor of Nandana and held that position at the time of Mahmūd's death.

Mahmūd was next attracted by the wealth of the sacred city of Thānesar, between Ambāla and Karnāl, and in 1014 marched from Ghaznī. When Jaipāl heard of his intention he sent a mission to

---

[1] Situated in 30° 43′ N. and 73° 17′ E.

Ghaznī, offering to send him fifty elephants annually if he would spare so sacred a place, but Mahmūd rejected the offer and required of Jaipāl a free passage through his territory. Jaipāl perforce assented, but warned Bijayapāl, the Towār raja of Delhi, of the approach of the invader, thus enabling him to summon others to his assistance.

Mahmūd marched with such rapidity through the Punjab as to forestall Bijayapāl's preparations, and found the shrine at Thānesar undefended. He entered it without encountering serious opposition[1], plundered it of its vast treasures, and destroyed its idols, except the principal object of worship, which was sent to Ghaznī to be buried in a public thoroughfare, where it might be trodden underfoot by the people. After this easy success Mahmūd wished to march on Delhi, but was over-ruled by his advisers, who were averse from advancing so far into India until the annexation of the Punjab should have furnished a base of operations within its borders.

In 1015 Mahmūd invaded Kashmīr and besieged Lohkot or Loharkot, but the weather was so inclement and the garrison so constantly received reinforcements that he was compelled to raise the siege and retire. This was his first serious reverse in India. His army lost its way in the unfamiliar highlands and its retreat was interrupted by flooded valleys, but at length, after much toil, it debouched into the open country and returned to Ghaznī in disorder.

In 1016 and 1017 Mahmūd was occupied in Khvārazm and in the northern provinces of his empire, and it was not until 1018 that he was able again to turn his attention to India. He now prepared to penetrate further into the country than on any former occasion, and to plunder the rich temples of Hindūstān proper. With an army of 100,000 horse raised in his own dominions and 20,000 volunteers from Turkistān, Transoxiana, and the confines of Khūrāsān, soldiers of fortune eager to share in the rich spoils of India, he marched from Ghaznī in September, before the rainy season in India was well past, and, guided by the Lohara raja of Kashmīr, crossed with some difficulty the Indus and the rivers of the Punjab. On December 2 he crossed the Jumna and pursued his march southwards. Avoiding Delhi, he followed the eastern bank of the Jumna until he reached Baran, the modern Bulandshahr,

---

[1] According to al-'Utbī, one of the earliest authorities, the Hindus had assembled, and it was only after overcoming a desperate resistance that Mahmūd entered the shrine, but al-'Utbī's topography is faulty, and he appears to be confounding this expedition with another.

the first strong place which lay in his path. Hardat, the governor, fled from the fortress and left the garrison to make what terms they might with the invader. They propitiated him by the surrender of a great quantity of treasure and thirty elephants, and he passed thence to Mahāban, on the eastern bank of the Jumna. Kul Chandra, the governor of this place, drew up his forces and made some attempt to withstand the Muslims but his army was put to flight and he first slew his wife and son and then committed suicide. Besides much other spoil eighty elephants were taken by Mahmūd at Mahāban, and he crossed the river in order to attack Muttra, the reputed birthplace of Krishna and one of the most sacred shrines in India. The city, though fortified and belonging to Bijayapāl, the raja of Delhi, undefended, and Mahmūd entered it and plundered it without hindrance. His hand was not stayed by his admiration of its marble palaces and temples, unsparingly expressed in the dispatch in which he announced his success, and the temples were rifled and, as far as time permitted, destroyed. The plunder taken was enormous, but it is difficult to believe stories of a sapphire weighing over sixteen pounds and a half and of five idols of pure gold, over five yards in height, though the quantity of gold taken may very well have been over 548 pounds, as is recorded.

Mahmūd continued his march and on December 20 arrived before Kanauj, the capital of Rāhtor Rājputs, whose raja, Jaichand, terrified by the numbers, the discipline and achievements of the invading army, withdrew from his strong city, the ramparts of which were covered by seven detached forts, and left it open to Mahmūd, who occupied both the city and the forts. The raja returned and preserved his city from destruction by making submission to the conqueror and surrendering eighty-five elephants, much treasure and a large quantity of jewels.

From Kanauj Mahmūd marched to Manaich, afterwards known as Zafarābād, near Jaunpur. The fortress was strongly garrisoned and well furnished with supplies, but a vigorous siege of fifteen days reduced the defenders to such despair that they performed the rite of jauhar[1], first slaying their wives and children and then rushing out to perish on the swords of the enemy.

---

[1] This Hindī word signifies 'taking one's own life' and is applied to a rite performed by Rajputs when reduced to the last extremity. First the women and children are destroyed, or destroy themselves, usually by fire, and the men, arrayed in saffron robes, rush on the enemy sword in hand and fight until all are slain. Instances of the performance of this rite, the object of which is to preserve the honour of the women from violation by the enemy, are common in Indian history.

After plundering Manaich, Mahmūd attacked Asnī, a fortress in the immediate neighbourhood, defended by deep ditches and a dense jungle, that is to say an enclosure of quickset bamboos, similar to that which now surrounds the city of Rāmpur in Rohilkhand and forms an impenetrable obstacle. Asnī was the stronghold of a powerful chief named either Chandpāl or Chandāl Bor, who had recently been at war with Jaichand. On hearing of Mahmūd's approach he fled, leaving his capital a prey to the invader.

From Asnī Mahmūd marched westwards to a town which appears in Muslim chronicles as Sharva and may perhaps be identified with Seūnza on the Ken, between Kālinjar and Banda or Sriswagarh on the Pahūj not far from Kūnch. This town was the residence of another Jaichand, who is said to have been long at enmity with Jaichand of Kanauj and even now held his foe's son in captivity. Jaichand of Kanauj, who wished to terminate the strife and had sent his son Bhīmpāl to arrange marriage between his sister and Jaichand of Sharva, wrote to the latter dissuading him from rashly attempting to measure his strength against that of the invader, and Jaichand of Sharva followed this advice and left his capital, taking with him into the forest in which he took refuge the greater part of his army and his elephants. Mahmūd, not content with the plunder of Sharva, pursued him by difficult and stony tracks into the forest, suddenly attacked him shortly before midnight on January 5, 1019, and defeated him. Jaichand's elephants were captured, specie and jewels rewarded the exertions of the victors, and captives were so numerous that slaves could be purchased in the camp at prices ranging from two to ten *dirhams*.

After this victory, the last exploit of a most laborious and adventurous campaign, Mahmūd returned to Ghaznī, and the booty was counted. It is impossible to reconcile the conflicting accounts of the enormous quantity of treasure taken, but the plunder included over 380 elephants and 53,000 human captives. Of these poor wretches many were sold to foreign merchants, so that Indian slaves became plentiful in Transoxiana, 'Irāq and Khurāsān, 'and the fair, the dark, and rich and the poor were commingled in one common servitude.'

It was after this most successful raid that Mahmūd founded at Ghaznī the great Friday mosque[1] known as 'the Bride of Heaven'

---

[1] In a Muslim city each quarter has its mosque for the daily prayers, but it is the duty of the faithful to assemble on Fridays at a central mosque in order that the whole congregation may make a united act of worship. This mosque is known as the *Masjid-i-Jāmi'*, 'the mosque which gathers all together.' The expression 'Friday mosque' is not a literal translation, but is a convenient English equivalent.

and the college which was attached to it. His example was eagerly followed by his nobles, who had been enriched by the spoils of India and were amply supplied with servile labour ; and mosques, colleges, caravanserais, and hospices sprang up on every side.

The date of Mahmūd's next expedition is given by some historians as ·1019, but those authorities are to be preferred which place it in 1021. Its occasion was the formation of a confederacy, headed . by Nanda, raja of Kālinjar, for the purpose of punishing Jaichand of Kanauj for his pusillanimity and ready submission to the invader. Nanda led the army to Kanauj and defeated and slew Jaichand, whose death Mahmūd resolved to avenge, and an army greater than any which he had hitherto led into India was assembled at Ghaznī for the purpose. Jaipāl II, who had tamely acquiesced in Mahmūd's passage through the Punjab, was now dead, or had abdicated the throne, and had been succeeded by his more spirited son, Bhīmpāl the Fearless, who joined the Hindu confederacy but, instead of rashly opposing Mahmūd on his western frontier where he would have been beyond the reach of help from his allies, withdrew to the banks of the Jumna, where they might have supported him. Here Mahmūd found him encamped, and hesitated to attempt the passage of the swollen river in the face of his army, but eight Muslim officers, apparently without their king's permission or knowledge, suddenly crossed the river with their contingents, surprised the Hindus and put them to flight. The eight officers continued to advance and occupied a city which cannot now be identified[1], and Mahmūd, whose way was cleared before him, crossed the Jumna and the Ganges, and found Nanda awaiting him on the banks of the Sai with an army of 36,000 horse, 105,000 foot, and 640 elephants. Before this host Mahmūd's heart failed him for a moment, and he repented of having left Ghaznī, but prayer restored his courage and he prepared for battle on the following day. In the night, however, Nanda was unaccountably stricken with panic and fled with a few attendants, leaving his army, his camp and his baggage at the mercy of the invader. The confusion which prevailed among the Hindus on the discovery of Nanda's flight was at first suspected by Mahmūd to be a stratagem to induce him to attack, but having ascertained that it was genuine he permitted his army to plunder the camp, and a vast quantity of booty was collected without a blow. Of Nanda's elephants 580 were taken and Mahmūd,

---

[1] Professor Dowson has suggested that it was Bārī, in the present state of Dholpur, but the identification is unconvincing. .

who was apprehensive of disturbances in the Punjab, returned, content with this victory, to Ghaznī.

Later in the same year he led an expedition into two districts disguised in Persian histories under the names of Qīrāt and Nūr and said to have been situated between the boundaries of India and Turkistan. The most probable conjecture identifies them with the districts of Dīr, Swāt, and Bajaur. The enterprise was successful and the command of the last named district having been bestowed upon 'Alī *bin* Qadr, a Saljūq Turk, Mahmūd again invaded Kashmīr and besieged Loharkot, but abandoned the siege after a month and retired from Kashmīr. He did not return at once to Ghaznī, but marched into the Punjab to chastise Bhīmpāl for having joined the confederacy of the rajas of Hindūstān. The army, instead of besieging Lahore, dispersed throughout the neighbouring country in order to subsist upon it and to prevent supplies from reaching the capital, and Bhīmpāl was reduced to such straits that he fled and sought an asylum with the Chauhān raja of Ajmer. His flight marks the formal annexation of the Punjab by Mahmūd, who may henceforth be regarded as an Indian ruler. Less than a century and a half after his death the Indian province of his great empire became the kingdom and the sole refuge of his descendants.

In the autumn of 1022 Mahmūd again invaded Hindūstān in order to inflict further punishment on Nanda of Kālinjar. He marched through the Doāb, crossed the Jumna below Delhi, and was attracted by the strong fortress of Gwalior, to which he laid siege but, finding that the operation was likely to be protracted, permitted the Kachhwāha raja to compound for a formal submission by a gift of no more than thirty-five elephants, and pursued his way towards his real objective, Kālinjar, to the reduction of which he was prepared to devote more time. After a protracted siege Nanda was permitted to redeem his stronghold for three hundred elephants which, instead of being formally delivered, were mischievously driven in a body towards the Muslim camp, in the hope that they would throw it into confusion ; but the Turks had by now some experience of elephants, and caught and managed them. According to a possibly mythical account of the event, their success compelled the unwilling admiration of Nanda, who addressed to Mahmūd an encomiastic poem which was so highly praised by learned Hindus in the Muslim camp that its author was rewarded with the government of fifteen fortresses, a grant probably as hollow as the flattery which had earned it. After this composition with Nanda, Mahmūd returned to Ghaznī with his spoils.

In 1023 he was occupied in Transoxiana and in the following year set out on his most famous expedition into India. There is a conflict of authority on the subject of the date of his departure from Ghaznī, but he appears to have left his capital on October 17, 1024, at the head of his own army and a body of 30,000 composed, as on a former occasion, of volunteers from Turkistān and other countries, attracted by the hope of booty.

It is said that the impudent vaunts of the Brāhmans attached to the wealthy religious establishment of Somnāth, on the coast of Kāthiāwār suggested to Mahmūd the desirability of striking a blow at this centre of Hinduism. The wealth and importance of the shrine far exceeded those of any temple which he had yet attacked. One thousand Brāhmans daily attended the temple, three hundred barbers were maintained to serve the pilgrims visiting it, and three hundred and fifty of the unfortunate women whom the Hindus dedicate nominally to the service of their gods and actually to the appetites of their priests danced continually before the idol, which was a huge *lingam* or phallus. These priests and attendants were supported from the endowments of the temple, which are said to have consisted of the revenues of 10,000 villages, the idol was washed daily with water brought from the Ganges, 750 miles distant, and the jewels of the temple were famed throughout the length and breadth of India.

The Brāhmans attached to this famous shrine boasted that their master Shiva, the moon-lord, was the most powerful of all the gods and that it was only owing to his displeasure with other gods that the invader had been permitted to plunder and pollute their shrines. This provocative vaunt suggested to Mahmūd the destruction of the temple of Somnāth as the readiest means to a wholesale conversion of the idolators.

He reached Multān on November 20 and decided to march across the great desert of India to Ajmer. In his arduous undertaking he made elaborate preparations. Each trooper was ordered to carry with him fodder, water and food for several days, and Mahmūd supplemented individual efforts by loading his own establishment of 30,000 camels with water and supplies for the desert march. These precautions enabled his army to cross the desert without mishap, and on its reaching Ajmer, or rather the Chauhān capital of Sāmbhar, for the modern city of Ajmer was not then built, the raja fled and the invaders plundered the city and slew many Hindus, but did not attempt the reduction of the fortress. From Sāmbhar the army marched towards Anhilvāra, now known as Pātan, in Gujarāt, capturing on its way an unnamed fortress which furnished it with water and supplies. Mahmūd, on arriving at Anhilvāra early in January, 1025, discovered that the raja, Bhīmdeo, and most of the inhabitants had fled, and the army, having plundered the supplies left in the city, continued its march to Somnāth. On his way thither Mahmūd captured several small forts and in the desert of Kāthīāwār encountered a force of 20,000, apparently part of Bhīmdeo's army, which he defeated and dispersed. Two days' march from Somnāth stood the town of Dewalwāra, the inhabitants of which, secure in the protection of the god, had refused to seek safety in flight and paid for this misplaced confidence with their lives.

On reaching Somnāth the Muslims perceived the Hindus in large numbers on the walls, and were greeted with jeers and threats. On the following day they advanced to the assault and, having driven the Hindus from the walls with well directed showers of arrows, placed their scaling ladders and effected a lodgement on the rampart. Many Hindus fell in the street-fighting which followed but by dusk the Muslims had not established themselves sufficiently to justify their remaining in the town during the night, and withdrew to renew the attack on the following morning. They then drove the defenders, with terrible slaughter, through the streets towards the temple. From time to time bands of Hindus entered the temple and after passionate prayers for the moon-lord's aid sallied forth to fight and to die. At length a few survivors fled towards the sea and attempted to escape in boats, but Mahmūd had foreseen this and his soldiers, provided with boats, pursued and destroyed them.

When the work of blood was finished Mahmūd entered the temple, the gloom of which was relieved by the light from costly lamps which flickered on the fifty-six polished pillars supporting the roof, on the gems which adorned the idol, and on a huge golden chain, the bells attached to which summoned to their duties the relays of attendant priests. As the eyes of the conqueror fell upon the hewn stone, three yards in height above the pavement, which had received the adoration of generations of Hindus, he raised his mace in pious zeal and dealt it a heavy blow. Some historians relate that when he commanded that the idol should be shattered the Brāhmans offered to redeem it with an enormous sum of money, and that their prayers were seconded by the arguments of his courtiers who urged that the destruction of one idol would not extinguish idolatry and that the money might be employed for

pious purposes. To both Mahmūd replied that he would be a
breaker, not a seller of idols, and the work of destruction went
forward. When the idol was broken asunder gems worth more
than a hundred times the ransom offered by the Brāhmans were
found concealed in a cavity within it and Mahmūd's iconoclastic
zeal was materially rewarded ; but this story appears to be an
embellishment, by later historians, of the earlier chronicles. Of the
fragments of the idol two were sent to Ghaznī to form steps at the
entrance of the great mosque and the royal palace, and two are
said to have been sent to Mecca and Medina, where they were
placed in public streets to be trodden underfoot.

Mahmūd was now informed that Bhīmdeo of Anhilvāra had
taken refuge in the island of Beyt Shankhodhar[1], at the north-
western extremity of the peninsular of Kāthīāwār, and pursued him
thither. If the chroniclers are to be credited it was possible in those
days to reach the island on horseback at low tide for native guides
are said to have pointed out the passage to Mahmūd and to have
warned him that he and his troops would perish if the tide, or the
wind rose while they were attempting it. Mahmūd nevertheless
led his army across and Bhīmdeo was so dismayed by his determination and intrepidity that he fled from the fortress in a mean
disguise and left it at the mercy of the invaders, who slew all the
males in the town and enslaved the women, among whom, according to one authority, were some of the ladies of Bhīmdeo's family.

From Beyt Shankhodhar Mahmūd returned to Anhilvāra, where
he halted for some time to refresh his troops. It is difficult to believe
that the climate and situation of the city and the reputed existence
of gold mines in its neighbourhood induced Mahmūd seriously to
propose that the court should be transferred thither. The historian
responsible for this statement adds that Mahmūd's proposal was
successfully combated by his counsellors, who impressed upon him
the impossibility of controlling from Anhilvāra the turbulent province of Khurāsān, the acquisition and retention of which had been
so difficult and so costly ; and Mahmūd prepared to return to Ghaznī.
The line of retreat chosen was through the desert of Sind to Multān,
for Mahmūd was loth to risk his booty in a battle with the raja of

---

[1] The stronghold is variously styled in Persian texts Kandana, Khandana, and
Khandaba, in which some resemblance to the last two syllables of the name of the
island can be traced, but the Persian script, being easily corruptible by ignorant or
careless scribes, is ill-suited for the preservation of the correct forms of proper names,
and it is the description of Bhīmdeo's retreat that enables us to identify it with Beyt
Shankhodhar.

Sāmbhar, who had closed with a great army the line by which he had advanced.

The army suffered much in its retreat, first through the arid desert of Sind and next through the Sind-Sāgar Doāb, where it was so harassed and delayed by the Jāts of that region that it was not until the spring of 1026 that it reached Ghaznī.

Mahmūd's vanity was flattered after his return by the receipt of complimentary letters from the Caliph al-Qādir Billāh conferring fresh titles on him, distinguishing his sons in the same manner, and formally recognizing him as ruler of Khurāsān, Hindūstān, Sīstān, and Khvārazm, the whole of which great empire, with the exception of India, where he held only one province, actually acknowledged his sway.

In the autumn of this year Mahmūd made his last incursion into India, a punitive expedition against the Jāts who had harassed his retreat. He marched to Multān and there prepared a fleet of 1400 boats, each armed with an iron spike projecting from the prow and similar spikes projecting from the gunwale on either side and carrying a crew of twenty men armed with bows and arrows and hand grenades of naphtha. The Jāts launched four, or, according to some authorities, eight thousand boats and attacked the Muslims, but their boats were pierced or capsized by the spikes and the victory was so complete that the Jāts, almost to a man, were drowned or slain. The Muslims then disembarked on the islands where the Jāts had placed their wives and families for safety and carried off the women and children as slaves.

The remainder of Mahmūd's reign was occupied by the suppression of the Saljūq Turks, whom he had incautiously encouraged too far and by the annexation of western Persia. He died at Ghaznī on April 21, 1030.

It is only in a limited sense that Mahmūd can be described as an Indian sovereign, for it was not until the later years of his reign that he annexed and occupied the Punjab, the only Indian province which he held, but he was the first to carry the banner of Islam into the heart of India and to tread the path in which so many followed him. He founded an Indian dynasty, for the later kings of his house, stripped of all their possessions in Persia, Transoxiana, and Afghānistān, were fain to content themselves with the kingdom of the Punjab, which had been but an insignificant province of his great empire.

To Muslim historians Mahmūd is one of the greatest of the champions of Islam. How far his Indian raids and massacres were inspired by a desire of propagating his faith, for which purpose they were ill adapted, and how far by avarice, must remain uncertain, for Mahmūd's character was complex. Though zealous for Islam he maintained a large body of Hindu troops, and there is no reason to believe that conversion was a condition of their service. The avarice most conspicuously displayed in his review of his riches before his death and in his undignified lamentations over the prospect of leaving them gave way to lavishness where his religion or his reputation was concerned. His patronage of architecture adorned Ghaznī with many a noble building and his no less munificent patronage of letters made his court the home of Firdausī, 'Asāirī, Asadī of Tūs, Mīnūchihrī of Balkh, 'Unsuri, 'Asjadi of Marv, Farrukhī, Daqīqī ; and many other poets of less note. His treatment of the first-named poet, whom he paid for his great epic in silver instead of the promised gold, is remembered to his discredit, though it was probably due less to his niggardliness than to a courtier's jealousy.

Some European historians, ignorant of the principles of oriental abuse and of the Islamic law of legitimacy have asserted, on the authority of the satire which Firdausī, after his disappointment, fulminated against his patron, that Mahmūd was a bastard, but Firdausī's charge against him is only that his mother was not of noble birth. He seems to have been the son of a concubine or handmaiden, but by the law of Islam the son of a concubine or handmaiden is as legitimate as the son of a regularly married wife.

The story of the contest between Mahmūd's two sons is a mere repetition of that of the contest between Mahmūd and his brother Ismā'īl. Mas'ūd, the abler of the two, was at Hamadān when his father died, and at once set out for Ghaznī, where a party of the nobles had, in obedience to Mahmūd's will, acknowledged Muhammad as their sovereign. Mas'ūd was joined during his advance by several of the leading nobles, including Ayāz, Mahmūd's favourite slave and confidential adviser, and on October 4 those who had hitherto supported Muhammad perceived that his cause was lost, imprisoned him, and joined his brother, who had reached Herat, but their tardy submission availed them little, and they were either executed or imprisoned for life. The unfortunate Muhammad was blinded, and was carried by Mas'ūd to Balkh, which for a time became the royal residence.

Mas'ūd never attempted to emulate his father's activity, but history now sheds more light on the administration of the Indian province of the empire. The government of the Punjab had been entrusted by Mahmūd to a Turkish officer named Ariyāruq, whom Mas'ūd summoned to Balkh. He was charged with oppression and extortion, with preventing his victims from having access to their sovereign, and with retaining with treasonable intent a large part of the revenue. His power was so great that it was considered unlikely that he would obey the summons of Mas'ūd, but he presented himself at Balkh with a large contingent of Indian troops and by ingratiating himself with the leading courtiers contrived to evade for some time an inquiry into his administration, but his enemies watched their opportunity and one day, when they knew that he was drunk, persuaded Mas'ūd to summon him to court. He was constrained to obey and Mas'ūd incensed both by his dilatoriness in appearing and by the unseemliness of his conduct, caused him to be arrested as a preliminary to an investigation. His Indian troops were disposed to attempt a rescue but were dissuaded by the threat that the first act of violence would be the signal for his execution and by the promise that they should not suffer by the change of masters, the royal officers were thus enabled to enter Ariyāruq's quarters, and seize his movable property, his treasure, and, more important than all, his accounts, which furnished ample evidence of his misconduct. He was sent to Ghūr, where he was put to death, and his friend Āsaftigīn Ghāzī shortly afterwards shared his fate.

Mas'ūd entered Ghaznī on May 23, 1031, and incurred much odium by requiring, against the advice of his counsellors, a refund of all the largesse which had been distributed by his brother on his proclamation as Amīr.

The affairs of the empire were now suffering from the loss of Mahmūd's strong guiding hand. Western Persia was disturbed and a new governor was sent thither, but the Punjab was in even greater confusion, for no governor had been appointed since the recall of Ariyāruq, and the officers sent to seize his property and conduct a local inquiry into his administration were unable to cope with the opposition of his relations and their dependants and partisans. There was nobody at court fit for the important post of governor of the Indian province, and Mas'ūd with some misgivings, appointed to it his father's treasurer, Ahmad Niyāltigīn, whose honesty was dubious and whose inexperience of civil and military affairs was notorious. It was believed that the retention of his son at Ghaznī as a hostage would ensure his fidelity and the instructions issued for the guidance of officials in India indicate the nature of the irregularities of Ariyāruq's administration. They were not to undertake, without special permission, expeditions beyond the limits of the Punjab, but were to accompany Ahmad on any expedition which he might undertake ; they were not to drink, play polo, or mix in social intercourse with the Hindu officers at Lahore ; and they were to refrain from wounding the susceptibilities of those officers and their troops by inopportune displays of religious bigotry.

Mas'ūd would have visited the Punjab in person had his presence not been more urgently required in the north, where the Saljūqs threatened Balkh, and in the west, where the governor of 'Irāq needed support and where the daily expected death of the Caliph, al-Qādir Billāh, might breed fresh disorders. The news of his death actually reached Balkh on November 9. Ahmad Niⱥ āltigīn, on arriving in India, at once quarrelled with Abu-'l-Hasan, 'the Shīrāzī *Qāzī*,' one of the officials who had been sent to collect the revenue and inquire into Ariyāruq's administration. Abu-'l-Hasan was in-clined to resent what he regarded as his supersession by Ahmad and the latter's success in collecting revenue which he himself had been unable to collect, but his opposition was based chiefly on the new-comer's treasonable designs. Ahmad's appointment had turned his head, and he encouraged the circulation of a rumour that his mother had been guilty of an intrigue with Mahmūd, of which he was the offspring, and planned an expedition to distant Benares, the wealth of which might enable him to establish himself as an independent sovereign in India. Abu-'l-Hasan advised him to devote his atten-tion to the civil administration and to delegate the actual command of the troops to a military officer, but was curtly told to mind his own business. Each party then reported the other to Mas'ūd, Ahmad complained that Abu-'l-Hasan was attempting to undermine his authority and Abu-'l-Hasan warned his master of Ahmad's designs. In this contest Abu-'l-Hasan was worsted. He was ordered to confine his attention to the collection of the revenue, which was his affair, and to leave the general civil and military administration to the governor.

Mas'ūd suffered for his neglect of the warning. Ahmad led his troops to Benares[1], indulged them with twelve hours' plunder of

---

[1] The date of this expedition coincides nearly with the date (June 19, 1033), assigned for the death of the mythical hero Sālār Mas'ūd, popularly known as Ghāzī Miyān, at Balrāich. Sālār Mas'ūd is said to have been the son of Sālār Sāhū and Māmal, sister of Mahmūd. The only work, pretending to be a history, which treats of him, is the Mir'āt-i-Mas'ūdī, written in the reign of Jahāngīr by 'Abd-ur-Rahmān Chishtī, who cites as his authority 'an old book written by Mullā Muhammad of Ghaznī, a servant of Sultan Mahmūd,' but no trace of this 'old book' is to be found and there is little reason for believing that it ever existed, save in the imagination of 'Abd-ur-Rahmān Chishtī, who seems to have been a crazy and credulous retailer of popular legends. The marvellous exploits of the young

the city and in 1034 returned to Lahore with enormous wealth. He reported his success in glowing terms to Mas'ūd, but his report was not accompanied by the expected remittance of spoil. Abu-'l-Hasan reported at the same time that Ahmad was employing the plunder of Benares in the raising of a large army recruited from the most turbulent and disaffected ruffians of Lahore and the Punjab, that he openly boasted of being the son of Mahmūd, and that he was on the point of repudiating his allegiance. This report was corroborated by Ahmad's conduct and it was decided to treat him as a rebel. There was an awkward pause when Mas'ūd asked who would undertake the task of crushing the rebellion. The Muslim nobles, who under-stood the difficulty of the enterprise and disliked the Indian climate, were mute, and their silence was the opportunity of the Hindu Tilak, who offered his services as a native who knew the country and for whom the climate had no terrors.

Tilak was of humble origin, being the son of a barber, but was handsome, enterprising and accomplished, speaking and writing well both Hindī and Persian. From the service of Abu-'l-Hasan he had been promoted to that of Mahmūd's minister and eventually to that of Mahmūd himself. He had deserved well of Mas'ūd, for he had, at considerable personal risk, consistently supported his cause against that of his brother, and had been rewarded, after his accession, with the chief command of the Hindu troops and the rank of a noble of the empire.

When Tilak reached India he found that the officers and troops who remained loyal to Mas'ūd had taken refuge in a fortress near Lahore, where they were besieged by Ahmad. He occupied Lahore, seized several Muslims known to be partisans of Ahmad, and caused their right hands to be struck off. This ruthless measure so terrified the rebellious troops that many of them deserted Ahmad and joined Tilak. Judicious bribery still further thinned the ranks of the rebel army, and when Ahmad was forced to stand and face his pursuers he was defeated, and was deserted by all save a body of three hundred horse. Instead of pursuing him Tilak offered the lately rebellious Jāts the royal pardon and a sum of 500,000 *dirhams* as the price of Ahmad's head. The Jāts surrounded the fugitive, slew

hero need not be related here, but he and his four mythical companions have become objects of worship to a peculiar sect, the *Pachpīriyas*, or followers of the five saints, which embraces ignorant Hindus as well as ignorant Muslims and is of great interest to students of folklore. There is probably some slender historical foundation for the myth, but it can no longer be traced. See *E. and D.* II, 513-549 and *The Heroes Five*, by the late Mr. R. Greeven, I.C.S. (Allahabad, 1898).

him, and demanded their reward. Tilak retorted that they had already received it from the plunder of Ahmad's camp, but after some chaffering Ahmad's head and his son, who had been taken alive, were surrendered in consideration of the royal pardon and 100,000 *dirhams*. Tilak presented his prizes to Mas'ūd at Marv and was rewarded by further tokens of his master's favour.

On August 29, 1036, Mas'ūd sent his second son, Majdūd, to India, as governor of the Punjab, and vowed, when he himself fell sick in the following year, that if he recovered he would lead an expedition into India and capture the fortress of Hānsī. On his recovery his advisers warned him in vain of the folly of engaging in a purposeless enterprise in India while the Saljūqs were threatening his northern and eastern provinces : Mas'ūd insisted on the fulfilment of his vow and on October 5, 1037, he left Ghaznī for India. On November 8 he reached the Jhelum and was detained there for a fortnight by an illness serious enough to startle his conscience into abjuration of the sin of wine-bibbing, and his wine was poured into the river and the use of intoxicants forbidden in his army. By November 29 he was able to take the field and on December 20 arrived before Hānsī and opened the siege of the fortress. In spite of an obstinate resistance the town was stormed on January 1, 1038, after the walls had been breached in five places, and was sacked ; the Brāhmans and the fighting men were put to the sword and the women and children were enslaved.

Mas'ūd returned to Ghaznī on February 11 to learn that the Saljūqs were besieging the ancient town of Rai, near the modern Tehrān, and had also invaded Khurāsān. He encouraged his officers with promises of speedy relief but lingered at Ghaznī until the following winter and by the time he had taken the field Chaghar Beg Dāūd the Saljūq was in possession of Nīshāpūr. The campaign against the Saljūqs was ended by a crushing defeat sustained by Mas'ūd in 1040 at Tāliqān, three marches from Marv, Khvārazm was lost, and Mas'ūd was compelled to retreat to Ghaznī while the Saljūqs besieged Balkh. It was during this campaign that the character of the Hindu troops was first impugned. The Muslim officers complained that five hundred of them could not be induced to face ten Turkmāns, and the Hindu officers retorted that while the Muslim troops had fared well their men were starved, and had received no flour for four months. When it was suggested that an Indian corps should be raised for the expulsion of the Saljūqs, Mas'ūd exclaimed, with petulant ingratitude, 'Never ! These are the men who lost us Marv.'

On November 13 Mas'ūd, overcome by craven fear, set out from
Ghaznī for Lahore, taking with him the women of his harem, what
remained of his father's treasure, and the brother whom he had
blinded years before. He was now an object of contempt to his
own troops, and when he reached the Marīgala pass, a few miles
east of Hasan Abdāl, his guards fell upon his treasure-laden camels,
divided the spoils, and gaining possession of the person of the blind
Muhammad, acclaimed him as their Amīr. Mas'ūd was arrested
and brought before the brother whom he had so cruelly mutilated,
and was overwhelmed with shame when Muhammad told him that
he bore him no malice and bade him choose his place of residence.
Mas'ūd chose the fortress of Girī and was sent thither, but was put
to death a few months later by order of Muhammad's son, Ahmad.

Mas'ūd's son Maudūd, who was at Balkh, marched to Ghaznī
on hearing of his father's deposition and Muhammad turned back to
meet him. In the winter of 1041-42 the two armies encountered
one another at Nangrahār, about half-way between Ghaznī and
the Indus, and after an obstinate conflict Maudūd was victorious
and avenged his father's fate by putting to death with torture
Muhammad and all his sons except two, 'Abd-ur-Rahīm, whom he
spared in return for consideration shown for the imprisoned Mas'ūd,
and Nāmī, who was governor of the Punjab. An officer sent to
India had no difficulty in defeating and slaying Nāmī, but there still
remained Maudūd's own brother, Majdūd, who had been appointed
by his father to the government of the Indian province and had
proved himself an energetic and capable commander. He had captured the important town of Thānesar and was now at Hānsī,
awaiting a favourable opportunity for attacking Delhi, but on learning that Maudūd had sent an army against him returned rapidly
to Lahore, and arrived there on July 27, 1042. Maudūd's troops
reached the city one or two days later and it appeared probable
that they would declare for the more capable and more popular
Majdūd, but on the morning of July 30 he was found dead in his
bed. No cause is assigned for his death, and it may have been due
to heat stroke, or some other rapidly fatal disease, but it is more
probable that agents of Maudūd had been at work.

Maudūd's authority was now established in the Punjab but it
commanded none of the respect which the Hindus had yielded to
the great Mahmūd, and two years later Mahīpāl, raja of Delhi, recaptured without difficulty Hānsī, Thānesar, and Kāngra, inflaming
the zeal of his troops by exhibiting to them at the temple in the
last-named fortress a replica of the famous idol carried off by

Mahmūd, now believed to have returned by a miracle to its former shrine.

Mahīpāl was encouraged by his success at Kāngra to advance even to the walls of Lahore, and besieged the city, but the nobles, who had been too deeply engaged in quarrels regarding precedence, fiefs, and titles to send relief to the three lost fortresses, showed a united front to the enemy at the gates, and Mahīpāl was obliged to retire.

In 1046 Maudūd's chamberlain renewed the feud with Ghūr by invading the small principality with a large force, and capturing two princes of the ruling house, who were carried to Ghaznī and put to death.

In 1048 Maudūd, in order to allay the strife between the nobles of the Punjab, appointed his two eldest sons, Mahmūd and Mansūr, to the government of Lahore and Peshāwar, and at the same time sent Bu ʿAli Hasan, *Kotwāl*[1] of Ghaznī, to India to curb the aggression of the Hindus, in which task he succeeded well and captured a fortress which cannot now be identified with any certainty, but he fell a victim to one of the intrigues so common in oriental courts, and was rewarded, on his return to Ghaznī, by being cast into prison, where his enemies anticipated the probability of his restoration to power by murdering him.

Maudūd died of an intestinal complaint on December 22, 1049, while preparing to visit his father-in-law, Chaghar Beg Dāūd the Saljūq, and in accordance, it was said, with his will, his infant son Masʿūd, aged three, was proclaimed Amīr by the servants of his household, who proposed that the boy's mother, the daughter of Chaghar Beg Dāūd, should exercise the powers of regency, but the nobles of Ghaznī, who had not been consulted, refused to ratify this arrangement, and on December 29 deposed the child and proclaimed his uncle, ʿAli Abu-'l-Hasan, who married his brother's widow, the Saljūq princess.

ʿAlī proved to be a feeble ruler, and in 1052 his uncle, ʿIzz-ud-daulah ʿAbd-ur-Rashīd, the sixth son of Mahmūd, was released from the fortress in which he had been imprisoned, advanced on Ghaznī, deposed his nephew, and ascended the throne; while the daughter of Chaghar Beg Dāūd, bitterly resenting her husband's deposition, left Ghaznī and returned to her father.

ʿAbd-ur-Rashīd was a scholar with a taste for theology, but was as little fitted as ʿAli to hold the reins of government in troubled times. He appointed to the government of the Punjab Nūshtigīn,

---

[1] The *Kotwāl* of a large city corresponded to the officer whom we designate Commissioner of Police, and exercised also extensive magisterial powers.

an able and active officer who recovered the fortress of Kāṅgra and restored order, but in Tughril 'the Ingrate', another servant, who had been a slave of Mahmūd, he was less fortunate. Tughril was sent to Sīstān and reduced that province to obedience, but it was his own authority and not his master's that he established. His successes, which appear to have included some victories over the Saljūqs[1], who now ruled Khurāsān, enabled him to raise and maintain a large army, with which he marched to Ghaznī, defeated and put to death 'Abd-ur-Rashīd and nine other members of the royal house, and ascended the throne. His treachery was generally abhorred, and he was assassinated, after a reign of forty days, by the royal guards. Nūshtigīn, who had left India on hearing of Tughril's usurpation, arrived at Ghaznī a few days after his death and took counsel with the nobles regarding the filling of the vacant throne. There still survived, imprisoned in a fortress, Farrukhzād and Ibrāhīm, two sons of Mas'ud I, and the nobles elected the latter, but, on discovering that he was in feeble health, transferred their suffrages to his brother. Almost immediately after Farrukhzād's enthronement the kingdom was invaded by Chaghar Beg Dāūd who, after being defeated by Nūshtigīn, summoned to his assistance his more famous son Alp Arsalān, against whom Farrukhzād took the field in person. Alp Arsalān gained an indecisive victory and retired with his prisoners, leaving in Farrukhzād's hands those taken from Chaghar Beg Dāūd by Nūshtigīn. An exchange formed the basis of a treaty of peace, and on Farrukhzād's death in March, 1059, his brother Ibrāhīm, who succeeded him, renewed the treaty and arranged a marriage between his son Mas'ūd and the daughter of Malik Shāh, Alp Arsalān's son. The treaty was faithfully observed by the Saljūqs during Ibrāhīm's long reign, and the security of his northern and western frontiers enabled him to devote his attention to India. In 1079 he crossed the southern border of the Punjab and captured the town of Ajūdhan, now known as Pāk Pattan. In the course of the same campaign he is said to have taken a town named Rūpāl, which was perhaps the place of that name in Mahī Kāntha, as he appears to have advanced towards the western coast and to have come upon a settlement of Pārsīs which may be identified with Nāvsārī in Gujarāt. This is the only supposition by which it is possible to explain a Muslim historian's obviously in-

---

[1] According to another account of Tughril's career in Sistān he temporarily transferred his allegiance to the Saljūqs, and, having acquired the art of war according to their system, utilized his knowledge for the destruction of his master, but he does not appear to have been acting, in his rebellion, as an agent of the Saljūqs.

accurate statement that he reached a town populated exclusively by Khurāsānīs who had been deported to India by Afrāsiyāb.

Ibrāhīm died on August 25, 1099, after a comparatively peaceful reign of forty-two years, and was succeeded by his twenty-third son, 'Alā-ud-Daulah Mas'ūd III, surnamed al-Karīm, who had married the daughter of Malik Shāh. The chief events of his peaceful reign of seventeen years were an expedition beyond the Ganges, led by Tughātigīn of Lahore, of whose exploits no details are given, and the appointment of Husain, son of Sām, to the government of Ghūr, which is interesting as evidence that the Shansabānī princes were still vassals of Ghaznī. Mas'ūd III died in 1115 at the age of fifty-seven, and was succeeded by his son Shīrzād, who was deposed in the following year by his brother Arsalān 'Abd-ul-Malik. Arsalān's half brother Bahrām, who was the son of the Saljūq princess, fled for refuge to his uncle, Sultān Sanjar, in Khurāsān, and Arsalān was foolish enough to treat his stepmother with indignity, and even to offer her a gross insult. His folly incensed Sanjar, who was already disposed to espouse the cause of his nephew Bahrām, and he advanced on Ghaznī with a large army. Arsalān was defeated within a few miles of the city and fled to India, and Sanjar placed Bahrām on the throne and returned to Khurāsān. Arsalān, on learning of his departure, returned to Ghaznī and expelled Bahrām. In 1117 Sanjar, who had succeeded, on the death of his brother Muhammad, to the sovereignty of all the dominions of the Great Saljūqs, was too much occupied with his own affairs to be able to send assistance to Bahrām, but in 1118 he provided him with troops, and he marched to Ghaznī and defeated and captured his brother. He was at first disposed to spare his life, but, on discovering that he was hatching schemes for the recovery of the throne, put him to death.

Shortly after his accession Bahrām marched into India to reduce to obedience Muhammad Bāhlīm, who, having been appointed governor of the Punjab by Arsalān, refused to acknowledge his successor. Bāhlīm was defeated and captured on January 22, 1119, but Bahrām, with culpable leniency, not only pardoned but reinstated him, and returned to Ghaznī. Bāhlīm displayed great energy in subduing the minor Hindu chieftains on the borders of the Punjab and established himself in Nāgaur, where he again repudiated his allegiance to Bahrām. Bahrām marched from Ghaznī against the rebel, who foolishly advanced northward and met him in the neighbourhood of Multān, where he was defeated, and in attempting to escape was swallowed up, with two of his sons, in a quicksand. He deserves to be remembered, because he established Muhammadan rule over provinces which had never acknowledged the authority of the greatest of the Ghaznavids. Nāgaur is situated more than 300 miles to the south of Lahore, and it is said that Bāhlīm was accompanied, on his march against Bahrām, by ten sons, each of whom ruled a province or district.

The later years of Bahrām's reign were overshadowed by the menace of the growing power of the Shansabānī princes of Ghūr, who had husbanded their resources while the Ghaznavids and the Saljūqs were at strife. Qutb-ud-dīn Muhammad of Ghūr, having quarrelled with his brother, fled to Ghaznī and married a daughter of Bahrām, who, after harbouring him for some time, suspected him of plotting against him and removed him by poison. Qutb-ud dīn's next brother, Saif-ud-dīn, prince of Ghūr, invaded the Ghaznavid dominions to avenge his brother's death, defeated Bahrām, drove him to India, and occupied Ghaznī, appointing his brother Bahā-ud-dīn Sām his lieutenant in Ghūr. In 1149 Bahrām returned suddenly from India, surprised Saif-ud-dīn, and put him to flight. He was pursued and overtaken and was induced to surrender by a promise that his life should be spared, but the perfidious Bahrām, having secured his enemy, first publicly exposed him to the derision of the populace and then put him to death. Bahā-ud-dīn Sām is said to have died of grief for his brother, and another brother, 'Alā-ud-dīn Husain, succeeded to the principality and in 1151 took a terrible revenge for Saif-ud-dīn's death. He invaded the Ghaznavid kingdom, defeated Bahrām in three successive battles, captured Ghaznī, and burnt it to the ground. The flames raged for seven days and the outrage earned for its author the name of 'Jahānsūz,' 'the World-burner.' The remains of the kings, except Mahmūd, Mas'ūd I and Ibrāhīm, were torn from their graves and burnt, and their tombs were destroyed, the male inhabitants, except the Sayyids[1], who were carried to Ghūr to be put to death there, were slaughtered and the women and children carried off into slavery, and 'Alā-ud-dīn, after leaving Ghaznī, marched through other provinces of the kingdom, destroying the monuments of the taste and munificence of its former rulers.

Bahrām had fled to India after his defeat, but ventured to return to Ghaznī when the World-burner, shortly after his victories, incurred the wrath of Sultān Sanjar the Saljūq and was defeated and temporarily imprisoned by him. Bahrām, who died shortly

---

[1] Sayyids are descendants of Muhammad through his daughter Fātima, who was married to his cousin 'Alī. They had two sons, Hasan and Husain, from one or other of whom all Sayyids claim descent.

afterwards[1], is favourably known as a patron of literature. The famous poet Sanāī resided at his court and another writer made for him a Persian translation of the Arabic version of the story *Kalīlah wa Damnah*, the better known translation of which, the *Anvār-i-Suhailī*, by Mullā Hasan Wāʿiz, al-Kāshifī, was made in the reign of Sultān Hasan the Timurid.

Bahrām was succeeded by his son Khusrav Shāh, a feeble ruler in whose reign a horde of the Ghuzz tribe of Turkmāns invaded Khurāsān and defeated and captured Sultān Sanjar, who died in their hands in 1157. From Khurāsān the Turkmāns advanced on Ghaznī, and Khusrav Shāh fled before them to Lahore, where he died in 1160. The Punjab was all that now remained to the descendants of Sabuktigīn of the wide domains of their ancestors. The Ghuzz Turkmāns retained possession of Ghaznī for ten years and it then fell into the hands of the princes of Ghūr.

Khusrav Shāh was succeeded by his son Khusrav, who bore the title of Malik. He was a mild and voluptuous prince to whom authority was irksome. The governors of the districts of his small kingdom behaved as independent rulers, but he recked nothing, so long as the means of indulgence was at hand. The districts fell one by one, as will be related in the following chapter, into the hands of Muʿizz-ud-dīn Muhammmand *bin* Sām, the World-burner's nephew, who occupied Ghaznī and ruled the southern portion of the country now known as Afghānistān as the lieutenant of his elder brother, Ghiyās-ud-dīn Muhammad, who governed the now extensive dominions of his family from his capital, Fīrūzkūh in Ghūr. In 1181 Muʿizz-ud-dīn Muhammad appeared before Lahore and compelled Khusrav Malik to surrender, as a token of submission, his finest elephant, and as a hostage, his son. Muhammad then marched to Siālkot, built the fort there and placed one of his own officers in command of it. After his departure Khusrav Malik plucked up courage and besieged Siālkot, but could not take it and returned to Lahore. In 1186 Muhammad again appeared before Lahore and Khusrav sued for peace. He left the city, under a safe conduct, to arrange the terms, but Muhammad violated his engagement, seized him, and occupied Lahore. Khusrav Malik was sent to Ghiyās-ud-dīn at Fīrūzkūh, where he remained a prisoner until 1192, when Ghiyās-ud-dīn and his brother were preparing for hostilities against Sultān Shāh Jalāl-ud-dīn Mahmūd of Khvārazm and put him and his son Bahrām to death as dangerous incumbrances.

[1] According to another account Bahrām, regarding the date of whose death there are several discrepancies, died in 1152, before the burning of Ghazni, and had been succeeded by Khusrav Shah. The T.N. is followed here.

CHAPTER III

MU'IZZ-UD-DĪN MUHAMMAD *BIN* SĀM OF GHŪR AND THE EARLIER SLAVE KINGS OF DELHI

THE history of the Ghaznavids has given us occasional glimpses of the princes of Ghūr and of the circumstances in which, during the conflicts of their powerful neighbours, they gradually rose to prominence. They have usually been described, on insufficient grounds, as Afghāns, but there is little doubt that they were, like the Sāmānids of Balkh, eastern Persians. In 1163 Saif-ud-dīn Muhammad, son and successor of the World-burner, was slain in battle against the Ghuzz Turkmāns, and was succeeded by his cousin, Ghiyās-ud-dīn Muhammad, son of Bahā-ud-dīn Sām, who in 1173 expelled the Ghuzz Turkmāns from Ghaznī and appointed his younger brother Shihāb-ud-dīn, afterwards known as Mu'izz-ud-dīn Muhammad, to the government of that province.

The relations between the brothers exhibit a pleasing contrast to the almost invariable tale of envy, jealousy, and fratricidal strife furnished by the records of other Muslim dynasties. Ghiyās-ud-dīn commanded, until his death, the loyal assistance of his brother, and in return reposed in him a confidence which was never abused and permitted to him a freedom of action which few other eastern rulers have dared to tolerate in a near relation. Muhammad acquired territory and wealth which would have enabled him, had he been so minded, to overthrow his brother and usurp his throne, and was described on his coins 'as the great and victorious Sultan', but the place of honour was always assigned to his brother's name, which was distinguished by epithets denoting his superiority.

In 1175 Muhammad led his first expedition into India. Ismā-'īlian heretics, long freed from the restraining hand of a powerful and orthodox ruler, had for some years borne sway in Multān. Muhammad captured the city, appointed an orthodox governor, and marched to the strong fortress of Uch, which he took by a stratagem. He promised to make the raja's wife, who was on bad terms with her husband, the principal lady in his harem if she would deliver the fortress to him. She declined the honour for herself but secured it for her daughter, caused her husband to be put to death, and surrendered the city. She gained little by her unnatural treachery, for she and her daughter were sent to Ghaznī, ostensibly that they might learn the doctrines and duties of Islam, and there she died soon afterwards, justly scorned by the daughter whom she had sold. The unfortunate girl herself died two years later, never having been Muhammad's wife but in name.

In 1178 Muhammad sustained his first reverse on Indian soil. He rashly led an army by way of Multān, Uch, and the waterless Indian desert against Anhilvāra, or Pātan, the capital of Bhīm the Vāghela, the young raja of Gujarāt. His army arrived before Anhilvāra exhausted by its desert march and utterly unfit to encounter the fresh and numerous army of Bhīm. His troops fought with the valour which religious zeal inspires but were defeated, and compelled to retrace their steps across the inhospitable desert. The sufferings of the retreat far exceeded those of the advance and it was but a miserable remnant of the army that reached Ghaznī.

He was nevertheless able, in the following year, to lead an army to Peshāwar, which he wrested from the feeble grasp of the governor placed there by Khusrav Malik, and in 1181 he led to Lahore the expedition of which the result was the establishment of a fortress at Siālkot.

The later successors of the great Mahmūd had been unable to maintain their position in India by the strength of their own arm and the hostility of the rajas of Jammū had compelled them to ally themselves to the Khokars. The support of Khusrav Malik enabled these tribesmen to repudiate their allegiance to Chakra Deo of Jammū and to resist his demands for tribute and the raja avenged himself by inviting Muhammad to invade the Punjab and promising him his assistance. Muhammad accepted the offer with an alacrity which did little credit to his zeal for Islam, reduced Khusrav to submission as has already been described, and at Chakra Deo's suggestion built the fortress of Siālkot for the purpose of curbing the Khokars. It was at the instance and with the assistance of these tribesmen that Khusrav Malik attacked the fortress after Muhammad's departure, and it was owing to Chakra Deo's aid to the garrison that the siege was unsuccessful. In 1186, when Muhammad invaded the Punjab for the second time, Vijaya Deo, the son and successor of Chakra Deo, aided him against Khusrav Malik, who was treacherously seized and carried to Ghaznī as already described. 'Ali Karmākh, who had hitherto been governor of Multān, was appointed to Lahore, and Muhammad, having thus established himself in India, proceeded, by a series of operations differing entirely from Mahmūd's raids, to the conquest of further territory in that country.

In the winter of 1190-91, the south-eastern boundary of his dominions being then probably the Sutlej, he captured Bhātinda, in the kingdom of Prithvī Rāj[1], the Chauhān raja of Delhi and placed in command of it Qāzī Ziyā-ud-dīn with his contingent of 1200 horse. Muhammad was preparing to return when he heard that Prithvī Rāj was advancing with a vast army to attack him. He turned to meet him and encountered him at Tarāorī, near Karnāl. The Muslims were overpowered by sheer weight of numbers, and both their wings were driven from the field, but the centre still stood fast and Muhammad, leading a furious charge against the Hindu centre, personally encountered the raja's brother, Govind Rāi, and shattered his teeth with his lance, but Govind Rāi drove his javelin through the sultan's arm, and Muhammad, fearing to sacrifice his army by falling, turned his horse's head from the field. The army was now in full flight, and Muhammad, faint from pain and loss of blood, would have fallen, had not a·young Khalj Turk, with great presence of mind, sprung upon his horse behind him until he reached the place where the fugitive army had halted. Here a litter was hastily constructed for him and the army continued its retreat in good order. Prithvī Rāj advanced to Bhātinda and besieged it, but the gallant Ziyā-ud-dīn held out for thirteen months before he capitulated.

Muhammad's sole care, after reaching Ghaznī, was to organise and equip such an army as would enable him to avenge his defeat, and in 1192 he invaded India with 12,000 horse. He was not in time to relieve Bhātinda, but he found Prithvī Rāj encamped at Tarāorī, and adopted tactics which bewildered the Rājput, a slave to tradition. Of the five divisions of his army four, composed of mounted archers, were instructed to attack, in their own style, the flanks and, if possible, the rear of the Hindus, but to avoid hand to hand conflicts and, if closely pressed, to feign flight. These tactics were successfully employed from the morning until the afternoon, when Muhammad, judging that the Hindus were sufficiently perplexed and wearied, charged their centre with 12,000 of the flower of his cavalry. They were completely routed and Prithvī Rāj descended from his elephant and mounted a horse in order to flee more rapidly, but was overtaken near the river Saraswatī and put to death. His brother was also slain and his body was identified by the disfigurement which Muhammad's lance had inflicted in the previous year.

This victory gave Muhammad northern India almost to the

---

[1] Called Rāi Pithaura by Muslim writers.

gates of Delhi. Hānsī, Sāmāna, Guhrām and other fortresses surrendered after the battle of Tarāorī, and the sultan marched to
Ajmer, which he plundered, carrying away numbers of its inhabitants as slaves, but the city, isolated by the desert, was not yet a safe
residence for a Muslim governor, and a son of Prithvī Rāj was
appointed, on undertaking to pay tribute, as governor.

Muhammad appointed as viceroy of his new conquests Qutb-
ud-dīn Aibak, the most trusty of his Turkish officers, who made
Guhrām his headquarters. Qutb-ud-dīn, the real founder of Muslim
dominion in India, had been carried as a slave in his youth from
Turkistān to Nīshāpūr, where he was bought by the local governor
and, being again sold on the death of his master, passed eventually
into the hands of Muhammad. He first attracted his new master's
attention by his lavish generosity, and rose to the highest rank in his
service. His name, Aibak, which has been the subject of some
controversy, means either 'Moon-lord,' and may indicate that he was
born during an eclipse, or 'Moon-face,' an epithet which in the East
suggests beauty, though we learn that he was far from comely. He
was also nicknamed *Shal* ('defective' or 'paralysed') from an injury
which deprived him of the use of one little finger. He was active
and energetic, an accomplished horseman and archer, and sufficiently
well learned, and the lavish generosity which had distinguished his
youth earned for him in later years, when wealth had augmented his
opportunities, the name of *Lak-bakhsh*, or giver of tens of thousands.
Muhammad trusted Aibak as he himself was trusted by his brother,
and left him untrammelled, not only in his administration of the new
conquests, but also in his discretion to extend them.

Towards the close of the rainy season of 1192 an army of Jāts
under a leader named Jatwān, who owed allegiance to Rāja Bhīm of
Anhilvāra, invaded the Hānsī district and compelled Nusrat-ud-dīn,
the Muslim governor, to take refuge in the fortress. Aibak marched
to his relief and in September appeared before Hānsī. The Jāts had
fled, but he followed them so closely that they were compelled to
turn and meet him and were defeated and lost their leader. Aibak
returned to Guhrām and almost immediately set out for Meerut,
captured the fortress from the Hindu chieftain who held it, and thus
established an outpost to the east of the Jumna.

Delhi still remained in the hands of the Chauhān Rājputs and
was a nucleus of aggressive national and religious sentiment and a
formidable obstacle to the progress of the Muslim arms. From
Meerut, therefore, Aibak marched thither, and in December, 1192,

or January, 1193, captured the city which was destined to be the capital of the Islamic power in India. In 1193 he made it his head-quarters, but allowed himself no repose there.

Meanwhile an officer subordinate to Aibak had been carrying the banner of Islam further afield. This was Ikhtiyār-ud-din Muhammad, son of Bakhtyār, of the Turkish tribe of Khalj, which was settled in the Garmsīr between Sīstān and Ghaznī. His mean and unprepossessing appearance and his ungainly build, which enabled him, while standing upright, to reach with his hands the calves of his legs, had long debarred him from employment commensurate with his ambition and his merits, and he had entered the service of Hijabr-ud-dīn Hasan Adīb, an adventurous officer who had con-quered Budaun even before Muhammad had taken Bhātinda, and afterwards that of Malik Hisām-ud-dīn Āghūl Bak, another leader of the vanguard of Islam, who had established himself in Oudh, where Ikhtiyār-ud-dīn received some fiefs between the Ganges and the Son. From this advanced base he led raids into Bihār and Tirhut and took so much booty that large numbers of his own tribe, eager to serve under so fortunate a leader, joined him. With this accession of strength he invaded Bihār, took its capital, Odantapurī, put to death the Buddhist monks dwelling in its great monastery, and returned with his plunder, which included the library of the monastery, to make his obeisance to Aibak, now, in the summer of 1193, established at Delhi. The honours bestowed upon him aroused much envy and jealousy, and intriguers and backbiters were able to freeze the stream of Aibak's favour into the ice of suspicion and aversion ; but their malice overreached itself, for to compass Ikhtiyār-ud-dīn's destruction they attributed to him a foolish boast, that he could overcome an elephant in single combat, and persuaded Aibak that the vaunt should be made good. It had never been uttered, but Ikhtiyār-ud-dīn would not decline the challenge and, against the expectation of all, put the beast to flight. His success regained the favour of Aibak, who dismissed him with fresh honours to Bihār, after conferring on him as a fief his past and future conquests.

After his departure Aibak marched into the Doāb and captured Koil, and a month or two later joined his master with 50,000 horse. Muhammad had invaded India for the purpose of attacking Jai-chand, Raja of Kanauj and Benares, who according to Hindu accounts, had been his ally against Prithvī Rāj, but on discovering that the Muslims were determined to annex northern India, had repented of his unpatriotic alliance and was preparing to attack the intruders. Muhammad halted near Kanauj and sent Aibak to meet Jaichand, who was encamped at Chandwār, now Fīrūzabād, on the Jumna, between Agra and Etāwah. The armies met on the banks of the river, and the Muslims were on the point of giving way when a fortunately aimed arrow struck Jaichand in the eye and he fell dead from his elephant, whereupon the Hindus broke and fled, and were pursued with great slaughter. Jaichand's body, crushed beyond recognition, was found with difficulty, but his attendants recognised it by means of the teeth, which had either been stopped with gold or were false teeth fastened with gold wire. The victorious army pressed on to the fortress of Āsī, near Manaich, where Jaichand had stored his treasure, which was plundered. Thence it marched to Benares where it destroyed several temples and took much booty, and Muhammad then returned to Ghaznī.

Muhammad's policy in Ajmer was not entirely successful. The son of Prithvī Rāj whom he had installed there was illegitimate, and the Rājputs, who resented his subservience to the foreigner, made his birth a pretext for disowning him and elected in his place Hemrāj, the brother of Prithvī Rāj. Hemrāj had molested Aibak when he was besieging Meerut, but had been defeated and driven off. In 1194 Rukn-ud-dīn Hamza, Qavām-ul-Mulk, who had captured and held Ranthambhor, reported that Hemrāj was in rebellion and was marching to attack him. Aibak marched from Delhi to the relief of the fortress, but Hemrāj eluded him and took refuge in the hills of Alwar, the district then known as Mewāt. From this retreat he attacked and captured Ajmer, compelling his nephew to flee for refuge to Ranthambhor, and from Ajmer he dispatched a force under a leader named Jhat Rāi against Delhi. A demonstration by Aibak was sufficient to drive Jhat Rāi back to Ajmer, whither Aibak followed him. Hemrāj came forth to meet his enemy but was defeated and driven back into the city, where he mounted a funeral pyre and perished in the flames, and a Muslim officer was appointed to the government of the city and province.

In 1195 Aibak formed the ambitious design of avenging his master's defeat in Gujarāt and punishing Rāja Bhīm for having molested Nusrat-ul-dīn at Hānsī, and marched to Anhilvāra. Kunwar Pāl, the commander of Bhīm's army, retired before him but was compelled by a close pursuit to turn and stand. He was defeated and slain, and while Bhīm took refuge in a remote corner of his kingdom Aibak plundered his capital and the neighbouring country and returned with much booty to Delhi by way of Hānsī. Muhammad, on receiving Aibak's dispatch announcing his success, summoned him to Ghaznī, where he received him with every demonstration of approval and formally appointed him viceroy of the Muslim dominions in India. Aibak was detained for some time at Ghaznī by a serious illness and shortly after his arrival at Delhi, towards the end of 1196, was called upon to meet his master, who had led an expedition into India, at Hansī. During this campaign Bayāna was captured and was placed under the command of a Turkish slave named Bahā-ud-dīn Tughril, and Muhammad advanced to Gwalior. He found the fortress too strong to be taken by a *coup de main* and he could not spare the time for a regular siege, but the raja was prepared to purchase immunity for himself and his dominions, and in consideration of a promise to pay tribute and the immediate payment of a first instalment he was permitted to retain possession of his state and his fortress.

In the hot season of 1197, when Aibak was at Ajmer, the Mers, who inhabited the neighbourhood of that city, rose in rebellion and invited Rāja Bhīm of Gujarāt to aid them in expelling the Muslims. Aibak heard of these communications, and in spite of the great heat of the season marched from Ajmer and attacked the Mers early one morning before their ally had joined them, but their superior numbers enabled them to maintain the conflict throughout the day, and when the battle was renewed on the following day Bhīm's army arrived and overpowered the Muslims, driving them back into the city. Here Aibak was besieged until the news that a large army was marching from Ghaznī to his relief caused the Mers and Rāja Bhīm's army to retreat. The reinforcements reached Ajmer late in the year, and in December Aibak marched on Anhilvāra by way of Sirohī to avenge his defeat. He found Bhīm's army awaiting him at the foot of the Abū hills in a position so strong that he hesitated to attack it, and his caution enticed the Hindus from the position which constituted their strength. Aibak, now on equal terms with his enemy, attacked shortly after dawn and was obstinately resisted until midday, when the Hindus broke and fled. They suffered severely : 15,000 were slain and 20,000 captured and twenty elephants and much other plunder were taken. Aibak advanced, unopposed, to Anhilvāra, plundered the city and returned with much wealth, of which he transmitted a due proportion to Muhammad and to Ghīyās ud-din.

During the next five years the two brothers were much occupied with the affairs of Khurāsān, and Muhammad had so little leisure to spare for India that the northern provinces enjoyed a period of comparative repose, welcome to the troops after nine years' warfare, and beneficial to the country. We may imagine that the conquerors employed this interval of peace for the establishment of their simple system of government, but of this no details are given, for Muslim historians are concerned almost exclusively with war and court intrigue. There is no reason to believe that the system established by the earlier conquerors differed from that which we find in existence at a later date under Muslim rulers. Military fief-holders were responsible for the preservation of order, for the ordinary executive duties of government, and for the collection of the revenue when it was necessary to use any degree of force, but in matters of detail full use was made of indigenous institutions. Hindu accountants kept the registers in which was recorded the landholder's or cultivator's normal liability to government, Hindu village officials ordinarily collected such revenue as could be collected without the employment of force, and Hindu caste tribunals decided most of the disputes to which Hindus only were parties. Disputes between Muslims were decided by Muhammadan *qazīs* and *muftīs*, and differences between Hindus and their conquerors either by these officials or by the strong hand of the fief-holder or his deputy, whose natural predilection for their co-religionists would be restrained sometimes by a sense of justice but more often by their interest in repressing misconduct likely to lead to disorders.

It must not be supposed that this description applies uniformly to the whole of the territory over which the Muslims pretended to dominion. Extensive tracts often remained under the rule of Hindu rajas or landowners who were permitted to retain their authority on promising to pay tribute or taxes, which they paid when the central authorities was strong and withheld when it was weak. Both the extent and the boundaries of fiefs held by Muslim officers were uncertain and a strong or ruthless fief-holder would extinguish all vestiges of Hindu authority in his fief, and even beyond its borders, while another, weak or accommodating, might deal with lesser Hindu proprietors as the central government dealt with the rajas and great landholders. The history of northern India exhibits, until the middle of the sixteenth century, many instances of the extent to which Hindus regained their power under a weak government, as well as of their sufferings under despots strong enough to indulge their bigotry without restraint.

The five years' interval of peace was limited to the provinces in north-western India under Aibak's immediate control, for Ikhtiyār-ud dīn's activity was not abated. After returning, in 1193, from Delhi to Bihār he hatched schemes of conquest which should extend the dominion of the faithful to the sea on one side and beyond the great mountain barrier of the Himālaya on the other. Lower Bengal was now ruled by Lakshman, of the Sen dynasty, who, having been a posthumous son, had succeeded at his birth to his father's kingdom and was now an aged man dwelling peacefully at Nabadwīpa or Nadiya, which his grandfather had made the capital of Bengal. In 1202[1] Ikhtiyār-ud-dīn left Bihār with a large body of horse, and marched so rapidly on Nadiya that he arrived at the city with no more than eighteen companions. Nadiya was partly deserted at this time, many of its wealthier inhabitants having retired and settled further to the east, owing, it is said, to predictions in ancient books that the city would be captured by the Turks[2], but their flight may be more reasonably attributed to authentic stories of the activity and rapacity of the Muslims than to ancient prophecy. Lakshman Sen, whether from apathy or from confidence, had refused to leave his capital, and when the intruders, who had been permitted to pass through the city under the impression that they were horsedealers from the north, reached his palace gates he was sitting down to a meal. The Muslims cut down the guards and bystanders, burst into the palace, and at once all was uproar and confusion. The raja, in the half-naked state in which a Hindu of high caste is obliged to eat, left his unfinished meal and escaped by boat, and the adventurers were able to hold their own until the rest of the army arrived, when they plundered the treasury of the accumulations of a peaceful reign of eighty years and sacked and destroyed the city[3]. Ikhtiyār-ud-dīn retired to Gaur or Lakhnāwati, where he established himself firmly as governor of Bengal, founded mosques, colleges, and caravanserais, and caused the *Khutba*[4] to be recited in the name of Mu'izz-ud-dīn Muhammad, who had succeeded as sole ruler on the death of his elder brother, Ghiyās-ud-dīn, on February 11, 1203.

Lakshman Sen escaped to Vikrampur, near Sonārgāon and eight miles south-east of Dacca, and from this town, which had been the

---

[1] This date is not quite certain. Some authors place the expedition a year later and one some years earlier.

[2] The predictions, as recorded by Muslim historians, were strangely minute in matters of detail, but these historians wrote after the event, and the original texts which they cite cannot be traced.

[3] Some suspicion rests on the details of this account, which is drawn from Muslim sources.

[4] This is a homily and bidding prayer recited in mosques on Fridays and festivals and contains the name of the ruling sovereign, whose title it formally acknowledges. Among Muslims it is one of the two symbols of sovereignty, the other being the minting of money.

favourite residence of his great-grandfather Balāl Sen, ruled the narrow remnant of his kingdom, in which he was succeeded by his son Mādhav Sen, who, again, was succeeded by his own son Sū Sen, the last of the line.

The peace in northern India was broken by Aibak, who in 1202 attacked Parmāl, the Chandel raja of Kālinjar, whose ancestor had paid tribute to Mahmūd. Parmāl was defeated, and in order to retain possession of his fortress accepted the position of a vassal, but while he was collecting the stipulated tribute suddenly died, and his minister Aja Deo, who aspired to his throne, refused to abide by the treaty and, trusting to a spring which had never been known to fail, resolved to stand the chances of a siege, but a few days after he had closed the gates the hitherto inexhaustible spring dried up, and the citizens, confronted with the prospect of death from thirst incautiously admitted the besiegers without making fresh terms. Aibak punished Aja Deo's treachery by treating the city as one taken by storm. Plunder amounting to far more than the promised tribute was taken, 50,000 captives, male and female, were carried off as slaves, and the temples in the city were converted into mosques. After capturing Kālinjar, Aibak reduced without difficulty Mahoba, the civil capital of the Chandel state, and on his way towards Budaun received Ikhtiyār-ud-dīn, who presented to him the spoils of Nadiya.

Muhammad *bin* Sām sustained at the hands of the Turkmāns of 'Alā-ud-dīn Muhammad Khvārazm Shāh, near Andkhūī, in 1205, a defeat which dealt a fatal blow at his military reputation in India. It was reported, and for some time believed, that he had been killed, and his old enemies the Khokars and some other tribes to the north of the Salt Range rose under the leadership of Rāi Sāl, a petty raja who, having been converted to Islam, had since relapsed. The rebels defeated the deputy governor of Multān and plundered Lahore, and by closing the roads between that city and Ghaznī prevented the remittance of revenue from the Punjab. Muhammad, intent on avenging his defeat at the hands of Khvārazm Shāh, ordered Aibak to deal with the rebellion in India, but this step confirmed the rebels in their belief that the reports of his death were true, for they did not understand the difficulties which confronted him in Central Asia and could not believe that he would entrust to a subordinate a task so important as the suppression of their rebellion. Muhammad at length perceived the necessity for taking the field in person, and on October 20, 1205, set out from Ghaznī for India. He left Peshāwar on November 9 and fell suddenly on the Khokars in a position of their own choosing between the Jhelum and the Chenāb. They withstood him from daybreak until the afternoon with such obstinacy that the tide of battle was only turned by the arrival of Aibak with the army of Hindūstān. The Muslims pursued the Khokars with great slaughter and took so many alive that five Khokar slaves sold in the camp for a *dīnār*. Of the two leaders of the Khokars one, Sarka, was slain and the other, Bakan, made his way to a fortress in the Salt Range but, being pursued thither, saved his life by surrendering. A body of the more determined rebels fled from the fortress into a dense jungle where they perished miserably when the forest was fired by the Muslims.

Muhammad arrived at Lahore on February 25, 1206, and gave his troops permission to return to their homes in order that they might be ready to accompany him on his projected expedition to Khvārazm. On his return towards Ghaznī he was assassinated, on March 15, on the bank of the Indus.

The circumstances of his death are a vexed question. The legend which attributes it to Prithvī Rāj who, according to the bards of the Rājputs had not been slain at Tarāorī but was wounded and taken prisoner and remained, after having been blinded, a captive for the rest of his life, is mentioned by one Muslim historian but may be dismissed without hesitation as a fabrication. Other authorities attribute the deed to some of the Khokars whose homes had so recently been made desolate, but though these were perhaps privy to the design, and, if so, certainly furthered it, the actual assassins appear to have been fanatical Shiahs of the heretical Ismā'īlī sect. A few years before this time these heretics had again established themselves in Khurāsān, where they are still numerous, and held possession of that province until Muhammad crushed them in 1199, and restored his brother's authority. A number of these bound themselves by an oath to slay the persecutor of their faith, and found on this occasion their opportunity.

The body of the murdered sultan was carried to Ghaznī and there buried. His nominal successor was 'Alā-ud-dīn, of the Bāmiyān branch of his family, who was almost immediately supplanted by Mahmūd, the son of Ghiyās-ud-dīn, but these princes were mere pageants, and the real successors were the provincial viceroys, Tāj-ud-dīn Yildiz, governor of Kirmān, and Qutb-ud-dīn Aibak, who assumed the title of Sultan at his master's death and was acknowledged as sovereign by Ikhtiyār-ud-dīn of Bengal and by Nāsir-ud-dīn Qabācha who, having distinguished himself at the disastrous battle of Andkhūī, had in 1205 been appointed governor of Multān and Uch, and had married Aibak's daughter.

We may now conveniently revert to the course of events in Bengal, where Ikhtiyār-ud-dīn, having firmly established himself in Lakhnāwatī, had begun to indulge in dreams of carrying his arms beyond the Himālaya. He had already extended his influence to the foot of these mountains among the Mongoloid tribes, Koch, Mech, and Kachārī, and one chieftain, known after his conversion as 'Alī the Mech, had exchanged his animistic belief for the doctrines of Islam. 'Alī undertook to guide Ikhtiyār-ud-dīn through the great mountains and about the middle of the year 1205 he set out, with an army of 10,000 horse, on his perilous adventure. The interest which this enterprise might have possessed is unfortunately diminished by the impossibility of tracing the adventurer's footsteps, for the vague accounts of historians ignorant of geography preserved in corrupted texts afford us no means of following his course. Having entered into a treaty with the raja of Kāmrūp, who agreed to refrain from molesting him and to assist him, at least with advice, he marched from Debkot in the modern district of Dinājpur, to the banks of a great river which seems to have formed the boundary between his territory and Kāmrūp and followed its course northwards for ten days until he reached a city, perhaps Burdhankot, in the raja's dominions. Here the river was spanned by a stone bridge, and Ikhtiyār-ud-dīn, leaving a force to hold the bridge, set out, against the advice of the raja, who counselled him to wait for the spring, for Tibet. In what direction he marched, or what part of Tibet was his objective, is uncertain, but after fifteen days' marching he reached a strong fortress standing in open country which was well cultivated and thickly populated. The inhabitants joined the garrison of the fortress in opposing the invader and though Ikhtiyār-ud-dīn held his ground throughout the day his losses were very heavy and information received from prisoners, who reported that large reinforcements from a neighbouring city were confidently awaited, convinced him of the necessity for an immediate retirement. During his retreat he paid the penalty of his rashness in advancing so far into an unknown country without securing his communications. The natives had destroyed or obstructed the roads and burnt all vegetation, so that neither fodder nor fuel was procurable and the army was reduced to living on the flesh of its horses. When the river was reached it was discovered that the inhabitants had taken advantage of quarrels between the officers left to secure at least this point to destroy the bridge, that the river was unfordable, and that no boats were at hand. The raja of Kāmrūp perfidiously attacked the retreating army and drove it into the river. Ikhtiyār-ud-dīn succeeded in reaching the opposite bank with about a hundred horsemen, with which sorry remnant of his army he returned to Lakhnāwatī.

This was the greatest disaster which had yet befallen the Muslim arms in India. Armies had been defeated, but Ikhtiyār-ud-dīn's force had been all but annihilated, and it would have been well for him to have perished with it, for he could not show his face in the streets of Lakhnāwatī without encountering the gibes and reproaches of the wives and families of those whom he had led to their death and early in 1206 he took to his bed and died, of grief and mortification, as some authorities assert, but he was in fact murdered by 'Ali Mardān, a leading member of the Khaljī tribe.

On Ikhtiyār-ud-dīn's death the government was assumed by Muhammad bin Shīrān, a Khaljī officer who had acted as one of his deputies during his absence in Tibet. 'Alī Mardān was imprisoned, but escaped and fled to Lahore, where he persuaded Aibak, from whom he concealed his share in Ikhtiyār-ud-dīn's death, to depute an officer from Oudh to make a fresh distribution of fiefs among the officers in Bengal. In the course of the dissensions which arose in connection with this redistribution Muhammad bin Shīrān, 'Alī Mardān's principal enemy, was slain, and 'Alī Mardān persuaded Aibak to appoint him governor.

Nāsīr-ud-dīn Qabācha's acknowledgement of his father-in-law, Aibak, as his sovereign aroused the resentment of Tāj-ud-dīn Yildiz, governor of Kirmān, who claimed the succession to Muhammad in Ghaznī and, in consequence, the sovereignty of the Punjab. He sent an army against Qabācha and drove him from Multān but was in turn attacked by Aibak, defeated, and driven back to Kirmān. Aibak, elated by his success, entered Ghaznī as a conqueror in 1208-09 and celebrated his victory with wine and revelry, while his troops robbed and ill-treated the citizens. They secretly informed Yildiz of the state of affairs and he suddenly marched on Ghaznī and so completely surprised Aibak that he fled to Lahore without striking a blow.

Early in November, 1210, Aibak's horse fell upon him as he was playing chaugān or polo and the high pommel of the saddle pierced his breast, inflicting a wound so severe that he died almost immediately. The nobles, in order to avoid the confusion and strife

inseparable from a delayed or disputed succession, hurriedly proclaimed Ārām Shāh, sometimes described as Aibak's adopted son
but usually believed to have been a son of his body.

The death of Aibak affords us an opportunity of turning again
to the course of events in Bengal. 'Alī Mardān, on receiving the
news, adopted the style of royalty and the title of Sultan 'Alā-ud-
dīn. To his own subjects he was a ruthless and bloody tyrant, and
the Hindu rulers on his borders stood in such awe of him that the
tribute with which they conciliated him filled his treasury. The
rapid growth of his power and prosperity so unhinged his mind
that he believed himself to be monarch of all the known world and
bestowed upon his subjects and suppliants grants of the most
distant kingdoms and provinces. To a poor merchant of Isfahān
who had been robbed of his goods in Bengal he made a grant of
his native city and province, and none dared to suggest that the
grant was but breath and paper. The violence of his temper
increased with his mania until neither the Khaljī noble nor the
humble trader of the bazar was secure, and when he had reigned
for about two years a party among the nobles conspired and slew
him and raised to the throne Hisām-ud-dīn 'Iwaz, governor of the
frontier district of Debkot.

On Aibak's death Qabācha also declared himself independent
in Multān, and nothing was left to Ārām Shāh but Hindūstān and
a part of the Punjab, where the turbulence of the Hindus threatened
his rule and alarmed the stoutest hearts among the Muslims. From
Lahore the new king marched to Delhi but the nobles who had
remained in the capital when Aibak marched to Lahore, and had
had no voice in the election of Ārām, Shāh were loth to accept so
feeble a ruler, and invited Shams-ud-dīn Iltutmish, son-in-law of
Aibak and the foremost of his slaves, to ascend the throne. Iltutmish
marched from Budaun to Delhi, defeated and captured Ārām Shāh,
who met him in the plain before the city, and ascended the throne
in the latter half of 1211. Of Ārām Shāh, who reigned for less than
a year, nothing more is heard.

The new king, who is usually, but incorrectly, styled Altamsh
by European historians, was a Turk of the Ilbarī tribe who, though
of noble birth, had, like Joseph, been sold into slavery by his
brothers. When he and another slave named Aibak Tamghāj were
first carried to Ghaznī Muhammad would not pay the price
demanded for them, but afterwards permitted Qutb-ud-dīn Aibak
to purchase them at Delhi. Tamghāj was slain when Yildiz drove
Qutb-ud-dīn Aibak from Ghaznī, but Iltutmish advanced rapidly

in his master's favour and held in succession the fiefs of Gwalior, captured in 1196, Baran (Bulandshahr) and Budaun.

It was but a remnant of Aibak's wide dominions that Iltutmish gained by his victory over Ārām Shāh. 'Alī Mardān was independent in Bengal, Qabācha seemed likely, besides retaining his independence in Multān and Sind, to extend his authority over Lahore and the upper Punjab, and Yildiz, who held Ghaznī, pretended, as Muhammad's successor, to suzerainty over all the Indian conquests and asserted his claim by issuing to Iltutmish a commission as viceroy. The position of Iltutmish was so precarious that he dared not at once resent the insult, but he neither forgot nor forgave it. Many of the Turkish nobles, even in Hindūstān, chafed against his authority and he was for some time occupied in establishing it in the districts of Delhi, Budaun, Oudh, and Benares, and in the submontane tract of the Himālaya.

In 1214 'Alā-ud-dīn Muhammad Khvārazm Shāh drove Yildiz from Ghaznī, and the fugitive took refuge in Lahore and expelled the officer who held the town for Qabācha. Iltutmish protested against this act of aggression, and when the protest was disregarded marched towards Lahore. Yildiz accepted the challenge and on January 25, 1216, the armies met on the already famous field of Tarāorī. Yildiz was defeated and taken, and after being led through the streets of Delhi was sent to Budaun, where he was put to death in the same year.

After the overthrow of Yildiz, Qabācha again occupied Lahore, but in 1217 Iltutmish expelled him from the city and recovered the upper Punjab.

In 1221 the effects of the raids of the heathen Mughuls which afterwards became a source of constant anxiety to the sultans of Delhi, first made themselves felt in India. These savages, under their leader, the terrible Chingiz Khān, drove 'Alā-ud-dīn Muhammad Khvārazm Shāh from his throne, and his son, Jalāl-ud-dīn Mangbarnī, took refuge in Lahore and sent an envoy to Iltutmish to beg for an asylum in his dominions. The fugitive and his 10,000 troops were most unwelcome guests on the frontier, and Iltutmish, having put the envoy to death on the pretext that he was attempting to stir up sedition, replied that the climate of Lahore was likely to be prejudicial to Mangbarnī's health and offered him a residence near Delhi. The offer was declined and Mangbarnī retired towards the Salt Range, where he first attacked and defeated the Khokars but afterwards found it to his advantage to enter into an alliance with them, and by a marriage with the daughter of their chief, who had long been at enmity with Qabācha, acquired an interest in an intestine feud. With his new allies he attacked Qabācha and compelled him to comply with an exorbitant demand for tribute. Rumours that Chingiz had discovered his retreat and purposed to follow him thither seriously perturbed him, and by extorting a further sum from Qabācha and plundering Sind and northern Gujarāt he amassed treasure sufficient to enable him to flee, in 1224, to Persia.

The defeat and humiliation of Qabācha had profited Iltutmish, who was at leisure, after Mangbarnī's flight, to turn his attention to Bengal, where Hisām-ud-dīn 'Iwaz had assumed the title of Sultan Ghiyās-ud-dīn, and in 1225 he led his army through Bihār. On his approach 'Iwaz submitted to him, abandoned the use of the royal title, acknowledged his sovereignty and presented to him, as tribute, thirty-eight elephants and much treasure, and Iltutmish, after appointing his eldest son, Nāsir-ud-dīn Mahmūd, governor of Oudh, and establishing his own governor in Bihār, returned to Delhi.

In 1226 Iltutmish recovered Ranthambhor, which, in the confusion which followed Aibak's death, had fallen into the hands of the Hindus, and in the following year took Mandāwar, a strong fortress eight miles north of Bijnor held by Rahup, an Agarwāl Baniya who had captured it from a prince of the Parihar dynasty. Having thus established his authority in Hindūstān and Bengal he decided that the time had come to deal with Qabācha, who still maintained his independence in Sind and the lower Punjab and had not abandoned his pretensions to the upper province. He marched first towards Uch, and Qabācha withdrew to Ahrāwat[1] on the Indus and moored his boats near his camp, leaving his minister to defend Uch. As Iltutmish approached Uch his lieutenant, Nāsir-ud-dīn Aiyitim, advanced from Lahore and besieged Multān, and Qabācha took to his boats and fled to the island-fortress of Bakhar, in the Indus, leaving his minister to follow him with the treasure stored at Uch. On February 9, 1228, Iltutmish arrived at Uch and opened the siege, at the same time dispatching a force under his minister, Kamāl-ud-dīn Muhammad Junaidī, entitled Nizām-ul-Mulk, in pursuit of Qabācha, who in his despair sent 'Alā-ud-dīn Bahrām Shāh, his son by Aibak's daughter, to make terms. Bahrām was successful, and in accordance with the treaty Uch was surrendered on May 4, but Junaidī was either not informed of the

---

[1] This place cannot now be identified and is not to be sought on the Indus, which has changed its course considerably since the thirteenth century.

treaty or wilfully disregarded it, for he continued- to besiege Bakhar, and Qabācha was drowned in the Indus. The circumstances of his death are variously related ; some writers say that he was accidentally drowned in attempting to escape, and others that he committed suicide by throwing himself into the river. His death ended the campaign, and his troops transferred their services to Iltutmish, who returned to Delhi in August, leaving Junaidī to complete the conquest of lower Sind. Malik Sinān-ud-dīn Chatīsar, eleventh of the Sūmra line, a Rājput dynasty the later members of which accepted Islam, submitted and was permitted to retain his territory as a vassal of Iltutmish, whose dominions were thus extended to the sea.

Iltutmish, as a good Muslim, had, while still employed in establishing his authority, sought from the 'Abbasid Caliph of Baghdād confirmation of his title and he was gratified by the arrival, on February 8, 1229, of the Caliph's envoy, who invested him with a robe of honour and delivered to him a patent which conveyed the Caliph's recognition of his title as Sultan of India.

After the retirement of Iltutmish from Bengal in 1225 'Iwaz rebelled, expelled the king's governor from Bihār and ill-treated those who had acknowledged his authority. The governor fled to Oudh and in 1227 Mahmūd, the son of Iltutmish, invaded Bengal from that province to punish the rebel. 'Iwaz being absent on an expedition; he occupied Lakhnāwatī without opposition, and when 'Iwaz returned he defeated him, captured him, put him to death, and imprisoned the Khaljī nobles who had formed a confederacy to oppose the suzerainty of Delhi[1].

Mahmūd now governed Bengal as his father's deputy, and made the most of an opportunity which was closed by his early death in April, 1229, for he defeated and slew raja Britu, possibly the raja of Kāmrūp, who had, until that time, defeated the Muslims on every occasion on which they had attacked him. On Mahmūd's death Balkā, the son of 'Iwaz, caused himself to be proclaimed king of Bengal under the title of Ikhtiyār-ud-dīn Daulat Shāh Balkā, and it was not until the winter of 1230-31 that Iltutmish was able to lead an army into Bengal to crush the rebellion. Balkā was captured and probably put to death, and 'Alā-ud-dīn Jānī was appointed governor of Bengal.

---

[1] According to another account 'Iwaz had died before this time and it was his son Nāsir-ud-dīn who invaded Bihār and was afterwards defeated and slain by Mahmūd, but this account and another, which describes Nāsir-ud-dīn as Balkā, seem to be based on a confusion of the events of 1227 with those of 1229-31.

The king's next task was the recovery of his fief, Gwalior, which, since the death of Aibak, had been captured by the Hindus, and was now held by the raja Mangal Bhava Deo, son of Māl Deo[1], and in February, 1232, he invested the fortress, which he besieged until December 12, when the raja fled by night and succeeded in making his escape. Iltutmish entered the fortress on the following morning and, enraged by the stubborn resistance which he had encountered and by the raja's escape, sullied his laurels by causing 700 Hindus to be put to death in cold blood. On January 16, 1233, he set out on his return march to Delhi, where, in this year, he purchased the slave Bahā-ud-dīn Balban, who eventually ascended the throne as Ghiyās-ud-dīn Balban.

Iltutmish had now established his authority throughout the dominions which Aibak had ruled, and in order to fulfil the duty of a Muslim ruler towards misbelieving neighbours and to gratify his personal ambition set himself to extend those dominions by conquest. In 1234 he invaded Mālwa, captured the city of Bhīlsa, and advanced to Ujjain, which he sacked, and, after demolishing the famous temple of Mahākālī and all other temples in the city, carried off to Delhi a famous *lingam*, an image of Vikramāditya, and many idols. The *lingam* is said by some to have been buried at the threshold of the Friday mosque of Old Delhi, and by others to have been buried at the foot of the great column of red sandstone built by Iltutmish.

This famous column, known as the Qutb Minār, was founded in 1231-32 in honour of the saint, Khvāja Qutb-ud-dīn Bakhtyār Kāki, of Ūsh, near Baghdād, who, after residing for some time at Ghaznī and Multān, settled at Delhi, and lived at Kilokhrī, highly honoured by Iltutmish, until his death on December 7, 1235. The name of the column has no reference, as is commonly believed, to Qutb-ud-dīn Aibak, the master and patron of Iltutmish.

After the king's return from Mālwa a serious religious disturbance broke out at Delhi, where a large community of fanatics of the Ismā'īlī sect had gradually established itself. They may have been irritated by persecution but they appear to have believed that if they could compass the king's death they might be able to establish their own faith as the state religion. They plotted to assassinate Iltutmish when he visited the great mosque for the Friday prayers, which he was wont to attend unostentatiously and without guards. One Friday, accordingly, while the congregation was at prayers, a large body of Ismā'īlīs ran into the mosque armed,

<hr>

[1] Otherwise Bīrbal Deo.

drew their swords, and attempted to cut their way through the
kneeling multitude to the Sultan, but before they could reach him
he made his escape and, the alarm having been given, the people
crowded the roofs, walls, and gateways of the mosque and with
a shower of arrows and missiles annihilated the heretics. Such
adherents of the sect as remained were diligently sought and were
put to death.

In the winter of 1235-36 Iltutmish led an expedition against
the Khokars, whose hostility to the Muslim rulers of India had
survived the extinction of the dynasty of Ghūr, but on his way he
was stricken with an illness so severe that it was necessary to carry
him back to Delhi in a litter. As his life was ebbing the courtiers,
desirous of averting the horrors of a disputed succession urged him
to name his successor. Mahmūd, the only one of his sons who,
having reached maturity had shown any promise, was dead, and
the dying monarch named his daughter Raziyya. The courtiers,
scandalised by this suggestion, urged the insuperable objection of
her sex, and the king, languidly replying that they would find her
a better man than any of her brothers, turned his face to the wall
and died, on April 29, 1236[1], after a reign of twenty-six years.

Iltutmish was the greatest of all the Slave Kings. His achievements were hardly equal to those of his master, but he never had,
as Aibak had, the moral and material support of a great empire.
What he accomplished he accomplished by himself, often in the
face of great difficulties, and he added to the dominions of Aibak,
which he found dismembered and disorganised, the provinces of
Sind and Mālwa. That he was even more profuse than his master
is little to his credit, for the useless and mischievous prodigality of
eastern rulers is more often the fruit of vanity than of any finer
feeling, and at a court at which a neat epigram or a smart repartee
is almost as profitable as a successful campaign the resources of a
country are wasted on worthless objects.

The courtiers, disregarding their dying master's wishes, raised
to the throne his eldest surviving son, Rukn-ud-dīn Fīrūz, who had
proved himself, as governor of Budaun, to be weak, licentious and
worthless. The nobles assembled at the capital returned to their
fiefs with well-founded misgivings, and Fīrūz, relieved of the restraint of their presence, devoted himself entirely to pleasure, and
squandered on the indulgence of his appetites the treasure which

---

[1] The oldest extant authority is here followed. Other historians give dates
corresponding with April 17, May 2, and May 5. One gives a date corresponding
with May 19, 1237, but this is certainly incorrect, and is probably due to a scribe's
error.

his father had amassed for the administration and defence of the empire. He took a childish delight in riding through the streets on an elephant and scattering gold among the rabble, and so neglected public business that the direction of affairs fell into the hands of his mother, Shāh Turkān, who, having been a handmaid in the harem, now avenged the slights which she had endured in the days of her servitude. Some of the highly born wives of the late king were put to death with every circumstance of indignity and those whose lives were spared were subjected to gross and humiliating contumely.

The incompetence and sensuality of Fīrūz and the mischievous activity of his mother excited the disgust and indignation of all, and passive disaffection developed into active hostility when the mother and son barbarously destroyed the sight of Qutb-ud dīn, the infant son of Iltutmish. Nor was intestine disorder the only peril which threatened the kingdom, for the death of Iltutmish had been the opportunity of a foreign enemy. Malik Saif-ud-dīn Hasan Qarlugh, a Turk who now held Ghaznī, Kirmān and Bāmiyān, invaded the upper Punjab and, turning southwards, appeared before the walls of Multān. Saif-ud-dīn Aibak, governor of Uch, attacked and routed him and drove him out of India, but to foreign aggression the more serious peril of domestic rebellion immediately succeeded. Ghiyās-ud-dīn Muhammad, a younger son of Iltutmish, rebelled in Oudh, detained a caravan of treasure dispatched from Bengal, and plundered many towns to the east of Jumna, and 'Izz-ud-dīn rebelled in Budaun. In the opposite direction the governors of Multān, Hānsī and Lahore formed a confederacy which, to within a distance of ninety miles from Delhi, set the royal authority at naught. In Bengal no pretence of subordination remained. In 1233 'Izz-ud-dīn Tughril Taghān Khān had succeeded Saif-ud-dīn Aibak as governor of the province, but Aor Khān, who held the fief of Debkot, had established his independence in the country to the north and east of the Ganges and had recently attempted to expel Tughril from Lakhnāwatī. He had been defeated and slain, but neither antagonist had dreamt of appealing to Delhi, and Tughril, who now ruled the whole of Bengal, was bound by no ties, either of sentiment or interest, to the unworthy successor of Aibak and Iltutmish.

When Fīrūz awoke to a sense of his danger his situation was already desperate. He turned first to attack the confederacy which threatened him from the north-west, but as he was leaving Delhi he was deserted by his minister Junaidī, who fled and joined 'Izz-ud-dīn Jānī at Koil, whence both marched to join the confederates of the Punjab. Fīrūz continued his march, but had not advanced beyond the neighbourhood when the officers with him and the slaves of his household murdered two of his secretaries and other civil officials, including Junaidī's son, and at the same time the news of a serious revolt at Delhi recalled him to the capital. His mother had made preparations for putting to death his half-sister Raziyya, whose abilities she regarded as a menace to his authority, but the populace, aware of the high esteem in which the princess had been held by her father, rose in her defence, and before Fīrūz could reach Delhi his mother was a prisoner in the hands of the victorious rebels. Those who had defied his authority at Tarāorī deserted him and joined the people of Delhi in raising Raziyya to the throne, and Fīrūz, who took refuge in Kilokhrī was seized and put to death on November 9, 1236, after a reign of six months and seven days.

The task which lay before the queen would have taxed even her father's powers. Junaidī and the governors of Multān, Hānsī, Lahore and Budaun, who were marching on Delhi, had all been implicated in excluding her from the throne, and still declined to recognise her. She summoned to her aid Nusrat-ud-dīn, who had been appointed to Budaun after the defection of 'Izz-ud-dīn Jānī, but before he could cross the Ganges he was defeated by the confederates, in whose hands he died, and they besieged her in her capital, but she marched out and encamped on the banks of the Jumna. She was not strong enough either to give or accept battle, but she turned her proximity to their camp to good account and by means of dexterous intrigues fomented distrust and dissension among them. She induced 'Izz-ud-dīn Jānī and Ayāz of Multān to visit her and to treat for the betrayal of some of their associates, and then circulated in the rebel camp an account of all that had passed at the conference. Consternation fell upon all, no man could trust his neighbour, and Saif-ud-dīn Kūjī of Hānsī, 'Alā-ud-dīn Jānī of Lahore, and Junaidī, who were to have been surrendered to her, mounted their horses and fled, but were pursued by her cavalry. Jānī was overtaken and slain near Pāel, Kūjī and his brother were taken alive and put to death after a short imprisonment, and Junaidī fled into the Sirmur hills, where he died.

Raziyya's astuteness thus dissolved the confederacy and established her authority in Hindūstān and the Punjab, where Ayāz was rewarded for his desertion of his associates with the government of Lahore in addition to that of Multān, and Khvāja Muhazzib-ud-dīn Husain, who had been assistant to the fugitive minister, Junaidī, succeeded him in his office and in his title of Nizām-ul-Mulk. The queen's energy and decision secured for her also the adhesion of the governors of the more distant provinces of Bengal and Sind, who voluntarily tendered their allegiance, but she found it necessary to send a force to the relief of Ranthambhor, where the Muslim garrison had been beleaguered by the Hindus since the death of Iltutmish. Qutb-ud-dīn Husain, who commanded the relieving force, drove off the Hindus, but for some unexplained reason withdrew the garrison and dismantled the fortress.

Raziyya now laid aside female attire, and appeared in public, both in the court and in the camp, clothed as a man and unveiled. This seems to have given no cause for scandal, but she aroused the resentment of the nobles by the appointment of an African named Jalāl-ud-dīn Yāqūt to the post of master of the horse, and by distinguishing him with her favour. Later historians suggest or insinuate that there was impropriety in her relations with him, but the contemporary chronicler makes no such allegation, and it is unnecessary to believe that she stooped to such a connexion, for the mere advancement of an African was sufficient to excite the jealousy of the Turkish nobles, who formed a close corporation.

Notwithstanding the vindictive zeal with which Iltutmish had pursued Ismā'īlian and Carmathian heretics, some appear to have escaped death, and Delhi now again harboured large numbers of these turbulent fanatics, who had assembled from various provinces of the kingdom and were excited by the harangues of a Turk named Nūr-ud-dīn, a zealous preacher and proselytizer. On Friday, March 5, 1237, the heretics made a second organised attempt to overthrow the established religion, and to the number of a thousand entered the great mosque from two directions and fell upon the congregation. Many fell under their swords and others were killed by the press of those who attempted to escape, but in the meantime the Turkish nobles assembled their troops and, aided by many of the congregation who had gained the roof of the mosque and thence hurled missiles on their foes, entered the courtyard and slaughtered the heretics to a man.

Discontent in the capital bred disaffection in the provinces. By the death of Rashīd-ud-dīn 'Alī the command of the fortress of Gwalior had devolved upon Ziyā-ud-dīn Junaidī, a kinsman of the late minister. He was believed to be ill-disposed towards the government, and on March 19, 1238, both he and the historian Minhāj-ud-dīn were compelled by the governor of Baran to leave Gwalior for Delhi. The historian cleared his reputation and was restored to favour, but of Junaidī nothing more is heard. A more formidable rebel was Ayāz, governor of the Punjab, who, resenting Yāqūt's influence at court, repudiated his allegiance to the queen. Towards the end of 1239 Raziyya marched into the Punjab to reduce him to obedience, and Ayāz submitted without a contest, but was deprived of the government of Lahore and compelled to retire to Multān. From this district he was shortly afterwards expelled by Saif-ud dīn Hasan Qarlugh, who, having in 1230 been driven by the Mughuls from Kirmān and Ghaznī, had retired into Sind, where he had been awaiting an opportunity of establishing himself to the east of the Indus.

Raziyya returned to Delhi on March 15, 1240, but on April 3 was again compelled to take the field. The Turkish nobles, headed by the lord chamberlain, Ikhtiyār-ud-dīn Aitigīn, resented the power and influence of Yāqūt and instigated Ikhtiyār-ud-dīn Altūniya, governor of Bhātinda, to rebel. When the army reached Bhātinda the discontented nobles slew Yāqūt, imprisoned Raziyya, whom they delivered into the custody of Altūniya, and directed their confederates at Delhi to raise to the throne Mu'izz-ud-dīn Bahrām, third son of Iltutmish and half-brother of Raziyya. Bahrām was proclaimed on April 22, and when the army returned to Delhi on May 5, its leaders formally acknowledged him as their sovereign, but made their allegiance conditional on the appointment of Aitigīn as regent for one year. Aitigīn married the king's sister and usurped all the power and most of the state of royalty, and Bahrām, chafing under the regent's arrogance and the restraint to which he was subjected, on July 30 incited two Turks to stab, in his presence, both Aitigīn and the minister, Nizām-ul-Mulk. Aitigīn was killed on the spot, but the minister was only wounded, and made his escape. To save appearances the assassins suffered a brief imprisonment, but were never brought to punishment, and Bahrām appointed as lord chamberlain Badr-ud-dīn Sunqar, a man of his own choice.

Meanwhile Altūniya was bitterly disappointed by the result of his rebellion. The courtiers had made him their catspaw, and had appropriated to themselves all honours and places, leaving him unrewarded. Aitigīn was dead, Nizām-ul-Mulk was discredited, and there was nobody to whom the disappointed conspirator could turn. He released Raziyya from her prison, married her, and, having assembled a large army, marched to Delhi with the object of replacing his newly-wedded wife on her throne, but on October 13 Bahrām defeated him near Kaithal, and on the following day he and Raziyya were murdered by the Hindus whom they had summoned to their assistance.

The situation at court was now extremely complicated. Sunqar, the new lord chamberlain, was as arrogant and as obnoxious to his master as his predecessor had been. Nizām-ul-Mulk, who had condoned the attempt on his life and still held office as minister, resented, equally with Bahrām, Sunqar's usurpation of authority, and allied himself with the king. Sunqar perceived that his life would not be safe as long as Bahrām reigned and conspired to depose him, but committed the error of confiding in Nizām-ul-Mulk. He would not believe that the minister had really forgiven Bahrām and could not perceive that he was subordinating his resentment to his interest. He received Sunqar's emissary apparently in privacy, but as soon as he had departed dispatched a confidential servant who had been concealed behind a curtain to acquaint Bahrām with what he had heard. Bahrām acted with promptitude and decision ; he rode at once to the meeting to which Nizām-ul-Mulk had been summoned and compelled the conspirators to return with him to the palace. Sunqar was dismissed from his high office, but his influence among the great Turkish nobles, or slaves, who were now known as 'the Forty' saved his life for the time, and his appointment to Budaun removed him from the capital. Three other leading conspirators fled from the city, and in November, 1241, Sunqar's return from Badaun without permission gave the king a pretext for arresting him and putting him to death. This necessary act of severity greatly incensed the Forty.

The consideration of the position of the Forty affords a convenient opportunity for an explanation of the name by which the dynasty under which they acquired their influence is known, for to most Europeans the appellation 'Slave Kings' must appear to be a contradiction in terms. In an eastern monarchy every subject is, in theory, the slave of the monarch and so styles himself, both in conversation and in correspondence. To be the personal slave of the monarch is therefore no disgrace, but a distinction, and, as eastern history abundantly proves, a stepping-stone to dignity and power. The Mamlūk or Slave Sultans of Egypt are a case in point. The Turks were at this time the most active and warlike people of Asia, and the Ghaznavids, themselves sprung from a Turkish slave, the princes of Ghūr, and other houses, surrounded themselves with slaves of this nation who, often before they received manumission, filled the highest offices in the state. Loyal service sometimes earned for them a regard and esteem which their master withheld from his own sons, born in the purple and corrupted from their cradles by flattery and luxury. A faithful slave who had filled with credit the highest offices was sometimes rewarded with the hand of his master's daughter in marriage, and was preferred to an unworthy or degenerate son or nephew. Alptigīn had been the slave of 'Abd-ul-Malik the Sāmānid and Sabuktigīn the slave and son-in-law of Alptigīn. Qutb-ud-dīn Aibak was Muhammad's viceroy in India for some time before he received manumission, and succeeded his master in the Indian conquests. He was indeed succeeded by his son, but Ārām Shāh was almost immediately compelled to make way for Iltutmish, Aibak's son-in-law and the ablest of his slaves. During the reign of Iltutmish the leading Turks formed themselves into a college of forty, which divided among its members all the great fiefs of the empire and all the highest offices in the state. The commanding genius of Iltutmish preserved the royal dignity intact, but in the reigns of his children the power of the Forty was ever increasing. Raziyya lost her throne by her preference for one who was not of their number and her brother Bahrām was no more than their nominee. There can be no doubt that the throne itself would ordinarily have been the prize of one of the Forty had not the jealousies of all prevented them from yielding precedence to one. They were thus content to own the nominal authority of one or other of the offspring of Iltutmish, but their compact with Bahrām at the time of his accession clearly indicated their determination to retain all authority for themselves, and the king, by destroying one of their number, sealed his fate.

Bahrām was friendless, for the crafty Nizām-ul-Mulk, who had assumed the mask of loyalty for the purpose of destroying an enemy, so dexterously concealed his betrayal of Sunqar's plot that he retained the confidence of the Forty, whose resentment against Bahrām was so strong that it was not even temporarily allayed by the invasion of a foreign enemy who deprived the kingdom of a province. The Mughuls, who had expelled the Qarlugh Turks from Ghaznī, now appeared before Multān under their leader, Bahādur Tāir, the lieutenant of Chaghatai Khān and of his grandson Hulāgū. Kabīr Khān Ayāz, who had expelled Saif-ud-dīn Hasan Qarlugh and re-established himself in Multān, confronted them with such resolution that they turned aside and marched to Lahore, a more tempting prey. The citadel was ill-furnished with stores, provisions, and arms and the citizens were not unanimous in opposition to the invaders, for the merchants, who were accustomed to trade in Khurāsān and Turkistān, were largely dependent on the goodwill of the Mughuls and held their passports and permits, which were indispensable in those countries and might even protect them at

Lahore. The garrison was weak and the governor relied on assistance from Delhi which never reached him.

The feeble-minded king had now entrusted his conscience to the keeping of a *darvīsh* named Ayyūb, at whose instigation he put to death an influential theologian who was highly esteemed by the Forty, and thus still further estranged that influential body. On learning of the Mughul invasion he ordered his army to march to the relief of Lahore, but the nobles, fearing lest their absence from the capital should give him an opportunity of breaking their power, hesitated to obey. Procrastination served them for a time but they were at length compelled to depart, and Nizām-ul-Mulk employed their resentment and their apprehensions for the purpose of avenging the king's attempt on his life. When the army reached the Sutlej he secretly reported that the Turkish nobles were disaffected and sought the king's sanction to their destruction. The shallow Bahrām, suspecting no guile, readily consented, and the minister exhibited to the Forty his order approving their execution, and easily persuaded them to return to Delhi with a view to deposing him.

Qarāqush, the governor of Lahore, defended the city to the best of his ability, but the dissensions among the citizens and the misconduct of his troops caused him to despair of success, and after burying his treasure he fled by night, leaving the city on the pretext of making a night attack on the besiegers' camp. On the following day, December 22, 1241, the Mughuls took the town by storm. They suffered heavy losses, including that of their leader, in the street fighting which ensued, but before retiring they annihilated the citizens and razed the walls to the ground. Qarāqush returned, recovered his treasures and retired to Delhi.

The army, in open rebellion, arrived at Delhi on February 22, 1242, and besieged the king in the White Fort until the month of May. He had received an accession of strength by the adhesion of Qarāqush and one other faithful Turkish noble but he had fallen under the influence of a slave named Mubārak Farrukhī, at whose instance he committed the supreme folly of imprisoning these two nobles, and the same pernicious influence restrained him from coming to terms with the Forty, who were ready, after more than two months' fighting, to secure their safety by an honourable composition. Nizām-ud-dīn seduced from their allegiance, by large bribes, the ecclesiastics, who were the king's principal supporters, and on May 10 the city and fortress were captured by the confederate nobles, and Bahrām was put to death five days later.

On the capture of the city 'Izz-ud-dīn Balban, entitled Kishlū Khān, caused himself to be proclaimed king, but his action was repudiated by his associates, who assembled at the tomb of Iltutmish to determine the succession. Their choice fell upon 'Alā-ud-dīn Mas'ūd, the son of Fīrūz Shāh, and Qutb-ud-dīn Husain was appointed regent. Nizām-ul-Mulk was permitted at first to retain office as minister, but so disgusted the nobles by his arrogance that on October 28 he was put to death, and Qarāqush was made lord chamberlain. Kishlū Khān was consoled for his disappointment with the fiefs of Nāgaur, Mandāwar, and Ajmer, and the gift of an elephant.

At the beginning of Mas'ūd's reign the governor of Budaun conducted a successful campaign against the Rājputs of Katehr, the later Rohilkhand, but was shortly afterwards poisoned while revolving schemes of wider conquest, and Sanjar, entitled Gurait Khān, having ensured the obedience of the native landholders of Oudh, invaded Bihār, where the Hindus had taken advantage of the dissensions among their conquerors to re-establish their dominion. He plundered the province, but was slain before the walls of its capital. While these events were occurring in the eastern provinces the Qarlugh Turks again attacked Multān and were repulsed, but in this achievement the kingdom had no part, for Ayāz, after turning aside, unaided, the Mughul, had renounced his allegiance to Delhi and his son, Abu Bakr, now ruled Multān as an independent sovereign. The kingdom had thus lost Bengal and Bihār on the east and on the west and north-west Multān, Sind, and the upper Punjab, wasted by Mughuls and occupied by the Khokars.

After the death of Nizām-ul-Mulk the office of minister was allotted to Najm-ud-dīn Abu Bakr and that of lord chamberlain, with the fief of Hānsī, on Bahā-ud-dīn Balban, who was afterwards entitled Ulugh Khān and eventually ascended the throne. He will henceforth be designated Balban, the ambitious 'Izz-ud-dīn Balban being described by his title, Kishlū Khān.

In December, 1242, Tughril, governor of Bengal and the most powerful of the satraps, who resented Kurait Khān's invasion of Bihār, though it had temporarily passed out of his possession, marched to Kara, on the Ganges above Allahabad, with the object of annexing to his government of Bengal that district and the province of Oudh, but the historian Minhāj-ud-dīn, who was accredited to his camp as the emissary of Tamar Khān, the new governor of Oudh, succeeded in persuading him to return peaceably to Bengal.

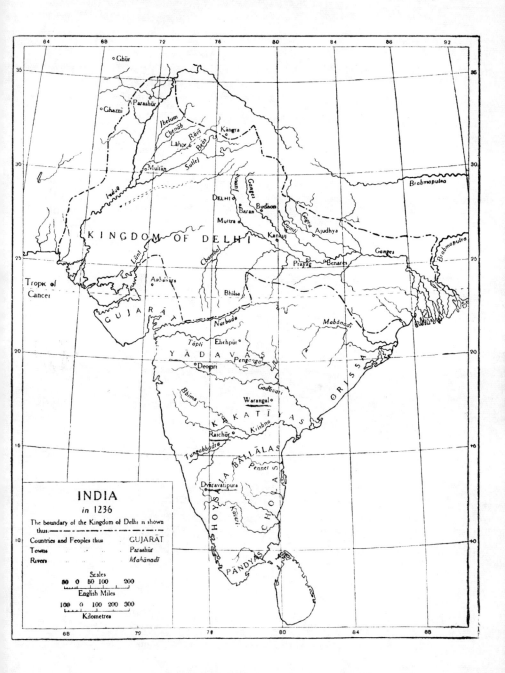

INDIA
in 1236

The boundary of the Kingdom of Delhi is shown
thus
Countries and Peoples thus   GUJARĀT
Towns   .   .   Parashūr
Rivers   .   .   .   Mahānadī

Scales
50 0 50 100   200
English Miles
100 0 100 200 300
Kilometres

Mas'ūd now released from confinement his two uncles, Nāsir-
ud-dīn Mahmūd[1], who afterwards ascended the throne, and Jalāl-
ud-dīn, and appointed one to the government of Bahrāich and the
other to that of Kanauj, in which situations they acquitted themselves well.

Towards the end of 1243 the raja of Jaipur in Cuttack, called
Jājnagar by Muslim historians, invaded and plundered some of the
southern districts of Bengal, and in March, 1244, Tughril marched
to punish him and met the Hindu army on April 16, on the northern
bank of the Mahānadī. The Hindus were at first driven back, but
rallied and defeated the Muslims, among whom a supposed victory
had, as usual, relaxed the bonds of discipline. Tughril was followed,
throughout his long retreat to his capital, by the victorious Hindus,
who appeared before the gates of Lakhnāwatī[2], but retired on
hearing that Tamar Khān was marching from Oudh to the relief of
Tughril.

Tamar Khān arrived before Lakhnāwatī on April 30, 1245, and,
alleging that his orders authorised him to supersede Tughril, demanded the surrender of the city. Tughril refused to comply and
on May 4 was defeated in a battle before the walls and driven into
the town. Peace was made by the good offices of Minhāj-ud-dīn,
and Tughril surrendered the city but was permitted to retire with
all his treasure, elephants, and troops, to Delhi, where he was
received with much honour on July 11 and was appointed, a month
later, to the government of Oudh, vacated by Tamar He died in
Oudh on the day (March 9, 1247) on which Tamar, who was then
in rebellion, died at Lakhnāwatī.

Later in 1245 a large army of Mughuls under Manqūta invaded
India, drove from Multān Hasan Qarlugh, whose second attempt
at ousting Abu Bakr had been successful, and besieged Uch, but
raised the siege and retired when they heard that the king, who
was marching to its relief, had reached the Beās.

The character of Mas'ūd had gradually succumbed to the
temptations of his position, and he had become slothful, impatient

---

[1] Not to be confounded with his elder brother, also named Mahmūd, whohad
died, as governor of Bengal, during the reign of his father, Iltutmish.

[2] This is the event regarding which so many historians, both Eastern and Western
have been misled by a misreading in the *Tabaqāt-i-Nāsiri*, due to the ignorance or
carelessness of a scribe, who substituted for the Persian words meaning 'the misbelievers of Jājnagar' a corruption which might be read 'the infidels of Chingīz
Khān.' Much ink has been spilt over the question, and much ingenuity has been
displayed in conjectures as to the route by which the Mughuls reached lower Bengal,
but the question has now been laid to rest. Chingīz Khān had, by this time, been
dead for eighteen years, and neither he nor any of his Mughuls ever invaded Bengal.

of the tedium of business, and inordinately addicted to drink, sensuality, and the chase. Rebellions, which he lacked the strength or the energy to suppress, rendered him apprehensive and suspicious of all around him, and his severity and lack of discrimination in punishment alienated from him the Forty, who now turned their eyes towards his uncle, Nāsir-ud-dīn Mahmūd, a youth of seventeen or eighteen, who was nominally governor of Bahrāich. When their invitation reached him his mother, an ambitious and resourceful woman, spread a report that her son was sick and must go to Delhi for treatment. She placed him in a litter and sent him from Bahrāich with a large retinue of servants. When night fell the prince was covered with a woman's veil and set on a horse, and the cavalcade pressed on to Delhi with such caution and expedition that none but the conspirators was aware of his arrival in the city.

On June 10, 1246, Mas'ūd was deposed and thrown into prison, where he perished shortly afterwards, doubtless by violence, and Mahmūd was enthroned in the Green Palace.

Of Mahmūd, who was an amiable and pious prince, but a mere puppet, absurd stories are told by the later historians. He is said to have produced every year two copies of the Koran, written with his own hand, the proceeds of the sale of which provided for his scanty household, consisting only of one wife, who was obliged to cook for him, as he kept no servant. This story, which is told of one of the early Caliphs, is not new, and, as related of Mahmūd, is not true, for he is known to have had more than one wife. His principal wife was Balban's daughter, who would certainly not have endured such treatment, and as he presented forty slaves, on one occasion, to the sister of the historian Minhāj-ud-dīn it can hardly be doubted that his own household was reasonably well supplied in this respect. The truth seems to be that the young king possessed the virtues of continence, frugality and practical piety, rare among his kind, and had a taste in calligraphy which led him to employ his leisure in copying the Koran, and that these merits earned for him exaggerated praise.

On November 12 Mahmūd, on the advice of Balban, his lord chamberlain, left Delhi in order to recover the Punjab. He crossed the Rāvī in March, 1247, and after advancing to the banks of the Chenāb sent Balban into the Salt Range. Balban inflicted severe punishment on the Khokars and other Hindu tribes of those hills and then pushed on to the banks of the Indus, where he despoiled Jaspāl Sehra, raja of the Salt Range, and his tribe. While he was encamped on the Jhelum a marauding force of Mughuls approached the opposite bank but, on finding an army prepared to receive them, retired. There now remained neither fields nor tillage beyond the Jhelum, and Balban, unable to obtain supplies, rejoined the king on the Chenāb, and on May 9 the army arrived at Delhi.

In October Balban led an expedition against the disaffected Hindus of the Doāb, took, after a siege of ten days, a fortress near Kanauj, and then marched against a raja[1] whose territory had formerly been confined to some districts in the hills of Bundelkhand and Baghelkhand, but who had recently established himself in the fertile valley of the Jumna. Balban attacked him so vigorously in one of his strongholds that he lost heart, and retired by night to another fortress, further to the south. The Muslims, after pillaging the deserted fort, followed him through defiles described as almost impracticable, and on February 14, 1248, captured his second stronghold, with his wives and children, many other prisoners, cattle and horses in great numbers, and much other plunder. Balban rejoined Mahmūd, now encamped at Kara, and on April 8 the army set out for Delhi. At Kanauj Mahmūd was met by his brother, Jalāl-ud-dīn, who was now appointed to the more important fiefs of Sambhal and Budaun. He warned Mahmūd against the ambition of Balban, whom he accused of secretly aiming at the throne, but the warning was unheeded, and after Mahmūd's return to Delhi Jalāl-ud-dīn, fearing that his confidence had been betrayed, fled from Budaun and joined the Mughuls in Turkistān.

In 1249 Balban was employed in chastising the turbulent people of Mewāt, the district to the south of Delhi, and in an unsuccessful attempt to recover Ranthambhor, which had been restored by the Hindus since it had been dismantled by Raziyya's troops, and was now held by Nāhar Deo. He returned to Delhi on May 18, and on August 2, the king married his daughter and he became almost supreme in the state. Mahmūd appointed him lieutenant of the kingdom and his place as lord chamberlain was taken by his brother, Saif-ud-dīn Aibak, Kashlī Khān. In the early months of 1250 Balban was again engaged in restoring order in the Doāb.

In this year the north-western provinces of the kingdom were thrown into confusion by a complicated dispute between the great fief-holders. Kishlū Khān of Nāgaur demanded that the fiefs of Multān and Uch should be bestowed upon him and though there was some difficulty in ousting Ikhtiyār-ud-dīn Kuraiz, who had expelled the Qarlughs from the province, his request was granted

---

[1] The name of this raja is uncertain. It appears to have been either Dhalkī or Dhulkī, of Mahalkī.

on condition of his relinquishing Nāgaur and his other fiefs to Kuraiz. Ignoring this condition he marched from Nāgaur, expelled Kuraiz from Multān and Uch and occupied those places. Hasan the Qarlugh immediately attacked him at Multān and although he was slain his followers concealed his death and persuaded Kishlū Khān to surrender the city. Sher Khān Sunqar then marched from his headquarters at Bhātindā, expelled the Qarlughs, and replaced his lieutenant Kuraiz in Multān. The situation was anomalous and complicated. The governor appointed by royal authority had surrendered the city to a foreign enemy, and Sunqar held it by right of conquest from that enemy, and Kuraiz, his deputy, strengthened his claim by capturing, in December, from a force of Mughul marauders a large number of prisoners, whom he sent as a peace offering to Delhi. Kishlū Khān, on the other hand, had defied the royal authority by failing to surrender Nāgaur, whither he had again retired after his discomfiture at Multān, and early in 1251 Mahmūd marched to Nāgaur to enforce the fulfilment of this condition. After much prevarication Kishlū Khān submitted, and retired to Uch, still held by one of his retainers, and Kashlī Khān, Balban's brother, was installed in Nāgaur, but meanwhile Sunqar had marched to Uch and was besieging the fortress. Kishlū Khān, who was related to Sunqar, incautiously placed himself in his power while attempting to effect a composition and was imprisoned, compelled to issue orders for the surrender of Uch, and sent to Delhi. Balban, who was related to both Sunqar and Kishlū Khān, adjusted the quarrel by appointing the latter to Budaun.

In November Balban led an expedition against Chāhad the Achārya, raja of Chanderī and Narwar and the most powerful Hindu chieftain in Mālwa. He is said to have been able to place in the field 5000 horse and 200,000 foot, but he was defeated and his capital was taken, though no permanent settlement was made in Mālwa, and the army returned to Delhi on April 24, 1252, with much booty and many captives.

During Balban's absence those who were jealous of his great power, including Mahmūd's mother and Raihān, a eunuch converted from Hinduism, who had already shown some aptitude for factious intrigue, poisoned the king's mind against him, and found many sympathisers and supporters among the Forty, who resented the excessive predominance of one of their number. Balban's condonation of the offences of his disobedient cousin, Sunqar, furnished xt for the exhortations of the intriguers, who succeeded in uading Mahmūd that it was necessary to vindicate his authority

by punishing Sunqar, and in the winter of 1252-53 Balban was compelled to accompany his master on a punitive expedition and to
submit to the daily ·increasing arrogance of his enemies. At the
Sutlej the conspirators attempted his assassination, but fortune,
or his own vigilance, befriended him, and having failed in their
attempt they persuaded Mahmūd to banish him to his fief of Hānsī,
hoping that an overt act of disobedience would furnish a pretext
for his destruction, but they were disappointed, for Balban obeyed
the order in dignified silence. The expedition had been merely
an excuse for his humiliation, and the army retired to Delhi immediately after his dismissal.

The rancour of the vindictive eunuch was not yet sated, and
he persuaded the king to transfer the fallen minister from
Hānsī to Nāgaur, and so confidently anticipated resistance that he
sent the royal army, in June, 1253, to enforce obedience, but again he
was disappointed, for Balban retired without a murmur to his new
fief. Hānsī was bestowed nominally upon an infant son of the king
by a wife other than the daughter of Balban, but was occupied by
a partisan of Raihān as the child's deputy.

Kashlī Khān shared his brother's disgrace, and was deprived of
his office and sent to the fief of Kara, all real power at court was
usurped by the eunuch, and even the leading members of the Forty
were fain to content themselves with minor offices. Sunqar, dismayed by his patron's sudden fall, had fled to Turkistān, leaving
his three fiefs, Bhātinda, Multān and Uch, in the hands of deputies
whose surrender enabled the king to bestow them on Arsalān Khān
Sanjar Chast, one of the Forty who was then hostile to Balban.

Balban displayed, meanwhile, an equivocal activity. He invaded
the Hindu state of Būndī, attacked and defeated Nāhar Deo of
Ranthambhor, and returned to Nāgaur with much booty, prepared,
apparently, either to take credit for his exploits or to devote his
spoils to the improvement of his own military strength, as circumstances should dictate. Mahmūd, under the guidance of Raihān,
led a successful expedition against the Hindus of Katehr and
returned to Delhi on May 16, 1254. Five months later he learnt
that his fugitive brother Jalāl-ud-dīn and Balban's cousin Sunqar
had returned from Turkistān and joined forces in the neighbourhood
of Lahore with the object of establishing themselves in the Punjab
under the protection of the Mughuls.

Meanwhile the rule of Raihān at Delhi was daily becoming
more intolerable, and the Turkish nobles whose jealousy of Balban
had associated them with the eunuch felt keenly, as his insolence

increased, the disgrace of their subservience to him. He maintained a gang of ruffians to molest those who were not well affected towards him and the historian Minhāj-ud-dīn complains that for a period of six months or more he dared not leave his house to attend the Friday prayers for fear of these bullies. Nearly all the great nobles of the kingdom sent messages to Balban imploring him to return to the capital and resume his former position. A confederacy was formed, and Balban from Nāgaur, Arsalān Khān Sanjar of Bhātinda, Bat Khān Aibak of Sunām, and Jalāl-ud-dīn and Sunqar from Lahore assembled their troops at Bhātinda. In October the king and Raihān marched from Delhi to meet them, and an indecisive affair of outposts, which threw the royal camp into confusion, was fought near Sunām. After celebrating, the 'Id-ul-Fitr (November 14) at this place Mahmūd retired, a week later, to Hānsī, and the confederates advanced to Guhrām and Kaithal. They were loth to attack the king and endeavoured to attain their object by means of intrigue and secret negotiations. Jalāl-ud-dīn expected that his brother would be deposed and that he would be raised to the throne, but Balban, who seems to have entertained a genuine affection for his weak and pliant son-in-law, was not prepared to gratify this ambition. The Turkish nobles in the king's camp favoured, almost unanimously, the cause of the confederates, and on December 5, while the army was retreating from Hānsī towards Jīnd, the eunuch was dismissed from his high office and invested with the fief of Budaun. On December 15 Bat Khān Aibak was sent to thank Mahmūd for this act and to request an audience for the confederate nobles, but the imminent reconciliation was nearly frustrated by the malice of the eunuch, who arranged to have the emissary assassinated. The design was fortunately discovered and Raihān was at once dismissed to Budaun, and on December 30 Balban and his associates were received by the king. Balban at once resumed his former place at the head of affairs and on January 20, 1255, returned with Mahmūd to Delhi. Jalāl-ud-dīn was rewarded for his services to the confederacy and consoled for the disappointment of his ambition by his brother's formal recognition of his independence in Lahore.

After Balban's return another ramification of the conspiracy against him came to light. Qutlugh Khān of Bayāna, one of his leading opponents, now outwardly reconciled, had secretly married the king's mother, who had formerly exercised much influence over her son and had been Raihān's chief ally. Mahmūd's eyes were opened to the network of intrigue by which he had been surrounded, and Qutlugh and his wife were dismissed to Oudh, in order that they might be as far as possible from the court. Raihān was transferred, at the same time, from Budaun to Bahrāich, a less important fief, but it was discovered a few months later that he was in dangerous proximity to Qutlugh Khān, and Sanjar Chast was sent to remove him from Bahrāich. He was arrested and imprisoned by Qutlugh Khān but in August made his escape, attacked Bahrāich with a small force, defeated and captured the eunuch, and put him to death.

Early in 1256 Mahmūd and Balban marched to punish Qutlugh Khān, who advanced to Budaun and defeated a detachment sent against him. As the main body of the army approached he retired and contrived to elude Balban's pursuit and on May 1 the army returned to Delhi. After its return Qutlugh attempted to conquer his old fief, Kara-Mānikpur, but was defeated by Sanjar Chast and endeavoured to retreat into the Punjab in order to seek service at Lahore under Jalāl-ud-dīn. He followed the line of the Himālaya and marched to Santaurgarh[1], where he gained the support of Ranpāl, raja of Sirmūr, but on January 8, 1257, Balban marched from Delhi and Qutlugh fled. Balban continued his advance, driving both Qutlugh and the raja before him and, after plundering Sirmūr[2], returned to Delhi on May 15.

Kishlū Khān had been reinstated in Multān and Uch during Raihān's ascendency and had since thrown off his allegiance to Delhi and acknowledged the suzerainty of the Mughul Hulāgū, whose camp he visited and with whom he left a grandson as a hostage for his fidelity. When the army returned from Sirmūr to Delhi he was in the neighbourhood of the Beās and marched north-eastwards until he was joined by Qutlugh Khān, when their combined forces marched southwards towards Sāmāna. Balban marched from Delhi to meet them and came into contact with them in the neighbourhood of Kaithal. A faction of discontented ecclesiastics had written from Delhi, urging the rebels to advance fearlessly and seize the capital, but the intrigue was discovered and at Balban's instance the traitors were expelled from the city. The rebels followed, however, the advice of their partisans, eluded Balban, and, after a forced march, encamped on June 21 before Delhi, hoping to find the city in friendly hands, but were disappointed to learn that the loyal nobles were exerting themselves to assemble

---

[1] In the hills below Mussoorie, lat. 30° 24′ N. long. 78° 2′ E.

[2] The ancient capital of the state of Sirmūr, 'now a mere hamlet surrounded by extensive ruins, in the Kiārda Dūn.' Nāhan, the modern capital, was not founded until 1621.

troops and repair the defences, and that the governor of Bayāna was approaching the city with his contingent. Balban remained for two days in ignorance of the rebels' march to Delhi but they knew that he might at any moment cut off their retreat, and many disaffected officers who had joined them now deserted them and made their peace with the king, and on June 22 Kishlū Khān and Qutlugh Khān fled towards the Siwāliks, whence the former, with the two or three hundred followers who still remained to him, made his way to Uch.

In December an army of Mughuls under the Nūyīn Sālīn invaded the Punjab and was joined by Kishlū Khān. They dismantled the defences of Multān and it was feared that they were about to cross the Sutlej. On January 9, 1258, the king summoned all the great fief-holders, with their contingents, to aid him in repelling the invaders, but the Mughuls, whether alarmed by this demonstration or sated with plunder, retired to Khurāsān. Their retreat was fortunate, for the condition of the kingdom was so disordered that the army could not safely have advanced against a foreign foe. Two fief-holders, Sanjar of Oudh and Mas'ūd Jānī of Kara, had disobeyed the royal summons, the Hindus of the Doāb and the Meos of Mewāt, to the south of the capital, were in revolt and the latter had carried off a large number of Balban's camels, without which the army could hardly have taken the field. For four months the troops were occupied in restoring order in the Doāb and in June marched to Kara against the two recalcitrant fief-holders. The latter fled, but received a promise of pardon on tendering their submission, and after the return of the army to Delhi appeared at court and were pardoned. Shortly afterwards Sanjar received the fief of Kara and Mas'ūd Jānī was promised the government of Bengal, from which province Balban Yūzbakī, the governor, had for some time remitted no tribute, but the latter, on hearing that he was to be superseded, secured his position by remitting all arrears. He died in 1259, but the promise to Mas'ūd Jānī was never fulfilled.

Early in 1259 the disorders in the Doāb necessitated another expedition, and after the punishment of the rebels the principal fiefs in the province, as well as those of Gwalior and Bayāna, were bestowed upon Sunqar.

In 1260 the Meos expiated by a terrible punishment a long series of crimes. For some years past they had infested the roads in the neighbourhood of the capital and depopulated the villages of the Bayāna district, and had extended their depredations eastwards nearly as far as the base of the Himālaya. Their impudent robbery of the transport camels on the eve oı a projected campaign had aroused Balban's personal resentment, and on January 29 he left Delhi and in a single forced march reached the heart of Mewāt and took the Meos completely by surprise. For twenty days the work of slaughter and pillage continued, and the ferocity of the soldiery was stimulated by the reward of one silver *tanga* for every head and two for every living prisoner. On March 9 the army returned to the capital with the chieftain who had stolen the camels, other leading men of the tribe to the number of 250, 142 horses, and 2,100,000 silver *tangas*. Two days later the prisoners were publicly massacred. Some were trampled to death by elephants, others were cut to pieces, and more than a hundred were flayed alive by the scavengers of the city. Later in the year those who had saved themselves by flight returned to their homes and ventured on reprisals by infesting the highways and slaughtering wayfarers. Balban, having ascertained from spies the haunts and movements of the bandits, surprised them as before by a forced march, surrounded them, and put to the sword 12,000 men, women and children.

A most gratifying mission from the Mughuls now arrived at Delhi. Nāsir-ud-dīn Muhammad, son of Hasan the Qarlugh, had been negotiating a marriage between his daughter and Balban's son, and had sent Balban's agent to Hulāgū's court at Tabrīz, where he was received with great honour. On his return to Delhi he was accompanied by a Mughul officer of high rank from the north-western frontier of India, who was authorised to promise, in Hulāgū's name, that depredations in India should cease.

The contemporary chronicle closes here, and there is a *hiatus* in the history of Muhammadan India, which later historians are unable to fill, from the middle of the year 1260 to the beginning of 1266. In attempting to explain the abrupt ending of the *Tabaqāt-i-Nāsirī* some say that the author was poisoned by the order of Balban, whose displeasure he had incurred, others that he was thrown into prison and starved to death, but these tales rest on no authority and are probably pure conjecture.

The next historical fact of which we are aware is that Mahmūd Shāh fell sick in 1265 and died on February 18, 1266[1]. He is said to have designated his father-in-law as his successor but, as no male heir of the house of Iltutmish survived, the accession of the powerful regent followed as a matter of course, and he ascended the throne under the title of Ghiyās-ud-dīn Balban.

---

[1] One authority alone says that he fell sick in 1264 and died on March 1, 1265, but the text is not satisfactory.

CHAPTER IV

GHIYĀS-UD-DĪN BALBAN, MU'IZZ-UD-DĪN KAIQUBĀD, AND SHAMS-UD-DĪN KAYŪMARS

THE Forty could ill brook the elevation of one of their own number to the throne. The disorders of the late reign had been largely due to revolts against Balban's supremacy, and the jealousy of one noble had reft the Punjab from the kingdom, but in the absence of an heir of the line of Iltutmish the recognition of Balban's sovereignty was the only alternative to anarchy. Balban, on the other hand, was resolved on founding a dynasty and, as a necessary step to that end, on destroying the confederacy whose strength lay in the weakness of the crown.

His first, and probably his most unpopular reform, was the establishment of a rigid ceremonial at his court, which differed entirely from that of his meek and unassuming predecessor. His maxim was that the freedom which came naturally and easily to one born to a throne could not be safely used by a monarch who had acquired one, and was surrounded by courtiers who had formerly been his equals ; but his policy ministered to his pride, for though his original position among the royal slaves had been extremely humble he claimed descent from Afrāsiyāb of Tūrān, and pretended, on this ground, to an innate right to sovereignty. His court was an austere assembly where jest and laughter were unknown, whence wine and gaming, to which he had formerly been addicted, were banished, partly because they were forbidden by the Islamic law but chiefly because they promoted good fellowship and familiarity, and where no detail of punctilious ceremony was ever relaxed. He atoned for former laxity by a rigid observance of all the ceremonial ordinances of his faith, and at meals his favourite companions were theologians and his favourite topic the dogmas of Islam. His justice knew no respect of persons, if we except a prejudice against the Forty. Malik Baqbaq, a great noble who maintained from the revenues of his fief of Budaun 4000 horse, caused one of his servants to be beaten so unmercifully that he died under the lash. When Balban next visited Budaun the man's widow demanded justice, and Malik Baqbaq was flogged to death and the news-writer who had suppressed the circumstance was hanged over the city gate. Haibat Khān, who held the great fief of Oudh, slew a man in a fit of drunken rage, and when the victim's relations appealed to Balban he caused Haibat Khān to be flogged with five hundred stripes and then delivered him to the widow, saying, 'This murderer was my slave, he is now yours. Do you stab him as he stabbed your husband.' Haibat Khān found intercessors who induced the woman to stay her hand, and purchased his freedom for 20,000 *tangas*, but was so overcome with shame that to the day of his death he never left his house. Balban more than once announced that he would treat his own sons in like manner in similar circumstances. An officer who was defeated by rebels was hanged over the gate of the city which was the seat of his government. This was not a proper punishment for incapacity or ill fortune, but the officer was, like Baqbaq and Haibat Khān, one of the Forty. Balban was occasion- ally, as will be seen from the chronicle of his reign, capricious as well as cruel in his punishments. A virtue eulogised by Muslim historians was his capacity for weeping at sermons, but he could remain unmoved by the sight of cruel executions.

The informers or news-writers formed a branch of the public service to which he devoted special attention and were an important feature of Muslim rule in India, as of all despotic rule over large areas in which extensive delegation of authority is necessary. They were appointed by the king and were independent of local governors, the affairs of whose provinces it was their duty to report and on whose actions they were, in some sort, spies. Their position was extremely delicate and Balban took great pains in selecting and exercised great caution in promoting them.

His ambition of emulating Mahmūd of Ghaznī and Sultān Sanjar the Saljūq was restrained by the ever present menace of a Mughul invasion. To the courtiers who urged him to conquer Gujarāt and recover Mālwa and other provinces lost to the kingdom he replied that he had the will to do far more than this but had no intention of exposing Delhi to the fate of Baghdād. His energies found a vent in the hunting field, where his strenuous expeditions, in which he was accompanied by large bodies of horse and foot, were com- mended by the Mughul Hulāgū as useful military exercises. Balban was much gratified by this commendation and complacently ob- served that those whose business it was to rule men knew how to appreciate in others the qualities of a ruler.

The record of his reign is chronologically less exact than that of preceding reigns, for our principal authority is Ziyā-ud-dīn Baranī, an interesting and discursive but unmethodical writer with no taste for chronology. He seldom troubles to assign a date to an event and never troubles to see that it is correct.

One of the first to recognise that the accession of Balban had inaugurated a new era was Arsalān Tātār Khān, now governor of Bengal, who had latterly withheld from Mahmūd material recognition of his sovereignty, but at once sent Balban a gift of sixty-three elephants.

The Meos had recovered from their severe chastisement and infested the jungle which had been permitted to grow unchecked round Delhi. They plundered travellers on the roads, entered the city by night, and robbed the inhabitants in their houses, and even by day robbed and stripped water-carriers and women drawing water from the large reservoirs just within the city walls, so that it became necessary to shut the gates on the western side of the city immediately after the hour of afternoon prayer. During the year following his accession Balban was occupied in exterminating the robbers. The jungle was cleared, the Meos lurking in it were put to death, a fort was built to command the approaches to the city from the west, and police posts were established on all sides.

A recrudescence of turbulence among the Hindus of the Doāb, who had entirely closed the roads between Bengal and Delhi, necessitated measures of repression and precaution, and all important towns and villages in this region were granted as fiefs to powerful nobles, who cleared the jungles which harboured gangs of brigands, slew large numbers of Hindus and enslaved their wives and children. Balban himself remained for many months in the districts of Patiyālī, Kampil, Bhojpur, and Jalālī, extirpated all highway robbers, built forts at those places, garrisoned them with Afghāns, who received lands in their vicinity for their maintenance, and by these measures secured the tranquillity of the roads between Delhi and Bengal for a century.

While he was thus engaged he learnt that the Hindus of Katehr had risen and were overrunning and plundering that province in such force that the governors of Budaun and Amroha were unable to take the field against them. He hastily returned to Delhi, assembled his best troops and, having misled his enemy by announcing his intention of hunting, made a forced march and appeared in Katehr sixty hours after he had left the capital. The rebels in arms, taken completely by surprise, fled, and Balban terribly avenged his outraged authority. All males over the age of eight were put to death, the women were carried off into slavery, and in every village through which the army passed huge heaps of corpses were left, the stench of which poisoned the air as far as the Ganges. The region was plundered and almost depopulated, and those of the inhabitants who were spared were so cowed that for thirty years order reigned in the province and the districts of Budaun, Amroha, Sambhal, and Gunnaur had peace.

In 1268-69 Balban led his army into the Salt Range with the object, primarily, of preparing for the re-establishment of the royal authority in the Punjab, and, secondarily of obtaining a supply of horses for his army. His operations were successful ; the Hindus were defeated and plundered and so many horses were taken that the price of a horse in his camp fell tc thirty or forty *tangas*.

In the course of this campaign a grave abuse inseparable from the lax feudal system of India and constantly recurring in the history of Islamic kingdoms in that country was first brought to Balban's notice. Iltutmish had provided for the king's personal troops by grants of land in fee, on condition of service. Most of the actual grantees were now dead and the survivors were unfit for service, but the immunity which they had enjoyed under the feeble Mahmūd encouraged them to advance the impudent claim that their fiefs had been granted unconditionally and in perpetuity. It appeared likely that an inquiry would arouse discontent and disaffection and even Balban was obliged to leave the question at rest for the time, but in 1270, in the course of an expedition during which he restored the city of Lahore and re-established a provincial government in the upper Punjab the quality of the contingent supplied by the grantees necessitated the investigation of the matter, and he discovered, on his return to Delhi, that there was a general tendency on the part of the actual holders of the lands to evade their personal liability for service and that many of the able-bodied, as well as those who were too young or too old to take the field, sent as substitutes useless and unwarlike slaves. The grants were resumed and the grantees were compensated beyond their deserts by the allotment of subsistence allowances, not only to themselves but to their descendants, but this did not satisfy them and they carried their grievance to the aged Fakhr-ud-dīn, *Kotwāl* of Delhi, who worked on Balban's feelings by the irrelevant argument that old age was no crime and that if it were he, the *Kotwāl*, was one of the chief offenders. The emotional king failed to detect the fallacy and, after weeping bitterly, rescinded the reasonable orders which he had issued and wasted the resources of the state by confirming the grants unconditionally.

Balban's intention of founding a dynasty and his attitude towards the Forty were no secret, and his own cousin, Sher Khān Sunqar, the most distinguished servant of the kingdom, who now held the fiefs of Bhātinda, Bhatnair, Sāmāna, and Sunām, had avoided Delhi since his accession. Sunqar's courage and abilities, no less than his mistrust, rendered him an object of suspicion to his cousin, now about sixty-five years of age, and his sudden death at this time is attributed to poison which Balban caused to be administered to him. His fiefs of Sāmāna and Sunām were bestowed upon Tātār Khān of Bengal, one of the Forty, but less formidable than Sunqar, and Tughril was appointed to Bengal in his place.

Balban soon discovered that in attempting to protect the interests of his posterity he had endangered the peace of his kingdom. Sunqar had been dreaded by the Mughuls and by the Khokars and other turbulent Hindu tribes, and his death revived the courage of both foreign and domestic enemies. Owing to the renewed activity of the Mughuls the king transferred his elder son, Muhammad Khān, entitled Qā'ān Malik, from his fief of Koil to the government of Multān. This prince was the hope of his line. He was gentle and courageous, able and learned, a diligent student and a munificent patron of letters. The poets Amīr Khusrav and Amīr Hasan began their literary careers as members of his household, and he invited the famous Sa'dī of Shīrāz to visit him at Multān, and was disappointed of the honour of entertaining him only by reason of the poet's extreme age. His table and intimate circle were adorned by the presence of the learned and the wise, and though wine was in use it was drunk for the purpose of stimulating, not of drowning, the intellect. No obscenity or ribald conversation was heard in that society, nor did cheerfulness and merriment ever transgress the bounds of decorum. Eastern historians and poets are wont to associate the names of princes with fulsome and almost blasphemous adulation, but in all that has been written of Muhammad Khān affection, as well as admiration, may be traced. In him were centred all the hopes of the stern old king ; for him the Forty were doomed, and for him the blood of near kinsmen was shed. The relations between father and son were of the most affectionate character, and Muhammad Khān used to travel every year from Multān to visit Balban, to enjoy his society, and to profit by his counsels. Before his departure he was formally designated heir-apparent and was invested with some of the insignia of royalty.

The character of Balban's second son Mahmūd, entitled Bughrā Khān, was a complete contrast to that of his brother. He was slothful, addicted to wine and sensual pleasures, and devoid of generous ambition. His father, though well aware of his faults and the weakness of his character, regarded him with natural tenderness and attempted to arouse in him a sense of responsibility by bestowing on him the fief of Sāmāna. Bughrā Khān, who dreaded his father's critical scrutiny and found the restraint of his society irksome, was well content to leave the capital ; but for the general advice which had been deemed sufficient for Muhammad Khān, Balban substituted, in the case of his younger son, minute and detailed instructions, accompanied by special warnings against self-indulgence and intemperance and a threat of dismissal in case of misconduct.

About the year 1279 the Mughuls again began to appear in north-western India, and in one of their incursions even crossed the Sutlej, but though they harried the upper Punjab Delhi had little to apprehend from them, for domestic enemies had now been crushed, and a force of seventeen or eighteen thousand horse composed of the contingents of Muhammad Khān from Multān, Bughrā Khān from Sāmāna, and Malik Bektars from Delhi so severely defeated them as to deter them from again crossing the Sutlej.

- In the same year Balban learnt with indignation that Tughril was in rebellion in Bengal. The allegiance of the governors of this distant and wealthy province to the reigning king had usually depended on circumstances. A strong ruler was gratified by frequent, though seldom regular remittances of tribute, one less strong might expect the compliment of an occasional gift, but with any indication of the king's inability to maintain his authority nearer home remittances ceased entirely. Lakhnāwatī had thus earned at Delhi the nickname of Balghākpur, 'the city of rebellion.' Tughril was encouraged by Balban's advancing age and by a recrudescence of Mughul activity on the north-western frontier, to withhold tribute, and Balban ordered Malik Aitigīn the Longhaired, entitled Amīn Khān, to march against him from Oudh. Amīn Khān was defeated, many from his army joined Tughril, and those who attempted to save themselves by flight were plundered by the Hindus. Balban, whom the first news of the rebellion had thrown into such paroxysms of rage that few durst approach him, was now nearly beside himself, and caused Amīn Khān to be hanged over the gate of the city of Ajodhya. In the following year an army under Malik Targhī shared the fate of its predecessor, and Tughril was again reinforced by deserters. Balban now gnawed his own flesh in his fury, and when his first outburst of rage was spent prepared to take the field in person. Fleets of boats were collected on the Jumna and the Ganges, and Balban, accompanied by his second son, Bughrā Khān, set out from Delhi and marched through the Doāb. In Oudh he mustered his forces, which numbered, including sutlers and camp-followers, 200,000, and, although the rainy season had begun he crossed the Gogra and invaded Bengal. Here he was often compelled by the state of the weather and the roads to halt for ten or twelve days at a time, and when he reached Lakhnāwatī he found it almost deserted, for Tughril, on hearing of his approach, had fled with his army and most of the inhabitants to Jājnagar[1] in eastern Bengal. After a short halt Balban continued his march until he reached Sonārgāon, on the Meghna, near Dacca, where he compelled the raja, Bhoj, to undertake to use his utmost endeavours to discover Tughril and to prevent his escape by land or water. He dismayed his army by solemnly swearing that he would not rest nor return to Delhi, nor even hear the name of Delhi mentioned, until he should have seized Tughril, even though he had to pursue him on the sea. His troops, who had not yet even discovered the place of Tughril's retreat, wrote letters, in the deepest dejection, bidding farewell to their families at Delhi, and the search for Tughril began. One day a patrol under Sher Andāz of Koil and Muqaddir encountered some grain merchants who had been abroad on business. When two had been beheaded to loosen the tongues of the rest, Sher Andāz learned that he was within a mile of Tughril, who was encamped with his army beside a reservoir. After sending word to Bektars, commanding the advanced guard, he rode cautiously on, found the rebel army enjoying a day's halt after the fashion of undisciplined troops and, fearing lest an incautious movement should give the alarm, formed the desperate resolution of attacking the enemy with his party of thirty or forty horsemen. As they galloped into the camp with swords drawn, shouting aloud for Tughril, the rebels were too astonished to reckon their numbers or to attempt resistance and they rode straight for his tent. Amid a scene of the wildest confusion he fled, and, mounting a barebacked horse, endeavoured to escape, but was recognised and pursued. Malik Muqaddir brought him down with a well aimed arrow and was thenceforward known as *Tughril-Kush*, 'the Slayer of Tughril'[2]. Bektars then arrived on the scene and, receiving Tughril's head from Muqaddir, sent it to Balban with news of the success which had been gained. Balban summoned the adventurous officers to

---

1 Not to be confounded with Jājpur in Orissa, also called Jājnagar by the Muslims.

2 From the printed text of Baranī it would appear that Muqaddir and Tughril-Kush were distinct persons, but this text is confused and corrupt, and in the list of Balban's nobles which precedes the account of his reign Malik Muqaddir is entitled Tughril Kush.

his presence and after severely reproving their rashness generously rewarded their success. The army passed at once from despair to elation ; their master's vow was fulfilled and the remainder of their task was a labour of love. The rebel's demoralised force was surrounded and nearly the whole of it was captured. The army then set out on its return march to Lakhnāwatī where Balban proposed to glut his revenge. On either side of the principal bazar, a street more than two miles in length, a row of stakes was set up and the family and the adherents of Tughril were impaled upon them. None of the beholders had ever seen a spectacle so terrible and many swooned with terror and disgust. Such was the fate of Tughril's own followers, but those who had deserted from the two armies sent against him and had joined his standard were reserved for what was designed to be a yet more appalling spectacle at the capital.

Before leaving Bengal Balban appointed Bughrā Khān to the government of the province and after repeating the advice which he had given him on appointing him to Sāmāna added a brief and impressive warning. 'Mahmūd,' he said, after the punishment of the rebels, 'didst thou see ?' The prince was silent and the question was repeated. Still there was no answer. 'Mahmūd,' repeated Balban, 'didst thou see the punishment inflicted in the great bazar ?' 'Yes,' at length replied the trembling prince, 'I saw it.' 'Well,' said Balban, 'take it to heart, and whilst thou art at Lakhnāwatī remember, that Bengal can never safely rebel against Delhi.' He then proceeded, with strange inconsistency, to advise his son, if he should ever find himself in arms against Delhi, to flee ‹ some spot where he might baffle pursuit and remain in hiding until the storm should have passed.

The only cloud overshadowing the rejoicings which marked Balban's triumphant return to Delhi was the impending fate of his wretched captives, most of whom had wives and families in the city. These repaired in their grief to the qāzī of the army, a pious and gentle man, and besought him to intercede for the lives of those dear to them. He gained the royal presence and, after a harangue on the blessedness of mercy which reduced Balban to tears, applied his arguments to the fate of the doomed men. His efforts were successful ; the double row of stakes which had been set up from the Budaun gate of the city to Tilpat was removed, and the prisoners were divided into four classes. The common herd received a free pardon, those of slightly greater importance were banished for a time, those who had held respectable positions at Delhi suffered a term of imprisonment, and the principal officers were mounted on buffaloes and exposed to the jeers and taunts of the mob. This act of mercy blotted out the remembrance of the atrocity perpetrated at distant Lakhnāwatī and irom all parts of the kingdom congratulations poured in.

Balban, now eighty years of age, was at the height of his prosperity and glory when he received a blow which darkened the brief remainder of his days. The Mughuls, under Tamar Khān, invaded the province of Multān in great force and Muhammad Khān attacked and defeated them, but was surprised by an ambush and slain on March 9, 1285. The historian Baranī gives an affecting account of the behaviour of the aged king in his affliction. He would in no way compromise his dignity, and gave audiences and transacted business with his usual stern and grave demeanour, though the weight of the blow which had fallen on him was manifest to all ; but at night, and in the privacy of his chamber, he rent his clothes, cast dust upon his head, and mourned for his son as David mourned for Absalom. The dead prince was henceforward always known as *Shahīd,* 'the Martyr,' and his youthful son Kaikhusrav was sent from Delhi with a large staff and a numerous force to take his father's place as warden of the marches.

Bughrā Khān, whom Balban now designated as his heir, was summoned from Bengal in order that his presence at the capital might avert the evils of a disputed succession, but the worthless prince had always chafed under the restraints of his father's austere court and declined, even for the sake of a throne, to endure existence under the cloud of gloom which now overhung it. Leaving the city on the pretext of a hunting excursion, he returned without permission to Bengal, but before he reached Lakhnāwatī his father was on his deathbed. Balban summoned a few trusted counsellors and disinherited his unworthy son, designating as his heir Kaikhusrav, the son of the Martyr Prince. When he had issued these injunctions the old king breathed his last.

His counsellors disregarded his last wishes, and enthroned Kaiqubād, a youth of seventeen or eighteen, son of Bughrā Khān. The historian Baranī says that for a reason which could not be mentioned without disclosing the secrets of the harem they had been on bad terms with the Martyr, and feared to raise his son to the throne. These expressions may indicate a former lapse from virtue on the part of the otherwise blameless prince, or a suspicion that Kaikhusrav was not the son of his putative father, but their import cannot be accurately determined.

Nizām-ud-dīn, nephew and son-in-law of the aged *Kotwāl* Fakhr-ud-dīn, acquired on Kaiqubād's accession in 1287 a prominent position at the capital, and the son of Balban's brother Kashlī Khān, who bore his father's title but was more generally known as Malik Chhajjū, received the important fief of Sāmāna. Bughrā Khān tamely acquiesced in his supersession by his son, but assumed in Bengal the royal title of Nāsir-ud-dīn Mahmūd Bughrā Shāh.

The young king had been educated under the supervision of his grandfather in the straitest paths of virtue, and his guardians and tutors, trembling under the old despot's eye, had subjected him to the most rigid discipline. As a natural consequence of this injudicious restraint the youth, on finding himself absolute master of his actions, plunged at once into a whirlpool of debauchery. The unrestrained indulgence of his appetites was his sole occupation, and to the duties of his station he gave not a thought. The Arabic saying, 'Men follow the faith of their masters' found ample confirmation during his brief reign, and as in the reign of Charles II in England the reaction from the harsh rule of the precisians and the evil example of the king produced a general outburst of licentiousness, so in that of Kaiqubād at Delhi the reaction from the austere and gloomy rule of Balban and the example of the young voluptuary inaugurated among the younger generation an orgy of debauchery. The minister, Khatīr-ud-dīn, abandoned in despair the task of awakening his young master to a sense of duty and the ambitious Nizām-ud-dīn was enabled to gather into his own hands the threads of all public business and, by entirely relieving Kaiqubād of its tedium, to render himself indispensable. His influence was first exhibited in the course followed with Kaikhusrav, whose superior hereditary claim was represented as a menace to Kaiqubād. The prince was summoned to Delhi and, under an order obtained from Kaiqubād when he was drunk, was put to death at Rohtak. Nizām-ud-dīn then obtained, by means of a false accusation, an order degrading the minister, who was paraded through the streets on an ass, as though he had been a common malefactor. This treatment of the first minister of the kingdom and the execution, at Nizām-ud-dīn's instigation, of Shāhak, governor of Multān, and Tūzakī, governor of Baran, alarmed and disgusted the nobles of Balban's court, and caused them gradually to withdraw from participation in public business, and the power of Nizām-ud-dīn, the object of whose ambition could not be mistaken, became absolute. All who endeavoured to warn the king of what all but he could see were delivered to Nizām-ud-dīn to be dealt with · as sedition-mongers.

The aged *Kotwāl* attempted to restrain his nephew, but he had already gone so far that he could not safely recede. Even the slothful and self-indulgent Bughrā sent letters to his son warning him of the inevitable consequences of his debauchery and neglect of business, and, more guardedly, in view of Nizām-ud-dīn's control of the correspondence, of the danger of permitting a subject to usurp his authority. A ¡roposed meeting between father and son, on the frontiers of their kingdoms, was postponed by an irruption of the Mughuls under Tamar Khān of Ghaznī, who overran the Punjab, plundered Lahore, and advanced nearly as far as Sāmāna. Amid the general demoralisation of the court and the capital Balban's army still remained as a monument of his reign, and a force of 30,000 horse under the command of Malik Muhammad Baqbaq, entitled, perhaps for his services on this occasion, Khān Jahān, was sent against the invaders, who were overtaken in the neighbourhood of Lahore and utterly defeated. Most of their army were slain, but more than a thousand prisoners were carried back to the capital. The description of these savages by the poet Amīr Khusrav, who had been a prisoner in their hands for a short time after the battle in which his early patron, the Martyr Prince, was slain, is certainly coloured by animosity, but is probably as true as most caricatures, 'Their eyes were so narrow and piercing that they might have bored a hole in a brazen vessel, and their stench was more horrible than their colour. Their heads were set on their bodies as if they had no necks, and their cheeks resembled leathern bottles, full of wrinkles and knots. Their noses extended from cheek to cheek and their mouths from cheekbone to cheekbone. Their nostrils resembled rotten graves, and from them the hair descended as far as the lips. Their moustaches were of extravagant length, but the beards about, their chins were very scanty. Their chests, in colour half black, half white, were covered with lice which looked like sesame growing on a bad soil. Their whole bodies, indeed, were covered with these insects, and their skins were as rough-grained as shagreen leather, fit only to be converted into shoes. They devoured dogs and pigs with their nasty teeth...Their origin is derived from dogs, but they have larger bones. The king marvelled at their beastly countenances and said that God had created them out of hell fire.'

Numbers of these prisoners were decapitated and others were crushed under the feet of elephants, and 'spears without number bore their heads aloft, and appeared denser than a forest of bamboos.' A few were preserved and kept in confinement. These were sent from city to city for exhibition, and, as the poet again observes, 'sometimes they had respite and sometimes punishment'.

It was after this irruption of the Mughuls that Nizām-ud-dīn persuaded Kaiqubād to put to death the 'New Muslims.' These were Mughuls who had been captured in former campaigns and forcibly converted, or who had voluntarily embraced Islam and entered the royal service, in which some had attained to high rank. They were, for many years after this time, a source of anxiety, for it was believed that they, like the 'New Christians' of Spain and Portugal, were not sincere in their change of faith, and they fell under the suspicion of treasonable correspondence with their unconverted brethren. The accusations against them were vague, and were not substantiated by any trial or enquiry, but they were proscribed and put to death, and those who had been on friendly terms with them and had permitted them to intermarry with their families were imprisoned.

Meanwhile Bughrā had advanced with his army to the frontier of his kingdom and was encamped on the bank of the Gogra[1]. His intentions were undoubtedly hostile. He had acquiesced in his son's elevation to the throne, but the latter's subsequent conduct and the prospect of the extinction of his house, had aroused even his resentment. Kaiqubād, on learning that his father had reached the Gogra, marched from Delhi in the middle of March, 1288, to Ajodhya, where he was joined by his cousin Chhajjū from Kara.

The armies were encamped on the opposite bank of the Gogra, and the situation was critical, but Bughrā hesitated to attack his son's superior force and contented himself with threatening messages, but when they were answered in the same strain changed his tone and suggested a meeting. This was arranged, but it was stipulated that Bughrā should acknowledge the superior majesty of Delhi by visiting his son. He consented, and crossed the river. Kaiqubād was to have received his father seated on his throne, but as Bughrā approached his natural feelings overcame him, and he descended from the throne and paid to him the homage due from a son to his father, and their meeting moved the spectators to tears. A friendly contention regarding precedence lasted long and was concluded by the father taking the son by the hand, seating him on the throne, and standing before him. He then embraced his son and returned to his own camp. Kaiqubād celebrated

---

[1] The account of the meeting between Kaiqubād and his father given by Amīr Khusrav has been generally preferred to that given by Baranī. Amīr Khusrav was an eye witness and Baranī writes only from hearsay.

the reconciliation, in characteristic fashion, with a drinking bout at which he and his courtiers got drunk. He exchanged complimentary presents with his father and three more meetings took place between them. Bughrā took his son to task for putting to death Kaikhusrav and so many of the old nobles and advised him to substitute a council of four for a single adviser. At the last meeting he whispered in his son's ear, as he embraced him, a caution against Nizām-ud-dīn and advised him to put him to death. The two parted with tokens of affection and returned to their capitals. 'Alas!' cried Bughrā, 'I have seen the last of my son and the last of Delhi.' His counsels induced Kaiqubād to make a faint effort to reform his ways, but before he reached Delhi he had returned like a dog to his vomit and a washed sow to her wallowing in the mire. The rejoicings with which his hardly expected return was celebrated were the occasion of general licence, in describing which the aged and toothless Baranī, writing more than half a century later, is beguiled into rhapsodical and unseemly reminiscences of his own misspent youth.

In the midst of his debauchery Kaiqubād bore in mind his father's warning and one day summoned up courage to inform Nizām-ud-dīn abruptly that he was transferred to Multān and must leave Delhi at once He so delayed his departure on various pretexts that the king concluded that he intended to defy his authority, and, caused him to be poisoned. Baranī, who condemns the minister's unscrupulous ambition, praises him for his judicious selection of subordinates, and justly observes that but for his unremitting attention to public business the authority of Kaiqubād could not have been maintained for a day. His sudden removal dislocated the machinery of the administration and the king, incapable of personal attention to business, summoned to Delhi the most powerful and capable noble in the kingdom, Malik Jalāl-ud-dīn Firūz Khaljī, who, since the transfer of Chhajjū to Kara, had held the important fief of Sāmāna, transferred him to Baran, and appointed him to the command of the army. His advancement gave great offence to the Turkish nobles and to the people of the capital, who affected to despise his tribe and feared both his power and his ambition. Almost immediately after he had taken possession of his new fief incontinence and intemperance did their work on Kaiqubād, who was struck down with paralysis and lay, a helpless wreck, in the palace which he had built at Kilokhrī, while Firūz marched with a large force from Baran to the suburbs of Delhi.

The Turkish nobles and officers, headed by Aitamar Kachhan and Aitamar Surkha, were in a dilemma. Fīrūz, though his designs were apparent, had not declared against Kaiqubād and had done nothing which his official position, which required him to keep the peace, would not justify, and they were debarred by the king's physical condition from the usual expedient of carrying him into the field and so arming themselves with his authority. They there-fore, although Kaiqubād still lived, carried his three year old son into the city and enthroned him under the title of Shams-ud-dīn Kayūmars.

Kaiqubād lay unheeded in his palace at Kilokhrī while the two parties contended for the mastery. Neither wished to be the first to appeal to arms, and Kachhan visited Fīrūz to invite him to discuss the situation with the Turkish nobles in the city, but Fīrūz having ascertained that the invitation was a snare, and that pre-parations had been made to murder him and his Khaljī officers, caused Kachhan to be dragged from his horse and slain. The sons of Fīrūz then dashed into Delhi, carried off Kayūmars, and defeated a force sent in pursuit of them, slaying Surkha, its leader, and capturing the sons of Fakhr-ud-dīn, the *Kotwāl*. The success of the unpopular party so incensed the people that they rose and streamed out of the city gates, with the intention of attacking Fīrūz in his camp, but the *Kotwāl*, who was a man of peace, and trembled for the fate of his captive sons, quelled the disturbance and dispersed the mob. Fīrūz was now master of the situation, and most of the Turkish nobles, who had lost their leaders, openly joined him, and the rest, with the populace of Delhi, maintained an attitude of sullen aloofness. Meanwhile the wretched Kaiqubād was an unconscionable time a-dying, and, with the approval of Fīrūz, an officer whose father had been executed by the sick man's orders was dispatched to his chamber to hasten his end. The ruffian rolled his victim in the bedding on which he lay, kicked him on the head, and threw his body into the Jumna[1]. At the same time Chhajjū, whose near relationship to Kaiqubād might have encouraged him to assert a claim to the throne, was dismissed to his fief of Kara, and on June 13, 1290, Fīrūz was enthroned in the palace of Kilokhrī as Jalāl-ud-dīn Fīrūz Shāh.

The early Muhammadan kingdom of Delhi was not a homo-geneous political entity. The great fiefs, of which the principal were, on the east, Mandāwar, Amroha, Sambhal, Budaun, Baran-

---

[1] According to a less authentic account Kaiqubād died of hunger and thirst in a prison into which Fīrūz had thrown him.

(Bulandshahr), Koil and Oudh ; on the south east Kara-Mānikpur ;
on the south Bayāna and Gwalior ; on the west Nāgaur, recently
abandoned ; and on the north-west and north, Hānsī, Multān, Uch,
Lahore, Sāmāna, Sunām, Guhrām, Bhātinda and Sirhind, were
nuclei of Muhammadan influence, the holders of which discharged
some of the functions of provincial governors, but the trans-
Gangetic fiefs of Mandāwar, Amroha, Sambhal, and Budaun were
mere outposts of dominion against the territory of Katehr, where
the independence of the Hindus was only occasionally disturbed
by punitive expeditions which usually engaged the sovereign with
the greater part of his available military strength ; and similarly
the fiefs to the south, south-west, and west were outposts against
Rājput chieftains who might have been strong enough, had union
been possible to them, to expel the foreigners. Gwalior had been
taken by Aibak, but lost during the reign of his son and with
difficulty recovered by Iltutmish ; the fortress of Ranthambhor
had been dismantled and abandoned by Raziyya and occupied and
restored by the Rājputs ; and Nāgaur, at one time held by Balban
as his fief, was also in their hands. On the north-west Lahore, Uch
and Multān were exposed to the constant inroads of the Mughuls
of Ghaznī, and the ties which bound them to Delhi were now
relaxed. The fiefs or districts in the heart of the kingdom were
interspersed with tracts of country in the hands of powerful Hindu
chieftains or confederacies. Immediately to the south of Delhi
Mewāt, which incl ed part of the modern districts of Muttra and
Gurgāon, most of Alwar, and part of the Bharatpur State, had
never been permanently conquered, and the depredations of its
inhabitants, the Meos, extended at times to the walls of Delhi and
beyond the Jumna into the Doāb. The rich fiefs of the latter
region supported strong Muslim garrisons but the disaffection of
the Hindu inhabitants was, for long after the period of which we
are writing, a menace to domestic peace, and the ferocious punishment inflicted on them by Muhammad Tughluq exasperated without taming them. After his time Etāwah became a stronghold of
Rājput chieftains who gathered round themselves the most turbulent elements in the indigenous population, were frequently in
revolt, and seldom recognised the authority of Delhi otherwise than
by a precarious tribute.

The rhapsodies of Muslim historians in their accounts of the
suppression of a rising or the capture of a fortress, of towns and
villages burnt, of whole districts laid waste, of temples destroyed
and idols overthrown, of hecatombs of 'misbelievers sent to hell,'

or 'dispatched to their own place,' and of thousands of women and children enslaved might delude us into the belief that the early Muslim occupation of northern India was one prolonged holy war waged for the extirpation of idolatry and the propagation of Islam, had we not proof that this cannot have been the case. Mahmūd the Iconoclast maintained a large corps of Hindu horse ; his son Mas'ūd prohibited his Muslim officers from offending the religious susceptibilities of their Hindu comrades, employed the Hindu Tilak for the suppression of the rebellion of the Muslim Ahmad Niyāltigīn, approved of Tilak's mutilation of Muslims, and made him the equal of his Muslim nobles ; Mu'izz-ud-dīn Muhammad allied himself with the Hindu raja of Jammū against the Muslim Khusrav Malik of Lahore, and employed Hindu legends on his coinage ; all Muslim rulers in India, from Mahmūd downwards, accepted, when it suited them to do so, the allegiance of Hindu rulers and landholders, and confirmed them, as vassals, in the possession of their hereditary lands ; and one of the pretexts for Tīmūr's invasions of India at the end of the fourteenth century was the toleration of Hinduism. Neither the numbers nor the interest of the foreigners admitted of any other course. Their force consisted in garrisons scattered throughout the land among the indigenous agricultural population vastly superior in numbers to themselves and not unwarlike. On this population they relied not only for the means of support but also, to a great extent, for the subordinate machinery of government ; for there can be no doubt that practically all minor posts connected with the assessment and collection of the land revenue and with accounts of public and state finance generally, were filled, as they were many generations later, by Hindus. Among those who met Balban at each stage on his triumphal return from the suppression of Tughril's rebellion were *rāis*, *chaudharīs* and *muqaddams*. The first two classes were certainly Hindu landholders and officials of some importance, and in the third we recognise a humbler class of Hindu revenue officials which in many parts of India retains its Arabic designation to this day. The Hindu husbandman is not curious in respect of high affairs of state, and cares little by whom he is governed so long as he is reasonably well treated. He is more attached to his patrimony than to any system of government, and while he is permitted to retain enough of the kindly fruits of the earth to satisfy his frugal needs, concerns himself little with the religion of his rulers ; but oppression or such extortion as deprives him of the necessaries of life may convert him into a rebel or a robber, and there was at that time no lack of warlike leaders and communities of his own faith ready to welcome him in either character. The Rebellion and overt disaffection were repressed with ruthless severity, and were doubtless made occasions of proselytism, but the sin was rebellion, not religious error, and there is no reason to believe that the position of the Hindu cultivator was worse under a Muslim than under a Hindu landlord. The disaffected were those of the upper and recently dominant class of large landholders and petty chieftains.

It was certainly possible for Hindus to obtain justice, even against Muslims, for Baranī tells us that the Multānīs and money-lenders of Delhi, the former term being evidently employed much as the local designation Mārwārī is used to-day, were first enriched by the profusion and improvidence of the nobles of Balban's court, who not only borrowed largely but were defrauded by dependants who borrowed in their names. As the usurers could not have been enriched by lending money which they could not recover it is evident that even the grandees of the court were not permitted to plunder the Hindus indiscriminately, nor to withhold from them their just dues.

That there was in other respects some sympathetic intercourse between Muslims and Hindus we may infer from Hindī nicknames by which some of the nobles were beginning to be known. One of the two Aitamars was known as Kachhan, and Balban's nephew 'Abdullāh as Chhajjū.

On the whole it may be assumed that the rule of the Slave Kings over their Hindu subjects, though disfigured by some intolerance and by gross cruelty towards the disaffected, was as just and humane as that of the Norman Kings in England and far more tolerant than that of Philip II in Spain and the Netherlands.

CHAPTER V

THE KHALJĪ DYNASTY AND THE FIRST CONQUEST
OF THE DECCAN

THE repugnance of the populace to Fīrūz was due to the belief that his tribe, the Khaljīs, were Afghāns, a people who were regarded as barbarous. They were, in fact, a Turkish tribe but they had long been settled in the *Garmsīr*, or hot region, of Afghānistān, where they had probably acquired some Afghān manners and customs, and the Turkish nobles, most of whom must now have belonged to the second generation domiciled in India, refused to acknowledge them as Turks[1]. It was owing to this hostility of the people that Fīrūz elected to be enthroned in Kaiqubād's unfinished villa at Kilokhrī rather than at Delhi, and for some time after his elevation to the throne he dared not enter the streets of his capital. The more prominent citizens waited on him as a matter of course, and swore allegiance to him, and the people in general repaired to Kilokhrī on the days appointed for public audiences, but they were impelled less by sentiments of loyalty than by curiosity to see how the barbarian would support his new dignity, and were compelled reluctantly to admit that he carried it well, but their disaffection did not at once abate, and Fīrūz completed the buildings and gardens left unfinished by Kaiqubād, named Kilokhrī *Shahr-i-Nau*, or the New City, and ordered his courtiers to build themselves houses in the neighbourhood of his palace. The order was unpopular, but there was a large class whose livelihood depended on the court, and villas and shops rose round the palace of Kilokhrī.

The court of Fīrūz differed widely from that of the Slave Kings. Balban had undermined, if he had not destroyed, the power of the Forty and the character of the Turkish nobles was changed. They were now represented largely by men born in the country, in many instances, probably, of Indian mothers, and though, as their hostility to Fīrūz proves, they retained their pride of race, they lost for ever their exclusive privilges, which were invaded by Khaljīs and by

1 The late Major Raverty, an authority from whom it is seldom safe to differ, protested vigorously against the common error of classing the Khaljīs as Afghāns or Pathāns, but the people of Delhi certainly fell into the error which he condemns. He also inveighs, with much acrimony and less reason, against the plausible identification of the Khaljīs with the Ghilzais, a tribe which claims a Turkish origin and occupies the region originally colonized by the Khaljīs. If the Ghilzais be not Khaljīs it is difficult to say what has become of the latter.

all whom it was the king's pleasure to promote. The change was inevitable. It would have been impossible for a small number of native courtiers to have maintained for ever a claim based on a remote foreign ancestry, and Fīrūz, though he did not exclude the Turks from office, completed very thoroughly the work which Balban had begun. The fief of Kara-Mānikpur was considered an ample provision for Chhajjū, the sole survivor of the former royal family, and Fīrūz had his own relations to consider. His eldest son, Mahmūd, was entitled Khān Khānān, his second Arkalī Khān, and his third Qadr Khān ; his brother was entitled Yaghrush Khān and was appointed to the command of the army, and his two nephews, 'Alā-ud-dīn and Almās Beg, received important posts, the latter being entitled Ulugh Khān. Another relation, the blunt and out-spoken Malik Ahmad Chap, held the unsuitable post of Master of the Ceremonies.

The popular prejudice against Fīrūz was soon discovered to be groundless. Save for an occasional outburst of wrath no milder monarch ever sat upon the throne of Delhi. His treatment of Kaiqubād belied his boast that he had never shed the blood of a Muslim, but throughout his reign he displayed the most impolitic tenderness towards rebels and other criminals. His mildness and his conduct when he first ventured into Balban's Red Palace in the city gained him the adherence of many of those who had opposed him as a barbarian. He declined to ride into the courtyard, but dismounted at the gate, and before entering the throne room wept bitterly in the antechamber for Balban and his offspring and lamented his own unworthiness of the throne and his guilt in aspiring to it. The few old nobles of Balban's court and the ecclesiastics of the city were moved to tears and praised his sensibility, but the soldiers and those of his own faction murmured that such self-abasement was unkingly, and Malik Ahmad Chap openly remons-trated with him.

In the second year of the reign Chhajjū assumed the royal title at Kara and was joined by Hātim Khān, who held the neighbouring fief of Oudh. The rebels advanced towards Delhi, where they were confident of the support of a numerous faction not yet reconciled to the rule of the Khaljī, but Fīrūz marched to meet them, and his advanced guard under his son Arkalī Khān encountered them near Budaun and defeated and dispersed them. Two days after the battle Chhajju was surrendered by a Hindu with whom he had taken refuge, and he and the other captives were sent, with yokes on their necks and gyves on their wrists, to Budaun. Fīrūz seated

upon a cane stool, received them in public audience and when he
saw their bonds wept in pity. He caused them to be loosed and
tended and entertained them at a wine party. As they hung their
heads with shame he cheered them and foolishly praised them for
their loyalty to the heir of their old master. The indignant courtiers,
headed, as usual, by Ahmad Chap, protested against this encouragement of rebellion and demanded that he should consider what his,
and their, fate would have been had the rebels been victorious,
and the old man, who seems to have entered upon his dotage
when he seized the throne, could find no better reply than that he
dared not, for the sake of a transitory kingdom, imperil his soul by
slaying fellow-Muslims.

Arkalī Khān's victory was rewarded with the fief of Multān,
and Chhajjū was delivered into the custody of his conqueror, who
was known to be opposed to his father's mild policy. The fief of
Kara was bestowed upon 'Alā-ud-dīn, who lent a willing ear to the
counsels of Chhajjū's principal adherents, whom he took into his
service. Domestic griefs helped to warp his loyalty, for his wife,
the daughter of Fīrūz, and her mother, who perhaps suspected the
trend of his ambition, were shrews who not only embittered his
private life, but constantly intrigued against him at court. 'Alā-
ud-dīn's original intention seems to have been to escape their
malignity by leaving his uncle's dominions and establishing a
principality in some distant part of India, but the course of events
suggested to him a design yet more treasonable.

Fīrūz Shāh's lenity and the simplicity of his court were most
distasteful to the Khaljī officers, who were disappointed of the
profit which they had expected from confiscations and murmured
against a prince who would neither punish his enemies nor reward
his friends. Their strictures on his attitude towards criminals were
just, as in the case of the *Thags*[1], those miscreants whose religion
was robbery and murder and who were the dread of wayfarers in
India within the memory of the last generation. A few of these
fanatical brigands were captured at Delhi and one gave information
which led to the arrest of over a thousand. Not one was punished
but the whole gang was carried in boats down the Jumna and
Ganges and set free in Bengal. Such culpable weakness would
have again thrown the kingdom into complete disorder had the
reign of Fīrūz been prolonged.

The discontent of the nobles found expression at their drinking
parties when the deposition of the old king was freely discussed.

[1] This is the word used by the contemporary historian Baranī.

Firūz, though aware of this treasonable talk, at first paid no heed to it, but at one drinking bout many nobles swore allegiance to Tāj-ud-dīn Kūchī, a survivor of the Forty, and boasted of how they would slay Fīrūz He sent for the drinkers and, after upbraiding them, threw a sword towards them and challenged any one of them to attack him. They stood abashed until the tension was relieved by the effrontery of his secretary, Nusrat Sabbāh, who, though he had boasted as loudly as any, now told Fīrūz that the maunderings of drunkards were beneath his notice, that they were not likely to kill him, for they knew that they would never again find so indulgent a master, and that he was not likely to kill them, for he knew, in spite of their foolish talk, that he would nowhere find servants so faithful. Firūz called for a cup of wine and handed it to the impudent apologist, but the boasters were dismissed from court for a year and were warned that if they offended again they should be delivered to the tender mercies of Arkalī Khān, who was fettered by none of his father's scruples.

Fīrūz Shāh's solitary departure from his policy of leniency was unfortunate. A religious leader named Sidī Maulā, originally a disciple of Shaikh Farīd-ud-dīn Ganj-i-Shakar of Pāk Pattan or Ajūdhan had, in 1291, been established for some time at Delhi, where his mode of life attracted general attention. He accepted neither an allowance from the state nor offerings from disciples or admirers, but all might enjoy at the hospice which he had built for himself the most lavish hospitality. His wealth was attributed by the vulgar to his discovery of the philosopher's stone, but it has been suggested that he was a patron and a pensioner of the *Thags*. The most frequent guests at his private table were the Khān Khānān and some of the old nobles of Balban's court, who had enrolled themselves as his disciples, and their meetings naturally attracted suspicion It was discovered, one historian says, by Fīrūz himself, who attended a meeting in disguise, that there was a plot to raise Sidī Maulā to the throne as Caliph, and he and his principal disciples were arrested. Scruples, suggested by the theologians, regarding the legality of the ordeal by fire, disappointed the populace of a spectacle, and Sidī Maulā was brought before Fīrūz, who condescended to bandy words with him and, losing his temper in the controversy, turned, in the spirit of Henry II of England, to some fanatics of another sect and exclaimed, 'Will none of you do justice for me on this saint?' One of the wretches sprang upon Sidī Maulā, slashed him several times with a razor, and stabbed him with a packing-needle. Arkalī Khān finished the business by bringing up

an elephant which trampled the victim to death.   One of those dust-
storms, which, in northern India, darken the noonday sun immediately arose and was attributed by the superstitious to the divine
wrath, as was also a more serious calamity, the failure of the seasonal
rains, which caused a famine so acute that bands of hungry and
desperate wretches are said to have drowned themselves in the Jumna.
Shortly after the execution of Sidī Maulā the suspiciously opportune
death of the Khān Khānān, his principal disciple, was announced,
and Arkalī Khān became heir-apparent and remained at Delhi as
regent while his father led an expedition against Ranthambhor.   On
his way he captured the fortress and laid waste the district of Jhāīn,
but a reconnaissance of Ranthambhor convinced him that the place
could not be taken without losses which he was not prepared to
risk, and he returned to Delhi to endure another lecture from his
outspoken cousin, Ahmad Chap, to whose just strictures he could
oppose no better argument than that he valued each hair of a true
believer's head more than a hundred such fortresses as Ranthambhor.
     In 1292 a horde of Mughuls between 100,000 and 150,000 strong,
under the command of a grandson of Hulāgū, invaded India and
penetrated as far as Sunām, where it was met by Fīrūz.   The
advanced guard of the invaders suffered a severe defeat and they
readily agreed to the king's terms.   Their army was to be permitted
to leave India unmolested, but Ulghū, a descendant of Chingīz,
and other officers, with their contingents, accepted Islam and entered
the service of Fīrūz, who gave to Ulghū a daughter in marriage.
The converts settled in the suburbs of Delhi and though many,
after a few years' experience of the Indian climate, returned to
their homes, a large number remained and become known, like
their predecessors, as the New Muslims.   The recapture of Mandāwar from the Hindus and a raid into the Jhāīn district completed
the tale of Fīrūz Shāh's activities in 1292, but in the same year his
nephew 'Alā-ud-dīn, having received permission to invade Mālwa,
captured the town of Bhīlsa, whence he brought much plunder to
Delhi, and received as a reward the great fief of Oudh, in addition
to that of Kara.   Nor was this all that he gained by his enterprise,
for he had heard at Bhīlsa of the wealth of the great southern
kingdom of Deogīr, which extended over the western Deccan, and
his imagination had been fired by dreams of southern conquest.
Without mentioning these designs to his uncle he took advantage
of his indulgent mood to obtain from him permission to raise

additional troops for the purpose of annexing Chanderī and other fertile districts of Mālwa.

At this period two Hindu kingdoms existed in the Deccan, as distinct from the Peninsula ; Deogīr[1] in the west and Warangal or Telingāna in the east. The former was ruled by Rāmachandra, the seventh of the northern Yādava dynasty, and the latter by Rudramma Devī, widow of Ganpati, fifth raja of the Kākatīya dynasty.

On his return from Delhi 'Alā-ud-dīn made preparations for his great enterprise, and, having appointed Malik 'Alā-ul-Mulk his deputy in Kara, with instructions to supply the king with such periodical bulletins of news as would allay any anxiety or suspicion, set out in 1294 at the head of seven or eight thousand horse After marching for two months by devious and unfrequented tracks he arrived at Ellichpur in Berar, where he explained his presence and secured himself from molestation by letting it be understood that he was a discontented noble of Delhi on his way to seek service at Rājamahendri (Rajahmundry) in southern Telingāna. After a halt of two days he continued his march towards Deogīr, where fortune favoured him. Rāmachandra was taken by surprise and the greater part of his army was absent with his wife and his eldest son, Shankar, who were performing a pilgrimage, but he collected two or three thousand troops and met the invader at Lāsūra, twelve miles from the city He was defeated and compelled to seek the protection of his citadel, which he hastily provisioned with sacks taken from a large caravan passing through the city, only to discover, when it was too late, that the sacks contained salt instead of grain Meanwhile 'Alā-ud-dīn, who now gave out that his troops were but the advanced guard of an army of 20,000 horse, which was following him closely, plundered the city and the royal stables, from which he obtained thirty or forty elephants and some thousands of horse, and Rāmachandra sued for peace. 'Alā-ud-dīn agreed to desist from hostilities on condition of retaining what plunder he had and of extorting what more he could from the citizens. He collected over 1400 pounds of gold and a great quantity of pearls and rich stuffs, and prepared to depart on the fifteenth day after his arrival, but Shankar, who had heard of the attack on Deogīr, had hastened back, and arrived within six miles of the city as 'Alā-ud-dīn was starting on his homeward march. His father in vain implored him not to break faith with the invaders and he marched to attack them. 'Alā-ud-dīn detached Malik Nusrat, with a thousand horse,

[1] Since known as Daulatābād.

to watch the city and himself turned to meet Shankar. He was on the point of being overwhelmed by the superior numbers of the Hindus when Malik Nusrat came to his relief. His force was taken for the army of which 'Alā-ud-dīn had boasted and the Hindus broke and fled in confusion. 'Alā-ud-dīn now again invested the citadel and treated his captives and the citizens with great severity, and the garrison, on discovering that the place had been provisioned with salt instead of grain, was obliged to sue humbly for peace. 'Alā-ud-dīn's terms were now naturally harder than at first, and he demanded the cession of the province of Ellichpur, which was to be administered at his convenience and for his benefit either by Rāmachandra's officers or his own, and the payment of an extravagant indemnity, amounting to 17,250 pounds of gold, 200 pounds of pearls, 58 pounds of other gems, 28,250 pounds of silver, and 1000 pieces of silk.

The booty was enormous, but it was the reward of an exploit as daring and impudent as any recorded in history. 'Alā-ud-dīn's objective, the capital of a powerful kingdom, was separated from his base by a march of two months through unknown regions inhabited by peoples little likely to be otherwise than hostile. He knew not what forces might oppose his advance, and he was unable to secure his retreat, which, by reason of the wealth which he carried with him, was more perilous than his advance, but fortune befriended him and his own resourcefulness and high courage sustained him, and he reached Kara safely with all his treasure.

His lieutenant at Kara had succeeded, by means of false and temporising messages, in explaining to the satisfaction of the doting Fīrūz the absence of reports from his nephew. The king's advisers were less credulous, but were unable to shake his confidence in 'Alā-ud-dīn, whom he loved, he said, as a son.

Late in the year 1295 Fīrūz went on a hunting tour to Gwalior and there learned that his nephew was returning from the south to Kara, laden with such spoils as had never been seen at Delhi. The news delighted him, and he debated whether he should return to Delhi to await 'Alā-ud-dīn's arrival, remain at Gwalior to receive him, or advance to meet him. Ahmad Chap, without pretending to conceal his suspicions, advocated the last course, which would take the ambitious adventurer by surprise, and bring him to his knees, but Fīrūz rebuked him for his jealousy of 'Alā-ud-dīn, whereupon Ahmad Chap struck his hands together in despair and left the council chamber, exclaiming, 'If you return to Delhi you slay us with your own hand.'

'Alā-ud-dīn was well served at court by his brother Ulugh Khān, who exerted such influence over Fīrūz that he refused to listen to any warnings, and who kept his brother informed of all that passed at court. It was by his advice that 'Alā-ud-dīn assumed an attitude of apprehensive penitence, declaring that his actions and designs had been so misrepresented that he feared to appear at court. Ulugh Khān drew a pitiable picture of his brother's fear and anxiety and so worked on his uncle's feelings by describing his hesitation between taking poison and fleeing to a distant country that he persuaded the old man to visit Kara in person, and himself carried to 'Alā-ud-dīn the assurance of his uncle's forgiveness and the news of his approaching visit.

Fīrūz, disregarding the warnings of his counsellors, set out from Delhi and travelled down the Ganges by boat, escorted by his troops, which moved by land under the command of Ahmad Chap. 'Alā-ud-dīn crossed from Kara to Mānikpur and, as the royal barge came into sight, drew up his troops under arms and sent his brother to lure Fīrūz into the trap set for him. 'Alā-ud-dīn was represented as being still apprehensive and the king was implored not to permit his troops to cross to the eastern bank of the river, and to dismiss all but a few personal attendants. The murmurs of the courtiers were met with the explanation that 'Alā-ud-dīn's troops were drawn up to receive the king with due honour, Fīrūz Shāh's complaints of 'Alā-ud-dīn's obstinacy were silenced by the excuse that he was occupied in preparing a feast and in arranging his spoils for presentation, and Ulugh Khān even persuaded his uncle to order his few personal attendants to lay aside their arms. As Fīrūz landed 'Alā-ud-dīn advanced to meet him and bowed to the ground. The kindly old man raised him up, embraced him, and chid him for his fears, and then took his hand and led him towards the boat, still speaking affectionately to him. 'Alā-ud-dīn gave a preconcerted signal and one of his companions, Muhammad Sālim, struck two blows at the king with a sword, wounding him with the second. Fīrūz attempted to run towards his boat, crying " Alā-ud-dīn, wretch, what have you done ?' But another assassin, Ikhtiyār-ud-dīn, came up behind him, struck him down, severed his head from his body, and presented it to 'Alā-ud-dīn. The few attendants of the king were murdered and the royal umbrella was raised above the head of 'Alā-ud-dīn, who was proclaimed king in his camp on July 19, 1296. The unnatural wretch caused the head of his uncle and benefactor to be placed on a spear and carried through Mānikpur and Kara, and afterwards through Ajodhya. The faithful Ahmad

Chap would not acknowledge the usurper but returned by forced marches, and led the army, exhausted by a most arduous march in the rainy season, into Delhi.

'Alā-ud-dīn, doubting his power to cope with the adherents of Fīrūz Shāh's lawful heir, was hesitating whether he should march on Delhi or retire into Bengal when his difficulty was solved by his old enemy, his mother-in-law. Arkalī Khān, the heir, was at Multān, and Fīrūz Shāh's widow, 'the most foolish of the foolish,' deeming that a king *de facto* was necessary, in such a crisis, to the security of Delhi, proclaimed the younger son of Fīrūz as king, under the title of Rukn-ud-dīn Ibrāhīm. Arkalī Khān sulked at Multān and his partisans at Delhi refused to recognise his brother. These divisions encouraged 'Alā-ud-dīn to march on Delhi and his spoils provided him with the means of conciliating the populace. At every stage a *balista* set up before his tent scattered small gold and silver coins among the mob. At Budaun he halted, for an army had been sent from Delhi to bar his way, but no battle was fought, for the nobles were lukewarm in the cause of Ibrāhīm and 'Alā-ud-dīn's bursting coffers justified a transference of allegiance. He was thus enabled to advance on Delhi at the head of an army of 60,000 horse and 60,000 foot, and Ibrāhīm, after a feeble demonstration, fled towards Multān with his mother and the faithful Ahmad Chap, and on October 3, 1296, 'Alā-ud-dīn was enthroned in the Red Palace of Balban, which he made his principal place of residence.

The new king, having gained the throne by an act of treachery and ingratitude seldom equalled even in oriental annals, conciliated the populace by a lavish distribution of his southern gold, but his example was infectious and attempts to follow it disturbed the early years of his reign. These and other causes, irruptions of the Mughuls and the necessity for subjugating the Hindu rulers of Rājputāna, Mālwa and Gujarāt protected the Deccan for a while from a second visitation, for the king of Delhi could not conduct war after the fashion of the desperate adventurer who had been ready to risk all on a single throw.

Ulugh Khān and Hijabr-ud-dīn were sent with an army of 40,000 to Multān to secure the persons of Arkalī Khān, Ibrāhīm, and their mother. The city surrendered at once and the princes and their few remaining adherents fell into the hands of Ulugh Khān, and by the king's instructions they, their brother-in-law Ulghū Khān the Mughul and Ahmad Chap were blinded when they reached Hānsī, and the widow of Fīrūz was kept under close restraint.

During the early years of his reign 'Alā-ud-dīn was ably and faithfully served by four men, his brother Ulugh Khān, Nusrat Khān, who was rewarded for his services at Deogīr with the post of minister, Zafar Khān, who had served him well at Kara, and Alp Khān of Multān.   'Alā-ul-Mulk, his faithful lieutenant at Kara, received the post of *Kotwāl* of Delhi, being now too gross for more active employment.

'Alā-ud-dīn had been no more than a few months on the throne when a large horde of Mughuls invaded his kingdom.   Zafar Khān, who was sent against them, defeated them with great slaughter near Jullundur, and his victory was celebrated with rejoicings at Delhi, but his military genius rendered him an object of jealousy and suspicion to his master.

After the repulse of the Mughuls the king considered the case of those nobles whom his own bribes had seduced from their allegiance to his predecessor.   It ill became him to condemn them but it was evident that they were not to be trusted, and cupidity and policy pointed in the same direction.   They were despoiled by degrees, first of their hoards and then of their lands, and when nothing else remained they suffered in their persons.   Some were put to death, some were blinded, and some were imprisoned for life, and the families of all were reduced to beggary.   All deserved their fate, but none was so guilty as he who decided it.

In 1297 'Alā-ud-dīn resolved to undertake the conquest of the Hindu kingdom of Gujarāt which, though frequently plundered, had never yet been subdued, and had long enjoyed immunity, even from raids.   Ulugh Khān and Nusrat Khān were selected for the task and invested and took its ancient capital, Anhilvāra, now Pātan, captured the wife of raja Karan, its ruler, and sent to Delhi as a trophy the idol which had been set up at Somnāth to replace that destroyed by Mahmūd.   Raja Karan and his daughter, Deval Devī, fled, and found an asylum for a time with Rāmachandra of Deogīr.   Nusrat Khān plundered the wealthy merchants of the port of Cambay and obtained, with much other booty, a Hindu eunuch nicknamed at first Kāfūr and afterwards *Hazārdīnārī*, 'the thousand *dīnār* Slave' from the price which he had originally been bought. This wretch became successively the king's vile favourite, lieutenant of the kingdom, and, for a short time before and after 'Alā-ud-dīn's death, its ruler.

After establishing a Muslim government in Gujarāt Ulugh Khān and Nusrat Khān set out for Delhi, and at Jālor distributed the plunder taken in the expedition.   The allotment of the greater part of it caused grave discontent, and the new Muslims mutinied and slew Nusrat Khān's brother and a nephew of 'Alā-ud-dīn. The great drums were sounded, the troops responded to the call to arms, and the mutineers, outnumbered, took to flight and were pursued with great slaughter. Those who escaped took refuge with various Hindu chieftains principally with Hamīr Deo, raja of Ranthambhor, but were unable to escape vicarious punishment, for the fierce tyrant of Delhi put their wives and families to death in circumstances of revolting brutality, and Nusrat Khān avenged his brother's death by delivering the wives of the murderers to the embraces of the scavengers of Delhi, an unspeakable degradation.

The historians of India attribute to 'Alā-ud-dīn the introduction of the barbarous practice of visiting the sins of rebels on the heads of their innocent wives and children ; but the accusation is not strictly just, for there are instances of the practice before his time. It was he, however, who first elevated it into a political principle.

In this year the Mughuls again invaded India and took the fortress of Sibī, which Zafar Khān recaptured after a short siege, and took their leader with 1700 of his followers and their wives and daughters, and sent them to Delhi ; but the success was another step towards his ruin.

Hitherto 'Alā-ud-dīn had prospered in everything to which he had set his hand, and his success had turned his brain. He detected an analogy between himself with his four faithful servants and the founder of his faith with his four companions and successors, Abu Bakr, 'Usmān, 'Umar, and 'Alī, and dreamed of spiritual as well as material conquests. In the latter he sought to surpass Alexander of Macedon and in the former Muhammad. He would ask his boon companions, over the wine-cups, why he should not surpass both. His suggestion that he should declare himself a prophet was received in silence by his associates but his proposal to emulate Alexander was applauded.

These projects had been considered at the royal *symposia* for some time before 'Alā-ud-Mulk the *Kotwāl*, who by reason of his corpulence was excused from attendance at court oftener than once a month, was commanded to deliver his opinion upon them. After demanding that the wine should be removed and that all but the king's most intimate associates should withdraw he deprecated 'Alā-ud-dīn's wrath and proceeded to speak his mind. Innovations in religion, he said, were for prophets, and not for kings. Their success depended not on might, nor on power, but on the will of the Lord of Hosts. It was useless for a king, however great, to

attempt the foundation of a new religion, for unless he were truly
inspired of God he would not long be able to deceive himself, much
less the world.

'Alā-ud-dīn remained for some time sunk in thought, and at
length, raising his head, acknowledged the justice of the rebuke
and declared that he had abandoned his impious design. Against
the second project 'Alā-ul-Mulk had no moral objections to urge,
but he observed that a great part of India remained yet unconquered, that the land was a constant prey to marauding Mughuls,
that there was no Aristotle to govern the realm in the king's absence
and that there were no officers to whom the government of conquered
kingdoms could be entrusted. Waxing bolder he exhorted 'Alā-ud-
dīn to avoid excess in wine, and to devote less of his time to the
chase and more to public business. The king professed himself
grateful for this candid advice and generously rewarded his honest
counsellor, but he could not forgo the petty vanity of describing
himself on his coins as 'the Second Alexander.'

In 1299 an army of 200,000 Mughuls under Qutlugh Khvāja
invaded India. Their object on this occasion was conquest, not
plunder ; they marched from the Indus to the neighbourhood of
Delhi without molesting the inhabitants, encamped on the banks
of the Jumna, and prepared to invest the city. Refugees from the
surrounding country filled the mosques, streets, and bazars, supplies
were intercepted by the invaders, and famine was imminent. The
king appointed 'Alā-ul-Mulk to the government of the city and led
his army out to the suburb of Sīrī, where he summoned his nobles
to join him. The timid *Kotwāl* ventured to resume the character
of adviser, and implored 'Alā-ud-dīn to temporise with the Mughuls
instead of risking all by attacking them at once, but the king refused, in his own phrase, to sit on his eggs like a hen. 'Man,' he
said, with good-humoured contempt, to the unwieldy *Kotwāl*, 'you
are but a scribe, the son of a scribe ; what should you know of
war ?' On the morrow he attacked the Mughuls. The bold and
impetuous Zafar Khān charged the enemy's left with such vigour
that he drove it before him and pursued it until he was lost to the
sight of the rest of the army. Other bodies of the enemy turned
and followed him, so that he was surrounded and slain, after refusing to surrender. Even in this moment of peril 'Alā-ud-dīn and
Ulugh Khān saw with satisfaction that the object of their jealousy
had rushed to certain death, made no attempt to support or succour
him, and contented themselves with a languid demonstration against
the diminished army which remained opposed to them ; but the

valour of Zafar Khān had so impressed the invaders that they retreated precipitately in the night, and when the sun rose 'Alā-ud-dīn, finding that they had decamped, returned to Delhi, hardly less thankful for the death of Zafar Khān than for the flight of the enemy. It is said that the name of Zafar Khān was for some years afterwards used by the Mughuls as that of Richard of England is said to have been used by the Saracens of Palestine, and that they would urge their weary beasts to drink by asking whether they had seen Zafar Khān, that they feared to slake their thirst.

The strength of Ranthambhor, formerly an outpost of the Muslims, but long since a stronghold of the Hindus, had defied Balban's arms and daunted Fīrūz ; its ruler, Hamīr Deo, who boasted descent from Prithvī Rāj, had recently insulted 'Alā-ud-dīn by harbouring the rebellious New Muslims, and the king resolved to punish him. Ulugh Khān and Nusrat Khān were sent against him and, having first reduced Jhāīn, encamped before Ranthambhor. The death of Nusrat Khān, who was slain by a stone from a *balista*, discouraged the army, and a sortie by Hamīr Deo drove Ulugh Khān back to Jhāīn. 'Alā-ud-dīn marched from Delhi to his aid but halted for some days at Tilpat to enjoy his favourite recreation, the chase. After a long day's sport he and his small escort were benighted at a distance from his camp, and when he rose in the morning he ordered his men to drive some game towards him while he awaited it, seated on a stool. His absence had caused some anxiety, and as he awaited the game his brother's son, Ākat Khān, arrived in search of him with a hundred horse, New Muslims of his own retinue. Ākat Khān's ambition was suddenly kindled by the sight of his uncle's defenceless condition and he ordered his Mughul archers to draw their bows on him. The king defended himself bravely, using his stool as a shield, and a faithful slave named Mānik stood before him and intercepted the arrows, but he was wounded in the arm and fell. Some foot soldiers of his escort ran up and, drawing their swords, stood round him, crying out that he was dead. Ākat Khān, without waiting to ascertain whether they spoke the truth, galloped back to the camp, announced that he had slain 'Alā-ud-dīn, and demanded the allegiance of the army. He held a hurried and informal court, at which some officers rashly came forward and offered him their congratulations, but when he attempted to enter the harem the more cautious guards refused to admit him until he should produce his uncle's head.

In the meantime stray horsemen, to the number of sixty or seventy, had gathered round 'Alā-ud-dīn and dressed his wounds,

and on his way towards the camp he was joined by other small
bodies of horse, which brought his numbers up to five or six hundred.
Ascending a knoll he caused the royal umbrella to be raised over
his head, and the sight drew the troops and the courtiers out to join
him. Ākat Khān, finding himself deserted, fled, but was pursued,
taken, and beheaded. The tedium of 'Alā-ud-dīn's convalescence
was alleviated by the punishment of Ākat Khān's associates, who
were put to death with torture, and when he had recovered he
marched on to Ranthambhor, where Ulugh Khān, encouraged by
the news of his approach, had already opened the siege.

While the siege was in progress news reached him that his
sister's sons, Amīr 'Umar and Mangū Khān, had raised the standard
of revolt in Budaun and Oudh, but loyal fief-holders speedily overpowered and captured the young men, and sent them to their uncle,
in whose presence their eyes were cut out.

This rebellion had hardly been suppressed when a serious revolt
in the capital was reported. 'Alā-ul-Mulk ; the fat Kotwāl, was
now dead, and the oppressive behaviour of his successor, Tarmadī,
aroused the resentment of the populace, who found a willing leader
in the Person of Hājī Maulā, an old officer who resented his supersession by Tarmadī. Encouraged by rumours of discontent in the
army before Ranthambhor he assembled a number of dismissed
and discontented members of the city police and others, and by
exhibiting to them a forged decree purporting to bear the royal
seal, induced them to join him in attacking Tarmadī. On reaching
his house they found that he, like most Muslims in the city, was
asleep, for the faithful were keeping the annual fast, which fell in
that year in May and June, the hottest months of summer. He
was called forth on the pretext of urgent business from the camp,
and was at once seized and beheaded. The crowd which had been
attracted by the disturbance was satisfied by the exhibition of the
forged decree, and Hājī Maulā, having caused the gates of the city
to be shut, attempted to deal with Ayāz, the Kotwāl of Sīrī, as he
had dealt with Tarmadī, but Ayāz had heard of Tarmadī's fate and
refused to be inveigled from the fortress of Sīrī. Hājī Maulā then
marched to the Red Palace, released all the prisoners, broke into
the treasury, and distributed bags of money among his followers.
He seized an unfortunate Sayyid, with the suggestive name of
Shāhinshāh, who happened to be descended through his mother
from Iltutmish, enthroned him nolens volens, and, dragging the
leading men of the city by force from their houses, compelled them
to make obeisance to the puppet. The dregs of the populace, lured

by the hope of plunder, swelled the ranks of the rebels, but the more respectable citizens halted between the fear of present violence and the apprehension of the royal vengeance. In the seven or eight days during which Delhi was in the hands of the rebels, several reports of their proceedings reached 'Alā-ud-dīn, but he set his face, concealed the news from his army, and continued the siege.

On the third or fourth day after the rebellion had broken out Malik Hamīd-ud-dīn, entitled Amīr-i-Kūh, assembled his sons and relations, forced the western gate of the city, marched through to the Bhandarkāl gate and there maintained himself against the determined attacks of the rebels. His small force was gradually swelled by the adhesion of some loyal citizens, and by a reinforcement of troops from some of the districts near the capital, and he sallied forth from his quarters at the Bhandarkāl gate, defeated the rebels, and slew Hājī Maulā with his own hand. The troops recaptured the Red Palace, beheaded the unfortunate Sayyid, and sent his head to the royal camp. 'Alā-ud-dīn still remained before Ranthambhor but sent Ulugh Khān to Delhi to see that order was thoroughly restored.

These successive rebellions convinced 'Alā-ud-dīn that something was wrong in his system of administration, and after taking counsel with his intimate advisers he traced them to four causes :

(1) The neglect of *espionnage*, which left him ignorant of the condition, the doings, and the aspirations of his people ;

(2) The general use of wine, which, by loosening the tongue and raising the spirits, bred plots and treason ;

(3) Frequent intermarriages, between the families of the nobles which, by fostering intimacy and reciprocal hospitality, afforded opportunities for conspiracy ; and

(4) The general prosperity which, by relieving many of the necessity for working for their bread, left them leisure for idle thoughts and mischievous designs.

He resolved to remedy these matters on his return, and in the meantime brought the siege of Ranthambhor to a successful conclusion. Hamīr Deo, the New Muslims who had found an asylum with him, and his minister, Ranmal, who had, with many other Hindus, deserted him during the siege and joined 'Alā-ud-dīn, were put to death. It was characteristic of 'Alā-ud-dīn to avail himself of the services of traitors and then to punish them for the treason by which he had profited. After appointing officers to the government of Ranthambhor he returned to Delhi to find that his brother Ulugh Khān, who had been making preparations for an expedition to the Deccan, had just died,

'Alā-ud-dīn now addressed himself, in accordance with the decision at which he had arrived, to the enactment of laws for the prevention of rebellion, and, with the severity which was part of his nature, framed regulations which might have been designed to punish actual rather than forestall potential rebels. Private property was the first institution which he attacked, and he began by confiscating all religious endowments and all grants of rent-free land, both of which supported numbers of useless idlers. Tax-collectors were appointed and were instructed to extort gold, on any pretext that could be devised, from all who possessed it. The result of this ordinance, as described by the contemporary historian, was that gold was not to be found save in the houses of the great nobles, the officers of state, and the wealthiest merchants, and that excepting lands of an annual rental of a few thousand *tāngas* in the neighbourhood of Delhi all rent-free grants in the kingdom were resumed.

The second ordinance established an army of informers, whose business it was to spy upon all and to report to the king anything deemed of sufficient importance for his ear. Everything which passed in the houses of the nobles and officers of state was known, and was reported the morning after its occurrence, until the victims of the system hardly dared to converse in open spaces otherwise than by signs. Even the gossip and transactions of the market place reached the king's ear.

By the third ordinance the use of intoxicating liquor and drugs was prohibited, and those who used them were banished from the city, thrown into prison, or heavily fined. The king himself set the example of obedience by causing his wine vessels to be broken and the wine to be poured out near the Budaun gate, but the habit could not be eradicated. Stills were set up in private houses and liquor was distilled and sold in secret, or smuggled into the city on pack animals, under other merchandise, but the system of *espionnage* made all attempts at evasion dangerous, and many were compelled to cross the Jumna and travel twenty or twenty-five miles to satisfy their craving, for the suburbs were as closely watched as the city itself. Offenders were cruelly flogged and confined in pits so noisome that many died in their fetid and polluted atmosphere, and those who were dragged forth alive escaped only with constitutions permanently shattered. At length 'Alā-ud-dīn learnt that the use of intoxicants cannot be prevented by legislation, and the ordinance was so far relaxed as to permit the private manufacture and consumption of strong drink, but its sale and convivial use remained forbidden.

The fourth ordinance prohibited social gatherings in the houses of the nobles and marriages between members of their families without special permission. Fear of the informers ensured obedience, and even at court the nobles were so closely watched that they dared not exchange whispered complaints of the tyranny under which they lived.

'Alā-ud-dīn next framed a special code of laws against Hindus, who were obnoxious to him partly by reason of their faith, partly by reason of the wealth which many of them enjoyed, and partly by reason of their turbulence, especially in the Doāb. The Hindu hereditary officials enjoyed a percentage on revenue collections and the wealthier Hindus and those of the higher castes were inclined to shift to the shoulders of their poorer brethern the burdens which they should themselves have borne. All this was now changed, and it was decreed that all should pay in proportion to their incomes, but that to none was to be left sufficient to enable him to ride on a horse, to carry arms, to wear rich clothes, or to enjoy any of the luxuries of life. The government's share of the land was fixed at half the gross produce, and heavy grazing dues were levied on cattle, sheep, and goats. The officials and clerks appointed to administer these harsh laws were closely watched, and any attempt to defraud the revenue was severely punished. Hindus throughout the kingdom were reduced to one dead level of poverty and misery, or, if there were one class more to be pitied than another, it was that which had formerly enjoyed the most esteem, the hereditary assessors and collectors of the revenue. Deprived of their emoluments, but not relieved of their duties, these poor wretches were herded together in droves, with ropes round their necks, and hauled, with kicks and blows, to the villages where their services were required. The Muslim officials, under Sharaf Qāī, the new minister of finance, earned the hatred of all classes, and were so despised that no man would give his daughter in marriage to one of them. This measure of 'Alā-ud-dīn's is remarkable as one of the very few instances, if not the only instance, except the *jizya*, or poll-tax, of legislation specially directed against the Hindus.

It was not until these repressive and vexatious laws were in full operation that 'Alā-ud-dīn, disturbed possibly by murmurs which had reached his ears, began to entertain doubts of their consonance with the Islamic law, and sought the opinion of Qāzī Mughīs-ud-dīn of Bayāna, one of the few ecclesiastics who still frequented the court, on the ordinances and other questions. The fearless and conscientious *qāzī* replied that an order for his instant

execution would save both time and trouble, as he could not consent
to spare the king's feelings at the expense of his own conscience, but,
on being reassured, delivered his opinion on the questions propound-
ed to him. The first was the persecution of the Hindus, which he
pronounced to be not only lawful, but less rigorous than the treatment sanctioned by the sacred law for misbelievers. The apportion-
ment of the plunder of Deogīr was a more delicate question, and
though 'Alā-ud-dīn defended himself by maintaining that the
enterprise had been all his own, and that nobody had even heard
the name of Deogīr until he had resolved to attack it, the *qāzī*
insisted that he had sinned in appropriating the whole of the plunder
and in depriving both the army and the public treasury of their
share. Last came the question of the cruel punishments decreed
for various offences, and the *qāzī* rose from his seat, retired to the
place reserved for suppliants, touched the ground with his forehead,
and cried, 'Your Majesty may slay me or blind me, but I declare
that all these punishments are unlawful and unauthorised, either by
the sacred traditions or by the writings of orthodox jurists.' 'Alā-
ud-dīn, who had displayed some heat in the discussion, rose and
retired without a word, and the *qāzī* went home, set his affairs in
order, bade his family farewell, and prepared for death. To his
surprise he was well received at court on the following day. The
king commended his candour, rewarded him with a thousand
tangas, and condescended to explain that although he desired to rule
his people in accordance with the Islamic law their turbulence and
disobedience compelled him to resort to punishments of his own
devising.

During the winter of 1302-03 'Alā-ud-dīn marched into the
country of the Rājputs, and without much difficulty captured Chitor
and carried the Rānā, Ratan Singh, a prisoner to Delhi. At the
same time he dispatched an expedition under the command of
Chhajjū, nephew and successor of Nusrat Khān, from Kara into
Telingāna. For some obscure reason this expedition marched on
Warangal, the capital of the Kākatīya rajas, by the then unexplored
eastern route, through Bengal and Orissa. Unfortunately no detailed
account of the march has been preserved, but the expedition was
a failure. The army reached Warangal, or its neighbourhood, but
was demoralised by the hardships which it had endured in heavy
rain on difficult roads, and, after suffering a defeat, lost most of its
baggage, camp equipage, and material of war and returned to Kara
in disorder.

The Mughuls had missed the opportunity offered by the siege

of Ranthambhor and the simultaneous disorders of the kingdom, but the news of 'Alā-ud-dīn's departure for Chitor, the siege of which appeared likely to be protracted, encouraged them to make another attempt on Delhi, and Targhī, their chief, led an army of 120,000 into India and encamped on the Jumna, in the neighbourhood of the capital, but 'Alā-ud-dīn had already returned from Chitor. He had lost many horses and much material of war in the siege and during his retirement, the army of Kara was so disorganised by the unsuccessful campaign in Telingāna that before it could reach Baran and Koil the Mughuls had closed the southern and eastern approaches to the capital, and the movements of the invaders had been so rapid that they were threatening the city before the great fief-holders could join the king with their contingents. He was thus unable to take the field and retired into his fortress of Sīrī, where he was beleaguered for two months, while the Mughuls plundered the surrounding country and even made raids into the streets of Delhi. Their sudden and unexpected retreat, attributed by the pious to the prayers of holy men, was probably due to their inexperience of regular sieges, the gradual assembly of reinforcements, and the devastation of the country, which obliged them to divide their forces to a dangerous degree in their search for supplies.

This heavy and humiliating blow finally diverted 'Alā-ud-dīn's attention from vague and extravagant designs of conquest to the protection of the kingdom which he had so nearly lost. On his north-western frontier and between it and the capital he repaired all old fortresses, even the most important of which had long been shamefully neglected, built and garrisoned new ones, and devised a scheme for increasing largely the strength of his army. This was no easy matter, for his subjects were already taxed almost to the limit of their endurance, but he overcame the difficulty by means of his famous edicts which, by arbitrarily fixing the prices of all commodities, from the simple necessaries of life to slaves, horses, arms, silks and stuffs, enabled him to reduce the soldier's pay without causing hardship or discontent, for the prices of necessaries and of most luxuries were reduced in proportion. Strange as the expedient may appear to a modern economist, it was less unreasonable than it seems, for the treasure which he had brought from the south and had so lavishly distributed had cheapened money and inflated prices. The fall in the purchasing value of money was, however, in those days of defective and imperfect means of transport and communication, largely restricted to the capital and the suburban area, which were the centre of wealth to a degree hardly comprehensible by those who use railways. Nevertheless, so drastic a measure necessarily met with much opposition, which 'Alā-ud-dīn overcame, in the case of the grain-merchants, by prohibiting the purchase of grain elsewhere than at the state granaries, until the merchants were fain to agree to sell their stocks at a rate lower than originally fixed, and after surmounting a few initial difficulties he was able to maintain, through good years and bad, and without any real hardship to sellers, the scale of prices fixed by him. In the districts around the capital the land revenue was collected in kind, so that when scarcity threatened, in spite of edicts, to enhance price, the king was enabled to flood the market with his own grain, and in the provinces the governors possessed the same power.

These measures, crude as was the conception of political economy on which they were based, attained · so well the object at which they aimed that 'Alā-ud-dīn was able to raise and maintain a standing army of nearly half a million horse. Nevertheless in 1304 a-horde of Mughuls invaded India under 'Alī Beg, a descendant of Chingīz, and another leader, whose name is variously given[1]. The invasion was a mere raid, undertaken with no idea of conquest. The Mughuls evaded the frontier garrisons and marched in a south-easterly direction, following the line of the Himālaya until they reached the neighbourhood of Amroha, plundering, slaying, ravishing and burning as they advanced. The king sent the eunuch Kāfūr Hazārdīnārī, who was already in high favour, and Malik Ghiyās-ud-dīn Tughluq, master of the horse, against them. These two commanders intercepted them on their homeward journey, when they were burdened with plunder, and defeated them. The two leaders and 8000 others were taken alive and sent to Delhi, together with 20,000 horses which the invaders had collected. 'Alā-ud-dīn held a court in the open air, beyond the walls of the city, and the two chiefs were trampled to death by elephants in view of the people. The other prisoners were decapitated and their heads were built into the walls of the fortress of Sīrī, where the king habitually dwelt.

As a reward for his success on this occasion Tughluq was appointed, in 1305, governor of the Punjab, and at the same time Alp Khān was made governor of Gujarāt, and 'Ain-ul-Mulk, governor of Multān, was sent on an expedition to Jālor and to Ujjain and

---

[1] The variants are Tarzāk, Tiriyāk, Barmāk, Tiriyāl, Tiriyāq, and Tartāq. They exemplify the unsuitability of the Persian script for the preservation of proper names.

Chanderī in Mālwa. As he advanced into Mālwa the raja Koka, or Haranand, came forth at the head of an army of 40,000 horse and 100,000 foot to oppose him. The armies met on December 9, and the Hindus, after a determined resistance, were routed. This victory, the news of which was received with great joy at Delhi, made the Muslims masters of Ujjain, Māndū, Dhār, and Chanderī, and so impressed Kaner Deo, the Chauhān raja of Jālor, that he accompanied 'Ain-ul-Mulk on his return to Delhi and swore allegiance to 'Alā-ud-dīn.

The Rānā had been imprisoned at Delhi ever since the fall of Chitor, two years before this time, and was so weary of his confinement that when 'Alā-ud-dīn demanded of him the surrender of his beautiful wife Padmani as the price of his liberty he was disposed to comply. His *thākurs*, or nobles, who were wandering as outlaws in the hills and jungles of Mewār, heard of his intention and sent him messages beseeching him not to disgrace the name of Rajput. They offered to send him poison, which would enable him to avert dishonour, but the fertile brain of his daughter devised a scheme for restoring him to liberty without the sacrifice of his honour or his life. He and his nobles were to feign compliance with the demand, and a train of litters, ostensibly containing the Rānā's wife and her retinue, but filled with armed men, was to be sent to Delhi, escorted by a large force of horse and foot. The cavalcade reached Ratan Singh's prison in safety, the armed men sprang from their litters, slew the guards, and carried off their master. Bodies of Rajputs had been posted at intervals along the road to cover his flight, and though they were defeated one by one they so delayed the pursuers that Ratan Singh reached his country in safety and assembled in the hills a force which enabled him to raid even the environs of Chitor. 'Alā-ud-dīn avenged his discomfiture by removing from the government of Chitor his own son, Khizr Khān, an indolent and self-indulgent youth, and appointing in his place Ratan Singh's sister's son Arsī, who had entered his service, and thus sowed the seeds of dissension among the Rājputs. Many of the *thākurs* transferred their allegiance from Ratan Singh who had forfeited their respect, to Arsī, who remained loyal to 'Alā-ud-dīn and until his death attended regularly at court to present his tribute.

In 1306 the Mughuls invaded India to avenge 'Alī Beg. A horde under Kabk crossed the Indus near Multān, marched towards the Himālaya, plundered the country, and was returning homewards in the hot weather when it found the passage of the Indus barred by a large army under Tughluq, who now bore the title of Ghāzī[1] Malik. Faint and weary, and well nigh perishing for want of water, they were compelled to attack the foe who stood in their path, and of fifty or sixty thousand no more than three or four thousand escaped. Kabk and many others were taken alive and carried by Ghāzī Malik to Delhi, where they were thrown under the feet of elephants. Traces of the column built of their heads on the plain outside the Budaun gate are said to have been visible more than two hundred and fifty years later, in the reign of Akbar. Their wives and children were sold as slaves in Delhi and in the principal cities of northern India. During 'Alā-ud-dīn's reign the Mughuls only once again ventured to invade his kingdom. In 1307-08 a chieftain named Iqbālmand led a horde across the Indus and was defeated and slain. The captives were, as usual, sent to Delhi and crushed to death, and this last defeat deterred the barbarians from invading India until the disorders arising from the misgovernment of 'Alā-ud-dīn's son, Qutb-ud-dīn Mubārak, invited their aggression.

In 1306-07 'Alā-ud-dīn observed that Rāmachandra oi Deogīr had for three successive years failed to remit to Delhi the revenues of the Ellichpur province, and a large army was sent under the command of Kāfūr Hazārdīnārī, now entitled Malik Nāib, or lieutenant of the kingdom, to punish his negligence and reduce him to obedience. The expedition had a secondary object. The wife of raja Karan of Gujarāt, Kamala Devī, longed for the society of her daughter, Deval Devī, who had been carried off by her father to Deogīr, and Malik Nāib was instructed to secure her and bring her to Delhi.

Karan, after his flight from Gujarāt, had not remained an idle guest at Rāmachandra's court, but had rebuilt the town and fortress of Nandurbār and ruled, as Rāmachandra's vassal, a small principality. Malik Nāib passed through Mālwa and entered the Deccan, and Alp Khān, governor of Gujarāt, who had been ordered to co-operate with him, attacked Karan, who for two months offered a most determined resistance.

Shankar Deo, the eldest son of Rāmachandra, had for some time been a suitor for the hand of Deval Devī, but Karan's Rajput pride

---

[1] *Ghāzī*, 'one who defeats and slays infidels in war.' Ibn Batūtah mentions an Arabic inscription of Tughluq on the Friday mosque of Multān, which ran as follows : 'I have encountered the Tātārs on twenty-nine occasions and defeated them : hence I am called *Malik-ul-Ghāzī*.' From this inscription it appears that there was never peace on the frontier. The historians record only invasions in force, in the course of which the Mughuls evaded or overcame the frontier garrisons and advanced for some distance into India.

would not consent to his daughter's union with one whom he stigmatised as a Marāthā[1]. Shankar took advantage of Karan's difficulties to renew his suit, and sent his younger brother Bhīm Deo with an escort to convey Deval Devī to Deogīr. Karan could not but prefer for his daughter an alliance with the Yadava prince to captivity with the unclean foreigners, and surrendered her to Bhīm Deo, who carried her off towards Deogīr.

Alp Khān, ignorant of Deval Devī's departure, attempted to capture her by overwhelming her father with his whole force, defeated him, and pursued him towards Deogīr. In the neighbourhood of that fortress he granted leave to three or four hundred of his men to visit the wonderful cave temples of Ellora, situated in the hills above the town. While they were inspecting the temples they perceived, marching towards them, a Hindu force which they suspected of the intention of cutting them off, and accordingly received with a flight of arrows. The force was, in fact, Deval Devī's escort, commanded by Bhīm Deo, and one of the arrows wounded the horse on which the princess rode. As the pursuers came up with her, her attendants revealed her identity and besought them to respect her honour. She was at once escorted to Alp Khān, who retired to Gujarāt and dispatched her thence to Delhi, where she rejoined her mother and was married, in the summer of 1307, to Khizr Khān, the king's eldest son. The story of their loves is told by Amīr Khusrav in a long poem. The enmity between Malik Nāib and Alp Khān, which had fatal results for the latter at the end of the reign, undoubtedly arose from his forestalling the eunuch on this occasion.

Malik Nāib obviated any future default in the remittance of the revenues of Ellichpur by appointing Muslim officers to administer the province, and advanced to Deogīr, where Rāmachandra, profiting by past experience, was prepared to make his submission. Leaving his son Shankar Deo in the citadel he went forth with his principal officers of state to make obeisance to the king's representative. He was courteously received and was sent to Delhi with a letter of recommendation from Malik Nāib. The gifts which he offered in place of the arrears of tribute due from him and as a peace offering included 700 elephants, and the king, with a

---

[1] The Yādavas of Deogir, like the Jādons of Sindkhed, who claimed descent from them, boasted a Rājput lineage, but the undoubted Rājputs of Rājasthān and Gujarāt, who suspect the Hindus of the south of a strain of Dravidian blood, are loth to admit such claims. It was on account of his nebulous claim to Rājput descent that Jādon Rāo of Sindkhed regarded the marriage of his daughter, Jīji Bai, to Shahjī the Marāthā, father of Shivajī, as a *mesalliance.*

generosity which was attributed to a superstitious regard for Deogīr and its ruler as the origin of his wealth and power, freely pardoned him, bestowed on him the title of *Rāi-i-Rāyān* ('Chief of chiefs') and appointed him to the government of Deogīr as a vassal of Delhi.

While Malik Nāib was engaged in restoring Muslim supremacy in the Deccan an army from Delhi was besieging Siwāna in Mārwār, described later, in the *Āīn-i-Akbarī*, as one of the most important strongholds in India. The siege progressed languidly until 'Alā-ud-dīn himself appeared on the scene and infused such vigour into the operations that Sītal Deo, the raja, sued for peace. In order to escape the humiliation of appearing before his conqueror as a suppliant he caused a golden image of himself to be made and sent it, with a hundred elephants and many other gifts to 'Alā-ud-dīn, but he was disappointed, for the king retained all the gifts and returned a message to the effect that no overtures would be considered until Sītal Deo made them in person. After his submission 'Alā-ud-dīn parcelled out Mārwār among his own nobles and swept the fort clean of everything that it contained, 'even the knives and needles,' but permitted the raja to retain the empty stronghold.

Kāner Deo of Jālor had been permitted to return to his dominions, though he had once aroused the king's wrath by the foolish vaunt that he was prepared at any time to meet him in the field. The boast was not forgotten, and on the raja's exhibiting signs of contumacy 'Alā-ud-dīn sent against him, in bitter contempt, an army under the command of one of the female servants of his palace, named Gul-i-Bihisht ('the Rose of Paradise'). The woman was a capable commander, the Kāner Deo was on the point of surrendering to her when she fell sick and died. Her son Shāhīn, who succeeded her in the command, had less military ability than his mother, and was defeated and slain, but after the arrival of reinforcements under Kamāl-ud-dīn Gurg ('the Wolf') Jālor was taken and Kāner Deo and his relations were put to death.

In 1308 'Alā-ud-dīn made a second attempt to establish his authority in Telingāna, and a large army under the command of Malik Nāib and Khvāja Hājī was dispatched from Delhi by way of Deogīr. He had no intention of annexing more territory than could be conveniently administered from Delhi, and Malik Nāib's instructions were to insist upon no more than the formal submission of the raja of Warangal and an undertaking to pay tribute. Rāmachandra hospitably entertained the whole army during its halt at Deogīr, and when it advanced towards Telingāna supplied it with an efficient commissariat.

Malik Nāib, after passing Indūr, the frontier town between the kingdoms of Deogīr and Warangal, wasted the country with fire and sword, driving its inhabitants before him towards Warangal. The reigning king at this time was Pratāparudradeva II, the seventh known raja of the Kākatīya dynasty, who had succeeded to the throne when his grandmother Rudramma Devī, alarmed, in 1294, by the news of 'Alā-ud-dīn's descent on Deogīr, abdicated in his favour. The statement of the historian Budaunī, who says that the dynasty had reigned for 700 years before its final extinction in 1321, is corroborated by Hindu tradition, but so far as our knowledge at present extends the first of the line was Tribhuvanamalla Betmarāja, who reigned in the first half of the twelfth century.

Rudramma Devī had surrounded the city of Warangal with an outer wall of earth, which enclosed an area about two miles in diameter, and within this was an inner wall of stone, with a circumference of four miles and six hundred and thirty yards, which had been designed by her husband Ganpati and completed under her supervision, and formed an inner line of defence. The invaders, after numerous assaults in which the garrison suffered heavy loss, carried the outer line of defence and captured large numbers of the citizens with their families, and the raja tendered his submission, offering, as an immediate indemnity, three hundred elephants[1], seven thousand horses, and large quantities of coined money and jewels, and, for the future, the payment of an annual tribute. The terms were accepted, and Malik Nāib returned towards Delhi, where the news of his success, which preceded him, relieved the prevalent misgivings as to his fate, for during the siege the Hindus had intercepted the postal runners between the army and the frontier of Telingāna.

Reports which he brought of the great wealth of the temples and the Hindu rulers of the extreme south excited the king's cupidity, and in 1310 Malik Nāib and Khvāja Hājī were again sent southwards with a large army to plunder the kingdom of the Hoysāla Ballālas, which lay to the south of the Krishna, and to explore the southern extremity of the peninsula. The army marched again by way of Deogīr, where Shankar Deo had succeeded his father who had, in the words of an uncompromising historian, 'gone to hell' either late in 1309 or early in 1310. Historians are not agreed on Shankar's attitude to the Muslims. Some describe him as being as loyal as his father, but one says that his fidelity was not above suspicion, and that Malik Nāib deemed it prudent to protect

---

[1] The number is given by most historians as 3000, but an exaggeration may be suspected, and the more probable number has been given.

his communications by establishing a military post at Jālna, on the Godāvarī. From Deogīr he took the direct route to Dvāravatīpura, the capital of the Hoysāla Ballālas, called by Muslim historians Dhorasamundar, the ruins of which are still to be seen at Halebid, in the Hassan district of the Mysore State. The rapidity of his advance took the Hindus by surprise ; Vīra Ballāla III, the tenth raja of the dynasty, was captured in the first attack on his capital, and the city itself fell, with great ease, into the hands of the invaders. Thirty-six elephants, the plunder of the great temple, and all the raja's treasures rewarded them, and a dispatch announcing the victory was sent to Delhi. From Dvāravatīpura Malik Nāib marched to the kingdom of the Pāndyas in the extreme south of the peninsula, to which the attention of 'Alā-ud-dīn had been attracted by recent events. Sundara Pāndya had slain his father, Kulashekharadeva, and attempted to seize his throne, but was defeated by his brother, Vīra Pāndya, and in 1310 fled to Delhi. Malik Nāib advanced to Madura, which Vīra had evacuated, plundered and destroyed the great temple, and thence marched eastwards to the coast. Here he founded, either at Rāmeswaram on the island of Pāmban or on the mainland opposite to it, a mosque which he named after his master.

According to Muslim historians Malik Nāib found two rajas ruling kingdoms in this region. One was Vīra Pāndya, and the other was probably Ravivarman or Kulashekharadeva of Kerala. Both were defeated and plundered, and a Muslim governor was left at Madura. An interesting fact recorded of the expedition into the kingdom of Dvāravatīpura is the encounter of Malik Nāib army at Kadūr with some Moplahs, who are described as half Hindus, and lax in their religious observances, but as they could repeat the *Kalima*, or symbol of Islam, their lives were spared.

Malik Nāib left Madura on April 24 and reached Delhi on October 18, 1311 with the enormous spoils of his enterprise, which included 312 elephants, 20,000 horses, 2,750 pounds of gold, equal in value to 100,000,000 *tangas*, and chests of jewels. No such booty had ever before been brought to Delhi : the spoils of Deogīr could not compare with those of Dvāravatīpura and Madura, and the king, when receiving the leaders of the expedition in the Palace of the Thousand Pillars at Sīrī, distributed largesse to them and to the learned men of Delhi with a lavish hand.

'Alā-ud-dīn's power, having reached its zenith, began to decline. He had hitherto shown considerable administrative capacity, and, though headstrong and self-willed, had usually sought and frequently followed the advice of others, even to the abandonment of some of his most cherished dreams ; but his intellect was now clouded and his naturally fierce temper embittered by ill-health, and though he was physically and mentally less capable than formerly of transacting business of state, he rejected the counsels even of his own chosen ministers, and insisted on administering his vast dominions by the light of his own unaided intelligence, with the result that the affairs of the kingdom fell into such disorder that his declining years were darkened by rebellions and disturbances.

The new Muslims had been a perpetual source of trouble and anxiety during the reign. It was they who had rebelled when the army was returning from the conquest of Gujarāt, and the followers of Ākat Khān had been New Muslims. They were generally discontented, not entirely without cause. They had exchanged the cool highlands of the north for the burning plains of Hindūstān, and their change of domicile and change of faith had not been adequately rewarded. Their prince, Ulghū Khān, had been treated with distinction by Fīrūz, but he had been blinded by 'Alā-ud-dīn, and if he was still alive was living in captivity and misery. No other Mughul appears to have attained to wealth or high place, which is not surprising, for though a few leaders may have received some veneer of civilisation the mass of the tribe was probably not far removed in habits and customs from the ignorant and filthy savages described with such warmth of feeling and language by their sometime captive, the poet Amīr Khusrav. 'Alā-ud-dīn dismissed all New Muslims from his service. They were permitted to enter that of any noble who would employ them, but those who could not obtain or would not accept such employment were told that they might depart whither they would. Many were too proud to serve the courtiers, and remained without employment until they could surreptitiously creep back into the royal service in inferior positions and on insufficient wages. They waited in vain for signs of relentment in the king, and at length in their despair hatched a wild plot to assassinate him while he was hawking near Delhi. The plot was discovered and the vengeance taken was characteristic of 'Alā-ud-dīn. Orders were issued that every New Muslim, wherever found, whether at Delhi or in the provinces, should be put to death, and obedience was ensured by a promise that the slayer of a New Muslim should become the owner of all that his victim had possessed. Between twenty and thirty thousand were massacred, and their wives, children, and property were appropriated by their murderers.

In 1312 Khizr Khān was invested with an umbrella and designated heir-apparent. 'Alā-ud-dīn had paid no attention to his son's education, and the young man had grown up weak, self-indulgent, thoughtless and slothful. Between him and the favourite, Malik Nāib, there existed hatred and mistrust. The able and enterprising minister might well despise the weak and indolent prince, and Khizr Khān would have been worthless indeed had he felt anything but contempt for a creature so vile as the eunuch.

Malik Nāib was so resentful to Khizr Khān's advancement and so weary of his quarrels with the prince's mother that he begged that he might be sent back to the Deccan, where the presence of an officer of high rank happened to be required. Pratāparudradeva of Warangal had complained of the great distance to which he was obliged to send the tribute demanded of him, and had requested that an officer empowered to receive it might be posted at a reasonable distance from Warangal ; and Shankar of Deogīr had been guilty of some acts of defiance of the royal authority. He was accordingly dispatched, in 1313, to Deogīr, where he put Shankar to death and assumed the government of the state. In order to establish his authority in its more remote districts he led an expedition southwards, captured Gulbarga, and annexed the tract between the Krishna and the Tungabhadra, after taking its chief fortresses, Rāichūr and Mudgal. After overrunning some of the southern districts of Telingāna he marched westwards, took the seaports of Dābhol and Chaul, and then invaded for the second time the dominions of Vīra Ballāla III. Thence he returned to Deogīr and dispatched to Delhi the spoils and tribute which he had collected.

'Alā-ud-dīn's excesses had now so undermined his health that he was compelled to take to his bed. Neither his wife nor his eldest son bestowed much attention on him. The former, whom he had neglected, amused herself with arranging and attending marriages and other festivities of the harem, and the latter could spare no time from his wine parties, polo matches, music, dancing, and elephant fights. 'Alā-ud-dīn summoned Malik Nāib from Deogīr and Alp Khān from Gujarāt, and complained bitterly to the former of the heartless conduct of his wife and son. The eunuch perceived an opportunity of destroying all his enemies at once, and assured his master that his wife and son were in league with Alp Khān to take his life. An inopportune proposal by the wife that her second son, Shādī Khān, should be permitted to marry the daughter of Alp Khān, confirmed 'Alā-ud-dīn's suspicions. Khizr Khān was banished to Amroha,˚ but on hearing that his father's health was restored returned to Delhi, in accordance with a vow, to offer thanks at some of the shrines near the capital. The act of disobedience was represented as a wilful defiance of authority, and though Khizr Khān's filial piety at first regained his father's affection, Malik Naīb's persistence and his skilful distortion of facts confirmed the king's belief in the existence of the conspiracy. Khizr Khān and Shādī Khān were sent to Gwalior, now apparently used for the first time as a state prison, their mother was removed from the harem and imprisoned at old Delhi, Alp Khān was put to death, and Kamāl-ud-dīn Gurg was sent to Jālor to slay his brother, Nizām-ud-dīn, who commanded that fortress.

These tyrannical acts caused widespread discontent. Alp Khān's troops in Gujarāt rose in rebellion, and when Kamāl-ud-dīn Gurg was sent to restore order they seized him and put him to death with horrible tortures. The Rānā of Chitor seized many Muslim officers who held fiefs in his dominions and threw them, bound, from the battlements of his fortress. In Deogīr Harpāl Deo, a son-in-law of Rāmachandra, proclaimed himself independent and occupied most of the fortified posts established by the Muslims.

The news of these successive rebellions augmented the king's disorder, remedies failed of their effect, and he wasted away daily until, on January 2, 1316, he died, his end, according to the generally accepted belief, having been hastened by his favourite, who, two days later, assembled the nobles present in the capital and read to them his will. This document, possibly authentic, but certainly procured by misrepresentation and undue influence, disinherited Khizr Khān and made Shihāb-ud-dīn 'Umar, a child of five or six heir to his father. The infant was enthroned and Malik Naīb acted as regent. He caused Khizr Khān and Shādī Khān to be blinded and, eunuch though he was, he pretended to marry 'Alā-ud-dīn's widow, possessed himself of all her jewellery and private property, and then again imprisoned her. His object was to destroy the whole of 'Alā-ud-dīn's family and ascend the throne himself. He had already imprisoned Mubārak Khān, 'Alā-ud-dīn's third son, a youth of seventeen or eighteen years of age, and now sent some men of the corps of infantry on guard at the Palace of the Thousand Pillars, which he had chosen as his residence, to blind him. The prince reminded the soldiers of the duty which they owed to his house, bribed them with some jewellery, and sent them back to the palace on another errand. That night, thirty-five days after the death of 'Alā-ud-dīn, they slew Malik Nāib and his companions. The nobles then recognised Mubārak as regent for his infant brother, and for two months he acquiesced in this obviously temporary arrangement, but on April 1 blinded the unfortunate child and ascended the throne with the title of Qutb-ud-dīn Mubārak Shah.

The new king, who had but lately been a prisoner trembling for his eyesight, if not for his life, began his reign by releasing all prisoners, by recalling all those who had been banished from the capital by his father, and by showing clemency and mercy to all except the murderers of Malik Nāib. Like his father, he could inspire and profit by treachery, but he could not endure the sight of his instruments. The soldiers, however, brought their fate on themselves. They adopted an attitude similar to that of the Praetorian Guards of the Roman Emperors, and demanded extravagant honours. Their two principal officers, Bashīr and Mushīr, were put to death, and the crops was drafted, in small detachments, to distant garrisons.

Mubārak gained much popularity in the early days of his reign by the rescission of all his father's harsher enactments. The compulsory tariff was abolished, with the result that the prices of all commodities rose suddenly, to the great satisfaction of the mercantile community. Some of the lands and endowments resumed by the despot were restored to the original grantees, and the possession of wealth by private persons ceased to be regarded as a crime. The sudden removal of all the harsh restraints which the people had suffered produced an outburst of licentiousness similar to that which had disgraced the short reign of Kaiqubād, and once again the king's example encouraged the extravagance of his subjects, for his morals were no better than his father's and from the earliest days of his reign he was entirely under the influence of a vile favourite. This wretch was by origin a member of one of those castes[1] whose touch is pollution to a Hindu, whose occupation is that of scavengers, and whose food consists largely of the carrion which it is their duty to remove from byre and field. He was nominally a Muslim, and received at his conversion the name of Hassan and from his infatuated master the title of Khusrav Khān and the office of chief minister of the kingdom.

[1] He is described as a Parwārī, a word much mutilated in the Persian texts of Muslim historians. It is a polite name for the Mahār and Dher caste of western India, the lowest of all village menials except the Māngs, and so unclean that they are not permitted to live within the village, but must dwell apart in a separate quarter.

As soon as Mubārak was firmly established on the throne he took steps to restore order in the rebellious provinces of Gujarāt and Deogīr. 'Ain-ul-Mulk Multānī was sent to the former province, and after he had quelled the rebellion Mubārak's father in-law, who received the title of Zafar Khān, was appointed its governor. The other task Mubārak reserved for himself and, having appointed as regent in the capital a slave named Shāhīn, upon whom he conferred the title of Vafā Malik, he set out in 1317 for the Deccan. The usurper Harpāl was not a formidable foe, and fled from Deogīr as the army approached it, but was pursued and captured, and after he had been flayed and decapitated his skin was stretched upon, and his head placed above, one of the gates of the city. Mubārak spent the rainy season of 1318 at Deogīr, once more parcelled out Mahārāshtra among Muslim officers, and appointed military governors to Gulbarga and Sāgar, and even to distant Dvāravatīpura. During his sojourn at Deogīr he built the great mosque which yet stands within the walls of Daulatābād, as the town was afterwards named, using in its construction the materials of demolished temples, the pillars of which are still recognisable as Hindu handiwork. When the rains abated he appointed Malik Yaklakī to the government of Deogīr, sent his favourite, Khusrav Khān, on an expedition to Madura, and set out 'for Delhi. On his way thither a serious conspiracy against his life was formed by his cousin Asad-ud-dīn, the son of Yaghrush Khān, brother of Fīrūz Shāh. Mubārak was to have been assassinated in the camp, but the plot had ramifications in the capital, for two coins struck at Delhi in A H. 718 (A.D. 1318-19) bear the title of Shams-ud-dīn Mahmūd Shāh, which was either that which Asad-ud-dīn intended to assume or, more probably, that of a ten-year old son of Khizr Khān, whose elevation to the throne was, according to Ibn Batūtah, the object of the conspiracy. It was arranged that Mubārak should be attacked in his harem on an occasion on which he diverged, for the distance of a few marches, from the route followed by the army, and took a different road attended only by a small guard, but one of the conspirators lost heart and disclosed the design to Mubārak, and Asad-ud-dīn and his confederates were seized and executed. Mubārak at the same time caused all the family and descendants of his grand-uncle, Yaghrush Khān, at Delhi, to the number of twenty-nine, some of whom were mere children, to be put to death.

From Jhāīn Mubārak dispatched an officer to Gwalior to put to death Khizr Khān, Shādī Khān, and Shihāb-ud-dīn 'Umar. As the three princes had already been blinded their murder was wanton and superfluous, but Mubārak coveted Deval Devī, the wife of his eldest brother, and after the murder of her husband the unfortunate princess was brought to Delhi and placed in his harem.

The murder of his brothers appears to have whetted Mubārak's appetite for blood, and on his return to Delhi he summoned from Gujarāt his father-in-law, Zafar Khān, and for no apparent reason put him to death. He also executed Shāhīn, who had been left as regent at Delhi, and though historians allege no specific crime against this victim it can hardly be doubted that he had been implicated in the recent conspiracy.

Mubārak now indulged in the grossest licentiousness and the most disgusting buffoonery. He delighted to appear before his court tricked out in female finery and jewels. Harlots and jesters were assembled on his palace roof and greeted the great nobles, such men as 'Ain-ul-Mulk Multānī and Qarā Beg, who held no fewer than fourteen offices, with lewd gestures and foul abuse, and, descending from the roof, ran naked among the courtiers, et gestu turpi et obscoeno in vestes nobilium honoratorum mingebant. Yet the degraded youth who could organise and enjoy such scenes as these assumed a character to which no former ruler of Delhi had ventured to aspire. Others had eagerly sought recognition by, and proudly owned allegiance to the Caliphs, and even 'Alā-ud-dīn had readily abandoned his brief and impious dream of posing as a prophet. It remained for his son, who inherited his vices without his genius, to arrogate to himself the titles of Supreme Pontiff and Vicegerent of the God of heaven and earth, and to assume the pontifical title of al-Wāsiq-billāh.

Hisām-ud-dīn , half-brother of Khusrav Khān, and partner with him in the king's affections, was sent to Gujarāt in the place of Zafar Khān, and his first act there was to attempt to raise a rebellion against his master, but the nobles of the province refused to follow such a leader, seized him, and sent him to Delhi, where, for his own sake and that of his brother, he was not only pardoned, but restored to favour.

Malik Yaklakī, encouraged by reports of the demoralisation of the court, raised the standard of rebellion in Deogīr and proclaimed his independence, but was defeated and captured by an army sent against him and carried, with his associates, to Delhi, where Mubārak's perverted sense of justice permitted him to put the subordinates to death while he inflicted on Yaklakī no heavier punishment than mutilation of the nose and ears, and shortly afterwards appointed him governor of Sāmāna.

Khusrav Khān was meanwhile active in the south. Having collected much booty in the Madura district he returned to Telingāna, where he was detained by the rainy season and beguiled the tedium of inaction with ambitious dreams. He discussed with his intimates the possibility of establishing himself as an independent ruler in the south, and would have put the design into execution had not some of the officers of the army reported it to the king and compelled him to lead them back to Delhi. Mubārak ignored the report and, in his impatience to embrace his favourite, ordered him to travel from Deogīr to the capital in a litter and by posting relays of bearers on the road enabled him to perform the journey of nearly 700 miles in seven days. Khusrav Khān at once resumed his former ascendency and persuaded his master that the reports sent from the camp were false and malicious. When his accusers reached Delhi, prepared to substantiate their charges and expecting at least commendation for their fidelity, they were dismissed from their posts and forbidden the court, and one of them, Malik Talbagha of Kara, was thrown into prison.

Khusrav Khān's treasonable design had failed principally because he had, although he was in chief command, no personal troops to support him against the nobles of whose contingents his army was composed, and so deeply was the king infatuated that, notwithstanding the revelation of his favourite's treachery, he lent a sympathetic ear to his complaints and permitted him to raise in Gujarāt a corps of 40,000 horse, largely composed of and exclusively commanded by members of his despised tribe. The long meditated treason was now nearly ripe for execution and, after a design for assassinating Mubārak in the hunting field had been abandoned as too dangerous, it was decided that he should be put to death in his palace.

Khusrav Khān, by complaining that his nightly attendance prevented him from meeting his relations, obtained possession of the keys of the palace gates, and was enabled to admit large numbers of his relations and of his corps of horse to the palace, in the lower story of which they used nightly to assemble. A warning given to Mubārak on the eve of his death by his former tutor was repeated to Khusrav Khān, and served only as a text for hypocritical protestations, which entirely disarmed suspicion. On the night of April 14, 1320, all was ready and he who had uttered the warning to the king was cut down as he was inspecting the guard. The uproar which ensued disturbed Mubārak in the upper story of his palace and he asked Khusrav Khān to see what was amiss. Khusrav, having ascertained from a glance into the courtyard that the work was already begun, told him that the men were trying to catch some horses which had broken loose. Even as he spoke the assassins were ascending the stairs and Mubārak, as they burst into his room, sprang up in terror and ran towards the female apartments, but Khusrav seized him by the hair and held him while Jāharya, one of the Parwārīs, stabbed him to death. His head was severed from his body and thrown into the courtyard, as a signal to all that the throne was vacant, and the outcastes broke into the harem, murdered the children of the royal family, and outraged the women. When Mubārak's head was recognised the royal guards on duty at the palace fled, and left all in the hands of Khusrav's tribesmen. The palace was illuminated and all the great nobles then present in the capital were summoned to court, and hastened thither in ignorance of what had happened. They were detained until the morning and were then forced to attend a court at which the outcaste was proclaimed king under the title of Nāsir-ud-dīn Khusrav Shāh. The proclamation was followed by a massacre of many of the old servants of 'Alā-ud-dīn and Mubārak, whose known fidelity rendered them dangerous to the usurper ; and the Khaljī dynasty, which had reigned for no more than thirty years, but had given to the Muslim empire in India its first administrator, was wiped out. Khusrav possessed himself of the person of the unfortunate princess Deval Devī, who had been successively the wife of Khizr Khān and of his brother and murderer Mubārak. Against the union with the foul outcaste who became her third husband 'her proud Rājput blood must indeed have risen.'

In the distribution of honours and rewards with which Khusrav, following the usual custom, inaugurated his reign his own near relations and those of his tribe who had most distinguished themselves in the late tumult were the most favoured, but an attempt was made to conciliate those powerful nobles who had been entrapped and compelled unwillingly to countenance by their presence the enthronement of the outcaste, and Wahīd-ud-dīn Quraishī was entitled Tāj-ul-Mulk and permitted to retain office as minister. 'Ain-ul-Mulk Multānī received the titles of 'Ālam Khān and Amīr-ul-Umarā, but Khusrav applied himself especially to the conciliation of the son of the powerful Ghāzī Malik, Fakhr-ud-dīn Muhammad Jauna, whom he appointed master of the horse. Ghāzī Malik himself

had always avoided the intrigues of the capital, and seems never to
have visited Delhi during Mubārak's brief and profligate reign, but
he was dreaded by the gang of outcastes and pseudo-Muslims now
in power both as a loyal adherent of the Khaljī dynasty and as a
rigid Muslim, and his son was valuable either as a supporter or as a
hostage. The attempt to secure him failed, and he escaped from
Delhi at midnight with only two or three followers, and took the
road to Dīpālpur, his father's headquarters. A force sent in pursuit
of him failed to overtake him, and Jauna was joyfully welcomed by
his father at Dīpālpur. The governor of Multān hesitated to support
Ghāzī Malik against the king *de facto*, but was slain by a less
scrupulous officer, Malik Bahrām Aiba, who led the army of Multān
to Dīpālpur and joined the old warrior who stood forth as the
champion of Islam.

Islam stood in sore need of a champion. None of Khusrav's
tribe was a Muslim in more than name, and only a few had made
profession of the faith. Muslim historians record with indignation
the open celebration of idolatrous worship at court and the gross
insults offered to their faith. Mosques were defiled and destroyed
and copies of the scriptures of Islam were used as seats and stools.

Ghāzī Malik now set out for Delhi. He was first opposed by
Yaklakī, the noseless and earless governor of Sāmāna, but swept the
feeble obstacle from his path. Yaklakī fled to Sāmāna and was
preparing to join Khusrav at Delhi when the landholders of the
district rose against him and cut him to pieces. At Sirsa Ghāzī
Malik defeated and put to flight an army under the command of
Hisām-ud-dīn, the usurper's half-brother, and continued his march
to Delhi. Khusrav prepared to meet him near the old fort at
Indarpat, and in attempting to secure the fidelity of his troops by
donations varying in amount from four to two and a half years' pay
and to conciliate by means of gifts the most respected professors of
the religion which he and his followers had outraged, completely
emptied the treasury. His profusion availed him little, for 'Ain-ul-
Mulk, who was hardly less powerful than Ghāzī Malik, deserted him
and withdrew with his troops into Mālwa.

The armies met on September 5, and though 'Ain-ul-Mulk's
defection had damped the spirits of the usurper's faction his troops
fought bravely until they were overpowered by Ghāzī Malik's
veterans. Khusrav attempted to save himself by flight, but was
found lurking in a garden, and was brought before the conqueror
and beheaded. Ghāzī Malik halted for the night at Indarpat, where

he received from some of the leading citizens the keys of the gates of Siri, and on the following day he entered the Palace of the Thousand Pillars and wept as he beheld the scene of destruction of his old master's family. He asked whether there yet remained any descendant of 'Alā-ud-dīn who might claim his allegiance, but was informed that the whole family had been extinguished and was urged to ascend the throne. After a decent profession of reluctance he was proclaimed king on September 8, under the title of Ghiyās-ud-dīn Tughluq Shāh.

CHAPTER VI

THE REIGNS OF GHIYĀS-UD-DĪN TUGHLUQ AND MUHAMMAD TUGHLUQ, AND THE SECOND CONQUEST AND REVOLT OF THE DECCAN

TUGHLUQ's[1] ascent of the throne recalls that of Jalāl-ud-dīn Fīrūz Khaljī. Both were aged warriors called upon to restore the dominion of Islam, menaced by the extinction of the dynasties which they had long served, but here all similarity between them ends. The powers of Fīrūz were failing when he was called to the throne, and his reign would have closed the history of his family but for the usurpation of his unscrupulous but vigorous nephew. Tughluq on the other hand, though old, was in full vigour of mind, and during his short reign displayed none of the contemptible weakness of Fīrūz. He was able to enforce many of the salutary laws of ' Alā-ud-dīn and to enact others which restored order in a kingdom which had nearly passed from the grasp of Islam. He enjoyed the advantage of pure Turkish lineage, his elevation excited no jealousy among the nobles who had formerly been his equals, and he was able, within a week of his accession, to pacify the capital and within forty days his sovereignty was everywhere acknowledged.

One of his first acts was to provide for surviving females of the Khaljī house by suitable marriages. He pursued and punished with great severity all who had been in any way concerned in marrying the beautiful Deval Devī to the vile upstart Khusrav; he provided with lands and employment all old officials who had faithfully served the fallen dynasty, and he distributed appointments among his own adherents, the chief of whom, Fakhr-ud-dīn Muhammad Jauna Khān, his eldest son, received the title of Ulugh Khān and was designated heir apparent ; he recovered the treasure which had been lavished by the usurper or had been plundered during the confusion of his short reign, and thus replenished his empty treasury. In giving effect to this unpopular measure he encountered much difficulty and opposition. Khusrav, in order to

---

[1] This, a tribal name, is usually transliterated ' Tughlaq.' Mr. Stanley Lane Poole prefers Taghlak, Sir Aurel Stein (*Ruins of Desert Cathay*) gives the name of the tribe, which inhabits the neighbourhood of Khotan, as Taghlik, doubtless representing faithfully the modern pronunciation. I follow the traveller Ibn Batūtah, who is explicit on the point and must have known how the word was pronounced at Delhi in his day, seeing that Muhammad Tughluq was his patron. See *J.R.A.S.*, July, 1922. But Professor D. S. Margoliouth points out that it is also a personal name.

conciliate the professors of the dominant religion, had made large gifts, ostensibly for charitable purposes, to the leading *shaikhs*, or religious teachers. Three of these had refused to touch any money coming from a source so polluted and most of those who had feared to refuse the gift had prudently kept the money in deposit and restored it when called upon to do so, but Shaik Nizām-ud-dīn Auliyā, the most renowned of them all, who had received as much as half a million *tangas*, replied that he had at once distributed in charity all that he had received and was not in position to make restitution. Public opinion forbade, in the case of a religious leader so prominent and so renowned for sanctity, the torture or duress to which humbler delinquents were subjected and the king was obliged to accept the explanation instead of the money, but the Shaikh was a marked man, and was almost immediately denounced for indulgence in the ecstatic songs and dances of *darvīshes*, a form of devotion regarded as unlawful by rigid Sunnis of the established religion. Tughluq summoned him before an assembly of fifty-three theologians, and though he was forced to bow to their decision that these religious exercise were not unlawful relations between him and the Shaikh remained strained until his death, in which it is not improbable that the Shaikh was implicated.

The odium incurred by the forcible recovery of the usurper's gifts was dissipated by the king's judicious liberality and his care for the welfare of his subjects. Unlike his son he did not seek to conciliate the few and astonish the many by enormous gifts to favoured individuals, but on occasions of public rejoicing his bounty, widely diffused, earned popularity and the only malcontents were the rapacious, whose avarice was disappointed by his settled policy of promoting the welfare of the public and discouraging the accumulation of great wealth by individuals.

Private property confiscated under the harsh rule of ' Ala-ud-dīn and still retained by the state was restored to its former owners ; all the usurper's decrees were revoked ; public works of utility, such as forts in which peaceful husbandmen might seek a refuge from brigands, and canals to irrigate their fields were undertaken, and highway robbery was suppressed ; but Tughluq devoted his attention above all to the encouragement of agriculture. Gardens were planted, the land tax or rent due to the state was limited to one-tenth or one-eleventh of the gross produce, which was to be assessed by the collectors in person, and not estimated from the reports of informers and delators ; the revenue was to be collected with due regard to the cultivator's power to pay, and all officials were reminded that the surest method of improving the revenue was the extension of cultivation, not the enhancement of the demand, and thus ruined villages were restored, waste land was reclaimed, and the area under cultivation was extended. Fief-holders and local governors were held responsible for the observance of this policy and it was ordained that the emoluments of the collectors of the revenue should consist in the exemption of their holdings from taxation, and should not be derived from extortion. Some privileges were accorded to the nobles, place-seekers were forbidden to haunt the public offices, and torture was prohibited in the recovery of debts due to the state and was restricted to cases of theft and embezzlement.

One class was subjected to repressive legislation. Tughluq not unreasonably, considering the circumstances of his elevation to the throne, decreed that while it should be possible for Hindus to live in moderate comfort none should be permitted to amass such wealth as might nurture ambition. The decree, though harsh, was not altogether unnecessary, and it has benefited posterity by causing the concealment of portable wealth which, discovered in after ages, has shed much light on history.

Tughluq personally was a rigid Muslim, punctilious in the observance of all the ordinances of his faith, and especially in avoiding intoxicants. He forbade the manufacture and sale of wine and enforced, as far as possible, the observance of the Islamic law. He was devoid of personal pride and vanity and his elevation to the throne made no difference in his relations with his family, his associates, and his immediate attendants.

The security and order which reigned in the kingdom within a short time of his accession were due hardly less to his admirable system of communications than to his other measures of adminis-trative reform. Postal systems had from time immemorial existed in India, but during recurring periods of disorder, such as Khusrav's reign, shared the general disintegration of all administrative machi-nery, and Tughluq may be credited with the inauguration of the perfect system found existing in the reign of his son and successor, and minutely described by the Moorish traveller, Ibn Batūtah.

Posts were carried by horsemen, called *ulāq* (*ulāgh*), or by runners, called *dāwat*. For the former, horses were posted at distances of seven or eight miles along the roads, but the stages travelled by the latter were but the third of a *kurūh*, or about two-thirds of a mile. Ibn Batūtah mistranslates the word *dāwat*, properly *dhāwat*, as 'the third of a *kurūh*,' but it means simply 'a runner.' He says that these occupied huts, without the villages, at every third part of a *kurūh* on the roads, and were always ready to start at a moment's notice. Each carried a staff tipped with copper bells, and when he left a post town he took his letters in his left hand and his staff in his right, shaking it so that the bells jingled, and ran at full speed towards the next post-house, where a runner, warned of his approach by the sound, awaited him, took the letters from him, and ran at full speed in like manner towards the next post-house.

In parts of India a modification of this system still exists. The staff, or short spear, with its cluster of bells, is still carried, but the runner's stage is about five miles, which he is expected to cover, at his peculiar jog-trot, in an hour, but these runners carry bags containing the public mails. Tughluq's apparently carried only a few official dispatches and, as Ibn Batūtah says, ran at full speed. Five minutes would therefore be a liberal allowance of time for each stage, and, as there was no delay at the post-houses, it may be calculated that news travelled at the rate of nearly two hundred miles in twenty-four hours. News of Ibn Batūtah's arrival at the mouth of the Indus reached Delhi, between eight hundred and nine hundred miles distant by the postal route, in five days. The king was thus in close touch with the remotest corners of his kingdom, and the service was rapid even for heavier burdens. In the next reign fresh fruit was transported from Khurāsān and Ganges water for the royal table from Hindūstān to Daulatābād on the heads of postal runners.

The province of the Deccan, under the rule of Malik Qavām-ud-dīn, who had been appointed to its government with the title of Qutlugh Khān, remained loyal to the new dynasty, but Pratāparud-radeva of Warangal appears to have believed that his fealty to Delhi was dissolved by the extinction of the Khaljīs, and in 1321 Tughluq sent his eldest son, Ulugh Khān, to reduce him again to obedience.

The prince met with no opposition during his advance, and opened the siege of Warangal. The earthern rampart of Rudram-madevī was stoutly defended, but the Hindus were outmatched in the combats which were daily fought beneath it, and so many were slain that Pratāparudradeva attempted to purchase peace by promises of tribute, hoping to obtain terms similar to those to which Malik Nāib had agreed, but the offer was rejected. In the meantime, however, the Hindus, as in the former siege, had been engaged in cutting the communications of the besiegers, and the absence of news from Delhi suggested to 'Ubaid the Poet and the Shaikhzāda of Damascus, two turbulent and mischievous favourites of the prince, the fabrication of false news, with the object of facilitating their master's usurpation of the throne, and Ulugh Khān suffered himself to be led astray.

A report of the king's death was circulated in the camp and the army was called upon to swear allegiance to the prince as their new sovereign, but the leading nobles with the expedition knew that the report was fabricated and withdrew their contingents. One even suggested that the prince should be put to death as a traitor, but to this the others would not agree. The siege was raised and the army, marching in separate divisions, retired to Deogīr, pursued and harassed by the Hindus.

Before the troops reached Deogīr they learned by posts from Delhi that the king still lived, and the treason of the prince and his counsellors became apparent to all, but the great nobles who had opposed him were apprehensive of his vengeance, or of his influence with his father, and fled, with his evil advisers. One died in Gondwāna, another was slain by a Hindu chieftain who flayed his body and sent the skin to the prince, and the others were captured and sent to the prince.

Ulugh Khān travelled post haste to Delhi with the horsemen and by some means made his peace with his father and betrayed both his associates and his enemies, who were put to death[1].

So successful was Ulugh Khān in persuading his father of his innocence or his penitence that in 1323 he was permitted to lead another expedition into Telingāna, and on this occasion he observed the precaution, which he had formerly neglected, of securing his lines of communication. His first objective was Bīdar, the ancient Vidarbha, and having captured that fortress he marched on War-angal and opened the siege with more vigour than on the first occasion. The efforts of his troops were supported by such artillery as that age possessed, catapults and *balistae*, and their valour, thus aided, reduced both the outer and the inner lines of defence. Pratāparudradeva and his family, the nobles of the kingdom with their wives and children, and the elephants, horses and treasure of the state, fell into the hands of the victors, and Telingāna, for the first time, was directly subjected to Muslim rule. The country was

---

[1] In this account of Ulugh Khān's rebellion Ibn Batūtah has been followed. Baranī's confused and perplexing account, which has been followed by other Indian historians is coloured by his own and Fīrūz Shāh's regard for Muhammad's memory. Vide *J.R.A.S.*, for July, 1922.

divided into fiefs and districts which were allotted to Muslim nobles
and officers, and Warangal, now renamed Sultānpur, became the
capital of a province of the empire. The news was received at
Delhi with great rejoicings and Ulugh Khān remained for some
time at Sultānpur-Warangal to establish the administration of the
province. His restless activity led him into the ancient Hindu
kingdom of Utkala in Orissa, called by Muslim historians Jājnagar,
the ancestors of whose rulers had stemmed the advance of the earlier
Muslim governors of Bengal. His expedition was a mere raid,
undertaken with no design of permanent conquest, and its only
immediate result was the capture of forty elephants, but the raja,
who had lived for some time at peace with the quasi-independent
rulers of Bengal, of the line of Balban, was disturbed by the discovery
that the Turks were in a position to menace his southern as well as
his northern frontier.

During the prince's absence in the south an army of Mughuls
invaded the kingdom of Delhi from the north-west, but was defeated,
its two leaders being captured and brought to Tughluq's court.
Almost immediately after this event the king received reports from
Bengal which led him to form the resolution of invading that country
in person for the purpose of restoring order and asserting the
supremacy of Delhi, and he called his son from Telingāna to act as
regent during his absence.

It was a civil war arising from conflicting claims to the throne
that summoned Tughluq to Bengal. Shams-ud-dīn Fīrūz Shāh of
that country, third son of Nāsir-ud-dīn Mahmūd Shāh Bughrā and
grandson of Balban, had died in 1318, after a reign of sixteen years,
leaving five sons, of whom the three eldest only need occupy our
attention. These were Shihāb-ud-dīn Bughrā, who succeeded his
father on the throne at Lakhnāwati, Nāsir-ud-dīn, and Ghiyās-ud-
dīn Bahādur, who, having been appointed by his father governor of
Sonārgāon, or Eastern Bengal, had proclaimed his independence in
that province in 1310 and, on his father's death, disputed the title of
his elder brother, Shihāb-ud-dīn Bughrā, and in 1319 overcame him
and usurped his throne, the succession to which was then claimed
by Nāsir-ud-dīn, who appealed to Tughluq. The king eagerly
seized so favourable an opportunity of intervention in Bengal, the
allegiance of which to Delhi had been severely shaken by the
downfall of the Khaljī dynasty and the rulers of which were bound
by no ties either to Khalj or to Tughluq, but had, on purely
hereditary grounds, a better claim than either to the throne of
Delhi.

Tughluq Shāh marched to Bengal by way of Manaich, the town which had been stormed by Mahmūd of Ghaznī. In the year following his accession he had appointed to the government of this district Tātār Malik, whom he had entitled Zafar Khān. The governor's first task had been to crush the local Rājput chieftain who, during the short interval of Hindu supremacy, had established himself in the district. According to tradition the Rājput was invited to a conference at which the merits of Islam and Hinduism were discussed and, being convinced of the truth of the former, accepted it and submitted, thus rendering unnecessary an appeal to arms. Zafar Khān renamed Manaich Zafarābād[1] and was firmly established in the district when the king passed through it on his way to Bengal. He accompanied the royal army into Tirhut, where Nāsir-ud-dīn waited upon Tughluq and did obeisance to him, and was sent in command of the force dispatched against Lakhnāwati. All opposition was crushed and Ghiyās-ud-dīn Bahādur was captured and brought before the king with a rope around his neck. The elephants from the royal stables at Lakhnāwati were appropriated by Tughluq and his army took much plunder, but Nāsir-ud-dīn was placed as a vassal monarch on the throne of Western Bengal. Eastern Bengal, which had for thirteen years been independent under Bahādur, was annexed and administered as a province of the kingdom af Delhi.

Meanwhile disquieting news of his son's behaviour in the capital reached Tughluq. Ulugh Khān had purchased vast numbers of slaves and had formed a party by extravagant gifts and grants to those who he believed could be converted by this means into adherents. His chief crime appears to have been his intimate association with the obnoxious Shaikh Nizām-ud-dīn Auliyā, whose disciple he had become, and who was believed to have prophesied, in one of his ecstatic trances, his imminent accession to the throne. It was also reported that astrologers had prophesied that the king would never return to the capital alive. Reports of these conversations and machinations reached Tughluq in his camp, and enraged him. He wrote to the astrologers, menacing them with his displeasure ; to his son, threatening to deprive him of his office and to exclude him from any participation in public business ; and to the Shaikh, to whom he addressed the threat that when he returned from Bengal Delhi would be too small to hold both of them. The Shaikh is said to have replied with the prophetic menace, which

---

[1] Zafarābād is situated in 25° 42′ N. and 82° 44′ E., in the Jaunpur District of the United Provinces.

has since become proverbial, *Hanūz Dihlī dūr ast*, 'Delhi is yet afar off,' and so it proved to be.

Tughluq sent Bahādur a prisoner to Delhi and himself set out for Tughluqābād, the capital which he had built for himself to the south of Old Delhi. He attacked on his way the raja af Tirhut, whose loyalty was doubtful, and reduced him to submission, and from Tirhut travelled towards the capital by forced marches, leaving the army to follow at its leisure.

Tughluqābād was elaborately decorated and Ulugh Khān prepared a welcome for his father by building for his reception at Afghānpur[1], a few miles from the city, a temporary kiosk, where he might take rest and refreshment after his toilsome journey and before his state entry into his capital.

Ulugh Khān caused this building, which was chiefly of wood, to be erected from his own designs, employing in the construction of it one Ahmad, son of Ayāz, known as Malikzāda, an inspector of buildings whom, on his accession to the throne, he made his minister, with the title of Khvāja Jahān. The building was so designed as to fall when touched in a certain part by the elephants, and it appears that the device was a projecting beam. Ulugh Khān welcomed his father at the kiosk, and entertained him at a meal, at the conclusion of which he begged that the elephants from Bengal might be paraded and driven round the building. His father acceded to his request and Ulugh Khān, before the elephants were brought up, suggested to Shaikh Rukn-ud-dīn, for whom he had a special regard, that he should leave the kiosk for his prayers. Immediately after the Shaikh's departure the elephants were brought up, came into contact with that part of the building which had been designed to effect its collapse and the whole structure fell on the old king and crushed him. Diggers were summoned, but their arrival was purposely delayed, by Ulugh Khān, and the king's body was discovered, when the *debris* was removed, bending over that of his favourite sen, Mahmūd Khān, as though to protect him. It was commonly believed that the king still breathed when his body was discovered and was dispatched under the orders of his son. He was buried at night in the tomb which he had selected for himself at Tughluqābād and Ulugh Khān ascended the throne under the title of Muhammad Shāh[2].

[1] Probably the village, about five and a half miles to the south-east of Tughluqābād, which appears in the Indian Atlas as Aghwanpur.

[2] This account, which differs from that of the contemporary Baranī and Indian historians who have followed him, is taken from the narrative of Ibn Batūtah, whose informant was Shaikh Rukn-ud-dīn. Vide *J.R.A.S.*, for July, 1922.

The death of Ghiyās-ud-dīn Tughluq occurred in February or March, 1325, and Shaikh Nizām-ud-dīn soon followed him, dying on April 3[1]. Almost at the same time died the greatest of all the poets of India who have written in Persian, Yamīn-ud-dīn Muhammad Hasan, known as Amīr Khusrav, at the age of seventy-two. He was of Turkish origin, his father having been a native of 'the green-domed city' of Kash, in Turkistān, who, driven from his home early in the thirteenth century by the horde of the Mughul, Chingīz Khān, had found an asylum in India. The poet was born at Patiāla in A.H. 651 (A.D. 1253) and entered the service of 'Alā-ud-dīn Khaljī as court poet, but later in his life became the disciple of Shaikh Nīzām-ud-dīn Auliyā, abandoned the court and worldly ambitions, and lived in religious retirement, but still wrote poetry. He was a most prolific writer and estimated the number of couplets which he had written at more than 400,000 but less than 500,000, dividing his poems into four classes, youthful effusions; poems of early middle age, written when he was putting off childish things and turning his thoughts to religion; poems written when he had attained the dignity of a religious teacher; and the poems of his old age. Each of the four classes bears, as might be expected, the impress of his views on this world and the next during the period of his life in which it was produced, but in the second class there are to be found poems sufficiently courtly to be acceptable to the vanity of a royal patron.

Amīr Khusrav had a deep veneration for Sa'dī, whom he entertained when he visited India, and the great poet of Persia repaid his admirer by recommending him very warmly to 'Alā-ud dīn. As Khusrav himself says in one of his verses, with a play upon words which cannot be preserved in translation :

> The volume of my verse hath the binding of Shīrāz.

Amīr Khusrav was survived by another poet, Shaikh Najm-ud-dīn Hasan, known as Hasan-i-Dihlavī, whose works, less widely known than Khusrav's, were much admired. Both poets are honourably mentioned in the *Tazkirat-ush-Shu'arā* and in the *Ātashkada*. Hasan died in 1338 at Daulatābād in the Deccan, and was buried there. The celebrated Jāmī refers in highly complimentary terms to these two poets of Delhi, and they are among the few Indian-born writers of Persian verse whose works have been read and admired beyond their own country.

---

1 Ibn Batūtah says that the Shaikh died before the king's return from Bengal, and that Ulugh Khān incurred his father's wrath by helping to bear the corpse to the grave.

Tughluq, following the example of other founders of dynasties at Delhi, had left an interesting monument of his short reign in the fortress capital of Tughluqābād, which he built for himself on a rocky eminence nearly ten miles to the south of the site afterwards selected by Shāh Jahān for his city. He founded this town immediately after his ascent to the throne and completed it before he received the news of the conquest of Telingāna. ' Here,' said Ibn Batūtah, ' were Tughluq's treasures and palaces, and the great palace which he had built of gilded bricks, which, when the sun rose, shone so dazzlingly that none could gaze steadily upon it. There he laid up great treasures, and it was related that he constructed there a cistern and had molten gold poured into it so that it became one solid mass, and his son Muhammad Shāh became possessed of all of it when he succeeded him.' Tughluq's mausoleum in red sandstone and white marble, connected with his town by a bridge carried on arches, and the massive walls of his fort still remain, but no palace now dazzles the eye, and the once brilliant town is entirely deserted.

Muhammad, after remaining for forty days at Tughluqābād, went in state to the old city of Delhi and there took his seat on the throne in the palace of the former kings. The city was decorated for his reception and the acclamations of the people were stimulated by a lavish distribution of gold and silver coins.

The delineation of a character so complex and contradictory as that of Muhammad Tughluq is no easy task. He was one of the most extraordinary monarchs who ever sat upon a throne. To the most lavish generosity he united revolting and indiscriminate cruelty ; to scrupulous observance of the ritual and ceremonial prescribed by the Islamic law an utter disregard of that law in all public affairs; to a debasing and superstitious veneration for all whose descent or whose piety commanded respect a ferocity which when roused respected neither the blood of the prophet nor personal sanctity. Some of his administrative and most of his military measures give evidence of abilities of the highest order, others are the acts of a madman. His protégé Ziyā-ud-dīn Baranī, the historian, whom he admitted to a considerable degree of intimacy and whom he often deigned to consult, attributes many of the atrocities which he commanded or sanctioned to the evil influence of twelve wicked counsellors, stigmatized as 'miserable,' 'accursed,' or 'most accursed,' whose delight was to shed the blood of Muslims, but Muhammad Tughluq was no weakling, and was never a tool in the hands of his counsellors. If his advisers were vile and bloodthirsty men it was he that chose them, and if he followed evil counsels he did so because they commended themselves to him. In like manner Baranī attributes his disregard of the Islamic law in administrative and punitive measures to his early association with Sa'd, the heretical logician, 'Ubaid, the infidel poet, and 'Ālim-ud-dīn, the philosopher, but this is mere special pleading. His association with these freethinkers never diminished his faith in Islam, his careful regard in other respects for its laws, or his veneration for its traditions. It was not the fault of logicians, poets, or philosophers that he scandalised the orthodox by deliberately preferring human reason to divine revelation as a guide in mundane matters, and by openly avowing his preference. His private judgement misled him, but this was due to his temperament. His peculiar vice as a judge and administrator was his inordinate pride, which deprived him of the power of discriminating between offences. All his commandments were sacred and the slightest deviation from an impracticable regulation and the most flagrant act of defiance and rebellion were alike punished by a cruel death. This policy acted and re-acted with cumulative effect on the monarch and his people. Disgusted by their sovereign's barbarity they grew ever more refractory ; exasperated by their disobedience he grew ever more ferocious. His wide dominions were seldom free from rebellion during his reign, and at his death the whole kingdom was in a ferment.

Baranī, notwithstanding his gratitude and his fears, is surprisingly frank. So overweening, he says, was the king's pride that he could not endure to hear of a corner of the earth, hardly even of a corner of heaven, which was not subject to his sway. He would be at once a Solomon and an Alexander ; nor did mere kingship content him, for he aspired to the office of prophet as well. His ambition was to make all the kings of the earth his slaves, and Baranī would liken his pride to that of Pharaoh and Nimrod, who claimed divinity as well as royalty, but that his scrupulous personal observance of the law and firm adherence to the faith of Islam cleared him of the suspicion of blasphemy and infidelity. He would compare him with Bāyazīd of Bustām and Husain, son of Mansūr-ul-Hallāj, who, in the ecstacy of their devotion, believed themselves to have been absorbed into the Godhead, but that his barbarous cruelty deprived him of any claim to sanctity.

Against his overweening pride must be set the grovelling servility with which he received at his court the great-great-grandson of the Abbasid Caliph al-Mustansir of Baghdād, the miser

Ghiyās-ud-dīn, whom he received with more than royal honours, whom he compelled, much against his will, to place his foot upon his neck, and on whom he lavished wealth with astonishing profusion ; his abasement before Hājī Sa'īd Sarsarī, envoy from the phantom Abbasid Caliph al-Mustakfī of Egypt, whose name appeared on the currency of his kingdom and of whose envoy's utterances he spoke as though they were divine revelations ; and the extravagant veneration for the temporal, as well as the spiritual authority of the Caliphate which led him to strike from the formal Friday sermon the names of all his predecessors but such as had been formally recognised by one of the Caliphs.

Against his barbarous punishments and indiscriminate bloodshed may be set a few instances, related by Ibn Batūtah, of a fantastic display of reverence for abstract justice and the forms of law. On one occasion a Hindu complained to the *qāzī* that the king had slain his brother without a cause, and the king, having previously ordered the magistrate not to rise at his entrance, appeared unarmed in court and made his obeisance. He heard with humility and obeyed with promptitude the sentence directing him to compensate the complainant. In another cause a Muslim complained that the king had unjustly retained some of his property, and in obedience to the *qāzī's* order restitution was made. In a third case a young man, son of one of the great officers of the kingdom, complained that the king had arbitrarily caused him to be beaten for no fault, his complaint was found to be true, and according to the Islamic law of retaliation he was permitted to take his revenge. A stick was placed in his hand and he gave the royal offender twenty-one strokes. The chastisement was probably purely formal, but the king's head-dress fell to the ground.

These rare displays, made probably in the early years of the reign, and possibly collusive, cannot palliate the arbitrary cruelty of a monarch whose punishments were as revolting as they were frequent, and whose gateway was seldom unpolluted by the corpse of a freshly slain victim, but they illustrate some of the extraordinary contradictions of his character. It may be that Muhammad thus compounded with his conscience for many barbarities. The severest condemnation of his cruelty is the remorse of his old servant Baranī, who bitterly laments his own cowardice and that of his fellow-courtiers. 'We were traitors,' he says, 'who were prepared to call black white, though not devoid of that knowledge which ennobles a man. Avarice and the desire of worldly wealth led us into hypocrisy, and as we stood before the king and witnessed punishments forbidden by the law, fear for our fleeting lives and our equally fleeting wealth deterred us from speaking the truth before him.'

A catalogue of the atrocities committed by Muhammad during his reign, such as that given by Ibn Batūtah, would be tedious and revolting, but it will be necessary from time to time to refer to the punishments inflicted by him. One of the early acts of his reign was the murder of his brother, Mas'ūd, whose only offence seems to have been that he was handsome and popular. Muhammad professed to suspect him of treasonable designs, and the unfortunate prince discovered, as did so many of the tyrant's victims, that it was better to court a speedy death by a false confession than to suffer day by day the barbarous tortures devised by the perverted ingenuity of Muhammad.

Against this unnatural act may be set a display of foolish generosity. In the year of his accession Muhammad permitted Ghiyās-ud dīn Bahādur, the worthless and turbulent prince whom his father had brought in chains from Bengal, to return to Sonārgāon, where he was associated in the government of Eastern Bengal with Tātār Khān, who had been entitled Bahrām Khān and left at Sonārgāon as governor by Ghiyās-ud-dīn Tughluq. In the following year Nāsir-ud-dīn, who was reigning at Lakhnāwati as Muhammad's vassal, died, and Qadr Khān was appointed by Muhammad governor of Western Bengal.

Muhammad may be compared, in his devotion to the details of administration, with Philip II of Spain, and one of his earliest acts was to order the compilation of a register of the revenue and expenditure of the provinces of his kingdom. The governors of provinces were directed to send to the capital all the materials for the compilation of such a register, and during the first few years of the reign a large number of clerks and officials was employed in the Palace of the Thousand Pillars at Delhi in the work of compilation. The object of the measure seems to have been to introduce a uniform standard of land revenue and to ensure that no village in the kingdom remained unassessed or unvisited by collectors. The register already maintained for the districts in the neighbourhood of the capital served as a model for the larger work, and the revenue exacted from these districts as a standard for the assessment of the more distant provinces, but we have unfortunately no details of the principles on which allowance was made for the different classes of soil, for distance from markets and the other considerations which affect the assessment of the land revenue in India.

In ᴜᴇ second year of the reign a most serious rebellion broke out in the Deccan. Bahā-ud-dīn Gurshāsp, sister's son to Ghiyās-ud-dīn Tughluq, and therefore first cousin to Muhammad, held the fief of Sāgar, about ten miles north of Shorāpur, and enjoyed great influence among the Muslim officials of the Deccan. He refused to recognise the new king and appears to have believed that he might be able to establish a claim to the throne, though relationship in the female line seldom counts for much in the east. He exerted all his influence, and the whole of the Deccan was soon aflame. The rebels advanced towards Deogīr, but were met by the minister, Khvāja Jahān, and the brutal Mujīr-ud-dīn, Abu Rijā, who defeated them. Gurshāsp fled to Sāgar and thence to Kampalī, on the Tungabhadra, where he took refuge with the raja. The imperial troops sustained a reverse before this place, but were reinforced, and the noble raja, seeing that he could no longer protect his guest, sent him to Dvāravatīpura with a letter commending him to the protection of Vīra Ballāla III, and performed the awful rite of *jauhar*. After the women had been destroyed the raja led his bravest warriors in a charge on the royal army, in which all the Hindus perished. Khvāja Jahān then entered Kamplī and carried off the principal inhabitants, including the dead raja's eleven sons, into slavery. The Hindu princes were forced to accept Islam, but were otherwise treated with the distinction due to their high birth and their father's valour. Ibn Batūtah, while at Muhammad's conrt, met three of these princes and describes one of them as an intimate friend of his own.

Vīra Ballāla was made of less stern stuff than the raja of Kamplī, and tamely complied with Khvāja Jahān's demand for the surrender of the fugitive, who was carried to Deogīr where Muhammad had now arrived, to receive his punishment. After being subjected to the insults of the women of the harem he was flayed alive. His flesh was cooked with rice and offered to the elephants, after portions of it had been sent to his wife and children, and his skin was stuffed with straw and exhibited in the principal cities of the kingdom.

It was probably the rebellion of Gurshāsp that impressed upon Muhammad the desirability of a more central situation than that of Delhi for the capital of a kingdom which included the Deccan and the Peninsula, and it was now, in 1327, that he decreed that Deogīr, which he renamed Daulatābād, or the abode of wealth, should replace Delhi as the capital. Not only the great officers of state and the courtiers but apparently also provincial governors were commanded to build for themselves houses at Daulatābād, to send their families thither, and to make it their home. The king spared neither pains nor expense to beautify his new capital and to make it a worthy substitute for Delhi. Spacious bazars were laid out and handsome buildings erected, and Ibn Batūtah, who visted Daulatābād several years later, described it as a great and magnificent city equal to Delhi. But the king's greatest work was the marvellous citadel, an ancient stronghold of the rajas of Deogīr, which was strengthened and improved by him. The fort, probably as Muhammad left it, was described as follows, more than three centuries later, by 'Abu-ul-Hamīd Lāhori, the official chronicler of Shāh Jahān's reign. 'This lofty fortress, the ancient names of which were Deogīr, and Dhārāgīr, and which is now known as Daulatābād, is a mass of rock which raises its head towards heaven. The rock has been scarped throughout its circumference, which measures 5000 legal yards, to a depth which ensures the retention of water in the ditch at the foot of the escarpment. The escarpment is so smooth and even that neither an ant nor a snake could scale it. Its height is 140 cubits, and around its base a ditch forty cubits in width and thirty in depth has been dug in the solid rock. Through the centre of the hill a dark spiral passage like the ascent of a *minār*, which it is impossible to traverse, even in daylight, without a lamp, had been cut, and the steps in this passage are cut out of the rock. It is closed at the foot of the hill by an iron gate, and after passing through this and ascending the passage one enters the citadel. At the head of the passage is a large grating of iron which is shut down in case of necessity, and when a fire is lighted upon it the ascent of the spiral passage becomes impossible owing to the intense heat. The ordinary means of reducing fortresses, such as mines, covered ways, batteries, etc., are useless against this strong fortress.'

This passage still exists, and is the only work the attribution of which to Muhammad is doubtful, for Ibn Batūtah, who visited Daulatābād late in 1342 or early in 1343, records that access to the citadel was then gained by means of a leathern ladder.

Besides officers of state and courtiers numbers of tradesmen and others who gained their livelihood by serving or supplying the court followed it to Daulatābād, and encouragement was given to any who could be persuaded voluntarily to transfer their domicile to the new capital, but the steps taken in this year must not be confounded, as some historians have confounded them, with those adopted two years later, when the whole of the population of Delhi was transported, as a punitive, not an administrative measure, to Daulatābād.

From the new capital as a base of operations it was possible to establish order more completely in the Deccan, and Muhammad's troops were occupied for eight months in the siege of the strong fortress of Kondhāna, now known as Sinhgarh. The fort, which was held by a Kolī chieftain, surrendered at the end of that time.

Muhammad was not allowed to repose long at Daulatābād. In 1328 he was disturbed by news of the rebellion of Malik Bahrām Aiba, Kishlū Khān, the governor of Multān and Sind. The position of this governor was peculiar. He had been on terms of the closest intimacy with Ghiyās-ud-dīn Tughluq, had co-operated most cordially with him in the campaign against the usurper Khusrav, and had had a friendly contest with his comrade, in which each had urged the other to ascend the throne. Kishlū Khān had eventually prevailed by warning Tughluq that if he hesitated his ambitious son would certainly forestall him, and his old friend left him in virtual independence at Multān. The circumstances of Tughluq's death had not improved the relations between Muhammad and Kishlū Khān, who rose in arms against his sovereign. Of the circumstances of his rebellion there are two accounts. According to one he incurred the king's wrath by decently interring the stuffed skin of the unfortunate Gurshāsp instead of sending the miserable relic on for exhibition in another province, and according to the other Muhammad ventured to send 'Alī, a collector of revenue, to Multān to inquire when Kishlū Khān proposed to obey the order to build for himself a house at Daulatābād and to send his family thither. 'Alī's insolence in delivering this message so inflamed the wrath of Kishlū Khān's son-in-law that he slew the messenger, and Kishlū Khān raised the standard of revolt.

Muhammad hastened in person from Daulatābād to crush the rebellion, marching by way of Delhi. Kishlū Khān marched eastward from Multān and the armies met in the desert plain of Abohar[1], where Muhammad defeated his adversary by means of a stratagem. Shaikh 'Imād-ud-dīn, who closely resembled him in personal appearance, was placed in the centre of the army, under the royal umbrella, and Muhammad himself, with 4000 horse, lay in ambush. The rebels naturally directed their chief efforts against the centre of the royal army, and in an impetuous charge broke the line and slew the Shaikh. The army retired in real or feigned confusion and the rebels dispersed to plunder the camp. The king then

---

[1] In 30° 8′ N. and 74° 11′ E.

emerged from his ambush, fell upon Kishlū Khān, who was but scantily attended, slew him, and severed his head from his body. The positions were now reversed, and the rebels broke and fled. Muhammad marched on to Multān, about 160 miles distant, occupied the city, and prepared to take punitive measures against the inhabitants, whom he condemned as the accomplices of Kishlū Khān. He seized the *qāzī*, Karīm-ud-dīn, caused him to be flayed alive, and ordered a general massacre, but this calamity was averted by the intercession of the saint, Shaikh Rukn-ud-dīn. Muhammad sent his minister, Khvāja Jahān, towards the coast of Sind, to repress disorders which had arisen in that province, and was almost immediately recalled to Delhi by the news of disturbances in the Gangetic Doāb. Before leaving Multān he distinguished the house which he had occupied by hanging over its gate the head of the rebel, Kishlū Khān, which was seen by Ibn Batūtah when he visited Multān five years later.

In 1328, or early in 1329, very shortly after Muhammad's return to Delhi, his dominions were invaded by Tarmāshīrīn the Mughul, who may be identified with the Chaghatāī, 'Alā-ud-dīn Tarmāshīrīn, who reigned in Transoxiana from 1322 until 1330 or 1334. The invader passed through Lahore and Sāmāna to Indrī[1], and thence to the borders of the Budaun district, traversing the Doāb to the banks of the Ganges and plundering and devastating the country on their way. The incursion was a mere raid and it is probable that the invaders lost no time on their homeward journey, but Muhammad pursued them as far as Kalānaur, a few miles south of the Rāvī, afterwards to become famous as the town where the youthful Akbar ascended the imperial throne, and to have left Abu Rijā there to destroy the fort which had afforded a refuge to the marauders, while he returned to Delhi. According to another account he was on this occasion mean spirited enough to bribe the Mughuls to retire, but the inconsistency of such conduct with his character is sufficient to discredit the record.

After the retirement of the Mughuls the king remained for some time at Delhi, where he had an account to settle with his people. The citizens were enraged against their sovereign, whose removal of the court to Daulatābād had gone far towards ruining Delhi and depriving those who had preferred to remain of their livelihood. Open resistance to a bloodthirsty tyrant who could count on the fidelity of his troops was not to be thought of, and the citizens vented their spleen by the characteristically oriental

---

1 A *pargāna* town in 29° 53′ N. and 77° 5′ E., near the western bank of the Jumna.

means of anonymous letters, filled with reproaches, invective, and abuse, which were thrown a night into the hall of audience. The tyrant avenged himself by issuing the monstrous decree that every soul should leave Delhi and migrate to Daulatābād, more than six hundred miles distant to the south. Some attempt was made to provide funds for the journey and accommodation on the way, but the decree was rigorously enforced and these measures were utterly inadequate to relieve the sufferings of the inhabitants of a whole city. 'The king ordered all the inhabitants to migrate from Delhi to Daulatābād, and on their hesitating to obey, issued a proclamation that nobody should remain in the city for more than three days longer, and the greater part of them moved out, but some of them hid themselves in their houses, and he ordered a search to be made for those who had remained, and his slaves found in the narrow streets of the city two men, one of whom was a cripple and the other blind, and they brought them before him, and he ordered that the lame man should be cast from a *balista* and that the blind man should be dragged from Delhi to Daulatābād, which is forty days' journey, and he was rubbed to pieces on the way, so that nothing but his foot reached Dulatābād. When he did this all the people departed from Delhi and left their goods and their wealth, and the city was left without inhabitants and deserted[1]' Large numbers perished by the way and the greater part of those who reached their journey's end never ceased to mourn for their old homes. It was nothing to them that they dwelt in a city of which the courtly poet sang that the heavens were the anvil of the knocker of its door, that its gates were the eight gates of paradise, and much more in the same strain of exaggeration. To them the city was a foreign land, and the magnificence of its buildings, the fertility of the soil, and the beauty and majesty of the landscape could not appease their longings for the imperial city of the Jumna. After the wretched citizens had been driven forth on their perilous and toilsome journey the king, standing by night on the roof of his palace and looking over the city which he had made desolate rejoiced to see that no smoke rose and that neither lamp nor fire shone in its deserted dwellings. 'Now,' said he, 'is my heart content and my soul appeased.'

His vindictive wrath had blazed against his people, not against his city, and efforts were made, by persuading or compelling the people of other towns and of the surrounding country to move to Delhi, to repopulate the city, but these efforts were not successful.

[1] Ibn Batūtah.

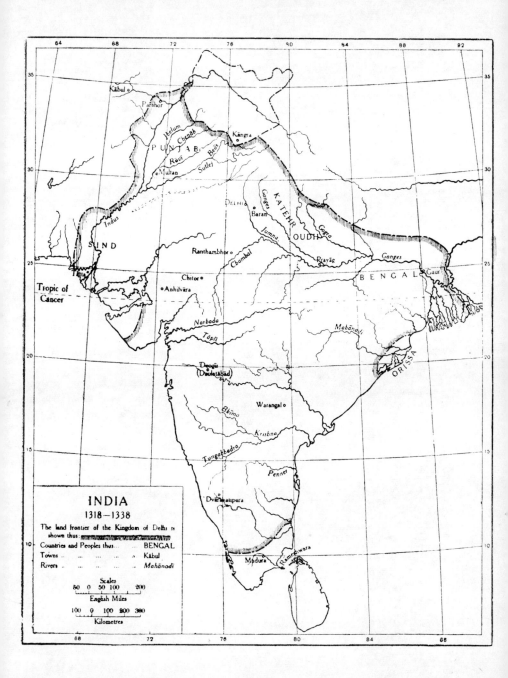

INDIA
1318—1338

The land frontier of the Kingdom of Delhi is
shown thus
Countries and Peoples thus ... ... BENGAL
Towns .. .. ^ Kābul
Rivers .. .. Mahānadi

Scales
50 0 50 100　　　200
English Miles
100 0 100 200 300
Kilometres

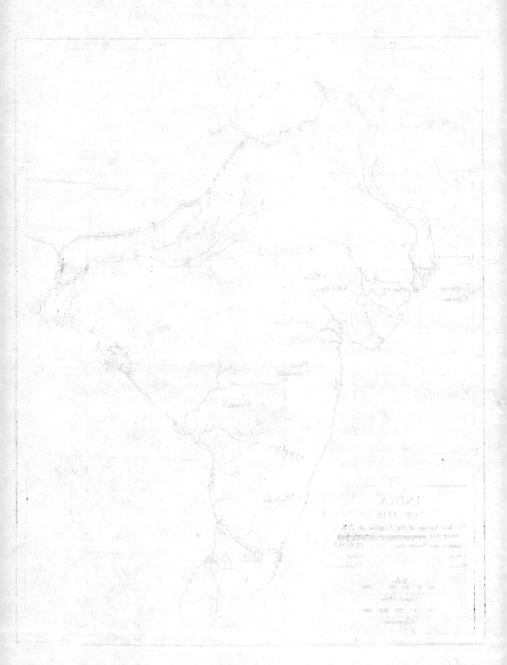

INDIA
1410–1450

Ibn Batūtah, who arrived at Delhi five years later, describes the splendours of the royal palace and the pomp of the court, but of the city itself he says, 'When I entered Delhi it was almost a desert. ...Its buildings were very few and in other respects it was quite empty.'

The transportation of the population of Delhi has been described as a punitive rather than an administrative measure. A measure adopted in the following year, the enhancement of the assessment on land in the Doāb and the introduction, with a view to further taxation, of a census of the houses and cattle, partook of both characters. The Hindus of the Doāb were disaffected and turbulent, but it is inconceivable that they should have been guilty of the folly, imputed to them by Muhammad, of inviting the Mughuls to invade the country. They had had experience of Mughul raids, and would not have prepared a scourge for their own backs, but the measure was designed to replenish the treasury as well as to punish the people, and it failed of both its objects.

The extent of the enhancement is uncertain. The statement that the demand was increased ten fold and twenty-fold is almost certainly hyperbolical, and the statements of Firishta, who says that it was increased three-fold and four-fold, and of Budaunī, who says that it was doubled, are probably nearer the truth ; but whatever the extent of the enhancement may have been the cultivators were unable to meet the demand, and abandoned their holdings and took to brigandage, so that the treasury suffered and the guilty went unpunished. The reprisals ordered by the king converted one of the richest and most fertile provinces of the kingdom into the seat of a war between the royal troops and the inhabitants.

Some means of replenishing the treasury had to be devised, and it was now that Muhammad conceived the idea of his famous fictitious currency. He may have heard of the paper currency of Khubilāī Qā-ān in China, and the fictitious money of the Mughuls in Persia, and it was perhaps in imitation of these fiscal measures that he issued brass or copper tokens which were, by his decree, to pass current for the silver *tanga* of 140 grains. Mr. Thomas, in his *Chronicles of the Pathan Kings of Delhi*[1] has contended that Muhammad's vast power and the great wealth of his dominions justified, or almost justified, this measure, and that its failure was due to unforeseen causes, but the contemporary historian Baranī asserts that it formed a part of the kings' extravagant design of bringing under his away the whole habitable world, for the execution

[1] Edition of 1871, pp. 239-47.

of which boundless wealth would be necessary, and from this statement it would appear that Muhammad had no clear notion of the uses and limitations of a fictitious currency, but believed that he could, by his decree, virtually convert brass and copper into silver and gold. He was rudely undeceived. With the almost worthless tokens the people purchased the gold and silver coins for which they were legal tender. The revenue was paid in the tokens, which were also freely used by foreign merchants in their disbursements but refused by them in payment for their goods, but the principal factor in the collapse of the scheme was the wholesale counterfeiting of the tokens. As Mr. Thomas says, 'There was no special machinery to mark the difference of the fabric of the royal mint and the handiwork of the moderately skilled artisan. Unlike the precautions taken to prevent the imitation of the Chinese paper notes there was positively no check on the authenticity of the copper tokens, and no limit to the power of production of the masses at large.' The justice of these remarks will be appreciated by those acquainted with the appearance and workmanship of the copper coinage of India before the introduction of European methods of minting. An artisan with a few simple tools and a moderate degree of skill in their use could sell at the price of silver any brass or copper which fell into his hands, and this result might have been foreseen. The enormous extent to which counterfeiting was carried on is described in graphic terms by all the historians, and Baranī merely paints the picture in somewhat vivid colours when he writes that every Hindu's house became a mint.

The tokens were not current for more than three or four years, and as an oriental despot, who is, in fact, the state, cannot be expected to understand that public funds are held in trust for the public, some credit is due to Muhammad for his prompt acknowledgement of his error by the recall of the tokens, though it is doubtful whether he had any conception of the cost of the measure. It was proclaimed that silver coins would be issued to the public from all treasuries in exchange for brass and copper tokens, so that the state began by buying copper at the price of silver and ended by virtually distributing silver *gratis*, for so vast was the quantity of tokens which poured in that no use could be found even for the metal. Mountains of them arose at the treasuries and lay there for years. The remains of them were still to be seen, a century later, in the reign of Mu'izz-ud-dīn Mubārak Shāh. As Budaunī says, ' After all, copper was copper, and silver was silver.'

Discontent now manifested itself among a very different class of

Muhammad's subjects. It was three years since he had compelled his courtiers to transfer their families to Daulatābād, and he had already been absent for two years and a half from his new capital. Those in attendance on him began to murmur that they might as well have been permitted to keep their families at Delhi if they themselves were to be compelled to live there, but Muhammad was probably obeying his own impluse rather than their importunity when he returned, in 1330, to Daulatābād.

In the following year Ghiyās-ud-dīn Bahādur rose in rebellion at Sonārgāon, but the rising was crushed by Bahrām Khān, and the rebel was put to death. His skin, like that of Gurshāsp, was stuffed with straw and exhibited in the principal cities of the kingdom.

The following year, 1331-32, passed uneventfully at Daulatābād, but the king's tyranny was bearing its fruit in the Doāb, and in 1333 he returned to Delhi and led a punitive expedition into that region, which he treated in all respects as a hostile country. Baran, now Bulandshahr, was first attacked, and the whole district was plundered and laid waste. The inhabitants were slaughtered like sheep, and rows of Hindu heads decked the battlements of the city of Baran. Those who escaped fled into the jungles, where they were hunted like wild beasts. Continuing his march in a south-easterly direction the king plundered and devastated, in like manner, the districts of Kanauj and Dalmau[1], where he was still engaged when Ibn Batūtah arrived at Delhi late in 1333 or early in 1334.

The Moorish traveller's account in his *Tuhfat-un-Nuzzār fī Gharāib-il-Amsār*, of his journeys and sojourn in India, throws much light on the condition of the country, the character of its sovereign, and many details. He arrived at the mouth of the Indus on September 12, 1333, and his arrival, as he was a foreigner, had to be reported to Qutb-ul-Mulk, the governor of the city of Multān. He describes a rebellion at Sihwān, not mentioned in the general histories of the reign, which had been suppressed shortly before his arrival. The king had appointed to the government of Sihwān a Hindu named Ratan, who was well skilled in accounts, and whom he entitled 'Azīm-us-Sind. The appointment gave great offence to Wunār, chief of the Sūmras, and to a noble named Qaisar-ur-Rūmī living at Sihwān, who resented the appointment of a Hindu governor over them. Having involved him in hostilities with some brigands or tribesmen in the neighbourhood of Sihwān, they attacked him by night, slew him, and afterwards plundered the treasury.

---

[1] The town of Dalmau is situated in 25° 4' N. and 81° 6' E.

'Imād-ud-Mulk Sartīz, governor of Sind, marched against the rebels, and Wunār fled to his tribe, but Qaisar sustained a siege of forty days in Sihwān and eventually surrendered on receiving an assurance that his life would be spared, but 'Imād-ul-Mulk broke faith with him, and put him and large numbers of his followers to death. Many were flayed, and their skins, stuffed with straw, were suspended from the walls and public buildings of the city. The sight of these miserable relics so horrified Ibn Batūtah, who was compelled by the heat of the weather to sleep in the open air, as to hasten his departure from the city. After some stay at Multān he travelled by way of Abohar, Pākpattan, Sirsa, and Hānsī to Delhi. His account of the journey illustrates Muhammad's lavish hospitality to foreigners visiting his dominions and the disorder prevailing in the country.

When he reached Delhi Muhammad was in the Kanauj district, but the minister, Khvāja Jahān, saw that he and his fellow travellers were well received at the capital. The king's generosity to these strangers, who had no claims on him, was fantastic. Ibn Batūtah himself received 6000 *tangas* in cash, a grant of three villages within thirty miles of Delhi which gave him an annual income of 5000 *tangas*, and ten Hindu slaves.

Some months later Muhammad returned from Kanauj, and on June 8, 1334, reached Tilpat. Ibn Batūtah was among those who went forth to meet him, and describes the king's kindly reception of himself and others, his ceremonial entry into the capital, and the great honour shown to foreigners, whom he was ever solicitous to attract to his court. They were offered appointments, which few were prepared to accept, for they were, for the most part, mere beggars, who had visited India with the object of amassing wealth as quickly as possible and carrying it back to their own countries. Ibn Batūtah, to whose original grant two other villages were added and whose annual stipend was fixed at 12,000 *tangas*, was willing to work for his bread, but hesitated to accept the post of *qāzī* of Delhi on the ground of his ignorance of the language of the country and of his attachment to the Mālikī sect of the Sunnis whose practice differed somewhat from that of the Hanafī sect, whose religion was established in India. The king removed both obstacles by offering to appoint two assistants, who would perform the duties of the post while Ibn Batūtah enjoyed the stipend.

The king had enjoyed but a brief period of repose at Delhi when he was summoned southward by the news of a serious rebellion. He had appointed Sayyid Jalāl-ud-dīn Ahsan of Kaithal to the government of Ma'bar, the most southerly province of his kingdom. Ahsan now raised the standard of rebellion at Madura, proclaimed his independence under the style of Jalāl-ud-dīn Ahsan Shāh, and struck coin in his own name. On January 5, 1335, Muhammad left Delhi for southern India, travelling by way of Daulatābad, where he levied heavy contributions to the expense of equipping his army. He marched thence for Madura by way of Bīdar and Warangal, but at the latter place his further progress was stayed by a pestilence, probably cholera, which broke out in his army. The disease raged in the camp, smiting alike the great noble and the humble camp follower, and the mortality was appalling. The king himself fell sick and his health was not restored for several months. All thought of a further advance was abandoned, and Muhammad, leaving Malik Qabūl at Warangal as governor of Telingāna, began to retrace his step. He never had another opportunity of recovering the lost province of Ma'bar, which remained a petty kingdom for the next forty years. All that is known of its history is to be ascertained from its coins[1], from the narrative of Ibn Batūtah, who was son-in-law to its founder, and from a few inscriptions, and may be related in the course of a brief digression.

Jalāl-ud-dīn Ahsan Shāh, having declared his independence in A.H. 735, was slain in A.H. 740 by one of his officers, who usurped the throne under the title of 'Alā-ud-dīn Udaujī but had not reigned a year when he was slain by a stray arrow which penetrated his head when he had removed his helmet after a victory over the ' infidels,' that is to say the subjects either of the Pāndya or of the Kerala kings, and was succeeded by his son-in-law, Qutb-ud-dīn Fīrūz Shāh, who was slain in a revolt after a reign of forty days. On his death the throne was seized by Ghiyās-ud-dīn Dāmaghānī, who had been a trooper in the service of Muhammad Tughluq, and now assumed the title of Ghiyās-ud-dīn Muhammad Dāmaghān Shāh. He married a daughter of Ahsan Shāh, and thus became the brother-in-law of the wife of Ibn Batūtah, who was a guest at his court after leaving that of Muhammad Tughluq, and records some of the atrocities committed by him, such as the torture and massacre of a great number of Hindu captives, men, women, and children. He also records Dāmaghān Shāh's victory over Vīra Ballāla III of Dvāravatīpura, who was over eighty years of age and was captured, strangled, and flayed by his adversary, who had learnt some lessons at the court at Delhi, and hung the stuffed skin of the raja on the wall of Madura. The death of Dāmaghān Shāh's

---

[1] See *J.A.S.B.*, Pt. I, lxiv, 49, and *J R A S*, 1909, p. 667.

only son from cholera on his return to Madura and his own death
a fortnight later from the effects of an aphrodisiac were regarded
as the due punishment of his cruelties.

He was succeeded in A.H. 745 (A.D. 1344) by his nephew, Nāsir-
ud-dīn, who had been a domestic servant at Delhi before his uncle's
elevation to the throne of Madura, and now assumed the title of
Mahmūd Ghāzī Dāmaghān. He slew all the officers, of the kingdom
likely to disturb his possession of the throne, and among them the
husband of his predecessor's daughter, whom he married immediately after her husband's death. It was during his reign that Ibn
Batūtah, though pressed by him to stay, left the court of Madura.

He was succeeded by 'Ādil Shāh, whose coins were dated A.H.
757 (A.D. 1356), and he by Fakhr-ud-dīn Mubārak Shāh, whose
earliest coins are dated in A.H. 761 (A.D. 1360), and who apparently
reigned until A.D. 1368-69, or perhaps until A.D. 1372-73, when he
was succeeded by 'Alā-ud-dīn Sikandar Shāh, whose latest coin is
dated in A.H. 778 (A.D. 1377-78). The rising power of the great
Hindu kingdom of Vijayanagar had, some years before, begun to
overshadow the small Muslim state of Madura, and an inscri tion
of Sangama I, the founder of the first dynasty of Vijayanagar,
records a victory over 'that proud lord of Madura, the valiant
Turushka.' In another inscription of 1371 Goppana, commanding
the army of Bukka I, son of Sangama and third raja of Vijayanagar,
claims a victory over the Turks of Madura, and the date of
Sikandar's latest coin is probably that of the extinction of the
Muslim dynasty of Madura by Bukka I.

We now return to the movements of Muhammad Tughluq, who
retired from Warangal to Bīdar, of which city and province he
appointed Shihab-ud-dīn governor, conferring on him the title of
Nusrat Khān. This appointment marks the introduction of the
pernicious system, which was soon to become general, of farming
the revenue. Muhammad's lavish profusion and wild and disastrous
schemes of conquest so impoverished him as to render him desperate, and the system of farming the revenue was introduced with
the object of wringing from the wretched cultivator the utmost
farthing. His experience in the Gangetic Doāb should have taught
him the axiom that there is a point beyond which demands cannot
be raised, and that human beings will not labour to till the soil
unless they are allowed to retain a proportion of its fruits sufficient
to maintain life. In the later years of the reign no experienced and
conscientious official would enter into the unholy competition for

governorships, for the government of districts and provinces was virtually put up to auction, and he who promised to pay the largest annual sum to the treasury obtained the prize. The successful bidders were usually men of mean origin, devoid of knowledge, experience, and compassion, who, without staying to consider what men could or would pay, made the most extravagant promises, only to discover that they could not meet their obligations. It was well known that the king would make no allowance for circumstances, and the defaulter was left with no remedy but rebellion.

Nusrat Khān agreed to pay the treasury, for the districts placed under his charge, the annual sum of ten millions of *tangas*, and Muhammad continued his retreat. At Bīr he suffered from a severe toothache, and his vanity caused to be erected over the spot where the tooth, when extracted, was buried, a domed tomb, which is still standing and is known as the Dome of the Tooth.

Reports of the king's sickness at Warangal had been exaggerated into rumours of his death, which had been believed by Malik Hūshang of Daulatābād, a noble with whom he had been on terms of peculiar affection and intimacy. Hūshang had risen in rebellion, but on learning that Muhammad was alive and was returning to Daulatābād fled and sought an asylum with a Hindu chieftain in the Western Ghāts, who subsequently surrendered him. The rebel, strange to say, was pardoned.

Muhammad had for some time past deliberately encouraged foreigners of all nations to settle in his dominions. He cherished the insane design of subjugating the whole world. His knowledge of geography was scanty and he could form no conception of the magnitude of the task which he proposed to himself, but he understood that the first step to be taken would be the conquest of the neighbouring countries of Transoxiana and Persia, and with this object in view he encouraged wealthy and influential Mughuls and natives of Khurāsān to enter his service in the hope that they would assist him in the conquest of their native lands. Later in his reign, when he had succeeded in obtaining the formal recognition of al-Hākim II, the Abbasid Caliph in Egypt, he obliged these foreigners to swear allegiance to him as the only lawful Muslim sovereign.

For the conquest of Persia he raised an enormous army, the maintenance of which so depleted his treasury that in the second year of the army's existence no funds remained for its payment, and it melted away.

Not all the foreigners so freely welcomed and so liberally remunerated proved to be faithful, and during the king's absence in the south Hulāgū, a Mughul noble at Lahore, proclaimed his independence, appointed Gul Chandar, Chief of the Khokars, his minister, and slew the governor, Tātār Khān the elder. Khvāja Jahān, the minister, assembled an army at Delhi and marched towards Lahore, taking with him, among others, Ibn Batūtah, who has left an account of the expedition which, though brief, is the most circumstantial which has come down to us. Hulāgū and Gul Chandar marched to meet Khvāja Jahān, and the two armies met and fought on the banks of one of the great rivers of the Punjab, probably the Sutlej. Hulāgū was defeated and fled, and large numbers of his army were drowned in the river. Khvāja Jahān advanced to Lahore, where he punished, after his master's manner, the remnant of the rebels and their partisans. Many were flayed alive and many were slain in other ways, and three hundred of the widows of the victims were sent into imprisonment at Gwalior.

Before leaving Daulatābād the king gave general permission to those who had been transported from Delhi eight years before to return to their former home, and most of them returned joyfully, but some had become attached to the land of their exile, and remained there.

During Muhammad's absence from Delhi a heavy calamity had befallen northern India, and famine was sore in the land. It lasted, like that recorded in the Book of Genesis, for seven years, and was the most severe famine of which we have any record in India. It is attributed by historians to natural causes, and Budaunī goes as far as to say that 'for seven whole years not a drop of rain fell from the heavens.' This is, of course, mere hyperbole, and must be interpreted to mean that the rainfall was deficient for seven years, but it is certain that the famine was not due to natural causes alone, or the province of Oudh would not have been able to afford relief during that period to the inhabitants of Delhi and the Doāb. Muhammad's exactions, which extinguished cultivation in large tracts of the Doāb, and his severity, which destroyed those who might have cultivated the land, contributed in no small measure to the calamity, which is always mentioned in connexion with, though not directly attributed to, his ill-treatment of his subjects in the Doāb.

His way to Delhi lay through the usually fertile province of Mālwa, and here he had an opportunity of observing the havoc which famine had wrought upon his people. Towns and whole districts were depopulated and even the postal runners were constrained to abandon their posts, so that the royal mails no longer

ran between Delhi and Daulatābād. A pound of grain cost twenty-
two or twenty-three grains of silver, and the people were reduced
to eating unnatural and loathsome food. Ibn Batūtah saw some
women cutting strips from the skin of a horse which had been dead
for some months, and eating them, cooked hides were exposed for
sale in the bazars, and people thronged round the butchers to
catch and drink the blood of slaughtered cattle. Some travellers
resting in the deserted city of Agroha, now Hissar, found a man
cooking a human foot, and as the famine grew ever more severe
human flesh became a common article of food.

Muhammad was not regardless of the sufferings of his people.
A daily ration of grain was issued for six months to all the citizens
of Delhi, and cooked food was distributed at the wealthy college
which his eccentric piety had endowed at the tomb of the worthless
Qutb-ud-dīn Mubārak, and at other shrines in the city. Large
sums of money were advanced to enable husbandmen to buy seed
and plough-cattle, to sink wells, and to improve and extend their
holdings, but the king insisted on the application of these grants
or loans to the objects for which they were made, and to no other.
In some cases the starving people were too weak to carry out the
works for which the money was granted, in others they were convinced, by the continued failure of the rains of the futility of
spending money on tilling and sowing the parched land, and they
applied the grants to their own immediate needs. This was regarded
as contumacy and Muhammad punished the miserable transgressors
with such rigour that the tale of executions shocked and disgusted
even those accustomed to his barbarous severity, and this measure
of relief produced more misery than would have resulted from a
policy of inaction.

It was not only at Daulatābād that the news of the king's sickness in Telingāna had given rise to reports of his death. The
rumour had been circulated and had gained some credence at
Delhi and in its neighbourhood. Sayyid Ibrāhīm the Pursebearer,
son of Sayyid Jalāl-ud-dīn Ahsan of Madura, was a favourite of the
king, whose confidence in the son was so little shaken by the father's
rebellion that Ibrāhīm was left as governor of the districts of Hānsī
and Sirsa when Muhammad left Delhi for the south. He heard and
was inclined to credit the news of the king's death, and when a
large remittance of treasure of Sind reached Hānsī on its way to
Delhi he detained the convoy on the pretext that the roads were
unsafe, with the intention of seizing the treasure and establishing
his independence as soon as he should receive confirmation of the

news of the king's death, but on learning that the rumour was false he allowed the convoy to pass on to Delhi. No overtact of rebellion had been committed, and had Ibrāhīm kept his own counsel, he might have escaped suspicion, but he had incautiously mentioned his design in the presence of his servants, and the matter reaced the king's ears. Owing to the regard which he had for Ibrāhīm he hesitated to proceed to extremities against him, and he might have escaped had not a treasonable speech, rashly uttered, been reported at court. He was arrested and confessed, under fear of torture, his real object in detaining the treasure, and the king put him to death.

Nusrat Khān now discovered that he was not able to remit to Delhi even a quarter of the sum of ten millions of *tangas* which he had promised to pay annually from the revenues of Bīdar, and rose in rebellion. Reinforcements were sent to Qutlugh Khān at Daulatābād, and he marched against the rebel, besieged him in Bīdar, captured him, and sent him to Delhi.

Muhammad now decreed a fresh evacuation of Delhi, actuated on this occasion by a desire for the welfare of his subjects. The fertile province of Oudh had for many years prospered under the mild and paternal rule of its governor, 'Ain-ul-Mulk, and from its overflowing granaries the king purposed to relieve the misery of his people. Any attempt to transport grain through the starving and turbulent Doāb would have been foredoomed to failure, and since he could not bring food to his people he led his people to the food. On the western bank of the Ganges, near the site of the ancient city of Khor, in 27° 33′ N. lat. and 79° 35′ E. long. at a distance of 165 miles from Delhi, he caused a city of booths to be built, to which he gave the Sanskrit name of Sargadwārī (*Swarga-dwāra*), 'the Gate of Paradise,' and which he made his headquarters for the next six years. To this city he brought the inhabitants of Delhi, and here they were fed. 'Ain-ul Mulk and his brothers loyally supported him, encamped on the opposite bank of the river, and conveyed the hoarded grain of Oudh to Sargadwārī, the temporary booths of which were replaced in the following year by more permanent buildings, where the citizens of Delhi dwelt, not only in plenty, but in moderate comfort.

Neither his people's distress nor his preoccupation in relieving it could restrain the king from indulging his vain dreams of world-empire, and in 1337—38, the year after the foundation of Sargadwārī, he perpetrated one of his greatest acts of folly. The dream of conquering Transoxiana and Persia had faded, but there were other lands to subdue. Beyond the vast mountain chain which bounded his kingdom on the north-east lay the mysterious land of Tibet, and beyond that again the great empire of China, and an army which could traverse the mountains might, Muhammad believed, take those two countries by surprise. Of the nature of the country and the inhabitants, the narrow passes, the perilous mountain paths, the sheer precipices, and the bitter cold to be endured by troops bred in the scorching plains of India he could form no idea, and he persuaded himself that dread of his wrath would carry his troops over all obstacles. An army of 100,000 horse and a large number of foot was assembled at Delhi under the command of Malik Nīkpāī, who held the honorary post of chief of the inkstand-bearers, and was dispatched on the desperate adventure. The troops marched by way of Nāgarkot, or Kangra, the capture of which in this year is recorded in an ode of Badr-i-Chāch, and entered the mountains after plundering and devastating the villages on their lower slopes. They advanced by a narrow road, which would admit no more than one horseman at a time, along the precipitous mountain side, but safely reached the stronghold, which Ibn Batūtah call Warangal, of the local chieftain, where they halted after their toilsome journey. Here they were overtaken by the heavy and drenching rains of the mountains, which spread disease among men and horses and destroyed large numbers of both. The officers sought and received permission to lead their men back to the plains, there to await the end of the rainy season, when a second attempt might be made to traverse the mountains, and they set out with all their plunder, but the mountaineers had assembled to harass their retreat and occupied the gorges and defiles. Great stones and felled trees were hurled from the heights on the retreating host, laden with its plunder, stragglers were cut off, the passes were held and stoutly defended, and the highlanders so thoroughly performed their task that they destroyed the army almost to a man, and recovered all the plunder. Nīkpāī, two other officers, and about ten horsemen were all who returned to Delhi and the king was deeply humiliated. He was obliged to conclude with the mountaineers who had destroyed his army a treaty of peace, in which the only condition to his advantage was an undertaking to pay tribute for the land cultivated by them in the plains, which was at all times liable to be overrun by his troops.

The effects of this campaign on the kingdom were disastrous. Not only had a great army and the enormous quantity of treasure which accompanied it been lost, but Muhammad's reputation had received such a blow that disaffection in the regions groaning under his tyranny blazed into rebellion, and he was never again able to place himself at the head of such a host as he had assembled for the conquest of China.

In 1338-39 Bahrām Khān, governor of Eastern Bengal, died, and an officer of his troops proclaimed his independence in that province under the title of Fakhr-ud-dīn Mubārak Shāh. The tortuous course of events in Bengal which resulted in the death of Qadr Khān, governor of Lakhnāwati and in the establishment of Fakhr-ud-dīn Mubārak in the eastern and of Shams-ud-dīn Iliyās in the western province and finally, in 1352, as sultan of all Bengal will be traced in Chapter XI. Muhammad's activities were para-lysed by the blow which he had received in the Himālaya and by the havoc which famine had wrought in his dominions, and he could take no steps to restore his authority in the eastern provinces, so that Bengal was permanently lost to him.

In the following year, 1339-40, came news of another serious rebellion in the Deccan. 'Alī Shāh Kar (' the Deaf'), an officer serving under Qutlugh Khān, was sent to collect and escort to Daulatābād the revenue due from the province of Gulbarga, the defencelessness of which tempted him to rebellion. He attacked and slew Bhairon, the Hindu officer who held Gulbarga, raised a force by means of the treasure which he should have conveyed to Daulatābād, marched to Bīdar, slew the governor, and occupied the town. Here, however, he was defeated by Qutlugh Khān, surrendered to him, and was sent to Delhi.

The king himself was now embarrassed by a rebellion. 'Ain-ul-Mulk, governor of Oudh, had for many years governed his province with ability and clemency and had acquired great influence and popularity. The successful victualling of Sargadwārī was due entirely to his prudence and foresight and to his admirable arrange-ments for the conveyance of grain to the temporary city. Many of the respectable inhabitants of Delhi, fearing the king's tyranny, had withdrawn from the city and had settled in Oudh, where they received generous treatment at the hands of 'Ain-ul-Mulk, who attached them to himself and ensured the extension of cultivation in his province by granting them villages in fee. With these immigrants had come others, less desirable fugitives from justice, who were harboured on the immoral eastern principle that it is dishonourable to surrender to justice even a malefactor who has sought an asylum with a protector. 'Ain-ul-Mulk was humiliated by a demand for their surrender, but the chief cause of his estrange-

ment from the king was the latter's design of transferring him to
the government of the Deccan in the place of Qutlugh Khān. The
avowed reason for the transfer was 'Ain-ul-Mulk's efficiency and
success as a provincial governor, from which some improvement in
the situation in the Deccan might be expected, but it was generally
known that the deplorable condition of the southern provinces was
due not to any fault of Qutlugh Khān, who was a loyal and able
governor, but to the pernicious system of farming the revenues,
and 'Ain-ul-Mulk feared, probably with justice, that the king's real
motive in transferring him from Oudh was jealousy of his power
and influence, and that the object of appointing him to a government in which Qutlugh Khān had failed was to ensure his disgrace
and destruction.   His brothers, who had loyally assisted him in the
government of Oudh now urged him not to submit to the caprice
of an ungrateful master, but to rely on the support of the people
by whom he was so well beloved.   Opportunity favoured him, for
the elephants, horses, pack animals and cattle of the royal army
had been sent across the Ganges into Oudh for grazing, and the
rebellion was precipitated by the seizure of those animals, while
'Ain-ul-Mulk fled from the camp and joined his own army on the
east of the Ganges.   He assumed the title of Sultān 'Alā-ud-dīn,
and Muhammad, for the first time in his reign, had cause to tremble
for his throne and his life.   The disaster to his army in the Himālaya
had impaired his prestige and his severity and cruelty had alienated
the nobles in his camp, on whose fidelity he could no longer rely.
The rebel army, though composed of poor material, was more
numerous than his own, and he desired to avoid an immediate
battle.   Hastily summoning reinforcements from Delhi and other
towns, he marched rapidly towards Kanauj, seeking the protection
of its walls.   The rebels on the eastern bank marched from Bangarmau, and it seemed that Muhammad's only hope of safety lay in
outstripping them.   When it became known that they had crossed
the river he was much alarmed, for he did not believe that they
would have ventured on this step without encouragement from
traitors in his own camp.   The rebels, to the number of 50,000,
attacked his outposts by night, and the battle soon became general.
Notwithstanding the overwhelming numerical superiority of the
enemy, the Persians, Turks and Khurāsānīs in the royal army
fought valiantly, and at dawn the rebels were in full flight and
were pursued for twenty miles.   Many, including two of 'Ain-ul-
Mulk's four brothers, were slain in the battle or the pursuit, or
drowned in the Ganges.   Malik Ibrāhīm, one of 'Ain-ul-Mulk's

accomplices in rebellion, seized him and carried him before the minister, Khvāja Jahān, in the hope of earning a pardon, and the minister, after causing 'Ain-ul-Mulk to be stripped, carried him before the king. The captive was naked save for a small loin-cloth, and was mounted on an ox. Following him was a large number of other prisoners, and the sons of the courtiers disgraced themselves by crowding round the unfortunate prisoners, heaping abuse on 'Ain-ul-Mulk, spitting in his face, and beating with their fists his companions in misfortune.

Few rebels who fell into the hands of Muhammad Tughluq escaped a cruel death, but the tyrant had the grace to remember the long and faithful service of 'Ain-ul-Mulk, and the captive, instead of being executed, was condemned to imprisonment in sackcloth and chains.

From Kanauj Muhammad marched to Bangarmau, and thence performed a pilgrimage to the shrine of the half-mythical hero Sālār Mas'ūd, said in story to have been sister's son to Mahmūd of Ghaznī, and one of his bravest warriors. From Bahrāich, where the hero's tomb stands, he sent Khvāja Jahān with a sufficient force to intercept the remnant of 'Ain-ul-Mulk's army and to prevent the fugitives from entering the kingdom of Bengal. The minister was also entrusted with the task of collecting all those who had migrated from Delhi into Oudh, and of conducting them to their homes. This measure, strange to say, was conceived in clemency and the fugitives were kindly treated instead of being dealt with as rebels.

From Bahrāich the king returned to Delhi after an absence of two and a half years, and here found 'Alī Shāh Kar and his brothers, who had been sent from the Deccan by Qutlugh Khān. With rare clemency he contented himself with banishing them to Ghaznī, but 'Alī Shāh afterwards returned to India without permission, and was captured and executed. At the same time 'Ain-ul-Mulk was pardoned, released from prison, and reinstated in the government of Oudh.

Muhammad's active but inconstant mind had conceived at Sargadwārī the notion that no sovereign could legitimately wield authority unless he were commissioned by God's vicegerent on earth, the Caliph and Commander of the Faithful, and set himself diligently to inquire who the Caliph was and where he was to be found. He ascertained from travellers that there still existed in Egypt a puppet of the house of 'Abbās, who claimed the dignity. Their information was not very recent, for they styled him al-

Mustakfī, while he who bore that title had died or had been deposed a year earlier, but the coins of A.H. 740 (A.D. 1340-41) bear the title of al-Mustakfī and the ceremonial performance of the Friday prayers and the observation of the great festivals of Islam were suspended until the king should have received the Caliph's recognition, which he sought by means of a humble petition, accompanied by costly gifts, but three years passed before a reply could be received. This act of humility indicated no change in the king's nature, and neither his arrogance nor his impatience of contradiction or disobedience was diminished.

Had he only had patience he might have maintained at his court, like the Mamlūks of Egypt, a submissive Caliph of his own, for in this year there arrived at Delhi from Transoxiana, where he had been living under the protection of the Mughul Khān, 'Ala-ud-dīn Tarmāshīrīn, Ghiyās-ud-dīn Muḥammad, son of 'Abd-ul-Qāhir, son of Yūsuf, son of 'Abd-ul-'Azīz, son of the Abbasid Caliph al-Mustansir of Baghdad, who reigned from 1226 to 1242. His descent having been verified he was received with great honour. To the two messengers who arrived at the court seeking permission for their master to visit it the king gave 5000 *tangas*, to which were added 30,000 *tangas* for Ghiyās-ud-dīn himself. The leading ecclesiastics and theologians of the court were sent as far as Sirsa to meet him, and the king himself met him at Mas'ūdābād, now Bahādurgarh. After a ceremonious interchange of gifts he held Ghiyās-ud-dīn's stirrup while he mounted and they rode together, the royal umbrella being held over the heads of both. Ghiyās-ud-dīn received extraordinary privileges at court, and the profusion of the king's liberality to him is not to be reconciled with sanity. The vessels in his palace were of gold and silver, the bath being of gold, and on the first occasion of his using it a gift of 400,000 *tangas* was sent to him ; he was supplied with male and female servants and slaves, and was allowed a daily sum of 300 *tangas,* though much of the food consumed by him and his household came from the royal kitchen ; he received in fee the whole of 'Ala-ud-dīn's city of Sīrī, one of the four cities (Delhi, Sīrī, Tughluqābād, and Jahanpanāh) which composed the capital, with all its buildings, and adjacent gardens and lands and a hundred villages ; he was appointed governor of the eastern district of the province of Delhi ; he received thirty mules with trappings of gold ; and whenever he visited the court he was entitled to receive the carpet on which the king sat. The recipient of all this wealth and honour was but a well-born beggar, mean and miserly almost beyond belief. He

ate alone, not from pride or arrogance, but because, as he confessed
to Ibn Batūtah, he could not bear to see other mouths eating his
food and grudged even a lamp in his palace, preferring to sit in
darkness. He personally collected sticks in his garden for firewood,
and stored them, and compelled his personal servants to till his
land. He was dishonest as well as parsimonious, and Ibn Batūtah
vainly demanded payment of a debt which the descendant of the
Caliphs owed him.

Multān was the scene of the next rebellion. Malik Shāhū Lodī,
an Afghān noble who had a considerable following of his own tribe,
had risen in that province, slain Malik Bihzād, its governor, expelled another officer, and seized the city. The king assembled his
army and set out from Delhi, but had travelled no more than two
or three stages when he heard of the death of his mother. This
was a real loss to the kingdom, for she was charitable and generous,
not with the insane profusion of her son, but in due measure. The
people, no less than the king, deplored her loss, for her counsels
had to some extent restrained her son's ferocity, and after her
death no such acts of clemency as the pardoning of 'Ain-ul-Mulk,
'Alī Shāh Kar, Hūshang, Nusrat Khān, and other rebels are
recorded.

Muhammad would not permit his mourning for his mother to
interrupt the expedition which he had undertaken, but when he
reached Dīpālpur he received a petition from Shāhū expressing
contrition, and learnt at the same time that the rebel and all his
followers had fled beyond his reach into the mountains of Afghānistān, and accordingly returned to Delhi. The subsequent rebellions
in Gujarāt and the Deccan were partly due to the severity of the
restrictions placed upon Afghāns in India in consequence of Shāhū's
revolt.

When the king returned to Delhi the famine was at its worst,
and the people were eating human flesh. He had been engaged,
since his return from Sargadwārī, in devising schemes to restore
prosperity to the land which his tyranny had done so much to
devastate. To the regulations which he framed he gave the name
of *uslūb*, or 'methods' and by their means, says Baranī, with probably unconscious irony, agriculture would have been so improved
and extended that plenty would have reigned throughout the earth,
and so much money would have poured into the treasury that the
king would have been able to raise an army capable of conquering
the world—had they been practicable.

A department to deal with all questions relating to agriculture
was created and placed under the charge of a minister called, for

no apparent reason, *Amīr-ī-Kūhī*, or 'Mountain Lord,' and it was ordained that the kingdom should be divided into districts thirty by thirty leagues, or about 1800 square miles, in area, in which not one span of land was to be left uncultivated, and crops were to be sown in rotation. This ordinance was the conception of a mere theorist. No allowance was made for forest, pasture, or unculturable land, and though the order relating to rotation appears to indicate some knowledge of the principle of scientific agriculture it is clear, from the examples given, that these principles were not understood. Barley, for instance, was to follow wheat; sugarcane, a most exhausting crop, after which the land should have been allowed to lie fallow for at least a year, was to follow barley; and grapes and dates were to follow sugarcane. To these districts were appointed superintendents who, to borrow a term from Anglo-Irish history which literally translates their designation, were styled 'undertakers,' who undertook to see not only that the regulations were carried out to the letter, but also to re-people the land and make every square mile maintain a fixed number of horse soldiers. None but irresponsible adventurers would have entered into such an agreement, and even these would have held aloof but for the immediate inducements offered. The king, who was as bad a judge of men as he was of affairs, would not see a favourite scheme baulked at the outset, and undertakers were induced to come forward by gifts of caparisoned horses, rich robes of honour, and estates to reward them for their promises and large sums of money to enable them to inaugurate the scheme. These gifts were, as the historian says, their own blood money, for when they perceived the impossibility of meeting their engagements they appropriated to their own use all that they had received and trusted to events to enable them to escape an almost inevitable fate. More than seventy millions of *tangas* were thus disbursed in gifts to the undertakers and at the end of the stipulated term of three years so little of what had been promised had been performed that Baranī speaks of the performance as not one hundredth, nay, not one thousandth part of the promise, and adds that unless Muhammad had died when he did, in his expedition to Sind, not one of the undertakers would have survived his resentment.

The second regulation encouraged Mughuls to settle in India. These fierce nomads might furnish a mobile and efficient army, but they could not replace the industrious peasantry whose labours had filled the coffers of the state and who had been, in many tracts, dispersed and destroyed by famine and oppression. The Mughuls were attracted to India by enormous gifts, and by favours of every description, so that at the beginning of every winter numbers of commanders of tens of thousands and of thousands arrived with their wives, their families, and their followers, received great sums of money, horses, and jewels, and were entertained at princely banquets. This expenditure on an unproductive class maintained at great cost necessitated further schemes for the improvement and development of the resources of the state, and the third regulation was framed to this end. Of the details of the scheme nothing is recorded, nor is it easy to divine what sources of revenue the king could have tapped other than those which he had already exploited to the utmost, but as the regulation is said to have been enforced by clemency mingled with severity it perhaps provided for the levy of forced loans and benevolences, which led naturally to the framing of the fourth regulation, enhancing the severity of the penal code. The frequency and cruelty of the punishments inflicted by the king bred seditions and rebellion which still further inflamed his wrath and increased his severity, and even suspects were seized and cruelly tortured until in their agony they confessed to imaginary crimes and were executed on their confessions.

Baranī relates an interesting conversation which he had with the king on political offences and their punishment. The occasion was Muhammad's halt at Sultānpur, about two years after this time, on his way to suppress the rebellion in Gujarāt. The king, referring to the disorders and revolts in all parts of his dominions, expressed a fear lest men should attribute them all to his severity, but added that he should not be influenced by irresponsible opinion. He asked Baranī, as one versed in history, for what offences kings of old had been wont to inflict death. Baranī admitted the necessity for capital punishment, without which order could not be maintained, and said that the great Jamshīd of Persia had inflicted it for seven offences, viz. apostasy, wilful murder, adultery by a married man with another's wife, high treason, rebellion, aiding the king's enemies, and such disobedience as caused injury to the state, trivial acts of disobedience being expressly excepted. Muhammad then asked for what crimes capital punishment was sanctioned by the Islamic law, and Baranī replied that there were only three for which it was provided, apostasy, wilful murder of a Muslim, and rape of a chaste woman, but that it was understood that kings might, for the maintenance of peace and order, inflict it for the other four crimes for which it had been sanctioned by Jamshīd.

Muhammad replied that Jamshīd's code had been framed for earlier times, when men were innocent and obedient, and that in the latter times wickedness had increased upon the earth and a spirit of disaffection was everywhere abroad, so that it had become necessary to punish with death acts of disobedience which would formerly have been regarded as venial, lest the infection should spread and disaffection breed open rebellion.   In this course, he said, he would persevere until his death, or until his people became submissive. His reply embodies his whole theory of penal legislation. He regarded his people as his natural enemies, and the penal laws as a means of visiting his personal displeasure on them. They accepted the challenge, and the hideous rivalry continued until his death.

On July 22, 1342, Ibn Batūtah left Delhi. Favoured foreigner though he was his life had been twice in danger. In terror for his own life, he was sickened by the daily spectacle of the king's cruelty. 'Many a time,' he writes, 'I saw the bodies of the slain at his gate, thrown there.   One day my horse shied under me and I saw something white on the ground and asked what it was, and my companions told me that it was the breast of a man who had been cut into three pieces. The king slew both small and great, and spared not the learned, the pious or the noble. Daily there were brought to the council hall men in chains, fetters, and bonds, and they were led away, some to execution, some to torture, and some to scourging. On every day except Friday there was a gaol delivery, but on Friday the prisoners were not led out, and it was on that day only that they took their ease and cleansed themselves. May God preserve us from such calamities !

Muhammad took advantage of Ibn Batūtah's desire to leave India and intention of continuing his travels to appoint him his envoy to China. During the expedition into the Himālaya a temple or shrine to which Chinese pilgrims resorted had been destroyed, and the emperor of China had sent a mission seeking leave to rebuild it. Muhammad was prepared to grant this permission on condition that the worshippers paid *jizya*, the poll-tax levied from idolators, and Ibn Batūtah, with a hundred followers, was deputed to accompany the Chinese mission on its return and to deliver this decision. He was accompanied to the port of embarkation by an escort of 1000 horse, without which it would have been unsafe to travel through Muhammad's dominions, and his account of his journey discloses the deplorable condition of the country. The Gangetic Doāb was seething with revolt. The town of Jalālī, near

Koil ('Alīgarh) was besieged by 4000 Hindu rebels, and seventy-eight of the mission's escort were killed on the way thither. Ibn Batūtah was himself taken prisoner by a band of Hindus, and escaped with great difficulty, after suffering many hardships. It was no unusual thing for Muslim governors to be besieged in their cities by bands of Hindu rebels, and they were sometimes obliged to appeal to Delhi for assistance. Ahmad Khān, governor of Gwalior, offered to entertain Ibn Batūtah with the spectacle of the execution of some Hindus, but the Moor had had his fill of horrors at Delhi, and begged to be excused.

In 1343 Muhammad was called to the districts of Sunām, Sāmāna, Kaithal, and Guhrām where the Hindus had entirely abandoned agriculture and deserted their villages, assembling in large camps in the jungles, where they lived by brigandage. The rebellion spread as far east as the lower slopes of the Himālaya and called for extensive operations and vigorous action. Muhammad performed the congenial task thoroughly. The camps of the rebels were plundered and broken up, and the gangs were dispersed, but the ringleaders were treated with unusual leniency. They were deprived of their ancestral lands, but were brought into Delhi and settled there with their wives and families. Many became Muslims, and as many were also ennobled it may be assumed that their conversion was the price of their preferment.

On his return to Delhi in 1344 Muhammad received Hājī Sa'īd Sarsarī, the envoy sent from Egypt by the Abbasid-al-Hākim II in response to his prayer for pontifical recognition. The envoy was received with the most extravagant honours, and the arrogant Muhammad's self-abasement before him verged on the grotesque. The king, all the great officers of state, the Sayyids, holy and learned men, and all who could pretend to any importance went forth from Delhi to meet the envoy, who bore the Caliph's decree of recognition and a robe of honour for Muhammad. The king walked several bowshots barefoot as the envoy approached, and, after placing the decree and the robe of honour on his head in token of reverence, kissed his feet several times. Triumphal arches were erected in the city and alms were lavishly distributed. On the first Friday after the envoy's arrival the long discontinued Friday prayers were recited with great pomp and the names of such previous rulers of India as had failed to secure the formal recognition of one of the Abbasid Caliphs were omitted from the formal sermon. The most exaggerated respect was paid to the envoy. His utterances were recorded and repeated as though they had been inspired and, as Baranī says, 'Without the Caliph's command the king scarcely ventured to drink a draught of water.' The festivals of Islam were now again observed, the legends on the coins were corrected and Muhammad sent Hājī Rajab Burqa'ī to Egypt as envoy to the Caliph.

In 1344 a rebellion broke out in Kara. This rich district had been farmed for an immense sum to a worthless debauchee, who bore the title of Nizām-ul-Mulk. He discovered, when he attempted to fulfil his promise to the king, that he could not collect the tenth part of what he had contracted to pay to the treasury and, in his drunken despair, raised the standard of rebellion, styling himself Sultān 'Alā-ud-dīn. The king was assembling troops at Delhi when news was received that 'Ain-ul-Mulk had justified the clemency with which he had been treated by marching from Oudh and capturing and slaying Nizām-ul-Mulk, and the news was confirmed by the arrival of the rebel's skin. The Shaikhzāda of Bastām, who had married the king's sister, was sent to complete the work and to restore order in the Kara district, and stamped out the embers of rebellion with great severity.

The king's attention was now turned to the Deccan where the revenue collections had fallen by ninety per cent. The decrease was probably due to the introduction of the farming system and to consequent rebellions, but Muhammad was easily persuaded to attribute it to the sloth and peculation of the collectors appointed by Qutlugh Khān. On December 8, 1344, the poet Badr-i-Chāch was sent from Delhi to recall Qutlugh Khān from Daulatābād, and his brother, Maulānā Nizām-ud-dīn, a simple man devoid of administrative experience, was sent from Broach to succeed him, but with restricted powers. Muhammad, ever ready to remedy disorders by new devices, now divided the Deccan into four revenue divisions (*shiqq*) to each of which was appointed a governor upon whom the enforcement of new regulations and the extortions of the uttermost *tanga* of the revenue were strictly enjoined. The removal of the mild and pious Qutlugh Khān, whose benevolent rule and readiness to stand between the people and the king's wrath had won the love of Hindu and Muslim alike, excited the gravest apprehensions, and a discontent which might at any moment burst into the flame of rebellion ; and the king's avowed intention of collecting annually 670 millions of *tangas* from the four divisions, and the selection of the agents who were to enforce the demand, increased the people's alarm. Mālwa was included in the Deccan and formed with it one *shiqq*, to the government of which was

appointed 'Azīz Khammār[1], a low born, unscrupulous and extortionate official who had won an evil reputation as revenue collector in
the 'thousand' of Amroha, a tract containing about 1,500 villages,
and whose propensity to cruelty was now stimulated by the express
injunctions of the king, whose fury stigmatised all officials and
farmers in the Deccan, but above all the 'centurions,'[2] as traitors and
rebels.   In respect of this class 'Azīz received special instructions.
Impelled by the hope of plunder and profit the 'centurions,' said the
king, were the instigators and fomenters of every revolt and rebellion,
and 'Aziz, liberally supplied with troops and funds, was to use his
utmost endeavour to destroy them.   These injunctions fell upon
willing ears, and 'Azīz, immediately after his arrival at Dhār, the
seat of his government, caused eighty-nine 'centurions' to be put to
death before his official residence.   This barbarous act excited
among the 'centurions' of Gujarāt and the Deccan a horror which
was enhanced by the king's official approval of it.   Not only did
Muhammad himself send 'Azīz a robe of honour and a *farmān* prais-
ing his services to the state, but the courtiers and great officers at
the capital were commanded to follow their master's example.

This insane policy produced its inevitable result.   The king had
declared war against a whole class of his servants and the 'centurions'
of Dabhoi and Baroda in Gujarāt were the first to take up the
challenge.   Taking advantage of the dispatch by Muqbil, governor
of Gujarāt, of the annual remittance of revenue from his province
they fell upon the caravan and were enriched not only by the tribute
but by quantities of merchandise which the merchants of Gujarāt
were sending to Delhi under the protection of the convoy.

When the news of the rebellion reached Delhi the king appointed
a council of regency consisting of his cousin Fīrūz, Malik Kabīr,
and Khvāja Jahān and towards the end of Ramazān, A.H. 745, left
Delhi, never to return.   He halted for some days at Sultānpur,
about twenty-two miles west of Tughluqābād, in order to avoid
marching during the fast, and on Shawwāl 1 (February 5, 1345)

---

[1] In the *Bibliotheca Indica* edition of the text of Baranī's *Tārīkh-i-Fīrūz Shāh*. 'Azīz
is always styled *Himār* ('the ass').   In the Cairo text of Ibn Batūtah the *Bibliotheca
Indica* text of Budaunī, and the Bombay text of Firishta he is called *Khammār*
('the Vintner'), which seems to have been his correct designation.   Between the two
words, as usually written, there is a difference of only one dot, the omission of which
may be due to a scribe's carelessness or may be an author's deliberate pleasantry.

[2] This term literally translates the '*amīrs* of hundreds' or *yūzbāshī*, who were not,
however, purely military officers, but revenue officials responsible for the collection
of taxes in groups of about a hundred villages each, who were entitled to a commission of five per cent. on their collections.

continued his march towards Gujarāt. While at Sultānpur he was
disturbed by the news that 'Azīz had marched against the rebels.
In oppressing the poor, in plundering the rich, in torturing and
slaying the helpless, 'Azīz had few equals, and was a servant after
his master's heart, but Muhammad knew that he was no soldier
and learnt to his vexation, but without surprise, that the rebels
had defeated and captured him and put him to death with
torture.

The king marched from Sultānpur to Anhilvāra (Pātan) in
Gujarāt, and, leaving Shaikh Mu'izz-ud-dīn and other officers in
that town to reorganise the administration of the province, passed
on to Mount Ābū, whence he sent an army to Dābhoī and Baroda
against the 'centurions,' who were defeated with heavy loss and,
after collecting their wives and families, retired towards Daulatābād.
The king then marched to Broach and thence sent a force to intercept them. His troops came up with them on the bank of the
Narbada, again defeated them, captured their wives and families,
camp equipage and baggaged and slew most of the men. A few of
their leaders contrived to escape on barebacked horses, and took
refuge with Mān Singh, raja of Baglāna, who imprisoned them and
took from them such money and jewels as they had succeeded in
carrying off. The royal troops halted on the Narbada, and there
their leader, Malik Maqbūl, received and promptly executed an
order to arrest and execute the 'centurions' of Broach, who had
accompanied him. There is no suggestion that these officers had
failed in their duty, but they were 'centurions' and that was enough
for Muhammad. The few who escaped the executioner's sword fled
to Daulatābād, where their account of the king's ferocity added
fuel to the fire of sedition in the Deccan.

At Broach Muhammad found such employment as suited his
temper. The collection of the revenue had been neglected for some
time past, and the tale of arrears was heavy. Extortionate collectors
were appointed, no excuse was accepted and what was due was
exacted with the utmost severity. Inability to pay, as well as
obstinacy in refusing payment, was punished with death, and the
ghastly list of executions was increased by means of a minute and
careful investigation of the past behaviour of the people. Whoever
had in any way helped the rebels, whoever expressed sympathy
with them, whoever bemoaned their fate, was put to death, and as
though the rumours of his proceedings in Gujarāt were not
sufficient to exasperate his subjects in the south, the king appointed
two notorious oppressors to conduct an inquisition into the conduct

and opinions of his people at Daulatābād. One of these reached the city, and the other, Zain Banda, Majd-ul-Mulk, travelling less expeditiously, had not passed beyond Dhār when it became evident that a rebellion was on the point of breaking out at Daulatābād. Th actual outbreak was accelerated by an act of ill-timed severity. Two officers were sent from Broach to Daulatābād with orders to Maulānā Nizām-ud-dīn, the feeble governor, to collect 1500 horse and to send the 'centurions' of his province to Broach under escort. The escort was assembled and the 'centurions' were dispatched from Daulatābād, but at the end of the first day's march took counsel together and, preferring the chances of a rebellion to the certainty of death, slew Malik 'Alī and Malik Ahmad Lāchīn, who were conducting them to court, and returned to Daulatābād. Here they imprisoned Nizām-ud-dīn, seized the fort, with the treasure which had accumulated in it owing to the insecurity of the roads, which had rendered remittances to Delhi impossible, and proclaimed one of their number, Ismā'īl Mukh[1] the Afghān, king of the Deccan, under the title of Nāsir-ud dīn Shāh. The treasure was distributed to the troops, and Mahārāshtra was parcelled out into fiefs which the 'centurions' divided among themselves. The rebellion was at its height when the remnants of the 'centurions' of Dābhoī and Baroda, who had been imprisoned in Baglāna, escaped and joined their fellows at Daulatābād.

Muhammad at once assembled a large force at Broach and marched to Daulatābād. The rebels came forth to meet him, but were defeated with heavy loss and, with their wives and families, took refuge in the citadel which Muhammad himself had made impregnable, while Hasan the centurion, entitled Zafar Khān, the rebels from Bīdar, and the brothers of Ismā'īl Mulk retired to Gulbarga with a view to consolidating their position in the outlying districts of the province since the neighbourhood of Daulatābād was no longer safe.

The royal troops were permitted to sack the city of Daulatābād and plunder the defenceless inhabitants, the Muslims among whom were sent as prisoner to Delhi with dispatches announcing a great victory over the rebels. The king then opened the siege of the citadel and sent 'Imād-ul-Mulk Sartīz, who had been governor of Ellichpur when the rebellion broke out and had fled to court, to Gulbarga to crush the rebellion in that region.

Meanwhile the provinces of the extreme south were slipping

---

[1] This name appears in the texts of various histories as Mukh, Mugh, and Fath, the *Blibilothecea Indica* text of Baranī has been followed here.

from the king's grasp. Vīra Ballāla III of Dvāravatīpura established his independence ; Kamplī was occupied by one of the sons
of its valiant raja, who apostatised from Islam and restored Hindu
rule southward of the Tungabhadra ; and Krishna or Kānhayya
Nāik, apparently a scion of the Kākatīyas, expelled all Muslim
officers from Telingāna and established himself at Warangal.

Muhammad had been besieging the citadel of Daulatābād for
three months when he received news of another serious rebellion
in Gujarāt, where Taghī, a cobbler, had assembled a band of rebels
who promised to become formidable owing to the disaffection which,
the king had excited throughout the province. Taghī, despite his
humble antecedents, was a man of ability and energy. He attached
to his cause the remnant of the centurions of Gujarāt and some of
the Hindu chieftains of the hilly country on the east of the province,
and attacked Pātan, where he captured and imprisoned the governor,
Shaikh Mu'izz-ud-dīn, and some of his officers, and put to death his
assistant, Malik Muzaffar. From Pātan he marched to Cambay,
and, after plundering that town, ventured further southward, and
laid siege to Broach, recently the king's headquarters. On hearing
that Broach was besieged Muhammad decided that his presence was
more urgently required in Gujarāt than in the Deccan. Appointing
Khudāvandzāda Qavām-ud-dīn, Malik Jauhar, and Shaikh Burhān
Bilārāmī to the command of such troops as he could leave before
Daulatābād, and to the government of the province, he set out for
Broach. Taghī, on learning of his approach, raised the siege and
fled towards Cambay with no more than 300 horse, and Muhammad
sent Malik Yūsuf Bughrā with 2000 horse in pursuit of him. Yūsuf
came up with the rebels neer Cambay, and, notwithstanding his
superiority in numbers, was defeated and slain. Muhammad now
marched against Taghī in person, but the latter retired before him
to Asāwal, now Ahmadābād, and put to death Shaikh Mu'izz ud-dīn
and his other prisoners. As the king advanced to Asāwal, Taghī
again retired to Pātan, but, emboldened by a relaxation of the
pursuit, the royal army having been obliged by the poor condition
of its horses and the heavy rains to halt for nearly a month at
Asāwal, advanced as far as Kadī, apparently with the object of
attacking the king. Incensed by this insolence Muhammad marched
to meet him. Taghī, in order to encourage his troops to meet an
army commanded by the king in person, had plied them with liquor,
under the influence of which they charged so recklessly that they
succeeded in penetrating the centre of the royal army, but here
they were overpowered by the elephants, and the survivors fled to

Pātan, leaving their camp and baggage in the hands of the enemy, who slew the baggage guard of 500 men. The son of Yūsuf Bughrā was placed in command of a force detached to pursue the rebels and Taghī caused his followers to collect their wives, followers and dependants at Pātan and to remove them to Khambāliya[1], whither he retired. Thence he fled further into Kāthiāwār and took refuge with the raja of Gunar (Junagarh) who afforded him 'wood and water' in the hills and forests of his small kingdom.

Muhammad meanwhile advanced to Pātan, where he received the submission of the Hindu chieftains of the province, and from the raja of Mandal and Pātrī[2] an offering of the heads of some of the rebels who had taken refuge with him. While at Pātan he received the news that the Deccan, where everything had gone ill with his cause since his departure, was lost to him. The 'centurion' Hasan, who had received from the Afghān king the title of Zafar Khān, had marched to Bīdar and, with the help of reinforcements received from Daulatābād and from Kānhayya Nāik of Warangal, had defeated and slain 'Imād-ul-Mulk Sartīz and dispersed his army. His victory was the death-blow to the royal cause in the Deccan, and as Hasan approached Daulatābād the royal troops raised the siege and hastily retreated on Dhār. Nāsir-ud-dīn Ismā'īl Shāh left the citadel and met the conqueror at Nizāmpur, about three and a half miles from the fortress, where he entertained him for fourteen days. Ismā'īl, an old man who loved his ease, clearly perceived that Hasan was the man of the hour, and resolved to descend gracefully from a throne which he had not sought and professed not to desire. Summoning his officers, he announced to them his intention of abdicating and professed his readiness to swear allegiance to any, worthier than himself, on whom their choice might fall. The election of Hasan was a foregone conclusion. It was he who had driven the royal troops from the Deccan, and his claim to descent from the half-mythical hero, Bahman son of Isfandiyār, seemed to mark him out for the honour of royalty. On August 3, 1347, he was acclaimed by the assembled nobles of the Deccan under the title of Abu'l-Muzaffar 'Alā-ud-dīn Bahman Shāh[3], and founded a dynasty which ruled the Deccan for nearly a hundred and eighty years.

---

[1] Situated in 22° 9'N. and 69 40'E.

[2] Two towns immediately to the east of the Little Rann, Mandal is in 23° 16'N. and 71° 55'E. and Pātrī in 25° 10' N. and 71° 48'E.

[3] That this was his title is proved by a contemporary inscription and legends on coins, as well as by independent historical evidence. European historians have hitherto accepted unquestioningly Firishta's absurd legend of his having assumed the title 'Alā-ud-dīn Hasan Kankū *Bahmanī* in honour of one Gangu, a Brāhman whose slave

The king had aleardy summoned Khvāja Jahān and other nobles from Delhi with a large army, with a view to dispatching them to the Deccan, but the news of Bahman Shāh's success deterred him from attempting the recovery of the southern provinces while Taghī was still at large in Kāthiāwār and disaffection was rife throughout his dominions, and he resolved to restore order in Gujarāt before attempting to recover his lost provinces. The local officials and chieftains who had come from the Daulatābād province to wait on him, on learning this decision, returned in a body to Daulatābād, where they settled down quietly as loyal subjects of Bahman Shāh.

The loss of the Deccan was a bitter blow to Muhammad, and after his custom he sought counsel and consolation of Baranī, the historian. He sadly likened his kingdom to a sick man oppressed by a variety of diseases, the remedy of one of which aggravated the rest, so that as soon as he had restored order in one province another fell into disorder, and he appealed to Baranī for historical precedents for the course to be followed in such a case. Baranī could give him but little comfort. Some kings so situated, he said, had abdicated in favour of a worthy son and had spent the rest of their lives in seclusion, while others had devoted themselves to pleasure and had left all business of state in the hands of their ministers. The king replied that he had intended, had events shaped themselves according to his will, to resign the government of his kingdom to his cousin Fīrūz, Malik Kabīr, and Khvāja Jahān, and to perform the pilgrimage to Mecca, but that the disobedience of his people had so inflamed his wrath and his severity had so aggravated their contumacy that he could not escape from the vicious circle, and must continue, while he lived, to wield the sword of punishment.

Having definitely abandoned the idea of recovering the Deccan he was able to devote the whole of his attention and resources to the suppression of Taghī's rebellion and to the re-establishment of his authority in Gujarāt and Kāthiāwār. He spent the rainy season of 1348 at Mandal and Pātrī, engaged in re-organising his army and in improving the administration of Gujarāt. At its close he marched into Kāthiāwār with the object of subjugating the raja of Girnār, who had harboured the rebel. The raja, with a view to averting his vengeance, was preparing to seize and surrender Taghī, but the latter, being apprised of the design, fled from Kāthiāwār to Sind. The rainy season of 1349 was spent in the neighbourhood

he had formerly been. His regal name was Bahman, and it is only to his successors that the epithet Bahmani is properly applied. The meaning of the addition Lankū has not been established, but it is probably a corruption of Kaīkāūs, the name of Bahman Shāh's father.

of Girnār, which fortress Muhammad captured, establishing his
authority in all the ports of the Kāthiāwār coast. Not only the
raja of Girnār, but Khengār, raja of Cutch, whose dominions extended into Kāthiāwār, and the minor chieftains of the peninsula
appeared before him and made their submission to him, acknowledging him as their over-lord. From Girnār he marched to Gondāl,
in the centre of Kāthiāwār, where he was attacked by a fever which
prostrated him for some months. Here he spent the rainy season
of 1350, and here he received news of the death of Malik Kabīr at
Delhi, which deeply grieved him. Khvāja Jahān and Malik
Maqbūl were sent to Delhi to carry on the administration of the
kingdom and Muhammad ordered the nobles at Delhi to join him
with their contingents, to reinforce the army with, which he purposed to invade Sind and punish the Jām, who had harboured the
rebel Taghī. Contingents were likewise summoned from Dīpālpur,
Multān, Uch, and Sehwān, so that it was at the head of a great
host that the king, in October, 1350, set out for Sind. Aster crossing
the Indus he was joined by a force of four or five thousand Mughul
auxiliaries under Ūltūn Bahādur, who had been sent by the Amīr
Farghan to his assistance. He then marched on towards Tattah,
and was within thirty leagues of that town on Muharram 10, 752
(March 9, 1351) which, being a day of mourning, he observed by
fasting, He broke his fast with a hearty meal of fish, and the fever
from which he had suffered in the previous year returned. He still,
however, travelled on by boat, but was obliged to rest when within
fourteen leagues of Tattah, and as he lay sick fear fell upon his great
army, held together by his personal authority alone. Far from
home, encumbered with their wives and families, within reach of
the enemy, and attended by allies whom they feared hardly less,
they knew not what should become of them on the death of their
leader. On March 20, 1351, the event which they dreaded came to
pass, 'and so,' says Budaunī, 'the king was freed from his people
and they from their king.'

Enough has perhaps been said of the extraordinary character
of Muhammad Tughluq. He was a genius, with an unusually large
share of that madness to which great wit is nearly allied, and the
contradictions of his character were an enigma to those who knew
him best. Both Baranī and Ibn Batūtah are lost in astonishment
at his arrogance, his piety, his humility, his pride, his lavish
generosity, his care for his people, his hostility to them, his preference for foreigners, his love of justice and his ferocious cruelty,
and can find no better description of their patron than that he was
a freak of creation.

CHAPTER VII

THE REIGN OF FĪRŪZ TUGHLUQ, THE DECLINE AND EXTINCTION OF THE DYNASTY, AND THE INVASION OF INDIA BY TAIMŪR

THE death of Muhammad left the army without a leader and threw it into confusion. Some historians allege that on his death-bed he designated his cousin, Fīrūz, the son of Rajab, as his heir, but these are the panegyrists of Fīrūz, who made no attempt to claim the throne but merely associated himself with other officers in the endeavour to extricate it from a perilous situation. Its Mughul allies under Ūltūn Bahādur were regarded with apprehension and, having been rewarded for their services, were requested to retire to their own country. They were already retreating when they were joined by Naurūz Gurgīn, a Mughal officer who had served Muhammad for some years and now deserted with his contingent and disclosed to Ūltūn the confusion which reigned in the army. The army had already begun a straggling and disorderly retreat when it was attacked in flank by the Mughuls and in rear by the Sindīs and plundered, almost without opposition, by both. The dispirited and demoralised host had been at the mercy of its enemies for two days when the officers urged Fīrūz, now forty-six years of age, to ascend the throne, but the situation was complicated by his professed unwillingness to accept their nomination and by the presence of a competitor, a child named Dāvar Malik, whose claims were vehemently urged by his mother, a daughter of Ghiyās-ud-dīn Tughluq. She was silenced by the objection that the crisis required a man, not a child, at the head of affairs, and on March 23, 1351, the nobles overcame the protests of Fīrūz by forcing him on to the throne and acclaiming him. Having ransomed the captives taken by the Mughuls and the Sindīs he attacked and drove off the enemy, so that the army was able to continue its retreat to Delhi without molestation, while a force was left in Sind to deal with the rebel Taghī.

On his way towards Delhi Fīrūz learned that the aged minister, Khvāja Jahān, had proclaimed in the capital, under the title of Ghiyās-ud-dīn Muhammad, a child whom he declared to be the son of Muhammad Tughluq, but whom the historians represent as supposititious. We have, however, no impartial chronicle of this reign

and there is much to justify the belief that the child was Muhammad's son and that the allegation that he was not was an
attempt by panegyrists to improve their patron's feeble hereditary
title[1].

To the people of Delhi the boy's relationship, whether genuine
or fictitious, to their old tyrant was no recommendation, and numbers fled from the city to join Fīrūz. The king was relieved of much
anxiety by the receipt of the news of the death of Taghī in Sind,
and by the adhesion to his cause of Malik Maqbūl, the ablest noble
in the kingdom, a Brāhman of Telingāna who had accepted Islām
and whom he made his minister.

The cause of the child king was hopeless and Khvāja Jahān repaired as a suppliant to the camp and was kindly received and
pardoned, against the advice of the officers of the army, but as he
was retiring to Sāmāna, where be proposed to spend the rest of his
life in seclusion, he was followed by an officer entitled Sher Khān,
who put him to death.

On August 25, 1351, Fīrūz entered Delhi without opposition and
ascended the throne. He conciliated his subjects by remitting all
debts due to the state and by abstaining from any endeavour to
recover the treasure which had been lavished by Khvāja Jahān in
his attempt to establish his nominee. For the first year of his reign
he was fully employed in restoring peace and order in the kingdom,
which had been harried and distracted by the freaks and exactions
of his predecessor. Bengal and the Deccan were lost, and he made
no serious attempt to recover either, but in the extensive territory
still subject to Delhi he did his best to repair Muhammad's errors.
He appointed Khvāja Hisām-ud-dīn Junaid assessor of the revenue,
and within a period of six years the assessor completed a tour of
inspection of the kingdom and submitted his report. Fīrūz reduced
the demand on account of land revenue so as to leave ample provision for the cultivator and further lightened his burdens by
abolishing the pernicious custom of levying benevolences from provincial governors, both on first appointment and annually. The
result of these wise measures was an enormous expansion of the
cultivated area, though the statement that no village lay waste and
no culturable land remained untilled is certainly an exaggeration.
In fertile tracts thriving villages inhabited by a contented peasantry
dotted the country at intervals of two miles or less, and in the
neighbourhood of Delhi alone there were 1200 garden villages in
which fruit was grown and which paid yearly to the treasury 180,000

[1] See *J.R.A.S.*, for July, 1922.

langas. The revenues from the Doāb, which had been nearly depopulated by the exactions of Muhammad amounted to 8,000,000
tangas, and that of the crown lands of the whole kingdom to
68,500,000 *tangas,* each worth about twenty pence. At a later period
of his reign, in 1375, Fīrūz abolished some twenty-five vexatious
cesses, mostly of the nature of *octroi* duties, which had weighed
heavily upon merchants and tradesmen. The immediate loss to the
public exchequer was computed at 3,000,000 *tangas* annually, but
the removal of these restrictions on trade and agriculture naturally
produced a fall in prices, so that wheat sold in Delhi at eight
jītals and pulse and barley at four *jītals* the *man,* the *jītal* being
worth rather more than one-third of a penny. These rates
were virtually the same as those fixed by 'Alā-ud-Dīn Khaljī, but in
the reign of Fīrūz there was no arbitrary interference with the law
of supply and demand, except in the case of sweatmeats, the manu-
facturers of which were justly compelled to allow the consumer to
benefit by the fall in the price of the raw material.

It was not only by lightening the cultivator's burden that Fīrūz
encouraged agriculture. He is still remembered as the author of
schemes of irrigation, and traces of his canals yet remain. Of these
there were five, the most important being the canal, 150 miles long
which carried the waters of the Jumna into the arid tract in which
he founded his city of Hisār-i Fīrūza (Hissār). He also sank 150
wells for purposes of irrigation and for the use of travellers and
indulged a passion for building which equalled, if it did not surpass
that of the Roman Emperor Augustus. The enumeration of three
hundred towns founded by him must be regarded as an exaggeration
unless we include in the number waste villages restored and re-
populated during his reign, but the towns of Fīrūzābād, or New
Delhi, Fathābād, Hissār, Fīrūzpūr near Budaun, and Jaunpur were
founded by him, and he is credited with the construction or restoration of four mosques, thirty palaces, two hundred caravanserais, five
reservoirs, five hospitals, a hundred tombs, ten baths, ten monumental pillars, and a hundred bridges.

While resting at Delhi after his return from Sind Fīrūz performed the quaintly pious duty of atoning vicariously for the sins
of his cousin. In his own words he caused the heirs of those who
had been executed during the reign of his late lord and master,
and those who had been deprived of a limb, nose, or eye to be
appeased with gifts and reconciled to the late king, so that they
executed deeds, duly attested by witnesses, declaring themselves
to be satisfied. These were placed in a chest, which was deposited

in the tomb of Muhammad in the hope that God would show him mercy.

Bengal had for some years ceased to acknowledge the authority of Delhi. In 1338 Mubārak, styling himself Fakhr-ud-dīn Mubārak Shāh, had established himself in Eastern Bengal, and had been succeeded in 1349 by Ikhtiyār-ud-dīn Ghāzī Shāh; and in 1339 'Alā-ud dīn 'Alī Shāh had assumed independence in Western Bengal. In 1345 Hājī Iliyās, styling himself Shams-ud-dīn Iliyās Shāh, had made himself master of Western Bengal, and in 1352 had overthrown Ghāzī Shāh and established his dominion over the whole of Bengal. Emboldened by success, and by the indifference of Fīrūz, Iliyās had rashly invaded Tirhut with the object of annexing the south-eastern districts of the new restricted kingdom of Delhi, but Fīrūz was now free to punish this act of aggression, and in November, 1353, marched from Delhi with 70,000 horse to repel the invader. Iliyās retired before him into Tirhut, and thence to his capital. Pāndua, but mistrusting the strength of this stronghold, continued his retreat to Ikdāla, a village situated on islands in the Brāhmaputra and protected by the dense jungle which clothed the river's banks, whither Fīrūz followed him. Fīrūz failed to reduce Ikdāla and Iliyās endeavoured to detain the invaders in Bengal until the advent of the rainy season, in the hope that the unhealthiness of the climate and the difficulty of communicating with Delhi would place them at his mercy, but Fīrūz preferred an undignified retreat to almost certain disaster. Iliyās followed and attacked him, but was defeated with some loss and Fīrūz continued his retreat without further molestation and on September 1, 1354, entered Delhi.

After his return he founded on the banks of the Jumna immediately to the south of the present city of Delhi, a new capital which he called Fīrūzābād, a name which he had already vauntingly bestowed on the city of Pāndua. The new town occupied the sites of the old town of Indarpat and eleven other villages or hamlets, and contained no fewer than eight large mosques. A regular service of public conveyances, with fixed rates of hire connected it with Old Delhi, ten miles distant. In the following year Fīrūz, when visiting Dīpālpūr, gave directions for the cutting of a canal from the Sutlej to Jhajjar, a town within forty miles of Delhi, and in 1356 he founded Hissār on the sites of two villages Larās-i-Buzurg and Larās-i-Khurd. The neighbourhood was arid, and the new town was supplied with water by two canals, one from the Jumna, in the neighbourhood of Karnāl, and the other from the Sutlej,

near the point at which it emerges from the mountains. The canal
from Dīpālpūr to Jhajjar also passed at no great distance from the
new town.

In December, 1356, the king was gratified by the receipt of a
robe of honour and a commission recognising his sovereignty in
India from the puppet Abbasid Caliph in Egypt, but the envoy
also bore a letter which commended to him the Bahmanī dynasty
of the Deccan in terms which made it clear that the Caliph recognised its independence. At the same time envoys arrived with
complimentary gifts from Iliyās, and obtained from Fīrūz recognition of the independence of Bengal.

Throughout this reign the country was remarkably free from
irruptions of the Mughuls of which only two are recorded, both of
them being successfully repulsed.

In 1358 a plot was formed against the life of Fīrūz. His cousin
Khudāvandzāda, who had unsuccessfully claimed the throne for
her son, now lived at Delhi, and she and her husband arranged
that the king should be assassinated by armed men on the occasion
of a visit to her house, but the plot was frustrated by her son,
Dāvar Malik, who was not in sympathy with his stepfather, Khusrav
Malik, and contrived to apprise Fīrūz by signs that his life was in
danger, thus causing him to depart sooner than was his wont, and
before the arrangements for his assassination were complete. On
returning to his palace he sent troops to surround the house, and
the men who were to have slain him were arrested and disclosed
the plot. Khudāvandzāda was imprisoned, her great wealth was
confiscated, and her husband was banished.

Iliyās was now dead, and had been succeeded in Bengal by his
son, Sikandar Shāh, and in 1359 Fīrūz, regardless of his treaty
with the father, invaded with a large army the dominions of the
son. The transparently frivolous pretext for the expedition was
the vindication of the rights of Zafar Khān, a Persian who had
married the daughter of Fakhr-ud-dīn Mubārak Shāh of Eastern
Bengal and whose hopes of sitting on the throne of his father-in-law
had been shattered by the conquest and annexation of Eastern
Bengal by Iliyās. On the conquest of the country Zafar Khān had
fled to the coast and embarked on a ship which carried him round
Cape Comorin to Tattah, whence he had made his way to the
court of Fīrūz, who appointed him, in 1357, deputy minister of the
kingdom.

Fīrūz halted for six months at Zafarābād on the Gumti and
founded in its neighbourhood a city which became known as

Jaunpur. Muslim historians derive the name from Jauna, the title
by which Muhammad Tughluq had been known before his acces·
sion, but the city of Fīrūz was not the first town on the site and
Hindus derive the name, which occasionally takes the form of Jamna-
pur, from Jamadagni, a famous *rishi*.

At the end of the rainy season Fīrūz continued his march into
Bengal, and Sikandar, following his father's example, retired to
Ikdāla. The second siege was no more successful than the first,
and Sikandar was able to obtain peace on very favourable terms.
He is said to have promised to surrender Sonārgāon, the capital
of Eastern Bengal, to Zafar Khān, but the promise, even if made,
cost him nothing, for Zafar Khān preferred the security and emolu·
ments of his place at court to the precarious tenure of a vassal
throne. From partial historians we learn that Sikandar agreed to
pay an annual tribute of forty elephants, but the same historians
are constrained to admit that he obtained from Fīrūz recognition
of his royal title, a jewelled crown worth 80,000 *tangas* and 5,000
Arab and Turkish horses.

Fīrūz halted at Jaunpur during the rainy season of 1360, and
in the autumn led an expedition into Orissa. It is not easy, from
the various accounts of the operations, to follow his movements
with accuracy, but his objective was Purī, famous for the great
temple of Jagannāth. As he advanced into Orissa, which is described as a fertile and wealthy country, the raja fled and took
ship for a port on the coast of Telingāna. Fīrūz reached Purī,
occupied.the raja's palace, and took the great idol, which he sent
to Delhi to be trodden underfoot by the faithful. Rumours of an
intended pursuit reached the raja, who sent envoys to sue for
peace, which he obtained by the surrender of twenty elephants
and a promise to send the same number annually to Delhi, and
Fīrūz began his retreat. He attempted to reach Kara on the
Ganges, where he had left his heavy baggage, by a route more
direct than, that by which he had advanced. traversing the little
known districts of Chota Nāgpur. The army lost its way, and wandered for six months through a country sparsely populated, hilly,
and covered with dense jungle. Supplies were not to be had, and
numbers perished from the hardships and privations which they
suffered, but at length the troops emerged from the hills and
forests in which they had been wandering into the open plain.
Meanwhile the absence of news from the army had caused at Delhi
unrest so grave that Maqbūl, the regent, had considerable difficulty
in maintaining order, but news of the army allayed the excitement

of the populace, and the king was received on his return with great rejoicing.

In 1351 Fīrūz marched from Delhi with the object of attempting to recover the fortress of Daulatābād, but his progress was arrested by reports that the raja of Kāngra had ventured to invade his kingdom and plunder some of the districts lying at the foot of the mountains, and he marched to Sirhind with the object of attacking Kāngra. On his way to Sirhind he observed that a canal might be cut to connect the waters of the Saraswatī with those of another river, probably the Markanda, which rises near Nāhan and flows past Shāhābad, to the south of Ambāla. The two streams were divided by high ground, but the canal was completed by the labours of 50,000 workmen. In the course of the excavation large fossil bones were discovered, some of which were correctly identified as those of elephants, while others were ignorantly supposed to be those of a race of prehistoric men. The records of the reign have proved useful as a guide to later and more scientific investigators, and led to the discovery of the fossil bones of sixty-four *genera* of mammals which lived at the foot of the Himālaya in Pliocene (Siwālik) times, of which only thirty-nine *genera* have species now living. Of eleven species of the elephant only one now survives in India, and of six species of *bos* but two remain.

Fīrūz enriched Sirhind with a new fort, which he named Fīrūzpur, and continued his march northwards towards Kāngra by way of the famous temple of Jwālamukhī, where he dealt less harshly than usual with the Brāhman priests. A panegyrist defends him from the imputation of encouraging idolatory by presenting a golden umbrella to be hung over the head of the idol, which he seems, in fact, to have removed ; but he ordered that some of the sacred books, of which there were 1300 in the temple, should be translated, and one in particular, treating of natural science, augury, and divination, was rendered into Persian verse by a court poet, A'azz-ud-dīn Khālid Khānī, and named by him *Dalā'il-i-Fīrūz Shāhī*. Firishta describes the book as a compendium of theoretical and practical science, and even the rigidly orthodox Budaunī admits that it is moderately good, free neither from beauties nor defects, which is high praise from him. Budaunī mentions also some ' unprofitable and trivial works on prosody, music, and dancing,' which were translated. There seems to be no reason for crediting the statement, made with some diffidence by Firishta, that Fīrūz broke up the idols of Jwālamukhī, mixed their fragments with the flesh of cows, and hung them in nosebags round the Brāhmans' necks, and that he sent the principal idol as a trophy to Medina. The raja of Kāngra surrendered after standing a very short siege, and was courteously received and permitted to retain his territory as a fief of Delhi.

The enforced retreat from Sind and the insolence of the Sindīs had rankled in the memory of Fīrūz ever since his accession, and in 1·362 he set out for that country with an army of 90,000 horse and 480 elephants. He collected on the Indus a large fleet of boats, which accompanied the army down-stream to Tattah, the capital of the Jāms of Sind, which was situated on both banks of the river. The ruler was now Jām Mālī, son of Jām Unnar, and he was assisted in the government by his brother's son, Bābaniya. Both were resolute in defending the city, and the royal army was exposed to the *sorties* of the garrison and suffered from a severe famine and from an epizootic disease which carried off or disabled three-quarters of the horses of the cavalry. The garrison, observing their plight, sallied forth and attacked them in force, and though they were driven back within the walls Fīrūz, who was humiliated at the same time by the capture of his entire fleet, decided to retreat for a time to Gujarāt, where his troops might recruit their strength and replace their horses.

The troops suffered more severely during the retreat than during the siege. The disease among the horses lost none of its virulence, and grain still rose in price. The starving soldiery fell out by the way and died, and the survivors were reduced to eating carrion and hides. The principal officers were obliged to march on foot with their men, and treacherous guides led the army into the Rann of Cutch, where there was no fresh water, so that thirst was added to their other privations, and they suffered terrible losses. Once again no news of the army reached Delhi for some months, and Maqbūl, the regent, had great difficulty in restraining the turbulence of the anxious and excited populace, and was at length reduced to the expedient of producing a forged dispatch. The execution of one of the treacherous guides induced the others to extricate the army from its perilous position and it emerged at length from the desert and salt morass into the fertile plains of Gujarāt. Dispatches to Delhi restored order in the city, and the governor of Gujarāt, Nizām-ul-Mulk, who had failed to send either guides or supplies to the army, was dismissed from his post, Zafar Khān being appointed in his place.

During the rainy season of 1363 Fīrūz was employed in Gujarāt in repairing the losses of his army. Officers and men received liberal grants to enable them to replace their horses, the revenues of the province were appropriated to the reorganisation of the army, and requisitions for material of war were sent to Delhi. The king was obliged to forgo a favourable opportunity for interference in the affairs of the Deccan, where Bahman Shāh had died in 1358 and had been succeeded by his son, Muhammad I. His son-in-law, Bahrām Khān Māzandarānī, who was governor of Daulatābād, resented the elevation of Muhammad, against whom he openly rebelled three years later, and now invited Fīrūz to recover the Deccan, promising him his support, but the king would not abandon his enterprise in Sind, and Bahrām was disappointed.

Fīrūz Shāh's return to Sind was unexpected, and the people, who were quietly tilling their fields, fled before him destroyed that portion of Tattah which stood on the eastern bank of the Indus, and took refuge behind the fortifications of mud on the western bank. Fīrūz, hesitating to attempt the passage of the river under these defences, sent two officers with their contingents up the Indus, which they crossed at a considerable distance above the town and, marching down the western bank, made an unsuccessful attack on the town. After this failure they were recalled and the king sent to Delhi for reinforcements and, while awaiting their arrival reaped and garnered the crops, so that his army was well supplied while the garrison of Tattah began to feel the pinch of famine. When the reinforcements arrived the Jām lost heart and sent an envoy to sue for peace. Fīrūz was inclined to leniency, and Bābaniya and the Jām, on making their submission to him, were courteously received, but were informed that they would be required to accompany him to Delhi and that an annual tribute of 400,000 *tangas*, of which the first instalment was to be paid at once, would be required. These terms were accepted and the Jām and Bābaniya accompanied Fīrūz to Delhi as guests under mild restraint. The rejoicings on the return of the army were marred by the lamentations of those who had lost relations during the disastrous retreat to Gujarāt, and Fīrūz, who had already, while wandering in the Rann, sworn never again to wage war but for the suppression of rebellion, now publicly expressed regret for having undertaken the expedition to Sind, and ordered that the estates and property of the deceased should descend, rent-free, to their heirs.

In 1365—66 envoys from Bahrām Khān Māzandarānī, who was now in rebellion against Muhammad Shāh Bahmanī, arrived at court and besought Fīrūz to come to the aid of those who wished to return to the allegiance of Delhi, but were curtly told that whatever they suffered was the just and natural punishment of their rebellion against Muhammad Tughluq, and were dismissed.

In 1372—73 the faithful minister, Maqbūl Khānjahān, died, and was succeeded in his honours and emoluments by his son, who received his father's title of Khānjahān ; and in the following year Zafar Khān, governor of Gujarāt, died, and was succeeded by his son, Daryā Khān, who also received his father's title.

The affectionate disposition of Fīrūz received a severe blow from the death of his eldest son, Fath Khān, on July 23, 1374, and we may attribute to his grief the gradual impairment of his faculties, evidence of which may be observed shortly after his son's death. At first he withdrew entirely from public business, and when he resumed its responsibilities one of his first acts was entirely foreign to his previous character. Shams-ud-dīn Dāmaghānī, a meddle-some and envious noble, insisted that the province of Gujarāt was assessed for revenue at too low a rate, and offered, if placed in charge of it, to send annually to Delhi, in addition to the revenue for which the province had been assessed, 100 elephants, 400,000 *tangas*, 400 slaves, and 200 horses. Fīrūz was loth to disturb Zafar Khān, but demanded of his deputy, Abū Rijā, the additional con-tributions suggested by Dāmaghānī. Abū Rijā declared that the province could not bear this impost and Fīrūz ordinarily solicitous to alleviate the burdens of his subjects, dismissed him and his master, Zafar Khān, and appointed Dāmaghānī governor of Gujarāt. On his arrival in the province the new governor encountered the most determined opposition to his extortionate demands and, finding himself unable to fulfil his promise, raised the standard of rebellion, but was overpowered and slain by the centurions of Gujarāt, who sent his head to court. Fīrūz then appointed to the government of Gujarāt Malik Mufrih, who received the title of Farhat-ul-Mulk.

In 1377 Fīrūz was engaged in repressing a rebellion in the Etāwah district, where the revenue could seldom be collected but by armed force; and two years later found it necessary to take precautions against a threatened inroad of the Mughuls, which his preparations averted. In the same year his usually mild nature was stirred to a deed of vengeance worthy of his predecessor. Kharkū, the raja of Katehr, had invited to his house Sayyid Mu-hammad, governor of Budaun, and his two brothers, and trea-cherously slew them. In the king's pious estimation the heinousness of the crime was aggravated by the descent of the victims and in the spring of 1380 he marched into Katehr and there directed a massacre of the Hindus so general and so indiscriminate that, as one historian says, 'the spirits of the murdered Sayyids themselves arose to intercede'. Kharkū fled into Kumaun and was followed by the royal troops who, unable to discover his hiding place, visited their disappointment on the wretched inhabitants, of whom vast numbers were slain and 23,000 captured and enslaved. The approach of the rainy season warned Fīrūz to retire from the hills of Kumaun, but his thirst for vengeance was not yet sated. Before leaving for Delhi he appointed an Afghān to the government of Sambhal, and ordered him to devastate Katehr annually with fire and sword. He himself visited the district every year for the next five years and so supplemented the Afghān's bloody work that 'in those years not an acre of land was cultivated, no man slept in house, and the death of the three Sayyids was avenged by that of countless thousands of Hindus.'

In 1385, the last year of these raids, Fīrūz founded near Budaun a strong fort which he named Fīrūzpur[1], but the miserable inhabitants called it in derision Ākhirīnpūr ('the last of his cities') and the gibe was fulfilled, for Fīrūz now lapsed into a condition of senile decay, and could no more found cities or direct the ship of state. As a natural consequence of the failure of his intellect his minister, Khānjahān, became all powerful, and soon abused his power. In 1387 he persuaded Fīrūz that Muhammad Khān, his eldest surviving son, was conspiring with Zafar Khān and other nobles to remove him and ascend the throne. Fīrūz, without inquiring into the matter, authorised the minister to arrest those whom he had accused, and Zafar Khān was summoned from his fief of Mahoba on the pretext that his accounts were to be examined, and was confined in Khānjahān's house. The prince evaded, on the plea of ill-health, attendance at a *darbār* at which he was to have been arrested, but privately gained access to the royal harem by arriving at the gate in a veiled litter which was supposed to contain his wife. His appearance, fully armed, in the inner apartments at first caused consternation, but he was able to gain his father's ear, and easily persuaded him that the real traitor was Khānjahān, who intended to pave his own way to the throne by the destruction of the royal family. Armed with his father's authority, he led the household troops numbering ten or twelve thousand, and the royal elephants to Khānjahān's house. The minister, on hearing of his approach, put Zafar Khān to death and sallied forth with his own troops to meet his enemies. He was wounded

---

[1] Perhaps the village about three miles south of Budaun, which appears in the Indian Atlas as Fīrūzpūr Iklehrī.

and retired into his house, whence he made his escape by an unguarded door and fled into Mewāt, where he took refuge with a
Rājput chieftain, Koka the Chauhān. His house was plundered
and his followers were slain, and Muhammad Khān returned to
the palace. Fīrūz, no longer capable of governing, associated his
son with himself not only in the administration, but also in the
royal title, and caused him to be proclaimed, on August 22, 1387,
under the style of Nāsir-ud-dīn Muhammad Shāh.

One of Muhammad's first acts was to send Sikandar Khān,
master of the horse, into Mewāt to seize Khānjahān, with a promise
of the government of Gujarāt as the reward of success. Khānjahān
was surrendered by Koka, and Sikandar Khān, after carrying his
head to Delhi, set out for Gujarāt. Muhammad was hunting in
Sirmūr when he heard that Farhat-ul-Mulk and the centurions of
Gujarāt had defeated and slain Sikandar Khān, whose broken troops
had returned to Delhi. He returned at once to the capital, but
instead of taking any steps to punish the rebels neglected all
public business and devoted himself entirely to pleasure. For five
months the administrative machinery, which had been adjusted by
Fīrūz in the earlier years of his reign, worked automatically, but
the apathy and incompetence of Muhammad became daily more
intolerable, and many of the old servants of the crown assembled
a large force and rose against him nominally in the interests of
Fīrūz. An envoy who was sent to treat with them was stoned and
wounded, and Muhammad was forced to take the field against
them, but, when hard pressed, they succeeded in forcing their way
into the palace and, after two days' indecisive fighting, placed the
decrepit Fīrūz in a litter and carried him into the field. The device,
which is of frequent occurrence in Indian history, succeeded. The
troops with Muhammad believed that their old master had deliberately taken the field against his son and deserted Muhammad, who
fled into Sirmūr with a few retainers. Fīrūz promoted his grandson,
Tughluq Khān, son of the deceased Fath Khān, to the position
lately held by Muhammad, and conferred on him the royal title.
On September 20, 1388, Fīrūz died, at the age of eighty-three, after
a reign of thirty-seven years.

Indian historians praise Fīrūz as the most just, merciful, and
beneficent ruler since the days of Nāsir-ud-dīn Mahmūd, son of
Iltutmish, and there is some similarity between the characters of
the two, though Fīrūz was in almost every respect superior. Both
were weak rulers, but Fīrūz was far less weak and vacillating than
Mahmūd, and both were benevolent, but the benevolence of Fīrūz

was more active than that of Mahmūd. Fīrūz possessed far more
ability than Mahmūd, and his weakness consisted largely in an
indolent man's distaste for the details of business and in unwillingness to cause pain. His benevolence was indiscriminate, for he
showed as much indulgence to the corrupt official as to the indigent
husbandman, and his passion for constructing works of public utility
was due probably as much to vanity as to benevolence. The dis-
continuance of the practice of demanding large gifts from placeholders was intended to relieve the poorer classes, on whom the
burden ultimately fell, and was perhaps not wholly without effect,
but placeholders continued to enrich themselves, and many amassed
large fortunes. Fīrūz Shāh's connivance at corruption and his
culpable leniency destroyed the effect of his own reforms. Old and
inefficient soldiers were not compelled to retire but were permitted
to provide substitutes of whose fitness they were the judges, and the
annual inspection of cavalry horses was rendered futile by the many
evasions devised by the king himself. One story is told of his over-
hearing a trooper bewailing to a comrade the hardship of being
compelled to submit his horse for inspection. He called the man
to him and asked him wherein the hardship lay, and he explained
that he could not expect that his horse would be passed unless he
offered the inspector at least a gold *tanga*, and Fīrūz gave him the
coin. The perversity of the act is not perceived by the historian
who records it, and he merely praises Fīrūz for his benevolence.
Similar laxity prevailed in the thirty-six departments of state, and
in the checking and auditing of the accounts of fiefs and provincial
governments. There was a great show of order and method, and a
pretence was made of annually scrutinising all accounts, but notwithstanding all formalities 'the king was very lenient, not from
ignorance of accounts and business, which he understood well, but
from temperament and generosity.' The working of the mint supplies an instance of the fraud and peculation which were rife. In
1370-71 Fīrūz extended his coinage by minting, for the convenience
of the poorer classes, pieces of small denominations, and the integrity
of the officers of the mint was not proof against the opportunity
for peculation offered by this large issue. Two informers reported
that the six *jītal* pieces were a grain short of standard purity, and
the minister, Maqbūl Khānjahān, whose anxiety to hush the matter
up suggests his complicity, sent for Kajar Shāh, the mintmaster,
who was the principal offender, and directed him to devise a means
of establishing, to the king's satisfaction, the purity of the coin.
Kajar Shāh arranged that the coins should be melted before the

metal was assayed, approached the goldsmiths whose duty it would be to conduct the experiment in the king's presence, and desired them secretly to cast into the crucible sufficient silver to bring the molten metal to the standard of purity. They objected that in accordance with the ordinary precautions on such occasions they would be so denuded of clothing that they would be unable to secrete any silver on their persons, but offered to do what was required if the silver could be placed within their reach. Kajar Shāh accordingly arranged that the necessary quantity of silver should be concealed in one of the pieces of charcoal used for heating the crucible, and the goldsmiths succeeded in conveying it into the vessel without being observed, so that the king was hoodwinked and the metal when assayed, was found to be of the standard purity. Kajar Shāh's presumed innocence was publicly recognised by his being carried through the city on one of the royal elephants, and the two informers were banished, but both the investigations and the public justification of the mintmaster were mere sops to public opinion, for Kajar Shāh was shortly afterwards dismissed. The comments of the contemporary historian are even more interesting, as an example of the view which an educated and intelligent man could then take of such an affair, than his simple record of the facts. He can see nothing wrong in the concealment of a crime, in the punishment of the innocent and the vindication of the guilty, or in the deception practised on the simple Fīrūz, but commends Maqbūl Khānjahān for having dexteriously averted a public scandal The same historian, who has nothing but approval for whatever was established or permitted in the reign of Fīrūz, applauds another serious abuse. Of the irregular troops some received their salaries in cash from the treasury but those stationed at a distance from the capital were paid by transferable assignments on the revenue. A class of brokers made it their business to buy these drafts in the capital at one-third of their nominal value and to sell them to the soldiers in the districts at one-half. Shams-i-Sirāj 'Afīf has no word of condemnation for the fraud perpetrated on the unfortunate soldier, and nothing but commendation for a system which enabled so many knaves to enrich themselves without labour.

Some of the measures introduced by Fīrūz for the welfare of his subjects may be described as grandmotherly legislation. One of them was a marriage bureau and another an employment bureau. The marriage of girls who have reached marriageable age is regarded in India, with some reason, as a religious duty, and Fīrūz charged himself with the task of seeing that no girl of his own faith remained unmarried for want of a dowry. His agency worked chiefly among the middle class and the widows and orphans of public servants, and was most efficient. The employment agency, unlike those of our day, was concerned chiefly with those who desired clerical and administrative employment, for at this time the extension of cultivation and the construction of public works provided ample employment for labourers and handicraftsmen. It was the duty of the *kotwāl* of Delhi to seek those who were without employment and to produce them at court. Here Fīrūz personally made inquiry into their circumstances and qualifications, and after consulting, as far as possible, their inclination, provided them with employment. Whether there was any demand for their services lay beyond the scope of the inquiry, for the business was conducted on charitable rather than on economic principles and probably provided sinecures for many a young idler.

The interest of Fīrūz in public works was not purely utilitarian, and he is remembered for two feats of engineering which appear to indicate an interest in archaeology, but may be more justly attributed to vanity. These were the removal to Delhi, from the sites on which they had been erected by Asoka, of two great inscribed monoliths. The first, known as the *Mināra-yi-Zarīn*, or golden pillars, was transferred from a village near Khizrābād, on the upper Jumna, to Delhi, where it was re-erected near the palace and great mosque at Fīrūzābād, and the second was transported from Meerut and set up on a mound near the *Kūshk-i-Shikār*, or hunting palace, near Delhi. The curious may find, in the pages of Shams-i-Sirāj 'Afīf, an elaborate and detailed description of the ingenious manner in which these two great pillars were removed and erected in their new positions. The difficult feat elicited the admiration of the Amīr Tīmūr when he invaded India, and the pillars, which are still standing, attracted the attention, in 1615, of 'the famous unwearied walker,' Tom Coryate, who erroneously supposed the Sanskrit and Prākrit inscriptions of Asoka to be Greek, and referred them to the time of Alexander the Great.

The harsher side of Fīrūz Shāh's piety was displayed in the persecution of heretics, sectaries, and Hindus. His decree abolishing capital punishment applied only to those of his own faith, for he burnt to death a Brāhman accused of trying to propagate his religion, and the ruthless massacres with which he avenged the murder of the three Sayyids in Budaun prove his benevolence to have been strictly limited. In general it seems to have been due to weakness of character and love of ease, but he could be firm when a question of principle arose. In the course of years Brāhmans had acquired, probably by the influence of Hindu officials, exemption from the *jizya*, or poll-tax, leviable by the Islamic law from all non-Muslims, and Fīrūz was resolved to terminate an anomaly which exempted the leaders of dissent from a tax on dissent, but the exemption had acquired the character of a prescriptive right, and his decision raised a storm of discontent. The Brāhmans surrounded his palace and loudly protested against the invasion of their ancient privilege, threatening to burn themselves alive, and thus to call down upon him, according to their belief, the wrath of heaven.[1] Fīrūz replied that they might burn themselves as soon as they pleased, and the sooner the better, but they shrank from the ordeal, and attempted to work on his superstitious fears by sitting without food at his palace gates. He still remained obdurate, but they had better success with the members of their own faith, and it was ultimately arranged that the tax leviable from the Brāhmans should be borne, in addition to their own burden, by the lower castes of the Hindus.

The reign of Fīrūz closes the most brilliant epoch of Muslim rule in India before the reign of Akbar. 'Alā-ud-dīn Khaljī, who, though differing much from Akbar in most respects, resembled him in desiring to establish a religion of his own devising, had not only extended the empire over almost the whole of India, but had welded the loose confederacy of fiefs which had owned allegiance to the Slave Kings into a homogeneous state. The disorders which followed his death failed to shake seriously the great fabric which he had erected, and the energy of Tughluq and, at first, of his son Muhammad gave it solidity. The latter prince possessed qualities which might have made him the greatest of the rulers of Delhi had they not been marred by a disordered imagination. The loss of the Deccan and Bengal, occasioned by his tyranny, was not an unmixed evil. The difficulty of governing the former, owing to its distance from the centre of administration, had been acknowledged by the

---

[1]This is an extreme example of the practice of *dharna*, so common at one time in India that it was found necessary to make it an offence under the Penal Code. The aggrieved person sits at the door of his enemy and threatens to starve himself to death, in the belief, common to both, that his enemy will be held responsible for his death and thus become the object of divine wrath. By the Brāhmanical law the slaying of a Brāhman involves an infinitely greater degree of guilt than any other crime, and it is difficult to persuade a Brāhman that his person is not more sacred than that of other men. Lord Macaulay's description, in his essay on Warren Hastings, of the scene at the execution of Nanda Kumār is, like much else in his historical writings, pure fiction, but it was certainly only by slow degrees that Hindus learned the principles of a law which is the same for the Brāhman as for the outcaste.

ill-considered attempt to transfer the capital to Daulatābād, and the allegiance of the latter had seldom been spontaneous and had depended chiefly on the personality of the reigning sovereign of Delhi, an uncertain quantity. What remained of the kingdom was more than sufficient to engross the attention of a ruler of ordinary abilities, and Fīrūz had, in spite of two great defects of character, succeeded in improving the administration and in alleviating the lot and winning the affection of his subjects. Military capacity and diligence in matters of detail are qualities indispensable to an oriental despot, and Fīrūz lacked both. After two unsuccessful expeditions into Bengal he was fain to recognise the independence of that country, and his rashness twice imperilled the existence of his army. His easy tolerance of abuses would have completely destroyed the efficiency of that mainstay of absolute power, had it not been counteracted by the vigilance and energy of his officers, who were carefully selected and entirely trusted by him. His judgement of character was, indeed, the principal counterpoise to his imaptience of the disagreeable details of government, and the personal popularity which he enjoyed as the kindly and genial successor of a capricious tyrant secured the fidelity of his trusted officers, but his extensive delegation of authority to them undermined the power of the crown. No policy, however well devised, could have sustained this power under the feeble rule of his successors and the terrible blow dealt at the kingdom within ten years of his death, but his system of decentralisation would have embarrassed the ablest successors, and undoubtedly accelerated the downfall of his dynasty.

Fīrūz was succeeded at Delhi by his grandson, who took the title of Ghiyās-ud-dīn Tughluq Shāh II, while his uncle, Nāsir-ud-dīn Muhammad, in his retreat in the Sirmūr hills, prepared to assert his claim to the throne. Tughluq sent against him an army under the command of Malik Fīrūz 'Ali, whom he had made minister with the title of Khānjahān, and Bahādur Nāhir, a Rājput chieftain of Mewāt who had accepted Islām and now became a prominent figure on the political stage. Muhammad retired to a chosen position in the hills, but was defeated and fled to Kāngra, and Khānjahān, who shrank from attacking the fortress, returned to Delhi, satisfied with his partial success.

Tughluq, thus temporarily relieved of anxiety, plunged into dissipation and sought to secure his tenure of the throne by removing possible competitors. By imprisoning his brother, Sālar Shāh, he so alarmed his cousin Abu Bakr that that prince was constrained, in self-defence, to become a conspirator. He found a willing supporter in the ambitious Rukn-ud-dīn, Khānjahān's deputy, who had much influence with the household troops. Their defection transferred the royal power from Tughluq to Abu Bakr and Tughluq and Khānjahān fled from the palace by a door opening towards the Jumna. They were overtaken and slain by a body of the household troops led by Rukn-ud-dīn, and on February 19, 1389, the nobles at Delhi acclaimed Abu Bakr Shāh as their king. The appointment of Rukn-ud-dīn as minister followed as a matter of course, but he was almost immediately detected in a conspiracy to usurp the throne, and was put to death. This prompt action established for a time Abu Bakr's authority at Delhi, but a serious rebellion broke out in the province immediately to the north of the capital. The centurions of Sāmāna rose against their governor, Khushdil, a loyal adherent of Abu Bakr, put him to death at Sunām, and sent his head to Nāsir-ud-dīn Muhammad, whom they invited to make another attempt to gain the throne. Muhammad marched from Kāngra to Sāmāna, where he was proclaimed king on April 24, 1389. He continued his march towards Delhi, and before reaching the neighbourhood of the city received such accessions of strength as to find himself at the head of 50,000 horse, and he was able to take up his quarters in the Jahānnumā palace in the old city. On April 29 some fighting took place at Fīrūzābād between the troops of the rival kings, but the arrival of Bahādur Nāhir from Mewāt so strengthened Abu Bakr that on the following day he marched out to meet his uncle and inflicted on him so crushing a defeat that he was glad to escape across the Jumna into the Doāb with no more than 2000 horse. He retired to Jalesar, which he made his headquarters, and sent his second son, Humāyūn Khān, to Sāmāna to rally the fugitives and raise fresh recruits. At Jalesar he was joined by many discontented nobles, including Malik Sarvar, lately chief of the police at Delhi, whom he made his minister, with the title of Khvāja Jahān, and Nasir-ul-Mulk, who received the title of Khizr Khān, by which he was afterwards to be known as the founder of the Sayyid dynasty. Muhammad was thus enabled, by July, again to take the field with 50,000 horse, and marched on Delhi, but was defeated at the village of Khondlī and compelled to retire to Jalesar. Notwithstanding this second blow his authority was acknowledged in Multān, Lahore, Sāmāna, Hissār, Hānsī and other districts to the north of Delhi, and was confirmed by executions of those disaffected to him, but the general effect of the prolonged struggle for the throne was temporary eclipse of the power and authority of the dominant race. Hindus ceased to pay the poll-tax and in many of the larger cities of the kingdom menaced Muslim supremacy. In January, 1390, Humāyūn Khān advanced from Sāmāna to Pānīpat and plundered the country as far as the walls of Delhi, but was defeated and driven back to Sāmāna. Abu Bakr had hitherto been detained in Delhi by the fear that his enemies in the city would admit Humāyūn in his absence, but this success encouraged him to attack Muhammad in his stronghold, and in April he left Delhi. As he approached Jalesar Muhammad, with 4000 horse, eluded him, reached Delhi by forced marches, and occupied the palace. Abu Bakr at once retraced his steps, and as he entered the city Muhammad fled and returned to Jalesar. Abu Bakr's success was, however, illusory and transient ; his authority was confined to the capital and the district of Mewāt, where Bahādur Nāhir supported his cause, and even at Delhi his rival had many partisans. In August Islām Khān, a courtier who had great influence in the army, opened communications with Muhammad and placed himself at the head of his adherents in Delhi. The discovery of the conspiracy so alarmed Abu Bakr that he retired with his partisans to Mewāt, and Muhammad, on August 31, entered the capital and was enthroned in the palace of Fīrūzābād. He ordered the expulsion from Delhi of all the household troops of Fīrūz Shāh, whose share in the late revolutions had proved them to be a danger to the State. Most of these troops joined Abu Bakr in Mewāt and those who claimed the right, as natives of Delhi, of remaining in the city were required to pronounce the shibb leth *khārā* ('brackish'). Those who pronounced it *khārī*, after the manner of the inhabitants of eastern Hindūstān and Bengal were adjudged to be royal slaves imported from those regions, and were put to death.

The nobles from the provinces now assembled at Delhi and acknowledged Muhammad as king, and Humāyūn Khān was sent into Mewāt to crush Abu Bakr and his faction. The army arrived before Bahādur Nāhir's stronghold in December 1390, and, being fiercely attacked by the enemy, suffered considerable loss, but eventually drove Bahādur Nāhir into the fortress. Muhammad himself arrived with reinforcements and Abu Bakr and Bahādur Nāhir were compelled to surrender. The latter was pardoned, but Abu Bakr was sent as a prisoner to Meerut, where he soon afterwards died. Muhammad, on his return to Delhi, learnt that Farhat-ul-Mulk, who had been left undisturbed in Gujarāt after his victory over Sikandar Khān, refused to recognise his authority and sent to

Gujarāt as governor Zafar Khān, son of Wajīh-ul-Mulk, a convert·
ed Rajput.

In 1392 the Hindus of Etāwah, led by Nar Singh, Sarvadhāran
the Rāhtor, and Bir Bhan, chief of Bhansor, rose in rebellion, and
Islām Khān was sent against them, defeated them, and carried
Nar Singh to Delhi ; but as soon as his back was turned the
rebellion broke out afresh and Sarvadhāran attacked the town of
Talgrām[1]. Muhammad now marched in person against the rebels,
who shut themselves up in Etāwa, and when hard pressed escaped
from the town by night and fled. The king dismantled the fortifications of Etāwah and marched to Kanauj and Dalmau, where
he punished many who had participated in the rebellion, and
thence to Jalesar, where he built a new fortress, which he named
Muhammadābād.

In June, while he was still at Jalesar, the eunuch Malik Sarvar,
Khvāja Jahān, who had been left as regent at Delhi, reported that
Islām Khān, who had been appointed minister, was about to leave
Delhi for Lahore, in order to head a rebellion in the Punjab. Mu·
hammad hastily returned and taxed Islām Khān with harbouring
treasonable designs. He protested his innocence, but the faithless-
ness of his conduct towards Abu Bakr was fresh in the memory of
all, his nephew appeared as a witness against him, and he was put
to death.

In 1393 the Rājputs of Etāwah again rebelled, but the governor
of Jalesar enticed their leaders, by fair words, into Kanauj, and there
treacherously slew all except Sarvadhāran, who escaped and took
refuge in Etāwah. In August of the same year the king marched
through the rebellious district of Mewāt, laying it waste, and on
reaching Jalesar fell sick, but was unable to enjoy the repose which
he needed, for Bahādur Nahir again took the field and Muhammad
was compelled to march against him, and defeated him. From
Jalesar he wrote to his son, Humāyūn Khān, directing him to
march into the Punjab and quell the rebellion of Shaikhā the
Khokar. The prince was preparing to leave Delhi when he heard
of the death of his father at Jalesar on January 20, 1394, and on
January 22 he ascended the throne at Delhi under the title of 'Alā·
ud-dīn Sikandar Shāh. His reign was brief, for he fell sick almost
immediately after his accession and died on March 8.

1 Bilgrām is another reading, but it is far more probable that Talgrām in the
Doāb was the town attacked, for the Hindus were attempting to establish themselves
in the Doāb, and it is difficult to see why they should have crossed the Ganges and
attacked Bilgrām.

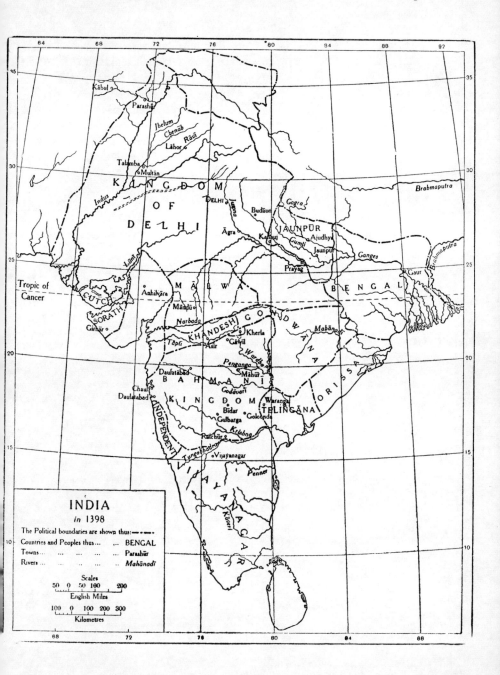

INDIA

in 1398

The Political boundaries are shown thus:—·—·—

Countries and Peoples thus... ,.. BENGAL

Towns... ... ... Parashūr

Rivers ... ... Mahānadī

Scales

50 0 50 100   200

English Miles

100 0 100 200 300

Kilometres

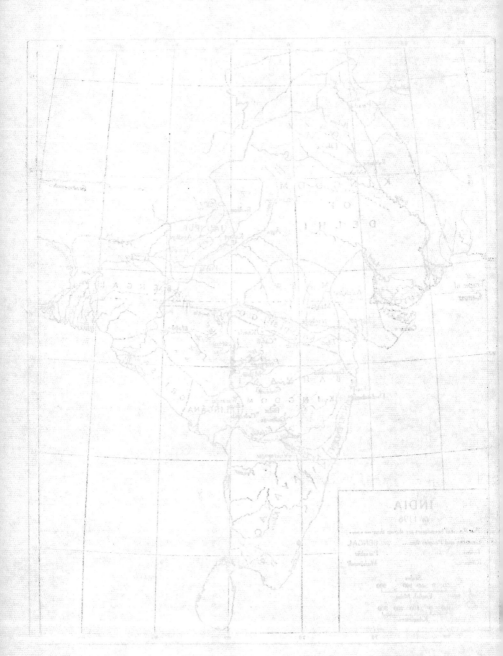

So little respect did the royal house now command that the provincial governors, who had assembled their troops at Delhi for the expedition to Lahore, would have left the capital without waiting for the enthronement of a new king, had not Malik Sarvar induced them to enthrone, under the title of Nāsir-ud-dīn Mahmūd, Humāyūn's brother, the youngest son of Muhammad.

The kingdom was now in a deplorable condition. The obedience of the great nobles was regulated entirely by their caprice or interest, and they used or abused the royal authority as occasion served. In the eastern provinces the Hindus, who had for some years past been in rebellion, threw off all semblance of obedience, and the eunuch Malik Sarvar persuaded or compelled Mahmūd to bestow upon him the lofty title of *Sultān-ush-Sharq*, or King of the East, and to commit to him the duty of crushing the rebellion and restoring order. He left Delhi in May, 1394, punished the rebels, and after reducing to obedience the districts of Koīl, Etāwah, and Kanauj, occupied Jaunpur, where he established himself as an independent ruler. The day on which he left Delhi may be assigned as the date of the foundation of the dynasty of the Kings of the East, or of Jaunpur.

Meanwhile Sārang Khān, who had been appointed on Mahmūd's accession to the fief of Dīpālpūr, was sent to restore order in the north-western provinces. In September, 1394, having assembled the army of Multān as well as his own contingent, he marched towards Lahore, which was held by Shaikhā the Khokar. Shaikhā carried the war into the enemy's country by advancing into the Dīpālpūr district and forming the siege of Ajūdhan (Pāk Pattan) but, finding that this counterstroke failed to arrest Sārang Khān's advance, hastily retraced his steps and attacked Sārang Khān before he could reach Lahore. He was defeated, and fled into the Salt Range, and Sārang Khān appointed his own brother, Malik Kandhū, governor of Lahore, with the title of 'Ādil Khān.

During the course of these events the king visited Gwalior, where Mallū Khān, a brother of Sārang Khān, plotted to overthrow Sa'ādat Khān, a noble whose growing influence over the king's feeble mind had excited the jealousy of the courtiers. The plot was discovered and some of the leading conspirators were put to death, but Mallū Khān fled to Delhi and took refuge with the regent, Muqarrab Khān, who resented the ascendency of Sa'ādat Khān and, on the king's return to the capital, closed the gates of the city against him. For two months Delhi was in a state of siege but in November Mahmūd, whose authority was disregarded by both parties, grew weary of his humiliating position at the gates of his capital, and fled to the protection of Muqarrab Khān. Saʿādat Khān, enraged by his desertion, summoned from Mewāt Nusrat Khān, a son of Fath Khān, the eldest son of Fīrūz, and proclaimed him in Fīrūzābād under the title of Nāsir-ud-dīn Nusrat Shāh. There were thus two titular kings, one at Delhi and the other at Fīrūzābād, each a puppet in the hands of a powerful noble. Saʿādat Khān's arrogance exasperated the old servants of Fīrūz who adhered to Nusrat Shāh, and they expelled him from Fīrūzābād. He fled, in his extremity, to Delhi, and humbled himself before his enemy, Muqarrab Khān, who gave him an assurance of forgiveness, but a few days later treacherously caused him to be put to death.

The various cities which had at different times been the capital of the kingdom were now held by the factions of one puppet or the other. Muqarrab Khān and Mahmūd Shāh were in Delhi, Nusrat Shāh and the old nobles and servants of Fīrūz in Fīrūzābād, Bahādur Nāhir, whose allegiance had been temporarily secured by Muqarrab Khān, was in Old Delhi, and Mallū, who owed his life to Muqarrab Khān and had received from him the title of Iqbāl Khān, was in Sirī, but neither Nāhir nor Mallū was a warm partisan, and each was prepared to shape his conduct by the course of events. For three years an indecisive but destructive strife was carried on in the names of Mahmūd and Nusrat, but the kingdom of the former, who had been first in the field, was bounded by the walls of Delhi, though Muqarrab Khān reckoned Old Delhi and Sirī as appanages of this realm, while the upstart Nusrat Shāh claimed the nominal allegiance of the districts of the Doāb, Sambhal, Pānīpat, Jhajjar, and Rohtak. The great provinces were independent.

In 1395-96 Sārang Khān of Dīpālpūr quarrelled with Khizr Khān the Sayyid, governor of Multān, expelled him from that city, and annexed his fief. Emboldened by this success he marched, in June, 1397, to Sāmāna, and there besieged the governor, Ghālib Khān, who fled and joined Tātār Khān, Nusrat's minister, at Pānīpat. Nusrat Shāh sent a small reinforcement to Tātār Khān, who on October 8 attacked and defeated Sārang Khān and reinstated Ghālib Khān at Sāmāna.

At the close of this year a harbinger of the terrible Amīr Tīmūr appeared in India. Pīr Muhammad, son of Jahāngīr, the eldest son of the great conqueror, crossed the Indus and besieged Uch, which was held for Sārang Khān by ʿAlī Malik. A force was sent to the relief of Uch, but Pīr Muhammad attacked it and drove it into Multān, where Sārang Khān then was. In May, 1398, he was compelled to surrender and Pīr Muhammad occupied Multān.

In June, 1398, the deadlock at Delhi was brought to an end by a series of acts of extraordinary perfidy and treachery, Mallū, resenting the dominance of his benefactor, Muqarrab Khān, deserted Mahmūd and joined Nusrat, whom he conducted in triumph into Jahānpanāh, after swearing allegiance to him on the Koran. Two days later he suddenly attacked his new master and drove him to Fīrūzābād and thence to Pānīpat, where he took refuge with Tātār Khān. Although Nusrat had thus disappeared from the scene the contest was maintained for two months by Mallū on the one hand and Muqarrab Khān, with Mahmūd, on the other. At length Mallū feigned a reconciliation with Muqarrab Khān, who entered Jahānpanāh in triumph with Mahmūd Shāh while Mallū remained in Sirī. Almost immediately afterwards Mallū treacherously attacked Muqarrab Khān in his house at Jahānpanāh, captured and slew him, and, having gained possession of the person of Mahmūd Shāh exercised the royal authority in his name.

There still remained Tātār Khān and Nusrat Shāh to be dealt with, and in August Mallū, carrying Mahmūd with him, marched to Pānīpat. Tātār Khān eluded him and marched to Delhi by another road, but while engaged in a vain attempt to force an entry into the capital learnt that Mallū had captured Pānīpat, taken all his baggage and elephants, and was returning towards Delhi. Tātār Khān fled and joined his father Zafar Khān, who had, two years before this time, proclaimed his independence in Gujarāt, and was now known as Muzaffar Shāh, and Nusrat Shāh found an asylum in the Doāb.

This was the state of affairs at Delhi when, in October, 1398, news was received that Tīmūr the Lame, 'Lord of the Fortunate Conjunction,' Amīr of Samarqand and conqueror of Persia, Afghānistān, and Mesopotamia, had crossed the Indus, the Chenāb, and the Ravī, taken Talamba, and occupied Multān, already held by his grandson. Tīmūr seldom required either a pretext or a stimulus for his depredations, but India supplied him with both. The pretext was the toleration of idolatry by the Muslim rulers of Delhi and the stimulus was the disintegration of the kingdom, unparalleled since its earliest days. The invader's object was plunder, for if he ever had any idea of the permanent conquest of India he certainly abandoned it before he reached Delhi.

Tīmūr had left Samarqand in April, but had been delayed on his way to India by an expedition in Kāfiristān, by the construction of fortresses on the road which he followed, and by the business of his vast empire. He left Kābul on August 15, crossed the Indus

13—2

on September 24, and two days later reached the Jhelum, where he was delayed by the contumacy of a local ruler, Shihāb-ud-dīn Mubārak, styling himself Shāh, who, having submitted to Pīr-Muhammad, had changed his policy when that prince appeared to be in difficulties and ventured to oppose Tīmūr, who drove him from his island fortress on the Jhelum. Mubārak and his whole family perished in the river and Tīmūr crossed the Jhelum and the Rāvī and on October 13 encamped before Talamba. He agreed to spare the ancient town in consideration of a ransom, but differences regarding its assessment or undue harshness in levying it provoked resistance and furnished him with a pretext for a massacre.

His advance was delayed by the necessity for disposing of Jasrat, brother of Shaikhā the Khokar, who had re-established himself in Lahore when Sārang Khān was overcome by Pīr Muhammad. Jasrat had entrenched himself in a village near the north bank of the Sutlej and menaced the invader's communications. His stronghold was taken and he fled, and on October 25 Tīmūr reached the northern bank of the Sutlej, where he met his baggage train and the ladies of his harem. On the following day he was joined by Pīr Muhammad, whose movements had been retarded by an epizootic disease which destroyed most of the horses of his army. Tīmūr's resources, replenished by plunder, enabled him to supply 30,000 remounts for his grandson's troops and Pīr Muhammad accompanied him and commanded the right wing of his army during the rest of the Indian campaign.

The camp was situated on the Sutlej about midway between Ajūdhan (Pāk Pattan) and Dīpālpūr, both of which towns had incurred Tīmūr's resentment by rising against Pīr Muhammad. He marched to Pāk Pattan, where he visited the tomb of Shaikh Farīd-ud-dīn Ganj-i-Shakar, dispatched his harem and heavy baggage by way of Dīpālpūr to Sāmāna, started from Pāk Pattan on November 6, and by the morning of the following day arrived, after a march of eighty miles, at Bhatnair, where the fugitives from Dīpālpūr and Pāk Pattan had taken refuge. The ruler of Bhatnair was a Bhātī Rājput named Dul Chand, but his tribe was already undergoing the process of conversion to Islām, and his brother bore the Muslim name of Kamāl-ud-dīn. The city was captured, with great loss to the Hindus, and on November 9 Dul Chand, who had shut himself up in the citadel, surrendered. The refugees were collected and 500 of the citizens of Dīpālpūr were put to death to avenge their slaughter of Pīr Muhammad's garrison in that town. The citizens of Pāk Pattan were flogged, plundered,

and enslaved. The assessment and collection of the ransom of
Bhatnair again provokẹd resistance on the part of the inhabitants,
and after a general massacre the city was burnt and laid waste, 'so
that one would have said that no living being had ever drawn breath
in that neighbourhood.'

On November 13 Tīmūr left this scene of desolation, already
offensive from the putrefying bodies of the dead, and marched
through Sirsa and Fathābad, pursuing and slaughtering the inhabitants, who fled before him. Aharwān was plundered and burnt,
at Tohāna about 2000 Jāts were slain, and on November 21 Tīmūr
reached the bank of the Ghaggar, near Sāmāna, where he halted for
four days to allow his heavy baggage to come up. On November 25,
near the bridge of Kotla, he was joined by the left wing of his army,
which had marched from Kābul by a more northerly route and had
captured and plundered every for'ress which it had passed. On
November 29 the whole army was assembled at Kaithal and on
December 2 Tīmūr marched through a desolate country, whence
the inhabitants had fled to Delhi, to Pānīpat. On December 7 the
right wing of the army reached Jahānnumā, north of Delhi and
near the northern extremity of the famous Ridge, overlooking the
Jumna. On December 9 the army crossed the river and on the
following day captured Lonī, the Hindu inhabitants of which were
put to death. The fortress, which was surrounded by good pasture
land, was made the headquarters of the army.

The invader's rapid and davastating advance struck terror and
dismay into the hearts of Mahmūd Shāh and Mallū, for the limits
and resources of what remained to them of the kingdom were so restricted that no adequate preparations for resistance were possible,
but such troops as remained were collected within the walls of the
city which was also crowded with the host of fugitives who had
fled before Tīmūr's advance. On December 12, as Tīmūr, who had
led a reconnaissance in force across the river, was returning to Lonī,
Mallū attacked his rearguard. Two divisions were promptly sent to
its assistance, Mallū was defeated and driven back into Delhi, and
the only fruit of his enterprise was a terrible massacre. Tīmūr had
collected in his camp about 100,000 adult male Hindu captives, and
when Mallū delivered his attack these poor wretches could not
entirely conceal their joy at the prospect of a rescue. The demonstration was fatal to them, for Tīmūr became apprehensive of the
presence in his camp of so large a number of disaffected captives,
and caused them all o be put to death.

On December 15 Tīmūr, disregarding both the warnings of his

astrologers and the misgivings of his troops, whose inexperience
was not proof against absurd fables of the terrors of the elephant in
battle, crossed the Jumna, and early on the morning of the 17th
drew up his army for the attack, while Mallū and Mahmūd led
their forces out of Delhi. The Indian army consisted of 10,000
horse, 40,000 foot, and 120 elephants, which are described as being
clad in armour, with their tusks armed with poisoned scimitars, and
bearing on their backs strong wooden structures occupied by javelin
and quoit throwers, crossbow-men and throwers of combustibles.
The mention of poison is probably a figure of speech, for poisoned
weapons were not a feature of Indian warfare.

The fighting line of the invading army entrenched itself with a
ditch and screens of thatch, before which buffaloes were hobbled
and bound together to break the onslaught of the elephants, and
the infantry carried calthrops. The Indian attack on the advanced
guard and right wing was vigorously met and failed utterly when
it was taken in rear by a detached force which circled round its
left flank ; while the attack of Tīmūr's left on the Indian right,
after repulsing a few ineffectual counter-attacks, was entirely successful, and the Indian army broke and fled. The dreaded elephants
were driven off, according to Tīmūr's memoirs, like cows. Mallū
and Mahmūd reached the city and that night fled from it, the
former to Baran and the latter to Gujarāt, where he sought the
hospitality of Muzaffar Shāh. They were pursued, and two of
Mallū's sons, Saif Khān and Khudādād, were captured, besides
many other prisoners and much spoil.

On the following day Tīmūr entered the city and held at the
'Īdgāh a court which was attended by the principal citizens, who
obtained, by the mediation of the Sayyids and ecclesiastics, an
amnesty which proved, as usual, to be illusory. Within the next
few days the licence of the soldiery, the rigour of the search for fugitives from other towns, who had not been included in the amnesty,
and the assessment of the ransom led to disturbances, and the
people rose against the foreigners and in many instances performed
the rite of jauhar. The troops, thus freed from all restraint, sacked
the city, and the work of bloodshed and rapine continued for several
days until so many captives had been taken that, in the words of
the chronicler, 'there was none so humble but he had at least
twenty slaves.' Pillars were raised of the skulls of the slaughtered
Hindus, 'and their bodies were given as food to the birds and the
beasts and their souls sent to the depths of hell.' The artisans
among the captives were sent to the various provinces of Tīmūr's

empire, and those who were stonemasons to Samarqand for the construction of the great Friday mosque which he designed to raise in his capital.

We are indebted to Tīmūr for an interesting description of Delhi as he found it. 'Alā-ud-dīn's palace-fortress of Sirī, some traces of which are still to be found to the east of the road from modern Delhi to the Qutb Minār, was enclosed by a wall, and to the south-west of this, and also surrounded by a wall, stood the larger city of old Delhi, that is to say the town and fortress of Prithvī Rāj, which had been the residential capital of the Muslim kings until Kaiqubad built and Fīrūz Khaljī occupied Kilokhrī. The walls of those two towns were connected by parallel walls, begun by Muhammad Tughluq and finished by his successor, the space between which was known as Jahānpanāh, 'the Refuge of the World,' and the three towns had, in all, thirty gates towards the open country. Fīrūzābād, the new city on the Jumna built by Fīrūz Tughluq, lay some five miles to the north of Jahānpanāh.

The three towns of Sirī, Old Delhi, and Jahānpanāh were laid waste by Tīmūr, who occupied them for fifteen days and on January 1, 1399, marched through Fīrūzābād, where he halted for an hour or two, to Vazīrābād, where he crossed the Jumna. On this day Bahādur Nāhir of Mewāt arrived in his camp with valuable gifts and made his submission. At Delhi Tīmūr had already secured the adhesion of a more important personage, Khizr Khān the Sayyid, who had been living since his expulsion from Multān under the protection of Shams Khān Auhadī at Bayāna, and, having joined Tīmūr, accompanied his camp as far as the borders of Kashmīr.

Meerut refused to surrender to the invader but was taken by storm on January 9, the Hindu citizens being massacred ; a detachment plundered and destroyed the towns and villages on the eastern bank of the Jumna, and Tīmūr himself marched to the Ganges. After a battle on that river on January 12, in which he captured and destroyed forty-eight great boat-loads of Hindus, he crossed the river near Tughluqpur on January 13, defeated an army of 10,000 horse and foot under Mubārak Khān, and on the same day attacked and plundered two Hindu forces in the neighbourhood of Hardwār. The course which he followed lay through the Siwālik, the outermost and lowest range of the Himālaya, and his progress was marked by the almost daily slaughter of large bodies of Hindus who, though they assembled in arms to oppose him, were never able to withstand the onslaught of the Mughul horse and, as they fled, were slaughtered like sheep. On January 16 he captured Kāngra, and between January 24 and February 23, when he reached the neighbourhood of Jammū he fought twenty pitched battles and took seven fortresses. Continuing his career of plunder and rapine towards Jammū he arrived before that city on February 26, and sacked it on the following day. Both Jammū and the neighbouring village of Bāo were deserted, and he was disappointed of human victims, but an ambuscade which he left behind him to surprise the Hindus when they should attempt to return to their homes intercepted and slew large numbers and captured the raja, who was carried before Tīmūr and saved his life by accepting Islām and swearing allegiance to the conqueror.

Shaikha the Khokar had sworn allegiance to Tīmūr after the defeat of his brother Jusrat, but had broken his promise to join the invading army, had given it no assistance, and had insolently ignored the presence in Lahore of Hindū Shāh[1], Tīmūr's treasurer, who had come from Samarqand to join him in India. An expedition was sent to Lahore, the city was captured and held to ransom, and Shaikhā was led before Tīmūr, who put him to death.

On March 6 Tīmūr held a court for the purpose of bidding farewell to the princes and officers of the army before dismissing them to their provinces, and on this occasion appointed Khīzr Khān the Sayyid to the government of Multān, from which he had been expelled by Sārang Khān, Lahore, and Dīpālpūr. Some historians add that he nominated him as his viceroy in Delhi, but this addition was probably suggested by subsequent events.

On March 19 Tīmūr recrossed the Indus, and two days later left Bannū, after inflicting on India more misery than had ever before been inflicted by any conqueror in a single invasion. Mahmūd's tale of slaughter from first to last probably exceeded his, but in no single incursion did he approach Tīmūr's terrible record.

After his departure the whole of northern India was in indescribable disorder and confusion. Delhi, in ruins and almost depopulated, was without a master, and the miserable remnant of the inhabitants was afflicted with new calamities, in the form of famine and pestilence. Famine was the natural consequence of the wholesale destruction of stores of gain and standing crops by the invading army, and the pestilence probably had its origin in the pollution of the air and water-supply of the city by the putrefying corpses of the thousands of victims of the invader's wrath. So complete was

1 Hindū Shāh was an ancestor of the historian Firishta.

the desolation that 'the city was utterly ruined, and those of the inhabitants who were left died, while for two whole months not a bird moved wing in Delhi.' The kingdom was completely dissolved. It had been stripped of some of the fairest of its eastern provinces by the eunuch Khvāja Jahān, who ruled an independent kingdom from Jaunpur ; Bengal had long been independent ; Muzaffar Shāh in Gujarāt owned no master ; Dilāvar Khān in Mālwa forbore to use the royal title, but wielded royal authority ; the Punjab and Upper Sind were governed by Khizr Khān as Tīmūr's viceroy; Sāmāna was in the hands of Ghālib Khān and Bayāna in those of Shams Khān Auhadi; and Kālpī and Mahoba formed a small principality under Muhammad Khān. Mallū remained for the present at Baran, but Nusrat Shāh, the pretender whom he had driven from Delhi and who had since been lurking in the Doāb, again raised his head, and with the assistance of 'Ādil Khān became for a space lord of the desolate capital. Mallū's influence with the Hindus of the Doāb enabled him to defeat a force sent against him from Delhi, and by the capture of its elephants and material of war he obtained such superiority over Nusrat Shāh that he expelled him from Delhi and forced him to take refuge in Mewāt, his old home, where he soon afterwards died. In 1399 Mallū defeated Shams Khān Auhadi of Bayāna, who had invaded territory considered to belong to Delhi, led an expedition into Katehr, and compelled the turbulent Hindus of Etāwah to pay him tribute, but failed to convince them of his supremacy and was obliged, in the winter of 1400—01, to take the field against them. He defeated them near Patiālī and marched on to Kanauj with the object of invading the kingdom of Jaunpur, where Malik Qaranful had succeeded his adoptive father, the eunuch Khvāja Jahān, under the title of Mubārak Shāh. On reaching Kanauj he found Mubārak encamped on the opposite bank of the Ganges, but for two months neither army ventured to attack the other and a peace was concluded. He had been accompanied on this expedition by Shams Khān Auhadī and Mubārak Khān, son of Bahādur Nāhir, but he regarded both with suspicion, and during his retreat from Kanauj took the opportunity of putting them to death.

In 1401, after his return to Delhi, Mallū perceived that the prestige of the fugitive Mahmūd Shāh would be useful to him, and persuaded him to return to the capital. The wanderer's experiences had been bitterly humiliating. Muzaffar Shāh of Gujarāt would not compromise his newborn independence by receiving him as king of Delhi, and was at no pains to conceal from him that his presence was distasteful until, after repeated slights, he retired to Mālwa, where Dilāwar Khān Ghūrī, mindful of his obligations to Mahmūd's father, received him with princely generosity and assigned to him a residence at Dhār. In this retreat he was probably happier than in his gilded bonds at Delhi, but he could not refuse the invitation to return, and Mallū, after receiving him with every demonstration of respect interned him in one of the royal palaces and continued to govern the remnant of the kingdom with as little restraint as though Mahmūd had never returned from Malwa.

In 1402 the death of Mubārak Shāh and the accession of Ibrāhīm Shāh in Jaunpur appeared to Mallū to offer another opportunity for the recovery of this territory, and he marched to Kanauj, carrying Mahmūd with him, but again found the army of Jaunpur confronting him on the opposite bank of the Ganges. Mahmūd, chafing at his subjection to Mallū, fled from his camp by night and took refuge with Ibrāhim Shāh, from whom he hoped for better treatment, but he was so coldly received that he left Ibrāhim's camp with a few followers who remained faithful to him, expelled Ibrāhīm's governor from Kanauj, and made that city his residence. Here several old servants of his house assembled round him, and Mallū, who was considerably weakened by his defection, returned to Delhi. Ibrāhīm acquiesced in Mahmūd's occupation of Kanauj and returned to Jaunpur.

Latter in this year and again in the following year Mallū attempted to recover Gwalior, which had been captured during the confusion arising from Tīmūr's invasion by the Tonwār Rājput Har Singh, and was now held by his son Bhairon, but although he was able to defeat Bhairon in the field and to plunder the country he could not capture the fortress, and was compelled to retire. Bhairon harassed him by lending aid to the Rājputs of Etāwah, and in 1404 Mallū besieged that city for four months, but was fain to retire on receiving a promise of an annual tribute of four elephants, and marched to Kanauj, where he besieged Mahmūd Shāh. Here also he was baffled by the strength of the fortifications, and returned to Delhi. In July, 1405, he marched against Bahrām Khān, a turbulent noble of Turkish descent who had established himself in Sāmāna. On his approach Bahrām fled towards the Himālaya, and was pursued as far as Rūpar, where a pious Shaikh composed the differences between the enemies and Bahrām joined Mallū in an expedition against Khizr Khān. Their agreement was of short duration, for on their march towards Pāk Pattan Mallū

caused Bahrām to be flayed alive. As Mallū approached Khizr
Khān advanced from Dipālpur and on November 12 defeated and
slew him in the neighbourhood of Pāk Pattan.

On Mallū's death the direction of affairs at Delhi fell into the
hands of a body of nobles headed by Daulat Khān Lodī and
Ikhtiyār Khān, at whose invitation Mahmūd Shāh returned, in
December, to the capital. Daulat Khān was appointed military
governor of the Doāb and Ikhtiyār Khān governor of Fīrūzābād.

In 1406 Mahmūd sent Daulat Khān to reduce Sāmāna where,
since Bahrām's death, another of Fīrūz Shāh's Turkish slaves,
Bairam Khān by name, had established himself as Khizr Khān's
deputy, and himself marched to Kanauj with the intention of punishing Ibrāhīm Shāh of Jaunpur for his contemptuous treatment of him
when he had fled to his camp from that of Mallū. Ibrāhīm again
marched to the Ganges and encamped opposite Kanauj, and after
some days of desultory fighting a peace was concluded, and each
monarch set out for his capital, but Ibrāhim immediately retraced
his steps and besieged Kanauj. Malik Mahmūd Tarmatī, who commanded the fortress for Mahmūd Shāh, held out for four months and
then, seeing no prospect of relief, surrendered, and Ibrāhīm, who
spent the rainy season at Kanauj, was joined by some discontented
nobles of the court at Delhi. This accession of strength encouraged
him, in October, 1407, to take the offensive against Mahmūd Shāh,
and he marched to Sambhal, which was almost immediately surrendered to him by Asad Khān Lodī. Having placed Tātār Khān in
command of Sambhal he marched towards Delhi, and was on the
point of crossing the Jumna when he learnt that Muzaffar Shāh of
Gujarāt, having invaded Mālwa and captured Hūshang Shāh, who
had succeeded his father, Dilāvar Khān, in that country, intended
to pursue his career of conquest towards Jaunpur. He therefore
retreated towards his capital, leaving a garrison in Baran, but in
the summer of 1408 Mahmūd Shāh recovered both Baran and
Sambhal.

In the meantime Daulat Khān had, on December 22, 1406, driven
Bairam Khān from Sāmāna to Sirhind and had, after a short siege,
compelled him to surrender. He befriended and patronised his
defeated adversary and established himself at Sāmāna, but on the
approach of Khizr Khān fled into the Doāb, while most of his partisans
deserted to Khizr Khān. Besides Sāmāna Khizr Khān captured
and annexed Sirhind, Sunām, and Hissar, so that beyond the walls
of Delhi only the Doāb, Rohtak, and Sambhal remained subject to
Mahmūd Shāh.

In 1408 Mahmūd recovered Hissar, but the temporary success profited him little, for on January 28, 1409, Khizr Khān appeared before the walls of Fīrūzābād and besieged the city, and at the same time sent his lieutenant, Malik Tuhfa, to ravage the Doāb. The country, wasted and impoverished by several years of famine, was no longer capable of supporting an army, and Khizr Khān was therefore compelled to retire, and in the following year was employed in recalling to his allegiance Bairam Khān of Sirhind, who had again allied himself to Daulat Khān ; but in 1410 he reduced Rohtak after a siege of six months, during which the mean-spirited Mahmūd made no attempt to relieve the town, though it was within forty-five miles of the capital. In the following year Khizr Khān marched to Nārnaul, plundered that town and three others to the south of Delhi, and then, turning north-wards, besieged Mahmūd Shāh in Sirī. Ikhtiyār Khān prudently joined the stronger party, and surrendered Fīrūzābād to Khizr Khān, who was thus enabled to cut off all supplies from the direction of the Doāb, but Mahmūd was once more saved by famine, for Khizr Khān was again compelled, by the failure of supplies, to raise the siege and retire. In February, 1413, Mahmūd died at Kaithal after a nominal reign of twenty years, during which he had never wielded any authority and had more than once been a fugitive from his capital, and with him died the line of Ghiyās-ud-dīn Tughluq.

On his death the nobles transferred their allegiance to the strongest of their number, Daulat Khān Lodī, whose first act as ruler of Delhi was to march into the Doāb and compel the Rājputs of Etawāh and Mahabat Khān of Budaun to own him as their sovereign. His progress was checked by the discovery that Ibrāhīm Shāh of Jaunpur was besieging Qādir Khān, son of Mahmūd Khān, in Kālpī, and in order to avoid an encounter with the superior forces of Ibrāhīm he returned to Delhi.

In December, 1413, Khizr Khān invaded Daulat Khān's territory and, leaving a large force to besiege Rohtak, marched into Mewāt, where he received the submission of Bahādur Nāhir's nephew, Jalāl Khān. Thence he marched across the Doāb to Sambhal, plundered that town, and in March, 1414, returned to Delhi with an army of 60,000 horse and besieged Daulat Khān in Sirī. Daulat Khān held out for four months, when some of his officers treacherously admitted the besiegers, and he was forced to throw himself on his enemy's mercy. On May 28 Khizr Khān entered Delhi as its sovereign and founded a new dynasty, known as the Sayyids; and Daulat Khān was imprisoned in Hissar.

The empire of Muhammad Tughluq had included the whole continent of India, with the exception of Kashmīr, Cutch and a part of Kāthīāwār, and Orissa. On the death of his grand nephew Mahmūd the extent of the kingdom was defined by the contemporary saying :

حکمِ خداوندِ عالم از دهلی تا پالم

'The rule of the Lord of the World extends from Delhi to Pālam'— a small town little more than nine miles south-west of the capital. Independent kingdoms had been established in Bengal and the Deccan before Muhammad's death, and the rebellion of the royal officers in the south had enabled the Hindus to found the great kingdom of Vijayanagar and had facilitated the establishment in Telingāna of a Hindu state in subordinate alliance with the kingdom of the Deccan, not with Delhi. During the reigns of the feeble successors of Fīrūz the province of Oudh and the country to the east of the Ganges as far as the borders of Bengal were formed into the independent kingdom of Jaunpur ; the great provinces of Gujarāt and Mālwa and the smaller province of Khāndesh severed their connexion with Delhi and became separate states ; a Hindu principality was established in Gwalior and Muslim principalities in Bayāna and Kālpī ; the nominal allegiance of Mewāt was transferred from one prince to another at the caprice of the local chieftain ; the Hindus of the Doāb were almost continually in revolt and the ruler of Delhi had to be content with the small contributions which he could extort from them by armed force when he was not otherwise engaged ; and the ruin of the state was completed by the invasion of Tīmūr, who established in the Punjab a power which eventually absorbed the kingdom of Delhi.

CHAPTER VIII

THE SAYYID DYNASTY

THE claim of Khizr Khān, who founded the dynasty known as the Sayyids, to descent from the prophet of Arabia was dubious, and rested chiefly on its causal recognition by the famous saint Sayyid Jalāl-ud-dīn of Bukhārā. He assumed no title associated with royalty, but was content with the position of viceroy of Shāh Rukh, Tīmūr's fourth son and successor, to whom he is said to have remitted tribute, and with the title of *Rāyāt-i-A'lā*, or 'the Exalted Standards.' His success reunited the Punjab to Delhi, but the turbulent governors and fief-holders who had withheld their allegiance from a lawful master hesitated at first to acknowledge an upstart, until by degrees many of the old nobles of the late dynasty submitted to him and were permitted to retain their former offices and emoluments.

The Hindus of the Doāb and Katehr withheld payment of tribute, and in the year of his accession Khizr Khān found it necessary to send an army under Tāj-ul-Mulk to reduce to obedience Har Singh, the rebellious raja of Katehr. The raja fled into the forests of Āonla, but a rigorous blockade compelled him to submit and to give an undertaking to pay tribute in future. Mahābat Khān, governor of Budaun, also made his submission, and Tāj-ul-Mulk recrossed the Ganges and compelled the fief-holders and Hindu chieftains of the lower Doāb, among them Hasan of Rāprī[1], Raja Sarwar of Etāwah, and the raja of Kampil, to own allegiance to their new master. In Chandwār he restored Muslim supremacy, which had been subverted by the Hindus, and returned to Delhi with the tribute, or plunder, which he had collected in the course of his expedition.

The chronicles of the Sayyid dynasty are chiefly a history of expeditions of this nature. Khizr Khān was the most powerful ruler of a house the influence and dignity of which decayed with an unvarying and unchecked rapidity seldom surpassed in the most ephemeral of eastern dynasties, and even in his reign military force was the normal means of collecting the revenue. Recalcitrants were not treated as rebels, and the only punishment inflicted was the exaction of the taxes due from them and of a promise, which they usually violated on the first opportunity, to make regular

[1] In 26° 58′N. and 78° 36′E. Then an important town.

remittances in the future. Thus, in July, 1416, a most inconvenient season for the collection of revenue, Tāj-ul-Mulk was sent to Bayāna and Gwalior, not with a view to the reduction of these fortresses but merely to recover, by plundering at random the unfortunate cultivators, the equivalent of the tribute which should have been paid. With this, and with arrears of tribute which he collected from Kampila and Patiālī, he returned to Delhi.

In 1415, Malik Sadhū Nādira had been sent to Sirhind as the deputy of Khizr Khān's son Mubārak, on whom that district had been bestowed, and in the following year the Turkish landholders, kinsmen and dependants of Bairam Khān, the former governor, rose under the leadership of Malik Tughān, put him to death, and occupied the fortress. Zīrak Khān was sent against them and pursued them across the Sutlej and as far as the lower slopes of the Himālaya, but did not venture to continue the pursuit into the mountains, and returned to Delhi.

In the same year Khizr Khān himself took the field with the object of chastising Ahmad I of Gujarāt who, by pursuing his rebellious uncles to Nāgaur, which was nominally, at least, subject to Delhi, had violated the fronties of the kingdom. Ahmad, on learning of his approach, fled into Gujarāt, and Khizr Khān retired, receiving on his homeward march tribute from Iliyās Khān, the Muslim governor of Jhāīn, the raja of Gwalior, and his own former protector, Shams Khān Auhadī of Bayāna, whom he might well have spared.

On his arrival at his capital he learnt that Tughān and his followers had returned to Sirhind and were besieging Malik Kamāl Badhan, who had been appointed deputy of Mubārak in the place of the murdered Nādira. On this occasion Zīrak Khān was more successful, for he overtook the fugitive Turks at Pāel, where Malik Tughān submitted and surrendered his son as an hostage for his good behaviour, for which subservience he was rewarded with the fief of Jullundur.

Early in 1418 Har Singh of Katehr was again in revolt, and was on this occasion brought to pay and suffered a complete defeat at the hands of Tāj-ul-Mulk. He fled, and was pursued into the hills of Kumāon, where Tāj-ul-Mulk, unable to seize the object of his pursuit, contented himself with the ignoble but customary satisfaction of plundering the people amongst whom the rebel had found an asylum, and returned to the plains. From Katehr he marched to Etāwah, and there besieged Raja Sarwar, who was again in rebellion. Unable to reduce the fortress, he plundered the inhabitants of the district and returned to Delhi in May, but his devastating progress, which had resembled rather the raid of a brigand chief than an expedition for the permanent establishment of order, had so exasperated the people of the region through which he had passed that before the end of the year Khizr Khān found it necessary to follow in the tracks of his lieutenant, and the record of his progress exhibits both the frailty of the bond between him and his subjects and the futility of the means which he employed for the establishment of his authority. He was compelled to use force against the people of Koïl, within eighty miles of his capital, and then, crossing the Ganges, laid waste the district of Sambhal. His proceedings so alarmed Mahābat Khan of Budaun, who was in his camp and was, perhaps, conscious of shortcomings in his administration or apprehensive of the discovery of his traffickings with the rebels, that he fled and shut himself up in Budaun, which Khizr Khān besieged for six months without success. For the history of this and the following reign the sole original authority is an encomiast of the Sayyids, and it is impossible to fathom the undercurrent of politics or to estimate the difficulties with which Khizr Khān was confronted, but Mahābat Khān was an old noble of the late dynasty, and there were in the royal camp several of his former comrades who had formally submitted to the new order of things, and in June, 1419, Khizr Khān discovered the existence among them of a conspiracy to which Mahābat Khān was doubtless a party, and, in order to separate his enemies, raised the siege and returned towards Delhi. On June 14 he halted on the banks of the Ganges and put the leading conspirators, Qavām-ul-Mulk and Ikhtiyār Khān, to death.

In the following year he was reminded of his early misfortunes by the appearance in Bajwāra, near Hoshiārpur, of an impostor who pretended to be that Sārang Khān who had expelled him from Multān. The real Sārang Khān had died in captivity shortly after his surrender to Pīr Muhammad, and this fact must have been widely known, but interest may lead the intelligent, as ignorance leads the vulgar, to espouse the cause of a pretender; and the name of the man who had driven before him, as chaff before the wind, the occupant of the throne of Delhi was well chosen by the impostor. Khizr Khān was, however, well served. A family of the Lodī clan of the great Ghilzai or Khaljī tribe had recently been domiciled in India, and its leader, Malik Sultān Shāh Bahrām, subsequently styled Islām Khān, by which title he may now conveniently be known, had been appointed governor of Sirhind. He was dispatched against the pretender, who marched to the Sutlej to meet him but was defeated and compelled to retire. After the battle Islām Khān was joined by Zīrak Khān of Sāmāna and Malik Tughān of Jullundur, and before their overwhelming force the impostor fled, by way of Rūpar, which he had made his head-quarters, into the mountains. He was ineffectually pursued but emerged and fell a victim to the perfidy of Malik Tughān, who inveighed him into his power and treacherously put him to death, being prompted to this act rather by cupidity than by loyalty, for the impostor had amassed great wealth.

In the same year Tāj-ul-Mulk was dispatched on another foray. dignified by the name of an expedition against rebels, into the districts of Koïl and Etāwah. Raja Sarwar was besieged in his fortress, but no important military success was gained. The wretched inhabitants of the country were, as usual, plundered and Sarwar purchased the retreat of the raiders by a contribution to the royal coffers and one of his oft-repeated promises to pay with more regularity in the future. On returning from Etāwah Tāj-ul-Mulk plundered Chandwār and invaded Katehr, where he compelled Mahābat Khān to pay the tribute due from him.

In August news was received at the capital that Malik Tughān, whose resources had been replenished by the plunder of the pre-tender, was again in rebellion and had marched from Jullundur to Sirhind where, having plundered the country, he was besieging the fortress. Malik Khair-ud-dīn was sent to its relief and, marching by way of Sāmāna, was there joined by Zīrak Khān. Tughān raised the siege of Sirhind and retreated, and Khair-ud-dīn and Zīrak Khān pursued him across the Sutlej and compelled him to seek refuge with Jasrat the Khokar, the son of that Shaikhā who had established his independence in the reign of Mahmūd Shāh. Jasrat had been carried off into captivity by Tīmūr, with his father, but on the conqueror's death had regained his freedom and returned to his country, where having established for himself an independent principality of considerable extent, he had gained over the army of Kashmīr[1] a victory which fostered in his mind extravagant notions of his power and importance and inspired in him the belief that the throne of Delhi was within his reach. Tughān's fief of Jullundur was bestowed upon Zīrak Khān.

In 1421 Khizr Khān marched into Mewāt to assert his authority in that province, captured and destroyed the former stronghold of Bahādur Nāhir and received the submission of most of the inhabitants.

[1] See Chapter XII.

He then turned to Gwalior, and on January 13, during his march thither, his faithful minister, Tāj-ul-Mulk, died, and his office was bestowed upon his son, Malik Sikandar Tuhfa, who received the title of Malik-ush-Sharq. The raja of Gwalior took refuge within his fortress and by means of the usual dole and the usual empty promise relieved his subjects from the depredations of the royal troops. Thence the king marched to Etāwah, where Sarwar Singh had lately died and his son was prepared to purchase peace on the customary terms, and here he fell sick and hastened back to Delhi, where he died on May 20, 1421, having designated his son Mubārak Khān his heir. He is extolled as a charitable ruler but his charity was confined within the narrow limits of his territories and to the members of his own faith.

Mubārak, beside whose weakness that of his father assumes the appearance of strength, found it no longer necessary to feign vassalage to any of the rulers who now governed the fragments of Tīmūr's vast empire, and freely used the royal title of Shāh, which his father had never assumed. On his coinage he was styled Mu'izz-ud-dīn Mubārak Shāh, and another unmistakable claim to complete independence was exhibited in his profession of allegiance to the puppet Caliph alone. He confirmed most of the nobles in the fiefs and appointments which they had held during the late reign, but, conscious of his own weakness, pursued the fatuous policy of perpetually transferring them from one fief to another. He perhaps attained his object of preventing any one noble from acquiring a dangerous local influence in any district of the kingdom, but it was attained at the cost of efficient administration, and the discontent of the nobles, harassed by these vexatious transfers, led finally to his downfall. In pursuance of this policy Malik Rajab Nādira, son of the late Sadhū Nādira, was transferred from Fīrūzā-bād and Hānsī to Dīpālpūr, to make room for the king's nephew, Malik Bada, who eventually succeeded him as Muhammad Shāh.

The early days of the reign were disturbed by the activity of Jasrat the Khokar, who, with the interests of the fugitive Tughān as a pretext and the throne of Delhi as a lure, crossed the Sutlej and attacked Rāi Kamāl-ud-dīn, a vassal of Delhi, at Talwandī. Rāi Fīrūz, a neighbouring fief-holder, fled towards the Jumna, and Jasrat occupied Lūdhiāna, ravaged the country eastwards as far as Rūpar, and returning across the Sutlej, besieged Zīrak Khān in Jullundur, when a composition not very creditable to either party was effected. Zīrak Khān betrayed the interests of his master by the surrender of the fortress and Jasrat betrayed his guest by

sending his son to Delhi as an hostage for his father's good behaviour, and his former adversary, Zīrak by seizing and imprisoning him   With Jullundur as a base Jasrat again crossed the Sutlej
and on June 22 appeared before Sirhind, now held for Mubārak
Shāh by Islām Khān Lodī. In July, although the rainy season was
at its height, Mubārak Shāh marched to the relief of Sirhind, and
as he approached Sāmāna Jasrat, after releasing Zīrak Khān, who
rejoined his master, retreated to Lūdhiāna, whither Mubārak Shāh
followed him.   Jasrat, having collected all available boats, crossed
the flooded river and encamped in security on the opposite bank.
As the rains abated Mubārak Shāh retired, in real or feigned
apprehension, along the bank of the river to Qabūlpūr, while
Jasrat, who had failed to observe that a force had been dispatched
up stream to search for a ford, followed him.   The two armies were
still facing one another when Jasrat learnt that this force had
crossed the river and, fearing lest his retreat should be cut off,
retreated precipitately towards Jullundur, but was unable to rest
there owing to the vigour of Mubārak's pursuit, during which the
fugitives suffered heavy losses, and retired to the lower slopes of
the Kashmīr highlands.   Bhīm, raja of Jammū, guided the royal
army to the principal stronghold of the Khokars, which was
captured, with heavy loss to the defenders, and destroyed, but
Jasrat escaped.   From the hills Mubārak Shāh marched to Lahore
ruinous and deserted since its capture by Tīmūr's troops and spent
a month in replacing its once formidable defences by a mud fort.
On returning to Delhi he left Malik Mahmūd Hasan, who had distinguished himself at the passage of the Sutlej and was henceforward the ablest and most active of his nobles, with a force of
2000 horse to hold the restored outpost of the kingdom.   By May,
1422, Jasrat had reassembled his army, descended from the hills,
and attempted to carry the new citadel by assault, but was repulsed
and forced to retire.   For more than a month he harassed Mahmūd
Hasan by desultory skirmishes, but, finding his labour vain, retired
to Kalānaur, his principal place of residence in the plains. Here
he met Raja Bhīm of Jammū, who was marching to the assistance
of Mahmūd Hasan, and after one battle made peace with him and
retired towards the Beās.   In the meantime Mubārak Shāh had
dispatched to the aid of Mahmūd Hasan the minister, Sikandar
Tuhfa, who crossed the Rāvī, once more drove Jasrat into the hills
and marched to Lahore, where he was welcomed by Mahmūd Hasan
on September 28.   Malik Rajab Nādira of Dīpālpur arrived at
Lahore at the same time, and the three nobles marched to Kalānaur,

where they were met by Raja Bhīm, to punish Jasrat's presumption. They invaded the Khokar country, but Jasrat had escaped into the higher ranges, and after plundering the homes of his tribesmen the three nobles returned to Lahore.

During the absence of the minister, Sikandar Tuhfa, from the capital the governor of Delhi, Sarvar-ul-Mulk, induced the feeble king to order, for the benefit of himself and his son, a redistribution of various important offices. Sikandar Tuhfa was dismissed from the office of minister, to make way for Sarvar-ul-Mulk, who was succeeded as governor of Delhi by his son Yūsuf. Sikandar Tuhfa received the fief of Lahore as compensation for the loss of the first post in the kingdom, but his transfer thither necessitated the removal of Mahmūd Hasan, who was transferred to Jullundur, but was ordered for the time to wait on Mubārak Shāh with the contingent maintained from his fief. These changes bred much discontent; to which may be traced the assassination of Mubārak Shāh which took place twelve years later.

In 1423 Mubārak Shāh once more invaded Katehr, collected tribute from the people in the usual fashion, and, crossing the Ganges, entered the lower Doāb, where he treated the Rajputs with great severity and behaved as though he were in an enemy's country. Zīrak Khan was left as governor of Kampil, but his illtreatment of the Hindus so alarmed the son of Sarvar Singh that he fled from the camp to Etāwah and successfully defended the town against Malik Khair-ud-dīn Tuhfa, brother of Sikandar Tuhfa, who was fain to raise the siege on receiving the usual nugatory promise of tribute.

Recent successes encouraged Jasrat the Khokar again to invade the kingdom. He had defeated, and slain in battle his old enemy, Raja Bhīm of Jammū and now overran and plundered the districts of Dīpalpūr and Lahore. Sikandar Tuhfa marched against him, but retired before him leaving him free to prepare for more extensive aggressions. At about the same time it was reported that 'Alā-ul-Mulk, governor of Multān, had died and that Shaikh 'Alī, the deputy in Kabul of Suyurghātmish, the fourth son of Shahrukh, who had succeeded to the greater part of Tīmūr's empire, proposed to invade and ravage the western Punjab and Sind. Malik Mahmūd Hasan was sent to Multān, and restored some degree of confidence to the people who had been plundered by Shaikh 'Alī's troops.

Towards the end of the year Mubārak was obliged to march to the aid of Gwalior, which was besieged by Hūshang Shāh of Mālwa.

Hūshang, on learning that Mubārak was marching towards Dholpur, raised the siege and marched to the southern bank of the Chambal, so that when Mubārak reached the northern bank he found most of the fords held by the troops of Mālwa, but he discovered an unguarded ford, crossed the river, and permitted his advanced guard to attack some outlying parties of Hūshang's army. A trivial advantage was gained and some prisoners and plunder were taken, but neither party desired a general engagement or a protracted campaign, and negotiations ended in the retreat of Hūshang to Māndū. Mubārak returned to Delhi in June, 1424, and in the following cold weather marched to Katehr, extorted three years' arrears of tribute from the raja, Har Chand, plundered the country as far as the foot of the Kumāon hills, and, marching down the banks of the Rāmgangā, crossed the Ganges and entered the Doāb. It had been his intention to remain in the neighbourhood of Kanauj, and to establish his authority to the south of that district, but the country had suffered from famine and would neither repay rapine nor support the troops, and he was compelled to return. He turned aside with the object of crushing a rebellion in Mewāt, but the rebels laid waste their villages in the plains and retired into their mountain fastnesses, and the king was obliged to retire, but returned in 1425, when the rebels under Jallū, or Jalāl Khān, and Qaddū, or 'Abd-ul-Qādir repeated their tactics of the preceding year. Mubārak on this occasion followed them into the hills, drove them from one stronghold, and pursued them to Alwar, where they surrendered. Jalāl Khān escaped, but Qaddū was carried prisoner to Delhi.

In 1426 Mubārak traversed Mewāt, plundering the people, on his way to Bayāna to attack Muhammad Khān, a rebellious member of the Auhadī family. Most of the rebel's men deserted to the royal standard and Muhammad Khān was sent, with all the members of his family, to Delhi, where he was interned in Jahānnumā. The district of Bayāna was divided into two fiefs. Bayāna itself being granted to Muqbil Khān and Sīkrī, later to be known as Fathpūr, to Khair-ud-dīn Tuhfa. Mubārak marched from Bayāna to Gwalior and returned to Delhi, which he reached in March, 1427, by way of the eastern bank of the Jumna. Shortly after his arrival at Delhi Muhammad Khān Auhadī and his family escaped from the capital and took refuge in Mewāt where many of his former followers assembled around him. Muqbil was absent from Bayana on an expedition, and Khair-ud-dīn Tuhfa held the fortress with an inadequate garrison. Muhammad Khan was joined by all classes of the inhabitants and Khiar-ud-dīn was obliged to evacuate the fortress and retire to Delhi. Malik Mubāriz was sent from Delhi to recover Bayāna and besieged the place, but the garrison defended it obstinately while Muhammad Auhadī withdrew to Jaunpur to seek help of Ibrāhīm Shāh. Mubārak Shāh recalled Mubāriz and marched in person to Bayāna, but before he could form the siege was disturbed by an appeal from Qādir Khān of Kālpī, who implored his aid against Ibrāhīm Shāh, who was marching on Kālpī with the intention of annexing it. Mubārak abandoned for the time all intention of reducing Bayāna and turned against Ibrāhīm, who having plundered the district of Bhongāon near Mainpurī, was preparing to march on Budaun. Mubārak crossed the Jumna, and, on reaching Atraulī, sixteen miles from Koil, learnt that Mukhtass Khān, Ibrāhīm's brother, was threatening Etāwah. Mahmūd Hasan was detached against him and forced him to join forces with his brother, and the army of Jaunpur traversed the Doāb and crossed the Jumna near Etāwah with a view to supporting the garrison of Bayāna. Mubārak crossed the river near Chandwār (now Fīrūzābād) and Ibrāhim, in February, 1428, marched towards Bayāna and encamped on the banks of the Gambhir, while Mubārak encamped at a distance of ten miles from him. Neither was anxious to risk a battle and for some time the operations were confined to affair of outposts, but on April 2 Ibrāhim drew up his army for battle, and Mubārak, who lacked even the ordinary merit of physical courage, deputed his nobles to lead his army into the field. The two armies fought, with moderate zeal and without any decisive result, from midday until sunset, when each retired to its own camp, but on the following day Ibrāhīm retreated towards Jaunpur. He was followed for some distance, but Mubārak would not permit the pursuit to be pressed, and ordered that it should be abandoned. His encomiast praises his forbearance towards fellow Muslims, but we may believe that he did not choose to provoke too far an adversary whose strength he had not fully gauged.

Mubārak then marched to Gwalior on his usual errand, and, after collecting an instalment of tribute, returned towards Delhi by way of Bayāna, still held by Muhammad Auhadī, who, on May 11, evacuated the fortress and retired into Mewāt. Mahmūd Hasan was invested with the fief of Bayāna and Mubārak returned to Delhi, where he found that his prisoner Qaddū, the grandson of Bahādur Nāhir, had been in secret correspondence with Ibrāhīm during the late campaign. He was put to death and his execution led to a fresh rebellion in Mewāt headed by his brother, Jalāl

Khān. Sarwar-ul-Mulk, the minister, who was appointed to suppress it, followed the rebels into the hills in which they had after their manner, taken refuge and returned to Delhi on their paying him the empty compliment of a formal submission to his master.

Jasrat the Khokar was again active, and in August news was received that he was besieging Kalānaur and had driven back to Lahore Sikandar Tuhfa, who had attempted to relieve the beleaguered town. Emboldened by his success he attacked Jullundur, and though he failed to capture the town he plundered the district and carried off into slavery large numbers of its inhabitants. Zīrak Khān from Sāmāna and Islām Khān Lodī from Sirhind marched to support Sikandar Tuhfa at Lahore, but before they could reach him he had succeeded in effecting a junction with Raī Ghālib, the defender of Kalānur, and had defeated Jasrat, driven him into the hills, and recovered all his spoil.

Mahmūd Hasan, having restored the royal authority in Bayāna, returned to Delhi, and thence to Hissar, his former fief, and Mubārak invaded the plains of Mewāt, where Jalāl Khān and other chieftains of the country presented their tribute and were received at court.

In July, 1429, Rajab Nādira died at Multān and Mahmūd Hasan received the title of 'Imād-ul-Mulk and was transferred to that province, the government of which he had formerly held. In the cold weather Mubārak marched to Gwalior and thence against the contumacious raja of Athgāth[1], who was defeated and compelled to take refuge in the hills of Mewāt. His country was plundered and many of his people carried off into slavery, and Mubārak marched to Rāprī, expelled the son of Hasan Khān, and bestowed the fief upon Malik Hamzah. On his way back to Delhi he learnt of the death, at Bhātinda, of Sayyid Sālim, who had served his house for thirty years. Mubārak, who seems to have been unacquainted with the true character of the Sayyid, and was certainly ignorant of that of his offspring, rewarded the father's long service by bestowing on his elder son the title of Sālim Khān and on the younger that of Shuja'-ul-mulk. The Sayyid had been both rapacious and parsimonious, and during his long tenure of the lucrative fief of Bhātinda had amassed enormous wealth. The central situation of this district in the province of which Khizr Khān had enjoyed the virtual sovereignty for some time before his establishment on the throne of Delhi had secured it from attack from without and from demands for contributions to the defence of the frontiers. The customary law of Muhammadan states in India, which made the ruler the heir

1 On the Chambal, in 26° 48′ N. and 78° 46′ E.

of his officials, was especially formidable to those who had defrauded
their sovereign and oppressed his subjects, and Sālim Khān and
Shujā'-ul-Mulk, who were in the king's power, attempted to secure
their wealth by instigating Fūlād, a Turkish slave of their late
father, to rebel in Bhātinda. Their complicity in the rebellion was
discovered, they were thrown into prison, and Yūsuf, son of Sarvar-
ul-Mulk, and Rāi Hansū Bhatī were sent to treat with Fūlād and
to induce him to surrender the treasure, but Fūlād, who had no
intention of surrendering it either to the king or to his late master's
heirs, amused the envoys for a time with fair words and promises
and, having thrown them off their guard, made a sudden attack on
their troops, defeated them and was further enriched by the plunder
of their camp. Zīrak Khān, Malik Kālū, and Islām Khān Lodī
were then sent to besiege the rebel in Bhātinda. Fūlād announced
that he was prepared to consider terms of submission provided that
negotiations were conducted through 'Imād-ul-Mulk of Multān, in
whom he had confidence, and 'Imād-ul-Mulk was summoned and
arrived at court in August, 1430. He was sent to Bhātinda, but it
was discovered that the rebel's offer to treat with him had been
merely a device to gain time, the negotiations broke down, and he
returned to Multān after urging the officers before Bhātinda to
continue the siege.

Fūlād, after holding out for six months, sent a large sum of
money to Shaikh 'Alī of Kābul and summoned him to his aid. In
January, 1431, he left Kābul and marched to Bhātinda, and on his
arriving within twenty miles of the town Mubārak's nobles hurriedly
raised the siege and fled to their fiefs. Fūlād issued from the fortress
to meet him, paid him 200,000 tangas as the price of his assistance,
and entrusted his family to his care, in order that they might be
removed to a place of safety. A passing remark of the historian of
this reign throws much light on the position of affairs in the Punjab
during Mubārak's futile attempts to establish his authority in the
Doāb, the trans-Gangetic region, and the south-eastern districts of
his kingdom. Sikandar Tuhfa paid to Shaikh 'Alī 'the sum which
he had been wont to pay him annually,' and thus induced him to
refrain from molesting Lahore during his retreat. From the reference to the yearly payment of blackmail it is clear that the
kingdom had been exposed, during its intestine troubles, to the
danger of invasion from the direction of Lahore. In the direction
of Multān the worthless Mubārak was better served, and when
Shaikh 'Alī, during his retreat, attacked a fortress within the limits
of that province. Imād-ul-Mulk marched to Talamba and forced

him to relinquish his prey. Unfortunately 'Imād-ul-Mulk received
orders to retire to Multān, and Shaikh 'Alī, attributing his retreat
to cowardice or a consciousness of weakness, crossed the Rāvī near
Khatībpur, plundered the country along the banks of the Chenāb,
and marched to within twenty miles of Multān. 'Imād-ul-Mulk
sent Islām Khān Lodī to stem his advance, but Islām Khān's
force, while still on the march, came unexpectedly on the invaders
and was defeated before it could form for attack or defence. Islām
Khān was slain, and the remnant of his force fled back to Multān.
Shaikh 'Alī advanced to Khairābād, near Multān, and encamped
there on May 15, 1431. On the following day he advanced to
attack one of the gates, but his troops were repulsed by a sortie
of the garrison, and he did not resume the offensive until June 8,
when he made a second attempt to carry the place by assault, but
was again repulsed with heavy loss, and thereafter contented himself with harassing the garrison in a series of skirmishes until the
arrival of a strong relieving force which attacked him and drove
him within his entrenched camp, whence he fled across the Rāvī.[1]
He was pursued, and numbers of his army perished in the river
and by the swords of the pursuers, but he eventually threw himself
into Shorkot, leaving all his horses, camels, and equipment in the
hands of the victors. 'Imād-ul-Mulk and the army which had
marched to his relief followed the fugitives to Shorkot and Shaikh
'Alī fled with a small force to Kābul, leaving his nephew, Amīr
Muzaffar, with the remainder of his army in Shorkot. Further
operations were stayed by the receipt of orders from the king,
recalling to Delhi the relieving force, and most imprudently removing from Multān the able and energetic 'Imād-ul-Mulk, who
was relieved by Khair-ud-dīn Tuhfa. Misfortunes now fell thick
and fast on Mubārak. Jasrat the Khokar again rebelled and
marched on Jullundur. Sikandar Tuhfa, marching against him,
met him on the Dhaulī Waīn, but was defeated and taken alive,
and Jasrat marched to Lahore and besieged the city, which was
defended by Sayyid Najm-ud-dīn, Sikandar's lieutenant, and Malik
Khushkhabar, his slave. Meanwhile Shaikh 'Alī of Kābul had
again invaded the Multān province and on November 13 captured
Talamba, occupied the citadel, threw the leading citizens into prison,
and plundered all the surrounding country. At the same time

[1] Yahyā b. Ahmad and his copyists have 'the Jihlam,' but the Jhelum, or Chenāb,
as it is called below its confluence with that river, has always flowed to the west of
Shorkot, to reach which Shaikh 'Alī must have crossed the Rāvī. Had he crossed
the Chenāb he would have placed that river between himself and Shorkot.

Fūlād, who still held Bhātinda, led an expedition against Rāi Fīrūz, whose fief lay in the neighbourhood, slew him and plundered the district which he had governed.

Mubārak, on receiving news of these calamities, acted with unusual vigour and decision, and, having dispatched Sarvar-ul-Mulk in advance, with a force sufficient to check, if not to crush, Fūlād, left Delhi, in January, 1432, for Lahore. The sudden flight of his enemies occasioned a modification of his plans. Jasrat raised the siege of Lahore and fled into the mountains, carrying with him his captive, Sikandar Tuhfa, and Shaikh 'Alī evacuated Talamba and retreated to Shorkot. Mubārak advanced no further, but bestowed the fief of Lahore on Nusrat Khān Gurgandāz and sent Sarvar-ul-Mulk to Lahore to escort the family of Sikandar to Delhi.

In August Jasrat was again active. He issued from his stronghold, plundered some districts in the plains, and attacked Gurgandāz in Lahore, but, being worsted by him, retired again into the mountains. Mubārak, who had marched as far as Pānīpat on hearing of his renewed activity, returned to Delhi on learning of his retreat, and sent 'Imād-ul-Mulk into the districts of Bayāna and Gwalior In September he again left the capital to quell some disturbances in the Sāmāna district, but returned to Delhi on hearing of his mother's illness and arrived in time to be present at her obsequies. Having rejoined his army he sent Sarvar-ul-Mulk with a large force against Fūlād, and Sarvar-ul-Mulk, after completing all dispositions for the siege of Sāmāna, left Zirak Khān in charge of the operations and returned to the royal camp at Pānīpat. Mubārak now abandoned his intention of taking the field in person, and sent Malik Ilāhdād Lodī to supersede Gurgandāz in the fiefs of Lahore and Jullundur, but as he was approaching the latter town Jasrat fell upon him at Bajwārā, near Hoshiārpur, defeated him, and drove him into the lower slopes of the mountains.

In November Mubārak invaded Mewāt, where Jalāl Khān was again in revolt, and drove him from one stronghold to another, compelling him to purchase peace on the usual terms of a present payment and promise of amendment. He was joined by 'Imād-ul-Mulk on his return from his successful foray into the Bayāna district and dispatched Kamāl-ud-dīn and other officers on similar raids into the districts of Etāwah and Gwalior, returning, in January, 1433, to Delhi, where he learnt that Shaikh 'Alī was again preparing to march to the relief of Bhātinda, and dispatched 'Imād-ul-Mulk with reinforcements for the besieging army. This measure curtailed the extent of Shaikh 'Alī's activity, but he issued from

Shorkot, plundered the villages on the banks of the Rāvī, enslaved their inhabitants, and marched on Lahore, which was held for the king by Yūsuf, son of Sarvar-ul-Mulik, and Malk Ismā'īl.

These two officers, after enduring a short siege, discovered that the fidelity of the citizens, which had been sorely tried by constant attacks against which the royal garrison could ill protect them, was uncertain, and fled from the city with their troops. During their flight they suffered heavy losses at the hands of a force dispatched in pursuit of them by Shaikh 'Alī, who plundered Lahore, placed a garrison of 10,000 horse in the city, marched to Dīpālpūr, where Yūsuf had taken refuge, and besieged that town. 'Imād-ul-Mulk, who was still besieging Bhātinda sent his brother, Malik Ahmad, to the relief of Yūsuf, and Shaikh 'Alī raised the siege of Dīpālpūr, but occupied all the towns lying between that place and Lahore.

Mubārak at length perceived that affairs in the north-western provinces of his kingdom demanded his personal attention, and marched to Sāmāna, where he was joined by Kamāl-ud-dīn and the other officers who had been sent to Etāwah and Gwalior, and advanced to Talwandī, where 'Imād-ul-Mulk joined him from Bhā-tinda. The officers who still remained before that town were summoned to the royal camp, and Mubārak advanced to the Rāvī. Here Sikandar Tuhfa, who had escaped from Jasrat's custody, appeared before him and received the ill-deserved title of Shams-ul-Mulk and a grant of the fiefs of Lahore, Dīpālpūr, and Jullundur. In the meantime Shaikh 'Alī had retreated across the Chenāb, and, as Shams-ul-Mulk advanced to take possession of his new fiefs, fled precipitately, leaving most of his horses, and his baggage, camp equipage, and booty, which were already bestowed in boats for transport across the Chenāb, in his enemy's hands. Mubārak crossed the Rāvī at Talamba and besieged Shorkot, which, after the lapse of a month, was surrendered to him by Amīr Muzaffar, Shaikh 'Alī's nephew, who secured his safety by large gifts, and by bestowing a daughter in marriage on Muhammad Khān, the nephew and adopted son of Mubārak. The king then retired towards Multān after dispatching Shams-ul-Mulk to Lahore, where the garrison left by Shaikh 'Alī purchased for itself a safe retreat by the surrender of the town and citadel. Mubārak, after retiring to Dīpālpūr, wisely removed Shams-ul-Mulk from the important fiefs which he had recently bestowed upon him to Bayāna, and conferred Lahore, Dīpālpūr, and Jullundur on 'Imād-ul-Mulk. On his return to Delhi he discovered that Sarvar-ul-Mulk had for some time past been remiss in the performance of his duties as minister of the kingdom, and appointed Kamāl-ud-dīn as his co-adjutor in the hope that the two would work in harmony. He was disappointed, for the influence of the abler and more energetic Kamāl-ud-dīn soon eclipsed that of Sarvar-ul-Mulk, who, resenting his virtual supersession in office, formed a faction consisting of some discontented Khatrīs, Mīrān Sadr, the deputy muster-master-general, Qāzī 'Abd-us-Samad Khān, a royal chamberlain, and others, and conspired against the king's life.

On November 1 the king founded Mubārakābād, on the Jumna, and while superintending the building of this town learnt that the protracted siege of Bhātinda had at length been brought to a success-ful conclusion. The news was confirmed by the receipt of the head of the rebel, Fūlād, which had been severed from his body after his capture by Mīrān Sadr. He marched to Bhātinda and, after ex-tinguishing the smouldering embers of disaffection, learnt that a dispute had arisen between Ibrāhīm Shāh of Jaunpur and Hūshang Shāh of Mālwa regarding the town and district of Kālpī, which had ever been included, in name at least, in the dominions of Delhi, and that they were marching to decide the question by an appeal to arms. He could not but resent an insult so gross and returned to Delhi to assemble his forces. On his way to Kālpī he turned aside to visit Mubārakābād, and here, on February 19, 1434, Sarvar-ul-Mulk found the opportunity which he had been seeking. Mīrān Sadr relieved the royal bodyguard with a force of his own troops, and while the king was preparing for prayers entered his apartment on the pretext of taking leave of him, posting Sidhāran, one of the Khatrīs, at the door to prevent the entrance of any person not privy to the plot. While he engaged the king in conversation Sidhū Pāl, another Khatrī, cut him down with his sword, and Rānū and other Hindus rushed in and completed the bloody work.

On the death of Mubārak Shāh, who had left no son, the nobles at Delhi raised to the throne Muhammad, the son of his brother Farīd. Sarvar-ul-Mulk's complicity in the murder of the late king could not be concealed, but as he held possession of the royal treasury, armoury, and elephants he was too powerful to be touched and though he was suspected of designs on the throne it was neces-sary, for the time, to confirm him in his office, and he received the title of Khānjahān, while his accomplice, Mīrān Sadr, received that of Mu'īn-ul-Mulk. Kamāl-ud-dīn, whose appointment had been the cause of Sarvar-ul-Mulk's disaffection, and other of Mubārak's nobles were desirous of avenging his death, but were compelled to bide their time, and Sarvar-ul-Mulk, with a view to intimidating them executed one officer of high rank and imprisoned others, seized all the vacant fiefs in the kingdom and distributed them among his creatures. Bayāna, Amroha, Nārnaul, Guhrām, and some districts in the Doāb were granted to Sindhāran, Sidhū Pāl, and their relatives who had been personally concerned in the murder of the late king. Sidhū Pāl sent his slave Rānū, another assassin, to Bayāna to collect the revenue, but Yūsuf Khān Auhadī marched from Hindaun to meet him, and when Rānū attempted to take possession of the fort attacked, defeated, and slew him.

The nobles who still held their fiefs made preparations for overthrowing Sarvar-ul-Mulk. Malik Ilāhdād Lodī, now governor of Sambhal and Āhār, Malik Chaman of Budaun, Amīr 'Alī Gujarātī Amīr Kambal, and others agreed to stand or fall together and raised the standard of revolt. Sarvar-ul-Mulk assembled an army to crush them, and appointed to its command Kamāl-ul-dīn, who had dissembled his hostility, associating with him his own son Yūsuf, Sayyid Khān, and Sidhāran the Khatrī. This force advanced from Delhi to Baran and Ilāhdād Lodī retired, but halted at Āhār on learning that Kamāl-ud-dīn favoured his cause. His hostility to the minister and sympathy with the faction in arms against him could no longer be concealed, and Sarvar-ul-Mulk sent from Delhi to the army his slave Hūshyār, nominally as Kamāl-ud-dīn's assistant, but in fact as a spy upon his actions and a coadjutor of Yūsuf and Sidhāran. Malik Chaman of Budaun now joined Ilāhdād Lodī at Āhār and Kamāl-ud-dīn's attitude became so menacing that Yūsuf and Sidhāran returned to Delhi. On their departure Ilāhdād and his allies joined Kamāl-ud-dīn, marched with him on Delhi, defeated Sarvar-ul-Mulk's troops in a battle before the city, and besieged him for three months in Sirī. Sarvar-ul-Mulk discovered, in the course of siege which lasted for three months, that the king was in sympathy with the besiegers, and attempted to slay him as he had slain his predecessor, but Muhammad was prepared for the attempt and his armed attendants slew Sarvar-ul-Mulk, and seizing the sons of Mīrān Sadr, executed them on the spot. Kamāl-ud-dīn and the confederates were then summoned into the city and the remaining conspirators retired to their houses. Sidhū Pāl imitated the Rajput custom of *jauhar*, set fire to his house; immolated his family, and died fighting, but Sidhāran and the other Khatrīs were taken alive and put to death, and Hūshyār the slave and Mubārak, police magistrate of the city, were executed at the *Lāl Darwāza*, or Red Gate.

The confederates repeated the ceremony of enthroning Muhammad Shāh ahd swore allegiance to him, and in the new distribution of offices and fiefs Kamāl-ud-dīn became minister and received the title of Kamāl Khān, Malik Chaman was entitled Ghāzī-ul-Mulk and was confirmed in the fiefs of Budaun and Amroha, Ilāhdād Lodī, who would accept no title for himself, obtained that of Daryā Khān for his brother, who succeeded him in Sambhal, Malik Khoīrāj retained Hissar, and Hājī Shudanī was entitled Hisām Khān and appointed governor of the capital.

In October Muhammad Shāh made a pilgrimage to Multān to visit the shrines of the saints, and in 1436 marched to Sāmāna and dispatched thence an army which is said to have laid waste the country of the Khokars.

Muhammad had been, until the fall of Sarvar-ul-Mulk, the victim of factions and the sport of circumstances, but when he had an opportunity of displaying his fitness for rule he so abused it as to lose both the affection and the confidence of those who had freed him from his enemies. After his return to Delhi from Sāmāna his counsellors were perturbed by the news of successive calamities. In Multān the Langāhs, an Afghān tribe recently settled in the district, rebelled against Muhammad Shāh's governor ; in the opposite direction Ibrāhīm Shāh of Jaunpur invaded and annexed some of the south-eastern districts of the kingdom ; and to the south of Delhi the raja of Gwalior and other Hindu chieftains openly repudiated their liability to pay tribute. Even the forays undertaken in his uncle's reign would have been preferable to inaction, but Muhammad remained in his capital, sunk in indolence and pleasure, until his nobles, losing heart, clearly perceived that if the ancient prestige of Delhi were to be preserved they must seek another leader. It was during this period that the commanding qualities of Malik Buhlūl Lodī[1], nephew and adopted son of Islām Khān and now governor of Sirhind, first attracted attention. As the king's weakness and meanness of spirit became more apparent he gradually extented his influence over the whole of the Punjab, and began to withhold the revenue due to the royal treasury. The condition of the remnant of the kingdom of Delhi was deplorable. Muhammad's nominal authority did not extend beyond Pānīpat to the north ; on the south and south-east the raja of Gwalior, who had during the previous reign periodically acknowledged the sove-

---

[1] In English histories this name is usually written Bahlol,' as it is also pronounced by the vulgar in India. Buhlul is the correct form. The word is Arabic, and means one who laughs or smiles, or a prince endowed with every accomplishment.

reignty of Delhi, no longer made any pretence of fealty, and the
king of Jaunpur had invaded and annexed the districts bordering
on his kingdom. The Hindus of the Doāb, always refractory, disregarded with impunity an authority which was never asserted,
and the turbulent tribesmen of Mewāt plundered the country to
within a short distance of the wall of the city. The Nobles of Delhi,
despairing of a king who was content to loiter in his palace while his
kingdom dissolved, had recourse, in 1440—41, to Mahmūd Shāh
Khaljī of Mālwa, an active and warlike prince who had in 1436 seized
the throne of that kingdom[1], and sent repeated messages to him
representing the miserable plight of the once glorious kingdom and
imploring him to march to Delhi for the purpose of restoring peace
and order. Mahmūd set out, and Muhammad Shāh, roused at
length from his disgraceful torpor, prepared to oppose him. Assembling such troops as he could muster, he sent an appeal for help
to Buhlūl Lodī, whose readiness to respond had its origin not in
loyalty to Muhammad, but in the resolve to preserve the kingdom
for himself. He would not, however, lend his aid unconditionally,
and demanded as its price the death of Hisām Khān, governor of
the capital, in whom he recognised either a dangerous rival or too
staunch and powerful a champion of hereditary right. The
condition was fulfilled, and Buhlūl led his forces to the support of the
king.

Meanwhile Mahmūd, marching from Mālwa by way of Hindaun,
was there joined by Yūsuf Khān Auhadī and continued his advance
to Delhi. Muhammad marched forth to meet him, and the two
armies confronted one another between Tughluqābād and the city.
Here Muhammad, who had already proved himself to be devoid
of the qualities of a leader of men, sank to the lowest depths of
contempt by showing that he lacked the mere physical courage
expected of the humblest soldier. He would not take the field
in person, but entrusted the command of his troops nominally to
his son 'Alā-ud-din, with whom he associated Sayyid Khān Daryā
Khān Lodī, Qutb Khān, and other officers. Like Muhammad, but
for a different reason, Mahmūd Khaljī refrained from personally
engaging in the conflict. His courage was never impugned, and he
was, indeed, brave to rashness, but he would not deign to take the
field against Muhammad's officers, and was resolved to show that
his own subordinates were well able to cope with them. Retaining
for the protection of his person a small force of picked cavalry he
entrusted the command of the rest of his army to his two sons

1 See Chapter XIV.

Ghiyās-ud-dīn and Nusrat Khān. The battle began at noon and lasted, without any decisive advantage to either side, until nightfall, when each army returned to its own camp. The pusillanimous Muhammad, dreading the alternative prospects of being obliged to take the field or falling into the hands of the enemy, hastened to make undignified proposals for peace, which might have been rejected with contempt, had not Mahmūd received reports which necessitated an immediate return to his capital. A mob at Māndū had removed the royal umbrella suspended over the tomb of Hūshang Shāh and had raised it over the head of a pretender whom they had proclaimed king of Mālwa as representative of the Ghūrī family[1]. Accordingly he welcomed the overtures for peace and on the following day began his retreat. With flagrant disregard of the agreement between the two kings Buhlūl Lodī followed and attacked the retreating army, and obtained a trivial advantage over its rearguard and some plunder. It need not be assumed that Muhammad was privy to this act of treachery, for Buhlūl was beyond his control, but he participated in its guilt by becoming, in legal phrase; an accessory after the fact. The perfidious Afghān was received on his return with extravagant demonstrations, his mean and petty triumph was magnified into a victory over the army of Mālwa, and the king distinguished him by styling him his son, and conferred on him the title of Khān Khānān.

Buhlūl now consulted his interest by feigning loyalty to Muhammad and in the following year the king marched to Sāmāna and there formally bestowed on him, in addition to the fiefs which he already held by grant from the crown, Dīpālpūr and Lahore, which were no longer his to bestow. Buhlūl deigned to accept a commission to attack Jasrat the Khokar, but, on discovering that Jasrat was inclined to favour his designs on the throne of Delhi, made peace with him on easy terms and withdrew to Sirhind, where he strengthened himself by annexing the districts adjoining those which he already held, and by enlisting large numbers of Afghāns, especially of his own tribe[2], in his army. He picked a quarrel, on trivial grounds, with Muhammad Shāh, marched to Delhi, and besieged it, but failed to capture it, or perhaps, for he returned unmolested to his own dominions, where he styled himself Sultān Buhlūl, was bought off, or retired on realising the magnitude

[1] Some historians attribute the retreat of Mahmūd Khaljī to a report that Ahmad I of Gujarāt had invaded or was about to invade his dominions, but the account of the circumstances given in the text is to be preferred.

[2] The Lodīs were Khaljīs or Ghilzāis, Turks by origin, but so long resident in Afghānistān that by the fifteenth century they could be correctly described as Afghāns.

of the task with which he would be confronted after taking the city.

After the siege of the capital the disorders of the kingdom increased daily, and when Muhammad Shāh died, in 1444, no point on his frontier was more than forty miles distant from Delhi, and the kingdom inherited by his son 'Alā-ud-dīn, who assumed the title of 'Ālam Shāh, consisted of the city and the neighbouring villages.

The new king was even more feeble and vacillating than his father, and although Buhlūl humoured the nobles of Delhi by formally acknowledging his accession he sedulously continued his preparations for seizing the throne when the time should be ripe.

Shortly after his accession 'Ālam Shāh marched towards Sāmāna, apparently with no other purpose than that of showing that a king of Delhi yet dared to leave his palace, but was recalled by a rumour that Mahmūd Shāh of Jaunpur was marching on the city. The report, which he had not taken the trouble to verify, proved to be false, and an outspoken courtier incurred his displeasure by upbraiding him for his undignified and unnecessary retreat. In 1447 he marched to Budaun, where he was received with respect, and found the city so attractive that he resolved to reside there rather than at Delhi. Having prepared a dwelling for himself he returned to Delhi, where the same blunt courtier remonstrated with him on the folly of the step which he contemplated, but gained nothing but his own removal from office. The king appointed one of his wife's brothers governor of the capital and in 1448 retired permanently to Budaun, where he abandoned himself entirely to the pursuit of pleasure.

It is now proper to examine the condition of the territories over which Khizr Khān had established his authority. The province of Multān had elected a ruler of its own, who never recognised, even formally, the royal authority ; and the rest of the Punjab, as far south as Pānīpat and Hissar, was in the possession of Buhlūl, whose relative, Daryā Khān Lodī, held the district of Sambhal, the western limit of which he had pushed forward as far as the ford of Khvāja Khizr, on the Jumna near Delhi. Adjoining this petty state on the south, within the limits of the Doāb, was the state of Koīl, held by 'Isā Khān the Turk, and south of this state Hasan Khān, another Afghān, held Rāprī. The lower central Doāb, including Bhongāon, Patiālī, and Kampil, was held by the Rājput, Raja Partāb and to the west of the Jumna Dāūd

Khān Auhadī was independent in Bayāna. All these rulers were partisans of Buhlūl. Gwalior was an independent Hindu state, and such tracts of Mewāt as did not acknowledge the rule of Dāūd Auhadī were held by native chieftains whose power extended almost to the gates of Delhi.

'Alam Shāh, on his way to Budaun, took counsel with Qutb Khān, cousin of Buhlūl, 'Isā Khān, and Raja Partāb, regarding the possibility of rehabilitating the royal power. Hamīd Khān, who was now minister, was obnoxious to Raja Partāb, for his father, Fath Khān, had formerly devastated Partāb's fief and carried off his wife. The three courtiers promised to add to 'Alam Shāh's small kingdom forty *parganas* on condition that he put Hamīd Khān to death. He was imprisoned, but escaped and fled to Delhi.

After the king's departure from the capital a quarrel broke out between his two brothers-in-law, one of whom had been left there as governor and the other as chief of the city police, and one of them had been killed in a fight between their factions. The mob, at the instigation of Hisām Khān, had risen against the survivor and put him to death, and Hisām Khān and Hamīd Khān remained arbiters of the destinies of Delhi. The restoration of 'Alam Shah was out of the question, and both desired to find a substitute who would be content with no more than the royal title and would permit them to govern in his name. The claims of the kings of Jaunpur and Mālwa were considered and rejected, for the former was connected by marriage with 'Alam Shāh and might attempt to avenge his wrongs and the latter was so attached to his distant kingdom that it was improbable that he would transfer his affections to Delhi. Their choice fell ultimately upon Buhlūl, though there was little probability of his becoming a pliable instrument in their hands, and he was invited to Delhi. He responded with such alacrity that he arrived with a force insufficient to establish his authority, but he formally received from Hamīd Khān, in exchange for conciliatory promises, the keys of the city, and wrote to 'Alam Shāh a letter as masterly as it was insincere, in which he explained that he was actuated solely by jealous zeal for the royal authority, which he had seen set at naught. Buhlūl seated himself on the throne on April 19, 1451, and set out at once to Dīpālpūr to collect the troops which in his haste he had left behind. His letter to 'Alam Shāh elicited the desired reply. The mean-spirited King, content with the ease and freedom from care which his residence in Budaun afforded, replied that he had had neither fruit nor profit of sovereignty, that his father had styled Buhlūl his son and that he himself freely and cheerfully resigned his throne to Buhlūl as to an elder brother. Thus Buhlūl, on his return to Delhi, ascended the throne not merely as the creature of a successful faction, but as the heir designate of a king who had voluntarily abdicated. The contemptible 'Ālam Shāh remained contentedly in Budaun, where the revenue of the small territory which he had been permitted to retain sufficed to defray the cost of his pleasures.

15—2

... ...

CHAPTER IX

THE LODĪ DYNASTY

THE condition of the kingdom over which Buhlūl was called to
rule has already been described, but he differed from its late feeble
sovereign in being already, at the time of his elevation to the throne,
a powerful ruler. The greater part of the Punjab owned his sway,
and one of his kinsmen was virtual ruler of the country to the
east of Delhi, the northern Doāb, and the province now known as
Rohilkhand.

The new king was just such a ruler as the distracted state required. With sufficient political acumen to serve his purpose he
was active and warlike and had formed the resolution of restoring
the kingdom to its pre-eminence among the Muhammadan States
of Northern India. Among his Afghān kinsmen he was little more
than *primus inter pares*, and was well content with that position,
but he would tolerate no interference by strangers, and one of his
first acts was to overthrow the powerful Hamīd Khān, by whom
he had been called to the throne and whose influence in Delhi
might at any time be sufficient to initiate a formidable movement
for the restoration of the old order of things, when everybody
was his own master. The Afghāns, acting under their leader's
instructions, behaved with grotesque boorishness at all his formal
meetings with Hamīd Khān. The men-at-arms crowded into the
hall of audience on the pretext that all soldiers and fellowtribesmen
were equals, and their conduct, while it excited the surprise and
disgust of Hamīd Khān, encouraged him to believe that he had
to deal with a horde of mere rustic simpletons. The Afghān troops
were soon numerous enough to crush any disturbance which might
arise in the city, and their numbers at court were always sufficient
to enable Buhlūl to carry out any act of violence. At one
audience Qutb Khān Lodī, Buhlūl's cousin and brother-in-law, produced a chain and, casting it down before Hamīd Khān, informed
him that it was considered necessary for reasons of state that he
should be confined for a few days, but that in consideration of the
services which he had rendered his life would be spared. How this
promise was kept we do not know, but Hamīd Khān disappears
henceforth from the scene.

Shaikh Yūsuf, the popularly elected governor of Multan, who had been expelled from that city by the Langāhs[1] and had taken refuge at Delhi, urged Buhlūl to recover the lost province, and late in 1451 he left the capital for Multān, but as soon as his back was turned some of the old nobles of 'Ālam Shāh, who found the energetic personal rule of the new king little to their taste, invited Mahmūd Shāh of Jaunpur to attack the city and expel the Afghāns. Mahmūd responded to the appeal, and on his march towards Delhi was joined by Buhlūl's relative, Daryā Khān Lodī, who remained at heart loyal to his kinsman, and whose adherence to the invader was a matter of necessity rather than choice. Mahmūd advanced to Delhi and besieged Buhlūl's eldest son, Khvāja Bāyazīd, who had been left in charge of the city; and Buhlūl, who had reached Dīpālpur, immediately retraced his footsteps and was within thirty miles of the capital before Mahmūd had succeeded in making any impression on its defences. He was fortunate enough to capture large numbers of Mahmūd's transport animals, which were at pasture but immediately after this successful stroke was attacked by Mahmūd's principal lieutenant, Fath Khān of Herat, with 30,000 horse and thirty elephants. In the battle Qutb Khān Lodī, who was an expert archer, checked the onset of Fath Khān's elephant by wounding it with an arrow, and this mishap shook the ranks of the Jaunpur troops. Qutb Khān was able to convey a message to Daryā Khān Lodī, urging him to desert the enemy and join his kinsmen, and Daryā Khān at once led his troops from the field. The rest of the army of Jaunpur, demoralised by his defection, broke and fled, and Fath Khān was taken alive and was beheaded by Raja Khān, a Hindu officer of Buhlūl's who had a blood feud with him.

Mahmūd, on the defeat of his army in the field, raised the siege and returned to Jaunpur. His expedition convinced Buhlūl that the settlement of the trivial disorders in the Punjab, where Lodī supremacy was assured, might, well be postponed until the turbulent fief-holders of the Doāb and the petty princes of Mewāt, who had long been independent, were once more brought into subjection to the kingdom of Delhi and the power of the king of Jaunpur which, during the reigns of Mubārak, Muhammad, and 'Ālam Shāh, had always equalled and frequently over-shadowed that of the king of Delhi, had been broken. Buhlūl, whose reputation had been greatly enhanced by his victory, marched to Mewāt, where he received, without a battle, the submission of Ahmad Khān, who

---

[1] See Chapters VIII and XIX.

surrendered seven *parganas* to him, agreed to holding the remainder of his territory as a fief of Delhi, and placed his uncle,
Mubārak Khān, at Buhlūl's court, nominally as his agent, but in
fact as a hostage.

From Mewāt Buhlūl crossed the Jumna and marched to Baran,
where Daryā Khān Lodī waited on him and compounded for his
late adhesion to Mahmūd of Jaunpur by the surrender of seven
parganas of his great fief to the crown. It was Buhlūl's policy to
conciliate the great fief-holders of the Doāb, whose disobedience to
Delhi and subservience to Jaunpur had been forced upon them
by circumstances, and all were treated with leniency. 'Īsa Khān,
Mubārak Khān, and Raja Partāb submitted to him and were permitted to retain the fiefs of Koīl, Suket and Bhongāon, and even
Qutb Khān[1], son of Hasan Khān, who defended the fortress of
Rāprī against the royal troops, was permitted to retain his fief after
his submission.

From Rāprī Buhlūl marched to Etāwah and received the submission of the raja, but this assertion of his authority provoked
Mahmūd of Jaunpur, who claimed the allegiance of Etāwah and
invaded the district for the purpose of contesting Buhlūl's claim.
Neither king was in a position to proceed to extremities against the
other, and after one day's desultory fighting they concluded a truce,
in accordance with the terms of which the boundaries between the
two states were to be those which had been recognised in the reign
of Mubārak Shāh of Delhi, seven elephants taken from Fath Khān
were to be restored to Jaunpur, and Buhlūl was to be permitted,
after the rainy season, to wrest Shamsābād from Jaunān Khān, who
held it nominally as a fief of Jaunpur.

Mahmūd returned to Jaunpur and Buhlūl drove Jaunān Khān
from Shamsābād and placed his own vassal, Raja Karan, in possession of the fief. Mahmūd, though Buhlūl had violated none of the
conditions of the treaty, marched against him, and as the army of
Jaunpur approached Shamsābād it was attacked by night by a
force under Qutb Khān Lodī and Daryā Khān Lodī. The attack
failed and Qutb Khān was captured and sent to Jaunpur, where
he remained a prisoner for seven months. Just as the main bodies
of the two armies were about to join battle Mahmūd died, in 1457,
and his son Bhīkan was raised to the throne under the title of
Muhammad Shāh, and made peace with Buhlūl, whose right to
retain Shamsābād he acknowledged. Buhlūl returned towards
Delhi, but on reaching Dhankaur received a message from Qutb

[1]Not to be confounded with Qutb Khān Lodī, Buhlūl's cousin and brother-in-law

Khān's sister, reproaching him for having left her brother in captivity and urging him not to rest until he had liberated him, whereupon he at once turned back to meet Muhammad Shāh, who marched with equal promptness to Shamsābād, expelled Raja Karan, and restored the fief to Jaunān Khān. His success attracted to his standard the raja of Etāwah, who openly transferred his allegiance from Delhi to Jaunpur, and Muhammad marched to Saraswati while Buhlūl marched to the neighbouring town of Rāprī. After some desultory fighting between the two armies intestine discord deprived that of Jaunpur of the power of offensive action[1], and Muhammad was deserted by one of his brother, who led away a force of 30,000 horse and thirty elephants and halted on the banks of the Jharna. Buhlūl, who regarded this move as a tactical manoeuvre against himself, followed them, and on his way captured Jalāl Khān, a third brother of Muhammad, who was attempting to join the deserter, and detained him as a hostage for the safety of Qutb Khān Lodī.

Muhammad retreated towards Kanauj, and was followed as far as the Ganges by Buhlūl, but his brother Husain had already been acclaimed as king at Kanauj and Muhammad was deserted by the few courtiers who had remained with him, and was put to death.

Husain Shāh ascended the throne of Jaunpur in 1458, and at once concluded a four years' truce with Buhlūl. Qutb Khān Lodī was exchanged for Husain's brother, Jalāl Khān, and peace reigned between Delhi and Jaunpur for the period for which the truce had been concluded.

During this period Buhlūl's attention was fully occupied in the administration of his dominions and late in 1472 he marched towards Multān, to reduce to obedience Husain Shāh Langāh, who had succeeded his father in that small kingdom.

In 1473 Husain Shāh of Jaunpur, instigated by his wife Jalīla, who was a daughter of 'Ālam Shāh, marched on Delhi with a large army, and this menace to his capital recalled Buhlūl, who however, sent his third son, Bārbak Shāh, and Tātār Khān Lodī, governor of Lahore, to Multān, where they suffered a crushing defeat at the hands of Husain Langāh, and were compelled to retreat.

Buhlūl, on reaching Delhi, was dismayed by the imminence of his peril and hastily sent a mission to Mahmūd Khaljī II of Mālwa, imploring him to come to his aid and promising to cede to him the whole country west of Bayāna, but Husain had reached the banks of the Jumna, a short distance to the south-east of Delhi, before a

[1] For the details of these disputes see Chapter X.

reply could be received from Mahmūd, and Buhlūl attempted to purchase peace by the most humiliating submission. Were he allowed, he said, to retain Delhi and the country for thirty miles around it he would cheerfully hold it in Husain's name. The offer was haughtily rejected and Buhlūl marched forth at the head of 18,000 Afghān horse, to meet his powerful enemy. The armies were encamped on opposite banks of the Jumna and for several days neither ventured to cross the river in force to attack the other until one day Husain who, in his contempt of his opponent neglected all military precautions, permitted the whole of his army to disperse for the purpose of plundering the fertile lands of the Doāb. His camp was left unprotected, and Buhlūl crossed the river by a ford and fell upon it. Even now Husain's insensate pride blinded him to his danger and it was not until the Afghāns were actually plundering his tents that he sought safety in flight, then the only course left open to him. The ladies of his harem, including his wife Jalīla, were captured by Buhlūl, who generously sent them unharmed to Jaunpur.

A new treaty, in which a truce of three years was agreed upon, was concluded and Buhlūl, besides turning his attention once more to the improvement of his administration and the consolidation of his power, marched into Mewāt for the purpose of dealing with Ahmad Khān, a great fief-holder who had joined Husain Shāh in his recent expedition. Ahmad Khān fled and joined Husain in Jaunpur, thus furnishing him with a pretext for renewing hostilities, to which course he was constantly urged by his wife Jalīla.

Husain, after capturing Etāwah, marched on Delhi with an army of 100,000 horse and 100 elephants, and Buhlūl again stooped to supplication and promised, if Husain would refrain from molesting him, to attend him in the field whenever in future he might require assistance. Husain vouchsafed no answer to this piteous appeal and Buhlūl was compelled to take the field. He again defeated the army of Jaunpur, but was not strong enough to profit by his success, and was fain to make peace. Shortly afterwards Husain again marched against Buhlūl, who marched from Delhi and en- countered him at Sikhera, about tewenty-five miles east of the city. Husain was defeated but was again able to make peace on equal terms and retired to Etāwah, where Qutb Khān Lodī and the son of the raja of Gwalior waited on him. Qutb Khān, learning that Husain still entertained designs on Delhi, ingratiated himself by disparaging Buhlūl, and promised Husain that he would never rest until he had conquered for him the country as far north as Delhi.

Husain was duped, and allowed Qutb Khān to leave his camp. He at once joined his cousin at Delhi, and warned him against Husain, whose military strength was still great and who had not abandoned the design of annexing Delhi to his dominions.

Husain once more assembled his army for an attack on Delhi, and in March, 1479, arrived at the bank of the Jumna. This was the most promising of all his campaigns and the effect of his numerical superiority was everywhere apparent, but Qutb Khān Lodī, by an appeal to the memory of Husain's mother, who had be-friended him during his captivity in Jaunpur, so played upon the invader's feelings that he induced him to make peace on obtaining from Buhlūl formal recognition of his tenure of all districts east of the Ganges, corresponding to the modern province of Rohilkhand After concluding this treaty Husain began a leisurely retreat and Buhlūl perfidiously attacked him and captured a large number of elephants and horses laden with spoil and treasure, Husain's minister, and about forty of his principal nobles. This success, disgracefully obtained, marks the turn of the tide in favour of Delhi, and Buhlūl pursued the demoralised army of Jaunpur and occupied the *parganas* of Kampil, Patiālī, Shamsābād, Suket, Koīl, Mārhara and Jalesar. Husain, hard pressed by Buhlūl's pursuit, turned and faced him, but was again defeated and was now obliged to acquiesce in Buhlūl's retention of the large tract of territory which he had recovered and to agree that the frontier of the kingdom of Jaunpur should be withdrawn to Chhibrāmau in the district now known as Farrukhābād. Husain retired to Rāprī and Buhlūl to Delhi, but the former, after a brief period of repose, again took the field to recover his lost territory and met Buhlūl at Senhā, where he suffered the heaviest defeat he had yet experienced. The plunder which fell into the hands of Buhlūl and the prestige which he gained with his victory established the superiority of Delhi and Buhlūl encamped at Chhibrāmau and shortly afterwards took the offensive against Husain and defeated him at Rāprī. Husain fled towards Gwalior, and after losing some of his wives and children in the passage of the Jumna, was attacked near Athgāth by the Bhadauriyas, a predatory tribe, who plundered his camp. Kirat Singh of Gwalior was still faithful to him, supplied him with money, troops, and transport, and escorted him as far as Kālpī on his way to Jaunpur. Buhlūl, after capturing Etāwah, which surrendered to him after a siege of three days, marched to attack Husain, who turned to meet him at Rāigāon Khāgā[1], where

1 In 25° 53′N. and 81° 16′E.

his front was protected by the Ganges, which postponed Buhlūl's attack for some months until Raja Tilok Chand of Baksar[1] joined his army and led it across the river by a ford, when Husain retreated rapidly to Phāphāmau[2], the raja of which place provided him with money, horses, and elephants, and escorted him in safety to Jaunpur. Buhlūl marched straight on Jaunpur and Husain fled towards Kanauj by way of Bahrāich, an unnecessarily circuitous route. Buhlūl followed him, overtook him on the banks of the Rahab, attacked him, and defeated him, capturing one of his wives. He then returned to Jaunpur, which he captured, and placed Mubārak Khān Lohānī in the city as governor. He also placed a garrison under the command of Qutb Khān Lodī in Majhaulī[3], beyond the Gogra and then marched to Budaun, which had been nominally subject to Husain since the death of 'Ālam Shāh in 1478. Husain took advantage of his absence to re-assemble his army and march to Jaunpur, compelling Mubārak Khān to with- draw to Majhaulī. Husain marched thither, and Buhlūl's officers, who could not risk a battle, gained time by feigning to negotiate, and while Husain was thus permitting himself to be delayed, Buhlūl returned rapidly from Budaun, sent a force under his son Bārbak to relieve Majhaulī, and re-occupied Jaunpur. Husain, in despair, fled into Bihār, and Buhlūl followed him as far as Haldī, on the Ganges near Ballia, where he heard of the death of Qutb Khān Lodī at Majhaulī and, after halting to mourn for him, returned to Jaunpur, where in 1486 he placed his eldest surviving son Bārbak on the throne of that kingdom and permitted him to coin money and to use the royal title. He then marched, by way of Chandwār, to Dholpur where the raja, as earnest of his submission, presented to him a large quantity of gold. From Dholpur he marched eighteen miles westward to Bārī, where Iqbāl Khān, the Muslim governor, also made his submission, and was permitted to retain his fief. Thence he marched to 'Ālampur, near Ranthambhor, plun- dered that district, and destroyed all the standing crops. Returning to Delhi he enjoyed some well-earned repose there and at Hissar and, thus refreshed, marched to Gwalior, where Kirat Singh had for many years virtually maintained his independence by paying tribute to Jaunpur. Buhlūl was ill-prepared for such an enterprise as the siege of the fortress, and Kirat Singh was well content to purchase peace and liberty by the payment of eight millions of rupees. From Gwalior Buhlūl returned to Etāwah, where he made

1 Thirty-four miles south-east of Unao town.   2 In 25° 32′N. and 81° 56′E.
3 In 26° 17′N. and 83° 57′ E., on the Little Gandak river.

some administrative changes, and, on returning towards Delhi, was overtaken, near Suket, by his last illness, which produced a crop of intrigues regarding the succession. Buhlūl himself, who had provided for his second and eldest surviving son, Bārbak, by placing him on the throne of Jaunpur, seems to have intended that his third son, Nizām Khān (Sikandar Shāh) should succeed him, but the Afghān nobles objected to him on the ground that his mother, a favourite wife or concubine, was the daughter of a goldsmith, and prevailed upon the dying king to summon him to the camp, lest he should usurp the throne in Delhi; but the prince's mother and a few who favoured his cause were in the camp and secretly warned him that if he obeyed the order he would certainly be imprisoned by his father. Nizām Khān temporised and the nobles, who were almost unanimous in opposing his succession, some supporting Bārbak Shāh of Jaunpur, and others Aʻzam-i-Humāyūn, son of Khvāja Bāyazīd, Buhlūl's eldest son, urged Buhlūl to assert his authority, and an order was sent to Nizām Khān, warning him that if he did not immediately obey the summons his father would march to Delhi and punish him. Nizām Khān pitched his camp beyond the walls and announced that he was about to set out, but needed a few days in which to prepare for the journey. Meanwhile Buhlūl suddenly died, in the second week of July, 1489. Zībā, the goldsmith's daughter, boldly confronted the Lodī nobles with an assertion of her son's claim to the throne, and was abused to her face by ʻĪsā Khān, Buhlūl's first cousin, who brusquely told her that the son of a goldsmith's daughter was not the man to fill a throne. His discourtesy injured his cause by exciting sympathy for the widow, and Khān Khānān Qarmalī rebuked him. ʻĪsā Khān angrily replied that a servant had no right to interfere in the family affairs of the Lodīs, and the Khān Khānān retorted that if he was a servant he was the servant of Sikandar Shāh, the title by which Nizām Khān was already known to his adherents, and of none other. The army moved to Jalālī, where it was met by Nizām Khān, who, on July 17, 1489, was proclaimed king under the title of Sikandar Shāh.

Sikandar was undoubtedly the fittest of all Buhlūl's sons to fill his father's throne, and his promptitude in joining the army settled the question of the succession, but some of the courtiers withdrew in sullen disaffection to their fiefs and Sikandar soon found it necessary to attack his uncle[1], ʻĀlam Khān, who was making

---

[1] According to Nizām-ud-dīn Ahmad ʻĀlam Khān was Sikandar's brother but he may be satisfactorily identified with the ʻĀlam Khān (Jalāl Shāh) who was a younger brother of Buhlūl.

pretensions to independence in Rāprī and Chandwār. 'Ālam Khān, after enduring a few days' siege in Rāprī, fled and took refuge in Patiālī with Īsā Khān, who was in rebellion in consequence of the insult which he had hurled at the king's mother. Sikandar conferred the fief of Rāprī on Khān Khānān Lohānī and retired to Etāwah, where he spent seven months in reorganising the administration of the provinces, which had been thrown into confusion by governors and fief-holders appointed during the late reign and disaffected to his rule and in conciliating those who were prepared to accept his succession as an accomplished fact. He succeeded in persuading 'Ālam Khān to leave the protection of 'Īsā Khān and endeavoured to secure his fidelity by bestowing on him the fief of Etāwah, and he sent an embassy to his brother Bārbak in Jaunpur with the object of concluding a permanent treaty between that kingdom and Delhi, and marched in person against 'Īsā Khān in Patiālī. 'Īsā met him in the field, but was defeated, and so severely wounded that he survived his reconciliation with his nephew but a few days. Raja Ganesh, a Hindu officer who had espoused Bārbak's cause, submitted to Sikandar and was rewarded with the fief of Patiālī.

The mission to Jaunpur failed. Husain Sharqī, from his retreat in Bihār, had assiduously instigated Bārbak to attack his brother, in the hope that their quarrels would open a way for his return to Jaunpur, and Sikandar, apprised of his brother's designs, marched to attack him. Bārbak advanced to Kanauj to meet him and suffered a defeat, in consequence of which he fled to Budaun. Sikandar pursued him, besieged him in that city, and after a few days compelled him to surrender. He was treated with great leniency and was replaced on the throne of Jaunpur, but merely as a king in name, for Sikandar distributed the rich fiefs of the kingdom among his own adherents, and even placed confidential agents in Bārbak's household.

After this success Sikandar marched to Kotala and Kālpī, dispossessed his nephew, A'zam-i-Humāyūn, who had been a cadidate for the crown, of these fiefs, and bestowed them upon Muhammad Khān Lodī. He next attacked, in Jhatra, Tātār Khān Lodī, who had been one of his bitterest opponents, compelled him to submit and generously restored him to his fiefs. Marching thence to Gwalior he received the submission of Raja Kirat Singh, invested him with a robe of honour as governor of the fortress and district, and marched to Bayāna, where the governor, Sharaf, son of Ahmad Jalvānī, appeared before him and, by a feigned submission, obtained a promise of the fiefs of Jalesar, Chandwār, Mārhara, and Suket on condition of his surrendering the keys of Bayāna. He was permitted to return for the keys but had no sooner regained the shelter of the fortress than he prepared to stand a siege. Sikandar marched to Āgra, which was held by Haibat Khān, a dependant of Sharaf, and, having entrusted the siege of that town to some of his officers, returned to Bayāna and after a short siege compelled Sharaf to surrender. He was permitted to retire to Gwalior, the fief of Bayāna was granted to Khān Khānān, and the king returned to Delhi.

He had rested for no longer than four days in the capital when he received news of a serious rebellion in Jaunpur, where the Hindu landholders assembled an army of 100,000 horse and foot and put to death Sher Khān, brother of Mubārak Khān Lohānī, governor of Kara. Mubārak himself escaped from Kara, but was seized by his Hindu boatmen at a ford near the present city of Allahabad and delivered to the raja of Phāphāmau, who imprisoned him. Bārbak Shāh of Jaunpur was utterly unable to cope with this formidable insurrection, which seems to have been due to the intrigues of Husain Sharqī, in Bihār and withdrew to Daryābād, between Lucknow and Gonda, whence he joined Sikandar, who was marching on Jaunpur, at Dalmau on the Ganges. The raja of Phāphāmau, alarmed at Sikandar's approach, released Mubārak Khān and sent him to the royal camp, but the king's advance on Jaunpur was opposed by the rebel army, but he attacked it, defeated it with great slaughter, dispersed it, and took much plunder, and, continuing his march to Jaunpur, reinstated his brother and retired towards Oudh, where he proposed to enjoy the chase, but was almost immediately recalled by the news that Bārbak was helpless before the rebels. The facts of the case are obscure, but it appears that Bārbak had been coquetting with the rebels and also with Husain. Sikandar dealt promptly with him by sending some of his principal nobles to Jaunpur to arrest him, and he was brought before the king and delivered into the custody of Haibat Khān and 'Umar Khān Shirvānī. From the neighbourhood of Jaunpur Sikandar marched to Chunār, where a number of Husain's nobles were assembled. He defeated them but was not strong enough to attempt the siege of the fortress, and marched to Kuntit, on the Ganges, a dependency of Phāphāmau, where Bhīl, the raja of Phāphāmau, made his obeisance, and was confirmed in the possession of Kuntit, as a fief. Sikandar marched on to Arāīl, opposite to Allahabad, and the raja, who accompanied him, became apprehensive for his personal safety and fled, leaving his camp and baggage in the king's hands. Sikandar, to reassure him, courteously sent his property after him. Araïl was laid waste, and the army marched to Dalmau by way of Kara, and thence to Shamsābād, where Sikandar halted for six months, visited Sambhal, and returned to Shamsābād, de. stroying on the way the inhabitants of two villages who had been guilty either of rebellion or brigandage.

In October, 1494, after spending the rainy season at Shamsābād he marched against Bhīl of Phāphāmau, who remained obdurate, laid waste his territory, and defeated his son Narsingh in the field. The raja fled in the direction of Sundha[1], but died on the way, and Sikandar, unable, owing to scarcity of provisions, was obliged to push on to Jaunpur, where most of the horses of his army died, from the hardships of the campaign according, to the chroniclers, but in fact owing to the improvident habit of destroying both crops and stores of grain in a hostile province. The rebellious landholders, at whose head was Lakhmī Chand, a son of Raja Bhīl, urged Husain Sharqī to attack Sikandar, assuring him that nine-tenths of the latter's cavalry horses had perished, and Husain marched from Bihār with all the forces which he could assemble and 100 elephants. Sikandar, whose losses had been exaggerated and had not proved to be irreparable, marched southward, crossed the Ganges by the fort at Kuntit, placed a garrison in Chunār, and advanced to Benares, sending Khān Khānān to conciliate Sālibāhan, another son of Raja Bhīl. Thence he marched to attack Husain, who was within thirty-six miles of the city, and on his way was joined by Sālibāhan, whose adhesion had been secured by the promise of his father's territory. He had repaired his losses, and he inflicted a crushing defeat on Husain, and pursued him towards Patna with 100,000 horse. On learning that Husain had continued his flight from Patna he marched with his whole army to Bīhār, and Husain, leaving Malik Kandū in the fortress of Bihār, fled to Kahalgāon (Colgong). Sikandar, after detaching a force which drove Kandū from Bihār, left some officers to complete the subjugation of that province and marched into Tirhut, where he received the allegiance of the raja and, having left Mubārak Khān Lohānī to collect the tribute imposed upon him, returned to Bihār.

. This invasion of Bihār which, though held by the kings of Jaunpur in the day of their strength, had always been regarded as a province of Bengal, aroused the hostility of 'Alā-ud-dīn Husain Shāh, the active and warlike king of that country, who resented

[1] In 82° 38′E. and 25° 17′N.

both the pursuit of his protege and the violation of his frontiers. He hesitated to march in person against the king of Delhi, and sent his son Dāniyāl with an army to Bārh, where he was met by a force under Mahmūd Khān Lodī and Mubārak Khān Lohānī. Neither party had anything to gain by proceeding to extremities and the treaty executed by both contained the usual stipulation, meaning- less when boundaries fluctuate and are ill defined, that neither the king of Delhi nor the sultan of Bengal was to invade the dominions of his neighbour, but the latter's promise to abstain from harbouring Sikandar's enemies was an admission that he had erred in espousing Husain's cause.

Sikandar remained for some time in Bihār and his army suffered from famine, perhaps the result of climatic conditions, but more probably caused and certainly aggravated by the devastation cam- paign in which it had been engaged. Grain became so dear that one of the taxes levied under the Islamic law was remitted, and Sikandar marched to Sāran, asserted his authority by removing some of the landholders from their fiefs and appointing nobles of his own clan in their place, and returned to Jaunpur, where he reorganised the administration of the distracted province and, having accomplish- ed this task, demanded a daughter in marriage from Sālibāhan of Phāphāmau. He met with a refusal and attacked Sālibāhan's strong- hold, but failed to capture it and returned to Jaunpur, where he demanded from Mabārak Khān Lodī, to whom the collection of the revenue had been entrusted since the imprisonment of Bārbak, an account of his stewardship. Mubārak Khān, who had been guilty of wholesale peculation, was much alarmed and sought the inter- cession of several influential courtiers with a view to avoiding an inquiry, but his anxiety betrayed his guilt, and he was ordered to pay into the treasury the large sums which he had embezzled.

During the king's stay at Jaunpur the turbulent conduct of some of his nobles aroused his displeasure and his suspicions. One accidentally struck another on the head with his stick while playing polo with the king and the injured man's brother promptly attacked Haibat Khān the unintentional offender, and a disturbance arose. The combatants were separated, but renewed their combat on the polo ground on the following day, and the king caused one of them to be flogged. Being apprehensive of the effect of this punishment on his nobles, and of the temper of men who did not hesitate to belabour one another with sticks in his presence, he took precau- tions to secure his personal safety. Selecting a number of nobles on whom he believed he could rely, he placed them on a roster for the duty of mounting guard over his palace and person at night. These nobles, either originally disaffected or rendered so by an irksome duty, conspired to depose him and to raise to the throne his younger brother Fath Khān, the seventh son of Buhlūl. The young prince privately repeated their proposals to his mother and a holy man, who advised him to disclose the matter to the king without delay. This he did, and the conspirators, twenty-two in number, were banished from court.

In 1499 Sikandar left Jaunpur for Sambhal, where he remained for four years, engaged in organising the administration of the trans-Gangetic province, and in pleasure, sport, and polo. Shortly after his arrival at Sambhal he received complaints of the oppressive behaviour of Asghar, whom he had left at Delhi as governor of the city, and ordered Khavāss Khān, who held the fief of Māchiwāra, in the present district of Lūdhiāna, to march to Delhi, seize the offender, and send him to court. Before Khavāss Khān could reach the city Asghar left it and submitted himself to the king, who caused him to be imprisoned and Khavāss Khān occupied Delhi without opposition and assumed the vacant office of governor.

Sikandar had an opportunity while at Sambhal of displaying the bigotry which was a prominent feature of his character. A Brāhman of Bengal excited some interest and, among precisians, much indignation, by publicly maintaining that the Muhammadan and Hindu religions were both true, and were but different paths by which God might be approached. A'zam-i-Humāyūn, governor of Bihār, was directed to send the daring preacher and two rival doctors of the Islamic law to court, and theologians were summoned from various parts of the kingdom to consider whether it was permissible to preach peace. They decided that since the Brāhman had admitted the truth of Islam he should be invited to embrace it, with the alternative of death in the event of refusal. The decision commended itself to Sikandar and the penalty was exacted from the Brāhman, who refused to change his faith.

An incident which happened at this time throws some light on the nature of the dominion of the Lodīs in the Punjab, the province in which they had originally established themselves. They should certainly have been able, had they commanded the resources of this province, to crush at once the kingdom of Jaunpur, which for a long time contended with them on equal terms, to establish themselves as undisputed lords of the Doāb, and to recover the fortress and province of Gwalior, which had been a Muhammadan possession for more than a century and a half until, in the troublous times of

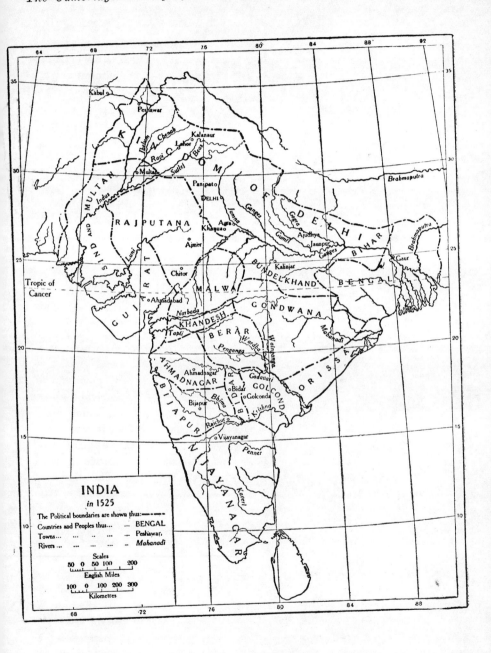

INDIA
in 1525

The Political boundaries are shown thus:— · — · —
Countries and Peoples thus... ... **BENGAL**
Towns... ... ·· .. *Peshawar,*
Rivers ... ... *Mahanadi*

Scales
50 0   50 100   200
English Miles
100 0 100 200 300
Kilometres

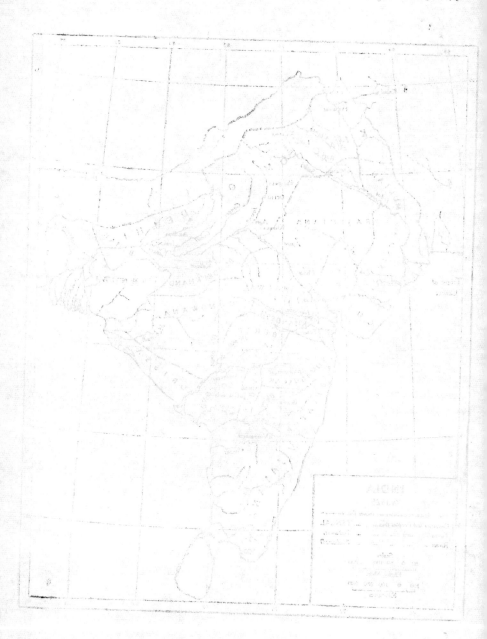

Tīmūr's invasion, it was annexed by the Tonwar Rājputs; but the hold of the Lodīs on the Punjab was precarious. It was held for them by their relations and dependants, but solidarity has never been an Afghan characteristic, and the Lodīs seem never to have ventured to tax the loyalty of their officials in the Punjab too highly. In the discontents of the next twenty-five years the Punjab was the only part of their dominions to welcome a foreign invader, and Buhlūl, Sikandar, and Ibrāhīm were content with such acknowledgement of their supremacy as was indicated by occasional remittances of tribute or revenue, and did not call upon their officers in the Punjab to furnish large contingents for the subjugation of Hindustān. In 1500 Sa'īd Khān Shirvānī came from Lahore to Sambhal to pay his respects to the king, but was banished on suspicions of disaffection and, with some other discontented nobles took refuge with Mān Singh, raja of Gwalior. The raja, with a view to deprecating Sikandar's wrath, sent as envoy to his court a eunuch named Raihān, with valuable presents, but the envoy was less conciliatory than his master, and returned impudent answers to some questions put to him by Sikandar. He was accordingly dismissed with an intimation that the raja would do well to look to himself.

Sikandar soon found the opportunity which he sought. Khān Jahān Qarmalī, governor of Bayāna, died, and though his two sons were for a short time permitted to manage the affairs of their father's fief their experience was not equal to the task, and they were summoned to Sambhal, where less important fiefs were bestowed upon them. Khavāss Khān, governor of Delhi, was appointed to Bayāna, and his son Ismā'īl Khān succeeded him in the capital. His hands were strengthened in his new post by the appointment of Safdar Khān as governor of Āgra, then a dependency of Bayāna, and 'Ālam Khān, governor of Mewāt, and Khān Khānān Lohānī, governor of Rāprī, were ordered to co-operate with him against Bināyik Deo, raja of Dholpur. A combined attack was made on Dholpur, but the royal officers were repulsed with loss and Sikandar marched, on March 15, 1502, from Sambhal towards Dholpur. On his approach Bināyik Deo fled to Gwalior, leaving his officers to defend Dholpur, but they followed their master's example and Sikandar occupied the fortress and sacked the town. The conquerors committed a senseless act of revenge by destroying the groves of trees which extended for a distance of fourteen miles round it.

Sikandar halted for a month at Dholpur, placed Ādam Khān Lodī there as governor, and marched towards Gwalior. He crossed the Chambal and halted for two months on the banks of the Āsan, where the army suffered so much from a pestilence, probably cholera, that all thought of advancing to Gwalior was abandoned. The Muslim chroniclers state that Mān Singh expelled from Gwalior Sikandar's nobles who had taken refuge with him, visited the camp to make his submission, and left his son Bikramājit, or Vikramāditya, in attendance on the king, but as Sikandar was in no position to bring pressure to bear upon Mān Singh, and found it necessary to receive Bināyik Deo and to reinstate him in Dholpur it is improbable that Mān Singh visited the royal camp. If he sent his son thither it was in the capacity of an envoy and the reinstatement of Bināyik Deo was demanded as the price of the expulsion of the refugees, for Sikandar was at the moment eager for peace, though the peace which he made was illusory, for on his return to Āgra he transferred his capital from Delhi to that city, in order to facilitate the prosecution of his designs against Gwalior. This is the first occasion on which Āgra, which acquired such importance under the Mughul emperors, comes prominently into notice, for it had hitherto been a dependency of the more important fortress of Bayāna.

The account of Sikandar's subsequent operations illustrates the strength of the raja of Gwalior and the extent of his territories, for the king did not venture to attack Gwalior itself, but attempted the systematic reduction and conquest of fortresses and districts subject or tributary to Mān Singh. The first of these was Mandrāel[1], for the siege of which he prepared by devastating the villages between it and Gwalior. In March, 1505, he marched against Mandrāel, which surrendered to him. He destroyed Hindu temples in the town and erected mosques on their sites, and plundered and laid waste the districts surrounding the fortress. This success emboldened him to remove Bināyik Deo from Dholpur on his return to Āgra and to appoint Malik Qamar-ud-dīn governor of that fortress and district.

On July 6 a most destructive earthquake occurred in Āgra. The area affected by it was extraordinarily large. It was general throughout India, it is mentioned by Bābur in his memoirs, and it is said by Budaunī to have extended to Persia.

In October, after the rainy season, Sikandar renewed hostilities against Gwalior. After a short halt at Dholpur he established his headquarters on the banks of Chambal, and, leaving his camp there, led an expedition into Gwalior country. The direction in which he marched is uncertain, but the Hindus, who fled to the hills and jungles, were slaughtered and enslaved in large numbers, and the country was laid waste. The work of devastation was so

---

[1] In 77° 18′ E. and 26° 18′ N.

complete that the invaders suffered from scarcity of food until a
large caravan of Banjāras, carrying grain and other provisions, was
captured. Mān Singh was not inactive, and Sikandar, as he approached his camp, observed precautions not habitual to him and
threw out an advanced guard on the march and outposts when
halted, suspecting some sudden manœuvre. His precautions were
opportune for, as he was retiring towards his camp on the Chambal,
Mān Singh laid an ambush for his army. The officers whose troops
were exposed to the sudden and unexpected attack displayed great
valour, and held the enemy until succour arrived from the main
body of the army, when the Hindus were defeated with great
slaughter. As the rainy season was approaching, in which operations
were difficult, the only result of this success was to secure Sikandar's
retreat, and he retired to Āgra, but as soon as the rains abated
marched to besiege the fortress of Utgīr. The siege was pressed with
such vigour that the walls were soon breached in many places and
the fortress was carried by assault, the Hindus fighting desperately
to the last. Utgīr shared the fate of Mandlāer, and Makan and
Mujāhid Khān, the latter of whom had remained at Dholpur, were
appointed to the command of the new acquisition, but it was discovered, after the capture of the fortress, that Mujāhid had been in
correspondence with the raja of Utgīr, and had undertaken, in
consideration of a bribe, to dissuade Sikandar from attacking it.
Mullā Jaman, one of his principal followers, who was with the army,
was arrested, and orders for the arrest of Mubārak Khān himself
were sent to Dholpur. After the capture of Utgīr, Sikandar again
retired to Āgra, and by some extraordinary error the army was led
by a route in which it endured the torments of thirst, and when
water was found many of the sufferers drank so greedily of it as to
cause death. The usual routes from Utgīr to Āgra were well supplied with water, and the selection of a waterless route suggests
apprehensions of another attack by Mān Singh.

Sikandar again spent the rainy season at Āgra, and early in 1508
marched to attack Narwar, usually included in the kingdom of
Mālwa, but now, apparently, subject to Gwalior. He first sent Jalāl
Khān Lodī, governor of Kālpī, against the fortress, and followed
him from Āgra. On his arrival at Narwar Jalāl Khān drew up his
army to receive him, and he was so impressed by its strength and
warlike appearance as to become jealous of its leader's power and
apprehensive of his motives, and resolved to degrade him.

Some days' desultory fighting was followed by a general attack
on the fortress, which was repulsed with heavy loss, and Sikandar

invested the place with the object of reducing it by famine. During this period of comparative leisure he was occupied in compassing the ruin of Jalāl Khān. Having attracted all his best officers into his own service he broke up his contingent, and sent him in custody in Utgīr.

Under the stress of famine and want of water the garrison of Utgīr surrendered on terms and Sikandar entered the fortress and, after his custom, destroyed Hindu temples and on their sites raised mosques, which he endowed with lands in the district.

At this time Shihāb-ud-dīn, son of Nāsir-ud-dīn Khaljī of Mālwa, who had been in rebellion against his father[1] and, having been defeated by him, was now a fugitive, arrived at Siprī, near Narwar, and expressed his readiness to enter Sikandar's service. Sikandar sent him a horse and a robe of honour, but negotiations proceeded no further.

Sikandar, on leaving Narwar, encamped on the banks of the Sindh, in its neighbourhood. Considering the importance of the fortress, and its distance from his capital, he judged it expedient to strengthen its defences, and encircled it with a fresh line of fortifications. He then marched to the district of Athgāth, which was disturbed by Hindu rebels, against whom he carried out some successful and destructive operations, and, after establishing military posts throughout the district, returned, in the summer of 1509, to Āgra.

At the close of the rainy season he indulged in a tour to Dholpur, bent only on sport and pleasure, but while he was thus employed fortune added another province to his kingdom. 'Alī Khān and Abu Bakr, brothers of Muhammad Khān, the independent ruler of the small state of Nāgaur, had conspired against their brother and, on their guilt being detected, fled to Sikandar's court and endeavoured to enlist his aid by stories of Muhammad's tyranny, but he adroitly forestalled them by sending gifts to Sikandar and acknowledging him as their sovereign.

Dūngar, lately raja of Utgīr, had, after the capture of his stronghold, accepted Islam, and was now suffering at the hands of his former co-religionists. Sulaimān, son of Khān Khānān Qarmalī, was directed to go to his aid, but demurred, ostensibly on the ground that he was unwilling to serve at a distance from court. Sikandar, incensed by his pusillanimity, dismissed him in disgrace to the *pargana* of Indrī, in the Sahāranpur district, which was assigned to him for his maintenance, and permitted the army to plunder his camp.

1 See Chapter XIV.

Troubles in Mālwa now supplied Sikandar with a pretext for interfering in the affairs of that kingdom. Sāhib Khān, the eldest son of Nāsir-ud-dīn Khaljī, had been proclaimed king by a faction, and had at first maintained himself against his younger brother, Mahmūd II, but had eventually fled before him and was now, in 1513, under the protection of Bahjat Khān, governor of Chanderī, who had proclaimed him under the title of Muhammad Shāh[1] and sought aid of Sikandar. Sikandar recognised the prince as king of Mālwa, but Sa'īd Khān and 'Imād-ul-Mulk, whom he sent to his aid with 12,000 horse, demanded that Bahjat Khān should cause the *Khutba* to be recited in the name of the king of Delhi, and, on his hesitating to comply with the request, retired, leaving him exposed to the wrath of Mahmūd II, who, however, accepted his conditional surrender and recognised Sāhib Khān as governor of the districts of Rāisen, Bhīlsa, and Dhāmonī ; but Sāhib Khān mistrusted Bahjat Khān and, on November 8, fled from Chanderī and took refuge with Sikandar.

Sikandar sent Sa'īd Khān Lodī, Shaikh Jamāl Qarmalī, Rāi Jagar Sen Kachhwāha, Khizr Khān, and Khvāja Ahmad to Chanderī to establish his authority there and to govern the province nominally on behalf of Muhammad Shāh of Mālwa, but actually as a fief of Delhi.

Husain Khān Qarmalī, governor of the recently acquired district of Sāran, now fell into disfavour for some reason not recorded, and, having been dismissed in favour of Hājī Sārang, fled to Bengal and took refuge with 'Alā-ud-dīn Husain.

Sikandar had provided for 'Alī Khān of Nāgaur, who had fled from the wrath of his brother, Muhammad Khān, by giving him a fief on the borders of the district of Ranthambhor, which was then held for Mahmūd II of Mālwa by Daulat Khān, a prince of the Khaljī family. Alī Khān tampered with Daulat Khān and, having induced him to promise that he would transfer his allegiance to Delhi, reported his success to Sikandar, who marched in a leisurely manner towards Ranthambhor. At Bayāna he was visited by Daulat Khān and his mother, but discovered, when the topic of the surrender of the fortress was broached, that 'Ali Khān was playing a double game, and had secretly urged Daulat Khān not to surrender it. 'Alī Khān was punished by being removed from his fief, which was conferred on his brother Abu Bakr, and Daulat Khān suffered nothing worse than reproaches for his duplicity.

[1] See Chapter XIV.

From Bayāna Sikandar returned by way of Dholpur to Āgra, where he fell sick. He suffered from a quinsy and from fever, but struggled against his malady and insisted on attending as usual to business of state. He was choked in attempting to swallow a morsel of food, and died on November 21, 1517.

He was the greatest of the three kings of his house and carried out with conspicuous success the task left unfinished by his father. We hear little of the Punjab during his reign and he drew no troops from it to aid him in his eastern campaigns, but there are indications that it was more tranquil and more obedient to the crown than it had been in his father's reign. His vigorous administration amply justified the choice of the minority which, in the face of strong opposition, raised him to the throne, and his selection saved the kingdom from becoming the plaything of an oligarchy of turbulent, ignorant, and haughty Afghāns. His weakest action was his support of his hopelessly incompetent brother Bārbak, but this weakness was an amiable trait in a character by no means rich in such traits. He seems to have had a sincere affection for his brother, and to have felt that he owed him some reparation for having supplanted him in his birthright, but when he discovered that leniency was a mistaken policy he knew how to act.

The greatest blot on his character was his relentless bigotry. The accounts of his conquests, doubtless exaggerated by pious historians, resemble those of the raids of the protagonists of Islam in India. The wholesale destruction of temples was not the best method of conciliating the Hindus of a conquered district and the murder of a Brāhman whose only offence was the desire for an accommodation between the religions of the conquerors and the conquered was not a politic act, but Sikandar's mind was warped by habitual association with theologians.

After his death the choice of the Lodī nobles fell upon his eldest son, Ibrāhīm, who was raised to the throne at Āgra on November 21, 1517, but a turbulent faction advocated, for its own selfish ends, a partition of the kingdom, and secured the elevation of Jalāl Khān, who was either a younger brother of Ibrāhīm or his uncle, the youngest son of Buhlūl, to the throne of Jaunpur, and carried him off to that city. Before he was established there the influence of Khānjahān Lohānī, governor of Rāprī, who vehemently condemned the suicidal policy of dividing the kingdom, secured an order for his recall, the delivery of which was entrusted to prince Haibat Khān, 'the Wolf-slayer'. His efforts were powerless to induce Jalāl Khān, who was loth to forgo a kingdom, and naturally sus-

pected Ibrāhīm, to leave Jaunpur, and the envoy was reduced to
the necessity of tampering with the fidelity of Jalāl Khān's adherents in Jaunpur. With these his efforts and the profusion of
Ibrāhīm were more successful, and they forsook the prince's cause.
Jalāl Khān, on discovering their defection, retired from Jaunpur,
where he could no longer maintain himself, to Kālpī, where he
caused the *khutba* to be recited in his name and pretended to
independence. Here he found himself in proximity to A'zam-i-
Humāyūn Shirvānī, who was besieging Kālinjar in Ibrāhīm's interest, though he was lukewarm in his cause. Jalāl Khān's position,
which interrupted A'zam-i-Humāyūn's communications with the
capital, enabled him to deal on very favourable terms with him,
and he experienced little difficulty in securing his adherence. The
two agreed that their first step should be the recovery of Jaunpur
and with this object in view they attacked Sa'īd Khān, governor
of Oudh, who, having no force sufficient to oppose them, retired
to Lucknow and reported his situation to Ibrāhīm, who secured
his position at Delhi by placing his brothers in confinement in
Hānsī, and led a large army against the rebels. Before he had
reached Kanauj his anxiety was allayed by the news that A'zam-i-
Humāyūn had quarrelled with Jalāl Khān and was hastening to
make his submission. He received him well, and at the same time
was enabled to welcome Malik Qāsim Khān, governor of Sambhal,
who had suppressed a rebellion headed by a Hindu landholder in
the Koīl district. He also received at Kanauj most of the fief-
holders of the province of Jaunpur, and dispatched A'zam-i-
Humāyūn and other officers against Jalāl Khān, who was at Kālpī.
Before the arrival of this army Jalāl Khān, leaving a garrison in
Kālpī, marched with 30,000 horse and a number of elephants on
Agra. The royal troops captured Kālpī after a few days' siege,
and sacked the city, and Jalāl Khān announced his intention of
avenging its wrongs on Āgra, but Ibrāhīm dispatched a force under
Malik Ādam to cover the approach to Āgra. This detachment was
not strong enough to try conclusions with Jalāl Khān's great army,
but its leader was a host in himself, and contrived, by opening
negotiations to delay Jalāl Khān until reinforcements arrived,
when he changed his tone and demanded that the prince should
surrender his insignia of royalty and make his submission, promising, in return for compliance with the demand, to commend
him to Ibrāhīm and to recommend his retention of the government
of Kālpī. Jalāl Khān, who suspected the fidelity of his troops,
complied, but Ibrāhīm refused to ratify the terms half promised

by his lieutenant, and marched to attack the prince, who fled and took refuge with the raja of Gwalior.

The king halted in Āgra, and found sufficient occupation in the task of restoring order in the south-eastern districts of the kingdom, which, owing to the prince's rebellion, had been in confusion since Sikandar's death. Here he received the submission of the rebellious nobles ; those, that is to say, who had either overtly or covertly supported Jalāl Khān or had refrained from opposing him. He also secured his communications with Delhi and sent Shaikhzāda Manjhū to Chanderī to control the policy and behaviour of the puppet Muhammad Shāh, who had failed, since Sikandar's death, to acknowledge in an adequate manner the sovereignty of Delhi. He also imprisoned Miyān Bhoda, one of his father's leading nobles, against whom the only offence alleged was that he was careless of forms and acted as he thought best in his master's interests without always troubling to obtain formal approval of his proceedings. This seems to have been the earliest of those encroachments on the liberties and privileges of the great nobles which ultimately lost Ibrāhīm both his throne and his life. The imprisoned noble's son was generously treated, and was installed in the position which his father had held, but the old man died in prison and his death sapped his son's fidelity.

Ibrāhīm now resolved to pursue his father's design of annexing Gwalior. The occasion was favourable, for the brave and generous Mān Singh, who had so long withstood Sikandar, had recently died, and had been succeeded by his son, Bikramājīt Singh, who lacked his father's military and administrative capacity but, fearing an attack, had considerably strengthened the defences of his fortress-capital. A'zam-i-Humāyūn Shirvānī who had been rewarded for his defection from Jalāl Khān with the government of Kara, was ordered to take the field with 30,000 horse and 300 elephants, and a large army was sent from Āgra to co-operate with him. On the approach of the imperial troops Jalāl Khān fled from Gwalior and took refuge with Mahmūd II in Mālwa.

The siege of Gwalior was opened vigorously and an important outwork was captured. While the siege was still in progress Jalāl Khān, who had furnished the pretext for the attack on Bikramājīt Singh, fell into Ibrāhīm's hands. He had fled from the court of Mālwa into the Gond principality of Katangī, and the Gonds sent him as a prisoner to Ibrāhīm, who condemned him to imprisonment in Hānsī, where the other Lodī princes were confined, but he was murdered on the way thither.

Ibrāhīm now gave rein to those groundless and unreasonable suspicions of his nobles which prompted acts of capricious tyranny, and at length drove those who might have been the staunchest defenders of his throne into the arms of an invader. Immediately before the surrender of Gwalior he summoned A'zam-i-Humāyūn Shirvānī and his son Fath Khān to Āgra and threw them into prison. The tyrant was gartified by the fall of Gwalior, but his elation was short-lived, for Islām Khān, another son of A'zam-i-Humāyūn, headed a rebellion in Āgra, assumed command of his father's troops and defended his property, and defeated Ahmad Khān, the governor, as he was preparing to assert his authority. As Ibrāhīm was assembling his army for the suppression of this rebellion A'zam-i-Humāyūn Lodī and Sa'īd Khān Lodī, two nobles whose importance was due no less to the strength of the forces at their command then to their influence in the clan, deserted him, marched to Lucknow, which they held as a fief, and sent to Islām Khān a message assuring him of their sympathy and support. The King sent an army against the rebels, but it fell into an ambush and was driven back with heavy loss. Ibrāhīm seriously damaged his own cause by sending to the officers of his army a message bitterly reproaching them, and warning them that if they failed to crush the rebellion they would themselves be treated as rebels. Fortunately for himself he did not confine his resentment to this tactless and provocotive message, but took the field at the head of 40,000 horse. The danger in which he stood is veiled in Muslim chronicles under the statement that when the two armies were within striking distance Shaikh Rājū of Bukhārā intervened to avert strife, but is displayed in the attitude of the rebellious nobles, who demanded the release of A'zam-i-Humāyūn Shrivānī as the price of their return to their allegiance. Ibrāhīm declined to accede to this condition and, after summoning reinforcements to his standard, attacked and defeated the rebels, slew Islām Khān, captured Sa'īd Khān, and rewarded those who had remained faithful to him by bestowing on them the fiefs which the rebels had held.

His triumph over his enemies served only to direct his thoughts towards the disloyalty of those whom he had trusted, his suspicion increased, A'zam-i-Humāyūn Shirvānī and other nobles died at this time in prison, in circumstances which caused a fresh outburst of disaffection, and Daryā Khān Lohānī, governor of Bihār, Khānjahān Lodī, Miyān Husain Qarmalī, and others raised the standard of rebellion. Their resentment against the tyrant was increased by his procuring the assassination in Chanderī of Shaikh Hasan Qarmalī governor of that district and a relative of one of their number. Daryā Khān Lohānī, the leader of the revolt, died, and his son Bahādur Khān was proclaimed king in his father's fief of Bihār, and assumed the usual prerogatives of eastern royalty. This bold act of defiance attracted many malcontents to his standard, and he was soon at the head of an army of 100,000 horse, with which he occupied the country to the east of the Ganges as far north as Sambhal. Nasīr Khān Lohānī, governor of Ghāzīpur, who had rebelled on his own account, joined him, and he assumed the title of Muhammad Shāh and was able, for several months, to set Ibrāhīm at defiance.

In this position of affairs Ghāzī Khān, son of Daulat Khān Lodī, the powerful governor of Lahore, visited Ibrāhīm at Delhi, and was so impressed by the discontent which had alienated from him the leading nobles of the kingdom that he returned to the Punjab a bitter enemy of Ibrāhīm's rule, and warned his father that should the king be successful in his campaign against the rebels in Hindūstān and Bihār he would not leave him long in possession of Lahore. From this time date Daulat Khān's virtual assumption of independence and his intrigues with Bābur, which will be described in Chapter I of Volume IV, and which led to Ibrūhīm's overthrow and to the establishment of a new and foreign dynasty on the throne of Delhi.

Daulat Khān died while Bābur was yet on the way to his great conquest, and at the same time died Bahādur Khān, or Sultān Muhammad, the *de facto* king of Bihār, but Ibrāhīm Shāh Lodī was defeated and slain by Bābur at Pānipat on April 18, 1526, after a reign of nine years, as will be related in the account of Bābur's conquest of India.

CHAPTER X

THE KINGDOM OF JAUNPUR

THE eunuch Malik Sarvar, Khvāja Jahān, having, as minister, placed on the throne of Delhi, in March, 1393, Nāsir-ud-din Mahmūd, son of Muhammad and grandson of Fīrūz Tughluq, and suppressed the Hindu rebellions in the Gangetic Doāb and Oudh, threw off his allegiance to Delhi, and established himself at Jaunpur. He extended his authority not only over Oudh, but also over the Gangetic Doāb as far west as Koïl and, on the east, into Tirhut and Bihār. His advance in this direction alarmed the king of Bengal, who propitiated him with the tribute of elephants, due under the treaty with Fīrūz Tughluq, to the king of Delhi, who was no longer strong enough to assert his claim to the tribute or to resent its diversion to Jaunpur.

Khvāja Jahān sent no aid to Delhi when it was attacked by Timūr, and it is not recorded that he paid any attention to the invaders. He died in 1399, leaving his dominions intact to his adopted son, Malik Qaranful, who adopted the royal style of Mubārak Shāh, and struck coin and caused the *khutba* to be recited in his name.

An account of the abortive expedition undertaken by Mallū and Mahmūd Shāh of Delhi, who hoped, on Khvāja Jahān's death, to recover Jaunpur, has already been given in Chapter VII. Jaunpur was again menaced in 1401, and Mubārak prepared to repel an invasion, but died suddenly in 1402, and was succeeded by his younger brother, who ascended the throne under the title of Shams-ud-dīn Ibrāhīm Shāh.

Ibrāhīm was a cultured prince and a liberal patron of learning, which was then in sore need of a peaceful retreat, and found it at his court, from which issued many works on theology and law. The second expedition of Mallū and Mahmūd Shāh of Delhi against Jaunpur ended, as has been already related, in Mahmūd's flight from his overbearing minister. Ibrāhīm's pride forbade him to treat his guest as his sovereign, and Mahmūd was so chagrined by his reception that he surprised Ibrāhīm's governor in Kanauj, expelled him from the town, and made it his residence. Ibrāhīm hesitated to take up arms against him, and returned to Jaunpur, while Mallū returned to Delhi. In 1405 he was slain in battle by Khizr Khān the Sayyid and Mahmūd Shāh returned to Delhi, leaving Malik Mahmūd in command of Kanauj. Ibrāhīm attempted to expel him, but Mahmūd Shāh marched to his relief, and Ibrāhīm retired, but returned again in 1407 and, after a siege of four months, forced Malik Mahmūd to surrender and marched on Delhi. He was deterred by a report that Muzaffar I of Gujarāt had marched from Mālwa to the assistance of Mahmūd Shāh from attacking the city, but annexed the district of Sambhal, east of the Ganges, and appointed his son governor there.

Between 1409 and 1414 Ibrāhīm was persuaded by the saint Qutb-ul-Ālam to invade Bengal with the object of punishing Raja Gānesh who, having acquired in that kingdom more power than its nominal ruler, was persecuting Islam. Ganesh, on discovering that his persecution of Muslims was raising up enemies against him on all sides promised to desist from it, and permitted Qutb-ul-'Ālam to convert his son Jaimal to Islam, and the saint, satisfied with this success, persuaded Ibrāhīm Shāh to retire.

Ibrāhīm's abortive attempt, early in 1428, to restore Muhammad Khān Auhadī to Bayāna has been described in Chapter VIII. It added nothing to his reputation.

In 1433 the idea of annexing the town and district of Kālpī occurred simultaneously to Ibrāhīm and to Hūshang Shāh of Mālwa. Each had advanced his frontier in this direction, and the district lay between their dominions and was separated from Delhi, to which it nominally owed allegiance, by the turbulent district of Etāwah. The two kings met in the neighbourhood of Kālpī and hostilities were imminent when Ibrāhīm was obliged to retreat by the news that Mubārak Shāh of Delhi was marching on Jaunpur. His anxiety was relieved by the assassination of Mubārak, but before he could return Hūshang had profited by his absence to receive the surrender of Sādir Khān, the governor, and had added Kālpī to his dominions.

Ibrāhīm died in 1436 and was succeeded by his son Mahmūd Shāh, who in 1443 opened with Mahmūd Shāh Khaljī a friendly correspondence followed by measures which involved the two states in hostilities. Hūshang Shāh, Mahmūd Khaljī's cousin, had left Qādir Khān at Kalpī as governor of the fortress and district and he profited by the disputes regarding the succession to the throne of Mālwa to assume independence, and even styled himself Qādir 'Shāh' Qādir was now dead and had been succeeded by his son, who styled himself Nasīr Shāh, and so conducted himself as to scandalise all good Muslims. He destroyed a flourishing and populous town and handed over many Muslim girls to Hindus in order that they might be taught to posture and dance, accomplishments held in the East to be disreputable. Mahmūd of Jaunpur was among those to whom Nasīr's behaviour gave offence, and he sent a mission to Mahmūd Khaljī to complain of his lieutenant's misconduct. The king of Mālwa admitted that he had heard the reports which were confirmed by the letter of Mahmūd Sharqī[1], and gave him permission to punish Nasīr. He marched to Kālpī, attacked Nasīr, and expelled him from the town, and, Nasīr, assuming now the character of a vassal of Mālwa, wrote to Mahmūd Khaljī and complained that the king of Jaunpur had expelled him from a fief which had been bestowed upon his father by the king of Mālwa, and intended to annex not only Kālpī, but Chanderī. Mahmūd Khaljī sent a message to Mahmūd Sharqī, suggesting that as Nasīr had expressed contrition he should be left in possession of the sub-district of Rāth in the Kālpī district, but Mahmūd Sharqī, impelled either by ambition or by a just appreciation of the offences of which Nasīr had been guilty, refused to stay his hand, and on November 14, 1444, Mahmūd Khaljī marched against him. The armies met near Īrij, and an indecisive battle was fought, but Mahmūd Sharqī occupied a strong position from which he refused to be drawn, and desultory operations continued for some months, until Mahmūd Khaljī and his protégé Nasīr withdrew to Chanderī for the rainy season. While they were in quarters at Chanderī peace was concluded, Mahmūd Sharqī agreeing to place Nasīr at once in possession of Rāth and to restore the rest of the Kālpī district within four months, provided that Mahmūd Khaljī had retired, by that time, to Māndū. After some hesitation on the part of Mahmūd Khaljī these terms were accepted, and were observed, and by the end of the year each monarch had returned to his own capital and the district of Kālpī had been restored to Nasīr, whose chastisement was deemed to have been sufficient.

Mahmūd Sharqī's adventure against Buhlūl Lodī of Delhi in 1452 and its unfortunate results for Jaunpur, have already been described in Chapter IX. His rash attack on Delhi served but to open Buhlūl's eyes to the danger with which the existence of an independent kingdom of Jaunpur menaced him, and to convince him of the necessity for its destruction.

After this unfortunate enterprise Mahmūd turned his attention to the Chunār district, the greater part of which he annexed.

1 The dynasty of Jaunpur is known as the Sharqī, or Eastern, dynasty, both from the title of Malik-ush-Sharq ('King of the East') held by its founder, and from the situation of its dominions, to the east of those of Delhi.

Nizām-ud-dīn Ahmad gives him credit for an expedition against the idolators of Orissa, whom, he says, he plundered, destroying their idol-temples, but he may be acquitted of the folly of pursuing purposeless adventures in foreign lands when the defence of his own kingdom demanded all his energies.

The death of Mahmūd in 1457, just as he was about to meet Buhlūl Lodī in the field, and the accession of his son Bhīkan, who assumed the title of Muhammad Shāh, have been described in the preceding chapter. Buhlūl, having made peace with Muhammad and retreated as far as Dhankaur, near the Jumna, about twenty-eight miles south-east of Dehi, was reminded that he had left his kinsman, Qutb Khān Lodī, in captivity at Jaunpur, and suddenly returned to compel Muhammad Shāh to release him. Muhammad turned with equal promptitude and marched to Shamsābād[1], from which fief he expelled Raja Karan, Buhlūl's vassal, and installed in his place Jaunān Khān, his own. His success attracted to his standard Raja Partāb of Etāwah who openly transferred his allegiance from Delhi to Jaunpur. The two opposing armies marched to the neighbourhood of Rāprī[2], on the Jumna, where, after some desultory and inconclusive fighting that of Jaunpur was demoralised by intestine strife. Muhammad Shāh, who, after his elevation to the throne, had evinced a violent and bloodthirsty disposition, had sent an order directing the chief magistrate of Jaunpur to put to death Hasan Khān, a younger son of Mahmūd Shāh, and Qutb Khān Lodī. The magistrate replied that he could not carry out the order as the king's mother was protecting the condemned men, and Muhammad enticed his mother from the city by persuading her that he wished to consult her regarding the assignment of a share of the kingdom to his brother, Hassan Khān. She had no sooner left Jaunpur than Hassan Khān was murdered, and as she remained at Kanauj to mourn her son, Muhammad insulted her grief by the brutal taunt that she would save herself trouble by mourning at the same time for her other sons, who would presently follow Hasan to the grave. The threat put the princes on their guard, and by persuading the tyrant that Buhlūl was about to make a night attack on his camp they induced him to place at their disposal 30,000 horse and thirty elephants, wherewith to meet it. With this force Hussain Khān, the king's elder surviving brother, withdrew from the camp, followed by Buhlūl, who perceived in the movement a menace to his lines of communication. He intercepted Hussain Khān's younger

---

[1] In 27° 32′ N. and 79° 30′ E

[2] In 26° 58′ N. and 78° 36′ E

brother, Jalāl Khān, who was attempting to join him, and detained him as a hostage for Qutb Khān Lodī, who had by some means escaped assassination. Muhammad Shāh, now aware of the defection of his brothers, retreated towards the Ganges, followed by Buhlūl, but, on approaching Kanauj, discovered that his power was gone, and that his brother Husain had there been acclaimed as king. Muhammad was deserted by the few nobles who remained with him and was slain while attempting, with a few personal adherents, to defend himself against an attack from the army which had lately been his own.

Husain Shāh surrendered Qutb Khān Lodī to Buhlūl, receiving in return his brother, Jalāl Khān, and the two monarchs concluded a four years' truce, which both observed, Husain because his ambition found another outlet, and Buhlūl because he required a period of peace in which to consolidate his power and develop his resources.

Husain's military strength far exceeded that of Buhlūl, for, if the historians are to be believed, he was able, after concluding peace, to assemble an army of 300,000, with 1,400 elephants, for a predatory incursion into Orissa, where Kapileshwar Deva, of the Solar line, had established his authority in 1434. The numbers may be exaggerated, but without a very numerous army Husain could not have risked an advance to distant Orissa through or along the frontier of the intervening kingdom of Bengal, still less a retreat, laden with spoil. His first step was to crush the now virtually independent landholders of Tirhut, which province was devastated and plundered. He then marched on to Orissa, where the depredations of his great army overawed the raja and induced him to purchase peace by the payment of an immense ransom in elephants, horses, money, and valuable goods, which is represented by Muslim vanity as the first instalment of an annual tribute.

In 1466, after his return from Orissa, he sent an army to capture the fortress of Gwalior, where Raja Mān Singh still maintained his independence of both Jaunpur and Delhi, but the expedition was only partly successful, and after a protracted siege the army retired on the payment of an indemnity by the raja.

The four years' truce with Delhi, concluded on the king's accession in 1458, was long expired, and in 1473 Husain, urged by his wife Jalīla, a daughter of 'Alam Shāh, the last Sayyid king of Delhi, now living contentedly in inglorious retirement at Budaun, entered upon a series of campaigns, having for their object the conquest and annexation of Delhi.

He marched with a large army to the eastern bank of the Jumna, a few miles to the south-east of Delhi, and Buhlūl, who could put into the field no more than 18,000 horse, was so dismayed by the imminence of his peril that he attempted to secure peace by offering to retain only the city of Delhi and the country for thirty-six miles round it, and to govern this district as Husain's vassal. The offer was rejected, and Buhlūl marched from the city to meet his powerful enemy. The armies were encamped on opposite banks of the Jumna, which, for some days, neither ventured to cross in force, but Husain Shāh, in his contempt of his opponent, neglected all military precautions, and was accustomed to permit nearly the whole of his army to disperse for the purpose of plundering the rich villages of the Doāb. Buhlūl, observing this, crossed the river in force and suddenly attacked his camp. There was no force to oppose him, and Husain was compelled to flee, leaving not only his camp, but the ladies of his harem, in the victor's hands. The latter were generously sent by Buhlūl unharmed to Jaunpur.

A new treaty was now made, and a truce of three years was agreed upon, but was broken in the following year by Husain, who, at the instigation of his wife, marched with an army of 100,000 horse and 1000 elephants to Etāwah, held by Qutb Khān Lodī. Etāwah was captured at once, and Husain marched on Delhi. Buhlūl again sued, in the humblest guise, for peace, but his entreaties were disregarded, and when he took the field he again defeated Husain, but was not strong enough to profit by his success and was fain to agree to peace. Shortly afterwards Husain marched on Delhi for the third time, but was defeated at Sikhera, about twenty-five miles east of the city, and retreated to Etāwah. Qutb Khān Lodī had been permitted to retain his fief on swearing fealty to Husain, and now waited on him. On learning that Husain still entertained the design of conquering Delhi the wily Afghān went about to mislead him, and, after disparaging Buhlūl, promised that he would never rest until he had conquered Delhi for Jaunpur. Husain was completely deceived and allowed Qutb Khān to leave his camp. He joined Buhlūl at Delhi and put him on his guard against Husain, of whose determination he warned him.

The fugitive 'Alam Shāh, Husain's father-in-law, now died, and his death supplied Husain with a pretext for visiting Budaun, of which district he dispossessed his brother-in-law, 'Alam Shāh's son. From Budaun he marched to Sambhal, captured Tātār Khān Lodī, who held the district for Buhlūl, and sent him a prisoner to Sāran, in Tirhut. He then again assembled his army for an attack on

Delhi, and in March, 1479, encamped on the eastern bank of the Jumna. This appeared, of all Husain's campaigns, to offer the fairest prospect of success. He had been victorious on the east of the Ganges, his numbers were overwhelming, and Buhlūl Lodī and his officers were even more depressed than on former occasions. Qutb Khān was, however, enabled to serve his kinsman by appealing to Husain's filial affection. He invoked the memory of Bībī Rājī, Husain's mother, who had befriended him when he was a prisoner at Jaunpur, and conjured the invader to leave Delhi unmolested. Husain was so affected that he agreed to retire on obtaining Buhlūl recognition of his tenure of his new conquests to the east of the Ganges, corresponding to the modern province of Rohilkhand. The recognition was readily accorded and Husain began a leisurely retreat towards Jaunpur. He had so frequently violated treaties that Buhlūl considered himself justified in following his example, and perfidiously attacked the retreating army and captured a large number of elephants and horses laden with spoil and treasure, and the persons of Husain's minister and about forty of his principal nobles.

This success marks the turn of the tide in favour of Delhi, and Buhlūl pursued the demoralised army of Jaunpur and occupied and annexed the sub districts of Kampil, Patiālī, Shamsābād, Suket, Koīl, Mārahra, and Jalesar. Husain, when hard pressed by Buhlūl's pursuit, turned and faced him, but was defeated, and when peace was made was obliged to acquiesce in Bahlūl's retention of the considerable tract which he had recovered, and to withdraw the frontier of his kingdom to Chhibrāman, sixteen miles south of the modern town of Farrukhābād.

Buhlūl returned to Delhi and Husain retired to Rāprī, but was soon in arms again to recover his lost territory, and met Buhlūl at Suhnuh[1]. On this occasion he suffered the heaviest defeat which he had yet experienced, and the plunder which fell into Buhlūl's hands, and the military renown which he acquired with his victory turned the scale in favour of Delhi. Buhlūl encamped at Chhibrāmau and shortly afterwards resumed the offensive against Husain and defeated him at Rāprī. Husain fled towards Gwalior, and, after losing some of his wives and children in his passage of the Jumna, was attacked near Athgāth on the Chambal by the Bhadauriyas, a predatory tribe, who plundered his camp. Kirat Singh of Gwalior, who still retained confidence in his cause, supplied him with a large sum of money, a contingent of troops, tents, horses, elephants, and

[1] In 27° 21′ N. and 78° 48′ E.

camels, and personally escorted him as far as Kālpī on his way back
to Jaunpur.

Buhlūl marched, after his victory, on Etāwah, which was still
tributary to Jaunpur, captured the fort after a siege of three days,
and then turned to attack Husain, who awaited him opposite Rāigāon
Khāgā[1], on the Ganges, and was still strong enough to deter him for
some months from attempting to force the passage of the river, until
Raja Tilok Chand, whose estate lay on the north of the Ganges
joined him, and led his army across by a ford. Husain then retreated to Phāphāmau, six miles north of Allahabad, the raja of which
place escorted him in safety to Jaunpur Buhlūl marched directly on
Jaunpur, and Husain fled by a circuitous route towards Kanauj, but
Buhlūl pursued him, attacked him before he could reach that city,
and defeated him, capturing one of his wives. He then returned to
Jaunpur, took the city, placed Mubārak Khān Lohānī there as
governor, established a garrison under the command of Qutb Khān
Lodī at Majhaulī[2], beyond the Gogra, and marched to recover
Budaun, which was still nominally subject to Husain. Husain took
advantage of his absence from the neighbourhood of Jáunpur to
reassemble his army and march on that city, and Mubārak Khān,
who was not strong enough to withstand him, withdrew to Majhaulī
and joined Qutb Khān. Husain followed him thither, and the Afghān
officers, who hesitated to risk a battle, feigned to negotiate, and thus
gave Buhlūl time to return from Budaun and reoccupy Jáunpur. A
force under his son Bārbak had already relieved the garrison of
Majhaulī, and Husain, at length despairing of recovering his
kingdom, fled into Bihar, followed by Buhlūl as far as Haldī, on the
Ganges near Ballia.

With Hussain's flight the line of the Sharqī kings of Jaunpur
came to an end. Buhlūl established his son Bārbak as governor of
Jaunpur, and gave him permission to use the royal title and to coin
money, specimens of which, issued by him before his father's death,
are extant.

Husain lived in Bengal under the protection of Shams-ud-dīn
Yūsuf Shāh and his successors on the throne of that kingdom until
1500, but made no attempt to recover his throne beyond fomenting
the strife between Bārbak and his younger brother, Sikandar, who
succeeded their father on the throne of Delhi in 1489. His hope
that the quarrel might open a way for his return to his former
kingdom was frustrated, for Sikandar overcame Bārbak and Jaunpur

---

[1] In 25° 53′ N. and 81° 16′ E.

[2] In 26° 17′ N. and 83° 57′ E.

was absorbed in the kingdom of Delhi, and Husain died in exile in circumstances not widely different from those in which his father-in law, the former king of Delhi, died at Budaun.

The Sharqī dynasty reigned in Jaunpur for rather more than eighty years, and in that period produced one king of happy memory, Ibrāhīm, the patron of learning and of architecture. For a dynasty whose rule was so brief the Sharqīs have left very creditable memorials in their public buildings, and the enlightenment which earned for Jaunpur in Ibrāhīm's reign, the title of 'the Shīrāz of India' is surprising in one of negro blood. Malik Sarvar, who founded the dynasty, was a eunuch, and could therefore have no heirs of his body. His two successors were his adopted sons, the brothers Mubārak Shāh and Ibrāhīm Shāh, probably slaves. Mubārak's name, before he assumed the royal title, was Qaranful, 'the Clove,' a contemptuous term of endearment appropriated to African slaves. No portraits of the period are known to exist, but there appears to be no reason to doubt that the kings of Jaunpur were of negro descent. The character of Husain, the last of the line, is perplexing and disappointing. He was a man of ideas, with wide opportunities, and resources commensurate with both, ever on the point of realising some great scheme of aggrandisement and ever missing his opportunity through carelessness, folly, and perhaps physical cowardice.

CHAPTER XI

THE KINGDOM OF BENGAL

It must not be supposed that the province of Bengal, conquered for Muhammad *bin* Sām and Qutb-ud-dīn Aibak by Muhammad Bakhtyār the Khalj, was conterminous with the Lower Provinces of Bengal which were governed until 1905 by a Lieutenant Governor. Before the Muhammadan conquest Bengal was divided into five regions, (1) Rādha, the country west of the Hughlī and south of the Ganges ; (2) Bāgdī, the delta of the Ganges and Brāhmaputra ; (3) Banga, the country to the east of the delta ; (4) Bārendra, the country to the north of the Padma and between the Karatoya and the Mahānandā rivers ; and (5) Mithila, the country west of the Mahānandā. Muhammad Bakhtyār took possession of the south-eastern parts of Mithila, Bārendra, the northern district of Rādha, and the north-western district of Bāgdī. The Muhammadan province and kingdom of Bengal was long confined to this territory, which was commonly known, from the name of its capital, as Lakhnāwatī, but was subsequently extended into Banga and the western districts of Rādha, which included Jhārkhand, or Chota Nāgpur.

The course of events in Bengal during the period of its dependence on Delhi, which was its normal condition until 1338, has already been traced. Although the country was regarded until that time as a province the loyalty of its governors was always, owing to the distance which separated Lakhnāwatī from Delhi, and climatic conditions which rendered military operations impossible for many months in each year, a very uncertain quantity. It depended almost entirely on the king's ability to command obedience, and the dubious attitude of the governors of Lakhnāwatī to the central authority became a byword at Delhi. The royal title was occasionally assumed, as by 'Alī Mardān, who obtained the government from Qutb-ud-dīn Aibak after the death of Muhammad Bakhtyār, and by Ghiyās-ud-dīn the Khalj, who succeeded 'Ali Mardān. The first serious rebellion against a strong king of Delhi was that of Tughril against Balban, and the first instance of the unquestioned use of the royal title in Bengal was that of Nāsir-ud-dīn Mahmūd, the contemptible father of the still more contemptible Mu'izz-ud-dīn, Balban's successor on the throne of Delhi. The father was content with the sovereignty of Bengal, and outlived the son, who was unfit to wield the sceptre of Delhi. Mahmūd, on his death in 1291, was succeeded by his next surviving son, Rukn-ud-dīn Kaikāūs, who, though he used the royal title and coined money in his own name, owned allegiance to 'Alā-ud-dīn Khaljī of Delhi.

Kaikāūs died in 1302, and was succeeded by his next brother, Shams-ud-dīn Fīrūz, who reigned obscurely until his death in 1318, when his eldest son, Shihāb-ud-dīn Bughrā and his third son,

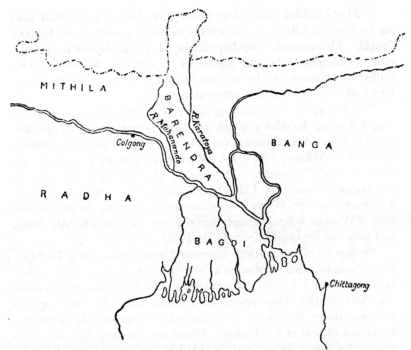

SKETCH MAP OF THE ANCIENT DIVISIONS OF BENGAL

Ghiyās-ud-dīn Bahādur, contended for the kingdom. The Muslims had by this time extended their rule into Bang, or Eastern Bengal, and Bahādur had established himself, before his father's death, at Sonārgāon, in the present district of Dacca, and when Bughrā ascended the throne in Lakhnāwatī he attacked and defeated him. Bughrā died, or was slain, and his next brother, Nāsir-ud-dīn, who was older than Bahādur, ascended the throne and in 1324 sought the assistance of Ghiyās-ud-dīn Tughluq[1] of Delhi against his

—————————
[1] See Chapter VI.

brother. Tughluq marched into Bengal, established Nāsir-ud-dīn on the throne of Lakhnāwatī, and carried Bahādur a captive to Delhi.

Muhammad Tughluq, immediately after his accession, restored Bahādur to the government of Sonārgāon, or Eastern Bengal, but associated with him, as a precautionary measure, Tātār Khān, better known by his later title of Bahrām Khān. Shortly afterwards Muhammad appointed Malik Bīdār Khaljī, Qadr Khān, to the government of Lakhnāwatī and 'Izz-ud-dīn A'zam-ul-Mulk to that of Satgāon.

In 1330 Bahādur rebelled in Sonārgāon, but was defeated and put to death and Bahrām Khān remained sole governor of Eastern Bengal. Muhammad Tughluq displayed the vindictive temper for which he afterwards became notorious by causing Bahādur's skin, stuffed with straw, to be exhibited throughout the provinces of the kingdom as a warning to disaffected governors.

The history of Bengal during the period immediately preceding and following Bahrām's death in 1336 is extraordinarily obscure. Bahrām either died a natural death or was slain by his chief armour-bearer, who had acquired great influence in the state and on his master's death assumed in Sonārgāon the royal title of Fakhr-ud-dīn Mubārak Shāh. In 1339 Qadr Khān died at Lakhnāwatī, and the muster-master of his forces caused himself to be proclaimed king of Western Bengal under the title of 'Alā-ud-dīn 'Alī Shāh, and removed his capital from Lakhnāwatī to Pāndua.

Neither rebel had much to apprehend from Muhammad Tughluq, whose long course of tyranny was now bearing fruit in these rebellions which led to the disintegration of his kingdom, and 'Alā-ud-dīn 'Alī's transfer of his capital to Pāndua seems to have been a strategic move calculated to bring him within striking distance of his rival's capital at Sonārgāon. Hostilities between the two continued for some years, and in 1349 Mubārak disappears from the scene. He can hardly have been defeated and put to death, as stated by the chroniclers, who place the event some years earlier, by 'Alī, for he was succeeded in Eastern Bengal by his son, Ikhtiyār-ud dīn Ghāzī Shāh, and 'Alī himself was no longer reigning in 1349, for his foster-brother, Malik Iliyās, who had been contending with varying success for the crown of Western Bengal ever since 'Alī had assumed the royal title, caused him to be assassinated in 1345, and ascended the throne under the title of Shams-ud-dīn Iliyās Shāh. He was nicknamed *Bhangara* from his addiction to the preparation of hemp known as *bhang*. There is some authority for the statement that he captured and slew Mubārak of Sonārgāon, but he did not obtain possession of Sonārgāon until 1352, when Ghāzī Shāh was expelled. Iliyās is also said to have invaded Jājnagar, as the Muslim historians style the kingdom of Jājpur[1] in Orissa, and there to have taken many elephants and much plunder. He also invaded the south-eastern provinces of the kingdom of Delhi and overran Tirhut, thus incurring the resentment of Fīrūz Tughluq, whose punitive expedition against him has already been described[2]. Iliyās was compelled to leave his capital, Pāndua, at the mercy of the invader, and to retire to Ikdāla, where he offered a successful resistance. The victory described by the sycophantic historians of Delhi was infructuous, for Fīrūz was obliged to retreat without obtaining from Iliyās even a formal recognition of his sovereignty, and, though he is said to have remitted tribute to Fīrūz in 1354 and 1358, the truth seems to be that he merely accredited envoys to Delhi who bore with them the complimentary presents which eastern custom demands on such occasions. In December, 1356, Fīrūz formally recognised the independence of Bengal, and the gifts borne by his mission were at least as valuable as those received by him from Iliyās. These gifts, however, never reached their destination, for the envoy, Saif-ud-dīn, heard when he reached Bihār of the death of Iliyās and the accession of his son Sikandar, and applied to his master for instructions regarding their disposal. Fīrūz, notwithstanding his treaty with Iliyās, directed that they should be distributed among the nobles of Bihār and recalled Saif-ud-dīn to Delhi to assist in the preparations for an invasion of Bengal. Some pretext for this breach of faith was furnished by a refugee who had recently arrived at his court. This was Zafar Khān, son-in-law to Mubārak of Eastern Bengal, whom, according to his own account, he had had some expectation of succeeding. The conquest of Eastern Bengal by Iliyās had compelled him to seek safety in flight, and after many vicissitudes he reached Delhi, where he was well content with the position of a courtier until his wrongs suggested themselves to the king as a pretext for invading and conquering Bengal. His advance to Bengal has already been described in Chapter vii, and while he halted at Zafarābād, engaged in superintending the building of Jaunpur, he received envoys from Sikandar, bearing valuable gifts. These he meanly retained, while persisting in his design of invading Bengal. Sikandar, like his father, took refuge in Ikdāla, and so completely

---

[1] In 20° 51′ N. and 80° 20′ E.
[2] See Chapter VII.

baffled Fīrūz that when he opened negotiations for peace he demanded and obtained most favourable terms. He is said to have been obliged to agree to send to Delhi an annual tribute of forty elephants and to surrender Sonārgāon to Zafar Khān. The latter condition was never fulfilled, owing, as the Delhi historians say, to Zafar Khān's preferring the security of Delhi to the precarious tenure of a fief in Sikandar's dominions, and if the tribute was ever paid Sikandar obtained an equivalent in the formal recognition of his independence, a jewelled crown worth 80,000 *tangas*, and 500) Arab and Turkmān horses ; and Bengal was no more molested.

Sikandar had seventeen sons by his first wife, and only one, Ghiyās-ud-dīn A'zam, the ablest and most promising of them all, by his second. A'zam's stepmother, in order to secure the succession of one of her own sons, lost no opportunity of traducing him to his father, and at length succeeded in arousing his apprehensions to such an extent that in 1370 he fled to Sonārgāon and assumed the royal title in Eastern Bengal. Sikandar, who had never believed the calumnies against A'zam, left him unmolested for several years, but in 1389 marched against him. The armies of the father and the son met at Goālpāra, and although A'zam had given orders that his father was to be taken alive, Sikandar was mortally wounded, and died, after the battle, in his son's arms, forgiving him with his latest breath. The throne was the victor's prize, and one of A'zam's first acts after his accession was to blind all his stepbrothers and send their eyes to their mother. He is more pleasantly remembered as the correspondent of the great poet Hāfiz[1], who sent him the ode beginning.

ساقی حدیث سرو وكل ولالہ میرود ٭ وین بحث با ثلا ثۀ غسالہ میرود

Of the circumstances in which the ode was composed and sent a graceful story is told. A'zam, stricken down by a dangerous malady, abandoned hope of life and directed that three girls of his hare.n, named 'Cypress,' 'Rose,' and 'Tulip' should wash his corpse and prepare it for burial. He escaped death and, attributing his

[1] Dr Stanley Lane-Poole, at p. 307 of *The Mohammadan Dynasties*, gives 1389 as the date of A'zam's accession in Pāndua, but Hāfiz died in 1388 so that unless A'zam's accession in Pāndua is antedated it must be assumed that he enjoyed royal honours in Sonārgāon before his father's death. There is no doubt as to the identity of the king addressed by Hāfiz, for the poet, after saying that he is sending some Persian sugar to Bengal for the parrots of India, closes his ode thus;

حافظ زشوق مجلس سلطان غیاث دین ٭ خامش مشوك كارتو از نالہ میرود

recovery to the auspicious influence of the three girls, made them his favourites. Their advancement excited the jealousy of the other inmates of the harem, who applied to them the odious epithet *ghassāla*, or corpse-washer. One day the king, in merry mood with his three favourites, uttered as an impromptu the opening hemistich for the ode, 'Cupbearer, the tale now runs of the Cypress, the Rose, and the Tulip,' and finding that neither he nor any poet at his court could continue the theme satisfactorily, sent his effusion to Hāfiz at Shīrāz, who developed the hemistich into an ode and completed the first couplet with the hemistich :

'And the argument is sustained with the help of three morning draughts.'

the word used for 'morning draught' being the same as that used for 'corpse-washer'[1]. The *double entendre*, said to have been fortuitous, was more efficacious even than the king's favour, and secured the three reigning beauties from molestation.

Another story also exhibits A'zam in a pleasing light. One day, while practising with his bow and arrow he accidently wounded the only son of a widow. The woman appealed for justice to the *qāzī*, who sent an officer to summon the king to his court. The officer gained access to the royal presence by a stratagem and unceremoniously served the summons. A'zam, after concealing a short sword beneath his arm, obeyed the summons and, on appearing before the judge, was abruptly charged with his offence and commanded to indemnify the complainant. After a short discussion of terms the woman was compensated, and the judge, on ascertaining that she was satisfied, rose, made his reverence to the king, and seated him on a throne which had been prepared for his reception. The king, drawing his sword, turned to the *qāzī* and said, 'Well, judge, you have done your duty. If you had failed in it by a hair's breadth I would have taken your head off with this sword !' The *qāzī* placed his hand under the cushion on which the king was seated, and, producing a scourge, said, 'O king! You have obeyed the law. Had you failed in this duty your back should have been scarified with this scourge !' A'zam, appreciating the *qāzī*'s manly independence, richly rewarded him. If this story be true Bengal can boast of a prince more law-abiding than Henry of Monmouth and of a judge at least as firm as Gascoigne.

It is said that A'zam, alarmed by the growth of the power of the eunuch Khvāja Jahān of Jaunpur remitted to him the arrears of tribute due to the king of Delhi, but there is no evidence that

1 The analogy is apparent.

tribute had ever been remitted to Delhi, and the sum sent to Khvāja Jahān was perhaps a complimentary present.

Little more is known of A'zam except that he died in 1396, and even the manner of his death is uncertain. Most historians mention it casually, as though it were due to natural causes, but one author asserts that it was brought about by Raja Ganesh of Dinājpur, a Hindu chieftain who is styled Raja Kāns by most Muslim historians and ultimately ruled Bengal for several years. A'zam was, however, peaceably succeeded by his son, Saif-ud-dīn Hamza Shāh, the obscurity of whose reign ill accords with the grandiose title of *Sultān-us-Salātīn*, or king of kings, bestowed upon him by some chroniclers, though it does not appear on his known coins. He was defeated in 1404 by Ganesh, but continued to reign until his death in 1406, though it appears that the influence of Ganesh was dominant in Bengal from the time of his victory. Shams-ud-dīn, a son or adopted son of Hamza, was permitted to ascend the throne, but exercised no power, and died after a reign of little more than three years. Muslim historians describe Ganesh as a sovereign ruling Bengal in his own name, but he has left neither coins nor inscriptions, and it would seem that he was content with the power of royalty without aspiring to its outward tokens, for coins prove that the puppet Shams-ud-dīn was succeeded by another puppet Shihāb-ud-dīn Bāyazīd, whose parentage is doubtful. There is no less difference of opinion regarding the character than regarding the status of Ganesh. According to some accounts he secretly accepted Islam, and according to one tolerated it and remained on the best of terms with its professors, while remaining a Hindu, but the most detailed record which has been preserved represents him as a Hindu bigot whose persecution of Muslims caused Qutb-ul-'Ālam, a well-known Muslim saint of Bengal, to invoke the aid of Ibrāhīm Shāh of Jaunpur. Ibrāhīm invaded Bengal, and Ganesh is said to have sought, in his terror, the intercession of Qutb-ul-'Ālam, who refused to intercede for a misbeliever. Ganesh considered conversion as a means of escape from his difficulties, but eventually compounded with Qutb-ul-'Ālam by surrendering to him his son, Jadu or Jatmall, in order that he might be converted to Islam and proclaimed king, by which means the country might escape the horrors of a religious war. Qutb-ul-'Ālam accepted the charge, but discovered, after he had, with great difficulty, prevailed upon Ibrāhīm Sharqī to retire, that he had been the dupe of Ganesh, who treated the proclamation of his son as a farce, persecuted Muslims more zealously than ever, and attempted to reclaim the renegade. The

ceremonial purification of the lad was accomplished by the costly
rite of passing him through golden images of cows, which were
afterwards broken up and distributed in charity to Brāhmans, but
the young convert obstinately refused to return to the faith of his
fathers, and was imprisoned. The discredited saint suffered for his
folly by being compelled to witness the persecution of his nearest
and dearest, but in 1414 death came to the relief of the Muslims of
Bengal and the convert was raised to the throne under the title of
Jalāl-ud-dīn Muhammad, and persecuted the Hindus as his father
had persecuted the Muslims. The Brāhmans who had arranged or
profited by the ineffectual purification of the new king were permanently defiled by being obliged to swallow the flesh of the animal
which they adored, and hosts of Hindus are said to have been forcibly converted to Islam.

The general attitude of the Muslim rulers of Bengal to their
Hindu subjects was one of toleration, but it is evident, from the
numerical superiority in Eastern Bengal of Muslims who are certainly not the descendants of dominant invaders, that at some period
an immense wave of proselytisation must have swept over the
country, and it is most probable that that period was the reign of
Jalāl-ud-dīn Muhammad, who appears to have been inspired by the
zeal proper to a convert, and by a hatred of the religion which had
prompted his imprisonment, and had ample leisure, during a reign
of seventeen years, for the propagation of his new faith.

On his death in 1431 he was succeeded by his son, Shams-ud-
dīn Ahmad, who reigned until 1442, but of whose reign little is
known, except that Bengal suffered at this time from the aggression
of Ibrāhīm Sharqī of Jaunpur. Ahmad is said to have appealed
to Sultān Shāhrukh, son of Tīmūr, who addressed to Ibrāhīm a
remonstrance which proved effectual. Towards the end of Ahmad's
reign his tyranny became unbearable, and he was put to death by
conspirators headed by Shādī Khān and Nāsir Khān, two of his
principal officers of state, who had originally been slaves and owed
their advancement to his favour. Each had designs upon the throne,
but Nāsir Khān forestalled his confederate and, having put him to
death, assumed the sovereignty of Bengal under the title of Nāsir-
ud-dīn Mahmūd. He claimed descent from Iliyās, and in his person
the line of the house which had compelled Delhi to recognise the
independence of Bengal was restored.

Mahmūd reigned peacefully for seventeen years, for the warfare
between Jaunpur and Delhi relieved Bengal of the aggressions of
its western neighbour, and left the king leisure for the indulgence of

his taste in architecture. He rebuilt the old capital, Gaur, and built a mosque at Satgāon, but we know little else of him. He died in 1459, and was succeeded by his son, Rukn-ud-dīn Bārbak, who died in 1474. He was the first king in India to advance African slaves in large numbers to high rank, and is said to have had no less than 8000 of these slaves, who afterwards became a danger to the kingdom. He was succeeded on his death by his son Shams-ud-dīn Yūsuf, a precisian who insisted on the rigid observance of the Islamic law and prohibited the use of wine in his dominions. On his death in 1481 the courtiers raised to the throne his son Sikandar, a youth whose intellect was so deranged that he was almost immediately deposed in favour of his great-uncle, Jalāl-ud-dīn Fath Shāh, a son of Mahmūd. Fath Shāh was a wise and beneficent ruler, but incurred the hostility of the African slaves who thronged the court by curbing their insolence and punishing their excesses. The malcontents elected as their leader a eunuch named Sultān Shāhzāda, and took advantage of the absence from court, on a distant expedition, of Indīl Khān, who, though an African, was a loyal subject of Fath Shāh and an able military commander, to compass the king's death. The guard over the palace consisted of no less than 5000 men, and it was the king's custom to appear early in the morning at the relief of the guard and receive the salutes of both guards. The eunuch corrupted the officers of the palace guards, and one morning in 1486, when the king came forth, as usual, to take the salute, caused him to be assassinated and usurped the throne under the title of Bārbak Shāh.

Indīl Khān, at his distant post, heard of the tragedy and was considering on what pretext he could lead his troops to the capital to avenge his master's death when he received a summons from Bārbak. He welcomed the opportunity and hastened with his troops to Gaur, where his influence and the armed force at his command rendered his position secure. He found that the eunuch's rule was already unpopular, and allowed it to be understood that he was a partisan of the old royal house, which was not yet extinct. Bārbak was apprehensive of his designs, and when he appeared at court insisted that he should take an oath not to injure or betray him. A copy of the Koran was produced, and Indīl Khān, who could not refuse the oath, added to it the reservation that he would not injure Bārbak so long as he was on the throne; but he interpreted the reservation literally, and, having bribed the ushers and doorkeepers of the court, awaited an opportunity of avenging the murder of Fath Shāh. This soon presented itself when the eunuch fell into a drunken slumber. Indīl Khān forced his way into the royal apartment, but finding that Bārbak had fallen asleep on the cushions which composed the throne, hesitated to violate the letter of his oath, and was about to withdraw when the drunkard rolled heavily over on to the floor. Indīl Khān at once struck at him with his sword, but the blow failed of its effect, and Bārbak, suddenly waking sprang upon him and grappled with him. His strength and weight enabled him to throw his adversary and sit on his chest, but Indīl Khān called to Yaghrush Khān, a Turkish officer whom he had left without, and who now rushed in with a number of faithful Africans. The lamps had been overturned and extinguished in the struggle, and Indīl's followers hesitated to strike in the darkness, lest they should injure their master, but he encouraged them by shouting that their knives would not reach him through the eunuch's gross body, and they stabbed Bārbak repeatedly in the back. He rolled over and feigned death, and they retired, satisfied that their task was done. After they had left a slave entered to relight the lamps, and Bārbak, fearing the return of Indīl Khān, lay still. The slave cried out that the king was dead, and Bārbak recognising his voice, bade him be silent and asked what had become of Indīl Khān. The slave replied that he had gone home, and Bārbak, who believed the man to be faithful to himself, issued an order for the execution of Indīl Khān. The slave left the chamber, but instead of delivering the order to any who might have executed it, went at once to Indīl Khān and told him that his enemy yet lived. Indīl Khān returned to the palace, stabbed Bārbak to death, and, sending for the minister, Khānjahān, consulted him regarding the filling of the vacant throne, the rightful heir to which was a child of two years of age. In the morning the courtiers waited upon Fath Shāh's widow, who urged the avenger of her husband's blood to ascend the throne. Indīl Khān, after a decent display of reluctance, accepted the charge, and was proclaimed, a few months after the assassination of Fath Shāh, by the title of Saif-ul-dīn Fīrūz. His elevation established an unfortunate precedent, and historians observe that it was henceforth an accepted rule in Bengal that he who slew a king's murderer acquired a right to the throne.

Fīrūz had already distinguished himself as a soldier and administrator, and during his short reign of three years he healed the disorders of the kingdom and restored the discipline of the army. His fault was prodigality, and despite the warnings and protests of his counsellors he wasted the public treasure by lavishing it on beggars.

On his death in 1489 the nobles raised to the throne, under the title of Nāsīr-ud-dīn Mahmūd II, the surviving son of Fath Shāh. Owing to the king's youth the administration was necessarily carried on by his counsellors, and all power in the state fell into the hands of an African entitled Habash Khān, whose monopoly of power excited the discontent of the other courtiers, one of whom, an African known as Sīdī Badr the Madman, slew him and took his place. Sīdī Badr's ambition was purely selfish, and in 1490 he caused the young king to be put to death and himself ascended the throne under the bombastic title of Shams-ud-dīn Abu-Nasr Muzaffar Shāh. This bloodthirsty monster, in the course of a reign of three years, put most of the leading men in the kingdom to death. The only measure in which he displayed wisdom was his choice of a minister, which rested on 'Alā-ud-dīn Husain, a Sayyid of a family which came from Tirmiz, on the Oxus, and a man respectable alike by reason of his lineage, his ability, and his personal character. He probably restrained Muzaffar's violence, and he served him faithfully as long as it was possible to do so, but the African developed the vice of avarice, fatal to a ruler whose authority depends upon the sword. and committed at once the crime of enhancing the burdens of his people and the blunder of diminishing the emoluments of his army. Sayyid Husain could no longer maintain his master's authority, and, wearied by protests against the tyranny with which his position in a measure identified him, withdrew his supports, and immediately found himself the leader of a revolt. The troops, placing him at their head, besieged the king for four months in Gaur. The contest was terminated by the death of the king, who perished in a sortie which he led from the fortress. The nobles, after some consultation, elected Sayyid Husain king in 1493, on receiving from him guarantees which bore some resemblance to a European constitution of 1848.

The new king's full title appears from inscriptions to have been Sayyid-us-Sādāt 'Alā-ud-dīn Abu-'l-Muzaffar Shāh Husain Sultān bin Sayyid Ashraf al-Husainī, and it is possible that to his father's name Ashraf may be traced the belief of some historians that he was descended from or connected with the Sharīfs of Mecca. He proved to be worthy of the confidence reposed in him, and inaugurated his reign by issuing orders for the cessation of plundering in Gaur. The orders were not at once obeyed, and the punishment of the refractory was prompt and severe, though the statement that he put 12,000 plunderers to death on this occasion is probably an exaggeration. The booty recovered from those who suffered for their disobedience enriched the royal treasury.

Husain Shāh transferred his capital from Gaur to Ikdāla probably with the object of punishing the people of Gaur for their support of Muzaffar's cause, but his successor restored Gaur to its former pre-eminence.

Husain was, with the exception of Iliyās, the greatest of the Muslim kings of Bengal. Among his earliest reforms were two very necessary measures, the first of which was the destruction of the power of the large force of *pāiks*, or Hindu infantry, which had long been employed as the guards of the palace and of the royal person, and had gradually, during several preceding reigns, acquired a position analogous to that of the Praetorian Guards at Rome. A great part of the corps was disbanded, and the remainder was employed at a distance from the capital, and the duty of guarding the king's person was entrusted to Muslim troops. The second reform was the expulsion from the kingdom of all Africans, whose numbers had greatly increased and whose presence, since some of them had tasted the sweets of power, was a danger to the throne. During the seventeen years preceding Husain's accession three kings of this race had occupied the throne, and there was some reason to fear that the negroes might become a ruling caste. The exiles in vain sought an asylum in Delhi and Jaunpur, where they were too well known to be welcome, and most of them ultimately drifted to the Deccan and Gujarāt, where men of their race had for many years been largely employed.

In 1495 Husain Shāh, the last of the Sharqī kings of Jaunpur, having been driven from his kingdom by Sikandar Lodī of Delhi, fled for refuge to Bengal, and was hospitably accommodated by 'Alā-ud-dīn Husain Shāh at Kahalgāon (Colgong), where he lived in retirement until his death in 1500.

Husain, having established order in the neighbourhood of the capital, carried his arms into those districts which had formerly been included in the kingdom of Bengal, but had, during the disorders of the six preceding reigns, fallen away from a trunk too feeble to support branches. He recovered the lost provinces as far as the borders of Orissa to the south, and, having thus established his authority at home, turned his attention to foreign conquest, and in 1498 invaded the kingdom of Assam, then ruled by Nilāmbar, the third and last reign of the Khen dynasty. Husain led his army as far as Kāmrūp and, after a long siege, captured Kāmalapur, Nilāmbar's capital, by stratagem. Other rulers Rūp

Nārāyan, Māl Kunwar, Gosāl Khen, and Sachhmī Nārāyan, are mentioned by a Muslim historian as having been overcome in this campaign. They were probably governors of provinces of Nilāmbar's kingdom.

Husain, on returning to his capital, placed one of his sons in command of his new conquest, but the raja, who had fled to the hills, took advantage of the rainy season, when the state of the roads and rivers rendered the arrival of reinforcements and supplies impossible, to descend into the plains and attack the foreign garrison, which he put to the sword. Husain made no attempt to avenge this defeat or to recover Assam, but devoted his attention to securing his frontiers, and to the building of mosques and almshouses, for the maintenance of which he provided by endowments of land. He died a natural death in 1518, after a reign of twenty-five years and was succeeded by his eldest son, Nasīb Khān, who assumed the title of Nāsir-ud-dīn Nusrat Shāh.

Nusrat Shāh, who had, before his accession exercised almost regal power as governor of Bāgdī, or the Ganges delta, and had coined money in his own name, was a prince of gentle disposition and strong natural affections, for he not only refrained from following the barbarous eastern custom of slaying, mutilating, or imprisoning his brothers, but doubled the provision which his father had made for them. Early in his reign he invaded Tīrhut, attacked, defeated, and slew the raja, and appointed 'Alā-ud-dīn and Makhdūm-i-Ālam, his own brothers-in-law, to the government of the reconquered province.

Nusrat had occupied the throne for seven years when Bābur invaded India, and having defeated and slain Ibrāhīm Lodī, seated himself on the throne of the kingdom of Delhi. Numbers of the Afghān nobles of Delhi and many of the late royal family fled to Bengal, and were well received by Nusrat, who bestowed fiefs upon them for their support, and married the daughter of Ibrāhīm Lodī. He made a demonstration against Bābur by sending Qutb Shāh, one of his nobles, to occupy Bahrāich, but when Bābur established his authority in Jaunpur attempted to conciliate him with gifts which would not have turned him from his purpose had the time been ripe for the invasion of Bengal. In 1532, after Bābur's death, Nusrat was alarmed by rumours of the hostile intentions of Humāyūn, and sent an envoy to Bahādur Shāh of Gujarāt in Māndū to form an alliance. The envoy was well received, but his mission was fruitless.

The Portuguese now made their first appearance in Bengal. In

1528 Martim Affonso de Mello Jusarte was sent by Nuno da Cunha, governor of the Portuguese Indies, to gain a foothold in Bengal, but was shipwrecked, and fell into the hands of Khudā Bakhsh Khān of Chakiria, south of Chatgāon (Chittagong), where he remained a prisoner until he was ransomed for £1500 by Shihāb-ud-dīn, a merchant of Chittagong. Shihāb-ud-dīn was soon afterwards in difficulties with Nusrat Shāh, and appealed to the Portuguese for help. Martim Affonso was sent in command of a trading expedition to Chittagong, and sent a mission, with presents worth about £1200 to Nusrat Shāh in Gaur. The misconduct of the Portuguese in Chittagong, and their disregard of the customs regulations incensed the king, and he ordered their arrest and the confiscation of their property. The governor of Chittagong treacherously seized their leaders at a banquet to which he had invited them, slew the private soldiers and sailors who had not time to escape to the ships, confiscated property worth £100,000, and sent his prisoners to Gaur. Nusrat Shāh demanded a ransom so exorbitant that the Portuguese authorities refused to pay it, but punished the king by burning Chittagong. This measure of reprisal in no way benefited the captives, who had from the first been harshly treated, and were now nearly starved.

Nusrat Shāh's character deteriorated towards the end of his reign, probably as a result of his debauchery, and his temper became violent. One day in 1533, as he was paying a visit to his father's tomb at Gaur he threatened with punishment for some trivial fault one of the eunuchs in his train. The eunuch, in fear of his life, persuaded his companions to join him in an attempt to destroy the tyrant, and on returning to the palace the king was put to death by the conspirators. He was succeeded by his son 'Alā-ud-din Fīrūz, who had reigned for no more than three months when he was murdered by his uncle, Ghiyās-ud-dīn Mahmūd, who had been permitted by Nusrat to wield almost royal power throughout a great part of the kingdom.

Mahmūd usurped his nephew's throne in 1533, and was almost immediately involved in trouble by the rebellion of his brother-in-law, Makhdūm-i-'Ālam, who held the fief of Hājīpur in Bihār and was leagued with the Afghān, Sher Khān Sūr of Sasseram, who had established himself in Bihār on the death of Muhammad Shāh, the Afghān who had been proclaimed by the refractory Lodī nobles king in Eastern Hindūstān. The two rebels defeated and slew Qutb Khān, governor of Monghyr who was sent against them by Mahmūd, and Sher Khān captured the elephants, material of war, and treasure of the defeated army, by means of which he was enabled immediately to increase his power and extend his influence.

The successful issue of this rebellion and the great profit reaped by Sher Khān emboldened Makhdūm-i-'Alam again to rise against Mahmūd without seeking, on this occasion, a partner who might again appropriate all the spoils, but the task was beyond his power, and he was defeated and slain. Sher Khān resolved to avenge the death of his former confederate, sent his advance guard towards Bengal, and followed it with all his available forces. The position which Mahmūd elected to defend was the narrow passage between the Rājmahall hills and the Ganges, which is strengthened by the fortress of Teliyagarhī on the south and Sikrīgalī on the north bank of the Ganges, and was known as the gate of Bengal, and he turned for assistance to his Portuguese captives, all of whom, except four, preferred action with a chance of freedom to their lingering captivity.

In this chosen position the troops of Bengal were able to stem the advance of Sher Khān's army for a whole month, and the Portuguese were the life and soul of the defence, but the invaders at length forced the position and advanced against the main body of Mahmūd's army, which met them at some spot between Teliyagarhi and Gaur, and was defeated. Mahmūd fled to Gaur, whither Sher Khān followed him, and the capital was invested. The siege, which was vigorously pressed, suffered little interruption from a rising in Bihār, for Sher Khān, who returned to suppress the disorder, was able to leave his son Jalāl Khān and Khavāss Khān, one of his officers, iṅ charge of the operations, which did not languish in their hands, and the garrison was reduced to such straits by famine that on April 6, 1538, Mahmūd led them forth and attacked the besiegers. He was defeated and put to flight, his sons were captured, and Gaur was sacked and occupied by Jalāl Khān.

Sher Khān, having restored order in Bihār, returned to Bengal and pursued Mahmūd, who, when closely pressed, turned and gave him battle, but was defeated and grievously wounded. Sher Khan entered Gaur in triumph and assumed the royal title, while Mahmūd fled for protection to Humāyūn, who, in response to an appeal from him, had taken advantage of Sher Khān's preoccupation in Bengal to capture Chunār from his officers, and had now advanced to Darvīshpur in Bihār. Sher Khān sent Jalāl Khān and Khavāss Khān to hold the gate of Bengal, and Humāyūn sent Jahāngīr Qulī Beg the Mughal to attack it. Jahāngīr Qulī's force was surprised at the end of a day's march and routed, the commander himself being wounded. Humāyūn then advanced in force to attack the position, and during his advance Mahmūd, the ex-king of Bengal, died at Kahalgāon, after learning that Sher Khān had put his two sons to death.

Jalāl Khān, who feared to encounter the whole strength of Humāyūn's army, avoided it by escaping into the hills to the south of his position, and fled thence to Gaur, where he joined his father, while Humāyūn advanced steadily towards the same place. Sher Khān, alarmed by his approach, collected his treasure and fled into Rādha, and thence into the Chota Nāgpur hills. Humāyūn entered Gaur without opposition, renamed the place Jannatābād, caused the *khutba* to be recited and coin to be struck in his name, and spent three months there in idleness and pleasure while his officers annexed Sonārgāon, Chittagong, and other ports in his name. He foolishly made no attempt to pursue Sher Khān, and lingered aimlessly at Gaur until the climate bred sickness in his army and destroyed many of his horses and camels. In the meantime Sher Khān descended from the Chota Nāgpur hills, captured the fortress of Rohtas, raided Monghyr, and put the Mughul officers there to the sword. At the same time, in 1539, Humāyūn received news of Hindāl Mīrzā's rebellion at Delhi, and was overwhelmed by the accumulation of evil tidings. After nominating Jahāngīr Qulī Beg to the government of Bengal and placing at his disposal a contingent of 5000 picked horse, he set out with all speed for Agra, but Sher Khān intercepted his retreat by marching from Rohtas to Chausa, on the Ganges. Here he was able to check Humāyūn's retreat for three months, and extorted from the emperor, as the price of an undisturbed passage for his troops, the recognition of his sovereignty in Bengal. Having thus lulled Humāyūn into a sense of security, he fell upon his army and defeated and dispersed it.

On his return to Bengal he was harassed for some time by the active hostility of Humāyūn's lieutenant, Jahāngīr Qulī Beg, but ultimately disposed of his enemy by inveigling him to an interview and causing him to be assassinated. He thus became supreme in Bengal, and the increasing confusion in the newly established Mughul empire enabled him to oust Humāyūn and ascend the imperial throne.

When he marched from Bengal in 1540 to attack Humāyūn he left Khizr Khān behind him as governor of the province. Khizr Khān's head was turned by his elevation, and though he refrained from assuming the royal title he affected so many of the airs of royalty that Sher Shāh, as soon as he was established on the imperial throne, marched into Bengal with the object of nipping his lieutenant's ambition in the bud. Khizr Khān, who was not strong enough to try conclusions with the conqueror of Delhi, welcomed his master with the customary formality of the East, and was immediately seized and thrown into prison. Sher Shāh obviated a recurrence of his offence by dividing Bengal into a number of small prefectures, the governors of which were responsible, for the regular collection and remittance of the revenue, to Qāzī Fazīlat of Agra, who was appointed supervisor of the now disintegrated kingdom of Bengal.

The independence of Bengal, due partly to the weakness and preoccupation of the sovereigns of Delhi between 1338 and 1539, and partly to the existence, between 1394 and 1476, of the buffer state of Jaunpur, dated from the later days of the reign of Muhammad Tughluq, and endured, despite the two abortive attempts of Fīrūz Tughluq to subvert it in the reigns of Iliyās and his son Sikandar, until Humāyūn destroyed it by establishing himself, for three months in 1539, on the throne of Gaur. It was restored by Sher Khān's defeat of Humāyūn at Chausa, but again destroyed by Sher Shāh after his ascent of the imperial throne.

The annals of Bengal are stained with blood, and the long list of Muslim kings contains the names of some monsters of cruelty, but it would be unjust to class them all as uncultured bigots void of sympathy with their Hindu subjects. Some certainly reciprocated the attitude of the lower castes of the Hindus, who welcomed them as their deliverers from the priestly yoke, and even described them in popular poetry as the gods, come down to earth to punish the wicked Brāhmans. Others were enlightened patrons of literature. At the courts of Hindu rajas priestly influence maintained Sanskrit as the literary language, and there was a tendency to despise the vulgar tongue, but Muslim kings, who could not be expected to learn Sanskrit, could both understand and appreciate the writings of those who condescended to use the tongue in which they themselves communicated with their subjects, and it was the Muslim sultan rather than the Hindu raja that encouraged vernacular literature. Nāsir-ud-dīn Nusrat Shāh, anticipating Akbar, caused the *Mahābhārata* to be translated from Sanskrit into Bengali, and of the two earlier versions of the same work one possibly owed something to Muslim patronage and the other was made to the order of a Muslim officer at the court of Sayyid 'Alā-ud-dīn Husain Shāh, Nusrat's father, who is mentioned in Bengali literature with affection and respect.

CHAPTER XII

THE KINGDOM OF KASHMĪR

ISLAM was introduced into Kashmīr at the beginning of the four-teenth century of the Christian era by Shāh Mīrzā, an adventurer from Swāt, who in 1315 entered the service of Sinha Deva, a chief-tain who had established his authority in the valley of Kashmīr. Sinha Deva was overthrown and slain by Rainchan, a Tibetan who also was in his service and is said to have accepted Islam, probably at the suggestion of Shāh Mīrzā, whom he made his minister, en-trusting him with the education of his children. On Rainchan's death Udayana Deva, a scion of the old royal house, who had found an asylum in Kishtwār during the usurpation, returned to the valley married Kota Devī, Rainchan's widow, and ascended the throne. He died after a reign of fifteen years, and his widow called upon Shāh Mīrzā to place upon the throne her son, but the minister, during his long tenure of office, had formed a faction of his own, and was no longer content with the second place in the state. The circumstances in which he obtained the first are variously related. According to one account he proposed marriage to the widowed queen, who committed suicide rather than submit to the alliance, but the more probable story is that on Shāh Mīrzā's hesitating to obey her command she assembled her forces, attacked him, and was defeated. Shāh Mīrzā then forcibly married her, and before she had been his wife for twenty-four hours imprisoned her and ascended the throne in 1346, under the title of Shams-ud-dīn Shāh.

The new king used wisely and beneficently the power which he had thus acquired. The Hindu kings had been atrocious tyrants, whose avowed policy bad been to leave their subjects nothing beyond a bare subsistence. He ruled on more liberal principles, abolished the arbitrary taxes and the cruel methods of extorting them, and fixed the state's share of the produce of the land at one-sixth. He was obliged, however, during his short reign, to suppress a rebellion of the Lon tribe of Kishtwār. He died, after a reign of three years, in 1349, leaving four sons, Jamshīd, 'Alī Sher, Shīrāshāmak, and Hindāl, the eldest of whom succeeded him, but reigned for no more than a year, being dethroned in 1350 by his next brother, 'Alī Sher, who ascended the throne under the title of 'Alā-ud-dīn.

'Alā-ud-dīn, with a confidence rare among oriental rulers, made his next brother, Shīrāshāmak, his minister, and seems to have had no reason to repent his choice. The events of his reign, which are very briefly chronicled, included a severe famine, a conspiracy which was frustrated, and the promulgation of a law, said to have been effectual, depriving women of light character of any share in the property left by their husbands.

'Alā-ud-dīn died in 1359[1], and was succeeded by his brother, Shīrāshāmak, who assumed the title of Shihāb-ud-dīn, which was probably his real name, for that by which he was known before his accession means 'the little milk-drinker', and was probably a childish nickname.

Shihāb-ud-dīn has left a reputation both as an administrator and as a warrior. He founded two towns and caused landed estates to be carefully demarcated, to prevent encroachments on the crown lands. At the beginning of his reign he led an army to the borders of Sind, and defeated the Jām on the banks of the Indus. Returning thence, he gained a victory over the Afghāns at Peshāwar, and marched through Afghānistan to the borders of the Hindū Kush, but was compelled to abandon his enterprise, whatever its object may have been, by the difficulties which he encountered in attempting to cross that range. Returning to India he established a cantonment in the plains, on the banks of the Sutlej, where he met, in 1361, the raja of Nagarkot (Kāngra), returning from a raid on the dominions of Fīrūz Tughluq of Delhi. The raja, who is said to have conciliated Shihāb-ud-dīn with a liberal share of his spoil, suffered for his temerity[2], and received no assistance from Shihāb-ud-dīn, who returned to Kashmīr.

For reasons which have not been recorded Shihāb-ud-dīn disinherited and banished to Delhi his two sons, Hasan Khān and 'Alī Khān, and designated as his heir his brother Hindāl, who succeeded him, under the title of Qutb-ud-dīn, on his death in 1378. A rebellion of some of his predecessor's officers obliged him to send an expedition, which was successful, for the recovery of the fortress of Lokarkot[3].

Qutb-ud-dīn was for a long time childless and, recalling from Delhi his nephew Hasan Khān, made him his heir, but Hasan's impatience exceeded his gratitude, and he conspired with a Hindu courtier against his patron. The plot was discovered, and Hasan and his accomplice fled to Loharkot, but were seized by the landholders of that district and surrendered to Qutb-ud-dīn, who put

1 The chronology of the kings of Kashmīr is bewildering. See *J R.A.S.*, 1918, p.451
2 See Chapter VII.
3 In 33° 50′ N. and 74° 23′ E.

the Hindu to death and imprisoned his nephew, of whom no more is heard.

Two sons were born to Qutb-ud-dīn in his late years, Sikandar known before his accession as Sakār or Sankār, and Haibat Khān.

Qutb-ud-dīn died in 1394 and his widow, Sūra, placed Sikandar, on the throne and to secure his undisputed retention of it put to death her daughter and her son-in-law. It was probably at her instigation that Rāi Madārī, a Hindu courtier, poisoned Sikandar's brother, Haibat Khān, but this act incensed the young king, who called the Hindu to account for it. Rāi Madārī, in order to escape an embarrassing inquiry, sought and obtained leave to lead an expedition into Little Tibet. He was successful, and, having occupied that country, rebelled. Sikandar marched against him, defeated and captured him, and threw him into prison, where he committed suicide by taking poison.

In 1398 the Amīr Tīmūr, who was then at Delhi, and proposed to retire by the road which skirted the spurs of the Himālaya, sent his grandson Rustam and Mu'tamad Zain-ud-dīn as envoys to Sikandar. They were well received, and when they left Kashmīr Sikandar sent with them as his envoy Maulānā Nūr-ud-dīn, and left Srīnagar with the intention of waiting personally on the conqueror. The envoys reached Tīmūr's camp in the neighbourhood of Jammū on February 24, 1399, and the rapacious courtiers, without their master's knowledge, informed Nūr-ud-dīn that Tīmūr required from Kashmīr 30,000 horses and 100,000 golden *dirhams*. The envoy returned to his master and informed him of this extravagant demand. Sikandar, whose gifts did not approach in value those required by the courtiers, turned back towards Srīnagar, either in despair or with a view to collecting such offerings as might be acceptable, and Tīmūr, who was expecting him, failed to understand the delay in his coming. The members of Nūr-ud-dīn's mission who were still in the camp informed him of the demand and he was incensed by the rapacity of his courtiers, and sent Mu'tamad Zain-ud-dīn with the returning mission to request Sikandar to meet him on the Indus on March 25, without fear of being troubled by exorbitant demands. Sikandar again set out from Srīnagar, but on reaching Bāramūla learnt that Tīmūr had hurriedly left the Indian frontier for Samarqand, and returned to his capital.

Hitherto the Muslim kings of Kashmīr had been careless of the religion of their subjects, and free from the persecuting spirit, but Sikandar amply atoned for the lukewarmness of his predecessors. He was devoted to the society of learned men of his own faith, whom his generosity attracted from Persia, Arabia, and Mesopotamia, and it was perhaps the exhortations of bigots of this class that aroused in him an iconoclastic zeal. He destroyed all the most famous Hindu temples in Kashmír, and the idols which they contained, converting the latter, when made of the precious metals, into money. His enthusiasm was kept alive by his minister, Sinha Bhat, a converted Bráhman with all a convert's zeal for his new faith, who saw to it that his master's hostility extended to idolators as well as to idols. With many innocuous Hindu rites the barbarous practice of burning widows with their deceased husbands was prohibited, and finally the Hindus of Kashmír were offered the choice between Islam and exile. Of the numerous Bráhmans some chose the latter, but many committed suicide rather than forsake either their faith or their homes. Others, less steadfast, accepted Islam, and the result of Sikandar's zeal are seen to-day in Kashmír, where there are no more than 524 Hindus in every 10,000 of the population. The ferocious bigot earned the title of Butshikan, or the Iconoclast.

He died in 1416, leaving three sons, Núr Khán, Sháhí Khán and Muhammad Khán, of whom the eldest succeeded him under the title of 'Alí Sháh. The renegade Bráhman, Sinha Bhat, retained his office until his death, and the persecution of Hindus was not relaxed. Shortly before the end of the reign Sinha Bhat died, and 'Alí Sháh appointed his own brother, Sháhí Khán, minister, and shortly afterwards desiring, in an access of religious zeal, to perform the pilgrimage to Mecca, nominated him as regent and left Srínagar. He had not, however, left the country before his father-in-law, the raja of Jammú, and the raja of Rájáorí succeeded in convincing him of the folly of leaving a kingdom which, after his absence in a far land, he could never expect to recover, and provided him with an army which expelled Sháhí Khán and restored him to his throne.

Sháhi Khán fled and took refuge with Jasrat, chief of the turbulent Khokar tribe, who had incurred the resentment of Tímúr by failing to keep his promise to aid him during his invasion of India and by plundering his baggage, and had been carried off to Samarqand, whence he had escaped on Tímúr's death, which occurred on February 28, 1405.

'Alí Sháh marched against Jasrat and Sháhí Khán, but foolishly exhausted his army by a forced march, and Jasrat, on being informed of its condition, suddenly attacked it in the hills near the Tattakutí Pass, and overwhelmed it. 'Alí Sháh's fate is uncertain. According to one account he escaped, but as he is no more heard of it is more probable that, as is stated in other records, he was captured by Jasrat's troops.

Shāhī Khān ascended the throne of Kashmīr in June, 1420, under the title of Zain-ul-'Ābidīn, and was not unmindful of his benefactor, whose successes in the Punjab, which slipped from the feeble grasp of the Sayyid king of Delhi, were due in part to support received from Kashmīr.

Zain-ul-'Abidīn may be regarded as the Akbar of Kashmir. He lacked the Mughul's natural genius, spirit of enterprise, and physical vigour, and his outlook was restricted to the comparatively narrow limits of his kingdom, but he possessed a stock of learning and accomplishments from which Akbar's youthful indolence had, to a great extent, excluded him, his views were more enlightened than the emperor's, and he practised a tolerance which Akbar only preached, and found it possible to restrain, without persecution, the bigotry of Muslim zealots. He was in all respects, save his love of learned society, the antithesis of his father, the Iconoclast, and in the one respect in which he most resembled him he most differed from him in admitting to his society learned Hindus and cultural Brāhmans. His learning delighted his hearers, and his practical benevolence enriched his subjects and his country. He founded a city, bridged rivers, restored temples, and conveyed water for the irrigation of the land to nearly every village in the kingdom, employing in the execution of these public works the malefactors whom the ferocious penal laws of his predecessors would have put to death. Theft and highway robbery were diminished by the establishment of the principle of the responsibility of village communities for offences committed within their lands, and the authoritative determination of the prices of commodities, economically unsound though it was, tended, with other regulations framed with the same object, to prevent the hoarding of food supplies and imported goods.

The fierce intolerance of Sikandar had left in Kashmīr no more than eleven families of Brāhmans practising the ceremonies of their faith. The exiles were recalled by Zain-ul-'Ābidīn, and many of those who had feigned acceptance of Islam now renounced it and returned to the faith of their ancestors. The descendants of the few who remained in Kashmir and of the exiles who returned are still distinguished as Malmās and Banamās. All, on undertaking to follow the rules of life contained in their sacred books, were free to observe all the ordinances of their faith which had been prohibited, even to the immolation of widows, which a ruler so enlightened might well have excluded from his scheme of toleration. Prisoners undergoing sentences inflicted in former reigns were released, but disobedience to the milder laws of Zain ul-'Ābidīn did not go unpunished. Alms was distributed in moderation to the deserving poor, and the *jizya*, or poll-tax on non-Muslims, was abolished. Accumulations of treasure in conquered territory were allotted to the troops as prize-money, and the inhabitants were assessed for taxes at the moderate rates which satisfied a king who was able to meet most of the expenses of the administration from the produce of the royal mines. The currency, which had been debased by the indiscriminate conversion into coin of idols composed of metal of varying degrees of fineness, was gradually rehabilitated, and the king's decrees, engraved on sheets of copper and terminating with imprecations on any of his descendants who should depart from them, were distributed to the principal towns of the kingdom.

Zain-ul-'Ābidīn was proficient in Persian, Hindī, and Tibetan, besides his own language, and was a munificent patron of learning poetry, music, and painting. He caused the Mahābhārata and the *Rājatarangiṇī*[1], the metrical history of the rajas of Kashmir, to be translated from Sanskrit into Persian, and several Arabic and Persian works to be translated into the Hindī language, and established Persian as the language of the court and of public offices. He shared Akbar's scruples with regard to the taking of life, forbade hunting, and abstained entirely from flesh during the month of Ramzān ; and in other relations of life his morals were unquestionably superior to Akbar's, for he was faithful throughout his life to one wife, and never even allowed his eyes to rest on another woman. In other respects he was no precisian, and singers, dancers, musicians, acrobats, tumblers, and rope-dancers amused his lighter moments. A skilled manufacturer of fireworks, whose knowledge of explosives was not entirely devoted to the arts of peace, is mentioned as having introduced firearms into Kashmīr.

The enlightened monarch maintained a friendly correspondence with several contemporary rulers. Abu Sa'īd Shāh, Bābur's grandfather, who reigned in Khurāsān from 1458 to 1468, Buhlūl Lodī, who ascended the throne of Delhi in 1451, Jahān Shāh of Azarbāijān and Gīlān, Sultān Mahmūd Begarha of Gujarāt, the Burjī Mamlūks of Egypt, the Sharīf of Mecca, the Muslim Jām Nizām-ud-dīn of Sind, and the Tonwār raja of Gwalior, between whom and the king of Kashmir love of music formed a bond, were among those with whom he exchanged letters and complimentary gifts.

---

[1] This, which is believed to be the only genuinely historical work in the Sanskrit language, has been admirably translated by Sir Aurel Stein.

Early in his reign Zain-ul-'Ābidīn associated with himself in the government, and even designated as his heir, his younger brother Muhammad, but Muhammad predeceased him, and though the king admitted his son Haidar Khān to the confidential position which his father had held the birth of three sons of his own excluded his nephew from the succession. These were Adam Khān, Hājī Khān, and Bahrām Khān, three headstrong young men whose strife embittered his declining years. Hājī Khān, his father's favourite, was the least unworthy of the throne, and Bahrām employed himself chiefly in fomenting dissensions between his two elder brothers.

Ādam Khān recovered Bāltistān, or Little Tibet, and Hājī Khān the fort and district of Loharkot, both of which provinces had revolted. Adam Khān returned first to the capital, and, as the brothers were clearly seeking an opportunity to measure their strength against each other, his father detained him at Srīnagar. Hājī Khān then returned from Loharkot with the object of attacking both his father and his brother, who marched from the capital to meet him. He was defeated, and fled to Bhimbar, where the main road from the plains of the Punjab enters the Kashmīr mountains, and Zain-ul-'Ābidīn celebrated his victory with a ferocity foreign to his character by massacring his prisoners and erecting a column of their heads.

Adam Khān now remained at Srīnagar with his father for six years, participating largely in the administration of the kingdom. He slew many of the adherents of his fugitive brother and persecuted their families. At this period Kashmīr suffered from a severe famine, and the king was obliged temporarily to reduce the land tax, in some districts to one-fourth and in others to one-seventh of its normal amount.

After the famine Adam Khān was entrusted with the government of the Kamrāj district, but complaints of his rapacity and cruelty earned for him from his father a rebuke which provoked him to rebellion, and he assembled his troops and marched against his father. Zain-ul-'Ābidīn succeeded in recalling him to a sense of his duty, and permitted him to return to Kamrāj, but recalled from exile at the same time Hājī Khān. The news of his brother's recall again provoked Ādam Khān to rebel, and he attacked and slew the governor of Sopur and occupied that city. His father marched against him and defeated him, but he remained encamped on the northern bank of the Jhelum, opposite to the royal camp, until he heard of Hājī Khān's arrival at Bāramūla, when he fled to the Indus. Zain-ul-'Ābidīn and his second son returned to Srīnagar, where Hājī Khān atoned by faithful service for past disobedience and was rewarded by being designated heir to the throne.

Shortly after this time the king fell sick, and a faction persuaded Ādam Khān to return to the capital, but his arrival at Srīnagar was distasteful to his father, and he was ill received. Others, with better intent, endeavoured to bring about a reconciliation between the two elder brothers, but the attempt was foiled by Bahrām Khān, and Ādam Khān retired to Qutb-ud-dīnpur, near the city.

As the old king grew weaker his counsellors, dreading a fratricidal war, begged him to abdicate in favour of one of his sons, but he rejected their advice, and the three princes remained under arms. It is needless to recite at length their intrigues. Hājī Khān was supported by his brother Bahrām, and by the majority of the nobles, and Ādam Khān was obliged to leave Kashmīr, so that when Zain-ul-'Ābidīn died, in November or December, 1470, Hājī Khān ascended the throne without opposition as Haidar Shāh.

With the death of Zain-ul-'Ābidīn the power of the royal line founded by Shāh Mīrzā declined, and the later kings were mere puppets set up, pulled down, and set up again by factious and powerful nobles, who were supported by their clansmen. The most powerful and most turbulent of these tribes was the Chakk clan, who even in the reign of Zain-ul-'Ābidīn, became such a menace to the public peace that he was obliged to expel them from the Kashmīr valley, but under his feebler successors they returned, and, after exercising for a long time the power without the name of royalty, eventually usurped the throne.

Haidar Shāh was a worthless and drunken wretch who entirely neglected public business and permitted his ministers to misgovern his people as they would. His indulgence of their misconduct was tempered by violent outbursts of wrath which alienated them from him, and his elder brother Ādam Khān, learning of his unpopularity, returned towards Kashmīr with a view to seizing the throne, but on reaching Jammū was discouraged by the news of the death of Hasan Kachhī and other nobles on whose support he had reckoned, and who had been put to death on the advice of a barber named Lūlī. He remained at Jammū, and, in assisting the raja to expel some invaders from his dominions, received a wound from the effects of which he died.

The nobles now conspired to raise to the throne Bahrām Khān, Haidar Shāh's younger brother, but Hasan Khān, his son, who had been raiding the Punjab, returned to maintain his claim to the throne, and when his father, in December, 1471, or January, 1472, slipped, in a drunken fit, on a polished floor, and died of the injuries which he received, Ahmad, Aswad, one of the most powerful of the courtiers, caused him to be proclaimed king under the title of Hasan Shāh.

Bahrām Khān and his son Yūsuf Khān, who had intended to contest Hasan's claim to the throne, were deserted by their troops, and, leaving the valley of Kashmīr, took refuge in the hills of Kama, to the west of Kamrāj. Shortly afterwards a faction persuaded them to return, but they were defeated by Hasan Shāh's army, and both were captured. Bahrām was blinded and died within three days of the operation.

Ahmad Aswad, who had been entitled Malik Ahmad, acquired great influence over Hasan Shāh, who, though less apathetic than his father, displayed little devotion to business. He sent an expedition under Malik Yārī Bhat to co-operate with the troops of the raja of Jammū in ravaging the northern districts of the Punjab, where Tātār Khān Lodī represented the military oligarchy over which his cousin Buhlūl presided at Delhi. The town of Siālkot was sacked, and Malik Yārī Bhat returned with as much plunder as enabled him to form a faction of his own, and when Hasan Shāh required tutors and guardians for his two young sons he confided Muhammad, the elder, to Malik Naurūz, son of Malik Ahmad, and Husain, the younger, to Yārī Bhat. This impartiality encouraged both factions, and their passions rose to such a height that Malik Ahmad forfeited his master's favour by permitting his troops to become embroiled, in the royal presence, with those of his rival, and was thrown into prison, where he presently died.

The mother of the two young princes was a Sayyid, and the king, after the death of Malik Ahmad, selected her father as his minister. The Sayyids became, for a time, all powerful in the state, Malik Yārī Bhat was imprisoned and many other nobles fled from the valley of Kashmīr. Among these was Jahāngīr, chief of the Mākū clan, who established himself in the fortress of Loharkot.

In 1489 Hasan Shāh, whose constitution had been enfeebled by debauchery, died, and the Sayyid faction raised to the throne his elder son, Muhammad in whose name they ruled the kingdom, but their arrogance so exasperated the other nobles that they chose as their candidate for the throne Fath Khān, the son of Hasan's uncle, Ādam Khān, and succeeded, before the child Muhammad had occupied the throne for a year, in establishing Fath Shāh. Muhammad was relegated to the women's quarters in the palace, where he was well treated.

The history of Kashmīr for the next half century is no more than a record of the strife of turbulent nobles, each with a puppet king the least important actor on the stage, to place on the throne. Their intrigues and conflicts are of little interest.

One solitary event during this period is worthy of record. This was the appearance in Kashmīr, during the first reign of Fath Shāh (1489-1497) of a preacher from Tālish, on the shores of the Caspian, named Shams-ud-dīn, who described himself as a disciple of Sayyid Muhammad Nūr Bakhsh of Khurāsān, and preached a strange medley of doctrines. He named his sect *Nūr Bakhsh* ('Enlightening'), after his master, but its tenets resembled in no way any doctrines ever taught by Sayyid Muhammad. Shams-ud-dīn professed to be an orthodox Sunnī, like the majority of the inhabitants of the valley of Kashmīr, but the doctrines set forth in his theological work entitled *Ahwatah*, or 'most comprehensive,' are described as a mass of infidelity and heresy, conforming neither to the Sunnī nor to the Shiah creed. He insisted on the duty of cursing the first three orthodox Caliphs and the prophet's wife, 'Āyishah, a distinctively Shiah practice which strikes at the root of Sunnī orthodoxy and accentuates the chief difference between the sects. He differed from the Shiahs in regarding Sayyid Muhammad Nūr Bakhsh as the promised Mahdī, who was to appear in the last days and establish Islam throughout the world, and taught much else which was irreconcilable with the doctrines of any known sect of Islam.

Mīrzā Haidar the Mughul, who conquered Kashmīr in 1541, found the sect strongly represented at Srīnagar, and, obtaining a copy of the *Ahwatah*, sent it to the leading Sunnī doctors of the law in India, who authoritatively pronounced it to be heretical. Armed with this decision Mīrzā Haidar went about to extirpate the heresy. 'Many of the people of Kashmīr,' he writes, 'who were strongly attached to this apostasy, I brought back, whether they would or no, to the true faith, and many I slew. A number took refuge in Sūfī-ism, but are no true Sūfīs, having nothing but the name. Such are a handful of dualists, in league with a handful of atheists to lead men astray, with no regard to what is lawful and what is unlawful, placing piety and purity in night watches and abstinence from food, but eating and taking without discrimination what they find : gluttonous and avaricious, pretending to interpret dreams, to work miracles, and to predict the future.' Orthodoxy was safe in Mīrzā Haidar's hands.

The enthronement of Fath Shāh was a blow to the Sayyids, but within the next few years the chiefs of the popular party quarrelled among themselves, and in 1497 Muhammad Shah, now about sixteen years of age, was restored by Ibrāhīm Mākarī, whom he made his minister, designating Iskandar Khān, the elder son of Fath Shāh, as his heir; but in 1498 Fath Shāh regained the throne, only to be expelled again in 1499, when he escaped to the plains of India, where he died.

Muhammad Shāh was the first to raise a number of the Chakk tribe to high office, by appointing as his minister Malik Kājī Chakk, with whose assistance he retained the throne, on this occasion, until 1526. The Mākarīs and other clans resented the domination of the Chakks, and made more than one attempt to raise Iskandar Khān to the throne, but the pretender fell into the hands of his cousin Muhammad, who blinded him. This action offended Kājī Chakk, who deposed Muhammad, and raised to the throne his elder son, Ibrāhīm I.

Abdāl Mākarī fled into the Punjab after the failure of the last attempt to raise Iskandar to the throne, and there found Nāzuk, the second son of Fath Shāh, with whom, after obtaining some help from Bābur's officers in the Punjab, he returned to Kashmīr. Malik Kājī Chakk and Ibrāhīm I met him at Naushahra (Nowshera), and were utterly defeated. Kājī Chakk fled to Srīnagar, and thence into the mountains, but Ibrāhīm appears to have been slain, for he is no more heard of. He reigned for no more than eight months and a few days.

Abdāl Mākarī enthroned Nāzuk Shāh at Nowshera in 1527, and advanced on Srīnagar, which he occupied. After dismissing his Mughal allies with handsome presents he sent to Loharkot for Muhammad Shāh, and in 1529 enthroned him for the fourth time. Malik Kājī Chakk made an attempt to regain his supremacy, but was defeated and fled to the Indian plains. He returned shortly afterwards, and joined Abdāl in defending their country against a force sent to invade it by Kāmrān Mīrzā, the second son of Bābur. The Mughuls were defeated and retired into the Punjab.

Abdāl Mākarī and Kājī Chakk again fought side by side in 1533, when a force sent by Sultān Saʿīd Khān of Kāshghar and commanded by his son Sikandar Khān and Mīrzā Haider invaded the Kashmīr valley from the north, and by their ravages inflicted terrible misery on the inhabitants. The battle was indecisive, but the army of Kashmīr fought so fiercely from morning until evening that the invaders were fain to make peace and withdraw from the country, relinquishing some of their plunder. Their departure was followed by a severe famine, during which large number died of hunger and many more fled the country.

Muhammad Shāh died in 1534, having reigned four times, and was succeeded by his surviving son, Shams-ud-dīn II, who died in June or July, 1540, when Nāzuk Shāh was restored.

In this year Mīrzā Haidar the Mughal again invaded Kashmīr. He was with Humāyūn at Lahore, and obtained some assistance from him on promising, in the event of success, to govern Kashmir as his vassal. He had with him no more than 400 horse, but was joined by Abdāl Mākarī and Zangī Chakk, who, having rebelled in Kamrāj, had been defeated by Kājī Chakk. His allies engaged Kājī Chakk's attention by threatening a frontal attack while he marching by Pūnch, where the passes were undefended, turned the enemy's right flank and, on November 22, 1540, entered Srīnagar unopposed.

Mīrzā Haidar, aided by Abdāl Mākarī and Zangī Chakk, occupied himself with the administration of his easily won kingdom, while Kājī Chakk fled to Delhi and sought aid of Sher Shāh, who placed at his disposal 5000 horse. He returned to Kashmīr in 1541, but was defeated by Mīrzā Haidar and found an asylum in Baramgalla, where he was joined, in 1543, by his kinsman Zangī Chakk, who had become suspicious of Haidar's attitude towards him. An attempt to recover Srīnagar was defeated in 1544, and they were compelled to return to Baramgalla, where, in 1545, Kājī Chakk and his son Muhammad died of fever. In the following year Zangī Chakk and his son Ghāzī attacked a force under Haidar's officers, and both were killed. These opportune casualties among his enemies allowed Haidar leisure to receive with due honour a mission from Kāshghar, his own country, and to lead into Kishtwār an expedition which was compelled to retreat after suffering heavy losses and accomplishing nothing. Expeditions to Rājāorī and the region beyond Bāltistān were more successful, and these districts were annexed in 1548.

In 1549 the Chakk tribe gave offence to Islām Shāh Sūr of Delhi by harbouring Haibat Khān and other Niyāzī Afghāns who had rebelled against him. They made their peace with Delhi, but attempted to utilise Haibat Khān as a counterpoise to Mīrzā Haidar in Kashmīr. Mīrzā Haidar was strong enough to frustrate this design, but was obliged, in order to strengthen his position, to conciliate Islām Shāh by a remittance of tribute.

The affection of racial superiority by the Mughuls gave great offence to the natives of Kashmīr, and in 1551 Haidar's officers at

Bāramūla, where a mixed force proceeding to restore order in the eastern districts was encamped, warned him that the Kashmīrī officers were meditating mischief. Mīrzā Haidar, though he received confirmation of their report from the Mākarīs, always his staunch allies, committed the fatal error of mistrusting his own officers, whom he accused of contentiousness. The force continued its march from Bāramūla, the Mughuls were surrounded in the mountains, eighty officers were slain, others were captured, and a few escaped to Baramgalla. The outrage was followed by a rising throughout the provinces, where Mughul officers were either slain or compelled to flee.

Mīrzā Haidar was now left with a handful of Mughuls at Srīnagar, and to oppose the united forces of the Kashmīr nobles, who were now returning from Bāramūla he hastily raised a force from the lower classes in the capital, who were neither well affected nor of any fighting value. With no more than a thousand men he marched from the city and attempted to counterbalance his moral and numerical inferiority by surprising the enemy in a night attack on his camp, but was slain in the darkness by some of his own men. The remnant of the Mughuls was pursued to the citadel of Srīnagar, and after enduring a siege of three days was fain to purchase, by a timely surrender, a safe retreat from Kashmīr.

Thus, late in 1551, ended ten years of Mughul rule in Kashmīr, whose turbulent nobles were now free to resume their intrigues and quarrels. Nāzuk Shāh was seated, for the third time, on the throne, and the chiefs of the Chakk tribe extended their influence by judicious intermarriage with other tribes. An invasion by Haibat Khān, at the head of a force of Niyāzī Afghāns, was repelled, and the victory helped Daulat, now the most prominent Chakk, to acquire the supreme power in the state. In 1552 he deposed Nāzuk Shāh, who had reigned for no more than ten months, and enthroned his elder son, Ibrāhīm II, whose short reign of three years was marked by a victory over the Tibetans, who had invaded the kingdom, and by a great earthquake which changed the course of the Jhelum, as well as by a quarrel between Daulat Chakk and another chieftain of the same tribe, Ghāzī Khān son, of Kājī Chakk.

Ghāzī Khān, whose success secured for him the position which Daulat had held, deposed Ibrāhīm II in 1555, and placed on the throne his younger brother, Ismā'īl Shāh. The quarrels between chieftains of the Chakk tribe continued throughout his brief reign of two years and that of his son and successor, Habīb Shāh, who was raised to the throne on his father's death in 1557, but Ghāzī

Khān retained his supremacy and in 1558 crushed the serious rebellion of Yūsuf Chakk, who was supported by Shāh Abu-'l-Ma'ālī,
recently escaped from Lahore, where he had been imprisoned by
Akbar, and Kamāl Khān the Gakhar. In 1559 Ghāzī Khān executed
his own son Haidar, who was conspiring against him and had murdered the agent whom he had sent to advise him to mend his ways ;
and in the following year crushed another serious rebellion supported by Mughuls and Gakhars from the Punjab.

In 1561 Ghāzī Khān dethroned and imprisoned Habīb Shāh,
and, finding that it was no longer necessary to veil his authority
with the name of a puppet, ascended the throne under the title of
Ghāzī Shāh.

The house of Shāh Mīrzā had held the throne for 215 years,
from 1346 to 1561, but his descendants since 1470 had exercised
no authority in the state.

In 1562 Ghāzī Shāh sent his son Ahamd Khān in command of
an expedition into Tibet. His advanced guard was defeated, and
instead of pressing forward to its support he fled with the main
body of his force—an act of cowardice which cost him a throne.
Ghāzī Shāh set out in the following years to retrieve the disaster,
but was obliged by his disease to return. He was a leper, who had
already lost his fingers and on this expedition lost his sight. He
learnt that disturbances were impending in the capital owing to
the animosity of two factions, one of which supported the claim of
his son, Ahmad, and the other that of his half-brother, Husain, to
the throne. He returned at once to Srīnagar and, being no longer
physically fit to reign, abdicated in favour of his half-brother who
in 1563-64, ascended the throne as Nāsir-ud-dīn Husain Shāh.

Ghāzī Shāh could not at once abandon the habits formed during
a long period of absolute power and so resented a measure taken
by his brother to remedy an act of injustice committed by himself
that he attempted to revoke his abdication, but found no support,
and was obliged to retire into private life.

Husain's was a troubled reign. His elder brother, Shankar
Chakk, twice rose in rebellion, but was defeated, and a powerful
faction conspired to raise his nephew Ahmad to the throne, but
he inveigled the conspirators into his palace and arrested them.
Ahmad and two others were afterwards blinded, and Ghāzī Shāh's
death is said to have been hastened by grief for his son.

In 1565 the minister, Khān Zamān Khān, fell into disgrace, and
was urged by some of his supporters to seize the royal palace while
the king was hunting, and to raise Ahmad, who had not yet been

blinded, to the throne. Khān Zamān attacked the palace, but his
son, Bahādur Khān, was slain by the king's servants while attempting to force an entry and he himself was captured and suffered death by impalement, his ears, nose, hands, and feet having
first been amputated.

In 1568 a religious disturbance gave Akbar's envoy, Mīrzā
Muqīm, a pretext for interfering in the domestic affairs of the
kingdom. Qāzī Habīb, a Sunnī was severely wounded with a sword
by one Yūsuf, a fanatical Shiah who was seized and brought before
the doctors of the law, who adjudged him worthy of death, despite
the protests of his victim, who said that so long as he lived his
assailant could not lawfully be put to death. Yūsuf was stoned to
death and Husain Shāh replied to the protests of the Shiahs that
he had but executed a sentence passed by the doctors of the law.
Mirzā Muqīm, who was a Shiah, demanded the surrender of the
wounded man and those who had pronounced the illegal sentence,
but the latter defended themselves by asserting that they had
passed no sentence of death, but had merely expressed the opinion
that Yūsuf might be executed in the interests of the public tranquillity. Husain escaped the clamour of the contending sects by a
river tour, and the jurists were delivered into the custody of Fath
Khān Chakk, a Shiah, who, after treating them with great harshness, put them to death by Mīrzā Muqīm's order, and caused their
bodies to be dragged through the streets of the city.

The affair caused Husain Shāh much anxiety and, believing
that his hesitation to punish the doctors of the law would give
offence to Akbar, he sent him, by Mīrzā Muqīm, a daughter and
many rich gifts, but Akbar was offended by his envoy's display of
religious bigotry, and put him to death. It was reported in Kashmīr
that the emperor was sending back the princess, and this gross
indignity so preyed upon the king's spirits as to increase the weakness and depression caused by an attack of dysentery from which
he was already suffering. While he was in this feeble state of
health his brother 'Ali Khān assembled his troops with the object
of seizing the throne. Husain's conduct during the recent troubles
had alienated most of his supporters, and he found himself deserted,
and, surrendering the crown to his brother, retired to one of his
villas, where he died three weeks later.

'Alī Shāh, who ascended the throne in 1569-70, was happier in
his relations with Akbar than his brother had been. In 1578 he
received two envoys, Maulānā 'Ishqī and Qāzī Sadr-ud-dīn, whom
he sent back to the imperial court with rich gifts and a report,

19—2

gratifying to the emperor, that the *khutba* had been recited in Kashmīr in his name. His reign of nearly nine years was troubled by the usual rebellions, and by one severe famine in 1576. He died in 1579 from the effects of an accident at polo similar to that which caused the death of Qutb-ud-dīn Aibak of Delhi, the high pommel of his saddle entering his belly, and was succeeded by his son, Yūsuf Shāh.

The early years of Yūsuf's reign were even more than usually full of incident. He was immediately called upon to quell a serious rebellion headed by his uncle, Abdāl Chakk, and had no sooner suppressed it than Mubārak Khān, a leading Sayyid, rose in rebellion and usurped the throne. A counter-rebellion displaced the Sayyid, who approached Yūsuf and owned him as his sovereign, but the reconciliation came too late, for Lohar Chakk, Yūsuf's cousin, seized the throne.

Yūsuf left Kashmīr, and on January 2, 1580, appeared before Akbar at Fathpur-Sīkrī, and sought his aid. In August he left the court armed with an order directing the imperial officers in the Punjab to assist him in regaining his throne. His allies were preparing to take the field when many of the leading nobles of Kashmīr, dreading an invasion by an imperial army, sent him a message promising to restore him to his throne if he would return alone. He entered Kashmīr and was met at Baramgalla by his supporters. Lohar Chakk was still able to place an army in the field and sent it to Baramgalla, but Yūsuf, evading it, advanced by another road on Sopur, where he met Lohar Chakk and, on November 8, 1580, defeated and captured him, and regained his throne.

The remainder of the reign produced the usual crop of rebellions, but none so serious as those which had already been suppressed. His chief anxiety, henceforth, was the emperor. He was indebted to him for no material help, but he would not have regained his throne so easily, and might not have regained it at all, had it not been known that Akbar was prepared to aid him. The historians of the imperial court represent him, after his restoration, as Akbar's governor of Kashmīr, invariably describing him as Yūsuf *Khān*, and he doubtless made, as a suppliant, many promises of which no trustworthy record exists. His view was that as he had regained his throne without the aid of foreign troops he was still an independent sovereign, but he knew that this was not the view held at the imperial court, where he was expected to do homage in person for his kingdom. In 1581 Akbar, then halting at Jalālābād on his return from Kābul, sent Mīr Tāhir and Sālih Dīvāna as

envoys to Kashmīr but Yūsuf, after receiving the mission with
extravagant respect, sent to court his son Haidar, who returned
after a year. His failure to appear in person was still the subject
of remark and in 1584 he sent his elder son, Ya'qūb, to represent
him. Ya'qūb reported that Akbar intended to visit Kashmīr, and
Yūsuf prepared, in fear and trembling, to receive him, but the
visit was postponed, and he was called upon to receive nobody
more important than two new envoys, Hakīm 'Alī Gīlānī and Bahā-
ud-dīn.

Ya'qūb, believing his life to be in danger, fled from the imperial
camp at Lahore, and Yūsuf would have gone in person to do homage
to Akbar, had he not been dissuaded by his nobles. He was treated
as a recalcitrant vassal, and an army under raja Bhagwān Dās
invaded Kashmīr. Yūsuf held the passes against the invaders, and
the raja, dreading a winter campaign in the hills and believing
that formal submission would still satisfy his master, made peace
on Yūsuf's undertaking to appear at court. The promise was fulfilled on April 7, 1586, but Akbar refused to ratify the treaty which
Bhagwān Dās had made, and broke faith with Yūsuf by detaining
him as a prisoner. The raja, sensitive on a point of honour, committed suicide.

Ya'qūb remained in Kashmīr, and though imperial officers were
sent to assume charge of the administration of the province, attempted to maintain himself as regent, or rather as king, and carried
on a guerrilla warfare for more than two years, but was finally
induced to submit and appeared before Akbar, when he visited
Kashmīr, on August 8, 1589.

Akbar's treatment of Yūsuf is one of the chief blots on his
character. After a year's captivity the prisoner was released and
received a fief in Bihār and the command of five hundred horse.
The emperor is credited with the intention of promoting him, but
he never rose above this humble rank, in which he was actively
employed under Mān Singh in 1592 in Bengal, Orissa, and Chota
Nagpur.

CHAPTER XIII

GUJARĀT AND KHĀNDESH

THE great empire of Muhammad Tughluq was dismembered partly by his own ferocious tyranny and partly by the weakness of his successors. Bengal revolted in 1338 and the Deccan in 1347, during Muhammad's lifetime. There were no further defections in the reign of his successor Fīrūz, who had some success in Bengal, but failed to recover the province, but the twenty-five years which followed the death of Fīrūz witnessed the accession of one weakling after another to the throne of Delhi, the destruction of such power as still remained in the hands of the central government by the invasion of Tīmūr, and the establishment of independent principalities in Sind, Oudh, Khāndesh, Gujarāt, and Mālwa.

Malik Ahmad, the founder of the small principality of Khāndesh was not, however, a rebel against the king of Delhi, but against the Bahmanī dynasty of the Deccan. In 1365 he joined the rebellion of Bahram Khān Māzandarānī against Muhammad I, the second king of that line, and when he was compelled to flee from the Deccan established himself at Thālner, on the Tāptī. By 1382 he had conquered the surrounding country and ruled his small territory as an independent prince. He was known both as Malik Raja and Raja Ahmad, but he and his successors for some generations were content with the title of Khān, from which circumstance their small principality became known as Khāndesh, 'the country of the Khāns.' His dynasty was distinguished by the epithet Fārūqī, from the title of the second Caliph, 'Umar, al-Fārūq, or 'The Discriminator,' from whom Ahmad claimed descent.

The kingdom of Gujarāt was established in 1396. Farhat-ul-Mulk, who had been appointed governor of the province by Fīrūz Shāh, had long ceased to pay any heed to orders received from Delhi and the inhabitants groaned under his yoke. In 1391 Muhammad Shāh, the youngest son of Fīrūz, appointed Zafar Khān to the government of Gujarāt, and sent him to establish his authority there. The new governor was the son of a Rajput convert to Islam, Wajīh-ul-Mulk of Dīdwāna, governor of Nāgaur. On January 4, 1392, he defeated and mortally wounded Farhat-ul-Mulk at Gāmbhū, eighteen miles south of Pātan, and gradually reduced to obedience all disorderly elements in the province. In 1396 the strife between two rival kings Mahmūd Shāh and Nusrat Shāh, and the impossibility of determining to whom allegiance was due, furnished him with a pretext for declaring himself independent, and he was joined in the following year by his son Tātār Khān, who, having espoused the cause of the pretender Nusrat Shāh, had been compelled to flee from Delhi. Zafar Khān was preparing to march to Delhi when he was deterred by tokens of Tīmūr's impending invasion, and devoted the whole of his attention to his campaign against the Rājput state of Īdar, which he subdued in 1400.

In 1399 Mahmūd Shāh of Delhi and large numbers of fugitives fleeing before Tīmūr arrived in Gujarāt. They were hospitably received, but Mahmūd considered that Zafar Khān's attitude to him was not sufficiently deferential, and retired to Mālwa, where he took refuge with Dilāvar Khān Ghūrī, the governor.

In 1403 Tātār Khān, learning that Iqbāl Khān, or Mallū, who had driven him from Delhi, had so humiliated Mahmūd Shāh that the latter had fled from him, urged his father to march on Delhi and assume control of the situation, but Zafar Khān was well stricken in years and shrank from the enterprise. He so far yielded to his son's importunity as to place a force at his disposal in order that he might wreak his vengeance on his former antagonist, but Tātār Khān, finding himself at the head of an army, rose against his father, seized him and imprisoned him at Asāwal, and caused himself to be proclaimed king under the title of Nāsir-ud-dīn Muhammad Shāh. Having thus secured his father he appointed his uncle Shams Khān regent of the kingdom, with the title of Nusrat Khān, and set out for Delhi in order to carry out his original project, but as soon as he had left Asāwal Zafar Khān persuaded the regent, his brother, to follow the rebel and privily compass his death. Shams (Nusrat) Khān set out for Tātār's camp and there poisoned him in a draught of wine, and on his return released his brother and restored him to his throne, which he now ascended under the title of Sultān Muzaffar.

In 1407 Muzaffar invaded Mālwa and besieged the king, Hūshang Shāh, in Dhār. The pretext for this attack was his resolve to avenge the death of his old friend and comrade, Dīlāvar Khān, who had been poisoned by his son Hūshang. Dhār fell, and Hūshang was captured and imprisoned, and Muzaffar established his own brother, Nusrat Khān (Shams Khān) in Dhār.

After capturing Dhār Muzaffar learnt that Ibrahīm Shāh of Jaunpur, having annexed some districts to the east of the Ganges, intended to attack Delhi ; he thereupon marched from Mālwa to the support of Mahmūd Shāh Tughluq, carrying with him the captive Hūshang. The menace deterred Ibrāhīm from prosecuting his enterprise and Muzaffar returned to Gujarāt.

Nusrat Khān had made himself so odious by his exactions in Mālwa that the army expelled him, and elected Mūsā Khān, a cousin of Hūshang as their governor, and Muzaffar, who was not prepared to permit the army of Mālwa to rule the destinies of that country, sent his grandson Ahmad, son of Tātār Khān, to restore Hūshang who was sent with him. Ahmad reinstated Hūshang in Mālwa and returned to Gujarāt where he was designated heir to the kingdom by his grandfather.

Muzaffar died in June, 1411, and Ahmad was confronted on his succession, by a serious rebellion, headed by his four uncles, Fīrūz Khān, Haibat Khān, Sa'ādat Khān, and Sher Khān, who resented their nephew's elevation to the throne. He succeeded, without bloodshed, in inducing them to acknowledge him as their sovereign, and was enabled to turn his arms against Hūshang Shāh of Mālwa whom he had summoned to his aid but who had determined, instead of assisting him, to profit by his difficulties. Hūshang who had hoped to find him fully occupied with the rebels, retreated precipitately when he learnt that the rebellion had been extinguished and that Ahmad was marching against him, but his retirement was followed by a fresh rising of the rebels, who were however, defeated and dispersed. The rebellion of the raja of Jhālāwar then called Ahmad into Kāthīāwār, and during his absence in that region Hūshang at the invitation of Ahmad's uncles, again invaded Gujarāt, and Ahmad, returning from Jhālāwar sent his brother Latīf Khān against their uncles and 'Imād-ul-Mulk Sha'bān one of his nobles, against Hūshang who, finding that he was not supported retired to Mālwa, while Latīf Khān dispersed the rebels and compelled them to seek refuge with the Chudasama chief of Girnār in Sorath. Ahmad proceeded to chastise the raja for harbouring them, defeated him in the field, and besieged him in his fort on the Girnār hill. He purchased peace by a promise to pay tribute, and Ahmad, who was suddenly called away by a report of the invasion of Nandurbār, left two of his officers to collect the tribute and returned to his new city of Ahmadābād, which he had built on the site of Asāwal, to assemble troops for the expulsion of the invader.

Raja Ahmad of Khāndesh had died on April 29, 1399, leaving two sons, Nasīr and Hasan, to inherit his dominions. Nasīr had

received the eastern and Hasan the western districts, and the
former had founded, in 1400, the city of Burhānpur, and had captured from a Hindu chieftain the strong fortress of Asīr, while the
latter had established himself at Thālner. Such a division of the
territories of the small state held no promise of permanence, and
in 1417 the elder brother, Nasīr, having obtained assistance from
Hūshang of Mālwa, who had married his sister, captured Thālner
and imprisoned Hasan before a reply could be received to the
latter's appeal for aid to Ahmad of Gujarāt. Nasīr, with a view to
forestalling Ahmad's intervention and to repairing the discomfiture
of his father, who had made an unsuccessful attempt to annex the
south-eastern districts of the kingdom of Gujarāt, attacked Nandurbār. A relieving force sent by Ahmad compelled Nasīr to retreat
to Asīr, and besieged him in that fortress. Peace was made on
Nasīr's swearing fealty to Ahmad, and promising to abstain in
future from aggression, and Ahmad in return recognised Nasīr's
title of Khān. Nasīr's brother Hasan retired to Gujarāt, where he
and his descendants for generations found a home and intermarried
with the royal house.

From this treaty dates the estrangement between Khāndesh
and Mālwa, which had hitherto been allies. Nasīr Khān resented
Hūshang's failure to support him adequately against Ahmad Shāh
and friendly relations were broken off. In 1429 Nasīr, in spite of
the old animosity of his house towards the Bahmanids, attempted
to form an alliance with the Deccan by giving his daughter in
marriage to 'Alā ud dīn Ahmad, son of Ahmad Shāh, the ninth king
of that dynasty, but the union engendered strife, and Khāndesh,
after a disastrous war with her powerful neighbour, was at length
driven into the arms of Gujarāt.

Ahmad himself had advanced as far as Nandurbār, sending
Malik Mahmūd, one of his officers, to besiege Asīr, and while at
Nandurbār he heard from his uncle Fīrūz, who had taken refuge
in Nāgaur, that Hūshang Shāh was about to invade Gujarāt. This
report was followed immediately by the news that Hūshang, in
response to invitations from the rajas of Īdar, Chāmpāner, Mandal,
and Nāndod, had crossed his frontier and reached Modāsa[1]. Ahmad,
although the rainy season of 1418 had begun, at once marched
northward, traversed the country of the disaffected rajas, and appeared before Modāsa. Hūshang beat a hasty retreat, but Ahmad
had no rest. He was obliged to send expeditions to quell a rebellion in Sorath, and to expel Nasīr Khān from the Nandurbār

[1] In 23° 28' N. and 73° 18' E.

district, which he had invaded in violation of his promise. Both expeditions were successful, and Nasīr was pardoned on its being discovered that the real culprit was Hūshang's son, Ghaznī Khān, who had not only instigated him to invade the district but had supplied him with troops.

It was now evident that the real enemy was Hūshang, and Ahmad, having pardoned the rebellious rajas on receiving from them double tribute and promises of better behaviour, set out in March, 1419, to invade Mālwa.

Hūshang came forth to meet him, but was defeated in a fiercely contested battle and compelled to take refuge in Māndū. Ahmad's troops devastated the country, but as the rainy season was at hand he returned to Ahmadābād, plundering on his way the districts of Chāmpāner and Nāndod.

In 1420 Ahmad marched to Songarh[1], and thence, in a north-easterly direction, towards Māndū, 'punishing' on his way, 'the infidels' of the Sātpūras. Hūshang, dreading another invasion, sent envoys to crave pardon for his past conduct, and Ahmad retired, and in 1422 reduced the raja of Chāmpāner to vassalage. In 1422, during Hūshang's absence on his famous raid into Orissa, Ahmad invaded Mālwa, capturing Maheshwar on the Narbada on March 27. He appeared before Māndū on April 5, and besieged it ineffectually until the beginning of the rainy season, when he retired into quarters at Ujjain. In the meantime Hūshang returned to Māndū, and on September 17 Ahmad reopened the siege, but, finding that he could not reduce the fortress, retired by Ujjain to Sārangpur, with the object of continuing his depredations in that neighbourhood, but Hūshang, marching by a more direct route, met him near Sārangpur on December 26. Neither was anxious to risk a general action and after desultory and inconclusive hostilities of two and a half months' duration Ahmad began his retreat on March 17. He reached Ahmadābād on May 15, and in considera-tion of his army's labours refrained for more than two years from embarking on any military enterprise and devoted himself to administrative reforms. From 1425 until 1428 he was engaged in hostilities against Īdar, which ended in the reduction of Harī Rāi, the raja, to the condition of a vassal of Gujarāt.

In 1429 Kānhā, raja of Jhālāwar, fled from his state and took refuge with Nasīr Khān of Khāndesh, who, not being strong enough to protect him, sent him to the court of Ahmad Shāh Bahmanī at Bīdar, who dispatched a force into the Nandurbār district to ravage

[1] In 21° 10′ N. and 73° 36′ E.

the country. This force was expelled and driven back to Daulatābād, whereupon Ahmad of the Deccan sent an army under his son 'Alā-ud-dīn Ahmad to invade Gujarāt and re-establish Kānhā in Jhālāwar. This army, which assembled at Daulatābād, was there joined by Nasīr Khān of Khāndesh, and against the allied forces Ahmad of Gujarāt sent an army under his eldest son, Muhammad Khān. This prince defeated the allies at Mānikpunj, about thirty-eight miles north-west of Daulatābād, and 'Alā-ud-dīn Ahmad fled to Daulatā-bād while Nasīr and Kānhā fled into Khāndesh. Muhammad Khān of Gujarāt perceiving that it would be useless to besiege Daulatā-bād, laid waste part of Khāndesh and retired to Nandurbār.

In 1430 Khalaf Hasan of Basrah, an officer of the army of the Deccan attacked Mahīm the southernmost port of the kingdom of Gujarāt and Ahmad of Gujarāt sent his younger son, Zafar Khān, to the relief of the town, while 'Alā-ud-dīn Ahmad marched to the support of Khalaf Hasan. Mahīm was taken, but Zafar Khān not only besieged the army there, but also took Thāna, a port belonging to the kingdom of the Deccan. The campaign was decided, however by a battle in which the army of the Deccan was completely defeated and was forced to evacuate Mahīm and retreat.

Ahmad of the Deccan was much chagrined by the news of this defeat, and led an army in person to invade Baglāna, the small Rājput state between Gujarāt and Deccan which was protected by the former, but, on hearing that Ahmad of Gujarāt was march-ing against him retired to Bīdar. Ahmad of Gujarāt returned to Ahmadābād and Ahmad of the Deccan again advanced and besieged the fortress, of Batnols which was gallantly defended by Malik Sa'ādat, an officer of Gujarāt. Ahmad of Gujarāt marched to the relief of the fortress, and Ahmad of the Deccan, raising the siege, turned to meet him. A battle was fought in which each army held its ground but Ahmad of the Deccan, dismayed by the extent of his losses, retreated in the night.

In 1433 Ahmad led a raid into the Dūngarpur state, compelled the Rāwal to pay a ransom, and left an officer at Kherwāra to collect tribute. He continued his depredations in Mārwār, compelled his Kinsman Fīrūz Khān[1], now governor of Nāgaur, to pay an in-demnity, and returned to Ahmadābād.

In 1436 Mas'ūd Khān of Mālwa arrived at Ahmadābād as a suppliant seeking redress. His father, Ghaznī Khān, had ascended the throne of Mālwa in 1435 and had been poisoned in the following year by his cousin, Mahmūd Khaljī, who had ascended the throne

---

[1] Fīrūz was the son of Ahmad's grand-uncle, Shams Khān.

and deprived him of his inheritance. Ahmad welcomed the opportunity of intervening and in 1438 invade Mālwa with a view to seating Mas'ūd on the throne of that kingdom. After many months of fruitless campaigning he was obliged to retire owing to an outbreak of pestilence in his army, and died on August 16, 1442, before he could fulfil his promise to restore Mas'ūd. He was succeeded in Gujarāt by his eldest son, who ascended the throne under the title of Mu'īzz-ud-dīn Muhammad Shāh. Soon after his accession to the throne Ahmad had begun to build the town of Ahmadābād on the site of the old city of Asāwal, and in spite of the constant military activities of his reign he was able to devote much of his time to the establishment of this city, which even to-day bears witness to the taste and munificence of its founder.

While Ahmad had been engaged in espousing the cause of Mas'ūd Khān in Mālwa Nasīr Khān of Khāndesh had involved himself in hostilities with the Deccan. His daughter had complained that her husband 'Alā-ud-dīn Ahmad, who had succeeded his father in 1435, was neglecting her for a beautiful Hindu girl, and Nasīr, to avenge his daughter's wrongs, invaded Berar, the northernmost province of the Bahmanī kingdom. His son-in-law sent against him a large army under Khalaf Hasan, who defeated him at Rohankhed[1] and drove him into his frontier fortress, Laling[2], where he besieged him. Nasīr Khān, joined by a large force under his nobles, made a sortie, but suffered a severe defeat, died on September 20, and was succeeded by his son, 'Ādil Khān I. Khalaf Hasan, hearing that a force was advancing from Nandurbār to the relief of Laling retired to the Deccan with his plunder, which included seventy elephants and many guns.

'Ādil Khān I reigned in Khāndesh without incident until 1441, when he died and was succeeded by his son Mubārak Khān, who reigned, likewise without incident, until his death on June 5, 1457, when he was succeeded by his son 'Ādil Khān II.

In 1446 Muhammad Shāh of Gujarāt, who was surnamed Karīm or 'the Generous,' marched against Īdar, to reduce its ruler, Raja Bīr, son of Pūnjā, to obedience. Bīr appeared before him and made submission, giving him his daughter in marriage, and at her intercession, Īdar was restored to him. Muhammad next attacked, at Bāgor, Rānā Kūmbha, of Mewār, who fled and took refuge with the Rāwal of Dūngarpur, the chief of his house, but afterwards appeared before the invader and purchased peace with a heavy indemnity.

---

[1] In 23° 37′ N. and 76° 11′ E.　　　　[2] In 20° 49′ N. and 74° 44′ E.

In 1449 Muhammad attacked Chāmpāner, with the object of expelling the raja, Gangādās, and annexing his state. Gangādās was defeated in the field with great slaughter, and driven into the hill fortress of Pavagarh, above the city. Muhammad indicated his intention of permanently occupying the city by constructing a fine cistern, which was named the Shakar Talāo, and by founding a palace and some public buildings. Gangādās appealed for help to Mahmūd Khaljī of Mālwa, who marched to his relief, but on reaching Dahod learnt that Muhammad, in spite of a severe illness contracted at Chāmpāner, had advanced as far as Godhra to meet him. He retreated at once to Māndū, and Muhammad, oppressed by his sickness, was obliged to return to Ahmadābād where he died on February 10, 1451.

Three days after his death the courtiers enthroned his eldest son, Qutb-ud-dīn Ahmad, and the young king was at once called upon to cope with a serious invasion of his kingdom. Mahmūd Khaljī, on learning the seriousness of Muhammad's malady, resolved to seize the opportunity of conquering Gujarāt, and after his return to Māndū assembled an army of 100,000 horse and 500 elephants, · and invaded the Nandurbār district. 'Alā-ud-dīn Suhrāb, who commanded the fortress of Nandurbār, made no attempt to hold it against such a force, but surrendered it at once, and consulted his own safety by swearing allegiance to the invader and entering his service. After capturing Nandurbār Mahmūd learnt of the death of Muhammad and marched on Broach, where he summoned Marjān, the governor, to surrender. Marjān refused, and Mahmūd was about to besiege the town when, by the advice of 'Alā-ud-dīn Suhrāb, he decided, instead, to attack the capital at once, and marched to Baroda, where he was joined by Gangādās of Ghāmpāner and other chiefs. Crossing the Māhī river he advanced to Kapadvanj, where 'Alā-ud-dīn deserted him and joined his old master, who received him with great favour and conferred on him the title of 'Alā-ul-Mulk, Ulugh Khān. Qutb-ud-dīn advanced from Ahmadābād with 40,000 horse and encamped six miles from Kapadvanj. On the night of April 1, 1451, Mahmūd Khaljī left his camp with the object of making a night attack on Qutb-ud-dīn, but lost his way, and, after wandering about all night, found himself by daylight before his own camp. Disappointed of surprising the enemy, he drew up his army, and Qutb-ud-dīn, who had intelligence of what had passed, advanced to the attack. At a critical moment of the battle which ensued Qutb-ud-dīn threw in his reserves, the great army of Mālwa was utterly defeated, and Mahmūd fled, leaving eighty-one elephants and all his baggage in the hands of the victors. He halted at a short distance from the field until five or six thousand men of his scattered host had assembled round him, and at midnight began his retreat on Māndū, during which he was much harassed by the Kolīs, who inflicted heavy losses on the remnant of his army.

In 1453 Mahmūd Khaljī opened an abortive campaign against Nāgaur, which was held by Fīrūz Khān, the kinsman of Qutb-ud-dīn, but was compelled to retire to Mālwa without having effected anything. In the same year Fīrūz Khān died, and his brother Mujāhid Khān took possession of Nāgaur, expelling Shams Khān, the son of Fīrūz Khān, who sought aid of Rānā Kūmbha of Chitor. The Rānā promised to restore him to his inheritance on condition that he destroyed three of the bastions of Nāgaur, as a symbol that the disgrace of the defeat of Mūkal, the Rānā's father, by Fīrūz Khān was wiped out. Shams Khān agreed to the condition and was restored, but when he had recovered his patrimony his nobles refused to allow him to destroy any part of the fortifications, and Kūmbha returned to Mewār to assemble an army for the reduction of Nāgaur. Shams Khān fled to Ahmadābād and, by giving a daughter in marriage to Qutb-ud-dīn, induced him to send an army to the defence of Nāgaur, but the Rānā defeated and almost destroyed the army, and overran the whole of the Nāgaur territory, though he failed to take the fortress.

In 1456 Qutb-ud-dīn marched to Kumbhalgarh to punish Kūmbha, and on his way thither captured and destroyed the town of Sirohī and expelled the raja, Sains Mal. He laid waste all the lowlands of the Rānā's territory, defeated him in the field, and besieged him in Kumbhalgarh. The fortress was not taken, but Kūmbha was obliged to purchase peace by the payment of ample compensation to Shams Khān for all the injuries which he had inflicted on him, and a heavy indemnity to Qutb-ud-dīn.

On returning to Ahmadābād Qutb-ud-dīn learned that Ghiyās-ud-dīn, the son of Mahmūd Khaljī, had led a raid into his dominions as far as Sūrat, but had hurriedly retreated on hearing of his return, and later in the year Mahmūd sent a mission to propose a treaty of peace between the two kingdoms, in order that both might be free to wage holy war against the Hindus of Rājputāna. These overtures were favourably received, and Mahmūd marched to Dhār and Muhammad to the frontier of Mālwa in the neighbourhood of Chāmpāner, where they halted while plenipotentiaries concluded a treaty binding each to abstain from aggression on the other, and allotting to Gujarāt the western and to Mālwa the eastern districts

of the Rānās dominions as the theatre in which each was to be free
to attack the misbelievers.

In 1457 Qutb-ud-dīn again invaded the dominions of Rānā
Kūmbha. He had in his camp the chief of Ābū, who had been
expelled from his mountain fortress by the Rānā, and his first care
was to restore him. Having accomplished this he attacked and
burnt Kumbhalgarh, and slaughtered both men and cattle throughout the neighbourhood, but though he burnt the fortress he was
unable to take it, and, having devastated the country round about
Chitor, he returned to Ahmadābād, where he died, after a short
illness, on May 18, 1458.

Qutb-ud-dīn was a young man, and as he had hitherto enjoyed
good health his sudden illness and death aroused suspicions of
poison. He had been addicted to strong drink, and when under its
influence had been violent and quick to shed blood. Suspicion fell
upon his wife, the daughter of Shams Khān of Nāgaur, who was
supposed to have instigated his daughter to administer poison to
her husband in the hope of succeeding to the throne of Gujarāt.
Qutb-ud-dīn's officers at Nāgaur put Shams Khān to death, and
the king's mother subjected his widow to torture and ultimately
handed her over to her jealous co-wives who avenged the preference formerly shown for her by cutting her to pieces.

On Qutb-ud-dīn's death the great officers of state raised to the
throne his uncle Dāūd, but his prince immediately displayed such
depravity and proceeded to fill the places of those who had enthroned
him with favourites so unworthy that he was deposed after a reign
of no more than twenty-seven days, and his younger brother, Abu-'l-
Fath Mahmūd was raised to the throne on May 25. Sultān
Mahmūd, a mere youth, was at once involved in the meshes of a
conspiracy to raise his brother Hasan Khān to the throne. The
courtiers who entertained this design approached him and informed
him that the minister, 'Imād-ul-Mulk Sha'bān, was conspiring to
depose him and to place on the throne Mahmūd's son, Shihāb-ud-
dīn, an infant in whose name he would be able to govern the whole
country as regent. Mahmūd, new to political intrigue, believed
them, and permitted them to arrest the minister and imprison him
over one of the gates of the palace. During the night Malik
'Abdullāh, the superintendent of the elephant stables, who had
access to the young king, informed him privately of the real state
of affairs, and warned him that his throne was in danger. Mahmūd
consulted his mother and a few of his immediate attendants, and
at once decided on a course of action. Going in person to the

Tarpūliya gate, where the minister was confined, he easily gained admission, for the outer precincts of the gate were held by 500 of his own guards, whom he had lent for the purpose, but he found more difficulty in removing the scruples of the minister's gaolers, who were the creatures of the conspirators. By stamping his foot and demanding in a loud and angry tone the immediate surrender of the traitor that he might suffer instant death he succeeded both in overawing the gaolers by a display of the divinity that doth hedge a king, and in beguiling them into the belief that compliance with his commands would accomplish their master's design, but as soon as their prisoner was in the king's power they perceived their error. He begged his minister to excuse the mistake which he had made, and to resume his post. The conspirators, supported by their troops, assembled in the morning at the Tarpūliya gate in the expectation of removing their enemy by a summary execution, but to their dismay found the king holding an audience with his minister, who was standing in his accustomed position behind the throne. Trusting to numbers, they attempted to assume control of the situation, but were deserted by many of their troops and by the city mob, who hesitated openly to take up arms against the king. They fled, and some gained secure places of refuge, but others were captured and publicly executed. Among the latter was one who had attempted to flee, but was too corpulent to use the necessary expedition, and was discovered lurking in his hiding place. Before him lay the obvious fate of being trampled to death by an elephant, and the populace was regaled with the unctuous spectacle.

The conspiracy having been thus frustrated the minister resumed office, but shortly afterwards retired. Haj Sultānī, one of Mahmūd's confidants, was appointed in his place, with the title of 'Imād-ul-Mulk, and Mahmūd assumed charge of the administration of his kingdom. 'Imād-ul-Mulk Sha'bān did not long survive his retirement.

In 1462 Mahmūd, while on a hunting expedition, received an appeal for help from the guardians of the infant Nizām Shāh of the Deccan, whose dominions had been invaded by Mahmūd Khaljī of Mālwa. Mahmūd of Gujarāt marched to Nandurbār, where a second messenger informed him that Mahmūd Khaljī had defeated the army of the Deccan near Kandhār. Mahmūd of Gujarāt therefore marched eastward into Khāndesh and cut off his retreat by that road, so that he was compelled to retire through the Mahādeo hills in northern Berar, where the army of Mālwa suffered severely both from want of water and from the attacks of the Korkus.

In the following year Mahmūd Khaljī again invaded the Deccan, but had penetrated no further than the northern confines of Telingāna when the news that the sultan of Gujarāt was again marching to the help of Nizām Shāh caused him to retreat. Nizām Shāh sent an envoy to thank his deliverer for the assistance which he had given him, and Mahmūd of Gujarāt wrote to Mahmūd Khaljī saying that it was unfair to molest a child who had not reached maturity, and warning him that if he invaded the Deccan again he would find his own country overrun by the army of Gujarāt. The threat was effectual, and Mahmūd Khaljī refrained from further acts of aggression.

In 1464 Mahmūd of Gujarāt attacked the Hindu chief of Pardī, near Damān, who had been guilty of piracy. As he was ascending the hill to capture the fort the chief met him with the keys, and the stronghold was restored to him on his undertaking to pay tribute and promising amendment

In 1466 Mahmūd invaded the territory of Mandalak Chudāsama, raja of Girnār, his object being to compel the raja to pay tribute. The state was pillaged, and a number of Hindus perished in the defence of a famous temple, which was sacked. On the receipt of this news Mandalak agreed to pay tribute and Mahmūd retired ; but in the following year, learning that Mandalak was in the habit of using the insignia of royalty, wrote and commanded him to discontinue their use, and the raja, dreading another invasion, obeyed.

On May 31, 1469, Mahmūd Khaljī of Mālwa died and was succeeded by his eldest son, Ghiyās-ud-dīn. The question of the invasion of Mālwa was at this time discussed at the court of Gujarāt, but Mahmūd showed that the warning which he had addressed to Mahmūd Khaljī when the latter was attacking Nizām Shāh of the Deccan had its origin in principle, and declined to invade a state which had just suffered the misfortune of losing its ruler. Later in the year, however, he committed an act as wanton by leading into Sorath a large army against Mandalak of Girnār. It was in vain that the raja pleaded that he had remitted tribute regularly and had been an obedient vassal. Mahmūd replied that he has come neither for tribute nor for plunder, but to establish the true faith in Sorath ; and offered Mandalak the choice between Islam and death. The answer admitted of no argument, and Mandalak could only prepare to defend himself. He retired to his citadel, Uparkot, and was there closely besieged. When reduced to straits he attempted to purchase peace by offering an enomous indemnity, but to no purpose, and, finding that he could no longer defend Uparkot, he fled with his Rājputs to his hill fort on the Girnār mountains, but was followed by Mahmūd, who again closely besieged him until at last, on December 4, 1470, he was compelled to surrender. He accepted Islam and received the title of Khān Jahān, and the long line of Chudāsama chiefs of Girnār came to an end. Mahmūd incorporated Girnār in his dominions, and at the foot of the hill founded the city of Mustāfā-ābād, which became one of his capitals.

Mahmūd now learned that while he had been besieging Girnār Jai Singh, the son of Gangādās of Chāmpāner, had been committing systematic brigandage and highway robbery in the country between his stronghold and Ahmadābād. He therefore sent Jamāl-ud-dīn Muhammad to govern this tract, conferring on him the title of Muhāfiz Khān, and he put down thieving and highway robbery with such a firm hand that the inhabitants, we were told, slept with open doors.

He had intended at this time to reduce the fortress of Chāmpāner, but he was interrupted by complaints from southern Sind, where Muslims were said to be persecuted by Hindus. He crossed the Rann of Cutch by forced marches, and arrived in what is now the Thār and Parkār district with no more than 600 horse. An army of 24,000 horse which he found before him appears, if it were not that of those who had appealed, at least to have had no hostile intentions, for its leaders readily entered into negotiations with him. It proved to be composed of Sūmras, Sodas, and Kalhoras, and its leaders told him that they were professing Muslims but knew little of their faith or its rules, and were wont to intermarry with and to live as Hindus. He invited those who would to enter his service, and to return with him to Gujarāt, and many accepted his invitation and received grants of land in Sorath, where teachers were appointed to instruct them in the faith of Islam.

In 1472 it was reported to Mahmūd that 40,000 rebels had risen against Jām Nizām-ud-dīn, the ruler of Sind, whose daughter was the mother of Mahmūd. According to Frishta these rebels were Balūchīs of the Shiah persuasion, and according to the author of the Zafar-ul-Wālih they were pirates who dwelt on the sea coast, owing allegiance to none, and skilled in archery. Mahmūd again crossed the Rann by forced marches, and appeared in Sind with his army. The rebels dispersed on hearing of his approach, and Mahmūd halted, and before he returned received gifts and a letter of thanks from the Jām, who also sent his daughter, who was married to

Qaisar Khān, grandson of Hasan Khān Iftikhār-ul-Mulk of Khān-desh, who had taken refuge in Gujarāt.

On his return from Sind Mahmūd marched, on May 14, 1473, to Jagat (Dwārkā), the holy town on the coast in the north-western corner of Kāthīāwār, which was sacked by Mahmūd of Ghaznī. Mahmūd Samarqandī, a learned poet and merchant sailing from a port of the Deccan, had been driven ashore at Dwārkā, where the Hindus had robbed him of all that he had. He appeared at Sultān Mahmūd's court to demand redress, and the king resolved to chastise the idolators. He marched to Dwārkā, from which the Hindus, with their king, Bhīm fled on his approach, plundered and destroyed the temple, and built a mosque in its place. He then marched to Arāmura, at the extreme north-western point of the peninsula, where the army was much troubled by lions, and by venomous reptiles and insects, to attack the island fortress of Bet Shan-khodhar, where Bhīm and his people had taken refuge. The Hindus were defeated in a sea-fight and were compelled to· surrender, as their fortress, though well stored with merchandise, had not been provisioned. The plunder was carried to the mainland and trans-ported to Mustafā-ābād. Mahmūd Samarqandī was summoned and called upon to identify his goods ; all that he identified was deliver-ed to him, and over and above this rich presents were bestowed on him. Finally the king delivered to him his enemy, Raja Bhīm, that he might do with him what he would. Mahmūd Samarqandī thanked the king, but returned the raja, who was sent to Ahmadābād and impaled.

In October, 1473, Mahmūd, who had held his court at Mustafā-ābād since his capture of Girnār, returned after an absence of nearly five years to Ahmadābād. A fleet of Malabar pirates made a descent on his coasts, but they were driven off and some of their ships were captured. In January, 1474, he ravaged part of the Chāmpāner country and shortly afterwards returned to Mustafā-ābād (or Junāgarh) where he made a practice of spending part of each year, leaving his minister, Khudāvand Khān b. Yūsuf, who had married his sister, at Ahmadābād in charge of his son Ahmad.

Mahmūd's tireless energy and ceaseless activity were most wearisome to his courtiers and officers, and during his absence from his capital his minister, Khudāvand Khān, having on December 4, 1480, assembled at Ahmadābād, on the pretext of celebrating the festival '*Īd-ul-Fitr* at the end of the month's fast, the principal nobles, formed a conspiracy with the object of deposing Mahmūd and raising to the throne his son, Ahmad Khān. The minister desired to put to death 'Imād-ul-Mulk Hājī Sultānī, whose fidelity to Mahmūd was believed to be unalterable, but Rāi Rāyān, the chief Hindu noble and one of the leading spirits among the conspirators, was a personal friend of 'Imād-ul-Mulk, and refused to be a party to his death. He proposed to inform him of the plot and to gain his acquiescence, and, notwithstanding the minister's protests, carried out his intention. 'Imād-ul-Mulk feigned acquiescence, but secretly summoned his troops from his fiefs and took other steps to defeat the designs of the conspirators, and Qaisar Khān Fārūqī, who was at Ahmadābād, privately informed the king of the affair, so that it came to naught.

Mahmūd, instead of arraigning the conspirators, as might have been expected from the energy of his character, took steps to test the fidelity of his servants. He made all the necessary preparations for a sea voyage, and announced that he intended to perform the pilgrimage to Mecca, leaving his son Ahmad as regent of the kingdom. The nobles were summoned from Ahmadābād to Cambay to consider this proposal, and, perceiving that their plot had been discovered, urged the king to return to Ahmadābād and set the affairs of the kingdom in order before taking any irrevocable step. He accepted their advice and returned to Ahmadābād, where he kept them still on the rack. He desired, he said, to make the pilgrimage, but must leave the matter to the decision of his counsellors, and would neither eat nor drink until he had received that decision. The courtiers were in a quandary. They knew not how their advice would be accepted, but knew that they must either forgo the object of their conspiracy or be accounted hypocrites. So long did they hesitate that it became necessary to remind them that the king was hungry and awaited their decision. They had arrived at none, and sent Nizām-ul-Mulk Aisan, the oldest courtier, to the king as their spokesman. Nizām-ul-Mulk, who perceived that the king had outwitted the conspirator, adroitly suggested that just as the king was satisfied of his son's ability to guide the affairs of the kingdom, so he too had a son who was competent to advise and assist him, and requested that he himself might be permitted to accompany the king on his pilgrimage. It was now Mahmūd's turn to be at a loss, but he sent Nizām-ul-Mulk back to those who had sent him, saying tha the could not permit him to accompany him to Mecca and demanding a categorical answer. By the advice of 'Imād-ul-Mulk, Nizām-ul-Mulk was sent back to the king with the message that he would do well to conquer Chāmpāner before deciding to make the pilgrimage. This advice was accepted, but it was not convenient to attack Chāmpāner at once, and Mahmūd marched to Pātan and thence sent 'Imād-ul-Mulk and Qaisar Khān Fārūqī on an expedition to Sānchor and Jālor in Marwār. As the expedition was about to start the two sons of the minister, Khudāvand Khān, entered the tent of Qaisar Khān and murdered him for his share in discovering the plot to the king. The actual murderers escaped, but Khudāvand Khān was imprisoned, and Muhāfiz Khān was made chief *vazīr* in his place. 'Imād-ul-Mulk died in the same year, and was succeeded by his son, Buda 'Imād-ul-Mulk. From Pātan Mahmūd returned to Ahmadābād, and the country now suffered from a failure of the rains and famine.

In 1482 Mahmūd obtained the opportunity which he sought of attacking Chāmpāner. Mulik Sūdha, his governor of Rasūlabād, fourteen miles south-west of Chāmpāner, led a raid into the raja's territories, and plundered and laid them waste nearly to the walls of the fortress, slaying the inhabitants. As he was returning, the raja, Patāī, son of Udai Singh, followed him up, attacked and slew him, recovered all his booty, took two elephants, and sacked and destroyed Rasūlabād. Mahmūd, on hearing of this defeat, assembled his forces, and on December 4, 1482, marched from Ahmadābād to Baroda, on his way to Chāmpāner. From Baroda he sent an army to besiege Chāmpāner while he invaded the raja's territories to collect supplies for the besiegers, whom it was difficult, owing to the famine, to provision.

Raja Patāī came forth to meet his enemy, but was defeated and driven into Pavagurh, his hill fortress above Chāmpāner, while the besiegers occupied the town. Patāī succeeded in cutting off one convoy sent by Mahmūd to his army, but this was his sole success. When Mahmūd joined the besieging army in person Patāī made repeated offers of submission, but none was accepted, and Mahmūd displayed his determination to capture the place by building in the city the beautiful mosque which still adorns its ruins. This measure not only discouraged Patāī, but stimulated the Muslim officers, who now perceived that they would not be allowed to leave the fortress uncaptured, to exertions more strenuous than their former faint efforts. Patāī sent him minister, Sūrī, to seek help of Ghiyās-ud-dīn Khaljī of Mālwa, and Ghiyās-ud-dīn, assembling his troops, left Māndū and marched as far as Na'lcha. Mahmūd, leaving his officers to continue the siege, led a force as far as Dohad to meet Ghiyās-ud-dīn, but the latter, repenting of his enterprise, which, as he was advised by Muslim doctors at his court, was unlawful, retired to Māndū, and Mahmūd returned to Chāmpāner and continued the siege.

The operations lasted for a year and nine months, throughout which period Mahmūd, besides besieging the fortress, continued to plunder the country, so that there remained no town, no village, no house, of which the money was not taken into the royal treasury, the cloths and stuffs into the royal storehouses, the beasts into the royal stables, the corn into the royal granaries and kitchens. At the end of this time the Rājputs were reduced to extremities, and resolved to perform the dreadful rite of *jauhar*. The women were burnt, and the men, arrayed in yellow garments, went forth to die. On November 21, 1484, the Muslims forced the gate and met their desperate opponents. Of the seven hundred Rājputs who performed the rite nearly all were slain, but Raja Patāī and a minister named Dungarsī were wounded and captured. Mahmūd called upon them to accept Islam, but they refused and remained steadfast in their refusal during an imprisonment of five months, at the end of which time they were executed, together with the minister Sūrī. Patāī's son accepted Islam and in the next reign became *Amīr* of Īdar, receiving the title of Nizām-ul-Mulk.

Mahmūd now made Chāmpāner one of his principal places of residence, giving it the name of Muhammadābād, the other being Mustafā-ābād or Junāgarh. The kingdom of Gujarāt had reached its extreme limits. After this conquest Mahmūd held possession of the country from the frontiers of Māndū to the frontiers of Sind, by Junāgarh ; to the Siwālik Parbat by Jālor and Nāgaur ; to Nāsik Trimbak by Baglāna ; from Burhānpur to Berar and Malkāpur of the Deccan ; to Karkūn and the river Narbada on the side of Burhānpur ; on the side of Īdar as far as Chitor and Kūmbhalgarh, and on the side of the sea as far as the bounds of Chaul. It seems to have been after the conquest of Chāmpāner that Mahmūd was first styled *Begarha*.

In 1487, while he was hunting at Hālol, near Chāmpāner, a company of horsedealers complained to him that the raja of Ābū had robbed them of 403 horses, which they were bringing to Gujarāt for him by his order. Mahmūd paid them the full price of the horses and gave them a letter to the raja demanding restitution of the stolen property. The raja was terrified, and restored 370 horses, paid the price of 33 which had died, gave the merchants valuable gifts for Mahmūd, and begged them to intercede with him. Mahmūd content with this display of his power and the raja's humiliation, permitted the merchants to retain the horses as well as their price,

In 1491 Mahmūd received complaints of the exactions of Bahādur Gīlānī, who, during the troubles which had fallen upon the Bahmanī kingdom, had possessed himself of the whole of the Konkan and committed piracy at sea and brigandage on land, his depredations extending as far north as Cambay. Qīvām-ul-Mulk, who was sent with an army to punish him, discovered that he could not reach him without invading the Deccan, and returned to Ahmadābād to seek authority for this action, but Mahmūd was averse from any act of aggression against the southern kingdom, and contented himself with writing to Mahmūd Shāh Bahmanī, reminding him of the claims which Gujarāt had on the gratitude of his house and requesting him to suppress the marauder. Bahādur was in fact in rebellion against the feeble Bahmanīd, who had no control over him, but a reassuring reply was sent to Gujarāt and Mahmūd Bahmanī, or rather his minister Qāsim, Barīd-ul-Mamālik, with the help of Ahmad Nīzām Shāh, who was now virtually independent at Junnār, undertook a campaign against the pirate. The operations were protracted, and it was not until 1494 that Bahādur Gīlānī was defeated and slain and full reparation was made to Gujarāt. The ships which Bahādur had taken were restored to their owners, and gifts consisting of Arab horses, a large quantity of pearls, five elephants, and a jewelled dagger were sent to Mahmūd.

In 1492 Bahā-ud-dīn Ulugh Khān, son of Ulugh Khān, Suhrāb and governor of Modāsa, oppressed the people and appropriated the pay of his troops, so that they rose against him and he fled. Mahmūd sent Sharaf-i-Jahān to reassure him, but the mission was a failure, and Ulugh Khān, just as his father had joined Mahmūd Khaljī, sought an asylum with Ghiyās-ud-dīn Khaljī of Mālwa, who refused to receive him. He then went to Sultānpur, and besieged the governor, 'Azīz-ul-Mulk Shaikhan, but on the arrival of a relieving force fled into Baglāna, and was followed thither and defeated. After wandering for some time as a fugitive he submitted to the king and was pardoned and reinstated, but shortly afterwards, having murdered one of his officers, was thrown into prison, where he died in 1496.

On November 20, 1500, Ghiyās-ud-dīn Khaljī of Mālwa, had been deposed by his son, Nāsir-ud-dīn, and died in February 1501, not without suspicion of poison. Mahmūd resolved to punish the reputed parricide, and prepared to invade Mālwa, but Nāsir-ud-dīn succeeded in persuading him that his father had acquiesced in his deposition, and that he was innocent of his death, and the expedition was abandoned.

Vasco da Gama had appeared on the Malabar coast in 1498, and the Portuguese were now firmly established in more than one western port. In 1506 a strong fort was built at Cochin, which was their chief emporium, and in 1507 a settlement was made on the island of Socotra, near the entrance of the Red Sea. Thus, in less than a decade, they had diverted the greater part of the lucrative spice trade from the Red Sea and Egypt ; for the discovery of the direct sea route to Europe had deprived the Mamlūk Sultans of one of their chief sources of revenue, heavy dues being levied both at Jedda and Alexandria on goods in transit. The important ports of north-western India, such as Cambay and Chaul, which were held by the Muslims, were at the same time seriously affected, and thus the Portuguese incurred the hostility of all the Muhammadan powers surrounding the Arabian Sea, who determined to make a combined effort to oust the infidel intruders. It was finally arranged, by correspondence which passed between Qansauh-al-Ghaurī, sultan of Egypt, the king of Gujarāt, other local Muhammadan rulers, and the Zamorin of Calicut, who had been the most intimately associated with the Europeans, that a fleet should be equipped at Suez and dispatched to India, where it would be reinforced by such vessels as were available locally. The Egyptian fleet was under the command of Amīr Husain the Kurd, governor of Jedda, while the Indian contingent was commanded by Malik Ayāz, a Turkish subject who had found his way to the court of Gujarāt. Up to the year 1507 the Portuguese had confined their activities inland to the Malabar coast, though they had frequently harassed the trading vessels and pilgrim ships bound from Gujarāt, 'the Gate of Mecca' to Indian Muslims, for Jedda. The Portuguese Viceroy, Francesco de Almeida, in this year resolved to exploit the northerly coast of India, and dispatched his gallant son Lourenco with a squadron to explore the coast as far as Gujarāt. It does not appear that the Viceroy had any intimation of the attack which was to be made by the Egyptian fleet, although he was aware of the correspondence which had been passing between India and Egypt. Had he known that Amīr Husain was on his way it is unlikely that he would have sent so small a squadron under his son. Amīr Husain reached India at the end of 1507 and encountered Lourenco in the harbour of Chaul in January, 1508, when a fierce fight ensued in which the Portuguese were utterly defeated by Amīr Husain and Malik Ayāz, and Dom Lourenco died a hero's death. After this victory, which was the occasion of much jubilation and of mutual congratulations among the Muslims, Mahmūd returned to Chāmpāner.

We must revert to the history of Khāndesh, in the affairs of which Mahmūd was now, not unwillingly, entangled. We have already traced its history, in outline, to the succession of 'Ādil Khān II in 1457.

'Ādil Khān II was one of the most energetic and most powerful rulers of Khāndesh. He consolidated his authority in that region, and extended it over Gondwāna, he suppressed the depredations of the Kolīs and Bhīls, thus ensuring the safety of travellers in his dominions, and carried arms as far as Jhārkhand, the modern Chota Nāgpur, from which circumstances he is known as *Jhār-Khāndī Sultān*. Since Khalaf Hasan's invasion the rulers of Khāndesh had regarded the king of Gujarāt as their natural protector, and had paid him tribute, but 'Ādil Khān II, in his career of victory, had scorned dependence, and had omitted to send the usual tribute. A demonstration of force by Mahmūd in 1499 or 1500 had sufficed to bring him to his senses, and from that time until his death, more than a year later, he was on cordial terms with his suzerain and visited his court

On September 28, 1501, 'Ādil Khān II died without issue and was succeeded by his younger brother, Dāūd Khān. There was, however, another aspirant belonging to the Fārūqī family, named 'Ālam Khān, who had enjoyed the protection of the king of Gujarāt. This 'Ālam Khān was the great-great-grandson of Hasan Khān, who had been expelled from Khāndesh by his elder brother, Nasīr Khān. and had fled to the court of Ahmad Shāh of Gujarāt. All Hasan Khān's descendants, with the exception of one, who married a daughter of Jām Nizām-ud-dīn of Sind, had married princesses of the royal house of Gujarāt, and 'Ālam Khān was the grandson of Mahmūd Begarha. It thus came about that Mahmūd induced 'Ādil Khān II to nominate his youthful kinsman as his heir, to the exclusion of his brother Dāūd, but in 1501 Mahmūd was not in a position to press his grandson's. claim, and Dāūd succeeded without opposition to the throne of Khāndesh. He was a feeble but reckless prince, who contrived to embroil himself with Ahmad Nizām Shāh of Ahmadnagar, who invaded Khāndesh and could not be expelled until Dāūd had purchased the aid of Nāsir-ud-dīn Khaljī of Malwa by the humiliating concession of causing the *Khutba* to be recited in his name. His death on August 28, 1508, ended an inglorious reign, and he was succeeded by his son Ghaznī Khān, who was poisoned after a reign of ten days. Ahmad Nizām Shah now again invaded Khāndesh with the object of placing on the throne another scion of the Fārūqī house also named 'Ālam

Khān, who had taken refuge at his court. Mahmūd Begarha was at this juncture reminded of his pledge to support his grandson's claim, and he too invaded Khāndesh with the object of placing the other 'Adam Khān on the throne. Khāndesh was divided into two factions, the one supporting the Gujarāt claimant and the other the Ahmadnagar claimant. The adherents of the former, under Malik Husain the Mughul, established themselves in Burhānpur, where they were joined by Ahmad Nizām Shāh and the king of Berar, while Malik Lādan, the leader of the Gujarāt party, shut himself up in Asīrgarh, where he was besieged. Meanwhile Mahmūd Begarha, with his grandson, was marching on Thālner, and when news of his arrival reached Burhānpur Ahmad Nizām Shāh and the king of Berar withdrew, leaving a force of 4000 to support the Ahmadnagar candidate and Malik Husain. When they heard that Mahmūd had sent a force to attack them these troops fled from Burhānpur, carrying the pretender with them and Malik Husain, thus deserted, was obliged to submit to Mahmūd. All opposition being thus removed, the king of Gujarāt held a court at Thālner and installed his candidate on the throne of Khāndesh with the title of 'Ādil Khān III. After Mahmūd's return to Gujarāt an envoy from Ahmad's son and successor, Burhān Nizām Shāh, waited on him and demanded that some provision should be made for 'Ālam Khān, but was compelled to convey to his master the humiliating message that the sultan of Gujarāt recognised no royalty in the rebellious slave of the kings of the Deccan, and that if Burhān dared again to address a king otherwise than as a humble suppliant he should repent it.

'Ādil Khān III of Khāndesh cemented his alliance with Gujarāt by marrying a daughter of Sultān Muzaffar, Mahmūd's son, who afterwards succeeded his father as Muzaffar II. One of his first acts was to cause Malik Husain, who was again plotting with the king of Ahmadnagar, to be assassinated. The dispatch from Gujarāt of a large force averted a danger which threatened the state from the direction of Ahmadnagar, and the reign of 'Ādil Khān III was not marked by any noteworthy event. On his death, on August 25, 1520, he was succeeded by his son, Muhammad I, generally known as Muhammad Shāh, from his having been summoned to the throne of Gujarāt, which he never lived to occupy.

From Thālner Mahmūd returned to Chāmpāner, where, in 1510, he was gratified by the arrival of a mission from Sikandar Lodī of Delhi, who tendered him his congratulations on his success in Khāndesh. A mission in the following year from Shāh Ismā'īl I

Safavī, of Persia, was less favourably received. The envoy, Yādgār Beg Qizilbāsh, was commissioned to invite Mahmūd to embrace the Shiah faith, but Mahmūd, whose health was failing, had refreshed his orthodoxy by visits to the shrines of saints at Pātan and Sarkhej, and sent a message to the heretics bidding them begone. He had already designated his son Muzaffar as his heir, and feeling the approach of death summoned him from Baroda. Muzaffar arrived only in time to assist in bearing his father's coffin from Ahmadābād to his tomb at Sarkhej, for Mahmūd I, the greatest of the sultans of Gujarāt, had breathed his last on November 23, 1511.

Mahmūd Begarha was not only the greatest of the sultans of Gujarāt. He holds a prominent place among the warrior princes of India. Succeeding to the throne at an age when even Akbar was under tutelage, he at once assumed the management of affairs, overcame an extensive conspiracy backed by armed force, and administered his kingdom with complete freedom, whether from the dictation of a minister or from the more pernicious influence of the harem. He was, in short, a prodigy of precocity. When he grew to manhood his appearance was striking. Tall and robust, with a beard which descended to his girdle and a heavy moustache which twisted and curled upwards, his mien struck awe into his courtiers. His elder brother, Qutb-ud-dīn Ahmad Shāh, had died by poison, and wonderful fables are related of the means by which Mahmūd protected himself from a like fate. He is said gradually to have absorbed poisons into his system until he was so impregnated with them that a fly settling on his hand instantly died, and he was immune from the effects of any poison which might be administered to him. It is to him that Samuel Butler refers in *Hudibras*, first published in 1664 :

> The prince of Cambay's daily food
> Is asp and basilisk and toad[1].

Physicians will estimate the practicability and efficacy of such a course of prophylactic treatment, but whatever foundation there may be for these strange legends there is no reason to doubt that Mahmūd profited from the general belief in his immunity from poison, and Butler's description of his diet is at least incomplete, for his voracious appetite demanded large supplies of more wholesome food. His daily allowance was between twenty and thirty pounds' weight, and before going to sleep he placed two pounds or more of boiled rice on either side of his couch, so that he might

[1] Part II, Canto i,

find something to eat on whichever side he awoke. When he rose in the morning he swallowed a cup of honey, a cup of butter, and from 100 to 150 bananas.

His martial exploits and the expansion of his dominions which they brought about have been recounted. He was mild and just to his own servants, and his fierce intolerance of Hinduism is counted to him by historians of his own religion as a merit. Of his nickname Begarha two explanations have been given, but there can be no doubt that the true interpretation is *be garh*, or 'two forts,' and that it had reference to his capture of the two great Hindu strongholds of Girnār and Chāmpāner.

The naval victory over the Portuguese at Chaul in 1508, which had so elated the Muslims, was without lasting results, for in the following year Almeida sailed up the west coast with his whole fleet to Diū, where he found the Egyptian fleet with its Indian auxiliaries lying between the island and the mainland. In the desperate battle which followed the Muslims were totally defeated and the Egyptian fleet almost entirely destroyed. No mention of this Portuguese victory is made by the Muslim historians, but it is alluded to by the Arabic historian of the Zamorins of Calicut. Full and circumstantial accounts are, however, to be found in the Portuguese chronicles. After this failure to drive the Portuguese from the Indian seas Mahmūd Begarha ordered Malik Ayāz to make peace, and to return the prisoners taken at Chaul. In the following year the Portuguse first obtained possession of Goa and transferred their headquarters from Cochin to that city. Mahmūd offered them a site for a factory at Diū, and almost immediately after the accession of Muzaffar II in 1511 a Portuguese mission arrived to seek permission for the construction of a fort to protect the factory. This request was not granted, and the mission left. Yadgar Beg, the ambassador from Shāh Ismā'īl Safavī whom Mahmūd Begarha had refused to receive, was favourably received by Muzaffar, and was lodged at Ahmadābād, and afterwards at Chāmpāner.

Mahmūd II, who had ascended the throne of Mālwa in 1510, was the younger son of his father, Nāsir-ud-dīn, whom he had deposed, and the elder son, Sāhib Khān, entitled Muhammad Shāh, now sought refuge with Muzaffar and begged him to help him to expel his brother and gain his throne. He joined Muzaffar's camp at Baroda, on the way from Ahmadābād to Chāmpāner, and Muzaffar sent an agent into Mālwa to investigate the situation and report upon it. The agent, Qaisar Khān, returned with a report favourable to Sāhib Khān's claim, and Sāhib Khān was impatient for his host to take the field. Muzaffar bade him have patience and promised to invade Mālwa at the end of the rainy season, but before the time came to redeem his promise Sāhib Khān had left Gujarāt in consequence of the gross misconduct of the Persian ambassador, who invited him to dinner and assaulted him. The prince's servants attacked the ambassador's suite and plundered his lodging, but the affair was noised abroad, and Sāhib Khān was so overcome with shame that he fled from Gujarāt and attempted to take refuge with 'Ādil Khān III of Khāndesh, but while he was travelling to that court the governor of a frontier district of the kingdom of Mālwa attacked and defeated him, and he fled, with a following of 300 horse, to 'Alā-ud-dīn 'Imād Shāh of Berar, who would not offend the sultan of Mālwa by offering the fugitive armed assistance, but assigned to him lands for his maintenance.

Nāsir-ud-dīn of Mālwa had employed in his army a large number of Rājputs from eastern Hindūstān, who had become so powerful in the kingdom that Mahmūd II was a puppet in their hands. Muzaffar II marched to Godhra with a view to invading Mālwa and restoring Mahmūd's authority by crushing the Rajputs, but at Godhra he received disturbing news from Īdar. 'Ain-ul-Mulk Fūlādī, governor of Pātan, was marching with his contingent to join him at Godhra, but on the way learned that Bhīm Singh of Īdar, taking advantage of Muzaffar's preoccupation with the affairs of Mālwa, had raided the whole country to the east of the Sābar-matī river. He turned aside to punish him, but the raja defeated him, slew his brother and 200 of his men, and compelled him to flee. Muzaffar, on receiving the news, marched in person to Modāsa, drove Bhīm Singh to the hills and sacked his capital, destroying the temples and other buildings. Bhīm Singh was fain to purchase peace, and permission to return to Īdar by a payment of 800,000 rupees and the delivery of 100 horses.

Having thus settled affairs on his north-eastern frontier Muzaffar, in 1513, marched to Godhra, sent his son Sikandar to Chāmpāner as governor, dispatched a force under Qaisar Khān to Deolī[1] near the Māhī, and followed him with his army. He had now changed his intention of aiding Mahmūd by crushing the Rājputs, and had formed the design of conquering and annexing Mālwa. He sent a force to occupy Dhār, the governor of which offered no resistance on receiving an assurance that the city should not be sacked nor its inhabitants massacred.

[1] In 22° 57′ N. and 74° 58′ E.

Muzaffar now learnt that Mahmūd was at Chanderī, endeavouring to crush a rebellion of the Rājput troops under their
leader, Medeni Rāi, and he once more changed his mind. For this
second instance of vacillation two reasons are assigned. The first
more favourable to Muzaffar's character, was the reflection that
to attack a brother Muslim who was in straits owing to the misconduct of infidels would be both unlawful and ungenerous, and
the second was the defeat of a detachment sent by him to Na'lcha,
which he regarded as an evil omen. The former reason may be
accepted as the true one, first because it is conformable to the whole
course of Muzaffar's behaviour towards Mahmūd Khaljī, and
secondly because the fact that his troops were defeated   not established. He retired to his own dominions and relieved the anxiety
which oppressed Mahmūd, beset on all sides by difficulties.

In 1515 Raja Bhīm Singh of Īdar died, and should have been
succeeded by his son Biharī Mal, but his cousin german contested
the succession, and Sangrama Singh, Rānā of Mewār, the Sāngā or
Sānkā of Muslim historians, welcomed the opportunity of asserting
his ill-founded claim to supremacy over all Rājput princes and
supported the pretender, who was his brother-in-law. He invaded
Īdar and enthroned Rāi Mal, expelling Bihārī Mal, who took refuge
with Muzaffar. Muzaffar would not brook this interference in a
state which had for many years owned allegiance to Gujarāt, and,
marching to Ahmadnagar, sent Nizām-ul-Mulk to Īdar to expel
Rāi Mal and establish Biharī Mal as raja. The selection of Nizām-
ul-Mulk for the duty was not merely fortuitous, for he was the
son of Raja Pataī of Chāmpāner, and had embraced Islam after
the fall of that stronghold. He expelled Rāi Mal from Īdar and
restored Biharī Mal. He then followed Rāi Mal into the Bichabhera
hills and attacked him. The battle was indecisive, many lives being
lost to no purpose, and Muzaffar rebuked Nizām-ul-Mulk for his
inconsiderate rashness ; and shortly afterwards Nizām-ul-Mulk was
stricken with paralysis and was relieved at his own request,
Nusrat-ul-Mulk being sent to Īdar in his place. Nizām-ul-Mulk
was so eager to return to Chāmpāner that he started from Īdar
before Nusrat-ul-Mulk could arrive, leaving Zahīr-ul-Mulk with
no more than a hundred men to hold Īdar.

Rāi Mal marched on Īdar and Zahīr-ul-Mulk went forth with
his small force to meet him, and was defeated with the loss of more
than a quarter of his men. Nusrat-ul-Mulk, who was at Ahmadnagar, pressed on, drove off Rāi Mal, and made Ahmadnagar his

headquarters, maintaining order in the plains by harrying the brigands of the Vajinagar hills.

Mahmūd II of Mālwa was so weary of the dominance of his Rājput officers that he secretly left his capital and arrived at Bhāgor[1], where he was received by the Gujarāt noble, Qaisar Khān. As soon as Muzaffar heard of his arrival he sent him tents, treasure, and elephants, and shortly afterwards joined him with an army and entertained him at banquet to celebrate the occasion. When Medenī Rāi heard of these doings he set out for Chitor, in order to seek help from Rānā Sangrama, leaving a garrison to protect Māndū, against which Mahmūd and Muzaffar were marching. The Rājput garrison was twice defeated before the walls, and Muzaffar formed the siege of the fortress. Pithaura, who commanded the garrison, had heard from Medenī Rāi that the Rānā was coming to his aid, and strove by feigned negotiations, as well as by force of arms, to hold out as long as possible. Muzaffar II was now joined by his nephew and son-in-law, 'Ādil Khān III of Khāndesh, whom he sent with Qivām-ul-Mulk to check the progress of the Rānā and Medenī Rāi, who had already reached Ujjain.

On February 23, 1518, the day of the Hindu festival of the Holī, Māndū was carried by escalade, the Rājput garrison performed the rite of *jauhar*, and Muzaffar, on entering the city, ordered a general massacre of the surviving Rājputs. Nineteen thousand were put to the sword, and the streets ran with blood, which streamed from the drains which carried rainwater into the ditch.

Muzaffar now prepared to march against the Rānā and Medenī Rāi, but learned that they had been so terror-stricken by the news of the massacre that they at once turned and fled, riding fifty-four miles on the first night of their flight. Muzaffar restored Māndū to Mahmūd, who entertained him sumptuously and accompanied him on his homeward way as far as Deolī, and Āsaf Khān with 10,000 horse was left in Mālwa to aid Mahmūd against his enemies. In connexion with the siege of Māndū we first hear of 'Imād-ul-Mulk, Khush Qadam, who played such an important part in the affairs of Gujarāt at this time.

Muzaffar, after returning to Chāmpāner, learned that Rāi Mal had been ravaging the Pātna district, and marched to punish him, remaining for some time in Īdar while Rāi Mal and his confederates were pursued in hills.

In 1519, after his return to Chāmpāner Muzaffar heard of the defeat and capture of Mahmūd II by Rānā Sangrama near Gāgraun,

[1] In 22° 53′ N. and 74° 36′ E.

and of the heavy losses suffered by his own contingent of 10,000 horse. He sent reinforcements into Mālwa, but they were not required, for the Rānā generously restored his vanquished foe to his throne.

Mubāriz-ul-Mulk was now sent to relieve Nusrat-ul-Mulk at Īdar, where he was so annoyed by hearing the praise of the valour and generosity of the Rānā that he named a dog Sangrama, and tied it up at one of the gates of the town. The Rānā, on hearing of this insult, assembled his army and marched on Īdar, where Mubāriz-ul-Mulk's officers were so enraged with him for having by his contemptible act endangered them and the city that they dissuaded the king from sending assistance to him, and retired to Ahmadnagar, carrying him with them. The Rānā occupied Īdar and marched on to Ahmadnagar, where he defeated Mubāriz-ul-Mulk with heavy loss and compelled him to retreat to Ahmadābād. After plundering Ahmadnagar he marched to Vadnagar, the inhabitants of which town, being Brāhmans, escaped molestation thence he marched to Visnagar, plundered the town after defeating Malik Hātim, who gallantly came forth to meet him with the small force at his disposal, and then returned to his own country.

After his departure Mubāriz-ul-Mulk returned with a small force to Ahmadnagar and buried the dead. Here he was attacked by the Kolīs of Īdar, whom he defeated.

In January, 1521, Muzaffar sent an army of 100,000 horse and 100 elephants under the command of Malik Ayāz, governor of Sorath, to chastise the Rānā for his raid into Gujarāt. Bākor[1], Gāliākot[2], Dūngarpur[3], Sagwāra[4], and Bānswāra[5] were ravaged and laid waste. At Bānswāra a large force of Hindus lying in ambush was attacked and put to flight after suffering losses. Malik Ayāz then marched to Mandasor, and besieged that town. Rānā Sangrama marched to its relief, but would not venture within twenty miles of the muslim camp, and sent agents to Malik Ayāz offering to pay tribute to Muzaffar II if he would raise the siege, but his prayers were unheeded. Mahmūd II joined Malik Ayāz, and Mandasor might have been captured and Sangrama defeated, but for the jealousy of Malik Ayāz, who feared lest Qivām-ul-Mulk, his principal lieutenant, should gain the credit for the victory. He therefore made peace with the Rānā on his promising to pay

---

[1] In 23° 21′ N. and 73° 37′ E.   [2] In 23° 21′ N. and 74° 1′ E.
[3] In 23° 50′ N. and 73° 43′ E.   [4] In 23° 40′ N. and 74° 2′ E.
[5] In 23° 33′ N. and 74° 27′ E.

tribute, to place a son at Muzaffar's court as a hostage, to wait in person on the king and to be obedient to his orders. Qivām-ul-Mulk was strongly opposed to this treaty and persuaded Mahmūd Shāh to join him in an attack on the Rānā, but Malik Ayāz was informed of this design, used his authority over the army of Gujarāt to prevent its execution and marched b ck to Ahmadābād. Muzaffar was so deeply disappointed by this termination of a promising campaign that he would not see Malik Ayāz, but sent him straight back to Sorath, where he died in the following year and was succeeded by his son Ishāq.

Muzaffar himself was preparing in 1522, to march against the Rānā but before he could start from Ahmadābād Sangrama's son arrived with gifts from his father, and the expedition was abandoned.

In 1524 'Ālam Khān, son of Buhlūl Lodī of Delhi, who was a refugee at Muzaffar's court, informed him that according to information received by him from Delhi there was much dissatisfaction with his nephew, Sultān Ibrāhīm Lodī, and the chances of his obtaining his father's throne appeared to be good. Muzaffar accordingly supplied him with a sum of money and a small force and dismissed him.

Late in 1524 Muzaffar's second son, Bahādur, demanded equality of treatment with his eldest brother, Sikandar, but the king who had designated Sikandar as his heir, feared to place more power in the hands of the ablest and most energetic of his sons, and put him off with fair words. Bahādur fled disgusted from his father's court and repaired first to Udai Singh of Dūngarpur, then to Sanggrama Singh at Chitor, and next to Mewāt, where the local Muhammadan ruler, Hasan entertained him hospitably. He eventually proceeded to Delhi, but it is not quite clear at what precise date. In all probability it was at the beginning of 1526, for the people of Delhi were then expecting the approach of Bābur with his invading army. Bahādur was well received by Ibrāhīm Lodī who was doubtless glad to obtain the services of this young but experienced soldier. Ibrāhīm was encamped at Pānīpat when Bahādur joined him, and skirmishes had already begun with the advanced guard of the Mughul army. It was in one of these skirmishes that Bahādur so greatly distinguished himself that the jealousy of Ibrāhīm Lodī was roused, and Bahādur deemed it prudent to withdraw, and set out for Jaunpur, possibly selecting this town in response to an invitation received from the local nobles, who are said to have offered him the throne. The battle of Pānīpat, in which Bābur defeated

Ibrāhīm, was fought on April 18. Abū Turāb, a contemporary writer, tells us that Bahādur was present at this battle, but took no part in the fighting. If this refers to the decisive action Bahādur must have left for Jaunpur as soon as the issue of the day had been decided. On April 7 his father Muzaffar died, and it was while he was on his way to Jaunpur that Bahādur received an invitation to return, and immediately turned back in the direction of Gujarāt, travelling by way of Chitor.

The nobles of Gujarāt were now divided into three factions, supporting the claims of Sikandar, Bahādur, and Latīf, the eldest, second, and third sons of Muzaffar. Sikandar, who had been designated heir by his father, was immediately proclaimed by 'Imād-ul-Mulk Khush Qadam and Khudāvand Khān al-Ijī, and marched from Ahmadābād to Chāmpāner. The new king was feeble and ill-advised. He alienated the old nobles of his father's reign by advancing his own personal servants beyond their merits, and by his untimely profusion. There was general dissatisfaction, and an impression prevailed that Bahādur would soon return to seize the throne, but the immediate danger was from Latīf Khān, who was assembling, his forces at Nandurbār. A force under Sharza Khān was sent against him, but he retired into Baglāna and when Sharza Khān followed him thither he was attacked, defeated, and slain by the raja, and the Rājputs and Kolīs followed the defeated army and slew 1700 of them. The superstition of the time regarded the termination of the first enterprise of the reign as an augury of the future fortune of the king. Another army, under Qaisar Khān, was assembled, but the choice was an indication either of the ignorance and folly of the king or of the treachery of the nobles, for Qaisar Khān was Latīf's principal adherent ; but before the expedition could start 'Imād-ul-Mulk Khush Qadam had caused Sikandar to be assassinated during the midday slumbers, and had raised to the throne Mahmūd, an infant son of Muzaffar II, whom on April, 12, 1526, he caused to be proclaimed as Mahmūd II.

His object in selecting an infant son, was, of course, that the government of the kingdom might remain entirely in his hands, but it may be doubted whether he expected to maintain his puppet against Bahādur, or even against Latīf. The adherents of the former had been writing to urge him to return without delay to Gujarāt, and he had eagerly responded to their solicitations. The old nobles of the kingdom, disgusted with the rule of the freedman, 'Imād-ul-Mulk, who was as lavish of titles and robes of honour as he was niggardly of more substantial favours, fled from Chāmpāner, and Tāj Khān Narpālī led a force to escort Bahādur back to Gujarāt.

'Imād-ul-Mulk in his terror sent large sums of money to Burhān Nizām Shāh I of Ahmadnagar and Udai Singh, raja of Pālanpur, to induce the former to invade Nandurbār and the latter to advance on Chāmpāner in support of the infant king, and wrote also to Bābur, requesting him to send a force to Dīū with the same object, and promising him a gift of 10,000,000 *tangas* and the allegiance of Gujarāt. This last promise was reported to Khudāvand Khān and Tāj Khān, and only served to increase the general detestation in which 'Imād-ul-Mulk was held. Burhān Nizām Shāh accepted the money sent to him, but did nothing in return. Udai Singh did indeed march to Chāmpāner, but his aid alone was of little consequence, and he almost immediately transferred his allegiance to Bahādur.

Bahādur at once returned to Gujarāt by way of Modāsa and Pātan and, as he advanced, was everywhere welcomed and joined by the nobles and officers of his father's court. On July 11 he ascended the throne at Ahmadābād, and immediately continued his journey to Chāmpāner. The feeble efforts of 'Imād-ul-Mulk to delay or hamper his advance were ineffectual ; he entered Chāmpāner without opposition and at once went about to punish those who had murdered his brother and prepared his own way to the throne. 'Imād-ul-Mulk Khush Qadam, Saif-ul-Mulk, and the actual assassins of Sikandar were immediately put to death. Latīf Khān, who was lurking in the city in the hope of events taking a turn favourable to his pretensions, wisely accepted the advice of his friends and fled to Pālanpur, and thence to Nandurbār, where he was joined by a number of his partisans. His adherents at Chāmpāner were arrested, and their houses were plundered by the mob. Ghāzī Khān, who was upholding Bahādur's cause in the Nandurbār district, reported that Latīf Khān had raised the standard of revolt, that he had defeated him and dispersed his followers, and that Latīf was a wounded prisoner in his hands. He was ordered to see that his prisoner received proper treatment and to send him to court, but the prince died on his way thither and Bahādur was left without a competitor except his infant brother Mahmūd, who was secretly put to death within the year. Another brother, Chānd Khān, had taken refuge with Mahmūd Khaljī at Māndū, and Mahmūd's refusal to surrender him dissolved the friendship which had once saved his kingdom for him. The murder of the child Mahmūd II alienated Udai Singh of Pālanpur, who sacked the town of Dohad, but Tāj Khān Narpālī led a punitive expedition against him and chastised him severely.

Malik Ishāq, who had succeeded his father, Malik Ayāz, in the important government of Sorath, lost his reason in 1527, and attacked without any justification the Hindu chief of Dwārkā, who was an obedient vassal of Bahādur. After his return to Junāgarh he became so violent that it was found necessary to put him in prison, where he died shortly afterwards. He was succeeded by his brother, Malik Tūghān, famous for his stature and great bodily strength, who in order to watch the Portuguese made Diū his principal place of residence. The adventurers would not abandon their design to build at Diū a fort for the protection of their trade and merchandise, and sought to execute it at times by means of negotiations and at times by force, but for several years had no success. At length, on September 21, 1534, Bahādur permitted them by treaty to build a fort.

Towards the end of 1527 Bahādur received an appeal for help from 'Alā-ud-dīn 'Imād Shāh of Berar and Muhammad I of Khāndesh. The kings of Ahmadnagar and Berar had quarrelled over the possession of the town and district of Pāthrī on the Godāvarī, which belonged to the latter but were coveted and had been annexed by the former. 'Alā-ud-dīn had enlisted the aid of Muhammad and had marched to recover the district, but Burhān Nizām Shāh of Ahmadnagar and his ally, Amīr 'Alī Barīd of Bīdar, had attacked and defeated them, captured their artillery and elephants, pursued them through Berar, and expelled 'Alā-ud-dīn from his kingdom, compelling him to take refuge in Khāndesh. Bahādur marched to Nandurbār, where he was met by his cousin, Muhammad of Khāndesh, and by the Rāhtor raja of Baglāna, who did homage to him and entertained him in his fortress of Sālher. Bahādur gave his sister in marriage to Muhammad, upon whom he conferred the title of Shāh, and after the rainy season of 1528 marched on Ahmadnagar by way of Berar, where he was joined by 'Alā-ud-dīn 'Imād Shāh, sending a force with the raja of Baglāna, whom he ordered to advance on Ahmadnagar by the more direct route of his own principality.

Burhān's army, with a contingent of 6000 horse furnished by Ismā'īl 'Ādil Shāh of Bījāpur and 3000 furnished by Amīr 'Alī Barīd, was in the hilly country about Bīr, and Amīr 'Alī Barīd inflicted two defeats on detachments of Bahādur's army between Paithan and Bīr, but the army of Gujarāt continued to advance, and occupied Ahmadnagar for forty days, while Burhān Nizām

Shāh, who had first retired from Bīr to Parenda, was pursued to Junnār. Meanwhile the army of Ahmadnagar had been engaged in cutting off Bahādur's supplies, and the invaders had already begun to suffer from famine when Bahādur marched to Daulatābād and opened the siege of the fortress, while Burhān and Amīr 'Alī Barīd occupied the neighbouring hills. They attempted to relieve Daulatābād but were driven back into the hills, and then opened negotiations with Sultān Bahādur's allies, and found no difficulty in seducing 'Alā-ud-dīn 'Imād, Shāh, who was beginning to suspect that Bahādur did not intend to leave the Deccan, and regretted having summoned him to his aid. He sent a quantity of supplies into the fortress and hurriedly retired into Berar, leaving his camp standing.

Bahādur's situation gave him some cause for anxiety. He had no prospect of capturing Daulatābād, one of his allies had deserted him, the other, Muhammad of Khāndesh, desired peace, and the rainy season of 1529 was approaching. He therefore permitted Muhammad to open negotiations, and after some discussion agreed to peace on terms sufficiently humiliating to Burhān Nizām Shāh. Both he and 'Alā-ud-dīn 'Imād Shāh were to cause the *khutba* to be recited in Bahādur's name in their dominions, and were to appear before him as vassals ; all the elephants taken from 'Alā-ud-dīn and Muhammad were to be restored, and Pāthrī and Māhūr were to be ceded again to Berar. Burhān fulfilled the first condition by causing the *khutba* to be recited on one occasion in Bahādur's name, but it was only with great difficulty that Muhammad of Khāndesh recovered his elephants, and those of 'Alā-ud-dīn were never restored, nor were Pāthrī and Māhūr ceded to him.

Bahādur returned to Gujarāt in the spring of 1529, and his relative, the Jām Fīrūz of Sind, who had been expelled from his country by Shāh Beg Arghūn, took refuge at his court.

In 1530 the Portuguese, having already assembled at Bombay a great fleet, sailed for Damān and captured that town, and in February, 1931, arrived before Diū, which they attacked, but Bahādur had already visited the place in 1530, and had made all provision for its defence, and the Portuguese, having failed to take the town, sailed back to Goa, leaving a fleet in the Gulf of Cambay to harass the trade and shipping of Gujarāt.

Bahādur returned from Diū to Chāmpāner, where he received some of the nobles of the late Ibrāhīm Shāh Lodī of Delhi, who had reached his court with 300 followers. From Chāmpāner Bahādur marched to Modāsa and thence led an expedition into Bāker and

Bānswāra. The Rānā, Ratan Singh II, who had succeeded San-grama after the battle of Sīkrī, interceded for the two chiefs, and Bahādur stayed his hand.

Mahmūd II of Mālwa was now pursuing a suicidal policy. He had sent a force to ravage the southern districts of the territories of the Rānā, he had so alienated by his sinister and deceitful course of conduct the nobles of Mālwa that some had taken refuge with the Rānā and others with Bahādur, and he was harbouring at his court a son of the late Sultān Muzaffar of Gujarāt, Chānd Khān, a pretender to Bahādur's throne, whose claims he was understood to favour. The old friendship between Mālwa and Gujarāt was thus entirely dissolved. Bahādur, less bigoted than his father, and sensible of Ratan Singh's claims of his friendship, which were based on Sangrama's reception of him when he was a fugitive, was inclined to deprecate wanton attacks on his territories, was bitterly resentful of the harbourage offered to Chānd Khān, and was inclined to regard Mahmūd, who owed his tenure of his throne to the capture of Māndū from rebellious Rājputs by Mahmūd Begarha, as a vassal : Mahmūd, on the other hand, was perturbed by Bahādur's harbourage of malcontents from Mālwa, and suggested a meeting at which differences could be settled. Bahādur haughtily replied that he had been awaiting a request for an interview at which Mahmūd could appear before him and explain matters. This had not been Mahmūd's intention, but he found it difficult to recede from his suggestion, and could hardly propose that Bahādur should wait upon him. He feigned to be eager to pay his respects to the sultan of Gujarāt but always discovered a pretext for evading a meeting. Ratan Singh of Mewār marched as far as Sārangpur and threatened Ujjain, to which city Mahmūd advanced. Bahādur entered Mālwa and awaited Mahmūd's arrival at his camp, but an envoy from Mahmūd made his excuses by explaining that his master had broken his arm whilst out hunting. In private he informed Bahādur that Chānd Khān was the real difficulty, as Mahmūd did not wish to surrender him, but feared to refuse. Bahādur bade the envoy reassure his master on this point, and marched slowly towards Māndū, accompanied by Muhammad Shāh of Khāndesh, expecting Mahmūd at each stage ; but Mahmūd had washed his hands of kingship, and had withdrawn into his seraglio at Māndū, meeting the remonstrances of his courtiers with the answer that he knew that his reign was drawing to its close, and that he intended to enjoy life while it lasted. He had thoughts of abdicating and installing his son Ghiyās-ud-dīn, but seemed to be unable to execute any plan. Meanwhile Bahādur marched to Na'lcha and formed the siege of Mandū, being joined by many of the nobles and officers of Mālwa. The sloth and carelessness of Mahmūd infacted his army, and on the night of March 17 the besiegers scaled an unguarded section of the wall and entered the city unopposed. Mahmūd formed the intention of imitating the Rājputs and performing the rite of *jauhar*, but, on receiving a message from Bahādur that his life and honour were safe, abandoned it and waited on Bahādur with seven of his officers. The *khutba* was recited at Māndū in the name of Bahādur, Mālwa was annexed to Gujarāt, and Mahmūd and his family were sent towards Chāmpāner, where Bahādur proposed to imprison them, but on April 12, 1531, the camp of Āsaf Khān; in whose custody the prisoners were, was attacked by Bhīls and Kolīs, and Mahmūd's guards, fearing a rescue, put him to death, and he was buried near Dohad. His seven sons were sent to Chāmpāner, where they were imprisoned.

Bhādur remained awhile at Māndū and marched in June to Burhānpur, where he was entertained by Muhammad Shāh of Khāndesh, who persuaded him, with some difficulty, to receive the learned and pious Shāh Tahir, who had come as an envoy from Burhān Nizām Shāh I of Ahmadnagar. Burhān had not fulfilled the conditions of the treaty of Daulatābād, and Bahādur was consequently ill-disposed towards him, but Shāh Tāhir undertook that his master should wait on him at Burhānpur and, returning to Ahmadnagar, persuaded Burhān, to carry out this promise, which he had made at Daulatābād. The humiliating circumstances of the reception were somewhat alleviated by an artifice of Shāh Tāhir, who bore a copy of the Koran for presentation to Bahādur, and thus obliged the latter to descend from his throne to do reverence to the holy book. Both Bahādur and Burhān remained for a short time at Burhānpur as the guests of Muhammad Shāh, and before they parted Bahādur gratified Burhān's vanity by recognising his title of Shāh.

The Rājput Silāhdi, who held the districts of Rāisen, Bhīlsa, and Sārangpur, nominally as fiefs of Mālwa but actually as a small principality, had been permitted by Bahādur to visit Rāisen after the fall of Māndū, but showed no disposition to fulfil his promise to return, aud Nassan Khān, who was sent to Rāisen and brought him to court, privately informed the king that he was disloyal, and if permitted again to leave the court would ally himself to the Rānā. He was therefore arrested at Dhār, his troops were plundered and dispersed, and his elephants were confiscated.

Early in January, 1532, Bahādur sent 'Imād-ul-Mulk Malikjī, son of Tawakkul, to arrest Sīlāhdī's son Bhopat, who had remained at Ujjain when his father came to court and had since occupied Sārangpur. 'Imād-ul-Mulk reported that he had fled to Chitor to seek help of the Rānā, and the king marched by Bhīlsa, which he occupied, to Rāisen, still held by Sīlāhdī's brother, Lakhman Singh. He was attacked as he approached the town on January 26, but drove the Rājputs into the fortress and formed the siege.

Bahādur's artillery, under Mustafā Rūmī Khān, who had succeeded Tūghān as governor of Diū, did much execution, and Sīlāhdī conciliated Bahādur by perfidiously feigning to accept Islam, and thus obtained permission to meet his brother, ostensibly with the object of arranging for the surrender of the fortress, but when he and Lakhman Singh met they agreed to await the relieving force expected from Chitor, and sent 2000 men under Sīlāhdī's youngest son to hasten its arrival. This force, was, however, intercepted by the besiegers and defeated, Sīlāhdī's son being slain, and Bahādur, on learning of Sīlāhdī's perfidy, sent him in custody to Māndū and dispatched a force under Muhammad Shāh of Khāndesh and 'Imād-ul-Mulk Malikjī to meet the Rānā and Bhopat. This force met and put to flight at Kamkera another force of 2000 Rājputs under Pūran Mal, another of Sīlāhdī's sons, and Bahādur, learning that the Rānā was at the head of a large army left his officers to continue the siege and marched against him. Vikramāditya, who had succeeded his father Ratan Singh would not face Bahādur in the field, but retired to Chitor, and Bahādur returned to Rāisen. Lakhman Singh, despairing of relief, offered to surrender on condition that Sīlāhdī was pardoned, but when Sīlāhdī, having been recalled from Māndū, was again permitted to enter Rāisen, he was persuaded to perform the rite of *jauhar* rather than incur the disgrace of being implicated in the surrender. Over 700 women were burnt, and the men sallied forth, according to custom, in garments died yellow, but exhibited little of the spirit of the Rājput, for though all were slain the losses of the Muslims amounted to no more than four or five.

Muhammad Shāh of Khāndesh, who was sent to establish Bahādur's authority over the outlying districts of Mālwa, captured Gāgraun[1] and Kanōr[2], both of which had been treacherously surrendered by Medenī Rāi, who had held them of the king of Mālwa, to the Rānā of Mewar, and Bahādur, having appointed as governor of Rāisen Sultān 'Ālam, chief of Kālpī, who had fled from his prin-

---

[1] In 24° 38′ N. and 76° 12′ E.　　　　[2] In 24° 26′ N. and 74° 16′ E.

cipality before Bābur, overran part of Gondwāna, captured many elephants, appointed Alp Khān governor of that region, and, turning westward, captured Islāmābād and Hoshangābād, and met Muhammad Shāh, of Khāndesh at Sārangpur, where the Rānā's governor of Gāgraun was presented to him. Then returning to Māndū he sent 'Imād-ul-Mulk Malikji and Ikhtiyār Khān to take Mandasor, formerly spared at the intercession of Sangrama Singh, whose successor's writ no longer ran either in Mālwa or in Gujarāt. The town and fortress were taken, the Rānā's officer fled, and Bahādur dismissed Muhammad Shāh to Khāndesh, visited Diū, and on his return thence spent the rainy season at Chāmpāner considering the punishment of the Rānā. The occasion was opportune, for Vikramāditya was the Commodus of Rājputānā and disgusted his haughty nobles by his preference for the society of gladiators, wrestlers, and professional swashbucklers.

Bahādur, having been joined by Muhammad Shāh of Khāndesh, marched from Chāmpāner on November 6, 1532, and on February 14, 1533, the two kings arrived before Chitor. Ten days later the queen-mother, the widow of Sangrama Singh, purchased peace with what remained of the plunder taken by her husband when he captured Mahmūd Khaljī II of Mālwa, including the jewelled crown of Hūshang and Bahādur retired, but returned again in 1534.

On this occasion he received in his camp Muhammad Zamān Mīrzā, a prince of the house of Tīmūr, whose pretensions had so incensed his kinsman, the emperor, that he had been sentenced to imprisonment in the fortress of Bayāna and to the loss of his eyes, which he saved by flight. Humāyūn whose relations with Bahādur had hitherto been perfectly friendly, took umbrage at his harbouring the fugitive and his followers, and a correspondence ensued which led to a permanent rupture between the two monarchs. Two of the letters which passed between them have been preserved in their entirety and offer a striking picture of the diplomatic methods of that day. Humāyūn pointed out that although his ancestor Tīmūr had desisted from attacking the Ottoman Sultan Bāyazīd while he was engaged in fighting the Franks he protested against Bāyazīd's harbouring princes who had rebelled against himself. He therefore demanded that the prince should be either surrendered or expelled. To this Bahādur, who is said to have dictated his reply when in his cups, sent a most insulting answer, in which he ironically suggested that Humāyūn had boasted of the exploits of 'his sire seven degrees removed' because he himself had achieved nothing worthy of record.

So shocked were Bahādur and his nobles when they considered the tone of this letter on the morrow that an effort was made to overtake the courier, but without success, and their only solace was the reflection that nothing more could be done, and that what was decreed must come to pass.

Bahādur gained an easy victory over Vikramāditya at Loicha[1] ; in the dominions of Surjan, Rāo of Būndī, for the Rānā was deserted by most of his vassals, who marched to the defence of Chitor, and Bahādur, after his successs turned in the same direction and formed the siege. Burhān-ul-Mulk now held Ranthambhor, which he had captured for Bahādur when he had first appeared before Chitor in the preceding year, and Bahādur sent Tātār Khān Lodī, a grandson of Buhlūl Lodī of Delhi who had entered his service, with a vast sum of money, in order that he and Burhān-ul-Mulk might attack the Mughul empire. Tātār Khān raised an army and captured the fortress of Bayāna, but Humāyūn's youngest brother immediately recovered it, and slew him. Meanwhile the siege of Chitor continued. According to Rājput legend Jawāhir Bāi, the queen-mother, of Rāhtor race, sent Humāyūn a bracelet, in accordance with the chivalrous custom of Rājasthān, adopting him as her champion against Bahādur, but the legend is inconsistent with the Muslim chronicles and with the conduct of Humāyūn, who, despite the gross provocation which he had received, would not attack a brother Muslim while he was engaged in fighting the misbelievers.

Bahādur was seriously perturbed by the news of the defeat and death of Tātār Khān Lodī and by apprehensions of being attacked by Humāyūn, and would have raised the siege but for the confident assurance of Sadr Khān, one of his officers, that Humāyūn would never attack him while he was besieging Chitor. After a lapse of three months an extensive breach was made in the rampart, which had never before been exposed to artillery fire. It was stoutly defended but with a terrible sacrifice of life, and the valiant, Jawāhir Bāi led a sortie from the fortress and was slain at the head of her warriors. The garrison lost hope. The infant heir, Udai Singh, was conveyed by Surjan prince of Būndī, to a place of safety, and the surviving Rājputs performed the rite of *jauhar*. Thirteen thousand women, so the legend says, headed by Karnavatī, the mother of the young prince, voluntarily perished in an immense conflagration fed by combustibles, and the survivors of the slaughter in the breach, led by Bāghjī, prince of Deola, rushed on the Muslim and

[1] In 25° 17′ N. and 75° 34′ E.

were exterminated. Chitor was for the moment a possession of the king of Gujarāt, and received a Muslim governor.

Bahādur had now to think of his return to his capital, and had reason to repent the folly which had prompted him to insult the emperor ; for Humāyūn, though he had scrupulously abstained from attacking him while he was engaged with the misbelievers, had advanced to Mandasor, and was there awaiting him. Bahādur had already taken a step which proclaimed his despair by sending to Mecca, under the charge of a certain Āsaf Khān, both the ladies of his harem and his treasury. His army, as it approached the emperor's position at Mandasor, was disheartened by the defeat of its advanced guard and by the defection of Sayyid 'Alī Khān Khurāsanī, who deserted to the emperor. Bahādur was beset by conflicting counsels. Sadr Khān urged that an immediate attack should be delivered, while the army was still flushed with its victory at Chitor, but Rūmī Khān, who commanded the artillery, was of opinion that it should entrench itself and rely on its great superiority in guns. Unfortunately the advice of the artilleryman was followed. The light armed troops of Gujarāt dared not face the Mughul archers in the field, and the imperial troops, beyond the range of the guns, were able to cut off the supplies of the entrenched camp. A reinforcement from Rāisen only increased his difficulties by consuming his supplies, and after enduring a siege of two months, during which losses from famine were heavy, he basely deserted his army by night on April 25, 1535, and fled with Muhammad Shāh of Khāndesh, Mallū Qādir Khān, governor of Mālwa, and three other nobles, to Māndū. His army dispersed, only a few of the principal officers being able to lead off their contingents.

Humāyūn pursued him and besieged him in Māndū. A division escaladed the walls of the fortress at night, and Bahādur, who was asleep at the time, escaped with difficulty to Chāmpāner with no more than five or six followers. Sadr Khān and Sultān 'Ālam, governor of Rāisen, retired into the citadel, Songarh, but were forced to surrender after the lapse of two days, when the former entered the emperor's service and the latter, guilty of being a member of the Lodī clan, was mutilated by the amputation of his feet. Sadr Khān was not the only one who changed his allegiance. Mustafā Rūmī Khān, to whom the government of Ranthambhor had been promised during its siege, so resented his master's failure to keep his word that he entered Humāyūn's service after the defeat at Mandasor.

After reducing the citadel of Māndū Humāyūn pursued Bahādur, who fled from Chāmpāner to Cambay. Humāyūn followed him thither, but arrived at the port on the day on which he had taken ship for Diū. The remnant of the fugitive's army was staunch and made a night attack on the imperial camp, but a traitor had betrayed their design and the imperial troops, having vacated their tents, allowed the enemy to plunder them and then, falling on them, put them to the sword. They also slew, lest they should be rescued, Sadr Khān and Fīrūz, formerly Jām of Sind, who had fallen into their hands.

Bahādur induced Humāyūn to withdraw from Cambay by sending Mahmūd Lārī, Muhtaram Khān, to interview Mustafā Rūmī Khān. Hājī Dabīr reports the interview as it was related to him by Muhtaram Khān, who conveyed such bitter reproaches from Bahādur that Rūmī Khān sweated with shame, and added, 'If this attack on Diū is your suggestion, then employ some device to deter him : if it is not your suggestion then try to shake his purpose.' Rūmī Khān, stung by these reproaches, went to Humāyūn, who happened to be suffering from the effects of the climate and advised him to postpone the attack on Diū, as the sea air was bad for his health. Humāyūn agreed, and at the same time news of disturbances in Ahmadābād was received, and he withdrew to Chāmpāner.

Chāmpāner was still held by Ikhtiyār Khān for Bahādur, and Humāyūn besieged the fortress. Selecting the most inaccessible part of the wall as likely to be the most lightly guarded he led to the spot 300 men armed with steel spikes, by means of which, driven into the mortar between the stones, they escaladed the wall and, on August 9, 1935, opened the gates to the rest of the army. Ikhtiyār Khān fled to the citadel, but almost immediately surrendered, and Humāyūn was master of Chāmpāner.

The treasure found at Chāmpāner relieved the imperial troops of the duty of dispersing themselves throughout the country for the collection of revenue, and the fief-holders sent to Bahādur in Kāthīāwār a message expressing their unaltered loyalty and their readiness to pay the land tax, if officers could be sent to collect it. Bahādur selected 'Imād-ul-Mulk Malikjī for this duty, and he, assembling an army of 50,000 horse, encamped before Ahmadābād and sent out detachments to collect the revenue. Humāyūn, who would have been better employed in his own dominions, was intoxicated by his new conquest and bent on including it in his empire. He marched towards Ahmadābād and his advanced guard defeated 'Imād-ul-Mulk between Nadiād and Mahmūdābād. The victory encouraged him to distribute the fiefs of Gujarāt among his officers, as though the conquest were complete and permanent, and the kingdom assumed for a short time the appearance of a settled province of the empire. Bahādur, at Diū, was trembling at the prospect of an attack by land on that port and wrote to Nunho da Cunha, governor of Portuguese India, imploring his aid. Da Cunha visited Diū and on October 25 concluded a treaty by which he undertook to assist Bahādur against his enemies by land and sea, and received in return confirmation of the cession of the port of Bassein to the king of Portugal and permission to build a fort at Diū, the customs dues of the port being retained, however, by Bahādur.

Humāyūn, fired with the lust of conquest, marched into Khāndesh and visited Burhānpur. Muhammad Shāh wrote, begging him to spare his small kingdom the horrors of an invasion, and at the same time wrote to Ibrāhīm 'Ādil Shāh I of Bījāpur, Sultān Qulī Qutb Shāh of Golconda, and Daryā 'Imād Shāh of Berar, proposing a league for the defence of the Deccan but Humāyūn's operations were confined to a military promenade through Khāndesh, whence he returned to Māndū.

While he had been indulging in dreams of conquest Sher Khān Sūr, the Afghān, had risen in rebellion in Bengal, the nobles of Gujarāt, with the aid of the Portuguese, had recovered some posts from the Mughuls, and 'Askarī Mīrzā, at Ahmadābād, was meditating his own proclamation as king of Gujarāt. Tardī Beg, the Mughul governor of Chāmpāner, refused to admit into the fortress the officers who, having been driven from their posts by Bahādur's troops, desired to take refuge there, for he believed them to be partisans of 'Askarī and disaffected towards Humāyūn. They accordingly besieged him in Chāmpāner and Humāyūn hastily returned towards Āgra, where his presence was urgently required, and was joined on the way by 'Askarī and those who had besieged Chāmpāner who now made their peace with him. His ill-timed expedition into Gujarāt had lasted for thirteen months and thirteen days.

Bahādur had closely followed the retreating Mughuls, and as he approached Chāmpāner Tardī Beg evacuated it and Bahādur reoccupied it on May 25, 1536. He apologised to his nobles for having at Mandasor followed the advice of Mustafā Rūmī Khān, who had since deserted to Humāyūn, to which error all the subsequent misfortunes of Gujarāt were to be traced. Mallū Qādir Khān returned to Māndū as governor of Mālwa.

Bahādur, having regained his kingdom, repented of his bargain with the Portuguese, and sought to expel them from Diū. Manoel de Sousa, who commanded the fort, was aware of this design, and when the king visited Diū late in 1536 would not wait upon him, lest he should be treacherously assassinated. Nundo da Cunha, in response to an invitation from Bahādur, visited Diū towards the end of December, but having been warned by de Sousa that it was the king's intention to send him in a cage to the sultan of Turkey, feigned sickness and refused to land. He persisted in his refusal until the king lost patience and decided, on February 13, 1537, against the advice of all his counsellors, to visit him on board his ship. He made his visit accompanied by thirteen officers of high rank, and after remaining a short time on board expressed a desire to return. The Portuguese attempted to detain him, ostensibly that he might inspect the gifts which they had brought for him from Goa, but doubtless with a view to obtaining a pledge that he would abandon his designs against them and to extorting further concessions from him. He is said to have cut down a priest who attempted to bar his way, and when he entered his barge the Portuguese boats closed round it and swords were drawn. Manoel de Sousa was killed, and the king and Khvāja Safar leaped into the water. A Portuguese friend drew the Khvāja aboard his boat, but the king was drowned and all his other companions were killed.

Bahādur was one of the greatest and may be reckoned the last of the kings of Gujarāt, for his three actual successors were mere puppets in the hands of a turbulent and factious nobility. His one great error was committed at Mandasor, when he entrenched himself instead of falling at once on the imperial army. His disgraceful flight was almost a necessary consequence, for in it lay his only chance of saving his kingdom. If we except these two actions and his meditated treachery towards his Portuguese allies, which was not regarded as reprehensible in his faith and in that age, we shall be inclined to agree in the praise bestowed upon him by Hāji Dabīr, author of the *Zafar-ul-Wālih*[1], who describes him as liberal, generous, and valiant, with a loftier spirit and wider ambitions than any of his line, and reckons as his conquests the places in which he caused the *khutba* to be recited in his name ; Gujarāt, the Deccan, Khāndesh, Mālwa, Ajmer, the Aravalli Hills, Jālor, Nāgaur, Junāgarh, Khānkot, Rāisen, Ranthambhor, Chitor, Kālpī, Baglāna, Īdar, Rādhanpur, Ujjain, Mewāt, Satwās, Ābu, and Mandasor.

Bahādur left no son, and Muhammad Zamān Mīrzā, the kinsman and brother-in-law of Humāyūn, impudently claimed the throne

[1] Vol. I, p. 263.

on the ground that Bahādur's mother had adopted him as her son, but 'Imād-ul-Mulk Malikjī hastened from Diū to Ahmadābād and agreed to call to the throne Muhammad Shāh of Khāndesh, whose wife, mother, grandmother, and two more remote ancestresses had all been princesses of Gujarāt. Descent in the female line seldom counts for much in questions of succession in Muslim states, but Muhammad had been for years the loyal vassal and faithful companion in arms of Bahādur, whose recognition of his title of Shāh was understood to indicate a wish that he should succeed him. Muhammad Shāh obeyed the summons and set out from Burhānpur to ascend the throne of Gujarāt, but died on May 24, on his way to Chāmpāner.

There now remained only one possible successor, the last descendant of Muhammad Karīm, Mahmūd Khān, son of Bahādur's brother Latīf Khān, who, during his uncle's reign, had been placed in the custody of Muhammad of Khāndesh, and was a state prisoner in a fortress in that state. The nobles of Gujarāt summoned him to the throne, but Mubārak II, who had succeeded his brother in Khāndesh, and had almost certainly hoped to receive a summons to the throne of Gujarāt, would not surrender him until a force led by Ikhtiyār Khān invaded Khāndesh. Ikhtiyār Khān carried Mahmūd with him to Ahmadābād, where he was enthroned on August 8, 1587, as Sa'd-ud-dīn Mahmūd Shāh III.

The part which Ikhtiyār Khān Siddīqī had played in bringing the new king from Khāndesh and placing him on the throne gained for him the regency, for Mahmūd was but eleven years of age. Ikhtiyār Khān was learned and accomplished and his surname indicates descent from Abū Bakr as-Siddīq ('the truthful'), the first successor of the prophet Muhammad, but his father had held the comparatively humble post of *qāzī* of Nadiād and his advancement was resented by many of the nobles, now divided into factions quarrelling over the part which each had borne in attempting to overcome the calamities which had recently fallen upon the kingdom and over the compensation due to each for his sufferings and his losses.

Two nobles of the second rank, Fattūjī Muhāfiz Khān and Daryā Khān Husain, urged 'Imād-ul-Mulk Malikjī, son of Tawakkul, who had long taken a prominent part in the affairs of the kingdom and now found himself relegated to the third place, that of deputy minister, to remove Ikhtiyār Khān by assassination, and his jealousy and ambition succumbed to the temptation. He stepped into Ikhtiyār Khān's place and appropriated the title of Amīr-ul-Umarā, but 'Abd-ul-Latīf Sadr Khān, the minister, grieved deeply for his old friend, and taxed 'Imād-ul-Mulk with having been accessory to his death. The new regent's denial of his complicity was not believed, and Sadr Khān voluntarily resigned his post, and explained to the king the grounds for his action. He informed both the king and the regent that Daryā Khān aspired to the first place in the kingdom, and privately warned 'Imād-ul-Mulk that the life of none would be safe if ambitious subordinates were permitted to foment discord between the great officers of state and to persuade them to remove rivals by assassination. Daryā Khān obtained the post vacated by Sadr Khān, but the latter's warning was not lost upon 'Imād-ul-Mulk who regarded his late accomplice with suspicion, which was rewarded with secret intrigue and open hostility.

In 1517 the last of the Mamlūk Sultans had been overthrown, and Egypt became part of the Ottoman Empire, but it was not until 1538 that the new rulers of Egypt made any further attempt to drive the Portuguese from the Indian Ocean. In 1537, however, when news reached Egypt of the tragic death of Bahādur and the consequent strengthening of the Portuguese position in India, the Ottoman Sultan, Sulaimān I, grew apprehensive and ordered the equipment at Suez of a powerful fleet, which eventually set sail under Sulaimān Pāshā al-Khādim, governor of Cairo, and then an old man of eighty-two. His objective was Diū, which was now in the sole possession of the Portuguese. His public announcement that he was setting out on a 'holy war' against the Franks did not prevent his behaving with the utmost treachery and cruelty towards his co religionist at Aden, where he called on his way to India. News of his disgraceful behaviour at Aden travelled quickly to India, and was doubtless the real cause of his failure against the Portuguese, for when he reached Muzaffarābād Khvāja Safar, Khudāvand Khān, whom Mahmūd III had placed in command of a large force intended to co-operate with the Pāshā, and who was at first inclined to join him, was deterred by his friends, who reminded him of the fate of the governor of Aden, and although he sent many gifts to the Pāshā he persistently evaded a personal interview. But though co-operation between the land and sea forces was thus incomplete the Portuguese were reduced to great straits. They were driven by Khvāja Safar from the city into the fort, which they held with their wonted determination. Garcia de Noronha, the newly arrived viceroy, either could not or would not understand the situation, and failed to send relief; the defences were almost destroyed, and of the original garrison of 600 only forty men remained fit to bear arms. Sulaimān Pāshā, who had been attacking by sea, was unaware, owing to the army's failure to co-operate with him, of the desperate situation of the defence and was so discouraged by repeated failure and by his losses that when Khvāja Safar, disgusted by the arrogance of the Turks, which had convinced him that Gujarāt had nothing to gain by their taking the place of the Portuguese at Diū, sent him a fabricated letter, announcing that the viceroy was about to arrive from Goa with a formidable fleet, he sailed away on November 5. Some of his officers remained behind and entered the service of Gujarāt. Among these were Āqā Farahshād the Turk, afterwards entitled Fath Jang Khān, Nāsir the African, afterwards entitled Habash Khān, and Mujāhid Khān, who occupied Junāgarh. Khvāja Safar, on Sulai-mān Pāshā's departure, set fire to the town of Diū and retired.

'Imād-ul-Mulk was now to discover the wisdom of Sadr Khān's warning. His relations with Daryā Khān had been growing ever more strained and the latter's influence over the feeble king ever stronger. He accompanied the king on an excursion, ostensibly for the purpose of hunting, but when well beyond the city walls carried him off to Chāmpāner, and sent to 'Imād-ul-Mulk a royal letter directing him to retire to his fiefs in Kāthīawār. 'Imād-ul-Mulk assembled his troops and attempted to obtain possession of the king's person in order to re-establish his influence over him, but the proceeding so closely resembled rebellion that many of his officers deserted him for the royal camp, and he was obliged to return to Ahmadābād, whence he retired, with Sadr Khān, to Morvī, his principal fief. In 1540 Daryā Khān, carrying with him the king marched against 'Imād-ul-Mulk, defeated him at Bajāna[1], where Sadr Khān was slain, and drove him into Khāndesh. Daryā Khān followed him, and at Dāngrī[2], near the Tapti, met Mubārak II, who was prepared to oppose any attempt to enter his kingdom. Daryā Khān was again victorious, and 'Imād-ul-Mulk fled to Māndū, where Mallū Nāsir Khān, appointed governor by Bahādur was now independent, styling himself Nāsir Shāh. At this point Daryā Khān and Mahmūd III abandoned the pursuit and returned to Gujarāt.

Daryā Khān was now absolute in the kingdom, but Mahmūd had sufficient spirit to be sensible of the humiliation of his situation, and enlisted the aid of a humble attendant, one Chīrjī, a fowler, to escape from it. Chīrjī had horses ready one night under the city wall, and the king, leaving his palace at midnight, mounted and

[1] In 23° 7′ N. and 71° 47′ E. [2] In 21° 9′ N. and 75° 4′ E.

rode to Dhandhūka, the fief of 'Ālam Khān Lodī, nearly sixty miles south-west of Ahmadābād.

'Ālam Khān received him with every demonstration of loyalty, and summoned to his aid his brother-in-law, Nāsir-ud-dīn Ulugh Khān of Junāgarh, Mujāhid Khān of Pālitāna, and other fief-holders. Daryā Khān, on discovering that the king had escaped him and found a powerful protector, renounced the struggle to maintain his ascendancy and sent to the king a mission with the royal insignia, elephants, horses, and his own letter of resignation ; but his old accomplice, Fattūjī Muhāfiz Khān, coming into the city from his fief of Viramgām, met the mission at Sarkhej, turned it back, and persuaded Daryā Khān to strike a blow for the recovery of his lost supremacy. It was necessary to oppose a puppet to the actual king, and a child of obscure origin was accordingly proclaimed and carried by Daryā Khān with the army which he led against Mahmūd III and his new protectors.

The armies met to the south west of Ahmadābād, in a confused conflict which had a strange result. 'Ālam Khān Lodī charged with great impetuosity, cut his way through the centre of Daryā Khān's army, rode to Ahmadābād with only five or six of his men, and took possession of the city in the name of Mahmūd III. Daryā Khān, convinced that 'Ālam Khān's small force had been cut to pieces, continued the action with apparent success until it was confidently reported that 'Ālam Khān had entered the royal palace, proclaimed his victory over the rebels, and let loose a mob of plunderers into his house. He hesitated, and was lost. His army fled, and Mahmūd marches on into the city, Muhāfiz Khān and the child who had been proclaimed king fleeing before him. Daryā Khān fled to Burhānpur and Muhāfiz Khān, with his puppet, to Chāmpāner, whither he was followed by Mahmūd III and 'Ālam Khān. He was glad to purchase life by a speedy surrender and disappeared from the kingdom.

Mahmūd III now returned to Ahmadābād to discover that he had but changed one master for another. He insisted, in his gratitude, on promoting Chīrjī the fowler to the rank lately held by Fattūjī and conferred on him all Fattūjī's possessions, and his title of Muhāfiz Khān, but the advancement profited the humble bird-catcher little, for when he took his seat among the nobles of the kingdom 'Ālam Khān Lodī protested, and when Chīrjī, with the king's support, persisted in asserting his right, compassed his death. The manner in which the minister's decision was executed indicates the estimation in which the king and his wishes were held by his

new master. Ashja 'Khān, 'Ālam Khān's brother, entered the royal
presence with a dagger in his hand, laid hold of the wretched
Muhāfiz Khān, dragged him forth, and as soon as he had crossed
the threshold of the hall of audience stabbed him to death. 'Ālam
Khān became, of course, lieutenant of the kingdom, and Nūr-ud-dīn
Burhān-ul-Mulk Bambānī was appointed minister. 'Imād-ul-mulk
Malikjī returned from Māndū and received Broach as his fief.

The domination of 'Ālam Khān was even less tolerable than
that of Daryā Khān. The latter had, at least, observed some
moderation in the pomp with which he surrounded himself, but
the former encroached, in this respect, on the royal prerogative.
A minister whose power was absolute might well have avoided this
indiscretion and should have understood that a king deprived of
his power will cling all the more jealously to its outward symbols.
Nor was this his greatest error. The assassination of the recently
ennobled fowler wounded the king's affections as well as his honour,
and in crushing one presumptuous minister he had learned how
to deal with another. By a private appeal to the loyalty of some,
who, though nominally 'Ālam Khān's followers were no less disgusted than the king with his arrogance and presumption, he
succeeded in ridding himself of his new master. On a night when
Mujāhid Khān was on duty at the palace the king persuaded him
to assemble his troops, and at break of day rode forth with the
royal umbrella above his head and proclaimed by a crier that
'Ālam Khān's palace might be sacked. The mob broke in, and
'Ālam Khān, roused from a drunken slumber, fled in confusion and
made the best of his way to Māndū, where he joined his former
enemy, Daryā Khān.

Mujāhid Khān now became lieutenant of the kingdom, with
'Abd-us-Samad Afzal Khān as minister. Muharram *bin* Safar was
entitled Rūmī Khān, and others who afterwards became prominent
in the state received titles. 'Ābd-ul-Karīm became I'timād Khān,
Bilāl Jhūjhār Khān, and Abu Sulaimān Mahalldār Khān.

Daryā Khān and 'Ālam Khān now appeared at Rādhanpur[1]
with 'Ālā-ud-dīn Fath Khān of the royal line of Sind, whose mother
had been a princess of Gujarāt, and proclaimed him king, but
Mahmūd attacked and defeated them, and they fled again to Māndū,
while Fath Khān, who had merely been an instrument in their hands,
made his excuses to Mahmūd and was well received at his court.

Mahmūd, now freed from the domination of ambitious ministers,
turned his attention to the portuguese. Khvāja Safar, Khudāvand

[1] In 23° 49′ N. and 71° 39′ E.

Khān, was governor of Cambay, and was ordered to construct a fort at Sūrat for the protection of the maritime trade, which had been much harassed by the Portuguese ever since their establishment at Diū. Though much hampered by the Portuguese, who attempted, first by force and afterwards by bribery, to prevent its construction, the fort was successfully completed according to the principles of fortification then obtaining in Europe, and was armed with many guns which had belonged to Sulaimān Pāshā's fleet, and had been carried to Junāgarh by Mujāhid Khān.

Mahmūd had not forgotten the death of his uncle, Bahādur, nor its authors, and his failure to expel the Portuguese from Diū in 1538 had not discouraged him. Khvāja Safar, who maintained an outwardly friendly correspondence with them, and was well acquainted with their affairs, encouraged his master to make another attempt to recover Diū, but before resorting to arms endeavoured to gain possession of the fortress by treachery. The plot was discovered and Khvāja Safar opened the siege. The fort was small, and would accommodate only a small garrison, and Safar's bombardment caused heavy losses, but the Portuguese fought with unflinching valour. They were encouraged by the death, on June 24, 1546, of Khvāja Safar, whose head was taken off by a gunshot. He was succeeded in the command by his son, Muharram Rūmī Khān, who made desperate efforts to take the place, one assault being repulsed with the loss of 2000 men and of Bilāl Jhūjhār Khān, his second in command, but the numbers of the Portuguese were reduced to 200, until a timely reinforcement of 400 men under Alvaro de Castro encouraged them to sally forth and attack the enemy. They were repulsed with heavy loss, but on November 7 a fleet of nearly 100 sail, under the command of João de Castro, governor of Portuguese India, appeared off Diū.

On November 10 the Portuguese attacked in force, and drove the Muslims into the city, where they massacred men, women, and children without discrimination. The Muslims rallied, but after a bloody fight were defeated with the loss of 1500 killed, 2000 wounded, and many prisoners. Muharram Rūmī Khān and many other officers were among the slain and Jhūjhār Khān was captured. The loss of the Portuguese was no more than 100, and their booty included many standards, forty heavy and a hundred and sixty field and light guns, and much ammunition.

Jahāngīr Khān fled from the field and carried the mournful news to the king, who wept with rage and mortification, and caused twenty-eight Portuguese prisoners to be torn to pieces in his presence.

João de Castro celebrated his victory by a triumph at Goa, his prisoners following him in chains, in imitation of the Roman custom, which drew from Queen Catherine of Portugal the remark that he had conquered like a Christian and triumphed like a heathen.

The failure of the attack on Diū led to the dismissal, on February 21, 1547, of the minister, Afzal Khān, in whose place 'Abd-ul-Halim Khudāvand Khān was appointed.

In September, 1547, Jorge de Menezes landed at Broach, burned both the fortress and the city, destroyed such guns as he could not carry away, and put the inhabitants to the sword. Later in the year the governor, João de Castro, with 3000 men, formed the foolhardy resolve of landing near Broach and attacking Mahmūd, who had assembled a force of 150,000 men, and eighty guns either in order to renew the attack on Diū or to protect his ports from raids, but was dissuaded from the rash act. He sailed off and plundered and destroyed some ports on the coasts of Kāthiāwār and the Konkan, carrying much booty back to Goa ; and Mahmūd, unwilling at length to exasperate a power which could at all times descend with impunity on his coasts refrained from renewing the attacks on Diū, and in 1548 executed a treaty most advantageous to the Portuguese.

In the same year disputes between Mujāhid Khān and Afzal Khān had given rise to internal troubles, and it was resolved to recall Āsaf Khān, who had been in Mecca ever since 1535, when Bahādur had sent him away in charge of his harem and treasure. His first reform on assuming office was the formation of a powerful bodyguard recruited from the foreign legion and composed of Turks, Africans, Javanese. and others, numbering in all 12,000. By this means the king's authority was firmly established.

In 1549 the king made Mahmūdābād on the Vātrak his ordinary place of residence. The town had been built by his ancestor, Mahmūd Begarha, and he conceived a liking for its air and surroundings. He enlarged the existing royal palace and parcelled out land among his nobles, bidding them build palaces and houses for themselves. Mallū Qādir Shāh of Mālwa, who had been expelled from his kingdom by Shujā'at Khān, Sher Shāh's governor, was now at his court, and described in detail the beauties of the deer-park of Māndū, inspiring Mahmūd to lay out a replica of it. Here he lived in great splendour and luxury, indulging, besides the usual lusts of an oriental prince, his propensity for powerful and poisonous drugs, which he took not only for their intoxicating and stupefying effect, but also as aphrodisiacs.

The raja of Īdar had, since Humāyūn's invasion, behaved as an independent monarch, remitting no tribute, and when, in 1549, a small force was sent to demand the arrears due he opposed the royal troops and compelled them to retire, but a larger force under 'Imād-ul-Mulk Aslān Rūmī, who had been appointed to the command of the foreign legion, captured Īdar and compelled the raja to pay tribute. Farahshād, one of the Turkish officers who had deserted Sulaimān Pāshā on his withdrawal, acted as 'Imād-ul-Mulk's standard bearer and behaved with great gallantry, for which he was rewarded with the title of Fath Jang Khān. In the following year a similar expedition was dispatched to Sirohī, the country round about which was plundered ; but there was no design, apparently, of reducing Sirohī to the condition of a vassal state paying regular tribute. In 1551 it was necessary to suppress the predatory Rājputs who infested the heart of the kingdom and had murdered a doctor of the law travelling from Pātan to Ahmadābād. A massacre reduced the survivors to temporary obedience.

One of Mahmūd's immediate attendants, Burhān-ud-dīn, a man who made pretensions to piety, and one of whose duties it was to lead the prayers when the king was in the field, offended him one day by disrespectful behaviour, and Mahmūd in his wrath sentenced him to death by being bricked up in a wall. The barbarous sentence was put into execution, but Mahmūd happened to pass while the wretch's head yet protruded, took pity on him, and caused the structure to be pulled down. He was much lacerated and injured by the pressure of the mortar and rubble, but with care he recovered, and lived to resent his sufferings rather than to be grateful for his life. His resentment exhibited itself again in disrespect, and the king used language which left no doubt that he would not escape the punishment to which he had once been sentenced, but the celebration of the prophet Muhammad's birthday, on February 15, 1554, temporarily diverted Mahmūd's attention from the matter. At the conclusion of the feast which marked the occasion Mahmūd, stupefied with wine and drugs, withdrew to his bedroom, where he was attended by Daulat, the nephew and accomplice of Burhān-ud-dīn, who had also taken the precaution of corrupting the royal bodyguard, known as the Lion-slayers. It was an easy matter for Daulat to cut the king's throat as he lay on his bed, and Burhān-ud-dīn issued summonses in the king's name to all the chief officers of state. Most obeyed, and were assassinated by the royal guards, ten being slain in this manner, including the famous *vazīr*, Āsaf Khān, but 'Abd-ul-Karīm I'timād Khān suspected mischief, and remained at home. Burhān-ud-dīn then bestowed titles upon the soldiers of the guard and the menial servants of the palace, promised to promote them to the principal offices in the kingdom, and in the morning caused the royal umbrella to be raised over his head and proclaimed his accession.

The surviving nobles led their troops to the palace and attacked the usurper, who fell at their first onslaught, and then proceeded to determine the succession, which was no easy matter, for Mahmūd, who had a nervous dread both of providing an heir who might be put forward as a competitor for the throne and of a disputed succession after his death, had taken the barbarous precaution of procuring an abortion whenever a woman of his harem became pregnant. Inquiries were made in the harem and it was reported that one child, Khalīl Shāh, had escaped the cruel law. After the burial of Mahmūd the nobles demanded the delivery of Khalīl Shāh, that he might be enthroned, but were informed that a mistake had been made, and that there remained no heir to the throne. It would appear that some fraud had been intended, but that when the moment arrived the conspirators lost heart and abandoned their design.

Inquiries were made and a young prince entitled Razī-ul-Mulk, the great grandson of Shakar Khān, a younger son of Ahmad I was raised to the throne under the title of Ahmad Shāh II.

The leaders of the nobles who placed Ahmad II on the throne were I'timād Khān and Sayyid Mubārak Bukhārī, and it was the former who assumed the office of regent, while the later retired to Mahmūdābad, which he occupied as his fief. All the nobles of the kingdom were virtually independent, and each lived on his estate, leaving I'timād Khān to carry on a pretence of administering the whole country in the name of the youthful king.

The port of Damān was held by one Sayyid Abu-'l-Fath, who, as he neither paid taxes nor materially acknowledged the central government, could except no support when, in 1559, the Portuguese viceroy, Constantino de Braganza, attacked him, drove him first from Damān and then from Pārdī, and established the Portuguese firmly in Damān and Bulsār, securing native support by assigning the customs of the former port to the governor of the island of Salsette, which was within the dominions of Ahmadnagar.

Ahmad II was virtually a prisoner in the hands of I'timād Khān, and after passing five years in this condition he reached an age at which he became sensible of the restraint to which he was subjected, and of the minister's usurpation of his rights. He fled and threw himself on the protection of Sayyid Mubārak Bukhārī at Mahmūdābād, where a number of nobles, influenced more by the Sayyid's prestige and by hostility to I'timād Khān than by loyalty to a sovereign whom they hardly knew, assembled. I'timād Khān and his partisans marched against his confederacy, and the death of Sayyid Mubārak from an arrow involved the defeat and dispersal of the army assembled round the king. Ahmad wandered for some days a helpless fugitive in the jungles, until he was obliged to return to his master, who carried him back to Ahmadā-bād and imprisoned him in the palace.

'Imād-ul-Mulk Aslān and Tātār Khān Ghūrī, disgusted with I'timād Khān's monopoly of power, dragged forth their guns and bombarded his house at Ahmadabād, and the regent fled to Hālol, near Chāmpāner, taking the young king with him. Here he began to assemble his army, and civil war was on the point of breaking out when peacemakers intervened and effected a composition whereby I'timād Khān retained the office of regent and the custody of the king and the other nobles parcelled out the kingdom among themselves, 'Imād-ul-Mulk Aslān, I'timād Khan's principal opponent, receiving Broach, Chāmpāner, Nāndod, and other districts between the Māhi and Narbada rivers. To the king was assigned land sufficient for the maintenance of 1500 horse, but this was no more than a concession to his vanity, for he remained almost as closely guarded as before.

I'timād Khān could not, however, entirely seclude him, and he used to amuse himself by hatching, with those officers who gained access to him, boyish plots for the assassination of the regent, and by drawing his sword and severing the soft stem of a plantain tree, with the childish boast that he could thus cleave in two his tyrant. All this was reported to I'timād Khān, who, though he well knew that the boy was incapable of any desperate deed, began to fear lest some officer should earn the king's gratitude and the coveted post of regent by giving effect to wishes so unreservedly expressed. He therefore, in July 1562, caused Ahmad to be assassinated and his body to be flung out of the citadel into the open space between the river and the house of a noble entitled Vijīh-ul-Mulk Abūjī Tānk, and when it was discovered gave out that Ahmad Shāh must have gone secretly to Vajīh-ul-Mulk's house on some amorous adventure and have been slain by some injured person before he could be recognised.

The death of Ahmad II revived the question of the succession, now more complicated than ever, as no scion of the royal house was known to exist. I'timād Khān solved it by producing a child named Nathū and swearing that he was the son of Mahmūd III by a concubine. He explained his birth by saying that Mahmūd, when he discovered that the concubine was pregnant, handed her over to him with instructions to procure an abortion, but that he, discovering that the girl was in the sixth month of her pregnancy, could not find it in his heart to subject her to an operation which would almost certainly be fatal, and retained her in his house, concealing the birth of the child and bringing him up in secret. The story was in the last degree improbable, for greater facilities for carrying out Mahmūd's unnatural orders must have existed in the royal harem than elsewhere, and no explanation of the preference shown for a collateral when Ahmad II was enthroned was offered, but an heir had to be found, for none of the nobles would have submitted to any one of their order, and I'timād Khān's oath was accepted and the child was enthroned as Muzaffar III.

The history of Muzaffar's ten years' reign is but a record of perpetual strife between the great nobles, each of whom was independent in his fief, while I'timād Khān retained the office of regent.

The whole of northern Gujarāt, as far south as Kādī, was divided between Mūsā Khān and Sher Khān Fūlādī, two Afghāns, and Fath Khān, a Balūch; the country between the Sābarmātī and the Māhī was held by I'timād Khān, and Dholka and Dhandhūkā by Sayyid Mīrān, son of Sayyid Mubārak Bukhārī; Chingīz Khān, son of I'timād Khān's enemy, 'Imād-ul-Mulk Aslān Rūmī, held Sūrat, Nāndod, and Chāmpāner, and his brother-in-law, Rustam Khān, Broach; and Kāthīāwār was held by Amīn Khān Ghūrī.

A very brief sketch of the conflicts between these factious nobles will suffice.

In 1563 the Afghāns Mūsā Khān and Sher Khān expelled Fath Khān from northern Gujarāt, and drove him to take refuge with I'timād Khān, who attacked the Afghāns but was defeated and driven back to Ahmadābād. The Afghāns then marched to attack him, and he was defeated at Jotāna and fled and sought aid of Chingīz Khān, who accompanied him to Jotāna. No further fighting took place, a peace being arranged, but after the nobles had returned to their fiefs Chingīz Khān wrote to I'timād Khān, casting doubts on the king's birth. The regent replied that his oath had been accepted and that Chingīz Khān's father, had he been alive, would have corroborated it. Chingīz Khān then openly demanded

more land for the support of his troops. I'timād Khān evaded the
demand by advising him to recover the district of Nandurbār,
which had formerly belonged to Gujarāt and was now held by
Muhammad II of Khāndesh. Chingīz Khān fell into the trap and
in 1566 marched to Nandurbār, which he occupied, and, encouraged
by his success, advanced towards Thālner, but was attacked and
defeated by Muhammad II and Tufāl Khān of Berar, and compelled
to flee to Broach, where he proceeded, in 1568, to reorganise his
army, in which work he was assisted by the rebellious Mīrzās,
Akbar's kinsmen, who had fled from the empire and sought a refuge
in Gujarāt. He now resolved to avenge himself on I'timād Khān
for the trick which he had played him, and marched on Ahmadābād, requesting the regent to withdraw to his fiefs, as he was coming to pay his respects to the king, and it was undesirable that they
should meet in the capital. I'timād Khān and the king marched
towards Nadiād, near which place the armies met. There was no
battle, for I'timād Khān, who had heard much of the war-like disposition of the Mīrzās, was smitten with sudden panic, and fled to
Dūngarpur, whence he sent a message to Akbar, who was then before Chitor, inviting him to invade Gujarāt.

The rest of the army dispersed, the Sayyids of Bukhārā going
to Dholka, Ikhtiyār-ul-Mulk to Ma'mūrābād, and Ulugh Khān and
Marjān Jhūjhār Khān with the young king to Virpur[1]. Sher Khān
Fūlādī, jealous of the power so suddenly acquired by Chingīz Khān,
hinted that he required a share of the spoils, and Chingīz Khān,
anxious to conciliate him, ceded to him all territory to the west of
the Sābarmatī.

Muhammad II of Khāndesh profited by these disputes to assert
his claim to the throne of Gujarāt, which was certainly less open
to suspicion than that of Muzaffar III, and invaded the kingdom
with an army of 30,000 horse, but was defeated before Ahmadābād
by Chingīz Khān and the Mīrzās and driven back to his own country. Chingīz Khān rewarded the Mīrzās with extensive fiefs in the
Broach district, but in a short time it was discovered that they were
encroaching on the land of their neighbours and had been guilty of
cruelty and oppression on their estates. They defeated a force sent
against them by Chingīz Khān, but retired into Khāndesh.

Meanwhile Muhammad Ulugh Khān and Marjān Jhūjhār Khān,
who had been awaiting help from I'timād Khān or from Sher Khān
Fūlādī, were disappointed and, joining Ikhtiyar-ul-Mulk, marched

[1] In 23° 11' N. and 73° 29' E.

with him to Ahmadābād to make their peace with Chingīz Khān. A redistribution of fiefs was agreed upon, and Chingīz Khān promised to treat the other nobles as his equals in all respects, but neither party trusted the other, and Ulugh Khān was warned that Chingīz Khān was meditating his assassination. He provided for his safety by inducing Jhūjhār Khān to decapitate Chingīz Khān with his sword[1] as the three were riding together to the polo ground, and he and his partisans took possession of the citadel while their troops plundered those of Chingīz Khān, and Rustam Khān rode off, with his brother-in-law's corpse, to Broach.

Ulugh Khān and Jhūjhār Khān, who were joined by Sher Khān Fūlādī, invited I'timād Khān to return to Gujarāt, and he assumed the office of regent, but there was little confidence between the parties, and I'timād Khān refused to leave the capital when the other nobels marched to expel the Mīrzās, who had returned to Broach and resumed possession of their former fiefs. His suspicions were so bitterly resented that those who had recalled him to power agreed to divide his fiefs among themselves, but they quarrelled over the division of the spoil, and I'timād Khān succeeded in detaching Jhūjhār Khān and inducing him to join him at Ahmadābād. Ulugh Khān joined Sher Khān Fūlādī at Ghiyāspur, opposite to Sarkhej, on the Sābarmātī, and the king, taking advantage of these dissensions, fled from Ahmadābād and joined the camp at Ghiyāspur. I'timād Khān wrote to Sher Khān, impudently repudiating his own solemn oath and asserting that Muzaffar III was not the son of Mahmūd III, and that he had therefore deposed him and invited the Mīrzās from Broach in order that one of them might ascend the throne. The Mīrzās arrived, and when the quarrels between the two parties had continued for some time without any definite result I'timād Khān again invited Akbar to invade the country.

Sher Khān Fūlādī was besieging Ahmadābād when the imperial army reached Pātan, and fled, carrying with him Muzaffar III, when he heard of its arrival. The Mīrzās at the same time fled to Baroda and Broach, and on Akbar's arrival at Ahmadābād I'timād Khān, Ulugh Khān, Jhūjhār Khān, and Ikhtiyār-ul-Mulk submitted to him and entered his service.

In 1572 Muzaffar III fled from the camp of Sher Khān Fūlādī, who had not treated him well and on November 15 was found by two of the imperial officers lurking in the neighbourhood of Akbar's

---

[1] For this crime Akbar afterwards, on the complaint of Chingīz Khān's mother, caused Jhūjhār Khān to be crushed to death by an elephant.

camp at Jotāna. On November 20 he appeared before Akbar, who detained him as a political prisoner, and Gujarāt was formally annexed to the empire.

Some time after the annexation Muzaffar was permitted to live in retirement in Kāthiāwār, but in 1583 a rebellion appeared to offer him an opportunity of recovering his throne, and he joined the rebels. After ten years of hopeless adventure, during the greater part of which time he was a fugitive, he fell into the hands of the imperial troops in 1593, and committed suicide by cutting his throat.

CHAPTER XIV

THE KINGDOM OF MĀLWA

MĀLWA, like Gujarāt, became independent of Delhi on the dissolution of that kingdom after the invasion of Tīmūr, at the end of the fourteenth century.

The date of the appointment of Dilāvar Khān Ghūrī, the Afghān governor, is not precisely known, but he was certainly in Mālwa in 1392, and was probably appointed by Fīrūz Shāh of Delhi, who died in 1388. He remained quietly in Malwa while Tīmūr sacked Delhi, and when Mahmūd Shāh Tughluq, fleeing before the conqueror, sought an asylum and was disappointed by his reception in Gujarāt, Dilāvar Khān received him as his sovereign, and entertained him with princely hospitality until he was able, in 1401, to return to his capital.

Alp Khān, Dilāvar Khān's son and heir, strongly disapproved of the deference shown to Mahmūd, which he considered to be incompatible with the independence of Mālwa, and, while the royal guest remained at Dhār, withdrew to Māndū, where he occupied himself in perfecting the defences of that great fortress city.

Dilāvar Khān never assumed the style of royalty, though he could maintain no pretence of dependence on Delhi, whose nominal lord was a prisoner in the hands of an ambitious minister, but in 1406 Alp Khān, impatient for his inheritance, removed his father by poison, and ascended the throne under the title of Hūshang Shah.

In the following year Muzaffar I of Gujarāt invaded Mālwa on the pretext of avenging the death of his old friend, defeated Hūshang before Dhār, drove him into the citadel, forced him to surrender, and carried him off a prisoner to Gujarāt, leaving in Mālwa, as governor, his own brother Nusrat Khān.

Nusrat Khān treated Mālwa as a conquered country, and his rule was so oppressive and extortionate that the army expelled him, and elected as their ruler Hūshang's cousin, Mūsā Khān, who, fearing the vengeance of the king of Gujarāt, established himself in Māndū, the fortifications of which were now complete. Hūshang, on hearing of this usurpation, implored Muzaffar to restore him to his throne, swearing on the Koran that he was guiltless of his father's death, and Muzaffar, who had his own outraged authority to assert, sent his grandson Ahmad Khān, with an army to restore Hūshang.

His orders were executed, and Ahmād Khān, after restoring Hūshang at Dhār, then the capital of Mālwa, returned to Gujarāt, but Mūsā Khān, who still held Māndū, was not inclined to submit, and most of the nobles of the kingdom, who were at Māndū with him, though they favoured Hūshang's cause feared to join him, as their wives and families would be left exposed to Mūsā's wrath.

Hūshang marched to Māndū, and some combats took place between his troops and those of his cousin, but he had no means of reducing the fortress and marched off, but took possession of the kingdom by establishing military posts in the principal towns. Malik Mughīs Khaljī, said to have been descended of the elder brother of Jalāl-ud-dīn Fīrūz Khaljī of Delhi, and Malik Khizr, sons of Hūshang's paternal aunts, left Mūsā Khān and joined Hūshang, and Mūsā, who could not maintain an army without the revenues of the country, which his rival was collecting, was induced by Mughīs to vacate Māndū, which was promptly occupied by Hūshang.

Hūshang's two abortive invasions of Gujarāt, undertaken for the purpose of supporting rebels against Ahmad I, who succeeded his grandfather on the throne of that kingdom in 1411, have already been described in Chapter XIII. He gained neither credit nor advantage from these attacks on a former benefactor, and he estranged his brother-in-law, Nasīr Khān of Khāndesh, by his tardiness in assisting him when Ahmad attacked him in 1417. Another invasion of the north-eastern districts of Gujarāt in 1418 ended in a disgraceful retreat, and Ahmad, exasperated by these unprovoked attacks, in 1419 invaded Mālwa, defeated Hūshang in a battle fought near Māndū, drove him into that fortress, plundered his country, and retired to Gujarāt at the beginning of the rainy season.

In 1422 Hūshang undertook a most adventurous enterprise. Believing that elephants were required to make good his military inferiority to his neighbour of Gujarāt he resolved to lead a raid into Orissa, and to capture a number of these beasts from the raja He cannot have understood the nature of the expedition on which he embarked, for he had to traverse the forests of Gondwāna, then an unknown country to the Muslims, but his objective was Jājpur[1], the capital of Orissa, distant more than 700 miles in a straight line from Māndū.

Leaving his cousin Mughīs as his regent in Mālwa he set out at the head of 1000 horse, carrying with him some horses and merchandise which might enable him to pass as a merchant. He

[1] In 20° 51′ N. and 86° 20′ E.

travelled expeditiously, and in due course arrived before Jājpur, though it is difficult to believe that he was no more than a month on the road. At Jājpur the raja, one of the line founded by Chora Ganga of Kalinganagar, sent a message to Hūshang, at the spot where he was encamped, and asked him why he did not bring his caravan into the city. Hūshang replied that his men were too numerous to find accommodation, and the raja promised to visit his encampment, to inspect his merchandise and to pay, either in cash or elephants, for anything that he might purchase. On the day appointed the raja came forth attended by 500 horse, and Hūshang had the stuffs which he had brought with him spread on the ground for his inspection. They were damaged by a shower of rain which fell, and by the hoofs of the horses of the raja's escort, and the damage supplied the pretended merchants with a pretext for quarrelling with the Hindus, whom they attacked and put to flight, the raja himself being taken prisoner. Hūshang then disclosed his identity and informed the raja that he had come to Orissa in search of elephants. The leading men of Jājpur sent an envoy to ask him to formulate his demands, and on learning that he required elephants sent him seventy-five. He then set out for his own country, but carried the raja with him as far as the frontier of the Jajpur state. On his homeward way he learnt that Ahmad I had invaded Mālwa and was besieging Māndū, but he found time to capture Kherla[1] and carry off the raja as his prisoner. As he approached Māndū Ahmad withdrew his troops from the trenches in order to oppose his entry, but he contrived to evade his enemy and entered the fortress.

The rest of this campaign has already been described in the preceding chapter. Hūshang was again unfortunate, and after his defeat returned to Māndu and, having allowed his army a brief period of repose, marched to Gāgraun[2], and besieged and captured that town. Thence he marched to Gwalior, and had been besieging the fortress for a month when Mubārak Shāh of Delhi advanced by way of Bayāna to attack him. He raised the siege and marched towards the Chambal, but Mubārak had gained his object by relieving Gwalior, and hostilities were averted by a treaty, under which each king agreed to return to his own capital.

The raja of Kherla, since he had been made prisoner by Hūshang in 1422, had acknowledged him as his overlord and paid him tribute, thus giving offence to his former suzerain, Ahmad Shāh Bāhmanī of the Deccan, who still claimed his allegiance and, in 1428, besieged

[1] In 21° 56′ N. and 78° 1′ E.   [2] In 24° 38′ N. and 76°12′ E.

Kherla, but on Hūshang's marching to its relief retired southwards
for three stages, closely followed by Hūshang. He then halted to
receive Hūshang's attack, which at first succeeded, but his army
was attacked, at the moment when victory seemed assured, by
Ahmad Shāh Bahmanī, who had been lying in ambush, and was
put to flight. Its rout was so complete that the ladies of Hūshang's
harem fell into the hands of the victors, while the army of Mālwa
fled headlong to Māndū. The scrupulous and pious Ahmad sent
his prisoners to their lord under an escort of 500 horse.

Hūshang's campaign against Qādir Khān of Kālpī has been
described in Chapter X. Kālpī was captured, but Qādir Khān,
whose chief offence against Hūshang had been the assumption of
the royal title, was reinstated on swearing fealty. Hūshang was
much annoyed on his homeward march by the quarrels of his four
sons, Ghaznī Khān, Usmān Khān, Fath Khān, and Haibat Khān,
graceless and worthless youths.

After his return to Mandū he was engaged in punishing robbers
and when he had completed this task he founded the city of Hoshangābād, on the Narbada. Here he was alarmed by an accident
which he took for an omen of death. A ruby fell one day from his
jewelled crown, and though his courtiers endeavoured to reassure
him, an attack of diabetes confirmed his fears. He left Hoshangābād and returned to Māndū, and on his way thither designated his
eldest son as his heir. A number of the nobles, to whom Ghaznī
Khān was obnoxious, supported the pretensions of 'Usmān Khān,
who had been imprisoned for having grossly insulted his elder
brother, and intrigues were set on foot for his liberation, to which
the king would not consent.

Hūshang died on July 6, 1435, within a day's march of Māndū,
and Ghaznī Khān, who had the powerful support of his cousin
Mughīs and his son Mahmūd Khān, was proclaimed under the title
of Muhammad Shāh.

He was a confirmed drunkard, and left the administration almost
entirely in the hands of Mughīs and Mahmūd Khān, but displayed
a malignant activity in putting to death his three brothers and
blinding his nephew and son-in-law, Nizām Khān, and his three
young sons. This barbarity alienated Mahmūd Khān, who began
to scheme to depose the tyrant and to seize the throne for himself.
His design was revealed to the king, who made arrangements to
have him assassinated, but Mahmūd discovered the preparations
a nd to protect himself took precautions so marked that they could
not pass unnoticed, and the king took him into his harem and in

the presence of his wife, who was Mahmūd's sister, conjured him to be faithful to him. Mahmūd swore that he harboured no designs against him and begged the king to slay him if he suspected him. The king excused himself for his suspicions, and outward harmony was restored, but mutual distrust remained and increased, and Mahmūd, shortly after the interview in the harem, caused his master's death by a dose of posion administered in his wine.

A faction among the nobles raised to the throne Muhammad's son Mas'ūd Khān, a boy of thirteen years of age, and, believing Mahmūd Khān to be yet ignorant of the late king's death, summoned him to the palace in Muhammad Shāh's name, and, when he refused to attend, went to his house in a body to arrest him ; but he had concealed armed men in the house, and when the nobles entered it they were arrested and imprisoned. Those of their faction who had remained with Mas'ūd Khān assembled the royal troops and raised an umbrella over his head, and Mahmūd marched on the palace to secure the persons of Mas'ūd and his younger brother, 'Umar Khān. Some fighting occurred between the royal troops and those of Mahmūd, and lasted until the evening, when the two boys were so terrified that they persuaded their attendants to allow them to flee from the palace by night. Masūd Khān sought the protection of a holy Shaikh, and found his way to Gujarāt, and in the morning his supporters, having nothing left to fight for, dispersed, and Mahmūd took possession of the royal palace. He offered the crown to his father, Malik Mughīs, then engaged in hostilities against the Hāra Rājputs of Harāotī, but he hastened to Māndū, declined the honour, and urged his son to ascend the throne. Mahmūd was accordingly proclaimed on May 13, 1436.

There was still much disaffection among the nobles, who resented the usurpation of the throne by one of their number, and Mahmūd was obliged, immediately after his accession, to cope with a rebellion which assumed serious dimensions owing to the presence in the rebel ranks of Ahmad Khān, a surviving son of Hūshang. The rebellion was crushed, and the leading rebels, including Ahmad Khān, were pardoned and received fiefs, but they rebelled again, and Malik Mughīs was employed to crush them. Ahmad Khān, the most formidable of them, was poisoned by a musician at the instigation of Mughīs, and operations against the others were in progress when Ahmad I of Gujarāt invaded Mālwa with the object of placing Mas'ūd Khān on his father's throne. The course of this campaign has been traced in the preceding chapter. Ahmad Shāh was compelled to retire to Gujarāt, and died, in 1442, before he could fulfil his promise to Mas'ūd Khān.

Mahmūd Shāh's troubles were not ended by Ahmad Shāh's retreat. 'Umar Khan, the younger son of Muhammad Shāh had fled from Gujarāt to Chitor, whence he had again crossed the frontier of Mālwa and was welcomed by the garrison of Chanderī, who acknowledged him as king. He had been slain during Ahmad Shāh's invasion, but the garrison had proclaimed another pretender, Malik Sulaimān, under the title of Shihab-ud-dīn Shāh. Mahmūd besieged Chanderī for seven months, during which period the pretender died, and finally carried it by assault, but during the siege Raja Dongar Singh the Tonwār, of Gwalior, had invaded Mālwa and laid siege to a town named Shahr-i-Nau, not now traceable. Mahmūd invaded Gwalior, plundered and devastated the country, defeated the Hindus, and drove them into the fortress, which he besieged. Dongar Singh raised the siege of Shahr-i-Nau and retired into his own dominions, and Mahmūd, whose sole object had been the expulsion of the invader, returned to Māndū, where he completed the great mosque founded by Hūshang.

The feeble Sayyid, Muhammad Shāh, now occupied the throne of Delhi, the affairs of which kingdom were in the utmost confusion, and a faction among the nobles, who admired the energy and enterprise of Mahmūd Shāh of Mālwa, and were, perhaps, affected by the consideration that he was a member of a family which had already ruled India, not without glory, invited him to Delhi, and offered him the throne. In 1440 he marched northwards and encamped before Tughluqābad, within eight miles of the city, but his partisans were either too weak to afford him any assistance or had repented of the advances made to him, for the royal army, commanded nominally by Muhammad Shāh's son 'Alā-ud-dīn, and actually by Buhlūl Lodī, marched forth to meet him. Mahmūd retained one division of his army in reserve, and sent two, under his sons Ghiyās ud-dīn and Qadr Khān, against the enemy. The battle, which lasted until nightfall, was indecisive, and Muhammad Shāh proposed terms of peace, of which the principal condition was Mahmūd's retirement. The offer was readily accepted, for Mahmūd had learnt that during his absence the mob had risen in Māndū removed the gilded umbrella from the tomb of Hūshang, and raised it over the head of a pretender. The nobles of Delhi were, however, deeply disgusted with the meanness of spirit which permitted an invader thus to depart in peace, and when Buhlūl Lodī violated the treaty by following the retreating army and taking some plunder the exploit was magnified into a great victory, and honour was satisfied.

On reaching Māndū, on May 22, 1441, Mahmūd found that the rebellion had been suppressed by his father, and rested for the remainder of the year, but marched in 1442 to punish Kumbha, the Rānā of Chitor, for the assistance which he had given to 'Umar Khān, the son of Muhammad Shāh Ghūrī. On his way he learnt that Nasīr Khān, son of Qādir Khān, governor of Kālpī, had assumed the royal title, styling himself Nasīr Shāh, and had, moreover, adopted strange heretical opinions, which he was spreading in his small state. He was minded to turn aside and punish him, and actually marched some stages towards Kālpī, but was persuaded by his courtiers to pardon the offender, who had sent an envoy with tribute and expressions of contrition, and to pursue the object with which he had left Māndū.

After entering the Rānā's dominions he captured a fort and destroyed a temple, and advanced to Chitor, the siege of which he was forming when he learnt that the Rānā had retired into the hills. He followed him thither, and the Rānā returned to Chitor.

While Mahmūd was preparing again to form the siege of Chitor his father, Malik Mughīs, who had led an expedition against Mandasor, died, and he retreated to Mandasor, followed by the Rānā, who, in April, 1443, attacked him, but was defeated, and suffered a second defeat in a night attack which Mahmūd made on his camp. The Rānā then retired to Chitor and Mahmūd, who had decided to postpone until the following year the siege of that fortress, returned to Māndū.

Immediately on his return he received a mission from Mahmūd Shāh Sharqī of Jaunpur, who complained of the misconduct of Nasīr Khān of Kālpī, and sought permission to attack him, which was granted. Mahmūd afterwards repented of having acceded to the request of Mahmūd Sharqī, and desired him to desist from molesting Nasīr Khān, who had fled to Chanderī and sought his assistance. Mahmūd Sharqī evaded a decided answer and on January 12, 1445, Mahmūd Khaljī marched for Chanderī. Thence he marched on Kālpī, avoiding the army of Jaunpur, which was drawn up at Erij to meet him. An indecisive battle was fought near Kālpī, and desultory fighting, in which neither gained any decided advantage, continued for some months, at the end of which period peace was made[1]. Nasīr Khān, who promised amendment, was to be restored by degrees to the districts comprising the small

---

[1] See Chapter X.

state of Kālpī, and Mahmūd Khaljī returned to Māndū, where he occupied himself in building a hospital.

In October, 1446, he again invaded the Rānā's dominions He halted at Ranthambhor, removed Bahār Khān from the command of that fortress, appointed Malik Saif-ud-dīn in his stead, and next halted on the Banās, while his army besieged the Rānā in Māndalgarh. The siege was raised on the Rānā's promising to pay tribute for the fortress, and Mahmūd marched on Bayāna. When he was within two leagues of the fortress the governor, Muhammad Khān, sent to him his younger son, Auhad Khān, with 100 horses and 100,000 *tangas* as tribute, and Mahmūd, having sent complimentary gifts in return, halted until he had ascertained that Muhammad Khān had substituted his name for that of 'Alam Shāh of Delhi in the *khutba* and had struck coin in his name, and then retired by way of Ranthambhor, near which place he captured a minor fortress, and continued his journey towards Māndū, sending Tāj Khān with 8000 horse and twenty-five elephants to besiege Chitor. Before reaching Māndū he collected 125,000 *tangas* as tribute from the raja of Kota.

Towards the end of 1450 Mahmūd, as has been already recorded in the preceding chapter, invaded Gujarāt in support of Kanak Dās, raja of Chāmpāner, but retired to Māndū without effecting anything or gaining anything beyond an instalment of tribute from Kanak Dās. His invasion of Gujarāt in the following year, which has also been described, ended in a disastrous defeat, which was not retrieved by a raid on Surat, carried out by his son in 1452.

In 1454 he led a punitive expedition against the rebellious Hāra Rājputs on his northern frontier, put many of them to the sword, and sent their children into slavery at Māndū. Marching on to Bayāna, he collected tribute from the governor, Dāūd Khān, who had succeeded his father, Muhammad Khān, confirmed him in the government, and composed a long-standing dispute between him and Yūsuf Khān of Hindaun. On his return to Māndū he appointed his younger son, Fidāī Khān, entitled Sultān 'Alā-ud dīn, to the command of the fortress of Ranthambhor and the government of Harāolī, the district of the Hāra Rājputs.

Later in the same year Mahmūd invaded the Deccan at the invitation of two rebellious nobles, and laid siege to the fortress of Māhūr, but raised the siege and retired when 'Alā-ud-dīn Ahmad Shāh Bahmanī marched to the relief of the fortress.

In 1455 he again attacked the Rānā, marching to Chitor and ravaging his dominions. Kumbha attempted to purchase peace by a large indemnity, but as the money sent bore his own name and device it was indignantly returned, and the devastation of the country continued. Māhmūd retired to Māndu for the rainy season, but returned, when it was past, to Mandasor, and began the systematic conquest of that region. He occupied a standing camp, and sent his troops in all directions to lay waste the country. While he was thus employed it was suggested to him that it would be a work of merit to recover from the idolators the city of Ajmer, which contained the holy shrine of Shaikh Mu'īn-ud-dīn Chishtī, and he marched rapidly on the city and invested it. Gajānhar, the Rājput commander, made daily sorties, all of which were unsuccessful, and on the fifth day of the investment ordered a general sortie, which was driven back into the city. The pursuers entered with the pursued, and the city was won after great slaughter in the streets. Mahmūd paid his devotions at the shrine, appointed Khvāja Ni'matullāh, whom he entitled Saif Khān, governor of the city, founded a mosque, and marched to Māndalgarh. Temples were destroyed and the country was devastated in the neighbourhood of this fortress, the siege was opened, and the approaches were carried up to the walls. On October 19, 1457, the place was carried by assault, with great slaughter. A remnant of the garrison shut itself up in the citadel, but was compelled by want of water to surrender, and the lives of the men were redeemed by a promise to pay 1,000,000 *tangas*. The temples in the fortress were overthrown, a mosque was built of their stones, Mahmūd turned again towards Chitor, sending columns in different directions to harass the Rājputs and reduce them to obedience. Būndī was captured by one column, various districts were harried and placed under contributions of tribute by others, and heavy idemnities were exacted from the raja of Kūmbhalgarh and the raja of Dungarpur, whose fortresses were too strong to be taken without tedious sieges, to which Mahmūd was not disposed to devote his time.

After this protracted and successful campaign he returned to Māndū and in 1461 was induced to embark on a disastrous expedition to the Deccan.

Nizām-ul-Mulk Ghūrī, who was perhaps related to Mahmūd, was a noble at the court of Humāyūn Shāh, known as the Tyrant— the most brutal and depraved of the line of Bahman. He was traduced at his master's court, and the tyrant caused him to be assassinated. His family escaped to Māndū and besought Mahmūd to avenge his death, and the invitation was welcomed by Mahmūd, who composed a recent quarrel with 'Ādil Khan II of Khāndesh and invaded the Deccan. The tyrant Humāyūn had been removed, and had been succeeded by his infant son, Nizām Shāh, who was carried into the field by his nobles. When the two armies met, that of the Deccan gained some slight advantage, but the precipitate action of a slave named Sikandar Khān, who had charge of the person of the child king, decided the fate of the day. He conceived his master's life to be in danger, carried him from the field, and delivered him to his mother, who was at Fīrūzābād, in the south of his dominions.

After his victory Mahmūd occupied Berar and the northern Deccan, entered Bīdar, the capital, and besieged the citadel, but meanwhile the guardians of the young Nizām Shāh had sought aid of Mahmūd Bīgarha of Gujarāt, who had arrived on the frontiers of the kingdom with 80,000 horse. Mahmūd Gāvān, one of Nizām's two ministers, marched by Bīr to meet him and assembled a force of 20,000 horse. Mahmūd Bīgraha placed a similar force at his disposal and Mahmūd Khaljī found his direct line of retreat barred. He retired hastily by way of eastern Berar, followed by Mahmūd Gāvān, who cut off his supplies and so harassed him that he abandoned his elephants, after having blinded them, and burnt his heavy baggage. His retreat soon became a rout, and to avoid his pursuers he plunged into the forests of the Malghāt, where his army was nearly destroyed. Over 5000 perished of thirst, and the Korkūs fell upon the remnant and slaughtered large numbers. Mahmūd put the Korkū chieftain to death, but his vengeance could not save his army, few of whom returned to Māndū.

He learnt little from this disaster and later in 1462, again invaded the Deccan with 90,000 horse, but the army of the Deccan was drawn up to meet him at Daultabād, and the sultan of Gujarāt once more marched to Nandurbār. On this occasion Mahmūd Khaljī retired before it was too late, and again traversed the Melghāt on his homeward way, but his march was now leisurely, and his troops suffered from nothing more serious than the difficulty of the roads.

In 1465 Mahmūd was much gratified by the arrival at Māndū of Sharaf-ul-Mulk, an envoy from al-Mustanjid Billāh Yūsuf, the puppet 'Abbāsid Caliph of Egypt, who brought for him a robe of honour and a patent of sovereignty. The honour was an empty one, such patents being issued chiefly for the purpose of filling the coffers of the needy pontiffs who were in theory the Commanders of the Faithful, and in practice obsequious courtiers of the Mamlūk

Sultans of Egypt, but it was highly prized by the lesser sultans in India.

Nizām-ul-Mulk, an officer of Nizām Shāh of the Deccan, now led a large army against the fortress of Kherla. Sirāj-ul-Mulk, who held it for Mālwa, was helplessly drunk when the enemy arrived before the fortress, but his son attempted to withstand the invader. He was defeated and fled, and Nizām-ul-Mulk occupied Kherla. Mahmūd retaliated by sending Maqbūl Khān against Ellichpur, the capital of Berar, and though he failed to capture the city he laid waste the fertile district in which it stood and returned to Māndū with much spoil, but in the following year a treaty of peace was concluded with Muhammad III, who had succeeded his brother Nizām on the throne of the Deccan and Mahmūd's possession of Kherla was confirmed but the integrity of Berar, with that exception, was maintained.

In the same year Mahmūd marched to Kūmbhalgarh and besieged Rānā Kumbha, who was then in that fortress. Learning that Chitor was denuded of troops, Mahmūd ordered his officers to assemble an army, as quietly and unostentatiously as possible, at Khaljīpur, hard by Mandasor, in order that a sudden descent might be made on the Rānā's capital, but Kumbha discovered the design and sallied from Kūmbhalgarh to attack him. He was defeated, but succeeded in making good his retreat to Chitor, and as the opportunity of surprising the fortress had been lost Mahmūd returned to Māndū. While he had been thus engaged Sher Khān, a Turkish officer in his service, had captured Amrelī in Kāthīāwār and slain its raja, Chītā.

Muhammad III of the Deccan had broken the treaty of 1466 by tampering with the loyalty of Maqbūl Khān, Mahmūd's governor of Kherla, who transferred his allegiance to the southern kingdom and surrendered the fortress to the son of the raja whom Mahmūd had imprisoned. Mahmūd's sons, Tāj Khān and Ahmad Khān, made a forced march to Kherla, defeated the raja's son, put him to flight, and re-occupied the fortress. The Gonds with whom he took refuge, on hearing that Tāj Khān was preparing to attack them, sent the fugitive to him in chains. Mahmūd visited Kherla, and marched thence to Sārangpur, where he received Khvāja Kamāl-ud-dīn Astarābādī, an envoy from Tīmūr's great-grandson, Sultān Abu-Saʿīd, king of Transoxiana, Khurāsān, and Balkh. When the envoy departed he was accompanied by Shaikhzāda ʿAlā-ud-dīn, whom Mahmūd sent as his ennoy to Abu-Saʿīd.

In 1468 the landholders of Kachwāra raided some of the

districts of Mālwa, and Mahmūd at once marched to punish them. His son Ghiyās-ud-dīn built, in an incredibly short space of time, a fortress which he named Jalālpur, on the border of Kachwāra, which was occupied by a garrison which curbed the predatory tendencies of the rebels.

In the same year Mahmūd marched to Chanderī, and thence sent Sher Khān and Fath Khān to capture the town of Karahra, 160 miles distant from his camp. They invested the place and pushed forward their parallels until they were able to throw lighted combustibles into one quarter of the town. The fire spread, and destroyed 3000 houses, and the town was captured without difficulty, no fewer than 7000 prisoners being taken. Mahmūd was informed at Chanderī of the outbreak of the conflagration, and is said to have ridden in one night from that town to Karahra in order to witness the discomfiture of the unbelievers, but this is hardly credible.

In the course of this expedition Mahmūd received, on February 20, 1469, Shaikhzāda Muhammad Qarmali Qutb Khān Lodī, and Kapūr Chand, son of Karī Singh, raja of Gwalior, who came as envoys from Buhlūl Lodī, king of Delhi, to seek his help against Husain Shāh of Jaunpur, whose repeated attempts to gain possession of Delhi gave its master no rest and appeared, at this time, to be certain of success. Bayāna was held out as the bait, and Mahmūd promised, in return for the cession of this district, to supply Buhlūl with 6000 horse whenever he might have need of them.

After the dismissal of this mission Mahmūd returned to Māndū, exhausted with unceasing warfare. He was now sixty-eight years of age, and during a reign of more than thirty-three years he had preferred the song of the lark to the cheep of the mouse, and to be worn out rather than rusted out. In the course of his return march to his capital he suffered severely from the fierce heat of an Indian summer, and on June 1, 1469, shortly after his arrival at Māndū, he expired.

He was the greatest of the Muslim kings of Mālwa, which reached its greatest extent during his reign. His ambition may be measured by his attempts to conquer Delhi, Gujarāt, Chitor, and the Deccan, in all of which he failed but against his failures must be set his signal successes against the Rānā Kumbha and many minor Rājput chieftains, his enlargement of the frontiers of his kingdom, and the high estimation in which he was held by his contemporaries. His recognition by the phantom Caliph, worthless though it was, proved, at least, that his fame had reached distant

Egypt, and the mission from Sultan Abu-Saʿīd conveyed to him the more valuable regard of a king in fact as well as in name. He earned a reputation as a builder, and one of his works was a column of victory an Māndū, erected to commemorate his successes against Rānā Kumbha of Chitor. The more famous column of victory at Chitor is said to commemorate victories over Mahmūd of Gujarāt and Mahmūd of Mālwa. If this is so it, 'like some tall bully lifts its head and lies.' Mahmūd I failed to capture Chitor, but the Rānā never gained any important victory over him. The successes of the Gahlots against Mālwa were gained by Sangrama Singh, not by Kumbha, against Mahmūd II, not Mahmūd I.

Mahmūd was a good Muslim. He substituted the unpractical and inconvenient lunar calendar, sacred to Islam, for the solar calendar in all public offices, he destroyed temples and idols and slew or enslaved their worshippers, and he was so scrupulous about meats that when he was besieging the citadel of Bīdar he harassed the saint Khalīlullāh Butshikan, son of Shāh Niʿmatullāh of Māhān, with questions regarding a supply of lawful vegetables for his table. The saint expressed surprise that one who was engaged in attacking a brother Muslim and slaying his subjects should be so scrupulous in the matter of his food. Mahmūd acknowledged, with some embarrassment, the justice of the rebuke, but pleaded that the laws of the faith had never sufficed to curb the ambition of kings.

Mahmūd I was succeeded by his eldest son, Ghiyās ud-dīn, who took his seat on the throne two days after his father's death. He earned the gratitude of his servants by retaining in their posts all those whom his father had appointed, and displayed a confidence in the loyalty of his near relations rarely found in an eastern king. His next brother, Tāj Khān, was confirmed in his fiefs and received the title of ʿAlā-ud-dīn, and his younger brother, Fidāī Khān, was permitted to retain the government of Ranthambhor and other districts. His declaration of policy resembled that of the Roman emperor Augustus. His father, he said, had extended his sway over the whole land of Mālwa, and it should be his care to hold what had been acquired, not to molest his neighbours. So averse was he from war that when Buhlūl Lodī raided Pālampur, near Ranthambhor, he would not take the field himself, but ordered Sher Khān, governor of Chanderī, to obtain satisfaction from the invader, which task was sufficiently well performed, and when, in 1484, he marched from Māndū in response to an appeal from the raja of Chāmpāner, who had sought his aid against Mahmūd Begarha, he was suddenly smitten with compunction, and consulted the doctors of the law on the legality of aiding an infidel against a Muslim, and, on their delivering the opinion that such assistance was unlawful, at once returned to Māndū.

At the beginning of his reign he conferred on his eldest son, 'Abd-ul-Qādir, the title of Nāsir-ud-dīn Sultān, designated him as his heir, and associated him with himself in the business of government.

Ghiyās-ud-dīn found his own chief amusement in the administration of his harem, which it was his fancy to organise as a kingdom in miniature, complete in itself. Its army consisted of two corps of Amazons, of 500 each, one of African and one of Turkish slave girls, who at public audiences were drawn up on either side of the throne. The harem contained, besides these, 1600 women, who were taught various arts and trades, and organised in departments. Besides the musicians, singers, and dancers, usually found in a royal seraglio there were goldsmiths, blacksmiths, shoemakers, weavers, potters, tailors, makers of bows, arrows, and quivers, carpenters, wrestlers, and jugglers, each, of whom received fixed wages. their officers, also women being paid at higher rates, also women who supervised the various crafts and administrative departments. These women were recruited, at great trouble and expense, from all parts of India, but a case in which one of his agents abducted a girl from her parents led him to order the cessation of recruitment in his own dominions. A replica in miniature of the great bazar in the city was erected within the precincts of the palace, and was filled with the artists, artisans and craftswomen of the harem. The king himself regulated with meticulous nicety the pay and allowances of all, even to the quantities of grain, fodder and meat allotted to the various animals employed or domesticated within the extensive premises set apart for the harem, decided disputes, and generally wasted in these futile pursuits the time and energy which should have been devoted to the administration of his kingdom.

When not thus employed he devoted himself to the ceremonies of his faith, and to inventing others, to add to the list of those with which the daily life of a devout Muslim is encumbered. He insisted on being aroused every night, shortly after midnight, even if force should be necessary, for the recitation of the voluntary night prayers, and he abstained, not only from all intoxicants, but from all food of the legality of which there was the slightest doubt, and from wearing clothes of materials not sanctioned by the law of Islam.

.His folly and profusion were practised upon by rogues and impostors, whose fraudulent tricks needed but to be connected in some way with professions of religion to receive unmerited rewards. A beggar from Delhi picked up a handful of wheat from a heap lying in the courtyard of the palace and carried it into the royal presence. When asked the meaning of his action he explained that he was one who had committed to memory the whole of the Koran, which he had recited over each single grain of the wheat in his hand, which he now offered to the king. Honours and favours were showered upon him.

Another rogue brought to the king the hoof of an ass, which he asserted to be a hoof of the ass on which our Lord had entered Jerusalem. He received 50,000 *tangas* and was, of course, followed by three other rogues, each bearing the hoof of an ass, of which he told the same story and for which he received the same reward. As though this were not enough, a fifth appeared, with a fifth hoof, and the king commanded that he likewise should receive 50,000 *tangas*. The courtiers protested against this folly, and asked their master whether he believed that the Messiah's ass had five legs. 'Let him have the reward,' replied the crowned fool, 'perhaps he is telling the truth and one of the others made a mistake.'

At such a court as this beggars of all classes of course abounded, and the taxes wrung from a thrifty and industrious people were squandered on rogues, vagabonds and idlers.

Ghiyās-ud-dīn's declining years were embittered by a violent quarrel between his two sons, 'Abud-ul-Qādir, Nāsir-ud-dīn and Shujā'at Khan 'Alā-ud-dīn, whose mother, Rānī Khurshīd, daughter of the raja of Baglāna, favoured the cause of the younger. The miserable king, whose naturally feeble intellect was now impaired by old age, was incapable of composing the strife, and vacillated between his heir and his wife's favourite. Murders were committed on either side, and both appealed to arms. Nāsir-ud-dīn marched out of the capital and assembled an army, and both his father and his mother attempted to persuade him to return, the former that the prince might resume the government of the kingdom, which had latterly fallen entirely into his hands, and the latter that she might find an opportunity of putting him to death. Nāsir ud-dīn's first attempt to storm the capital was unsuccessful, but the greater part of the nobles and the army was on his side, and he was eventually admitted by the Bālāpur gate. He seized his mother and brother, imprisoned the one and put the other to death, and on October 22, 1500, ascended the throne with the consent of his father. He caused those of the nobles who had opposed him to be put to death and designated his second son, Miyān Manjhla, as his heir, conferring on him the title of Shihāb-ud-dīn.

Many of the nobles in the provinces, including Sher Khān the powerful governor of Chanderī, and Muqbil Khān, governor of Mandasor, declined to believe that the new king had ascended the throne with his father's conscent, and took up arms against him. After one unsuccessful attempt to crush this rebellion, and another attempt, equally unsuccessful, to conciliate the rebels, he took the field against them, and assembled his army at Na'lcha, leaving his son Shihab-ud-dīn in charge of the capital. At Dhār he received news of the death of his father, on February 28, 1501, from poison, administered, as it was generally believed, by his orders. He encountered the rebels at Sārangpur and utterly defeated them. Sher Khān fled to Chanderī, and thence to Erij and Bhānder[1], and Nāsīr-ud-dīn occupied Chanderī, but discovered that a faction in the town had invited Sher Khān to return and promised him their active support. He sent a force against the rebel who was advancing on Chanderī and who was defeated and so severely wounded that he died in the course of his retreat. The king marched as far as the spot where the body had been buried, exhumed it, and carried it back to Chanderī, where it was exposed on a gallows. He then appointed Bihajat Khān governor of Chanderī and returned to Māndū, when by deep drinking he aggravated the natural ferocity of his disposition and by his violent and irascible temper alienated his nobles.

In 1503 he led a marading expedition into the dominions of the Rānā, and later in the year sent a force to the aid of Dāūd Khān of Khāndesh, whose dominions had been invaded by Ahmad Nizām Shāh of Ahmadnagar.

In 1510 Shihāb-ud-dīn, his son and heir apparent, rose in rebellion, and was joined by most of the nobles in the provinces and many in the capital, who were disgusted by the king's tyranny. Nāsir-ud-dīn marched against him and met him, with greatly inferior numbers, at Dhār. Shihāb-ud-dīn, encouraged by his numerical superiority, attacked his father, but was defeated and fled to Chanderī, and, when he was pursued thither, to Siprī. His father followed him, and having vainly attempted to persuade him to return to his allegiance set out for Māndū, but died on his way thither.

Of the manner of his death there are two accounts. According

[1] In 24° 31′N. and 73° 45′E.

to one he contracted a fever and insisted on bathing in cold water, which so aggravated his illness that it terminated fatally. According to the other he gave expression to his suspicions of many of his nobles, whom he believed to have been secretly in correspondence with Shihāb-ud-dīn, and uttered menaces, until they became so apprehensive that they poisoned him. Immediately after his death they unanimously raised to the throne, on May 2, 1511, his son 'Alā-ud-dīn Mahmūd II, who was in the camp, and sent Nāsir-ud-d´n's body to Māndū for burial.

Shihāb-ud-dīn, on hearing of his father's death, returned to Mālwa and marched on Māndū, but Mahmūd II outstripped him and arrived there first, and when Shihāb-ud-dīn reached the city the gates were shut in his face. After attempting, without success, to persuade the governor of the city, Muhāfiz Khān, to admit him, he retired to the fortress of Asīr, in Khāndesh.

Mahmūd II confirmed in his post his father's minister, a Hindu named Basant Rāi, but the Muslim nobles so resented his tenure of his high place that they murdered him. The intrigues of Muhāfiz Khān, governor of Māndū, drove Iqbāl Khān and Mukhtass Khān, two of the leading nobles, into rebellion and they fled to the Narbada and sent Nusrat Khān, the former's son to Asīr, to summon Shihāb-ud-dīn to the throne of Mālwa. The prince was so overjoyed that he set out at once, riding hard, in the great heart, to join his adherents, but he succumbed, and on July 29, 1511, died on the road. The rebels sent his body to Māndū for burial, proclaimed his son King under the title of Hūshang II, and marched into the central districts of Mālwa. A force was sent against them and defeated them, and Hūshang took refuge in Sehore, but the leaders convinced the king that they were loyal at heart, and had rebelled only in consequence of the intrigues of Muhāfiz Khān. This officer had already angered the king by proposing that he should put to death his eldest brother, Sāhib Khān, and the quarrel became so acute that Muhāfiz Khān attacked the king in his palace. He was defeated and driven off, and avenged himself by proclaiming Sāhib Khān king under the title of Muhammad II[1]. Mahmūd II escaped from Māndū and withdrew to Ujjain, where he was joined by Iqbāl Khān, Mukhtass Khān, and Dastur Khān. Sāhib Khān advanced to Na'lcha and Mahmūd retired to Dipālpur, where most of the nobles, whose wives and families were in Māudū deserted him. He asked Bihjat Khān governor of

---

[1] Muhammad II reigned nominally from A.H. 917 to A.H. 921 (A.D. 1511—1516). His extant coins bear the latter date.

Chanderī, to give him an asylum in that fortress, but Bihjat Khān replied that he was the servant of the king who held Māndū. Mahmūd knew not where to turn, and remained irresolute for some days, until he bethought himself of Mednī Rāi the Purbiya, a Rājput of eastern Hindūstān, who held the military government of a small district in Mālwa and was noted for his valour. He responded to the king's call, and came to his aid, and his accession induced Bihjat Khān of Chanderī to change his attitude, so that he sent his son Shiddat Khān to the king with offers of service.

Mahmūd, thus reinforced, marched to meet his brother, who advanced from Māndū. The armies met in the evening, and while they were encamped for the night Afzal Khan deserted the prince, taking half of the army with him to Mahmūd's camp and Muhammad fled without fighting. Mahmūd at once marched on Māndū, being joined on the way by the remnant of Shihāb-ud-dīn's supporters from Sehore, and on November 28 found his brother, who had assembled a number of troops, barring his way to the capital. Muhammad was defeated, and fled into the fortress, and Mahmūd, after an inffectual attempt to induce him to submit, opened the siege of the palace. On January 6, 1512 he was admitted into the fortress, by some of his partisans and Muhammad and Muhāfiz Khān fled, with such jewels and treasure as they could collect and carry with them, and threw themselves on the protection of Muzaffar II of Gujarat, who was then encamped at Baroda. The course of Muhammad's subsequent wanderings has been traced in the preceding chapter. He found a home, for a time in Berar, under the protection of 'Alā-ud-dīn 'Imād Shāh.

Mahmūd was now established at Māndū, and soon had occasion to repent of having summoned the Purbiya Rājputs to his aid. Mednī Rāi assumed the office of minister, dismissed from their posts all the old nobles of the kingdom, in whose places he appointed men of his own faith and race, and induced the king to sanction the assassination of Afzal Khān and Iqābl Khān, whom he accused of entering in correspondence with Muhammad. The Muslim nobles viewed with mingled disgust and apprehension the supremacy of the idolators in the state, and Sikandar Khān, governor of Satwās and one of the most important of the great fief-holders, raised the standard of revolt. Bihjat Khān of Chanderī excused himself from obeying his sovereign's command to march against the rebel, and Mansūr Khān of Bhīlsa, who obeyed the royal summons, was so ill supported that he abandoned the attempt to crush the rebellion, and joined Bihjat Khān at Chanderī. Mednī

Rāi reduced Sikandar Khān to obedience, and by confirming him in his fiefs induced him to renew his allegiance to Mahmūd.

Bihjat Khān of Chanderī was still contumacious, and when Mahmūd marched in person to Āgar sent letters to Sāhib Khān, or Muhammad Shāh, in Berar, and to Sikandar Shāh Lodī of Delhi, begging the former to join him and received the crown of Mālwa, and seeking the assistance of the latter against a king who was dominated by infidels.

While Mahmūd was awaiting the return of a mission which he had sent to Bihjat Khān for the purpose of recalling him to his obedience, he was perturbed by the news of a revolt in his capital, and of the invasion of his kingdom by Muzaffar II of Gujarāt, but the revolt was immediately suppressed and Muzaffar was recalled to Gujarāt by domestic disturbances. No sooner had Mahmūd been reassured by this news than he learnt that Sikandar Khān was again in rebellion, and had defeated and slain a loyal officer who had endeavoured to reduce him to obedience. At the same time he learnt that his brother had reached Chanderī and had been proclaimed king by Bihjat Khān and Mansūr Khān. He retired to Bhilsa and remained for some time in that neighbourhood. His inaction encouraged the rebels to send a force to Sārangpur, but the governor of that district defeated them, and the news that a contingent sent to their help by Sikandar Shāh Lodī had retired restored Mahmūd's spirits, and disheartened, in a corresponding degree, his enemies. An attempt of Muhāfiz Khān to return to Māndū was defeated, and the rebels were ready to come to terms. The king was no less weary of the conflict, which, as he now understood, was being prolonged only in the interest of the Purbiya Rājputs, and ceded to his brother the districts of Rāisen Bhīlsa, and Dhamonī, besides remitting to him a substantial sum for his immediate needs. The retention of the money by Bihjat Khān excited the apprehensions of Muhammad, who believed that he was about to be betrayed to his brother, and fled to the protection of Sikandar Shāh Lodī, thus enabling his host to make an unqualified submission to Mahmūd, who, on December 18, 1513, was received at Chanderī by Bihjat Khān, who endeavoured, without success, to free him from his subservience to Mednī Rāi.

Early in 1514 the king returned to Māndū, where he fell entirely under the influence of the Rājput minister, and at his instigation put many of the old Muslim nobles of the kingdom to death. The rest left the court, and even menial servants were dismissed, until the king was entirely in their power. He made an effort to free himself by dismissing Mednī Rāi, but the minister refused to accept his dismissal, and the Rājputs were restrained from violence only by prudential considerations, and promised in future to abstain from what was their greatest offence in the eyes of Muslims — the keeping of Muslim women as concubines. One of their leaders, Sālibāhan, refused to make this promise, and the offence thus continued. Mahmūd then attempted to remove Mednī Rāi and Salibāhan by assassination, and succeeded in the case of the latter, but the former was only wounded, and the Rājputs attacked the king's small bodyguard of Muslims, but were defeated, chiefly owing to their fear of provoking the intervention of Muzaffar II of Gujarāt by proceeding to extremities.

In 1517 Mahmūd lost patience with his Hindu masters, and, leaving Māndū on the pretext of hunting eluded his Rājput escort and fled to the frontier of Gejarāt, where he sought aid of Muzaffar II, whose ready response to the appeal, and the capture of Māndū, the terrible massacre of the Rājputs, and Mahmūd's restoration to his throne have already been described in the preceding chapter.

The Rājputs had not all been in Māndū when it was taken by Muzaffar, and Mednī Rāi had established himself in the northren and eastern districts of the kingdom : his officers held Chanderī and Gāgraun, and his brother, Silahdī, Rāisen, Bhīlsa, and Sarangpur.

Mahmūd recalled all his old Muslim nobles and their troops, and by the advice of Āsaf Khān of Gujarāt, who had been left, with 10,000 horse, by Muzaffar II to assist him against his enemies, marched first to Gāgraun, which was held by Hemkaran for Mednī Rāi.

Mednī Rāi was himself with Rānā Sangrama, and, on hearing that Mahmūd had opened the siege of Gāgraun, implored the Rānā to save a town which contained all that was most precious to him. Sangrama responded to the appeal, and marched with a large army towards Gāgraun, and Mahmūd, on hearing of his advance, abandoned the siege and marched with great rapidity to meet him. His army encamped within fourteen miles of Sangrama, who, having ascertained that it was exhausted by its long march, attacked it at once. On his approach the Muslims took the field in small bodies, each division falling in as soon as it could arm and mount. The whole army was thus cut to pieces in detail and utterly defeated. Mahmūd himself was wounded and was captured, fighting valiantly, for he lacked not physical courage, and carried before Sangrama, who received him with the chivalrous courtesy which the Rājput knows how to show to a defeated foe, but compelled him to surrender all his crown jewels.

The Rānā was now in a position to annex Mālwa, but prudently refrained from a measure which would have raised against him every Muslim ruler in India, and, making a virtue of necessity, supplied Mahmūd with an escort which conducted him back to Māndū and replaced him on his throne.

Āsaf Khān's contingent of 10,000 cavarly fought in this battle, and shared the disaster which befell the army of Mālwa, and for this reason Sangrama's success is always represented in Hindu annals as a victory over the combined armies of Mālwa and Gujarāt.

Mahmūd's authority now extended only to the neighbourhood of his capital. The northern and eastern districts of the kingdoms remained, as already mentioned, in the hands of the Purbiya Rājputs, and Satwās and the southern districts in those of Sikandar Khān. A victory over Silahdī reduced him temporarily to obedience, but its effect was fleeting.

A few years later Mahmūd behaved with incomprehensible folly and ingratitude. When Bahādur Shāh, in July, 1526, ascended the throne of Gujarāt, his younger brother, Chānd Khān, fled to Māndū, and Mahmūd not only received him, but encouraged him to hope for assistance in ousting his brother from his kingdom. Three years later, having heard of the death of Rānā Sangrama, he raided the territories of Chitor and provoked Sangrama's successor, Ratan Singh, who invaded Mālwa and advanced as far as Sārangpur and Ujjain, to reprisals. He reaped the fruits of his ingratitude towards the king of Gujarāt as described in the preceding chapter. On March 17, 1531, Māndū was captured by Bahādur Shāh, and the Khaljī dynasty was extinguished. Bahādur's operations in Mālwa during the next two years, his defeat by Humāyūn, and the latter's capture of Māndū in 1535 have been described in the account of his reign. Humāyūn lingered in Mālwa until August, 1535, when he would have been better employed elsewhere, and was suddenly roused to activity by the rebellion of his brother 'Askarī. After his departure Mallū Khān, formerly an officer of the Khaljī kings, who had been permitted to retain the fief of Sārangpur and had received the title of Qādir Khān, reduced to obedience other fief-holders in Mālwa, from Bhīlsa to the Narbada, and, having established himself at Māndū, assumed the title of Qādir Shāh. When Sher Khān, hard pressed by Humāyūn in Bengal, demanded in language too peremptory for the occasion, assistance from Qādir Shāh, the latter returned an insolent reply, which was not forgotten, and Sher Shāh, now king of Delhi, invaded Mālwa in 1542. Qādir, who was not strong enough to oppose him, made his submission to him at Sārangpur, and was well received and appointed to the government of Bengal instead of that of Mālwa, but shortly afterwards, being apprehensive of Sher Shāh s intentions towards him, fled from his camp. The king imprisoned Sikandar Khān of Satwās, lest he should follow Qādir's example, and retired from Mālwa, leaving behind him as viceroy Hājī Khān, with Shujā'at Khān as governor of Satwās.

Nasīr Khān of Satwās attacked the new governor with the object of seizing his person and holding him as a hostage for his father, Sikandar Khān, but was defeated, though Shujā'at Khān was severely wounded in the battle. He had not recovered from his wounds when he was summoned by Hājī Khān to assist him against Qādir Shāh, who, having assembled an army in Bānswāra, was marching to attack him. Shujā'at Khān responded to the appeal, and Qādir was defeated, and fled to Gujarāt The credit of the victory rested with Shujā'at Khān, and Hājī Khān was recalled and Shujā'at Khān was appointed to succeed him as viceroy of Mālwa.

Puran Mal, the son of Silahdī, still retained possession of the fortress and district of Rāisen, and had recently, after occupying the town of Chanderī, massacred most of its inhabitants, and collected in his harem 2000 women, Muslims as well as Hindus. In 1543 Sher Shāh marched from Āgra against him and besieged him in Rāisen. He was induced by delusive promises to surrender, and Sher Shāh, when he had him in his power, attacked him and his followers with his elephants. The Rājputs performed the rite of *jauhar*, and, fighting bravely, were trampled to death.

Shujā'at Khān was on bad terms with Islām Shāh, Sher Shāh's son and successor, and in 1547 an Afghān, whom he had punished with mutilation for drunkenness and disorderly conduct, attempted, with the king's implied approval, to assassinate him. He was wounded, and so resented his master's behaviour that he fled from his camp at Gwalior.

Islām Shāh treated him as a rebel, and invaded Mālwa, but the viceroy would not fight against his king, and withdrew into Bānswāra. Islām Shāh was called to Lahore by the rebellion of the Niyāzīs, and at the instance of his favourite, Daulat Khān Ajyāra, who was Shujā'at Khān's adopted son, pardoned and reinstated the recalcitrant viceroy.

When Humāyūn recovered his throne in 1555 Shujāʻat Khān[1] abstained from acknowledging him, and demeaned himself in all respects as an independent sovereign. Later in the same year he died, and was succeeded by his son Miyān Bāyazīd, known as Bāz Bahādur, whose pretensions were opposed by his father's adopted son, Daulat Khān Ajyūra. Bāz Bahādur, having lulled his rival's suspicions by assenting to an arrangement by which Mālwa was partitioned, seized him and put him to death, and assumed the royal title. He then expelled his own younger brother, Malik Mustafā, from Rāisen, and captured Kelwāra from the Miyāna Afghāns. His next exploit was an expedition against the famous Rānī Durgāvatī, queen of the Gonds of Garha-Katanga, who defeated him and drove him back into his own country, where he forgot his disgrace in the arms of his famous mistress, Rūpmati. He sank into the condition of a mere voluptuary, and when Mālwa was invaded, in 1561, by the officers of the emperor Akbar, he was driven from his kingdom, which became a province of the Mughul empire.

[1] Shujāʻat Khān was vulgarly known as Sazāval or Sajāval Khān.

CHAPTER XV

THE KINGDOM OF THE DECCAN, 1347—1490

THE revolt of the centurions and the establishment by 'Alā-ud-dīn Bahman Shāh of the kingdom of the Deccan, not wholly recovered by Delhi for 340 years, have already been described in Chapter VI.

This kingdom was not conterminous with the southern provinces of Muhammad Tughluq's great empire, for the Hindus of the south had not failed to profit by the dissensions of their enemies. Kān-hayya Nāik of eastern Telingāna, who claimed to represent the Kākatīya dynasty, had readily assisted the rebels against the king of Delhi, but was not prepared to acknowledge Bahman Shāh as his master. Vīra Ballāla III of Dvāravatīpura had established his independence when the Muslim officers in the Deccan rose in rebellion, and having thrown off the yoke of Delhi was in no mood to bow his neck to that of Gulbarga. He pushed his frontier northward to the Tungabhadra river, which remained the extreme southern limit of Bahman's dominions, nor did his successors invariably succeed in retaining even this frontier, for the great kingdom of Vijayanagar, which rose on the ruins of Dvāravatīpura, claimed the Doāb between the Krishna and the Tungabhadra, with its two strong fortresses, Rāichūr and Mudgal, and this tract remained a debatable land while Bahman's dynasty endured.

Ibn Batūtah, in his account of his voyage down the western coast of India, mentions petty rulers of ports and their adjacent districts owning allegiance and paying tribute to Muhammad Tughluq, but this allegiance was withheld from Bahman Shāh, and only gradually recovered by his successors, whose authority over the Hindus of the Western Ghāts was always precarious.

The new kingdom included the province of Berar, which marched on the north-west and north with the small state of Khāndesh and the kingdom of Mālwa, and it was separated from Gujarāt by the small hilly state of Baglāna (Bāglān), which retained a degree of independence under a dynasty of native Rājput chieftains.

'Alā ud-dīn Hasan claimed descent from the hero Bahman, son of Isfandiyār, and his assumption of the title Bahman Shāh was an assertion of his claim[1]. Firishta relates an absurd legend connecting the title with the name of the priestly caste of the Hindus,

[1] *J.A.S.B.* Part *I*, vol. LXXIII, extra number, 1904.

but this story is disproved by the evidence of inscriptions and
legends on coins, and the name Kankū, which frequently occurs in
conjunction with that of Bahman, and is said by Firishta to represent Gangū, the name of the king's former Brāhman master, is
more credibly explained by Maulavī 'Abd-ul-Walī[1] as a scribe's
corruption of Kaikāūs, which was the name of Bahman's father as
given in two extant genealogies[2].

The lesser Hindu chieftains of the Deccan, who had been bound
only by the loosest of feudal ties to their overlord in distant Delhi,
had followed the example of Dvāravatīpura and Warangal, and
Bahman was engaged during his reign of eleven years in establishing his authority in the kingdom which he had carved out of
Muhammad's empire. He first captured the forts of Bhokardhan
and Māhūr from the Hindu chieftains who held them, and then
dispatched his officers into various districts of the Deccan to reduce
the unruly to obedience. 'Imād-ul-Mulk and Mubārak Khān advanced to the Tāpti and secured the northern provinces, and Husain
Gurshāsp received the submission of the remnants of Muhammad's
army which had been left to continue the siege of Daulatābād,
and which submitted readily on learning that Bahman Shāh was
prepared to pardon their activity in the cause of the master to
whom they had owed allegiance. Qutb-ul-Mulk captured the towns
of Bhūm, Akalkot, and Mundargi, and pacified, in accordance with
the principle approved by his master, the districts dependent on
them. Landholders who submitted and undertook to pay the taxes
assessed on their estates were accepted as loyal subjects, without
too rigorous a scrutiny of their past conduct, but the contumacious
were put to death, and their lands and goods were confiscated.
Qambar Khān reduced, after a siege of fifty days, the strong fortress of Kaliyāni, and Sikandar Khān, who was sent into the Bīdar
district, marched as far south as Mālkhed, receiving the submission
of the inhabitants of the country through which he passed, and
compelled Kānhayya Nāik of Warangal to cede the fortress of
Kaulās and to pay tribute for the territory which he was permitted
to retain.

Bahman had rewarded Ismā'īl Mukh, who had resigned to him
the throne, with the title of Amīr-ul-Umarā, the nominal command
of the army, and the first place at court, but afterwards transferred
this last honour to Saif-ud-dīn Ghūrī, father-in-law of Prince Muhammad, the heir-apparent, and the old Afghān, bitterly resenting

1. *Journal and Proceedings, A.S.B.*, vol. v. p. '463.
2. Preserved by Firishta and the author of the *Burhān-i-Ma'āsir*.

his supersession, conspired to assassinate the king, and paid the penalty of his crime, but Bahman was so sensible of his indebtedness to him that he appointed his eldest son, Bahādur Khān, to the post rendered vacant by his father's death.

Bahman was as yet far from being secure in his new kingdom and a pretence of loyalty to Delhi furnished Nārāyan, a Hindu who possessed the tract between the Krishna and Ghātprabhā rivers, and Muʿīn-ud-dīn, a Muslim who held a fief in the same neighbourhood, with a pretext for withholding tribute from a king who had renounced his allegiance to his former lord. Khvāja Jahān from Mīraj and Qutb-ul-Mulk from Mundargi besieged the rebels in Gulbarga, their chief stronghold, which was captured and occupied by the former, whose politic leniency immediately conciliated the inhabitants of the surrounding country. Khvāja Jahān, while he was at Gulbarga, received news of the mutiny of an army which had been sent to besiege Kanbari, one of Nārāyan's fortresses near Bījāpur. The troops, suspecting their leader of trafficking with the enemy, rose and slew him, and then, intoxicated by success, and by possession of the treasure-chest, marched to Sāgar, expelled the officers employed in that district and occupied the fortress. The news of the death of Muhammad Tughluq in Sind deprived the mutineers of a pretext for rebellion; and Bahman, who marched to Sāgar in person, received their submission. He then captured Kalabgūr, Kanbari, and Mudhol, pardoned Nārāyan, who surrendered to him, and marched to Mīraj, which he had formerly held as a fief from his old master, Muhammad Tughluq. Here he halted for some time, and after establishing his authority in the neighbourhood, returned to Gulbarga, which he made his capital, renaming it Ahsanābād. His leisure here was interrupted only by a rebellion of two Muslim officers at Kohīr and Kaliyāni.

After the suppression of this revolt he devoted himself to the adornment of his capital with suitable buildings and to the establishment of a system of provincial government in his kingdom, which he divided into four provinces, each of which was known as a *taraf*. The first, Gulbarga, extended on the west to the Ghāts, and later to the sea, on the north to the eighteenth parallel of latitude, on the south to the Tungabhadra, and on the east to the Banāthorā and a line drawn from its confluence with the Bhīma to the confluence of the Krishna and the Tungabhadra. To the north of Gulbarga lay the province of Daulatābād, bounded on the north and north-east by the petty state of Baglāna, Khāndesh, and the southern Pūrna river ; and north-east of this lay Berar, which, east of Burhānpur, was bounded on the north by the Tāpti and on the east by the Wardha and Pranhitā rivers, and extended on the south to the southern Pūrna and Godavri rivers and on the west approximately to its present limits. The fourth province was Bīdar, or Muhammadan Telingāna, which included the towns and districts of Bīdar, Kandhār, Indūr, Kaulās, Kotāgīr, Medak, and as much of Telingāna as was comprised in the Bahmani kingdom, extended eastward, at the end of Bahman's reign, as far as Bhongīr ; but the eastern border of this province, like the southern border of Gulbarga, where the Hindus of Vijayanagar often occupied the Raichūr Doāb, varied with the power of the Muslim kings to resist the encroachments or overcome the defence of the Hindus of Telingāna. The governors first appointed to these provinces were Saif-ud-dīn Ghūrī to Gulbarga ; the king's nephew Muhammad entitled Bāhram Khān, to Daulatābād ; Safdar Khān Sīstāni, to Berar ; and Saif-ud-din's son, who bore the title of A'zam-i-Humāyūn, to Bīdar. Muhmmad, the king's eldest son, received his father's former title of Zafar Khān, and the districts of Hūkeri, Belgaum, and Mīraj, which Bahman had formerly held of Muhammad Tughluq.

Rebellion never again raised its head during Bahman's reign, and having thus provided for the administration of his kingdom he was at leisure to extend its frontiers. He marched first into the Konkan where having captured the port of Goa, he marched northward along the coast, and took Dābhol, returning to his capital by way of Karhād and Kolhāpur, both of which towns he took from their Hindu rulers. After a period of repose at Gulbarga he led an expedition into Telingāna, captured Bhongīr, and remained in its neighbourhood for nearly a year, during which time he completely subjugated the country between it and Kohīr.

During one of his periods of repose the king, intoxicated with success in war and pride of race, indulged in extravagant dreams of conquest, similar to those which had once deluded 'Alā-ud-dīn Khaljī and Muhammad Tughluq, and imitated the former by assuming, in the legends on his coins the vain-glorious title of 'the Second Alexander.' He proposed to inaugurate his career of conquest by attacking the Hindu kingdom of Vijayanagar, which had suddenly risen to power, and carrying his arms to Cape Comorin, but, like his prototype, was recalled to sanity by the sober counsels of a faithful servant, the shrewd Saif-ud-dīn Ghūrī, who reminded him that there was work nearer home, and that there still remained in the northern Carnatic Hindu chieftains who had not acknowledged his sovereignty. Against these he dispatched an expedition, the success of which may be measured by its booty, which included 200,000 golden *ashrafīs* of 'Alā-ud-dīn Khaljī, large quantities of jewels, 200 elephants and 1000 singing and dancing girls, *murlīs* from Hindu temples.

Bahman next turned his eyes towards the southern provinces of the kingdom of Delhi, lying on the northern frontier of his kingdom, and set out for Mālwa with an army of 50,000 horse, but before he had traversed the hilly country of Southern Berar was persuaded by Raja Haran the Vāghelā, son of that Raja Karan of Gujarāt who had been expelled from his kingdom in the reign of 'Ala-ud-dīn Khaljī and had found an asylum with the Rāhtor raja of Baglāna, to attempt first the invasion of Gujarāt, which the raja promised, if restored, to hold as a fief of the kingdom of the Deccan. Bahman marched into that kingdom, but at Navsārī fell sick of fever and dysentery, brought on by his exertions in the chase and by excessive indulgence in wine and venison, and was compelled to abandon his enterprise. As soon as he had recovered sufficiently to travel he returned to Gulbarga, where he lay sick for six months and died on February 11, 1358[1]. He left four sons, Muhammad, Dāūd, Ahmad, and Mahmūd[2], the eldest of whom succeeded him.

Immediately after the accession of Muhammad I his mother performed the pilgrimage to Mecca and either visited or communicated with al-Mu'tadid, the puppet Caliph in Egypt, from whom, on her return to India in 1361, she brought a patent recognising her son as king of the Deccan, in consequence of which he assumed on his coins the title 'Protector of the People of the Prophet of the Merciful God.' His father before him seems to have sought and obtained this coveted recognition, for in 1356 the Caliph's envoy to Fīrūz Tughluq of Delhi had desired him to recognise and respect the Muslim king of the Deccan.

Muhammad I was a diligent and methodical administrator, and on ascending the throne carefully organised his ministry, his household troops, and the provincial administration which his father had inaugurated. His institutions demand more than passing notice, for they not only endured as long as the kingdom of his successors

---

[1] Rabi'ul-awwal 1, A.H. 759. This is the date given by Firishta. According to the *Tazkirat-ul-Mulūk* Bahman died in A.H. 761 (A.D. 1360). A coin of his, dated A.H. 760, exists, but is perhaps posthumous, although no coin of Muhammad I of an earlier date than A.H. 760 has been discovered. *J.A.S.B.*, new series, XIV, 475.
[2] *J.A.S.B.*, vol. LXXIII, extra number, 1904, pp. 4–6.

but were closely imitated in the smaller states which rose on its
ruins. The ministers were eight in number :

(1) Vakīl-us-Saltanah, the Lieutenant of the Kingdom ;
(2) Vazīr-i-Kull, the Superintending Minister ;
(3) Amīr-i-Jumlah, the Minister of Finance ;
(4) Vazīr-i-Ashrāf, the Minister of Foreign Affairs and Master
     of the Ceremonies ;
(5) Nāzir, the Assistant Minister of Finance ;
(6) Pīshvā, who was associated with the Lieutenant of the King-
     dom, and whose office was in later times almost invariably
     amalgamated with his ;
(7) Kotwāl, the Chief of Police and City Magistrate in the
     capital ; and
(8) Sadr-i-Jahān, the Chief Justice and Minister of Religion and
     Endowments.

The guards were commanded by officers known as *Tavājī*, many
of whom acted as aides-de-camp to the king and gentlemen ushers
at court, in which capacity they were styled *Bārdār*. The whole
bodyguard, known as *Khāss-Khail*, consisted of 200 esquires to
the king (*Aslihadār*) and 4000 gentlemen troopers (*Yaka-Javān*),
and was divided into four reliefs (*Naubat*), each consisting of
50 esquires and 1000 troopers, and commanded by one of the great
nobles at the capital, with the title of *Sar-Naubat*. The tour of
duty of each relief was four days, and the whole force was commanded by one of the ministers, entitled, as commander of the
guards, *Sarkhail*, who performed his ordinary military duties by
deputy.

The Hindu kingdom of Vijayanagar has already been mentioned.
The founder of the dynasty which ruled it from 1339 to 1483 was
Sangama I, a petty chieftain of Anagundī, on the north bank of
the Tungabhadra and near the site of Vijayanagar. Sangama had
never submitted to Muhammad Tughluq, but had maintained a
rude independence in his stronghold, and was at first probably
little more than a brigand chief ; but the subjection of the Kākatīyas of Warangal, the destruction of the kingdom of Dvāravatīpura
by the Sayyid sultan of Madura, and the rebellion in the Deccan,
which left the Peninsula free from Muslim aggression, were the
opportunity of Sangama and his successors, and there are few
examples in history of a large and powerful state being established
by adventurers in the short time which sufficed for the establishment of the kingdom of Vijayanagar. Unfortunately we lack the
means of tracing the process by which the insignificant chieftains

of Anagundī became, within the short space of thirty years, the unquestioned rulers of this great and wealthy kingdom, but we may form some idea of the course of events by imagining a great Hindu population exasperated by the sacrilegious oppression of foreign warriors with whom they had been powerless to cope, deprived of their hereditary rulers, and suddenly relieved of the hostile yoke by the intestine feuds of their enemies, joyfully acclaiming a national hero.

Sangama I was succeeded, in 1339, by his son, Harihara I, who again was succeeded, in 1354, by his brother, Bukka I. It cannot be determined what share each of these rulers had in establishing the kingdom, but before 1357 it was so powerful that the sagest counsellor of Bahman Shāh dissuaded him from molesting it. Muhammad I came into conflict with this great power in consequence of a measure of domestic policy, adopted in no spirit of aggression. His father had minted few or no gold coins, but Muhammad, who objected both on religious and political grounds to the circulation of Hindu money in his dominions, coined gold in considerable quantities. Bukka I and Kānhayya of Warangal, without any justification, resented this measure as tending to limit the circulation of their gold, and received support from the bankers and money-changers in Muhammad's dominions, native Hindus of the Deccan, who melted down all his gold coin falling into their hands, and either hoarded the metal, which was purer than that of the Hindu coins, or supplied it to the mints of Vijayanagar and Warangal. Repeated warnings were disregarded, and on one day in May or June, 1360, the Hindu bankers and money-changers in all towns of the kingdom were, by royal decree, put to death. Their place was taken by Hindus of the Khatri caste of northern India, who had accompanied the various armies which had invaded the Deccan, and now enjoyed a monopoly of the business of banking and money-changing until, in the reign of Fīrūz Shāh Bahmanī (1397-1422), the descendants of the slaughtered men were permitted, on payment of a large sum of money, to resume the business of their forefathers.

The rajas of Vijayanagar and Warangal feigned to regard Muhammad's determination to establish his own gold currency as an assertion of suzerainty, and, knowing that his treasury had been depleted by the profusion customary at the beginning of a new reign, addressed arrogant and provocative messages to him. Bukka demanded the cession of the Rāichūr Doāb, and threatened, failing compliance, to concert measures with the king of Delhi for a combined attack on the Deccan. Kānhayya of Warangal demanded the retrocession of Kaulās, and threatened war. Muhammad, on one pretext and another, detained the bearers of these insolent demands for eighteen months, by which time his preparations were complete, and, with an effrontery surpassing that of his enemies, haughtily inquired why his vassals, the rajas of Vijayanagar and Warangal, had not made the customary offerings on his accession, and demanded that they should atone for their negligence by immediately sending to him all the elephants fit for work in their dominions, laden with gold, jewels, and precious stuffs. Kānhayya's reply to this insult was the dispatch of an army under his son Venāyek Deva against Kaulās, and Bukka supplied a contingent of 20,000 horse for the enterprise. The armies of Berar and Bīdar under Bahādur Khān defeated and dispersed the invaders, and while Bukka's contingent fled southwards Venāyek Deva took refuge in his fief of Vailampallam, on the sea coast. Bahādur Khān marched to the gates of Warangal, forced Kānhayya to ransom his capital by the payment of 100,000 gold *hūns*[1] and the surrender of twenty-six elephants, and returned to Gulbarga.

These hostilities permanently disturbed the friendly relations between Warangal and Gulbarga. In 1362 a caravan of horse-dealers arrived at Gulbarga, and to the king's complaint that they had no horse in their stock fit for his stable, replied that on their way through Vailampallam Venāyek Deva had compelled them to sell to him all their best horses, despite their protest that they were reserved for the king of the Deccan. Muhammad set out in person to avenge this insult, and led 4000 horse on a sudden raid to Vailampallam, performing a month's journey in a week, and arriving at his destination with only a quarter of his original force ; but his arrival was unexpected, and, having gained admission to the town by a stratagem, he captured Venāyek Deva as he attempted to flee from the citadel. Exasperated by the foul abuse which his captive uttered, he caused his tongue to be torn out, and hurled him from a *balista* set up on the ramparts into a fire kindled below.

He was gradually joined by the complement of his original force, but imprudently lingered too long at Vailampallam, and in the course of his long retreat was so harassed by the Hindus that he was forced to abandon all his baggage and camp equipage, and lost nearly two thirds of his men. Reinforcements which joined

[1] The *hūn* was the coin former by known by the British in southern India as the pagoda, and was worth four rupees.

him at Kaulās not only checked the pursuit, but carried the war into the enemy's country, and devastated the western districts of Telingāna.

During the king's absence his cousin, Bahrām Khān Māzandarānī, governor of Daulatābād, had rebelled, and had sought the assistance of Fīrūz Tughluq of Delhi[1]. His mission, which was accompanied by envoys from Kānhayya of Warangal, failed to accomplish its object, and Muhammad sent an army to suppress the rebellion in Daulatābād and marched in person into Telingāna to avenge his recent discomfiture. One force was sent against Golconda and another against Warangal, whence Kānhayya fled into the hills and jungles and vainly sued for peace. Muhammad remained for two years in Telingāna, ravaging and laying waste the country, while his troops continued to besiege Warangal and Golconda. Kānhayya at length succeeded in obtaining peace by swearing fealty, paying an indemnity of 1,300,000 *hūns*, surrendering 300 elephants, and ceding Golconda. To these concessions he added a throne studed with turquoises, which had originally been prepared as an offering to Muhammad Tughluq, but was now included in the regalia of the kingdom of the Deccan, where it was known as the *Takht-i-Fīrūza*, or turquoise throne.

On March 21, 1365, Muhammad took his seat on this throne at Gulbarga and made himself merry with wine, dance, and song. The singers and dancers had to be suitably rewarded, and the king, flushed with wine and success, ordered that they should be paid by a draft on the treasury of Vijayanagar. His ministers hesitated to execute an order issued, as they were persuaded, under the influence of strong drink, but the king was in earnest, and insisted on obedience. The order, delivered to Bukka by an accredited envoy, incensed the powerful raja beyond measure, its bearer was ridden round the city on an ass and ignominiously expelled, and Bukka crossed the Tungabhadra and besieged Mudgal, a fortress then held by no more than 800 Muslim troops. The place fell, and its garrison was massacred before relief could reach it, and Muhammad set out for the Doāb with no more than thirty elephants, crossed the flooded Krishna, and marched towards Bukka's great army of 30,000 horse and 900,000 foot[2], vowing that he would not

---

1 See Chapter VII.

2 The vast numbers of infantry led into the field by the rajas of Vijayanagar will frequently be noticed. They suggest a suspicion of deliberate exaggeration by Muslim historians for the purpose of magnifying the exploits of Muslim warriors but the suspicion is unjust. 'Abd-ur-Razzāq, an unprejudiced observer, who visited Vijayanagar in 1442, when the kingdom was at peace, says that the army consisted of 1,100,000 men. The Hindu infantry was of very poor fighting

sheathe the sword until he had avenged the massacre of the garrison of Mudgal by the slaughter of a hundred thousand misbelievers.

His impetuosity terrified Bukka, who fled with his cavalry towards Adonī, leaving the infantry, followers, and baggage animals to follow as best they could. The Muslims plundered the Hindu camp, taking a vast quantity of booty, and Muhammad, after slaughtering 70,000 Hindus of both sexes and all ages, retired for the rest of the rainy season into the fortress of Mudgal where he was joined by reinforcements from Daulatābād. He sent orders to all the forts in his kingdom, demanding a detachment of artillery from each, and sent the elephants which he had captured to Gulbarga, for the conveyance of the guns[1]. At the close of the rainy season he advanced towards Adonī, while Bukka retired, leaving his sister's son in command of that fortress.

Bukka reassembled his scattered army, and Muhammad, crossing the Tungabhadra at Siruguppa, advanced to meet him. Bukka detached an officer, Mallināth, with the flower of his army, consisting of 40,000 horse and 500,000 foot, to attack the Muslims, and Muhammad sent against him his cousin, Khān Muhammad, with 10,000 horse, 30,000 foot, and all the artillery, and followed him with the remainder of his army. Early in 1367 the forces met near Kauthal, and the first great battle between the Hindus of the Carnatic and the Muslims of the Deccan was fought. It raged with great fury from dawn until four o'clock in the afternoon, the commanders of the wings of the Muslim army were slain and their troops put to flight but the centre stood fast, encouraged by the news of the near approach of the king, and, by a timely discharge of the artillery, worked by European and Ottoman Turkish gunners, shook the Hindu ranks, and completed their discomfiture by a cavalry charge which prevented their artillery from coming into

quality and probably consisted of a host of lightly armed and half-trained rustics, of whom almost any number might have been collected.

[1] With reference to this statement, and the mention of guns as part of Bukka's armament, Firishta remarks that this was the first occasion on which the Muslims used guns in warfare in the Deccan. It is quite possible that a knowledge of the use of gunpowder in war had by this time reached southern India, for Ismā·Il b. Faraj, king of Granada, used artillery at the siege of Baza, in 1325, and cannon of brass, with iron balls, were made at Florence in 1326. Who the Europeans and Ottoman Turks, mentioned by Firishta as serving with the artillery, can have been, is not clear, for the Portugese did not reach India until more than 130 years after this time. It is not, however, improbable that Europeans from the Eastern Empire and Venice occasionally found their way to India by way of Egypt and Red Sea, or overland, either as independent adventurers or as the slaves of Muhammadan merchants. Both Europeans and Ottoman Turks were in great request at a later period, as gunners and artillerists.

action, and in which Mallināth was mortally wounded. His army broke and fled, and Muhammad Shāh arrived on the field in time to direct the pursuit, in the course of which the victors slaughtered every living soul whom they overtook, sparing neither women nor sucklings. Muhammad marched in pursuit of Bukka, who, after eluding him for three months, contrived to throw himself into Vijayanagar, which the Muslims were not strong enough to besiege, but Muhammad, by feigning sickness and ordering a retreat, enticed him from the fortress, and, having led the Hindus to a distance attacked their camp by night, slew 10,000 men, and again captured their treasure and elephants. Bukka again fled to Vijayanagar and Muhammad, without attempting to besiege him, ordered a general massacre of the inhabitants of the surrounding country. Bukka, urged by his courtiers, sent envoys to sue for peace, and even the Muslim officers were moved to beg that the slaughter might cease, but Muhammad replied that although he had slain four times the number of Hindus which he had sworn to slay, he would not desist until his draft on Bukka's treasury was honoured. To this the envoys consented, the draft was honoured, and the war ended. The Hindus, horrified by the massacre of 400,000 of their race, including 10,000 of the priestly caste, proposed that both parties should agree to spare non-combatants in future. Muhammad consented, and the agreement, though sometimes violated, mitigated to some extent the horrors of the long period of intermittent warfare between the two states.

Bahrām Khān and his confederate, Kondba Deva the Marāthā, were now stronger than ever in Daulatābād. The failure of their missions to Delhi had been more than counterbalanced by the withdrawal of the royal troops for the campaign in the south, and Bahrām was enriched by the accumulation of several years' revenue of the province and strengthened by the support of a numerous and well-equipped army, by an alliance with the raja of Baglāna, and by the adhesion of many of the fief-holders of southern Berar. To a letter from Muhammad promising him forgiveness if he would return to his allegiance he vouchsafed no reply, and Khān Muhammad was reappointed to Daultatābād and sent against him, the king following with the remainder of the army.

Bahrām and his allies advanced as far as Paithan on the Godāvari, and Khān Muhammad halted at Shivgāon, only thirteen miles distant, and begged his master, who was hunting in the neighbourhood of Bīı, to come to his assistance. On the news of the king's approach the rebels dispersed and fled, evacuating even the fortress of Daulatābād and were pursued to the frontiers of Gujarāt, in which province they took refuge.

After some stay at Daulatābād Muhammad I returned to Gulbarga, and devoted himself to the demestic affairs of his kingdom which enjoyed peace for the remainder of his reign. Highway robbery had for some time been rife, and he exerted himself to suppress it, with such success that within six or seven months the heads of 20,000 brigands were sent to the capital.

The provincial governors enjoyed great power. They collected the revenue, raised and commanded the army, and made all appointments, both civil and military, in their provinces, under a strong king, and as long as the practice, now inaugurated by Muhammad, of annual royal progresses through the provinces was continued, this system of decentralisation worked tolerably well, but as the limits of the kingdom extended and the personal authority of the monarch waned its defects became apparent, and an attempt to modify it in the reign of Muhammad III led indirectly to the dismemberment of the state.

It was in 1367 that Muhammad I completed the great mosque of Gulbarga, which differs from other mosques in India in having the space which is usually left as an open courtyard roofed in. The late Colonel Meadows Taylor was mistaken in the idea that it was an imitation of the great mosque, now the cathedral of Cordova, for it differs from it in the style of its architecture, but it is a noble building, impressive in its massive solidity.

In the spring or early summer of 1377 Muhammad I died, and was succeeded by his elder son, Mujāhid, remarkable for his personal beauty, his great physical strength, and his headstrong disposition. One of his earliest acts as king was to demand from Bukka I the cession of the extensive tract bounded on the north by the Ghātprabhā and on the south by the Tungabhadra, and stretching eastward nearly as far as Mudgal and westward to the sea. Bukka replied by demanding the return of the elephants captured in the previous reign, and Mujāhid at once invaded his dominions. Sending a force under Safdar Khān Sīstanī to besiege Adonī, he marched in person against Bukka, who was encamped on the bank of the Tungabhadra, near Gangāwatī, and retreated southward on his approach. For five or six months Mujāhid followed him through the jungles of the Carnatic, without succeeding in forcing a battle, and in the end Bukka eluded him and shut himself up in Vijayanagar. Mujāhid followed him, penetrated beyond the outer defences of the city, and defeated successive forces of Hindus sent against him. The failure of his uncle, Dāūd Khān, to hold a defile, the defence of which had been entrusted to him, imperilled his retreat, but he forced his way through the defile and retired at this leisure towards Adonī with sixty or seventy thousand captives, whose lives were spared under the pact into which his father had entered. Bukka feared to follow, and Mujāhid besieged Adonī for nine months, and was on the point of receiving its surrender when the rainy season began, replenished the water supply of the garrison, and caused much distress in the besiegers' camp. Saif-ud-dīn Ghūrī persuaded him to raise the seige, peace was made with Bukka, and Mujāhid set out for his capital

His uncle, Dāūd Khān[1], had taken grave offence at the rebuke which he had received for his desertion of his post at the battle of Vijayanagar, and entered into a conspiracy to destroy him. An opportunity occurred when Dāūl Khān's turn to mount guard over the royal tent came, and on the night of April 15, 1378, the conspirators entered Mujāhid's sleeping tent and slew him, and Dāūd was proclaimed king.

Safdar Khān, governor of Berar, and A'zam-i-Humāyūn, the new governor of Daulātābād, both partisans of Mujāhid, had preceded the army to the capital, and on learning of the success of the conspirators took possession of the royal elephants and returned to their provinces without waiting to tender their allegiance to the new king. Their defection menaced Dāūd's authority, but there was also a party in the capital which was prepared to oppose his enthronement, and the Hindus, on hearing of the death of Mujāhid, crossed the Tungabhadra and laid siege to Rāichūr. The aged regent, Saif-ud-dīn Ghūrī, averted the calamity of a rebellion at Gulbarga, but refused to serve the usurper, and retired into private life, and on May 20, 1378, Dāūd, at the instigation of Mujāhid's sister, Rūh Parvar Āghā, was assassinated at the public prayers in the great mosque. Khān Muhammad, Dāūd's principal supporter, slew the assassin and attempted to secure the throne for Dāūd's infant son, Muhammad Sanjar, but the child's person was in the possession of Rūh Parvar, who caused him to be blinded, and, with the concurrence of the populace raised to the throne Muhammad[2], son of Mahmūd Khān, the youngest son of Bahman Shāh.

---

[1] For a discussion of the question of the relationship between Mujāhid and Dāūd see *J. A. S. B.*, vol. LXXIII, part *I*, extra number, 1904, p. 5.

[2] Firishta wrongly styles this prince Mahmūd. He is refuted by the evidence of coins, inscriptions, and other historians, excepting those who are admittedly mere copyists, but has led all English historians astray. See *J. A.S.B.*, vol. LXXIII, part I, extra number, 1904, pp. 6, 7.

Muhammad II imprisoned Khān Muhammad in the fortress of Sāgar, where he shortly afterwards died, and punished his accomplices. The provincial governors who had refused to recognise the usurper returned to their allegiance to the throne, Saif-ud-dīn Ghūrī again became chief minister of state, and Bukka, on learning of the unanimity with which the young king was acclaimed, prudently raised the siege of Rāichūr and retired across the Tungabhadra.

Muhammad II was a man of peace, devoted to literature and poetry, and his reign was undisturbed by foreign wars. His love of learning was encouraged by the Sadr-i-Jahān, Mīr Fazlullāh Injū of Shīrāz, at whose instance the great poet Hāfiz was invited to his court. Hāfiz accepted the invitation and sent out from Shīrāz, but he possessed that horror of the sea which is inherent in Persians, and he was so terrified by a storm in the Persian Gulf that he disembarked and returned to Shīrāz, sending his excuses to Mīr Fazlullāh in the well-known ode[1] beginning :

دمی باغم به سر بردن جهان یکسر نمی ارزد *
به می بفروش دلق ما که بیش از این نمی ارزد

and the king was so gratified by the poet's attempt to make the journey that although the plentiful provision which he had sent for him had been dissipated, he sent him valuable gifts.

Between 1387 and 1395 the Deccan was visited by a severe famine, and Muhammad's measures for the relief of his subjects displayed a combination of administrative ability, enlightened compassion, and religious bigotry. A thousand bullocks belonging to the transport establishment maintained for the court were placed at the disposal of those in charge of relief measures, and travelled incessantly to and fro between his dominions and Gujarāt and Mālwa, which had escaped the visitation, bringing thence grain which was sold at low rates in the Deccan, but to Muslims only. The king established free schools for orphans at Gulbarga, Bīdar, Kandhār, Ellichpur, Daulatābād, Chaul, Dābhol, and other cities and towns, in which the children were not only taught, but were housed and fed at the public expense. Special allowances were also given to readers of the Koran, reciters of the Traditions, and the blind.

The peace of Muhammad's reign was disturbed in its last year by the rebellion of Bahā-ud-dīn, governor of Sāgar, who, at the instigation of his sons raised the standard of revolt. A Turkish

[1] No. 142 in Lt.-Colonel H. S. Jarrett's edition of Hāfiz.

officer named Yūsuf Azhdar was sent to quell the rebellion, and besieged Sāgar for two months, at the end of which time the garrison rose against their leader, decapitated him, and threw his head over the battlements as a peace offering. His sons were slain while making a last stand against the royal troops, and the rebellion was crushed.

On April 20, 1397, Muhammad II died of a fever, and on the following day Saif-ud-dīn Ghūrī, the faithful old servant of his house, passed away at the great age of 104 (solar) years, and was buried beside his master.

Muhammad was succeeded by his elder son, Ghiyās-ud-dīn, a resolute but indiscreet youth of seventeen. He angered Tughalchīn, the chief of the Turkish slaves, by refusing to appoint him governor of Gulbarga and lieutenant of the kingdom, and incautiously placed himself in his enemy's power, lured by his infatuation for his daughter. Tughalchīn blinded the young king and caused the leading nobles of the kingdom to be assassinated.

The unfortunate Ghiyās-ud-dīn, who had reigned but one month and twenty-six days, was blinded and deposed on June 14, 1397, and on the same day Tughalchīn raised to the throne his younger half-brother, Shams-ud-dīn Dāūd, and assumed the regency. He secured his position by playing on the vanity, the fears, and perhaps on the warmer sentiments of the young king's mother, who had been a maid-servant of Ghiyās-ud-dīn's mother, but his dominance in the state and the degradation of the royal family were deeply resented by the king's cousins, the brothers Fīrūz and Ahmad, sons of Ahmad Khān[1], one of the younger sons of Bahman Shāh, who had been brought up by their cousin Muhammad II and had each been married to one of his daughters, full sisters of Ghiyās-ud-dīn. The brothers, now young men of twenty-seven and twenty-six, do not seem to have been actuated at first by selfish motives, but desired only to protect the dignity of the throne and to serve the dynasty. Tughalchīn so aroused their apprehensions by poisoning the mind of the queen-mother against them that they fled from Gulbarga to Sāgar, where they were befriended by the governor, and demanded that the king should dismiss Tughalchīn. On receiving the reply that he was unable to exercise his authority they marched with a small force on Gulbarga, where they expected support from the minister's enemies, but they were disappointed, and Fīrūz, in order to encourage the faint-hearted among his

---

[1] See *J.A S.B.*, vol. LXXIII, part I, extra number, 1904, and *An Arabic History of Gujarāt*, text, edited by Sir E. Denison Ross, I, 160.

followers, assumed the royal title. Their troops were defeated by
the royal army, led by Tughalchīn and the puppet king, and they
fled to Sāgar. After·a short time they professed penitence, and
returned to Gulbarga, where they were received with outward
tokens of forgiveness, but continued to concert plans for the overthrow of the slave in which it was now clear that his puppet must
be involved.

On November 15, 1397, Fīrūz and Ahmad contrived to enter
the palace with a few armed adherents, on the pretext of paying
their respects to the king, and overpowered both him and Tughalchīn.
Fīrūz ascended the turquoise throne, and was proclaimed under the
title of Tāj-ud-dīn Fīrūz Shāh, and Sham-ud-dīn was blinded and
imprisoned, and eventually permitted to perform, with his mother,
the pilgrimage to the Hijāz, where he died. The blind Ghiyās-ud-
dīn was brought from Sāgar, a sword was placed in his hand and
Tughalchīn, who was compelled to sit before him, was cut to pieces
by his former victim.

Fīrūz, at the time of his accession, was an amiable, generous,
accomplished, and tolerant prince, possessed of a vigorous constitution and understanding, both of which he undermined by
indulgence in the pleasures of the harem.

His first task was to reorganise the administrative machinery of
the kingdom, and he appointed his brother, Ahmad Khān, minister,
with the titles of Amīr·ul-Umarā and Khānkhānān, and Mīr Fazlullāh Injū governor of Gulbarga and lieutenant of the kingdom,
and Brāhmans were more extensively employed in important posts.

In 1398 the long peace between the Deccan and Vijayanagar
was broken, the aggressor being Harihara II, who invaded the
Rāichūr Doāb with an army of 30,000 horse and 900,000 foot, while
the Hindu chieftain on the north bank of the Krishna headed
a rebellion of the Kolīs. Fīrūz first dealt with the latter, and after
defeating them in the field put to death large numbers of them
and crushed the rising, but was compelled to send back the armies
of Berar and Daulatābād, which he had summoned to his assistance
against Harihara in order that they might deal with Narsingh,
the Gond raja of Kherla, who had invaded Berar and ravaged
the eastern districts of that province as far south as Māhūr, on the
Penganga. No more than 12,000 horse remained to him, but he
ventured to advance to the Krishna. The rainy season of 1399 had
now set in, and Harihara's vast army held the southern bank of the
river. The tactics and discipline of the Hindus were contemptible.
They were scattered over an area which extended for some seventeen

miles along the bank of the river and the same distance in depth to the south of it, and this dispersion, necessary for purposes of supply, was sufficient to destroy their cohesion, but their mere numbers precluded any attempt to force the passage of the river, and Fīrūz chafed at his enforced inaction until his health suffered. At this juncture Qāzī Sirāj-ud-dīn, an inferior officer of his court, whose enterprise and hardihood became rather his military than his judicial office, suggested a bold adventure, which Fīrūz at first forbade, but afterwards sanctioned[1].

The Qāzī, a man of parts, had in the course of a riotous youth, acquired considerable proficiency in music, dancing and juggling, and he proposed that he should cross the river with a small band of performers who would readily be admitted into the disorderly camp of the enemy, and might, by assassinating either Harihara or his son, throw it into confusion and thus give the Muslim army an opportunity of crossing in the darkness.   ←

Fīrūz Shāh's preparations for crossing river attracted the attention and earned the ridicule of the Hindus, but were not connected by them with the appearance in their camp of a band of twenty-six wandering minstrels, who, having crossed the river lower down, had lodged in a liquor shop, and exhibited their skill before other professional entertainers whom they met there. The new-comers soon gained a high reputation, and some nights after their arrival were commanded to perform before Harihara's son. The Qāzī sent a secret message to Fīrūz, warning him to be prepared, and led his troupe to the prince's tents. Only the Qāzī and two others were required to dance, and the rest of the party remained outside, and were instructed to be ready to facilitate the escape of the performers. After the exhibition of some tricks Sirāj-ud-dīn called for arms for the performance of the sword and dagger dance, and the three gave an exhibition of sword and dagger play which amazed the half-inebriated Hindus. Then, suddenly rushing forward, Sirāj-ud-dīn fell upon and cut down the prince, while his two confederates disposed of the minister, the other spectators,

[1] For this extraordinary exploit, which reads more like romance than history, we have three distinct authorities, (1) Firishta, who cites the *Tuhfat-us-Salātīn and Sirāj-ut-Tawārikh*, (2) Nizām-ud-dīn Ahmad, and (3) Khāfī Khān, who for once is not a mere echo of Firishta but obtained his facts from an independent source, and is corroborated in many important details by Nizām-ud-dīn Ahmad's briefer summary. Khāfi Khān's account has been followed as the fullest, most credible of the three. The exploit will appear incredible to those who do not understand the proneness of the Oriental to panic on the loss of a leader. The Qāzi understood the failing and laid his plans accordingly.

and the torch-bearers. The three escaped in the darkness and joined their companions without, who, on the first symptoms of a disturbance, had attacked and slain the guard, so that the gang was enabled to escape to a place of safety and await the success of the enterprise. The camp of the Hindus was thrown into confusion, and the wildest rumours circulated. It was widely believed that the enemy had crossed in force, and slain the raja, and some of the Hindus mistook others, in the darkness, for enemies, and fell upon them. The slaughter was only stayed when a conflagration caused by the ignition of some tents discovered to the combatants their error ; others, not knowing whither to turn, stood to arms by their tents, but none knew where to strike.

During the tumult some three or four thousand horse crossed the river in relays under cover of the darkness, and the Hindu picquets on the river bank, attacked in front and alarmed by the uproar in their rear, turned and fled : those who had already crossed the river covered the passage of the remainder, and before daybreak Fīrūz and his whole force had gained the southern bank. At dawn they attacked the vast and scattered camp of the Hindus, which was still in confusion, and Harihara, who had left the conduct of affairs entirely in the hands of his son, was so overwhelmed with grief and dismay that he fled to Vijayanagar, carrying his son's body with him, and leaving his army to follow as best it could. Fīrūz pursued the flying mob, annihilating any small bands which attempted to stem his progress, and at last halted before Vijaya-nagar. His numerical weakness precluded any idea of siege operations, or of attempting to carry the great city by storm, and part of the army was detached to plunder and lay waste the populous tract to the south of it. The agreement to spare the lives of non-combatants was respected, but large numbers, including 10,000 Brāhmans, were enslaved, and the leading Brāhmans of Vijayanagar insisted on the conclusion of peace on any terms obtainable, and on the ransom of the captives. These objects were attained by the payment of an indemnity of about £330,000 sterling, and Fīrūz retired. On his return to Gulbarga he made the first departure from the provincial system of Bahman Shāh and Muhammad I by appointing Fūlād Khān military governor of the Rāichūr Doāb, which had hitherto formed part of the province of Gulbarga, from which it was now separated.

It was now necessary to formulate the foreign policy of the kingdom with respect to the territories on its northern frontier, Gujarāt and Mālwa, which had declared their independence of

Delhi in 1396 and 1401, and the small state of Khāndesh, which had been established in 1382 by Malik Raja, a partisan of Bahrām Khān Māzandarānī who had fled from the Deccan. The kingdom of the Bahmanids, freed from the menace of its southern neighbour, would have been stronger than any one of these states, stronger, perhaps, than all together, but as matters stood Mālwa was only slightly weaker than the Deccan and Gujarāt equal to it, or perhaps slightly stronger, while the small state of Khāndesh could not have stood alone under any conditions, and was formidable only by reason of the support which one or other of its powerful neighbours was ever ready to lend it.

The aggression of Narsingh to Kherla had been prompted by Dilāvar Khān of Mālwa and Nasīr Khān of Khāndesh, and the governors of Berar and Daulatābād had not only been unable to punish him, but had not even succeeded in restoring order in Berar. Fīrūz was thus compelled, after two or three months' rest at Gulbarga, again to take the field, and at the beginning of the winter of 1399 marched to Māhūr, where he received the submission of the governor, a Gond or Hindu who had declared for Narsingh. After halting there for a month he continued his march to Ellichpur, whence he dispatched a force under his brother Ahmad and Mīr Fazlullāh Injū to punish Narsingh. The Gonds, disappointed of the help which they had expected from Mālwa and Khāndesh, fought with such desperate valour that the centre of the Muslims was broken, and many of the leading officers, among them Shujā'at Khān, Dilāvar Khān, and Bahādur Khān, were slain[1].

Ahmad Khān and Fazlullāh Injū rallied the fugitives and saved the day by causing the great drums to be beaten and spreading the report that the king was hastening to the support of his army. They attacked the Gond centre, captured Kosal Rāi, Narsingh's son, who commanded it, slew 10,000 Gonds, and pursued the remainder to the gates of Kherla, which were shut only just in time to exclude the victors. The fortress endured a siege of two months, at the end of which time Narsingh was informed, in reply to his prayers for peace, that the besiegers were not empowered to treat, and that he must make his submission to Fīrūz Shāh at Ellichpur.

[1] The shrine at Ellichpur known as that of Shāh 'Abd-ur-Rahmān is probably the tomb of one or all of these officers. 'Abd-ur-Rahmān is said to have been a nephew and son-in-law of Mahmūd of Ghazni, and to have invaded Berar early in the eleventh century, during the reign of the eponymous raja II of Ellichpur. The absurd story is unknown to history, and is merely a clumsy imitation of the legends of Sālār Mas'ūd of Bahrāich, in Oudh. For the legend, and a discussion of it see *J.A.S.B.*, vol. LXX, part III, p. 10.

He was fain to comply, and after offering forty elephants, a considerable weight of gold and silver, and a daughter for the king's harem, and promising to pay tribute annually, 'as in the days of Bahman Sha h,' was invested with a robe of honour and dismissed. Mir Fazlullāh Iujū was appointed governor of Berar, and Fīrūz returned to Gulbarga.

In the interval of peace which followed the expedition to Kherla, Fīrūz built for himself and the 800 women of various nations who composed his harem the town of Fīrūzābād, on the Bhīma, the site of which had attracted him on his return from Vijayanagar. The new town was his Capua, but never superseded Gulbarga as the administrative capital of his kingdom.

In 1401 Fīrūz, disturbed by rumours that Tīmūr, who was now in Āzarbāijān, proposed to return to India and seat one of his sons on the throne of Delhi, is said to have sent to him an embassy, and to have obtained, in return for his gifts and promises, a decree bestowing on him the Deccan, Gujarāt, and Malwa. Chroniclers of Tīmūr's reign make no mention of this, but a mission from a ruler so remote and comparatively obscure may well have passed unnoticed by them, and it is only on the supposition that the mission was sent and the decree received that the events of the next few years can be explained. Muzaffar I of Gujarāt, Dīlāvar Khān of Mālwa, and Nasīr Khān of Khāndesh, alarmed and enraged by Tīmūr's grant, demanded of Fīrūz that he should keep the peace, and sent envoys to Harihara II promising to assist him, when necessary, by attacking the Deccan from the north. Harihara, emboldened by these offers, withheld the tribute which he had paid since Fīrūz Shāh's invasion of his kingdom, and Fīrūz, apprehensive of attacks from the north, dared not attempt to enforce payment. He had gained little by his sycophantic and costly mission.

In 1406 Harihara II died, and was succeeded by his son, Bukka II[1] and in the same year occurred the romantic episode of the goldsmith's daughter of Mudgal, a strange occurrence, but reasonably well attested. A poor goldsmith and his wife, living near Mudgal, are said to have had a daughter named Parthāl, of such surpassing beauty and brilliant accomplishments that her fame spread far and wide, and was carried by a Brāhman who had been her instructor to the court of Bukka, who sent messengers to demand her of her parents. They, regarding the proposal as an

---

[1] The authority of the learned author of *A Forgotten Empire* is to be preferred to that of B. Suryanārāyan Rāo, who has parodied the title of Mr Sewell's valuable work, but has failed to controvert his conclusions.

honour, were disposed to comply, but the girl, declined it. Bukka crossed the Tungabhadra with 5000 horse and sent a party to Mudgal to abduct the girl but news of the raid had preceded it, and by the time that the party reached Mudgal Parthāl and her parents had fled. The disappointed Hindus vented their spleen by plundering the inhabitants, and rejoined Bukka, but Fūlād Khān, governor of the Doāb, attacked him, and, after suffering a reverse, defeated the invaders, slew a thousand of them, and drove Bukka back to Vijayanagar.

In order to avenge this outrage, Fīrūz assembled the provincial armies at Gulbarga, and at the end of 1406 marched to Vijaya-nagar and attempted to carry the city by assault, but within the walls the Hindu infantry, contemptible in the field, was more than a match for the Muslim horse, who were driven out of the city. Bukka, encouraged by this success followed, attacked, and defeated them, wounding Fīrūz himself. They fell back for twenty-four miles, fortified their camp, and halted to enable their wounded to recover. Bukka attacked them no less than eight times, but was defeated on each occasion, and was further disappointed by the silence of the kings of Gujarāt, Mālwa, and Khāndesh, from whom he had demanded the fulfilment of their promises. Fīrūz on his recovery, sent his brother, Ahmad Khān, with 10,000 horse to plunder the country to the south of his enemy's capital, and Mīr Fazlullāh Injū to besiege Bankāpur. Both operations were suc-cessful, and Fazlullāh not only captured Bankāpur, but reduced to obedience the country lying between it and Mudgal, thus making the Tungabhadra, throughout its course, the southern boundary of the kingdom, and securing the frontier for which Mujāhid had con-tended.

Ahmad Khān's spoils included, 60,000 captive Hindu youths and children, and Fīrūz, recognising the impossibility of capturing Vija-yanagar, marched to Adonī, but before he could form the siege envoys from Bukka arrived in his camp to sue for peace. It was with difficulty that he could be persuaded to consider their pro-posals, and when he consented to treat he insisted on the humi-liating condition that Bukka should surrender a daughter to him for his harem. Bukka also ceded the fort and district of Bankāpur as the dowry of the princess, and delivered to Fīrūz 130 pounds of pearls, fifty elephants, and 2000 boys and girls skilled in singing dancing or music, and paid an indemnity of about £300,000.

The marriage was celebrated with great pomp but failed to pro-mote goodwill between the two kingdoms. Bukka, when escorting

Fīrūz from Vijayanagar to his camp, turned back too soon, and the two parted in anger.

After his return to Fīrūzābād the king sent to Mudgal ior the beautiful Parthāl and her parents. The girl was given in marriage to Hasan Khan, his son, and the parents received gifts in money and a grant of their native village. It was probably on this occasion that the goldsmiths of the Deccan were permitted once more to follow their ancestral calling as bankers and money-changers, from which they had been debarred by the edict of Muhammad I.

In 1412 Fīrūz led an expedition into Gondwāna. The Gond or Hindu governor of Māhūr was again in rebellion and Fīrūz, finding the fortress too strong to be reduced, plundered southern Gondwāna, slaying the inhabitants and capturing 300 wild elephants, but was eventually obliged to return to his capital, leaving the rebel unpunished.

After his return the famous saint Jamāl-ud-dīn[1] Husainī, nicknamed Gīsū Darāz ('Long ringlets'), arrived from Delhi and established himself at Gulbarga, where he was received with great honour. The cultured Fīrūz soon wearied of the society of the ignorant and unlettered saint, but the simpler and more pious Ahmad took much delight in his discourse, and gained his support, which contributed largely to his success in the impending contest for the throne. From this time both Ahmad and the saint, who was indiscreet enough to prophesy his disciple's success, became objects of suspicion and aversion to Fīrūz, who, though no more than forty years of age, was worn out by his pleasures and delegated much of his authority to others. . Ahmad, who had served his brother faithfully in the past, now lost his confidence, and the king's choice fell upon Hūshyār and Bīdār, two manumitted slaves whom he ennobled under the titles of 'Ain-ul-Mulk and Nizām-ul-Mulk, and into whose hands, as habits of indolence grew upon him, he gradually resigned the entire administration of the kingdom.

In 1417 he so far roused himself from his lethargy as to lead an expedition into Telingāna, the raja of which country had withheld payment of tribute. The suzerainty of Fīrūz was acknowledged, the arrears of tribute were paid, and amendment was promised for the future.

It is doubtful whether Fīrūz, after this campaign, returned to his capital or marched directly to Pāngul, situated about twenty-five miles to the north of the confluence of the Krishna and the Tungabhadra,

---

[1] In the *Burhān-i-Ma'āsir* he is styled Sadr-ud-dīn, but the authority of the Zafar-ul-Wālih is to be preferred.

in which neighbourhood he waged his last and most unfortunate war against the 'misbelievers'. Pāngul had been included in the district of Golconda, ceded by Kānhayya to Muhammad I but was now in the possession of Vīra Vijaya of Vijayanagar[1] by whom, or by whose father, Devarāya I, it had been occupied Fīrūz was opposed, on his way thither, by a division of the enemy's army which fought with great bravery and was not defeated until it had inflicted heavy losses on his troops. The siege of Pāngul exhibited the physical, mental and moral deterioration of Fīrūz. Its operations were protracted for a period of two years, until the insanitary condition of the standing camp bred disease among men and beasts, and disease caused panic and wholesale desertion. Vīra Vijaya, seizing this opportunity, made an offensive alliance with the raja of Telingāna and marched to the relief of the town. Fīrūz Shāh's vanity and the recollection of his early successes forbade him to follow the wise advice of those who counselled a present retreat and preparations for future vengeance, and he insisted on giving battle to Vīra Vijaya. Mīr Fazlullāh Injū was treacherously slain during the battle by a Canarese Hindu of his own household, and the Muslims were routed, and would have been annihilated but for the careful dispositions and patient valour of Ahmad Khān, which enabled them to retire in some sort of order towards Gulbarga. The Hindus occupied the southern and eastern districts of the kingdom and repaid with interest the treatment which they had received.

Ahmad succeeded in expelling the Hindu troops, but the humiliation and anxiety to which Fīrūz had been subjected had shattered a constitution enfeebled by excesses, and the management of affairs fell entirely into the hands of Hūshyār and Bīdār, who desired to secure the succession of the king's son, the weak and voluptuous Hasan Khān, and induced the king to order that his brother should be blinded. Ahmad withdrew, with his eldest son, 'Alā-ud-dīn Ahmad, to the hospice of Gīsū Darāz[2], where he spent the night in making preparations to flee from the capital, and early in the morning left Gulbarga with 400 horse. He was joined by a rich merchant, Khalaf Hasan of Basrah, who had long been attached to him, and

---

[1] The succession to the throne of Vijayanagar at this period is not free from obscurity and doubt. According to Mr. Sewell, who is here followed, Bukka II died in 1408, and was succeeded by his brother, Devarāya I, who died in 1413 and was succeeded by his son Vīra Vijaya, but some authorities identify Devarāya I with Bukka II.

[2] The practice of taking sanctuary at the hospice or shrine of a saint is of great antiquity, and survives in the east, though not in India, to this day. Few Muslim rulers would venture to violate the sanctity of such a building.

halted in a village near Kaliyāni. The two favourites hastily collected a force of three or four thousand horse, with elephants and pursued Ahmad, whose followers now numbered a thousand. Khalaf Hasan encouraged Ahmad to assume the royal title and withstand his brother's troops, and by circulating a report that the provincial governors had declared for him, and by a stratagem similar to that of the Gillies' Hill at Bannockburn, enabled his patron to defeat his enemy and pursue the favourites to Gulbarga. Here they carried Fīrūz, now grievously sick, into the field, and ventured another battle, but the king swooned, and a rumour that he was dead caused the greater part of the army to transfer its allegiance to Ahmad. The citadel was surrendered, and Ahmad, in an affecting interview with his brother, accepted his resignation of the throne and the charge of his two sons, Hasan Khān and Mubārak Khān.

Ahmad ascended the throne at Gulbarga on September 22, 1422, and on October 2, Fīrūz died. He was probably not far from death when Ahmad usurped the throne, but the event was too opportune to have been fortuitous, and of the three best authorities for this period two, citing early historians, say that he was strangled, and the third says that he was poisoned.

Hasan, who had inherited his father's vices without his virtues, was content with a life of voluptuous ease at Fīrūzābād, where his uncle's indulgence permitted him to enjoy such liberty as was compatible with the public peace, but Ahmad's son and successor blinded him as a precautionary measure.

Fīrūz holds a high place among the princes of his house. His character at the time when he ascended the throne has been described, and it was not until he had reigned for some years that the wise, spirited, and vigorous king became a jaded and feeble voluptuary. He was a sincere, but not a rigid Muslim, and though nominally an orthodox Sunni of the Hanafite school, he drank wine, while confessing the sinfulness of his indulgence, and availed himself of the licence, admitted by theologians of the laxer Malikī school, and by the Shiahs, of temporary marriage. In his harem were women of many nations, with each of whom he is said to have been able to converse fluently and easily in her own language. His curiosity regarding the marriage law of Islam was enlightened on one occasion by a woman taken in adultery, who pleaded with irrefutable logic, that as that law allowed a man four wives her simplicity was to be pardoned for believing that it allowed a woman four husbands. Her impudent wit saved her.

The new king's first care was to honour the saint to whose

patronage and blessing he attributed his success, and his gratitude took the form of extravagant endowments. The shrine of Gīsū Darāz is yet honoured above that of any saint in the Deccan, and the constancy of the mob has put to shame the fickleness of the king, who lightly transferred his favour from the successor of the long-haired saint to a foreigner, Shāh Nī'matullāh of Māhān, near Kirmān, in Persia.

Ahmad was eager to punish the insolence of Vīra Vijaya, but the need for setting in order the domestic affairs of the kingdom postponed the congenial task. The merchant to whose energy and devotion he owed his throne was appointed lieutenant of the kingdom, with the title of Malik-ut-Tujjār, or 'Chief of the Merchants,' and Hūshyār and Bīdār were rewarded for their fidelity to the master to whom they had owed allegiance, the former with the title and post of Amīr-ul-Umarā and the latter with the government of Daulatābād.

The status and power of the great officers of the kingdom were more precisely determined by Ahmad than by his predecessors. Each provincial governor ranked as a commander of 2000 horse, though his provincial troops were not restricted to this number, and were supplemented when the king took the field by large contingents from the great fief-holders.

After a demonstration in the direction of his northern frontier, which expelled a force which had invaded the Deccan from Gujarāt, Ahmad marched, with 40,000 horse, against Vīra Vijaya, who, with the help of the raja of Telingāna led an army, of which the infantry and gunners numbered nearly a million, to the southern bank of the Tungabhadra, where he purposed to oppose the passage of the Muslims. Ahmad marched to the northern bank, and, having for forty days attempted in vain to lure the enemy into attempting the passage, took the offensive. A division of 10,000 men was sent up stream by night, to cross the river above the enemy's camp and create a diversion by attacking him on the left flank, or in rear. The Hindus, expecting a frontal attack in the morning, bivouacked by the river bank, but Vīra Vijaya himself was pleasantly lodged in a garden of sugarcane in rear of the position. The division which had crossed the river in the night reached the garden shortly before dawn, on their way to attack the Hindus in rear, and the raja's attendants fled. The Muslims, who had still some time to spare, spent it in cutting sugarcanes for themselves and their horses, and Vīra Vijaya, fearing lest he should fall into their hands, crept out and concealed himself in the standing crop, where he was found

crouching by the troopers.   Taking him for the gardener they gave
him a sheaf of sugarcane to carry, and drove him on before them
with blows of their whips.   Meanwhile the main body of the Muslim
army had begun to cross the river, and the Hindus, momentarily
expecting their ouslaught and taken in rear by the force which had
all unknowingly, captured the raja, were seized by the panic which
always strikes an eastern army on the disappearance of its leader,
and dispersed.   The Muslims began to plunder the camp, and the
raja, exhausted by the unwonted exercise of running under a heavy
load, and smarting under the humiliation of unaccustomed blows,
seized the opportunity of making his escape.   He might even yet
have rallied his army, but his spirit was so broken and his bodily
powers so exhausted that he fled with it to Vijayanagar.

   The Hindus now had reason to repent their breach of the humane
treaty between Muhammad I and Bukka I for never, in the course
of a long series of wars, did either army display such ferocity as did
Ahmad's troops in this campaign.   His temper, not naturally cruel,
had been goaded by the spectacle of the atrocities committed by
the Hindus after the disastrous campaign of Pāngul, and he glutted
his revenge.   Avoiding Vijayanagar, the siege of which had been
discovered to be an unprofitable adventure, he marched through
the kingdom, slaughtering men and enslaving women and children.
An account of the butchery was kept, and whenever the tale of
victims reached 20,000 the invader halted for three days, and celebrated the achievement with banquets and beating of the great
drums.   Throughout his progress he destroyed temples and slaughtered cows, he sent three great brazen idols to Gulbarga to be
dishonoured, and omitted nothing that could wound the natural
affections, the patriotism, or the religious sentiments of the Hindus.
In March 1423, he halted beside an artificial lake to celebrate the
festival of the Naurūz and his own exploits, and one day, while
hunting followed an antelope with such persistence that he was led
to a distance of twelve miles from his camp, and was observed by
a body of five or six thousand of the enemy's horse.   Of his immediate bodyguard of 400 men half were slain in the furious onslaught,
but he contrived to find shelter in a cattle-fold, where his 200
foreign archers for some time kept the Hindus at a distance, but
they had thrown down part of the wall of the enclosure and were
endeavouring to force an entrance when aid unexpectedly arrived.
A faithful officer, 'Abd-ul-Qādir, whose family had served the king's
for three generations, had grown apprehensive for his master's
safety, and had led two or three thousand of the royal guards in

search of him.   This force now appeared and fell upon the Hindus, who stood their ground until they had slain 500 of their assailants, and then fled, leaving a thousand of their own number dead on the field.

'Abd-ul-Qādir was rewarded with the title of Khānjahān and the government of Berar, and his brother 'Abd-ul-Latīf, who had shared the merit of the rescue, with that of Khān A'zam and the government of Bīdar.   The defence made by the foreign mounted archers had so impressed upon Ahmad the importance of this arm that Malik-ut-Tujjār was ordered to raise a corps of 3000 of them— a measure which was destined to have a deep and enduring effect on the history of the Muslims in the Deccan.

Having effected all that arms could accomplish against a defenceless population, Ahmad marched on Vijayanagar, where Vīra Vijaya, appalled by the sufferings of his poeple, sued for peace, and was forced to accept the conqueror's terms.   Payment of the arrears of tribute for several years was the lightest of these, for the immense sum had to be borne to Ahmad's camp by the choicest elephants in the royal stables, escorted by the raja's son Devarāya with every demonstration of joy.   The prince was obliged to accompany Ahmad in his retreat as far as the Krishna, and the Muslims retained the vast number of captives whom they had taken.   Among these were two destined to rise to high rank.   One, a Brāhman youth, received the name of Fathullāh on his reception into the fold of Islam, was assigned to the new governor of Berar, succeeded his master in that province, and eventually became, on the dissolution of the kingdom, the first independent sultan of Berar ; and the other, Tīma Bhat, son of Bhairav, an hereditary Brāhman revenue official of Pāthrī, who had fled to Vijayanagar to avoid punishment or persecution, received the Muhammadan name of Hasan, rose, by a combination of ability and treachery, to be lieutenant of the kingdom, and left a son, Ahmad, who founded the dvnasty of the Nizām Shāhī kings of Ahmadnagar.

The king returned to Gulbarga shortly before the time when the fierce heat of the dry months of 1423 should have been tempered by the advent of the seasonal rains, but the rain failed, and its failure was followed by a famine.   He was in his capital at the same season of the following year, when the distress of his people was at its height and the usual signs of the appoach of the rainy season were still absent.   The calamity was attributed to the displeasure of heaven, and Ahmad imperilled his reputation, if not his person, by publicly ascending a hill without the city and praying, in the sight of the multitude, for rain. Fortune favoured him, the clouds gathered, and the rain fell. The drenched and shivering multitude hailed him as a saint, and he proudly bore the title.

At the end of 1424 Ahmad invaded Telingāna and captured Warangal, which he made his headquarters while 'Abd-ul-Latīf, governor of Bīdar, established his authority throughout the country. The raja was slain, and Ahmad, having extended his eastern frontier to the sea, returned to Gulbarga leaving 'Abd-ul-Latīf to reduce the few fortresses which still held out.

The governor of Māhūr was still in rebellion and late in 1425 Ahmad marched against him. Of his operations against the fortress we have two accounts, according to one of which he was obliged to retire discomfited after besieging the place for several months, and returned and captured it in the following year. According to the other, which is more probable, the raja was induced, by a promise of pardon for past offences, to surrender and Ahmad violated every rule of honour and humanity by putting him and five or six thousand of his followers to death. From Māhūr he marched northwards to Kalam, which was in the hands of a Gond rebel, captured the place, which was of no great strength, and led a foray into Gondwāna, where he is said to have taken a diamond mine, the site of which cannot be traced. He then marched to Ellichpur and remained there for a year, engaged in rebuilding the hill forts of Gāwīl and Narnāla, which protected his northern frontier. This task was undertaken in connection with a project for the conquest of Gujarāt and Mālwa, suggested by Tīmūr's grant of these two kingdoms to his brother, and he missed no opportunity of embroiling himself with the two states, and furnished himself with a pretext for interfering in their affairs by entering into a close alliance with the small state of Khāndesh, the allegiance of which was claimed by both.

Hūshang Shāh of Mālwa had already, in 1422, furnished him with a *casus belli* by disregarding the position which Narsingh of Kherla had accepted in 1399, and compelling him to swear allegiance to Mālwa. In 1428 Hūshang prepared to invade Kherla, to enforce payment of tribute, and Ahmad, in response to Narsingh's appeal, marched to Ellichpur. Hūshang nevertheless opened the siege of Kherla, and Ahmad marched against him, but was perplexed by scruples regarding the lawfulness of attacking a brother Muslim on behalf of a misbeliever, and contented himself with sending a message to Hūshang begging him to refrain from molesting Narsingh. As he immediately retired to his own dominions, Hūshang attributed his conduct to pusillanimity, and marched against him with an army of 30,000 horse, but Ahmad on reaching the Tāptī, decided that he had suffered enough for righteousness' sake, and resolved at least to defend his kingdom. Hūshang came upon his army unexpectedly, and was taken by surprise, but the troops of Mālwa fought bravely until their discomfiture was completed by a force which had lain in ambush, and under the leadership of Ahmad himself attacked their right flank. They broke and fled, leaving in the hands of the victors all their baggage and camp equipage, 200 elephants, and the ladies of Hūshang's harem. Narsingh issued from Kherla, fell upon the fugitives, and pursued them into Mālwa. Ahmad advanced to Kherla, where he was sumptuously entertained by Narsingh, and thence sent to Mālwa, under the immediate charge of his most trusted eunuchs and the protection of 500 of his best cavalry, the ladies who had fallen into his hands.

His return march to Gulbarga led him to Bīdar, a still important city occupying the site of the ancient Vidarbha, the capital of the ancient kingdom of the same name. It had been restored by Raja Vijaya Sena, one of the Valabhīs of the solar line, who succeeded the Guptas in A.D. 319, and on the establishment of the Bahmanī kingdom more than a thousand year later became the capital of one of its provinces. Ahmad halted for some time at this town, and was so impressed by the beauty of its situation, the salubrity of its climate, and perhaps by its legendary glories that he resolved to transfer his capital thither, and an army of surveyors, architects, builders, and masons was soon engaged in laying out, designing and erecting a new city under the walls of the ancient fortress, which received the name of Ahmadābād Bīdar.

As soon as he was settled in his new capital, in 1429, Ahmad sent a mission to Nasīr Khān of Khāndesh, to demand the hand of his daughter, Āghā Zainab, for his eldest son, 'Alā-ud-dīn Ahmad, whom he designated as his heir. The proposal was readily accepted by Nasīr Khān to whom an alliance with the powerful kingdom of the Deccan was at once an honour and a protection.

In 1430 Ahmad, in pursuance of his short-sighted policy of aggression against his northern neighbours, wantonly attacked Gujarāt[1]. Kānhā raja of Jhālawār, apprehending that Ahmad I of Gujarāt intended to annex his territory, fled to Khāndesh and conciliated Nasīr Khān by the gift of some elephants. Nasīr Khān, who was

---

[1] The account of the origin, progress, and result of this campaign given in Firishta's history of the Bahmanids is most misleading. The same historian gives the true version of these events in his history of the kingdom of Gujarāt.

not strong enough to support or protect the refugee, sent him with a letter of recommendation to Ahmad Bahmanī, who supplied him with a force which enabled him to invade Gujarāt and lay waste the country about Nandurbār. An army under Muhammad Khān, son of Ahmad of Gujarāt, defeated the aggressors with great slaughter, and drove them to take refuge in Daulatābād, whence they sent news of the mishap to Bīdar. A fresh army, under the command of 'Alā-ud-dīn Ahmad, assembled at Daulatābād, where it was joined by Nasīr Khān and by Kānhā, who had fled to Khāndesh, and advanced to Mānikpunj, where it found the army of Gujarāt awaiting its approach. The army of the Deccan was again defeated and again fled to Daulatābād, while Nasīr Khān and Kānhā shut themselves up in the fortress of Laling in Khāndesh, and Muhammad Khān of Gujarāt withdrew to Nandurbār, where he remained on the alert.

The effect of this second defeat was to arouse rather than to daunt the spirit of the sultan of the Deccan, and he sent a force under Malik-ut-Tujjār to seize and occupy the island of Bombay. For the recovery of this important post Ahmad of Gujarāt sent an army under his younger son, Zafar Khān, and a fleet from Diu. His troops occupied Thāna, thus menacing Malik-ut-Tujjār's communications, and succeeded in enticing him from the shelter of the fort and in inflicting on him such a defeat that the remnant of his troops with difficulty regained its protection. They were closely invested by the fleet and army of Gujarāt. Ahmad Bahmanī sent 10,000 horse and sixty elephants under the command of 'Alā-ud-dīn Ahmad and Khānjahān of Berar to their relief, and thus enabled them to escape from the fortress, but the army of the Deccan was again defeated in the field, and Malik-ut-Tujjār fled to Chākan and the prince and Khānjahān to Daulatābād.

Disappointment and defeat only increased the obstinacy of Ahmad Bahmanī and in the following year he invaded in person the hilly tract of Baglāna, the Rāhtor raja of which was nominally a vassal of Gujarāt, and at the same time besieged the fortress of Bhaul, on the Girna, which was held for Gujarāt by Malik Sa'ādat. Ahmad of Gujarāt was engaged in an expedition to Chāmpaner, but raised the siege of that place and marched to his southern frontier. A series of undignified manoeuvres exhibited the unwillingness of the two kings to try conclusions. Ahmad Bahmanī raised the siege of Bhaul and retired to Bīdar, leaving a force on his frontier to check the anticipated pursuit, but Ahmad of Gujarāt, greatly relieved by his enemy's flight, returned to his capital. Ahmad Bahmanī then returned to Bhaul, and resumed the siege, disregarding a mild protest addressed to him by Ahmad of Gujarāt, but Malik Saʿādat repulsed an attempt to carry the place by storm, and in a sortie inflicted such heavy losses on the besiegers that Ahmad Bahmanī, learning that Ahmad of Gujarāt was marching to the relief of the fortress, raised the siege and turned to meet him. The battle was maintained until nightfall, and is described as indecisive, but the sultan of the Deccan was so dismayed by his losses that he retreated hurriedly towards his capital.

In 1432 the citadel of Bīdar was completed, and Ahmad put to death his sister's son, Sher Khān, who, having originally counselled him to seize the sceptre from his brother's feeble grasp was now suspected of the design of excluding his sons from the succession and usurping the throne.

The exhaustion of the kingdom after the disastrous war with Gujarāt encouraged Hūshang Shāh to retrieve his late discomfiture by capturing Kherla and putting Narsing to death. Ahmad was unprepared for war, but could not ignore so gross an insult, and marched northward to exact reparation, but Nasīr Khān intervened, and composed the quarrel on terms disgraceful to Ahmad. Kherla was acknowledged to be a fief of Mālwa and Hūshang made, in the treaty, the insolent concession that the rest of Berar should remain a province of the Deccan.

After this humiliating peace Ahmad marched into Telingāna, which, though nominally under the government of one of his sons, was in a condition approaching rebellion. Some of the petty chieftains of the province, who had defied the prince's authority, were seized and put to death, and order was, for the time, restored.

The decline of Ahmad's mental and bodily powers had for some time been apparent. He had recently allowed the management of all public business to fall into the hands of Miyān Mahmūd Nizām-ul-Mulk, a native of the Deccan who had succeeded Malik-ut-Tujjār as lieutenant of the kingdom on the latter's transfer to the government of Daulatābād and shortly after this time he died[1], at the age of sixty-three or sixty-four.

The character of Ahmad was simpler than that of his versatile and accomplished brother, Fīrūz, whose learning, with its taint of scepticism, was replaced in Ahmad by superstition, with a tinge of fanaticism. The uncouth enthusiasm of the long-haired zealot, Gīsū

---

[1] There is some uncertainty as to the precise date of his death. The dates given by the best authorities range between February 18 and February 27, 1435. Other dates given are 1438 and 1444 or 1445, which are certainly wrong. In his tomb at Bidar the date is given as Ziʾl-Hijjah 29, in a year which may be variously read, in a copy of the inscription supplied to me, as 837 or 839. The former reading gives the date August 6, 1434, and the latter July 15, 1436.

Darāz, which had disgusted the cultured and fastidious Fīrūz, delighted the devout and simple mind of his brother. But Ahmad, though scantily endowed with wit and learning, depised neither, and his court, if less brilliant than that of Fīrūz, was not destitute of culture. Of the men of learning who enjoyed his patronage the foremost was the poet Āzarī of Isfarāyīn in Khurāsān, who was encouraged to undertake the composition of the *Bahman-nāma*, a versified history of the dynasty, now unfortunately lost. From fragments preserved in quotations it seems to have been an inferior imitation of the *Shāhnāma* of Firdausi. Āzarī returned to his own country before Ahmad's death, but in remote Isfarāyīn continued the history until his own death in 1462. It was carried on by various hands until the last days of the dynasty, and some of the poetasters who disfigured the work with their turgid bombast, impudently claimed the whole as their own.

Ahmad transferred his devotion from the successor of Gīsū Darāz to Ni'matullāh, the famous saint of Māhān, but failed to attract the holy man himself to India, and had to content himself with his son Khalīlullāh, surnamed *Butshikan*, 'the Iconoclast,' who visited Bīdar and whose shrine, a cenotaph, is still to be seen there. The saint's family were Shiahs, and it is clear, from the inscriptions in Ahmad's tomb, that they converted him to that faith, but his religion was a personal matter, and he wisely refrained from interfering with that of his subjects. The first militant Shiah ruler in India was Yūsuf, 'Ādil Shāh of Bījāpur.

The employment of foreign troops in the Deccan, already mentioned, raised a question which shortly after this time became acute, and remained a source of strife as long as any independent Muslim state existed in the south. This was the feud between the Deccanis and the Foreigners. The climate of India is undoubtedly injurious to the natives of more temperate climes who adopt the country as a permanent domicile, and the degeneracy of their descendants is, as a rule, rather accelerated than retarded by unions with the natives of the soil. In northern India such degeneracy was retarded by the influx of successive waves of conquest and immigration from the north-west, and the country, from the time of its first conquest by the Muslims, seldom acknowledged for long rulers who could be regarded as genuine natives of India ; but the Deccan was more isolated, and though a domiciled race of kings succeeded in maintaining their power for more than a century and a half they looked abroad for their ablest and most active servants and their bravest soldiers. Most of Bahman Shāh's nobles were foreigners. His Afghān minister was succeeded by a Persian from Shīrāz, and he again by a native of Basrah. As the descendants of foreigners became identified with the country they coalesced with the natives, and acquired their manners, the process being sometimes retarded by the avoidance of intermarriage with them ; and their places were taken by fresh immigrants, who were usually employed, in preference of the less virile and energetic natives, in difficult and perilous enterprises, in which they generally acquitted themselves well, and the Deccanis found themselves outstripped at the council board as well as in the field, and naturally resented their supersession ; but it was not until the reign of Ahmad, who was the first to enlist large numbers of foreigners in the rank and file of his army, that the line between them was clearly drawn. War was openly declared between them when Malik-ut-Tujjār attributed his defeat by the troops of Gujarāt to the cowardice of the Deccanis, and the feud thus begun was not confined to intrigues for place and power, but frequently found expression in pitched battles and bloody massacres, of which last the Foreigners were usually the victims, and contributed in no small measure, first to the disintegration of the kingdom of the Bahmanids, and ultimately to the downfall of the states which rose on its ruins.

The feud was complicated by religious differences. The native Deccanis were Sunnis, and though all the Foreigners were not Shiahs, a sufficient number of them belonged to that sect to associate their party with heterodoxy, so that although the lines of cleavage drawn by interest and religion might not exactly coincide, they approached one another closely enough to exacerbate political jealousy by sectarian prejudice.

One class of foreigners, however, the Africans, who were afterwards largely employed, stood apart from the rest. Their attachment to the Sunni faith, and the contemptuous attitude adopted towards them by other Foreigners, who refused to regard the unlettered and unprepossessing negro as the equal of the fair-skinned, handsome, and cultured man of the north, threw them into the arms of the Deccanis. To the negroes were added the *Muwallads*, a name applied to the offspring of African fathers and Indian mothers. T us in this disastrous strife the Foreign Party consisted of Turks, Arabs, Mughuls, and Persians, and the Deccani Party of native Deccanis, negroes, and *Muwallads*. Instances of temporary or permanent apostasy, due to religious differences, to self interest, or to gratitude to a benefactor, were not unknown, but were not frequent enough to affect the homogeneity of either party. Rarer still were disinterested endeavours to restore peace for the benefit of the state, for party spirit was stronger than patriotism.

CHAPTER XVI

THE DECLINE AND FALL OF THE KINGDOM OF THE DECCAN. A.D. 1436—1490

AHMAD the Saint was succeeded by his eldest son, 'Alā-ud-dīn Ahmad, who surrounded himself with Foreigners and provided for his brother Muhammad by sending him to recover five years' arrears of tribute due from Devarāya II of Vijayanagar. Muhammad recovered the arrears but his head was turned by his success, and he was led astray by evil counsellors who persuaded him that his father had intended to give him a share of the kingdom and demanded that his brother should either admit him to an equal share in the government, and the honours of royalty, or divide the kingdom, giving him half. His demands were rejected and his brother defeated him, but pardoned him and, on the death of their younger brother, Dāūd, appointed him to the government of the Rāichūr Doāb, where he remained faithful until his death.

Early in March, 1437, Dilāvar Khān was sent into the Konkan to establish the king's authority, and reduced the Hindu chieftains of that region to obedience. The raja of Sangameshwar, besides paying tribute, surrendered his beautiful and accompl shed daughter to 'Alā-ud-dīn, who married her and bestowed on her the name of Zībā Chihra ('Beautiful Face'). After this expedition Dilāvar Khān resigned the lieutenancy of the kingdom and was succeeded by the eunuch Dastūr-ul-Mulk.

The new minister, who had the faults of his unfortunate class, alienated the nobles by his arrogance, which led to his ruin. Humāyūn, the king's eldest son, a brutal youth who lived to become the disgrace of his house, desired him to attend to some particular business and when the eunuch procrastinated took him to task for his negligence. He insolently replied that he would not tolerate the prince's interference in affairs of state and Humāyūn employed one of the king's esquires to assassinate him, and protected the murderer. 'Alā-ud-dīn, who in the early days of his reign was averse from taking life, was content, at his son's intercession, to leave the assassin to his care.

The king's preference for his Hindu wife aroused the bitter jealousy of Āghā Zainab, who complained to her father, Nasīr Khān of Khāndesh, of the indignity to which she was subjected, and he invaded Berar to avenge his daughter's wrongs, and succeeded in seducing from their allegiance many of the officers serving in that province, whose fidelity to their master was not proof against their veneration for the descendant of the Caliph 'Umar.

Khān Jahān, governor of Berar, withdrew into the fortress of Narnāla, and was there besieged by the troops of Khāndesh ; and the Deccani faction, which had risen to power in the capital after the assassination of Dastūr-ul-Mulk and, as Sunnis, respected the descendant of the second Caliph, advised caution in dealing with the aggressor, lest he should be joined by the kings of Gujarāt and Mālwa, but Malik-ut-Tujjār, governor of Daulatābād and leader of the Foreigners, volunteered to take the field, provided that all the Foreign troops were placed at his disposal and that he was not hampered by native troops, to whose pusillanimity he attributed the mishap at Bombay. The Deccanis, resenting these aspersions, agreed that all the Foreign troops should be sent forward as an advanced guard, hoping that they would be destroyed, and that the king should follow with the rest of the army.

Malik-ut-Tujjār left Daulatābād with 7000 Foreign horse, and, leaving the Deccani troops to guard the frontier, entered Berar. He was joined at Mehkar by Khān Jahān, who had escaped from Narnāla and was sent to Ellichpur and Bālāpur to check the incursions of the Korkus, who were in alliance with Nasīr Khān, while Malik-ut-Tujjār marched northward to Rohankhed, where the hills of southern Berar descend into the valley of the northern Pūrna, and there attacked and defeated Nasīr Khān, who fled to Burhānpur and thence to Laling, where he took refuge. Malik-ut-Tujjār laid waste the rich plain of Khāndesh, destroyed the public buildings of Burhānpur, and followed Nasīr Khān to Laling. He had now no more than 4000 horse with him, and Nasīr Khān, who had assembled 12,000, attacked him, but was defeated with heavy loss. Malik-ut-Tujjār returned with the spoils of victory to Bīdar, where his success assured the supremacy of his party and gained for it the place of honour at court, on the right hand of the throne, the Deccanis and Africans being relegated to the left.

Devarāya II of Vijayanagar now reorganised his army by recruiting a large number of Muslims, to whom he gave special privileges, and by discarding the useless and ill-trained troops which had formerly swelled its numbers. It had consisted of 200,000 inferior cavalry and 800,000 worse infantry; but after its reorganisation it consisted of 10,000 mounted foreign archers, and 60,000 Hindu horse, trained to the use of the bow, and 300,000 tolerably well-trained infantry, and the pay of all arms was greatly improved.

With this force Devarāya, in 1443, invaded the Rāichūr Doāb, captured Mudgal, besieged Rāichūr and Bankāpur, encamped on the Krishna and laid waste the country as far as Bījāpur and Sāgar. On the approach of 'Alā-ud-dīn he withdrew to Mudgal, and Malik-ut-Tujjār, having compelled the raja's two sons to raise the sieges of Rāichūr and Bankāpur, rejoined 'Alā-ud-dīn before Mudgal, where, within a period of three months, as many battles were fought, the Hindus being victorious in the first and the Muslims in the second. In the third Devarāya's elder son was killed and his troops were driven headlong into the fortress, whither two Muslim officers, Fakhr-ul-Mulk of Delhi and his brother, followed them and were captured and imprisoned, but a message from their master to the effect that the lives of 200,000 Hindus would be required as the price of theirs, so alarmed Devarāya that he sued for peace, which was granted on his promising to make no default in future remittances of tribute.

'Alā-ud-dīn, though generally pious and benevolent, gradually overcame his repugnance to taking life. He used wine himself, but prohibited its use by his subjects, and gamblers and wine-bibbers had iron collars riveted on their necks and were compelled to work as scavengers or set to hard labour on the public works ; and those who persisted, despite this discipline, in the use of wine, had molten lead poured down their throats. A grandson of the saint Gīsū Darāz, convicted of brawling with a women of the town, received the bastinado in the market place, and his companion was expelled from the city. The king's benevolence was displayed in the establishment and endowment at Bīdar of a hospital where food, drugs, and medical treatment were supplied free of charge, and his piety in his love of long sermons and the destruction of idol-temples, from the materials of which mosques were built. He prided himself also on his love of justice, and added *al-ādil* ('the Just') to his titles. At the end of his reign an Arab merchant who had been unable to obtain payment for some horses sold to officers of the court, and had also been scandalised by the massacre of the Sayyids and other Foreigners at Chākan, sprang up on hearing the king thus described, and cried, 'No, by God ! Thou art not just, generous, clement, or compassionate. O tyrant and liar ! Thou hast slain the pure seed of the prophet and in the pulpit of the Muslims takest to thyself such titles as these !' The king, weeping bitterly, replied, 'They will hardly escape from the fire of God's wrath who give me, in this world and the next, a name as ill, as Yazīd's.' He then retired to his chamber and left it no more until he was borne

forth to the grave. Against his virtues must be set that gross
sensuality which his religion permitted, and which he carried to
such excess that most of his time was spent among the thousand
women collected in his harem, and he so neglected business as to
hold a public audience no oftener than once in four or five months.

During this seclusion the Deccanis regained most of the power
which they had lost, and Miyān, Minullāh, in order to compass the
destruction of the Foreigners, organised an expedition for the
subjugation of the northern Konkan. Malik-ut-Tujjār, who was
appointed to the command, fortified Chākan, which he selected as
his base, dispatched expeditions against several minor chieftains,
who were reduced to obedience, and personally led a force against
one Sirka, whose stronghold was in the neighbourhood, and who
was defeated and captured. Malik-ut-Tujjār offered him the choice
between Islam and death, and Sirka professed his readiness to
change his faith but declared that he could not make an open
profession so long as his enemy the raja of Sangameshwar, near
Kondhāna, was in a position to punish him. He promised to act
as guide and to lead the royal troops to Sangameshwar, and in
1446 Malik-ut-Tujjār set forth on the enterprise.

The march through the dense forest and over the precipitous
slopes of the Ghāts was intensely laborious and the climate was
deadly. Malik-ut-Tujjār himself suffered from a severe attack of
dysentery, and the army was entirely demoralised. Sirka treacherously informed the raja of Sangameshwar of its plight, and he,
with 30,000 men well skilled in mountain warfare, fell upon it at
night and slew seven or eight thousand men besides its leader.

The remnant of the army contrived, with infinite difficulty, to
extricate itself from the hills and jungles, and joined those Deccanis
who had refused to accompany the expedition to Sangameshwar.
They advised the fugitives to return to their fiefs and collect fresh
troops for the renewal of the war, but the Foreigners returned to
Chākan. Some of them had incautiously avowed their intention
of informing the king that the disaster had been due to the refusal
of the Deccanis to support Malik-ut-Tujjār, whereupon the Deccanis
at once concocted a dispatch attributing it to Malik-ut-Tujjār's
own rashness and imputing to the survivors the intention of transferring their allegiance to the enemy. The dispatch was delivered
to the king, when he was drunk, by Mushīr-ul-Mulk, the bitterest
of the Foreigners' enemies, who persuaded him to give him the
command of a force wherewith to punish the fugitives in Chākan.
He intercepted all messages which the Foreigners attempted to

transmit to the court, lured them from Chākan by means of a forged decree granting them a free pardon and murdered their officers at a banquet. At the same time 4000 Deccani horse fell upon their camp, put to the sword 1200 Sayyids, 1000 other foreigners, and five or six thousand children, and appropriated the wives, daughters, and goods of their victims. Qāsim Beg and two other Foreign officers, whose suspicions had led them to encamp at a distance from the rest, contrived to escape, and, after undergoing great difficulties and hardships, succeeded in conveying to the king a true report of all that had passed. 'Alā-ud-dīn, overcome by remorse, avenged the wrongs of the Foreigners by executing the leaders of the Deccani party and reducing their families to beggary, Qāsim Beg was appointed to the government of Daulatābād, vacant since the death of Malik-ut-Tujjār, and his two companions were promoted to high rank. The Foreign party completely regained its former ascendancy, and in 1451 the king received from the poet Āzarī, in Isfaṟāyīn, a letter urging him to abandon the use of wine and to dismiss all Deccani officials. He obeyed both injunctions, and henceforth attended personally to affairs of state.

In 1453 the king received an injury to his leg which confined him to his palace, and rumours of his death were circulated and credited. Jalāl Khān, a Sayyid who had married a daughter of Ahmad Shāh, rose in rebellion in Telingāna, with the object of establishing the independence of his son, Sikandar, in that province. He learned too late that the king yet lived, but might still have been recalled to his allegiance by his promise of forgiveness but for Sikandar, who, having been deeply implicated in the revolt of Muhammad Khān at the beginning of the reign, despaired of pardon for a second act of rebellion. He sought aid, therefore, of Mahmud I of Mālwa, assuring him that 'Alā-ud-dīn was dead, that the courtiers were concealing his death for their own ends, and that Berar and Telingāna might be annexed to Mālwa without difficulty or opposition. Mahmūd responded to the appeal, and in 1456 invaded Berar, where Sikandar joined him with a thousand horse.

'Alā-ud-dīn marched against Mahmūd I who, indignant at the deception of which he had been the victim, hastily returned to Mālwa, while Sikandar joined his father at Bālkonda, where both were besieged by Khvāja Mahmūd Gāvān of Gīlān, a foreigner who afterwards rose to the highest rank in the state. They were compelled to surrender and 'Alā-ud-dīn not only pardoned them but injudiciously permitted them to retain Bālkonda.

'Alā-ud-dīn died in 1458, having some time before designated as his heir his eldest son Humāyūn, who bore a reputation so evil that his father had been urged to reconsider his decision, which however, had never been revoked. On the king's death a party among the courtiers, headed by Saif Khān, Mallū Khān, and Shāh Habībullāh, the soldier son of Khalīlullah the Iconoclast, enthroned his younger son, Hasan Khān, and the populace assembled for the purpose of attacking Humāyūn in his house and putting him to death, but cowardice was not among the prince's many faults, and he came forth with his personal guard of eighty horsemen, and cut his way through the crowd to the palace, where the royal troops joined him. He secured his brother's person, caused Saif Khān to be tied to the leg of an elephant and dragged through the streets until he perished, and imprisoned Habībullāh, but Mallū Khān fled into the Carnatic.

Humāyūn bestowed his favours chiefly upon the Foreign faction, and appointed Mahmūd Gāvān lieutenant of the kingdom and governor of Bījāpur, conferring on him the title of Malik-ut-Tujjār, but the Deccanis were not entirely excluded from office, and received some appointments.

Sikandar Khān, who had been with Humāyūn when the mob threatened to overwhelm him, and had contributed materially to his success, was so disappointed at not receiving the government of Telingāna that he joined his father at Bālkonda, again rebelled, and defeated the army of Berar, under Khān Jahān, which was sent against him. Humāyūn marched in person to Bālkonda where Sikandar, on being summoned to surrender, insolently replied that if Humāyūn was son's son to Ahmad the Saint he was daughter's son, and demanded the cession of the eastern half of the kingdom. To this there could be but one reply, and Humāyūn sounded the attack. Sikandar was on the point of defeating the royal troops when he was thrown to the ground by an elephant and trampled to death by his own cavalry. His army broke and fled and Humāyūn captured Bālkonda after a week's siege and imprisoned Jalāl Khān.

The Hindus of Telingāna, and especially those of the district of Deūrkonda, had generally supported Sikandar, and early in 1459 Humāyūn marched to Warangal and sent a force to reduce Deūrkonda. The garrison obtained assistance from one of the rajas of southern Orissa and Khvāja Jahān the Turk and Nizām-ul-Mulk Ghūrī, who commanded the Muslims, were attacked simultaneously by the garrison and the relieving force, and were utterly defeated, and fled to Warangal. Here Khvāja Jahān basely attributed the disaster to his colleague, who had in fact recommended that the siege should be raised in order that the relieving force might be dealt with singly, and Humāyūn, without investigating thè facts, put Nizām-ul-Mulk to death, and the family of the unfortunate officer fled to Mālwa and threw themselves on the protection of Mahmūd I[1]. Khvāja Jahān was imprisoned and the king was preparing to march to Deūrkonda when he learned of a rising in his capital. Scald-headed Yūsuf, the Turk, had released the king's brothers, Hasan Khān and Yahyā Khān, Shāh Habībullāh, and Jalāl Khān. The *Kotwāl* had put to death the younger prince, and the aged Jalāl Khān, but the rest of the party, after an abortive attempt to seize the citadel, had fled to Bīr, where Hasan assumed the royal title and appointed Habībullāh and Yūsuf his ministers. Humāyūn left Mahmūd Gāvān in charge of affairs in Telingāna, and returned by forced maches to Bīdar, where he displayed the ferocity which brands his memory. The *Kotwāl*, who had done his best to suppress the rising, was confined in an iron cage and exhibited daily in the city for the remainder of his life, which was not of long duration, for the tyrant caused portions of his body to be cut off daily, and presented to him as his only food. The three or four thousand infantry to whom the defence of the city had been entrusted was put to death with various tortures, and a force was sent to Bīr to suppress the rebellion. The royal troops were defeated, but a second and larger army defeated Hasan, who fled with his adherents towards Vijayanagar. Sirāj Khān Junaidī, governor of Bījāpur, lured them into that fortress by professions of attachment to the prince's cause, and attacked them. Habībullāh was so fortunate as to fall fighting, but the rest were taken and sent to meet their fate at Bīdar, where all suffered in public. The prince was thrown to a tiger, some of his followers were beheaded, their wives and families were dragged from their houses and tortured to death and seven hundred innocent persons who were connected with Hasan or had been dependent on his bounty were impaled, thrown to beasts, boiled to death, or slowly cut to pieces, joint by joint, and nearly all the descedants of Bahman Shāh were put to death.

Humāyūn's behaviour for the rest of his reign was that of a homicidal maniac. 'The torchbearer of his wrath ever consumed both Hindu and Muslim alike, the broker of his fury sold at one price the guilty and the innocent, and the executioner of his punishment slew whole families for a single fault.' Nobles summoned to court made their wills and bade their families farewell

[1] See Chapter XIV

before leaving them, and the inmates of the harem were butchered in mere sportive brutality, but the most hideous of all his acts of oppression were the forcible abduction of the wives and children of his subjects and his exercise of the *droit du seigneur*. He earned the name of *Zālim*, 'the Oppressor,' by which he is still remembered by the Deccan, and tormented his subjects until 'God the Most High, the Most Merciful, and the Succourer of them that seek aid answered the prayerful cries of his people' and stretched the monster on a bed of sickness On September 4, 1461, the tyrant died and his people were 'freed from the talons of his tortures.' It was understood that he had succumbed to his illness, but the best authority for his reign relates the true story of his death. He recovered but the, inmates of the harem could no longer endure his barbarity and the eunuch Shihāb Khān suborned an African maid-servant to stab him to death when he was helpless with drink.

The dome of the Tyrant's tomb at Bīdar is split, and half of it has fallen away. It is locally believed that this occurred when the monster's body was placed in it, and that the Almighty refused his remains protection. The accident happened when the building was struck by lightning forty or fifty years ago, but the currency of the legend proves at least that his memory is still execrated.

He was succeeded by his infant son Nizām Shāh, whose mother, with the assistance of Klivāja Jahān and Mahmūd Gāvān, managed the affairs of the kingdom, but the neighbouring rulers regarded the reign of a child as their opportunity, and the Hindus of Orissa, who were joined by those of Telingāna, invaded the kingdom and advanced to within twenty miles of Bīdar, where they were met by the royal army. Their advanced guard, driven in on to the main body of their army threw them into a panic, and they fled headlong, but the raja of southern Orissa was compelled to pay half a million of silver *tangas* in order to secure his retreat from molestation. The young king had hardly been borne back to the capital when news was received that Mahmūd I of Mālwa, instigated by the family of the murdered Nizām-ul-Mulk, had invaded the kingdom with 28,000 horse[1] and that the Hindus of Orissa and Telingāna had reassembled their forces and were menacing the capital from the east and north-east.

The local troops in Telingāna were instructed to deal with the Hindus while the ministers with the rest of the royal army carrying with them the young king, met the army of Mālwa in the neighbourhood of Kandhār. The wings of the invading army were put

[1] See p. 357.

to flight and the day would have been won for the Deccan had not Mahmūd I of Mālwa happened to hit the elephant of Sikandar Khān, the young king's tutor, in the forehead with an arrow. The beast, maddened with pain, turned and fled, trampling down many in its flight, and Sikandar Khān bore the young king with him from the field. The army of the Deccan, no longer perceiving the royal elephant, began to retire in confusion, and, overtaking the king and Sikandar Khān, bore them back with them to Bīdar. Here Khvāja Jahān threw Sikandar Khān into prison, but his incarceration, owing to the number and influence of his supporters, created dissensions which encouraged Mahmūd of Mālwa to advance on the capital, and the queen-mother carried her son to Fīrūzābād, where he was out of danger. Mahmūd of Mālwa captured the town of Bīdar after a siege of seventeen days, but the citadel held out, and Mahmūd Begarha, in response to an appeal from the young king's ministers, appeared on the frontier with 80,000 horse, and was joined by Mahmūd Gāvān who, with 20,000 horse placed at his disposal by the king of Gujarāt and a force of equal strength assembled by himself threatened the communications of the army of Mālwa. Mahmūd of Mālwa, thus menaced, retreated, and was much harassed by Mahmūd Gāvān. His troops also suffered severely in their passage through the hills of the Melghāt, into which he plunged in order to shake off his pursuers.

This discomfiture failed to deter him from invading the Deccan in the following year with 90,000 horse, and he advanced as far as Daulatābād, but the reappearance of Mahmūd Begarha on the northern frontier compelled him to retire to Māndū without having effected anything.

The youthful Nizām Shāh died suddenly on July 30, 1463, and was succeeded by his brother, aged nine, who ascended the throne as Muhammad III.

The Foreign party retained its predominance in the state, and the kingdom was administered, as in the preceding reign, by the queen-mother, Khvāja Jahān, and Mahmūd Gāvān, but the ambition of Khvāja Jahān disturbed the harmony which had hitherto prevailed. He aimed at the chief power in the state, and undermined Mahmūd Gāvān's influence at the capital by employing him continually on the frontier. The queen-mother became suspicious of his designs and persuaded her son to put him to death. When he entered his master's presence two maidservants of the harem appeared and cried aloud, in accordance with preconcerted arrangements, 'The matter which was spoken of yesterday should now be taken in hand.' Muhammad turned to Nizām-ul-Mulk and, pointing to Khvāja Jahān said, 'This man is a traitor. Slay him.' Nizām-ul-Mulk seized Khvāja Jahān by the hand, dragged him forth, and cut him to pieces.

Mahmūd Gāvān, who had devoted such care to the young king's education that he was the most accomplished monarch who had sat on the throne since the days of Fīrūz, was summoned to the capital and received the titles of Khvāja Jahān and *Amīr-ul Umarā*. The queen-mother wisely retired from the management of public affairs when her son reached the age of fifteen, and left him in the hands of his advisers, but retained his respect, and was consulted by him throughout her life.

In 1467 Nizām-ul-Mulk was appointed to the command of the army of Berar and was sent against Kherla, which was in the possession of Mahmūd I of Mālwa. He induced or compelled the governor to surrender the place, but was himself murdered by two Rājputs of the garrison, and Muhammad gained nothing by the campaign, which was terminated by a treaty acknowledging Kherla to be a fief of Mālwa, as in the reign of Ahmad the Saint. The treaty was preceded by protracted negotiations, in the course of which Mahmūd taxed Muhammad with bad faith in violating the treaty which had secured Kherla to Mālwa, but was forced to admit the justice of the retort that he had first violated the treaty of peace between the two countries by twice invading the Deccan during the reign of Nizām Shāh.

Mahmūd Gāvān yet retained the government of Bījāpur, and in 1469 was sent into the Konkan to reduce to obedience the rajas of Khelna (Vishālgarh), Sangameshwar, and other districts, whose pirate fleets had inflicted much loss on Muslim merchants and pilgrims. The two leading rajas entered into a close alliance and fortified the Western Ghāts, but Mahmūd Gāvān went patiently to work and forced and occupied the passes one by one. He dismissed his cavalry, useless in mountain warfare, and assembled corps of infantry from Junnār, Dābhol, and Karhād. The jungle was burnt and the siege of Khelna was opened and continued for five months, when Mahmūd, wisely shunning the dangers of a campaign in the hills during the rainy season, withdrew into quarters at Kolhāpur, leaving garrisons to hold the passes.

When the rainy season was past he returned to Khelna and, by tampering with the fidelity of the garrison, succeeded in capturing and occupying the fortress. As the rainy season approached he again retired above the Ghāts, leaving a garrison in Khelna, and, returning when the rains were abated, took Sangameshwar, avenging as Fīrishta says, the sufferings of Khalaf Hasan of Basrah. Leaving officers to carry on the administration of his conquests he marched to Goa, then one of the best ports of the raja of Vijayanagar, attacked it by land and sea, and took it. The exploit was celebrated with great rejoicings at Bīdar, both as an important victory over the hereditary enemies of the kingdom and as a boon to Muslim pilgrims and merchants, for the western ports, which might be dominated from Goa, harboured pirates whom their nominal sovereigns might disown at will, while profiting by their depredations.

Mahmūd Gāvān returned to Bīdar, after more than two years, absence, in the early summer of 1472, and was received with the highest honours by the king and the queen-mother. His slave Khushqadam, who had ably seconded his efforts during the arduous campaign in the Konkan, received the title of Kishvar Khān and was manumitted and ennobled.

Before the great minister's return news had been received at the capital that the Hindu chieftain of southern Orissa who had vexed the kingdom during the reigns of Humāyūn and Nizām had died and had been succeeded by an adopted son, Mangal whose title to the throne was contested by the deceased raja's cousin, Hambar. Hambar, having been defeated by Mangal and driven into the mountains, sought aid of Muhammad III, in return for which he promised, on attaining to the throne, to pay tribute. Malik Hasan, surnamed Bahrī[1], the Brāhman of Pāthrī who had been captured during the invasion of Vijayanagar by Ahmad the Saint and brought up as a Muslim, received the title of Nizām-ul-Mulk, and was sent to the assistance of Hambar. The expedition was successful. Mangal was defeated and put to flight and Hambar was placed on the throne and assisted Hasan to reduce Rajamundry (Rājamahendri), the Hindu ruler of which had maintained his independence and had assisted the rajas of southern Orissa in their campaigns against the Muslims. Kondavīr also was captured,

[1] The origin and meaning of this epithet, which is applied both to Hasan and to his descendants, the Nizām Shāhī kings of Ahmadnagar, are obscure. As written by Muslim historians it is an Arabic adjective singifying 'of, or connected with, the sea,' but Hasan was in no way connected with the sea and the word is never explained as bearing its obvious etymological signification. It is said to be connected with a Hindi word for a falcon, and to have been given to Hasan owing to his having at one time kept the favourite falcon of Muhammad III, but the derivation is unconvincing and fanciful, and the story lacks confirmation. I believe it to be a corruption of an adjective *Bhiravi*, regularly formed from Bhairav, the name of Hasan's father, and Arabicized in accordance with a custom not uncommon in India.

and the kingdom of the Bahmanids for the first time extended from sea to sea.

Malik Hasan, on his return to the capital with his spoils, was received with every mark of distinction and was made governor of Telingāna, now the most extensive of the four provinces. At the same time Fathullāh 'Imād-ul-Mulk, the other Brāhman who had been captured in Ahmad Shāh's campaign, was made governor of Berar, and Yūsuf 'Ādil Khān, Savāī[1], a Turk[2], received the government of Daulatābād.

Honours were now fairly evenly divided between the Foreigners and the Deccanis. Of the four great provincial governments two, Gulbarga (with Bījāpur) and Daulatābād, were held by Mahmūd Gāvān and Yūsuf 'Ādil Khān, foreigners, and two, Telingāna and Berar, by Malik Hasan and Fathullāh 'Imād-ul-Mulk, Deccanis. The leaders of the Foreigners were well disposed towards the Deccanis, and of the latter Fathullāh was a lifelong friend of Yūsuf 'Ādil Khān and was on terms of intimacy with many of the Foreigners, but the crafty, unscrupulous, and ambitious Malik Hasan could not tolerate a Foreigner's tenure of the first post in the kingdom, and never rested till he had destroyed Mahmūd Gāvān. His ambition was purely selfish, for Mahmūd was free from party spirit, and it was Yūsuf that became the leader of the Foreigners, who flocked around him in Daulatābād and enabled him to complete the subjugation of the northern Konkan, which earned him higher honours than those which had been accorded to Hasan, and the bitter hostility of the latter and of his followers.

At the end of the same year the rajas of Belgaum and Bankāpur, instigated by Virupaksha of Vijayanagar, attempted to recover

1 The meaning of this title, corrupted by the Portuguese into *Sabaio* or *Cabaio,* is also obscure. It has been explained as *Sawāi,* 'the one and a quarter man,' i.e. he who is better by one quarter than others—a conceit common enough in northern India, where the Mahārāja of Alwar still bears the title, but peculiar to Hindus, and unusual, if not unknown, in the Deccan. It is otherwise explained as an adjective formed from Sāva, the town in northern Persia where Yūsuf's youth was spent, but the first syllable of *Sawāi* is short and the second long, whereas in Sāva the first is long and the second short. Moreover, the adjective formed from Sāva takes the form *Sāvaji.*

2 Yūsuf claimed to be a son of Murād II, of Turkey, saved from the customary massacre of the males of the imperial house by the affection of his mother, who caused him to be secretly conveyed from the palace on the accession of his elder brother, Muhammad II, and delivered to à Turkish or Persian merchant of Sāva, who brought him up as his adopted son. There is little or no evidence in support of this legend, and the most that can be said of it is that it involves no impossibilities and may be true ; but it is at least equally probable that Yūsuf was a Turk of Sāva. The principal objection to the legend that he was a scion of the imperial house of Turkey is that he was a bigoted Shiah, and was the first Muslim ruler in India to attempt to establish that faith as the state religion in his kingdom.

Goa and Muhammad III marched, with Mahmūd Gāvān, to punish them. Birkāna, raja of Belgaum, was besieged in his stronghold and, when the outer defences had been carried and only the citadel remained to him, escaped in disguise and appeared in the Muslim camp in the character of an envoy. It was not until he was in the royal presence that he disclosed his identity and begged for mercy. His life was spared, but Belgaum was annexed and granted to Mahmūd Gāvān, whose fiefs it adjoined, and Muhammad III on entering the fortress, assumed the title of *Lashkarī*, 'the Soldier,' by which he is known in history. After the fall of Belgaum his mother, who had served the state so well, died, and her body was sent to Bīdar for burial while he halted at Bījāpur as the guest of Mahmūd Gāvān.

The Deccan now suffered from a terrible famine, the result of the failure of the rains for two successive years. Large numbers died of hunger and of an epidemic of cholera, which usually accompanies or follows a famine in India, and the kingdom was further depopulated by the flight of a large proportion of its inhabitants to Gujarāt and Mālwa, which escaped the visitation. The land lay untilled and cultivation was not resumed until, in the third year, the rain once more fell in abundance.

As soon as this calamity was past news was received that the people of Kondavīr had risen against their Muslim governor, an oppressor belonging to the school of Humāyūn, had put him to death, and had delivered the town to Hambar, who, forgetful of his obligations to Muhammad, had accepted the offering and, doubtful of his ability to retain it, had sought help of the raja of Jājpur in Orissa, who invaded Telingāna and besieged Malik Hasan in Rajamundry.

Muhammad marched to Rajamundry and relieved Malik Hasan, while Hamber shut himself up in Kondavīr and the raja withdrew to the northern bank of the Godavari, secured his position there by seizing all the boats which could be found, and, finding that nothing was to be gained by lingering in the neighbourhood, retired to Orissa. Muhammad followed him, invaded Orissa in February, 1478, and spent six months in the country, which he laid waste. He was contemplating its annexation when envoys arrived from the raja, bringing numbers of elephants and other rich gifts and charged with expressions of contrition, but Muhammad refused to retreat until the raja, most unwillingly, had surrendered other twenty-five elephants, the best which his father's stables had contained On his return he besieged Hambar in Kondavīr, and on his

surrendering granted him his life, but destroyed the great temple
of Kondavīr, built a mosque on its site, and earned the title of
Ghāzī by slaying with his own hand some of the attendant Brāhmans.

He made Rajamundry his headquarters for nearly three years
and, having completely subjugated Telingāna, prepared to invade
the eastern Carnatic, but, before setting out, provided for the
efficient administration of Telingāna by dividing it into two provinces, and appointed Malik Hasan to the eastern, or Rajamundry,
division and A'zam Khān, son of the rebel Sikandar, to Warangal,
which became the capital of the western division. The kingdom
had outgrown the old provincial system established by the first two
kings of the dynasty. Its extension to the sea coast on the west
and on the east had doubled the area of the old provinces of
Gulbarga and Daulatābād, and very much more than doubled that
of Telingāna, the partition of which was part of a scheme for the
division of the other provinces ; but Malik Hasan, who had hoped
to assume the government of the whole vast province, bitterly
resented its dismemberment, and resolved to destroy Mahmūd
Gavān, the author of the scheme. He begged that he might be
permitted to accompany the king on his expedition into the
Carnatic and to leave his son Ahmad as the deputy at Rajamundry.
Ahmad bore a higher reputation as a soldier than his father and
had been provided with a fief in the Māhūr district of Berar
because it had been considered dangerous to employ father and
son in the same province, but Hasan's prayer was granted, and his
son was summoned from Māhūr and installed in Rajamundry.

Narasimha, whose territory Muhammad invaded, was probably
a viceroy or the decendant of a viceroy of the rajas of Vijayanagar,
who had extended his power at the expense of his former masters
until his territories included the eastern districts of their kingdom
and extended on the north to Machchhlīpatan (Masulipatam).
Muhammad made Kondapalli his headquarters, and leaving his
son Mahmūd with Mahmūd Gāvān, in that town led a raid to the
famous temple of Kānchī (Conjeveram). He rode so hard that of
6000 horse who had set out with him no more than forty, among
whom were Yūsuf 'Ādil Khān and Malik Hasan, were with him
when he arrived at his destination. Nothing daunted he rode
towards the temple, from which emerged 'many Hindus of devilish
appearance, among them a black-faced giant of the seed of demons,
mounted on a powerful horse, who, having regarded them fixedly,
urged his horse straight at the king.' While his companions were
occupied with other Hindus Muhammad slew this champion and

another, and entered the temple, plundered it, and slew the attendant Brāhmans.

After resting for a week in Conjeveram Muhammad sent 15,000 horse against Narasimha and, having captured Masulipatam, returned to Kandapalli, where Malik Hasan, Zarīf-ul-Mulk, and the Deccani party lost no opportunity of slandering Mahmūd Gāvān to him.

It was at Kondapalli that Mahmūd Gāvān's plan for the partition of the four great *tarafs* or provinces of the kingdom was completed. As Telingāna had been divided into the two provinces of Rajamundry and Warangal, so Berar was divided into those of Gāwīl, or northern, and Māhūr, or southern Berar ; Daulatābād into those of Daulatābād on the east, and Junnār on the west ; and Gulbarga into those of Belgaum on the west and Gulbarga on the east. At the same time the powers of the *tarafdārs* or provincial governors were curtailed in many ways. Many of the *parganas*, or sub-districts, in the provinces were appropriated as crown lands and removed from the jurisdiction of the governor, and all military appointments which had formerly been part of the governor's patronage, were, with the exception of the command of the principal fortress in each province, resumed by the king. Allowances for the maintenance of troops, whether in cash or in grants of land, had hitherto been calculated at the rate of 100,000 huns for five hundred and 200,000 for 1000 horse. These sums were now raised to 125,000 and 250,000, but on the other hand a system of inspection and control was introduced, and deductions were made on account of men not regularly maintained and mustered. These reforms were most unpopular. The older nobles disliked them because they curtailed the power and diminished the wealth of the provincial governors, and all resented the curtailment of opportunities for peculation. They rendered their author more odious than ever to the Deccani faction, headed by Malik Hasan, who had been the first to suffer by them.

The new governments were fairly divided, Fathullāh 'Imād-ul-Mulk retained Gāwīl, Yūsuf 'Ādil Khān Daulatābād, Malik Hasan Rajamundry, and Mahmūd Gāvān Belgaum, and to the four provinces of Māhūr, Junnār, Gulbarga, and Warangal Khudāvand Khān the African, Fakhr-ul-Mulk the Turk, Dastūr Dīnār the African, and A'zam Khān the Deccani were appointed. The Deccani faction thus held five of the eight provincial governments, but this advantage was neutralised by Malik Hasan's hostility to the interloper, A'zam Khān.

The absence of Yūsuf 'Ādil Khān with the field force encouraged Malik Hasan, Zarīf-ul-Mulk, and Miftāh the African, the leaders of the Deccani party, to prosecute their designs against Mahmūd Gāvān. They induced the keeper of his seals, an African, to affix his private seal to a blank paper, on which they wrote, above the seal, a letter to the raja of Orissa, informing him that the people of the Deccan were weary of the tyranny and perpetual drunkenness of their king and urging him to invade the country. The paper was read to the king when he was drunk, and he at once sent for Mahmūd Gāvān, who insisted on obeying the summons, notwithstanding the protests of his friends, who warned him that mischief was brewing. The king made no inquiries and did not even require the production of the messenger with whom the letter was said to have been found, but when Mahmūd appeared roughly demanded what was the punishment due to a traitor. 'Death by the sword,' replied the minister, confident in his innocence. The king then showed him the letter, and, having read it, he exclaimed, 'By God, this a manifest forgery! The seal is mine, but the writing is none of mine, and I know nothing of the matter.' The king, disregarding his protestations of innocence, rose to leave the hall and, as he did so, ordered an African named Jauhar to put him to death. The minister knelt down and recited the short symbol of his faith, and cried, as the sword fell, 'Praise be to God for the blessing of martyrdom!'

He was seventy-eight years of age when, on April 5, 1481, he was unjustly put to death, and had served the Bahmanī dynasty with conspicuous ability and unwavering loyalty for thirty-five years. He was generous, charitable, learned, accomplished, and blameless in his private life. His attitude towards the Deccanis might have healed the disastrous feud between them and the Foreigners, but for the inappeasable rancour of Malik Hasan, and his death deprived his master of the only counsellor who united fidelity to ability.

The troops and the mob were permitted to plunder his camp, but his own Foreigners rode with all speed to the field force, where they took refuge with Yūsuf 'Ādil Khān, who was also joined by most of the Forign nobles in the royal camp.

The king sent for Nizām-ud-dīn Hasan Gīlānī, the murdered man's treasurer, and discovered, to his chagrin, that Mahmūd, with all his opportunities for acquiring wealth, had left no hoard, having distributed his income, as he received it, in charity. The faithful servant boldly taxed the King with having shed innocent blood and challenged him to prove his minister's guilt. Muhammad, too late,

commanded his betrayers to produce the messenger with whom the
letter had been found, and on receiving no answer hurriedly left the
hall of audience, leaving the courtiers trembling with apprehension.
On reaching his chamber he gave way to paroxysms of grief and
remorse. The body was sent to Bīdar for burial, escorted by the
young prince Mahmūd, the king himself being unable to accompany
it owing to the refusal of the nobles to march with him. Fathullāh
and Khudāvand Khān, both members of the Deccani party, refused
even to see him for the purpose of discussing the punishment of the
conspirators, and bluntly replied to his summons that they would not
trust the murderer of such a minister as Mahmūd, but would shape
their conduct by the advice of Yūsuf 'Ādil Khān. Muhammad recalled Yūsuf, but he could not join the royal camp, and encamped
apart, with Fathullāh and Khundāvand Khān.

The wretched king thus deserted by the Foreigners and by the
respectable portion of the Deccani party, was thrown into the arms
of the late minister's betrayers and compelled to accede to their
demands. Malik Hasan became lieutenant of the kingdom and was
henceforth known as Malik Nāib, his son Ahmad received his
father's title of Nizām-ul-Mulk and the province of Daulatābād,
vacated by Yūsuf, who had decided to take possession of Mahmūd
Gāvān's fiefs of Belgaum and Bijāpur, and Qivām-ul-Mulk the
elder and Qivām-ul-Mulk the younger, two Turks who, from selfish
motives, had attached themselves to Malik Nāib's faction, were
appointed to Warangal and Rajamundry.

The king set out for his capital, but the great nobles, except
Malik Nāib and his friends, marched and encamped at a distance
from the royal troops and, on reaching Bīdar, refused to enter the
city and were dismissed to their provinces. Shortly afterwards he
commanded Fathullāh 'Imād-ul-Mulk and Khudāvand Khān to
accompany him to Belgaum, where he hoped to conciliate Yūsuf
'Ādil Khān, but they, though they obeyed the summons, would
neither march with the royal troops nor enter his presence, but
saluted him always from a distance and chose their own road. From
Belgaum he proposed to visit Goa, but the nobles refused to accompany him and when news was received that Vīra Nrisimha of
Vijayanagar was preparing to attack the port, Yūsuf 'Ādil Khān
was sent to its relief. Fathullāh 'Imād-ul-Mulk and Khudāvand
Khān returned to Berar without permission, and the king withdrew
to Fīrūzābād, where he endeavoured to drown his humiliation and
grief in drink, and formally designated the young Mahmūd heir to
the throne. Thence he returned to Bīdar where, on March 22, 1482,

he died at the age of twenty-eight from the effects of incessant drinking crying out in his last moments that Mahmūd Gāvān was slaying him.

He was an accomplished and high-spirited prince of great energy and possessed considerable military ability. He was better served than any of his predecessors, and might have been the greatest prince of his house but for his addiction to drink, which destroyed first his reputation and then his life. He may be considered the last king of his line, for though five of his descendants followed him on the throne none was more than a state prisoner in the hands of ambitious and unscrupulous ministers.

On the death of Muhammad, his son Mahmūd, a boy of twelve years of age, was seated on the throne by Malik Nāib, Qivām-ul-Mulk the younger, and Qāsim, Barīd-ul-Mamālik, another Turk who for selfish reasons had allied himself to Malik Nāib's faction. None of the Foreign Party or of the more respectable section of the Deccani Party was present at his enthronement, which was a mean spectacle, shorn of the magnificence to which courtiers and people were accustomed, and a superstitious populace augured ill of a reign thus ushered in.

Yūsuf 'Ādil Khān, with most of the Foreign and many Deccani officers, had been absent at Goa at the time of Muhammad's unexpected death, and on his return he marched to Bīdar to make his obeisance to the new king. Disregarding the rule which prohibited the attendance of armed retainers at court he entered the palace with 200 picked troops. Malik Nāib had drawn up 500 of the royal guards at the gate, but none ventured to oppose Yūsuf, who as a precaution against assassination, compelled Malik Nāib and Qāsim Barīd-ul-Mamālik to precede him in the royal presence, where he took his place above them, notwithstanding Malik Nāib's high office. On leaving the palace Yūsuf took Malik Nāib by the hand and compelled him to accompany him as far as the gate. He lodged in the city with a guard of a thousand men while Daryā Khān, with the rest of his army, remained on the alert without the walls. He resisted all Malik Nāib's attempts to induce him to bring his troops into the city, where the Deccanis might have surprised them, and when the nobles met for the purpose of apportioning the great offices of state acquiesced in the retention of the principal places in the capital by the Deccani faction. Malik Nāib remained lieutenant of the kingdom. Qivām-ul-Mulk the elder became minister, Qivām-ul-Mulk the younger master of the ceremonies, and Dilāvar Khān the African assistant minister of finance.

This concession did not blind Malik Nāib to the necessity for removing Yūsuf, his most formidable enemy, and to this end he summoned from Warangal 'Abdullāh 'Ādil Khān the Deccani, the deputy of Qivām-ul-Mulk the elder in that province. It had become customary to confer the same title on two men, usually a Deccani and a Foreigner, though the two bearing the title of Qivām-ul-Mulk were both Turks, and there was commonly much jealousy between two bearers of the same title. 'Abdullāh 'Ādil Khān's opportunities were, however, curtailed by the simultaneous arrival in the capital of Yūsuf's friend, Fathullāh 'Imād-ul-Mulk of Berar.

Malik Nāib first arranged that the troops of Bījāpur and Berar should be reviewed by the king and that at the review the Deccanis should fall upon the Foreigners. On the day appointed he seated the king on one of the bastions of the citadel while the troops paraded below. Yūsuf and Fathullāh were summoned to the royal presence and the young Mahmūd, tutored by Malik Nāib, ordered the Deccanis to punish the Foreigners for their insolence and in-subordination. Yūsuf would have rejoined his men, but Fathullāh, to save his life, detained him in the palace. Matters went ill with the Foreign troops until Daryā Khān marched into the city with the whole of the army of Bījāpur, when street fighting continued for twenty days, and 4000 fell on both sides before the *'Ulamā* could restore peace. Yūsuf 'Ādil Khān then returned with his troops to Bījāpur, leaving Malik Nāib supreme in the capital. He associated Fathullāh 'Imād-ul-Mulk with himself as minister, and Qāsim Barīd, who, though a Turk, had borne arms against the Foreigners, was rewarded with the post of *Kotwāl* of the city, and the three carried on the administration for the next four years. Dilāvar Khān the African, resenting his exclusion from the highest offices, attempted, in obedience to the secret orders of the young king, who chafed under the restraint to which he was subjected, to assassinate the ministers, but failed and was obliged to flee to Khāndesh, while the king was guarded more closely than before.

Fathullāh 'Imād-ul-Mulk grew weary of the atmosphere of treachery and intrigue which pervaded the capital, and returned to Berar, leaving Malik Nāib supreme in the capital, and he, in order to extend his influence in the provinces appointed two Deccanis, Wahīd-ud-dīn and Sharaf-ud-dīn, as deputies for his son Ahmad, to Daulatābād, conferred the government of Sholāpur and Parenda on Fakhr-ud-dīn the Deccani, whom he had entitled Khvāja Jahān, and sent Ahmad to Junnār. These measures were necessitated by the virtual detachment of all other provinces, where the royal seal no longer commanded respect, the governors being well aware that all orders issued in the king's name were in fact the decrees of the justly detested Malik Nāib. In 1486 Qivām-ul-Mulk the younger rebelled in Telingāna, and when Malik Nāib marched against him complained to the king of the oppressive conduct of his minister, but the complaint was fruitless, for it was handed by the king to the minister. Najm-ud-dīn Gīlānī, governor of Goa, died, and his servant, Bahādur Gīlānī, seized the fortress and repudiated his allegiance to Mahmūd Shāh. Malik Nāib's son Ahmad accused Yūsuf 'Ādil Khān of countenancing and abetting the rebel, and thus further estranged the Foreigners. Zain-ud-dīn 'Alī, governor of Chākan, refused, on the ground that the king was not master in his own kingdom, to recognise Ahmad as governor of Junnār, and when Malik Nāib ordered Khvāja Jahān of Parenda and Wajih-ud-dīn of Daulatābād to assist Ahmad in asserting his authority, Yūsuf 'Ādil Khān sent five or six thousand horse to the assistance of Zain-ud-dīn 'Alī. The news of this act of defiance reached Warangal, where Malik Nāib and the king were endeavouring to suppress Qivām-ul-Mulk's rebellion, and undermined the authority of the regent, whose arrogance had left him friendless. Qāsim Barīd, the African eunuch Dastūr Dīnār, and other nobles complained of his behaviour to the king, who replied that none could be more disgusted than he with his minister, and besought them to seek occasion to put him to death. Malik Nāib was informed of the conference and fled from the camp, but instead of following the prudent course of joining his son without delay made for Bīdar where Dilpasand Khān, one of his own creatures, commanded the citadel. He and Dilpasand Khān broke into the treasury and began to raise troops, and the king, on receiving this news, set out at once from Warangal. Malik Nāib, not being strong enough to meet him in the field, prepared to carry off the treasure to Junnār, and join his son, but Dilpasand Khān deceitfully dissuaded him from this course and secretly sent a message to the king, assuring him of his loyalty and his readiness to obey any orders that he might receive. The king replied that he would best show his loyalty by sending to him Malik Nāib's head. Dilpasand Khān accordingly strangled the regent at a private interview and sent his head to the king, who entered the city and plunged into debauchery, neglecting all public business.

Meanwhile the quarrel between the Deccanis and the Foreigners continued with unabated rancour, and the former, dissatisfied with the king's attitude, plotted to dethrone him. On the night of November 7, 1487, they entered the palace, where the king was drinking, and, shutting the gates behind them lest the Foreign troops should come to his assistance, entered the royal apartment. The few Turkish slaves in attendance held their ground against the conspirators until the king had escaped to the roof of the great bastion of the palace, and then followed him, holding the narrow stairway. Mahmūd found means to dispatch a messenger to the Foreign troops, and three or four hundred were soon assembled before the palace. Eight officers scaled the bastion and blew their whistles, and the conspirators, believing that all the Foreign troops had entered the palace, opened the gates to make their escape, but were driven back by some Persian troops. A large body of troops entered the building, and the royal servants, who had at first befriended the conspirators, now drove them, with fire and smoke, from the corner in which they were lurking, and slew them.

Meanwhile the citizens, hearing the tumult in the palace, rose and plundered the houses of the Foreigners, but the Foreign troops, supplied with horses from the royal stables, suppressed the disorder, and when the sun rose on a scene of indescribable confusion the king took his seat on his throne and ordered a general massacre of the Deccanis and Africans. The carnage continued for three days, and was only stayed at the earnest prayer of a son of Shāh Muhibbullāh.

The king now devoted himself entirely to pleasure, and the great provincial governors, perceiving that he would never exercise his authority, began to strengthen themselves in their provinces, and when they attended him in court or camp shunned his presence as they had been wont to shun that of his father in the last days of his reign.

In 1490 Malik Ahmad Nizām-ul-Mulk, who had built the city of Ahmadnagar and called it after his own name, sent envoys to Yūsuf 'Ādil Khān of Bījāpur and Fathullāh 'Imād-ul-Mulk of Berar, inviting them to join him in assuming the royal title and asserting their independence of Bīdar, and from this date these three rulers became independent sovereigns of the territory which they had hitherto held as viceroys of the king of the Deccan[1]. Their dynasties

---

[1] The founders of the dynasties seem seldom, if ever, to have used the royal title. The Portuguese did not accord it to Yūsuf 'Ādil Khān, or to his son Ismā'īl ; Sultān, Qulī Qutb-ul-Mulk, who became independent in Telingana in 1512 never used it, as is evident from the epitaph on his tomb. Ahmad could hardly have borne it, for if his courtiers had been accustomed to it they would not have murmured at his using an umbrella, and if these three did not assume it it is certain that Fathullāh did not. They were, however, in all respects independent, though they sometimes, when it suited their policy and convenience, took the field with the puppet king of Bīdar, or rather with his guardian, and their successors used the title of Shāh.

were known, from the titles borne by their founders, as the Nizām Shāhī, 'Ādil Shāhī, and 'Imād Shāhī dynasties, and later Qutb-ul-Mulk founded the Qutb Shāhī dynasty at Golconda and Barīd-ul-Mamālik the Barīd Shāhī dynasty at Bīdar.

These declarations of independence were not, except in the case of Ahmad, who never forgave Mahmūd Shāh for the murder of his father, prompted by disaffection towards the Bahmanī dynasty, for which Yūsuf and Fathullāh entertained to the end of their lives sentiments of loyalty and affection, but it was impossible to serve Mahmūd, for he would not be served, and had no sooner escaped from the toils of one master than he submitted to another, so that loyalty to the king became no more than subservience to an ambitious minister.

After the composition of the strife between the Deccanis and the Foreigners Qāsim Barīd-ul-Mamālik became lieutenant of the kingdom. He was a Turk, but he was a Sunni and had been a friend of Malik Nāib, so that he was acceptable to the Deccanis but odious to the Foreign Party. He held the king in thrall, and made no pretence of consulting his wishes. One of his earliest measures was to seize the government of the region about the capital, to take the field against the officers commanding its numerous fortresses, who refused to surrender what they held of the king, and to inflict several defeats on the royal troops. Dilāvar Khān the African returned from Khāndesh to help the king, drove Qāsim towards Golconda, and defeated him, but his troops, while pursuing those of Qāsim, were thrown into confusion by an unruly elephant, their victory was turned into a defeat, and Dilāvar Khān was slain. Qāsim returned to Bīdar and reduced the king to a condition of such impotence that some writers date the foundation of the Barīd Shāhī dynasty from this year.

Qāsim Barīd aimed at extending his power by reducing to obedience the provincial governors, and proceeded first against Yūsuf 'Ādil Shāh by inciting Sāluva Tīmma, the regent of Vijaya-nagar, to attack him. The Hindus invaded Rāichūr Doāb and captured both Rāichūr and Mudgal. Qāsim then induced Ahmad Nizām Shāh and Khvāja Jahān of Parenda to join him, and attacked Yūsuf near Gulbarga, but Ahmad disappointed him by taking no part in the action, and Qāsim and Khvāja Jahān were defeated.

Burhān I of Ahmadnagar was rebuked by Bahādur of Gujarāt, who afterwards recognised it, forusing it and it was never recognised by the Mughul emperors, who always addressed the rulers of Bijāpur, Ahmadnagar, and Golconda as 'Ādil *Khan*, Nizām-*ul-Mulk*, and Qutb-*ul-Mulk*.

In 1493 Mahmūd Bīgarha of Gujarāt complained that the pirate Bahādur Gīlānī had plundered many ships of Gujarāt and had sent his lieutenant, Yāqūt, to plunder the port of Bombay, and requested 'the King of the Deccan' to control his refractory vassal. Qāsim Barīd assembled the royal army and, carrying the king into the field, marched against the rebel Yūsuf, Ahmad, and Fathullah sent contingents to his aid, for it was to the interest of all that the king of Gujarāt should have no pretext for invading the Deccan.

Bahādur had established himself so firmly in the Konkan and the country above the Ghāts that both Yūsuf and Ahmad had been constrained to treat him with respect. When he heard that the royal army was marching towards his territory, and that an envoy was bearing a *farmān* to him, he forbade his road guards to permit the envoy to pass Mīraj, and his defiant attitude left the allies no choice but to advance. To Qutb-ul-Mulk the Deccani, now governor of Telingāna, was entrusted the siege of Jāmkhandi, but he was slain, and his title was conferred on Sultān Qulī, a Turk of Hamadān, who held fiefs in Telingāna. Sultān Qulī Qutb-ul-Mulk captured the fortress, handed it over to the officers of Yūsuf 'Ādil Shāh, and advanced to Mangalvedha, where Bahādur had taken refuge. Meanwhile the royal army had advanced to Miraj, and, after defeating Bahādur's troops before that place, captured the fortress but weakly permitted the garrison to join Bahā lur. The royal army marched from Mīraj to Panhāla, and some of the courtiers secretly informed Bahādur that the king was well disposed towards him, and that a submissive attitude would probably earn him a pardon. Negotiations were accordingly opened, but the terms offered by Qāsim Barīd were so generous as to encourage Bahādur to believe that his enemies despaired of crushing his revolt, and he loudly boasted that he would conquer both the Deccan and Gujarāt. Qāsim Barīd was loth to crush the rebel, whom he regarded as a useful counterpoise to the power of Yūsuf 'Ādil Shāh, but as Bahādur was not disposed to submit the war continued, and Khvāja Jahān besieged him in Panhāla, and reduced him to such straits that he sent an envoy to the king offering to submit on no other condition than that his life should be spared. The required assurance was given, but in the meantime Bahādur had escaped from Panhāla and demanded impossible conditions. Sultān Qulī Qutb-ul Mulk was therefore sent to continue the siege of Panhāla and Khvāja Jahān was sent against Bahādur. He defeated and slew the rebel, whose head was severed from his body and sent to the king, and his lands were bestowed on 'Ain-ul-Mulk Kan'ānī, whom Qāsim Barīd selected as one likely to be able to hold his own against Yūsuf 'Ādil Shāh. The king and Qāsim Barīd visited Dābhol and on their return towards Bīdar were entertained for some time at Bījāpur by Yūsuf 'Ādil Shāh.

In 1495 some changes were made in the provincial governments. On the death of Qutb-ul-Mulk the Deccani Dastūr Dīnār the African had been appointed governor of western Telingāna. He was now transferred to Gulbarga, his former fief, to make way for Sultān Qulī Qutb-ul-Mulk, to whom the reward of distinguished service was due· The African, resenting his supersession, rebelled, and occupied those districts of western Telingāna which adjoined Gulbarga. Qāsim Barīd was obliged to enlist the aid of Yūsuf 'Ādil Shāh against the rebel, and Dastūr was defeated, captured, and sentenced to death, but was almost immediately pardoned, and even reinstated in the fief of Gulbarga.

In 1497 the Deccanis again conspired to destroy the Foreigners at Bīdar, but the plot was discovered and Qāsim Barīd put the leading conspirators to death.

On May 3, 1494, during the expedition against Bahādur, a son, named Ahmad, had been born to the king, and in 1498 a marriage was arranged between the child and Bībī Satī, daughter of Yūsuf 'Ādil Shāh. Qāsim Barīd and the king, Yūsuf, Khvāja Jahān of Parenda, and Sultān Qulī Qutb-ul-Mulk assembled at Gulbarga to celebrate the betrothal. During the festivities a serious quarrel broke out between Dastūr Dīnār and Yūsuf, who claimed suzerainty over him. The support given to Dastūr Dīnār by Qāsim Barīd bred another quarrel between him and Yūsuf, Sultān Qulī supported Yūsuf, and the strife became general. Qāsim Barīd Dastūr Dīnār and Khvāja Jahān fled to Aland and were pursued by Yūsuf, who defeated them at Gunjotī, drove Qāsim Barīd, to Ausa and Khvāja Jahān to Parenda, and assumed that control of the king of which he had deprived Qāsim, but, having obtained from him such grants and dignities as he required, permitted him to depart for Bīdar, whither Qāsim Barīd immediately returned and resumed his former position.

At the end of this year Yūsuf attempted to compel Dastūr Dinār to acknowledge his suzerainty, but the African gained without difficulty the support of Ahmad Nizām Shāh as well as that of Qāsim Barīd, both of whom were interested in curbing Yūsuf's ambition, and he was content to abandon the enterprise on obtaining from Bīdar a decree prohibiting Ahmad from attacking him.

In 1504 Qāsim Barīd died, and was succeeded at Bīdar, as a matter of course, by his son, Amīr 'Alī Barīd, and Fathullāh died in Berar and was succeeded, in like manner, by his son, 'Alā-ud-dīn 'Imād Shāh. In the same year Yūsuf marched to Gulbarga, defeated Dastūr Dīnār, put him to death and annexed the province of Gulbarga to his dominions. He now believed himself to be strong enough to carry out a project which he seems to have cherished for some time, and established in his dominions the Shiah religion, to which he was devoutly attached. The *khutba* and the call to prayer were recited after the Shiah form, and the use of the Sunni form was prohibited. His decree raised a storm of discontent in his kingdom, where the majority of Muslims of the middle and lower classes was Sunni, and furnished all other rulers in the Deccan with a pretext for attacking the daring innovator. Mahmūd Shāh, under the instructions of Amīr 'Alī Barīd, commanded 'Alā-ud-dīn 'Imād Shāh, Khudāvand Khān, Ahmad Nizām Shāh, and Sultān Quli Qutb-ul-Mulk of Golconda to aid him in punishing the heretic, and the manner in which each received the order illustrates their political rather than their religious views. Ahmad Nizām Shāh responded with alacrity, both as a Sunni and as a personal enemy of Yūsuf, but 'Alā-ud-dīn 'Imād Shāh and Khudāvand Khān, though Sunnis, paid no heed to it, being well disposed towards Yūsuf and resentful of Amīr 'Alī Barīd's ascendancy at Bīdar. The Shiah Qutb-ul-Mulk, though he was a personal friend of Yūsuf obeyed the order without hesitation. His appointment to Golconda was recent, he still regarded orders from Bīdar, from whatever source they emanated, as binding on him, and he probably disapproved of Yūsuf's action as inopportune and likely to render his religion odious.

Yūsuf, unable to withstand the confederacy arrayed against him, fled to Berar and took refuge with 'Alā-ud-dīn 'Imād Shah, who was sympathetic, but could not protect him against his enemies and advised him to retire into Khāndesh. From Khāndesh Yūsuf sowed dissension among his enemies. He wrote to Ahmad and Qutb-ul-Mulk warning them against Amīr 'Alī Barīd, 'the Fox of the Deccan,' who desired to destroy him only that he might seize Bījāpur and dominate the whole of the Deccan. Having thus detached the two most powerful members of the confederacy he addressed to Mahmūd Shāh a petition seeking for pardon, to which an unfavourable answer was dictated by Amīr 'Alī Barīd, whereupon Yūsuf returned and with the assistance of 'Alā-ud-dīn 'Imād Shāh attacked Mahmūd Shāh and Amīr 'Alī Barīd āt Kalam in Berar. The king and his minister were defeated and fled to Bīdar, leaving their camp in the hands of the allies.

In 1509 Ahmad Nizām Shāh died and was succeeded by his son, Burhān I, and in the following year Yūsuf 'Ādil Shāh died and was succeeded by his son Ismā'īl, and Khvāja Jahān died at Parenda. In 1512 Sultān Qulī Qutb-ul-Mulk of Golconda, unable to maintain any longer the fiction of loyalty to Mahmūd Shāh, assumed independence in Telingāna. He did not use the royal title but is usually described by historians as Sultān Qulī Qutb Shāh[1].

In 1514 Amīr 'Alī Barīd conferred on Jahāngīr Khān, the adopted son of Dastūr Dīnār, the title of Dastūr-ul-Mamālik, and established him as provincial governor of Gulbarga In order to deter Ismā'īl 'Ādil Shāh from molesting him he obtained assistance from Sultān Qulī Qutb Shāh and Burhān Nizām Shāh, and invaded the kingdom of Bījāpur, carrying Mahmūd Shāh with him. Ismā'īl defeated the invaders, captured Mahmūd, who was wounded in the action, and his son Ahmad, and conciliated his captive by his courtesy and deference. He marched with him to Gulbarga, where Bībī Satī was delivered to her affianced husband, Prince Ahmad, and dispatched 5000 horse to escort Mahmūd to Bīdar. On the approach of this force Amīr 'Alī Barīd fled to Ausa, but, having obtained help from Burhān Nizām Shāh, returned to Bīdar, compelled the cavalry from Bījāpur to retire, and again resumed control of the king and what remained of his kingdom.

The miserable king made one more effort to free himself from this thraldom, and fled to Berar, where he sought an asylum with 'Alā-ud-dīn 'Imād Shāh, who readily espoused his cause and marched with him to Bīdar, but Amīr 'Alī Barīd had again obtained help from Burhān Nizām Shāh and drew up his army before Bīdar to oppose his master and 'Alā-ud-dīn. The latter could not take the field without Mahmūd, whose presence was his sole justification for appearing in arms before Bīdar, but Mahmūd, when he should have been at the head of his troops, was loitering in his bath, and was so annoyed by an impatient message which he received from 'Alā-ud-dīn that when he was dressed he rode to Amīr 'Alī Barīd's camp, and 'Alā-ud-dīn was compelled to retreat. Henceforth none would help the wretched puppet, who was interned in a villa at Kamthāna, two leagues from Bīdar.

---

[1] Some English and Hindu historians, ignorant of the meaning of his name, Sultan Qulī, have taken the first half of it to be a royal title, and described him as King Qulī Qutb Shāh. This is a mistake. The word Sultān was part of his name, which means 'the Slave of the King'. 'King Qulī' is nonsense.

In 1517 Amīr 'Alī Barīd, taking Mahmūd Shāh with him, marched to punish Sharza Khān, the son and successor of Khudā-vand Khān of Māhūr, who had plundered Kandhār and Udgīr. Sharza Khān and one of his brothers were slain in the field, and Māhūr was besieged, but 'Alā-ud-dīn 'Imād Shāh marched to its relief and compelled Amīr 'Alī Barīd to retire. He placed Ghālib Khān, another son of Khudāvand Khān, in Māhūr as his vassal, and thus established his authority in southern as well as northern Berar.

Mahmūd Shāh died, worn out with debauchery, on December 7, 1518, and his son Ahmad was placed on the throne by Amīr 'Alī Barīd. He died in 1521 and his brother 'Alā-ud-dīn was permitted to succeed.

'Alā-ud-dīn Bahmanī was a spirited prince, and chafed under the yoke of the *maire du palais*, of which he resolved to free himself. Having deceived him with specious expressions of his appreciation of his great services to the house of Bahman he arranged that the regent should be assassinated on the occasion of one of his monthly visits to him, but as he entered the royal apartment one of the assassins concealed behind the hangings sneezed, and Amīr 'Alī Barīd withdrew in alarm and sent the eunuchs to search the inner apartment. The conspirators were discovered and were executed in circumstances of great cruelty and 'Alā-ud-dīn was deposed and imprisoned, and shortly afterwards put to death.

Amīr 'Alī Barīd would not yet venture to ascend the throne, but proclaimed Walī-Ullāh, the brother of 'Alā-ud-dīn. The new king, after a nominal reign of three years, was detected in an attempt to rid himself of his minister, and was deposed and put to death by Amīr 'Alī Barīd, who married his widow and placed on the throne Kalīmullāh, the brother of the three preceding kings. Warned by the example of his predecessors he at first submitted meekly to the domination of the regent, but the news of the capture of Delhi by Bābur encouraged him to seek aid of the conqueror, and he secretly sent to his court one of his servants, bearing a letter in which he promised to surrender the provinces of Berar and Daulatābād in return for restoration to the remainder of the kingdom of his ancestors and liberation from the thraldom in which he lived. He received no answer and Amīr 'Alī Barīd's discovery of the secret mission so excited his apprehensions that in 1527 he fled to Bījāpur. Ismāīl 'Ādil Shāh received him coldly, and he left his court for that of Burhān Nizām Shāh I at Ahmadnagar.

Burhān received him with extravagant demonstrations of respect, treated him as his sovereign, and promised to recover Bīdar for him, but he soon discovered that his host had no intention of fulfilling his promise. Burhān's chief adviser, Shāh Tāhir, condemned the folly of according the honours of royalty to a stray mendicant, and the unfortunate Kalīmullāh was no longer admitted to court, but when he shortly afterwards died, not without suspicion of poison, his body was sent for burial to Bīdar, where it still rests. He was the last of his line, and on his flight from Bīdar Amīr 'Alī Barīd was free to assert openly that independence which he had long enjoyed in fact.

The relations of the Bahmanids with their subjects closely resembled those of their contemporaries and co-religionists with the peoples of northern India, and where it differed, differed, perhaps, for the worse. Little heed was paid to the interests of the Hindu peasantry, and the Russian merchant, Athanasius Nikitin, describes the poverty and misery of the children of the soil and the wealth and luxury of the nobles. Muhammad III who was reigning when he was sojourning in the Deccan was, even in 1474, described as being 'in the power of the nobles,' of whom the chief was Mahmūd Gāvān, Malik-ut-Tujjar, who kept an army of 200,000 men. Another kept 100,000 and another 20,000 men, and many khāns kept 10,000.

Drink was the curse of the race, and of the long line of eighteen kings there were few who were not habitual drunkards. Their addiction to this vice was the opportunity of informers, delators, and self-seekers, and inclined them to rash and inconsiderate action on the reports of such wretches. Such actions, as in the case of the murders of Nizām-ul-Mulk Ghūrī and Mahmūd Gāvān, were the proximate cause of the ruin of the dynasty and of the dismemberment of its kingdom.

Some of the line were bigots, but their carelessness of the welfare of their Hindu subjects is to be attributed neither to their bigotry nor to the apathy bred of habitual drunkenness. It was merely the fashion of an age in which subjects were believed to exist for their rulers, not rulers for their subjects, and the peasantry of the Hindu kingdom of Vijayanagar was equally neglected and equally miserable.

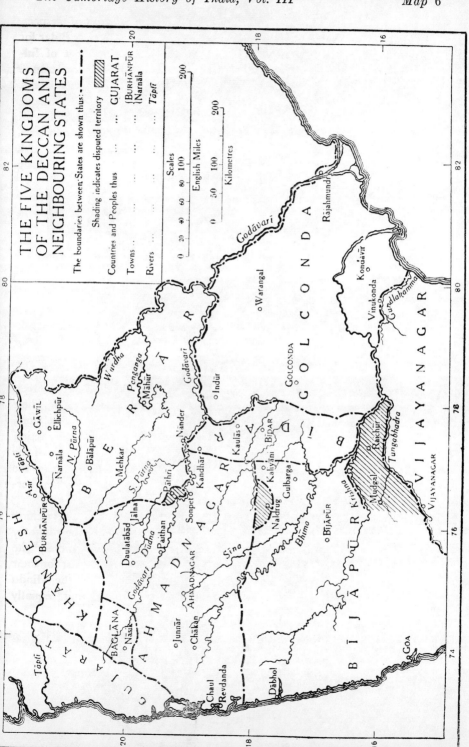

THE FIVE KINGDOMS
OF THE DECCAN AND
NEIGHBOURING STATES

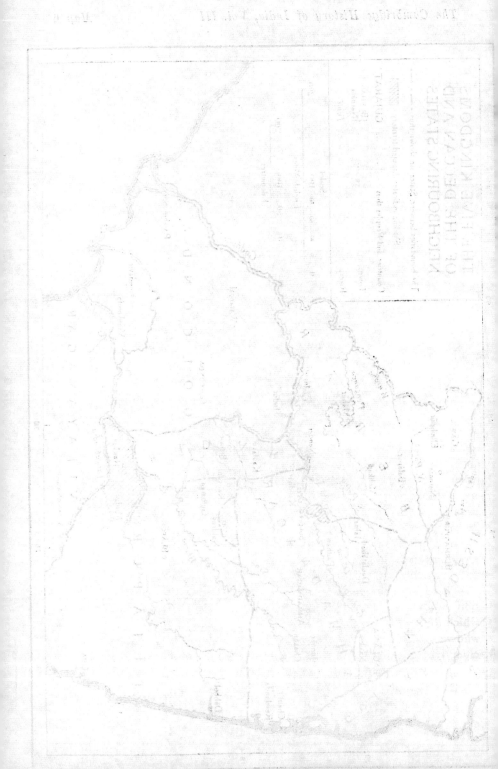

CHAPTER XVII

THE FIVE KINGDOMS OF THE DECCAN. A.D. 1527—1599

WHEN Kalīmullah, the last of Bahman Shāh's line, fled from Bīrdar. Amīr 'Alī Barīd, 'the Fox of the Deccan,' who had never ventured to offend his powerful neighbours by a formal assumption of independence, became independent by the act of his victim, and the tale of the five kingdoms of the Deccan was complete.

The history of these kingdoms is a record of almost continuous strife. Yūsuf 'Ādil Shāh and Sultān Qulī Qutb Shāh had always been Shiahs, Burhān, the son and successors of Ahmad Nizām Shāh, was converted to that faith, to which his successors adhered except during the brief reign of Ismā'il, and the small Sunni states of Berar and Bīdar, the former absorbed by Ahmadnagar in 1574 and the latter by Bījāpur in 1619, could not have disturbed the harmony which should have existed between them ; but community of religion, community of interests, and frequent intermarriages were alike powerless to curb the ambition of the rulers of the three greater states, each of whom aspired to the hegemony of the Deccan. Common jealousies not only prolonged the existence of the smaller states, but saved each of the larger from annihilation, and the usual course of warfare was a campaign of two of the larger states against the third, the smaller states ranging themselves as the policy of the moment might dictate. The assistance given to an ally was so measured as to restrain him from overwhelming his adversary, and a decisive victory was often forestalled by a shameless change of sides, the perfidy of which bred a new *casus belli*. The bitterness thus engendered led to alliances between Muslims and 'misbelievers' against Muslims, but this policy, apparently suicidal, produced a situation which enabled the petty kingdoms to succeed where the Bahmanids had failed, and to crush for ever the hereditary enemy.

There was not wanting subject-matter of dispute. The subjection of the weaker governors in the four pairs of provinces into which the Bahmani dominions had been divided by Mahmūd Gāvān, who were often supported by their powerful neighbours ; the mischievous grant to Ahmadnagar by Qāsim Barīd, acting in the name of Mahmūd Bahmanī, of Sholāpur and the district surrounding it, claimed by Bījāpur ; the refusal of the king of Berar to surrender peacefully Pāthrī, the ancestral home of the kings of Ahmadnagar, on whose border it lay; minor frontier disputes ; and the occasional defection of members of the 'Ādil Shāhī dynasty from the Shiah faith, reviving the old feud between Deccanis and Foreigners, with its intrigues and bloodshed, combined to banish peace from the Deccan. Even the attacks on Ahmadnagar by the Mughal emperors produced but a semblance of unity. Help came from the other kingdoms, but none put forth its full strength to avert a danger common to all. In later years, when only Golconda and Bījāpur remained to stem the tide of imperialism, sympathy, between the doomed states was more cordial but selfishness and cowardice so restricted the assistance given by the former to the latter that Aurangzīb, instead of meeting an alliance, was enabled to crush his victims singly.

The condition of Bījāpur at the time of the accession, at the age of thirteen, of Ismā'īl 'Ādil Shāh was deplorable. All power was in the hands of the minister, Kamāl Khān, a Deccani, who re-established the Sunni religion and was preparing to cede the old province of Gulbarga to Amīr 'Alī Barīd in order that he might establish his own independence in the rest of the kingdom. The Portuguese captured Goa on March 5, 1510, and the young Ism'āïl recovered it on May 20, but in November the Portuguese returned, recaptured it, and established themselves permanently in the port.

Kamāl Khān was assassinated, his plot was frustrated, and the Foreigners expelled by him returned from the neigbouring kingdoms in which they had taken refuge. Khusrav, a Turk of Lār, received the title of Asad Khān and the great fief of Belgaum, and a royal decree declared Deccanis, Africans, and even the children of Foreigners, born in India, to be incapable of holding office in the state.

Meanwhile events in Ahmadnagar followed a similar course. That state was in fact ruled by the minister, Mukammal Khān a Deccani, and the Foreigners, having been foiled in an attempt to place Rājājī, Burhān Nizām Shāh's brother, on the throne, fled to Berar and enlisted the aid of 'Alā-ud-dīn 'Imad Shāh, who espoused their cause and invaded the kingdom of Ahmadnagar, but was defeated at Rāhurī by Mukammal Khān, who drove him into Khāndesh and laid waste his kingdom.

The campaign of 1511 between Ismā'īl 'Ādil Shāh and 'Alī Barīd Shāh, in the course of which Mahmūd Shāh Bahmanī fell into the hands of the former, has already been described. Shortly after this campaign Ismā'īl was enabled to render to Shāh Ismā'īl

Safavī of Persia a service which earned for him a much prized honour. A persian ambassador had been unnecessarily detained and humiliated at Bīdar by the Sunni bigot Amīr 'Alī Barīd, and obtained his dismissal by means of the representations of Ismā'īl 'Ādil Shāh. In the letter acknowledging this courtesy the Persian monarch accorded to the ruler of Bījāpur the royal title, thus exalting him above his rivals, none of whom had received independent recognition of his royalty.

A fresh quarrel broke out between Ahmadnagar and Berar. The town of Pāthrī, north of the Godāvarī and in the latter kingdom had been the home of the Brāhman ancestors of Burhān Nizām Shāh, and their descendants wished to enjoy the protection and patronage of their royal kinsman. Burhān therefore begged that the town might be ceded to him, offering a favourable exchange of territory, but 'Alā-ud-dīn 'Imād Shāh rejected the offer and fortified the town, whereupon Burhān, in 1518, invaded his kingdom and captured Pāthrī.

On the death of Yusūf 'Ādil Shāh Krishnarāya of Vijayanagar had invaded the Bījāpur kingdom at the instigation of Amīr 'Alī Barīd and annexed the Rāichūr Doāb, and it was not until 1521 that Ismā'īl 'Ādil Shāh was in a position to attempt to recover the province. He led a small army from Bījāpur and encamped on the north bank of the Krishna, which he crossed one evening, in a fit of drunkenness, at the head of no more than 2,000 men. His followers were cut to pieces and he himself escaped with difficulty and retired to Bījāpur, where he forswore the use of wine until he should have recovered the Doāb.

Asad Khān Lārī, who directed the policy of Bījāpur, resolved to form an alliance with Ahmadnagar with the object of punishing Amīr 'Alī Barīd for his having incited the Hindu to attack a Muslim kingdom. The two kings met, in 1524, at Sholāpur, and Bībī Mariyam, the sister of Ismā'īl, was married to Burhān, but the alliance, instead of cementing friendship, bred enmity, for Ismā'īl's ministers had promised that the fortress of Sholāpur should be the dowry of the princess, but Ismā'īl, when its cession was demanded, professed ignorance of the obligation and refused to fulfil it, whereupon Burhān returned to Ahmadnagar and invited 'Alā-ud-dīn 'Imād Shāh and Amīr 'Alī Barīd to assist him in capturing the fortress. The three kings invaded Bījāpur in 1525 at the head of 30,000 horse, but were met near the frontier and gave way before the attack of the foreign mounted archers of Bījāpur. The day was decided by the collapse of Burhān, who, exhausted by heat and thirst, was borne fainting from the field, accompanied by his retreating army.

Ismā'īl gave his younger sister in marriage to 'Alā-ud-dīn of Berar and persuaded Sultān Qulī Qutb Shāh to aid him in recovering Pāthrī, but 'Alā-ud-dīn was not strong enough to retain it and in 1527 Burhān again took it and, aided by Amīr 'Alī Barīd, captured the stronger fortress of Māhūr and invaded Berar. 'Alā-ud-dīn and his ally, Muhammad I of Khāndesh, were defeated and driven into Khāndesh while the armies of Ahmadnagar and Bīdar ravaged Berar. The fugitives appealed to Bahādur of Gujarāt, who welcomed the opportunity of extending his influence in the Deccan and set out in 1528 for Ahmadnagar. The intervention of Gujarāt temporarily united Bījāpur and Ahmadnagar, and Burhān, who withdrew to Bīr, was joined by contingents of 6000 horse from Bījāpur and 3000 from Bīdar. Bahādur occupied Ahmadnagar, though his advanced guard suffered two defeats on the way thither, and Burhān and Amīr 'Alī Barīd retired to Parenda and thence to Junnār, from which place their light horse was able to cut off the invader's supplies. Bahādur, when provisions failed at Ahmadnagar, marched to Daultābād and besieged the fortress while the allies occupied the hilly country in the neighbourhood and repeated the tactics which had driven him from Ahmadnagar. It was evident by now that he was intent solely on his own aggrandisement, and 'Alā-ud-dīn of Berar and Muhammad of Khāndesh readily agreed to desert him in consideration of Burhān's promise to restore all that he had taken from them. The approach of the rainy season of 1529 warned Bahādur of the necessity for retreating before the roads became impassable, and Burhān obtained peace on paying an indemnity and causing the *khutba* to be recited in Bahādur's name. Burhān indemnified Muhammad of Khāndesh for his losses, but made no reparation to 'Alā-ud-dīn, and even retained Pāthrī and Māhūr.

The inveterate plotter Amīr 'Alī Barīd had endeavoured to tamper with the loyalty of the contingent sent from Bījāpur to the assistance of Ahmadnagar, and Burhān could not withhold his approval from Ismā'īl's proposal to punish him. Ismā'īl marched to Bīdar, and Amīr 'Alī, now an old man, retired, leaving the defence of the fortress to his sons, and sought aid of Sultān Qulī Qutb Shāh. Ismā'īl defeated a relieving force from Golconda and Amīr 'Alī withdrew to Udgīr and begged 'Alā-ud-dīn 'Imād Shāh to help him. 'Alā-ud-dīn would not oppose Ismā'īl, but marched to Bīdar and interceded with him, but he refused to hear of negotiations until Bīdar should have been surrendered. Amīr 'Alī sorrowfully withdrew to drown his troubles in drink, his troops followed his example, and Ismā'īl, hearing of their demoralisation, sent Asad Khān Lārī to attack his camp. He found all, even those on guard, in a drunken stupor, and he and his followers were able to enter Amīr 'Alī's tent, place the old man in a litter, and bear him away. The jolting of the litter gradually awoke him from his drunken sleep, and, starting up in terror, he cried that the *jinn* were carrying him off. He was undeceived by Asad Khān, who rebuked him for his gross indulgence and unsoldierly behaviour, and carried him before Ismā'īl. At the public audience the wretched old man was compelled to stand for two hours, bareheaded and neglected, in the burning sun, and was then led forward and sentenced to death unless Bīdar were immediately surrendered. To the order which he sent to his son the reply sent was that he was as old man, the short remainder of whose life would be dearly purchased by the surrender of such a fortress as Bīdar, but with this official reply his son sent a private message to the effect that he would surrender the place should all other means of saving his life fail. It was surrendered when Amīr 'Alī was about to be trampled to death by an elephant before the bastion on which his sons took the air, and Ismā'īl, after permitting his prisoner's sons to leave the fortress with their dependants, who smuggled out most of the jewels of the Bahmanids, entered the capital of the Deccan and took his seat upon the turquoise throne. He made Amīr 'Alī a noble of the kingdom of Bījāpur, and it was agreed that he and 'Alā-ud-dīn 'Imād Shāh should first aid him in recovering the Rāichūr Doāb, and that they should then march northwards to recover Mahūr and Pāthrī for 'Alā-ud-dīn.

Krishna Devarāya of Vijayanagar had recently died, and in the confusion which followed his death Ismā'īl was able to reduce both Rāichūr and Mudgal within three months. The recovery of the Doāb released him from his vow of abstinence and he celebrated the occasion by a select symposium, at which only 'Alā-ud-dīn and Asad Khān Lārī at first sat with him, but both begged him to admit Amīr 'Alī, and he consented, but when 'the Fox' entered quoted from the chapter 'The Cave' in the Koran the words, 'Their dog, the fourth of them.' Amīr 'Alī did not understand Arabic, but a burst of laughter from 'Alā-ud-dīn apprised him that he was the victim of a jest, and he wept with humiliation and resentment, while the others laughed. Ismā'īl pitied his distress and foolishly promised, in his cups, to restore Bīdar to him.

Disturbing rumours that Bahādur meditated another invasion of the Deccan postponed the joint expedition for the recovery of Māhūr and Pāthrī, and 'Alā-ud-dīn hastily returned to Berar, while Ismā'īl restored Bīdar to Amīr 'Alī on condition that he ceded Kaliyāni and Kandhār, a condition which he never fulfilled.

In 1531 Bahādur annexed the kingdom of Mālwa, and this accession of strength to Gujarāt so alarmed Burhān that he sent Shāh Tāhir, a famous theologian, to arrange a meeting between himself and Bahādur. Shāh Tāhir, as the envoy of an inferior, was at first ill-received, but ample amends were made to him when his merit was discovered. Burhān was received in the neighbourhood of Burhānpur, where Bahādur was visiting Muhammad, but it was only by means of Shāh Tāhir's ingenious trickery that he received permission to seat himself in Bahādur's presence. At the cost of some humiliation he obtained from Bahādur recognition of his royal title and the insignia of royalty captured from Mahmūd II of Mālwa. Bahādur's conciliatory attitude was adopted for the purpose of enlisting Burhān's aid in a campaign against Delhi, but failed of its object, for Burhān ceased not secretly to urge Humāyūn of Delhi to attack Gujarāt.

Ismā'īl's attempt, later in the year, to enforce his demand for the surrender of Kaliyāni and Kandhār drew from Burhān an insolent letter commanding him to abandon the enterpise. Ismā'īl's reply is an interesting example of the jealousy of the Muslim rulers of the Deccan regarding the use of the royal title. He twitted Burhān with the use of a title conferred by the leader of a gang of Gujarātīs and of the second-hand and soiled insignia of Mālwa, and vaunted his own title, conferred by the Shāh of Persia. War broke out and Burhān and Amīr 'Alī marched to the Bījāpur frontier, but Asad Khān Lārī inflicted on them near Naldrug a defeat which sent Burhān, in headlong flight, to Ahmadnagar. In the autumn of 1532 commissioners from both kingdoms met, and framed a treaty which permitted Burhān to annex Berar and Ismā'īl, who already claimed Bīdar, to annex Golconda, so that the whole of the Deccan would be divided between Ahmadnagar and Bījāpur, the latter receiving the lion's share.

In pursuance of this treaty Ismā'īl and Amīr 'Alī Barīd in 1534 besieged Nalgunda, about sixty miles south of Golconda, and repulsed the relieving force sent by Sultān Qulī Qutb Shāh. The garrison was on the point of surrendering when Ismā'īl fell sick and set out to recruit his health at Gulbarga, leaving Asad Khān Lārī to prosecute the siege, but on August 27, as he was starting in a litter, he

suddenly died.   Asad Khān sent the body to Gogī for burial, raised
the siege, and retired to Gulbarga, where, with many misgivings he
gave effect to his late master's will by raising to the throne his
eldest son, Mallū Khān, a worthless and debauched youth, and
retired to Belgaum, leaving the youth king's grandmother, Punjī
Khātūn, to manage the affairs of the kingdom as best she could.
Mallū's licentiousness, which did not spare the honour of the leading
families of the kingdom, soon convinced her of the futility of the
attempt and early in March, 1535, Mallū was deposed, with the
approval of Asad Khān, and his next brother was raised to the throne
as Ibrāhīm ʿĀdil Shāh I.

Ibrāhīm had imbibed the Sunni doctrines, and on his accession
established that religion in place of Shiah faith, dismissed the
Foreign officers and troops to make way for the less efficient but
more orthodox Deccanis and Africans, and struck a further blow at
foreign influence in the state by substituting the vernacular
languages, Canarese and Marathī, for Persian as the official
languages. This measure facilitated the employment of native
Brāhmans in the administration and excluded foreigners.

The first of Ibrāhīm's many wars was a campaign against
Vijayanagar, for which the intestine affairs of that state furnished
a pretext. For some years past the actual rulers had been the
ministers, and when Venkatarāya, the regent, attempted in 1530
to assume the style of royalty, public opinion obliged him to enthrone a child of the royal house, and to appoint as his guardian
his maternal uncle, Hoj Narmal Rāj.   While the regent was engaged
with a refractory chieftain in a remote part of the kingdom the
mob at Vijayanagar rose in the interests of their young raja, and
Hoj Narmal, intoxicated by the prospect of power, put his nephew
to death and usurped the throne.   The people, disgusted by this
outrage, opened communications with Venkatarāya and Hoj Narmal
sought aid of Ibrāhīm.   Venkatarāya, anxious to prevent, at all
costs, Muhammadan invasion, feigned submission to the usurper
and reminded him of the excesses committed in past time by their
hereditary enemies.   Hoj Narmal, beguiled by the regents professions and terrified by his warnings, assured Ibrāhīm that he had no
need of his services and bribed him with a large sum of money to
retire, and Venkatarāya marched on Vijayanagar.   Hoj Narmal's
fantastic tyranny had rendered him odious to all, and when he
discovered that he would probably be surrendered and called to
account for the murder of his nephew the wretched maniac ham-
strung the royal horses, blinded the elephants, ground the jewels to

powder, and plunged a dagger into his own breast. Venkataraya
ascended the throne of Vijayanagar without opposition, and Ibrāhīm,
on the pretext that he had broken faith with his late ally, sent an
army under Asad Khān Lārī to besiege Adonī, where he was defeated by Venkatādri, brother of Venkataraya. The story told by
Muslim chroniclers of a successful night attack on the Hindu camp,
which redeemed his defeat, is to be regarded with suspicion, for he
was obliged to obtain his master's sanction to a treaty of peace.

In 1537 Burhān Nizām Shāh was converted to the Shiah faith
by Shāh Tāhir, who had taken advantage of his successful treatment
of the dangerous illness of 'Abd-ul-Qādir, a favourite son, to influence a grateful father. The conversion did not improve Burhān's
relations with his Sunni neighbour, Ibrāhīm, and gave the enemies
of Asad Khān Lārī, one of the few Foreign Shiahs left in the
kingdom of Bījāpur, an opportunity of compassing his downfall
by accusing him of being in treasonable correspondence with the
Shiah Burhān. The accusation was false, but it suited Burhān to
assert its truth and in 1540 he marched, with Amīr 'Alī Barīd, to
Parenda, annexed Sholāpur, and advanced towards Belgaum. His
dexterous use of the false accusation paralyzed resistance, for
Ibrāhīm saw in his advance confirmation of Asad Khān's treason,
and Asad Khān was not strong enough to meet him in the field and
dared not, for fear of misconstruction, march to his master's assistance, and the only course left open to him was to join the invader
with a view to using his influence in his direction of peace.

Ibrāhīm retired to Gulbarga, where he was joined by Daryā
'Imād Shāh, who had succeeded his father in Berar in 1529, and
Burhān and Amīr 'Alī occupied and burnt the city of Bījāpur, but
abandoned the siege of its citadel in order to pursue Ibrāhīm.
As they approached Gulbarga, Asad Khān, with his 6000 horse,
deserted them and joined his master, and Ibrāhīm and Daryā thus
reinforced, compelled Burhān and Amīr 'Alī to retire towards Bīr,
and followed them closely. From Bīr they were driven to the
hills above Daulatābād where, in 1542, Amīr 'Alī Barīd died, and
was succeeded in Bīdar by his son 'Alī Barīd Shāh. Burhān purchased peace by the retrocession of Sholāpur and a promise never
again to molest Bījāpur.

Sultān Qulī Qutb Shāh of Golconda had reached the great age
of ninety-eight, and Jamshīd, his second surviving son, who had
grown grey in the expectation of succeeding him, caused him to be
assassinated on September 3, 1543, and ascended the throne.

Sultān Qulī had been in alliance with Burhān, who, eage to

avenge his recent defeat and humiliation, easily persuaded Jamshíd to renew the treaty, and, by inviting the raja of Vijayanagar to join the alliance against Ibráhím, committed an act of treachery and folly which he afterwards had cause to repent bitterly.

In 1543 the kingdom of Bíjápur was invaded by a Hindu army which besieged Ráichúr, by Jamshíd, who occupied the Gulbarga district and besieged Hippargí, and by Burhán and 'Alí Baríd Sháh, who besieged Sholápur. Ibráhím, thus beset, knew not whither to turn, but by means of flattery and concessions eventually succeeded in persuading Burhán and Sadáshivaráya of Vijayanagar to retreat, and left Asad Khán Lárí free to attack Jamshíd. He destroyed a fort which Jamshíd had built at Kakní, twice defeated him in the field, and drove him almost to the gates of Golconda, where he again defeated him and in single combat, after the manner of the Deccan, wounded him severely in the face. After such victories it was easy to enforce satisfactory terms.

In the following year the confederacy was renewed, and Burhán, at the instance of Sadáshivaráya, besieged Gulbarga, but was defeated by Ibráhím and driven from the kingdom. Burhán endeavoured to reconstruct the confederacy, but 'Alí Baríd Sháh had come to the conclusion that it was his duty to support the Sunni rather than the Shiah, and insulted Sháh Táhir, Burhán's envoy, who returned to Ahmadnagar breathing vengeance. Burhán then invaded the kingdom of Bídar and, in spite of the assistance which it received from Bíjápur, captured the fortresses of Ausa, Udgír, and Kandhár.

Ibráhím attributed these defeats to the treachery of his own servants, and put to death without trial seventy Muslim and forty Bráhman officials whom he suspected, so enraging his courtiers and officers that they entered into a conspiracy to depose him and raise to the throne his brother 'Abdulláh. Asad Khán, who had fallen under suspicion and retired to Belgaum, opened communications with the Portuguese of Goa, Burhán, and Jamshíd, with a view to enlisting their support. Ibráhím's discovery of the plot was followed by a number of ruthless executions, and 'Abdulláh fled to Goa and was well received by the Portuguese, who prepared to espouse his cause in consideration of the cession of the Konkan, which had been promised to them as the price of their support.

When Burhán and Jamshíd marched in person on Bíjápur Asad Khán refused to join them, fearing lest they should divide the kingdom between themselves, and while they retired to their own dominions the Portuguese withdrew their support from the pretender, whose party, both in Bījāpur and in Goa, dissolved, but the Konkan, disappointed of annexation by the Portuguese, revolted against Ibrāhīm, who crossed the Ghāts with a large army and crushed the rebellion. The veteran Asad Khān was reconciled to his master, who visited him on his deathbed on March 4, 1546.

In 1547 Burhān returned to the fatal policy of an alliance with Sadāshivarāya and besieged Sholāpur. By his ally's advice he determined to deal first with 'Alī Barīd Shāh, and, having raised the siege of Sholāpur, opened that of Kaliyāni. Ibrāhīm marched to its relief, but was surprised by Burhān on November 14, the festival which terminated the month of fasting, and his army, which had neglected every military precaution, fled in confusion. Kaliyāni fell, but Ibrāhīm, reassembling his army, marched on Parenda. His troops, finding the gates open, occupied the fortress, slew some of the garrison and put the rest to flight, and Ibrāhīm, leaving a Deccani officer in command of the place, retired to Bījāpur. Rumours of the approach of Burhān so terrified this officer that without awaiting an attack he fled precipitately, with the garrison, to Bījāpur, and was executed on his arrival there. According to the facetious account of the foreigner Firishta, 'the valiant Deccani was disturbed in the night by the buzzing of a mosqutio, imagined that he heard Burhān's trumpets, and, mounting his horse, rode for his life.'

In 1552 Burhān joined Sadāshivarāya in the Rāichūr Doāb, which was conquered and annexed to Vijayanagar, and afterwards took the fortress of Sholāpur. In the following year he and his ally besieged Bījāpur while Ibrāhīm withdrew to Panhāla, but a severe illness with which Burhān was smitten compelled him to return to Ahmadnagar, where he died on December 30, his last moments being embittered by open strife between his sons, two of whom, Husain and 'Abd-ul-Qādir, contested the succession to the throne. The former, with the aid of the foreign faction, was victorious, and the latter fled to Berar. Of his four other sons Haidar, with the aid of his father-in-law, Khvāja Jahān of Parenda, made an abortive attempt to seize the throne, and on its failure fled to Bījāpur, whither he was followed by his brothers 'Alī and Muhammad Bāqir, and Khudābanda, another son, fled to Bengal.

Jamshīd Qutb Shāh, after his defeat by Asad Khān Lārī, fell sick in Golconda, and his malady so embittered his temper as to render him obnoxious to his courtiers, who conspired to raise to the throne his brother Haidar. The conspiracy was discovered, and Haidar fled to Bīdar, while Ibrāhīm, the king's youngest brother,

fled to Vijayanagar and enjoyed the protection and hospitality of
Sadāshivarāya. Jamshīd died in 1550, and the Foreign party enthroned his son, Subhān Qulī, a child of two years of age, but
discovering that without royal support, which a child could not
give them, they were unable to cope with the Deccani faction,
invited Ibrāhīm to return. He responded with alacrity, entered
Golconda, and on October 28, 1550, deposed his young nephew and
ascended the throne.

Fresh strife was now brewing between Ahmadnagar and Bījāpur.
In 1554 Khvāja Jahān of Parenda, attacked by Husain Nizām
Shāh I, fled to Bījāpur, and at the same time Saif 'Ain-ul-Mulk, a
Turk who had espoused the cause of 'Abd-ul-Qādir, left Berar and
took refuge with Ibrāhīm 'Ādil Shāh, who bestowed on him the
fiefs of the late Asad Khān Lārī, so that he became the richest
and most powerful noble of Bījāpur. The two refugees easily persuaded Ibrāhīm to espouse the cause of his nephew 'Alī, half-brother
of Husain, who also had taken refuge at his court, and the prince
was supplied with a small force and was sent to invade his half-
brother's kingdom, where he hoped to find many partisans, while
Ibrāhīm besieged Sholāpur, but 'Alī was disappointed and Husain
marched with Daryā 'Imād Shāh to Sholāpur. Ibrāhīm sent Saif
'Ain-ul-Mulk, with the advanced guard, to check the advance of
Husain and Daryā, and the Turk rashly attacked the whole of
Husain's army. His small force was enveloped, and an officer, who
fled panic-stricken, falsely reported to Ibrāhīm that he had seen
Saif 'Ain-ul-Mulk dismount and do reverence to Husain, who had
received him kindly.

Ibrāhīm, without attempting to verify this story, retreated
towards Bījāpur, his march being accelerated by a report that Saif
'Ain-ul-Mulk, who was attempting to rejoin him, was pursuing him
with hostile intent. Husain, whose army had been severely handled,
retired to Ahmadnagar, and Saif 'Ain-ul-Mulk sent a message to
his master assuring him of his unwavering loyalty and asking for
an advance from the treasury to enable him to equip his exhausted
troops, but Ibrāhīm coldly replied that he had no longer any need of
his services, and 'Ain-ul-Mulk, thus summarily dismissed, became
a rebel and a free lance, and in March, 1555, occupied the fertile
Mān district, in the north-western corner of the kingdom, where he
supported his troops by levying taxes on the cultivators. He gained
more than one victory over the royal troops, declared for 'Abdullāh,
who was still at Goa, and at length singally defeated the royal army,
led by Ibrāhīm in person, followed the fugitives as far as Torwa,

within four miles of Bījāpur, and there proclaimed 'Abdullāh king. Ibrāhīm, in his extremity, appealed to Sadāshivarāya, who sent his brother Venkatādri, with 15,000 horse, to his assistance. 'Ain-ul-Mulk made a night attack on the Hindu army, but Venkatādri, accustomed to the tactics of Asad Khān Lārī, was on the alert, and 'Ain-ul-Mulk's force was nearly annihilated. Ibrāhīm captured 'Abdullāh and imprisoned him, and Saif 'Ain-ul-Mulk and his nephew Salābat Khān fled to the borders of Ahmadnagar and begged to be readmitted to the service of that kingdom. Husain treacherously returned a favourable answer, and caused 'Ain-ul-Mulk to be assassinated as he made his obeisance. Some of his followers saved their lives by accepting service under Husain, but the rest, including Salābat Khān, were murdered. The ladies of the murdered man's harem found an asylum at Golconda through the interest of his principal wife, who was a sister of Ibrāhīm Qutb Shāh.

During the last two years of his reign Ibrāhīm 'Ādil Shāh waged unsuccessful warfare against the Portuguese in the northern Konkan, and in 1558 died at Bījāpur. It had been his intention to disinherit his eldest son 'Alī, who was a Shiah, in favour of the younger, Tahmāsp, but on discovering that Tahmāsp was even a more bigoted Shiah than 'Alī he let matters take their course. 'Alī 'Ādil Shāh I re-established the Shiah religion and Foreigners were again encouraged to enter the service of the state, and regained their old ascendancy.

'Alī immediately sought the assistance of Sadāshivarāya for the recovery of Sholāpur, and Husain Nizām Shāh and Ibrāhīm Qutb Shāh invaded his kingdom and besieged Gulbarga, but Ibrāhīm, urged by Sadāshivarāya, who had claims on his gratitude, and suddenly doubtful of the wisdom of crushing Bījāpur, now once more a Shiah state, in the interests of Ahmadnagar, deserted Husain, who was obliged to raise the siege and retire. In the following year 'Alī endeavoured to persuade Husain to restore to him Sholāpur and Kaliyāni, but Husain, though embroiled at the time with the Portuguese and warned by his advisers that 'Alī was creating a powerful coalition against him, steadfastly refused to cede either fortress.

The Portuguese had sought permission to build a fort at Revdanda, near Chaul, but Husain detained their envoy and sent a force to build a fort on the site which they had chosen. Francisco Barreto, governor of Goa, caused the port to be blockaded until he could arrive with 4,000 Portuguese and a force af native troops, and Husain sued for peace, which was concluded on the condition that neither party fortified either Chaul or Revdanda.

'Alī Ādil Shāh had succeeded in drawing Golconda into the confederacy against Ahmadnagar, and Husain, who stood alone, looked round for an ally, but could find none better than his neighbour of Berar. He and Daryā 'Imād Shāh met at Sonpet on the Godāvarī, where he married Daulat Shāh, Daryā's daughter.

'Alī now addressed to Husain a more peremptory request for the surrender of Sholāpur and Kaliyāni, and on receiving an insulting reply prepared to enforce his demand. He marched northwards, accompanied by Sadāshivarāya with a large army, and was joined on his frontier by Ibrāhīm Qutb Shāh. As the allies advanced towards Ahmadnagar, Husain, leaving a garrison in the fortress, retired to Paithan, on the Godāvarī, and summoned to his aid Daryā 'Imād Shāh, who was, however, dissuaded from joining him by Khānjahān, brother of 'Alī Barīd Shāh of Bīdar, who joined 'Alī 'Ādil Shāh, while Daryā's minister, Jahāngīr Khān the Deccani, invaded Ahmadnagar with the army of Berar.

Meanwhile the invaders were laying waste the country which they occupied, and the Muslims of all the armies were scandalised by the insults offered by the Hindus to their religion. Mosques were used as stables, or destroyed, and Muslim women were violated and enslaved by misbelievers. Ibrāhīm Qutb Shāh again began to tremble for the balance of power, and entered into correspondence both with the garrison of Ahmadnagar, which he aided with supplies, and with Husain, whom he assured of his goodwill. This correspondence was discovered, and 'Alī and Sadāshivarāya bitterly upbraided Ibrāhīm, who deserted them by night and retired rapidly to Golconda, while one of his nobles joined the garrison of Ahmadnagar and eventually entered Husain's service.

Meanwhile Jahāngīr Khān of Berar received orders from his master to change sides, and proceeded to intercept all grain and provisions coming from the south for the allies. The invaders, reduced to great straits, raised the siege of Ahmadnagar and marched to Āshtī, whence an army was sent to besiege Parenda. Husain, with whom was his ally Daryā, sued for peace, and Sadāshivarāya, the dominant partner in the confederacy, insisted on three conditions, the surrender of Kaliyāni to 'Alī, the death of Jahāngīr Khān, whose interception of convoys had caused famine and much distress in his camp, and the personal submission of Husain. The second of these, the execution of an ally for faithful and efficient service, was impossible of acceptance but by one dead to all

sense of honour and of shame, but Husain accepted it and caused
Jahāngīr Khān to be put to death, while his master, being to some
extent in the murderer's power, could do nothing to save his servant,
but retired sullenly to Berar. Husain's humiliation before Sadāshivarāya was a fitting punishment for his turpitude. The haughty
Hindu refused to acknowledge his salutation otherwise than by
giving him his hand to kiss, and Husain in his wrath called for
water and washed his hands. The insult was returned by the in-
furiated Sadāshivarāya, who uttered the threat, in Canarese, that
if Husain had not been his guest the largest part of him that would
have been left whole would have been his finger tips. The quarrel
was composed, and Husain was compelled to surrender the keys of
Kaliyāni.

Sadāshivarāya, on his way back to Vijayanagar, treated 'Alī, as
his servant, and the result of this unfortunate campaign was an
increase of the bitterness between the Muslim kings and the
humiliation of all before the Hindu.

Husain's first thought on reaching his capital was revenge, and
his first act was to dismantle the mud fort of Ahmadnagar and to
build in its stead a stronger and more spacious structure of stone,
known as the *Bāgh-i-Nizām*. In 1561 he opened negotiations with Ibrāhīm Qutb Shāh, who had earned his gratitude in the late campaign
and in 1562 the two kings met before Kaliyāni, where Husain's
daughter, Jamāl Bībī, was married to Ibrāhīm and the siege of the
fortress was opened. 'Alī and Sadāshivarāya marched to its relief
and the armies of Berar and Bīdar set out to join them. Daryā
'Imād Shāh had died in 1561 and had been succeeded by his infant
son, Burhān, but Berar was ruled by the minister, Tafā'ul or Tufāl
Khān, who acted as regent and was in this campaign unanimously
supported by the nobles of Berar, who resented the murder of
Jahāngīr Khān.

Husain and Ibrāhīm raised the siege of Kaliyāni and marched
to meet their enemies. The rainy season of 1562 was now past, but
an unseasonable storm had filled the rivers and converted the
country into a quagmire. Husain's wonderful train of 700 guns
stuck fast in the mire, and he found it impossible to extricate more
than forty of them, with which, abandoning his intention of attacking
the enemy on that day, he returned to his camp. 'Alī's advanced
guard discovered the abandoned guns and waggons, and the armies of Bījāpur and Vijayanagar, having secured them, attacked the
camp of Ibrāhīm Qutb Shāh, who fled.

Having lost nearly all his artillery and discovered Ibrāhīm to be a broken reed, Husain was constrained to retire. His camp and that of Ibrāhīm were plundered, and their armies were much harassed during their retreat. At Ausa Ibrāhīm took his leave, but left the greater part of his army, under Murtazā Khān Ardistānī, with Husain, who continued his retreat to Junnār, leaving a garrison in Ahmadnagar, which was besieged by 'Alī and Sadāshivarāya. The Hindus repeated, on a more extensive scale, the outrages which they had committed during the former campaign. Mosques were desecrated, defiled, or destroyed, the palaces of Ahmadnagar were thrown down, and the wives and daughters of Muslims were violated. 'Alī, who was powerless to restrain his allies, persuaded Sadāshivarāya to raise the siege and join him in pursuing Husain, who retired to the hills as they approached Junnār, but detached his light troops to harass them and cut off their supplies.

The rainy season of 1563 was now approaching, and as Husain was inaccessible in his retreat in the Western Ghāts the allies returned to the siege of Ahmadnagar. Sadāshivarāya foolishly permitted his army to encamp in the dry bed of the river, and when the rains suddenly broke a flood carried away large numbers of his army. He was already weary of the campaign, and returned to his own country, while 'Alī retired to Naldrug and rebuilt that fortress.

The Barīd Shāhī kings, who first committed the error of inviting the intervention of Vijayanagar in the affairs of the Muslim kingdoms, could plead their own weakness and the neighbourhood of comparatively powerful states whose rulers they regarded as heretics; but the kings of Ahmadnagar and Bījāpur, who followed their example, had no such excuse. The arrogance of Sadāshivarāya had humiliated and disgusted both his allies and his enemies, the excesses of his troops had horrified all Muslims, and he now demanded the cession of extensive tracts of territory, from Bījāpur as the price of his assistance to 'Alī, and from Golconda as the penalty of Ibrāhīm's duplicity and hostility.

It was apparent to all that unless prompt measures were taken to curb his ambition the end of Muslim rule in the Deccan was at hand; but nothing could be effected without co-operation, and 'Alī was loth to approach Husain. Ibrāhīm acted as mediator and the differences between Ahmadnagar and Bījāpur were composed by two matrimonial alliances, Hadiyya Sultān, 'Alī's sister, being given in marriage to Murtazā, Husain's heir, and Chānd Bībī, Husain's daughter, to 'Alī. By this latter alliance the vexed question of Sholāpur was temporarily laid to rest, and the fortress con-

stituted the dowry of Chānd Bībī, 'the Noble Queen'. 'Alī Barīd
Shāh was drawn into the alliance and overtures were made to
Berar, but the murder of Jahāngīr Khān was not yet forgotten,
and Tufāl Khān would join no confederacy which included the
treacherous and ungrateful Husain.

The offensive alliance of the four kings was formed in the summer
of 1564, on December 12 they assembled at Sholāpur, and on
December 24 marched thence to Talikota, on the Khon river, near
the Krishna.

Sadāshivarāya had been fully informed of what was going
forward, and had not been idle. He sent his brothers, Tirumala
and Venkatādri, with 32,000 horse, 300,000 foot, and 1,500 elephants,
to hold the fords of the Krishna, and encamped with the rest of
his army, which brought the strength of the Hindus up to 82,000
horse, 900,000 foot and 2,000 elephants, at a distance of ten miles
from that river.

The allies, having discovered that there was no practicable ford
for a great distance, other than that held in force by the Hindus,
marched upstream and induced the enemy to follow them, leaving
the ford unguarded. After three days' march they suddenly turned
in their tracks, and not only covered, between sunrise and sunset,
the whole distance, but sent their advanced guard across the river
by the deserted ford. During the night the rest of the army crossed,
and advanced towards Sadāshivarāya's camp. The armies were
drawn up for battle on that day, but the Hindus failed to attack,
and on the following day, January 5, 1565, the allies again drew up
their forces. Their centre was commanded by Husain, their right
by 'Alī, and their left by Ibrāhīm and 'Alī Barīd Shāh. The Hindu
right, 20,000 horse, 200,000 foot, and 500 elephants, was commanded
by Tirumala, their centre by Sadāshivarāya in person, with 37,000
horse, 500,000 foot and 1,000 elephants, and their left by Venka-
tādrī, with 25,000 horse, 200,000 foot, and 500 elephants. The
Muhammadan heavy field and light artillery, the arm in which they
were strongest, was in the centre, under the command of Chalabī
Rūmī Khān, the master of Husain's ordnance.

Sadāshivarāya indulged both his pride and his infirmities by
being borne to the field in a magnificent litter, and when urged to
mount a horse declared that a horse was not necessary against an
enemy so contemptible. He ordered that Husain should be slain
and beheaded, but that 'Alī and Ibrāhīm should be taken alive.

The Hindu infantry, in the first line, opened fire with rockets,
matchlocks, and light guns, and their cavalry then charged the

Muslims, and pressed them so hard that 'Alī, Ibrāhīm and 'Alī
Barīd turned to flee, and were only arrested by encouraging
messages from Husain, who stood his ground. The first discharge
of his artillery did great execution among the Hindus, and Sadāshivarāya, perceiving that victory was to be contested, left his
litter and ascended a magnificent throne, which had been erected
for him beneath a rich canopy, behind the position of his army,
and here, surrounded by piles of jewels and gold and silver money,
he caused proclamation to be made that any notable success against
the enemy would be rewarded by him on the spot.

Chalabī Rūmī Khān caused the heavier guns to be loaded, for their
second discharge, with copper coin[1], and this ammunition tore great
gaps in the Hindu ranks, which were now at close quarters. Husain
followed up the advantage with a general charge of his cavalry,
which rode through the shattered ranks of the enemy, and Sadāshivarāya, now in personal peril, quitted his throne for his litter,
and though his guards offered a determined resistance they were
thrown into confusion by the repeated charges of the Muslim horse,
supported by the elephants. One of these, driven beyond the rest,
came up with the litter, and the driver, remarking its rich and
costly adornment, but not knowing whom it contained, drove the
elephant against it and overturned it, intending to secure it as
spoil. The raja fell to the ground, and an attendant Brāhman cried
to the driver, 'This is Sadāshivaraya. Save his life and he will
make you the greatest man in his kingdom ! The driver at once
caused the elephant to pick the raja up in his trunk and carried
him to Rūmī Khān, who led him before Husain Nizām Shāh. He
was beheaded on the spot, and the spectacle of his head, raised on
a spear, completed the rout of the Hindus, who fled, without striking
another blow, pursued by the victors as far as Anagondi. The
number slain in the battle and the pursued was computed at
100,000, and the spoil, which included large numbers of captives
consigned to slavery, enriched the whole of the Muslim armies, for
the troops were permitted to retain the whole of the plunder except
the elephants.

The victors destroyed Vijayanagar, which they occupied for six
months, plundered the country, and completed the reconquest of
the Doāb where Rāichūr and Mudgal held out for some time.
Venkatādri retired to Penukonda, nearly 120 miles south of the
former capital, and established himself beyond the reach of the

---

[1] The copper coinage of the Deccan consisted not of flat discs, but of small, thick
lumps, most suitable for Rūmī Khān's purpose.

victors, and Tirumala was permitted to establish himself in Anagondi as a vassal of Bījāpur. The head of the Hindu King[1], stuffed with straw, was sent as a warning to Tufāl Khān of Berar, who had not only stood aloof from the confederacy, but had, at the instigation of Sadāshivarāya, plundered Husain's kingdom as far as Ahmadnagar.

Talikota was one of the decisive battles of India, and broke for ever the power of the great kingdom of Vijayanagar, which had maintained for a century and a half an equal warfare with the Bahmanī kingdom and threatened to devour piecemeal the smaller kingdoms into which it had been divided. The victory of the Muslims against such overwhelming odds has the appearance of a miracle, but the superiority of their artillery and of their troops, especially the Foreigners helps to explain it. Their cavalry was better armed, better mounted, and excelled in horsemanship, and the mounted archers, of whom the Hindus seem to have had none remaining, were probably at least twice as efficient as cavalry equal to them in other respects but armed only with sword or lance. The main strength of the Hindu army was its infantry, ill-armed, ill-clad, ill-trained, and deficient in martial spirit. The capture of Sadāshivarāya was fortuitous, but no oriental army would have stood before the sight of its lifeless leader's head, carried before an enemy.

Husain died on June 6, 1565, shortly after his return, from the effects of debauchery, and was succeeded by his son, Murtazā Nizām Shāh I, a dissipated and self-indulgent young man who, for the first six years of his reign, left the management of all public business to his mother, Khānzāda or Khūnza Humāyūn, who caused much discontent by preferring the interests of her brothers, 'Ain-ul-Mulk-and Tāj Khān, on whom she bestowed vast estates, to those of the kingdom, but her power could not be broken without the aid of her son, who was too indolent to stir himself

In 1566 'Alī 'Ādil Shāh joined Murtazā Nizām Shāh with the object of punishing Tufāl Khān for his treason to the cause of Islam and his depredations in Ahmadnagar. The two kings invaded Berar and advanced as far as Ellichpur, the capital, laying waste the country. Tufāl Khān retired into fortress of Gāwīl and opened negotiations with 'Alī, whose heart was not in the campaign, and who, in consideration of fifty elephants and the equivalent of 40,000 in

---

[1] A stone representation of the head, which still exists, was set up on the wall of the citadel of Bījāpur and unless it is a gross libel, Sadāshivarāya had a heavy bestial face with a thick, coarse nose, practically no forehead, goggle eyes, and tusks like a boar.

cash, made the approach of the rainy season a pretext for returning to his own country and left Murtazā in the lurch.

In 1567 'Alī, provoked by Murtazā's persistent hostility, invaded his kingdom and captured the fortress of Kondhāna, now Sinhgarh, and sent a force under Kishvar Khān towards Bīr. Kishvar Khān defeated some of Murtazā's troops at Kāij and built there the fortress of Dhārūr.

Ahmadnagar was ill-prepared for war. The great fiefs were in the possession of the brothers and favourites of the queen-mother. who failed to maintain their contingents, and the situation was so desperate that even the Africans combined with the Foreigners to destroy her power, and were frustrated only by the king's cowardice and treachery. The principal conspirators, among whom was Sayyid Murtazā Sabzavārī, an able and energetic Persian, fled to Bījāpur and Gujarāt. A second attempt was, however, more successful than the first, and she was arrested and imprisoned in Shivner, and her brothers fled.

Murtazā, emancipated from his mother's control, exhibited unusual energy and spirit, and marched on Dhārūr with such speed that he arrived there without artillery. The suddenness of his appearance startled the garrison, but he would undoubtedly have been defeated had not one of his officers, Chingīz Khān, mortally wounded with an arrow Kishvar Khān, who was standing at a window or loophole. The death of the leader had the usual result, and the panic-stricken garrison evacuated the fortress and fled, pursued by the victors, who slaughtered many and took much booty.

Chingīz Khān was sent against 'Ain-ul-Mulk of Bījāpur, who was marching with 10,000 horse to relieve Kishvar Khān, and defeated and dispersed his troops, thus enabling Murtazā to invade the kingdom of Bījāpur. He was joined at Wākdari by Ibrāhīm Qutb Shāh, but Bījāpur was saved by a series of intrigues. Ibrāhīm, who was trimming as usual, sent a friendly letter to 'Alī 'Ādil Shāh. 'Alī suspected his minister, Shāh Abu-'l-Hasan, a son of Shāh Tāhir, of being in league with Murtazā, and of having instigated the invasion, and Abu-l-Hasan, who was innocent, sent Murtazā Nizām Shāh a message through Sayyid Murtazā Sabzavārī, begged him to avert, by retiring, the danger in which his master's suspicions placed him, and supported the request by warning him that his ally intended to play him false and sending him a copy of Ibrāhīm's letter to 'Alī. Murtazā in his wrath made a night attack on his ally's camp, captured his elephants, and drove him in headlong flight to Golconda, whither a detachment pursued him, but after returning to

Ahmadnagar repented of his hasty action and, fearing lest Ibrāhīm should ally himself with 'Alī, strove to conciliate him. He discovered that Ibrāhīm attributed the sudden and treacherous attack on his camp to the machinations of Mullā Husain Tabrīzī, Khān Khānān, lieutenant of the kingdom of Ahmadnagar, and, as the Mullā's recent conduct supplied a pretext, Murtazā conciliated Ibrāhīm by dismissing and imprisoning him, and appointed in his stead, in 1569, Shāh Haidar, a son of Shāh Tāhir.

In the same year 'Alī, Murtazā, and the Zamorin of Calicut formed an alliance for the purpose of expelling the Portuguese from India and dividing their possessions. In January, 1570, the siege of Goa was opened by 'Alī and that of Chaul by Murtazā, each placing in the field all his available forces. The indomitable viceroy, Dom Luiz de Atayde, Conde de Atouguia, not only maintained himself in Goa, but, in spite of the pressure brought to bear on him by his more timorous compatriots, sent aid to Chaul.

The account of the operations resembles a mediaeval romance. At Chaul an army of 150,000 men, under the eye of their king, besieged for nine months a garrison which never exceeded 3000 and slew considerably more than its own number of the enemy, compelling him to raise the siege. At Goa, besieged by an army more numerous than that before Chaul, the heroic viceroy, with a force which at first numbered 1600 and never exceeded 4000, withstood the enemy for ten months and finally compelled him to retreat after he had lost 12,000 men, 300 elephants, 4000 horses and 6000 oxen.

These victories were due no less to the skill with which the Portuguese exploited the corruption and dissensions of their enemies than to their valour and discipline. At Chaul most of Murtazā's nobles supplied the Portuguese not only with intelligence, but with provisions, and, despite the leniency with which such treachery was ordinarily regarded in the Deccan, even the foolish Murtazā was constrained to banish the highly respected Injū Sayyids. At Goa there were instances not only of information being sold to the Portuguese, but of a conspiracy headed by Nūrī Khān, commanding the army of Bījāpur, to assassinate 'Alī 'Ādil Shāh.

Through these mists of treachery, venality, and corruption the valour and steadfastness of Dom Luiz the Viceroy shone undimmed. He refused, in Goa's sorest straits, to abandon Chaul, and sent aid not only to that port, but to the southern settlements attacked by the Zamorin, to the Moluccas, and to Mozambique. He even refused to delay the sailing to Portugal of the annual fleet of merchantmen, whose crews would have formed a valuable addition to his garrison, and he carried the war into the enemy's country by a successful attack on Dābhol, led by Dom Fernando de Vasconcellos.

'Alī, after his defeat, concluded on December 17, 1571, a new treaty with the Portuguese, and Murtazā, after losing 3000 men in one day before Chaul, entered into an offensive and defensive alliance with Dom Sebastião, King of Portugal. Chingīz Khān, the only officer who had refrained, during the siege of Chaul, from treasonable correspondence with the Portuguese, became lieutenant of the Ahmadnagar kingdom, which received a further accession of strength by the return from Bījāpur of the able and energetic Sayyid Murtazā of Sabzāvār.

'Alī 'Ādil Shāh consoled himself for his defeat by capturing Adonī and annexing many other districts of the former kingdom of Vijayanagar, and Murtazā, alarmed by the increase of his rival's power and by an alliance which he had formed with Golconda, assumed a menacing attitude and advanced towards his frontier. 'Alī marched to meet him, but Chingīz Khān and Shāh Abu-'l-Hasan averted hostilities and concluded a treaty which permitted Ahmadnagar to annex Berar and Bīdar and Bījāpur to annex in the Carnatic the equivalent of those two kingdoms.

In pursuance of this treaty Murtazā sent an envoy to Tufāl Khān, demanding that he should resign his power to Burhān 'Imād Shāh, who was now of full age. His solicitude for the young king was rightly estimated by Tufāl Khān, who dismissed the envoy without an answer and prepared to resist invasion. Murtazā was already at Pāthrī, on the frontier, when the envoy returned and reported the failure of his mission.

Tufāl Khān first marched towards Bīdar, hoping to secure the co-operation of 'Alī Barīd Shāh, who was threatened, equally with himself, by the recent treaty, but 'Alī Barīd showed no inclination to assist him and after an indecisive action with Murtazā's advanced guard he retired rapidly on Māhūr, Murtazā, leaving a force at Kandhār to oppose an anticipated invasion from Golconda, started in pursuit of him and after another indecisive action he again retreated, and Murtazā, after masking the fortress of Māhūr, advanced into Berar. He received an unexpected reinforcement. In November, 1572, Akbar had conquered Gujarāt and captured its king Muzaffar III, and had subsequently been compelled to attack his rebellious cousins, 'the Mīrzās'. They were defeated, and many of their followers ensured their safety by entering Murtazā's service.

Tufāl Khān sought an asylum with Muhammad II of Khāndesh, but was expelled by him and shut himself up, with Burhān 'Imād

Shāh, in Narnāla sending his son, Shamshīr-ul-Mulk, to hold Gāwīl.

The siege of Narnāla was protracted until the end of April, 1574, and during its course the troops of Ibrāhīm Qutb Shāh invaded the kingdom of Ahmadnagar, but were defeated and expelled on May 11, 1573.

Long before Narnāla fell the vacillating Murtazā grew weary of the siege, and proposed to evacuate Berar and return to Ahmadnagar. His desire to return was shared, and perhaps prompted, by a new favourite, a boy named Husain, who had been a hawker of fowls in the camp and eventually received the title of Sāhib Khān and rose to a high position in the state, but his pretext was his longing to see his own infant son, Husain, at Ahmadnagar. Chingīz Khān was despairing of success in combating his master's resolve when a stratagem enabled him to bring the protracted siege to a successful conclusion. In April, 1574, a merchant from Lahore arrived in the camp with horses and other merchandise for Tufāl Khān, and was permitted to enter the fortress on agreeing to take with him Khvāja Muhammad Lārī, Murtazā's agent. The agent, who was well supplied with money, did his work so well that many of Tufāl Khān's officers deserted to the besiegers and the garrison lost heart. At the same time the artillery of Ahmadnagar was more vigorously served and a practicable breach encouraged Murtazā to order an assault. Tufāl Khān displayed great valour, but his men had no stomach for the fight, the besiegers entered the fortress, and he was forced to flee. He was pursued and captured, and his son, on learning his fate, surrendered Gāwīl, and the conquest of Berar was complete. Both father and son, with Burhān 'Imād Shāh and his family, were imprisoned in a fortress in the kingdom of Ahmadnagar, where all died shortly afterwards, not without suspicion of violence.

'Alī 'Ādil Shāh had meanwhile been pursuing a career of conquest in the western Carnatic, and on returning to his capital in 1575, after an absence of more than three years, he left Sayyid Mustafā Ardistānī at Chandraguni as governor of his southern conquests, which included, besides extensive tracts administered directly by his officers, the dominions of numerous petty rajas who enriched his treasury by the payment of tribute. After his return he besieged Bālkonda, where Venkatādri had established himself. Venkatādri escaped to Chandragiri, but left a garrison to hold the fortress, and when, after a siege of three months, it was on the point of surrendering owing to the failure of its supplies, he saved the place from falling into the hands of the Muslims by bribing 'Ali's

Marāthā troops, 9000 in number, to change sides. The defection of this large force, which immediately harassed its former comrades by cutting off their supplies, rendered the maintenance of the siege impossible and 'Alī returned to Bījāpur in 1578.

Murtazā's recent conquest aroused the hostility of Ibrāhīm Qutb Shāh and Muhammad II of Khāndesh, who regarded with apprehension the extension of his kingdom northward, its apparenlty imminent extension eastward, by the absorption of Bīdar, and the immediate proximity of a neighbour so much more powerful than themselves. A revolt in which the governor recently appointed by Murtazā lost his life encouraged Muhammad to intervene, and he sent an army under the command of his minister Zain-ud-dīn into Berar to support the cause of a pretender, probably a genuine scion of the 'Imād Shāhī family, who had taken refuge at his court. Zain-ud-dīn besieged Narnāla, and the officers left by Murtazā in Berar fled to his camp, now at Māhūr. He retraced his steps, and as he approached the Taptī Muhammad withdrew from Burhānpur to Asīr, his fortress-capital, whither the army of Ahmadnagar followed him, and he purchased peace by the payment of an indemnity of 1,000,000 *muzaffaris* of Gujarāt, of which 600,000 went into Murtazā's treasury and 400,000 to Chingīz Khān.

Ibrāhīm changed his policy at the same time, and with some reason began to regard 'Alī 'Ādil Shāh's southern conquests as a more real and present danger than the menace to Bīdar. Sayyid Shāh Mīrzā, his envoy, was authorized to conclude an alliance with Murtazā and to offer a subsidy of 20,000 *hūns* daily for any army invading the kingdom of Bījāpur, and an agent from Venkatādri promised a contribution of 900,000 *hūns* towards the expenses of a war on 'Alī. Sayyid Shāh Mīrzā found Chingīz Khān inaccessible to a bribe of 200,000 *hūns*, to be paid for a guarantee that Murtazā should be restrained from attacking Bīdar, and revenged himself by compassing his destruction. He found a willing confederate in Husain, the king's vile favourite, whom the minister had severely punished for some insolence, and who warned his master that Chingīz Khān was scheming to establish his independence in Berar, and, when the king scouted the malicious accusation, appealed for corroboration to Sayyid Shāh Mīrzā. The envoy, by ingeniously marshalling some specious evidence, persuaded the king of his minister's guilt, and Murtazā caused his faithful servant to be poisoned. He died in 1575, leaving a letter protesting his innocence and commending to his ungrateful master the foreigners in his service. His innocence was established after his death, and his master, overcome with grief and shame, expelled the envoy from his court and withdrew from affairs, on the ground that God had withheld from him the faculty of discriminating between truth and false-hood, and of executing righteous judgment, but his infatuation for the worthless Husain remained unchanged. The administration of the kingdom fell into the hands of Salābat Khān the Circassian and Sayyid Murtazā of Sabzavār.

Another pretender, styling himself Fīrūz 'Imād Shāh, arose in Berar, but was captured and put to death by Sayyid Murtazā, who was appointed to the government of the province. The Deccan was, however, almost immediately disturbed by Akbar's move-ments, which appeared to menace it. He left Āgra in 1576 on his annual pilgrimage to Ajmer, and in February, 1577, sent a force into Khāndesh to punish Raja 'Alī Khān, who, having succeeded his brother, Muhammad II, had withheld payment of tribute. Murtazā took the field and Berar was placed in a state of defence, one of the officers employed there being Akbar's rebellious kinsman, Muzaffar Husain Mīrzā, but Raja 'Alī Khān paid the tribute, the imperial troops were withdrawn, and the danger passed. The rest-less and turbulent Muzaffar Husain Mīrzā turned against those who had befriended him and attempted to make himself master of Berar, but Sayyid Murtazā defeated him at Anjangāon[1] and he fled into Khāndesh, where Raja 'Alī Khān seized him and surrendered him to Akbar.

The favourite Husain, who received the title of Sāhib Khān, became involved in a bitter quarrel with Husain Khān Turshīzī, one of the Foreign nobles in Berar, and shortly afterwards aroused the wrath of the whole of the Foreign party by his treatment of Mīr Mahdī, a Sayyid of the family to which the Shāhs of Persia belonged. After an unsuccessful attempt to abduct his daughter he attacked and captured his house and slew him. Dreading the vengeance of the Foreigners, he persuaded the king that they were conspiring to depose him, and to raise to the throne his son Husain, and many of the party, perceiving that they were suspected, left Ahmadnagar and retired to Golconda or Bījāpur, or to Berar, where they entered the service of Sayyid Murtazā Sabzavārī. A massacre of those who remained took place at Ahmadnagar, and the favourite endeavoured to persuade the king to order a general massacre throughout the kingdom, and especially in Berar, the Foreigners' stronghold, but even Murtazā was able to understand that such a measure was beyond his power, and that if it were possible it would

---

[1] In 21° 9′ N. and 77° 21′ E.

destroy the military strength of his kingdom, and Sāhib Khān, resenting his master's refusal to comply with his wishes, fled by night, with 3000 horse, towards Parenda. He was pursued and overtaken, but the infatuated king refused to punish him, and he sulked, and would not be reconciled until his master promised to capture Bīdar and appoint him to its government, and to cause Sayyid Murtazā and the Foreigners of Berar to be massacred when they joined the royal army.

Murtazā, by some means, persuaded Ibrāhīm Qutb Shāh to aid him in his design against Bīdar, and to send a contingent to join the small army of 20,000 horse destined for the enterprise, but 'Alī Barīd Shāh succeeded in obtaining, on humiliating conditions, the assistance of 'Alī Ādil Shāh. He was the owner of two handsome eunuchs, the possession of whom 'Alī 'Ādil Shāh had long coveted in vain, but their surrender was now made a condition of assistance, and he was obliged to comply. The assistance given by 'Alī to Bīdar was a violation of the treaty between Bījāpur and Ahmad- nagar, but Murtazā was compelled to raise the siege and endeavour- ed in vain to allay his favourite's resentment of the failure to fulfil the promise made to him. Sāhib Khān left the royal army during its retreat and retired to his fief, plundering and slaying his master's subjects on his way. He issued decrees in the regal manner, but Murtazā, in his infatuation, would take no steps against him, and mourned, in seclusion, his estrangement, until it began to be rumoured that the king was dead.

Burhān-ud-dīn, Murtazā's brother, had been confined in the fortress of Lohogarh, where he had married the daughter of his gaoler, Jūjār Khān, who released him and led him towards Ahmad- nagar, with a view to placing him on the throne. The capital became the goal of a race, which was won by the king, who, on his arrival, mounted an elephant and rode through the streets to con- vince his subjects that he still lived, but his brother was no more than three leagues distant when he entered the city, and on June 7, 1579, he marched out and defeated him, and Burhān fled to Bījāpur.

Murtazā would not take the field against his rebellious favourite, but ordered Sayyid Murtazā of Subzavār to take him alive or expel him from the kingdom. The foreign officers joyfully accepted the task and, having induced Sāhib Khān to receive them stabbed him to death and reported to the king that he had attacked them and had been slain in the combat that ensued. Murtazā mourned his favourite, while his subjects rejoiced at his death.

Alī 'Ādil Shāh was engaged, after the failure of his attempt to capture Bālkonda, in hostilities with the Marāthā officers who had played him false, and were now settled in the neighbourhood of Vijayanagar. Military operations against them were unsuccessful, and the king, not without difficulty, persuaded them to visit him at Bījāpur, where he blinded one of their leaders and put the rest to death with torture.

In November, 1579, 'Alī 'Ādil Shāh, who was childless, made Ibrāhīm, the son of his brother Tahmāsp, his heir, and on April 9, 1580, met his death. The two eunuchs from Bīdar felt their dishonour deeply, and the unfortunate creature first selected for presentation resented, with a spirit which demands respect, the proposals made to him, and, drawing a dagger which he had concealed about his person, inflicted on the king a mortal wound. He and his fellow were, of course, murdered, and the monster who had so richly deserved his fate is bewailed by Muslim historians as a martyr.

'Alī Barīd Shāh died in 1579, immediately after the raising of the siege of Bīdar, and was succeeded by his son, Ibrāhīm Barīd Shāh.

Ibrāhīm 'Ādil Shāh II was but nine years of age when he succeeded to the throne, and his education became the charge of Chānd Bībī, the widow of 'Alī I and sister of Murtazā Nizām Shāh, but the regency was assumed by Kāmil Khān the Deccani, who slighted her and treated her with disrespect. Chānd Bībī, a high-spirited woman had recourse to another Deccani, Hājī Kishvar Khān, son of that Kamāl Khān who had perished in Ismā'īl's reign. Kishvar Khān compelled Kāmil Khān to flee from the citadel, and in attempting to make his escape from Bījāpur he was intercepted and beheaded.

Bījāpur's troubles were Ahmadnagar's opportunity, and Salābat Khān sent an army to besiege Naldrug and induced Ibrāhīm Qutb Shāh to supply a contingent of 8000 horse, but committed a serious error in giving the command of the expedition to Bihzād-ul-Mulk, an inexperienced countryman of his own, to whom the veteran, Sayyid Murtazā, commanding the army of Berar, found himself subordinate. The interests of his king were of course, sacrificed to his private resentment, and he not only connived at the discomfiture of the army of Ahmadnagar, but cherished ever after the bitterest animosity against Salābat Khān.

Hājī Kishvar Khān sent from Bījāpur a force which intercepted and put to flight the contingent coming from Golconda and 'Ain-ul-

Mulk Kan'ānī, commanding the army sent to Naldrug, fell on the
enemy near Dhārāseo[1] just before dawn, when Bihzād-ul-Mulk
was still drinking. He and his boon companions displayed personal
courage, but the army was routed and fled towards the camp of
Sayyid Murtazā, who rejoiced in his rival's discomfiture and ordered
a retreat.

The success bred strife among the victors. Kishvar Khān
demanded the 150 elephants taken, and the officers in the field
resolved to compel him to relinquish the regency, but the Foreigners
and the Africans quarrelled over the reversion of the post, the
former demanding the reinstatement of Sayyid Mustafā Ardistānī
and the latter the appointment of one of their own number. They
parted in anger, 'Ain-ul-Mulk and the Foreigners returning to their
fiefs and the Africans marching to Bījāpur.

Kishvar Khān removed Sayyid Mustafā by assassination and
rendered himself odious to all parties in the state; and Salābat
Khān again sent an army from Ahmadnagar to besiege Naldrug,
but entrusted the command on this occasion to Sayyid Murtazā
Sabzavārī, to whose assistance Muhammad Qulī Qutb Shāh, who
had succeeded his father in Golconda on June 6, 1580, led a contingent of 20,000 horse.

No relief could be sent to Naldrug, but the fortress was strong
and its garrison faithful, and the besiegers suffered heavy losses.
The officer in command resisted all attempts to sap his fidelity and
rejected with scorn offers of wealth and high rank at Ahmadnagar.

Matters were going from bad to worse at Bījāpur. None resented more than Chānd Bībī the murder of the faithful Sayyid,
and Kishvar Khān attempted to carry things with a high hand,
and deported her to the fortress of Satāra, but his unpopularity
increased daily, and curses and abuse followed him as he rode
through the streets. The African nobles, Ikhlās Khān, Dilāvar
Khān, and Hamīd Khān assumed a menacing attitude and he left
the city with the young king on the pretext of a hunting tour, but
permitted him to return to the city and fled to Ahmadnagar,
whence, being ill-received there, he continued his flight to Golconda, where he was slain by a native of Ardistān in revenge for
his murder of Sayyid Mustafa.

Ikhlās Khān assumed the regency, but Chānd Bībī returned
from Satāra, dismissed him, and appointed Afzal Khān Shīrāzī in
his place. The Africans were, however, too strong for her, slew
Afzal Khān, and expelled the leading Foreigners from the city.

---

[1] Now Osmanābād, in 18° 11' N. and 76° 3' E.

Ikhlās Khān summoned 'Ain-ul-Mulk from his fief with the object of imprisoning or removing him, but he brought his whole contingent to the capital, seized the African nobles when they came out to meet him, and led them as prisoners through the streets, but was stricken with sudden panic by a rumour that the royal guards were about to rise on their behalf, and fled with his troops to Belgaum, leaving his prisoners, who were released and restored to power.

These disorders encouraged the army besieging Naldrug to advance on Bījāpur, and when it appeared before the walls no more than two or three thousand troops could be assembled for the defence of the city, but within a few days the Foreign nobles arrived from their fiefs with 600,000 men. Even in this extremity they would not make common cause with the Africans, but remained without the city, while 'Ain-ul-Mulk Kan'ānī and Ānkas Khān joined Sayyid Murtazā Sabzavārī. This was not treachery according to the code of the Deccan, but merely a justifiable precaution on the part of the leaders to ensure the ascendency of their party. Their apparent defection convinced the people that the Africans could not save the city, and the Africans furnished the only example of self-denying patriotism to be found in the history of this strife of factions by tendering their resignation to Chānd Bībī. The Foreigners of Bījāpur had, for the moment, gained their end. Marāthā and Canarese troops, skilled in the guerrilla warfare of the Deccan, were summoned to the aid of the beleaguered city, and 'Ain-ul-Mulk easily persuaded the Foreigners of Ahmadnagar and Golconda to retire before their armies were starved. The army of Golconda, which occupied Gulbarga during its retreat, was pursued and defeated, but that of Ahmadnagar retired unmolested.

The retirement of the enemy revived the strife of factions. Ikhlās Khān attacked Dilāvar Khān, the leader of the moderate party among the Africans, in the citadel, but was deserted by all his officers and captured and blinded by his rival, who became supreme in the state. Shāh Abu-'l-Hasan was blinded and shortly afterwards put to death, and the Shiah religion was suppressed and persecuted.

Dilāvar Khān remained in power from 1582 to 1590, and though he established the Sunni religion in Bījāpur he sought peace with the Shiah kingdoms, and endeavoured to secure it by means of matrimonial alliances. Ibrāhīm II married a princess of Golconda, and his sister Khadīja was given in marriage to Husain, son and heir of Murtazā Nizām Shāh, but this alliance bred nothing but strife, and the princess of Bījāpur was neglected until her brother, by invading Ahmadnagar and besieging the fortress of Ausa, compelled Murtazā to celebrate her marriage with Husain.

Murtazā, whose behaviour had always given indications of insanity, entirely lost his reason. He attempted the life of his son Husain by setting fire to his bedclothes, but the prince escaped, and shortly afterwards, on June 14, 1588, put his father to death by suffocating him in a heated bath. Ibrāhīm II, who was still before Ausa, upbraided the parricide, but retired to his own dominions in accordance with the treaty which he had made with Murtazā.

Husain II was a dissolute and bloodthirsty youth who had inherited his father's malady, and his deeds of violence and dark threats so alarmed his nobles that they deposed, imprisoned, and finally murdered him, and on April 1, 1589, raised to the throne his cousin Ismā'īl, the younger son of Burhān-ud-dīn, who had fled from the wrath of his brother Murtazā and was now in the service of the emperor Akbar.

During the short reign of Ismā'īl all power in Ahmadnagar was in the hands of Jamāl Khān, a native Muslim who was followed by the Deccani party. He belonged to a sect which then, in the closing years of the tenth century of the era of the *Hijra*, had some vogue. These heretics were the *Mahdavīs*, who confidently expected the manifestation, in the year 1000 of the Islamic era, of the *Mahdī*, the twelfth *Imām*, who was to establish Islam throughout the world. Jamāl Khān disestablished the state religion and persecuted both orthodox Sunnis and heterodox Shiahs.

Ibrāhīm II, moved by these innovations, and by the desire of liberating his widowed sister, to intervene in Ahmadnagar, sent Dilāvar Khān to invade that kingdom, and Jamāl Khān purchased peace by the surrender of Khadīja and the payment of 70,000 *hūns*.

The advancement of Ismā'īl to the throne aroused his father, Burhān, to the assertion of his rights, and he sought and obtained Akbar's permission to make an attempt to gain his throne. Akbar indeed pressed upon him, to serve his own ends, the co-operation of an imperial army, but Burhān wisely declined assistance which would render him odious in the eyes of his subjects and of the other kings in the Deccan and would involve him in humiliating obligations. He believed that his subjects longed for his return, and that he had only to appear in order to be acclaimed, but a premature invasion of Berar with an insufficient force ended in his defeat and his flight into Khāndesh. Here Raja 'Alī Khān assembled his army to assist him, and secured the co-operation of Ibrāhīm II, who sent an army under Dilāvar Khān to invade Ahmadnagar from the south. Jamāl Khān first faced this danger and, having inflicted a crushing defeat on Dilāvar Khān at Dhārāseo, turned northward to meet Raja 'Alī Khān and Burhān, who had invaded the kingdom from the north.

The armies met on May 7, 1591, at Rohankhed[1], and Jamāl Khān, who had exhausted his troops by a long forced march through the burning heat, was defeated and slain. The young Ismā'īl was captured, and Burhān marched on to Ahmadnagar and took possession of his kingdom under the title of Burhān Nizām Shāh II. He re-established the Shiah religion and recalled the Foreigners, who had been ruthlessly expelled.

Dilāvar Khān's defeat had led to his downfall, and he fled from Bījāpur and entered the service of Burhān II. Ibrāhīm II protested against his employment by Burhān and demanded the restitution of 300 elephants taken at Dhārāseo. Burhan's reply was a declaration of war, and on March 15, 1592, he invaded the kingdom of Bījāpur and restored the old Hindu fort to the south of the Bhīma. A force of Marāthā cavalry sent against him cut off his supplies and compelled him to retire towards his own frontier to revictual his troops, and the army of Bījāpur followed him and inflicted a severe defeat on him. Muhammad Qulī Shāh and Raja 'Alī Khān exerted themselves to restore peace, and Ibrāhīm accepted their conditions, which obliged Burhān to superintend in person the demolition of his works at Mangalvedha.

Burhān in spite of his brother's treaty with the Portuguese, assembled, in April, 1592, an army which attacked the weakly garrisoned fortress of Chaul. The Portuguese were hard pressed, but defended themselves with great vigour until reinforcements arrived from their other settlements on the coast, when they assumed the offensive and carried, with a loss of only twenty-nine men, a fortress held by the Muslims on the opposite bank of the creek, slaying ten or twelve thousand of Burhān's army. Farhād Khān, who commanded the Muslims, was captured, with his wife and daughter. His wife was ransomed, but he and his daughter were converted to Christianity and went to Portugal.

This disastrous defeat was attributed in great measure to the treachery of the officers, who, having learned that Burhān was engaged in intrigues with their wives and daughters at Ahmadnagar, betrayed their trust. They belonged to the Deccani faction and their master rejoiced in their defeat.

[1] In 20° 37' N. and 76° 11' E.

In 1594 Ismā'īl, the elder brother of Ibrāhīm II, rose in rebellion, and Burhān, who had assembled an army of Foreigners to attack the Portuguese, marched to his aid, but Ismā'īl was defeated and slain before Burhān had advanced beyond Parenda, and the army of Bījāpur, freed from its preoccupation with the rebel, attacked him and once more defeated him. He was in weak health, and this fresh disaster threw him into a state of nervous irritability. He designated as his heir his elder son, Ibrāhīm. whose mother had been an African, on which account his younger brother, Ismā'īl, had been preferred to him. Ismā'īl was still attached to the Mahdavī faith and the Deccani faction, and when his father put him to death for these offences the Deccanis with the army in the field suspected the Foreigners of complicity in the crime, and began to devise a fresh massacre of their opponents, but the Foreigners left the army and joined the king, who had already reached Ahmadnagar. Ikhlās Khān led the Deccanis back to the capital with the object of dethroning Burhān, but the king attacked him and drove him back to Parenda. The exertion and the heat were too much for a frame enfeebled by excess, disease, and mental anxiety, and on April 28, 1595, Burhān died.

Miyān Manjhū the Deccani, who became minister on the accession of Ibrāhīm Nizām Shāh, granted an amnesty to Ikhlās Khān and his faction, and Ikhlās Khān returned to the city and, although he was a member of the Deccani party and was under an obligation to the minister, arrayed himself against him. He persuaded the dissolute young king to declare war on Bījāpur, and, despite Miyān Manjhū's efforts to avoid actual hostilities, the armies met and Ibrāhīm was slain. His death was the signal for anarchy in the kingdom. Chānd Bībī, who had returned to the home of her youth, stood forth as the champion of order and supported Ibrāhīm's infant son, Bahādur, but Ikhlās Khān produced a man named Ahmad, whom he put forward as the son of the sixth son of Burhān Nizām Shāh I, Khudābanda, who had taken refuge in Bengal, and on August 16, 1595, proclaimed him king under the title of Ahmad Nizām Shāh II. Inquiries proved him to be an impostor, but he was supported by Miyān Manjhū, and civil war broke out.

The Africans and Deccanis who supported Ahmad soon quarrelled, and the former proclaimed as king, under the title of Motī Shāh, a child of unknown origin, and Miyān Manjhū appealed for help to Sultān Murād, Akbar's second son, who was now governor of Gujarāt.

Akbar, resenting the refusal of Burhān II to swear fealty to him, had already decided to attack the kingdom of Ahmadnagar, and the Khān Khānān in Mālwa as well as the prince in Gujarāt had been preparing for a campaign in the Deccan, and on receiving Miyān Manjhū's appeal both set their armies in motion.

Fighting continued at Ahmadnagar and Miyān Manjhū, having gained a success over the Africans, repented too late of his appeal to the prince, who, with the Khān Khānān, arrived before the city on December 26.

There were now four parties in the kingdom. (1) Miyān Manjhū and the Deccanis, acknowledging the pretender Ahmad II, were on the Bījāpur frontier, seeking help from Ibrāhīm II ; (2) Āhang Khān[1] and Habashī Khān, the Africans, acknowledging the third son of Burhān Nizām Shāh I, the old prince 'Alī, whom they had summoned from Bījāpur, were also on the southern frontier, with the same object ; (3) Ikhlās Khān, at the head of another African faction, acknowledging the child Motī Shāh, was in the neighbourhood of Daulatābād ; and (4) Chānd Bibī with the infant king Bahādur was in Ahmadnagar. All sent envoys to Ibrāhīm II who, perturbed by a peril which menaced the whole of the Deccan, begged them to sink their differences and to present a united front to the invader, and assembled, under the command of the eunuch, Suhail Khān, an army of 25,000 horse, besides a contingent of 6000 horse contributed by Muhammad Qulī Qutb Shāh.

Raja 'Alī Khān of Khāndesh had been obliged to join the imperial army, but his sympathies lay with the kingdoms of the Deccan, and his secret messages to the defenders of Ahmadnagar encouraged them in their resistance.

For this reason, and also owing to the jealousy and the disputes of Sultān Murād and the Khān Khānān, the siege progressed but slowly. Ikhlās Khān marched from Daulatābād with 10,000 horse to relieve the city, but was defeated at Paithan, on the Godāvarī. Āhang Khān then marched from the southern frontier with 7,000 horse, accompanied by Prince 'Alī and his son, Prince Murtazā, but was so stoutly opposed by the Khān Khānān's troops that he and the younger prince led no more than 400 horsemen into the city, after cutting their way through the enemy. The rest of his force, with the aged Prince 'Alī, fled back to the frontier.

Sultān Murād was much perturbed by the menace of the armies of Bījāpur and Golconda, which had reached Naldrug, and endeavoured to hasten the fall of the city by mining the defences,

1 Also described as Abhang Khān.

but treachery was at work, and secret information enabled the defenders to remove the charges by countermining, and render the mines harmless. One, however, remained intact and this, when exploded, killed many of the garrison and destroyed fifty yards of the curtain between two bastions, but the breach was so gallantly defended by Chānd Bībī in person that the assailants were repulsed and night permitted the defenders to repair the damage.

When Suhail Khān, responding to the urgent appeals of Chānd Bībī and encouraged by a treacherous message from the Khān Khānān, whose chief concern was to deprive the prince of the credit of capturing the city, was within thirty miles Sultān Murād sent an envoy to Chānd Bībī, offering to raise the siege in return for the cession of Berar. The garrison was suffering from famine, but it was with difficulty that the noble queen could be induced to save the capital by the surrender of the province. After some hesitation, she consented, and early in April the imperial army withdrew to take possession of its new conquest.

On the retirement of the besiegers Bahādur Shāh was proclaimed king Miyān Manjhū attempted to renew the civil war, but was summoned, with Ahmad II, to Bījāpur by Ibrāhīm, who took them both into the service.

The arrogance and oppressive behaviour of the new minister, Muhammad Khān, so alienated the nobles and enfeebled the state that Chānd Bībī was obliged to appeal for assistance to Ibrāhīm II, who sent a force under Suhail Khān, instructing him to place himself entirely at her disposal. Muhammad Khān, after being besieged for four months in Ahmadnagar, sent a message to the Khān Khānān, begging him to come to his aid, but the garrison on discovering this act of treason, arrested him and delivered him to Chānd Bībī, who appointed Āhang Khān lieutenant of the kingdom in his place.

War soon broke out again between the empire and Ahmadnagar. There were complaints on both sides. Gāwīl and Narnāla, the great fortresses of Berar, were still held by officers of Ahmadnagar. On the other hand the imperial troops had occupied the Pāthrī district, which, they plausibly contended, was part of Berar.

Āhang Khān again appealed to Bījāpur, and Suhail Khān was sent to his aid, but the armies of Bījāpur and Golconda were utterly routed by the Khān Khānān in the neighbourhood of Sonpet, on the Godāvarī, after a battle lasting for two days, on February 9, 1597.

Āhang Khān quarrelled with Chānd Bībī and besieged her in the fort of Ahmadnagar. The disputes between Murād and the

30

Khān Khānān continued until the latter was summoned to court and the former died of drink at Shāhpur, near Bālāpur in Berar. Shaikh Abu-'l-Fazl was sent to the Deccan, but could effect little, and Āhang Khān gained a success over the imperial officer who held Bīr.

In 1599 Akbar's youngest son, Dāniyāl, and Khān Khānān were appointed to the Deccan, and the emperor followed them and encamped at Burhānpur while his army besieged Asīr. The prince and the Khān Khānān advanced towards Ahmadnagar, and Āhang Khān, raising the siege, marched to meet them at Jeūr, but the sight of the imperial army approaching him overcame his resolution, and he fled in terror to Junnār, leaving Ahmadnagar to its fate.

Chānd Bībī at length lost heart. Summoning Jīta Khān, a eunuch who had been her confidant since Āhang Khān had turned against her, she sought his advice. He replied it was for her to take a decision, and she confessed that she could suggest nothing but a surrender on terms. Jīta Khān ran out crying that she had turned traitress, and wished to surrender the fortress to the Mughul, and a turbulent mob rushed into the inner apartments of the palace and slew her.

Dāniyāl and the Khān Khānān appeared before the city, and the mob who had found courage to murder their queen had little left for the defence of their homes. The defences were destroyed by mines and the place was carried by assault. The young king, Bahādur, was sent as a state prisoner to Gwalior and Ahmadnagar was garrisoned by a force of imperial troops.

CHAPTER XVIII

HINDU STATES IN SOUTHERN INDIA. A.D. 1000—1565

INDIA, south of the Vindhyas, always exhibited a tendency politically to fall' into two well-marked divisions, the boundaries of which varied at different periods of history. About the year A.D. 1000 this tendency was working itself out by a new shifting of the powers under two large political divisions. The kingdom of the Chālukyas, called for distinction the later Chālukyas or even the Chālukyas of Kalyāni, had its capital at Kalyāni in the Nizam's dominions. The Chālukyas may be regarded as a Deccan power whose original territory comprised the central and southern divisions of the Bombay Presidency and the western half of the Nizām's dominions. Along the Arabian Sea coast their territory extended well past Goa and varied from time to time in regard to its exact southernmost limit. In the north their territory extended even to Gujārat. But the simultaneous rise to power of the Paramaras of Mālwa kept them limited on this frontier to the region south of the Narbada, if not the Vindhya mountains themselves. The really uncertain and therefore the changing frontier was the eastern and southern. At the best, this frontier stretched so far as to take into the Chālukyan territory, the modern State of Mysore, and from there continued along the Tungabhadra till it joins the Krishna, proceeding north-eastwards through the middle of the Nizām's dominions across to the east of Nāgpur in the Central Provinces. The most vulnerable part of this frontier was the part extending along the Krishna from its junction with the Tunga-bhadra almost to its source, so that the region between the rivers Krishna and Tungabhadra constituted the bone of contention between the rival powers throughout the eleventh century.

The southern power contemporary with the Chālukyas was the great dynasty of the Cholas, coming into notice almost a century earlier than their rivals. They slowly forged their way up despite the crushing weight of the imperial power of the Rāshtrakūtas of the Deccan. When these were overthrown by the Chālukyas about the end of the tenth century the Cholas had put themselves on a footing of some permanence and power. The advent of Rājarāja. the Great, who was to have succeeded almost at the same time as the Rāshtrakūtas were overthrown, introduced a new spirit into the activities of the Cholas. They took advantage of the change of dynasties and consequent neglect of the southern frontier to go forward and occupy the territory of the Gangas by overthrowing them finally. This gave them southern and by far the greatest division of the territory of what is now the Mysore State, from which as a salient, they could carry on their war against the Chālukyas with advantage. This accession to the Chola territory took place in A.D. 1000 or 1001.

When the dynasty revolution was developing in the territory of the Rāshtrakūtas, the Eastern Chālukyas, whose territory included the part of the Madras Presidency north of Madras, had their own domestic troubles, which do not appear to have abated very much by the success of their cousins in the Deccan. Rājarāja took advantage of the opportunity and came to terms with them, supporting Vimalāditya on the throne and sealing the treaty by the marriage of his own daughter Kundavvai to the Chālukya prince. This treaty proved of a lasting character, and the Cholas had no trouble on this frontier except when outside powers like the Chālukyas tried to make a diversion. When Rājarāja's rule came to an end in about A.D. 1016 his frontier extended so far as to take into his territory the whole of the plain districts of the Mysore country and outside the State of Mysore, with the Tungabhadra marking the frontier. His son who ascended the throne nominally in A.D. 1011 and actually in 1016 had already seen considerable service under his father. He proceeded from this base to beat the Chālukyas back beyond the line of the Krishna, taking Banavāsi, Mālkhed and Kollippākkai, which were the key to the possession of the debatable land of the tract between the Krishna and the Tungabhadra. That done he could feel that he had reached a definitive frontier between the two powers and marched thence to invade the territory of Kalinga, extending from the mouths of the Ganges southwest and southwards along the coast to not far from the mouth of the Godāvarī. This invasion seems to have been undertaken with a view to bringing the Kalingas to such a sense of subordination to him that they might refrain from molesting him in his eastward expedition across the seas to the Malaya peninsula and the island of Sumatra, where he had to fight against the rising imperial power of Srī Bhoja in behalf of the various Tamil settlements in the island and along the coast of the peninsula opposite[1]. The wars of his successors had no further object in view than to maintain this frontier. They sometimes carried raids into the

[1] "Overseas Conquests of Dāiendra Chola" : *The Madras Christian College Magazine* for April 1921.

interior of the Chālukya territory even as far as Kolhāpur itself, where one of the Cholas claims to have planted a pillar of victory. Notwithstanding these occasional raids the frontier remained where Rājendra the Gangaikonda Chola had actually fixed it.

These powerful dynasties, the Cholas and the Chālukyas, were well matched in resources both material and personal ; each had a succession of capable rulers, and used its resources with a view to the attainment of a frontier which would put an end to perpetual wars. Further wars therefore resolved themselves into a fight for the possession of the Doāb and the State of Mysore. This war was ultimately decided in favour of the Chālukyas under their greatest ruler and his equally great contemporary among the Cholas. These two rulers were both of them usurpers in a sense, and used the power that they acquired to get a final settlement of the long-standing frontier problem. Vikramāditya VI, the second son of Sōmēsvara Āhavamalla, overthrew his brother, also a Sōmēsvara, after a short reign and ascended the throne in 1076. . His contemporary, the Chālukya-Chola Kulottunga, ascended the Chola throne in 1070. He was a grandson by the daughter of Rājendra, the Gangaikonda Chola, and was the legitimate ruler of the territory of the Eastern Chālukyas. He seems to have found this too small a patrimony, and would succeed to the imperial Chola throne and not remain content with his own territory. What exactly his title to this was, except through his mother, is not made clear. He seems to have bided his time and taken advantage of the machinations of his contemporary Vikramāditya to place himself on the throne of the Chālukyas. Sōmēsvara the father died in 1069, and Sōmēsvara II, the elder son, succeeded. Vikramāditya already held the position of viceroy of Banavāsi which included in it the wardenship of the southern marches of the Chālukya territory. While still viceroy of this province he concluded a treaty with the contemporary Chola, Vīra Rājendra, whose daughter he married. Vīra Rājendra died and was succeeded by his son, the brother-in-law of Vikramāditya, and Kulottunga found an opportunity of overthrowing this new ruler and of occupying the Chola throne. Vikramāditya was baulked in his ambition by this *coup* of his contemporary, and had to wait for yet another five years before he could put his own plans into execution. Both of them ruled for about half a century, Kulottunga's reign lasting from 1070 to 1118 at least, and that of Vikramāditya from 1076 to 1128. During the first decade of their rule Vikramāditya's efforts were so far successful that a considerable part of the territory of Mysore passed into his hands, and this progress continued till Chola rule in Mysore was put an end to by A D. 1117, about the end of the reign of Kulottunga Chola[1]. The chieftain who was responsible for this was the feudatory of the Chālukya emperor who laid the foundations of the greatness of the Hoysalas. The eleventh century for south India may therefore be regarded as the century of struggle for the fixing of a definitive frontier between the two contending empires.

The recurring frontier wars notwithstanding, this was a period of very successful administration both in the territory of the Cholas and that of the Chālukyas. It is the records of these two dynasties that enable us to see at their best the highly organised and systematic administration that obtained in the whole region. The civil administration was carried on largely by local agency, the central government retaining only oversight and control in cases of dispute. The ordinary routine of the administration was carried on by village and town organisations and as far as we can see from this distance of time, this administration was carried on with great success. The main duty of the imperial rulers was to assure to the people protection from external enemies and internal disturbances. Except on the fighting frontiers the whole country seems to have enjoyed this peace and protection in a very large measure. Large public works were undertaken, and considerable stimulus was given to learning and religion, in regard to the latter of which it was a period of great ferment. In spite of the financial enthusiasm of some of the religious leaders the movements were kept well under control and proceeded smoothly to work themselves out. With the passing away of these two rulers at the end of the first quarter of the twelfth century, the usual process of disintegration sets in. The kingdom of the Chālukyas underwent a dismemberment before the end of the century, and that of the Cholas continued almost intact until about the middle of the next century when it was overthrown by the revival of the Pāndyan state of Madura, which had been early reduced to subjection by the Cholas. At the period of the Muhammadan invasions of south India therefore, the political division of the country was very different from what it was in the eleventh century. In the working out of this transformation the feudatory dynasties of the Chālukyas played a very important part, and among these the chief distinction must be given to the Hoysalas of Dvārasamudra.

In the recesses of the Western Ghāts there is a small village, called Angadi since the days of Achyutarāya of Vijayanagar[2], in

---

[1] *Ancient India*, Ch. VI.   [2] *Ep. Car.* VI, p. 14 and v, Bl. 197.

the Mudegare taluk of the modern district of Kadur in Mysore.
It apparently derived its importance from its situation at the point
where the two roads from the Mysore State meet the road over the
Ghāts from Mangalore. These two roads are of considerable importance from the point of view of the coffee planting industry
now, and they seem to have enjoyed the same degree of importance even in those earlier days when the trade was in other commodities for which the region has always been famous. Before the
days of the Vijayanagar king Achyuta, the place seems to have
been generally known as Vāsantikāpura, apparently from the temple
of the village goddess now popularly called Vāsantamma, or more
formally Vāsantikādēvi. It had the alternative name Sasakapura
(hare-town) with it modern equivalent Sosevur, and it was here
that the Hoysalas had their origin.

The Hoysalas were a family of petty hill chiefs of the Western
Ghāts, and each ruler, even in the days of their highest prosperity
styled himself, "the man among the hill chiefs" (Malaparol-Ganda).
The first reference to the Hoysalas in inscriptions is found in a
Chola record of A.D. 1007. The first member of the family of any
note was Nripakāma, who is mentioned in 1022. The highest
achievement of this chief was the assistance that he rendered to
the chief of Banavāsi against his enemies, who are described by
name. The origin of his epithet, 'the Base,' has not been traced,
but it probably explains the omission of his name from the later
genealogies. In a record of 1026 he is said to have been defeated
by the Kongālva feudatory of the Cholas, Rājendra Chola Prithvi
Kongālva. He is himself given the title 'Rājamalla Perumānadi'[1]
in another record, a clear indication that he was a Ganga feudatory,
who bore his overlord's title. His son was Vinayāditya[2] the first
important member of the family to figure in the records of the
suzerain power, that of the Chālukyas. The period of Nripakāma
and his son was a period of wars between the Cholas and the
Chālukyas for the possession of Mysore. It was by distinguished
service in these wars that these chieftains rose to importance.
Vināyaditya's full style is Tribhuvana Hoysala, and later genealogies generally begin with his name. His headquarters were yet at
Sasakapura, while in the days of his grandson, his successor, the
capital was shifted to Belūr[3]. In the records of the great Chālukya
ruler Sōmēsvara Āhavamalla 1044—1069, Vināyaditya's name occurs
as the Mahāmandalēsvara of Gangavādi, 96,000. This vast province,

[1]*Ep. Car.* vi, Mg. 19.   [2]*Ibid.* v, Ag. 141.
[3]*Ibid.* vi, Cm. 160 and iv, Ng. 32.

which included almost the whole of the modern districts of Mysore, Bangalore and Kolar, was a province of the Cholas at the time, and was divided by them into three districts. The appointment of a Chālukya governor over this province at the time, with a capital far removed from the region itself, means that the governorship was the wardenship of the southern marches, where there would be ample opportunity for achieving distinction in war. It was from this struggle for the possession of what now constitutes the plateau of Mysore that the Hoysalas emerged into importance and succeeded ultimately in carving out for themselves from the dismembered Chālukya kingdom a state which became the most influential power in the succeeding period of South Indian history.

Reverting to the history of this struggle between the kingdoms, the Cholas had the upper hand to begin with, and carried all before them in the days of Rājarāja and his son, leaving to the Chālukyas the possession of only Banavāsi, one of the three divisions of what is now the State of Mysore. It has already been stated that Rājendra held possession of important fortresses on this frontier which are often described as 'the key to the south,' or 'the bolt against the south.' He seems to have inflicted a defeat upon his contemporary Chālukya Jayasimha, but does not appear to have pressed the enemy farther. When he died, in the forty fourth year of his reign, he was succeeded by three of his sons, one after another. His immediate successor carried the war into his enemy's country, as far north as Kolhāpur itself. By this time the Chālukya territories were under the rule of Sōmēsvara Āhavamalla (or 'the Great in War'). Sōmēsvara was able to hold up the Chola army at Koppa on the Krishna, a few miles south east of Kolhāpur, and after a strenuous fight the day went against the Cholas, Rājādhirāja falling in battle. His younger brother, who brought up reinforcements, retrieved the fortunes of the day, and claims to have set up a pillar of victory in Kolhāpur itself. The war continued between Sōmēsvara and the next Chola brother who succeeded these two with varying fortunes. In the course of one of the wars Sōmēsvara seems to have entrusted the southern division of his kingdom, the most vulnerable at the time, to his second and most talented son, who afterwards ascended the throne as Vikramāditya. This Prince did his utmost to maintain his position in the south and carried the war into the Chola country itself, but was checked on the banks of the Tungabhadra by the energetic Chola ruler Vīra Rājēndra. Vikramāditya tried diplomacy when war failed, and seems to have created a diversion against Vīra Rājēndra on the eastern Chālukya frontier. He ultimately succeeded in coming to an understanding with Vīra Rājēndra in regard to the debatable frontier, the treaty being sealed by the marriage of Prince Vikramāditya with Vīra Rājēndra's daughter. While these negotiations were still in progress, the Chālukya king Sōmēsvara had an attack of a malignant fever and died, in obedience to religious advice, by drowning himself in the Tungabhadra. His eldest son Sōmēsvara succeeded to the throne. At the same time the other enterprising Chālukya prince Kulot-tunga attempted to seize the Chola throne. Records bearing on this affair are laconic, merely stating that Vikramāditya entered the Chola capital Gangaikonda-Solapuram, a new foundation of Rājēn-dra, the Gangaikonda Chola, and placed on the throne his brother-in-law, who, however, was immediately deposed by his subjects. Whether Kulottunga, the Chālukya, prince, had any share in this is not known; but that he actually occupied the throne and suc-ceeded to the kingdom is undoubted. His father died seven years before this at Rājahmundry, his ancestral capital. There is nothing to show that Kulottunga ever occupied his father's throne at Rāja-mandri. He seems to have remained in the territory of the Cholas in the region round Kānchi, and let others govern the Eastern Chālukya territory, perhaps in his name. Kulottunga occupied the Chola throne from 1070 to 1118 at least, and his contemporary Vikramāditya ascended the throne six years later and continued to rule till 1128.

In all these transactions between the Cholas and the Chālukyas, both diplomatic and warlike, the Governors of Gangavādi and Nolambavādi have had their share. While inscriptions of Vīra Rājēndra claim for him the credit of having granted to Vikra-māditya, the Chālukya prince, the *Yauvarājya* or the position of heir-apparent to the Chālukya kingdom, Hoysala inscriptions of 1100 claim for Ereyanga the son of Vinayāditya the Hoysala governor of Gangavādi, that he caused Tribhuvanamalla's (Vikra-māditya's) eleder brother to sheathe his sword. His father-in law Irukkapāla similarly lays claim to having defeated Bhuvanaikamalla (the Chālukya king Sōmēsvara), and gave the kingdom to Vikra-māditya whose right-hand Ereyanga, the Hoysala prince, is described to have been. It becomes thus clear that, notwithstanding the statements in Bilhana's Vikramānka-dēvacharitam, Vikramāditya planned and carried out the usurpation, and, in this enterprise, he had the assistance of the southern chiefs Ereyanga seems to have taken part in the distant northern expeditions of the Chālukyas, as he claims a victory at Dhār in Malva, then under the successors of the great Bhoja. Ereyanga obviously died before his father and left three sons by his wife Echaladēvi, the daughter of the Nolamba chief referred to already.

Vinayāditya was succeeded in the governorship of Gangavādi 96,000, by his eldest grandson Ballāla I in 1101. His capital was at Bēlūr, with which the Hoysala dynasty was throughout the period of their rule associated, though Dvārasamudra became later on an alternative capital. The territorry under Ballāla I is given the same boundaries as that of his grandfather, and he is said to have paid a visit to the family capital Sosevur. In A.D. 1103 he made a re-grant of Sindagere to Mariāne *Dandanāyaka* as wages for wet-nursing his three daughters whom Ballāla married in the same pavilion at Bēlūr. The next year he led an expedition against the Changālva chiefs whose territory lay in the Hole-Narasipur taluk of the Hassan district of Mysore. He conducted a successful expedition the same year with his younger brother Vishnu into the neighbouring Pāndya dominions of Nolambavādi, and had to repulse an invader, Jagad-dēva, who had penetrated as far as Dvārasamudra. An inscription of Ballāla's time is dated in Chālukya Vikramāditya's era (K. 55).

Ballāla I was succeeded by his younger brother Bitti-dēva (Vishnu-dēva), better known by his later titles Vishnuvardhana. He was the founder of Hoysala greatness, and his titles are carried down in later inscriptions not only to his successors generally, some of them posthumously to his predecessors. His name is found mentioned for the first time in a record of 1100, associated with that of his brother Ballāla I. Records of Ballāla I do not go beyond 1105, at which date or soon after Vishnu must have ascended the throne. His real exploits however begin ten years later, according to the inscriptions, making it possible that Ballāla continued his reign even for some time after 1106. Notwithstanding all previous claims to conquest, Vishnu's signal achievements consist of the conquest of Gangavādi and the partial conquest of Nolambavādi, which together constitute his claim to greatness, as among one of the greatest of Vikramāditya's *Mahāmandalsēvaras*. A number of generals claim the conquest of Gangavādi, and inscriptions generally make a great deal of these conquests. Vishnu even assumes two special titles from this conquest namely, 'Vīra-Ganga' and 'Talakādu-gonda' (taker of Talakād). This conquest of Gangavādi took place before 1117. Vishnu took the province after overthrowing the Chola generals Adiyama, Dāmōdara and

Narasimhavarma. This conquest was apparently real, as Vishnu was able to undertake a tour through the territories of Gangavādi in the course of which at the Vijayāditya-mangala (mod₊ Betman-gala) his niece, the daughter of his brother Udayāditya, died. At about the same time he carried on a successful expedition against Nolambavādi and won a victory over the Pāndya ruler of the country at Dumme, on the borderland between Shimoga and Chittal-droog districts. By the year 1117, therefore, Vishnu had become master of Gangavādi 96,000, and had made himself felt in Nolamba-vādi also. Inscriptions of Vishnu mark the year as an epoch in the history of the Hoysala power. A number of inscriptions chiefly the one at Bēlūr, inscribed on the occasion of the dedication of the temple after Vishnu had adopted the teachings of Rāmānuja, the Vaishnava apostle, give an elaborate history of his conquests and sum up his achievements previous to the date by giving his territory the boundaries of the lower Ghāt of Nangali on the east, Kongu, Chēram and Ānaimalai in the south, Bārakanūr and other Ghāts of Konkana on the west, and Sāvimalai in the north. Of these Nangali is the pass through the Eastern Ghāts six miles east of Mulhagal on the Madras-Bangalore road. Kongu and Chēram are the well-known divisions in the middle across to the west coast, and Ānaimalai is a hill in the Coimbatore district belonging to the Western Ghāts. Bārakanūr is the Bārkālūr Ghāt in the Western Ghāts. So far the boundary gives him the boundary of the modern State of Mysore on three sides. The northern boundary of Sāvi-malai has not yet been satisfactorily identified. If it is a place on the Krishna in its upper reaches it can only be regarded as an anticipation of the conquests of his grandson. A record of the year 1118 describes him as in residence at Talakād, thus indicating full possession of the Gangavādi province by him. He is said in the year 1121 to be again at his headquarters at Dvārasamudra, and it was in this year that Kētamalla, probably a merchant, built the magnificent temple dedicated to Siva under the name Vishnu-vardhana-Hoysalēsvara at Halēbīd. In the same year he made a grant, with his queen-consort and the council of five ministers, to the temple of Jayangondēsvara, obviously a Siva temple of Chola foundation.

In 1123 Vishnu is again on the banks of the Kāveri while his northern boundary is described as the Pērddore, that is, the river Krishna. In 1128 he is in his royal residence at Yādavapura (Mēlkōtte), and makes a grant from there to Mārbalatīrtha, the Saiva shrine on the Chāmundi Hill in Mysore. It was in this year

that the Chālukya king Vikramāditya died, and his great contemporary Kulottunga died about a decade earlier and was succeeded
by his son Vikrama Chola. This last seems to have carefully checked
Hoysala aggression in the south so that Vishnu had to devote
himself to acquiring territory in the north. Vikramāditya was
succeeded by his son Sōmēsvara, with the title 'Bhūlōkamalla.'
During the first year of his reign the boundaries of the Hoysala
territory are defined exactly, as before, with Sāvimalai for the
northern limit. The new succession seems to have stimulated
Vishnu's activities afresh, and this renewed activity seems to have
frightened Sōmēsvara. Even while Vikramāditya was alive this
aggressive activity of the Hoysala chieftain attracted the attention
of the king, who deputed a number of his more loyal governors,
chief among them the Kadambas of Goa and the Sinda chieftain of
Elberga, to check the rising Hoysala. The Sinda chieftain Achugi II
who like the Hoysala Ereyanga, Vishnu's father, laid claim to
having rendered valuable services to Vikramāditya in his usurpation, seems to have inflicted a check if not a defeat on Vishnu's
general Gangarāja, which constrained him to suspend activities for
some time. These were renewed after the death of the great king.
In 1130 we find the Hoysalas supreme over the whole of the present
territory of Mysore with some territory in the region of Kongu
along the foothills of the Ghāts, together with portions of the
district of Dhārwār, Nolambavādi or Eastern Mysore being in large
part still out of the Hoysala territory. Even within the narrow
limits of this territory he had enemies yet to overcome, such as the
Chengālva and Kongālva chiefs along the Western Ghats. Gangarāja
seems to have been so devoted to the Jain faith that he is given
credit for having restored all the Jain shrines destroyed during
the repeated invasions of the Cholas, and made Mysore shine like
Kōpana (Koppal in the Nizām's dominions). For some year Vishnu
was chiefly engaged in the north against the chiefs on the frontier
for the final acquisition of Banavāsi and Nolambavādi. For, in spite
of the Mysore records, inscriptions of Sōmēsvara III show a series
of governors in charge of Banavāsi, and Vīra-Pāndya is said to
have been ruling from Uchangi-durga, the province of Nolambāvadi
32,000 Chālukya records of 1137 for the first time show Vishnuvardhana to be the *Mahāmandalēsvara* in charge of Gangavādi,
Nolambavādi and Banavāsi, constituting the whole of the present
State of Mysore. This year, therefore, may be regarded as marking
an epoch in the rise of the Hoysalas to independence, and the ten
years between the death of Vikramāditya and this must have been

a period of struggle to reach this assured position[1]. Even so, Bankāpur in Dhārwār must be regarded as the northern limit of his conquests, all Hoysala statements to the contrary notwithstanding. Vishnuvardhana then must be credited with having succeeded in uniting the whole of the modern Mysore State under his rule ; but he did not venture to assume the royal dignity. During the remaining years of his life he devoted himself to securing his position on the northern frontier where things were moving fast towards disruption. He marked his accession to royal power in this year by the performance of the royal act of '*tulā-purusha*[2].' He weighed himself against gold and distributed it among Brāhmans and other deserving recipients of charitable gifts. The next year he had to repulse an invasion of Dvārasamudra by Jagad-dēva and himself laid siege to Hangal in Dhārwār thereby making it clear that his position in the north was far from certain.

In this same year, 1138, the Chālukya Sōmēsvara III died and was succeeded by his son Jagadēkamalla in the Chālukya kingdom. Vishnu renewed his aggressions, taking advantage of the new succession, but was again baulked by the activities of the loyal governors of the kingdom. His activity ceased in 1141 or soon after, and though he was virtually independent he never ventured to assume the royal title. He was succeeded by his son Vijaya Narasimha, who is generally said to have been crowned at his birth[3]. He was a child of eight at his accession, and his territory could be preserved only by the efforts of his father's generals in the struggle that followed the disruption of the Chālukya kingdom.

Vikramāditya's long reign of fifty-two years was, as has already been remarked, one of peace, except for one invasion of the Chola territory and the occasional checks that had to be administered to the rising ambitions of the Hoysala feudatory in the last years of his reign. Vikramāditya had occasionally to carry on wars across the Narbada ; but these wars were not of frequent occurrence. At his death his kingdom extended from Broach to Erode and from Mangalore to the Sītābaldī hills in the Central Provinces. This vast territory was parcelled out into a number of viceroyalties ; the Seunas or Yādavas with a capital at Sinnar near Nāsik and later at Deogiri ; the Silāharas of the northern and southern Konkan-and of Kolhāpur, and the Kadambas of Goa and Hangal. East of these were the territories of the Sindas at Elberga, of the Guttas of Guttal in Dhārwār, and of the Rattas of Saundatti in

---

[1] *Ep. Car.* Bl. 17, cf. 1136.   [2] *Ibid*, vi, Cm. 161
[3] *Ibid* v, p. xviii.

Belgaum. Then came the royal domain, namely, all the Nizām's dominions except the most easterly part, the Khammamet division, and lastly the viceroyalty in the Central Provinces with its capital at Sītābaldī[1]. This leaves out Banavāsi, Nolambavādi and Ganga-vādi under the Hoysalas, although up to the last years of Vishnu-vardhana almost, other viceroys continued to be appointed for the two former. This great kingdom passed in 1128 to his son Sōmēs-vara III, who was succeeded in 1138 by his son Pērma Jagadēka-malla who ruled till 1150. In this reign comes to notice a young man of promise whose father was governor of Tardavādi 1000, a district round Bījāpur, an alternative capital of the Chālukyas. This was Bijjala. He became governor of the same province as his father, and later was appointed viceroy of Nolambavādi and Bana-vāsi, governing these provinces by deputies while he himself remained at the capital like the Sayyid brothers under the Mughul emperor Farrukhsiyar. This change in the position of Bijjala is already noticeable under Jagadēkamalla ; but when the latter was succeeded by his brother Taila III, his power grew perceptibly till in 1156 he became virtually ruler, though Taila reigned nominally till 1163.

Another enterprising ruler about this time was rising on the horizon of history on the eastern frontier. After the accession of Vikrama Chola the Eastern Chālukya dominions fell into disorder, and an enterprising chief between the two Chālukya kingdoms found his opportunity. Just within the frontier of the Eastern Chālukyas is the hamlet of Anamakonda, the ancestral capital of the Kākatīyas, known generally as the Kākatīyas of Warangal, which his son Prola founded and whither he had shifted the capital. This Prola lays claim to having defeated Tailapa some time in his reign, and it was very likely that this took place in 1155. This external shock combined with the loss of hold on the *Mahāmanda-lēsvaras* must have thrown Tailapa into the arms of Bijjala, who for the time proved the saviour of the empire. Bijjala having thus acquired power gradually assumed royal state. His usurpation was opposed alike by the loyal Sindas, in spite of their family alliance with him, and by the Pāndyas of Nolambavādi, but Bijjala succeeded, and he and his three sons continued to rule the kingdom for twenty years, from 1163 to 1183 when Bomma or Brāhma, son of Bijjala's general Kāmadeva or Kāvana, restored the son of Taila III under the title Sōmēsvara IV. Sōmēsvara IV ruled till 1189, and his rule was confined to the southern and south-western parts of his dominions. A combination of some of his chiefs against him and

[1] Fleet : *Bom. Gaz.* I, Pt. i, pp, 450-1.

his loyal feudatories the Sindas compelled him to retire to the
northern frontier of his dominions, and nothing more was heard of
him. In the scramble for territory that followed two leading powers
divided the kingdom, the Yādavas of Deogīr and the Hoysalas of
Dvārasamudra, the Kākatīyas of Warangal taking a humbler share
of the spoil.

Narasimha succeeded to the throne as a boy and ruled for thirty-
two years. His reign was co-eval with the reigns of Jagadekamalla
and Taila III, and ran into a part of the usurper Bijjala's reign.
Though Vishnuvardhana's title to Banavāsi and Nolambavādi had
been in a way recognised in 1137 or 1138 under Sōmēsvara III,
other royal officers continued to be appointed for the viceroyalty of
each of these provinces. These were included in the 'commissioner-
ship of the southern treasury' held by Bijjala himself. As a matter
of fact no Hoysala inscriptions have come from these provinces
dated before the reign of Vīra Ballāla II. During the reign of
Narasimha therefore these provinces may be taken to have been
outside his territory though his general Bokimayya or Bokana
brought under subjection to him the Tulu, the Changālva, the
Kongālva territories, and Bayalnādu (Wainād) in 1155. The same
general marched upon Bankapura, then in the occupation of the
Kadambas, and defeated them. It was during this period that
Bijjala was carrying out his scheme of usurpation, and Narasimha
obtained some successes both against other viceroys and Bijjala
himself by means of the opposition set up to Bijjala's usurpation.
In the course of this struggle Narasimha was gradually able to
impose his influence upon both Nolambavādi and Banavāsi, leaving
his son to complete the conquests of these provinces. Narasimha
died in 1173, and was succeeded by his son Vīra Ballāla II, who
ruled for forty-seven years, from 1173 to 1220.

Vīra Ballāla's reign coincided in the earlier part with the reign
of Bijjala's sons, extending from 1167 to 1186, and he took advantage
of the unpopularity of the usurpation to consolidate his own kingdom. Vīra Ballāla had already distinguished himself under his
father's general Tantrapāla Hemmādi in the conquest of the hill
territories and those of the Kongālva, Changālva and others. From
the date of his accession references to Chālukya overlordship disappear from inscriptions, as in fact it was the period of usurpation
by the Kalachūryas. Although Vīra Ballāla did not assume formal
independence and even recognised the overlordship of Sankama.
the third son of Bijjala, he was more or less independent. About
the year 1178 he brought under subjection the province of

Nolambavādi after capturing its capital Ucchangidurga. He restored
the capital to Vijaya Pāndya on his submission. The loyalist opposition to the usurpers does not appear to have died out, and the
Hoysalas seem to have acted against the Pāndyas of Nolambavādi
with the countenance of the last usurper. This brought on an invasion of the Hoysala territory by the loyalist general Bamma who
restored the Chālukya dynasty by setting Sōmēsvara IV on his
ancestral throne in 1183. Sōmēsvara was compelled to retire to the
southwest of his dominions before the rising power of the Yādavas
under Bhillama on the one side, and that of the Kākatīyas under
Prola and his son Pratāparudra I on the other. This extension of
the Yādava power brings the Hoysalas and the Yādavas face to face
on the banks of Mālprabhā and then the Krishna. It was in this
neighbourhood that a battle was fought, at Soratūr near Gadag,
where Bhillama Yādava was finally defeated, and the fort of Lokundi
in Dhārwār was occupied by Vīra Ballāla in 1190. He captured
besides other fortified places in the same neighbourhood, between
the present Mysore frontier and the Krishna. Sōmēsvara had disappeared before this as a reuslt of a defeat suffered by him from
his feudatories, and this victory gave Vīra Ballāla the occasion for
assuming formal independence, as no suzerain remained. The loyal
Sindas had already been overpowered, and there was no power
between the Hoysalas and the Yādavas. The Mālprabhā and the
Krishna formed the boundary between these two contending powers
on the western side of the Chālukya dominions, the eastern territory
passed into the hands of the Kākatīyas. Vīra Ballāla therefore
assumed in 1191-92 the titles of a paramount power, and signalised
the event by starting an era in his name. The remaining thirty
years of his reign were devoted to the work of settling a definitive
northern frontier for the Hoysalas and consolidating the territory
acquired by them.

During this period the Chola kingdom on the south remained
intact except for the loss of hold on the northern part of the territory which, during the period of the Kylachūrya usurpation, was
fast passing into the hands of the rising power of the Kākatīyas.
Vikrama Chola was followed by a succession of three rulers who
managed to keep their territory free from disturbance except for
the attempt of the Pāndyas in the distant south to regain their
independence. This was kept well under control on the whole till
the Pāndyas enlisted on their side the support of the powerful contemporary Celyon ruler Parākrama Bāhu[1]. With this new accession

[1] S. India and her Muhammadan Invadrs, Lect. I.

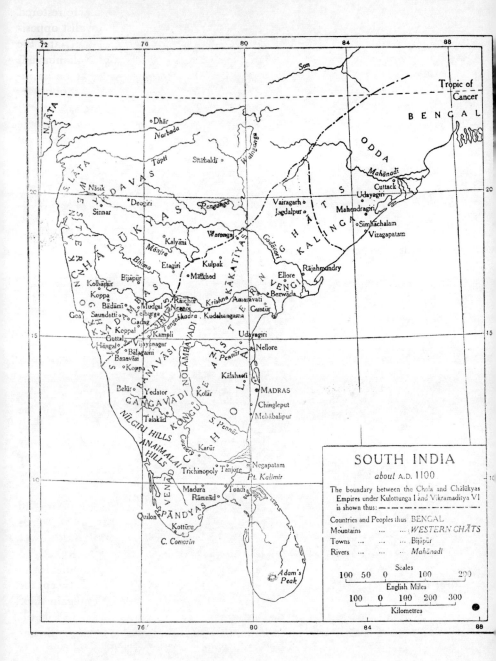

SOUTH INDIA

about A.D. 1100

The boundary between the Chola and Chálûkyas
Empires under Kulottunga I and Vikramaditya VI
is shown thus: — · — · — · —

Countries and Peoples thus BENGAL
Mountains   ...   . *WESTERN GHĀTS*
Towns   ...   . Bijāpūr
Rivers   ...   . *Mahānadi*

Scales
100 50 0   100   200
English Miles
100   0   100   200   300
Kilometres

of strength there was a greater effort on the side of the Pāndyas
to assert their independence, and this brought on a great war
between the Cholas and the Ceylonese. The Cholas managed ulti·
mately to turn the Ceylonese back into their island territory, and
punished the Pāndyas adequately for having thus brought on a
protracted war. While the war was still in progress the young
prince who distinguished himself in it succeeded to the throne under
the name of Kulottunga III, and ruled almost throughout the reign
of Vīra Ballāla II. Severe punishment quelled the Pāndyas, but
sowed the seeds of future bitterness[1]. During this war Vīra Ballāla
had so strengthened himself as to secure his dominions against
attack. Kulottunga died in 1216 and was succeeded by his son
Rājarāja III and Vīra Ballāla's reign continued up to A D. 1220.
The two families seem to have entered into a marriage alliance,
as one of the queens of Vīra Ballāla bore the name Chola Mahādēvi. The death of these great rulers created a new set of circumstances and gave the opportunity for a forward advance of the
Hoysalas.

    Kullottunga III was succeeded by his son Rājarāja. III who
reigned till 1246· Almost simultaneously with him came to the Pān·
dya throne an enterprising prince Māravarman Sundara Pāndya I
whose period of reign extended from 1216 to 1239 Almost the first
act of this Pāndya's reign seems to be the organisation of an advance
upon the Chola territory with a view to taking vengeance for the
disgrace to which Kulottunga had subjected his predecessors.
Records of his ninth year claim for him the credit of having captured
and burnt the towns of Tanjore and Uraiyūr in the course of a
successful invasion of the Chola territory. This invasion must have
taken place therefore before the year 1225. From the inscrip·
tional records of Rājarāja III himself it is clear that the first few
years of his reign were peaceful. The Pāndya invasion therefore
must have taken place somewhere about the year 1220. For the
next half-century the feature of the history of the Tamil country
is the effort of the Pāndyas not merely to reign their independence,
but to extend their authority over the Chola kingdom. This Chola-
Pāndya struggle provided the occasion for Hoysala intervention in
the Tamil country, and resulted in bringing about the dominance
of the Hoysala power in the south under their greatest ruler Vīra
Sōmēsvara. He fortified a permanent capital for himself ·at Kan-
nanūr-Vikramapura, five miles north of the island of Srīrangam
in the Chola country, and his authority, was acknowledged from

------

[1] *S India and her Muhammadan Invaders*, p. 11.

Pāndharpur in the Southern Marātha country to the extreme limit of the Tinnevelli district.

Vīra Ballāla continued to reign till 1220, and, according to the usual practice, he had his son Narasimha II anointed to the succession about the year 1217-18. With the accession of this ruler begins Hoysala intervention in the Chola country. From inscriptions in the Madura district and other sources we learn that he intervened to protect the dominions of the Cholas from the attacks of Māravarman Sundara Pāndya I, but his help profited his ally little, for by 1225 the Pāndya had destroyed the Chola cities of Tanjore and Uraiyūr and soon afterwards occupied the capital Mudikonda-Solapuram (Gangaikonda-Solapuram) and was anointed in the hall of the great temple at. Chidambaram, and it was only by submitting to the conqueror that Rājarāja III regained his kingdom. This must have happened before the year 1236-37, very probably before 1230. The weakening of the Chola power by this successful Pāndya invasion made it possible for the Chola feudatroy Kō-Perum Singa (*Sans*. Mahārāja Simha) of Sēndamangalam in South Arcot, the son and successor of the Pallava chieftain who was responsible for turning the Ceylonese out of the Pāndya territory in the war of Pūndya succession to declare his independence of his Chola overlord. He either invaded the Chola country or otherwise involved it in a war, and made Rājarāja III prisoner in his own capital of Sēndamangalam. This insolence called for the intervention of Hoysala Narasimha II who took the Magara or Magadai kingdom, the eastern part of the Salem district, and sent forward two of his generals to attack Sēndamangalam itself and release the Chola ruler, who was imprisoned there. They succeeded in this and restored Rājarāja III to his position of authority. It was probably in this war that Narasimha himself marched towards Srīrangam with a view to preventing the Pāndyas from invading the Chola country, carried the war into the Pāndya country, and is said to have set up a pillar of victory at Rāmēsvaram. In this southern campaign he seems to have associated with himself his young son Sōmēsvara who came to the throne in 1233 and ruled till 1264. In the course of these southern campaigns of Narasimha, the Yādavas had been active on the northern frontier and had gained some success as for south as Balagāmi in 1213, but they were easily beaten back during the reign of Narasimha.

Sōmēsvara's accession marks the beginning of a more vigorous reign both in the south and in the north. He carried on a successful war against the contemporary Yādava ruler Krishna Kandara, and extended his boundary northwards to the river Krishna as an inscription of his in Pandharpur near Sholapur of 1236 indicates. But his activities were chiefly along the Chola-Pāndya frontier which called for his presence so constantly that he erected for himself a royal city there and ruled his kingdom from that distant southern capital, except for one short interval in the middle of his reign when he is said to have been in his ancestral Hoysala territory proper. As early as 1236 we find him in residence in the Pāndyamandala which is said to have been acquired by his strength and valour. Probably about this time or earlier, in the reign of his father, the Hoysala entered into a marriage alliance with the Pāndyas, so that, in inscriptions of Māravarman Sundara Pāndya II of about this date, the Hoysala monarch is called 'uncle Sōmsēvara,' and a record of this Pāndya ruler in the Tinnevelli district names a village granted at the request of Sōmēsvara, Vikrama-Sōmi-Chaturvēdimangalam in honour of this uncle. It was about this time, or a few years later, that a younger brother of Rājarāja III, afterwards Rājēndra III, became so actively hostile to his elder brother that Sōmēsvara's intervention was called for as against this new rival. Rājēndra had under his rule all the northern territory of the Cholas, extending from the coast between Nellore and Kānchī across to the Hoysala frontier, and was the most important feudatory in the kingdom during the first twenty-five years of his brother's reign. He appears to have become hostile some time about 1242 or 1243, perhaps on account of Rājarāja's subserviency to the Hoysala, who dominated from his central position in Kannanūr both the Pāndya and the Chola kingdoms. As a matter of fact, the Chola power was little more than a feudatory of Sōmēsvara. Rājēndra therefore rose as a rival claimant and had to fight against Sōmēsvara rather than the nominal ruler, his brother. Both sides claim the victory. They seem however to have ultimately come to an understanding as Rājēndra is said to have let his brother rule for yet another three years, and at last killed him. With the accession of Rājēndra to power there was a change in the political relations between the Chola and the Hoysala, and the accession of another Pāndya to the throne in the person of Jaāvarman Tundara Pāndya I in 1251 brought the Pāndyas into hostility to Sōmēsvara. How actually this change of relations came about is not recorded, but soon after his accession the Pāndya set out on a campaign which lasted for more than ten years and carried the war successfully through the Chola country as far north as Nellore. According to a full *prasasti* which details the deeds of this great Pāndya, he began

by an invasion of the Travancore country and, having compelled
the Chera ruler to submit, marched into the Chola country. There
he defeated a number of Sōmēsvara's generals, and took Sēndamangalam. He expelled from Kānchī the Telugu Choda chieftains
and was anointed there. He then invaded the territory of the
Telugu Chodas themselves, defeated and killed in battle Gandago-
pala of Nellore, and placed one of his brothers, who submitted, on
the throne instead, thus carrying the war to the frontier of the
Kākatīya territory, whence he turned back towards his capital. On
the return journey we find him in occupation of the Hoysala
capital, Vikramapura, in 1264-65, and it was either in this year, or
the end of the previous one, that he defeated and slew Sōmēsvara
in battle and brought this victorious campaign to a close by
magnificent gifts to the great temple of Srīrangam, which according
to this record had suffered at the hands of the Hoysalas. They Hoysala Sōmēsvara is said to have built the front *gopura* of the Siva
temple at Jambukēsvaram. He was probably an ardent Saiva and
had neglected the Vishnu temple at Srīrangam. That is what is
hinted at in the first verse of the elaborate Sundara Pāndya inscription at Srīrangam. He is said to have weighed himself against
gold and jewels, mounting his elephant in full panoply of war, and
made a grant of the money which he himself appropriated for the
various works of extension and restoration to the great Vishnu
temple. He was anointed again in the Vishnu temple and crowned
with the crown *nagarodaya*.

Sōmēsvara had two sons of whom one, Narasimha III, the son
of queen Bijjala Rāni, was left in charge of the ancestral dominions
of the Hoysalas. Nearly ten years before his death he associated
with himself his other son Vira Rāmanātha, son of his queen Dēvala
Mahādēvi. The activities of the Yādavas probably called for this
division, and Narasimha III as regent of his father had to resist
more than one invasion. In 1276 the Yādava general Sāluva
Tikkama reached the capital, Dvārasamudra, but was beaten back
by the efforts of the prince. Vīra Rāmanātha continued to rule
from Kannanūr, and some of his inscriptions are found in Tanjore
Sendalai and Mannargudi, so that the Hoysala Rāmanātha may
be reckoned among the rulers of the south. Narasimha reigned till
1292 when he was succeeded by his son, Ballāla III. Ramanātha
ruled his extensive territory with an alternative capital Kundānī
in the Salem district and waged war against his own brother in the
south of Mysore. He died shortly after his brother, and was succeeded by his son Visvanātha, who seems to have ruled for three

years after the death of his father. When Visvanātha died the
southern territory also was again united under Vīra Ballāla III,
the last great Hoysala.

The accession of Vīra Ballāla marks a point in South Indian
History, when India south of the Vindhyas assumes, as it were, a
new political division and stands divided into four important kingdoms, two of which were situated in the Deccan and the other two
in the Peninsula. Of these four kingdoms three had formed part of
the Chālukya kingdom, the northern most being the kingdom of the
Yādavas, with their capital at Deogīr. The Yādavas and the Hoysalas contributed most to the dismemberment of the Chālukya
empire, and when dismemberment came benefited most by occupying compact blocks of territory. The river Krishna may roughly
be regarded as the frontier between the two, that being the frontier
for which the wars of the previous centuries were waged, whatever
were the dynasties actually ruling to the north and south of it.
The Yādava kingdom occupied the whole of the western half of the
Deccan, and its eastern frontier may be marked by a line drawn
roughly from somewhere east of Bījāpur through Gulbarga, Yādgīr,
Kalyāni, north east to Mahūr proceeding further north eastwards ;
all the territory west of it belonged to the Yādavas of Deogīr. The
territory on the eastern side extending to the lower course of the
river Krishna belonged to the Kākatīyas, who as feudatories of the
later Chālukyas had their territory in the Nizām's dominions with
a capital at Anamkonda, which later on they transferred to their
own fortified citadel of Warangal. Therefrom the dynasty extended
its territory chiefly at the expense of the waning power of the
Eastern Chālukyas. During the long reign of Ganapati, perhaps
the greatest among this dynasty, the southern frontier was settled
for them at the lower course of the river Krishna by the reduction
of the Telugu Choda chiefs of Nellore by Jatāvarman Sundara
Pāndya I. His daughter Rudrama or Rudrāmba, who succeeded,
was well able to maintain the territory bequeathed to her and hand
it over in fullness of time to her grandson Pratāparudra II, who
came to the throne about the same time as Vīra Ballāla III. With
the advent of Jatāvarman Sundara Pāndya the Chola territory had
been reduced to subordination to him. With the death of the
Hoysala Sōmēsvara, who had practically reduced the Cholas to a
position of complete insignificance and held their territory under
his own authority, so that under his son Vīra Rāmanātha what had
been the Chola kingdom was generally regarded as the territory of
the Hoysala Rāmanātha, the Hoysala hold was gradually slackening

while yet Vīra Rāmanātha was alive, chiefly from the pressure of the Pāndyas from the south. When the last great Pāndya, Mara-varman Kulasēkhara, ascended the throne in 1268 he seems to have gradually increased the pressure so much that he is often referred to as being in his capital Jayankonda-Sōlapuram, which is only about six miles from the regular Chola capital Gangaikonda-Sōla-puram. Under this great ruler, whose reign lasted till 1311, the Chola territory had definitely become Pāndyan, and the Telugu Chodas of Nellore, with their territory taking in the central block of the Nellore district and the Ceded Districts adjoining, constituted a buffer state between the Kākatīyas in the north and the Pāndyas in the south along the whole length of the Coromandel coast. The Hoysala frontier and the Pāndya frontier ran together along the whole length of it. Beginning from somewhere near Adonī, not far from the banks of the Krishna, this frontier ran close to the foot-hills of the Eastern Ghāts along the eastern frontiers of the present day Mysore territory, and proceeding westwards as far as the Nilgiris through the two Kongus, north and south. The Hoysalas as the central power remained in touch with the remaining three powers, and had to maintain their frontier against all three. While therefore they have had occasionally to go to war against their northern neighbours, more often against the Yādavas than against the Kākatīyas, they had to be considerably more active and con-stantly vigilant along the total length of their southern and eastern frontier. The position of these four powers was such and their interests so divided that when the first Muhammadan invasions deluged the territory of the Yādavas of Deogīr there was no common motive or interest among the four powers to adopt a con-certed policy, or take common action.

Such common action was hardly called for from the character of the first invasions under 'Alā-ud-din Khaljī. The first invasion was no more than a plundering raid ; and the next one under him was little more. It was the advent of Malik Kāfūr with more defi-nite instructions from his master to reduce the southern Hindu states to the position of tributaries that aroused these states to the real danger of the Muhammadan invasions. Even then the four kingdoms were so divided and separate in interests that the mis-fortune which befell one kingdom hardly evoked any active inter-vention on the part of the others. The Muhammadan conquests at first introduced hardly any sensible change in the political condi-tion of the kingdoms, involving no more than nominal subordination and the payment of tribute annually if it could be enforced. Hence

Deogīr fell and Warangal fell after two invasions and a raid was undertaken against the Hoysala capital of Dvārasamudra. The kings of the three kingdoms were treated almost similarly by 'Alā-ud-dīn. They were regarded as feudatories of high rank in the empire liable to tribute and subjected to occasional extortion when they gave cause by failure to send tribute. As often happened in Southern India, a pretext for intervention in the affairs of the Pāndya kingdom presented itself to the Muslims. Vīra and Sundara, the sons of the great Pāndya, Māravarman Kulasēkhara, contended for their father's throne, and Sundara, being worsted, appealed to 'Alā-ud-dīn Khaljī for help. Malik Kāfūr, then occupied with the Hoysalas, invaded the Tamil kingdom, placed Sundara Pāndya on the throne, and took advantage of the occasion to march through the Chola and Pāndya country as far south as Rāmēsvaram, his chief object being to secure the treasure accumulated in the temples of Southern India and gain possession of the elephants in the stables of the South Indian monarchs. Malik Kāfūr returned to the north after his magnificent march across peninsular India, carrying elephant loads of treasure unheard of before. This success confirmed his position at court. 'Alā-ud-dīn's illness and Malik Kāfūr's intrigues gave the south respite from foreign aggression, and enabled a Malabar ruler to descend from his mountains and carry his arms successfully across the whole of the Pāndya and Chola territory as far as Nellore. This was Ravivarman Kulasēkhara, who, starting from the Travancore country, defeated the Pāndya, and marched northwards occupying Tiruvadi in South Arcot, then Kānchī and then Poonamalle, going as far north as Nellore itself. He left inscriptions in all these places and was anointed in Tiruvadi and Kānchī, and, on his return journey, in Srīrangam. He was however expelled by the officers of Pratāparudra II, who penetrated as far south as Jambukēsvaram in the island of Srīrangam, where one of them left an inscription. Thus the four states of Southern India were left to themselves, and their tribute naturally fell into arrears.

When Mubārak ascended the throne he had virtually to reconquer India south of the Vindhyas. He showed great energy in the early years of his reign, marched to Deogīr and, having extinguished the ruling dynasty, made Deogīr the first Muhammadan province in the south, and planted along its southern frontier a number of Muhammadan garrisons in salient points. This seems to have given the first warning to the Hoysala monarch, who adopted the policy of the Indian reed, bending down when the flood runs high, and standing up again when it has passed. The Hoysala

replied to this menace by planting garrisons along his northern frontier, but so unobtrusively that his Muhammadan neighbours failed
to notice it. Muhammadan invasions under the Tughluqs continued
as before. The overthrow of the Kākatīyas and the accession of Muhammad Tughluq heralded a more aggressive policy in the Deccan.
Muhammad's activities in the south have been related in Chapter VI.

By 1328 he had occupied both Madura and its outer salient
Kannanūr, the Hoysala capital in the Chola country north of the
island of Srīrangam, and the Hoysala Vīra Ballāla replied by beginning the fortification of Hampi as a substitute for Kampli, which
had been destroyed during the rebellion of Bahā-ud-dīn Gurshāsp.
He further strengthened the garrisons along the northern frontier,
and moved southwards to occupy Tīruvannāmalai as a more suitable
centre from which to watch Muhammadan garrisons in the south
and Muhammadan movements from the north. This active movement of the Hoysala disconcerted the Muhammadan governor of
Ma'bar, and Muhammad had to send further contingents and other
governors. Jalāl-ud-dīn Ahsan Shāh, the last officer sent by him
ruled in the name of his master for about five years, and proclaimed
his independence in 1334. This rebellion was followed by others in
the north, so that the south was left entirely to itself, and Jalāl-ud-
dīn could enjoy a short period of independence. This interval of
difficulty to Muhammad the Hoysala took advantage of to the full
and gradually extended his authority southwards into the Chola
country, and was even prepared, about 1340, to plan and carry
out a sweeping movement as far south as Rāmēsvaram itself[1]. As a
provision against contingencies in this dangerous enterprise of his
he had his son anointed to the throne in the holy place of Hampi
under the designation of Vīra Virūpāksha Ballāla, in honour of the
god Virūpāksha of Hampi, one of the long established holy places
of the Hindus. His movements were so far successful that the
northern garrisons held their positions efficiently and prevented the
Muhammadans from coming into the south, if they ever made an
effort at all. On the south he was able to isolate Madura, and even
separate Kannanūr from it, so that in 1342 the garrison of Madura
felt that there was no alternative for them except to make a
desperate sally, as Kannanūr was so closely besieged that the fall
of the place, which was imminent, would mean inevitably the fall of
Madura. In a battle fought at Trichinopoly in 1342 Vīra Ballāla
was taken prisoner at the moment of victory, and put to death[2]. His
son apparently succeeded, and perhaps also fell, like his father, in

---

[1] *S. India and her Muhammadan Invaders.* p. 172 *et seq.*   [2] See p. 149.

battle two or three years after his succession to the throne. The rulers fell, but the officers who had charge of the various garrisons planted across the northern frontier, continued the good work. Among these, five brothers had charge of important garrisons along the northern frontier. The eldest, Harihara or Hariyana Odiyar, had the southern Marātha territory under his charge with his head-quarters at Bankāpur or Goa. What was hitherto Banavāsi 12,000 and the coast country over against Mysore on the west were under his authority. Hampi and Dvārasamudra with an alternative at Penukonda were in charge of the third brother Bukka. Nellore and Udayagiri with the dependent territory were in charge of the second brother Kampa. The two youngest of the five brothers were subordinate governors, one at Āraga near Tīrthalli in Mysore and the other at Penukonda. Behind all these at Mulbāgal was placed the young and enterprising son of Bukka, by name Kumāra Kampana. He is described in Indian chronicles as having held the position of door-keeper to the Hoysala monarch. The five brothers and this prince were the officers of the Hoysalas who were primarily responsible for the foundation of Vijayanagar.

Muhammad Tughluq's aggressive policy in the south menaced the Hindus with the complete destruction of their civilisation and religion. It was with difficulty that disaffection was suppressed even in the provinces directly under Muhammadan rule. The Kākatīya ruler had learned prudence by bitter experience; his young sons had no reason for the same caution. They seem to have thrown themselves heart and soul into the movement originated by the Hoysalas. With the death of the Hoysala monarchs, both father and son, the mantle of leadership fell upon their officers, and the five brothers and the son of one of them stood out as leaders of this movement, possibly with the active assistance of the Brāhman sage Vidyāranya, whose association with the movement gives a clear indication of its character.

Various stories are related of the foundation of Vijayanagar. The fortification of the city that afterwards became Vijayanagar must, however, be regarded as the deliberate work of the last great Hoysala ruler, Vīra Ballāla III. It was founded soon after the destruction of Kampli by the army of Muhammad and the immediately following invasion of the Hoysala capital of Dvāra-samudra. The fortifications were probably completed by about 1336, the traditional date ascribed to its foundation, and the fact that the Ballāla prince was anointed about the year 1340 in the holy place of Hampi, confirms this view. From 1335 onwards the

Hoysala power had to face the Muslim in two directions. The northern frontier was put into a state of defence and on the south the Muhammadan kingdom of Madura was attacked. In the early campaigns of 'Alā-ud-dīn Bahman Shāh, the founder of the Bahmanī kingdom, figure the names of three chieftains, Harihara, Bukka and Kampa, disguised as Harib (Hariyappa), Kapras (Bukkapparazu), and Kampras (Kamparazu). Earlier than this we have the state-ment of Ibn Batūta that the Muhammadan Sultan of Honowar was a subordinate of the Hindu chieftain Horaib (Hariyappa). It is thus clear that the arrangement made by Ballāla III continued through the reign of his son, and lasted even longer. The last known date of Hariyappa or Harihara is 1346, the year preceding that in which Bahman Shāh assumed independence. During the next five years the Bahmanī kingdom was open to attack from the north, and was not free for aggressive action on its southern frontier. When Bahman Shāh passed away Bukka was the sole representative of the Hoysala wardens of the marches, and succeeded to the kingdom and the responsibilities of the Hoysalas. His son Kumāra Kampana waged a successful war against the Sambuvarāya chieftains of the pālār basin and the Sultans of Madura. In the early years of Muhammad Shāh Bahmani I both the Muhammadan and Hindu powers alike had to keep watch on the movements of Fīrūz Shāh Tughluq, as his attitude towards the southern rebels, Muhammadan and Hindu, had not yet become clear. When Fīrūz definitely declared that he would not interfere in the affairs of the south[1], the two powers stood face to face, and then began the great duel which lasted practically all the time that the empire of Vijayanagar was in existence.

The earlier wars between the lately established kingdoms of the Deccan and Vijayanagar are described in Chapter xv. Muhammad I died in 1377, and Bukka followed him a year later. After the destruction of the Muhammadan kingdom of Madura in 1377[2] Vijayanagar was free to employ its whole strength against its northern neighbour, and, notwithstanding the victories of Mujāhid Shāh Bahmnī in that year, ventured to describe himself as 'emperor of the south' among other imperial titles; and claimed to be 'one that established the Vedas, and maintained the four castes and orders,' and as 'the publisher of the commentaries on the Vedas.' It was in this work of the founders of Vijayanagar that the Brāhmans, Vidyāranya and his brother Sāyana, had a share. The Hindu king-

<hr>

[1] S. India and her Muhammadan Invaders, p. 186, and Elliot, III, p. 339.
[2] See p. 150.

dom of Vijayanagar stood for all that constituted Hindu civilisation and culture in the south. The five brothers and prince Kampana continued the policy of the last Hoysalas, and Harihara II reaped the fruits of their labours. With him, therefore, the kingdom may be said to begin.

The first dynasty, which lasted up to the year 1487, a little over a century the formal assumption of the royal title by Harihara II, counted six rulers. As before in South Indian history the Rāichūr Doāb, the land between the river Krishna and the Tungabhadra, formed the bone of contention between the states to the north and the south of the former river.

With the accession of Harihara's successor, Dēvarāya I, began a period of wars which lasted for forty years, more or less continuously, and have been already described in Chapter XV. The accession of Devarāya II marked the zenith of the prosperity of Vijayanagar under the first dynasty.

When Devarāya II had been on the throne for about ten years a change of rulers took place in Orissa to the north of the territory of Warangal which exercised great influence upon the history of Vijayanagar during the next century. In 1435, the last year of the reign of Ahmad I, Bahmanī, the enterprising and ambitious Kapilesvaradeva ascended the throne of Orissa. By that time the territory of Warangal had been annexed by the Bahmanī kingdom, but the Telingana coast was as yet unconquered, and was open to the enterprise of rising power of Orissa. The Bahmanī kingdom had been involved in wars with the Sultan of Khāndesh, the Marātha chieftains on the western and south-western frontier, and the Gond chieftain, Raja Narsingh Kherla. Kapilēsvara took advantage of these difficulties to extend his territory gradually along the coast to the Godāvarī, and extended his raids as far south as Nellore and Udayagiri. A new danger thus threatened Vijayanagar. In the years immediately preceding 1440 Vijayanagar took the offensive and attacked the Bahmanī kingdom, but was worsted. An investigation of the causes of the defeat led to the conclusion that the superiority of the Muhammadan forces lay in their Turkish force of mounted archers, and Dēvarāya took steps immediately to remove the defect by enlisting a special force of 2000 Muhammadan archers, cantoning them in a special quarter of the city where they had a mosque and a separate slaughter-house, and respecting their sentiment so far as to place a copy of the Koran in front of his throne, so that the obeisance made before the monarch was offered to the Koran. This force was not the first Muhammadan contingent in the Vijayanagar armies. The last Hoysala is said to have had a contingent of 20,000 Muhammadans in the battle at Trichinopoly. Inscriptions state that Dēvarāya I, a predecessor of Dēvarāya II, employed a force of Muhammadan cavalry. Devarāya employed these troops to train other archers, so that in the course of the next few years he had a body of 60,000 archers ready to take the field[1]. With this reformed army he sent an expedition into the Bahmanī kingdom in 1443 which achieved considerable success against the Bahmanī forces. During the absence of the army an abortive attempt on Dēvarāya's life was made by one of his relatives. It was soon after this incident thât 'Abd-ur-Razzāq, the ambassador of Shāh Rukh from Samarqand, who had been for some time in Calicut, came to Vijayanagar and stayed a few months in the capital. From his account it appears that by 1442 the fortifications, temples, palaces, and public buildings of Vijayanagar had been completed. The city occupied a space of about sixty-four square miles, and had the seven enclosures—the accepted numbers of circuits for a first-class city. The three outermost enclosures contained only fields intended for cultivation, with the huts of those engaged on the land. The four inner enclosures were occupied by houses, the innermost containing the palace and its precincts. A number of channels had baen led into the city from the Tungabhadra; one of them yet goes by the name Rāya channel They were intended partly for the purpose of cultivation and partly for the water-supply of the city. Even allowing for exaggeration in Abd-ur-Razzāq's account, Vijayanagar under Dēvarāya II must have been a splendid city, and exceedingly well fortified. Dēvarāya II lived for six years after this date and died in February 1449, a brother of the same name having predeceased him by three years. Dēvarāya II, by far the greatest ruler of the first dynasty, was excelled only perhaps by Krishnadevarāya of all the kings of Vijayanagar. Under him the kingdom as a whole had been well knit together and brought under an ordered administration, chiefly through the genius of 'the great Danayak' of 'Abd-ur-Razzāq, the Brāhman minister Lakkana or Lakshmī-dhara. Lakkana and his brother Madana were governors of important divisions in the south and passed from province to province by way of official promotion. There were other governors besides, each in his own province, and all of them were kept well in hand by the ruler and his chief ministers. The only frontier that caused anxiety was the northern frontier, and that through the activities of the monarch of Orissa. When Dēvarāya II died,

[1] See p. 406.

therefore, the kingdom was in the most satisfactory condition and passed on without dispute to his eldest living son, Mallikārjuna.

Dēvarāya II had lost in the course of his lifetime one or two of his grown up sons in the wars against the Muslims. It is also said that in the massacre which ended in the attempt upon his life, one of his grown up sons was killed. It seems probable therefore that Mallikārjuna· succeeded to the throne comparatively young. The accession of this new ruler was taken advantage of by the two northern powers, the Bahmanī kingdom and the Hindu state of Orissa. They made a combined attack and laid siege to the capital. Young Mallikārjuna succeeded in repulsing them about the year 1450[1], and ruled for nearly ten years in peace. About the end of this period we hear of him in residence in Penugonda with his minister Timma 'on business connected with the administration of the kingdom of Narasimha.' This could only mean that he moved eastward from the capital and was for some time on the frontiers of the territory of the rising chieftain Sāluva Narasimha either to protect his own dominions, or, as is more likely, to be prepared to support Narasimha against the ruler of Orissa and his Muslim allies. Neither inscriptions nor other sources of information available to us so far tell us any more about him than that he continued to rule till 1467 or 1468. The kingdom appears to have continued intact during the whole of his reign.

It was during his reign that the Sāluva chieftain, whose ancestral territory lay around Chandragiri or Nārāyanavanām in the modern district of Chittūr, and whose ancestors for a few generations had been working loyally in behalf of the kingdom, comes into prominent notice. Mangū or Mangirāja of this family bore an honourable share in the southern campaigns of prince Kampana, and his successors, several of them held important positions in the state, and one of them had married into the royal family. Narasimha or Narasingha found an opportunity for signal achievement in the aggressive activities of the monarchs of Orissa who had penetrated certainly as far as Nellore, and either at this time or a little later, as far south as the South Arcot district. He developed his resources early and gradually extended his influence in the neighbouring provinces of the kingdom of Vijayanagar so as to be able to offer effective resistance to these aggressions. He was so far successful that his control was more or less acknowledged over the greater

---

[1] *Gangadasapratapavilasam*, India Office Catalogue of MSS. by Julius Eggeling, No. 1610. 'Alā-ud-dīn Ahmad Bahmanī was in no position to supply a large contingent for the prosecution of this campaign.

part of the kingdom. Having thus consolidated his position he marched into the southern possessions of Orissa and gradually pushed the invaders back so that when the attention of Muhammad Shāh Bahmanī III was drawn to the political condition of the Telingāna coast about 1476, he found Sāluva Narasimha posted in great strength on the banks of the Godāvarī at Rājahmundry. Muhammad's efforts to dislodge him do not appear to have been attended with success, and he had to content himself merely by carrying a raid across his territory as far south as Kānchī[1]. While Narasimha was opposing the Bahmanī king, a change had taken place in the kingdom of Vijayanagar ; either Mallikārjuna died, or was put to death by a younger brother, by name Virūpāksha. This latter, whether guilty of his brother's death or no, put to death all who could dispute his possession of the throne, and carried on the administration so inefficiently and oppressively that the eastern and southern provinces transferred their allegiance to Narasimha. On the west coast his maladministration caused the Arab horse-traders who had settlements on the west coast to transfer their places of business from the ports of the kingdom to those beyond the Vijayanagar frontier. Sāluva Narasimha decided that the only way of saving the kingdom was to depose Virūpāksha and seize the throne for himself, and in 1487 Narasa, who commanded his troops, deposed the tyrant and assumed the government of the kingdom on behalf of his master. This was the first usurpation in the kingdom, and Narasimha found his justification in the perils which menaced it. Virūpāksha's reign corresponded with the reign of Purushottama Gajapati of Orissa. Purushottama's records assert that he penetrated as far south as Kānchī, carried off a princess of Kānchī, and married her in peculiarly romantic circumstances. Narasimha ruled as king for six years, during which period he recovered most of the revolted provinces, but failed to conquer the Rāichūr Doāb, which was retained by the Bahmanī kingdom, or to recover Udayagiri, which remained in the possession of the raja of Orissa. On his death-bed he entrusted the kingdom and his two sons to Narasa, begging him to carry on the administration, to enthrone whichever of his two sons should prove the fitter for rule, and to recover Rāichūr, Umagal, and Udayagiri. Narasa placed one of Narasimha's young sons on the throne, but this prince died as the result of wounds that he received in an expedition into the Rāichūr Doāb. Narasa circumvented court intrigues, placed the second son of Narasimha upon the throne and carried on the

1 See pp. 417-419.

administration as before. He died in 1505, and it was his son, Vīra
Narasimha, that deposed the Sāluva ruler Narasimha II.

This second usurpation caused widespread rebellion and Narasimha was engaged during the four or five years of his reign in
attempting to recover the revolted provinces. He was successful
on the whole, but the enterprising Gangarāja Ummattūr remained
in rebellion, in the territory round Kānchī. Vīra Narasimha left
some infant sons and three grown up brothers, and charged his
faithful minister Sāluva Timma, as Nuniz records, to put out the
eyes of the ablest of his grown-up brothers, and place on the throne
one of his sons. The minister proved false to the dying sovereign
and remained true to the interests of the kingdom ; and placed
the youngest brother, marked for mutilation, upon the throne in
1509. Thus ascended the throne the great king Krishnadevarāya of
Vijayanagar.

Krishna ascended the throne at a critical moment in the history
of South India. The Portuguese had landed in India eleven years
before, and, just as he was settling himself on the throne at Vijayanagar, had taken possession of Goa, which has remained in their
possession since. The entry of this European nautical power created
an unsettling factor in the commercial relations of the kingdom
with the outer world. The kingdom itself was disturbed, and the
very heart of it was in the hands of a rebellious vassal. Although
the Bahmanī kingdom had broken up into five separate states there
was considerable activity on that frontier, chiefly from the direction
of Bījāpur. The rajas of Orissa sill held the east coast as far as
Nellore, and were in possession of the most important fortresses
in the Telugu country, extending north-westward from Udayagiri
in the Nellore District. Krishna came to the throne between May
and Novembr of the year 1509, and his coronation did not take
place until the following January. The delay seems to have been
due to a circumstance recorded by Nuniz. The young king's elder
brother ordered the Brāhman minister, Sāluva Timma, to bind
him, and the minister was inclined to obey the order until his pity
was moved by his master's entreaties. Sāluva Timma remained in
power, treated almost with deference by Krishnadevarāya, who
used to style him Āppājī ('reverend father'), and the relations
between the two gave rise to the stories of Rāyar and Āppājī
which are current in Southern India and resemble those related of
Hārūn-ur-Rashīd and Ghafūr, and of Vikramāditya and Bhattī.

Krishna remained at his capital for a few months after his
accession and there received the Portuguese embassy from Affonso

de Albuquerque, who desired to enter into a commercial treaty and sought aid against the Zamorin of Calicut. Krishna detained the embassy at the capital while he suppressed the rebellion in the region about Kānchī. Marching from Penukonda he reduced to obedience all the petty chieftains whose lands lay on his way, attacked the Raja of Ummattūr, defeated him in the field, and laid siege to his stronghold, the fortress of Sivasamudram. He drained off the Kāverī, which flowed round it, and captured it with all the treasure which it contained. He then marched to Srīrangapatam, thence to Ikkēri, and thence to the frontiers of Bījāpur. These operations were completed by the year 1512. He then marched along his northern frontier strengthening the garrisons in the fortresses, particularly in Mudgal, Rāichūr and Adonī.

Resolving wisely, on the advice of Sāluva Timma, to leave the Muslim Sultans alone for the time, he made preparations for an invasion of the territories of Orissa with a view to detaching the Gajapatiking from the alliance with the Muhammadans, and coming to terms with him if possible. He sent Sāluva Timma to the capital to make the necessary preparations, and himself went on a visit to the shrines of Tirupti and Srīsailam. When the minister had completed his preparations Krishna marched to invade the kingdom of Orissa. He first marched against Udayagiri, the southernmost fortress in the occupations of the Gajapati monarch, and took it after a protracted siege. This war occupied the years 1512 and 1513, and he carried back with him, together with much treasure and prisoners belonging to the royal family of Orissa, the image of Bālākrishna which he set up in a temple constructed for the deity, the ward of Vijayanagar in which the temple was built being named Krishnāpuram from this temple of Krishnasvāmi. This was completed in March 1514.

Krishna next attacked the fortress of Kondavīdu (Kondavir) and a number of fortified places of lesser importance held for the Raja of Orissa in the neighbourhood. These he reduced in spite of the assistance which they received from the Sultans of Bīdar and Golconda, and he finally carried the fortress of Kondavīdu itself by storm. Here he took prisoner the Gajapati prince Vīrabhadra and a number of Orissa noblemen of high rank. All this took place in the first half of the year 1515. After a raid into the kingdom of Golconda he broke up his camp at Bezwāda and besieged and took Kondapalli, capturing the officers who held it for the Raja of Orissa. He then marched north-eastwards as far as Simhāchalam in the Vizagapatam district, taking several fortresses on his way. Here he halted and opened negotiations with the raja of Orissa, who gave him a daughter in marriage and accepted the Krishna as the boundary between the kingdoms of Orissa and Vijayanagar, the retrocession of the territory to the south of that river being effected under the form of bestowing it on the princess as her dowry. Krishna's achievement was meagre. He had fulfilled only part of his father's behest, and had but recovered a province which had formerly belonged to the kingdom which he ruled : yet he was not ashamed to assume the vainglorious title of *Gajapatisaptan-gaharana*, appropriator of (Orissa's) seven elements of royalty. On his return journey he was on the banks of the Krishna in July—August, 1516. After his return from this war he made large grants to temples in southern India for the repair of the damages which they had suffered in the Muhammadan invasions and built the small town of Hospet in memory of his mother Nāgalādēvi giving it the name Nāgalāpura. At some time between the death of Yūsuf 'Ādil Shāh in 1510 and this period Krishna's troops, profiting by the discussions between the five kingdoms of the Deccan, had invaded and annexed the Rāichūr Doāb, and in 1520 Ismā'il 'Ādil Shāh attempted to recover it, but was defeated[1]. The battle, which is mentioned in one of Krishna's inscriptions, was fought on May 19, 1520, at a place named Kembhāvī ('Red Well') and a Telugu poem exults in the reddening of the well with the blood of the Yavanas, or Muslims.

The remainder of Krishna's reign was undisturbed by foreign wars, but in his declining years his kingdom was harassed by rebellion. He appears to have fallen sick in 1525, when his brother Achyuta, who afterwards succeeded him, acted for a short time as regent. It was about this time that Tirumala Rāya, another of his sons, died, and a rising, connected in some unexplained manner with the death, occurred, but was suppressed. At the end of Krishnas' reign, in 1528 or 1529, one of his most trusted officials, Vira Narasimha, who is styled Sellappā, 'the Dear One,' and was governor of the central districts of the kingdom, rebelled, and, fearful of the consequences, fled to the kingdom of Tiruvadi, or Travancore. At the same time Nāgama, an old officer of the kingdom who was placed in charge of the Madura district refused to obey the orders which he received from court, and persisted in his contumacy until his own son, Vishvanāth, who was sent against him, defeated him, and was appointed to the government of the district in his father's place. The central districts of the kingdom

[1] See p. 435.

were still disturbed when Krishna died in 1530, and almost the first act of his successor, Achyuta, was to lead a punitive expedition against the fugitive governor. Achyuta had marched as for south as Srīrangam when one of his brothers-in-law, Salakam Tirumala-rāzu, volunteered to lead the expedition. Achyuta remained in Srīrangam while his brother-in-law reduced to obedience the ruler of Tiruvadi, the rebel governor, and their Pāndya allies. Having concluded a treaty sealed by his own marriage with a Pāndya princess, Achyuta marched across to Srīrangapatam and Ikkēri, and thence towards the frontier of the Bījāpur kingdom, but effected nothing, and returned to his capital. Having begun his reign with so much promise he lapsed immedaitely into a life of luxury and sloth, and let the administration pass into the hands of his two brothers-in-law, both named Tirumala. This usurpation aroused the opposition of a party led by three brothers, Rama, Tirumala and Venkata of the Āravīti family, the first of whom is described as the son-in-law of Krishna or of one of his brothers, Narasimha or Ranga. This party seems to have had the countenance even of the widows of Krishna. The party of the brothers Tirumala had the upper hand to begin with, and the three brothers had to flee from court for safety. When they had gathered together sufficient force in their own districts and prepared to march upon the capital Tirumala, the elder of the two brothers, who is described as the mad Tirumala (Kanarese *Hucchu*, corrupted into Hoj, Tirumala), sought the assistance of Ibrāhīm 'Ādil Shāh I of Bījāpur. The intervention of Bījāpur served only to embitter the strife. When Ibrāhīm retired the three brothers marched upon the capital and the mad Tirumala destroyed the portable wealth in the treasury, hamstrang the royal horses, blinded the elephants, and committed suicide. In the course of these events, which followed the death of Achyuta, his son Venkata was placed upon the throne. Venkata was killed by the mad Tirumala and the three brothers now placed on the throne a nephew of Achyuta and Krishna, by name Sadā-shiva, son of Ranga, one of the four brothers. The date of the commencement of Sadāshiva's reign is 1542, and with his accession begins the *de facto* rule of the three brothers[1].

The abortive attempt of Ibrāhīm ' Ādil Shāh I to add the fortress and district of Adonī to his dominions has already been described[2]. This fact of aggression aroused the enmity of Sadāshivarāya, who

[1] This is the true version of the story which has already been related on pages 439 and 440.

[2] See p. 440.

eagerly embraced opportunity afforded by an   invitation from
Burhān Nizām Shāh I of Ahmadnagar of attacking Bījāpur. The
story of the intervention of Sadāshivarāya in the quarrels of the
Muslim kings of the Deccan, first as the ally of Ahmadnagar
against Bījāpur, and afterwards as the ally of Bījāpur against
Ahmadnagar, of the gratuitous insults offered to the Muhammadan
religion, of the foolish arrogance which united against him those
by whose differences he might long have continued to prosper, of
his defeat and death at Talikota, and of the destruction of his great
kingdom has been related in Chapter XVII[1], and little need be
added to that account. The evacuation of the strongly fortified
city of Vijayanagar has not yet been explained. It was due,
according to Caesar Frederick, who was at Vijayanagar two years
after the battle of Talikota, to the mutiny of two corps of Muhammadan mercenaries, each of which is said to have been 70,000
strong, employed in the army of Vijayanagar. The attitude of the
Hindus to Islam during the campaigns in the kingdom of Ahmadnagar had been such as to exasperate all Muslims, and it is not
surprising that the victory of their co-religionists should have
encouraged these mercenaries to turn their arms against their
former employers and to transfer their allegiance to the conquerors.

1 See pp. 441—450.

CHAPTER XIX

SIND AND MULTĀN

I. Sind

THE history of Sind from the period of the Arab conquest early in the eighth century to the time when it became a province is fragmentary and obscure. From the first conquest until A.D. 1010, when it was conquered by Mahmūd of Ghaznī it was ruled by a governor of governors who pretended to represent the 'Abbāsid Caliphs of Baghdād, but were more probably hereditary rulers who obtained the Cliph's recognition as a matter of form, and in some cases, doubtless, neglected even this formality. From its conquest by Mahmūd until 1053, in the reign of Farrukhzād, the tenth of his line, it was, at least nominally, a province of the empire of Ghaznī, but in that year, while the empire was still in confusion owing to the recent usurpation of Tughril 'the Ingrate,' the Sūmras, a native Rājput tribe of Lower Sind established themselves in that region, but failed to extend their authority over Upper Sind and Multān. The province was conquered by Mu'izz-ud-dīn Muhammad Ghūrī, and was governed by his lieutenant, Nāssir-ud-dīn Qabācha, who attempted, after his master's death to assert his independence but was conquered by Shams-ud-dīn Iltutmish. Of the nature and extent of the authority exercised by the later Slave king over the province little is known, but it probably varied with the personal character of the monarch and of the ruler of Sind. The province owned the authority of Ghiyās-ud-dīn and of the Khaljīs of Delhi, whose power preserved it from becoming the prey of the Mughuls, but retained so much autonomy, even during the reign of Muhammad Tughluq; whose empire included the whole of India except Kashmīr and some tracts in the neighbourhood of Cape Comorin in the extreme south and in Kāthīāwār in the extreme west, as enabled the Sammās, a Rājput tribe of Cutch and lower Sind, to oust the Sūmras and to usurp, without the interference of any central authority, the government of the country. There are many discrepancies as to the date of this event, and one authority places it in 1439, which is at least a century too late. From a consideration of all the circumstances it is safe to conclude that it occurred about 1336.

The Sammās, of whom Abu-'l-Fazl enumerates, in the *Āīn-i-Akbarī* sixteen, and Muhammad Ma'sūm, in the *Tārīkh-i-Sind*, seventeen, had adopted Islam, and propagated that religion in their dominions. They used, as rulers, the title of Jām, still retained by the chiefs of Nawanagar in Kāthīāwār, which is explained as an assertion of a claim to descent from Jamshīd, and the explanation, though not convincing, is the only one which has been offered.

The first three princes of this line acknowldged, by the payment of tribute, the supremacy of Muhammad Tughluq, but the third, by harbouring and protecting the rebel Taghī, repudiated his allegince to Delhi, and was enabled, by the opportune death of his suzerain and the defection of his allies, to escape the punishment of rebellion, but his successor, Timājī, was compelled by the arms of Fīrūz Tughluq to return to his allegiance, and to signalize his obedience by a protracted sojourn at the court of Delhi.

The chroniclers of Sind make no mention of the victory of Shihāb-ud-dīn of Kashmīr (1359—1378)[1] over the Jām of Sind on the banks of the Indus, the only authorities for which are the chronicles of Kashmīr, so vague on the point as to be worthless.

The disruption of Muhammad Tughluq's great empire after the death of Fīrūz, and the contraction of the kingdom of Delhi, after the invasion of Tīmūr, to a few districts round the capital absolved the Jāms of Sind from their allegiance to a central authority, and they ruled their principality as independent sovereigns until, in the reign of Jām Nizām-ud-dīn, commonly known as Nanda, who succeeded in 1439 and reigned for sixty years, the Mughuls of the Arghūn clan began to make their influence felt in Lower Sind, and the Sammās sought to increase their power by a close alliance with Gujarāt. Daughters were given in marriage to the kings of that country, and, in one instance, to one of their dependants, Qaisar Khān Fārūqī, who belonged to the ruling family of Khāndesh, and whose grandson succeeded to that principality, but in 1521 Shāh Beg Arghūn, driven from Qandahār by Bābur, conquered Sind and expelled Jām Fīrūz, the last of the Sammās, who found an asylum at the court of Gujarāt and gave his daughter in marriage to Sultān Bahādur of that country.

Shāh Beg Arghūn died in 1524, and was succeeded by his son, Shāh Husain, who in 1528, after a siege of more than a year's duration, took Multān, then nominally ruled by Sultān Husain Langāh II, devastated the city, carried the inhabitants between the ages of seven and seventy into captivity, and appointed Khvāja

[1] See Chapter XII.

Shams-ud-dīn its governor, with Langar Khān, who had formerly commanded the army of Multān, as his assistant. Shortly afterwards Langar Khān, having collected the scattered inhabitants and restored a measure of prosperity to the city, expelled Shams-ud-dīn and governed Multān as an independent ruler.

Shāh Husain Arghūn was reigning in 1541 when Humāyūn, fleeing from Lahore, took refuge in Sind. Sultān Mahmūd of Bukkur shut himself up in his island fortress and refused to assist in any way the fallen emperor, nor was Shāh Husain more inclined to protect the man whose father had expelled him from Qandahār. Humāyūn attempted to persuade him to join him in an attack on Gujarāt, but Shāh Husain, having kept his envoys in attendance for five or six months, dismissed them without a decided answer, and while Humāyūn was besieging Bukkur and Sehwān cut off his supplies. Humāyūn left Sind in May, 1542, and, having vainly endeavoured to obtain assistance from the rajas, Māldeo of Jodhpur and Lonkaran of Jaisalmer, returned to the country later in the year. His son Akbar was born at Umarkot on November 25, 1542, and Humāyūn fled through Sind towards Persia, crossing the Indus at Sehwān.

Shāh Husain Arghūn suffered from continued fever, and his health was so enfeebled that his nobles deserted him and elected as their sovereign Mīrzā Muhammad 'Isā Tarkhān, a member of the elder branch of the Arghūn clan. Shāh Husain and Sultān Mahmūd, the governor of Bukkur, were united in their opposition to 'Isā, but were compelled to sue for peace and to cede to him a great part of Sind, the whole of which fell into his possession on the death of Shāh Husain in 1556.

Muhammad 'Isā Tarkhān died in 1567, and was succeeded by his son, Mīrzā Muhammad Bāqī Tarkhān, who, after crushing the revolt of his younger brother, reigned peacefully until 1585, when he committed suicide in a fit of insanity. His son Mīrzā Pāyanda Muhammad Tarkhān, being likewise insane, was excluded from the succession, which passed to his son, Mīrzā Jānī Beg Tarkhān, the grandson of Muhammad Bāqī.

Akbar, who regarded Sind as a province of his empire, resented Jānī Beg's failure to appear at his court, and in 1591 sent 'Abd-ur-Rahīm Khān, Khān Khānān, to invade the country. He defeated Jānī Beg in two engagements, compelled him to surrender both Tattah and Sehwān, and carried him to Akbar's court at Lahore. Here he was well received, and was appointed governor of the Multān province, and shortly afterwards, owing to the clamours of the Arghūn clan for the return of their old ruler, was restored to Sind as governor of the province. He died at Burhānpur in 1599, and his son Mīrzā Ghāzī Beg Tarkhān was appointed to the government of Sind, the history of which was merged thenceforward in that of the Mughul empire.

II. Multān

Multān, regarded by the Arab conquerors as the principal city of Upper Sind, was the capital of a region which was often closely connected with Sind, but was ordinarily regarded as a province of the kingdom or empire of Delhi, whose claim to its obedience was established early in the thirteenth century by Shams-ud-dīn Iltutmish, when he defeated Nāsir-ud-dīn Qabācha, the governor who had been appointed by Mu'izz-ud-dīn Muhammad Ghūrī, and was retained, at least nominally, by his successors until the disruption of the kingdom after the invasion of Tīmūr Lang. The authority of the Sayyid dynasty, which acquired the throne in 1414, extended no further than the immediate neighbourhood of Delhi, and Muhammad Shāh, the third king of that line, failed even to observe the formality of nominating a governor to Multān, and the people were compelled to provide one for themselves. Their devotion to the local saint, Bahā-ud-dīn Zakariyā, who was born at Karor in 1182 and died at Multān on November 7, 1267, had always been conspicuous, and in 1438 they chose as their ruler Shaikh Yūsuf Quraishī, the guardian of the saint's shrine.

The Shaikh had the merits and the defects of one who had chosen a life of seclusion and devotion. His rule was mild and beneficent, but he was ill-equipped to combat, either by force or by art, the enemies of his rule. An Afghān chief, Sahra Langāh, of Sibī, beguiled him by professing devotion for him, gave his daughter in marriage, and made paternal affection a pretext for visits to Multān so frequent that they ceased to excite either comment or suspicion. In 1440 he succeeded by a stratagem in introducing his troops into the Shailkh's citadel, deposed him, and banished him to Delhi, where he was well received by Buhlūl Lodī.

Sahra, who assumed the title of Sultān Qutb-ud-dīn, founded the Langāh dynasty, which endured almost as long as Multān maintained her independence of Delhi. He died in 1456 after a reign of sixteen years, and was succeeded by his son, Sultān Husain I.

Shaikh Yūsuf constantly urged Buhlūl Lodī to recover Multān, and the Afghān king twice set out from Delhi with this object. In 1452 he was recalled by the advance of Mahmūd Shāh of Jaunpur, whom some disaffected nobles had invited to Delhi, and once again, after 1458, the menacing attitude of Husain Shāh of Jaunpur compelled him to retrace his steps.

Husain Langāh I was an energetic ruler, and annexed Shorkot and Karor. While he was engaged in suppressing the rebellion of his brother in Karor Buhlūl, moved once again by the importunity of Shaikh Yūsuf, sent his third son, Bārbak Shāh, to attempt to recover Multān, and ordered Tātār Khān Lodī, governor of the Punjāb, to support him. The two kinsmen advanced on Multān, but Husain returned by forced marches and utterly defeated them before the city, putting their armies to flight.

On the death of Buhlūl Lodī, on July 17, 1489, Husain I sent letters of condolence and congratulation to his son and successor, Sikandar Shāh, and the two monarchs concluded a treaty of peace. Husain I abdicated in his old age, nominating his son Fīrūz as his successor, but Fīrūz proved to be a dissolute and worthless ruler. He conceived unfounded suspicions of Bilāl, son of the minister, 'Imād-ul-Mulk, whom his father had chosen, and caused him to be assassinated. 'Imād-ul-Mulk avenged Bilāl's death by poisoning Fīrūz, and Husain, deeply grieved by his son's death, resumed the reins of power, and designated Mahmūd, the son of Fīrūz, as his heir. 'Imād-ul-Mulk's past services and the death of his son were not allowed to atone for his having compassed the death of his prince, and he was executed. On August 31, 1502, Husain himself died, after a reign of forty-six years, and was succeeded by his grandson, Mahmūd, the son of Fīrūz.

Mahmūd was a profligate youth, and his tyranny drove his minister, Jām, Bāyazīd, on whom Husain had bestowed the important fief of Shorkot, into rebellion. War broke out between the king and his vassal, who summoned to his aid Daulat Khān Lodī, governor of the Punjab. The combination was too strong for the king of Multān, who was compelled to relinquish his claims to sovereignty over the Shorkot district, and to acquiesce in Daulat Khān's decision that the Rāvi should be regarded as the northern frontier of the kingdom of Multān[1]. Shorkot was thus lost to Multān and became a fief in the province of the Punjab.

[1] A strange error is made in the *I.G.* (xviii, 26), where it is stated that in 1502 the Rāvi was fixed as the boundary between the territories of Delhi and those of Multān. This is impossible, for both Delhi and Multān lay then, as now, to the south of the Rāvi. See "The Mihrān of Sind," by Major H.G. Raverty, *J.A.S.B.*, vol. lxi. part 1, 1892.

In 1527 Mīrzā Shāh Husain Arghūn of Sind invaded the kingdom of Multān at the instigation of Bābur. Mahmūd vainly endeavoured to stay his advance by sending to him a mission charged with the duty of effecting a settlement by negotiation, and, on the failure of his efforts to secure peace, marched forth to a distance of two stages from the city. Here his mission rejoined him on its return, and immediately after receiving it he died, poisoned, as was supposed, by Langar Khān, the commander of his troops, who on his master's death, deserted to the enemy. The army returned to Multān and proclaimed Husain, the infant son of Mahmūd, king. Shujā'-ul-Mulk Bukhārī, son-in-law of the late king, became regent, and decided, against the advice of all his officers, to stand a siege. The city after enduring fearful privations, fell in 1528, after a resistance of a year and some months, the young king was imprisoned, and Shujā-ul-Mulk Bukhārī was tortured to death. The kingdom was annexed to Sind and Khvāja Shams-ud-dīn was appointed governor by Shāh Husain Arghūn, but was shortly afterwards removed by Langar Khān, who submitted to Kāmrān Mīrzā, brother of Humāyūn of Delhi, and governor of the Punjab on his behalf, thus re-uniting Multān to Delhi, from which it had been severed for a century.

CHAPTER XX

THE NATIVE STATES OF NORTHERN INDIA FROM A.D. 1000 TO 1526

ON no occasion were the earlier Muslim invaders of India called upon to meet a mighty Indian ruler. No Asoka, Kanishka, or Harsha arose to defend the rich and alluring plains. Such rulers were, indeed, rare phenomena in India, which has never been the home of a nation, and whose normal condition was that of a congeries of independent and mutually hostile states, fortunate if they could agree temporarily to sink their differences before a common foe.

When Muhammad b. Qāsim invaded Sind in 711 the Chālukyas, the Pallavas, and the Rāshtrakūtas were contending for supremacy in the Deccan, and the Arab geographers of a later date corrupted Vallabha Rāī, the title borne by many of the Rāshtrakūtas, imitating the Chālukyas, into Balharā, and used this word as a generic title for the leading ruler in India ; but in Northern India the empire of Harsha had dissolved on his death in the middle of the preceding century, and no power had succeeded to the hegemony. How Muhammad dealt with Dāhir, the local ruler of Sind, we have seen. The Chāvadas of Kāthīāwār, the Gahlots of Chitor, the Chauhāns of Sāmbhar, and probably other houses claim to have met and defeated the Arab invaders, but these chiefs ruled principalities contiguous to or not far distant from the conquered state, and their opposition to Muhammad was not a united effort. The claims may well be true, but the conflicts were of little importance. The Arabs had Sind, and if they ever contemplated an extension of their conquests in India they soon abandoned the idea.

At the time of Mahmūd's invasion India north of the Vindhyas was divided into a number of independent states. The Hindu Shāhiya dynasty, founded by Lulliya the Brāhman at the end of the ninth century, with its capital at Ūnd on the Indus existed on sufferance for some time after the establishment of the Turkish power in Ghaznī, but was extinguished by Mahmūd. Of the history of the kingdom of the Punjab, with its capital at Bhātinda, little is known. Its position compelled its kings, Jaipāl I, Anandpāl, Jaipāl II, and Bhīmpāl the Fearless to stand forth for a time as the principal champions of Hinduism, and though their end was unfortunate it was not dishonourable. On Bhīmpāl's flight to Ajmer in 1021 his kingdom became a province of Mahmūd's empire.

The other states in northern India at this time were Sāmbhar, or Ajmer, ruled by the Chauhān Rājputs; Delhi, lately founded by the Tomaras near the site of the ancient Indraprastha (Indarpat), Chitor, already possessed by the Gahlots, who were not prominent among the opponents of the invader; Kanauj, still held by the Gurjara Pratihāras, Harsha's desendants, whose power had waned before that of the Chandel rajas of Jijhoti (the modern Bundelkhand), chieftains of Gond origin, who had advanced northwards until they made the Jumna the boundary between their territory and that of Kanauj; and Gujarāt, ruled by the Chālukyas or Solankīs, who had superseded the Chāwaras. The Jāts inhabited the country on the banks of the Indus between Multān and the Sulaimān Range, and their chieftains seem to have owned allegiance to the Muslim rulers of Multān. To the south of Jijhoti lay Chedi, held by the Kālachurīs or Haihayas, another tribe of Gond origin, and to the west of Jijhoti and Chedi lay Mālwa, governed by a line of Paramāras or Pawārs which had been founded early in the ninth century. Bengal was ruled by the Pāla dynasty, founded in the eighth century by Gopāla, who was elected king of Bengal and founded the city of Odantapurī (Bihār). Kāmarūpa, or Assam, was ruled by an ancient family of Koch, or Tibeto-Chinese origin, which had become completely Hinduized. In Kashmīr the Karkota dynasty, founded in Harsha's lifetime by Durlabhavardhana, still reigned. The fortress of Gwalior was the capital of the Kachhwāha Rājputs, who were probably feudatories of Jijhoti.

The leading confederates of Jaipāl I in his campaign against Sabuktigin were Rājyapāla of Kanauj, styled Jaichand by Muslim historians, and Dhanga of Jijhoti. The confederacy formed against Mahmūd in 1001 was far more formidable, and Anandpāl of the Punjab was joined by Vīsaladeva, the Chauhān king of Sāmbhar or Ajmer, to whom was given the chief command, his vassal the Tomara raja of Delhi, Rājyapāla of Kanauj, Ganda of Jijhoti, Vajradāman Kachhwāha of Gwalior and Narwar, and the Pawār raja of Dhār, or Mālwa, all of whom shared in the disastrous defeat suffered by the Hindus on December 31, 1001[1].

Ganda Chandel, who had succeeded his father Dhanga in 999, and appears in Muslim annals as 'Nanda, raja of Kālinjar,' which was his principal fortress, succeeded Vīsaladeva of Sāmbhar as the

[1] See *ante*, p. 16.

leader of the Hindu confederacy, and, on Mahmūd's return to Ghaznī in 1019, from the expedition in which he plundered Muttra and Captured Kanauj, Manaich, and Asnī[1], took upon himself the probably congenial duty of punishing Rajyapāla for having in order to save Kanauj from pillage and destruction, betrayed the national cause by swearing fealty to the foreigner. Ganda's son, Vidhyādara, aided by the prince of Gwalior, invaded Kanauj and defeated and slew Rājyapāla, who was succeeded by his son, Trilochanapāla.

Mahmūd was not slow to avenge his vassal, and in 1021 invaded India to punish Ganda. The details of this invasion have already been given[2]. Gandā, with the confederate army of 36,000 horse, 105,000 foot, and 640 elephants, prepared to meet the invader on the Sai, between the Ganges and the Gumtī, but his courage failed him, and after his flight Mahmūd captured Bārī, the new Pratihāra capital, and returned to Ghaznī with the booty which he had taken from Ganda's camp. In 1022 he returned and compelled Ganda's son to surrender to him Kālinjar, which long remained a bone of contention between Hindu and Muslim in India, and was regarded as the key to the region south of the Jumna and east of Mālwa.

Hindu annals do not credit the Solankīs of Gujarāt with a share in the various confederacies formed to oppose the invader, but the considerations which led Mahmūd to undertake the most famous of all his expeditions, that to Somnāth, have been recorded[3]. Bhīm the Solankī then ruled Gujarāt, having his capital at Anhilvāra, in the neighbourhood of the modern Pātan. After the capture of Beyt Shankhodhar and the flight of Bhīm, Mahmūd, before returning to Ghaznī, made arrangements for the administration of Gujarāt. According to the legend related in some Muslim histories an ascetic named Dābshilīm, who had some claim to the throne, was brought to his notice as a fit person and was appointed by him to govern the country. At his request Mahmūd carried to Ghaznī for safe custody another Dābshilīm, a relative whose pretensions the newly made king dreaded, and detained him until king Dābshilīm was securely seated on his throne, when he sent him back to Gujarāt at the king's request. When the prisoner approached Anhilvāra the king, according to custom, went forth to meet him, and, arriving at the appointed spot before him, passed the time in hunting. At length, overpowered by the heat and by fatigue, he lay down under a tree to rest, covering his face with a red handkerchief. A bird of prey, taking the handkerchief for a piece of flesh, swooped down upon it and, driving his talons into the king's eyes, destroyed his

---

[1] See *ante*, pp. 18-20.　　　[2] See *ante*, p. 21.　　　[3] See *ante*, p. 23.

sight. One so injured was disqualified from reigning, and the prisoner Dābshilīm, arriving at that moment, was acclaimed by the popular voice as king, while the blinded man was confined in the dungeon under the throne-room which he had destined for his relative.

Dābshilīm is well known in Muslim literature as the king to whom the Brāhman, Pīlpāy, related the fables of the jackals Kalīla and Dimna, which have been translated into Arabic and Turkish, and twice into Persian, but the name is unknown in Indian history and it is difficult to connect it with any Indian king. It has been suggested that Maḥmūd, after the flight of Bhīm I, appointed his uncle, Durlabha, to the government, and that the two Dābshilīms represent Durlabha and his son, but Lt.-Colonel Tod's explanation appears to be more probable. He says[1] that the Dābhis were a well known tribe, said by some to be a branch of the Chāwaras, who had preceded the Solankīs on the throne of Gujarāt, and suggests that the name is a compound of Dābi Chāwara.

The remnant of the dominions of Rājyapāla of Kanauj had passed to his son, Trilochanapāla, who first transferred his capital to Bārī, which was taken by Maḥmūd, and afterwards resided much at Benares, which was attacked and plundered by Ahmad Niyāltigīn, the traitor who governed the Punjab for Mas'ūd, the son of Maḥmūd.

Hānsī, a possession of Mahīpāl, rāja of Delhi, was captured early in 1038 by Mas'ūd, but in 1044 Mahipāl recovered from Maudūd, Mas'ūd's son, not only Hānsī, but also Thānesar and Kāngra. In 1079 Ibrāhīm, the eleventh king of the Ghaznavid dynasty, led a raid into Western India, and early in the twelfth century Muhammad Bāhlīm, a rebellious governor of the Punjab under Bahrām, the fifteenth king, established himself as far south as Nāgaur, from which town he governed a large tract of country ; but the power of the Ghaznavids had long been declining, and, with the exceptions already mentioned, the Hindu states of India were not molested, and were left free to pursue their internecine strife.

After the submission of Rājyapāla of Kanauj to Maḥmūd the power of the Pratihāras declined, Trilochanapāla and his successors were styled rajas of Kanauj, but lived principally at Manaich, now Zafarābād, near Jaunpur, and more remote than their ancient capital from the menace of the Chandel. Shortly before 1090 Chandradeva, of the Gaharwār clan, acquired possession of Benares and Ajodhya, both of which had been included in the kingdom of

---

[1] Tod, i, 122 and note.

Kanauj, and extinguished the last vestiges of the authority of the Pratihāras by extending his dominions as far as Delhi, which he is said to have captured, and occupied, reducing the Tomaras to vassalage.

Gangeyadeva Kālachurī of Chedi, who reigned from 1015 to 1040, extended his ancestral dominions, and almost succeeded in becoming the paramount power in Northern India, but was not powerful enough to crush the Chandel kingdom. His son Karnadeva, who reigned from 1040 to 1100, invaded the Pāla kingdom of Magadha, or Bihār, in 1039, before his father's death, and defeated the reigning king, Nayapāla. In 1060 he and Bhīm II of Gujarāt attacked and crushed Bhoj, the learned king of Mālwa.

Mālwa had been ruled for two centuries and a half by chiefs of the Paramāra or Pawār tribe, whose capital was at first Ujjain and later Dhār. The line was honourably distinguished by its love for and encouragement of learning, and in this respect Bhoj was not the least distinguished of his house. The death of Bhoj broke the power of the Pawārs, who, however, ruled Mālwa until the beginning of the thirteenth century, when they were ousted by the Tomaras. The inclusion of the Deccan in the Muslim kingdom of Delhi between the years 1294 and 1347 made Mālwa a highway between the northern and the southern provinces, and destroyed the power of the Hindu rulers of the country; but the Tomaras were succeeded by the Chauhāns, who enjoyed some power and influence in Mālwa until the end of the fourteenth century, when it became an independent Muslim kingdom.

The victory over Bhoj of Mālwa benefited the Kālachurī but little. Some years later Karnadeva suffered several defeats at the hands of his enemies, the chief of whom were Kīrtivarman Chandel, who reigned from 1049 to 1100, and Vigrahapāla III, king of Bihār and Bengal ; and little more is heard of Chedi. After 1181 the Kālachurī rajas of northern Chedi disappear, having probably been supplanted by Bāghel chiefs of Rewa.

The Gahlot kingdom, which is still represented by the State of Udaipur, had been founded before the invasion of Sind by Muhammad b. Qāsim, and tradition credits its ruler with having met the Muslim in the field in those early days, but the state seems to have taken no part in the resistance offered to Mahmūd. The same may be said of the Pāla kings of Bengal and Bīhar, who apparently believed that they were not concerned in the fate of the Punjab and Hindūstān, though the dominions of Dharmapāla, the second of the line, are said to have extended from the Bay of Bengal to Delhi and Jullundur. They were devout Buddhists, and their religion perhaps set a gulf between them and their Brahmanical neighbours. Mahīpāla I was reigning in Bengal during the period of Mahmūd's raids, but before the next wave of invasion, destined to engulf Bengal, had broken over Northern India, and during a serious rebellion which broke out in the Pāla kingdom about the year 1080, Choragangā, king of Kalinga, extended his conquests to the extreme north of Orissa, and Sāmantasena, a chieftain from the Deccan, founded a principality at Kāsipurī, now Kasiārī, in the Mayūrbhanj State. His grandson, Vijayasena, established his independence about 1119, and took much of Bengal from the Pālas, his aggression being doubtless stimulated by religious antagonism, for all the Senas were Brahmanical Hindus. Vallālasena, or Ballāl Sen, Vijayasena's son and successor, was the most powerful of the line. He introduced Kulinism into Bengal, and is said to have founded Gaur, or Lakhnāwatī, but the city was probably built before his reign. About 1175 he was succeeded by his son, Lakshmanasena, who was driven from his capital, Nadiya, by Ikhtiyār-ud-dīn Muhammad b. Bakhtyār[1]. The capture of Nadiya (Nuddea) did not immediately extinguish the dynasty, which continued its existence for four generations after Lakshmanasena, but the rajas were mere vassals of the Muslim rulers of the country.

Rāmapāla, who reigned from about 1077 to 1120, was one of the most famous of the Pāla kings. His father, Mahīpāla II, was slain by rebels, and Rāmapāla was compelled to flee, but obtained assistance from many other princes, defeated and slew the rebel chief, and regained the throne. He extended his dominions and encouraged Buddhism, and it was not until the end of his reign that the Senas established themselves in Bengal. Rāmapāla has sometimes been regarded as the last of the Pālas, but he was succeeded by five kings of his family, who, though Bengal had been lost, retained Bihār. Indradyumnapāla, the last known raja of the line, was reigning at the time of the Muslim invasion of Bihār[2], in which he probably lost his life, as nothing more is heard of his house.

The Muhammadan kingdom of the Punjab had long ceased to be a menace to the Hindu princes of India, but they cannot have been ignorant of the rise of new powers beyond the Indus. No menace, however, sufficed to deter them from their internecine disputes.

A long line of princes of the Chauhān tribe had ruled the principality of Sāmbhar, of which Ajmer had become the chief town, and

<hr />

[1] See *ante*, p. 46.   [2] See *ante*, p. 42.

in the middle of the twelfth century Vigraharāja (Vīsaladeva or
Bīsal Deo) of this line extended his dominions in an easterly direction by capturing Delhi from a chief of the Tomara tribe, who had
founded the city in A.D. 993-94 by building the Red Fort where the
Qutb Minār now stands. The city was of no great importance but
Vigraharāja's victory extinguished a minor dynasty and might have
made for unity and strength, had there not been other competitors
for power in the field.

Vigraharāja's nephew and successor was Prithvī Rāj, known to
Muslim historians as Rāī Pithaurā, the most chivalrous warrior of
his time in India : but the most powerful of Indian princes at the
end of the twelfth century was Jaychandra, the Gaharwār raja of
Kanauj and Ajodhya, styled by the Muhammadans 'Jaichand, raja
of Benares'. He had a marriageable daughter, in whose honour he
held a *swayamvara*, the assembly to which, in accordance with
ancient custom, princes prepared to offer themselves as suitors for
the lady's hand were summoned, in order that she might make her
choice of a husband. The *swayamvara* was regarded as an assertion
of superiority and Prithvī Rāj failed to respond to the invitation
and to appear as a formal suitor, but his reputation had reached
the princess and he wounded Jayachandra's honour by carrying off
the not unwilling damsel. This romantic exploit bred bitter enmity
between the two leading powers of Northern India, and a victory
in 1182 over the Chandel raja, Parmāb, and the capture of the
important fortress of Mahoba, while they enhanced the reputation
of Prithvī Rāj, weakened the Hindu cause by sowing further dissension between the native princes.

These princes, however, sank their differences and united to
oppose the invader at the first battle of Tarāorī[1], in which Muhammad b. Sām was defeated, for the Muslim writers say that all the
rajas of Hindūstān were present at that battle ; but Jayachandra
of Kanauj seems to have found an alliance with his son-in-law too
high a price to pay even for national freedom, for he stood aloof
from the Hindu confederacy at the second battle of Tarāroī[2]
which laid the foundation of Muslim rule in Hindūstān, and if
Hindu legend is to be believed even allied himself to the national
enemy.

The operations of the Muslims after the second battle of Tarāorī,
in 1192, have been described in Chapter III. Muhammad b. Sām
marched at once on Ajmer, the Chauhān capital, and, after sacking
the city and enslaving many of its inhabitants, appointed Govinda-

[1] See *ante*, p. 40.   [2] *Ibid.*

rāja, the son of Prithvī Rāj, as its governor. According to the Muslim chroniclers the new raja was distasteful to his subjects by reason of his illegitimacy[1], but the truth was that he was a minor, and was not fit to contend with the enemies of his people. Harirāja, called Hemrāj by Muslim historians, who was the younger brother of Prithvī Rāj, accordingly deposed his nephew and usurped the throne. Govindarāja fled to the fortress of Ranthambhor, where, as will be seen, he carried on the line of his house, not without glory. He was succeeded by his son, Balhanadeva, who was reigning in 1215, and Balhanadeva was succeeded by his son Prahlād, who was killed by a lion. Vīra Narāyan, Prahlād's infant son, succeeded to the throne of Ranthambhor, and his uncle, Vegbhata, assumed the regency. The history of the Chauhāns of Ranthambhor will be resumed later.

The fate of Harirāja in Ajmer has already been recorded[2]. After suffering two defeats at the hand of Muhammad's lieutenant, Qutb-ud-dīn Aibak, he committed suicide, and Ajmer, the capital of the Chauhāns, became a Muslim city.

Jayachandra of Kanauj had, since the second battle of Tarāorī, acquiesced in all the acts of aggression committed by the invaders, but Muhammad b. Sām learned that he had repented of the alliance and was preparing to oppose him, and in 1193 he invaded India with the object of attacking him. It was probably the invasion of Bihār[3], the fate of its monks, and his own isolation that aroused in him, too late, a sense of the folly of his association with the enemies of his country. His fate has been recorded in Chapter III.[4] Benares was plundered, Kanauj was destroyed, and the kingdom of the Gaharwārs came to an end. The Muslims did not, however, immediately establish their authority in this region, and chiefs of the Chandel tribe from Mahobā ruled as local sovereigns in Kanauj for eight generations. The Gaharwārs were extinguished, and there is no evidence to support the legend that a remnant migrated to the country now known as Mārwār and became known as Rāhtors, or the claim of the Mahārāja of Jodhpur to descent from the old royal house of Kanauj.

The conquest of Bihār involved the destruction of the Pāla dynasty, which had borne sway in Bengal and Bihār for nearly four centuries, and in the latter country alone for nearly a hundred years. Indradyumnapāla, the last king of the line, was alive in 1197, but retained no power during the later years of his life.

[1] See *ante*, p. 43.   [2] See *ante*, p. 43.
[3] See *ante*, p. 42.   [4] See *ante*, p. 43.

C.H.I. III,   33

Ikhtiyār-ud-dīn Muhammad b. Bakhtyār, having extinguished the Pālas of Bihār, drove Lakshmanasena or Lakshman Sen of Bengal from his capital and established Muslim rule in Bengal[1]. Lakshmanasena, and, after him, his son and his grandson ruled at Vikrampur as vassals of the Muslim governor of Bengal, but the dynasty virtually came to an end with the capture of Nadiya (Nuddea). His conqueror died shortly after his disastrous expedition into Bhutān, or Tibet[2], where the destruction of his army was partly due to the treachery of the king of Kāmarūpa (Kāmrūp), or Assam. This kingdom successfully resisted all attempts of the Muslims to invade it, but the Hinduized Koch, who ruled it at this time, succumbed in 1228 to an invasion by the Āhoms, a Shān tribe, whose chiefs ruled the country until 1816, when they were conquered by the Burmese, who in 1824, during the first Burmese war, were expelled by British and Indian troops, and in 1826 Assam became a province of the British empire in India.

The extinction of the Kanauj dynasty and the disappearance of the Gaharwārs left the Chandels of Jijhoti the only formidable neighbours of the Muslims. Paramardī, or Parmāl, who had been defeated by Prithvī Rāj, was still reigning at Mahobā[3], which had superseded Khajrāho[4] as the residential capital of the Chandels. The principal fortress in their dominions was Kālinjar[5], which had been surrendered to Mahmūd of Ghaznī by the son of Ganda Chandel, and in 1202 Qutb-ud-dīn Aibak marched against the fortress, the account of his siege and capture of which has already been related[6]. After the death of Paramardī, the Chandels, as an important dynasty, disappeared, and the tribe dispersed, but petty chieftains of the race held lands in Mālwa, as local rulers, until the sixteenth century.

All the ruling houses of Hindūstān proper, except the Chauhāns of Ranthambhor and the Katehriya Rājputs of Katehr, the modern Rohilkhand, had now been extinguished or expelled, and the latter were held in check by the Muslim garrison of Budaun, their former capital, which had been one of the earliest conquests of Qutb-ud-dīn Aibak and remained ever after in Muslim hands ; but the Rājputs made Āonla[7] their capital, and Katehr virtually retained its independence until the Mughul empire was firmly established in the middle of the sixteenth century. A strong king at Delhi might cow the Rājputs into submission, but whenever the central authority

---

[1] See *ante*, p. 46.   [2] See *ante*, pp. 49, 50.
[3] In 25° 18′ N. and 79° 53′ E.   [4] In 24° 51′ N. and 79° 56′ E.
[5] In 25° 1′ N. and 80° 29′ E.   [6] See *ante*, p. 47.
[7] In 28° 17′ N. nd 79° 10′ E.

was weakened the Hindus rose and attacked the Muslims. The inhabitants of Katehr often suffered severely for the turbulence of
their chiefs, who themselves usually found an asylum in the hills of
Kumāon until the storm had passed.

But though the great ruling houses were extinct, the people
were not left leaderless. The history of the Doāb and the country
on either side of the Ganges contains evidence that the local Hindu
landholders, petty rajas, who were probably regarded as fief-holders
and paid tribute or rent when the central government could enforce
the demand, were ever ready to resist oppression, as in the reign of
Muhammad Tughluq, and to take advantage of the weakness of
their rulers, as during the reigns of the feeble Sayyids, or of their
dissensions, as in the struggle for supremacy between the kingdoms
of Delhi and Jaunpur.

The most turbulent of these petty chiefs were the leaders of the
Meos, inhabitants of Mewāt, the 'ill-defined tract lying south of
Delhi and including part of the British Districts of Muttra and
Gurgāon, and most of the Alwar and a little of the Bharatpur State';
the Hindu landholders of Baran, or Bulandshahr, and Etāwah ; and
various chiefs holding lands near the confluence of the Ganges and
the Jumna. The depredations of the Meos extended across the
Jumna into the Doāb, and northward even into the streets of Delhi.
The ruling family accepted Islam, and became known as Khānzādas;
and Bahādur Nāhar, whose tomb still stands at Alwar, and who
ruled Mewāt at the time of Tīmūr's invasion at the end of the fourteenth century, was one of the most powerful chiefs in the neighbourhood of Delhi.

The capture of Ranthambhor by Shams-ud-dīn Iltutmish[1] adds
little to the reputation of that great king. According to the Hindu
records he was defeated before the fortress in 1225, but succeeded
in persuading the young raja, Vīra Narāyan, to visit him at Delhi,
poisoned him, and took possession of his capital. Mālwa was still
independent under the Pawārs, and the raja then reigning at Dhār
attempted to win the favour of Iltutmish by attacking Vagbhata,
Vīra Narāyan's uncle, who had been regent at Ranthambhor, but
Vagbhata defeated him, and after the death of Iltutmish recovered
Ranthambhor from the officer who held it for Raziyya, and was
acclaimed by the Chauhāns as their king. Muslim historians allege
that he was defeated at Ranthambhor by Raziyya's troops, but are
constrained to admit that the troops evacuated the fortress after
dismantling it[2].

[1] See *ante*, p. 53.   [2] See *ante*, p. 59.

In 1249 Ghiyās-ud-dīn Balban, who afterwards ascended the throne of Delhi, attempted to recover Ranthambhor for his master, but was obliged to retire discomfited[1]. The Muslim histrorian styles Vagbhata Nāhar Deo, confusing him, perhaps, with a Meo chief, who had probably allied himself to Vagbhata, for Balban, before marching on Ranthambhor, had been engaged in an attempt to establish order in Mewāt. Vagbhata was succeeded by his son, Jaitra Singh, who abdicated, and was succeeded in 1282 by his son Hamīra, known to the Muslims as Hamīr.

Hamīra was warlike and enterprising. After subduing Arjuna, a minor chieftain of Mālwa, he attacked the Gond raja of Garha-Mandlā who submitted and paid tribute.

The Pawār had gained little by his attempt to ingratiate himself with the foreigner. In 1234 Iltutmish invaded Mālwa and sacked both Bhīlsa and Ujjain, and Hamīra, after succeeding his father at Ranthambhor, resolved to punish Bhoja II, the reigning king of Mālwa, for the crime of his predecessor. Bhoja was defeated, and Hamīra made a triumphal entry into Ujjain, the ancient capital of Mālwa. Not content with this success, he marched northward, compelled the Gahlot, Lachhman Singh, to acknowledge his supremacy, captured Ābū and restored it to its hereditary prince in return for a promise to pay tribute, and marched homeward through Ajmer, Pushkar, Sāmbhar, and Khandela, all of which places he captured.

This vainglorious expedition enhanced Hamīra's military reputation and was probably not without effect on the attitude of Jalāl-ud-dīn Fīrūz, the first king of the Khaljī dynasty, who, in 1291, marched to Ranthambhor, but decided[2], after reconnoitring the fortress, that it would be dearly captured at the price in human lives which he would have to pay, and turned aside to Jhāīn and Mandāwar.

Hamīra's defiance of 'Alā-ud-dīn Muhammad by harbouring the leaders of the mutiny which had broken out in Ulugh Khān's army at Jālor, as it was returning from the conquest of Gujarāt, cost him his kingdom and his life[3]. Ulugh Khān followed the fugitives into the territory of Ranthambhor and defeated the Rājputs under two officers named Bhīm and Dharma Singh, but was unable to undertake the siege of the fortress, and retired to Delhi. Hamīra emasculated Dharma Singh, and he and his brother fled to Delhi and besought 'Alā-ud-dīn to avenge this outrage. Ulugh Khān and Nusrat Khān were sent to open the siege of Ranthambhor, and, having first captured Jhāīn, encamped before the fortress, but

---

[1] See *ante*, p. 67   [2] See *ante*, p. 95.   [3] See *ante*, p. 101.

were unfortunate. Nusrat Khān was killed and Ulugh Khān was defeated and driven back to Jhāīn. 'Alā-ud-dīn then marched from Delhi to conduct the siege in person, and after some delay arrived before Ranthambhor. The siege was protracted for some months, and Ranamalla, or Ranmal, Hamīra's minister, and some of the principal officers of the garrison deserted to the Muslims. The assault was delivered on July 10, 1301, and according to the Hindu version of the affair both Hamīrā and Mīr Muhammad Shāh, the leader of the mutineers who had found an asylum at Ranthambhor, performed the rite of *jauhar* and were slain. The queen, Rangadevī, immolated herself, and Hamīrā's brother Virama and the heroes Jajar, Gangādhar Tak, and Kshetra Singh Pawār shared their master's fate. The traitor Ranamalla and his companions were put to death by 'Alā-ud-dīn. Thus ended Chauhān rule in Hindūstān. The Raja of Nimrāna, in the north of the Alwar State, claims descent from Prithvī Rāj.

Reference has been made to the conquest of Gujarāt by 'Alā-ud-dīn's officers, Ulugh Khān and Nusrat Khān. Bhīm II, 'the Simpleton,' who reigned from 1179 to 1242, was the king who de-feated Muhammad b. Sām, and though he was afterwards defeated by Qutb ud-dīn Aibak, who plundered his capital, Gujarāt was not occupied by the Muslims, but remained a Hindu state. Bhīm II was the last of his line, the Solankīs, of which his ancestor Bhīm I, the contemporary of Mahmūd, had been the second.

Gujarāt was the richest kingdom of India. 'It was to India what Venice was to Europe, the *entrepot* of the products of both the eastern and western hemispheres.' Its princes favoured sometimes the Jain and sometimes the Buddhist heresy. The court of Siddha-rāja Jayasingha, the seventh of the Solankīs, who reigned from 1094 to 1143 and was one of the most powerful of Indian rulers, was visited by the geographer al-Idrīsī. On Bhīm's death in 1242 his throne passed to Visaladeva Vāghela of Dholka, who was descended from Siddharāja Jayasingha, and who reigned from 1243 to 1261.

Karandeva, the Rāī Karan of the Muslims and the fourth of the Vāghela dynasty, was reigning in 1297, when 'Alā-ud-dīn Khalji sent his brother Ulugh Khān and Nusrat Khān to make an end of Hindu rule in Gujarāt. They were successful, and the Rājput Kingdom was overthrown[1]. 'The walls of Anhilvāra were demol-ished ; its foundations excavated, and again filled up with fragments of their ancient temples.'

---

[1] See *ante*, p. 100

The fate of Karan and his family has been related elsewhere. His wife was captured and became the wife or concubine of the Muslim king of Delhi. Karan himself fled, with his beautiful daughter Deval Devī, and took refuge with Rāmchandra of Deogīr, well content now that his daughter should wed his host's son, to whom, in his pride, he had formerly refused her ; but the prince of Deogīr never possessed his bride, who was captured by the Muslim officer Alp Khān near Ellora[1], and carried to Delhi, where she became the wife first of Khizr Khān, 'Alā-ud-dīn's eldest son, who was afterwards murdered by order of his brother, Qutb-ud-din Mubārak, into whose possession she passed, and at last she suffered the degradation of the embraces of the foul outcaste, Khusrav Khān, who murdered his master and usurped his throne. Karan established himself for a time in the Nandurbār district, on the borders of the small state of Baglāna, or Bāglān, but his line died with him.

In Western India, as in Hindūstān, Hindu rule, in the hands of minor chieftains, survived the extinction of the royal house. Chauhāns held Chāmpāner and Pavagarh until 1484, when Mahmūd Begarha of Gujarāt took their stronghold[2] and the survivors fled to Chota Udaipur and Deogarh Bāriya, still held by their descendants. On the north-eastern frontier the state of Sirohi was held, as at present, by another branch of the Chauhāns, known as Deora Rājputs from the name of an ancestor, Deorāj, who migrated westward when his clan was driven from its patrimony, Nādol, by Qutb-ud-dīn Aibak. The raja of Sirohi was ever ready to take advantage of the weakness of the kings of Gujarāt by raiding the northern districts of their kingdom.

The peninsula of Cutch, too, remained unmolested by the Muslim governors and kings of Gujarāt. Sammā Rājputs of Sind, fleeing from that country before the Sūmras, who had superseded them as its rulers, found an asylum with the Chāvada Rājputs who ruled Cutch, and in about 1320 overcame their host and took the kingdom from them. Those of the Sammā tribe who remained in Sind accepted Islam, and their kinsmen in Cutch, not prepared entirely to abandon the religion of their fathers, adopted a strange medley of the two faiths. The peninsula was divided between three branches of the two tribe, all known as Jādeja, or 'the sons of Jāda,' until 1540, when Khengār, the head of one branch with the help of Mahmūd III of Gujarāt reduced his kinsmen to obedience and became sole ruler. His uncle, Jām Rāwal, fled to Kāthīāwār, and

[1] See *ante*, p. 113.   [2] See *ante*, pp. 309, 310.

received from the Muslim king of Gujarāt the fief of Nawanagar, still held by his descendants. The raja of Cutch was nominally bound to furnish a contingent of 5000 horse to the army of the Sultan of Gujarāt.

The south-western region of the peninsula of Kāthīāwār was held by the Chudāsima Rājput chief of Girnār, the group of hills rising above the fortress of Junāgarh. His dominions included a great part of the ancient Surāshtra, or Sorath, in its modern form. This remote corner of India was not molested by the early Muhammadan invaders, but the raja reigning in the middle of the fourteenth century harboured the rebel Taghī, who had risen in Gujarāt against the authority of Muhammmad Tughluq, whose evil days were drawing to a close. Muhammad pursued the rebel, and attacked both the raja of Girnār and the raja of Cutch, who was his ally. Taghī evaded him and fled into Sind, but the fortress-capital of Girnār was taken, and both the raja and his ally were compelled to make obeisance to Muhammad[1], who was too intent on capturing Taghī to remain in Kāthīāwār, and left that country without any more material assertion of his authority.

The raja of Girnār appears to have been independent of the earlier Muslim kings of Gujarāt, or at least to have paid tribute irregularly, and only when it was levied by force, for in 1466 Mahmūd Begarha invaded his state, and by means of wholesale pillage and massacre, including the sacking of a temple and the slaughter of its defenders, compelled him to agree to pay tribute. In the following year a threat sufficed to deter him from using the insignia of royalty, which he had hitherto displayed[2], and in 1469 Mahmūd, judging that the time had come to crush the 'misbelievers,' invaded the Girnār state and offered the raja the choice between Islam and death. Protestations of loyalty were of no avail, and he was besieged in his fortress, Uparkot, and, when hard pressed there, fled to another stronghold in the mountains, where Mahmūd besieged him and compelled him, on December 4, 1470, to surrender. He accepted Islam and was entitled Khān Jahān. This raja is styled by Muslim historians 'Mandalak', as though this were his personal name, but the word is evidently no other than *Mandalika*, the Sanskrit term for a provincial governor[3].

At about the time when the Arabs were overrunning Sind Bāpā, the Gahlot chieftain, captured from the Paramāras or Pawārs the fortress of Chitor, which remained the capital of this ancient tribe until it was captured by Akbar in 1567, when Udaipur became

---

[1] See *ante*. pp. 171, 172.   [2] See *ante*, p. 305.   [3] See *ante*, pp. 305, 306.

their principal seat. Their legends claim for them the credit of having opposed in arms both the Arab invader of Sind and the Turkish conqueror of the Punjab, and though it is possible that they marched, or sent contingents, against both, they were not sufficiently important to be mentioned in Muslim histories, and their own legends are not sufficient to establish any historical fact.

During the interval of comparative peace between the raids of Mahmūd and the more systematic subjection of Northern India by Muhammad b. Sām 'the Chauhāns of Ajmer and the Gahlots of Chitor were alternately friends and foes.' The prince of Chitor, who had married a sister of Prithvī Rāj of Ajmer and Delhi, espoused his cause in his contest with Jayachandra of Kanauj for supremacy in Northern India. The Solankī in Gujarāt and the Pratihāra in Mandor[1] supported the claim of the Gaharwār, and, according to Rājput legend, both Kanauj and Gujarāt employed Muslim mercenaries whose presence in their armies was a source of useful information to Muhammad b. Sām. The Rājputs of Northern India richly deserved their fate.

The prince of Chitor, his son Kalyan Singh, and thirteen thousand of his troops are said to have been slain at the second battle of Tarāorī, and his widow, on hearing of his death, 'joined her lord through the flame.'

North-west of Mewār, the region in which the Gahlots bore sway, lay the desert tract of Mārwār, at this time ruled by the Pratihāras, who were afterwards expelled by the Rāhtors, the tribe to which the present Mahārāja of Jodhpur belongs. West of Mār-wār lies the present State of Jaisalmer, held by the Jādons, whose home, according to their own traditions, had in ancient times been Zābulistān, between Sīstān and Qandahār. Long before the rise of Islam they had been driven thence into the Punjab, where they domiciled for some time, and one branch of the tribe, the leader of which had retired in the eighth century into the desert of western Rājfontāna, acquired from an ancestor the name of Bhātī. A branch of the Bhātīs settled in the north of the modern State of Bikaner, and gave to the town now known as Hanūmangārh[2] its original name, Bhatner, which in 1398 was taken by Tīmūr from a Bhātī chief named Dul Chand. This clan, as well as those branches of the Jādons which remained in the Punjab, accepted Islam. The main body of the tribe, however, travelling westward, had founded the fortress of Tanot, in the extreme north-western corner of what is now the Jaisalmer State. They afterwards made Ladorva their

[1] In 26° 21′ N. and 73° 2′ E.   [2] In 29° 35′ N. and 74° 20′ E.

capital, and in 1156 Rāwal Jaisal founded the town of Jaisalmer. In Mārwār communities of Gohels, Chauhāns, and Pawārs disputed the authority of the Pratihāras or Parihārs.

The founder of the Rāthor dynasty of Mārwār was Siāhjī, whom the bards of the Rājputs represent as a prince of the Gaharwār house of Kunauj, who escaped when the rest of the family was slain, and, fleeing, established himself in Mārwār, where his tribe received the name of Rāthor. This they explain as a corruption of Rāshtrakūta, alleging that the Gaharwārs were Rāshtrakūtas from the Deccan, but there is little doubt that the whole story is fiction. The Gaharwār line was certainly extinguished, and there is no evidence that any escaped ; there is no reason to believe that the Gaharwārs were Rāshtrakūtas ; and an inscription dated A.D. 997, found in a town in the Jodhpur State, names four Rāthor Rajas who reigned there in the tenth century. It was probably from these local chieftains that Siāhjī was descended. He established himself, with a small number of followers, first in the north of Mārwār, where he received, as the price of assistance rendered to a Solankī chieftain, a bride with a dower. On a pilgrimage to Dwārkā he encountered and slew the brigand from whom he had delivered the Solankī. The exploit enhanced his reputation and, about 1212, he took up his abode in the fertile region watered by the Lūnī river, west of the Arāvallī Mountains. Here, by violence combined with treachery, he obeyed the Rājput maxim, 'Get land.' One Rājput chief and his followers he slew at a feast, another he defeated and killed in the field. The Brāhmans of Pālī besought his aid against the Mers and Mīnas who ravaged their lands. He drove off the marauders and, having settled at Pāli on land granted to him by the grateful Brāhmans, slew the leaders of the community and appropriated their lands. His son and successor, Asvatthāma, established his brother Soning in Īdar, a principality of the Dābhi Rājputs, by treacherously slaying the members of that clan while they were mourning for one of their princes ; and Aja, another brother, invaded Okhamandal, in the extreme west of Kāthīāwār, and established himself there by murdering the Chāvade ruler of the country. His descendants bear the surname which he assumed, and are still known as Vādhel, 'the Slayers'.

Rāīpal, the fourth of the line, slew the Parihār chief of Mandor, and Chhada and Tida, the seventh and eighth, harassed the jādons or Bhātīs of Jaisalmer and escaped chastisement only by giving the daughter of one of them in marriage to Rāwal Chāchakdeo I.

---

[1] In 25° 47′ N. and 73° 19′ E.

The Rāthors were as prolific as they were unscrupulous, and wide as the lands were which they had obtained by violence and fraud, they were now insufficient for their support. Chonda, their eleventh chief, after suffering many vicissitudes, was able to assemble a large army composed entirely of the various clans of his tribe and to attack the Parihār prince of Mandor. He was victorious, and planted his banner 'on the ancient capital of Maru.'

Chonda also added to his dominions the important city and district of Nāgaur, a Muslim stronghold which the dissolution of the Kingdom of Delhi, following Tīmūr's invasion of India, enabled him to acquire, and it was at this city that he met his death.

His fourth son, Aranyakanwal, had been betrothed to Karamdevī, daughter of Mānik Rāo of Aurint, chief of the Mohil Rājputs, but the damsel met and loved Sadhu, heir of Rāningdeo, the Bhātī lord of Pugal, a fief of Jaisalmer, and chose him as her husband. The slighted prince of Mandor attacked his rival, and the two met in single combat. Sadhu was slain, and Karamdevī, 'at once a virgin, a wife, and a widow,' sacrificed herself in the fire. Aranyakanwal died of his wounds, but Rāningdeo, not content with the death of his son's rival, led a raid into Chonda's territory to punish the Sānkhlas, whose prowess had discomfited the Bhātīs in the combat between Sadhu and Aranyakanwal. Having slain three hundred of his enemies Rāningdeo was returning with his spoil when he was overtaken by Chonda, who defeated and slew him.

Rāningdeo's two surviving sons, Tana and Mera, accepted Islam, as so many other Bhātīs had done, and thus obtained from Khizr Khān, then governor of Multān, a force with which to attack their enemy, but Kilan, son of the Rāwal of Jaisalmer; who joined them, ensured their success by guile. Professing a desire to end the feud, he offered a daughter in marriage to Chonda, but when the Rāthor came forth to receive his expected bride his suspicions were aroused by the appearance of the *cortège*, which consisted of an unusually large number of armed men, and he turned back towards Nāgaur. His enemies pursued him, and slew him at the gate of the town, 'and friend and foe entering the city together a scene of general plunder commenced.'

The death of Chonda occurred in 1408, and Nāgaur was then lost to the Rāthors. He was succeeded by his son Ranmall, who took advantage of the marriage of his daughter to Lakhā Rānā, the old chief of Chitor, to obtain a large grant of land from his son-in-law, to whose court he migrated, and was followed thither by his son, Jodha. An account of the growth of Rāthor influence at the court of Chitor, and of their expulsion from Mewār will be given in the history of that principality. Ranmall, with the aid of the forces of Mewār, captured the city of Ajmer by a stratagem, and thus temporarily added the ancient heritage of the Chauhāns to the domains of Mewār. He attempted, after the death of Lakhā Rānā, to usurp the throne of his infant son, but was slain in 1444 by Chonda, the old Rānā's firstborn, who expelled the Rāthors from Mewār. He was succeeded by Jodha, the eldest of his twenty-four sons, who in 1454 acquired Sojat, and in 1459 laid the foundation of Jodhpur, which has ever since remained the capital of the Rāthor State. On his death in 1488 he was succeeded by his second son, Sūja, or Surajmall, the eldest, Sāntal or Sātal, having been slain near Pokhāran, where he had established himself on the lands of the Bhātīs. Sūrajmall was the hero of the episode known as the Rape of the Virgins. In July, 1516, a predatory band of Muslims, probably from Ajmer, descended on the town of Pīpar during the celebration of the Tij festival, and carried off a hundred and forty Rājput maidens. Sūrajmall, to whom news of the outrage was carried, at once mounted, pursued the marauders, and rescued the maidens, but lost his own life in the fray. He was succeeded by his grandson, Ganga, the son of his eldest son, Bhaga, who had predeceased him, but his title was contested by his uncle, Saga, Sūrajmall's third son, who was supported by Daulat Khān Lodī. Saga and his ally were, however, defeated, and the former was slain.

Rāo Ganga sent a large contingent to join Sangrama Rānā in the battle of Khānūā, fought against Bābur in 1527, and on that day, so disastrous to the Rājputs, the young prince Rāimall, grandson of Ganga, and many other Rāthors fell. Ganga himself survived this event by nearly four years, and died in 1532.

The Rāthors are widely spread. We have followed one tribe of them in Okhamandal, where they are known as Vādhel, 'the slayers.' The origin of a family which ruled the small principality of Baglāna, or Bāglān, a country now represented by the Bāglān and Kalvān *tālukas*, north of the Sātmāla hills, is more obscure. They, like the Rāthors of Mārwār, claimed kinship with the Gaharwārs of Kanauj, but did not trace their descent to Siāhjī. They were perhaps descended from earlier Rāthors of Mārwār and merely imitated Siāhjī in claiming descent from the Gaharwārs. Their chief used the honorific title of Baharjī and possessed seven fortresses, two of which, Mulher and Sālher, were noted for their strength. They seem to have been tributary to the princes of Deogīr, and they assisted Karandeva, the last Raja of Gujarāt, when he fled, after the conquest of his country, to the Deccan. When the kingdom of the Yādavas was annexed by the king of Delhi the allegiance of Baharjī was transferred to the conqueror, but the country became independent after the revolt of the Deccan and the establishment of the Bahmanī dynasty. Later it became tributary to the Sultans of Gujarāt, and was invaded and laid waste by Ahmad Shāh Bahmanī I in 1429. It remained tributary to Gujarāt, but enjoyed virtual independence until that kingdom was conquered by Akbar in 1573. He failed to conquer Baglāna, and was obliged to acquiesce in a treaty with Pratāp Shāh, the reigning prince, in 1599.

The original title of the Gahlot princes of Mewār was Rāwal but early in the thirteenth century Rāhup of Mewār captured Mokal the Parihār Prince of Mandor, who bore the title of Rānā, and carried him to Sesoda, the temporary capital of the Gahlots, where he compelled him to forgo the title of Rānā and assumed it himself, instead of that of Rāwal. It was he, too, who changed the name of his clan from Gahlot to Sesodia, derived from his temporary capital.

The legend that the Gahlots had met and defeated the Arab invaders of Sind has already been mentioned. It is to the effect that they repelled an invasion of Mewār led by one Mahmūd, whom they defeated and captured. It is certain that no Arab invader from Sind ever reached Mewār, and the name Mahmūd suggests confusion between the Arabs of Sind in the eighth century and the Turks of Ghazni in the eleventh. It is possible that a Gahlot prince joined one of the confederacies against Mahmūd, or met that invader on his way to Gujarāt in the expedition in which he plundered Somnāth, but we have no record of the event. The fate of the prince of Chitor at the second battle of Tarāorī has been mentioned. The Gahlot legend, disfigured by some palpable falsehoods, represents him 'as the Ulysses of the host; brave, cool, and skilful in the fight; prudent, wise, and eloquent in council; pious and decorous on all occasions; beloved by his own chiefs and reverenced by the vassals of the Chauhan.'

Little more that is authentic is known of the history of the Gahlots or Sesodias until the reign of 'Alā-ud-dīn Khaljī, who, having already captured Ranthambhor from the Chauhāns, besieged and took Chitor in 1303[1]. The bard's account of this siege is most inaccurate and misleading. He antedates it by thirteen years, to a time when 'Alā-ud-dīn had not ascended the throne; he

[1] See *ante*, p. 108.

makes Lachhman Singh, a distant cousin of the ruling prince, Rānā
of Chitor at the time of the siege ; and he makes the fair Padminī,
whom 'Alā-ud-dīn coveted, the wife of the prince's uncle. These
gross inaccuracies entirely discredit a story improbable in itself, at
variance with known facts, and designed to minimize the disgrace
of the loss of a strong fortress, of treachery on the part of Alā-ud-
din. The facts were that Ratan Singh was Rānā of Chitor, and that
Lachhman Singh, Rānā of Sesoda, commanded the fortress on his
behalf. Their common ancestor was Karan Singh, Rāwal of Chitor,
from whom Ratan Singh was ninth and Lachhman Singh eleventh
in descent. Ratan Singh was apparently in the fortress when it
was besieged, but, though the rite of *jauhar* is said to have been
performed and Lachhman Singh and eight thousand other Rajputs
fell, he was taken alive and carried off to Delhi. The fair Padmini
did not perish in the fire, as related by the bard, but lived to be
the subject of negotiation between her husband and his captor, and
the object of the bard's fiction appears to be the concealment of
Ratan Singh's readiness to obey the ancient maxim which permits
a Rājput to surrender his wife in order to preserve his land.

'Ala-ud-din left Māldeo, Raja of Jālor, whom he had defeated
and who had sworn fealty to him, in command of Chitor, and the
towns of Mewār were held by Muslim garrisons, and the survivors
of the Sesodias, and those who remained faithful to them took
refuge at Kelwārā[1], in the heart of the Arāvallī Mountains, and
from this stronghold harried the lands of Mewār. Māldeo was
shortly afterwards relieved of the command of Chitor, and Khizr
Khān, the eldest son of 'Ala-ud-din, was appointed in his place, but
after the rescue of Ratan Singh[2] 'Alā-ud-dīn removed Khizr Khan
and appointed Arsi, or Ar Singh, to the command. Arsi was, according to the Hindu legend, the elder son of Ajai Singh, Rānā of
Chitor, and, according to the Muslim chronicles, sister's son to
Ratan Singh. The bards do not mention Arsi's appointment to the
command of the fortress, but the Muslim historians say that on
being appointed he swore fealty to 'Alā-ud-dīn, who by this means
sowed discord among the Rajputs, some of whom remained faithful
to Ratan Singh, while others submitted to Arsi. The history of
Chitor at this time is hopelessly confused, owing to the silence of
the Muslim historians and the discrepancies between the Hindu
legends and the few facts known. It is certain, however, that Chitor
was recovered by the Rājputs shortly after this time, and that
Hamīr, or Hamīra Singh, was the hero of the enterprise. The pre-

1 In 25° 7′N. and 73° 36′E.   2 See *ante* p. 111.

cise degree of relationship between Hamīr and the Rānā is uncertain. According to the bards he was the son of Arsi, the elder son of Ajai Singh, but it seems probable that he was the grandson of Ratan Singh. The bards, in recording the recovery of Chitor, assign no date to it, but assert that it occurred in the reign of 'Mahmūd Khaljī of Delhi,' a king unknown to history. Elsewhere to Rajputs are said to have recovered Chitor about 1312, four years before the death of 'Alā-ud-dīn, who reigned until 1316, to have thrown the Muhammadan officers from the ramparts, and to have asserted their independence, but from an inscription at Chitor it appears that the fort was not recovered until the time of Muhammad Tughluq, who reigned from 1325 to 1351. According to native annals the 'Mahmūd Khaljī in whose reign the fort was taken by Hamīr was marching to recover it when he was met, defeated, and captured by the Rānā, who imprisoned him for three months at Chitor, and would not liberate him until he had surrendered Ajmer, Ranthambhor, Nāgaur, and Suī Sopar, with five millions of rupees and five hundred elephants. No Muslim king of Delhi was ever a prisoner in Chitor, or ever surrendered the fortresses mentioned to a Rānā of Chitor, and the story appears to be a clumsy but wilful adaptation of the defeat and capture of Mahmūd Khaljī II of Mālwa by Sangrama about 200 years after this time. Hamīr's reputation stands in need of so much manipulation of history. His reign was long and glorious. He lived until 1364, recovered all the dominions of his ancestors, and laboured to restore their prosperity.

He was succeeded by his son Kshetra, or Khet Singh, who extended the dominions of his house and is credited by the bards with a victory over the Mughul emperor Humāyūn, considerably more than a century before the latter's birth. He was slain in a family brawl in 1382, and was succeeded by his son Laksh Singh, or Lākhā. He conquered the mountainous region of Merwara and destroyed its chief stronghold, Bairātgarh, on the site of which he built Badnor[1], but of greater importance than this conquest was his discovery of the mines at Jāwar, sixteen miles south of Udaipur city, in territory taken by his father from the Bhīls. These produced lead, zinc, and some silver, and the wealth thus acquired enabled him to rebuild the temples and palaces destroyed by 'Alā-ud-dīn, and to build dams to form reservoirs or lakes for irrigation. Lākhā also defeated the Sānkhla Rājputs of Nagarchal, a district lying in the north of the present State of Jaipur, but the bards are not con-

---

[1] In 25° 50′ N. and 74° 17′ E.

tent with these exploits, and credit him with a victory over an imaginary Muhammad Shāh Lodī of Delhi.

Lākhā's eldest son, Chonda, was to have been betrothed to the daughter of Ranmall the Rāthor, but being annoyed by an innocent pleasantry of his father, which he regarded as indelicate, refused to accept Ranmall's offer of his daughter, and, as it could not be rejected without giving grave offence, Lākhā himself accepted it, but insisted that Chonda should relinquish his right to the succession in favour of any issue which might be born of the Rāthor lady. He agreed and Lākhā was succeeded, on his death in 1397, by his son Mokaljī, aged five, for whom Chonda acted as regent until, incensed by the unjust suspicions of the child's mother, he retired from the kingdom. The bards are at fault regarding his destination, which they give as Māndū, the capital of the Muslim kingdom of Mālwa, while they place the grant of land which he received in the west of the peninsula of Kāthīāwār, which was never included in the kingdom. On Chonda's departure the rapacious Rāthor kinsmen of the young Rānā's mother flocked into the state. Her brother Jodha, who afterwards founded Jodhpur, came first, but was soon followed by their father, Ranmall, with a large contingent of that clan. They murdered Raghudeva, the younger brother of Chonda, and their designs on the throne were so evident that the mother, trembling for her child's life, begged Chonda to return. He obeyed the summons, and promised to join her and the young Rānā on the Diwalī festival, the feast of lamps, at Gosunda, seven miles south of Chitor. Chonda and his band obtained admission to Chitor in the guise of neighbouring chieftains who had assembled to escort their prince to his capital. They overpowered the garrison, slew Rāo Ranmall and a large number of the Rāthors, and would have slain Jodha, had he not saved himself by flight. Chonda pursued him, occupied Mandor, then the Rāthor capital, which was held by the Sesodias for twelve years, and annexed the fertile district of Godwār, which adjoined Mewār.

Jodha Rāthor was a wanderer for seven years, but eventually succeeded in assembling a force of Rājputs of his own and other tribes, and in expelling the Sesodias from Mandor, where the two sons of Chonda were slain.

Mokal's reign was not distinguished by any feats of arms. The bards attribute to him a victory over the king of Delhi, but no contemporary king of Delhi was in a position to attack the Rānā of Chitor, and if there is any foundation for the bard's story Mokal must be suspected of refusing an asylum to Mahmūd, the last of

the Tughluq dynasty, when he was fleeing from Delhi after his
defeat by Tīmūr. Mokal was assassinated in 1433 by two of his
uncles, natural sons of his grandfather, they having interpreted an
innocent question put by him as a reflection on their birth. He
was succeeded by his son Kūmbha, one of the greatest of the princes
of Chitor, a soldier, a poet, a man of letters, and a builder to whom
Mewār owes some of her finest monuments. The temples of Kūmbha
Sham at Mount Ābū and Rishabhadeva in the Sadri pass, 'leading
from the western descent of the highlands of Mewār, 'still stand as
memorials of his devotion. 'Of eighty-four fortresses for the defence
of Mewār, thirty-two were erected by Kūmbha. Inferior only to
Chitor is that stupendous work called after him' Kūmbhalgarh,
'the fort of Kūmbha.' He captured Nāgaur and gained many successes over his enemies in the intestinal feuds of the Rājputs, but
the ascription to him of a great victory over Mahmūd I of Mālwa,
whom he is said to have taken prisoner, and to have released after
six months of captivity, is an error. Kūmbha was not fortunate in
his campaigns against Mahmūd I, which have been described in
Chapter xiv, and if 'the Pillar of Victory' at Chitor does indeed
describe victories over that king it resembles the bardic chronicles.
Mewār's victory over Mālwa was gained by Sangrama, Kūmbha's
grandson, over Mahmūd II of Mālwa, whom he defeated and took
prisoner near Gāgraun in 1517. Kūmbha was stabbed to death in
1468, after a reign of thirty-five years, by his son Uda, but the
patricide was attacked and defeated by his brother Rāimall, and
is said to have fled to Delhi, and to have offered a daughter in
marriage to the Muslim king as the price of his aid in seating him
on his throne, but no mention is made by Muslim historians either
of this event or of a subsequent Muhammadan invasion of Mewār
described by the bards, and Buhlūl Lodī, who was then reigning at
Delhi, was otherwise too deeply engaged to embark on such a campaign. Uda is said to have been struck by lightning and killed, as
he was leaving the king's presence at Delhi, but however this may
be, no more is heard of him, and Rāimall kept the throne. He was
a warlike prince, but he certainly did not, as recorded in the Rājput
annals, carry on an interminable strife with Ghiyās-ud-dīn Khaljī
of Mālwa, a slothful and unwarlike prince who hardly ever left his
palace, but it is not improbable that Rāimall raided the frontiers
of Mālwa.

He had three sons, Sangrama or Sangā, Prithvī Rāj, and Jaimall,
whose ambition bred bitter strife between them until Sangrama
withdrew from Mewār and lived in concealment to avoid the violence

of Prithvī Rāj, and Prithvī Rāj was banished. Jaimall was now regarded as the heir, but in attempting to gain access of the damsel whom he was to marry ·was slain by her indignant father, and Prithvī Rāj was recalled from banishment and gained the hand of the maiden on whose account his brother had been slain. Another claimant to the throne arose in the person of Sūrajmall, the cousin of the three princes, but Prithvī Rāj defeated him and drove him from Mewār, and his great-grandson, Bika, founded the Partābgarh· Deolïa state. Prithvī Rāj was afterwards poisoned by his brother-in-law, Jaimall of Sirohi; whose title to Ābū had been confirmed by his marriage, and whom Prithvī Rāj had punished for ill treating his sister ; and on Rāimall's death in 1508 his eldest son, Sangrama, succeeded him without opposition.

Sangrama, destined to fall on the field of battle, was one of the greatest of the princes of Chitor. 'Eighty thousand horse, seven Rajas of the highest rank, nine Rāos, and one hundred and four chieftains bearing the titles of Rāwal and Rāwat, with five hundred war elephants, followed him into the field. The princes of Mārwār and Amber did him homage, and the Rāos of Gwalior, Ajmer, Sikrī, Rāisen, Kālpī, Chanderi, Bundī, Gāgraun, Rāmpura, and Ābū served him as tributaries or held of him in chief[1].' Sangrama, like some of his predecessors, is credited with victories for which there is no historical warrant over the king of Delhi, Ibrāhīm Lodī, but he profited by the weakness and distractions of his enemies to extend and secure his frontiers, and it was he who, as already described, defeated and captured Mahmūd II of Mālwa, whose army contained a contingent placed at his disposal by the Sultan of Gujarāt, so that the victor was able to boast that he had defeated the allied forces of two Muslim kings[2].

Sangrama had been in communication with Bābur while the latter was still at Kābul, and had agreed, in the event of his invading India, to attack Agra while he attacked Delhi, but had failed to fulfil his promise hoping, apparently, either that both Bābur and Ibrāhīm Lodī would be destroyed or that the victor would be so exhausted as to afford him an opportunity of establishing his supremacy and restoring Hindu rule in Northern India. Not content with failing to aid Bābur, he assembled a large army to attack him, and began operations by besieging Bayāna. Bābur marched to the relief of the fortress, and Sangrama raised the siege and marched

---

[1] Tod, i, 348, 349. This account, based on the statements of the bards, is somewhat highly coloured.

[2] See *ante*, pp. 368. 369.

to Khānua, near Sīkrī, where the fate of Northern India was decided.
A full account of the battle will be given in the records of Bābur's
reign. Sangrama displayed no eagerness to attack the Muslims, and
according to the Hindu annals the battle was preceded by negotiations, in which Silahdī the Tomār, chief of Rāisen, a fief of Mālwa,
but now virtually independent, was employed as the inter mediary.
He is said, on the same authority, to have made a private agreement with Bābur, in pursuance of which he deserted the Hindu
cause and joined the Muslims during the battle, but the extenuation
of defeat by allegations of treachery is as common in Hindu annals
as in those of other nations. The Rājputs suffered a crushing defeat.
Sangrama himself was severely wounded, and Rāwal Udai Singh of
Dūngarpur ; Ratan Singh, Rāwat of Salūmbar ; Rāimall Rāthor,
grandson and heir of the prince of Mārwār ; Khet Singh and Ratan
Singh of Mertha ; Rāmdās, Rāo of Jālor ; Uja Jhāla ; Gokuldas
Pawār; Mānikchand and Chandrabhān, Chauhāns ; and many others
of less note were slain.

Sangrama retired towards Mewāt, resolved not to return to his
capital until he had retrieved his defeat and crushed the invader ;
but his ministers shrank from the discomfort and hardships which
his decision imposed upon them, and he died at Baswa of poison
administered at their instigation.

He was succeeded by Ratan Singh II, his eldest surviving son,
who was secretly affianced to the daughter of the Kachhwāha,
Prithvī Rāj, Rāo of Amber, but delayed the marriage ceremony, and
Sūrajmall, Rāo of Būndī of the Hāra clan of the Chauhāns, sought
and obtained her hand in marriage. Sūrajmall and Ratan Singh met
and fought in 1531, when each killed the other, and Vikramāditya
or Bikramājīt succeeded his brother on the throne of Mewār. The
new Rānā was arrogant, passionate, and vindictive, and alienated
his nobles, and the cavaliers of Mewār, by his preference for the
society of wrestlers and athletes and for the infantry of his army,
which he devleoped at the expense of his cavalry. An open rupture
occurred between the prince and his nobles, and his cavalry refused
to perform their duties. Matters had reached this stage when Sultān
Bahādur of Gujarāt marched against Bikramājīt, then encamped
at Loicha, in the Būndī territory. The feudal forces of the state
deserted their sovereign and marched off to defend Chitor and the
infant Udai Singh, posthumous son of Sangrama. Bahādur gained
an easy victory over the *pāiks*, or foot-soldiers of Mewār[1], and turned
towards Chitor, to the defence of which the prince of Būndī, the

[1] See *ante*, p. 330.

Rāos of Jālor and Ābū, and many chiefs from all parts of Rājasthān
hastened. The siege has been described in Chapter XIII[1]. Chitor
fell in 1534, and became for a short time a possession of the kingdom
of Gujarāt, but Udai Singh, who had been crowned during the siege,
was carried off into safety by Surjan, prince of Būndi. There is no
truth in the Rājput story of the dispatch of the *rākhī* to Humāyūn
by the young Rānā's mother, and of the latter's chivalrous response,
for though he had received gross provocation from Bahādur he
punctiliously refrained from attacking him while he was engaged in
warfare against the 'misbelievers'. After the fall of Chitor, however,
Bahādur was compelled to retire before Humāyūn, and Bikramājīt
returned and almost immediately recovered the fortress. He had
learned no wisdom in adversity, and his insolence and arrogance
towards his nobles culminated in a blow inflicted in open court on
Karamchand of Ajmer, his father's protector and benefactor. On
the following day the nobles put the unworthy prince to death and,
dreading the rule of a minor at such a critical period, persuaded
Banbir Singh, natural son of Prithvī Rāj, Sangrama's younger
brother, to mount the throne. Banbīr immediately sought the life
of the infant, Udai Singh, but he was saved by a faithful nurse, who
carried him off, and, after some vicissitudes, delivered him to Āsā
Sāh, governor of Kūmbhalgarh, who ensured his safety by passing
him off as his nephew, and for three years kept the secret of his
presence with him. The rumour at length spread that the son of
Sangrama was at Kūmbhalgarh, and the nobles of Mewār
assembled there to do him homage. The pretensions of the bastard,
Banbīr, had offended them, and all deserted him. He still held the
capital, but his ministers admitted a thousand of the adherents of
the legitimate prince, and he was deposed, and Udai Singh was
enthroned in 1537.

The foundation of Jaisalmer by Rāwal Jaisal, the Bhātī, has been
mentioned. The Jādons, or Bhātīs, yet occupy their home in the
desert. The Rāthors were gaining power in the land of Kher, the
desert of the west, and the Jādons found them troublesome neighbours, rapacious and unscrupulous. Rāwal Chāchakdeo grandson
of Jaisal, who reigned from 1219 to 1241, made preparations to
chastise them, but their leaders conciliated him by giving him a
daughter to wife. Karan Singh I, who reigned from 1241 to 1271,
espoused the cause of a Hindu living near Nāgaur, whose only
daughter had been abducted by Muzaffar Khān, the Muslim ruler
or governor of that district, and defeated and slew the Khān and
three thousand of his men.

[1] See *ante*, p. 330.

The annals of Jaisalmer record a siege of the city by the troops of 'Alā-ud-dīn Khaljī of Delhi, which lasted for eight years, from 1286 to 1295. 'Alā-ud-dīn did not ascend the throne of Delhi until 1296, and no such siege as that sung by the bards ever took place. The account of the performance of the rite of *jauhar*, and of the death of 24,000 women in the flames, is detailed and circumstantial. Three thousaud eight hundred Rājput warriors rushed on the foe ; Mūlrāj III, the Jādon chief, and seven hundred of his kin fell, and Jaisalmer was occupied by a Muslim garrison which, after holding the place for two years, dismantled it and retired.

It is impossible to connect this legend with any historical event, but it may possibly be a wilful perversion of the defeat of the Jādons by the Rāthors, for the annals proceed to relate that after the retirement of the Muslim garrison Māloji Rāthor, chief of Mewa, made preparations for occupying and colonizing the deserted city, but was expelled by the Bhātī chiefs, Dūda and Tilak Singh, the former of whom was elected Rāwal, and reigned from 1295 to 1806. The bards of Jaisalmer, no whit inferior to those of other states in imagination, thus describe the end of Dūda's reign, 'He even extended his raids to Ajmer, and carried off the stud of Fīrūz Shāh from the Anasāgar (lake), where they were accustomed to be watered. This indignity provoked another attack upon Jaisalmer, attended with the same disastrous results. Again the *sakha* was performed, in which sixteen thousand females were destroyed ; and Dūda, with Tilak Singh and seventeen hundred of the clan, fell in battle, after he had occupied the *gaddī* ten years.' This statement is quoted merely in order to display the shameless mendacity of the bardic annals. Fīrūz Shāh was Jalāl-ud-dīn Fīrūz Khaljī, the uncle and predecessor of 'Alā-ud-dīn, who is said to have taken Jaisalmer in the previous year. It may be one more perversion of a defeat at the hands of the Rāthors.

Jaisalmer was again restored by Ghar Singh, who is said to have received it in fee from the king of Delhi for services rendered against Tīmūr, who did not invade India until nearly a century after this time, but if any such services were rendered the occasion was perhaps, as conjectured by Lt-Col. Tod, one of the many irruptions of the Mughuls which took place at this period. Ghar Singh was assassinated in 1335, and was succeeded by his adopted son, Kehar Singh. Kehar Singh's third son, Kailan, involved the Jaisalmer state in hostilities with the kingdom of Multān by establishing himself on the northern bank of the Sutlej, where he is said to have founded the town of Kahror[1]. The presence of the Bhātīs on the Multān side of the river was resented, and Chāchakdeo, who succeeded to Jaisalmer about 1448, is said to have resided at Marot in order the more readily to repel raids on his territories from the direction of Multān. He is credited in the annals of the state with two victories over the Muslim kings of Multān, besides others over the Dhundīs, the Rāthors, and even the Khokhars of the Punjab. He is said to have lost his life in battle with the king of Multān, but the native annals a most untrustworthy guide, are the only authority for his exploits. Even these fail us after Chāchakdeo's reign, and until the time of the Mughul emperors record nothing but a bare list of names.

The famous fortress of Gwalior was held, at the time of Mahmūd's incursions into India, by Kachhwāha Rājputs, probably feudatories of the Chandels of Jijhoti. Mahmūd's siege of the fortress in 1022 has already been noticed[2], and its strength at that time may perhaps be gauged by the easy terms on which he raised the siege. About 1128 the Parihār Rājputs ousted the Kachhwāhas, a scion of whom established himself in the neighbourhood of Amber. Qutb-ud-dīn Aibak captured the fortress, but it was recovered during the feeble reign of his son, Ārām Shāh, by the Parihār Bīrbal, or Māl Deo, whose son, Mangal Bhava Deo, was holding it in 1232, when Iltutmish attacked it. An account of his siege and capture of the place has already been given.[3] It remained in the hands of the Muslim until after Tīmūr's invasion, and was captured, when the kingdom of Delhi fell to pieces, by the Tomār, Har Singh, and was successfully defended by his son Bhairon against the attacks of Mallū in 1402 and 1403[4]. The sieges of Gwalior in 1416, 1427, and 1432 by kings of the Sayyid dynasty were rather expeditions for the purpose of collecting taxes, or tribute, then serious attempts to capture the fortress, and the raja could always rid himself of the invaders by a payment on account, and an illusory promise to make regular payments in future. In 1423 Hūshang Shāh of Mālwa attacked the fortress, but raised the siege when the Sayyid, Mubārak Shāh, marched to its relief.

During the protracted contests in the reign of Buhlūl Lodī between the kingdoms of Delhi and Jaunpur Mān Singh of Gwalior espoused the cause of the latter, and gave an asylum to its last king, Husain Shāh, when he was fleeing before his enemies.

Mān Singh profited by the strife between the Muslims to extend his dominions, and when Sikandar Lodī, provoked by his protection of a fugitive rebel, invaded them in 1505 and the following years, he did not venture to attack Gwalior itself, but contented himself with reducing Mandrāel, Utgīr, and other fortresses of less importance, and was eventually recalled from this campaign by other affairs, but in 1518 his son, Ibrāhīm Lodī, incensed by the raja's protection of the pretender, Jalāl Khān, besieged his capital, and Vikramāditya or Bikramājīt, the son and successor of Mān Singh, was compelled to surrender.

Raja Mān Singh, who reigned from 1486 to 1517, enriched Gwalior with the great palace which crowns the eastern face of the rock, and earned a name as a patron of music and musicians. The famous singer, Tān Sen, and the best musicians and singers at Akbar's court had been trained in the Gwalior school.

The Kachhwāhas of Amber and Jaipur claim descent from the ancient rajas of Gwalior, of that tribe. Tej Karan, known as Dulha Rāī, or the Bridegroom prince, who was eighth in descent from Vajradāman, the first Kachhwāha prince of Gwalior, left that city, for some undetermined reason, in charge of his sister's son, a Parihār, who usurped his throne. Tej Karan married the daughter of the Bargūjar Rājput chief of Daosa, and inherited that principality, then known as Dhūndhār, from the Dhūnd river. Maidal Rāo, Tej Karan's grandson, took the fortress of Amber from the Mīna chief Bhāto, and made it his capital. Maidal's great-grandson, Pajūn, married the sister of Prithvī Rāj of Ajmer and Delhi, and was killed with his brother-in-law at the second battle of Tarāorī. The Amber state, as it was known after the establishment of that town as the capital, was of little importance until the reign of Humāyūn. Towards the end of the fourteenth century Udai Karan, prince of Amber, added the Shekhāwati district to his dominions, but his house did not otherwise specially distinguish itself.

Gondwāna, the forest region between Berar on the west and Orissa on the east, was sparsely populated by the Gonds, Dravidians who had probably migrated northwards from the Deccan, but in the eleventh century the nothern and eastern tracts of this region, which were known as Chedi, were ruled by two families of Haihaya Bans Rājputs who were probably, like the Chandels of Jijhoti, Hinduized Gonds. One family, which retained its possessions until it was ousted by the Marāthās, had its capital at Ratanpur[1], in the present Bilāspur District; and the other at Tripuri, or Tewar,

[1] 22° 17′ N., 82° 11′ E.

about six miles from Jubbulpore. The Haihayas were also known as the Kālachurīs. Those of Tewar disappeared towards the end of the twelfth century, being supplanted, as is commonly believed, by Bāghels of Rewa, but according to Gond tradition by a Gond hero named Jādū Rāī, said to be the ancester of the Gond dynasty which was certainly reigning in that region, with its capital at Garha, not long after that time.

Tradition records the existence of a dynasty of Gāolī, or cowherd race, of whom nothing certain is known, at Deogarh, the old fortress which stands twenty-four miles south-west of Chhindwāra. This dynasty ended with the twin-brothers Ransūr and Ghansūr, who reigned jointly, and who befriended a Gond named Jātba. Jātba eventually slew his master and founded the Gond dynasty which reigned at Deogarh. The only indication of a date in the legend is the record of an imaginary visit paid by Akbar to Jātba, and even tradition is silent as to the history of his successors, of whom hardly anything is known until the time of Bakht Buland, who was reigning at Deogarh at the latter end of the seventeenth century.

Rather more than sixty miles west of Deogarh stands the fortress of Kherla, the foundation of which is attributed to a Rājput dynasty, whose capital it remained for a long period. The last of the line, Jaitpal, is said to have been killed ofter a twelve years' siege by the army of the king of Delhi. No such siege is recorded by the Muslim historians, but it is possible that the officials first placed in Berar by 'Alā-ud-dīn Khaljī extinguished the Rājput dynasty and built the present fort, which appears to be of Muham-mādan construction. It fell afterwards, probably during the rebel-lion of the Deccan in the latter years of Muhammad Tughluq's reign, into the hands of Gonds, who established a dynasty there.

Gond legend assigns a high degree of antiquity to the dynasty of Southern Gondwāna, the original eapital of which is said to have been Sirpur, near the Pranhitā River, in the 'Ādīlābād District of the Nizām's dominions. Ballālpur, higher up the river and on the opposite bank, was next selected as the capital, which was moved almost immediately to the newly founded city of Chānda[1], where the Gonds reigned until the dynasty was extinguished by the Marāthās.

There were thus, when Muslim rule was established both in Northern and in Southern India, four Gond kingdoms in Gondwāna —a northern kingdom with its capital at Garha; two central kingdoms with their capital at Deogarh and Kherla; and a southern kingdom with its capital at Chānda. There are no

1 19° 57′ N., 78° 58′ E.

materials for a detailed history of these kingdoms during the period of which we treat The northern kingdom known to the Muslims as Garha-Katanga, from its capital and another town, and afterwards as Garha-Mandla, was extended by Sangram Shāh, who succeeded about 1480, and developed the little state, consisting of four districts lying about Garha and Mandla, into a kingdom containing fifty-four districts, by annexing large portions of the Narbada valley, the districts now called Sangor and Dāmoh, and the present state of Bhopāl. He built the fortress of Chaurāgarh, he enriched his capital with buildings, and he obtained the fair Durgāvatī, daughter of the Chandel raja of Mahoba, as a bride for his son Dalpat, who succeeded him. The alliance suggests the origin of the Chandels.

Durgāwatī, as regent for her son, Bīr Narāyan, earned undying fame as the defender of his inheritance against the Muslim ruler of Mālwa and against Akbar, though she perished in the Mughul's unprovoked attack on the kingdom.

Of the history of the neighbouring kingdom of Deogarh nothing certain, as has been said, is known until the reign of Bakht Buland, late in the seventeenth century.

Of Kherla more is known. The fortress is situated near the highway between Hindūstān and the Deccan, and could not fail to attract attention. The Muslim kings of Deccan refrained from molesting this state until, in 1398, Narsingh, the Gond raja, taking advantage of Fīrūz Shāh's preoccupation with Vijayanagar, and instigated by the Muslim rulers of Mālwa and Khāndesh, invaded and ravaged Berar. He was driven out of that province and obliged to swear fealty to Fīrūz. Subsequent relations between the three states, the Deccan, Mālwa, and Kherla, have been described in Chapter xv. In the reign of Ahmad Shāh, brother and successor of Fīrūz, it was agreed that the allegiance of Kherla should be transferred to Mālwa, and the king of Mālwa afterwards captured the fortress and exterminated the Gond dynasty. Kherla appears in the Āin-i-Akbarī as a district in the province of Berar.

Of the southern kingdom, Chānda, yet more is known, but what little certain knowledge we possess is disfigured and obscured by a rank overgrowth of fiction. Despite the claims to antiquity made in the legends of this kingdom it seems to have risen on the ruins of the Vākātaka dynasty, whose capital was probably at Bhāndak, a village near Chānda, at the end of the eleventh or beginning of the twelfth century, and the names of nineteen kings who reigned between that time and 1751, when the Marāthas occupied the kingdom, have been preserved.

The first was Bhīm Ballār, or Ballāl, Singh, whose capital was at Sirpur and his chief stronghold Mānikgarh, in the hills of west of that town. His grandson was Hir Singh, who induced the Gonds to cultivate the land and introduced a primitive land revenue system. Hir Singh's grandson, Dinkar Singh, was a patron of learning, and was succeeded by his son, Rām Singh, a just ruler and a successful soldier, who extended the frontiers of his kingdom. Rām Singh was succeeded by his son, Surja Ballāl Singh, 'one of the most romantic figures of old Gondwāna.' Owing to the absence of any written record it is impossible to say precisely at what period he reigned. The early part of the fifteenth century has been assigned as his date, but it appears to be at least as likely that he lived early in the fourteenth century. The romantic circumstances of his supposed visit to Delhi need not be recorded here, but it is probable that he visited that city, though the fact has not been deemed worthy of mention by any trustworthy historian. From the absence of any such mention it may be inferred that the Gond story of his rendering the king of Delhi an important service by capturing the fortress of a Rājput named Mohan Singh which the Muslim officers had failed to take is fiction, as is also the story that the king rewarded him for the exploit with the title of Shāh, which no Muslim king of Delhi would have conferred. It is certain, however, that Surja Ballāl and all who succeeded him on the throne of Chānda used this title, in the form 'Sāh,' and it appears that Surja Ballāl, who was known after his visit to Delhi as Sher Sāh Ballāl Sāh, assumed it in imitation of the king of Delhi. Surja Ballāl was succeeded by his son Khāndkia Ballāl Sāh, who suffered from some disease which caused tumours and swellings on his body. Seeking a healthier capital than Sirpur he built the town of Ballālpur on the opposite side of the river. While hunting he accidentally discovered near the site on which Chānda stands a pool of water in a river bed, having drunk and washed himself in the water, found his disease alleviated. It was decided that the spot was the resting-place of the great god Achaleshwar, 'the Immovable One,' and Khāndkia, having been perfectly restored to health by further use of the water, built a new capital near the site, naming it Chandrapur, or Chānda (the Moon City). Its walls were completed by his son and successor, Hir Sāh, who induced or compelled his subjects to undertake the cultivation of fixed holdings and constructed many reservoirs for irrigation. His revenue from the land was assessed on the ploughs employed. He also built the citadel and the palace of Chānda, parts of which still stand. Of Hir Sāh it is recorded that he paid no tribute to any foreign king,

from which statement it may be inferred that his predecessors had
paid tribute, probably to the Bahmanī kings of the Deccan, but
the relations between that kingdom and the southern Gond state
are most obscure. The king of Chānda were not, like those of
Kherla, drawn into the disputes between the kings of the Deccan
and their northern neighbours, and seem wisely to have avoided
such entanglements ; but when Fīrūz Shāh, the eighth king of the
Bahmanī dynasty, marched northwards, in 1399 or 1400, to punish
Narsinga of Kherla for having invaded Berar, the fortress of Māhūr
was held by a 'misbeliever,' probably a Gond from Chānda who
had joined Narsing ; but he was permitted to retain the command
of the fortress a governor on behalf of Fīrūz, on making submission[1]. The same governor was again in rebellion in 1424, and in the
following year Ahmad Shāh, the successor of Fīrūz, dealt with him in
the manner already described[2]. Continuing his march northwards
Ahmad found the fortress of Kalam in the hands of a Gond chief,
whom he slew or expelled, and then led a raid into Gondwāna. He
probably crossed the Wardha on this occasion, and, if so, this is the
only recorded instance of the invasion of the Chānda kingdom by
a Muslim king.

Hir Sāh was succeeded by his two sons, Bhima and Lokbā, who
reigned jointly until they were succeeded by Kārn Sāh, the son of
one of them, who embraced and propagated the Hindu religion
and substituted the regular administration of justice for the primitive system under which each man avenged his own wrongs.

Kārn Sāh was succeeded by his son, Bābājī Ballāl Sāh, who
recovered the fortress of Bairāgarh and is mentioned in the *Āīn-i-
Akbarī*[3] as being able to place in the field 1000 horse and 40,000
foot. He paid no tribute.

The Gond language possesses no written characters, and a high
standard of civilization could hardly exist at the courts of the four
Gond kingdoms, but the kings were not mere barbarians. Their
architecture proves their taste, and if they possessed no native
literature many were enlightened enough to encourage Hindu
letters. The northern kingdom, Garha-Mandla, was rich, the rajas
of Deogarh and Kherla were warlike, but none could compare with
the greatness of the southern kingdom. 'Unlike the other Gond
kingdoms, the house of Chānda seems to have had a long succession
of good and intelligent rulers, who resisted the natural temptations
to inner strife and intrigue which brought destruction to the other
kingdoms'.

[1] See *ante*, p. 390.   [2] See *ante*, p. 399.
[3] Vol. ii, pp. 230, 232.

CHAPTER XXI

BURMA A.D. 1287–1531. THE PERIOD OF SNĀH IMMIGRATION

THE Great Khān accepted the conquest of Pagān, described in volume II, as an accomplished fact, and for the next two and a half centuries the princelets who ruled the various parts of Burma frequently held authority under the Chinese seal. Technically they were Chinese governors ; actually they were the native chieftains who would have ruled there in any case and they did as they pleased.

Since the Nanchao barrier states were henceforth the Chinese province of Yunnan, the road lay open and there was no longer any impediment to communication with China. That being so, we should expect a marked advance in Burmese culture. What we actually witness is a decline. The great palace vanished, and in its stead were several squabbling little courts of which the most important were Āva, Pegū, and Toungoo. Religion languished, and though pagodas continued to be built, none of them can compare with even the lesser temples of Pagān. When at length the darkness lifts, it is from the opposite direction to China that two rays of light appear : one a religious revival from Ceylon, the other the birth of vernacular literature.

Yet it was not the Tartars who destroyed the overlordship of Pagān. They did not wish to upset existing conditions, and gave the dynasty every support in re-establishing itself. It was washed away by a wave of migration which was beyond the control of a purely dynastic government. What we are now to witness is not so much a series of internal squabbles as a racial movement affecting all Indo-China : the Shāns swarm south, east, and west. In 1229 they founded the Āhom kingdom of Assam along the Brāhmaputra river ; about the same time they made themselves felt in Tenasserim, and in 1350 they founded the kingdom of Siam—Siam is the same word as Shān, and she is simply the greatest of Shān states. In Burma they overran the entire country, swamping Burman and Talaing alike. To-day they are most numerous race in Indo-China, numbering eighteen millions[1].

---

[1] Cochrane, 'The Shāns ; *Gazetteer of Upper Burma and the Shān States.*

(a) Ava 1287—1555

After killing his father, Thihathu proceeded to kill such of his brothers as were in reach, in accordance with that Massacre of the Kinsmen which convention permitted to a Burmese king at his accession[1]. As the Tartars were in occupation of the north, he went south and tried to establish himself in the Delta, but was killed whilst besieging Pegū which was held by its rebellious governor, Tarabya.

The surviving son Kyawswa (1287-98) returned to Pagán, where he paid annual tribute to China and in 1297 sent his son to receive investiture from the Emperor himself as prince of the Upper Burma state. This state, which lasted till 1555, ran from Myedu in Shwebo district to below Prome, and from Laungshe in Pakokku district to Kyaukse.

At the same time as he invested Kyawswa, the Emperor sent a seal to Athinhkaya as prince of Myinsaing in the Kyaukse district ; Hsenwi had been similarly recognised in 1289, and Mohnyin[2] in 1296. Athinhkaya was the eldest of the Three Shān Brothers (1298-1324) who now became the real rulers of Upper Burma ; the second was Yazāthinkyan, chief of Mokkayā ; the youngest Thihathu, chief of Pinle. Their towns, all in the Kyaukse district, command passes into the Shān hills and were exactly where a chieftain ruling hill and plain would fix his stronghold—to command the plain and afford easy escape to his ancestral highlands. They were the sons of a hill chief who, owing to some feud, had fled to Myinsaing, where there was already a Shān colony ; his daughter married no less a person than a son of the Pagán dynasty, so that the family gained favour at court and were entrusted with the administration of the Kyaukse canals. When the dynasty fell, they had every temptation to be disloyal, for, being in charge of the great canals and rice fields, they controlled the food supplies of the palace. In 1298 they plotted with the queen dowager, lured Kyawswa into a new monastery which they had built, and forced him to take the robe and dwell there under guard. They then reported to Yunnan that it had been necessary to dispose him because he was asking for armed assistance from Chiengmai and had intercepted envoys whom the new Talaing state of Pegu was sending to Yunnan. Finally they killed him[3] ; at his death he said :'None of my ancestors was ever executed

---

[1] See Harvey, *History of Burma*, p. 338.   [2]Parker, 'Précis'.

[3] He merges with Minrekyawswa to form the Minkyawswa Nat spirit ; Temple, *Thirty Seven Nats*, p. 56.

with the sword. Either throw me into the river or strangle me' ; so they strangled and cremated him and cast his remains into the Irrawaddy[1]. They killed also his son, his monk and principal followers, and seized the harem.

Survivors of the dynasty appealed to Yunnan. The Yunnan commandant obtained the Emperor's sanction, and with 12,000 men besieged the Brothers in three walled towns at Myinsaing. On their walls the Brothers mounted balistae, and in one assault the Tartars lost 500 men from the arrows blocks of stone, and beams which rained down on the stormers[2]. Finding the climate hot and malarious, the Chinese accepted the bribe, 800 taels (63 lb.) of gold and 2200 taels (183 lb.) of silver, and withdrew to Yunnan after letting their men help on the Kyaukse irrigation works, constructing the Thindwe canal. This is the end of Chinese interference in Burma resulting from the expedition of 1287.

Whether Pagān had hitherto been fertile or not[3], it was certainly unfertile now, and the soil of the Myingyan district assumed its present desolate and barren aspect. Denudation of the forests to provide fuel for pagoda bricks had doubtless lessened the rainfall, and extensive irrigation at Kyaukse might attract rainfall thither from Pagān. Crops grow there, but not in such quantity as to supply a city of 50,000 inhabitants who eat rice. Probably this was the reason, in addition to the belief that the luck of the site was exhausted, which now led to the removal of the palace from Pagān.

There was rice in the Delta but it was far away and the Delta was now under a hostile chief. There was rice in Kyaukse, but the capital could not be put there, so far from the country's own highway, the Irrawaddy. It was necessary to find a site which should be on the Irrawaddy and accessible to the rice of Kyaukse. The obvious site was Ava, in the Sagaing district, where the Myitnge river brought down the grain boats from Kyankes. But as the omens were adverse to Āva, Thihathu, the surviving Shān Brother, in 1312 set up his palace at Pinya, a bad site near by, for which the omens were favourable.

The Pagān dynasty continued to exist as *myosa* (governors) of Pagān until 1369 and then ceased save where it had merged, on

---

[1] For the taboo on shedding royal blood, and the convention whereby princes were drowned, see Harvey, *History of Burma*, p. 339.

[2] Huber, 'Fin de la dynastie de Pagan' in *Bulletin de l' Ecle Francaise d'Extreme Orient*, 1909.

[3] Mekenzie, 'Climate in Burmese History' in *Journal of the Burma Research Society*, 1913.

the distaff side, with the lineage of the Shān Brothers. The only specific mention of the Ari[1] after their overthrow by Anawrahta is that Sawyun, lord of Sagaing, a son of Thihathu, in 1314 enume-rated Ari among his armed retainers ; apparently they were like the warrior abbots of contemporary Christendom.

Even in its limited area the Upper Burma state was loosely knit, towns such as Sagaing, Sagu and Taungdwingyi doing as they pleased. The confusion was something more than brigandage : it was the result of a racial movement, nothing less than the Shān migration into the plains of Burma. In 1364 the Maw (Mogaung) Shāns[2] took Sagaing and Pinya, carrying off the princes, the white elephants, and numbers of the townsfolk. To escape being driven off in Shān raiders' slave gangs, the population of Upper Burma took to migrating to Toungoo.

After the Maw Shāns had departed, Thadominbya (1364—8), one of the Sagaing family, killed off such of his kinsmen as stood in his way there and at Pinya, drained the swamps round Āva, and built the town. It was usually the Burmese capital for the next five centuries ; till two generations ago the English, like the Chinese, referred to Burmah as Āva, and for the Shāns the king of Burma was to the end 'The Lord of the Golden Palace at Āva'. On his mother's side Thadominbya was descended from the Three Shān Brothers, and his father was a Shān notable who claimed descent from the primitive Pyusawti lineage. His habits were sufficiently primitive—thus, after killing a Toungoo rebel he ate a meal on the corpse's chest. Whilst trying to subject Sagu he was seized with small-pox. As he lay dying, a pagan who had no respect for Buddh-ism, he told an officer to return to the palace and kill his queen lest she should pass to his successor. The officer entered the palace and told her his errand so she then and there married him. As part of the regalia she had already been queen to four successive chiefs[3] of Pinya, and her union with the officer raised him to the throne. The pair massacred the royal kinsmen but the ministers would not accept them and hawked round the crown until finally Minkyiswas-awhe accepted it.

Minkyiswasawke (1368 —1401) was descended from the union of the Shān sister with the son of the Pagān dynasty, and as a child

[1] Douroiselle, 'The Ari of Burma and Tantric Buddhism' in *Annual Report of the Archaeological Survey of India*, 1915-16.

[2] For Maw, Mogaung, Pong, etc., see Harvey's *History of Burma*, p. 322.

[3] For the custom whereby queens passed to the next king, see Harvey's *History of Burma*, p. 324.

he had been carried off into captivity with his father, the lord of Thayetmyo, when Minhti, king of Arakan, raided it in 1333. On his release he became *thūgyi* (village headman) of Amyin in the Sagaing district and on becoming king he made an Arakanese monk his primate. He built the Zidaw weir in Kyaukse district and repaired the embankment of Meiktila lake.

Laukpya, lord of Myaungmya, hated his nephew Razadarit, and when Razadarit succeeded to the throne of Pegū in 1385, Laukpya wrote to Minkyiswasawke offering to hold Pegū as a vassal if Minkyiswasawke would help him to oust Razadarit. This started a war between Upper and Lower Burma which lasted till 1422. The fighting was almost entirely in the Delta and probably the war was a war of migration, Shān saturation of Upper Burma being sufficiently complete for Āva to swarm down on Pegū. The Burmese advance base was Prome, and their usual line of advance was down the Hlaing river to Dāgon (Rangoon), sometimes with another string of levies going down the Sittang valley from Toungoo. With them marched contingents from allied states, Mohnyin, Kale, and Yawnghwe ; indeed, the Talaing chronicles sometimes refer to the invaders as simply 'the Shāns.' Their total strength would usually be some 12,000 and the advance took place every year or so, both sides going home for the rains (June-November). The invaders would sit down in large stockades, and sally forth headhunting and slave raiding, sometimes besieging Hmawbi, Dalla, Dāgon (Rangoon), and other towns, or being besieged themselves. Occasionally some determined leader would bring about a battle, but the casualties mentioned are seldom a decimal per cent. of the numbers engaged, and it is difficult to avoid the impression that most of the fighting was of the type not uncommon in mediaeval countries when there was as much shouting as killing and the wretched villagers were the chief sufferers.

In addition to raiding the Delta, Āva had to defend herself against attacks from the Shān hill states and sometimes they tried to get her to join in their own quarrels. Thus in 1371 the *sawbwas* (chiefs) of Kale and Mohnyin each asked Minkyiswasawke to help oust the other, promising to become tributary in return, but he let them exhaust each other, and thus secured a nominal supremacy over both for a few years. But in 1373 Mohnyin raided the frontier at Myedu in Shwebo district and the king had so much trouble that in 1383 he sent an embassy to Yunnan. China thereupon graciously appointed him governor of Āva and ordered Mohnyin to behave. But Mohnyin in 1393 ravaged up to the walls of Sagaing.

In 1374 Arakan was distracted with civil war and some of the people asked Minkyiswasawke to send them a king ; he sent them his uncle, Sawmungyi. Sawmungyi ruled well, and on his death a few years later the Arakanese asked Minkyiswasawke to select a successor. Minkyiswasawke sent one of his sons but this son oppressed the people and soon fled to Āva.

Finding Pyānchs, chief of Toungoo, becoming friendly with Pegū in 1377, Minkyiswasawke told his brother, the lord of Prome, to inveigle Pyānchi into a visit and kill him. The king's brother wrote to Pyānchi : 'Come and marry your son to my daughter. Pyānchi accepted the invitation and came with his son to Prome where, during the night, his host did him to death and seized his retinue with much booty. The king rewarded this exploit with rich presents. and the chroniclers[1] who record the incident describe him as a king with a most upright heart. He died in the odour of sanctity at the age of 70 and after some palace murders was succeeded by a younger son, Minhkaung.

Minhkaung (1401—22) had been married by his father to a daughter presented by the chief of the Maw Shāns during a friendly mood about the same time as Razadarit put to death his own son, Bawlawkyantaw. A year later during her first pregnancy, she longed for strange food from the Delta, and the family asked Razadarit, though a foe, to send some. Razadarit consulted his ministers and they perceived that the unborn child was Bawlawkyantaw himself taking flesh again according to his dying prayer ; they sent mangoes from Dalla and other food, having bewitched it.

The child, prince Minrekyawswa, born in 1391, was already campaigning at the age of thirteen ; he accompanied the 1404 expedition which, in retaliation for an Arakanese raid on Yaw and Laungshe in the Pakokku district, marched over to the An Pass and occupied Launggyet while the raja, Narameikhla, fled to Bengal. The Burmese left behind as regent Anawrahtaminsaw, to whom next year was sent a bride aged thirteen, sister to Minrekyawswa, together with the five regalia (white umbrella, yaktail, crown, sword, sandals).

In 1406 the Burmese overran Mohnyin and killed the chief ; China expostulated[2] and they withdrew, as they would doubtless have done in any case. In 1407 they sent an embassy to Yunnan. In 1413 the northern Shāh state of Hsenwi ravaged the Āva villages

---

1 Hmannan, Vol. i, pp. 420, 440.

2 Parker, ' Précis ' ; Huber, 'Une ambassade chinoise en Birmanie en 1406' in *Bulletin de l'Ecole Franeaise d'Extreme Orient*, 1904.

and sent some prisoners to Pekin, but Minrekyawswa shattered the Hsenwi host at Wetwin near Maymyo, killing their leader in single combat. In 1414 Hsenwi again raided Āva at the instigation of Razadarit, whose envoys travelled viā Chiengmai carrying a considerable weight of gold as an inducement.

Taking advantage of the usual palace troubles which attended Minhkaung's accession, Razadarit made several raids, and in 1406 he came up the Irrawaddy river. It is characteristic of Burmese warfare that though he failed to reduce the Burmese garrisons at Prome, Myede and Pagān, he simply left them in his rear, pressed on to Sagaing, and camped there, raising the white umbrella and beating his drums in triumph. There was only the palace guard in Āva, and although there were plenty of men in the villages, it was not possible to summon them with the Talaings surrounding the city. Taken at a loss, Minhkaung called a great council. Nobody dared speak, for there was nothing to be said. But at last an eminent monk of Pyinya came forward saying he had eloquence enough to persuade any king in the universe. Minhkaung consented, and the monk went forth riding a tall elephant with a golden howdah, attended by 300 *thadinthon* (fasting elders) robed in white, 300 old men bearing gifts, and many elephants loaded with silks and rich presents. They met Razadarit on his great barge and the monk spoke holy words on the sin of bloodshed while Razadarit inclined his ear. He could not reduce a walled town, he could not remain for ever in a hostile country, and he consented to withdraw ; he even rebuked his men for taking the heads of forty pagoda slaves.

On returning home, Razadarit besieged Prome, and when Minhkaung came down to relieve it, defeated him so severely that he sued for terms. The two kings swore eternal friendship, mounting the steps of the Shwehsandaw pagoda, Prome, together hand in hand, and entering into a marriage alliance. Razadarit granted Minhkaung the customs revenue of Bassein ; this, and the fact that throughout the fifteenth century Tharrawaddy was subject to Prome and was held by a governor who was appointed, at least nominally, by Āva, suggest that one cause of the fighting was the need of Āva to trade along the Irrawaddy river as far south as possible.

But in 1407 Razadarit, having intercepted a letter from Minhkaung asking Chiengmai to join him in attacking Pegū and share the booty, supported a fugitive Arakanese prince, son of Narameikhla ; the prince marched into Arakan, gathering strength from his fellow countrymen as he went, occupied Launggyet, and captured the Burmese garrison, 3000 strong Anawrahtaminsaw[1] was executed and his little queen, Sawpyechantha, passed into Razadarit's harem.

The news so enraged Minhkaung that he insisted on invading the Delta in the rains, with the natural result that he was severely defeated at Pankyaw, north of Pegū. He fled to Āva, leaving his men to be cut to pieces and his Maw Shān queen[2] to be captured ; she joined her daughter Sawpyechantha in Razadarit's harem.

Now that both his mother and sister were captives, Minrekyawswa became a fiend. 'As a crocodile eats his victims, so will I rend the flesh of the Talaings,' he said[3]. His father Minhkaung went no more to war, for his nerves were shattered after the fight at Pankyaw. But Minrekywswa took charge. Year after year he carried fire and sword into the hapless Delta, defeating all comers, deporting the population wholesale, and making life so unbearable that in Myaungmya and Bassein men dared not work their fields, and in 1415 the whole west side paid him homage. Things came to such a pass that a hundred Talaings would run at sight of a couple of Shān-Burmans.

But in 1417 the vengeful re-incarnation of Bawlawkyantaw came to an end. Razadarit, trusting to Minrekyawswa's impetuosity, lured him out of his camp at Dalla until he was separated from his men, and dashed out on him at the head of some thirty Talaing lords on elephants. Minrekyawswa's elephant, maddened by a hundred gashes, shook him off and crushed his thigh ; he crawled away under a bush, but was found and taken to Razadarit's camp. There he repelled Razadarit's chivalrous advances and died during the night, uttering hatred with his last breath. He is now worshipped as the Minkyawswa spirit.

At the news of his death, the Burmese Delta garrisons fled in panic, and the war soon came to an end, for men were weary. Minhkaung, broken-hearted at his brave son's death, spent his declining years in piety ; the Ari-gyi-do-ahnwe (descendants of the great Ari) frequented his palace and drank there, sometimes to such excess that they had to be carried back to their monasteries.

---

[1] He is worshipped at the Shwenawrahta Nat spirit ; Temple, *Thirty-Seven Nats*, p. 56.

[2] She is worshipped as the Anaukmibaya Nat spirit; Temple, *Thirty-Seven Nats*, p. 56.

[3] Hmannan, Vol. ii, p. 12. The Burmese used to eat portions of the flesh of their prisoners of war alive, *ad terrorem*; see Harvey, *History of Burma*, p. 298.

He was succeeded by his son Thihathu (1422—26), who took his father's queen Shin-Bo-me and was so fond of her that his first wife retired into religion. But during a raid on the Delta he did so much damage that the Talaing chief presented him with his sister Shinsawbu to buy him off; he brought her to Āva and crowned her queen consort in great state, so Shin-Bo-me had him assassinated. The court set up his nine-year-old son ; Shin-Bo-me poisoned him and brought in a cousin of the royal house, Kalekyetaungnyo (1426-27), and when he was supplanted by a kinsman she married the kinsman Mohnyinthado (1427—40) ; this was her fifth crowned consort, but she died childless. Mohnyinthado's reign was spent in striving, with tolerable success, to retain his throne against the principal fief-holders and the Shān states of Hsipaw and Yawnghwe ; Hsipaw once drove him out of his palace for eight months, withdrawing only on payment of a large sum.[1] It was in his reign that the first European wandered into Burma—Nicolo de' Conti, a merchant of Venice ; Conti visited Tenasserim, Mrohaung and Āva. His note[1] is brief, but its references to the white elephant, to tattooing the thighs, and to what he imagined was a prayer to the Trinity (the Buddhist invocation of the 'Three names of Refuge'), suggest that Burmese civilisation was then the same as in the nineteenth century.

Mohnyinthado's sons, Minrekyawswa (1440—43) and Narapati (1443—69), overran Kale and Mohnyin for a time, and captured the Maw Shān chief Thonganbwa when he was being hard pressed by Yunnan. Narapati refused to surrender him and in 1445 drove off the Yunnan levies at Kaungton in the Bhamo district. But when in 1446 they appeared in strength before Āva, he yielded, Thonganbwa committed suicide, so only his dead body could be given up ; the Chinese removed the intestines, dried the body in the sun and at the fire, thrust an iron spit through it and took it away[2].

In 1451 they sent Narapati a golden seal as governor of Āva, and in 1454 they gave him some Shān territory in return for the surrender of a Mohnyin chief. At this time China enumerated in and near Burma eight states held by what she was pleased to consider her 'comforters' or governors, of which five can be identified— Āva, Kenghung, Hsenwi, Pegū, and the country round Viengchang.

Narapati was succeeded by his son Thihathura (1469—81), who fought Toungoo, Pegū, Prome and Yawnghwe. In 1474 he and his

---

[1] Major, *India in the Fifteenth Century.*
[2] Hmannan, Vol. ii, p. 97 ; Parker, *Burma, relations with China,* p. 44, and 'Precis , Pemberton, *Report on Eastern Frontier,* pp. 111-12.

queen made their hair into a broom, studded the handle with gems and sent it to sweep the floor of the Temple of the Tooth at Kandy in Ceylon[1].   In 1472 he asked China to give him Mohnyin. China warned Mohnyin not to obstruct the road between China and Burma, but she would not give his territory to Āva, as he had done nothing to merit eviction. Mohnyin remained on good terms with the Chinese frontier eunuch, presenting him with a jewelled girdle.

Jewels also helped the expansion of Momeik, the ruby mine state ; founded in 1238, the town was part of Hsenwi but in 1420 it received thirteen villages as a reward for helping Yūnnan to raid Chiengmai.   In 1465 its chieftainess Nang-han-lung sent ruby tribute separately from Hsenwi and her present of jewels completely won over the frontier eunuch. She even tried to ally herself with Annam.   She seized most of Hsenwi, and when China remonstrated, she said : 'Momeik is the baby elephant which has outgrown the mother elephant Hsenwi and can never enter the womb again,' and as, in addition to talking, she presented more rubies to the enquiring officers, they reported sympathetically on her case and she was left in possession.

Conceivably the continuance of Chinese interest in Burma is due to the fact that after Kubla Khan's dynasty (1206—1368) had passed away, China lost control of the route across Asia to Europe. She had to look for other outlets, and the trade route down the Irrawaddy was perhaps one of them[2].   Chinese porcelain[3] of the fifteenth century had been found in the bed of the Bassein river near Negrais, and it is recorded[4] that in 1450 the chief of Āva gave to a favourite 'the Chinese customs revenue,' probably Yūnnan frontier tolls.

Hitherto writing had been in Pali and Sanskrit but in this age vernacular literature makes its appearance. Its rise exposes the inadequacy of our material—pagoda inscriptions and court chronicles which, in their present form, are not even contemporary

---

[1] Religious missions with Ceylon are also mentioned in 1430 and 1456. The Tooth had been at Kandy since 1286. Gerson da Cunha, 'Memoir of the History of the Tooth Relic of Ceylon' in *Journal of the Bombay branch of the Royal Asiatic Society*, 1875, gives the history of the Tooth.   The silver gilt caskets in which it now rests are not unlike a Burmese pagoda in shape ; the metal of which they are made and the gems which encrust them are largely Burmese.

[2] For Chinese sea trade, see Chau Ju-kua ; Mayer's 'Chinese Explorations of the Indian Ocean during the Fifteenth Century' in *China Review*, Vol. iii; Rockhill, 'Trade of China with the Coast of the Indian Ocean during the Fifteenth Century' in *T'oung Pao*, 1914. 1915.

[3] Report of the Superintendent, Archaeological Survey Burma, 1915, p. 35.

[4] Hmannan Vol. ii, p. 99.

Away from the track of the chiefs and their rabble, people were probably happy enough, and in many a monastery life must have been calm and beautiful. As is usual in secluded countries, Burmese literature is narrow in range and, though quite voluminous according to mediaeval standards, small in quantity. It shows little development and no improvement has been made on the earliest poets. The prose consists largely of translations and paraphrases from scripture stories. The verse is more original and includes minor poetry of a high order but the condensation of its style and the obscurity of its dialect militate against its having a wide appeal. The usually accepted view, that the following are the first vernacular writers, is probably correct, but the finish of their style indicates that the vernacular had been practised for some generations previously. The earliest writers are three monks, Shin Uttamagyaw, Shin Thilawuntha, and Shin Maharattathara. Shin Uttamagyaw, the author of *Tawla*, a celebrated poem, was a valued councellor in the Āva palace. He was born on the same day as Shin Thilawuntha (1453—1520) and together they entered a monastery school at Taungdwingyi, Magwe district. Shin Thilawuntha was expelled for writing *Paramiganpyo*, as the monk considered poetry sinful ; he continued writing in a fine monastery built for him at Āva by the chief, Minhkaung (1401—22) ; *Yazawingyaw*, the earliest chronicle extant, is his ; it is a disappointing work, for instead of recording what went on round him—it would have been an invaluable picture—he merely reproduced scriptural traditions. Shin Maharattathara (1468—1529), a descendant of the Thihathu, the Shān Brother, wrote, *Koganpyo* and other poems. Probably it is in this period that Yaweshinhtwe lived ; she was a maid of honour and wrote verse on the 55 styles of hairdressing used by maids of honour in the Āva palace, styles some of which are still in popular use.

Thihathura was succeeded by his son Minhkaung (1481—1502), who, hearing that Bimbisara, the king of Buddha's period, had raised his son to the throne as joint king, decided to follow the precedent, gave his son the white umbrella, and shared the throne with him. He was continually attacked by Hanthawaddy and Prome in the south, and by the Shāns above Shwebo in the north. When his vassal of Toungoo was assassinated, he recognised the assassin as king, sending him the white umbrella, an act which the 1829 chroniclers[1] cite as an instance of statesmanship.

He was succeeded by his younger son Shwenankyawshin (1502—

---

[1] Hmannan, Vol. ii, pp. 127, 185.

27), as the elder son, the joint king, had died. Shwenankyawshin already had a wife whose sister was consort to the dead joint king ; yet now, on coming to the throne, it was not his own wife, but the joint king's widow, who became his chief queen, as she was already part of the regalia. His life was attempted by kinsmen who fled to Toungoo. He thereupon gave his daughter in marriage to Minkyinyo of Toungoo with the villages from Kyaukse to Toungoo as dowry ; he was giving his daughter to the harbourer of his assassins, and in giving away the rice area of Kyaukse he was giving away his crown. But he could not help himself—Prome and Salin were in revolt, Mohnyin was attacking the Shwebo border, and his own brothers were in the field against him. In 1527 Mohnyin encamped under the walls of Āva, the Shāns in the Āva garrison deserted to him, and Shwenankyawshin fell fighting on his elephant. The population fled in large numbers to Toungoo.

Mohnyin set up his son Thohanbwa (1527—43) as king in Āva. Thohanbwa said: 'Burmese pagodas have nothing to do with religion. They are simply treasure chambers,' and proceeded to plunder such as were in reach. Probably, as in 1756 and 1885, the monks led the people in resistance; he said: 'Monks surround themselves with followers and could rebel if they liked. They ought to be killed'; in 1540 at Taungbalu, just outside Āva, he covered a field with huts, slaughtered buffaloes, cows, pigs and fowls and invited the monks to feast. When they were all in the huts, he surrounded them with his braves and massacred them to the number of 360. The survivors fled to Toungoo. He then seized the manuscripts in the monasteries and made bonfires of them. Finally he was assassinated by one of his Burmese ministers who thereupon, though of royal blood, retired into a monastery rather than take the throne.

It therefore passed to Hsipaw, who ruled as Hkonmaing (1543 - 46). He joined six other *sawbwas* in the attack on Prome and was succeeded by his son Mobye Narapati (1546—52), who, weary of attacks from Mohnyin, fled to Bayinmaung, leaving Āva to its last *sawbwa*, Sithukyawhtin (1552—55), a nominee of Mohnyin.

Indeed for two and a half centuries the ruler of Āva had been *sawbwa* in all but name ; yet there was this difference between Āva and the other Shān states, that whereas they were so wild as to leave not even a record, the tradition of the Burmese palace gave Āva a veneer of civilisation, and her numerous monasteries contained monks who, if not learned, were at least literate ; and to them it is due that though the lamp of civilisation flickered and burnt low, it never went out;

(b) PEGU 1287—1539.

Wareru (1287—96), a Shān pedlar born at Donwun in the Thaton district, took service in thé elephant stables of the chief of Sukhotai, became Captain of the Guard, eloped with the chief's daughter and set up as lord of his native village.

He had a fair sister, and Aleimma, the Burmese governor of Martaban, wished to marry her. Wareru prepared a wedding feast and when Aleimma came to get his bride, Wareru assassinated[1] him, seized his governorship, and so became lord of Martaban in 1281. When he built its walls in 1287, a pregnant woman was crushed under the gate post as a foundation sacrifice[2].

The Pagān kingdom was now breaking up, and Wareru made common cause with Tarabya, the revolting governor of Pegū, each marrying the other's daughter. But in 1287, after they had expelled the Burmese governors and occupied the country south of Prome and Toungoo, Tarabya tried to ambush Wareru. He failed. Wareru, calling the spirits of earth and air to witness his innocence, and pouring libations of water from a golden bowl, mounted his elephant, fought with Tarabya in single combat, and took him prisoner. At the intercession of the monks he spared his life. Tarabya again plotted, but his wife warned her father Wareru in time. So Tarabya was executed, although she twined her tresses with his and dared the executioners to cut off his head.

Wareru now became sole prince of the Talaing[3] state in Lower Burma which lasted till 1539. In 1298 it received recognition from China, which henceforth chose to regard its rulers as governors appointed by herself. Its capital was Martaban till 1369, when a palace was set up at Pegū.

Wareru received recognition from his old master and father-in-law, the chief of Sukhotai, who in 1293 sent him a white elephant because it chose to eat Martaban grass ; no sooner did they hear of its arrival than the Shān Brothers of Kyaukse came raiding Martaban to get it, but were driven off.

To Wareru we owe the earliest law book in Burma that now survives. The Hindu colonists who came to the Delta a thousand years before had brought with them traditional laws ascribed to the ancient sage Manu ; these law books were handed down in the Talaing monasteries, and Wareru commissioned his monks

---

[1] Paklat Talaing chronicle.

[2] Razadarit Ayedawpon. The practice survived in Burma till a century ago ; see *History of Burma*, p. 320.

[3] Halliday, *The Talaings*.

to produce the standard collection called after him, the Wareru *dhammathat*. It forms the basis of Burmese law literature[1].

The Siamese kingdom, founded in 1350, included in its list of provinces Tenasserim, Moulmein and Martaban[2] ; it certainly held Tenasserim, founding the town in 1373, and building the Wutshin-taung pagoda there in 1380 ; but it did not hold Moulmein save through some nominal tribute-offering, and Pegū held the country down to Tavoy. There was little established government. If it was not dacoits it was royal kinsmen who revolted, and sometimes bands of Shān immigrants from Siam would add to the disorder.

Binnya U (1353-85) repaired the Shwedāgon pagoda, raising its height to 66 feet. He repelled raiders from Chiengmai who destroyed several towns in Thaton district ; on the site of his victory he built a pagoda, enshrining relics obtained by sending a mission to Ceylon. But his white elephant[3] died, after being 61 years in the palace, and while he was devoutly searching the forests for a successor, his kins-men seized the palace and invited the Chiengmai chief to join them. For six years he maintained himself at Donwun, and then, being driven out, he moved to Pegū and repaired its walls.

His eldest son Razadarit (1385—1423) was the greatest of Wareru's lineage. Fighting for his existence since the age of sixteen, with but little assistance from his father, who could not control the family feuds, Razadarit succeeded in seizing Pegū town soon after his father's death, subjected Bassein, and repelled successive Burmese invasions. Finally, in 1390, he captured Myaungmya with Laukpya inside ; in thank-offering he built shrines at the Shwemawdaw pagoda, Pegū feeding a thousand monks throughout a seven days' festival and offering his weight in gold.

Hearing that his son Bawlawykantaw was practising horseman-ship and sharpening his elephant's tusks, Razadarit feared he was about to rebel, and sent two lords to slay him. They announced their duty to the lad, who replied : 'I do but follow the custom of young princes in manly exercise. I do not plot against my father and there is no fault in me. Give me time to prepare for death.' They gave him time, and for three days at the Shwemawdaw pagoda he listened to the reading of *Abidhamma*, the holy scriptures. When it was finished, he offered his ruby bracelets and earrings to the pagoda, and thus he prayed : 'If I have wished ill to my father,

[1] Forchammer, *Jardine Prize Essay on Burmese Law*.

[2] Pallegoix, *Description du Royaume Thai ou Siam*, Vol. ii, p. 75.

[3] For the cult of the white elephant, see Harvey, *History of Burma*, pp. 274, 361.

yea though it be a little, then may I lie in Hell for ever, and never behold the coming Buddha. But if I have not wished ill to my father, then may I be born again among the kings of Burma and be the scourge of the Talaings.' Then he took the poison that had been prepared, and drank it and died.

When this was reported to Razadarit, he said : 'It was a terrible prayer,' and, gilding the pagoda from top to bottom, he prayed : 'If he become a prince in Burma and make war on me, may I on my elephant vanquish him.'

During the war that followed, though he ultimately repulsed them, the Burmese sometimes left Razadarit in possession of little but Pegū town itself. In 1414 he gained a brief respite by stirring up Hsenwi to attack Āva, but was himself never free from the fear of Shān inroads, as on several occasions when he was hard pressed from the north the princes of Ayuthia, Kampengpet and Chiengmai would raid him from the south.

He built the Danok pagoda near Twante, and to him is ascribed the traditional division of each of 'the Three Lands of the Talaings' (Pegū, Myaungmya, Bassein) into 32 'provinces,' i.e. village circles.

He was of great strength and personal courage, and several times killed his man in single combat. The chief of Āva never dared accept his challenge and meet him hand to hand.

When the news of Minhkaung's death in 1422 reached Pegū, the queens jeered, saying to Razadarit : 'Now you can pounce down on his palace and capture all his women.' But he rebuked them, saying: 'My sweet enemy is dead. It will fight no more, but spend my declining years in piety.'

A year later, at the age of fifty-four, while snaring elephants with his own hand in the Labut-tha-lut forest at the foot of the Pegū Yomas, north of Pegū, he was caught in the rope and injured so that he died on the way home. His queens came out to meet the body and buried it at Kamathameinpaik (Minkanyo), near Payagyi, north of Pegū. He has a chronicle all to himself, the *Razadarit Ayedawpon*, which ends with the word : ' This Lion King, so wise, so generous, so mighty in word and deed, could overcome all his enemies, but he too at the last must bow before King Death.'

Binnyakyan (1450—53) raised the height of the Shwedāgon pagoda to 302 feet. At his death, as a result of palace massacres, there was no male of the family left alive. The throne then passed by general consent to Razadarit's daughter Shinsawbu (1453—72). Village headmanships have been known to descend in the female line[1], and Shān hill states have been held by chieftainesses, but this is the only instance of a major state in Burma being held by a woman. Daughter, sister, wife and mother of kings, she ruled well, leaving behind so gracious a memory on earth that four hundred years later the Talaings could think of no fairer thing to say of Queen Victoria than to call her Shinsawbu re-incarnate.

Once, while being carried round the city in her great palanquin, sword in hand and crown on head, she heard an old man exclaim, as her retinue pushed him aside, 'I must get out of the way, must I ? You call me an old fool, do you ? I am not so old that I could not get a child, which is more than your old queen could do!' Thunder-struck at such irreverence, she meekly accepted it as a sign from heaven, and thereafter styled herself 'The Old Queen[2].'

When young she had been given in marriage to the then chief of Āva and two Talaing monks had gone there to teach her letters. As she was not happy in a Burmese palace, she ran away, and fled down the river to Pegū. Her flight was successful because the two monks helped her, and, by benefit of clergy, a boat carrying monks could not be challenged. She admired the two monks beyond all other men, and when, after being queen of Pegū seven years, she wished to retire, it was one of them that she chose as successor. But she did not know which to choose. Therefore one day, when they entered the palace as usual to receive the royal rice in their alms bowls, she secretly put into one of the bowls not rice but a layman's dress, together with little models of the five regalia; then, having prayed that the lot might fall on the worthier, she returned the bowls[3]. Dammazedi, to whom the fateful bowl fell, abandoned the Order, received her daughter in marriage, and assumed the government. The other in his disappointment took to plotting, and was executed. The ambitious lords also objected, but in the end became reconciled to Dammazedi because of his wisdom and justice; and when some of them continued to murmur that he was not of royal blood, she took a beam out of a bridge in the city and had it made into a Buddha image, and said ;'Ye say he is of common blood, he cannot be your king. See here this common wood—yesterday it was trodden in the dust of your feet, but to-day, is it not Lord and do ye not bow before it ?'

Shinsawbu spent the remaining years of her life in retirement at the Shwedāgon. Successive princes had added to the original

1 Furnivall, 'Matriarchy in Burma' in *Journal of the Burma Research Society,* 1912.
2 *Thatonhnwemun Yazawin.*
3 *Sayadaw Athwa,* Vol. ii, p. 131.

structure, and she made it practically what we see to-day. Round it she banked up the terrace fifty feet high, nine hundred feet wide, with a great stone balustrade and encircling walls, between which she planted palm trees ; she kept forty-four people continually tending the sacred lamps, dedicated five hundred prisoners of war as slaves, and offered her own weight (91 lb.) in gold for gilding the dome[1]. When, at the age of seventy-eight, she felt her end approaching, she had her bed placed where her eyes could rest on that wondrous spire, and thus she breathed her last.

Dammazedi (1472—92) gave four times the weight of himself and his queen in gold to the Shwedāgon as compensation for revoking some of its lands, which Shinsawbu had extended to Danok. At Pegū he built the Shwekugyi and Kyaikpon pagodas, and west of the Shwemawdaw he built a new stockaded town, and set up his palace and elephant stable there[2]. The masonry of his reign is excellent, and a mass of pious edifices sprang up on the beautiful plateau between the old and the new town, men vying with each in works of merit, for it was an age of religious revival.

Dammazedi himself sent a mission to Buddhagaya[3] in Bengal to take plans of the Holy Tree and of the temple as models for his buildings at Pegū. But his most important work was his mission of twenty-two monks to Ceylon[4] in 1475. It was a long and dangerous journey, and several died in shipwreck or during their wanderings when cast away on the coast of Madras. To the Tooth, the Footprint, and the Holy Trees, at Kandy, they presented a stone alms bowl studded with sapphires, and reliquaries of gold and crystal ; to the Cingalese monks, cloths and Chiengmai lacquer boxes ; to the king of Ceylon, rubies, sapphires, Chinese silks, fine mats, and a letter on gold leaf. Their object was to secure valid ordination from the clergy of the Mahāvihāra, the great monastery in Ceylon which, founded in 251 B.C. still exists. On their return they proceeded to transmit this ordination to the clergy throughout Lower Burma : it was so generally accepted as valid that monks flocked to receive it from all over Burma and even from Siam ; and thus religion in Burma, which for three centuries had been split into sects each with its own ordination, received a measure of unity from the standard Kalyāni ordination. It was and is

1 Halliday, 'Slapat Rajawan Datow Smin Ron' in *Journal of the Burma Research Society*, 1923 ; Forchammer, 'Notes on Early History and Geography.'

2 Shwemawdaw Thamaing.

3 Report of the Supt. Archaeological Survey, Burma, 1914, p. 11.

4 Taw Sein Ko, 'Kalyāni Inscriptions' in *Indian Antiquary*, 1893, 1894.

granted at the Kalyāni *thein* (ordination hall) near Pegū, so called because the original monks were ordained on the banks of the Kalyāni stream in Ceylon. Dammazedi recorded these events on ten inscribed stones at the *thein*, called the Kalyāni Inscriptions.

One of the principal monks in the mission was Buddhaghosa, who translated the wareru *dhammathat* into Burmese; later generations confused him with his namesake, the Father of the Church who lived a thousand years previously. Dammazedi himself was a wise judge, and a collection of his rulings survives, the Dammazedi *pyatton.* He died at the age of eighty and was succeeded by his son Binnyaran.

Binnyaran (1492—1526) was beloved for his kindness, although, like others before and after, he enforced the Massacre of the Kinsmen, making a clean sweep of all his brothers. His son Takayutpi (1526—39) was the last king of Pegū.

Soon after 1500 the opening of the sea routes brought the Talaings great prosperity. Burma lay off the beaten track and her goods could be bought in Malacca. Her spices were few, and her finished articles crude. But two places in Burma lay near the track: Martaban and Tenasserim. These commanded short cuts over the hills to Siam, saving a dangerous sea voyage. Martaban sold the produce brought down the Salween and Irrawaddy rivers, and in 1519 the Portuguese[1] founded a trading station there which lasted till 1613. Tenasserim[2], which belonged to Siam till 1760, commanded an even better overland route, and the Portuguese had a settlement there till 1641. The Portuguese imported European clothes and velvets, and exported rubies, lac, wax, ivory, horn, lead, tin, Pegū jars ('Martabans'), and long pepper, which grew in the moist forests of Tenasserim; they exported also pepper from Achīn, camphor from Borneo, and porcelain and scented woods from China, brought by the junks for sale in the Talaing ports. There was no coinage, but goods were weighed against lumps of *ganza*, an alloy of lead and tin which passed as currency. Nikitin[3], a Russian from Tver, who travelled in the East about 1470, mentions Pegū as 'no inconsiderable port, inhabited principally by Indian dervishes. The products derived from thence are sold by the dervishes,' which indicates that then, as now, the merchant community was largely foreign.

---

[1] Faria y Sousa (Stevens), *The Portuguese in Asia*; Couto, *Da Asia*; Whiteway, *Rise of the Portuguese Power in India.*

[2] Anderson, *English Intercourse with Siam*

[3] Major, *India in the Fifteenth Century.*

Pegū had peace between Razadarit's death in 1423 and the end of the monarchy in 1539. The dynasty was mild. The kings could indulge their peaceful proclivities because the Upper Burma hordes found all the fighting they wanted among themselves, and the states of Prome and Toungoo acted as a buffer. An Italian traveller in 1505 describes the reigning king, Binnyaran, as so gentle that a child might speak to him, and as wearing so many jewels that at night he shone like the sun[1]. It was the golden age of Pegū, and there can be little doubt that its civilisation was higher than that of the savage north. If few traces remain, that is because it was a simple civilisation, the steaming climate of the Delta hastens decay, and the Burmese conquerors touched nothing which they did not destroy

(c) TOUNGOO 1280—1531.

In 1280 two brothers built a stockade round their village on the hill-spur (*taunggnu*), and thus founded Toungoo ; the stockade was probably a necessity against the ferocious slave-raiders of Karenni. The Pāgān kingdom was then on its death-bed, and Toungoo grew up without even such slight traditions of loyalty as other towns possessed. In the next two centuries she was ruled by twenty-eight chiefs, of whom fifteen perished by assassination.

Other places, notably Prome, were equally independent, but Toungoo differed in this, that she remained predominantly Burmese. The Shāns made life so unbearable in Upper Burma that every now and then crowds of Burmese families would flock south and settle round Toungoo with its stronghold on the hill. The first migration took place when Pyanchi (1368—77) was lord of Toungoo ; he joined the chiefs of Āva and Pegū in making offerings at Pagān, and in an inscription[2] at the Shwezigon he and his lady record with natural pride that they gave refuge to the Burmese who fled after the Shān sack of Sagaing and Pyinya. These twain prayed that in their next existence they might be man and wife together again, and dwell in the land of Toungoo, and once more rule the people they loved so well.

The lords of Toungoo styled themselves kings and had a golden palace at Gyobinzeik village, with elephant stables, and even an occasional white elephant. And indeed the little throne sometimes descended from father to son. But as often as not they paid

---

[1] Badger, *The Travels of Ludovico di Varthema*, p. 219.

[2] Tun Nyein, *Inscriptions of Pagan, Pinya and Āva*, p. 149.

homage to Āva, and Āva sometimes sent her nominee to rule as governor.

Toungoo was usually on good terms with Pegū, and when she went raiding it was to the north, especially to Kyaukse. She always looked longingly on that prosperous hollow, growing three crops a year when she could grow only one, and the stronger she grew the more she encroached there. Her greatest chief, Minkyinyo (1486—1531), finally secured it when the chief of Āva gave him a daughter, and, as her dowry, Kyaukse itself together with the country leading up to it from Toungoo, such as the Yamethin villages Taungnyo, Pyagaung (Kyidaunggan), Shwemyo, Kintha, Talaingthe and Petpaing. He deported the population of these to fill the new town Dwayawadi (Myogyi near Toungoo) which he founded. In 1510 he moved and founded the present Toungoo, digging the lake within the walls and laying out orchards. When the Shāns finally took Āva in 1527 he sallied forth and deliberately devastated the country in the central zone, filling in the walls and breaking down the channels so as to place an impassable belt between himself and the Shāns. While he was doing this, the last great influx of Burmans came fleeing from the Shān terror ; the lords of Pyinya in Sagaing district, Myittha in Kyaukse, and Hlaingdet in Meiktila, with many a Burmese family, noble and commoner, fled south to take refuge at his feet. In delight he exclaimed : 'Now I know why the bees swarmed on the gate of Toungoo : it meant that my city would be populous '; it meant more than that, although he did not realise it - it meant that Toungoo would see the re-birth of the Burmese race.

Chiengmai as well as Pegū recognised Minkyinyo as an independent chief, and he was so strong that Karenni sent him propitiatory homage. He was a great fighter, and once, when taking Kyaungbya (south-east of Toungoo) from the Talaings, he killed its Shān governor by jumping on to his elephant and cutting him down. He could trace his descent indirectly through forbears of rank to the Pagān dynasty, and dying at the age of seventy-two he bequeathed a great name of Tabinshwehti, his son by the daughter of the headman of Penwegon, six miles north of Toungoo.

CHAPTER XXII

CEYLON A. D. 1215—1527

THE successive raids from Southern India, described in volume II of this history, which had thrown Ceylon into confusion during the first twelve years of the thirteenth century, reached their climax in the irruption of the wicked Kālingo prince Māgha, who, with an army of Keralas of Malabaris, overran the country, destroying all that lay in his way. He entered the capital, polonnaruva, took its ruler, Parakkama pandu, captive, and despoiled the city of its treasures. He then ascended the throne under the title of Kālinga Vijaya-Bāhu, and ruled over the north central part of the Island for twenty-one years (A. D. 1213 to 1234).

His domination was characterised by wanton cruelty, and the Sinhalese chronicles give a heartrending account of the destruction of sacred edifices, the expulsion of priests, and other outrages, extending even to the destruction of the literature of the Island.

While Māgha and his confederate, Jaya-Bāhu, were thus oppressing the inhabitants of Polonnaruva and the neighbouring districts, a few Sinhalese chieftains successfully defended the religion and liberties of the people in the less accessible highlands. At Subha-pabbata (now Yāpavu in the North-Western province) was the military commander Subha-senāpati; at Gangādoni-pabbata in the Manimekhalā district was Sankha, another military commander; in Rohana (Southern Ceylon) Bhuvaneka-Bāhu bore sway; and Prince Vijaya-Bāhu, leading a Sinhalese army from the Vanni district, drove the Tamils from the Māyā, or central region of the Island, and, having built for himself a stronghold at Jambudoni (Dambadeniya), reigned there, contemporaneously with Māgha, for four years, from about A. D. 1227 to 1231. His chief work was the restoration of the Buddhist church, the recovery of such literature as remained, and the revival of letters. He invited to his capital Vāchissara[1], and all other learned Buddhist monks who had fled from the tyranny of Māgha, brought the Tooth and Bowl relics of the Buddha from Kotmale, where they had been hidden, to his capital, and afterwards enshrined them with great ceremony

---

[1] See Mv, lxxxi, 18, B.M. Cat. of Sinh. MSS., pp. xvi, xvii, and Katikāvat-sangarā, p. 8.

on the top of the Beligala Rock. He convened a Council of Elders consisting of the well-known author Saingha-rakkhita, the two Theras named Medhankara, and other representatives of Buddhist fraternities, who sat in his own temple, Vijayārāma, and, after rehearsing the Buddhist canon, issued an ecclesiastical rescript (*Katikāvata*) for the guidance of the clergy. He also caused copies of important Buddhist works to be made, to replenish the temple libraries rifled by the invaders.

Vijaya-Bāhu III had one daughter and two sons, Parakkama-Bāhu and Bhuvaneka-Bāhu. The first son under the tutorship of the renowned Sangha-rakkhita Thera, made such progress in learning that he received the title Kalikāla Sāhichcha Sabbanna Pandita ('the Omniscient Pandit of the Kaliyuga epoch of Literature').

He succeeded his father on the throne at Dambadeniya as Parakkama-Bāhu II, probably in A D. 1231, while the usurpers Māgha and Jaya-Bāhu were ruling over pihiti-rata at Polonnaruva. As soon as he ascended the throne he set himself to restore order in the kingdom. He appointed his younger brother, Bhuvaneka-Bāhu, to the office of sub-king, and held a great festival in honour of the Tooth-relic. He then led a large army against the strongholds of the invaders and in the course of about three years succeeded in expelling them from Ceylon. With his nephew, Vīra-Bāhu, he repulsed a raid led by Chandrabhānu, a Jāvaka, of Malay chieftain, and, as soon as peace and order were restored to the land, turned his attention to the purification of the Buddhist church. He held a convocation of elders, and the canon was rehearsed, sinful priests were excommunicated, and a new rescript or *Katikāvata* was issued for the use of the clergy. He gave every encouragement to art and learning, and it appears from the glowing accounts of him in the *Dambadeni-asna* and the *Rājaratnākara* that his own accomplishments were many. His *Visuddhi-magga-sannaya* and *Vinaya-vinichchhaya-sannaya* (Sinh. *Vanavinisa-sanne*) which he entitled *Nissandeha* are remarkable for their comprehensiveness, and his *Kavsilumina* is a masterpiece of Sinhalese poetry, which has furnished the author of the Sinhalese grammar, *Sidatsangarā*, with an exemple establishing the existence in the Sinhalese language of the semi-nasal *sannaka*. His just rule and the facilities for study afforded by him, by Devapratirājā his chief minister, and by his other ministers, resulted in the production of many important works. Dhammakitti Thera continued the compilation of the *Mahāvamsa*, under the title *Chūlavamsa*, from the date on which Mahānāma had relinquished it to the end of the reign of Parakkama-Bāhu I (A.D. 1153—86), and was probably prevented only by death, or by political disorders, from continuing the chronicle to his own times (A.D. 1235—65). Among other contemporary writers may be mentioned Mayūrapāda Thera, the author of the well-known *Pūjāvaliya*, and of a medical work named *Yogārnava*, both in Sinhalese prose.

Parakkama-Bāhu II had five sons, (1) Vijaya-Bāhu, (2) Bhuvaneka-Bāhu (3) Tiloka-Malla, (4) Parakkama-Bāhu, and (5) Jaya-Bāhu, called Siri Vijaya-Bāhu in the *Rājāvaliya*, and the nephew, Vīra-Bāhu, mentioned above. They were all skilful and experienced soldiers, and the eldest, Vijaya-Bāhu, was entrusted with the government of the country while his royal father was devoting his time to literature.

This prince was a master of strategy and a great organiser. He placed his two youngest brothers, Parakkama-Bāhu and Jaya-Bāhu, with their father, sent Tiloka-Malla to command the Sinhalese army of the south, and placed Bhuvaneka-Bāhu in the fortress of Sundara Pabbata (Yāpavu) in order that he might defend the northern district of the Island. He himself, with his cousin Vīra-Bāhu, journeyed through the length and breadth of the country, put down evil-doers, and freed the Island of enemies. among those whom they vanquished being Chandrabhānu, who was making a second attempt to gain the sovereignty of Ceylon. After visiting many places of importance, including Vāta-giri, Adam's Peak, Gampola, Kurunagala, and Yāpavu, and restoring peace and prosperity to all, they remained for a time in Anurādhapura, where they restored the sacred buildings. They conciliated the Vanni princes, and went on to Polonnaruva, which they completely restored. Vijaya-Bāhu then invited his father from Dambadeniya to Polonnaruva, and in 1779 A.B (A.D. 1235) held in great splendour the second coronation festival, a record of which is contained in the *Attanagaluvamsa*, and in the *Mahāvamsa* (lxxxix, 10). The *Pūjāvaliya* which is a contemporary work, gives the duration of Parakkama-Bāhu's reign as thirty-three years, while the *Mahāvamsa* gives it as thirty-five. According to the *Nikāyasangraha* and the *Rājaratnākara* he appears to have died in 1809 A.B. (A.D. 1265).

His eldest son, Vijaya-Bāhu IV, also known as Bosat Vijaya-Bāhu, then ascended the throne at Dambadeniya, but had reigned for barely two years (A.D. 1266—68) when he was slain at the instigation of an officer named Mitta, who attempted to usurp the throne, but was put to death by the troops, who placed the murdered

king's brother, Bhuvaneka-Bāhu I of Yāpavu on the throne of
Dambadeniya. He ruled for about eleven years (A.D. 1268-79), and
was sedulous in promoting the interests of the Buddhist church.
Shortly after his death Ceylon was visited by a famine. Āryachakravarti, who was then reigning in Jaffna, invaded the country, and
succeeded in carrying away from Yāpavu the Tooth-relic, which he
delivered to his king, Kulacekhara, who has been identified with
tho Pāndyan king, Māravarman Tribhuvana-chakravartin Kula-
cekhara-deva (*c.* 1268—1308)[1]. For nearly a year after this incident
the land was in confusion, until Parakkama-Bāhu III, a son of
Vijaya-Bāhu IV, assumed sovereignty at Polonnaruva. He made
peace with Kulacekhara, and recovered the Tooth-relic, which he
afterwards deposited in a temple at Polonnaruva. He seems to have
reigned for about seven years (A.D. 1281—88) before Bhuvaneka-
Bāhu II, son of Bhuvaneka-Bāhu I, deposed him and reigned for
two years at Kurunagala. According to the *Daladāsirita* these
two kings reigned contemporaneously at their respective capitals
until the latter, for some reason or other, deposed the former, and
brought the Tooth-relic from Polonnaruva to Kurunagala.

Parakkama-Bāhu IV, called also Pandita Parakkama-Bāhu II
(*c.* A.D. 1291—1326), son of the preceding king, then ascended the
throne at Kurunagala. The duration of his reign is not given in
any known historical work, but it may be gathered from the colo-
phon to the *Daladāsirita* that he was reiging in A.D. 1325 (*Saka*
1246 expired 1869 A.B.), and in the inscription at Kitsirimevan-
Kalani-Vihāra it is stated that Vilgammūla Mahāthera, who translated the *Bodhivamsa* into Sinhalese at the request of this king,
was in A.B. 1876 (A.D. 1322, seven years after the compilation of the
Daladāsirita) still holding the position of Māhimi. The king's
death seems to have taken place between A.D. 1325 and 1332,
probably in 1326, after a reign of thirty-five years. He was a patron
of learning, and during his reign many religious and historical
works were composed. To the king himself is ascribed the authorship of the Sinhalese Jātaka book[2], a monumental work, and
the *Daladāsirita*[3]. The second section of the *Chūlavamsa*, from
Vijaya-Bāhu II to Parakkama- Bāhu IV (A.D. 1186—1326), also was
probably compiled during this period.

Of the next two kings, Bhuvaneka-Bāhu III, called also Vanni
Bhuvaneka-Bāhu, and Vijaya-Bāhu V, called in the *Mahāvamsa*

---

[1] See *Madras Epigraphy, Report* for 1907, p. 70, and Hultzsch, *J. R. A. S.*, 1913,
p. 531.

[2] Mv. xc, 83.   [3] Mv. xc, 79.

Jaya-Bāhu, and in Sinhalese works Savulu Vijaya-Bāhu, hardly anything is known. They seem to have reigned in Kurunagala for about twenty years, one ·after the other, from A.D. 1326 to 1346. Bhuvaneka-Bāhu IV then ascended the throne. His capital wa s Gangācrīpura (Gampola). The Lankātilaka inscription (British Museum copy) of this king's minister, Senālankādhikāra, gives *Saka* 1264 (A.D. 1342) as the date of his accession, but according to the *Mahāvamsa* and other historical works he succeeded in A.B. 1890 (A.D. 1346). The difference of four years may be explained by assuming that the first was the year of his accession to the rank of sub-king, and the second that of his assumption of sovereign power. The Vāgiri-devāle inscription is dated in the tenth regnal year, so that Bhuvaneka-Bāhu IV must have reigned for at least ten years, four years (1342—46) as Apā, and six years (1346—52) as king.

The next king was Parakkama-Bāhu V, called in Sinhalese Savulu Parakum-raja, probably a son of Vijaya-Bāhu V. From inscriptions and other sources it appears that he ruled at Gampola and Dadigama for at least eleven years— four years (1348—52) as Apā, and seven years (1352-59) as king. He was succeeded at Gampola by his nephew, Vikkama-Bāhu III, who reigned, according to inscriptions, for about eighteen years. He was sub-king for about three years (A.D. 1356—59), and paramount sovereign for fifteen years (1359—74). During his reign Niccanka Alagakkonāra of Amaragiri, otherwise called Alakecvara, an intrepid warrior of the Girivamsa lineage[1], who was allied by marriage to Senālankādhikāra Senevirat, a minister of Bhuvaneka-Bāhu IV, came into prominence, rose to the rank of minister and *Prabhu·rāja*, and dwelt in Perādeniya. With a view to checking the ever-growing domination of the Tamils under their ruler, Ārya Chakravarti of Jaffna, he prepared for war, and built strong fortresses at Rayigama, and Kōtte, near Colombo. In 1912 A.B. (A.D. 1368-69) he summoned a convocation of Buddhist priests under the presidency of the Elder Dhammakitti I, and inaugurated reforms in religion Towards the end of Vikkama-Bāhu's reign Alakecvara reviewed his army and, finding himself strong enough to cope with the Tamil king, defied him by hanging his tax-collectors. Ārya Chakravarti replied by sending his army in two divisions, one by land and the other by sea, against the Sinhalese. Bhuvaneka-Bāhu V, who had succeeded Vikkama-Bāhu III on the throne of Gampola, was struck with panic, fled from Gampola, and took refuge in the fortress of Rayigama. In the battles which ensued Arya Chakravarti's

---

[1] For a fuller account see Perera's contribution to the *J. C. B. R. A. S.*, 1904.

power was crushed. Bhuvaneka-Bāhu returned to Gampola, but his cowardly behaviour had made him so unpopular that the retired to Kōtte, and left the management of public affairs in the hands of his powerful minister, Alakecvara, who in *Saka* 1304 (A.D 1382) was still in power, and Alakecvara's brother, Atthanāyaka, was also a minister of state [*Attanagaluvamsa*]. Bhuvaneka-Bāhu V seems to have ruled as Apa both at Gampola and at Kōtte from A.D. 1359 to 1370, as *Yuva-rāja* from A D. 1370 to 1374, and as king from A.D. 1374 to 1390—about thirty years in all. The *Mahavamsa* gives the duration of his reign as twenty years.

After the Tamil war the *Prabhu-raja*, Niccanka Alakecvara, and his brother, Atthanāyaka, lived for a while at Rayigama, but afterwards the *Prabhu-rāja* settled for the remainder of his life at Kotte, the city which he had himself built, where Bhuvaneka Bāhu V also held his court, for the reason already explained. At Rayigama, the family seat of the clan, the *Prabhu-raja's* son, Kumāra Alakecvara, probably assumed the reins of government in the usual course, and shortly afterwards, perhaps on the death of the *Prabhu rāja* and his son (*c* A.D. 1381—86), his sister's son, Vira Alakecvara, became governor of Rayigama, and another nephew, Vīra-Bāhu, who had distinguished himself as a soldier, succeeded him as Apā of Bhuvaneka-Bāhu V, and lived at Gampola, but Vīra Alakecvara being the elder of the two nephews, challenged Vīra-Bāhu's right to the throne of Kōtte, and a civil war ensued, in which Vīra Alakecvara was vanquished and driven from the country. It may be added that Senālankādhikāra Senevirat, of the Mehenavara clan, a close relation of the royal family, probably married the *Prabhu-raja's* sister. The two nephews were the issue of this marriage, and hence are referred to as scions of the Mehenavara clan, and Vīra-Bāhu is styled *saleko* (Sinh. *suhurubadu*) of Bhuvaneka-Bāhu V. It is this last reference that lends some colour to the statement in the *Mahavamsa* and in the *Raja-ratnakara* that Niecanka Alagakkonāra became King Bhuvaneka-Bāhu V, but contemporary records, which are to be preferred, controvert this statement. On the death of this king, Vīra-Bāhu II ascended the throne of Gampola and Kōtte, and reigned for about six years, from A.D. 1390 to 1396. Under his patronage another convocation of Buddhist priests, presided over by the Mahāthera Dhammakitti II, author of the *Nikayasangraha* and other treatises, was held in A.D. 1395. Vīra-Bāhu had two sons, Vijaya Apā and Tunayesaya, but neither his fate nor theirs is wknon.

Vīra Alakecvara, probably called also Vijaya-Bāhu VI, having been defeated by his younger brother, Vīra-Bāhu II, fled into Southern India, but returned in about A. D. 1397 with a large army, and, having ousted his brother from Kōtte, ascended the throne there, and reigned for twelve years from A.D. 1397 to 1409. At this period the kings of Kōtte, owing, probably, to the great military achievements of the late *Prabhu-rāja*, were recognised as paramount sovereigns of the Island, and it is possible that Vīra Alakecvara, like many another Sinhalese sovereign, took the *biruda* Vīra-Vijaya-Bāhu, but the evidence at our disposal is insufficient to prove that he assumed this name, and neither the inscriptions nor the Sinhalese works of the period throw much light on the matter.

In A.D. 1405 the Chinese eunuch Tcheng Houo arrived in Ceylon, apparently for the purpose of carrying away the Tooth-relic, but his designs were frustrated and he was plundered by Alagakkōnāra, who may be identified with Vīra Alakecvara. Four years later, in A.D. 1409, he came again, this time with an army, and succeeded in capturing the king, with his queen and family[1]. He returned to China with his captives in A.D. 1411, and from 1409 to about 1414 Ceylon was without a king; but according to *Saddharma-ratnākara*, a grandson of Senālankādhikāra Senevirad, Parakkama-Bāhu by name, who held the rank of Āpā, ruled the Island during the interregnum. If this was so Parakkama-Bāhu was a member of the Alakecvara family, perhaps a son of the captive king, or of his brother, Vīra-Bāhu II. He may therefore be identified with the ruler appointed by the Chinese as their vassal, and also with the Alakecvarayā of the *Rājāvaliya*, who made several attempts to kill the young Lambakanna prince, a grandson of Parakkama-Bāhu V, whom Visidāgama had arranged to place on the throne as Parakkama-Bāhu VI. Vīra Alakecvara and the other captives were released about A.D. 1411-12 by the Chinese, but on the night after their return to Ceylon Vīra Alakecvara is said to have been murdered in his capital[2].

The Lambakanna prince, although he had been elected to the throne, could not venture within reach of Parakkama-Bāhu Āpā, but he established himself at Rayigama, and was at war with the Āpā until 1414, when he ascended the throne at Kōtte as Parakkama-Bāhu VI. These vicissitudes of the early years of his reign explain discrepancies between the various authorities as to the date of his accession. He reigned for nearly fifty-seven years from his

---

[1] *Spolia Zeylanica*, June 1912.
[2] See Perera on Alakecvara in *J.C.B.R.A.S.* for 1904.

election as king in. A.D. 1409 until his death in A.D. 1466. His long reign, during which Totagamuve Crī Rāhula Thera and his learned colleagues and pupils flourished, was a period of great literary activity and brilliancy. Crī Rāhula, who was the abbot of Vijaya-Bāhu Parivena, and belonged to the *Uttaramūlanikāya*, was the greatest scholar of the age, and was patronised and encouraged by the king, himself the author of a metrical vocabulary of Elu words entitled *Ruvanmal-nighantu*. Crī Rāhula's devotion to the royal family is exhibited in many affectionate references to members of it in his writings. He was an accomplished linguist, being master of six languages, and was also a poet of the first rank.

The king had two sons and one daughter, the Princess Uluku-dava Devī. His elder son was Senānāyaka Sapumal Kumāra, who invaded the kingdom of Jaffna, killed its Tamil king, Ārya Chakra-varti, and established himself as its ruler. The second son was the Prince of Ambulugala, who led a punitive expedition into the Kanda Uda-rata (the Kandyan district), which was then a subordinate principality, subdued its refractory ruler, and appointed another, a solar prince of the Gampola royal family, to rule over the district.

On the death of the king in A.D. 1466 his grandson, Jaya-Bāhu II, called also Jaya Vīra Parakkama-Bāhu, son of Ulukudaya Devī, ascended the throne in Kōtte, but did not long retain the sceptre, for in A.D. 1468 Prince Sapumal, the rightful heir, came from Jaffna with a large army, put his nephew to death, and ascended the throne under the title of Bhuvaneka-Bāhu VI. His brother, the prince of Ambulugala, quelled a rebellion in the south raised by Crīvardhana Pratirāja and Kūragama Himi. The Kalyāni Upasampadā ordination was held in this king's reign, and is recorded in the Kalyāni Inscription[1].

Bhuvaneka-Bāhu VI died in A.D. 1476 after a reign of seven years, and was succeeded by his adopted son, Parakkama-Bāhu VII, called also Pandita Parakkama-Bāhu, who reigned for about eight years (A.D. 1476—84). The Prince of Ambulugala then rose against him, defeated his army, and slew his principal officers in battle, and, entering Kōtte, slew him at midnight. The next morning the prince ascended the throne under the title of Vīra Parakkama-Bāhu, or Parakkama-Bāhu VIII. He had one daughter and six sons, namely, (1) Dhamma Parakkama-Bāhu, (2) Crī Rājasimha, (3) Sakkāyudha, (4) Rayigam Bandāra, (5) Taniyān Vallabha, and (6) Sakalakalā Vallabha. Of these the second and third lived at Manikkadavara, as associated husbands of a Kīravalle princess; the fourth at Rayi-

[1] See *Indian Antiquary*, Vol. xxii, 1893.

gama ; and of the fifth and sixth, who were sons by a second wife, the former lived at Mādampe, where his daughter had two sons, Vīdya-Kumāra and Tāmmita-Bandāra by a Malabaı prince, and the latter settled at Udugampola. All these princes played an important part in the history of the Island.

Parakkama-Bāhu VIII reigned for about twenty years, from A.D. 1485 to 1505, and at his death was succeeded by his eldest son, Dhamma Parakkama-Bāhu, or Parakkama-Bāhu IX, who reigned for about twenty-two years, from A.D. 1505 to 1527. It was in his reign, in September 1506, that the Portuguese, under Dom Lourenco de Almeida, son of the viceroy, Francisco de Almeida, first reached Colombo. On hearing of their arrival the king summoned to his presence his brothers and took counsel with them, and on the advice of his brother Sakkāyudha, who had secretly seen the strangers, he entered with the Portuguese, into a treaty of friendship and commerce, undertaking to pay tribute in cinnamon and elephants to the King of Portugal, who, in return, was to protect Ceylon from all enemies.

CHAPTER XXIII

THE MONUMENTS OF MUSLIM INDIA

SELDOM in the history of mankind has the spectacle been witnessed of two civilisations, so vast and so strongly developed, yet so radically dissimilar as the Muhammadan and Hindu meeting and mingling together. The very contrasts which existed beween them, the wide divergences in their culture and their religions, make the history of their impact peculiarly instructive and lend an added interest to the art and above all to the architecture which their united genius called in o being.

How much precisely this Indo-Islamic[1] art owed to India and how much to Islam, has been a moot point. The majority of writers, approaching the question from a western standpoint, have treated Indo-Islamic art merely as a local variety of Islamic art ; others, taking the opposite side and in sympathly with Indian rather than with Muhammadan ideals, have seen in it nothing more than a modified form of Hindu art. Much may be said in favour of either point of view. On the one hand, examples might be adduced of Muhammadan architecture so closely resembling the Hindu as to be all but indistinguishable from it ; or, on the other, of monuments so entirely devoid of any indigenous influence that they might almost equally well have been erected in Samarqand or Damascus. Such examples, however, would be misleading and the arguments based on them fallacious. Broadly speaking, Indo-Islamic architecture derives its character from both sources, though not always in an equal degree. In India, indeed, the history of Muslim architecture is closely akin to what it was in other countries. Wherever the Muhammadans established themselves—whether in Asia or in Africa or Europe—they invariably adapted to their own needs the indigenous architecture which they found prevailing there. In the lands first conquered by them—in Pales-

---

[1] Although the term 'Saracenic' as applied to the art of Islam has the advantage of being consecrated by long usage, the term 'Islamic' seems preferable for two reasons ; first, because it was mainly the religion of Islam which gave to the Muhammadan world its common bonds of culture and art ; secondly, because to the Muhammadans themselves the 'Saracen' meant nothing more than the Arab tribesmen who dwelt along the borders of the Syrian desert. Without, therefore, altogether excluding the word 'Saracenic,' Islamic will be used generally in this chapter.

tine, for example, or in Syria or in Egypt—this was inevitable, for the reason, as we shall presently see, that the Arabs themselves possessed little or no genius for the art of building, and, if their places of worship were to be as attractive as those of rival creeds, it was indispensable that they should impress into their service the builders and artists of the newly conquered territories. Later on this deficiency was made good by wholesale conversions among their subject races, and in no long space of time the followers of the Prophet found themselves heirs by blood as well as by the right of conquest to the arts and learning not only of the vast Sasanian Empire but of the greater part of the Graeco-Roman Orient as well as of Northern Africa and Spain. Under the sway of the Muslims the cultural development of all these countries received a powerful stimulus and, thanks to the freer intercourse and increasingly closer ties established between them, Islam was able to evolve for itself a new culture, which rapidly became common to the whole Muslim Empire, and at the same time to elaborate novel forms of architecture especially adapted to its religious and social needs. But though Islamic architecture thus acquired a fundamental character of its own and found expression in standardised forms and concepts in general use throughout the length and breadth of the empire, it still remained true that almost every country within that empire— from Spain in the West to Persia in the East—developed a local Muslim style of its own based primarily on indigenous ideals and stamped with a strong national individuality. Nowhere, for example, but in Spain could the romantic gateway of Toledo, or the fairy-like courts of the Alhambra have taken shape, and nowhere but in India could the Qnwwat-ul-Islām mosque of Old Delhi or the chaste and stately fabric of the Tāj Mahall have been designed.

By the close of the twelfth century, then, when the Muslims established their power permanently in India, it was no longer a case of their having to be tutored by their new subjects in the art of building ; they themselves were already possessed of a highly-developed architecture of their own, as varied and magnificent as the contemporary architecture of Christian Europe ; and the Muslims, moreover, who conquered India—men of Afghān, Persian and Turkī blood—were endowed with remarkably good taste and a natural talent for building. The picture that some writers have drawn of them as wild and semi-barbarous hill-men descending on an ancient and vastly superior civilisation, is far from the truth. That they were brutal fighters, without any of the chivalry, for example, of the Rājputs, and that they were capable of acts of savagery and gross intemperance, may be conceded. But these were vices common in those ages to most Asiatic nations and did not preclude them any more than they had precluded the Ghaznavids from participating in the prevalent culture and arts of Islam. Qutb-ud-dīn Aibak was ruthless enough to enslave *en masse* the population of Kālinjar, but he also had the genius and imagination to create a mosque as superb as any in Islam ; and though 'Alā-ud-dīn Khaljī slaughtered thousands of Mongols in cold blood at Delhi, he was the author of buildings of unexampled grace and nobility. Doubtless, it was due in a great measure to this inborn artistry, coupled with a natural catholicity of taste, that the newcomers were so quick to appreciate the talent and adaptability of the Indian craftsmen and to turn these qualities to account on their own buildings. Few things in the history of architecture are more remarkable than the skill with which, from the very outset, the Muhammadans transformed Hindu and Jaina temples into mosques for the Faithful, or the imagination which they displayed in employing Indian sculptors to adorn their edifices with designs incomparably more exquisite than their own. To create a successful building out of such alien materials, to reconcile two styles so characteristically opposed, without transgressing the standard formulas of Islamic art, might well have been deemed an impossible task. For the contrast between the Hindu temple and the Muslim mosque could hardly have been more striking. The shrine of the former was relatively small and constricted ; the prayer chamber of the latter was broad and spacious. The one was gloomy and mysterious ; the other light and open to the winds of heaven. The Hindu system of construction was trabeate, based on column and architrave ; the Muslim was arcuate, based on arch and vault. The temple was crowned with slender spires or pyramidal towers ; the mosque with expansive domes. Hinduism found concrete expression in the worship of images, and its monuments were enriched with countless idols of its deities ; Islam rigidly forbade idolatry or the portrayal of any living thing. Decorative ornament in Hindu architecture delighted in plastic modelling ; it was naturalistic as the Gothic and far more exuberant ; Islamic ornament, on the other hand, inclined to colour and line or flat surface carving, and took the form of conventional arabesques or ingenious geometric patterning. Yet, with all these conspicuous contrasts (and there are many more that might be added), there are certain factors common to both forms of architecture which materially assisted towards their amalgamation.   Thus, a characteristic feature of many Hindu temples, as well as of almost every Muslim mosque—a feature derived from the traditional dwelling-house of the East and as familiar in India as in other parts of Asia—was the open court encompassed by chambers or colonnades, and such temples, as were built on this plan naturally lent themselves, to conversion into mosques and would be the first to be adapted for that purpose by the conquerors.   Again, a fundamental characteristic that supplied a common link between the two styles, was the fact that both Islamic and Hindu art were inherently decorative. Ornament was as vital to the one as to the other ; both were dependent on it for their very being.   In the Indian architect this sense for the decorative was innate ; it came to him as a legacy from the pre-Aryan races and ran through the whole fabric of the art.   The Muslim, on the other hand, had inherited a vast wealth of rich and varied designs particularly from the Sasanian and Byzantine empires, and though his taste in the handling of ornament might not be so exquisite as the Indian, the value he attached to it was in no way less.   Thus it came about that when the conquest of India opened up new realms of art before his eyes, he at once gauged their vast possibilities and set about taking the fullest advantage of them.

In the fusion of the two styles which followed, Muhammadan architecture absorbed or inherited manifold ideas and concepts from the Hindu—so many, indeed, that there is hardly a form or motif of Indian architecture which in some guise or other did not find its way into the buildings of the conquerors. But more important than these visible borrowings of outward and concrete features is the debt which Indo-Islamic architecture owes to the Hindu for two of its most vital qualities ; the qualities of strength and grace.   In other countries Islamic architecture has other merits. There is nothing in India, for instance, to match the green and gold mosaics of Jerusalem and Damascus, or the superb colouring of Persian tilework, or the wonderful fantasies of Spanish design ; but in no other country are strength and grace united quite so perfectly, as in India. These are the two qualities which India may justly claim for her own, and they are the two which in architecture count for more than all the rest.

In a country as vast and diversified as India, it is not to be supposed, that architecture ever conformed to a universal type. The local styles of buildings which the Muhammadans encountered in different districts were almost as numerous and distinct one from another, as the peoples themselves or the languages they spoke. Some of the styles, as we have seen in the preceding volume of this history, were determined by the ethnic character of the population ; others were the outcome of differing religions ; others, again, resulted from foreign inspiration ; and others were conditioned by geographical surroundings or by the climate or geology of the neighbourhood. Whatever the underlying causes, each style represented a spontaneous development suited to the religious or social needs of the inhabitants and reflecting their specific habits and mentality. Out of these antecedent styles the Muhammadans evolved their own particular forms of architecture, adapting each to their requirements and modifying or transforming it according to its character or to the facilities which they possessed for giving expression to their own ideals. Thus, at Delhi, they built their first mosques out of the spoils of Hindu and Jaina temples, constructing them on Indian principles and enriching them with the handiwork of indigenous sculptors. At Delhi, however, the Muslims were in preponderating strength and better able, therefore, to maintain their own traditions. Hence at Delhi they quickly began to assert their own individuality and allowed Hindu craftsmanship only a very limited play. At Jaunpur, on the other hand, and in the Deccan, the local styles enjoyed greater ascendancy, while in Bengal the conquerors not only adopted the established fashion of building in brick, but adorned their struc tures with chiselled and moulded enrichments frankly imitated from Hindu prototypes. So, too, in western India they appropriated to themselves almost *en bloc* the beautiful Gujarātī style, which had yielded some of the finest buildings of mediaeval India ; and in Kashmīr they did the same with the striking wooden architecture which must long have been prevalent in that part of the Himālayas. But much as Muhammadan architecture owed to these older schools, it owed much also to the Muhammadans themselves ; for it was they who, in every case, endowed it with breadth and spaciousness and enriched it with new beauties of form and colour. Before their advent, concrete had been little used in India, and mortar scarcely ever ; by the Muhammadans these materials were employed as freely as by the Romans and became two of the most important factors of construction. Thanks to the strength of their binding properties it was possible for the Muslim builders to span wide spaces with their arches, to roof immense areas with their domes and in other ways to achieve effects of grandeur such as the

Indians had never dreamt of. Of the arch the Indian had not been
wholly ignorant; but without a cementing agent for the masonry,
his knowledge had been of little avail. With the Muhammadans,
on the contrary, the arch and dome had been from time immemorial
the key-notes of their construction, and, though in their newly-
adopted styles they frequently perpetuated the trabeate system, it
was the arch .and dome that they always regarded as peculiarly
their own and as symbolic of their Faith. Other characteristic
features which they introduced were the minar and minaret, the
pendentive and squinch arch, stalactite, honey-combing and half-
domed double portal. Elaborate decoration and brightly coloured
ornament were at all times dear to the heart of the Muslim, and
in both these spheres he introduced striking innovations. The rich
floral designs of the Indian artists he supplemented with flowing
arabesque or intricate geometric devices of his own, or sometimes
interwove with them (as only a Muslim calligraphist could do) the
graceful lettering of his sacred texts and historic inscriptions. Nor
was it enough that his buildings should be beautified merely with
a wealth of carvings executed in stone or brick or plaster; the
Muslim required colour also and colour he supplied by painting
and gilding, or by employing stones of various hues to accentuate
the architectural features. Later on, by the more laborious pro-
cesses of tesselating and *pietra dura,* he reproduced the designs
themselves in coloured stones and marbles. Still more brilliant
were the effects he attained by encaustic tiling, which he used
at first sparingly and in a few colours only, but later without
restraint to embellish whole buildings with a glistening surface of
enamel.

Of the many and various groups into which the Islamic monuments of India are divided, that of Delhi occupies the central and
pre-eminent place ; for it was at Delhi that the Muhammadans
erected their first splendid memorials, and it was at Delhi that
there afterwards arose a succession of buildings extending over the
whole six centuries of their rule. But before approaching Delhi we
must cast back for a moment to the older Muslim kingdoms of
Sin l and Afghānistān and see what contribution, if any, they made
to the development of Islamic art in India. With the Arabs, who
in the beginning of the eighth century possessed themselves of
Sind, our concern is small. Like other Semitic peoples they showed
but little natural instinct for architecture or the formative arts.
Though the Caliphs retained Sind for more than a century and a
half and though Muslim rule endured there until the close of the

tenth century, the sole surviving relics of it are the foundations of some small mosques unearthed a few years ago in the buried city of Mansūra[1], which, so far as can be judged from their remains, possessed no artistic merit. But if the Arabs were negligible factor, it was far otherwise with the Ghaznavids of Afghānistān, who overran Northern India in the first quarter of the eleventh century. At that time Persia occupied an all-important place in the world of Islamic art. Her genius was of the mimetic rather than the creative order, but she possessed a magic gift for absorbing the artistic creations of other countries and refining them to her own standard of perfection. Situated as she was in the heart of the Middle East, she became the crucible in which the arts of Turkistān and China on the one side, of Mesopotamia, Syria and the Byzantine Empire on the other, were fused together and transmuted into new forms and from which they issued afresh with the indelible stamp of Persian beauty set upon them[2]. And the channel by which this stream of art flowed southward into India was Ghaznī. Ghaznī, however, was more than a mere medium for the dissemination of Islamic art. All the culture and magnificence which in the ninth and tenth centuries had belonged to the Sāmānid dynasty of North-Eastern Persia, had passed, as if by the natural right of inheritance, to the Ghaznavids, and under Mahmūd the Great and his immediate successors, Ghaznī became famous among all the cities of the Caliphate for the splendour of its architecture[3]. Most of its buildings, unfortunately, perished during the ruthless burning of the city by 'Alā-ud-dīn Husain Jahānsūz, the Ghūrid, and others fell victims to the ravages of time or of later vandals. To-day, the only monuments of note that are known to survive are the tomb of Mahmūd the Great and two minars or Towers of Victory, the one erected by Mahmūd himself and the other by one of his successors, Mas'ūd. For us the minars are especially interesting as being the prototypes of the famous Qutb minar at Delhi and analogous to the towers of Dāmghān in Persia and at Mujdan and Tāūq in Mesopotamia[4]. Up to half a century

---

[1] A.S.R., 1903-04, pp. 132 ff.

[2] These remarks apply rather to the architecture of Eastern than Western Persia. The former is distinguished by its essentially decorative character, the latter by its constructional forms and motifs, which link it up with the Islamic architecture of Mesopotamia and ultimately with the Hellnistic monuments of the Nearer East.

[3] No architectural remains of the Sāmānid dynasty are known to exist, but of the influence which its art and culture exerted on Ghaznī there can be no doubt. The architecture of Ghaznī also owed a great debt to the currents of art which flowed thither from Turkistān and from Central Asia generally.

[4] Cf. Gertrude Bell, *Palace and Mosque at Ukhaidir*, pp. 40-41.

ago they were standing to a height of about 140 feet, and at that time consisted of two storeys, the lower star-shaped in plan, the upper round, both built of brick and embellished with elaborate designs in terra-cotta[1]. The tomb of Mahmūd Yamīn ud-Daula (999—1030 A.D.) which was also of brick has been completely modernised by restoration, the only feature preserved intact being its richly carved doors which were brought from Ghaznī by the British in 1842 and are now in the Fort at Āgra. These doors are of deodar wood, divided into panels and adorned with six pointed stars and simple geometric figures ; the stars and figures, as well as the vertical styles between the leaves, being carved into a variety of interlacing designs or flowing arabesques, and the whole further enriched with decorative hinges and bands of ironwork. Along the lower edge of the lintel is an inscription in Kufic[2] lettering invoking the forgiveness of God and his blessings on 'Abū-l-Qāsim Mahmud,' son of Sabuk-tigīn, while round the framing of the doors is repeated in the same script the formula, 'the sovereignty belongs to God.' Assuming that these doors are of the same age as the tomb (and it is *prima facie* improbable that a later generation would have lavished so much care upon their carvings), they acquire a special interest from the exceptionally developed character of their arabesques, and interlaced designs, which resemble Cairens work of the later twelfth rather than of the eleventh century[3]. As more materials become available for the study of this period of Islamic art, it may well prove that in work of this kind, Afghānsitān, which was under the immediate influence of Persia, was a century ahead of Egypt.

To return, however, to Delhi. The city which the armies of Qutb-ud-dīn Aibak occupied in 1191 was the *Qal'a-i-Rāi Pithaura*, the oldest of the 'Seven Cities' of Delhi, within the perimeter of which was included the strongly-fortified citadel known as the 'Lāl Kot.' Inside this citadel the conquerors erected one of the most remarkable series of monuments of which Islam can boast.

---

[1] The upper storeys have since fallen and square bases have been added to the supports of the towers.

[2] The inscription is to the following effect :

In the name of God who is most merciful and compassionate. May there be forgiveness from God for the most exalted Amīr, the dignified king, born to become the chief of the state and the head of religion, Abū-l-Qāsim Mahmūd, the son of Sabuk-tigīn, upon whom be the mercy of God...His blessings for him.

[3] E.g. the doors from the mosque of As-Sālih Telāye (circa 1160 A.D.). Those of the Al-Azhar mosque bearing a Kufic inscription of the Fatimite Al'Hākim (circa 1010 A.D.) are far more primitive in style, and so too are the doors from the Fatimite palace at Cairo (circa 1057 A.D.).

Its nucleus in the Jāmi' or Quwwat-ul-Islām mosque founded in 1191 A.D. by Qutb-ud-dīn Aibak to commemorate the capture of Delhi and dedicated, as its name implies, 'to the Might of Islam.' Raised on a lofty plinth and approached through gateways set in three of its sides, its plan is typical of the majority of mosques ; it consists, that is to say, of an open quadrangle enclosed by colonnades of which the western one constituted the prayer chamber, the only unusual feature being the presence of entresol galleries at the four corners of the colonnades instead of at the sides of the prayer chamber. Seen from within or without, the building, as originally designed, presented an essentially Hindu appearance. Half of the plinth on which it stood had actually been the basement of a Hindu temple and the rest of the structure—walls, columns, capitals, architraves and ceilings—was composed of materials stripped from the shrines of the unbelievers, twenty-seven of which, so one of the inscriptions informs us, had gone to the making of this one mosque. Indeed, save for the five mihrābs in the back wall, there was scarcely a feature in the whole building to proclaim its Muslim character. A design so alien to their own traditions was hardly likely to satisfy the sentiments of the Muhammadans, and within two years of its completion (i.e. in 1198 A.D.) an arched screen of characteristically Muhammadan design was thrown across the whole front of the prayer chamber. It is this screen above all else that is the making of the Quwwat-ul-Islām masjid. Simple as it is in form—it consists merely of a lofty central arch (53 feet in height) flanked on either side by two lesser arches which once supported smaller ones above—it would be hard to imagine carvings more superbly ornate than these which enrich its facade : band on band of sacred texts, their Tughrā characters entwined with curling leaves, and sinuous tendrils, side by side with floral scrolls and flowing arabesques or geometric traceries of surpassing richness. No doubt it was a Muslim calligraphist who set out the scheme and penned in the texts, but it was only an Indian brain that could have devised such a wealth of ornament and only Indian hands that could have carved it to such perfection. In spite, however, of all its beauty it cannot be pretended that this screen is an architectural success. It is too obviously an afterthought, not an integral, organic part of the structure : too vast and over-powering to harmonise with the relatively low colonnades of the courtyard, and still more out of keeping with the slight elegant pillars of the hall behind. The pity is that the precedent set by this, the earliest mosque in Delhi, was destined to be followed in many subsequent buildings and to exercise a baneful influence on their style.

In 1230 A.D. the Emperor Iltutmish more than doubled the area of the Quwwat-ul-Islām mosque by throwing out wings to the prayer chamber and screen and by adding an outer court large enough to embrace within its surrounding colonnades the Great Minar begun by Qutb-ud-dīn Aibak.   Whether of set purpose or because there were no more temples to despoil, fresh materials were specially quarried for these extensions, and it is significant of the extent to which the Muhammadans were now asserting their own ideas at Delhi, that the new work was fundamentally Islamic in character and manifestly designed, if not executed, by Muslim craftsmen.   Shafts and capitals and architraves of a Hindu pattern were still used for the *liwān* and colonnades, but in the screen extensions, which were the outstanding features of the new additions, Indian influence is visible in little except the actual construction of the arches.   In Qutb-ud-dīn's screen the inscriptions were the only part of the surface ornament which were Muhammadan ; all the rest was Indian and modelled with true Indian feeling for plastic form.   In Iltutmish's work, on the other hand, the reliefs are flat and lifeless, stencilled as it were on the surface of the stone, and their formal patterns are identical with those found on contemporary Muslim monuments in other countries.   It is fair, however, to add that what this latter work loses in spontaneous charm and vitality, it more than gains in organic unity and tectonic propriety.

The last of the Delhi kings to enlarge the Quwwat-ul-Islām mosque was 'Alā-ud-dīn Khaljī.   In the spirit of megalomania which so often obsessed him he started reduplicating the prayer chamber toward the north, adding yet a third court more than twice the size of its predecessor, and erecting in it another minar as high again as the existing one.   Had these vast structures been completed, we may well believe that they would have transcended the other monuments of Delhi as much in beauty as in size, but, fortunately perhaps for the welfare of his subject, the death of the king 1315 A.D. put an end to his grandiose schemes.

Of the disposition of the mosque and other buildings composing this group a clear and graphic idea can be obtained from the skilful reconstruction drawn by Mr J. A. Page (Plate III).   The Qutb minar seems to have been intended as a *ma'zina* or tower from which the *mu'azzin* could summon the Faithful to prayer, though it soon came to be regarded as a tower of Victory, akin to those afterwards erected at Chitor and Māndū. As originally designed it stood some 225 feet in height and comprised four storeys divided one from another by richly decorated balconies and further embellished by vertical flutings and horizontal bands of inscriptions inwoven with foliate designs. Many of the inscriptions are Quranic texts and demonstrate the essentially sacred character of the fabric ; others contain panegyrics of the kings who built or repaired the minar, and from these as well as from architectural considerations it is evident that only a portion of the first storey was the work of Qutb-ud-dīn Aibak and that the rest was completed by his successor Iltutmish[1]. In an inscription on the lowest band of the first storey Qutb-ud-dīn is referred to under his usual viceregal titles of 'The Amīr, The Commander of the Army, The Glorious, The Great,' and on the adjacent bands are eulogies of his overlord Mu'izz-ud-dīn Muḥammad Ghūrī and of the latter's brother Ghiyās-ud-dīn, which leave no room for doubt that Qutb-ud-dīn was still Viceroy at Delhi when the minar was begun. Iltutmish's own inscriptions are engraved on the second and third storeys only, but there is another record concerning him on the fourth storey, which dates from the time of Fīrūz Shāh Tughluq. In the reign of that Emperor the minar was struck by lightning and the fourth storey being then apparently dismantled and replaced by two smaller ones, its height by this means was raised to 234 feet. This rebuilding is chronicled in an inscription on the fifth storey and is clearly apparent in the novel style of decoration as well as in the different materials employed in the new work ; for, whereas the three lower storeys are constructed of grey quartzite faced throughout with red sandstone, the fourth and fifth storeys are constructed of red sandstone faced largely with white marble. Finally, in 1503 A.D., during the reign of Sikandar Shāh Lodī, the minar was again restored and its upper storeys repaired, though what measures precisely were carried out on that occasion cannot easily be determined. On the strength of certain short Nāgarī records in the interior attempts have been made to prove that the minar was of Hindu origin and that the Muhammadans merely re-carved the outer surface. But the only Nāgarī record of a date earlier than 1199 A.D. is one on the soffit of a window lintel, in a position which leaves no doubt that this particular stone came from some older structure. As a fact, the whole conception of the minar and almost every detail of

[1] Two short Nāgarī records of 1199 A.D. carved on the lowest storey indicate that the minar was founded in or before that year.

its construction and decoration is essentially Islamic. Towers of
this kind were unknown to the Indians, but to the Muhammadans
they had long been familiar, whether as *ma'zinas* attached to
mosque or as free-standing towers like those at Ghaznī. Equally
distinctive also of Muslim art are the calligraphic inscriptions and
the elaborate stalactite corbelling beneath the balconies, both of
which can be traced back to kindred features in the antecedent
architecture of Western Asia and Egypt. Fergusson, who was no
mean judge, regarded the Qutb minar as the most perfect example
of a tower known to exist anywhere, and there is much to be said
in favour of his view. Nothing certainly, could be more imposing
or more fittingly symbolic of Muslim power than this stern and
stupendous fabric ; nor could anything be more exquisite than its
rich but restrained carvings. Nevertheless, with all its overwhelming strength, with all its perfection of symmetry and ornament—
nay, by reason perhaps of this very perfection—it seems to
miss the romance, the indefinable quality of mystery that clings
around some of its rivals : round the Campanile of Giotto, for
example, at Florence or round the towers of Victory and Fame at
Chitor.

The reaction against Indianisation which is so marked a feature
of the minar[1] is noticeable also in Iltutmish's extensions of the
Quwwat-ul-Islām screen and of the little tomb—said to be that of
Iltutmish—which stands behind the north-west corner of the
mosque. Here, however, the Muslim elements have been less
successful in dominating the Hindu, with the result that the style
is vacillating and nerveless, possessing neither the tectonic strength
and purposefulness of the former, nor the picturesque artistry of
the latter. In its form and dimensions the tomb is quite unpretentious ; a simple square chamber, less than 30 ft. across, of red
sandstone within and of grey quartzite relieved by red sandstone
without. In three of its sides are arched entrances, and on the
fourth a mihrāb flanked by two smaller ones, while thrown across
the corners are squinch arches supporting a domical roof, which
like many Syrian and Egyptian domes was probably constructed
in part of wood. But if the structure was simple, its decoration
could scarcely have been more elaborate. The lofty entrance bays
without and almost the entire surface of the walls within were
covered from floor to ceiling with Quranic texts in Naskh and

---

[1] Whether Qutb-ud-dīn or Iltutmish was mainly responsible for the design of
the minar as originally built, is uncertain. The style suggests that Iltutmish may
have modified Qutb-ud-dīn's design.

Tughrā and Kufic characters, or with formal arabesques and geometric diapers as bewildering as they were varied, and the ornate effect of the whole was further increased by picking out the background of the white marble reliefs in colours. Predominantly the ornamentation was Islamic. Only here and there are Indian features observable, but we cannot doubt that the craftsmen employed were Indian or that .they were working with designs to which they were little accustomed. That this tomb is the resting-place of Iltutmish is the common belief to which colour is lent by its location immediately behind Iltutmish's extension of the mosque. On the other hand, some doubt as to its identity is cast by a passage in the *Futūhāt-i-Fīrūz Shāhī*, where the Emperor speaks of having restored some fallen pillars and four towers at the 'Mausoleum of Iltutmish'—a description which manifestly does not apply to this tomb. Probably the writer of the memoir is at fault, the building to which he refers being not the tomb of Iltutmish himself, but one about two miles distant, now known as 'Sultān Ghārī,' which the Emperor built in 1231-32 for his son and which there is good reason, therefore, for regarding as the oldest building of its class in India. In this earlier tomb the pillars, capitals, architraves and most of the decorative motifs are purely Hindu, and though arches and domes figure prominently in its design, they are constructed, like all the arches and domes of this period, on the Hindu corbel principle. The plan, too, of the Sultān Ghārī is quite unlike that of Iltutmish's tomb and, indeed, unlike that of any other tomb in India. It stands in the middle of a square fortress-like enclosure with round turrets at the four corners and an arched entrance, approached by a flight of steps, on its eastern side. Walls and turrets alike are pierced by arched openings. At the back of the gateway is a pillared portico carried on Hindu pillars ; and opposite to it on the west is a second portico flanked by colonnades extending from side to side of the enclosure This second portico, which is square and covered by a dome, served as a mosque and was provided with a mihrāb in its back wall embellished with inscriptions in Naskh and Kufic characters. The or b in the centre—an octagonal chamber with flat roof supported on pillars—is sunk to about two-thirds of its height below the ground level, a fact to ·which it owes its name of 'Sultan of the Cave.' Most of the enclosure, let it be added, is of grey granite, but the mosque and entrance portico as well as the exterior facing of the tomb are of white marble.

Among other buildings associated with the name of Iltutmish, the most celebrated is the *Arhāī-din-ka-Jhompra* at Ajmer, which Qutb-ud-dīn Aibak had built in 1200 A.D. and which Iltutmish subsequently beautified with a screen. The story goes that Qutb-ud-dīn finished the original building in two-and-a-half days, whence its singular name of 'Two-and-a-half days hut,' but a more plausible explanation is that the name dates from Marāthā times, when an annual *melā* or fair was held there, lasting two-and-a-half days. Whatever the origin of the name, the mosque of Qutb-ud-dīn is more likely to have taken two-and-a-half years than two-and-a-half days to erect. In style and construction it closely resembles its older rival at Delhi, but its area is more than double as large and the several parts of the edifice are correspondingly more spacious and dignified. At Delhi, the planning of the prayer chamber had been done on makeshift lines, the colonnades being too constricted and the pillars in them too low and crowded. At Ajmer, these defects were remedied. A single broad aisle on three sides of the open court took the place of the two or three narrow ones at Delhi and the arrangement of domes and pillars in the prayer chamber was made strictly uniform and symmetrical. Both mosques were built out of the spoils of Hindu temples, but at Ajmer the architect went to work more boldly and, despite the multiplicity of his materials and their strange fantastic forms, he succeeded nevertheless in creating out of them a hall of really solemn beauty—fit setting for the exquisitely carved mihrāb of white marble set in its western wall (Pl. VI). A further note of distinction was given to this mosque by the addition of circular bastions, fluted and banded like the Qutb minar, at the two corners of its eastern facade. But if Qutb-ud-dīn's mosque at Ajmer was an improvement on its predecessor at Delhi, the same cannot be said of the screen, magnificent as it undoubtedly was, which Iltutmish threw across the front of the prayer chamber. It had the advantage of being a third again as broad as Qutb-ud-dīn's screen and vastly more massive ; its engrailed arches were a pleasing novelty, its decorative reliefs admirable of their kind, and its workmanship beyond reproach. Yet, with all its grandeur and perfection of technique, it missed the delicate and subtle beauty of its rival. Mathematically it was correct to the minutest detail, but mathematical precision is not architecture and no amount of accuracy with compass and ruler can make up for lack of natural artistry. The two minarets set meaninglessly on the top of the central archway, the inappropriate niches and tiny medallions in the spandrels, and the abrupt determination of the base mouldings sufficiently betray the limitations of the designer, who produced in this screen rather a *tour de force* of technical excellence than an artistic triumph.

Between the death of Iltutmish in 1236 and the accession of 'Alā-ud-dīn Khaljī the story of architecture at Delhi is all but a blank. The only monument of note that throws light on its progress in the interval is the tomb of Balban[1] (1266-86) which stands in the south-east quarter of the *Qal'a-i-Rāi Pithaura*. It is a simple structure comprising a square domed chamber, 38 inches across, with an arched entrance in each of its sides and a smaller chamber to the east and west, in one of which was the grave of Khān Shahīd, the son of the Emperor, who fell in battle against the Mongols (1285-86). Unfortunately, every trace of decoration has perished from the tomb and what is left of it is a mere shell, but the presence of arches built on true scientific principles is an innovation that deserves notice. In every building of Qutb-ud-dīn and Iltutmish that has been described, the arches were constructed not with voussoirs, as they ordinarily are, but in corbelled horizontal courses, the fact being that, in their ignorance of arch construction, the Hindu craftsmen engaged on these structures had to resort to their own traditional methods of dome building. The appearance, then of the true arch in the tomb of Balban marks a definite advance in construction and at the same time is symptomatic of a general reaction against Hindu influences. This reaction had already made itself felt during the reign of Iltutmish and, though we have no means of following it stage by stage, it is evident that it must have gathered considerable strength in the half century succeeding his death. For by the time the Khaljīs came upon the scene Muslim building traditions had already become firmly established on Indian soil, with the result that not only had methods of construction been revolutionised but ornament had come to be treated more as an integral factor and less as a quasi-independent accessory of architecture.

The effect of these developments upon the style of the Khaljī period is clearly evidenced in the two principal monuments of 'Alā-ud-dīn's reign : the Jamā'at Khāna Masjid at the *Dargah* of Nizām-ud-dīn Aulīyā and the 'Alāī Darwāza at the Qutb. The former is the earliest example in India of a mosque built wholly in accordance with Muhammadan ideas and with materials specially quarried for the purpose. It is of red sandstone and consists of

[1] For a minar built at Koil in the 'Aligarh District by Balban which was demolished in 1862, see '*Aligarh Gazetteer*, vol. v, p. 218.

three chambers : a square one in the centre and an oblong one on either side, each entered through a broad archway in the facade. All three entrances, as well as two smaller ones between them, are framed in bands of Quranic inscriptions and embellished with lotus cuspings. The central chamber is covered by a single dome (38 inches diameter) supported at the corners on fourfold squinch arches. Around the base of the dome, internally, are eight arched niches, four closed and four pierced through the thickness of the masonry. The side chambers, which are divided at their middle by a double arch and roofed by two small domes, differ from the central one in that their walls are of plastered rubble instead of sandstone, while their domes are supported on triangular pendentives instead of squinches. Originally, it is said, the building was intended by its author, Khizr Khān, son of 'Alā-ud-dīn, not as a mosque but as a tomb for Shaikh Nizām-ud-dīn and consisted of the central chamber only, the side wings being added in the early Tugluq period when it was converted into a mosque, while further alterations and repairs are mentioned in the *Thamarātu-l-Quds* as having been executed during the reign of Akbar. These last are patent at a glance and include, besides other items, the screens in the side portals (visible in Pl. VII) and the painted decorations in the interior of the prayer chamber, all of which are typical of the Mughul period. But that the side wings were a later addition is more than questionable ; the design of the whole facade is so homogeneous and so nobly planned, that it is well nigh incredible that it could have been the creation of two different epochs or that the new work could have been so cleverly dove-tailed into the old and the new carvings imitated so skilfully as to defy detection.

The 'Alāī Darwāza, built in 1311, was the southern gateway leading into 'Alā-ud-dīn's extension of the Quwwat-ul-Islām mosque. Though the only one of his buildings at Qūtb which has not fallen to ruin, its state of preservation is far from perfect, a pillared portico which once veiled its northern entrance having completely vanished and its walls being sadly damaged and incorrectly restored. In spite, however, of its mutilations the 'Alāī Darwāza is one of the most treasured gems of Islamic architecture. Like the tomb of Iltutmish, it consists of a square hall roofed by a single dome, with arched entrances piercing each of its four walls ; and like that tomb, also, it is of red sandstone relieved by white marble and freely adorned with bands of Quranic texts or formal arabesques. But there the likeness ends. In every feature whether structural or decorative, the 'Alāī Darwāza is incomparably the finer of the two monuments. Seen at a distance its well-proportioned lineaments are accentuated by the alternating red and white colour of its walls ; and an added dignity is given by the high plinth on which it stands. At closer range, the harmony of form and colour is enhanced by the wealth of lace-like decorations graven on every square foot of its exterior walls. Then, as one passes into the hall, this effect of warm sumptuous beauty gives place to one of quiet solemnity, to which every feature of the interior seems to contribute : the subdued red of the sandstone, the stateliness of the portals, the plain expanse of dome, the shapely horseshoe arches that support it, and the bold geometric patterning of walls and window screens. The key-notes of this building are its perfect symmetry and the structural propriety of all its parts. Whoever the architect may have been, he was a man of irreproachable taste, who was not satisfied merely with repeating traditional ideas, but who set himself to think out and perfect every detail of his creation.

Among other monuments of 'Alā-ud-dīn at Delhi two that merit notice are the City of Sirī—the second of the seven cities of Delhi —and the Hauz-i-'Alāī or Hauz-i-Khās tank on the banks of which the army of Tīmūr encamped after his defeat of Mahmūd Tughluq. To the latter there will be occasion to allude again in connexion with the buildings of Fīrūz Shāh Tughluq[1]. The former was built by 'Alā-ud-dīn about 1303 in order to protect the ever-growing population of the suburbs. Nothing is now left of this city except some fragments of the encircling walls, but even these few remnants, with their round and tapering bastions, their lines of loopholes, their flame-shaped battlements inscribed with the *Kalima*, and their inner berm supported on an arched gallery, are of value and interest for the light they throw on the military architecture of the period.

With the transfer of the throne of Delhi from the Khaljī to the Tughluq dynasty, the architecture of the Imperial capital entered on a new and more austere phase. The days of its first youthful splendour and prodigal luxuriance were over. Lavish display of ornament and richness of detail now began to give place to a chaste sobriety which, as time went on, developed into a severe and puritanical simplicity. At first the change was due to the urgent need for economy and to the general revulsion of feeling against the excesses of the Khaljī régime. Public opinion had been outraged by the reckless follies of 'Alā-ud-dīn and still more

[1] See p. 590 *infra*.

by the revolting vices of Qutb-ud-dīn Mubārak and his outcast minion Khusrav Khān. It was not, therefore, to be wondered at if Ghiyās-ud-dīn Tughluq sought to break away from the past and, even in the matter of architecture, to avoid anything which might savour of the wanton extravagance of his predecessors. Later on, however, other causes contributed to intensify the plainness and severity of Tughluq architecture. One of these was the extreme religious bigotry of Muhammad bin Tughluq and his cousin Fīrūz Shāh, which led them to discountenance any but the most scrupulously orthodox and austere forms of religious architecture. Another was the loss of State revenues consequent on the defection of the outlying provinces which made it increasingly difficult to finance vast building schemes such as those projected by Fīrūz Shāh. Yet a third cause which severely handicapped the architects was the decay of skilled craftsmanship during the reign of Muhammad bin Tughluq, when the whole population of Delhi was forcibly transferred to Daulatābād and the city itself given over to desolation. Writing some years after the event Ibn Batūta tells us that the capital was 'empty and abandoned with but a small population,' and from all we know of its condition after Fīrūz Shāh's succession to the throne, it is clear that Delhi was still suffering from the consequences of this disastrous migration which resulted in the dispersal of her skilled craftsmen and artisans, in the effectual loss of their traditions, and in the general neglect and ruin of her monuments. Thus the architects of the Tughluq period were beset on every hand by restrictions and difficulties which made it impossible for them to emulate the works of their predecessors under the Slave and Khaljī kings. All this is clearly demonstrated in the buildings they have left us. Ghiyās-ud-dīn reigned only four years (1321-25), and there are but two monuments of his of any consequence, namely, the city of Tughluqābād — the third of the Seven Cities—and the sepulchre which he built for himself beneath its walls. But both of these monuments are eloquent of the rapidly changing spirit of Imperial architecture. Few strongholds of antiquity are more imposing in their ruin than Tughluqābād. Its cyclopean walls, towering grey and sombre above the smiling landscape ; colossal, splayed-out bastions ; frowning battlements ; tiers on tiers of narrow loopholes ; steep entrance-ways ; and lofty narrow portals : all these contribute to produce an impression of unassailable strength and melancholy grandeur. Within the walls all is now desolation, but, amid the labyrinth of ruined streets and buildings, the precincts of the Royal Palace once roofed with tiles of glittering gilt are still discernible ; and so too is the citadel rising high above the rest of the town and protected by its own double or triple lines of defence But, with all their seeming impregnability, the fortifications of Tughluqābād were in reality but very poorly built, consisting of nothing but a core of loose rubble with a facing of ashlar granite, and it is only too evident that they must have been put together in great haste, owing perhaps to some imminent peril from the Mongols.

Though almost equally simple and massive, the tomb of the Emperor is of less forbidding aspect. Let the reader picture to himself an island castle set (as it used to be) in the midst of a lake and forming an outwork, as it were, to the overshadowing city, with which it was connected by a narrow causeway. Above its embattled ramparts and in sharp contrast with their monotonous grey, rises the red and white fabric of the mausoleum. The marble and sandstone of which it is built are treated in a strikingly novel fashion. Up to the springing of the arches the structure is wholly of red sandstone, but above that point the red walls are relieved by bands and panels of marble ; and the crowning dome is entirely of marble. The effect of the treatment and particularly of the glistening expanse of white dome is to impart a certain lightness and diversity to the structure ; but the impression nevertheless conveyed by its battering walls and sturdy proportions is essentially one of simplicity and strength Assuredly no resting-place could have been devised more befitting the stern warrior who founded the Tughluq dynasty ! That there are defects in its design, need hardly be said. The sloping pilasters, for example; the unduly small merlons; the crudely disposed panels and bands of marble : all these are features that might easily have been improved on. These, however, are but minor blemishes and, clearly as they show the incipient tendencies of the new style, they do not seriously impair the solemn grandeur of the Tomb[1].

Muhammad bin Tughluq, the son of Ghiyās-ud-dīn, was the author of few monuments at Delhi. In the first two years of his reign he founded the small fortress of 'Ādilābād and the city of Jahānpanāh, and on the transfer of the capital to Daulatābād he must have thrown himself wholeheartedly into the lay-out and

---

[1] By the side of Ghiyās-ud-dīn there also rests in this sepulchre his son Muhammad bin Tughluq. It was at the grave of the latter that Fīrūz Shāh performed an act of almost quixotic piety. Having brought together all the victims he could find of his cousin's misdeeds or their descendants, he compensated them for what they had suffered, and taking their duly attested receipts deposited them in the grave of the dead Emperor.

construction of his new city, of which more will be said when we
come to deal whith the monuments of the Deccan. After the failure
of his plans in the south, however, he seems to have lost all interest
in Delhi, nay, even to have conceived a positive aversion to it, and
he did nothing further to beautify or improve it. 'Ādilābād, which
was merely an outwork of the larger city of Tughluqābād and
almost identical with it in style, calls for no comment. Jahānpanāh
(the 'World Refuge') he made by linking up the walls of Old Delhi
on the one side and Sirī on the other and so enclosing the suburbs
that had grown up between them. The fortifications themselves of
this new city (they are some 12 yards in thickness and constructed
of rough rubble in lime) are now all but level with the ground and
in some places barely traceable; but an interesting object connected
with them is a double-storeyed bridge of seven spans, with subsidiary arches and a tower at each end, which served as a regulator
for drawing off the waters of a lake inside the walls. Then, at a
little distance within the walls, there is the Bijai Mandal, a terraced
tower-like structure which evidently formed part of a small palace
and which is noteworthy for the presence of horse-shoe arches
copied somewhat indifferently from Khaljī prototypes, as well
as of intersecting vaulting which was afterwards to become a
characteristic feature of Tughluq architecture. Lastly, there is,
immediately below the Bijai Mandal and probably of about the
same age, a square nameless tomb of rough rubble and plaster,
crowned by a low Byzantine-looking dome and fenestrated drum,
which for beauty of proportions, both inside and out, is unsurpassed
by any other example of Tughluq architecture.

Fīrūz Shāh, the third of the Tughluq kings, was an indefatigable
builder. Shams-i-Sirāj enumerates a long list, and Firishta a still
longer, of the cities, forts, palaces, embankments, mosques, tombs and
other edifices of which he was the author; and the former supplies
us with the names of the two chief architects, Malik Ghāzī Shahna
and 'Abdu-l-Haqq, who assisted him in carrying out his schemes.
One of the best known of his palace-cities, which he founded on his
way to Bengal, was Jaunpur; others, hardly less famous, were
Fathābād and Hisār Fīrūza. At Delhi he built the palace-fort of
Fīrūzābād, which henceforth became his official residence at the
capital, and for the convenience of Muslim travellers he provided
no less than 120 rest-houses. But most valuable of all his public
works were the canals (one of which, the 'Old Jumna Canal,' is
still in use) by which he brought water to his new settlements and
at the same time irrigated the intervening tracts. Nor did these

undertakings, numerous as they were, exhaust the sum of his activities. With a piety all too rare among Oriental potentates, he renovated or rebuilt many of the monuments of former times which had fallen into disrepair, and even went so far, as he tells us in his autobiography[1], as to give these works precedence over his own building schemes.

Operations on such a vast scale necessarily demanded an organised system of financial control, and we learn from the *Ta'rīkh-i-Fīrūz Shāhī* that a plan of every proposed edifice had to be made by the architect and scrutinised by the financial officer (Dīwān-i-Wizārat) responsible for the provision of funds. Whether the Finance Department was at liberty to modify the designs submitted to it is not stated, but it is quite clear that the strictest economy was enforced, and the effect of this economy coupled with the other restrictions under which the architects of Fīrūz Shāh had to struggle is only too apparent in their buildings. Like the monuments of the first Tughluq, these are virile and strong, wholly sincere in purpose and free from sham ; but, with few exceptions, their construction is cheaper and their appearance incomparably colder and more vacuous. Red sandstone and marble, which had previously been used with telling effect, are now rarely seen; even in the most important edifices their place is taken by rubble and plaster. Local granite, to be sure, is employed for short heavy pillars and a few other members, but it too is generally plastered over or whitewashed and little attempt is made to turn its colour or texture to account. When first erected, these buildings of Fīrūz Shāh, like any Indian edifices of to-day, were dazzling white and, needless to say, had nothing in their aspect of the dark and sombre melancholy which age has imparted to them. Yet even their pristine whiteness could not atone for the monotonous bareness of their walls. What little surface ornament there was generally took the form of inscribed borders, medallions in the arch spandrels and such-like simple and conventional devices. Of the rich imaginative designs in which the Indian fancy rejoices, there were none ; nor, on the other hand, was there, save in rare cases, that sense of aerial spaciousness which is able on occasion to compensate for the absence of decorative beauty. The virtues of this architecture reside in its vigour and straightforwardness ; in its simple broad effects ; and in the purposefulness with which it evolved new

---

[1] The description of these archaeological repairs in the *Futūhāt-i-Fīrūz Shāhī* contains interesting information concerning the ancient monuments of Old Delhi.

structural features or adapted old ones to its needs—the multi-domed roofing, for example, or the tapering minaret-like buttresses at the quoins. Its faults are seen in the monotonous reiteration of these self-same features, in the prosaic nakedness of its ideas, and in the dearth of everything that might make for picturesque charm or elegance. How much this architecture suffered from the lack of Hindu craftsmanship can best be gauged by comparing it with the work of the Lodī or early Mughul periods, when the magic touch of Hindu genius had again endowed it with life and warmth The fact, however, that under the Tughluq dynasty Hindu influence was from one cause or another reduced to its lowest ebb, must not be taken to imply that it was altogether a negligible factor. The architects who designed these Tughluq buildings and the workmen who constructed them, though possessed, perhaps, of no exceptional skill, and though hampered by many restrictions, had nevertheless been born and bred amid Indian surroundings, and could not help expressing themselves in terms of Indian thought. Try as they might to adhere to the established formulas of Muslim art, they inevitably fell back on the forms and motifs with which they were familiar. Thus it came about that the flat lintel frequently usurped the place of the pointed arch, and that pillars, brackets, balconied windows, caves and railings, besides a score of other features of Hindu origin, took their place naturally in an otherwise Muhammadan setting ; and thus, too, it happened that much of the mentality underlying and controlling the design was fundamentally Hindu. It cannot be strongly emphasised that the longer the Muhammadans remained in India, the more deeply imbued did their art become with Indian feeling. Even though every individual detail of a building might be derived from an external source (a contingency that rarely happened), it still remained true that the brain which conceived the whole was working in obedience to Indian precept. Had Indian imagination been allowed freer play at this period in the development of Indo-Islamic architecture, a much higher level of aesthetic beauty would undoubtedly have resulted. As it is, we must be grateful that this imagination was not wholly absent.

Of the many monuments of Fīrūz Shāh which have survived at Delhi, the most considerable is the Kotla Fīrūz Shāh : the palace-fort or citadel which the Emperor built whithin his new city of Fīrūzābād[1]. If credence can be given to the description of Shams-

---

[1] The tendency at Delhi, as in many ancient cities of the east, was to extend the city always in the direction of the prevailing cool winds, that is, towards the north.

i-Sirāj, the city was more than double the size of Shāhjahānābād, extending from the ridge on the north almost as far as the Hauz-i Khās on the south and embracing a large part of modern Delhi. Among other edifices it is said to have boasted eight public mosques and one private mosque, besides three palaces and serveral royal hunting boxes. It is not unlikely, however, that the size and magnificence of the city were much overstated by contemporary historians ; for their accounts find little confirmation in the few monuments that chance has preserved, while, on the other hand they are discounted by the fact that Old Delhi and its extensions were still the centre of civic life in the time of Tīmūr. Of the Kotla and its various buildings, as they once appeared, a graphic picture is afforded by Mr Page's bird's-eye view (Pl. IX) Noteworthy features of its fortifications are the machicoulis which now for the first time make their appearance in India, and the absence of any raised berm or gallery to give access to the double lines of loopholes—a phenomenon that can only be accounted for on the assumption that the berms were constructed, or intended to be constructed, of wood. Within the walls the best preserved monuments are the *Jāmi' Masjid* and a pyramidal structure crowned by a pillar of Asoka. The former was an imposing building of two storeys, with arcades and chambers on three sides of the ground floor and with deep triple aisles (now fallen) around the open court of the mosque above. Its other features—rubble and plaster masonry, high bare walls, multiplicity of small domes, squinch arches, battlemented neckings and crestings—all these are typical of the prevailing style and call for no particular remark. The pillar of Asoka which stood in front of the mosque came from the village of Tobrā in the Ambāla district and was one of two such pillars which Fīrūz Shāh erected at Delhi ; the other, which was brought from the neighbourhood of Meerut, being set up in the *Kūshk.i Shikār* palace on the ridge. The methods adopted for lowering, transporting and re-erecting this famous monolith are described at length by Shams-i-Sirāj, who relates how it was lowered on to beds of silk cotton, encased in reeds and raw skins, and hauled to the banks of the Jumna on a carriage with 42 wheels ; how the Sultan came to meet it in person and how it was then transferred to boats and so taken to Firūzābād. He tells, too, of how it was lifted, stage by stage, on to the top of the pyramid, and there with the help of windlasses and stout ropes raised to the perpendicular. Evidently the shifting and setting up of this pillar was regarded as a remarkable feat of engineering, and considering the indifferent mechanical appliances then available, the engineers had every reason to be proud of their achievement. It may be remarked, however, that the weight of the pillar was less than 40 tons—a very insignificant bulk compared with the 700 or 800 ton blocks handled with no better contrivances by the Romans at Baalbek, or the still heavier blocks used by the ancient Egyptians.

A smaller, but architecturally more striking, group of monuments is that forming the College[1] and Tomb which Fīrūz Shāh built for himself at the Hauz-i-Khās on the remains of an older structure of 'Alā-ud-dīn Khaljī. Much of the College is now in ruins and its interior planning is too intricate to admit of detailed description here ; it must suffice, therefore, to observe that the tomb is at the south-east corner of the lake and that the College buildings extend some 250 feet on its western and over 400 feet on its northern side ; that the latter are double storeyed on the lake front, single storeyed behind ; and that for the most part they consist of arcades or colonnades, two or three bays deep, interrupted at intervals by square domed halls. The happy grouping of these buildings as seen from the lake (Fig. 19), the effective combination in their facades of Hindu column and Muslim arch, and their exceptionally decorative appearance, all combine to place them on a higher plane than the other monuments of Fīrūz Shāh's reign and to make of them, indeed, one of the most attractive groups at Delhi. The tomb of the Emperor, which is the central and dominating feature of the whole, is a square structure (44 ft. 6 in. externally) with slightly battering walls and is surmounted by a single dome raised on an octagonal drum. Its marble and sandstone cornice, battlements adorned with floral reliefs, and coloured plaster decorations of the interior, are part of the repairs executed by Sultān Sikandar Lodī at the beginning of the sixteenth century, but even without these later embellishments its simple dignity and unpretentiousness must always have commanded admiration.

Another mausoleum of exceptional interest both on historic and on architectural grounds is that of Khān-i-Jahān Tilangānī, the Prime Minister of Fīrūz Shāh, who died in 1368-69. It is situate a little south of the Dargah of Nizām-ud-din, alongside the *Kālī* (or *Sanjar*) *Masjid*, which Khān-i-Jahān Jauna Shāh built two years after his father's death. The enclosure in which it stands is of the

---

[1] The theory that this College was originally intended as a palace is supported neither by the plan of the building, which is unsuited to a palace, nor by the presence of the tomb, which would be out of place in a palace but to which the College is a natural adjunct.

usual fortress-like character. But the tomb itself marks an entirely
new departure. Instead of being square, like all its predecessors at
Delhi, the tomb chamber is octagonal surmounted by a single dome
and encompassed ay a low arched verandah. Thus its form generally
resembles that of the Dome of the Rock (*Qubbat-us-Sakhra*) at
Jerusalem, from which it may, indeed, have been ultimately derived.
But the very dissimilar materials of which it is built—grey granite
and red sandstone, white marble and plaster—and the essentially
Indian character of its component parts produce an effect widely
different from that of its tile-enamelled prototype. Being the first
attempt of its kind, it need hardly be said that its architecture is
far from being faultless. The domes, for example, both central and
subsidiary, are too squat, the verandah arches too low, and in other
respects the elevation lacks symmetry and finish. These defects,
however, are not without interest, since they show us more clearly
than anything else could have done the difficulties which the architect had to face in essaying this novel type of funeral monument.
In the century following, the Tilangānī tomb became the standard
pattern for the royal tombs of the Sayyid and Afghān dynasties,
and one by one we shall trace the steps by which the initial defects
were removed and the design gradually improved upon and elabo-
rated until it reached its final consummation in the magnificent
mausoleum of Sher Shāh. The mosques of Fīrūz Shāh's reign are
for the most part remarkably uniform in style. Constructed of
rubble and plaster, with pillars, caves and brackets of local grey
granite, they are characterised by boldly projecting gateways,
multi-domed roofs, tapering turrets engaged at the quoins and
Hindu caves and brackets. But while these are factors common
to almost all buildings of this class, here and there may be found
an example distinguished by features of an exceptional kind. Thus
the Kālī Masjid which Jauna Shāh built in connexion with his
father's tomb is planned on quite unusual lines. Instead of the
area in front of the prayer chamber being an open court, it is
divided into four by arcades crossing it at right angles, one arcade
linking the eastern entrance with the middle bay of the prayer
chamber, the other linking the northern and southern entrances.
A still finer and better preserved masjid designed on the same
cruciform plan and also attributed to Jauna Shāh is in the village
of Khirkī in Jahānpanāh. But though this treatment of the courtyard had the advantage of affording shelter to the worshippers and
incidentally of relieving the nakedness of the interior, it failed to
supplant the more orthodox plan, and was not repeated at the

other mosques of this period such as the Begampurī mosque in Jahānpanāh or the Kalān Masjid in Shahjahānābād, which Jauna Shāh himself afterwards erected. Again, in the Kalān and Khirkī examples there is a lower *tahkhāna* storey resembling that in the *Jāmi' Masjid* at Fīrūzābād ; and at the Begampurī mosque, which was the principal place of worship in Jahānpanāh, there is a heavy arched screen in front of the central *liwān* of the prayer chamber, which in point of organic unity is as inappropriate as the screen in front of the Quwwat-ul-Islām mosque. Finally, in the mosque of Shāh 'Ālam at Tīmūrpur, there occurs the earliest example at Delhi of a ladies' gallery in the rear corner of the prayer chamber, which henceforth was to become the orthodox position for these galleries.

The only other monument of the Tughluq period that need be mentioned is the tomb of the Saint, Kabīr-ud-dīn Auliyā, locally known as the Lāl Gumbad, which there is reason to believe was erected in the reign of Nāsir-ud-dīn Mahmūd Shāh (1389—92). In general form as well as in materials it is clearly a copy, and a very indifferent copy, of the tomb of Tughluq Shāh. Nevertheless it possesses a certain interest if only because it indicates a reviving sympathy for the more animated colouristic style of the Khaljī and early Tughluq periods, which had then been out of fashion for more than half a century. Happily the new movement which this tomb seems, as it were, to inaugurate, was destined to find expression in something more than the slavish imitation of antique models. Out of the universal chaos which followed on the invasion of Tīmūr, there emerged a vigorous and catholic spirit of design—a spirit replete with creative energy and imagination—which under the Sayyid and Lodī dynasties gave encouragement once more to the latent genius of Hindūstān and at the same time derived new inspiration from the never failing source of Islamic art in Persia. To revive again the fresh, spontaneous beauty of thirteenth-century architecture was no longer feasible. Through mutual reaction and other causes Muslim and Hindu ideals alike had undergone too much change in the interval. However much the new generation might strive to emulate the old models, however much it might elaborate their form or improve upon their colour, it could never hope to recapture their poetry. The prosaic formality or Tughluq architecture, and the habit which had grown up of designing buildings largely in accordance with set conventional rules, had left an indelible mark on Indo-Saracenic architecture. Henceforth, in spite of its returning animation, the style could not escape being more or less laboured and self-conscious. It struggled hard to find scope for inventiveness and individuality, and in a large measure it succeeded, but it could never wholly shake off the deadening effect of the Tughluq period.

In the shrunken empire to which the Sayyid and Lodī kings succeeded the resources at their command were too limited to permit of any vast and ambitious schemes of building, and we shall find that, with few exceptions, the chief and best examples of architecture during this period are the tombs of the kings and noble. Of the royal tombs, all those that can now be identified with certainty[1] follow the model of the Tilangānī tomb described above, but each successive structure marks an advance on the design of its predecessor. The earliest of the series is the mausoleum of Mubārak Shāh Sayyid situated in the village of Mubārakpur. Here, the central dome was raised substantially higher than in the original prototype, pinnacles (*guldastas*) were added at the angles of the polygonal drum, and the summit was crowned with a novel and striking feature in the form of an arched lantern in place of the usual finial. The height of the verandah, too, was increased, and the eight subsidiary domes, which in the Tilangānī tomb had proved too low and insignificant, were replaced by pillared kiosks (*chhatrīs*). In the next example—the tomb of Muhammad Shāh, which is reputed to have been erected by his son and successor 'Alā-ud-dīn 'Ālam Shāh—the architects went a step further, increasing still more the height of the central dome and subordinate kiosks, adding a second range of pinnacles on the angles of the verandah cresting and in other ways developing the symmetry and cohesion of the several parts. Many of the details of this Sayyid architecture, both constructional and decorative, were, it need hardly be said, inherited from the preceding age, and a few of them, like the effective patterning of the pierced stone screens, can be traced as far back as the early thirteenth century. On the other hand, some of its distinctive traits—the use of blue enamelled tiling to give emphasis to decorative features, the elaborate and highly refined treatment of surface ornament incised on plaster and embellished with colours, the lotus finials on the domes and certain other Hindu or quasi-Hindu motifs—all these were innovations, and destined to exert an important influence on the subsequent development of this school. In the mausoleum of Sikandar Lodī, which is believed to have been erected by his son and successor

---

[1] The tomb of Buhlūl Shāh, the founder of the dynasty, is said to be a low square building of somewhat mean appearance at Raushan Chiragh, Delhi ; but its identity is far from certain.

Ibrāhīm Lodī in 1517-18, the use of enamelled tiles was much extended, the tiles of several colours—green, yellow, bright azure, and dark blue—being disposed in a variety of patterns both inside and outside the building, and in other respects also there was a marked tendency towards a richer and more lavish display of ornament. But a still more important feature of this tomb was the use made in it of the double dome[1]. This structural expedient, which originated probably in Syria, and passed thence through 'Irāq to Persia and India, was invented in order to preserve the symmetry and relative proportions of the interior as well as of the exterior. So long as the dome was not hidden from view by the sub-structure projecting in front of it, no difficulty was experienced in fashioning it to suit the proportions of the body of the building. Indeed, the single domes of some of the Khaljī and Tughluq monuments are as perfectly formed as any in the world. But when the design of the structure was such as to necessitate the dome being elevated on a lofty drum, the interior forthwith became stilted and disproportionately high in comparison with its width. It was with a view to correct this fault that the separate inner and outer domes were devised. The invention, which at Delhi made its appearance for the first time in the tomb of Shihāb-ud-dīn Tāj Khān (A.D. 1501) and a little later was repeated in this tomb of Sikandar Shāh, played, as we shall see later, an all-important part in the evolution of Mughul architecture, which but for it could never have achieved such wonderful symmetry.

While the royal tombs of this period thus follow an established and more or less uniform pattern, the contemporary tombs of the nobles branch out into a new and distinctive type, which, though more common place and prosaic, is nevertheless not without much dignity and strength. Among the host of monuments of this class with which the plains of Delhi are bestrewn, the finest examples are the tombs of Bare Khān and Chhote Khān, the Barā Gumbad (A.D. 1494), the Shīsh Gumbad, the tomb of Shihāb-ud-dīn Tāj Khān (1501) and the two tombs known as the Dādī-ka-Gumbad and Polī ka Gumbad. From the illustrations reproduced in Plate XIII the general characteristics of the whole class can readily be gauged. They are square solid looking buildings with domes carried on squinch arches and an octagonal pillared kiosk rising from each corner of the roof.

---

[1] Another noteworthy feature of Sikandar Lodi's tomb is the spacious and quasi-ornamental character of its walled enclosure which occupies a place midway between the fortified enclaves of the Tughluq tombs and the decorative gardens of the Mughul, for which it seems clearly to be preparing the way.

In the middle of each side is a high arched bay projecting slightly from the body of the building and for the rest the facades are, as a rule, divided into two or three storeys and further relieved by a series of shallow arched recesses or of window openings pierced through the thickness of the walls. In other respects they resemble the octagonal tombs described above ; their grey granite walls embellished with red sandstone and enamelled tilework, their lofty drums and domes, their battlemented parapets, their pinnacles and lotus finials, their brackets and mouldings and decorative designs incised on plaster and picked out in colours— all these being similar in character and following the same course of development as the corresponding features in the tombs of the kings. It is to be observed, however, that unlike the royal mausolea, these square tombs possess no walled enclosures around them, though on the other hand there are several instances of mosques being appended. At the tomb of Tāj Khān, for example, there is an open 'Īdgāh—a simple battlemented wall provided with a mihrāb and flanked by turrets at the corners—though whether it was erected along with the tomb is open to question, since the tomb itself is furnished with its own mihrāb, which takes the place of the doorway on the western side. Attached to the Barā Gumbad again was a walled court with a highly ornate mosque on one side and a low arched structure corresponding to it on the other. The mosque is particularly interesting ; for while its tahkhāna basement and tapering turrets at the rear quoins are strongly reminiscent of the Tughluq style, in other respects it presents striking differences, notably in the diversified treatment of the five arched bays into which the facade is divided, in the increased size of its domes, in its effective balconied windows, and above all in the exquisitely fine plaster ornament with which the eastern facade and whole interior of the prayer chamber are covered.[1] Another and much more imposing masjid of the same period is the Moth-kī-Masjid built by the Prime Minister of Sikandar Shāh. Not only is it the largest structure of its class erected during this period (the prayer chamber measures 124 ft. 6 in. from end to end), but it epitomises in itself all that is best in the architecture of the Lodīs. It cannot aspire to the poetic refinement which characterised some of the Slave and Khaljī monuments ; nor can it pretend to the rhythmic perfection

---

[1] The surface decoration in this mosque is of exceptional value for the reason that there are so few buildings in which the plaster work has survived, though many must once have been embellished in the same manner.

found in the later Mughul style ; but, if it lacks these qualities, and if it betrays a certain organic looseness, it displays on the other hand a freedom of imagination, a bold diversity of design, an appreciation of contrasting light and shade and a sense of harmony in line and colour, which combine to make it one of the most spirited and picturesque buildings of its kind in the whole range of Islamic art. The storeyed open towers at the rear corners of the building are especially happy adjuncts in place of the usual slender minarets ; the interior of the prayer chamber, though hardly spacious enough, is dignified ; the domes are better spaced and the arched openings of the facade are better proportioned than in the Barā Gumbad mosque ; in addition to which the surface decoration of both the mosque and gateway gains in effectiveness by being more restrained, while the freer use of white marble and coloured tiling in combination with red sandstone imparts a more animated note to the whole.

PROVINCIAL STYLES

Multān.

When, in a subsequent volume of this history, we came to deal with the sumptuous monuments of the Mughuls, we shall see what a profound influence the work of the Lodīs exerted on the shaping of their style. But before we follow up the further progress of this architecture at the Imperial capital, we must hark back for a while and consider how it had meanwhile been developing in the out-lying provinces of the Empire and in the various independent kingdoms that came into being between the thirteen and fifteenth centuries. Of these lesser centres of Indo-Muslim power, the first to claim attention is Multān ; not because its few surviving monu-ments are either as ancient or as magnificent as many elsewhere, but because it was one of the earliest cities to be occupied by the Muhammadans and for this and other reasons was relatively little under the influence of Hinduism.

Thrice conquered by the Arabs in the eighth and ninth centuries, Multān never again reverted into Indian hands. For a hundred years (A.D. 879-980) it was the capital of an independent Arab State, and from the Arabs it passed in turn to the Karma-tians, the Ghaznavids, a second time to the Karmatians, and then to the Ghūrids ; after which it was incorporated in the principality of Nāsir-ud-dīn Qubācha and was finally annexed by Iltutmish. From that time onwards it remained feudatory to Delhi, reasserting its independence only between the years 1457 and 1525, when the

Langāhs were in power. During these several centuries of continuous Muslim rule, many monuments of note must have been
erected in the city. As early, indeed, as A.D. 712 a mosque with
minarets is said to have been built by Muhammad ibn Qāsim, and
in 985 we hear of the far-famed temple of Āditya, the Sun-God,
being demolished by the Karmatians and of another mosque being
reared on its ruins. But of these early structures no vestige is now
left, and, strangely enough, Multān does not possess a single mosque
that can be referred to pre-Mughul times. Such monuments—
they are only five in number—as are reputed to have been founded
before 1526, are all tombs of saints, and two out of the five have
been so extensively renovated as to be little more than mere
semblances of their former selves, while a third—the shrine of
Shāh Yūsuf Gardīzī, said to date from A.D. 1152—has been wholly
reconstructed and modernised. Yet in spite of their renovations
the two tombs in question are not devoid of interest. One is the
resting-place of Bahāu-l-Haqq, who died in 1262, and according to
popular belief was built by the saint himself, but it was seriously
damaged during the siege of 1849 and since then has been completely restored. The other is the tomb of Shams-ud-dīn (dec.
1276), who is locally known as Shams-i-Tabrīzī, but is not to be
confused with the more famous Persian saint of that name. The
original structure is said to have been erected by his grandson a
generation or more after his death, but having fallen into ruin it was
rebuilt in A.D. 1780 by one Seth Mihr 'Alī, a disciple of the family.
Both monuments are designed on the same lines and consist of a
square tomb chamber, with walls battering on the outside, surmounted by a lofty octagon and crowned by a hemispherical dome.
Concealed as their fabrics are beneath modern plaster and glazed
tilework, it is not possible to determine how much of them has
been restored, but comparing them one with the other, and also
with other tombs in the neighbourhood, it can hardly be doubted
that their present form is substantially that of the originals and
that they represent an earlier stage than the tomb of Shāh Rukn-
i-'Ālam in the development of the local Multān style. In this connexion, the tomb of Shādnā Shahīd, who died a martyr's death in
1270, is particularly instructive ; for though relatively insignificant
(it is only 18 ft. 6 in. square inside), its original fabric has not been
greatly interfered with, and, denuded as it now is of its plaster
facing, it affords an excellent illustration of the methods of construction then in vogue. Here also the form of the structure is
identical with that of the two tombs already described, though the

dome, be it noted, is somewhat lower and more in accord with what we should expect at this period. On the other hand, the tomb of Rukn-i-Ālam, the grandson of Bahāu-l-Haqq, which Ghiyās-ud-dīn Tughluq caused to be built between the years 1320 and 1324, exhibits a marked advance on its predecessors. Taken all in all, indeed, this tomb of Rukn-i-'Ālam is one of the most splendid memorials ever erected in honour of the dead. Its height, measured to the top of its crowning finial, is 115, its diameter 90 feet. Instead of being square, however as the earlier examples were, the body of the tomb is an octagon—a feature which vastly enhances the symmetry of the whole, while any suggestion of weakness, to which the octagonal form might have giving rise, is cleverly avoided by buttressing the outer quoins with engaged and tapering minarets. The superb surface decorations which distinguish this building have been widely renovated in the course of the centuries, but though many of the details have undoubtedly been changed, there is no reason to suppose that their general character—the bands of carved timbering let into the walls, the elaborately chiselled brickwork, and the richly coloured tilling—is markedly different from the original Compared with the memorials of the Sayyid and Lodī kings at Delhi, or with the still more magnificent tomb of Sher Shāh at Sahsarām, it must be conceded that in the matter of surface ornament and particularly of brilliant colour effects, the tomb of Rukn-i-'Ālam has the advantage. On the other hand, what it gains in these respects it loses in rhythmic grace and in the poetry of composition. The difference between these monuments is the difference largely between the Persian and the Indian ideals. For despite the presence of many obviously Indian features in the tomb of Rukn-i-'Ālam, and despite the local character of much of its craftsmanship, based on pre-Muslim traditions the spirit underlying its design is largely Persian, while that of Sher Shāh's tomb has gone far to becoming Indian.

Bengal.

In India, as in Persia and 'Irāq, brick had been used as a building material almost from time immemorial, and even as early as the Gupta period the art of chiselling wall surfaces and of beautifying them with carvings in relief had reached a high state of perfection. We need not wonder, therefore, at the exquisite craftsmanship which the early Muhammadan buildings of India exhibit in their brickwork. But there is one all-important feature, as we have already seen, in which the indigenous architecture of the Peninsula, whether of brick or stone, differed fundamentally from Islamic. Save on the rarest occasions it made no use of any other binding material for its masonry but, mud, and as a consequence found itself unable to aspire to any of those spacious effects which the arch and vault and dome subsequently made possible. In Multān and Delhi, fortunately, and wherever else Islamic traditions established themselves in sufficient strength, these limitations of indigenous building made little or no impression upon the succeeding styles of the Muslims. But in the more distant parts of the Empire, where the conquerors were relatively few in number and little in touch with the outer world of Islam, their architecture took its character largely from the pre-existing monuments of the locality. This is a fact that comes out prominently if we turn our eyes from the plains of the Punjab to the far-off Province of Bengal which was annexed by Muhammad Bakhtyār Khān as early as 1198-99, within five years, that is to say, of the conquest of Delhi itself. In this low-lying and tropical country, the destructive forces of nature and the still more destructive agency of man have spared few monuments of the Hindu period, but on the strength of such scanty remains as have survived and from the indications afforded by later examples it may safely be inferred that, although stone was freely employed wherever it could be procured, brick, timber and bamboo were the principal building materials in use ; and that among the most salient features of this older Bengal architecture were a peculiar form of curvilinear roof, commonly known as Bengali, square brick pillars of stunted proportions as well as more slender ones of stone, and carved or moulded surface decorations of almost ultra-refined elegance. It is safe to infer also that pointed arches of small dimensions constructed on the corbel system were not unknown to the Bengalis in the pre-Muslim days. These were the main characteristcis of the style which the Muhammadans found prevalent on their arrival, and which, with the help of their own traditions, they proceeded forthwith to develop and expand.

Considering the almost unexampled opportunities which the riches of Bengal opened out to the conquerors, the inborn artistry and adaptability of its craftsmen, and the immense superiority of Islamic methods of construction, it might well have been thought that the resulting school of architecture would have been second to none in India. As a fact, it proved one of the least successful. Seen in the mass the wide-flung ruins of Gaur and Pāndua, where the Muhammadans successively established their capital, make an imposing array and convey an impressive idea of the wealth and luxury of their authors. But, with few exceptions, the individual buildings are disappointing. They lack the imagination necessary to adapt the form to the size; their component parts are often out of proportion; their pillars sometimes too cumbersome, sometimes unduly slight; and the form of their Bengali roofs, originally intended for bamboo and timber construction, shows less appropriately in brick or stone. The low relief work of their wall surfaces, too, though exquisite in itself and admirably adapted to interior details, is generally too delicate and hyper-refined for the decoration of exterior facades, while the designs and application of their enamelled tiles betray a singular poverty of imagination. Yet, in spite of its manifest shortcomings, there is an originality about this Bengal school—a certain spontaneous artistry and freedom from convention which can hardly fail to command admiration; and, though the style as a whole does not rise to the same high level as some other local styles, nevertheless it was capable on rare occasions of producing results, such as the Dākhil Darwāza, which are unsurpassed by anything of their kind in the East.

It was at Gaur, or Lakhnāutī, the former capital of the rich Pāla and Sena dynasts, where the Muslims established their seat of government, that their first building operations in Bengal were started. Mosques, palaces and the like they must have provided for themselves immediately after their arrival, doubtless by appropriating and, if necessary, ruthlessly despoiling the buildings of the Hindus; and before twenty years had elapsed we hear of the Sultān Ghiyās-ud-dīn (Hisām-ud-dīn 'Iwaz) constructing raised causeways across the low marshy country to serve as military roads and erecting a madrasah, caravansarais and other edifices at his capital. Curiously enough, however, it is not at Gaur, but at Tribeni in the Hughli District, that the oldest remains of Muslim buildings have survived. These are the tomb and mosque of Zafar Khān Ghāzi. The former is built largely out of the materials taken from a temple of Krishna, which formerly stood on the same spot but is now so mutilated as to have lost most of its architectural value. The neighbouring mosque is reputed to have been built, at any rate in its present form, during the reign of Sultān 'Alā-ud-dīn Husain Shāh (1493—1518)[1]. Be this date correct or not, the mosque is certainly much later than the neighbouring tomb; but framing the central mihrāb, and obviously transferred here from some older

[1] The mosque has been wrongly thought by some writers to be contemporary with the inscription of A.D. 1298; cf. *J.A.S.B.* vol. VI, 1910, p. 23.

monument, is a stone border bearing an Arabic inscription which records the conquest of Southern Bengal by Zafar Khān in A.D. 1298 during the reign of Sultān Rukn-ud-dīn Kai-kāūs.   Slightly later than these remains at Tribeni is the Sālik mosque at Basīrhāt in the Twenty Four Parganas, which was founded originally in A.D. 1305, but has been completely renovated in modern times.   With these unimportant exceptions, however, the history of this Bengal style is a blank until we come to the reign of Sikandar Shāh (1358—89), and by a strange concidence the first monument that we then meet —the far-famed Ādīna *Masjid* which the Emperor erected in the new capital of Pāndua—was also the most ambitious structure of its kind ever essayed in Eastern India.   In area, this *masjid* was almost as big as the Great Mosque of Damascus[1]: 507½ feet from north to south by 285½ from east to west.   But though it was regarded in Bengal as one of the 'Wonders of the World,' its design was far from being worthy of its size.   Imagine an immense open quadrangle, more than twice as long as it was broad, bounded on its four sides by arched screens, every archway (and there were 88 in all visible from the court) identical with its fellows and every one surmounted by an identical dome, with nothing to relieve the monotony of the whole save a single archway which, rising higher and wider than the rest, fronted the vaulted *liwān* in the middle of the western side.   Even the domed gateways, which usually interrupt the long lines of cloisters, are absent, the only entrances into this remarkable masjid being two small doorways in the back wall for the use of the king, a small arched opening for the public in the middle of the east side, and another public entrance, probably added as an afterthought, at the south-east corner. Imagine, too, the interior of the cloisters divided into 375 bays—five deep on the western and three deep on the other sides—each a replica of its neighbour and each roofed by a precisely similar dome, with no variation whatsoever except where a royal gallery (*bādshāh-kā-takht*) extending over eighteen bays in the northern wing of the prayer chamber is carried on ponderous pillars of Hindu pattern. Surely no place of worship was ever devised of such magnitude and with so little sense for the beautiful ! Considered by themselves, the several parts and the details are admirable enough : the arcaded aisles, for instance, are dignified; the vaulted *liwān* is well proportioned and pleasing and the mihrāb is as exquisite a piece of carving as can be found in India.   But no amount of perfection

---

[1] Fergusson was incorrect in stating that the dimensions and ground plan of the two mosques were identical.

in its parts can compensate for the lack of organic composition
and due proportion in the economy of the whole. Its design, as
Cunningham rightly observed, is more suitable for a caravansarai
than a mosque. It is monotonous and commonplace. Fortunately
for the Bengal school, the experiment of building on so gigantic
a scale was not afterwards·repeated, and though the charge of
monotony could legitimately be brought against some other members of the same group, the defect is never so glaringly apparent as
it is in the Ādīna *Masjid.*

To the reign of Sikandar Shāh are also ascribed several other
monuments including the mosque and minar at Chhotā Pāndua
in the Hughli District and the mosque and tomb of Akhī Sirāj-
ud-dīn at Gaur. But though the two former are supposed to have
been erected by Shāh Saif-ud-dīn, a nephew of Fīrūz Shāh Tughluq,
it is obvious that their style belongs to the fifteenth rather than
the fourteenth century ; while the two latter were so extensively
restored in 1510 as to have lost practically all value as examples
of fourteenth-century work.

Whatever buildings may have been erected under the short-
lived dynasty of Rāja Kāns, which interrupted the Iliyās Shāh
succession between the years 1409 and 1438, the only one of note
now generally assigned to it is the Eklākhī tomb at Pāndua.
According to tradition, as recorded in the *Riyāz-us-Salātīn*, this
is the tomb of Jalāl-ud-dīn Muhammad Shāh, the proselyte son of
Rāja Kāns, who was converted to Islam by the Saint Nūr Qutb-i-
Ālam. Be this tradition correct or not, the tomb is one of the
finest in Bengal and peculiarly interesting as the prototype on
which, strange to say, many mosques in this part of India were
subsequently modelled. Its design is simple : a square, rather low
structure 75 feet each way, with gently curving cornice and octagonal turret at each corner—the whole surmounted by a single
domes, which is carried on squinch arches and supported besides by
pillars. The fabric is of brick, helped out with slabs of dark horn-
blende taken from Hindu temples ; and, as usual, the decoration of
the exterior is executed in moulded terracotta or carved brick,
glazed tiles being employed only in the overhanging cornices. The
interior was originally decorated with painted flowers and other
devices, but only faint traces of this ornamentation are now visible.
Compared with the tomb of Rukn-i-ʿĀlam at Multān, or the con-
temporay monuments of the Sayyid kings of Delhi, the Eklākhī
tomb connot be pronounced a great achievement Its general lines
are not unpleasing; there is merit in the treatment of the curved,

overhanging cornice the corner turrets are effective ; and there is great beauty and variety in the low terracotta relief work. It fails, however, because it lacks the height and dignity so essential to monuments of this kind, and—more important still—because too much thought has been given to surface decoration, too little to structural formative beauty. This is a weakness common to most buildings of the Bengal school, and one which they share with the generality of the monuments of Eastern Persia. In both places the architects were apt to regard the fabric of a structure rather as a vehicle for ornament than as a thing of beauty in itself ; and as often as not they seem incapable of thinking freely of three dimensions. In the few rare instances in Bengal, such as the *Dākhil Darwāza* at Gaur, where structural and decorative beauty went hand in hand, the result was as perfect an example of brick architecture as can be found anywhere in the world.

After the expulsion of Rāja Kāns's House in 1438, the buildings of the restored Iliyās Shāh dynasty become more numerous. Besides other monuments of lesser note, there are the *Sāth Gumbad* mosque and tomb of Khān-i-Jahān 'Alī at Bagerhāt, both dating from about 1459 ; while at Gaur there is the Dākhil Gate-way, believed to have been built by Bārbak Shāh (1459—74), the Tāntīpāra, Daras Bārī and Lotan *masjids* ascribed to his son, Yūsuf Shāh (1474—81), and the Gunmant mosque erected probably a few years later. Of these the first mentioned—the *Sāth Gumbad* mosque—is noteworthy for its cornet turrets, which are strongly reminiscent of Tughluq architecture, and for the unusual treatment of its frontal cornice, which instead of being curvilinear, slopes away in straight lines from a small triangular pediment over the central bay. The interior is a fine spacious apartment albeit some-what marred by the exaggerated slenderness of its stone pillars. The *Dākhil Darwāza*—the most striking of several gateways at Gaur—is a superb example of what can be achieved in brick and terracotta. Sixty feet in height by 113 feet from back to front, it consists of a central arched passage with guard rooms on either side. At each of its four corners is a five-storeyed tapering turret, once crowned by a dome. Walls and turrets alike are relieved by string courses and mouldings, and adorned further with sunk panels, niches and rosettes and other motifs of Hindu origin, among which the chain and bell, battlement and quatrefoil are conspicuous. But the outstanding merit of this gateway is the surprising bold-ness of its design and the masterly skill with which its facades have been broken up and diversified by alternating effects of light and

shade. Between the Dākhil Gateway and the Tāntipāra *masjid*
erected (if we may accept the traditional dates) only ten years
later, there is a marked divergence of style. The latter—an oblong
brick structure of two aisles divided by stone pillars down the
centre—has suffered sadly from the effects of time. Its roof has
gone entirely and large sections of its walls have collapsed. Yet,
even in its ruin, it is still an object of beauty. Cunningham considered it the finest edifice of all in Gaur, and if perfection of
detail were the criterion of good architecture, his opinion would
be fully justified. In the matter of superficial ornament, indeed,
the Tāntipāra *masjid* marks the zenith of the Bengal school. In
other respects, however, it shows signs of incipient decadence.
Where the Dākhil Gateway is virile, the *masjid* is effeminate ;
where the former is free and spontaneous, the latter is mannered
and formal ; and even its lace-like ornamentation, beautiful as it is
in itself, must be admitted to be verging on the meretricious. The
same remarks apply also to the decoration of the Daras Bārī mosque
which belongs to about the same age but is even more sorely
battered than the Tāntipāra. The Lotan *masjid* which is another
of the monuments ascribed to Yūsuf Shāh is the best surviving
example of type of mosque peculiar to Bengal. It is said to take
its name (otherwise Lattan or Nattan) from Nattu, a favourite
dancing girl of the Emperor. Like the Chamkhan *masjid*, which
appears from its style to be somewhat older but is neither so large
nor so well preserved, it is constructed of brick and consists of a
square prayer chamber—manifestly built on the model of the
Eklākhī tomb—with an arched verandah added on to its eastern
side, the whole structure measuring 72½ feet long by 52 feet wide.
Inside and out, the brickwork was once covered with glazed tiles
of blue, white yellow, and green. Much of this tilework has now
perished, but what remains it does not suggest that it could ever
have been very attractive. Here and there were a few effective
ornaments, such as blue and white lotus medallions in the spandrels,
but most of the decoration took the form of narrow alternating
bands of colour, which are merely restless and bewildering to
the eye. Such decoration has little to commend it. It misses the
picturesque and imaginative colouring of the tile-enamelled buildings of Persia and equally it misses the charm of reticence and
restraint which characterise the use of coloured tilework at Multān
and Delhi. That it could have appealed much to taste of artists
who were capable of desiging the Dākhil Gateway or the Tāntīpāra *masjid* is *prima facie* unlikely, and its presence can only be

accounted for on the supposition that coloured tiling was considered the fashionable thing at the moment for mosques, and that no better tiles than these were obtainable in Bengal. Glazed tilework was used also in the the Gunmant mosque at Gaur, but here the coloured decoration was supplemented by reliefs on stone or plaster, and it is significant that the latter was employed in the most conspicuous part of the building, i.e., in the main hall of the prayer chamber, whereas the tilework was relegated to a subordinate position in the wings. The ground plan of this masjid is not unlike that of Ādīna. It consists, that is to say, of a central vaulted hall (51×17 feet) flanked to right and left by an arcaded wing, each wing divided into twelve bays (viz. three aisles with four openings to the front) and roofed with as many domes. The wings are in no way remarkable, but the central hall, with its stone masonry and decorative reliefs embossed on the soffit of the vaulted roof, is a fresh departure inaugurating, as we shall see, a new phase in the history of this school. Both stonework and reliefs, to be sure, had long before been anticipated in the Ādīna masjīd ; but in those early days the stone had been stripped from Hindu temples, and when the supply from this source had failed, its place had been taken by brick. From now onwards stone again comes into fashion, being specially quarried in the distant Balasore and Rājmahal Hills and conveyed to Gaur by water. Although, too, the reliefs in the Gunmant mosque were doubtless inspired by those in the Ādīna, the new work was very different from the old. This will be apparent at a glance if the reader will compare the illustrations of the Ādīna masjīd carvings (Figs. 33 and 34) with those of the Gunmant and Chhotā Sonā masjid (Figs. 38 and 41). Technically and artistically the former are far superior. They exhibit all the refinement and natural spontaneity of the old Hindu school of Eastern India which for five centuries and more had been producing carving of this kind in stone. The latter are careful, painstaking efforts and by no means unattractive, but in a great measure imitative of the terracotta relief work which for some generations had supplanted stone sculpture and which being moulded out of soft clay was little adapted for reproduction in the harder material.

The obscurity which envelops the authorship of most of the buildings described above extends also to the single important monument, which on the authority of the *Riyāz-us-Salātīn* is commonly accredited to the short-lived Habashī dynasty (1487—93). This is the Fīrūza (or *Chirāgh*) minar at Gaur, which, like the minars at the Qutb and at Daulatābād, was designed

perhaps to do duty both as a Tower of Victory and the *ma'zina* of
a mosque that has since disappeared. It was a five-storeyed tower
about 84 feet in height—excluding a high masonry plinth on which
it formerly stood—and ascended by a spiral staircase within. The
three lower storeys were twelve-sided and of equal dimensions,
separated one from the other by bands of simple ornament. Then
came a projecting balcony and above it two circular storeys diminishing in size, the topmost being pierced with four arched openings
and surmounted by a dome, like the crowning cupolas of Tughluq
buildings. Besides its surface decorations in brick and terracotta,
the body of the tower was also embellished with blue and white
tiles, many of which were found in the debris at its foot. According
to the *Riyāz-us Salātīn*, the author of the minar was Saif-ud-dīn
Fīrūz Shāh (A.D. 1487—89) and this date is probably correct. On
grounds of style Cunningham was in favour of placing it nearly a
century earlier, ascribing it to Saif-ud-dīn Hamza Shāh (1396-
1406). As a fact, however, the style of the minar accords far better
with the close of the fifteenth rather than of the fourteenth century,
and this date is confirmed both by other details of its decoration
and by the presence of the glazed and coloured tiling referred to
above which had not been introduced into Bengal at the time proposed by Cunningham.

With the monuments of the Husain Shāh period (1493—1552)
we are on firmer ground, the dates of the most important among
them being established by the presence of inscriptions. These
monuments include the *Chhotā Sonā Masjid* (Small Golden mosque)
at Gaur, built by Walī Muhammad during the reign of Husain
Shāh (A.D. 1493—1519); a mosque at Bāghā in the Rājshāhī district
dating from 1523; the *Barā Sonā Masjid* (Great Golden mosque)
at Gaur, completed by Nusrat Shāh in 1526; and the *Qadam
Rasūl* mosque, completed by the same Emperor in 1530. Of these
the mosque at Bāghā and the *Qadam Rasūl* are of brick and
terracotta, and mainly interesting as illustrating the progressive
decadence of buildings of that class, which become more and more
flamboyant as time goes on, until eventually they are smothered in
a medley of mechanical and tasteless patterns. The other two
monuments are of brick, faced on the outside entirely, and on the
inside partially with stone. Both derive their name of 'golden'
from the gilding which once enriched their domes, and they resemble one another in other features too; notably, in the half
stone, half brick arcading of the interior, in their multi-domed roofs,
and in the schematic treatment of the mouldings on their exterior

facades. There, however, the correspondence between them ends. The older mosque, though far the smaller, is the more elaborate of the two. Its length is less than half that of the other, and it possesses only five arched openings in front against the other's eleven ; but the mouldings of its cornice are duplicated and enriched, the monotony of the domes is broken by the insertion of a Bengali roof in their middle and the bareness of the stone walls is relieved by a wealth of foliate patterns carved in low relief. It must be confessed, however, that the effect produced by the addition of the Bengali roof is not a happy one, and the rich relief work, albeit in itself exquisitely executed, is too flat and characterless to redeem the design from mediocrity. The *Barā Sonā Masjid* has the merit of greater simplicity and impressiveness (Fergusson, indeed, calls it 'perhaps the finest memorial now left in Gaur') but the architect has made the mistake so commonly met with in Dravidian architecture of supposing that increased grandeur in a fabric can be produced by the mere reiteration of its parts ; and, though the interior is not lacking in dignity, the building as a whole will not bear comparison with the great mosques in Hindūstān and Western India. Let it be added that the quadrangle in front of this mosque was some 200 feet square and was entered through arched gateways on its north, south and east sides, the stone facing of which was sparingly adorned, as was the masjid proper, with glazed tiles of various colours—green and blue, white and yellow and orange.

Gujarāt.

It will help us better to appreciate the merits and faults of this Bengal architecture, if we betake ourselves directly from the eastern to the western side of India, and consider the instructive analogies and contrasts presented by the provincial architecture of Gujarāt, where traditions of a pre-existing school were equally strong but strikingly dissimilar from those prevailing in Bengal. When the armies of 'Alā-ud-dīn Khaljī overran Gujarāt and annexed it to the Delhi Sultanate, they found still flourishing there a singularly beautiful style of architecture. The history of this style—conveniently designated 'the style of Western India'—has already been told in the second volume of this history. Its zenith had been reached some two centuries before the coming of the Muhammadans, but at the close of the thirteenth century the school of Western India was still full of vitality and the Indian architects and craftsmen whom the conquerors pressed into their service were hardly less gifted than their forefathers who designed the

far-famed temples at Somnāth and Siddhāpur, at Modhera and
Mount Ābū. The particular style which they favoured was distinguished by a breadth and spaciousness unusual in pre-Muhammadan
India, and with these qualities it combined a chaste and graceful
elegance that could not fail to appeal strongly to Muslim taste.
Fortunately for the future of this school the annexation of Gujarāt
took place at the very moment when the Imperial architecture of
Delhi had reached its highest expression under 'Alā-ud-dīn Khaljī,
and the builders who came from Delhi to the new province must
have been deeply imbued with the spirit of that architecture ;
indeed it is more than likely that some of them had personally
participated in the building of the splendid structures erected by
'Alā-ud-dīn at the *Dargāh* of Nizām-ud-dīn and the Qutb. This point
which has hitherto escaped notice, had an intimate bearing on the
subsequent development of the Gujarāt school. It meant that the
sense for symmetry and proportion and the almost faultless taste
which had characterised Khaljī architecture became, from the outset, the key-notes of the Gujarāt style also. The effect of this
influence from Delhi is well evidenced in the noble facade of the
Jamī' Masjid at Cambay, which was erected as early as 1325, i.e.
within fifteen or twenty years of the Jamā'at Khāna at Nizām-ud-
dīn ; and it is also evident a little later (1333) in the mosque of
Hilāl (or Buhlūl) Khān Qāzī at Dholka, which in spite of its insignificant minarets and other shortcomings, is imbued nevertheless
with the same breadth of conception and purity of taste. Although'
however, the foundations of this Gujarāti style were thus well and
truly laid in the fourteenth century, the times were altogether too
unsettled, and conditions under the provincial Government of Delhi
in other respects too unpropitious for architecture to make much
headway ; and it was not until the establishment of independence
under the Ahmad Shāhī dynasty that the greatness of this school
really began. Like most Indian potentates the Ahmad Shāhī rulers
sought to display their wealth and power in the magnificence of
their buildings, each in turn endeavouring to outdo the efforts
of his predecessors. Ahmad Shāh, from whom the dynasty takes
its name, commemorated his accession by founding the city of
Ahmadābād, and later on in his reign he built the forts of Songarh,
Dohad and Ahmadnagar. Among the monuments with which he
beautified his new capital were the Ahmad Shāh and *Jāmi' Masjids*,
and to his reign also belong the fine gateway known as the *Tīn
Darwāza* and the mosques of Haibat Khān and Sayyid 'Ālam. Each
and every one of these buildings, as well as a multitude of others

erected by succeeding kings, is distinguished by some particular traits of its own. Space, however, would fail to tell of them all, and we must be content, therefore, to pick out a few of the most typical examples. Of Ahmad Shāh's buildings, the two most instructive are the *Tīn Darwāza* (Triple Gateway) and the *Jāmiʿ Masjid*. The former (Pl. XXIV) was the principal entrance to the outer court-yard of the palace, where feudatories and foreign ambassadors assembled before making their way to the Royal presence. It is 37 feet in thickness and pierced by three openings (the central one 17½ feet wide), connected one with the other by three cross passages. The charm of this gateway springs from its perfectly proportioned and delicately framed archways set off against highly ornate buttresses on the faces of the intervening piers, though the latter, be it said, are not entirely homogeneous in feeling with the rest of the design. The *Jāmiʿ Masjid* is a far more magnificent creation. By the collapse of its two minars in the earthquake of 1819 it has been shorn of a prominent feature, but it is question-able whether the minars ever added materially to its beauty. As it now stands, it is one of the most superb, as it is also one of the most imposing structures of its class, in the world. The defect of most mosques planned on a large scale is, as we have seen in con-nexion with the Adīna *Masjid* at Pāndua, the dull monotony of their composition. In the *Jāmiʿ Masjid* at Ahmadābād there is no such weakness. The prayer chamber is 210 feet in width by 95 feet in depth, but its façade is so admirably composed, so broken up and diversified, and so well proportioned in its parts, that its vastness only serves to enhance the beauty and impressiveness of the whole. The low flanking wings on either side with their pseudo-arched fronts are unusual adjuncts, but the other features of the facade—its shapely expansive arches, its engaged minars blended more harmoniously than in the foregoing example with the rest of the design, its carved mouldings and string courses and battlements—all these are familiar characteristics of the Gujarātī style. The same is true also of the interior with its 260 graceful columns, now emerging into an established architectural order, its narrow aisles, its clerestory galleries, its symmetrically arranged domes built on the Hindu corbel system its traceried windows and its rich arabesques. Most of these features are derived from the old pre-Muslim school, and all are repeated time and again in sub-sequent buildings, though seldom with better effect than here. The mode of lighting and ventilating the interior, which was an inven-tion of the Gujarāt architects, is a specially happy solution of a well-known problem but one, strangely enough, that has never found favour in other parts of India. It consists in carrying the upper roof well beyond the one below it, the overlapping portion being supported on dwarf columns and the outside of the gallery thus formed being closed with perforated screens, the advantage of this arrangement being that all the light and air required can be admitted, while the direct rays of the sun and the rain are effectually excluded.

The excellent taste and originality displayed by the architects of Ahmad Shāh are equally evident in the few monuments left by his successor Muhammad Shāh II (1442—57), notably in the mausoleum of Sultān Ahmad, where he himself and his son Qutb-ud-dīn are interred, in the 'Tombs of the Queens' (*Rānī-kā-Hujra*), and in the mosque and tomb of Shaikh Ahmad Khattrī at Sarkhej. Of these the two last mentioned are by far the most important, not only because of their own intrinsic merit, but because the style they ushered in was subsequently adopted for the whole of this admirable group of monuments at Sarkhej. Both buildings were begun in 1446 by Muhammad Shāh and finished five years later by Qutb-ud-dīn. The mausoleum (104 feet square) is the largest of its kind in Gujarāt. It comprises a square central chamber, surmounted by a single large dome with four aisles of slender columns on each face, roofed by smaller domes. The aisles are closed from without by perforated screens of stone, and the central chamber is separated from the verandahs by panels of brass, fretted and chased and tooled into an infinite variety of patterns. The mosque, which has an area of rather less that half that of the *Jāmi' Masjid* at Ahmadābād, differs from its predecessors in that it possesses neither arched facade nor minars and that its roof is of the same uniform height throughout. Its beauty, like that of the tomb and of the exquisite little pavilion in front of it, is due to its chaste simplicity and classic restraint ; and indeed, considered on its merits as a pillared hall, it is difficult to imagine how it could have been improved upon. But whether a hall such as this, constructed on purely Hindu principles, fulfils the Muslim ideal of a *masjid*, is open to question. Such a design may perhaps be admissible in a quasi-private mosque, such as this, attached to a *Dargāh* ; it would certainly not be suitable, for a public place of worship.

Qutb-ud-dīn (1451—59) did not add much to the beauties or amenities of the capital. He built the Hauz-i-Qutb Tank at Kankariyā as well as the Qutb-ud-dīn mosque in Ahmadābād

and he is said also to have been the author of the mosque and
tomb in Rājāpur which was erected to the memory of the wife of
Sayyid Buddhā bin Sayyid Yāqūt. The mosque which bears his
name and which was completed in 1449 before his father's death, is
a dull soulless affair without any claim to distinction ; and the
Rājāpur mosque also, though one of the largest in the suburbs (it
is 150 feet in length by 53½ feet in depth), is not in the best of
taste, the central bay with its two heavy flanking minarets being
out of all proportion to the long low wings, and the facade in other
respects lacking unity and cohesion. If, however, the buildings
associated with the name of the king are of little merit, there is
one, erected by one of his nobles, that furnishes an important
landmark in the history of the Gujarātī style. This is the tomb of
Daryā Khān (1453) which, like the somewhat later mosque of Ala
Khān at Dholka, is permeated with a strong Persian spirit. It is
an imposing square structure with a lofty central dome and lower
domed verandahs on its four sides, and is constructed throughout
on the arcuate principle, which was destined to play an increasingly prominent part in Gujarāt, the arch henceforth being
employed not merely as a characteristic symbol of the Faith, but
as a structural expedient more practicable than the horizontal
beam in districts where stone was not easily procurable.

With the accession of Mahmūd Begarha, the architecture of
Gujarāt entered upon its most magnificent stage. In the course of
his long reign, which lasted for more than half a century (1459—
1511), this powerful Sultan founded the new cities of Mustafābād
at Junāgadh, of Mahmūdābād near Khedā and of Muhammadābād
at Chāmpānīr. Ahmadābād, his capital, he enclosed with additional
lines of fortification and beautified with broad streets and a
multitude of splendid edifices. For Chāmpānīr, which he captured
in 1484, the Sultan seems to have conceived an especial fondness ;
for on the spot where his camp had stood he afterwards caused a
city and a palace citadel to be built ; and up to the time of his
death this remained his favourite place of residence. Of the outer
city, which once reached almost to Halol, 3½ miles away, little is
now left ; but the strong walls of the citadel with their bastions
and happily proportioned gateways (Pl. XXV), the fine custom
house, the imposing mosques and richly carved tombs—all bear
eloquent witness to the grandeur of Mahmūd Begarha's new
capital, which at one time threatened almost to rival Ahmadābād
itself. Outstanding amid these monuments of Chāmpānīr is the
great *Jami' Masjid* (completed only two years before the death of

the Sultan). It has been described as second to none of the mosques of Gujarāt, and undoubtedly it is a most striking edifice, a particularly fine effect being produced in the interior of the prayer chamber by three tiers of columns rising one above the other and supporting the dome, with richly carved balconies between the tiers and an equally rich frieze beneath the ribbed soffit of the ceiling. But, considered as an organic whole, it will not bear comparison with its older namesake in Ahmadābād. Its parts are neither so well proportioned nor so successfully co-ordinated. The elevation of the prayer chamber is too cramped ; the minarets flanking the main archway overpoweringly heavy ; and the transition from the side wings to the central hall altogether too abrupt. The truth is that by the end of the fifteenth century the faculty for composition on a grand scale which distinguished the architecture of Ahmad Shāh and which had come down as a legacy from Khaljī times had all but exhausted itself. For con-structional purposes, it is true, the arch and dome were now play-ing an increasingly important part ; but though the architects of Mahmūd Begarha and his successors made free use of these features, and could handle them, on occasion, with consummate skill and taste, still they were never so much at home with them as they were with their own traditional pillar and lintel system ; nor could they bring themselves, as their predecessors had done, to design in the broader and bolder manner that the arch and dome rendered possible. For perfection of detail and sheer decorative beauty the *Jāmiʿ Masjid* and other mosques at Chāmpānīr can challenge comparison with almost any Muhammadan building in the East, but they fail conspicuously in point of synthetic unity. The same phenomenon is equally observable among the contem-porary monuments at Ahmadābād as well as at Dholka, Mahmūdā-bād, and other less known centres ; for though Chāmpānīr had become the favourite residence of Mahmūd Begarha, and though its population must have been largely recruited from Ahmadābād, its growing popularity does not seem to have greatly diminished the importance of the older capital, which at this period was reckoned among the foremost and wealthiest cities in Asia. If we consider, for example, the remains of the palace (it is but a skeleton now) which Mahmūd erected for himself on the banks of his great reservoir at Sarkhej, with its stepped *ghāts* and terraces, its pillared verandahs and balconied windows, we cannot but be struck by its uniform excellence. It is less pure in style, less elegant in its proportions than the earlier buildings of Muhammad Shāh II, but its parts nevertheless are entirely appropriate and in keeping with their fellows, and the whole is not only pleasing to look upon but admirably adapted to its purpose as a cool and refreshing dwelling house. It is the same also with the exquisitely carved sluice heads that emptied their waters into the lakes at Sarkhej and Kankariyā, insignificant structures in themselves but finished with that perfection of taste which can make the commonest things beautiful ; and it is the same also with the impressive step-wells or *wāvs* such as that built in 1499-1500 by Bāī Harīr, the Superintendent of the royal haram, or the still more magnificent example in the village of Adālaj. Though larger and more elaborate, these step-wells are designed on essentially the same lines as the older step-wells of the Hindus, of which the finest extant specimen is that of Mātā Bhavānī, dating from about the eleventh century. They consist, that is to say, of a circular or octagonal well-shaft approached on one side by a broad stairway which descends flight upon flight to the water's edge ; on the landings between the flights are pillared galleries, whose tiers are multiplied as the depth increases and which serve at once as supports to counteract the inward thrust of the long side walls and as cool resting-places in the heat of summer. There are no other wells in the world that, structurally and decoratively, can compare with these step-wells of Western India, and it was because their builders were content to keep to the established traditions of the country that they were able to attain such perfection. So long as the Muslims could do this, the ground was safe and their success assured. Their difficulties began when the customs of Islam or other considerations necessitated the introduction of alien and incongruous elements— a contingency which inevitably happened over their tombs and mosques. To the Muslim a tomb was indissolubly associated with the idea of dome and arch construction, but in Gujarāt the old trabeate system was much too deeply rooted in the soil to make way for the arcuate, and hence the builders generally insisted on following their own principles of design, modified by little more than the use of structural domes in place of the older corbelled roofs. Were it not for these domes and the increased spaciousness which they facilitated the tomb, for example, of Mahmūd Begarha at Sarkhej, of Sayyid 'Usmān in Ahmadābād (1460), or of Bībī Acht Kūkī (1472) would show relatively little trace of Islamic influence. On the other hand, there are a few tombs in which greater size and dignity were achieved by adopting the arch and vault. Such are the tombs of Shāh 'Ālam and of Mubārak Sayyid at Mahmūdābād ; but even in these cases it is manifest that the architects were still working under the spell of their ancient tradition and still thinking more in terms of trabeate than of arcuate construction, with the result that their creations never attained the same sublimity and grandeur as the great tombs of Northern India and the Deccan.

But if the difficulty of compromising with Islamic ideals was felt over their tombs still more was it felt over the designing of their mosques, where an added stumbling-block was provided by the minaret—a feature which the Gujarātī architect never managed to handle with complete success. Even at the *Jāmiʿ Masjid* of Ahmad Shāh the minarets, when they existed, were in doubtful taste, and half a century later these features had become still heavier and more cumbersome in relation to the rest of the structure. This is a blemish that we have already noticed at Mahmūd Begarha's great *masjid* at Chāmpānīr, but it is just as conspicuous in contemporary mosques at Ahmadābād,' such as those of Miyān Khān Chīshtī (1465), Bībī Achut Kūkī (1472) or Bāī Harīr (1500). In all of these, as well as in most other mosques of this period, the minarets were placed on either side of the central archway, as they had been in earlier examples ; but in this position they so impaired the symmetry of the facade that in some later examples they were omitted altogether, while in others they were shifted from the centre to the front corners of the building So long, however, as their old dimensions were preserved, this last solution was no better than the first ; for whether the mosque took the form of a pillared hall like that of Sayyid ʿUsmān (1460) or an arched and vaulted one like that of Shāh ʿĀlam, the towering minars at the corners were bound to overpower the rest of the structure. The fact was that minars of such dimensions could not by any conceivable means be brought into harmony with the design of the prayer chamber, unless the latter was to be radically altered. This is the reason why in some of the later mosques, such as that of Muhāfiz Khān, we find the height of the minarets reduced and that of the prayer chamber increased—much to the advantage of the composition as a whole. It was not, however, until the minaret was transformed into a merely ornamental and symbolic appendage that the problem from an aesthetic standpoint was successfully solved and then only at the expense of utility. Mosques with this form of ornamental minaret first made their appearance at Ahmadbād in the opening years of the sixteenth century, the best example and one of the earliest being that of Rānī Sīparī ·(1514) which belongs to the reign of Muzaffar Shāh II, while another was the mosque of

Shāh Khūb Sayyid (1538). The former was judged by Fergusson to be one of the most exquisite structures in the world, and his judgement was not exaggerated. East or West, it would be difficult to single out a building in which the parts are more harmoniously blended or in which balance, symmetry and decorative rhythm combine to produce a more perfect effect. The mosque is a small one—only 48 feet by $19\frac{1}{2}$ feet—but this very smallness is an asset in its favour, since the delicate traceries and jewel-like carvings of Gujarāt, suggestive as they are of an almost feminine grace, show to less advantage in bigger and more virile structures. Another relatively small but equally famous monument of Mahmūd Begarha's reign[1], in which these traceries are seen to perfection, is the mosque of Sidī Sayyid. In form this mosque is unusually plain and chaste : merely an inarched chamber, five bays wide and three bays deep, its arches supported on squared pillars, or pilasters ; plain octagonal minarets (now level with the roof) at the two fore corners; and the interior lighted by demilune windows of pierced stone work. Anything more simple and unassuming, or more unlike the richly adorned mosque of Rānī Sīparī could hardly be imagined. But though such simplicity is rare enough in Gujarāt, there is no mistaking the Gujarātī genius in the graceful well proportioned arches and superbly designed window screens (Pl. XXIX). It is these screens that have made the mosque of Sidī Sayyid world-famous. Ten of them, namely, three in each of the side walls and two in the end bays of the rear wall, are divided into small square panes, filled with ever varying foliate and geometric patterns. The other two—one to the right and one to the left of the central mihrāb—are adorned with free plant and floral designs, the like of which does not exist in any other monument of India. What makes these windows so supremely beautiful is the unerring sense for rhythm with which the artist has filled his spaces and the skill with which he has brought the natural forms of the trees into harmony with their architectural setting. Such half conventionalised designs, it is true, are familiar enough in India. They are found commonly on textiles, silver and brass relief work and the like, but this is the only instance of their elaboration in stone and the wonder is that so exquisite a method of screening window openings, having once been hit upon, was never afterwards repeated.

---

[1] Local tradition assigns this mosque to Ahmad Shāh's reign, but its style is that of the latter part of Mahmūd Shāh Begarha's reign.

Dhar and Māndu.

Considering how effectually local tradition dominated the Indo-Islamic architecture of Gujarāt, it is surprising how relatively little it affected the architecture of Māndū, which is not 200 miles distant. The reason is that though Māndū was an ancient stronghold of the Paramāras and, like Dhār, a flourishing centre of Hindu power, there is no evidence of any vigorous school of architecture having existed there, not vigorous enough at any rate to force its character upon the monuments of the new comers. Temples and other buildings the Muhammadans found in abundance at both places and appropriated or despoiled for their own purposes. Craftsmen, too, there were in plenty whom they enrolled into their service and to whom they gave no little latitude in the working up of details. But in its main essentials the architecture which the Muslims evolved at Māndū was modelled on the architecture with which they had grown familiar at the Imperial capital. Many of their monuments reverted back a century to the virile style of the early Tughluqs, with its battering walls and narrow lofty archways ; others favoured the later style of Fīrūz Shāh's reign ; and others again were influenced by contemporary buildings of the Sayyid and Lodī kings. But though the Muslims turned to Delhi for their prototypes, this must not be taken to imply that their creations were the outcome of slavish copying or were lacking in originality. On the contrary, their monuments were truly living and full of purpose, as instinct with creative genius as the models themselves from which they took their inspiration. Part of their distinctiveness they owe no doubt to their impressive size and part to the remarkable beauty of their stone work which under the transforming effects of time and weather takes on exquisitely beautiful tints of pink and orange and amethyst ; but in a large measure their distinctive character is due to peculiarities of construction and ornament, to the happy proportions of their component parts or to other more subtle refinements that do not readily admit of analysis.

Taken all in all, Māndū[1] is of all the fortress cities of India the most magnificent. The plateau on which it stands—an outlying spur of the Vindhyās—rises a thousand feet and more above the plains of Narbadā, its sides steeply scarped and broken by wild chasmal ravines. Crowning its edges and extending over a length of more than 25 miles are battlemented walls of grey basalt,

---

1 Māndū or Māndugarh appears in Sanskrit inscriptions of the Paramāra period as Mandapa-durga. To the Muhammadans of the fifteenth and sixteenth centuries it was known as Shādīābād.

pierced at ten points by arched and vaulted gateways, or rather series of gateways, which guard the steep approaches. Within the walls is a broad expanse of rolling jungle, sparse on the hills, deep and dense in the valleys, interrupted by smiling lakes or dark pools. Pīpal and banyan and teak mingle their shade with the dark *khirnī* and the brilliant 'flame of the forest'; and outstanding among them all are the gaunt misshapen baobab[1] trees which centuries ago the Abyssinian guards of the Mālwa kings probably introduced from Africa. Such is the natural setting amid which the splendid monuments of the Mālwa kings are placed and to which they seem as it were to give solemnity by their own intrinsic beauty. Once the whole plateau within the walls covered with buildings either of the Muhammadans or of the Paramāras who had occupied Māndū before them. But the vast majority—shops and houses and all small civic structures—are now levelled with the ground; the only ones that have survived the ravages of time and the devastating jungle being the royal palaces or mosques or tombs. Of these the oldest is the mosque of Dilāwar Khān Ghurī (1401-05), the founder of the Mālwa dynasty. Like the *Lāt Masjid* in Dhār, which was erected by the same king, it is chiefly interesting for the many members—pillars and architraves and carved ceilings—stripped from Hindu temples and for the manner in which they are turned to account. Dilāwar Khān himself first established his capital at Dhār, the small fort of which had been built, so it is said, by Muhammad Tughluq, but realising the imperative need of larger and stronger defences, he lost no time in transferring it to Māndū. Hūshang, his son, known also as Alp Khān, to whom the task of fortifying the new city was entrusted, seems to have had ideas of building at once as sound and as lordly as his contemporary Ahmad Shāh I of Gujarāt. It was Hūshang who planned and began the magnificent *Jāmi' Masjid* afterwards to be finished by Mahmūd Khaljī; it was he probably who built the remarkable Darbār hall now known as the *Hindolā Mahall*, and it was he, too, who was doubtless responsible for the vast scale of the fortifications. Whether these works are the offspring of his own or of his architect's imagination is not known. Whosoever they were, they do unbounded credit to their author. The style on which they were modelled was the robust and massive style of the early Tughluqs, but among all the monuments at Delhi of that period there is not one that can equal the impressive grandeur of the *Hindolā Mahall* or the *Jāmi' Masjid* at Māndū. The former

[1] *Adamsonia digitata*

of these two buildings is unique of its kind. Its plan is T-shaped, the stem of the T forming the Darbār hall, and the cross a group of smaller apartments in two storeys intended for the Zanāna and furnished wherever necessary with lattice screens. In length the *Mahall* measures 160 feet, in width nearly 100 feet, and the reader may judge from the illustrations of it what a noble effect is produced from without by its plain battering walls, well proportioned archways, bracketed dripstone and oriel windows[1], and what an equally noble effect is produced within by its wide spanned arches, slightly ogee in form, which supported the wooden and concrete roof[2] Though there is no reason for supposing that this *Mahall* was ever meant for defensive purposes, it is not fanciful to see in its massive strength a reflection of the disturbed and insecure conditions which then prevailed in Mālwa, with warfare incessantly in the air and enemies threatening the kingdom on every side. The *Jāmi' Masjid* is almost as simple as but less vehement in style than the *Hindolā Mahall*. All the ornamental adjuncts that it possesses are intrinsically good in themselves and worthy of the places they occupy ; but they are wholly subordinate to the structural unity of the fabric, and might, indeed, be stripped away without greatly impairing its majesty[3]. Like many of its predecessors at Delhi, the *masjid* is raised on a lofty plinth, fronted at ground level with ranges of arcaded chambers. From east to west it measures 288 feet, from north to south some 20 feet less, but projecting from the middle of the eastern side is an imposing entrance porch with ascending steps which adds another 100 fee and more in this direction, while outside the northern wall are two other entrance porches of smaller dimensions. The interior court— a square of 162 feet—is bounded on all four sides by eleven arched bays, each identical in form with its neighbour and each surmounted by a similar small dome, but there is this difference between the four sides that while the eastern *dālan* has only two aisles, the northern and southern have three and the prayer chamber on the west five. The prayer chamber, moreover, is further distinguished from the other sides by the presence of three large domes, one in the centre covering the principal mihrāb and

---

[1] The pardau wall above the eaves is a later addition of Mughul date.

[2] Both the *Hindolā Mahal* and the *Jāmi' Mosjid* were built largely of stones taken from older buildings, but in every case the stones were recut to suit their new positions and did not in any way condition or qualify the character of the design.

[3] In this respect the architecture of Māndū offers a striking contrast to that of Ahmadābād in which ornament constitutes an integral and essential part of the main aesthetic purpose.

mimbar, and one over each of the royal galleries which occupy the
rear corners. Compared with Ahmad Shāh's Great Mosque at
Ahmadābād, with which it was contemporary, the *Jāmi' Masjid* of
Māndū is lacking in poetry and creative inspiration. It is too cold
and formal and calculated to take rank among the really great
architectural creations of India. On the other hand it is far from
being open to the charge of dull monotony in the sense in which
the Ādīna *Masjid* at Pāndua is open to that charge. Even within
its courtyard, the heroical simplicity of its arcades, its spaciousness
and perspicuity of detail produce an effect not of barren vacuity
like the Ādīna *Masjid* but of impressive solemnity ; and if we
contemplate the exterior with its arcaded facade, and harmoniously
proportioned porticos aglow with weathering tints of pink and
orange, it is impossible not to feel the eloquence of its forceful,
silent appeal.

Whether Hūshang's tomb which stands at the rear of the
Jāmi' Masjid was begun by himself and finished by Mahmūd
Khaljī or whether, as Firishta states, it was entirely the work of
the latter is doubtful, but considerations of style are in favour of
Hūshang himself having been the author. Whoever it may have
been, the conception marked a new departure ; for it was the first
great tomb in India made wholly of white marble and in other
respects also it differed from its predecessors, one specially pleasing feature of its design being the broad expanse of dome in
relation to the interior of the tomb chamber, and another the
happy transition, effected by means of an intervening terrace,
helped out by corner engaged cupolas, between the extrados of
the dome and the square sub-structure below[1]. The murder of
Muhammad Ghaznī Khān in 1436 by his *Wazīr* and the transfer of
the sovereignty from the Ghūrī to the Khaljī line did not affect
the continuity of the local school of architecture. Mahmūd was as
energetic a builder as Hūshang had been. Already in 1432 his
father, Mughīs-ud-Dunyā (Malik Mughīs) had erected the elegant
mosque still known by his name, constructing it with skill and
taste largely out of Hindu materials. Mahmūd himself, as we have
seen, completed the *Jāmi 'Masjid* and the tomb of Hūshang, but
besides these he also commemorated his conquest of Chitor in

[1] Fergusson was wrong in stating that light was admitted only through the doorway and two small windows at its side, there being, as a fact, three large screened
windows on the north. He was wrong, too (as so frequently on points of fact), in
stating that the entrance gateway on the north and the elegant Dharmasla to the
west of the tomb were built of stones from older Hindu or Jaina buildings. All the
members of these structures were carved by the Muhammadans themselves.

1443[1] by erecting a vast group of buildings opposite the front of the *Jāmiʿ Masjid*, comprising a College, a Tower of Victory and a mausoleum for the Khaljī family. The tomb[2], like that of Hūshang, was of white marble within and without and probably of much the same form, but freely adorned with carving and coloured tilework and with inlays of black and yellow marble, jasper and agate and cornelian It stood in the middle of a lofty plinth, some ninety yards square by nine in height with a smaller projection on its western side. At each of the four corners of the plinth was a tower, the one at the north-west corner larger than the other three ; and ranged along the sides of the plinth were long series of apartments screened in front by arched colonnades. These apartments constituted the College of Mahmūd, and the great tower of seven storeys (*haft manzil*) at the north-west corner was his 'Tower of Victory.' Tower and tomb crumbled to ruin long ago and the remains that have lately been exhumed (Pl. XXXIV) are too fragmentary to be reconstructed in all their original detail. They suffice, however, to show that Mahmūd's work, though closely akin in style, tended to be more elaborate than that of his predecessor and they suggest that it was he rather than Hūshang who was the author of the *Jahāz Mahall*[3] (figured in Pl. XXXIV) which, with its fine arched halls, its roof pavilions and boldly designed reservoirs still forms one of the most conspicuous landmarks in Māndū.

Of the building enterprises of Ghiyās-ud-din Khaljī (1475-1500) nothing certain is known, but as he is reputed to have been the most pleasure-loving of all the kings of Mālwa, it is not unlikely that he was responsible for the Turkish baths, arcaded well, and other structures designed to increase the luxury of the royal seraglio at Māndū. Of Nāsir-ud-dīn, his son, our information is more exact. As it now turns out, he was the builder of the palace so long associated with the romantic name of Bāz Bahādur. This fact has been established by the finding of an inscription dated in the year 1508-09 on the entrance of the palace itself, which thus provides another fixed and interesting landmark in the history of the Māndū school. The palace is a well-designed structure, pleasing and unpretentious in appearance, free from shams or meretricious ornament and adequately adapted to its needs, but it has little of

---

[1] Cf. Firishta. The tower is also referred to in the Āīn-i-Akbarī and diary of Jahāngīr.

[2] In the tomb were buried Mahmūd himself, his father, Malik Mughī and his successors Ghiyās-ud-dīn, and Nāsir-ud-dīd besides other members of his family.

[3] Or 'Ship Palace'—so called because it stood between two lakes. The palace was largely repaired and added to during the reign of Jāhāngīr.

the bold epic quality of Hūshang's or Mahmūd's work. It illustrates, indeed, the decline of the Māndū style at the moment when it had lost most of its original dynamic energy, but still remained unaffectedly sincere in purpose.

To describe only those monuments of the Muslims that are situated at the main centres of their political power—at Delhi, for example, or Gaur or Ahmadābād or Māndū—is to give but an incomplete picture of their architectural achievements ; for besides the capital groups whose history we have been sketching and others to be dealt with anon, there are scores of edifices in less important places that are well worthy of attention both from the historian and from the architect. Thus, at Bayāna, in the Bharatpur State, there is the *Ukha Mandir*—one of the earliest mosques erected (largely out of the spoils of Hindu shrines) by the Muslim conquerors, and afterwards converted into a temple ; while hard by it is the *Ukha Masjid* built in the reign of Qutb-ud-dīn Mubārak Shāh (1316—20) and a worthy example of Khaljī architecture. In Mewār, again, there is the fine arched bridge over the Gamberi River at Chitor built by 'Alā-ud-dīn Khaljī, when he besieged and took that city in A.D. 1303 ; and further west, in the Jodhpur State, are several buildings of no little merit. One of these is the *Atarkin-ka-Darwāza* in the old town of Nāgaur —a lofty gateway embellished, in the manner of the Arhāī-dīn-ka-Jhomprā screen at Ajmer, with a medley of geometric and flowing arabesques. The original structure appears to date from the first half of the thirteenth century, but to have been restored during the reign of Muhammad bin Tughluq (1325—51) and again added to in the sixteenth century[1]. Another is the *Shams Masjid*, also at Nāgaur, which according to local tradition was founded by the Governor Shams Khān, but which, to judge by its sharply tapering minarets, lofty narrow archways and clerestory gallery under the central dome (a feature manifestly borrowed from Gujarātī architecture), must in its present form be assigned to the fifteenth rather than the thirteenth century. A third is the Fort Mosque at Jalor erected by Muzaffar Shāh II in the graceful Gujarātī manner of the early sixteenth century ; and a fourth the *Top Khāna Masjid* in the same spot, with its magnificent but unfinished screen—also a work of the Gujarātī kings. Nor must mention be omitted of the highly interesting group of buildings at Chanderī in the Gwalior

[1] Garrick (*C.S.R.* vol. XXIII, p. 69) speaks of an inscription of the year A.H. 630 (A.D. 1233) which records the repair of the gateway by Muhammad ibn Tughluq (*sic*). The date (which he elsewhere gives as A.H. 633) is manifestly a mistake.

State. In the fifteenth and early sixteenth centuries Chanderī was in possession of the Ghūrī and Khaljī kings of Māndū, and such few monuments as have survived the ravages of time bear witness alike in their construction and their decoration to the close connexion between the two places. Most important among these few is the *Kūshk Mahall* at Fathābād, about two miles south-west of Chanderī. In 1445, so Firishta tells us, Mahmūd Shāh I of Mālwa passed through Fathābād on his way back from Jaunpur and gave orders for a seven-storeyed palace to be erected there. It is with this building that the *Kūshk Mahall* is popularly identified, and, though there is no inscription to prove the truth of the identification, colour is lent to it by the style of the structure, which is not unworthy to be ranked with those of Mahmūd in Māndū itself. Moreover, although only the remains of four storeys now exist, the vast mass of debris, with which the *Kūshk Mahall* was until recently choked, warrants the supposition that there were once additional storeys above. The plan of the structure is simple : a square of 115 ft. 8 in. divided internally into four equal quadrants by two arched passages crossing each other at right angles. Tier upon tier of triple arches open on to these passages from the four quadrants, and air and light are also admitted from the outside through windows and balconies alternating one above the other in the successive storeys. Like the college and tomb of Mahmūd and the *Jāmiʿ Masjid* at Māndū, the *Kūshk Mahall* depends for its charm upon its virile proportions well co-ordinated parts and unaffected simplicity. Almost every detail of its design and construction—its clean-cut intersecting vaults, its arches with their delicate reflex curves, its cornices, brackets, balconies and pierced screen-work—all suggest that the architect, and probably many of the craftsmen as well, came from Māndū. This influence of Māndū is observable also in some of the later buildings at Chanderī though in their case the presence of other elements from the schools of Gwalior and Ahmadābād has had the effect of sapping the Māndū style of much of its strength. The *Jāmiʿ Masjid*, for example, which in other respects is characteristic of Mālwa, is cramped in its proportions and enfeebled by the rows of weak serpentine brackets supporting the eaves. The same meaningless brackets, which subsequently found their way into Mughul architecture at Fatehpur Sikri and Bayāna, also contribute to mar the appearance of the two tombs known as the Madrasa and Shāhzādīkā. In the *Badal Mahall* Gateway, which may be presumed to have served as a commemorative arch, the process of degeneration has gone still further, and, though care has ben lavished upon its details, its design as a whole is weak and ungainly.

These and many other monuments scattered through the Central India and Rajputāna States, though they can rarely boast the grandeur of contemporary buildings in the capital cities, are nevertheless of very real value in filling in *lacunae* in the history of the style to which they belong. As more attention comes to be paid to them it will be possible to trace much more accurately than at present the streams of influence that issued from Delhi, Mālwa and Gujarāt and mingled or conflicted one with the other in the contested territories between these three kingdoms; and it will also be possible to gauge more precisely the part played by the neighbouring Hindu principalities in the shaping of the Muslim styles.

What has been said above about Rajputāna and Central India is equally true of other parts of the Peninsula, where the Muslim power established itself. In the cities of Hindūstān which were subject to the Imperial Sultanate there are many edifices that help to supplement and illumine the history of the Delhi style. At Badaun, for example, in the United Provinces, the name of the Emperor Shams-ud-dīn Iltutmish is still kept alive by three monuments : the *Hauz-i-Shamsī*, the *Shamsī-'Idgāh* and the *Jāmi' Masjid*, the first two of which were probably founded by him during his governorship of the Province between A.D. 1203 and 1209, and the third in 1223, twelve years after he had ascended the throne of Delhi. Besides being one of the most ancient, the *Jāmi' Masjid* at Badaun is also one of the largest and most massive mosques in India, measuring 280 feet from north to south and constructed up to a height of twelve feet mainly of sandstone blocks plundered from Hindu temples. But, restored and renovated as it has been from time to time, there is little except its general form that can now be ascribed to the time of Iltutmish[1]. Thus, the older parts of the arcaded cloisters round the quadrangle and the tapering turrets engaged in their outside quoins are evidently part of a restoration effected in 1326 during the reign of Muhammad Shāh Tughluq while the domes over the prayer chamber were rebuilt in their present shape during the reign of Akbar, having perhaps been destroyed in the great fire which swept Badaun in

---

[1] Sir A. Cunningham's statement that the whole surface of the inner walls of the *masjid* was originally covered with raised ornamentation in blue glazed tiles is open to grave doubt. If glazed tiles were used in the manner stated, they probably belong to the Tughluq restoration.

1571-72. Even the eastern gateway which is figured in Sir A. Cunningham's report for 1875-76[1] and which was then the one truly
authentic part of the original structure still surviving, has since
been dismantled, and the rest of the structure has been sadly
modernised. The village of Rāprī, again, not far from Shikohābād,
boasts of an imposing *'Īdgāh* which was built in A.D. 1311 during
the reign of 'Alā-ud-dīn Khaljī ; and at Fathābād in the Hissar
District of the Punjab stands the well-known mosque and pillar on
which the lineage of Fīrūz Shāh Tughlaq—the founder of the
city—is set forth in an elaborate inscription of *Tughrā* lettering.
To the reign of another Tughluq (Mahmūd Shāh II) belongs the
Jāmi' Masjid at Irich[2], with its highly ornate mihrab, which was
originally built in A.D. 1412 but renovated in the late seventeenth
century. Then, when we come to the period of the Lodīs, there is
at Kālpī[3] in the United Provinces the fine mausoleum known as
the *Chaurāsī Gumbaz*—an arcaded structure set in the midst of a
cloistered quadrangle—which is reputed to be the resting-place of
one of the Lodī kings, but of which one there is no record. At
Lalitpur, too, an unpretentious but pleasing example of Lodī
architecture is afforded by the local *Jāmi' Masjid*, while at Hansi
in the Hissar District of the Punjab there is the tile-enamelled
tomb of 'Alī, a structure manifestly referable to the late fifteenth
century, though hitherto ascribed to the thirteenth[4].

To return, however, to the local styles of architecture evolved
under the independent Muslim rulers—we have seen, in the case of
Bengal, Gujarāt and Mālwa, that their architecture did not take
definite shape until their rulers had thrown off their allegiance to
Delhi And we shall find that the same is true of all the local
styles. Jaunpur, which is the next centre to claim attention, was
founded in 1359-60 by Fīrūz Shāh Tughluq when he was encamped
with his armies at Zafarābād, and for a generation afterwards—
until Khvāja-i-Jahān assumed independence in 1394—this city
constituted a valuable bulwark of the Delhi Empire.

Unfortunately, many of its finest monuments were ruthlessly
destroyed or mutilated by Sikandar Lodī after his defeat of Husain
in 1395, and of those which have survived there are three only of
note that can claim to have been founded during the fourteenth
century. These are the *Masjid* and Fort of Ibrāhīm Nāib Bārbak,
which were built respectively in 1376 and 1377, and the Atala
Masjid, founded in the latter year by Khvāja Kāmil Khān. Of

[1] Vol. XI, pp. 1—11, pl. iii.   [2] About 40 miles north of Jhansi
[3] In the Jalaun District.   [4] Cf. *C.S.R.*, vol. XXIII, 16.

these theree, however, neither the Fort nor the Mosque of Nāib Bārbak is distinguished by any architectural feature worthy of remark ; and on the other hand the Atala *Masjid*, though founded as far back as 1377, seems to have progressed little further than its foundations until the reign of Ibrāhīm Shāh Sharqī, who brought it to completion in 1408 and who was indubitably responsible for the character of its design.

Constituting, as it does, the earliest and finest example of the Jaunpur style, this Atàla *Masjid* merits particular description. The site on which it stood had been the site of a temple of Atala-devī, and it was out of the materials of that temple that the mosque was largely built ; but the structure, as it stands, is entirely of the Muslim period and the stones taken from its predecessor were cut and sculptured afresh to suit the new requirements. Its plan is typical of most Indian mosques and many of its features are directly copied from the architecture of the Tughluqs. Seen, indeed, from the west and from without, the domes over the prayer chamber and its back wall, with its engaged and sharply tapering minarets, its *kangura* cornices and string courses, might have been transplanted almost bodily from the Imperial capital. On the other hand, the mosques of the Tughluqs are less ornate than the Atala *Masjid* or its successors at Jaunpur, nor is there anything in them to match the imposing propylon screens which adorn the latter. It is these features in particular,—the propylon screens and the surface decorations,—that give to the mosques of Jaunpur their distinctive character, but it is the former more than the latter that have become specially associated with the Jaunpur style. The idea of giving increased height and importance to the prayer Chamber by throwing an arched screen across its facade had been, as we have already seen, initiated, three centuries before, in the *Quwwat-ul-Islām* mosque at Delhi, and since then had frequently found favour and been repeated in various forms. It was left, however, for the architect of the Atala *Masjid* to make of the screen a feature so massive and imposing as to overshdow all else in the quadrangle. This he did by devising the screen in the form of a gigantic propylon, uncommonly like the propylons of ancient Egyptian temples, set in front of the central *liwān* of the prayer chamber and sufficiently lofty (75 feet) to hide from view the great dome behind it. The propylon consisted of two square and battering minarets with an immense arch between, the whole relieved by tier upon tier of smaller arched recesses or trellised windows. To right and left of it was a smaller propylon of similar pattern masking the two subsidiary domes of the prayer chamber and serving as a support to lessen the glaring disparity between the central propylon and the adjoining wings. The gateways that pierced the cloisters on three sides of the quadrangle were also designed to match the propylons, and extra height and mass were given to the cloisters themselves by making them five bays in depth and adding to them a second storey. If the object of the architect of the Atala *Masjid* was to accentuate the importance of the prayer chamber and at the same time produce something novel, there is no doubt he succeeded remarkably well, for there are few mosques in Islam so imposing in their proportions or so arresting in style. But whether his work deserves the lavish praise that critics have bestowed upon it is another matter, and one to which we shall revert anon, after considering the other surviving examples of the Jaunpur school.

Another mosque belonging to the reign of Sultān Ibrāhīm (1401—40) was built by two governors of Jaunpur, Maliks Khālis and Mukhlis, who have given their names to it ; and a third was the *Jhanjhrī Masjid* erected by Ibrāhīm himself in honour of Hazrat Saʾīd Sadr Jahān Ajmālī. The former is a simple plain structure, devoid of ornament and invested with little architectural interest. Of the latter only the main propylon screen is now standing—the rest having, it is said, been to a large extent destroyed by Sikandar Lodī. Yet even from this mutilated fragment it is evident that the *Jhanjhrī Masjid*, though smaller in scale, was very similar in design to the Atala;—so much so, indeed, that there seems every probability of its having been the creation of the same architect. Who this architect,—the father of the Jaunpur style,—was is not known, but he was certainly gifted with an originality and good taste far beyond that of his successors, who built the *Lāl Darwāza* and *Jāmiʿ Masjids*. The first of these, which dates from the reign of Mahmud Shāh (1440—56), is, indeed, but a small and pale edition of the Atala. True, there are differences between them. The style of the *Lāl Darwāza* is more markedly Hindu; its cloisters are only one storey in height by two bays in depth; the prayer chamber is provided with one instead of three domes; the ladies' galleries are placed alongside the central hall; and the single propylon is much lower in proportion to its width than that of Atala *Masjid*. These differences, howev are not enough to betoken originality on the part of the architect. On the contrary, in endeavouring to improve on his model, he has signally failed to reproduce its vigour and stylishness and succeeded only in giving us a dull and unimaginative substitute. It is much the same with the great *Jāmiʿ Masjid*, which was erected, a generation later, in the reign of Husain Shāh (*acc.* 1458), but in this case decidedly more inventiveness has been displayed over the planning and disposition of its parts. The prayer chamber of this mosque (which is 235 feet in length, over all) is divided into five compartments, viz. a square *liwān* in the centre surmounted by a lofty dome and fronted by the customary propylon ; on either side of it a low pillared chamber supporting a *zanāna* gallery, which thus looked down into the central *līwān* ; and beyond the *zanana* gallery, a vaulted hall 50 feet in length by 40 in depth. Though less chaste in its details than that of the Atala *Masjid*, which it closely resembles, the domed *līwān* is nevertheless a noble and imposing hall; and the vaulted wings are well conceived and, in cleverer hands, might have been developed into really effective features. As they are, however, no effort has been made to soften their hard straight silhouettes or to bring them into harmony with the central propylon which towers starkly abrupt above them. This weakness of composition and lack of rhythm is one of the most glaring defects of the Jaunpur school. Another (and this is a defect common to most Indo-Islamic architecture) is its failure to visualise the subject in more than two dimensions at once or to design a building in the mass and with reference to every angle of view. The propylon screen of a Jaunpur mosque was meant to be seen from the quadrangle only and in this direction it certainly presented an effective appearance. Looked at, however, from the side or back, it was an incongruous adjunct unconnected, structurally or artistically, with the rest of the building. Few things, indeed, in Muslim architecture are so anomalous as the juxtaposition of these flat, abruptly squared, propylons and of the graceful domes immediately behind them. It is an anomaly of which no architect imbued with the true spirit of Islamic art could have been guilty. The architect of the *Lāl Darwāza Masjid* is said to have been a Hindu, named Kamau, the son of Visadru, and it is likely enough that the architect of the Atala *Masjid* was a Hindu also,—a Hindu to whom the dome and arch meant little more than structural expedients of unavoidable symbolic accessories, and who had little understanding of their inherent beauty. However this may be, the defects of construction and composition are so fundamental and obtrusive in these mosques that it is impossible to place them, as Fergusson did, in the foremost rank of Indo-Islamic monuments. Certainly they are not to be mentioned in the same breath with the finest of the monuments at Delhi, Aḥmadābād, or Bījāpur.

When we turn from the north of India to the Deccan, Muslim architecture confronts us with an unexpected phenomenon. So long as the Deccan was part and parcel of the Delhi Empire, the Muslims settled there would naturally look to the northern capital for their ideas of art and culture, and whatever buildings they erected would be either put together out of dismantled Hindu shrines and the like, modelled on the Khaljī or Tughluq architecture in fashion at the time[1]. When once, however, the political connexion with ' Delhi had been severed, it might have been thought that the Muslims in that remote and little accessible country would rapidly have succumbed to the Hindu influences that surrounded them and that their architecture would have taken its complexion from the Hemādpanti, Chālukyan and Dravidian buildings which were daily before their eyes. As a fact, the very reverse happened No where else in India did the assimilation of indigenous art proceed so slowly as in the south. From 1347, when their independence was established, down to the close of the fourteenth century, the Bahmanīs based their architecture almost exclusively on that of the Imperial capital, and during the following century also they drew much of their inspiration from the same fountain head. From the beginning of the fifteenth century, however, other and more remote influences began to make themselves felt. At all times the Bahmanī dynasts were generous patrons of art and science and learning and their court was as attractive to poets, scholars and artists as their army was to soldiers of fortune. Thus it came about that much of their military architecture was introduced directly from Europe, and that Persia played a more important part in the development of their civil architecture than in that of any other contemporary Indian style. Some of the monuments erected by the Bahmanīs, such as the *Jāmiʿ Masjid* at Gulbarga, are definitely known to have been erected by Persian architects ; others, such as the Chānd Minar at Daulatābād (1435) and the College of Mahmūd Gāwān at Bīdar (1472), are so predominantly Persian in character as to leave no room for doubt that they were largely the work of architects and craftsmen from that country[2]; others, again, exhibit obvious Persian inspiration, but in a more partial and indirect form.

[1] Regarding the wholesale transportation of craftsmen and artisans from Delhi to Daulatābād by Muhammad bin Tughluq, see above, p. 144. The loss to Delhi must have been a great gain to the Deccan. [2] Māhmud Gāwān was himself a Persian.

To the period between 1294 when 'Alā-ud-dīn Khaljī invaded the country, and 1347, when Bahman established the Bhamanī dynasty, only two monuments can with confidence be ascribed, namely the *Jāmi' Masjid* at Daulatābād (circ. 1315) and the Deval Mosque at Bodhan of Muhammad Tughluq's reign (1325-51). Neither of these structures, however, was anything more than an adaptation of a Hindu shrine, slightly altered to suit the new exigencies, and neither of them, therefore, has any real bearing on the history of local Islamic architecture. During this provincial period, however, much sound work must have been put by the Muhammadans into the fortification of strongholds such as Devagiri (Daulatābād) which they had wrested from the Hindus. Unfortunately, the military architecture of the Deccan has attracted little or no attention from archaeologists, and the data at present available are insufficient to enable us to discriminate with confidence between successive periods of building or to determine which parts are attributable to the Hindu founders, which to the provincial governors from Delhi and which to the Bahmanī, Qutb Shāhī or other dynasties that followed them. In the case of Daulatābād, however, there can be no doubt that though some of its defences were devised by the Yādavas and others by the Bahmanīs or their successors, some also were the work of Muhammad Tughluq at the time (1339) when he transferred the population of Delhi to Daulatābād, and constituting, as this city does, one of the most striking example of fortification known to the mediaeval world, it rightly deserves special notice. Its inner citadel stands on an isolated conical rock 600 feet in height, with sides scarped sheer for 150 feet and a moat hewn out of the living rock at their base. The only entrance is through a devious tunnel which in times of siege was rendered impassable by an ingenious contrivance. At a bend in the tunnel which came near to the outer edge of the rock was small chamber provided with a flue pierced through the thickness of the wall and fitted, in addition, with a staging of iron plates. On these plates a charcoal fire was lit which, fanned by the wind blowing incessantly through the flue, would quickly fill the tunnel with its fumes and make any ingress impossible. Round about this almost impregnable acropolis, which be it added, possesses its own perennial springs of water, was a highly complex system of fortifications designed to protect the city. The outer wall has a perimeter of $2\frac{3}{4}$ miles and between it and the acropolis are three inner walls, each loopholed and battlemented and each furnished with fortified gateways, outworks and

bastions, all so disposed that with the help of salient and re-entrant
angles the maximum of fire could be directed against an assailant ;
in addition to which the outer wall is surrounded by a moat and
glacis in much the same manner as the mediaeval fortresses of
Europe. In the military architecture of Northern India—even
including that of the Mughuls—there is nothing at all comparable
for strength and ingenuity to these elaborate defences of Daulatābād. The Bahmanīs, indeed who were largely responsible for them,
seem to have done more for military engineering than any of their
contemporaries, though it was left, it is true, to their successors
the following century to make the radical changes in military
architecture which the introduction of artillery rendered necessary.
Threatened as they constantly were by powerful enemies on every
side—by the Rājas of Vijayanagar, Telingāna and Orissa, by the
Gonds; and by the Sultans of Khāndesh, Mālwa and Gujarāt, the
Bahmanīs were compelled to safeguard themselves by multiplying
the number and increasing the strength of their fortresses. On the
north, the *taraf* of Berar was defended by its capital Ellichpur as
well as by the two strongholds of Gāwīlgarh and Narnāla, the
former of which was built and the latter extensively repaired by
Ahmad Shāh Walī I between the years 1425—28. Māhūr, in the
modern district of Adilābād, served to keep in check the highland
chiefs of the Sātpuras and the wild tribes beyond the Wardha.
On the west, besides Daulatābād, there were the powerful fortresses
of Parenda, Naldrug and Panhāla and, a little farther south, the
capital Gulbarga itself. Nearer the centre of their dominions
stood Bīdar to which the capital was subsequently transferred ;
and, towards the east, Warangal and Golconda ; while in the
south-west corner, watching the ever-dangerous Vijayanagar border,
were Mudgal and Rāichūr. Some of these fortresses (and there
are many more of lesser note that might be added to their number)
had been taken over from the conquered Hindu states but so
transformed by the Muhammadans as to ratain little of their
original character. Such were Rāichūr built in 1294 by Gore
Gungāya Ruddivāru ; Mudgal, once the seat of local Yādava
governors ; Warangal, Gulbarga and Bīdar captured by Muhammad
bin Tughluq, and Golconda ceded to Muhammad Shāh I in 1364.
Some. again, stood in the open ; others like Māhūr and Naldrug,
were built on precipitous rocks are among the hills, and relied as
much on their natural as on their artificial defences Of those, like
Daulatābād, which possessed an elaborate system of fortification,
the most remarkable perhaps and second only to Daulatābād

itself, are Bīdar and Parenda[1]. The former was mainly constructed by Ahmad Shāh I in 1426—31, at the time when it supplanted Gulbarga as the Bahmanī capital. Its walls, which are some 50 feet in height and 3 miles in circumference, are furnished with battlements, bastions and outworks—all very solidly constructed, and are further protected by a triple ditch (75 feet wide and 45 feet deep) hewn out of the solid rock. The Parenda Fort is traditionally attributed to Mahmūd Gāwān, but whether the tradition has any basis in fact is questionable. Though relatively small in area, its defences are singularly efficient. They comprise an inner and outer wall separated by a covered passage, a moat from 80 to 110 feet in width, a second and broader covered passage outside the counterscarp and a glacis which rises to the height of the faussebraye. The outer or scarp wall is stengthened by 22 bastions and, like the inner, provided with loopholes, battlements and projecting galleries. The only entrance was by way of a drawbridge and gateway at the north-west corner, and thence through a narrow and devious vaulted passage to a second gateway defended by traverses and redoubts. Anyone familiar with the military architecture of mediaeval Europe will perceive at once the close resemblances between it and the system of fortification described above, which is followed not only in these but in many other Deccan forts of the period. So striking, indeed, are these resemblances that there can be no doubt but that the works in the Deccan were directly imitated from the European, and, though nothing is known of the engineers responsible for this imitation, it may be assumed that men well capable of planning such fortifications would not be difficult to find among the Turkish and other foreign mercenaries in the armies of the Bahmanī Sultans and their successors, by whom these fortresses were largely added to and impoved. This adoption of western principles of military engineering must not, however, be taken to imply that western influence also accounts for the architectural style of these forts. With a few notable exceptions, that style belongs essentially to the Deccan. It is a style which combines sincerity of purpose with an innate sense for the decorative. The Indian builders of these forts grasped what was required and designed their structures accordingly, not slavishly following established precedent nor matching one feature meticu-

---

[1] For the particulars of these two fortresses and for much else that follows concerning the monuments of the Deccan the writer is indebted to Mr. Ghulām Yazdani, M.A., the distinguished Director of Archaeology in H.E.H. the Nizam's Dominions.

lously against another as the later Mughul builders did, but
setting each where it was needed, making it of such size and
strength as was required, and giving to the whole that touch of
beauty that comes naturally and instinctively to the artists of
Southern India[1]. It is this quality of simple purposefulness in their
architecture that gave to these fortresses of the Deccan much of
their romantic charm—a charm which was denied to many a
building in which beauty was more consciously aimed at. What
this particular charm signified can perhaps best be appreciated by
comparing, for example, the dignified but unpretentious gateway
of Golconda (Fig. 90) with the highly ornate and conventionally
laboured Mahākālī gateway of the Narnāla Fort erected in 1486
during the reign of Shihāb-ud-dīn Mahmūd Shāh and manifestly
inspired by the contemporary Lɔdī architecture of Delhi.

As stated above, the capital of the Bahmanīs was established
first at Gulbarga and afterwards at Bīdar and it is in these two
cities that the most valuable materials are to be found for the
study of their civil architecture. At Gulbarga, the two groups of
royal tombs are particularly instructive. In the first group, which
is situated near the south gate of the fort, are the tombs of 'Alā-ud-
dīn Hasan, Bahman Shāh (d. 1358), Muhammad Shāh (d. 1375)
and Muhammad Shāh II (d. 1397), besides two anonymous tombs
of a later date; the second, which is known as the *Haft Gumbad*
or 'Seven Domes' and is situate to the east of the town, contains
the tombs of Mujāhid Shāh (d. 1378), Dā'ūd Shāh (d. 1378), Prince
Sanjar, Ghiyās-ud-dīn (d. 1397) and his family, and Fīrūz Shāh
(1422) and his family. In their general form all these tombs
present a striking family likeness; the single ones, that is to say,
are simple square chambers, crowned with battlements and corner
turrets and roofed by a single dome, the whole standing on a low
square plinth; while the double ones are merely a duplication of
the single ones, resulting in a building twice as long as it is broad
and covered by two domes instead of one. In their detail features,
however, they clearly reveal the phases through which the architecture of the Deccan passed during this period. Thus, the tomb
of the first king, Hasan, with its battering walls and low dome, its
fluted turrets, tall narrow doorways and band of blue enamel tiles
below the springers of the dome, is typical of the Tughluq style of

---

1 For an analysis of the fundamental differences between the art of the Dravidian South and the art of the Aryānised North of India, cf. the writer's article
'Influence of Race on Early Indian art,' in the *Journal of the Society of Arts*,
vol. lxxi, pp. 659—667.

Delhi ; and the tombs of Muhammad Shāh, Mujāhid Shāh, Dā'ūd Shāh and Prince Sanjar are direct products of the same style. In the tomb of Ghiyās-ud-dīn, on the other hand, which was built in the closing years of the fourteenth century, Hindu craftsmanship begins to show in the carvings of the prayer-niche ; and a generation later the splendid mausoleum of Fīruz Shāh and his family (153' × 78' externally) bears witness to the steadily growing strength of this Hindu influence as well as to the new fashion for Persian ornament, the former obtruding itself on the outside of the building in the carved and polished black stone pilasters of the entrance and in the dripstones and elegant brackets that support them; the latter, in the resplendent plaster and painted decorations of the interior which are closely akin to those found in the contemporary tombs of the Sayyid and Lodī kings at Delhi and call to mind the rich designs of Persian bookbinding and embroidery.

Muhammad Shāh Bahmanī, whose tomb has been noticed above, was the author also of two mosques at Gulbarga, the earlier and smaller of which is now known as the Shāh Bazār *Masjid*. Its gateway is an almost exact replica of the Sultan's tomb and in other respects also, notably in the tall stilted archways of its prayer chamber and in the austere simplicity of its style, imitates the Tughluq architecture of Fīrūz Shāh's reign at Delhi. The other mosque is the famous *Jāmi' Masjid* within the fort, which was built by one Rafī', 'the son of Shams, the son of Mansūr of Qazwīn,' whose Persian sympathies find expression in the stilted domes and narrow entrances, though in other respects, the style of this building appertains rather to Delhi than to Persia. Two features of this mosque call for particular remark. One is the design of the broad squat arches of the cloisters (Fig. 95) which now make their appearance for the first time, but are destined henceforth to become familiar adjuncts of the architecture of the Deccan; the other is the unique treatment of the courtyard, which instead of being left open to the sky, as usual, is covered in by 63 small domes carried on arched bays, the cloisters at the sides being roofed with corresponding vaults, and light and air being admitted to the interior through open archways in their outer walls. At the four corners of the building, which measures 216 by 176 feet over all, are four shapely domes, while a fifth and larger one dominating the whole is raised on a square clerestory above the prayer chamber. To single out for praise any particular feature of this mosque would be difficult ; yet there is about the whole a dignified simplicity and grandeur that place it in the first rank of such buildings and sufficiently account for the influence it exerted on the subsequent development of the Deccan style. The date of its erection, as stated in an inscription, was 1367—a few years, that is to say, before Jauna Shāh built the Kālī and Khirkī mosques at Delhi, and it is not unlikely therefore that Jauna Shāh's architect may have been acquainted with the design of this Gulbarga proto-type and sought to improve upon it by introducing open aisles across the closed court and thus obviating the need for the admission of light and air through the surrounding cloisters. The main drawback, however, to both the Gulbarga and the Delhi plans must have been that on important ceremonial occasions, most of the worshippers were obstructed from seeing the central *liwān* and *mimbar*—a drawback which was quite enough to account for their plans not being copied in later buildings.

The peculiar form of wide arch with low imposts initiated at the *Jāmi' Masjid* was subsequently imitated at Gulbarga in the stupendous archway over the entrance to the shrine of Banda Nawāz, which is traditionally ascribed to the reign of Tāj-ud-dīn Fīrūz Shāh (1397—1422) but which there are good reasons for referring to a later date. Whatever its age, this archway is eloquent of the fearless imagination of the architects of the Deccan, which led them to essay the construction of domes and arches as vast as any known to the mediaeval or ancient world.

Bīdar, where from the reign of Ahmad Shāh Vālī onwards the story of Deccan architecture continues to unfold itself, boasts, like Gulbarga, of two separate groups of royal tombs : one of the later Bahmanī kings, the other of the Barīd Shāhīs. The former are twelve in number and generally similar to their predecessors at Gulbarga, though their scale is larger, their domes loftier and more bulbous and their facades adorned with a greater multi-plicity of arched recesses or screened windows. The finest of them is the tomb of Ahmad Shāh Vālī, the interior of which is adorned with brilliantly coloured paintings in the Persian style and enriched with bands Kūfic, *Tughrā* and *Naskh* inscriptions worked out in letters of gold on a ground of deep blue or vermilion. This Persianising tendency which continued to gather strength during the fifteenth century found further expression during the reign of the next king 'Alā-ud-dīn Shāh, in the *Chānd Mīnār* at Daulatā-bād, the whole design of which is characteristically Iranian, as well as in the tomb of the same emperor, the facade of which is covered with a veneer of enamel tiles in various shades of blue. But of all the monuments of this period built in the Persian style the most remarkable is the *Madrasa* or College erected at Bīdar in 1472 by Mahmūd Gāwān, the mininster of Muhammad Shāh III. This building, which resembled, so it is said, the College of Ulugh Beg at Samarqand was of imposing appearance. Three storeys in height with towering minarets at its two front corners, it covered an area of 205 feet by 180. In it were a mosque, library, lecture halls, professors' quarters and students' cubicles, ranged about an open courtyard, a hundred feet this way and that. The mosque and library were to the front of the building on either side of the entrance ; the lofty lecture rooms (which rose to the full height of the three storeys) in the middle of the other sides ; and the professors' rooms in the corners—all planned for convenience and comfort and amply provided with light and air. In form the corner towers resembled somewhat the *Chānd Minār* at Daulatā-bād, but unlike that minar they were emblazoned, as was also the whole of the front facade between them with a glittering surface of encaustic tilework, which with its chevron patterning and deep bold bands of sacred texts would challenge comparison with anything of its kind in Persia. But with all its elegance of outline, its unimpeachable proportions, and refined details, there is little or no feeling in Mahmūd Gāwān's college for plastic form and mass, or for the values of contrasted light and shade. The architect has visualised his subject, as the architects of Eastern Persia habitually did, in two rather than in three dimensions, and has sought to achieve beauty by a glistening display of enamel, helped out by symmetry of outline and a nicely adjusted balance of parts. For sheer loveliness of colour the result could hardly be bettered ; but divest the building of it superficial ornament and little is left save a mathematically correct, tame, and highly stylised fabric. To the reign of Muhammad Shāh III there probably belongs also the *Solā Khamb* Mosque in the Bīdar Fort, and near by it an interesting group of palace buildings including the Gagan, Tarkash, Chīnī and Nagīna Mahals. Shorn of all ornament, modernised and converted to baser uses as record office, court and jail, these palace buildings are impressive even in their decay, and with their spacious halls, their water courses and cascades, still awaken echoes of their former splendour. The mosque, too despite its fallen domes and crumbling masonry, is a good example[1] of the Bahmanī style as illustrated in the royal tombs of Gulbarga and Bīdar—a style which is imposing but never pretentious, solemn in its simplicity but never austere.

[1] It measures 297 by 77 feet.

The Persianising tendency visible in much of the architecture of the Bahmanīs persisted, though in a less degree, under their successors, the 'Imād Shāhīs of Berar, the Barīd Shāhīs of Bīdar, the 'Ādil Shāhīs of Bījāpur, and the Qutb Shāhīs of Golconda, whose founder, Sultān Qulī was himself a Turk from Persia and endowed with that peculiar sympathy for ultra refinement in art and literature which belongs to the Persian temperament. By the end of the fifteenth century, however, the latent art of the Deccan was reasserting itself in increasing strength and when, in the following century, the 'Ādil Shāhīs set about their magnnificent monuments at Bījāpur and freely employed Indian artists and craftsmen on their construction, it was inevitable that Indian genius should rise superior to foreign influence and stamp itself more and more deeply on these creations. This later phase of Deccan architecture, however, when the style was attaining its full maturity, belongs to a subsequent period and to another volume of this history. To another volume also must be reserved our description of the monuments of the Fārūqi kings of Khāndesh at Thalner and Burhānpur, though it may be mentioned in passing that the few that have survived at the former place, including the inscribed tomb of Mīrān Mubārak I (dec. 1457) are strikingly akin in style to the monuments of Māndū.

Finally, there remains the remote valley at Kashmīr. When, in the fourteenth century, the Muhammadans entered into possession of this highland valley, they found there a legacy of many fine buildings left by their predecessors, some of stone, but the vast majority of wood, which has always been the principal building material in these well-wooded tracts of the Himālayas. The stone buildings, however,—imposing structures of peculiarly classic stamp—belonged to a bygone age, and the art of the stone-mason had been too long forgotten for the Muhammadans to revive it. True, they did convert a few of the stone temples of the unbelievers into mosques and tombs for themselves, but this they did merely by using such of the old architectural members as they could, and completing the rest of the structure in rubble or brick. One such reconstructed temple is the tomb of Mandanī, with mosque adjacent, which bears an inscription recording its erection in the year 1444—in the reign of Zain-ul-'Ābidīn ; but the remarkable tile decoration on its eastern face, for which this tomb is celebrated, belongs not, as is generally supposed, to the original edifice, but to a later restoration of the Mughul period. Another monument of Zain-ul-'Ābidīn's reign (1420—70) is the tomb of his mother, the wife of Sikandar Butshikan. In this case the builders left the enclosure wall and gateways of the desecrated temple much as they had found them, but of the temple itself they kept only the plinth, and on it erected an entirely new superstructure of brick and plaster, embellished here and there with glazed bricks. In style this tomb is typically Saracenic, if not purely Persian; nor is there anything in its design (nor indeed, in the design of any other brick or stone building of this period) to indicate that the old stone architecture of the Hindus exerted any appreciable influence upon it, beyond contributing some of the materials for their building. Far different is it with the wooden architecture of this epoch. Unfortunately, owing to their perishable nature, none of the old Hindu structures of wood have survived to the present day : but there can be no question that from time immemorial, wood had been, and under the Muhammadans still continued to be, the chief building material of the Kashmīrīs. Even in the reign of Akbar stone-masons had to be imported into Kashmīr to build the fort of Harī Parbat ; and two generations later wood was still, according to Bernier, preferred to stone 'on account of its cheapness and the facility with which it could be brought from the mountains by means of so many small rivers.' Although, however, in the matter of this wooden architecture the Muhammadans carried on the established tradition of the valley and adopted the architectural style of their predecessors, they were by no means content to perpetuate that style unchanged. They did in Kashmīr what they did everywhere else in India. They made the indigenous style the basis of their own ; but they gave it a new complexion by grafting on to it the structural forms and decorative motifs peculiarly associated with Islam, and—which was more important— they gave it a breadth and spaciouseness that could hardly have been dreamt of by the older Hindu builders. Of the style as we find it in the Muslim period, the most telling characterisitc is the treatment of the roof. Boldly projecting eaves, carried on several tiers of carved and overlapping brackets, and enriched with pendant drops at their corners ; sheets of growing irises or tulips covering the gently inclined roof; and crowning all a tall and graceful steeple—these are the features that first arrest the eye and give peculiar distinction to the mosques and tombs of Srīnagar. They are not, however, the only distinctive features ; for the well-finished timber work of the walls with its pleasing diaper of headers and stretchers ; the magnificent pillars of deodar in the larger halls, and the delicate openwork traceries of window screens and balustrades, skilfully put together out of innumerable small pieces of wood, all help to enhance the charm and accentuate the stylishness of this architecture. As a protection against the heavy rain and snows of Kashmīr, the use of birch bark nailed in multiple layers above the roofs and overspread, in turn, with turf and flowers could hardly have been improved upon ; and the planting of irises and tulips on the roofs was a singularly happy inspiration, not only because of their own intrinsic beauty, but because their tenacious roots gave added strength to the fabric of the roof covering. For the rest, however, it must be confessed that the construction of these buildings leaves much to be desired. The Muslim builder knew no more than the Hindu about trusses or struts or other devices familiar to the modern architect, and when there was an unusually large area to be roofed, the best he could do was to insert intermediate pillars for the support of the ceiling with ponderous piers of logs above the pillars to carry the sloping roof —as extravagant and cumbersome an arrangement as could well be imagined, and one which inevitably led to the premature collapse of the overweighted structure.

Of the few monuments in the wooden—or mainly wooden—style whose origin goes back to the pre-Mughul period, the most imposing is the *Jami' Masjid* at Srīnagar. Founded by Sikandar Butshikan (1390—1414) and extended by his son Zain-ul-Ābidīn, it was thrice burnt down and thrice rebuilt—once in 1479, a second time in 1620, and third time in 1674—and after again falling to ruin was extensively restored in recent years. In spite, however, of its many vicissitudes, the original design seems to have been more or less faithfully repeated by successive restorers, and though little of the first fabric is now left, the monument is still an instructive exemplar of the pre-Mughul style. Its plan is the orthodox one : a rectangular court closed by colonnades on its four sides, wherein the familiar method has been followed of screening the four colonnades from the court by an arched facade and setting a spacious hall in the middle of each—the hall on the west, which is the largest, constituting the prayer chamber, and the other three serving, as usual, for entrance gateways. But though there is nothing uncommon in the planning of this mosque, great and exceptional dignity is given to its elevation by the noble proportions of the four halls with their soaring spires, and this dignity is more than sustained as one enters the interior and gazes up at the timbered ceilings and lofty columns, each hewn from a single log, that support it.

A less pretentious but, in its own way, no less pleasing specimen of the wooden style is the mosque of Shāh Hamadān in Srīnagar. Unlike the *Jāmi‘ Masjid*, which is partly of timber, partly of brick and stone, this mosque is built exclusively of timber, and instead of being planned on the usual or orthodox lines, consists of nothing more than a single square hall, thus affording an interesting and instructive parallel with some of the pre-Mughul mosques of Bengal, which, as we have already seen, were all but indistinguishable from contemporary tombs. The qualities that distinguish these two mosques—the qualities of dignified simplicity and spaciousness on the one hand ; of grace of line and natural artistry on the other—are far from being peculiar to the Kashmīr school. They are qualities that were common at this epoch to the whole body of Indo-Islamic monuments, and are as conspicuous among those of Delhi as among those of Mālwa, Gujarāt and the Deccan, or wherever else Muslim genius came to resuscitate and enrich the older work of the Hindus. Vary as they might in individual expression, the local schools of Islamic architecture one and all derived their lineage from a common parentage and betray in their lineaments a family likeness that is unmistakable. In the case of Kashmīr this family likeness is specially significant ; for differently conditioned as the Kashmīr architecture was, fashioned out of dissimilar materials and cast in a mould unlike that of any other school, it would hardly have been surprising if its development had proceeded on radically different lines. That it did not do so ; that it exhibits, on the contrary, precisely the same fusion of Hindu and Muslim ideals, the same happy blend of elegance and strength, is eloquent testimony to the enduring vitality of Hindu art under an alien rule and to the wonderful capacity of the Muslim for absorbing that art into his own and endowing it with a new and grandeur spirit.

CHAPTER I

THE ARAB CONQUEST OF SIND

1. ORIGINAL SOURCES

Ibn Khurdādba. Kitāb-ul-Masālik wa'l Mamālik. Text and translation published by M. Barbier de Meynard in the Journal Asiatique, 1865.

Mas'ūdī. Murūj-udh-Dhahab. Text edited by M. de Meynard.

Al-Bilādūri. Futūh-ul-Buldān. De Goeje, Leyden.

Muhammad 'Alī Kūfī. Chach-nāma.

Mīr Muhammad Ma'sūm. Ta'rīkh-us-Sind.

Firishta, Muhammad Qāsim. Gulshan-i-Ibrāhīmī. Lithographed at Bombay, 1832.

Nizām-ud-dīn Ahmad. Tabaqāt-i-Akbarī. Bibliotheca Indica Series, Asiatic Society of Bengal, text and translation.

2. MODERN WORKS

Elliot, Sir H.M., and Dowson, Professor John. The History of India as told by Its own Historians. Trübner and Co., 1867-1877.

Haig, Major-General M.R. The Indus Delta Country, 1894.

Muir, Sir William. Annals of the Early Caliphate. Smith and Elder, 1883.

——The Caliphate, its Rise, Decline, and Fall. Religious Tract Society, 1892.

Raverty, Major H.G. The Mihrān of Sind and Its Tributaries. Journal of the Asiatic Society of Bengal, 1892.

The Imperial Gazetteer of India. 26 vols. Oxford, 1907-09.

CHAPTER II

THE YAMĪNĪ DYNASTY OF GHAZNĪ AND LAHORE, COMMONLY KNOWN AS THE GHAZNAVIDS

1. ORIGINAL SOURCES

Al-'Utbī. Ta'rīkh-i-Yamīnī.

Baihaqī, Abu-'l-Fazl. Ta'rīkh-i-Bihaqī. Bibliotheca Indica Series of the Asiatic Society of Bengal. Calcutta, 1862.

Budaunī, 'Abd-ul-Qādir. Muntakhab-ut-Tawārīkh, text. Bibliotheca Indica Series of the Asiatic Society of Bengal. Calcutta, 1868.
    Translation of vol. I by Lt-Colonel G.S.A. Ranking in the same series. Calcutta, 1898.

Hamd-Ullāh Mustaufī Qazvīnī. Ta'rīkh-i-Guzīda, text and abridged translation. E.J.W. Gibb Memorial Series, No. XIV, vols. I and II.

Hasan-un-Nizāmī. Tāj-ul-Ma'āsir.

Khvānd Mīr. Habīb-us-Siyar.

——Khulāsat-ul-Akhbār.

Minhāj-ud-dīn b. Sirāj-ud-dīn. Tabaqāt-i-Nāsirī, text. Bibliotheca Indica Series of the Asiatic Society of Bengal. Calcutta, 1864.
    Translation by Major H.G. Raverty in the same series. Calcutta, 1880.

Mīr Khvānd. Rauzat-us-Safā, text. Tehran, 1274 Hijrī.

Firishta, Muhammad Qāsim. Gulshan-i-Ibrāhīmī. See Bibliography to Chapter I.

Nizām-ud-dīn Ahmad. Tabaqāti-i-Akbarī. See Bibliography to Chapter I.

'Unsurī. Dīvān. Lithographed at Tehran. No date.

2. MODERN WORKS

Elliot and Dowson. The History of India as told by Its own Historians. See Bibliography to Chapter I.

Lane-Poole, Stanley. The Mohammadan Dynasties. Archibald Constable and Co. London, 1894.

——Mediaeval India under Mohammedan Rule. ("Story of the Nations" Series.) T. Fisher Unwin. London, 1903.

Smith, V.A. The Oxford History of India. Oxford, 1919.

Tate, G.R. Seistan. Calcutta, 1910.

Thomas, Edward. The Chronicles of the Pathan Kings of Delhi. Trübner and Co. London, 1871.

The Imperial Gazetteer of India. See Bibliography to Chapter I.

CHAPTER III

MU'IZZ-UD-DĪN MUHAMMAD *BIN* SAM OF GHŪR AND THE EARLIER SLAVE KINGS OF DELHI

1. Original Sources

Budaunī, 'Abd-ul-Qādir. Muntakhab-ut-Tawārīkh, text. Bibliotheca Indica Series of the Asiatic Society of Bengal. Calcutta, 1868.
> Translation of vol. ɪ by Lt-Colonel G.S.A. Ranking in the same series. Calcutta, 1898.

Ghulām Husain Salīm. Riyāz-us-Salātīn. Bibliotheca Indica Series of the Asiatic Society of Bengal. Calcutta, 1890.

Hamd-Ullāh Mustaufī Qazvīnī. Ta'rīkh-i-Guzīda, text and abridged translation. E J.W. Gibb Memorial Series, No. xɪv, vols. ɪ and ɪɪ.

Hasan-un-Nizāmī. Tāj-ul-Ma'āsir.

Khvānd Mīr. Habīb-us-Siyar.

——Khulāsat-ul-Akhbār.

Minhāj-ud-dīn b. Sirāj-ud-dīn. Tabaqāt-i-Nāsirī, text. Bibliotheca Indica Series of the Asiatic Society of Bengal. Calcutta, 1864.
> Translation by Major H.G. Raverty in the same series. Calcutta, 1880.

Mīr Khvānd. Rauzat-us-Safā, text. Tehran, 1274 Hijrī.

Firishta, Muhammad Qāsim. Gulshan-i-Ibrāhīmī. See Bibliography to Chapter ɪ.

Nizām-ud-dīn Ahmad. Tabaqāt-i-Akbarī. See Bibliography to Chapter ɪ.

Sayyid Ahmad Khān, Dr. Sir Asār-us-Sanādīd. Cawnpore, 1904.

2. Modern Works

Elliot and Dowson. The History of India as told by Its own Historians. See Bibliography to Chapter I.

Epigraphia Indo-Moslemica, 1911-12. Culcutta, 1914.

Lane-Poole, Stanley. The Mohammadan Dynasties. Archibald Constable and Co. London, 1894.

——Mediaeval India under Mohammedan Rule. ("Story of the Nations" Series.) T. Fisher Unwin. London, 1903.

Smith, V.A. The Oxford History of India. Oxford, 1919.

Tate, G.R. Seistan. Calcutta, 1910.

Thomas, Edward. The Chronicles of the Pathan Kings of Delhi. Trübner and Co. London, 1871.

The Imperial Gazetteer of India. See Bibliography to Chapter ɪ.

CHAPTER IV

GHIYĀS-UD-DĪN BALBAN, MU'IZZ-UD-DĪN KAIQUBĀD, AND SHAMS-UD-DĪN KAYŪMARS

1. ORIGINAL SOURCES

For Budaunī, Muntakhab-ut-Tawārikh ; Khvānd Mīr, Habīb-us-Siyar and Khulāsat-ul-Akhbār ; Mīr Khvānd, Rauzat-us-Safā ; Firishta, Gulshan-i-Ibrāhīmī ; and Nizām-ud-dīn Ahmad, Tabaqāt-i-Akbarī ; see Bibliography to Chapter II.

For Ghulām Husain Salīm, Riyāz-us-Salātin and Dr Sir Sayyid Ahmad Khān, Āsār-us-Sanādīd, see Bibliography to Chapter III.

Baranī, Ziyā-ud-dīn, Ta'rīkh-i-Fīrūz Shāhī. Bibliotheca Indica Series of the Asiatic Society of Bengal. Calcutta, 1862.

Amīr Khusrav. Poems, MSS.

2. MODERN WORKS

Elliot and Dowson. The History of India as told by Its own Historians. See Bibliography to Chapter I.

Lane-Poole, Stanley. The Mohammadan Dynasties. Archibald Constable and Co. London, 1894.

——Mediaeval India under Mohammedan Rule. ("Story of the Nations" Series). T. Fisher Unwin. London, 1903.

Smith, V.A. The Oxford History of India. Oxford, 1919.

Tate, G.R. Seistan. Calcutta, 1910.

Thomas, Edward. The Chronicles of the Pathan Kings of Delhi. Trübner and Co. London, 1871.

The Imperial Gazetteer of India. See Bibliography to Chapter I.

CHAPTER V

THE KHALJĪ DYNASTY AND THE FIRST CONQUEST OF THE DECCAN

1. ORIGINAL SOURCES

For Budaunī, Muntakhab-ut-Tawārīkh ; Khvānd Mīr, Habīb-us-Siyar and Khulāsat-ul-Akhbār ; Mīr Khvānd, Rauzat-us-Safā ; Firishta, Gulshan-i-Ibrāhīmī ; and Nizām-ud-dīn Ahmad, Tabaqāt-i-Akbarī ; see Bibliography to Chapter II.

For Ghulām Husain Salīm, Riyāz-us-Salātīn and Dr Sir Sayyid Ahmad Khān, Āsār-us-Sanādīd, see Bibliography to Chapter III.

Baranī, Ziyā-ud-dīn. Ta'rīkh-i-Firūz Shāhī. Bibliotheca Indica Series of the Asiatic Society of Bengal. Calcutta, 1862.

2. MODERN WORKS

Elliot and Dowson. The History of India as told by Its own Historians. See Bibliography to Chapter I.

Haig, Major T.W. Historic Landmarks of the Deccan. Allahabad, 1907.

Lane-Poole, Stanley. The Mohammadan Dynasties. Archibald Constable and Co. London, 1894.

—— Mediaeval India under Mohammedan Rule. ("Story of the Nations" Series.) T. Fisher Unwin. London, 1903.

Smith, V.A. The Oxford History of India. Oxford, 1919.

Tate, G. R. Seistan. Calcutta, 1910.

Thomas, Edward. The Chronicles of the Pathan Kings of Delhi. Trübner and Co. London, 1871.

The Imperial Gazetteer of India. See Bibliography to Chapter I.

Journal of the Asiatic Society of Bengal. 1895.

Journal of the Royal Asiatic Society. 1909.

CHAPTER VI

THE REIGNS OF GHIYĀS-UD-DĪN TUGHLUQ AND MUHAMMAD TUGHLUQ, AND THE SECOND CON-QUEST AND REVOLT OF THE DECCAN

1. ORIGINAL SOURCES

For Budaunī, Muntakhab-ut-Tawārīkh ; Khvānd Mīr, Habīb-us-Siyar and Khulāsat-ul-Akhbār ; Mīr Khvānd, Rauzat-us-Safā ; Firishta, Gulshan-i-Ibrāhīmī; and Nizām-ud-dīn Ahmad, Tabaqāt-i-Akbarī ; see Bibliography to Chapter II.

For Ghulām Husain Salīm, Riyāz-us-Salātīn and Dr Sir Sayyid Ahmad Khān, Āsār-us-Sanādīd, see Bibliography to Chapter III.

Badr-ud-dīn of Chāch. Qasā'id. Lucknow, A.H. 1301.

Baranī, Ziyā-ud-dīn. Ta'rīkh-i-Firūz Shāhī. Bibliotheca Indica Series of the Asiatic Society of Bengal. Calcutta, 1862.

Ibn Batūta. Tuhfat-un-Nuzzār fī Gharā'ib-il-Amsār. Cairo, A.H. 1322.

2. MODERN WORKS

Elliot and Dowson. The History of India as told by Its own Historians. See Bibliography to Chapter I.

Haig, Major T. W. Historic Landmarks of the Deccan. Allahabad, 1907.

Lane-Poole, Stanley. The Mohammadan Dynasties. Archibald Constable and Co. London, 1894.

—— Mediaeval India under Mohammedan Rule. ("Story of the Nations" Series.) T. Fisher Unwin. London, 1903.

Smith, V. A. The Oxford History of India. Oxford, 1919.

Tate, G. R. Seistan. Calcutta, 1910.

Thomas, Edward. The Chronicles of the Pathan Kings of Dehli. Trübner and Co. London, 1871.

The Imperial Gazetteer of India. See Bibliography to Chapter I.

Journal of the Royal Asiatic Society, July 1909 and July 1922.

CHAPTER VII

THE REIGN OF FĪRŪZ TUGHLUQ, THE DECLINE AND EXTINCTION OF THE DYNASTY, AND THE INVASION OF INDIA BY TĪMŪR

1. ORIGINAL SOURCES

For Budaunī, Muntakhab-ut-Tawārīkh ; Khvānd Mīr, Habīb-us-Siyar and Khulāsat-ul-Akhbār ; Mīr Khvānd, Rauzat-us-Safā ; Firishta, Gulshan-i-Ibrāhimī ; and Nizām-ud-dīn Ahmad, Tabaqāt-i-Akbarī ; see Bibliography to Chapter II.

For Ghulām Husain Salīm, Riyāz-us-Salātīn and Dr Sīr Sayyid Ahmad Khān, Āsār-us-Sanādīd, see Bibliography to Chapter III.

Baranī, Ziyā-ud-dīn. Ta'rīkh-i-Fīrūz Shāhī. Bibliotheca Indica Series of the Asiatic Society of Bengal. Calcutta, 1862.

'Afīf, Shams-i-Sirāj. Ta'rīkh-i-Fīrūz Shāhī. Bibliotheca Indica Series of the Asiatic Society of Bengal. Calcutta, 1891. .

'Alī, Sharaf-ud-dīn, of Yazd. Zafarnāma. Bibliotheca Indica Series of the Asiatic Society of Bengal. Calcutta, 1887.

Tīmūr, Amīr (ascribed to). Malfūzāt-i-Tīmūrī. MSS.

Ibn 'Arab Shāh. 'Ajā'ib-ul-Maqdūr fī Akhbāri Tīmūr. Calcutta, 1882.

Haidar, Mīrzā, Dughlāt. Ta'rīkh-i-Rashīdī. Translated by E. Denison Ross, with commentary, notes, and map by Ney Elias. London, 1898.

2. MODERN WORKS

Elliot and Dowson. The History of India as told by Its own Historians. See Bibliography to Chapter I.

Haig, Major T.W. Historic Landmarks of the Deccan. Allahabad, 1907.

Lane-Poole, Stanley. The Mohammadan Dynasties. Archibald Constable and Co. London, 1894.

—— Mediaeval India under Mohammedan Rule. ("Story of the Nations" Series.) T. Fisher Unwin. London, 1903.

Smith, V. A. The Oxford History of India. Oxford, 1919.

Tate. G. R. Seistan. Calcutta, 1910.

Thomas, Edward. The Chronicle of the Pathan Kings of Delhi. Trübner and Co. London, 1871.

The Imperial Gazetteer of India. See Bibliography to Chapter I.

Journal of the Royal Asiatic Society, July 1909 and July 1922.

CHAPTERS VIII, IX, X

THE SAYYID DYNASTY ; THE LODĪ DYNASTY ; AND THE KINGDOM OF JAUNPUR

1. Original Sources

For Budaunī, Muntakhab-ut-Tawārīkh ; Firishta, Gulshan-i-Ibrāhīmī ; and Nizām-ud-dīn Ahmad, Tabaqāt-i-Akbarī, see Bibliography to Chapter II.

2. Modern Works

For Elliot and Dowson, The History of India as told by Its own Historians, and The Imperial Gazetteer of India, see Bibliography to Chapter I.

For Stanley Lane-Poole, The Mohammadan Dynasties and Mediaeval India under Mohammedan Rule ; V.A. Smith, The Oxford History of India; and Edward Thomas, The Chronicles of Pathan Kings of Delhi, see Bibliography to Chapter II.

CHAPTER XI

THE KINGDOM OF BENGAL

1. ORIGINAL SOURCES

For Minhāj-ud-dīn, Tabaqāt-i-Nāsirī and Translation ; Budaunī, Munta-khabut-Tawārīkh and Translation ; Nizām-ud-dīn Ahmad, Tabaqāt-i-Akbarī ; and Firishta, Gulshan-i-Ibrāhīmī, see Bibliography to Chapter II.

For Ghulām Husain Salīm, Riyāz-us-Salātīn, see Bibliography to Chapter III.

For Baranī, Ta'rīkh-i-Fīrūz Shāhī, see Bibliography to Chapter IV.

For Ibn Batūta, Tuhfat-un-Nuzzār fī Gharā'ib-il-Amsār, see Bibliography to Chapter VI.

For Shams-i-Sirāj 'Afīf, Ta'rīkh-i-Fīrūz Shāhī, see Bibliography to Chapter VII.

'Abd-ur-Razzāq, Kamāl-ud-dīn, of Samarqand. Matla'-us-Sa'dain wa Majma'-ul-' Bahrain.

2. MODERN WORKS

For Elliot and Dowson, The History of India as told by Its own Historians, and The Imperial Gazetteer of India, see Bibliography to Chapter I.

For Stanley Lane-Poole, The Mohammadan Dynasties, and Edward Thomas, The Chronicles of the Pathan Kings of Delhi, see Bibliography to Chapter II.

Bhattasali, Nalina Kanta, M.A. Coins and Chronology of the Early Independent Sultans of Bengal. W. Heffer and Sons. Cambridge, 1922.

Danvers, F.C. The Portuguese in India. W.H. Allen and Co. London, 1894.

Journal of the Asiatic Society of Bengal for 1872 and 1873.

Stewart. The History of Bengal.

Whitehead, R.S. The Rise of Portuguese Power in India.

CHAPTER XII

THE KINGDOM OF KASHMĪR

1. ORIGINAL SOURCES

For Firishta, Gulshan-i-Ibrāhīmī ; Niẓām ud-dīn Ahmad, Tabaqāt-i-Akbarī ; and Sharaf-ud-dīn 'Alī Yazdī, Zafarnāma, see Bibliographies to Chapters I and VII.

Abu-'l-Fazl, Shaikh. Āīn-i-Akbarī, text. 3 vols. Bibliotheca Indica Series of the Asiatic Society of Bengal.

——Translation. Vol. I, Blochmann, vols. II and III, H.S. Jarrett. Bibliotheca Indica Series of the Asiatic Society of Bengal.

Haidar, Mīrzā, Dughlāt. Ta'rīkh-i-Rashīdī. Translated by E. Denison Ross, with commentary, notes, and map by Ney Elias. London, 1898.

Rājataranginī. Translation by M.A. Stein. Westminster, 1900.

2. MODERN WORKS

Bernier, Francois. Travels in the Mogul Empire. Edited by Archibald Constable. Westminster, 1891.

For The Imperial Gazetteer of India, see Bibliography to Chapter I.

Journal of the Royal Asiatic Society, July and October, 1918.

CHAPTERS XIII, XIV

GUJARĀT AND KHĀNDESH ; THE KINGDOM OF MĀLWA

1. ORIGINAL SOURCES

For Firishta, Gulshan-i-Ibrāhīmī, and Nizām-ud-dīn Ahmad, Tabaqāt-i-Akbarī, see Bibliography to Chapter I.

'Abdullāh Muhammad b. 'Umar al-Makkī. Zafar-ul-Wālih bi Muzaffar wa Ālih. (An Arabic History of Gujarāt.) Text, edited by Sir E. Denison Ross, C.I.E. John Murray, London. Vol. I, 1910, vol. II, 1921.

Abū Turāb Walī, Mir. Ta'rikh-i-Gujarāt. Edited by Sir E. Denison Ross, C.I.E. Bibliotheca Indica Series of the Asiatic Society of Bengal. Calcutta, 1908.

Khāfī Khān. Muntakhab-ul Lubāb, part III. Edited by Lt-Colonel Sir Wolseley Haig, K.C.I.E., etc. Bibliotheca Indica Series of the Asiatic Society of Bengal. Calcutta, 1923.

2. MODERN WORKS

For The Imperial Gazetteer of India, see Bibliography to Chapter I.

For Lane-Poole, The Mohammadan Dynasties, and Thomas, The Chronicles of the Pathan Kings of Delhi, see Bibliography to Chapter II.

For Danvers, The Portuguese in India, see Bibliography to Chapter XI.

CHAPTERS XV, XVI, XVII

THE KINGDOM OF THE DECCAN, A.D. 1347—1436 ; THE DE-
CLINE AND FALL OF THE KINGDOM OF THE DECCAN,
A.D. 1436—1490 ; THE FIVE KINGDOMS OF THE DECCAN,
A.D. 1527—1599

1. ORIGINAL SOURCES

For Firishta, Gulshan-i-Ibrāhīmī, and Nizām-ud-dīn Ahmad, Tabaqāt-i-
Akbarī, see Bibliography to Chapter I.

For Shaikh Abu-'l-Fazl, Āīn-i-Akbarī and translations, see Bibliography to
Chapter XII.

For Khāfī Khān, Muntakhab-ul-Lubāb, part III, and 'Abdullāh Muhammad b.

'Umar al-Makkī, Zafar-ul-Wālih bi Muzaffar wa Ālih, see Bibliography to Chapters XIII and XIV.

Abu-'l-Fazl, Shaikh. Akbarnāma. Text, in three vols. Bibliotheca Indica Series
of the Asiatic Society of Bengal.

> Translation of the same by H. Beveridge. Bibliotheca Indica Series of the
> Asiatic Society of Bengal. Calcutta, 1897-1921.

Abu-'l-Qāsim, Mīr, Mīr 'Ālam. Hadīqat-ul-'Ālam. Lithographed at Haidarābād,
Deccan, A.H. 1309.

'Alī Samnānī, Sayyid. Burhān-i-Ma'āsir, MSS. and translations, viz.

> (a). The History of the Bahmanī Dynasty, by Major J. S. King. Luzac
> and Co. 1900.

> (b) The History of the Nizām Shāhi Kings of Ahmadnagar, by Lt-
> Colonel Sir Wolseley Haig, K.C.I.E., etc. Indian Antiquary, 1920—1923.

Ibrāhīm Zubairī, Mīrzā. Basātīn-us-Salātīn. Lithographed at Haidarābād, Deccan.

Ta'rīkh-i-Muhammad Qutb-Shāhī.

2. MODERN WORKS

For The Imperial Gazetteer of India, see Bibliography to Chapter I.

For Whitehead, The Rise of Portuguese Power in India, and Danvers, The
Portuguese in India, see Bibliography to Chapter XI.

Cousens, Henry. Bījāpur Architecture. Archaeological Survey of India. 1916.

Duff, Captain James Grant. History of the Mahrattas. Reprinted at Bombay,
1878.

Haig, Major T.W. Historic Landmarks of the Deccan. Allahabad, 1907.

Journal of the Asiatic Society of Bengal. 1904.

CHAPTER XVIII

HINDU STATES IN SOUTHERN INDIA

For Elliot and Dowson, The History of India as told by Its own Historians, see Bibliography to Chapter I.

For King, The History of the Bahmanī Dynasty, see Bibliography to Chapters xv, xvi, and xvii.

Aiyangar, S. Krishnaswami. Ancient India.

——South India and her Muhammadan Invaders. Oxford University Press. 1921.

——A Little Known Chapter of Vijayanagar History.

——Krishnadevaraya of Vijayanagar.

——Sources of Vijayanagar History. Madras, 1919.

Briggs, Colonel J. A History of the Rise of Muhammadan Power. (Translation of the Gulshan-i-Ibrāhīmī of Firishta.)

Fleet, J.F. Dynasties of the Kanarese Districts in the Bombay Presidency.

Inscriptions relating to the period published in

    (1)   The Epigraphia Indica.

    (2)   The Epigraphia Carnatica.

    (3)   Nellore Inscriptions by Messrs Butterworth and Venugopal Chetti.

Longworth Damas, M. The Book of Duarte Barbosa. Hakluyt Society.

Major, R.H. India in the Fifteenth Century. Hakluyt Society.

Mysore Archaeological Reports, 1910—1921.

Rice, B.L. Mysore and Coorg from Inscriptions.

Sastri, Rai Bahadur H. Krishna. The Hoysalas in the Chola Country. A.S.R. 1909-10.

——The Dynasties of Vijayanagar, etc. A.S.R. 1907-8, 1908-9, 1911-12.

Sewell, R. A Forgotten Empire. London, 1900.

CHAPTER XIX

SIND AND MULTĀN

1. ORIGINAL SOURCES

For Firishta, Gulshan-i-Ibrāhīmī, and Nizām-ud-dīn Ahmad, Tabaqāt-i-Akbarī, see Bibliography to Chapter I.

For Shaikh Abu-'l-Fazl, Āīn-i-Akbarī, and Akbarnāma, and translations, see Bibliographies to Chapters XII, XV, XVI and XVII.

2. MODERN WORKS

For Elliot and Dowson, The History of India as told by Its own Historians ; and M.R. Haig, The Indus Delta Country, see Bibliography to Chapter I ; Raverty, The Mihrān of Sind and Its Tributaries.

CHAPTER XX

THE NATIVE STATES OF NORTHERN INDIA
FROM A.D. 1000 TO 1526

1. ORIGINAL SOURCES

For Abu-'l-Fazal Baihaqī, Ta'rīkh-i-Baihaqī ; Al-'Utbī; Ta'rīkh-i-Yamīnī ; Budaunī, Muntakhab-ut-Tawārīkh ; Hamd Ullāh Mustaufī Qazvīnī, Ta'rīkh-i-Guzīda ; Minhāj-ud-dīn, Tabaqāt-i-Nāsirī, and translation by Raverty ; Firishta, Gulshan-i-Ibrāhīmī ; Nizām-ud-dīn Ahmad, Tabaqāt-i-Akbarī ; see Bibliographies· to Chapters I and II.

For Shaikh Abu-'l-Fazl, Āīn-i-Akbarī, and translations by Blochmann and Jarrett, see Bibliography to Chapter XII.

2. MODREN WORKS

For Elliot and Dowson, The History of India as told by Its own Historians, see Bibliography to Chapter I.

Chatterton, Eyre, D.D., Bishop of Nagpur The Story of Gondwāna. Sir Isaac Pitman and Sons, Ltd. London, 1916.

Duff, C. Mabel. Chronology of India. Constable, 1899.

Indian Antiquary and Journals of the Asiatic Society of Bengal and the Royal Asiatic Society, *passim.*

Sarda, Har Bilas. Hammira of Ranthambhor, the last Great Chauhān Monarch. Ajmer, 1921.

Smith V. A. The Early History of India. 3rd edition, Oxford, 1914.

Tod, Lt-Col. James. Annals and Antiquities of Rajasthan, edited by William Crooke, C.I.E. Oxford, 1920.

CHAPTER XXI

BURMA A.D. 1287—1531

The main narrative, both for the Burmese homeland round Āva, and for Toungoo, to which they were driven, is the Hmannan Yazawin, the standard Burmese chronicle compiled in 1829 from earlier chronicles and from inscriptions. As only 207 out of its 1358 pages have been translated (Luce and Tin, 'The Glass Palace Chronicle.' Oxford University Press, 1923), my references are throughout to the original.

The Shāns were illiterate and had no records. The best books on them are Cochrane, 'The Shāns,' and the Gazetteer of Upper Burma and the Shān States.

The only surviving Talaing records are their MSS. chronicles of which the chief are Razadarit Ayedawpon, Thatonhnwemun Yazawin, and Sayadaw Athwa ; pagoda records, of which the chief, Slapat Rajawan Datow Smin Ron, is translated and in print ; and the Paklat Talaing chronicles, printed in Siam. The best study of the race is Halliday, 'The Talaings.'

All the above are court chronicles (see Harvey, 'History of Burma,' pp. xvii— xx, 103), and for social conditions we have nothing but inference. There are a number of inscriptions, all Burmese ; they have been printed, but inaccurately (see Harvey, 'History of Burma,' pp. xvi, 380), and only in vernacular ; I therefore refer only to Tun Nyein's small volume of selected translations. None of the inscriptions translated in Epigraphia Birmanica are as late as the period covered by this chapter.

Chinese records, which throw a scanty but invaluable light on the period, are found in Huber's great articles in the Bulletin de l'Ecole Francaise d'Extreme Orient, and in Parker's printed work which, save for ' Burma, relations to China,' is buried in the political files of the Rangoon Secretariat ; much of these files are, however, incorporated in the articles on the various Shān states in the alphabetical portion of the Gazetteer of the Shān States and Upper Burma.

* *indicates a vernacular work.*

Anderson. English Intercourse with Siam in the Seventeenth Century. Publ. Kegan Paul. London, 1890.

Badger. The Travels of Ludovico di Varthema. Publ. Hakluyt Society. London, 1863.

Chau Ju-kua. By Hirth and Rockhill. Publ. Imperial Academy of Sciences. St Petersburg, 1912.

Cochrane, The Shāns. Publ. Superintendent Government Printing. Rangoon, 1915.

Couto. Da Asia. Publ. His Majesty's Press. Lisbon, 1778-88.

Duroiselle. The Ari of Burma and Tantric Buddhism. In Annual Report of the Archæological Survey of India, 1915-16.

Faria y Sousa. The Portuguese in Asia. Trans. Stevens. Publ. London, 1695.

Forchammer. The Jardine Prize ; an Essay on the Sources and Development of Burmese law. Publ. Superintendent Government Printing. Rangoon, 1885.

—— Notes on the Early History and Geography of British Burma. Publ. Superintendent Government Printing. Rangoon, 1884.

Furnivall. Matriarchy in Burma. In Journal of the Burma Research Society, 1912. Publ. Rangoon.

Gazetteer of Upper Burma and the Shān States. Publ. Superintendent Government Printing. Rangoon, 1900.

Gerson da Cunha. Memoir on the History of the Tooth-Relic of Ceylon. In Journal of the Bombay Branch of the Royal Asiatic Society, 1875.

Halliday. The Talaings Publ. Superintendent Government Printing. Rangoon, 1917.

—— Slapat Rajawan Datow Smin Ron. In Journal of the Burma Research Society, 1923. Publ. Rangoon.

Harvey. History of Burma. Publ. Longmans. London, 1925.

*Hmannan Yazawin. Publ. Upper Burma Press. Mandalay, 1908.

Huber. Une Ambassade chinoise en Birmanie en 1406. In Bulletin de l'Ecole Francaise d'Extrême Orient, 1904. Publ. Hanoi and Paris.

—— Fin de la Dynastie de Pagān. Ibid. 1909.

Mackenzie. Climate in Burmese History. In Journal of the Burma Research Society, 1913. Publ. Rangoon.

Major. India in the Fifteenth Century. Publ. Hakluyt Society. London, 1857.

Mayers. Chinese Explorations of the Indian Ocean during the Fifteenth Century. In China Review, Vol. iii. Publ. Hong-Kong.

*Paklat Talaing Chronicle. Thudammawatiyazawuntha Thihayazadiyazawuntha. Printed at Paklat in Siam. 1910.

Pallegoix. Description du Royaume Thai ou Siam. Publ. Mission de Siam. Paris, 1854.

Parker. Burma with special reference to her relations to China. Publ. Rangoon Gazette Press. Rangoon, 1893.

—— ' Précis ' of Chinese records: Printed in the political files of the Rangoon Secretariat.

Pemberton. Report on the Eastern Frontier of British India. Publ. by Government. Calcutta, 1835.

*Razadarit Ayedawpon MS.

Report of the Superintendent Archaeological Survey, Burma. Publ. annually by the Superintendent Government Printing. Rangoon.

Rockhill. Notes on the Trade of China with the Coast of the Indian Ocean during the Fifteenth Century. In T'oung Pao, 1914, 1915. Publ. Leyden.

*Sayadaw Athwa. Burmese trans of his Talaing History of Pegū, used by Phayre, now in the British Museum. MS No. OR. 3462-4.

*Shwemawdaw Thamaing. Publ. Hanthawaddy Press. Rangoon, 1917.

Taw Sein Ko. The Kalyāni Inscriptions. In Indian Antiquary, 1893 and 1894.

Temple. The Thirty-Seven Nats, a phase of Spirit-Worship prevailing in Burma. Publ. Griggs. London, 1906.

*Thatonhnwemun Yazawin MS.

Tun Nyein. Inscriptions of Pagān, Pyinya, and Āva. Translation with notes. Publ. Superintendent Government Printing Rangoon, 1899.

Whiteway. The rise of the Portuguese Power in India, 1497—1550. Publ. Constable. London, 1899.

CHAPTER XXII

CEYLON A.D. 1215—1527.

The Mahāvaṁsa (*Mv.*) which includes the Chūlavaṁsa.   Pali.
Katikāvat-saṅgarā compiled by D. B. Jayatilaka.   Sinhalese.
Dambadeni-asna.   Sinhalese. MS.
Rājaratnākara.   Sinhalese.
Rājāvaliya.   Sinhalese.
Nikāyasangraha.   Sinhalese.
Attanagaluvaṁsa.   Pali and Sinahlese.
Pūjāvaliya.   Sinhalese.
Daladāsirita.   Sinhalese.
Bodhivaṁsa,   Sinhalese version.
Madras Epigraphy : Report for 1907.
Journal of the Royal Asiatic Society, 1913.
Journal of the Royal Asiatie Society, Ceylon Branch, 1904 and 1912
The Lankātilaka Inscription.   Sinhalese.
Saddharma-ratnākara.   Sinhalese.
Spolia Zeylanica.   June 1912.
Ruvanmal-nighaṇṭu.   Sinhalese.
Kitsirimevan Kälani inscription.
Vāgiri-devāle inscription.

CHAPTER XXIII

THE MONUMENTS OF MUSLIM INDIA

1. ARCHITECTURE

GENERAL

Choisy, A. Histoire de l'Architecture. 2 vols. Paris, 1899.

Fergusson, J. History of Architecture in all countries. 5 vols. 1893.

Fletcher, B.F. A History of Architecture on the Comparative Method. 6th edition. London, 1921.

Porter, A.K. Mediaeval Architecture. 2 vols. 1909.

Spiers, R.P. Architecture East and West. London, 1905.

Sturgis, R. and Frothingham. History of Architecture. 4 vols. New York, 1901.

2. MUSLIM ART AND ARCHITECTURE

GENERAL

Adamy, R. Architektonik des Muhamedanischen und Romanischen Stils. Hanover, 1883-89.

Bell (Miss), G.L. Amurath to Amurath. London, 1911.

——Palace and Mosque of Ukhaidir. London, 1914.

Berchem, Max von and Strzygowski. Amida. Heidelberg, 1910.

Borrmann, R. Die Baukunst...des Islams im Mittelalter. Leipzig, 1914.

Bourgoin, J. Les Arts Arabes. Folio. Paris, 1873.

——Les Eléments de l'Art Arabe : Le Trait des Entrelacs. Paris, 1879.

——Précis de l'Art Arabe. Paris, 1892.

Briggs, M.S. Saracenic Architecture in Egypt and Palestine. (In the J.R.I.B.A.)

Butler, H.C. Architecture and other Arts ; being Part II of the Publications of an American Archaeological Expedition to Syria in 1899-1900. New York, 1904.

Comité de Conservation des Monuments de l'Art Arabe. Annual Reports. Cairo, 1882-1925.

Coste, P.X. Architecture Arabe. Paris, 1893.

——Architecture Arabe aux Monuments du Caire. 2 vols. 4 to et folio. Paris, 1837-39.

——Monuments Modernes de la Perse. Paris, 1865-67.

Creswell, K.A.C. Brief Chronology of Muhammadan Monuments of Egypt to A.D. 1517. Cairo, 1919.

Diez, Ernst. Churasanische Baudenkmäler. Band I. Berlin, 1918.

——Die Kunst der Islamischen Völker. Berlin, 1915.

Franz, Pascha. Die Kunst des Islams. Darmstadt, 1896.

Gayet, A. L'Art Arabe. Paris, 1893.

Lane-Poole, S. Saracenic Art in Egypt. London, 1886.

Le Bon, G. La Civilisation des Arabes. Paris, 1884.

Migeon and Saladin. La Céramique dans l'Art Musulman. 2 vols. Paris.

——L'Art Musulman. 2 vols. Paris, 1907.

Musée Arabe, Caire. Arts Musulmans de l'Egypte : Collection des Monuments du Musée Arabe. Caire.

Musée de l'Art Arabe du Caire. La Céramique Egyptienne de l'Epoque Musulmane. Caire.

Olfusen, O. Old and New Architecture in Khiva, Bokhara and Turkestan. Copenhagen, 1904.

Parvillée, L. L'Architecture et Décoration Turques au xvᵉ siecle. Paris, 1874.

Pottier, E., Migeon and Dussaud. Syrie ; Revue d'Art Oriental et d'Archéologie. Tome I-VI. Paris, 1920-25.

Prisse d'Avennes. L'Art Arabe d'après les Monuments du Caire depuis le VIIᵉ siclèe jusqu'à la fin du XVIIIᵉ. Paris, 1877.

Rivoira, G. Γ. Moslem Architecture. London, 1919.

Sarre, F. Erzeugnisse Islamischer Kunst. Tome I-II. Berlin and Leipzig, 1906-9.

——Denkmäler Persischer Baukunst ; Geschichtliche Untersuchung und Aufnahme Muhamedanischer Backsteinbauten in Vorderasien und Persien. 2 Bände Berlin, 1910.

Schubert von Soldern, Z. Baudenkmäler von Samarkand. Architektonischer Reisebericht. Wien, 1898.

Simakoff, N. L'Art de l'Asie Centrale. St. Petersburg, 1883.

Vogüe (Le Comte de). Syrie Centrale. Architecture Civile et Religieuse du Iᵉ au VIIᵉ siècle. Tome I-II. Paris, 1865-77.

3. MUSLIM ART AND ARCHITECTURE IN INDIA

(a) GENERAL

Archaeological Survey of India Reports :

   (i) Cunningham, Alexander. Archaeological Survey of India. Vols. I—XXIII. Simla and Calcutta, 1865-77.

   (ii) Marshall, Sir John. Annual Report of the Director-General of Archaeology in India. Part I. 1902-3 to 1920-1. Calcutta, 1904-23.

   (iii) ——Annual Report of the Archaeological Survey of India. Part II. 1902-3 to 1915-16. Calcutta, 1904-22.

   (iv) ——ed. Memoirs of the Archaeological Survey of India. (1) Mosque of Shaikh Abdun-Nabi by M. Zafar Hasan, B.A. (Memoir No. 9.) 1921. (2) A Guide to Nizām-ud-Din by M. Zafar Hasan, B.A. (Memoir No. 10.) 1922. (3) The Drawings of Geometric Patterns in Saracenic Art by Dr. E.H. Hankin. (Memoir No. 15.) 1925. (4) The Jama Masjid at Budaun and other Buildings in the United Provinces by Mr J.F. Blakiston. (Memoir No. 19.) 1926. (5) Historical Memoir on the Qutb. Delhi by Mr. J.A. Page. (Memoir No. 22.) 1925.

   (v) —— Annual (Consolidated) Report of the Archaeological Survey of India. 1921-22, 1922-23, 1923-24. Simla and Calcutta.

Archaeological Survey of India : New Imperial Series Reports. Vols. I-XLVI. London and Calcutta. 1874—1926.

——Annual Report of the Archaeological Survey, Bengal. 1900-5. Calcutta, 1901-5.

——Annual Report of the Archaeological Survey, Eastern Circle. 1905-6 to 1920-21. Calcutta.

——Annual Report of the Archaeological Survey, Central Circle. 1919-20 and 1920-21. Patna.

——Annual Report of the Archaeological Survey, Frontier Circle. 1906-7 to 1920-21. Peshawar.

——Report of the Punjab Circle of the Archaeological Survey for 1888-89. Calcutta, 1891.

——Report of the Archaeological Survey, Punjab Circle. 1901-4. Lahore.

Archaeological Survey of India ; Annual Progress Report of the Superintendent of the Archaeological Survey, Punjab and United Provinces Circle, for the year ending 31st March 1905. Lahore.

—— Annual Progress Report of the Archaeological Survey, North Western Provinces and Oudh. 1887—1903. Allahabad.

——Annual Progress Report of the Archaeological Survey, Northern Circle. 1906-7. Allahabad.

—— Annual Report of the Archaeological Survey, Northern Circle Muhammadan and British Monuments, Agra. 1908-9 to 1920-21. Allahabad.

——Annual Progress Report of the Archaeological Survey, Southern Circle. 1881-82 to 1920-21. Madras.

—— Annual Progress Report of the Archaeological Survey, Western Circle. 1890-91 to 1920-21. Bombay.

Asiatic Researches : Transactions of the Society instituted in Bengal for enquiring into the History and Antiquities, the Arts, Sciences and Literature of Asia. Vols. I—XX. Calcutta, 1788—1836.

Cole, H.H. Reports of the Curator of Ancient Monuments in India for the years 1881-82, 1882-83, 1883-84. Simla and Calcutta.

Creswell, K.A.C. Indian Domes of Persian Origin. (In the Asiatic Review, new series. vol, v.) 1914.

Fergusson, J. History of Indian and Eastern Architecture. Revised and edited with additions. 2 vols. London.

Havell, E. B. Indian Architecture : Its Psychology, Structure and History, from the first Muhammadan invasion to the present day. London, 1913.

Indian Antiquary : A Journal of Oriental Research in Archaeology, History, Literature, Languages, Folklore, etc. Vols. I—LV. Bombay, 1872—1926.

Journal of the Asiatic Society of Bengal. Vols. I—LXXVII. Calcutta, 1832—1909.

Journal and Proceedings of the Asiatic Society of Bengal. Vols. I—XX. Calcutta 1905-25.

Journal of the Bombay Branch of the Royal Asiatic Society. Vols. I—XXVI Bombay, 1870—1923.

La Roche, Emanuel. Indische Baukunst. Folio. 3 vols. München, 1921.

Le Bon, G. Les Monuments de l'inde. Paris, 1893.

Preservation of National Monuments : Reports on the, by H. H. Cole, Curator of Ancient Monuments in India. Ahmadabad, Poona, Karli, Ambarnath, Bijapur, Kalburga, Mt Abu, Ajmir, Jaipur, Ulwar, Agra, Gwalior and Delhi. 1881-84. Calcutta and Simla.

Proceedings of the Asiatic Society of Bengal, edited by the Honorary Secretaries. 1865—1904. Calcutta.

Smith, E. W. Portfolio of Indian Architectural Drawings. Part I. London, 1897.

Smith, V.A. A History of Fine Art in India and Ceylon from the earliest times to the present day. Oxford, 1911.

Wetzel, F. Islamische Grabbauten in Indien aus der Zeit der Soldaten-Kaiser. 1320—1540. Leipzig, 1918.

(b) ASSAM

List of Archaeological Remains in Assam. Calcutta, 1902.

(c) BENGAL, BIHAR AND ORISSA

List of Ancient Monuments in Bengal, prepared in the Bengal Government Secretariat. Revised and corrected up to 31st August 1895. Calcutta, 1896.

Ravenshaw, J. H., Gaur : Its Ruins and Inscriptions ; edited by his widow. London.

(d) Bombay

Biggs, Col. and Theodore Hope and James Fergusson. Architecture at Ahmada-bad, the Capital of Goozerat, photographed by Biggs with Historical notes by Theodore Hope, and Architectural notes by James Fergusson. London, 1866.

Burgess, J. Memorandum on the Antiquities at Dabhol, Ahmadabad, Than, Junagadh, Gunar and Dhank. Bombay, 1875.

—— On the Muhammadan Architecture of Bharoch, Cambay, Dholka, Champanir and Mahmudabad in Gujarat. London, 1896.

—— The Muhammadan Architecture of Ahmadabad. Part I A.D. 1412—1520. Part II with Muslim and Hindu Remains in the vicinity. London. 1900-5.

Burgess, J. and Henry Cousens. The Architectural Antiquities of Northern Gujarat, more especially of the districts included in the Baroda State. London, 1903.

Cousens, H. Bijapur and its Architectural Remains ; with an Historical Outline of the 'Adil Shahi Dynasty. Bombay, 1916.

Hope, Theodore. Architecture at Ahmadabad, the Capital of Goozerat (with a note by James Fergusson). London, 1866.

(e) Central Provinces and Berar

Cousens, H. Lists of Antiquarian Remains in the Central Provinces and Berar. Calcutta, 1897.

(f) Central India

Barnes, E. Dhar and Mandu : A Guide. Bombay, 1902.

Creswell, K.A.C. The Vaulting System of the Hindola Mahal at Mandu. (In the J.R.I.B.A. 1918.) London.

(g) Delhi

Ahmad Khan, Sayid. Asar as-Sanadid. Cawnpore, 1904.

Cole, H.H. The Architecture of Ancient Delhi, especially the buildings around the Kutb Minar. London, 1872.

Fanshawe, H. C. Delhi : Past and Present. London, 1902.

Hearn, H.C. The Seven Cities of Delhi. London, 1906.

Journal of the Archaeological Society of Delhi. Delhi.

Keene. H. G. Keene's Handbook for Visitors to Delhi. Rewritten and brought up-to-date by E. A. Duncan. Calcutta, 1906.

Munshi, R. N. The History of the Kutb Minar (Delhi), with an account of the Inscriptions on the Minar. Bombay, 1911.

Sayyid Ahmad. Yadgar-i-Delhi ; being an account of the buildings of Historical and Archaeological interest in Delhi (Urdu). Delhi, 1905.

Sharp, Sir Henry. Delhi : Its Story and Buildings. Bombay, 1921.

Stephen, Carr. The Archaeology and monumental Remains of Delhi. Calcutta, 1876.

Zafar Hasan, M. List of Muhammadan and Hindu Monuments in the Province of Delhi. Vols. I—IV. Calcutta, 1916-22.

(h) Hyderabad Deccan

Archaeological Survey of H.E.H. the Nizam's Dominions : Annual Progress Reports. 1914-15 to 1922-23. Hyderabad. Deccan.

Cousens, H. List of Antiquarian Remains in H. H. the Nizam's Dominions. Calcutta, 1900.

Yazdani, G. Antiquities of Bidar. 1914.

(*i*) KASHMIR STATE

Archaeological Survey of Jammu and Kashmir State : Quinquennial Report on Archaeology and Research in Kashmir. April 1904 to April 1909. Jammu, 1911.

(*j*) MADRAS

Sewell, R. List of Antiquarian Remains in the Presidency of Madras with a list of Inscriptions and a Sketch of the Dynasties of Southern India. Parts I-II. Madras ,1882-84.

(*k*) MYSORE STATE

Archaeological Survey of Mysore : Annual Progress Reports. 1886—1925. Mysore.

(*l*) PUNJAB

Latif, Sayyid Muhammad. The Early History of Multan. Calcutta, 1890-91.

Rodgers, Chas. J. Revised List of Objects of Antiquarian Interest in the Punjab. Lahore, 1904.

(*m*) RAJPUTANA AND SIND

Cousens, H The Antiquities of Sind with Historical Outline. Calcutta, 1926.

Sarda, Harbilas. Ajmir : Historical and Descriptive. Ajmir, 1911.

Tod, J. Annals and Antiquities of Rajasthan or the Central and Western Rajput States of India. Revised and edited with an Introduction and Notes by William Crooke. Vols. I-III. London, 1920.

(*n*) U.P.

Fuhrer, A. The Monumental Antiquities and Inscriptions in the North Western Provinces and Oudh. Described and arranged. Allahabad, 1891.

——The Sharqi Architecture of Jaunpur ; with notes on Zafarabad, Sahet Mahet and other places in the North Western Provinces and Oudh. With Drawings and Architectural descriptions by Edmund Smith. Edited by J. Burgess. Calcutta, 1889.

Smith, E.W. Chaurasi Gumbaz, Kalpi, in the North Western Provinces of Agra and Oudh. (In the Journal of Indian Art, vol. v), 1893.

CHRONOLOGY

INDIA

A.D.

1016-7 Operations in Khvārazm and in the northern provinces of the empire of Ghaznī (p. 18).

1018-9 Mahmūd invades India, marches to Baran, Mahāban, Muttra, and Kanauj, captures Manaich, Asni, and Sharva, returns to Ghaznī with his booty, and founds the great mosque of Ghaznī (pp. 18—21).

1021 Mahmūd invades India, defeats a Hindu confederacy under Ganda of Kālinjar, and returns to Ghaznī (p. 21).

Invasion of Dīr, Swāt, and Bajaur, and of Kashmīr. Flight of Bhīm and annexation of the Punjāb (p. 22).

1022 Mahmūd invades India, receives the submission of the Kachhwāha raja of Gwalior and of Ganda of Kālinjar, and returns to Ghaznī (p. 22).

1023 Operations in Transoxiana (p. 23).

1024 Expedition to Somnāth, Mahmūd captures the town and plunders the temple (pp. 23-5).

1026 Mahmūd returns to Ghaznī (p. 26).

Expedition against the Jāts (p. 26).

1030 Death of Mahmūd (p. 26).

Mas'ūd blinds his brother Muhammad and ascends the throne (p. 27).

1034 Rebellion in the Punjāb crushed by Tilak (p. 30).

1037 Mas'ūd invades India and captures Hānsī (p. 31).

1039 Karnadeva Kālachurī invades the Pāla kingdom of Bihār (p. 510).

1040 Defeat of Mas'ūd by the Saljūqs. He retires from Ghaznī towards India. His deposition and death. Restoration of Muhammad (pp. 31-2).

Death of Gangeyadeva and accession of Karnadeva Kālachuri in Chedi (p. 510).

1042 Deposition and death of Muhammad, and accession of Maudūd (p. 32).

1044 Accession of Sōmesvara Āhavamalla, Chālukya (p. 471).

1046 Invasion of Ghūr (p. 33).

1049 Death of Maudūd and accession of Mas'ūd II. Deposition of Mas'ūd II and accession of 'Alī (p. 33).

1052 Deposition of 'Alī and accession of 'Abd-ur-Rashīd (p. 33).

1053 Usurpation and assassination of Tughril. Accession of Farrukhzād (p. 34).

1059 Death of Farrukhzād and accession of Ibrāhīm (p. 34).

1060 Karnadeva of Chedi and Bhīm II of Gujarāt crush Bhoj of Mālwa (p. 510).

1069 Death of Sōmesvara Āhavamalla, Chālukya (p. 471).

1070 Accession of Kulottunga, the Chālukya-Chola (p. 469).

1076 Accession of Vikramāditya VI, Chālukya (p. 469).

1077 Accession of Rāmapāla in Bihār (p. 511).

1079 Capture of Ajūdhan and invasion of Gujarāt by Ibrāhīm of Ghaznī (p. 34).

1090 The Gaharwārs gain possession of Benares and Ajodhya (p. 509).

1094 Accession of Siddharāja Jayasingha in Gujarāt (p. 517).

1099 Death of Ibrāhīm and accession of Mas'ūd III in Ghaznī (p. 35).

1101 Death of Vinayāditya Hoysala and accession of Ballāla I (p. 474).

1106 Death of Ballāla I and accession of Vishnu Hoysala (p. 474).

1115 Death of Mas'ūd III and accession of Shīrzād in Ghaznī (p. 35).

A.D.

1116 Deposition of Shīrzād and accession of Arsalān Shāh (p. 35).

1118 Deposition of Arsalān Shāh and accession of Bahrām Shāh (p. 35).
Death of Kulottunga, Chālukya-Chola (p. 469).

1119 Suppression of the rebellion of Bahlīm in the Punjāb (p. 35).
Vijaya Sena establishes his independence in Bengal (p. 511).

1120 Death of Rāmapāla in Bihār (p. 511).

1128 Death of Vikramāditya VI, Chālukya and accession of Sōmēsvara III (pp. 469-78).
The Parihārs oust the Kachhwāhas from Gwalior. The Kachhwāhas establish themselves in Amber (p. 533).

1138 Death of Sōm svara III and accession of Jagadekamalla, Chālukya (p. 477).

1141 Accession of Narasimha Hoysala (p. 479).

1143 Death of Siddharāja Jayasingha of Gujarāt (p. 517).

1149 Bahrām of Ghaznī captures Saif-ud-dīn Ghūrī and puts him to death (p. 36).

1150 Death of Jagadekamalla and accession of Taila III, Chālukya (p. 478).

1151 Burning of Ghaznī by Alā-ud-dīn Husain, *Jahānsūz* (p. 36).

1152 Death of Bahrām Shāh and accession of Khusrav Shāh (p. 37).

1160 Death of Khusrav Shāh and accession of Khusrav Malik (p. 37).

1173 Mu'izz-ud-dīn Muhammad b. Sām appointed governor of Ghaznī by his brother, Ghiyās-ud-dīn (p. 38).
Death of Narasimha Hoysala and accession of Vīra Ballāla II (p. 479).

1175 Muhammad invades India and captures Multān and Uch (p. 38).
Lakshmana Sena succeeds Vijaya Sena in Nadiya (Nuddea) (p. 511).

1178 Muhammad invades Gujarāt and is defeated (p. 39).

1181 Muhammad invades the Punjāb and builds and garrisons Siālkot (pp. 37-9).

1182 Prithvī Rāj captures Mahoba from Parmāb Chandel (p. 512).

1183 Restoration of Sōmēsvara IV (p. 478).

1186 Muhammad again invades the Punjāb and captures and imprisons Khusrav Malik. End of the Yamīnī dynasty (pp. 37 9).

1189 Death of Sōmsēvara IV, Chālukya (p. 478).

1190 Vīra Ballāla II defeats Bhillama Yādava (p. 480).

1190-1 Muhammad captures Bhātinda, but is defeated by Prithvī Rāj at Tarāorī (p. 40).

1192 Second battle of Tarāori. Defeat and death of Prithvī Rāj. Occupation of Hānsī, Sāmāna, and Guhrām, and appointment of Qutb-ud-dīn Aibak as governor (pp. 40-1).

1192-3 Capture of Delhi by Qutb ud-dīn Aibak, who makes it his capital.
Conquest of Bihār by Ikhtiyar ud-dīn (p. 42).

1194 Ajmer taken by the Hindus and recovered by Aibak (p. 43).

1195 Aibak invades Gujarāt and plunders Anhilvāra. He is appointed viceroy of the Muslim dominions in India (pp. 43-4).

1196 Muhammad invades India, captures Bayāna, and advances to Gwalior (p. 44).

1197 Aibak is defeated and driven into Ajmer by Raja Bhīm of Gujarāt (p. 44).

1198 Aibak again invades Gujarāt and plunders Anhilvār a (p. 44).

A.D.

1237   Suppression of a revolt of the Ismāʿīlīs (p. 59).

1239   Suppression of the rebellion of Ayāz in the Punjāb 'p. 60).
          Death of Māravarman Sundara Pāndya I (p. 481).

1240   Deposition of Raziyya and accession of Muʿizz-ud-dīn Bahrām.
          Death of Raziyya and rebellion of Sunqar (pp. 60-1).

1241   Death of Sunqar. Capture of Lahore by the Mughuls (pp. 61-3).
          Death of Rāwal Chāchakdeo of Jaisalmer and accession of Karan Singh I (p. 531).

1242   Mutiny of the army ; deposition and death of Bahrām, and accession of ʿAlā-ud-dīn Masʿūd (pp. 63-4).

1243   Death of Bhīm and accession of Vīsaladeva Vāghela in Gujarāt (p. 517).

1244   Defeat of Tughril in Bengal by the Hindus of Cuttack (p. 65).

1245   The Mughuls invade India and reach Multān and Uch (p. 65).

1246   Deposition and death of Masʿūd and accession of Nāsir-ud-dīn Mahmūd (p. 66).

1247   Mahmūd recovers the Punjāb from the Khokars (pp. 66, 67).

1247-8   Balban suppresses a rebellion in the Doāb (p. 67).

1249   Balban suppresses a rebellion in Mewāt (p. 67).

1251   Accession of Jatāvarman Sundara Pāndya I (p. 483).

1251-2   Balban invades Mālwa and defeats the raja of Chanderi and Narwar (p. 68).

1253   Balban is disgraced (p. 69).

1254   Expedition into Katehr (p. 69).

1255   Balban is restored to favour (p. 70).

1256-7   Suppression of the rebellions of Qutlugh Khān and Kishlū Khān. Invasion of the Punjāb by the Mughuls (pp. 71-2).

1258   Retreat of the Mughuls (p. 72).

1259   Suppression of disorder in the Doāb (p. 72).

1260   Punishment of the Meos (pp. 72-3).

1264   Death of Sōmēsvara Hoyṣala (p. 482).

1266   Death of Mahmūd and accession of Ghiyās-ud-dīn Balban (p. 73).

1268   Accession of Maravarman Kulasʹkhara Pāndya (p. 486).

1268—9   Suppression of disorders in the Punjāb (p. 77).

1270   Restoration of Lahore and re-establishment of provincial governmen in the Punjāb (p. 77).

1271   Death of Karan Singh I of Jaisalmer (p. 531).

1279   Mughul invasion repelled. Rebellion of Tughril in Bengal (pp. 79, 80).

1280   Suppression of Tughril's rebellion, Bughrā Khān, Balban's second son, appointed to the government of Bengal (pp. 80-1).

1282   Abdication of Jaitra Singh and accession of Hamīra in Ranthambhor (p. 516).

1285   Muhammad Khān, Balban's elder son, slain by the Mughuls (p. 82).

1287   Death of Balban and accession of Muʿizz-ud-dīn Kaiqubād. Mughul invasion repelled. Massacre of Mughuls and 'New Muslims' (pp. 82-5)

1288   Meeting between Kaiqubād and his father, Bughrā Khān of Bengal (pp. 85—6).

1290   Death of Kaiqubād and accession of Jalāl-ud-dīn Fīrūz Khaljī (pp. 87, 91).

A.D.

1291-2   Rebellion of Chhajjū suppressed (pp. 92—3).

Death of Nāsir-ud-dīn Bughrā and accession of Rukn-ud-dīn Kaikāūs in Bengal (p. 261).

1292   Mughul invasion. 'Alā-ud-dīn Khaljī invades Mālwa and captures Bhīlsa (p. 95).

Death of Narasimha III and accession of Ballāla III, Hoysala (p. 484).

1294   'Alā-ud-dīn invades the kingdom of Deogīr, in the Deccan (pp. 96-7).

1295   Dūda Singh Bhati is elected Rāwal of Jaisalmer (p. 532).

1296   Murder of Firūz and accession of 'Alā-ud-dīn Muhammad (p. 98).

1297   Conquest of Gujarāt (p. 100).

1299   The Mughuls invade India and are defeated before Delhi (p. 102).

1300   Siege of Ranthambhor. Rebellion of Ākat Khān suppressed. Rebellion of Hājī Maulā suppressed (pp. 103-4).

1301   Capture of Ranthambhor by 'Alā-ud-dīn Khaljī (p. 517).

1302-3   Capture of Chitor. Failure of an expedition to Warangal. Mughul invasion (pp. 108-9).

Death of Kaikāūs and accession of Shams-ud-dīn Fīrūz Shāh in Bengal (p. 261).

1306   Mughul invasion repelled by Tughluq (pp. 111-2).

1306-7   Expedition of Kāfūr (Malik Nāib) to Deogīr (p. 112).

'Alā-ud-dīn establishes his authority in Mārwār (p. 114).

1307-8   Mughul invasion repelled (p. 112).

1308   Expedition to Warangal. Pratāparudradeva II submits and pays tribute (pp. 114—5).

1310   Expedition, under Malik Nāib, into the Peninsula Capture of Dvāravatipura and Madura. Mosque built at Rāmeswaram. Submission of the Pāndya and Kerala kingdoms (p. 116).

Ghiyās-ud-dīn Bahādur assumes sovereignty in Eastern Bengal (p. 261).

1311   Death of Maravarman Kulasṣkhara Pāndya (p. 486).

1315   Shāh Mirzā enters the service of Sinha Deva of Kashmīr (p. 277).

1316   Death of 'Alā-ud-dīn and accession of Shihāb-ud-dīn 'Umar. Death of Malik Nāib. Deposition of 'Umar and accession of Qutb-ud-dīn Mubārak (pp. 119-20).

1317   Mubārak's expedition to Deogīr. Capture and death of Harpāl (p. 121).

1318-9   Rebellion of Asad-ud-dīn (p. 121).

Death of Fīrūz and accession of Shihāb-ud-dīn Bughrā in Western Bengal. Bughrā is deposed by Bahādur (p. 261).

1320   Murder of Mubārak and usurpation of Nāsir-ud-dīn Khusrav. Defeat and death of Khusrav and accession of Ghiyās-ud-dīn Tughluq (Ghāzī Malik) (pp. 124-6).

1321   Expedition to Warangal under Muhammad Jauna (Ulugh Khān).

Rebellion of Muhammad (pp. 130-1).

1323   Second expedition to Warangal under Muhammad. Capture of Pratāparudradeva II. Mughul invasion (pp. 131-2).

Nāsir-ud-dīn ascends the throne in Western Bengal (p. 261).

1324   Fīrūz Shāh's expedition to Bengal (pp. 132-3, 261-2).

1325   Death of Fīrūz and accession of Muhammad (pp. 134-5).

Ghiyās-ud-dīn Bahādur restored in Western Bengal (p. 262).

A.D.

1326   Rebellion of Gurshāsp (p. 140).

   Qadr Khān governor of Western Bengal (p. 262).

1327   Capital transferred from Delhi to Daulatābād (pp. 140-1).

1328   Rebellion of Kishlū Khān in Multān. Invasion of India by 'Alā-ud-dīn Tarmāshīrīn the Mughul (pp. 142-3).

1329   Transportation of the inhabitants of Delhi to Daulatābād. Issue of fictitious currency (pp. 144-6).

1330   Bahrām acquires the government of Eastern Bengal (p. 262).

1331   Rebellion of Ghiyās-ud-dīn Bahādur in Bengal (p. 147).

1333   Punitive expedition in the Doāb (p. 147).

1334   Rebellion of Sayyid Jalāl-ud-dīn Ahsan in Madura (p. 149).

1335   Muhammad leaves Delhi for Madura. He retires from Warangal. Rebellion in Lahore suppressed by Khvāja Jahān (pp. 149-52).

1336   Famine. Foundation of Sargadwāri. Rebellion of Nusrat Khān at Bīdar (pp. 152-4).

   Foundation of Vijayanagar (p. 489).

1337-8   Expedition into the Himālaya. Capture of Nagarkot. Failure of the expedition (p. 155).

1338-9   Fakhr-ud-dīn Mubārak Shāh proclaims his independence in Bengal (pp. 156, 262).

1339   Death of Jalāl-ud-dīn Ahsan Shāh and accession of 'Alā-ud-dīn Udaujī Shāh in Madura (p. 149).

   Death of Sangama I and accession of Harihara I in Vijayanagar (p. 378).

1339-40   Rebellion of 'Alī Shāh Kar in the Deccan (p. 156).

1340   Rebellion of 'Aīn-ul-Mulk in Oudh (pp. 156—8).

   Death of Udaujī Shāh and accession of Qutb-ud-dīn Fīrūz Shāh in Madura. Death of Fīrūz Shāh and accession of Ghiyās-ud-dīn Muhammad Dāmaghān Shāh in Madura (p. 149).

1340-1   Rebellion of Malik Shāhū Lodī in Multān (p. 160).

   Accession of 'Ala-ud-dīn 'Alī Shāh in Bengal (p. 262).

1342   Ibn Batūtah leaves Delhi on his mission to China (p. 163).

   Death of Vīra Ballāla III Hoysala, at Trichinopoly (p. 488).

1343   Muhammad's expedition into the districts of Sunām, Sāmāna, Kaithal, and Guhrām (p. 164).

   Accession of Hājī Shams-ud-dīn Iliyās, *Bhangara*, in Bengal (p. 262).

1344   Arrival in Delhi of the envoy of the Caliph al-Hākim III (p. 164). Rebellion in Kara (p. 165).

   Death of Ghiyās-ud-dīn Dāmaghān Shāh and accession of Nāsir-ud-dīn Dāmaghān Shāh in Madura (p. 150).

1345   Rebellion of the centurions in Gujarāt. Muhammad leaves Delhi for Gujarāt, and suppresses the rebellion (pp. 166-7).

1346   Kānhayya Nāik establishes his independence in Warangal. Vīra Ballāla III of Dvāravatipura founds Vijayanagar. Rebellion in Daulatābād : Ismā'īl Mukh proclaimed king of the Deccan. Muhammad besieges Daultābād (pp. 168-9).

   Shāh Mīrzā ascends the throne of Kashmīr under the title of Shams-ud-dīn (p. 277).

1347   Rebellion of Taghī in Gujarāt. 'Alā-ud-dīn Bahman Shāh proclaimed king of the Deccan (pp. 169-70, 372-3).

1348   Muhammad besieges Girnār in Kāthīāwār (pp. 171-2).

A.D.

1349   Capture of Girnār (p. 172).

Death of Shams-ud-dīn and accession of Jamshīd in Kashmīr (p. 277)

1350   Muhammad invades Sind (p. 72).

Deposition of Jamshīd and accession of 'Alā-ud-dīn in Kashmīr (p. 277).

1351   Death of Muhammad and accession of Fīrūz (pp. 172-3).

1353-4   Fīrūz Shāh's first expedition to Bengal (pp. 176, 263).

1354   Death of Harihara I and accession of Bukka I in Vijayanagar (p. 378).

1356   Foundation of Hissār (p. 176).

Death of Nāsīr-ud-dīn Dāmaghān Shāh and accession of 'Ādil Shāh in Madura (p. 150).

1357   Death of Iliyās and accession of Sikandar in Bengal (p. 263).

1358   Death of Bahman Shāh and accession of Muhammad I Bahmanī in the Deccan (p. 376).

1359   Fīrūz Shāh's second expedition to Bengal (pp. 177-8, 263-4).

Death of 'Alā-ud-din and accession of Shihāb-ud-dīn in Kashmīr (p. 278).

1360   Fīrūz Shāh's expedition to Orissa (pp. 178-9)

Death of 'Ādil Shāh and accession of Fakhr-ud-dīn Mubārak Shāl. in Madura (p. 150).

Muhammad I, Bahmanī, invades Telingāna (p. 379).

1361   Capture of Kāngra, or Nagarkot, by Fīrūz Shāh (p. 179).

1362   Fīrūz Shāh's first expedition into Sind (p. 180).

Muhammad I, Bahmanī, again invades Telingāna. Rebellion of Bahrām Khān Māzandarānī in Daulatābād (pp. 379-80).

1363   Fīrūz Shāh's second expedition into Sind (p. 181).

1364   Death of Rānā Hamīr Singh and accession of Khet Singh (p.526).

1365   Muhammad I, Bahmanī, invades Vijayanagar and defeats Bukka I. It is stipulated in the treaty of peace that in future wars non-combatants shall not be molested (pp. 381-3).

1366   Suppression of the rebellion of Bahrām Khān Māzandarānī (pp. 382-3).

1367   Completion of the great mosque at Gulbarga (p. 383).

1372-3   Death of Mubārak Shāh and accession of 'Alā-ud-dīn Sikandar Shāh in Madura (p. 150).

1377   Rebellions in Etāwah and Katehr (p. 182).

Extinction of the Muslim dynasty of Madura by Bukka I of Vija-yanagar (p. 150).

Death of Muhammad I and accession of Mujāhid Bahmanī (p. 383).

1378   Death of Shihāb-ud-dīn and accession of Qutb-ud-dīn in Kashmīr (p. 278).

Assassination of Mujāhid and accession of Dāūd Bahmanī. Assassination of Dāūd and accession of Muhammad II, Bahmanī (p. 384).

1380   Suppression of the rebellion in Katehr (p. 183).

1382   Independence of Rāja Ahmad, or Malik Rāja, in Khāndesh (p. 294).

Death of Rānā Khet Singh and accession of Lakhā Singh (p. 526).

1387   Fīrūz permits his son to be proclaimed under the title of Nāsir-ud-dīn Muhammad Shāh (p. 184).

1388   Deposition of Muhammad Shāh. Death of Fīrūz and accession of Ghiyās-ud-dīn Tughluq II (pp. 184, 189).

A.D.

1389   Death of Tughluq II and accession of Abū Bakr (p. 190).

1390   Expulsion of Abū Bakr and restoration of Muhammad (p. 191).

1391   Rebellion in Gujarāt. Zafar Khān appointed governor (pp. 191-2)

1392   Rebellion in Etāwah (p. 192).

            Dilāvar Khān governor of Mālwa (p. 349).

1393   Rebellions in Etāwah and Mewāt (p. 192).

            Malik Sarwar, Khvāja Jahān establishes his independence and founds the kingdom of Jaunpur (p. 251).

            Death of Sikandar and accession of Ghiyās-ud-dīn A'zam Shāh in Bengal (p. 264).

1394   Death of Muhammad and accession of 'Alā-ud-dīn Sikandar. Death of Sikandar and accession of Nāsir-ud-dīn Mahmūd. Rebellion in the Punjāb suppressed by Sārang Khān. Nusrat Khān proclaimed king under the title of Nāsir-ud-dīn Nusrat Shāh (pp. 192-4).

            Death of Qutb-ud-dīn and accession of Sikandar in Kashmir (p. 279).

1395-6   Rebellion of Sārang Khān in the Punjāb (p. 194).

1396   Muzaffar I establishes his independence in Gujarāt (p. 295).

            Rebellion of Bahā-ud-dīn of Sāgar in the Deccan (pp. 385-6).

1397   Death of Rānā Lakhā Singh and accession of Mokaljī (p. 527).

            Pīr Muhammad, son of Tīmūr, captures Uch (p. 194).

            Death of Muhammad II and accession of Ghiyās-ud-dīn Bahmanī. Deposition of Ghiyās-ud-dīn and accession of Shams-ud-dīn. Deposition of Shams-ud-din and accession of Fīrūz Shāh Bahmanī (pp. 386-7).

1398   Pīr Muhammad captures Multān (p. 194).

            Mallū becomes supreme in Delhi (p. 195).

            Tīmūr Lang crosses the Indus and invades India. He appears before Delhi, defeats Mahmūd and Mallū and plunders and devastates the city (pp. 195-9)

            Invasion of the Deccan by Harihara II of Vijayanagar and Narsingh of Kherla. Rebellion of the Kolīs in the Deccan crushed by Fīrūz Bahmanī (p. 387).

1399   Tīmūr's retreat (pp. 199, 200).

            Death of Nusrat Shāh. Suppressions of rebellions in Bayāna, Katehr, and Etāwah (p. 201).

            Death of Malik Sarwar and accession of Ibrāhīm Shāh to the throne of Jaunpur (p. 251).

            Death of Raja Ahmad and accession of Nasīr Khān in Khāndesh (p. 296).

            Fīrūz Bahmanī defeats Harihara II, invades Vijayanagar, and enslaves large numbers of the Hindu population (pp. 387-9).

            Defeat of Narsingh of Kherla (pp. 390-1).

1400   Mallū leads an expedition into Etāwah (p. 201).

            Fīrūz Bahmanī founds Fīrūzābād, on the Bhīma (p. 391).

            Har Singh Tomār captures Gwalior from the Muslims (p. 533).

1401   Mahmūd Shāh returns to Delhi (pp. 201-2)

            Pact between Muzaffar I of Gujarāt, Dilāvar Khān of Mālwa, Nasīr Khān of Khāndesh, and Harihara II of Vijayanagar against Fīrūz Bahmanī (p. 391).

1402   Death of Mubārak and accession of Ibrāhīm Shāh in Jaunpur (pp. 202, 251).

A.D.

Mahmūd establishes himself in Kanauj. Mallū returns from Kanauj to Delhi (pp. 202, 251).

Mallū attempts to recover Gwalior (p. 202).

1403 Mallū makes a second unsuccessful attempt to recover Gwalior (p. 202).

Rebellion of Tātār Khān in Gujarāt (p. 295).

1404 Mallū besieges Etāwah, and Kanauj (p. 202).

Usurpation of Ganesh in Bengal (p. 266).

1405 Death of Mallū. Mahmūd Shāh returns to Delhi at the invitation of Daulat Khān Lodī (p. 203).

1406 Expeditions to Sāmāna and Kanauj. Ibrāhīm Shāh of Jaunpur captures Kanauj (pp. 203, 252).

Death of Dilāvar Khān and accession of Hūshang Shāh in Mālwa (p. 349).

Death of Harihara II and accession of Bukka II in Vijayanagar. Fīrūz Bahmanī invades Vijayanagar, enslaves 60,000 Hindus, and compels Bukka to give him a daughter in marriage (pp. 391-3).

1407 Ibrāhīm Shāh of Jaunpur captures Sambhal and Baran (p. 203).

Muzaffar of Gujarāt invades Mālwa and captures Hūshang Shāh (pp. 295, 349).

1408 Mahmūd Shāh recovers Baran and Sambhal from Ibrāhīm Shāh and Hissār from Khizr Khān (pp. 203-4).

Death of Bukka II and accession of Devarāya I in Vijayanagar (p. 394).

Death of Chonda Rāthor and accession of his son, Ranmall (p. 522).

1409 Khizr Khān besieges Delhi (p. 204).

1410 Khizr Khān captures Rohtak (p. 204).

Death of A'zam and accession of Saif-ud-dīn Hamza in Bengal (p. 266).

1411 Khizr Khān captures Nārnaul, besieges Mahmūd Shāh in Siri, and captures Fīrūzābād (p. 204).

Death of Muzaffar I and accession of Ahmad I in Gujarāt (p. 296).

1412 Death of Hamza and accession of Shihāb-ud-dīn Bāyazīd in Bengal (p. 266).

Fīrūz Bahmanī invades and ravages Gondwāna (p. 393).

1413 Death of Mahmūd at Kaithal and failure of the house of Tughluq. Daulat Khān Lodī remains in authority at Delhi (p. 204).

Death of Devarāya I and accession of Vīra Vijaya in Vijayanagar (p. 394).

1414 Khizr Khān captures Delhi and ascends the throne (p. 204).

Death of Ganesh and accession of Jalāl-ud-dīn Muhammad Shāh in Bengal (p. 267).

1415 Suppression of the rebellion of Malik Tughān in Sirhind (p. 207).

1416 Malik Tughān again rebels, but submits (p. 207).

Death of Sikandar and accession of 'Alī Shāh in Kashmīr (p. 280).

1417 Fīrūz Bahmanī invades Telingāna (p. 393).

1418 Suppression of the rebellion of Har Singh of Katehr. Expedition to Etāwah. Expeditions to Koīl and Sambhal. Khizr Khān besieges Badaun (pp. 207-8).

Fīrūz Bahmanī invades Vijayanagar, but is defeated and expelled (pp. 393-4).

A.D.

1419 Khizr Khān raises the siege of Badaun (p.20 8).

Ahmad I of Gujarāt invades Mālwa and defeats Hūshang (pp. 298, 350).

1420 Islām Khān Lodī suppresses a rebellion in the Punjāb. Expedition to Koïl and Etāwah, and invasion of Katehr. Suppression of the rebellion of Malik Tughān in Sirhind (pp. 208-9).

Death of 'Alī Shāh and accession of Zain-ul-'Ābidīn in Kashmīr (p. 281).

1421 Expeditions into Mewāt and to Etāwah. Death of Khizr Khān and accession of Mu'izz-ud-dīn Mubārak Shāh. Rebellion of Jasrat the Khokar (pp. 209-11).

1422 Suppression of the rebellion of Jasrat (pp. 211-2).

Expedition of Hūshang of Mālwa to Orissa (pp. 298, 350).

Ahmad I of Gujarāt invades Mālwa and besieges Māndū (pp. 298, 351).

Rebellion of Ahmad Khān Bahmanī. He defeats the royal troops. Deposition of Fīruz and accession of Ahmad Shāh Bahmanī. Death of Fīrūz (pp. 394-5).

Ahmad I of the Deccan besieges Kherla, and is attacked by Hūshang of Mālwa, whom he defeats (pp. 351-2, 396).

1423 Invasion of Katehr. Jasrat again rebels. Shaikh 'Alī of Kābul plunders Multān. Mubārak marches to the relief of Gwalior, which is besieged by Hūshang of Mālwa (p. 212).

Ahmad Bahmanī invades Vijayanagar, massacres enormous numbers of Hindus, and compels Vīra Vijaya to pay tribute (pp. 397-8).

Famine in the Deccan (p. 398).

1424 Mubārak returns to Delhi and invades Katehr. Ahmad Bahmanī invades Telingāna and captures Warangal (p. 399).

1425 Suppression of the rebellion of Jalāl Khān and 'Abd-ul-Qādir in Mewāt (p. 213).

Ahmad Bahmanī recovers Māhūr and Kalam in Berar, and halts at Ellichpur (p. 399).

1426 Expedition into Mewāt and suppression of the rebellion of Muhammad Khān Auhadī of Bayāna (p. 213).

1427 Mubārak returns to Delhi. Muhammad Khān Auhadī escapes and recovers Bayāna. Expedition to Bayāna. Hostilities between Mubārak and Ibrāhīm Shāh of Jaunpur (pp. 213-4).

1428 Retreat of Ibrāhīm Shāh of Jaunpur. Expedition to Gwalior. Recovery of Bayāna. Rebellion in Mewāt. Jasrat the Khokar in rebellion (pp. 214-5, 252).

Ahmad Bahmanī marches to recover tribute from Kherla, but refrains from attacking Hūshang of Mālwa who is besieging the fortress. He retreats ; Hūshang follows, and is attacked and defeated by Ahmad (pp. 399, 400).

1429 Expeditions to Gwalior, Athgāth, and Rāprī. Rebellion of Fūlād Khān in Bhātinda (pp. 215-6).

War between the Deccan and Gujarāt (pp. 298-9, 400).

Ahmad Bahmanī transfers his capital from Gulbarga to Bīdar (p. 400).

1430 Siege of Bhātinda (p. 216).

Zafar Khān of Gujarāt defeats the army of the Deccan (pp. 299, 400-1).

A.D.

1431   Shaikh 'Alī of Kābul relieves Fūlād Khān in Bhāṭinda, and defeats and slays Islām Khān Lodī near Mulṭān. Shaikh 'Alī captures Talamba. Rebellion of Fūlād Khān (pp. 217-8).

        Death of Jalāl-ud-dīn and accession of Shams-ud-dīn Ahmad in Bengal (p. 627).

1432   Mubārak marches into the Punjāb and disperses his enemies. Jasrat again rebels. Rebellion of Jalāl Khān in Mewāt suppressed by Mubārak (p. 218).

        Completion of Bīdar, the new capital of the Deccan (p. 402).

1433   Shaikh 'Alī captures Lahore. Mubārak recovers the Punjāb. Capture of Bhātinda from Fūlād Khān (p. 220).

        Hūshang of Mālwa annexes Kālpī (pp. 252, 352).

        Assassination of Rānā Mokaljī and accession of Rānā Kūmbha (p. 528).

1434   Assassination of Mubārak and accession of Muhammad Shāh. Overthrow of the minister, Sarvar-ul-Mulk (pp. 220-1)

1435   Death of Hūshang Shāh of Mālwa and accession of Ghaznī Khān (p. 352).

1436   The country of the Khokars devastated (p. 222).

        Mahmūd Khaljī usurps the throne of Mālwa (pp. 223, 353).

        Death of Ibrāhīm and accession of Mahmūd Shāh in Jaunpur (p. 252).

        Death of Ahmad Bahmanī and accession of 'Alā-ud-dīn Ahmad (pp. 402, 405).

1437   'Alā-ud-dīn Ahmad Bahmanī establishes his authority in the Konkan (p 405)

1438   Ahmad I of Gujarāt invades Mālwa in the interests of Mas'ūd Khān Ghūrī (pp. 300, 353-4).

        Nasīr Khān of Khāndesh invades Berar, but is defeated by the army of the Deccan (pp. 405-6).

1440   Mahmūd I of Mālwa marches to Delhi, but is compelled to retire (pp. 223-4, 354-5).

        Usurpation of Sahra Langāh (Qutb-ud-din) in Multān (p. 503)

1441   Death of 'Ādil Khān I and accession of Mubārak Khān in Khāndesh (p. 300).

1442   Death of Ahmad and accession of Nāsir-ud dīn Mahmūd in Bengal (p. 267).

        Death of Ahmad I and accession o Muhammad I in Gujarāt (p. 300).

        Mahmūd I of Gujarāt invades the dominions of Kūmbha, Rānā of Chitor (p. 355).

1443   Muhammad I of Mālwa retreats from Chitor and is followed by Rānā Kūmbha, but defeats him (p. 355).

        Devarāya II of Vijayanagar invades the Deccan, but is expelled (p. 407).

1444   Death of Muhammad Shāh and accession of 'Ālam Shāh (p. 225).

        War between Mālwa and Jaunpur (pp. 253, 355).

        Death of Ranmall and expulsion of the Rāhtors from Mewār.

        Accession of Jodha Rāhtor (p. 523).

1445   Mahmūd I of Mālwa marches to Kālpī. Battle between his forces and those of Mahmūd of Jaunpur (pp. 355-6).

                                                            43—2

A.D.

1465 Mahmūd I of Mālwa besieges Rānā Kūmbha in Kūmbhalgarh (p. 359).

1466 Expedition of Husain Shāh of Jaunpur against Mān Singh of Gwalior (p 255).

Treaty of peace between Muhammad III of the Deccan and Mahmūd I of Mālwa (p. 359).

1467 Muhammad III of the Deccan unsuccessfully attempts to recover Kherla (pp. 359, 414).

Mahmūd I of Mālwa receives an envoy from Abū Sa'īd the Tīmurid (p. 359).

1468 Mahmūd I of Mālwa raids Kachwāra and captures Karahra (pp. 369-60).

Assassination of Rānā Kūmbha and accession of Jaimall (p. 528).

1469 Death of Mahmūd I of Mālwa and accession of Ghiyās-ud-dīn (pp. 305, 360).

Mahmūd Gāvān marches into the Konkan to re-establish the authority of Muhammad III Bahmanī (p. 414).

1470 Death of Zain-ul-Ābidīn and accession of Haidar Shāh in Kashmīr (p. 284).

Mahmūd Begarha of Gujarāt captures Girnār and compels the Chudāsama chief to accept Islam (p. 306).

1471 Mahmūd Begarah of Gujarāt invades Sind (p. 306).

1472 Buhlūl Lodī marches against Husain Shāh Langāh of Multān (pp. 231, 504).

Death of Haidar Shāh and accession of Hasan Shāh in Kashmīr (p. 285).

Mahmūd Gāvān returns to Bīdar after having re-established the authority of Muhammad III Bahmanī in the Konkan. Malik Hasan invades Orissa, re-establishes the Raja and captures Rajamundry for Muhammad III Bahmanī (pp. 415-6).

Belgaum is taken and the Raja, Birkāna, is deposed. Famine in the Deccan (pp. 416-7).

1473 Husain Shāh of Jaunpur appears before Delhi, but is defeated by Buhlūl Lodī (pp. 231-2, 256).

Mahmūd Begarha of Gujarāt destroys the temple of Dwārka (p. 307).

1474 Husain of Jaunpur again invades the kingdom of Delhi, but is defeated and compelled to retire (pp. 232, 256).

Death of Bārbak and accession of Shams-ud-dīn Yūsuf in Bengal (p. 268).

1476 Husain of Jaunpur again invades the kingdom of Delhi, but is defeated at Sikhera, and retires to Etāwah (pp. 232, 256).

Muhammad III, Bahmanī, invades Telingāna (p. 417).

1478 Death of 'Alam Shāh in Badaun (pp. 234, 256).

Muhammad III, Bahmanī, invades Orissa and compels the Raja of Jajpur to submit to him (p. 417).

Muhammad III recovers Rajamundry (p. 417).

1479 Husain of Jaunpur again invades the kingdom of Delhi, but is defeated and pursued by Buhlūl, who recovers Etāwah, invades Jaunpur, expels Husain and annexes the kingdom of Jaunpur (pp. 234, 257-8).

Muhammad III, Bahmanī, invades the Carnatic (pp. 418-9).

A.D.

1480   Subdivision of the four *tarafs*, or provinces, of the Deccan into eight. Conspiracy against Mahmūd Gavān (p. 419).

                Sangram Shāh, Gond, succeeds in Garha-Katanga (p. 536).

1481   Death of Yūsuf and accession of Sikandar. Deposition of Sikandar and accession of Jalāl-ud-dīn Fath Shāh in Bengal (p. 268).

                Murder of Mahmūd Gāvān in the Deccan (p. 420).

1482   Death of Muhammad III and accession of Mahmūd Bahmanī (p. 422).

1484   Mahmūd Begarha of Gujarāt captures Champaner (p. 310).

1486   Buhlūl places his son, Bārbak, on the throne of Jaunpur (p. 234).

                Assassination of Fath Shāh and usurpation of Bārbak, the eunuch, in Bengal. Death of Bārbak and accession of Malik Indīl, Fīrūz Shāh in Bengal (pp. 268-9).

                Mān Singh Parihār succeeds as Raja of Gwalior (p. 534).

1488   Death of Jodha Rāhtor and succession of Surajmall (p. 523).

1489   Death of Buhlūl and accession of Sikandar Shāh. Death of Fīrūz and accession of Nāsīr-ud-dīn Mahmūd in Bengal (p. 270).

                Death of Hasan Shāh and accession of Muhammad Shāh. Deposition of Muhammad Shāh and accession of Fath Shāh in Kashmir (p. 285).

1490   Murder of Mahmūd and usurpation of Sidī Badr, Muzaffar Shāh, in Bengal (p. 270)

                Ahmad Nizām-ul-Mulk of Ahmadnagar, Yūsuf 'Ādil Khān of Bījāpur. and Fathullāh 'Imād-ud-Mulk of Berar declare their independence (pp. 425-6).

                Qāsim Barīd becomes lieutenant of the Bahmanī kingdom (p. 427).

1491   Rebellion of Bahādur Gīlānī in the Konkan (pp 311, 427).

1493   Death of Muzaffar and accession of 'Alā-ud-dīn Husain in Bengal (p. 270).

                Mahmūd Begarha of Gujarāt complains to Mahmūd Bahmanī of the depredations of Bahādur Gīlānī (p. 427).

1494   Sikandar Lodī defeats Husain of Jaunpur and pursues him into Bihār (p. 238).

                Bahādur Gīlānī is defeated and slain in the Konkan (pp. 311, 427).

1497   Restoration of Muhammad Shāh in Kashmīr. (p. 287).

1498   Husain Shāh of Bengal invades Assam (pp. 271-2).

                Restoration of Fath Shāh in Kashmir (p. 287).

1499   Sikandar Lodī marches from Jaunpur to Sambhal (p. 240).

                Restoration of Muhammad Shah in Kashmīr (p. 287).

1500   Death of Husain, the deposed king of Jaunpur (p. 258).

                Abdication of Ghiyās-ud-dīn and accession of Nāsir-ud-dīn in Mālwa (pp. 311. 363).

1501   Death of 'Adil Khān II and accession of Dāūd Khān in Khāndesh (p. 313).

1502   Death of Husain I and accession of Mahmūd in Multān (p. 504).

1503   Nāsir-ud-dīn of Mālwa raids the dominions of the Rānā (p. 364).

1504   Death of Qāsim Barīd at Bīdar, and succession of his son, Amīr 'Alī Barīd Death of Fathullāh 'Imād-ul-Mulk in Berar, and accession of his son 'Alā-ud-dīn 'Imād Shāh. Yūsuf 'Ādil Shāh attempts to establish the Shiah religion in Bījāpur but is expelled from his kingdom by a confederacy (p. 429).

A.D.

1505 Sikandar Lodi captures Mandrāel. Earthquake in Āgra. Campaign in Gwalior. Sikandar Lodi captures Utgīr (pp. 242-3).

Yūsuf 'Ādil Shāh returns to Bījāpur (p. 430).

1506 The Portuguese established at Cochin (p. 312).

1507 The Portuguese established on Socotra (p. 312).

1508 Sikandar Lodi captures Narwar (pp. 243-4)

Death of Dāūd and accession of Ghaznī Khān in Khāndesh. Death of Ghaznī Khān and disputed succcssion until 'Ālam Khān ('Ādil Khān III) is installed by Mahmūd Begarha of Gujarāt (pp. 313—4).

Death of Rānā Raimall and accession of Sangrama Singh (p. 529).

1509 Death of Ahmad Nizām Shāh and accession of his son, Burhān Nizām Shāh I in Ahmadnagar (p. 430).

Accession of Krishnadevarāya of Vijayanagar (p. 495).

1510 Death of Yūsuf 'Ādil Shah and accession of his son, Ismā'īl 'Ādil Shāh, in Bījāpur. Death of Khvāja Jahān at Parenda (p. 430).

The Portuguese capture Goa. Ismā'īl 'Ādil Shāh recovers it, but is shortly afterwards expelled by the Portuguese (p 434).

Krishnarāya of Vijayanagar invades Bījāpur and annexes the Rāichūr Doāb (p. 435).

1511 Death of Mahmūd I (Begarha) of Gujarāt, and accession of Muzaffar II (pp. 315-6).

Death of Nāsir-ud-dīn and accession of Mahmūd II in Mālwa (pp. 316, 365).

1512 Dominance of the Rājputs and rebellion of the Muslim nobles in Mālwa (pp. 366—7).

Sultān Qulī Qutb-ul-Mulk declares his independence in Telingāna (p. 430).

1513 Sikandar Lodi sends an expedicion into Mālwa (p. 245).

1514. Mahmūd II returns to Māndū and submits to the dominance of the Rājputs (pp. 367-8).

Amīr 'Alī Barīd, Mahmūd Shāh Bahmanī, Burhān Nizām Shāh I, and Sultān Qulī Qutab Shāh invade Bījāpur, but are defeated by Ismā'īl 'Ādil Shāh, who captures Mahmūd Bahmanī, Amīr 'Alī Barīd recovers possession of Mahmūd (p. 430).

1516 'The Rape of the Virgins.' Death of Sūrajmall and accession of Ganga Rāhtor in Mārwār (p. 523).

1517 Death of Sikandar and accession of Ibrāhīm Shāh Lodi. Rebellion of Jalāl Khān (pp. 246-8).

Mahmūd II of Mālwa flees from Māndū and seeks the help of Muzaffar II of Gujarāt against the Rājputs (pp. 319, 368).

1518 Death of Husain Shāh and accession of Nāsir-ud-dīn Nusrat Shāh in Bengal (p. 272).

Muzaffar II of Gujarāt captures Māndū, massacres the Rājputs and restores Mahmūd II (pp. 319, 368).

Death of Mahmūd and accession of Ahmad Shāh Bahmanī in Bīdar (p. 431).

Burhān Nizām Shāh I invades Berar and captures Pāthrī (p. 435).

Ibrāhīm Lodi captures Gwalior from Bikramājīt Tomār (p. 534).

1519 Rānā Sangrama Singh defeats and captures Mahmūd II of Mālwa near Gāgraun (pp. 319-20, 368-9).

A.D.

1521   Muzaffar II of Gujarāt and Mahmūd II of Mālwa invade the
        dominions of Rānā Sangrama Singh and besiege Mandasor (pp.
        320-1).

        Death of Ahmad and accession of 'Alā-ud-dīn Shāh Bahmanī (p. 431).

        Ismā'īl 'Ādil Shāh attempts to recover the Rāichūr Doāb, but is
        defeated (p. 435).

        Shāh Beg Arghūn conquers Sind (p. 501).

1522   Deposition of 'Alā-ud-dīn and accession of Walī-Ullāh Shāh Bahmanī
        p. 431).

1524   Bahādur, son of Muzaffar II, leaves Gujarāt and visits Rājasthan,
        Mewāt, Delhi and Jaunpur (p. 321).

        Alliance between Ismā'īl 'Ādil Shāh and Burhān Nizām Shāh I
        (p. 435).

        Death of Shāh Beg Arghūn and accession of his son, Shāh Husain,
        in Sind (p. 501).

1525   Deposition of Walī-Ullāh and accession of Kalīmullāh Shāh Bahmanī
        (p. 431).

        Burhān Nizām Shāh I, 'Alā-ud-dīn 'Imād Shāh, and Amīr 'Alī Barīd
        invade Bījapur, but are defeated and expelled (p. 435).

1526   Battle of Pānīpat. Defeat and death of Ibrāhīm Lodī. Zahīr-ud-dīn
        Muhammad Bābur ascends the throne of Delhi (p. 250).

        Deposition of Muhammad Shāh and accession of Ibrāhīm I in
        Kashmīr (p. 287).

        Death of Muzaffar II in Gujarāt, and accession of Sikandar. Assas-
        sination of Sikandar and accession of Bahādur (pp. 322—4).

        Mahmūd II of Mālwa harbours the fugitive prince, Chānd Khān of
        Gujarāt (p. 369).

1527   Death of Ibrāhīm I and enthronement of Nāzuk Shāh in Kashmīr
        (p. 287).

        Flight of Kalīmullāh Shāh Bahmanī to Bījāpur, and, later, to
        Ahmadnagar. Accession of Amīr 'Alī Barīd Shāh in Bīdar (pp.
        431-2).

        Burhān Nizām Shāh I and 'Alī Barīd Shāh invade Berar and expel
        'Alā-ud-dīn 'Imād Shāh, who appeals for help to Bahādur of
        Gujarāt (p. 436).

1528   The Portuguese reach Bengal (p. 273).

        Bahādur of Gujarāt invades the Deccan (pp. 324—5, 436).

        Mīrzā Shāh Husain Arghūn captures Multān (p. 505).

1529   Deposition of Nāzuk Shah and restoration of Muhammad in Kashmīr
        (p. 287).

        Bahādur of Gujarāt retires from the Deccan (pp. 325, 436).

1530   [Death of Bābur and accession of Humāyūn.]

        The Portuguese capture Damān (p. 325).

        Ismā'īl 'Ādil Shāh captures Amīr 'Alī Barīd and recovers the Rāichūr
        Doāb (pp. 436-7).

        Death of Krishnadevaryāya and accession of Achyuta in Vijayanagar
        (p. 498).

1531   Failure of a Portuguese attempt to capture Diū (p. 325).

        Bahādur of Gujarāt, assisted by Muhammad of Khāndesh, captures
        Māndū and annexes the kingdom of Mālwa (pp. 326-7).

        Burhān Nizām Shāh I and Amīr 'Alī Barīd Shāh invade Bījāpur,
        but are defeated and expelled by Asad Khān Lārī (p. 438).

A.D.

1532   Operations against the Rājputs in Mālwa (p. 328).

1533   Assassination of Nusrat Shāh and accession of 'Alā-ud-dīn Fīrūz
        Shāh in Bengal (p. 273).

        Invasion of Kashmīr by Sultān Sa'īd Khān of Kāshghar and Mīrzā
        Haidar (p. 287).

        Bahādur of Gujarāt captures Chitoɪ (p. 329).

1534   Death of Muhammad Shāh and accession of Shams-ud-dīn II in
        Kashmīr (p. 288).

        Death of Ismā'īl and accession of Mallū 'Ādil Shāh (pp. 438-9).

        Accession of Rānā Udai Singh (p. 531).

1535   Humāyūn captures Māndū and invades Gujarāt (pp. 331-3).

        Deposition of Mallū and accession of Ibrāhīm 'Adil Shāh I. The
        Sunnī religion is established in Bijapur (p. 439).

1536   Humāyūn is compelled to retire from Gujarāt (p. 333).

        Qādir Khān assumes the royal title in Mālwa (p. 369).

        Asad Khān Lārī invades Vijayanagar, but is defeated (p. 440).

1537   Bahādur of Gujarāt is drowned at Diū. Accession of Muhammad II
        (of Khāndesh). Death of Muhammad II and accession of Mah-
        mūd III (pp. 334-5).

        Burhān Nizām Shāh I establishes the Shiah religion in Ahmadnagar
        (p 440).

1538   Sher Khān occupies Gaur and assumes the royal title in Bengal.
        Humāyūn occupies Gaur (pp. 274-5).

        The Ottoman fleet and the army of Gujarāt unsuccessfully besiege
        the Portuguese in Diū (pp 336-7).

1539   Humāyūn retires from Bengal and Sher Khān recovers the sovereign-
        ty (p. 275).

        [Sher Shāh ascends the throne of Delhi.]

1540   Khizr Khān assumes sovereignty in Bengal, but is overthrown and
        imprisoned by Sher Khān (pp. 275-6).

        Death of Shams-ud-dīn and restoration of Nāzuk Shāh in Kashmīr.
        Conquest of Kashmīr by Mīrzā Haidar (p. 288).

        Khengār is established as Rāo of Cutch, and Rāwal as Jām of
        Nawanagar (pp. 518-9).

1542   Sher Shāh invades Mālwa, receives the submission of Qādir Shāh,
        and appoints Hājī Khān governor of Mālwa. Hājī Khān is
        recalled and Shujā'at Khān is appointed governor of Mālwa
        (p. 370).

        Death of Amīr 'Alī Barīd and accession of 'Alī Barīd Shāh in Bīdar
        (p. 440).

1543   Assassination of Sultān Qulī and accession of Jamshīd Qutb Shāh in
        Golconda (pp. 440-1).

        Jamshīd, Burhān Nizām Shāh, 'Alī Barīd Shāh, and a Hindu army
        invade Bījāpur, but are expelled (p 441).

1544   Burhān Nizām Shāh I invades Bījāpur, but is defeated and expelled
        (p. 441).

1545   Death of Sher Shāh and accession of Islām Shāh in Delhi. Failure
        of a conspiracy to depose Ibrāhīm 'Ādil Shāh I and place his
        brother, 'Abdullah, on the throne (p. 441).

1546   Rout of the army of Gujarāt before Diū (p. 340).

        Death of Asad Khān Lārī (p. 442).

A.D.

1547   The Portuguese burn Broach and massacre the inhabitants (p. 341). Alliance between Burhān Nizām Shāh I and Sadāshivaraya of Vijayanagar. War between Ahmadnagar and Bījāpur (p. 442).

1550   Death of Jamshīd Qutb Shāh and accession of Subhān Qulī Qutb Shāh in Golconda. Deposition of Subhān Qulī and accession of Ibrāhīm Qutb Shāh (p. 443).

1551   Defeat and death of Mīrzā Haidar and restoration of Nāzuk Shāh in Kashmīr (P. 289).

1552   [Death of Islām Shāh aud accession of Muhammad 'Ādil Shāh in Delhi.]

Deposition of Nāzuk Shāh and enthronement of Ibrāhīm II in Kashmīr (p. 289).

Sadāshivaraya of Vijayanagar with the help of Burhān Nizām Shāh I recovers the Rāichur Doāb. Death of Burhān Nizām Shāh I and accession of Husain Nizām Shāh I in Ahmadnagar (p. 442.)

1553   [Accession of Ibrāhīm Shāh in Delhi.]

1554   [Accession of Sikandar Shāh in Delhi.]

Death of Mahmūd III and accession of Ahmad II in Gujarāt (pp. 342-3).

War between Bijāpur and Ahmadnagar (p. 443).

1555   [Humāyūn recovers the throne of Delhi.]

Deposition of Ibrāhīm II and accession of Ismā'īl in Kashmīr (p. 289).

Death of Shujā'at Khān and accession of Bāz Bahādur in Mālwa (p. 371).

Rebellion of Saif 'Ain-ul-Mulk in Bījāpur (pp. 443—4'.

1556   [Death of Humāyūn and accession of Akbar.]

Muhammad 'Īsā Tarkhān becomes ruler of Sind (p. 602).

1557   Death of Ismā'īl and accession of Habīb Shāh in Kashmīr (p. 289).

1558   Death of Ibrāhīm 'Ādil Shāh I and accession of 'Ali 'Adil Shāh I. Re-establishment of the Shiah religion in Bijāpur. 'Alī allies himself with Vijayanagar, and is attacked by Husain Nizām Shāh I and Ibrāhīm Qutb Shāh, of whom he rids his state. Husain Nizām Shāh I attacks Chaul, but makes peace with the portuguese (pp. 444-5).

1559—60   Aliyarāma Rāya of Vijayanagar, 'Ali 'Ādil Shāh I and Ibrāhīm Qutb Shāh invade Ahmadnagar. Humiliation of the Muslims (pp. 445-6).

1561   Deposition of Habīb and usurpation of Ghāzī Khān Chakk in Kashmīr (p. 290).

Akbar annexes Mālwa (p. 371).

Death of Daryā 'Imād Shāh and accession of Burhān 'Imād Shāh (p. 446.)

1562   Assassination of Ahmad II and accession of Muzaffar III in Gujarāt (pp. 344-5).

'Alī 'Ādil Shāh I and Aliyarāma Rāya defeat Husain Nizām Shāh I and Ibrāhīm Qutb Shāh (pp. 446-7).

1563   Aliyarāma Rāya and Ālī 'Ādil Shāh invade Ahmadnagar, but retire during the rainy season (p. 477).

1563-4   Abdication of Ghāzī Khān and accession of Nāsir-ud-dīn Husain Shāh in Kashmīr (p. 290).

A.D.

1564   Husain Nizām Shāh I, 'Alī 'Ādil Shāh I, Ibrāhīm Qutb Shah, and 'Alī Barīd Shāh from a confederacy against Vijayanagar. The four kings assemble at Sholāpur and march to Talikota (p. 448).

1565   Battle of Talikota. Overthrow of the kingdom of Vijayanagar (pp. 448-50).

      Death of Husain Nizām Shāh I and accession of Murtazā Nizām Shāh I (p. 450).

1566   'Alī 'Ādil Shāh I and Murtazā Nizām Shāh I invade Berar (pp. 450-1).

1567   War between Bijāpur and Ahmadnagar (pp. 451-2).

      Accession of Mīrzā Muhammad Bāqī Tarkhān in Sind (p. 502).

1568   The Mīrzās at Broach. I'timād Khān invites Akbar to invade Gujarāt (p. 346).

1569   League between 'Alī 'Ādil Shāh I, Murtazā Nizām Shāh I and the Zamorin of Calicut against the Portuguese (p. 452).

1569-70   Death of Husain and accession of 'Ali Shāh in Kashmīr (p. 291).

      'Alī 'Ādil Shāh I besieges Goa and Murtazā Nizām Shāh I besieges Chaul. Both are defeated (pp. 452-3).

1571   'Alī 'Ādil Shāh I and Murtazā Nizām Shāh I make treaties with Portugal (p. 453).

1572   Akbar annexes Gujarāt (p. 348).

1574   Murtazā Nizām Shāh I annexes Berar (pp. 453-4).

1575   Conquests of 'Alī 'Ādil Shāh I in the Carnatic (pp. 454-5).

1577   Akbar's troops invade Khāndesh. Submission of Rāja 'Alī Khān (p. 456).

1578   Murtazā Nizām Shāh I and Ibrāhīm Qutb Shāh attack Bīdar. 'Alī Barīd Shāh obtains the assistance of 'Alī 'Ādil Shāh I and the siege is raised (p. 457).

1579   Death of 'Alī and accession of Yūsuf in Kashmīr (p. 292).

      Rebellion of Prince Burhān-ud-din in Ahmadnagar. He flees and takes refuge at the court of Akbar (p. 457).

      Death of Alī Barīd Shāh and accession of Ibrāhīm Barīd Shāh in Bīdar (p. 458).

1580   Death of 'Alī 'Ādil Shāh I and accession of Ibrāhīm 'Ādil Shāh II in Bijāpur. War between Ahmadnagar and Bijāpur. Defeat of the army of Ahmadnagar. Death of Ibrāhīm Qutb Shāh and accession of Muhammad Qulī Qutb Shāh in Golconda. Disturbed condition of Bijāpur (pp. 458-60).

1582   Dilāvar Khan becomes supreme in Bijāpur. He establishes the Sunni religion (p. 460).

1585   Death of Mīrzā Muhammad Bāqī Tarkhān and accession of Mīrzā Jānī Beg Tarkhān in Sind (p. 502).

1588   Murder of Murtazā Nizām Shāh I and accession of Husain Nizām Shāh II in Ahmadnagar (p. 461).

1589   Deposition of Husain Nizām Shāh II and enthronement of Ismā'īl Nizām Shāh in Ahmadnagar (p. 461).

1591   Burhān-ud-dīn defeats his son, Ismā'īl Nizām Shāh and ascends the throne in Ahmadnagar as Burhān Nizām Shāh II (p. 462).

      'Abd-ur-Rahim, the Khān Khānān, conquers Sind (p. 502).

1592   Burhān Nizām Shāh II attacks the Portuguese in Chaul, and is defeated (p. 462).

1595   Death of Burhān Nizām Shāh II and accession of Ibrāhim Nizām Shāh. War between Ahmadnagar and Bījāpur and death of Ibrāhīm Nizam Shāh. Accession of Bahādur Nizām Shāh. Civil war in Ahmadnagar. Four parties, each acknowledging a different king. Akbar's intervention invited. Sultan Murād and the Khan Khānān open the siege of Ahmadnagar (pp. 463-4)

1596   Chāud Bībi cedes Berar to Akbar and the imperial army raises the siege of Ahmadnagar. Renewal of hostilities (pp. 465-6).

1599   Sultan Dāniyāl is appointed by Akbar to the command in the Deccan (p. 466).

1603   Murder of Chānd Bībī. The imperial troops take Ahmadnagar. Bahādur Nizām Shāh is imprisoned. Accession of Murtazā Nizām Shāh II (p. 466).

BURMA

1280   Establishment of the Toungoo State (p. 557).

1281   Wareru establishes himself in Martaban (p. 551).

1287   Kyawswa succeeds in Pagān (p. 540).

           Wareru founds the town of Martaban, overcomes and executes Tarubya governor of Pegu, and becomes ruler of the Talaing state of Pegū (p. 551).

1297   Investiture of Kyawswa by the Emperor of China (p. 540).

1298   The Three Shān Brothers establish their rule in Upper Burma. Kyawswa is compelled to take the robe (p. 540).

           Recognition of the Talaing state of Pegū by China (p. 551).

1312   Thihathu, the surviving Shāh Brother, establishes himself at Pinya (p. 541).

1353   Accession of Binnya U in Martaban (p. 552).

1364   The Maw Shāns capture Sagaing and Pinya. Thadominbya, after their departure, establishes himself at Ava (p. 542)

1368   Death of Thadominbya and accession of Minkyiswasawke (p. 542). Accession of Pyānchi, Lord of Toungoo (p. 557).

1374   Minkyiswasawke sends his uncle, Sawmungyi, to Arakan as king (p. 544).

1377   Murder of Pyānchi, Lord of Toungoo (p. 544).

1385   Death of Binnya U and accession of Razadarit, who establishes himself in Pegū (p. 552).

1390   Razadarit captures Myaungmya (p. 552).

1401   Death of Minkyiswasawke and accession of Minhkaung (p. 544).

1404   Minhkaung invodes Arakan (p. 544).

1406   The Burmese overrun Mohnyin (p. 544).

           Razadarit invades the kingdom of Ava, but retires (p. 545).

1407   Capture of the Burmese garrison of Launggyet and execution of Answrahtaminsaw. Minhkaung invades the Delta and is defeated (p. 546).

1413   Minrekyawswa defeats a marauding army from Hsenwi (p. 545)

1415   Minrekyawswa subjugates the Delta (p. 546).

1417   Death of Minrekyawswa. End of the war between Ava and Pegū (p. 546).

A.D.
1422 Death of Minhkaung and accession of his son Thihathu in Ava (p. 547).

1423 Death of Razadarit (p. 553).

1426 Assassination of Thihathu and accession of Kalekyetaungnyo in Ava (p. 547).

1427 Accession of Mohnyinthado in Ava (p. 547).

1440 Death of Mohnyinthado and accession of Minrekyawswa in Ava (p. 547).

1443 Death of Minrekyawswa and accession of Narapati in Ava (p. 547).

1450 Accession of Binnyakyan in Pegū (p. 553).

1453 Death of Binnyakyan and accession of Shinsawbu, ' the Old Queen, in Pegū (p. 553).

1469 Death of Narapati and accession of Thihathura in Ava (p. 547).

1472 Accession of Dammazedi in Pegū (pp. 554-5).

1475 Mission of 22 monks from Pegū to Ceylon (p. 555).

1481 Death of Thihathura and accession of Minhkaung in Ava (p. 549).

1486 Accession of Minkyinyo, Lord of Toungoo (558).

1492 Death of Dammazedi and accession of Binnyaran in Pegū (p. 556).

1500 Rise of Burmese vernacular literature.

1502 Death of Minhkaung and accession of Shwenankyawshin in Ava (p. 550).

1510 Foundation of the modern town Toungoo (p. 558).

1519 The Portuguese found a trading station at Martaban (p. 556).

1526 Death of Binnyaran and acccession Takayutpi in Pegū (p 556).

1527 Invasion of Ava by the Shāns. Death of Shwenankyawshin and accession of Thohanbwa (p. 550).

1531 Death of Minkyinyo, Lord of Toungoo (p. 558).

1539 Extinction of the Pegū kingdom (p. 557).

1543 Assassination of Thohanbwa and accession of Hkonmaing in Ava (p. 550).

1546 Death of Hkonmaing and accession of Mobye Narapati in Ava (p. 550).

1552 Flight of Mobye Narapati and accession of Sithukyawhtin in Ava (p. 550).

CEYLON

1213 The Kālinga prince Māgha ascends the throne in Polonnaruva under the title of Kālinga Vijaya-Bāhu (p. 559).

1227 Accession of Vijaya-Bāhu III in Jambudoni (Dambadeniya) (p. 559).

1231 Accession of Parakkama-Bāhu II in Dambadeniya (p. 560).

1234. Death of Kālinga Vijaya-Bāhu (p. 559).

1235 Second coronation festival, of Parakkama-Bāhu II in Polonnaruva (p. 561).

1265 Death of Parakkama-Bāhu II and accession of Vijay-Bāhu IV in Dambadeniya (p. 561).

1268 Assassination of Vijaya-Bāhu IV (Boast Vijaya-Bāhu) and accession of Bhuvaneka-Bāhu I to the throne of Dambadeniya (p. 562).

1279 Death of Bhuvaneka-Bāhu I. Famine in Ceylon (p. 562).

A.D.

1280   Removal of the Tooth-relic by Āryachakravarti of Jaffna and its delivery to Māravarman Tribhuvana-chakravartin Kulacekharadeva the Pāndya (p. 562).

1281   Accession of Parakkama-Bāhu III and recovery of the Tooth-relic (p. 562).

1288   Deposition of Parakkama-Bāhu III and accession of Bhuvaneka-Bāhu II (p. 562).

1291   Death of Bhuvaneka-Bāhu II and accession of Parakkama-Bāhu IV (Pandita Parakkama-Bāhu II) in Kurunagala (p. 562).

1326   Death of Parakkama-Bāhu IV and accession of Bhuvaneka-Bāhu III (Vanni Bhuvaneka-Bāhu) (p. 562).

1346   Accession of Bhuvaneka-Bāhu IV in Gangācrīpura (Gampola) (p. 563).

1352   Death of Bhuvaneka-Bāhu IV and accession of Parakkama-Bāhu V (p. 563).

1359   Death of Parakkama-Bāhu V and accession of Vikkama-Bāhu III (p. 563).

1374   Death of Vikkama-Bāhu III and accession of Bhuvaneka-Bāhu V (p. 563).

1390   Vīra-Bāhu II ascends the throne of Gampola and Kōtte (p. 564).

1395   Convocation of Buddhist priests, presided over by Dhammakitti II (p. 564).

1397   Vīra-Alakecvara (Vijaya-Bāhu VI) returns from Southern India, ousts his brother, Vīra-Bāhu II, from Kōtte and ascends the throne there (p. 565).

1405   The Chinese eunuch Tcheng Houo visits Ceylon for the purpose of removing the Tooth-relic, but is plundered by Vīra-Alakecvara (p. 565).

1409   Tcheng Houo returns to Ceylon with an army and captures Vīra-Alakecvara and his family (p. 565).

1411-2   Vīra-Alakecvara and his family are released by the Chinese, but are murdered on their return to Ceylon (p. 565).

1414   Parakkama-Bāhu VI ascends the throne at Kōtte (p. 565).

1466   Death of Parakkama-Bāhu VI and accession of Jaya-Bāhu II (Jaya Vīra Parakkama-Bāhu) in Kōtte (p. 566).

1468   Death of Jaya-Bāhu II and accession of Bhuvaneka-Bāhu VI in Kōtte (p. 566).

1476   Death of Bhuvaneka-Bāhu VI and accession of Parakkama-Bāhu VII (Pandita Parakkama-Bāhu) in Kōtte (p. 566).

1484   Death of Parakkama-Bāhu VII and accession of Parakkama-Bāhu VIII in Kōtte (p. 566).

1505   Death of Parakkama-Bāhu VII and accession of Parakkama-Bāhu IX (Dhamma Parakkama-Bāhu) in Kōtte (p. 567).

1506   Arrival of the Portuguese at Colombo (p. 567).

1527   Death of Parakkama-Bāhu IX (p. 567).

DYNASTIC LISTS AND GENEALOGICAL TABLES

1. The Yamīnī Dynasty of Ghaznī and Lahore.
2. The Shansabānī Dynasty of Ghūr.
3. The Slave Kings of Delhi.
4. The House of Balban.
5. The Khaljīs.
6. The Tughluqs.
7. The Sayyids.
   The Lodīs.
9. Governors of Bengal.
10. Kings of Bengal.
11. The Sultāns of Madura.
12. The Kings of Kashmīr, First Dynasty.
13. The Chakk Dynasty of Kashmīr
14. The Kings of Multān.
15. The Kings of Sind.
16. The Sharqī Dynasty of Jaunpur.
17. The Bahmanī Dynasty of the Deccan.
18. The 'Ādil Shāhī Dynasty of Bījāpur.
19. The Nizām Shāhī Dynasty of Ahmadnagar.
20. The Qutb Shāhī Dynasty of Golconda.
21. The 'Imād Shāhī Dynasty of Berar.
22. The Barid Shāhī Dynasty of Bīdar.
23. The Kings of Gūjarāt.
24. The Kings of Mālwa.
25. The Fārūqī Dynasty of Khāndesh.

1. THE YAMĪNĪ DYNASTY OF GHAZNĪ AND LAHORE
(Commonly known as the GHAZNAVIDS)

A.H.			A.D.
366	(1)	Sabuktigīn.	976
387	(2)	Ismā'īl.	997
388	(3)	Mahmūd, Yamīn-ud-Daulah.	998
421	(4)	Muhammad.	1030
421	(5)	Mas'ūd I.	1030
432	(6)	Maudūd.	1040
440	(7)	Mas'ūd II.	1049
440	(8)	'Alī, Bahā-ud-Daulah.	1049
444	(9)	'Abd-ur-Rashīd.	1052
444		Tughril 'the Ingrate.' (Usurper).	1052
444	(10)	Farrukhzād, Jamāl-ud-Daulah.	1053
451	(11)	Ibrāhīm, Zahīr-ud-Daulah.	1059
492	(12)	Mas'ūd III, 'Imād-ud-Daulah.	1099
508	(13)	Shīrzād, Kamāl-ud-Daulah.	1115
509	(14)	Arsalān Shāh, Sultān-ud-Daulah.	1116
512	(15)	Bahrām Shāh, Yamīn-ud-Daulah	1118
547	(16)	Khusrav Shāh, Mu'izz-ud-Daulah.	1152
555	(17)	Khusrav Malik, Tāj-ud-Daulah.	1160
—582			—1186

(Shansabānīs.)

THE YAMĪNĪ DYNASTY
GENEALOGY

(Numbers in brackets denote the order of succession.)

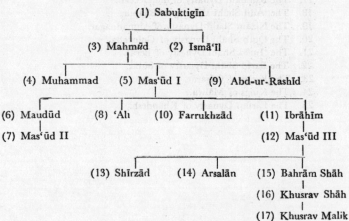

2. GENEALOGY OF THE SHANSABĀNĪ DYNASTY OF GHŪR, ETC.

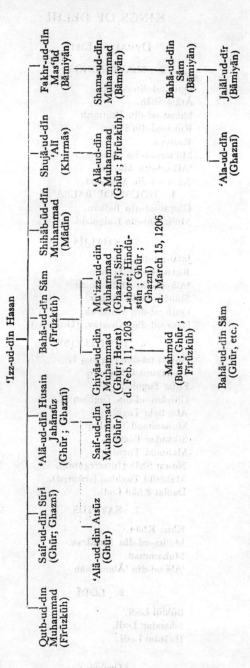

KINGS OF DELHI

DYNASTIC LISTS

A.H.	3. SLAVE KINGS	A.D.
602	Qutb-ud-dīn Aibak.	1206
607	Ārām Shāh.	1210
607	Shams-ud-dīn Iltutmish	1211
633	Rukn-ud-dīn Fīrūz.	1236
634	Raziyya.	1236
637	Mu'izz-ud-dīn Bahrām.	1240
639	'Alā-ud-dīn Mas'ūd.	1242
644	Nāsir-ud-dīn Mahmūd	1246

4. HOUSE OF BALBAN

664	Ghiyās-ud-dīn Balban.	1266
686	Mu'izz-ud-dīn Kaiqubād.	1287

5. KHALJĪS

689	Jalāl-ud-dīn Fīrūz.	1290
695	Rukn-ud-dīn Ibrāhīm.	1296
695	'Alā-ud-dīn Muhammad.	1296
715	Shihāb-ud-dīn 'Umar.	1316
716	Qutb-ud-dīn Mubārak.	1316
720	Nāsir-ud-dīn Khusrav. (Usurper.)	1320

6. TUGHLUQS

720	Ghiyās-ud-dīn Tughluq I.	1320
725	Muhammad Tughluq	1325
752	Fīrūz Tughluq	1351
790	Ghiyāsn-ud-dīn Tughluq II.	1388
791	Abū Bakr Tughluq.	1389
792	Muhammad Tughluq	1390
795	Sikandar Tughluq.	1394
795	Mahmūd Tughluq.	1394
797	Nusrat Shāh (Interregnum).	1396
801	Mahmūd Tughluq (restored).	1399
815	Daulat Khān Lodī.	1413

7. SAYYIDS

817	Khizr Khān.	1414
824	Mu'izz-ud-dīn Mubārak.	1421
837	Muhammad.	1434
847	'Alā-ud-dīn 'Ālam Shāh.	1444

8. LODĪ

855	Būhlūl Lodī.	1451
894	Sikandar Lodī.	1489
923	Ibrāhīm Lodī.	1517
—932		—1526

(*Timūrids.*)

3. THE SLAVE KINGS OF DELHI

GENEALOGY

(Numbers in brackets denote the order of succession.)

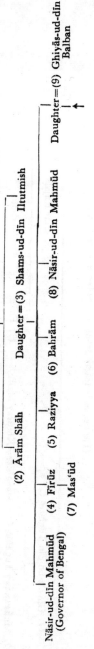

(1) Qutb-ud-dīn Aibak

Daughter=(3) Shams-ud-dīn Iltutmish

(2) Ārām Shāh

Nāsir-ud-dīn Mahmūd (Governor of Bengal)

(4) Fīrūz   (5) Razīyya   (6) Bahrām   (8) Nāsir-ud-dīn Mahmūd   Daughter=(9) Ghiyās-ud-dīn Balban

(7) Mas'ūd

4. THE HOUSE OF BALBAN
(DELHI AND BENGAL)

GENEALOGY

(Arabic numerals denote the order of succession in Delhi, small Roman numerals that in Bengal)

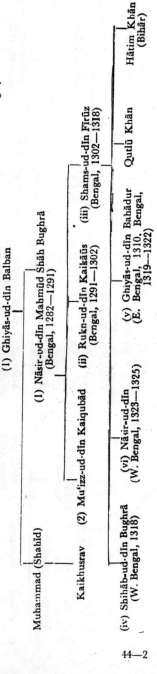

(1) Ghiyās-ud-dīn Balban

Muhammad (Shahīd)

(1) Nāsir-ud-dīn Mahmūd Shāh Bughrā (Bengal, 1282—1291)

Kaikhusrav   (2) Mu'izz-ud-dīn Kaiqubād

(ii) Rukn-ud-dīn Kaikāūs (Bengal, 1291—1302)

(iii) Shams-ud-dīn Fīrūz (Bengal, 1302—1318)

(iv) Shihāb-ud-dīn Bughrā (W. Bengal, 1318)

(vi) Nāsir-ud-dīn (W. Bengal, 1323—1325)

(v) Ghiyās-ud-dīn Bahādur (E. Bengal, 1310. Bengal, 1319—1322)

Qutlū Khān

Hātim Khān (Bihār)

44—2

5. THE KHALJĪS
GENEALOGY

(Numbers in brackets denote the order of succession.)

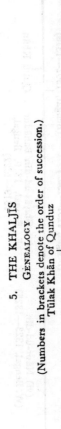

6. THE TUGHLUQS
GENEALOGY

(Figures in brackets denote the order of succession.)

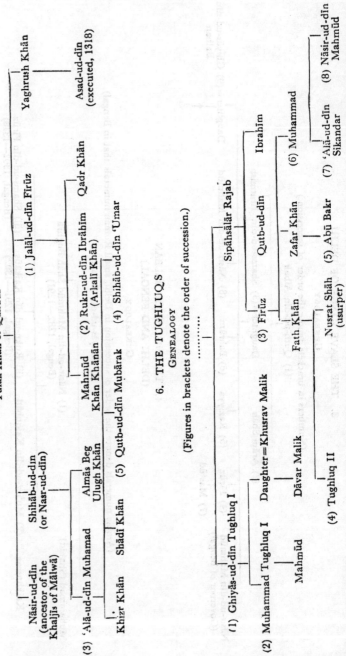

7. THE SAYYIDS

GENEALOGY

(Figures in brackets denote the order of succession.)

Malik Sulaimān
(Malik-ush-Sharq)
|
(1) Khizr Khān
|

(2) Mu'izz-ud-dīn Mubārak   Farīd

(3) Muhammad
|
(4) 'Alā-ud-dīn 'Ālam Shāh

8. THE LODĪS

GENEALOGY

(Figures in brackets denote the order of succession.)

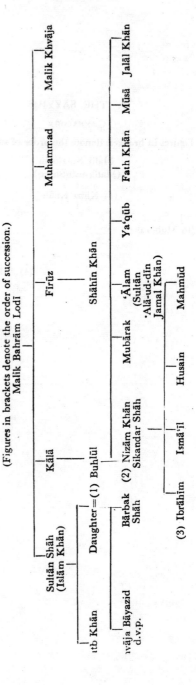

9. GOVERNORS OF BENGAL

A.H.		A.D.
599	Muhammad b. Bakhtyār, Khaljī.	1202
602	'Izz-ud-dīn Muhammad Shīrān, Khaljī.	1205
605	'Alā-ud-dīn 'Alī Mardān.	1208
608	Ghiyās-ud-dīn 'Iwaz Husain.	1211
624	Nāsir-ud-dīn Mahmūd.	1227
626	'Alā-ud-dīn.	1229
627	Saif-ud-dīn Aibak.	1230
631	'Izz-ud-dīn Tughril Taghān Khān.	1233
642	Qamar-ud-dīn Qarā Beg Tīmūr Khān.	1244
644	Ikhtiyār-ud-dīn Yūzbak.	1246
656	Jalāl-ud-dīn Mas'ūd Jānī.	1258
657	'Izz-ud-dīn Balban.	1259
657	Arsalān Khān.	1259
659	Muhammad Tātār Khān.	1261
674	Mughīs-ud-dīn Tughril.	1275
681	Nāsir-ud-dīn Bughrā.	1282
691	Rukn-ud-dīn Kaikāūs.	1292
702	Shams-ud-dīn Fīrūz Shāh.	1302
718	Shihāb-ud-dīn Bughrā Shāh (W. Bengal).	1318
710	Ghiyās-ud-dīn Bahādur (E. Bengal)	1310
719	Ghiyās-ud-dīn Bahādur (all Bengal).	1319
723	Nāsir-ud-dīn (W. Bengal).	1323
725	Ghiyās-ud-dīn Bahādur, restored, with Bahrām.	1325
731	Bahrām Shāh.	1330
726—740	Qadr Khān (Lakhnāwati).	1326—1339
724—746	'Izz-ud-dīn A'zam-ul-Mulk (Satgāon).	1324—1339
	(Kings of Bengal.)	

10. KINGS OF BENGAL

(1) *Eastern Bengal*

739	Fakhr-ud-dīn Mubārak Shāh.	1338
750	Ikhtiyār-ud-dīn Ghāzī Shāh.	1349
—753		—1352

(Iliyās of Western Bengal.)

(2) *Western Bengal and all Bengal*

742	'Alā-ud-dīn 'Alī Shāh.	1341
743	Hājī Shams-ud-dīn Iliyās, *Bhangara*.	1343
758	Sikandar Shāh.	1357
795	Ghiyās-ud-dīn A'zam Shāh.	1393
813	Saif-ud-dīn Hamza.	1410
815	Shihāb-ud-dīn Bāyazīd.	1412
817	Ganesh of Bhadūria ('Kāns Narāyan').	1414
817	Jadu, *alias* Jalāl-ud-dīn Muhammad Shāh.	1414
835	Shams-ud-dīn Ahmad Shāh.	1431
846	Nāsir-ud-dīn Mahmūd Shāh.	1442
864	Rukn-ud-dīn Bārbak Shāh.	1460

A.H.		A.D.
879	Shams-ud-dīn Yūsuf Shāh.	1474
886	Sikandar Shāh.	1481
886	Jalāl-ud-dīn Fath Shāh.	1481
891	Bārbak the Eunuch, Sultāh Shāhzāda.	1486
891	Malik Indīl, Fīıūz Shāh.	1486
894	Nāsir-ud-dīn Mahmūd Shāh.	1489
897	Sīdī Badr, Shams-ud-dīn Muzaffar Shāh.	1490
900	Sayyid 'Alā-ud-dīn Husain, Sha·īf-i-Makkī.	1593
924	Nasīr-ud-dīn Nusrat Shāh.	1518
939	'Alā-ud-dīn Fīrūz Shāh.	1533
939	Sultān Mahmūd.	15?3
945	Humāyūn, Emperor of Delhi.	1538
945	Sher Shāh Sūr.	1539
947	Khizr Khān.	1540
952	Muhammad Khān Sūr.	1545
962	Khizr Khān, Bahādūr Shāh.	1555
968	Ghiyās-ud-dīn Jalāl Shāh.	1561
971	(Son of preceding.)	1564
972	Tāj Khān, Kararānī.	1564
980	Sulaimān Kararānī.	1572
980	Bāyazīd Khān Kararānī.	1572
980	Dāūd Khān Kararānī.	1572
—984		—1576

(*Tīmūrids*.)

11. THE SULTANS OF MADURA

A.H.		A.D.
735	Sayyid Jalāl-ud-dīn Ahsan Shāh.	1334
740	'Alā-ud-dīn Udaujī Shāh.	1339
740	Qutb-ud-dīn Fīrūz Shāh	1340
740	Ghiyās-ud-dīn Muhammad Dāmaghān Shāh.	1340
745	Nāsir-ud-dīn Māhmūd Ghāzī Dāmaghān Shāh.	1344—45
757	'Ādil Shāh.	1356
761	Fakhr-ud-dīn Mubārak Shāh.	1360
774	'Alā-ud-dīn Sikandar Shāh.	1372—73
—779		—1377—78

(Rajas of Vijayanagar.)

12. THE KINGS OF KASHMÍR, FIRST DYNASTY

A.H.		A.D.
747	1. Shāh Mīrzā, Shams-ud-dīn.	1346
750	2. Jamshīd.	1349
751	3. ʿAlī Sher, ʿAlā-ud-dīn.	1350
760	4. Shīrāshāmak, Shihāb-ud-dīn.	1359
780	5. Hindāl, Qutb-ud-dīn.	1378
796	6. Sikandar Butshikan.	1393-94
819	7. Mīr Khān, ʿAlī Shāh.	1416
823	8. Shāhī Khān, Zain-ul-Ābidīn.	1420
875	9. Hājī Khān, Haidar Shāh.	1470
876	10. Hasan Shāh.	1472
894	11. Muhammad Shāh.	1489
894	12. Fath Shāh.	1489
903	11. Muhammad Shāh, *restored.*	1497-98
903-04	12. Fath Shāh, *restored.*	1498
904-05	11. Muhammud Shāh, *again restored.*	1499
932	13. Ibrāhīm Shāh, I.	1526
933	14. Nāzuk Shāh.	1527
935	11. Muhammad Shāh, *again restored.*	1529
941	15. Shams-ud-dīn Shāh II.	1534-35
947	14. Nāzuk Shāh, *restored.*	1540
947	16. Mīrzā Haidar, *usurper.*	1541
958	14. Nāzuk Shāh, *again restored.*	1551
959	17. Ibrāhīm Shāh II.	1552
962	18. Ismāʿīl Shāh.	1555
964	19. Habīb Shāh.	1557
—968		—1561

(*Chakks.*)

12. THE KINGS OF KASHMĪR, FIRST DYNASTY

GENEALOGY

(Figures in brackets denote the order of succession.)

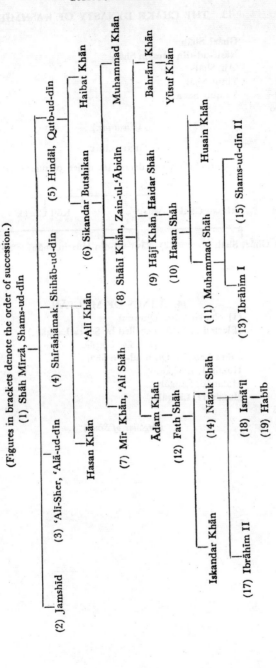

13. THE CHAKK DYNASTY OF KASHMĪR

A.H.		A.D.
968	Ghāzī Shāh.	1561
971	Nāsir-ud-dīn Husain Shān.	1563-64
977	'Alī Shāh.	1569-70
986	Yūsuf Shālı.	1578-79
993	Ya'qub Saah.	1585
—996		—1589

(*Tīmūrids.*)

GENEALOGY

(Figures in brackets denote the order of succession.)

....

```
                  ┌──────────────────┴──────────────┐
          Hasan Chakk=wife=                    Kājī Chakk
        ┌─────────┴───────┐        ┌──────────────────────────┐
 (1) Ghāzī Shāh     (2) Nāsir-ud-dīn Husain Shāh        (3) 'Alī Shāh
                                                              │
                                                        (4) Yūsuf Shāh
                                                              │
                                                        (5) Ya'qūb Shāh
```

14. KINGS OF MULTĀN

842	(1) Shaikh Yūsuf Quraishī.	1438
	(Elected in 1438 ; expelled by Sahra Langāh.)	
	(2) *The Langāhs*	
844	Sahra Langāh, Qutb-ud-dīn Shāh.	1440
861	Husain I, Langāh.	1456
908	Mahmūd, Langāh.	1502
933	Husain II, Langāh.	1527
—935		—1528

(*Arghūns of Sind.*)

15. KINGS OF SIND

A.H.	(1) *Sammā Jāms.* (Dates approximate)	A.D.
737	Jām Unar.	1336
741	Jām Jūna.	1340
745	Jām Banhatiya.	1344
760	Jām Timājī.	1359
773	Jām Salāh-ud-dīn.	1371
784	Jàm 'Alī Sher.	1382
790	Jām Karān.	1388
791	Jām Fath Khān.	1389
802	Jām Tughluq.	1399
830	Mubārak, the Chamberlain.	1427
830	Jām Sikandar.	1427
832	Jām Sanjar, known as Rādhan.	1428
841	Jām Nizam-ud-dīn, known as Naodā.	1437
900	Jām Fīrūz.	1494

(2) *Arghūns*

927	Mīrzā Shāh Beg, Arghūn.	1521
931	Mīrzā Husain, Arghūn.	1524

(3) *Arghūn Tarkhāns*

964	Mīrzā Muhammad 'Īsā, Tarkhān.	1556
975	Mīrzā Muhammad Būqī, Tarkhān.	1567
993	Mīrzā Jānī Beg, Tarkhān.	1585
—1001		—1591

(*Tīmūrids.*)

16. THE SHARQĪ KINGS OF JAUNPUR

796	Malik Sarvar, Khvāja Jahān.	1394
892	Malik Qaranful, Mubārak Shāh.	1399
804	Shams-ud-dīn Ibrāhīm Shāh.	1402
840	Mahmūd Shāh.	1436
862	Muhammad Shāh.	1458
862	Husain Shāh.	1458
—884		—1479

(Lodī Kings of Delhi.)

GENEALOGY

(Figures in brackets denote the order of succession.)

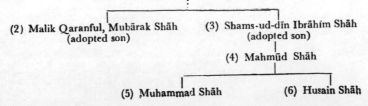

(1) Malik Sarvar, Khvāja Jahān

(2) Malik Qaranful, Mubārak Shāh
(adopted son)
(3) Shams-ud-dīn Ibrāhīm Shāh
(adopted son)

(4) Mahmūd Shāh

(5) Muhammad Shāh
(6) Husain Shāh

17. BAHMANĪ KINGS OF THE DECCAN

A.H.		A.D.
748	'Alā-ud-dīn Bahman Shāh.	1347
759	Muhammad I.	1358
776	Mujāhid.	1375
779	Dāūd.	1378
780	Muhammad II.	1378
799	Ghiyās-ud-dīn.	1397
799	Shams-ud-dīn.	1397
800	Tāj-ud-dīn Fīrūz.	1397
825	Ahmad, Valī.	1422
839	'Alā-ud-dīn Ahmad.	1436
862	Humāyūn Zālim.	1458
865	Nizām.	1461
867	Muhammad III, Lashkarī.	1463
887	Mahmūd.	1482
924	Ahmad.	1518
927	'Alā-ud-dīn.	1521
928	Walī-Ullāh.	1522
931	Kalīmullāh.	1525
—934		—1527

(Five Kingdoms of the Deccan.)

17. BAHMANĪ KINGS OF THE DECCAN
GENEALOGY
(Figures in brackets denote the order of succession.)

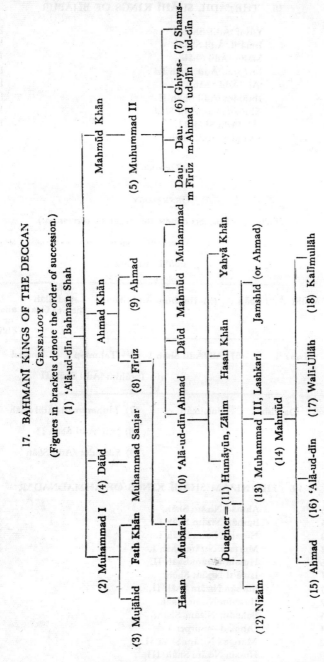

(1) 'Alā-ud-dīn Bahman Shah

18. THE 'ĀDIL SHĀHĪ KINGS OF BĪJĀPUR

A.H.		A.D.
895	Yūsuf 'Ādil Shāh.	1490
916	Ismā'īl 'Ādil Shāh.	1510
941	Mallū 'Ādil Shāh.	1534
941	Ibrāhīm 'Ādil Shāh I.	1534
965	'Alī 'Ādil Shāh I.	1558
988	Ibrāhīm 'Ādil Shāh II.	1580
1037	Muhammad 'Ādil Shāh.	1627
1068	'Alī 'Ādil Shāh II.	1657
1093	Sikandar 'Ādil Shāh.	1672
—1097		—1686

(*Tīmūrids.*)

GENEALOGY

(Figures in brackets denote the order of succession.)

(1) Yūsuf 'Ādil Shāh

(2) Ismā'īl 'Ādil Shāh

(3) Mallū 'Ādil Shāh   (5) Ibrāhīm 'Ādil Shāh I   Abdullāh   'Alī
                                                            (fled to Goa)   alias Allū
                                                                             or Annū
                                                                             (blinded)

Ismā'īl   (5) 'Alī 'Ādil Shāh I   Tahmāsp   Ahmad

(6) Ibrāhīm 'Ādil Shāh II

Darvīsh   Sulaimān   (7) Muhammad 'Ādil Shāh

(8) 'Alī 'Ādil Shāh II

(9) Sikandar 'Ādil Shāh

19. THE NIZĀM SHĀHĪ KINGS OF AHMADNAGAR

895	Ahmād Nizām Shāh.	1490
915	Burhān Nizām Shāh I.	1509
960	Husain Nizām Shāh I.	1553
973	Murtazā Nizām Shāh I.	1565
995	Husain Nizām Shāh II.	1586
997	Ismā'īl Nizām Shāh.	1589
999	Burhān Nizām Shāh II.	1591
1002	Ibrāhīm Nizām Shāh.	1595
1004	Bahādur Nizām Shāh.	1596
1004	(Ahmad—usurper.)	1596
1012	Murtazā Nizām Shāh II.	1603
1040	Husain Nizām Shāh III.	1630
—1043		—1633

(*Tīmūrids.*)

19. THE NIZĀM SHĀHĪ KINGS OF AHMADNAGAR

GENEALOGY

(Figures in brackets denote the order of succession.)

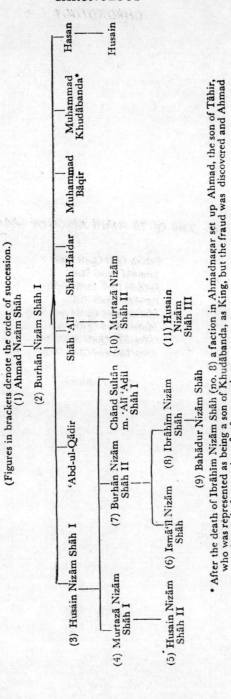

* After the death of Ibrāhīm Nizām Shāh (no. 8) a faction in Ahmadnagar set up Ahmad, the son of Tāhir, who was represented as being a son of Khudābanda, as King, but the fraud was discovered and Ahmad was deposed after a reign of a few months.

20. THE QUTB SHĀHĪ KINGS OF GOLCONDA

A.H.		A.D.
918	Sultān Qulī Qutb Shāh.	1512
950	Jamshīd Qutb Shāh.	1543
957	Subhān Qulī Qutb Shāh.	1550
957	Ibrāhīm Qutb Shāh.	1550
988	Muhammad Qulī Qutb Shāh.	1580
1020	Muhammad Qutb Shāh.	1612
1035	'Abdullāh Qutb Shāh.	1626
1083	Abu-'l-Hasan Qutb Shāh.	1672
—1098		—1687

(*Timūrids.*)

20. THE QUTB SHĀHĪ KINGS OF GOLCONDA

GENEALOGY

(Figures in brackets denote the order of succession.)

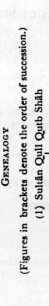
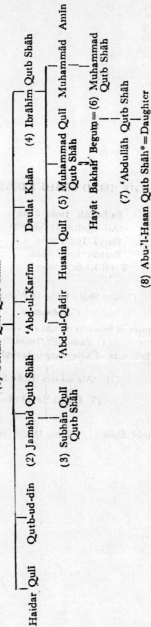

Haidar Qulī

(1) Sultān Qulī Qutb Shāh

Qutb-ud-dín   (2) Jamshīd Qutb Shāh   'Abd-ul-Karīm   Daulat Khān   (4) Ibrāhīm Qutb Shāh

(3) Subhān Qulī Qutb Shāh

'Abd-ul-Qādir   Husain Qulī   (5) Muhammad Qulī Qutb Shāh   Muhammad Amīn

Hayāt Bakhsh Begum = (6) Muhammad Qutb Shāh

(7) 'Abdullāh Qutb Shāh

(8) Abu-'l-Hasan Qutb Shāh* = Daughter

* Abu-'l-Hasan is said to have been descended of the royal family, but his descent is nowhere given.

45—2

21. THE 'IMĀD SHĀHĪ KINGS OF BERAR

A.H.		A.D.
895	Fathullāh 'Imād Shāh	1490
910	'Alā-ud-dīn 'Imād Shāh.	1504
937	Daryā 'Imād Shāh.	1529
970	Burhān 'Imād Shāh.	1562
	Tufāl Khān (usurper).	
—982		—1574

(Nizām Shāhī Kings of Ahmadnagar.)

GENEALOGY

(Figures in brackets denote the order of succession.)

(1) Fathullāh 'Imād Shāh

(A Brāhman of Vijayanagar brought up as a Muslim)

|

(2) 'Alā-ud-dīn 'Imād Shāh

|

(3) Daryā 'Imād Shāh

|

Burhān 'Imād Shāh   Dau., Daulāt Shāh—Husain Nizām Shāh I
                                                of Ahmadnagār

22. THE BARĪD SHĀHĪ KINGS OF BĪDAR

A.H.		A.D.
894	Amīr Qāsim Barīd.	1487
910	Amīr 'Alī Barīd.	1504
949	'Alī Barīd Shāh I.	1542
987	Ibrāhīm Barīd Shāh.	1579
994	Qāsim Barīd Shāh II.	1586
999	Amīr Barīd Shāh.	1589
1010	Mīrzā 'Alī Barīd Shāh.	1601
1018	'Alī Barīd Shāh II.	1609
—1028		—1619

('Ādil Shāhī Kings of Bījāpur.)

GENEALOGY

(Figures in brackets denote the order of succession.)

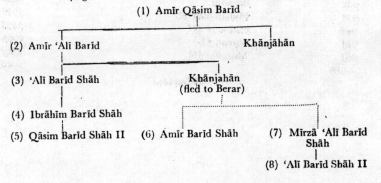

(1) Amīr Qāsim Barīd

(2) Amīr 'Alī Barīd   Khānjāhān

(3) 'Alī Barīd Shāh   Khānjahān (fled to Berar)

(4) Ibrāhīm Barīd Shāh

(5) Qāsim Barīd Shāh II   (6) Amīr Barīd Shāh   (7) Mīrzā 'Alī Barīd Shāh

(8) 'Alī Barīd Shāh II

23. THE KINGS OF GUJARÃT

A.H.		A.D.
798	Muzaffar I.	1396
814	Ahmad I.	1411
846	Muhammad I, Karim.	1442
855	Qutb-ud-din.	1451
862	Dãũd.	1458
862	Mahmũd I.	1458
917	Muzaffar II.	1511
932	Sikandar.	1526
932	Mahmũd II.	1526
932	Bahãdur.	1526
943	Muhammad II.	1537
943	Mahmũd III.	1537
961	Ahmad II-	1554
967	Muzaffar III.	1562
—980		—1572

(*Tĩmũrids.*)

23. THE KINGS OF GUJARAT

GENEALOGY

(Figures in brackets denote the order of succession.)

Wajīh-ul-Mulk of Nāgaur
(a Rājput convert)

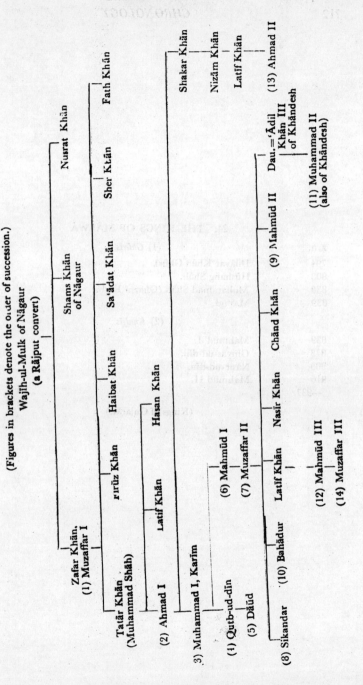

24. THE KINGS OF MĀLWA

(1) *Ghūris*

A.H.		A D.
794	Dilāvar Khān Ghūrī.	1392
808	Hūshang Shāh.	1405
838	Muhammad Shāh (Ghaznī Khān).	1435
839	Mas'ūd.	1436

(2) *Khaljīs*

A.H.		A D.
839	Mahmūd I.	1436
873	Ghiyās-ud-din.	1469
905	Nāsir-ud-dīn.	1500
916	Mahmūd II.	1510
—937		--1531

(Kings of Gujarāt.)

24. THE KINGS OF MĀLWA

Genealogy

(Figures in brackets denote the order of succession.)

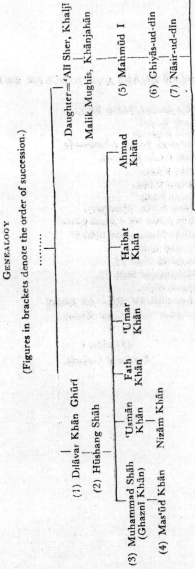

(1) Dilāvar Khān Ghūri

(2) Hūshang Shāh

(3) Muhammad Shāh (Ghaznī Khān)

(4) Mas'ūd Khān

'Usmān Khān

Fath Khān

Nizām Khān

'Umar Khān

Haibat Khān

Ahmad Khān

Shihāb-ud-dīn

Daughter = 'Alī Sher, Khaljī

Malik Mughis, Khānjahān

(5) Mahmūd I

(6) Ghiyās-ud-dīn

(7) Nāsir-ud-dīn

(8) Mahmūd II

25. THE FĀRŪQĪ KHĀNS AND KINGS OF KHĀNDESH

A.H		A.D.
784	Rāja Ahmad, Malik Rāja.	1382
801	Nasīr Khān.	1399
840	'Ādil Khān I:	1437
844	Mubārak Khān, Chaukanda.	1441
861	'Ādil Khān II, 'Ainā.	1457
907	Dāūd Khān.	1501
914	Ghaznī Khān.	1508
914	Hasan Khān.	1508
914	'Ālam Khān. (Usurper.)	1508
914	'Ādil Khān III ('Ālam Khān)	1509
926	Mīrān Muhammad Shāh I*	1520
943	Ahmad Shāh.	1537
943	Mubārak Shāh II.	1537
974	Muhammad Shāh II.	1566
984	Hasan Shāh.	1576-77
985	'Ādil Shāh IV (Rāja 'Alī Khān).	1577-78
1006	Bahādur Shāh (Qadr Khān).	1597
—1009		—1601

(*Tīmūrids.*)

* Also of Gujarāt.

25. THE FĀRŪQI KHĀNS AND KINGS OF KHĀNDESH

GENEALOGY

(Figures in brackets denote the order of succession.)

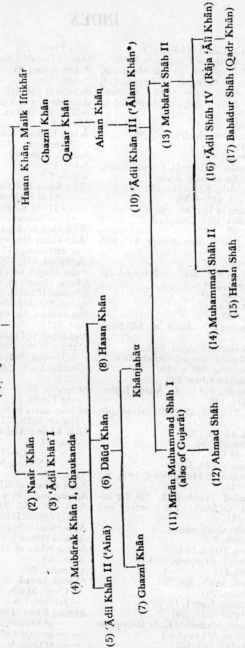

'Ain-ud-dīn Muhammad Khvāja Jahān

(1) Rāja Ahmad, Malik Rāja

Hasan Khān, Mailk Iftikhār

(2) Nasīr Khān

(3) 'Ādil Khān I, Chaukanda

Ghazni Khān

Qaisar Khān

(4) Mubārak Khān I, Chaukanda

Ahsan Khān

(5) 'Ādil Khān II ('Ainā)

(6) Dāūd Khān

(7) Ghaznī Khān

(8) Hasan Khān

Khānjahāū

(10) 'Ādil Khān III ('Ālam Khān*)

(11) Mīrān Muhammad Shāh I (also of Gujarāt)

(12) Ahmad Shāh

(13) Mubārak Shāh II

(14) Muhammad Shāh II

(15) Hasan Shāh

(16) 'Ādil Shāh IV (Rāja 'Ālī Khān)

(17) Bahādur Shāh (Qadr Khān)

* Not to be confounded with the usurper of the same name, who was a member of the family, but whose descent is not given, and was supported by Ahmad Nizām Shāh of Ahmadnagar.

INDEX

Detail of the star panels in the Ghaznī gate
at Agra Fort

2

Delhi : the Quwwat-ul-Islām *masjid* ; arched screen of Qutb-ud-dīn Aibak

3

Delhi : the Quwwat-ul-Islām mosque ; carvings on original screen of
Qutb-ud-din Aibak

4

Delhi : the Quwwat-ul-Islām mosque ; carvings on screen extension
added by Iltutmish

Delhi : bird's-eye view of Quwwat-ul-Islâm *masjid* and connected buildings (restored)

7

Interior of the Tomb of the Emperor Iltutmish

e

Delhi : the Qutb *Minār* from N. E.

8

Tomb of Sultān Ghārī.   Roof of subterranean tomb-chamber

9

Arhāī-dīn-kē-Jhomprā *masjid* at Ajmer.   Arched screen in front of prayer-chamber

11
Arhāī-dīn-kā-Jhomprā *masjid* at Ajmer.   Detail of
marble *mihrāb*

10
Arhāī-dīn-Jhomprā *masjid* at Ajmer.   Colonnades in
the prayer chamber

12

The Jamā'at Khāna *masjid* at the *dargāh* of Nizām-ud-dūin Auliyā

13

'Alāī Darwāza at the Qutb ; south facade

15

Tomb of Ghiyās-ud-dīn Tughluq : view from inside the castle walls

16

Tomb of Ghiyās-ud-dīn Tughluq, from the west

14

Interior of the 'Alāī Darwāza

Plate IX   *The Cambridge History of India, Vol. III*

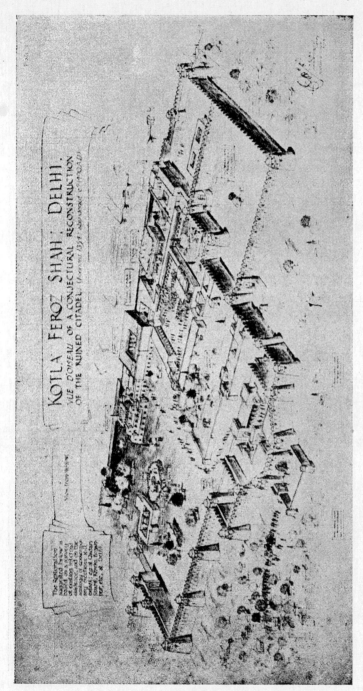

17

Conjectural restoration of the Kotla Fīrūz Shāh

Plate X   The Cambridge History of India, Vol. III

18
Aśoka's pillar with Fīrūz Shāh's pyramidal substructure in the
Kotla Fīrūz Shāh : from South-West

19
College and tomb of Fīrūz Shāh Tughluq at the Hauz-i-ʿAlāī

Plate XI   *The Cambridge History of India, Vol. III*

20

Tomb of Fīrūz Shāh Tughluq

21

Tomb of Khān-i-Jahān Tilangānī

Plate XII   *The Cambridge History of India, Vol. III*

22

The Kalān *masjid* in Shāhjahānābād

23

Tomb of Muhammad Shāh (Sayyid), from South-West

Plate XIII   *The Cambridge History of India, Vol. III*

24

Bare Khān kā *Gumbad*, from North-East

25

The *Barā Gumbad* and Mosque

Plate XIV   *The Cambridge History of India, Vol. II.*

26

Mosque of the *Barā Gumbad*

27

Interior of prayer-chamber of the *Moth-kī-masjid*
(built by the Prime Minister of Sikandar Shāh Lodī)

28

Tomb of Bahā-ul-Haqq at Multān, from East

29

Tomb of Rukn-i-'Alam at Multān, from South-West

Plate XVI *The Cambridge History of India, Vol. III*

30
Sectional drawing of the tomb of Rukn-i-'Alam at Multān

Plate XVII   The Cambridge History of India, Vol. III

31

Inscription on left of *mihrāb* of Zafar Khān Ghāzī mosque at Tribani

32

Adīna Masjid, Pānduah : the prayer-chamber as seen from the courtyard

Plate XVIII   The Cambridge History of India, Vol. III

33

A͞dīna Masjid, Pānduah : the niche and central *mihrāb*

34

Ādīna Masjid, Pānduah : corridor with royal gallery on right

Plate XIX   The Cambridge History of India, Vol. III

35

Sāth Gūmbaz mosque at Bagerhāt, from South-East

36

The Dākhil Darwāza at Gaur, from the North

Plate XX   The Cambridge History of India, Vol. III

Gunmant mosque, showing decoration of vaulted arch, at Gaur

38

Tantīpāra masjid at Gaur : details of terracotta decorations

37

Plate XXI   *The Cambridge History of India, Vol. III*

39
General view of *Chhotā Sonā Masjid* at Gaur, from East

40   41
Fīrūz *Minār* at Gaur   Details of central door of *Chhotā Sonā Masjid*
                                            at Gaur

42

Barā Sonā Masjid at Gaur, from North-East

43

Arcade in the prayer-chamber of the *Barā Sonā*
Masjid at Gaur.

Plate XXIII   The Cambridge History of India, Vol. III

44

The *Jāmiʿ Masjid* at Cambay

45

Dholkā; Balol Khēn Qēzī's *masjid*, entrance porch

Plate XXIV   The Cambridge History of India, Vol. III

46

Ahmadābād : *Tīn Darwāza.*   General view from East

47

The *Jāmiʿ Masjid* at Ahmadabad

Plate XXV   The Cambridge History of India, Vol. III

48
Chāmpāner : Halol gateway (inner) from East. North-West corner

49
Chāmpāner : *Jāmi' Masjid.* View from South-East

50
Chāmpāner : *Jāmi' Masjid.* General view from South- West

Plate XXVI   The Cambridge History of India, Vol. III

51
The Palace at Sārkhej

52
Adalaj : stepped well.   Interior view from second gallery

53
Ahmadābād : *masjid* of Sayyid 'Usmēn : tomb of Sayyid 'Usmān
in front of view from South-East (at 'Usmānpūra)

54

Ahmadābād : Shāh 'Alam's tomb. View frcm North-East

55

Ahmadābād : Bāī Harīr's *masjid* at Asarwa. View from East

56

Ahmadābād : Mosque of Shāh 'Ālam

Plate XXVIII   *The Cambridge History of India, Vol. III*

57

Mosque of Rānī Sīparī at Ahmadābād

Plate XXIX   The Cambridge History of India, Vol. III

58

Siddī Sayyid's mosque at Ahmadābād

59

Perforated stone window in Siddī Sayyid's mosque at Ahmadābād

Plate XXX   The Cambridge History of India, Vol. III

60

The Delhi Gate of Māndū, from within

61

Interior of the East entrance porch of the *Lāt Masjid* at Dhār

62

A corner of the Hindolā Mahall at Māndū

Plate XXXII   *The Cambridge History of India, Vol. III*

63

Interior of the Hindolā Mahall at Māndū

64

The *Jāmiʿ Masjid* at Māndū, from North-East

65

Interior of the *Jāmiʿ Masjid* at Māndū

Plate XXXIII   The Cambridge History of India, Vol. III

66

The tomb of Hūshang

67

Interior of mosque of Malik Mughīs (Mughīs-ud-Dunyā)

(typical of the Māndū style)

68

The ruined College and tomb of Mahmūd, with Tower of
Victory on the left

69

The Jahāz Mahall at Māndū

70

The palace of Bāz Bahādur with Rūpmati's pavilion
crowning the hill in the distance

Plate XXXV   The Cambridge History of India, Vol. III

The Ukha Masjid at Bayāna

72

The Ukha Mandir at Bayāna

71

73

The *Shams Masjid* at Nēgaur (Jodhpur)

74

The *Topkhāna* mosque at Jēlor (Jodhpur)

Plate XXXVII   *The Cambridge History of India, Vol. III*

75

Kūshk Mahall at Fathābād near Chanderī

76

Jāmiʿ Masjid at Chanderī

Plate XXXVIII   *The Cambridge History of India, Vol. III*

77

Jāmiʿ Masjid at Budaun

78

Bādal Mahall gate at Chanderī

79

The *Lāt* at Hissār

80
Chaurāsī Gumbad at Kālpī, from South-East

81
Atāla mosque at Jaunpur

82
Atāla mosque at Jaunpur

Plate XL   The Cambridge History of India, Vol. III

83
Jāmi‘ Masjid at Jaunpur

84
Jāmi‘ Masjid at Jaunpur.   Exterior colonnades on south side

Plate XLI   *The Cambridge History of India, Vol. III*

85

The citadel at Daulatābād, with Chānd *Minār* to the right

86

The entrance to the tunnel in the citadel at Daulatābād

Plate XLII   The Cambridge History of India, Vol. III

87
Rock-hewn moat around the citadel at Daulatābād

Plate XLIII — *The Cambridge History of India, Vol. III*

88

The *Gumbad* gate of Bidar Fort

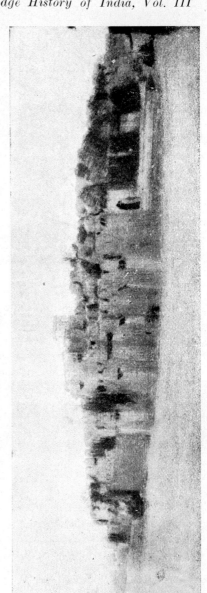

89

The Fort at Parenda

91

Mahākālī Gateway of Narnāla

90

The *Fath Darwāza*, Golconda Fort

92

Tomb of Bahman Shāh at Gulbarga, from North-East

93

Tomb of Fīrūz Shāh Bahmanī at Gulbarga, from North-West

Plate XLVI   The Cambridge History of India, Vol. III

94

The *Jāmi' Masjid* at Gulbarga, from North-East

95

Arcade in the *Jāmi' Masjid* at Gulbarga

Plate XLVII   *The Cambridge History of India, Vol. III*

96

Arch over entrance to *Banda Nawāz*, Gulbarga

97

Tombs of the later Bahmanī kings at Bīdar

Plate XLVIII   *The Cambridge History of India, Vol. III*

98

The *Chānd Minār* at Daulatābād

Plate XLIX   The Cambridge History of India, Vol. III

99

Madrasa of Mahmūd Gāwān at Bīdar

100

Tombs of the Fārūqī kings at Thālner, from North-East

Plate L   *The Cambridge History of India, Vol. III*

101

Tomb of the mother of Zain-ul-ʿĀbidīn (1417-1467)

102

Mosque of Madanī

Plate LI   *The Cambridge History of India, Vol. III*

103

Jāmiʿ Masjid, Srīnagar ; interior of cloisters

104

Mosque of Shāh Hamadān